PEOPLE, PENGUINS, AND PLASTIC TREES

Basic Issues in Environmental Ethics

Second Edition

Christine Pierce □ Donald VanDeVeer
North Carolina State University

Wadsworth Publishing Company
ITP™ An International Thomson Publishing Company

Belmont • Albany • Bonn • Boston • Cincinnati • Detroit • London • Madrid • Melbourne
Mexico City • New York • Paris • San Francisco • Singapore • Tokyo • Toronto • Washington

Philosophy Editor: Tammy Goldfeld
Editorial Assistant: Kelly Zavislak
Production Editor: The Book Company
Print Buyer: Randy Hurst
Permissions Editor: Robert Kauser

Designer: Cynthia Bogue
Copy Editor: Sonsie Conroy
Cover: William Reuter
Compositor: T:HTypecast, Inc.
Printer: Malloy Lithographing, Inc.

*This book is printed on
acid-free recycled paper.*

For more information, contact Wadsworth Publishing Group

Wadsworth Publishing Company
10 Davis Drive
Belmont, California 94002
USA

International Thomson Publishing Europe
Berkshire House 168-173
High Holborn
London, WC1V7AA
England

Thomas Nelson Australia
102 Dodds Street
South Melbourne 3205
Victoria, Australia

Nelson Canada
1120 Birchmount Road
Scarborough, Ontario
Canada M1K 5G4

International Thomson Editores
Campos Eliseos 385, Piso 7
Col. Polanco
11560 México D.F. México

International Thomson Publishing GmbH
Königswinterer Strasse 418
53227 Bonn
Germany

International Thomson Publishing Asia
221 Henderson Road
#05-10 Henderson Bldg.
Singapore 0315

International Thomson Publishing–Japan
Hirakawacho Kyowa Building, 3F
2-2-1 Hirakawacho
Chiyoda-ku, Tokyo 102
Japan

Library of Congress Cataloging-in-Publication Data
People, penguins, and plastic trees : basic issues in environmental
   ethics / [edited by] Christine Pierce and Donald VanDeVeer.—2nd
   ed.
      p.   cm.
   Includes bibliographical references and index.
   ISBN 0-534-17922-3
   1. Nature conservation—Moral and ethical aspects.   2. Nature
conservation—Philosophy.   3. Environmental protection—Moral and
ethical aspects.   4. Environmental protection—Philosophy.
I. Pierce, Christine.   II. VanDeVeer, Donald,
GE42.P46   1994
179'.1—dc20
                                                                94-13151

To Beth
C.P.

To Bob, Terry, Harry and Ladyce
D.V.

Contents

Preface to the Second Edition

When we began the preface to the first edition of *People, Penguins, and Plastic Trees* in 1986, we asked the question, "Why give a damn about the planet—or its nonhuman residents?" Reasoned answers to that question were just beginning to emerge in landmark essays from the United States, Europe, Australia, and other places. That first edition was a collection of some of the most influential and innovative of those critical essays.

Since that edition, however, environmental knowledge (and thus writing that addresses environmental issues) has increased almost exponentially. Consider the impact of just a few of the major environmental topics that have become news in the last decade: global warming, more species on the brink of extinction, the loss of vast areas of rain forests, the U.N. Conference on Environment and Development in Rio de Janiero in 1992 (with its declaration of governmental responsibilities for the planetary environment), lawsuits defending the territories of the spotted owl and the red cockaded woodpecker, the Prince William Sound oil spill of the Exxon Valdez, the nuclear disaster at Chernobyl, and the transport by ship of plutonium by the Japanese. All these events have altered public consciousness and public awareness.

Responses to these issues have included some new theories and points of view on our relationship with the rest of the natural world, responses such as ecofeminism and deep ecology, closer examination of the Native American land ethic, and critiques of industrialized nations by environmental theorists in less-industrialized countries. Essays that represent these emerging viewpoints are included in this second edition, as well as some of the essays from the 1970s and 1980s that remain influential in shaping our environmental ethics. We have also included essays on environmental racism and ecological sustainability—issues that were seldom discussed in 1986. Moreover, we have added a section on the ecological consequences of some of our personal choices. These essays about what we eat, what we plant in our yards, and how we create spaces in which to live might alternatively be labelled "sustainable ways of living."

This second edition, like the earlier one, does not attempt to be an introduction to ecology or any of the environmental sciences. It does contain essays by writers who find scientific data important in shaping their responses to fundamental ethical questions. Although the essays almost invariably exhibit some sort of positive concern for our planet, we have sought to focus on controversy and the questioning of fundamental assumptions about the relationship of humans to the rest of the natural world.

At times the essays explore specific policy issues—should we eliminate factory farming, for example—but more typically they focus on the ethical questions that underlie the policy decisions: Do nonhuman animals have moral standing? Do plants have interests? How about whole ecosystems? Does this generation have duties to future generations of people? These questions are not usually addressed in texts on economics or sociology or ecology, but they are the ones that texts in philosophy must address.

Some of the key topics are:

Moral relations with nonhumans

Biocentric views about intrinsic value

Cultural diversity and moral relativism

Ethical grounds for decision making

The moral standing of individuals and ecosystems

Animal liberation and environmental, holist views

The Deep Ecology Movement

Ecofeminism

Environmental racism/environmental justice

Population problems

Market solutions; efficiency

The value of land and landscape

Criticism of the values of developed countries

Ecological sustainability

Ethical implications of Darwin's thought

The good life in a sustainable society

We have sought to create a volume that:

Eases the reader into the material with useful previews

Is readable, with down-to-earth examples

Minimizes jargon

Is scientifically literate

Focuses on the evaluative assumptions behind environmental policy

Presents diverse views

Contains a judicious selection of important literature

What inspired our curious title? In an essay written in 1974 on valuing parts of the environment, author William Baxter claimed that penguins are important, if they are important at all, *only* because people like to watch them walk about on icy rocks. If that capacity to satisfy human desires were the only criterion for the valuing of nonhuman organisms, then perhaps there is no good reason to value living beings that do not immediately serve people. Taking such a view, it might be better

to replace real living trees with plastic ones in some places, such as along the freeway system in Los Angeles. Our title, then is a reminder of some of the fundamental issues of environmental ethics.

Answering the questions we confront in environmental ethics is both an intellectually intriguing and a practically compelling task. We can choose to abuse the earth and its resources, but we cannot choose to abuse the earth and then move elsewhere. When it comes to certain environmental choices, we all live downwind and downstream.

The second edition of *People, Penguins, and Plastic Trees* is the offspring of the first edition (1986), but so is another volume we have edited, *The Environmental Ethics and Policy Book* (1994). Many people will be interested in how the two volumes differ and how they are similar. The latter book, EEPB, in general is a larger, more comprehensive volume. It contains an extensive collection of essays on matters of environmental policy, namely:

Population problems

Pressure on resources

Justice across generations

Property rights and "takings" issues

Preservation of biodiversity

The concept of species

Forests and wilderness

Environmental racism (or justice)

Trash and pollution

Ozone depletion

Global warming

Environmental activism

The volume also contains essays of a theoretical nature about constructing an environmental ethic; they are, in fact, more inclusive than those in the new edition of *Penguins* (PPPT). The "Introduction to Ethical Theory" in EEPB is more thorough than the comparable materials in PPPT. In addition, EEPB contains a section entitled "Western Religion and Environmental Attitudes" and there is no comparable section in PPPT. EEPB also has more short editorial pieces entitled "Sidelights." In part, then, PPPT is somewhat more modest in scope, although similar in style, aim, and in its mode of ordering the materials.

Any good book in environmental ethics must include certain influential pieces and treat certain topics. This accounts for significant overlap in the two volumes. When feasible we have sought to make available new material in PPPT on certain topics that also appear in EEPB. Many readers and instructors will like the presence of new material in PPPT (and not in EEPB) on

Cultural diversity and moral relativism

The moral implications of Darwinism

The relation of animal rights and environmental ethics

Hunting

Whether ecosystems are purposive

Whether all living organisms have interests

Whether such interests are morally relevant

Attitudes toward land

Ecologically responsible personal choices

Other topics (ecological sustainability, environmental racism, etc.) may be noted in the table of contents. In brief we wanted to make this second edition a slightly leaner, more flexible volume than EEPB. This result will be useful to those who want a volume lower in absolute cost, and a volume more compatible with the use of other texts in a university course—since, after all, there are interesting and important volumes (usually philosophical) on the topics of animal rights, future generations, the preservation of species, environmental activism and so on, as well as many fine scientifically-oriented treatises. Prefer-

ences about what topics are most urgent, most interesting, or the most teachable in a certain course will vary. Some will have compelling reasons to use the one, some the other. *Chacun a son gout.*

For their help in creating this edition, we would like to thank those who did pre-revision reviews of the text: Chris Cuomo, University of Cincinnati; Richard Haynes, University of Florida; Kathie Jenni, University of Redlands; Robert Matthews, Rutgers University; Richard Sherlock, Utah State University; Charles Taliaferro, St. Olaf College; William Vitek, Clarkson University. We would also like to thank Traciel Reid, Anthony Weston, and Jacqueline Ariail for helping us discover or locate relevant materials. We especially want to thank Beth Timson for all-around advice from a landscape architect. Thanks also to Christine Cuomo, Victoria Davion, Claudia Card, and Gary Varner for their comments on proposed inclusions. Ann Rives, administrative secretary to our department, worked on this edition as well as the first. We continue to be in her debt for hours of typing, and, since we lack a *deus ex machina,* her crisis management. At Wadsworth, we want to acknowledge our Philosophy Editor, Tammy Goldfeld, for her enthusiasm for the project. We also want to thank our prior Philosophy Editor, Ken King, for his continued interest. In addition, we are grateful to Robert Kauser, Permissions Editor at Wadsworth, for his splendid help and good humor.

Finally, we add that we welcome suggestions or comments from instructors or students who use *Penguins* in college and university classes.[1]

1. Christine Pierce (E-mail: phil_rel@ncsu.edu)
Donald VanDeVeer (E-mail: don_vandeveer@ncsu.edu)
Department of Philosophy and Religion
North Carolina State University, Box 8103
Raleigh, NC 27695–8103
FAX 919–515–7856

GENERAL INTRODUCTION

1. THE ELUSIVE BROADER VIEW

Our lives overflow with familiar concerns: getting the car fixed, making a dental appointment, applying for another job, fighting the traffic ticket, paying the bills, or taking an aerobics class. Given such personal preoccupations, it is not easy to attend to more global issues. It is difficult to set aside temporarily one's personal aims and consider one's position as one of almost 6 billion members of *Homo sapiens* living in one very recent moment in the history of this planet.

To smooth the path to taking a broader view, recall that the earth is about 4.5 billion years old, that life on earth is estimated to have begun about 4 billion years ago, and that *Homo sapiens* appeared 250,000 or so years ago.[1] Historical records date back only about 5,000 years. In terms of our understanding of matters now taken for granted, it has been only in the last four centuries that we have known that the earth is not flat, about three centuries that we have known of the circulation of the blood, a little over one century that we have known of evolution, and about a quarter of a century since we began to understand nuclear fission and fusion and the biochemical dynamics of the genetic basis of life. In the span of human history, then, it is only in a most recent "moment" that we members of *Homo sapiens* have learned how to tinker, in profound ways, with the course of life on earth—by the employment, especially, of nuclear power and genetic engineering. A few members among the almost six billion members of our species, itself one among millions of species, now are capable of radically altering the fate of all species, and indeed the larger environment.

Against our concerns about the aerobics class, the dental appointment, or the traffic ticket, these global matters deserve attention and critical reflection—even though we view ourselves as comparatively more able to influence closer-to-home events and thus let others contemplate and consciously influence our larger environment and the future of life. However, it is not as if anyone could comply with the request, "Stop the world; I want to get off." What happens to our lives, our children's lives, the lives of others, and our planet depends on what we do. As a case in point, and ironically after an eight-year presidency in the United States in the 1980s during which the president did not officially voice the word "AIDS," it is predicted that 20 to 40 million people will die from the condition by the year 2000.

What we are doing and what we collectively will do depends in large part on what we believe about the way things are, will be, or can be and (importantly) what is good, what is right, or what it is permissible to do. Hence, if we are to think clearly about these earthly matters, we need the best scientific knowledge obtainable. We also need to be clear conceptually; that is, we need to know what we mean when we use terms such as *environment, nature, life, pollution, waste, trash, future generations, natural resources, wilderness, cost, benefit,* and *species*. Further, we need a rationally defensible ethical theory or viewpoint, for without one we can only understand what is, was, or will be and not have any rational basis for deciding how we ought, or ought not, treat others or our larger environment. We need, in short, a defensible environmental ethic. Whether it will be one that can be fashioned on the basis of established ethical

1

principles, or a more radical one requiring wholesale rejection of much traditional ethical theorizing, is itself a question of current controversy—a point evident in many of the articles in this volume. What is less controversial is that given the comparatively new scientific understanding of our environment, our new capacity to alter radically the environment (including the evolution of our own species) is more pressing than it has been since human life began. Given the risks and opportunities inherent in having such capacities, the need for a coherent, comprehensive, rationally persuasive environmental ethic is imperative.

The growing interest in ecologically sensitive ethics, thus, is propelled by urgent questions and problems of both a theoretical and an eminently practical nature. As much as we might prefer simple answers, and as much as our educational institutions tend to reward students for short and simple correct answers, our questions are diverse and complex. Simple answers are suspect. At the very least we must reassess traditional answers; indeed, we should go further and scrutinize critically whether we have been asking the right questions. Let us begin to sort out some fundamental issues in order to develop a general overview of the core of environmental ethics and perhaps to unearth matters too little noticed or even new issues on which this volume only touches. First, let us consider some matters concerning science.

2. SCIENCE AND ENVIRONMENTAL ETHICS

To what extent can scientific information or theory help us think about the environment? Does it help? Is it sufficient? Is it necessary? Does science ever hinder clear thinking about environmental issues? We shall comment briefly on some of these matters. We shall not explore just what makes a theory a scientific theory, but suffice it to say that the central province of science is the investigation of empirical claims, claims that we characterize here as any claims about how the universe, or some part of it is, was, or will be—claims that are not logically true or logically false.[2] To say any of the following is to make an empirical claim:

1. Mike Tyson is a strong man.
2. The University of Redlands is in California.
3. Methane is a "greenhouse gas."
4. Dinosaurs descended from birds.
5. An inch of topsoil takes hundreds of years to form.
6. Brass is made up of copper and tin.
7. The average height of the oceans will rise over six feet by the year 2100.
8. "Brains" beer is sold in Cardiff, Wales.
9. Men have more teeth than women.

Some of these claims are false; so we have *not*, please note, defined an "empirical claim" as a subclass of true claims. Further, not all of these claims are of the sort appropriate for scientific inquiry—partly because no special techniques are required to determine the truth or falsity of some of them, e.g., (8) as opposed to (3) or (6).

The primary concern of science, then, is with a subset of empirical claims—generally, with those whose truth or falsity is not obvious (but sometimes we need, of course, rigorously to test the "obvious") and for which special modes of inquiry are required. Aristotle apparently believed (9), although it is false, in spite of his thorough empiricism at other tasks; e.g., he drew a diagram of the insides of a frog that was so accurate that copies of it were used at Harvard University until the turn of the last century.

In England, at Oxford University, there is a doorway marked (in Latin) "school of natural philosophy." This building houses books for the sciences, however, and not what we today call "philosophy" in the academic world. The explanation for this is that until about the eighteenth century, only two basic modes of intellectual inquiry were recognized; roughly, philosophical on the one hand and religious on the other. In the medieval period, it was held by many that faith and/or divine revelation was one mode of obtaining knowledge and the other was philosophy. Philosophy so understood encompassed, then, logic, mathematics, and what today we call "the sciences." Thus in 1687, Sir Isaac Newton, one of the greatest physicists ("physics" is from *phusis*—transliterated Greek—which meant "nature"), entitled his work *Mathematical Principles of Natural Philosophy*. Note also that a person receiving a Ph.D. in chemistry today receives a "doctor of philosophy" degree. What today we call the sciences or the natural sciences was for centuries regarded as a kind of philosophical inquiry, "philosophical inquiry" thus carrying a meaning rather like "rational, secular inquiry" of various sorts. Indeed, the term "science" is derived from a Latin term that meant "knowledge." It seems, however, that we know much that is not based on science, e.g., that one editor has a mother whose name is "Evelyn," and much that we could not in any obvious sense "prove," e.g., that one editor dreamt about a relative the month of this writing. There is therefore good reason not to equate knowledge with science. And as we have characterized the central concerns of science here, paradigm devices of rational inquiry—namely, the principles of symbolic logic and mathematics—are not themselves science although they may function as crucial tools of science. Nevertheless, among the claims that seem most deserving of belief by rational persons are well-established scientific claims. Why that is the case and what constitutes the proper way of distinguishing real from pseudo-science are important matters in the philosophy of science and epistemology and far beyond our purview here. The ideal is not for us all to be scientists but to be

rational persons and to believe only what is worthy of belief. This latter category is not to be identified with what is established by science, but includes it as a subpart.

For reasons that will become increasingly evident, no environmental ethic can be respectable unless it is compatible with and embodies the best scientific understanding of the world, especially the deliverances of modern biology, ecology, and genetics. Crucial empirical assumptions enter as premises in moral arguments about what we ought to do, especially at the level of deriving rather specific conclusions about policy. For example, the reasoning in defense of widespread use of asbestos back in the 1940s no doubt assumed, either tacitly or explicitly, that asbestos particles posed no health hazard. This empirical assumption turned out to be false, and thus the associated argument for using asbestos was faulty. Better scientific data at the time might have helped authorities avoid accepting such reasoning and avoided the tragedies to which such a policy has led—namely, widespread lung cancer decades later in those who were exposed to such particles.

A second example of the importance of science in environmental thought is this: One cannot thoroughly investigate the relation of human beings to the rest of the living world without contemplating Darwin's theory of evolution, a theory accepted by virtually all modern biologists in its basic outlines. The theory entails that we humans are not unique in all the world, and that we, like the other animals on this planet, evolved from simpler organisms over an extremely long period of time. A recent estimate of the history of life on the planet is about 4 billion years, with the first human-like beings (hominids) coming to exist only a few million years ago. One cannot arrive at a considered perspective about the nature of our species, its relation to other living creatures, a reasonable conception of our origins, and where we are headed without some acquaintance with, for starters, modern biology—not to mention paleontology, geology, meteorology, ecology, and so on. Thus, in a very fundamental way, acquaintance with modern science will, and should, affect powerfully and comprehensively one's attitudes toward living things, our species, the earth, and our understanding of its processes, its thresholds, and its limits.

We note a difficulty here. In the eighteenth century David Hume, a famous Scottish philosopher, observed in the writings of many whom he studied that they went on for a time making claims about the nature of the world, the existence of God, what humans are like, etc.—i.e., claims about what *is, was,* or *will be* the case (what we call empirical claims) but then went on overtly, or more quietly and indirectly, to draw conclusions about what is right or wrong or about what people ought or ought not to do. This surprised Hume and he demanded that the authors explain and try to justify this step from "is" to "ought." It is most tempting to think that Hume is correct; surely one cannot rightly infer that rape is right solely from the fact that it has occurred, that it does occur, or that it will occur. There is some philosophical dispute about this matter, which we shall bypass, but if Hume is correct and if all or virtually all scientific claims are empirical ones, then nothing validly follows from science, so conceived, about what anyone, any corporation, or any government ought or ought not to do; nothing about what is good or bad, or right or wrong.[3]

If so, science as such cannot provide us with premises from which it logically follows that we ought to pollute less (or more), that we should be concerned about global warming, that we ought to increase it (or minimize it), that we ought to promote biodiversity or that we ought to minimize it, and so on. What are needed, so it seems, are normative or moral principles as well as empirical assumptions. Traditional ethical theorizing has aimed at ascertaining which of a number of competing moral principles are the most reasonable and which should therefore guide us in our moral decision making. If Hume is correct, science cannot provide us with an answer to the question of which are the justified principles of morality, and the assumptions (or empirical conclusions of) science do not give us any normative guidance without being supplemented by moral principles. All of this points to the conclusion that an adequate environmental ethic is going to require our best efforts at ascertaining the most reasonable scientific understanding of the world *and* our best efforts at ascertaining which principles of morality deserve our allegiance.

On reflection, not all moral principles are equally plausible. For example, consider (a) everyone should maximize the happiness of the editors' families (thus send your donations immediately), (b) everyone should maximize the happiness of all human beings, and (c) everyone should maximize the happiness of all sentient creatures. Hardly anyone seems to be tempted by (a), alas, and it is, we confess, arbitrary—in some contrast to (b) or (c). Especially in the last few decades, (b)—one familiar version of the principle of utility—has come in for severe criticism, partly from defenders of (c), which is actually a more inclusive version of the principle of utility. As this volume makes clear, there are serious objections to (c) as well, and serious intellectual work is required in order to assess the diverse arguments that can be and have been marshaled over the centuries in favor of and against, the more plausible, alluring principles of morality (and associated ethical theories)— that is, those that have survived the initial rounds of fire aimed at them by an unendangered, plentiful species: the critics.

Can one be thoroughly scientific and also a person of passionate commitment on say, environmental matters? Can one *not* be value-neutral and be totally committed to scientific research? Let us consider what appear to be two different matters: the relation of moral values to commitment to science and the relation of passion to scientific commitment. There are complexities here, but it is odd that some scientists seem to feel a bit of embarrassment, if not guilt, about subscribing to moral principles, "having values," or something other than being "value-neutral." Some people, indeed, seem to equate having values with being biased. Surely this assumption needs defense. Generally, scientists value discovery of truth and value knowledge and techniques for uncovering such; one would think that having such values would foster the aims of science, but if to have values is to be biased and if all biases thwart the aims of science, then scientists ought not to value truth or knowledge. This result ought to give one pause. Further, it seems that there is also widespread reasonable agreement that the ordinary killing of innocent persons, rape, and recreational torture are morally wrong; to so believe is *not* to be morally neutral on certain issues. Is the possession of such beliefs, or the espousal of them publicly, something that scientists, or anyone else, ought to be embarrassed about? On reflection, it seems that one ought to be embarrassed *not* to oppose the activities in question. Is it not the duty of any decent citizen to do so? Curiously, those who say, or hint, that reputable scientists ought not to take normative positions publicly (e.g., about loss of biodiversity, about global warming, about loss of wetlands, about pesticide usage, etc.) are, in so saying, taking a normative position ("expressing a moral value"), the very sort of thing they condemn, mildly or strongly. That one should be cautious in public pronouncements is reasonable, but that, of course, is not the issue.

Another possible reason for the temptation to be uncomfortable about the commitment to a moral or normative position is that in many well-known cases those with such commitments are not only passionate about them but attempt to shove them down others'

throats. So one may be wary of the passions and the passionate, e.g., the anti-abortion activist who murders the physician who carries out abortions, the member of the Irish Republican Army who places a bomb in a London underground stop, the followers of Columbus who were willing to convert or enslave the natives living in what has come to be called the Americas, and others who in the name of God (recall the Christian Crusades), civilization, communism (Stalin's activities devastated the lives of millions), the Aryan "race," or some other ideology (racism, sexism, etc.) have laid waste to the lives of vast numbers of innocent people. Arguably, the remedy for intolerable expressions of passion is not being calm, cool, or unconcerned, but rather to be passionate about the right things in the right way (the right way may require not acting or deciding on certain matters in the heat of passion, when impatient, and so on). Is it not desirable that those who are committed to discovering the truth are passionately dedicated to doing so? Passion can express itself in discipline and not just impulse. However, is it not a good thing that the courageous father quickly (impulsively?) runs into the flaming house to save his three-year-old daughter from being burned to death? That he values her life as well as his own? Is it not a good thing that a stranger is outraged and intervenes to stop the senseless beating of an 85-year-old man? Passion as such can be a fearful thing. However, sometimes its absence is a frightful thing (e.g., indifference toward the plight of the old man). Further, there seems to be no necessary connection between being passionate and being committed to certain moral principles. After all, one may be passionate about all sorts of matters that have little to do with moral values, e.g., playing video games, surfing, line-dancing, guitar playing, planting old roses, roller-blading, or rock climbing. In addition, one may be committed to certain moral principles or judgments without having any strong feelings or emotions about the matter, e.g., that homeless people deserve decent treatment, that the Welsh language be preserved, that more fetal tissue be made available to treat victims of Parkinson's disease.

Arguably, our passions can serve the aims of reason. What our aims ought to be individually or collectively is something we can reason about. Indeed what our aims ought to be with respect to how we think and act regarding our environment is the central focus of this volume. If we can discern the right values to have, we can try to align our daily lives and our habits accordingly. No doubt doing so will involve the usual struggle against our own contrary whims, our tendency to deceive ourselves, to do the easiest thing, or the most self-interested (short-term?) thing. These phenomena should be familiar to anyone who has tried to diet, to train rigorously for a sport, or perhaps to master various complex skills. It is not entirely obvious how we ought to live, and many seemingly innocuous habits that we have are seriously called in question when, as a result of good science, we come to be more fully aware of the global, perhaps long-term, consequences of what we are doing. We are often disinclined to admit, and fervently fight off, acknowledgment of such facts since they suggest that much that we love to do is suspect: drenching our ecosystem-destroying lawns with pesticides, indulging our hamburger habit (see the rain forest connection discussed in the Rifkin selection in Section V), and continuing our love affairs with our cars (as we nourish the hope that one billion Chinese do not develop the same sentiments).

3. THE CONCEPT OF MORAL STANDING: THE ANTHROPOCENTRIC PARADIGM

Reasonable people of good will agree that ordinarily it is wrong to murder or rape. However, it is not so easy to arrive at agreement about certain other questions, for example, whether one nation legitimately can intervene in the affairs of another nation to secure human rights, whether civil disobedience is justifiable, whether we ought to legalize physician-assisted suicide, or whether it is all right to let radically defective infants die. In cases of controversy over the ethical matters about what we ought to do (or avoid doing) or what it is permissible to do, it is natural to think that we can, and ought to, engage in discussion, debate, negotiation, or compromise in order to arrive at some mutually satisfactory solution to problems we confront. However, one rather obvious fact often gets overlooked: Those who do or can engage in such discussion, inquiry, or negotiation constitute only a small subset of those who will be affected by the views or policies agreed on or adopted as a matter of public policy. To emphasize a point, virtually all such discussants, or readers of this sentence, are characterizable as (1) adult, (2) competent, (3) literate, and (4) members of *Homo sapiens*. It typically is thought, however, that the boundaries of legitimate moral concern extend beyond those who satisfy conditions (1) through (4). How far beyond is one absolutely fundamental question of ethics and, hence, environmental ethics.

To make this central point even more vivid, let us make up a label for those who are literate (L), adult (A), competent (C), and members of *Homo sapiens* (H): LACHites. Although LACHites are the formulators, discussants, and adjudicators of ethical disputes or questions, they constitute only a small fraction of the population of *Homo sapiens*. It is commonly thought that LACHites possess certain rights or are owed certain duties (for example, they normally ought not to be caused pain, destroyed, raised for food, driven from their native habitat, and so on). It also is widely held that not only LACHites but all members of our species, that is, all humans, possess certain rights or are owed certain duties. Hence, we rightly concern ourselves with the well-being of children or incompetent adults as well. Thus, it is even clearer that the set of moral decision makers (discussants, theory formulators, and so on) is only a subset of the set of those thought to be owed certain duties. As some would put the matter, the class of *moral agents* (those capable of moral reflection and decision) is included in, but not identical to, the class of *moral patients* (those owed certain duties).

In order to formulate one important question central to environmental ethics it is useful to introduce here the important related concept of *moral standing*. Prior to defining the concept, it is worth explaining another concept to which it is analogous, namely the (different) concept of *legal standing*. These are quasi-technical matters, and will call for a certain amount of attention and patience until their usefulness is apparent.

Some people in a country (for example, illegal aliens) may have no legal standing as citizens; that is, they may enjoy none (or few) of the constitutional protections guaranteed to those who occupy the status of being a citizen. For certain purposes, at least, they are not owed certain legal duties and they lack certain rights. To have the legal standing of being a citizen, then, is to be regarded as a being whose interests must be positively weighed in governmental decisions about what may be done.[4] The state is thought to have at least a presumptive duty not to disregard or subvert the basic interests (say, in continued life, bodily integrity, or freedom of movement) of one who possesses legal standing. That these interests must be given positive weight in the decision making of others is a point usually implicit in claims that such interest bearers have rights or that we owe them certain duties.

Now let us turn to the concept of moral standing. Quite apart from what laws prevail at a given moment, or the shape of a particular nation's constitution (if it has one), we commonly think that the interest or well-being of certain things (normally, certain organisms)

must be positively weighed in deciding what it is permissible to do. Thus, it morally is wrong to kill LACHites for food when one is hungry. Similarly, it seems wrong to cause premature death to young (human) children to achieve the same goal. (Compare a simple taxonomy of the world: division into Edibles and Inedibles.) However, most people have few reservations about causing premature death to young nonhuman "children" (offspring) for culinary purposes. The different outlooks presupposed in these latter differential judgments may be couched in terms of moral standing.[5] Let us stipulate, for any thing, X,

> X has moral standing if and only if the continued existence of X or its interests in well-being have positive moral weight.

Explicitly or implicitly, one traditional view, often called the "anthropocentric paradigm," answers the basic question

> *Which things* have moral standing?

by proposing that

> All and only human beings have moral standing.

This latter view, in effect, assumes that the most defensible answer to another question

> What is the appropriate *criterion of moral standing?*

is

> Membership in *Homo sapiens.*

This proposed criterion has several virtues, one of which is reasonable clarity. However, there are hard cases: Does it include human fetal progeny, brain-dead yet breathing humans, recently dead humans, anencephalic babies? Also worrisome is what the anthropocentric criterion excludes; based on such a criterion, the well-being of nonhuman animals, nonhuman members or parts of the ecosystem, or even intelligent, personable, alien beings does not, in itself, count. If by "natural resource" we mean anything not a human being (or part of one), such things are, in the view under consideration, mere resources to be used to pursue human goals.[6] This pervasive and traditional outlook has come under sharp attack in the last decade—as the following essays demonstrate.

4. ENVIRONMENTAL DUTIES ACCORDING TO THE ANTHROPOCENTRIC CRITERION

Shortly, we shall return to questions about the implications of the anthropocentric criterion of moral standing and competing criteria. First, it is useful to reflect on the relation of questions of duty to the issue of moral standing. If we could settle the issue of what is the appropriate criterion of moral standing, then, in principle, we could ascertain which things have moral standing (technically, the extension of "things with moral standing"). Suppose these difficult problems were resolved. What would be the implications of recognizing that something has moral standing, that is, that its continued existence or interests in well-being have positive moral weight? A plausible answer is that, if so, then we moral agents (those who have the freedom and rational capacities to be responsible for choices) have a presumptive duty not to terminate, or undermine the interests of, those entities with moral standing. If this is right, matters are clarified somewhat. However, most of the important questions are left to be tackled, for reasons that will become clearer as we proceed.

If something lacks moral standing, its well-being does not itself morally count (by definition of "moral standing"). However, if something has moral standing its well-being

does count and is the basis of a presumptive duty to that thing. Presumptive duties, however, can be overridden under certain circumstances. Consider the fact that most of us think that ordinary persons have moral standing. Thus, we have a presumptive duty not to kill them—roughly, a duty not to kill them in the absence of morally compelling reasons for doing so. Most people, however, think that some killings in self-defense, or in defense of other innocents against aggressors, is morally justifiable. The contrary view, that we have an "absolute" or "categorical" duty never to kill persons (those paradigmatic beings with moral standing), is held by few (not even those who talk of the sanctity or infinite value of life or all human life) and is hard to defend rationally. It appeals to what most people think is not a compelling consideration. The more basic point is this: Even with regard to those paradigms of beings with moral standing (persons), there well may be important issues to be decided, regarding legitimate treatment of such beings, even if we take it as settled that such beings have moral standing. The moral of this story is twofold:

1. Whether we have a presumptive duty to some entity depends on settling the dispute over whether it has moral standing

and

2. However, even if we settle (1), there are still perplexities about just what reasons would serve to justify our going ahead and thwarting the interests of a being that has moral standing.

To stress a point, a necessary but not sufficient condition of formulating an adequate ethical theory (and, hence, an adequate environmental ethic) is determining the most defensible criterion of moral standing. Beyond that, there are other recalcitrant and challenging issues. The issue of moral standing, however, is more basic. Further, it is the one most neglected, because historically very few writers have questioned the anthropocentric position. Like other deeply entrenched assumptions, it often has functioned like a pair of lenses through which we view and conceptualize the environment, and not as itself an object in view, as something to be subjected to philosophical scrutiny.

Let us reflect again on the implications of the anthropocentric viewpoint and the assumption that all and only humans have moral standing. In such a view, only the well-being or the lives of humans in themselves count. Does this mean that it is all right to burn cats for recreational purposes? Or poison one's privately owned lake? Or blow up a small planet to entertain those with astronomical interests? Or fertilize our gardens with the cadavers of those who died a natural death (and, perhaps, earlier voiced no objection)? Or if I knew I was the last person on earth, would it be all right for me to trigger (if I could) all the nuclear weapons already in place—when I was ready to say "farewell," of course? After all, according to one view, the well-being of all and only humans counts! The answer to these questions (except perhaps the last one), according to the anthropocentric view, surely is: not necessarily.

To explain why not, it is useful to consider the distinction between (a) duties *to* something and (b) duties *regarding* something. If you have moral standing, then I have a presumptive duty to you not to harm you. Suppose that nonliving things lack moral standing, as the anthropocentric paradigm implies. Then a car lacks moral standing. I cannot have duties *to* it since, we may suppose, one can have (direct) duties only to (or toward) entities with moral standing. Still, the anthropocentric view reasonably can account for why it is wrong for me to destroy someone's car without his or her consent. Were I to do so, it would damage the legitimate interests of a being with moral standing, namely, the owner. Hence, I have duties *regarding* the car (for example, not to destroy it) even though its well-being in itself does not count; that is, it lacks moral standing.

In principle, then, even though the anthropocentric criterion of moral standing excludes everything nonhuman (mountains, penguins, real or plastic trees, blue whales, and so on) from possessing such standing, humans have certain duties to protect or not harm the nonhuman "furniture of the earth." A key feature, of course, is that according to this view any such duties will obtain only if they are derivative from duties we have toward human beings. Some writers make this (or a similar) point in terms of *intrinsic* versus *extrinsic* value. Certain things, for example, human beings (their existence or their well-being), are thought to be valuable in themselves, or intrinsically valuable; hence, certain duties are owed to them. In contrast, other things are thought to lack intrinsic value, and if valuable at all are valuable only if valued by beings that are intrinsically valuable. It is worth emphasizing that according to such views duties regarding certain things, or value being assigned to them, are contingent on their being valued by, or being objects whose existence is in the legitimate interest of, beings with moral standing. That certain animals, for example, are extrinsically valuable (so are humans) is noncontroversial. That no duties are owed to animals, that they utterly lack intrinsic value, is *not* uncontroversial. Similar points might be made with regard to mountains, oceans, redwood trees, and marshes. Such claims are among the central sources of contention in environmental ethics.

5. COMPETING CRITERIA OF MORAL STANDING

So far we have focused on only one proposed criterion of moral standing, albeit a pervasive and influential one: membership in *Homo sapiens*. As several of the selections to follow make clear, other views have been proposed as more defensible. A list of some of the leading competing candidates would include these (or some combination):

1. Personhood
2. Potential personhood
3. Rationality
4. Linguistic capacity
5. Sentience
6. Being alive
7. Being an integral part of an ecosystem
8. Being an ecosystem

The different criteria, generally, will select out different sets of beings (or entities) as possessing moral standing; some of the criteria clearly are more inclusive than others. Those who, like Albert Schweitzer, trouble to maneuver a housefly outside rather than kill it may be committed to, or presuppose, criterion 6 as the proper criterion. Criterion 7 promises to be even more inclusive since, according to this view, even things not themselves alive (for example, a mountain) may be part of an ecosystem. Some persons, of course, are inclined toward vitalism, understood as asserting that all things are, in some sense, alive. Others would insist that at least the earth's surface and atmosphere—the biosphere— should be thought of as a dynamic, living system or even like a gigantic, somewhat diffuse, organism. In recent years, the atmospheric chemist James Lovelock in his book, *Gaia*, has argued that the earth's biosphere behaves like "a single organism, even a living creature." This view revives, after a fashion, the predominant ancient conception of the earth as a goddess, as alive and a fitting referent of the expression "sister" or "earth mother" used both by Plato and St. Francis of Assisi.

Some contemporary environmentalists think it no small matter, and indeed of the greatest consequence, that a shift occurred (about the time of Descartes and Newton, in the seventeenth and eighteenth centuries) from conceptualizing the earth as alive, and a bountiful partner, to the earth as an object, as a wound-up clock to be tinkered with instead of affectionately tended by humans. Evidently, the implications of accepting *being alive* as the criterion of moral standing will vary depending on what is viewed as being alive. In contrast, the famous late-eighteenth-, early-nineteenth-century English utilitarian, Jeremy Bentham, defended sentience as the criterion of moral standing. He remarked that:

> The day *may come*, when the rest of the animal creation may acquire those rights which never could have been withholden from them but by the hand of tyranny. The French have already discovered that the blackness of the skin is no reason why a human being should be abandoned without redress to the caprice of a tormentor. It may come one day to be recognized, that the number of the legs, the villosity of the skin, or the termination of the *os sacrum*, are reasons equally insufficient for abandoning a sensitive being to the same fate. What else is it that should trace the insuperable line? Is it the faculty of reason, or, perhaps, the faculty of discourse? But a full-grown horse or dog is beyond comparison a more rational, as well as a more conversable animal, than an infant of a day, or a week, or even a month, old. But suppose the case were otherwise, what would it avail? the question is not, Can they *reason?* nor, Can they *talk?* but, Can they *suffer?*[7]

Thus, in Bentham's view the central question is whether a being can suffer or experience satisfaction—is it *sentient* (criterion 5)—not whether it possesses the capacity to reason (criterion 3) or the capacity to use language (criterion 4). The famous seventeenth-century French philosopher and mathematician René Descartes seems to have taken the view that nonhuman animals lack linguistic capacity and, for this reason, that they lack a mental or psychological life. Thus, animals are not sentient.[8] If so, of course, they cannot be caused pain, appearances to the contrary. Hence, there could be no duty not to cause them pain. In Cartesian language, they are mere *automata;* in modern language, they are like programmed robots. Thus, if Descartes is right, even if sentience is the most defensible criterion of moral standing, nonhuman animals fail to have such standing. Some people may side with Descartes in his denial of sentience to (any) animals, but his view seems indefensible.

It is worth noting that the criterion of sentience not only would include certain animals (those that are sentient; contrary to Descartes, we assume many are) but also would exclude nonsentient humans. Which humans are not sentient? Possibly the irreversibly comatose, some anencephalic (brainless or partly brainless) babies, first trimester fetuses, perhaps later fetal stages as well. In any case, the boundary around sentient creatures certainly does not coincide with the boundary around members of *Homo sapiens.* At least three reasons may be offered for accepting sentience, as opposed to membership in our species, as the most defensible criterion: (1) Drawing the line around our own species is entirely arbitrary, much like what, in effect, the racist or sexist does in favoring his (or her) own race or gender; (2) it is implausible to think that some humans, for example, the irreversibly comatose, have moral standing; (3) if suffering is an evil that *ceteris paribus* ought to be prevented, it is arbitrary to regard only human suffering as an evil. These points are somewhat controversial; to note them here is merely to hint at some of the debates that are part of the current reassessment of our dealings with animals. They are discussed in later essays.

Criterion 4, linguistic capacity, finds few defenders today. Even if it were the most defensible criterion of moral standing, two implications are of interest. First, it would imply that certain very seriously retarded humans lack moral standing. That we have no presumptive duties to such beings is a view many find repugnant. Second, a plausible case can be made that some nonhuman primates (at least) satisfy this condition, given the success in teaching Ameslan (American Sign Language) to certain gorillas and chimpanzees. Whether certain animals possess linguistic competence is a matter of current dispute, mainly because of conceptual disagreement over what counts as "possessing a language."

Criterion 3 is somewhat obscure also. What counts as being rational? If rationality is construed in a nonstringent fashion, it is likely that many animals will satisfy the condition (though not rocks or rivers). If the concept of rationality is construed stringently, it may exclude all animals and it is likely to exclude certain humans as well—for example, the severely retarded. Those who accept the sentience criterion or the anthropocentric one will find this an intolerable implication. Some philosophers who regard rationality as the proper criterion (as do some who accept sentience) do not hesitate to conclude that some members of *Homo sapiens* lack moral standing. Others, finding this implication repugnant, seek to avoid it by defending other proposals. According to one view, if something is a member of a species whose paradigm members (for example, normal adult members) are rational, then any member is classifiable as a rational creature. Thus, although no one would say of a human zygote (fertilized egg) that it can reason, one philosopher, Alan Donagan, viewed it as a rational creature, and, hence, deserving of the respect owed to rational creatures.[9] According to this view, of course it is clear that *actual* possession of the (allegedly) crucial trait, rationality, is not judged necessary for moral standing.

Donagan's view should be contrasted with various "potentiality principles." Suppose, for example, one were to propose that actual-rationality-or-potential-rationality (either trait or both) is the proper criterion of moral standing. Using this criterion, normal persons, infants, and embryos (maybe zygotes, too) have moral standing.[10] Embryos would have it, of course, because of their potential to become actually rational. Using this criterion, however, an anencephalic infant is not potentially rational, and thus lacks moral standing. Using Donagan's criterion, in contrast, such an infant probably possesses moral standing. So, Donagan's extension of moral standing (though he does not employ this terminology) to marginal members of *Homo sapiens* diverges from potentiality principles.

It is tempting to think that, although neonates or fetuses lack rationality or certain other complex psychological characteristics, they (or most of them) directly are owed certain duties, and, hence, to presuppose that they possess moral standing. Further, it is tempting to think that such standing is possessed because of their prospect of developing into beings who uncontroversially are agreed to have standing—namely, normal persons. Some claim that although certain adult primates may exhibit "more personality" or have capacities for rational choice not possessed by neonatal humans, a reason for attributing moral standing to such humans but not to such primates is that the former have a unique potential that the latter do not. According to this line of thought, it may not be thought that membership in *Homo sapiens* as such is the proper criterion of moral standing; rather, it is actual or potential personhood (or rationality, according to a variant view). This criterion tends to include virtually all humans (though not the most severely retarded, anencephalic infants, or those in persistent vegetative states) but probably no animals—at least, if the facts support the claim that no animals are rational or none exhibit the requisites of personhood. Such a view contrasts with the anthropocentric criterion; it also allows the possibility that nonhumans (for example, alien creatures) possess moral standing.

In spite of the intuitive appeal of regarding a creature's potentiality as morally significant, some deny its relevance. We note one objection here. Suppose that a sufficient condition for possessing moral standing is that an entity, X, possess a certain trait (P)—that is, is a person. Let MS stand for "moral standing." Then the supposition is that

1. For any X, if X has P, X has MS.

Defenders of the importance of potential personhood seem to assume that

2. For any X, if X potentially has P, X has MS.

Opponents of (2) wonder why we should accept (2). Claim (2) does not follow from (1). Nor does (2) follow from the weaker claim (3):

3. For any X, if X potentially has P, X potentially has MS.

To be less formal, consider some related examples. Although an acorn potentially is an adult oak tree, and adult oak trees are large, acorns are not large. Normal adult persons, it is commonly held (at least in the Western world), have a right to decide with whom to associate (or at least with whom not to associate); human zygotes are (generally) potential normal adults, but they, arguably, lack the right in question. Even though we may agree that a certain morally important trait (for example, having certain rights) is possessed by an entity in virtue of its having certain actual properties (for example, being an adult person), why think that an entity that only has the potential for these properties has the relevant trait? To press the point, infants are potentially adults. Actual adults (normally) have a right to vote. Why attribute such a right to the infant? Its potential adulthood does not seem a good reason. In short, there is a puzzle as to why *potential* possession of relevant properties is morally significant as opposed to *actual* possession. Getting clear about these matters is no easy task; here we call attention only to one source of contention. Further inquiry is in order.

Those new to the recent philosophical literature may be puzzled by the implicit contrast, in the above remarks, between humans and persons. Often we use "person" and "human" interchangeably. If the terms are synonymous, it is contradictory to talk of nonhuman persons or of humans who are not persons. Some philosophers (for example, Michael Tooley and Mary Anne Warren) suggest, however, that there is a sensible distinction worth making between (1) what is a human being (a member of the biological species, *Homo sapiens*) and (2) what is a person (when "person" is not used loosely simply to refer to humans in the biological sense). Concerning the view in question, to put matters roughly, it is suggested that something is a person if and only if it (a) is sentient, (b) is aware of itself as an entity existing over time (or self-aware and not just an organism that scans its environment), and perhaps (c) is capable (minimally) of reasoned choice. We have sketched the seeming implications of employing personhood as the criterion of moral standing.

A standard objection to this view is that such a position expresses an arbitrary strategy of some philosophers aimed at including, or allowing them to include, only those beings that they otherwise favor in the category of entities with moral standing. If one can define "personhood" as one wishes, the definer indeed has a "do-it-yourself construction kit" for setting the boundaries of the moral community (those possessing moral standing). Several responses to this point deserve reflection. Although dominant and influential, the anthropocentric criterion (membership in *Homo sapiens*) hardly seems self-evident in the light of current criticisms; it also needs defense

against the charge of arbitrariness as would other natural boundaries such as race or sex. Further, one conception of personhood as something with personality and psychological character (having beliefs about oneself, one's environment, having preferences, and capable of choice) hardly seems a new and stipulative use of the word '*person.*' According to this at least intelligible conception of person, it seems correct to say that human fetuses and neonates are not persons.

Another perspective is worth noting here. One might think that the most stringent duties of all are directly owed to persons (in the psychological as opposed to the biological interpretation), and yet other entities, say the merely sentient ones, also possess moral standing. Thus, one might think that there is a sort of moral hierarchy of entities; for example, all and only sentient creatures have moral standing but among these with such standing, the well-being or lives of some morally count more heavily than others. Thus, although there is a presumption against destroying or causing pain to any sentient creature, in certain conflicts of interest between persons and the merely sentient it is all right (or obligatory) to sacrifice the interests of the latter. If a baboon heart can be transplanted to a human baby to save the latter's life (but the baboon will die) it is, according to this view, proper that the transplant be carried out. Even some staunch advocates of animal liberation or animal rights (for example, Peter Singer or Tom Regan) accept this judgment. Why it should be accepted is, however, a matter of considerable controversy. If one includes both persons and others (say, the merely sentient) within the moral community but views some as, in some sense, second-class citizens, serious perplexities arise. *Is there a nonarbitrary basis for such differentiations within the set of beings possessing moral standing?* If so, what is it? And if rationality, for example, is invoked, will that not suggest that we can, or ought to, discriminate (differentiate) among humans according to possession (or not) of rationality (or even degrees of rationality)? Further, does such a view open the door to, or commit one to, a policy of invidious discrimination? If not, why not?

Much criticism in the last decade has been aimed at those who assume that it is only individual beings, of some sort, who possess moral standing. Instead, it is urged that it is rather more complex entities that possess moral standing (see criterion 8) or possess it in addition to individuals. Typical suggestions are that species or ecosystems possess moral standing—and perhaps even harder-to-characterize natural processes. There is a question about whether we can reasonably speak of the interests of such entities and, if we cannot, then it is not obvious that we can regard them as having moral standing. These matters are discussed, and anti-individualist views are articulated, in Sections IIIA, IIIB, and IIID.

6. HUMAN ORGANISMS

Talk of environmental ethics, ecological ethics, and the preservation of nature calls to mind concerns about protection of individual animals or rare species; preserving clean air, wilderness areas, groves of redwood trees; avoiding the destruction of the wonders of nature such as the Grand Canyon; or the sense of loss when woods and pastures are transformed into concatenations of steel, concrete, plastic, and neon. It is a bit surprising, then, when the suggestion is made that there is a link between some of the basic issues in environmental ethics and certain perplexing issues often classified as matters of biomedical ethics, e.g., abortion. Given our prior discussion, however, the link is more evident. If we agree that normal postnatal human beings have moral standing, whether "all things human" do is a matter of some dispute. Several sorts

of entities deserve special consideration: (1) human fetuses, (2) anencephalic or radically defective infants, (3) irreversibly comatose humans, (4) newly dead human bodies. Let us use *NPH* to stand for these nonparadigmatic humans. Do any or all NPHs have moral standing? If so, what sorts of duties are directly owed to NPHs? Must we make equally stringent efforts to preserve or protect (or somehow "respect") such beings as is required in our dealings with normal humans?

If the familiar contrast between "man" and "nature" is to be understood as one between normal neonatal humans and things that cannot be so classified—that is, everything else—then NPHs are a part of nature. As noted, according to one view what is part of nature (other than paradigm humans) can be used as a natural resource—for example, for the benefit of (paradigm) humans. Reasoning rather like this may be behind the view that we ought to put to good use, for example, aborted fetuses, the recently dead (where all respiratory and circulatory functions have irreversibly ceased), or those in a persistent vegetative state (sometimes described as being brain-dead). There is a great need for organs for transplantation, a need for blood, for growth hormone, and so on. Hence, some regard the failure to utilize NPHs (or some subset) as a shameful waste, given the scarcity of resources valuable to paradigmatic humans. Disputes about these matters depend in part on ascertaining the appropriate criterion of moral standing. As we have noted, if by "natural resource" what is meant is, "what it is morally permissible to use to benefit those with moral standing," one theoretical (and practical) connection of environmental ethics and biomedical ethics is clear. If we are to reassess or query *What's so important about animals?* (or rare species, jungles, wilderness, mountains, or redwoods), it is not out of place to consider, "*What's so important about people?*" Or nonparadigmatic humans as well.

7. TRADITIONAL ETHICAL THEORIES

Natural Law Morality and Judeo-Christian Morality

Traditional morality is often associated with the view that there is a certain natural and morally defensible hierarchy of beings. There is, it is claimed, a natural order according to which inanimate objects are to serve animate ones; further, plants are here for the sake of animals, and animals for the sake of humans. It is, thus, right and proper for the "higher" to use the "lower," as the former see fit. Throughout history, this view has rarely been questioned. It is a view implicit in much of natural law theory dating back to Aristotle (384–322 B.C.), and in Thomas Aquinas's (1225–1274) theological revision of Aristotelianism. In theological versions, of course, the natural order is seen as part of the divine order and people are around for the sake of God and are to function within the constraints laid down by divine purposes. In *The Politics*, Aristotle says,

> [P]lants exist for the sake of animals. . . . All other animals exist for the sake of man, tame animals for the use he can make of them as well as for the food they provide; and as for wild animals, most though not all of these can be used for food and are useful in other ways; clothing and instruments can be made out of them. If then we are right in believing that nature makes nothing without some end in view, nothing to no purpose, it must be that nature has made all things specifically for the sake of man.[11]

Elsewhere in *The Politics*, Aristotle compares the function of women to that of animals in an effort to explain the low position of each in the hierarchy of being:

> As between male and female the former is by nature superior and ruler, the latter inferior and subject. . . . Wherever there is the same wide discrepancy between two sets of human beings as there is between mind and body or between man and beast, then the inferior of the two sets, those whose condition is such that their function is the use of their bodies and nothing better can be expected of them, those, I say, are slaves by nature.[12]

In short, those with less rationality exist to serve the needs, interests, or good of those with more. One's place in the hierarchy of being reflects Aristotle's judgment concerning one's rational abilities.

Aquinas, like Aristotle, makes it clear that to kill and otherwise use animals for human purposes is part of the natural order of things. In the *Summa Contra Gentiles*, Aquinas says,

> [W]e refute the error of those who claim that it is a sin for man to kill brute animals. For animals are ordered to man's use in the natural course of things, according to divine providence. Consequently, man uses them without any injustice, either by killing them or by employing them in any other way. For this reason, God said to Noah "As the green herbs, I have delivered all flesh to you" (Genesis 9:3).[13]

In Aquinas's view, animals have no independent moral standing or intrinsic goodness. Aquinas thought that we ought not to be cruel to animals, not because animals have an interest in not suffering, but because if such cruelty is allowed, humans may learn callousness and inflict it on their fellow humans:

> Man's affections may be either of reason or of sentiment. As regards the former, it is indifferent how one behaves towards animals, since God has given him dominion over all as it is written, "thou has subjected all things under his feet." It is in this sense that St. Paul says

that God has no care for oxen or other animals. . . . As to affection arising from sentiment, it is operative with regard to animals. . . . And if he is often moved in this way, he is more likely to have compassion for his fellow men. . . . Therefore, the Lord, in order to stir to compassion the Jewish people, naturally inclined to cruelty, wished to exercise them in pity even to animals by forbidding certain practices savouring of cruelty to them.[14]

According to Genesis, God has given human beings dominion over the earth: "Be fruitful and multiply, and replenish the earth, and subdue it; and have dominion over the fish of the sea, and over the fowl of the air, and over every living thing that moveth upon the earth."[15] There is, in the recent literature on animal liberation and environmental ethics, a dispute over the interpretation of the biblical notion of dominion. Some say that dominion permits humans to do whatever they want with animals, plants, rivers, and rocks. Others claim that dominion means *stewardship*. According to this view, God expects us to exercise some responsibility toward the earth. The earth belongs to God and we are commanded to take care of it and the creatures that dwell therein.

A stewardship interpretation may be committed to an acceptance of a traditional private property view. That is, humans should not ruthlessly exploit the earth because the earth is God's. If we ought to treat the earth in a responsible and virtuous way, it is not because the earth and its creatures have independent moral standing or intrinsic goodness, but because it is God's property. It is important to note that this result, the lack of independent moral standing on the part of any being except humans, seems to follow from either interpretation of dominion. This is not a surprising outcome. In the history of ethics, Aristotle especially, and Aquinas, exemplify what is called *virtue ethics*. In this tradition, for example, one ought not to be cruel to animals because cruelty is a vice, a bad character trait for an agent to possess. It was too early in the history of thought for the notion of a right—that is, for the idea that there is something about the being or entity toward whom (or which) we act that must be respected; they are not simply to be thought of as the beneficiaries of our good character.

Natural Rights Theory

a. The Kantian Argument. It is generally accepted that persons are the sorts of being that have rights. Immanuel Kant, a German philosopher (1724–1804), provided the original argument that explains what persons are and why they have rights. Kant explicates what a person is by distinguishing persons from things. Persons are rational, autonomous beings who are capable of formulating and pursuing different conceptions of the good. That is, persons have ends of their own; "things" or objects in the world do not. For example, suppose I walk into a classroom and decide to break up all the chairs in order to use them for firewood. If I do this, it does not matter to the chairs.[16] Now, there may be many reasons why I should not destroy the chairs. The next class may be planning to sit on them. Presumably, somebody owns the chairs and does not want me to destroy them. However, I cannot give as a reason for refraining from breaking the chairs that it matters to the chairs. It can even be said that it is in the interests of chairs not to be broken (or in the interests of lawnmowers not to be left out in the rain), but this is not the same as claiming that chairs or lawnmowers have interests of their own if we mean by this that chairs or lawnmowers care about how they are treated. Persons care about how they are treated; things do not. According to Kant, things can be used to suit the purposes of persons, but persons are not to be used as if they were mere things, as if they had no ends or purposes of their own. Persons have rights because of their unconditional worth as rational beings, whereas the worth of things is relative to the ends of persons.

Conceptually, it is difficult, if not impossible, to extend rights to environmental objects such as rocks and streams on a Kantian analysis of rights. This is so for the following reason: According to this analysis, rights are designed to protect persons from being treated as things. Rocks and streams are paradigm cases of things or objects; they are incapable of formulating ends. *Thing*, in Kant's writing, is a technical term. Something is a *thing* if it is incapable of autonomy in the Kantian sense, which entails self-rule; that is, being able to formulate and follow rational principles. Hence, inanimate objects do not have rights in Kant's view. Nonetheless, we may have duties regarding inanimate objects. These duties, Kant maintained, are indirect duties toward human beings, as the following quotation shows:

> Destructiveness is immoral: we ought not to destroy things which can still be put to some use. No man ought to mar the beauty of nature; for what he has no use for may still be of use to some one else. He need, of course, pay no heed to the thing itself, but he ought to consider his neighbor.[17]

Animals are also considered "things" in Kant's scheme. In his *Lectures on Ethics*, he referred to animals as "man's instruments."[18] Despite Kant's innovative work on the subject of rights, many traditional views persisted in his philosophy. The idea that animals, like any tool, exist for the use of human beings is one example. Likewise, we find in Kant the idea that our treatment of animals is solely a matter of what fosters personal virtue. For example, in the *Lectures*, he says, "A master who turns out his ass or his dog because the animal can no longer earn its keep manifests a small mind."[19]

Some human beings are not autonomous, yet Kant accorded them rights. Since Kant defined persons as rational, autonomous beings and not merely as human beings, he had the philosophical ammunition, so to speak, to challenge the anthropocentric paradigm. That is, a little reflection shows that a rational being in the Kantian sense and a human being—that is, a member of the species *Homo sapiens*—are not one and the same. Some human beings are not rational: fetuses, infants, the permanently comatose; some rational beings may not be human beings. For example, some animals may be autonomous in the Kantian sense, even though Kant denied it. Moreover, as mentioned earlier, there may be extraterrestrial beings, like the movie character E.T., who are rational beings but are not members of our species. Not only did Kant treat "human being" and "rational being" as interchangeable (thereby attributing rights to all and only human beings); he also attributed all the traditional rights (liberty, property, and so on) to rational beings. Although autonomy may be necessary for possession of a right to liberty, one might ask why a being must be autonomous in order to have a right not to be tortured? The failure to take seriously the relevant criteria for the various rights is considered a serious weakness in classical rights theories by many contemporary philosophers.

b. Taking Qualifications Seriously. The new literature on animal liberation and animal rights has caused many to rethink the claim that humans have rights solely because they are human. If we no longer rely on this kind of argument, then right-holders must possess some morally relevant features that may turn out to be shared by humans, animals, and environmental objects alike. The method employed is to identify the morally relevant qualifications for the possession of specific rights in order to determine what rights, if any, a being or entity has. With respect to some rights, a plausible case can be made that certain qualifications are morally relevant. To do this, however, one needs to know the specific function of each right. For example, the right not to be tortured protects the basic interest certain beings have in not suffering. The right to liberty protects the interest in directing one's life as one sees fit without unjustified interference from others. If a being is capable of suffering, but not capable of autonomy or self-rule, it can have a right not to be tortured, but not a right to liberty. On this model, the right to life must protect some specific interest or desire. One plausible candidate, suggested by Michael Tooley, is a desire to continue into the future, that is, to continue to live.[20]

The desire for continued existence presupposes the capacity to have a *concept of one's self as a continuing self*, as an entity existing over time. Of course, each right, according to the view we have been developing, presupposes some morally relevant capacity. The right not to be tortured presupposes a capacity for suffering. The right to liberty presupposes a capacity for autonomy. Once we figure out the morally relevant capacity for any given right, only those beings or entities that have the relevant capacity have the right. Thus, only sentient beings have a right not to be tortured, only autonomous beings have a right to liberty, and only self-conscious beings have a right to life. Most adult human beings can meet the self-awareness or self-consciousness requirement, as may some animals. However, as Tooley points out, some adult human beings do not have the requisite capacity, nor do human fetuses or newborn infants. It is worth noting that the self-consciousness requirement is a fairly sophisticated one. According to a view like Tooley's, mere consciousness or sentience may be sufficient for having a right not to be tortured, but not for having a right to life.

According to the above approach to rights, many animals fare rather well. Some animals most certainly have a right not to be tortured, and quite possibly a right to life. Environmental objects, such as rocks and plants, however, appear to fare rather badly.

For example, it would be absurd to claim that rocks have a right not to be tortured if they are incapable of suffering. If environmental objects are not sentient or conscious, it is hard to see how they would qualify for many basic rights. Peter Singer claims that plants have no conscious experiences, and thus I do nothing seriously wrong if I pull out weeds from my garden.[21] Of course, some people believe that plants have feelings, and some, like Christopher Stone, think that the entire planet is at some level conscious.

So, there are matters of disagreement about who or what has certain capacities, but the important point here is that the challenge to the anthropocentric paradigm has changed the character of the rights debate into one about capacities and the moral relevance of capacities. All living things, from Siberian tigers to kudzu to the AIDS virus, have a capacity to live. So we must inquire whether they have a morally significant interest in continued life even if they lack self-awareness. Such matters receive attention in IIIA and IIID especially.

c. Rights and Duties.   Rights can be correlative with duties. For example, correlated with my duty not to kill you is your right not to have me kill you. Some philosophers claim there can be duties toward another without that other's possessing correlative rights; others claim that a being can possess rights without others owing that being duties. Moreover, some philosophers claim that only those who can perform duties or act from a sense of duty can have rights; others claim that beings or entities (such as animals and trees) can have rights even if they cannot act from a sense of duty.

It is doubtful that animals can act from a sense of duty. Promise-keeping is a paradigm of a duty or obligation. Suppose I say to my cat as I leave in the morning, "I want you to meet me here at 5:00 P.M." Can I seriously expect her to make and keep such a promise?

Animals kill and eat one another (and occasionally us). As unfortunate as this may be, it does not seem to make sense to say that animals have *duties* not to do this.

In arguments about the correlativity of rights and duties, it is often pointed out that infants and retarded persons may be incapable of duties, yet they may have rights. If this is so, an animal's inability to perform duties does not imply that it cannot have rights. If the only requirement for rights is to be capable of having certain interests, then beings that have those interests have rights whether or not they can meet additional requirements for being able to perform duties. Rights and duties are two different things. Acting out of a sense of duty presupposes certain rational capacities, whereas possession of the right not to be tortured, for example, presupposes only a capacity to suffer.

If animals cannot perform duties, it is even less plausible to suggest that the "environment" (or "Nature") can be morally responsible for the disasters 'it' causes. Rivers overflow and damage property, forest fires destroy lives, sinkholes swallow up Porsches. The interest argument, which tenably can provide a basis for attributing rights (or, at least some rights) to animals, cannot do the same, with comparable ease, for certain environmental objects. Trees and streams not only lack the rational capacity required for duties, they appear to lack interests as well, at least in the sense of caring about how they are treated. If a wilderness is destroyed to make a home for Mickey Mouse, it does not consciously matter to the wilderness.

Utilitarianism

Utilitarian theory prescribes that what is right is to act so as to bring about the greatest possible balance of good consequences over bad consequences for all concerned. John Stuart Mill (1806–1873), a leading exponent of classical utilitarianism and follower of Jeremy Bentham (see below), interpreted "good" as "happiness" or "pleasure." According to Mill,

> "Utility" or "the greatest happiness principle" holds that actions are right in proportion as they tend to promote happiness; wrong as they tend to produce the reverse of happiness. By happiness is intended pleasure and the absence of pain, by unhappiness, pain and the privation of pleasure.[22]

a. Quantifying Goodness. Jeremy Bentham (1748–1832), as well as Mill, interpreted utility in a hedonistic manner. Hedonism, as technically understood in moral philosophy, is the view that pleasure and pleasure alone is intrinsically good. Typically, pain is viewed as an intrinsic evil. If the right goal is to increase the sum of pleasure in the world, its accomplishment will be facilitated if pleasures can be measured and compared with one another. Bentham devised a "pleasure measure" known as the *hedonic calculus* in order to help perform this task. To assist us in remembering how to measure the value of a pleasure or pain, Bentham wrote the following poem:

> *Intense, long, certain, speedy, fruitful, pure*
> Such marks in *pleasures* and in *pains* endure.
> Such pleasure seek, if *private* be thy end:
> If it be *public*, wide let them *extend*.
> Such *pains* avoid, whichever be thy view:
> If pains *must* come, let them *extend to few*.[23]

Mill was critical of the results of Bentham's method. According to Bentham's account, only *quantitative* differences between pleasures matter in establishing the value of activities. Bentham claimed that pushpin is as good as poetry if the amount of pleasure in each experience is equal. In more contemporary terms, he might have said that playing video games is as good as studying Shakespearean plays if the amounts of pleasure are equal. Mill introduced the idea of considering quality as well as quantity in determining the value of pleasures. In arguing that pleasures of the mind are superior to those of the body, Mill maintained that it is better to be Socrates dissatisfied than a pig satisfied.

In contemporary economic theory, utility is often interpreted as the satisfaction of individual preferences, or want-satisfaction, as it is sometimes called. Some of the theoretical difficulties with classical utilitarianism are reflected in contemporary versions of utilitarianism. One such problem is the following: One often does not know what is going to make people happy. (This is why Mill worried about pushpin and poetry.) What if a junky environment makes people happy? Worse yet, what if unjust social institutions bring about the greatest happiness? This is not an implausible suggestion. After all, it may be that unjust social institutions have persisted through the centuries because some people benefit from them. If the benefits are great enough for enough people, maximization of utility may require certain kinds of injustice.

Mark Sagoff vividly describes the possible implications of preference-based utilitarianism for environmental quality: "Schlock on every block, K-Mart lowers the price . . . crowds for every Ho Jo, Go Go, Disco, and peep show that can be built."[24] If the value of the environment depends on what our preferences are or what we want, what objection can be made to a world of pizza parlors, pinball arcades, and plastic trees if that is what people want? According to a utilitarian view, there isn't anything wrong with plastic trees. As Tom Regan puts it, "If a *reductio* is possible in assessing theories relating to our duties regarding the environment, hedonistic utilitarianism falls victim to this form of refutation."[25]

Reductio is short for *reductio ad absurdum*, a Latin phrase that means reducing to the absurd. Elementary logic textbooks classify the reductio as one way of refuting an argument. The idea is to show that your opponent's views entail claims (presumably unnoticed by him or her) that are absurd. The hope is that your opponent will be sufficiently embarrassed upon this discovery to give up his or her original views. Reductios, however, do not always persuade, for some people are willing to live with implications that others find absurd.

Preference-based utilitarianism may sanction plastic trees because only human preferences are taken into account. It has been suggested that animals and some natural objects have wants that must be counted along with human wants. That some animals have wants is uncontroversial; that trees and streams have wants is regarded by some as, at best, a metaphorical way of speaking. Christopher Stone maintains that "natural objects can communicate their wants (needs) to us, and in ways that are not terribly ambiguous."[26] He says, for example, the lawn tells me that it wants water and a smog-endangered stand of pines wants the smog stopped.[27] If animals and trees have wants, such wants must be determined by some method other than observing their consumer behavior, the standard way economists determine a certain range of wants or preferences among humans. A golden retriever does not go to Ben and Jerry's to purchase an ice cream cone. This problem, along with many others, is discussed in Part IV (which is devoted to an analysis of economic methodology and related ethical assumptions).

b. Utility and Moral Standing.   If maximizing happiness and minimizing pain is what morality is all about, it seems reasonable to suppose that sentience is the criterion of moral standing. Peter Singer, a contemporary utilitarian, follows Bentham in claiming that "If a being suffers, there can be no moral justification for refusing to take that suffering into consideration."[28] Nor is there any justification for the claim that human interests and consideration of suffering outweigh nonhuman interests and suffering simply because they are human. The only requirement for having an interest is the capacity for suffering and enjoyment. Thus, animals have interests, according to Singer's view; at the very least, they have an interest in not suffering.

In order to reach a solution to a moral problem, utilitarians advocate weighing the interests of all relevant parties in an attempt to discover which alternative will maximize happiness on balance. For example, cosmetics, shampoos, food colorings, and the like are tested on animals before they are introduced into the market. Singer reports that in Great Britain alone almost 100 new cosmetics and toiletries are produced every week.[29] When we weigh the interest that animals have in not suffering against the interest humans have in having more and more choices with respect to cosmetics and shampoos, it is hardly obvious that such testing maximizes utility. Utilitarian arguments do not guarantee (prior to calculating) that the interests of animals necessarily will win out over the interests of humans, or that human interests should prevail over those of animals. Although utilitarian theory insists that animal interests be taken into account, it does not necessarily support an outcome favorable to those interests. The outcome depends upon which course of action in fact contributes most to the general happiness.

c. Utility and Rights. The appeal to maximization of utility takes priority over all other considerations in the theory of utilitarianism. Mill once put the point this way: "It is proper to state that I forgo any advantage which could be derived to my argument from the idea of abstract right as a thing independent of utility. I regard utility as the ultimate appeal on all ethical questions."[30] Many utilitarians claim there are no moral rights. Bentham, for example, referred to rights as "nonsense on stilts." Mill does not rule out the possibility of rights. However, he makes it clear that if any rights exist, they are somehow to be derived from the principle of utility.[31] According to this view, rights cannot override considerations of the general happiness. Those who align themselves with the (competing) rights tradition are critical of the utilitarian ideal that the basic interests or rights of individuals can be sacrificed for the sake of the greatest good. As we have seen, it may be that certain kinds of injustice can be justified if doing so contributed more to the general happiness than not doing so. On the other hand, utilitarians confront rights theorists with cases that cast doubt on a tough-minded opposition to the sacrifice of individual rights. One such imaginative example, used by John D. Arras, is taken from the movie *Dr. Strangelove*.[32] The situation is this: A nuclear war can be prevented only if someone phones the president, but the person who can make the call does not have a dime. He sees a soft drink machine and frantically kicks it to get a dime, to make a call, to save the world. However, a clever utilitarian will point out to a rights theorist that the property rights of the soft drink company must be infringed in order to get the money to make a call and save the world. Hence, there seem to be some cases in which the greater good takes precedence over rights. However, another interpretation is that the property rights of the soft drink company must be infringed to protect the rights of others.

8. TWO FUNDAMENTAL QUESTIONS

To not lose sight of the ethical forest because we have looked at some trees, we emphasize that two questions stand out as absolutely basic. Any proposed solution to an environmental problem must take a stand on these questions, explicitly or otherwise. First, what sorts of things have moral standing? That is, what sorts of things are such that their continued existence or welfare is valuable in themselves? To answer this question one must defend a particular criterion of moral standing. If we can settle on an answer to the first basic question, then we need to determine what are acceptable principles to invoke to help decide what are permissible (or obligatory) trade-offs in the many cases in which the lives or welfare of some things that possess moral standing conflict with the lives or welfare of other entities possessing moral standing. Some environmental proposals or positions make no effort to grapple with these perplexities. Others address one but make little or no effort to respond to the other. Reasonably addressing these two issues, however, must be viewed as a benchmark of any plausible environmental ethic.

9. THE IMPORTANCE OF THEORY

Part of the solution to environmental disputes involves the acquisition of more empirical information; for example, discovering whether sulfur or nitrogen, or neither, plays the dominant role in the causation of *Waldsterben,* the destruction of forests in various industrial nations. However, part of the solution must be found in ascertaining the most rationally defensible moral ground for evaluating this or that environmental alternative. To decide which is the most plausible view, one starting point is to be familiar with, and comparatively assess, the different ethical theories. In the Western tradition, the major ethical theories are natural rights theory and utilitarianism and, perhaps, natural law theory. Furthermore, critical acquaintance with such theories is essential to deciding whether some quite nontraditional position must be formulated in order to arrive at an adequate environmental ethic. Some essays in this volume argue for, or presuppose, some traditional theory or a variation of one; others, especially in Section IIIA, insist that a radically new ethic is needed.

Whether we should heed these new voices and whether an adequate environmental ethic requires a wholesale rejection of more traditional principles are questions that demand a careful analysis of the arguments. Attempting to identify the contours of the right theory is no easy, or brief, task. Reflecting on the essays that follow will take us a few steps toward clarity and toward rational convictions about how we should deal with other lives on earth and, indeed, the planet itself. If, and only if, we know what to *believe* about such matters can we know how to *act*—in order to shape responsibly our private lives and public policies. The price of our not thinking about these matters—of a certain intellectual neglect or recklessness—collectively will affect the fate of the earth. We do well to avoid that popular all-American anti-intellectualism that naively doubts that abstract ideas have consequences. We do well not to be impressed by the mindless cynicism embodied in remarks about "environmentalist do-gooders," "tree-huggers," "Bambi-lovers," and so on. We need not buy into those counsels of despair that assume that analytic or theoretic inquiry is useless because the path to practical, political change commonly is strewn with further obstacles.

NOTES

1. See the essays on "Life" (volume 12) and "*Homo sapiens*" (volume 8) in the *Encyclopaedia Brittanica* (Chicago: The University of Chicago Press, 1981).

2. Some claims are said to be logically true or logically false because their structure and/or the meaning of the key terms alone allows us to determine their truth or falsity. For example, "some bachelors are married" is false, given the ordinary meanings speakers of English assign to the terms in such a sentence. Similarly "the judge is a female or is not" is true, given linguistic considerations alone. Similarly we know that "some red things are colored" is true without any observation of particular red things.

3. What shall we count as a scientific claim? Any claim uttered by a scientist? Hardly. Suppositions such as "knowledge is valuable," "we ought to freely share scientific data," "the future will be like the past," "nonscientific claims are not to be trusted," "our sensory perceptions are reliable"? A host of questions arise; consult your personal philosopher of science or epistemologist—but not the kind that advertise in newspapers.

4. Given the high moral tone of many exhortations to obey the law, one should recall the legal rights and duties that sometimes have prevailed: for example, that women could not vote, that slaves must be

returned to their masters in the United States at one time, that Jews in Nazi Germany had to wear arm bands, and gay people had to wear pink triangles.

5. The term "moral standing" is not used invariably in the same way in the literature. Sometimes "moral status," "possesses inherent value," and "being morally considerable" are used in an equivalent fashion, sometimes not. Readers beware!

6. Compare also the possible lack of clarity of "nature" in "man and nature" as well as the ambiguity of "man."

7. As cited in Tom Regan and Peter Singer, eds., *Animal Rights and Human Obligations* (Englewood Cliffs, NJ: Prentice-Hall, 1976), p. XXX.

8. On Descartes' actual position see the unconventional but tempting view of Peter Harrison, "Descartes on Animals," *The Philosophical Quarterly* 42, no. 167 (April 1992), pp. 219–27.

9. Alan Donagan, *The Theory of Morality* (Chicago: The University of Chicago Press, 1977), p. 83.

10. The term "maybe" is used because a zygote may split in the first week and become twins. But if one twin is normal and the other is anencephalic, should we say that the zygote was potentially rational or not? Or partially rational, or . . . ?

11. Aristotle, *The Politics*, tr. by T. A. Sinclair (Baltimore: Penguin Books, 1962), p. 40.

12. Aristotle, *The Politics*, pp. 33, 34.

13. Thomas Aquinas, *Summa Contra Gentiles*, Book III, Part II, 112, 12, tr. by Vernon J. Bourke (Notre Dame: University of Notre Dame Press, 1975), p. 119.

14. Thomas Aquinas, *Summa Theologica*, II, Part I, 102, 8, tr. by David Bourke and Arthur Littledale (New York: McGraw-Hill, 1969), p. 225.

15. Gen. 1:28.

16. Mary Anne Warren puts the point this way in "The Abortion Issue," *Health Care Ethics*, ed. Donald VanDeVeer and Tom Regan (Philadelphia: Temple University Press, 1986). See also Edward Johnson, "Treating the Dirt: Environmental Ethics and Moral Theory," *Earthbound: New Introductory Essays in Environmental Ethics*, ed. Tom Regan (New York: Random House, 1984), p. 347. Johnson is not talking about rights, but he raises the following issue: "But does morality require us to pursue a creature's good, if that creature does not *care* about its good?"

17. Kant, *Lectures on Ethics*, tr. by Louis Infield (Indianapolis: Hackett Publishing Company, 1979), p. 241.

18. Kant, *Lectures on Ethics*, p. 240.

19. Kant, *Lectures on Ethics*, p. 241.

20. Michael Tooley, "In Defense of Abortion and Infanticide," *The Problem of Abortion*, 2nd ed., ed. by Joel Feinherg (Belmont, CA: Wadsworth Publishing Company, 1984).

21. Peter Singer, *Practical Ethics* (Cambridge: Cambridge University Press, 1979), p. 92.

22. J. S. Mill, *Utilitarianism*, ed. by George Sher (Indianapolis: Hackett Publishing Company, 1979), p. 7.

23. Oliver Johnson, *Ethics*, 4th ed. (New York: Holt Rinehart and Winston, 1978), p. 259.

24. Mark Sagoff, "Do We Need a Land Use Ethic?" *Environmental Ethics* 3, (Winter 1981), p. 299.

25. Tom Regan, "The Nature and Possibility of an Environmental Ethic," *All That Dwell Therein: Essays on Animal Rights and Environmental Ethics* (Berkeley: University of California Press, 1982), p. 196. Some think that Martin Krieger's article, "What's Wrong With Plastic Trees," is a reductio of utilitarian ethics. See also Laurence Tribe, "Ways Not to Think About Plastic Trees: New Foundations for Environmental Law," *Yale Law Journal* 83, no. 7 (June 1974), pp. 1315–46; an excerpt is reprinted in the first edition of *People, Penguins, and Plastic Trees: Basic Issues in Environmental Ethics* (Belmont, CA: Wadsworth Publishing Co., 1986).

26. Christopher D. Stone. *Should Trees Have Standing? Toward Legal Rights for Natural Objects* (Los Altos: William Kaufmann, Inc., 1974), p. 24.

27. Ibid.

28. Peter Singer, *Practical Ethics* (Cambridge: Cambridge University Press, 1979), p. 50.

29. Peter Singer, *Animal Liberation: A New Ethics for Our Treatment of Animals* (New York: Random House, A New York Review Book, 1975), p. 52.

30. J. S. Mill, *On Liberty*, ed. by Elizabeth Rapaport (Indianapolis: Hackett Publishing Company, 1978), p. 10.

31. On this point, see L. W. Sumner, *The Moral Foundations of Rights* (Oxford: Clarendon Press of Oxford University, 1987). Sumner is a utilitarian.

32. John D. Arras, "The Right to Die on the Slippery Slope," *Social Theory and Practice* 8 (Fall 1982), pp. 320–21.

I

WHAT WE ARE DOING [▭▭▭▭▭▭]

"[T]he natural background rate of extinction during the past 600 million years . . . has been on the order of only one species every year or so. . . . Today the rate is surely hundreds of times higher, possibly thousands of times higher."[1] In his "Tropical Forests and Their Species: Going, Going . . . ?" which we reprint here, noted scientist Norman Myers explains in rich detail a mass extinction episode that we are witnessing now due to worldwide deforestation.

In this first section, two scientists, Norman Myers and Edward O. Wilson; and a journalist, Karl Grossman; deal with some of the most important environmental problems confronting us today: population growth, depletion of tropical rain forests, the extinction of vast numbers of species, climactic change, and pollution. Norman Myers asks the following crucial questions: What are the repercussions of deforestation and loss of species for the future of evolution? What is the relationship between tropical forests and climatic change? Biologist Edward O. Wilson provides us with vivid descriptions of what human beings are doing to the earth, as well as a basis for ranking the seriousness of various environmental problems. Karl Grossman addresses the question of how environmental burdens get distributed among different populations.

Most fundamentally, Edward O. Wilson argues that there really are formidable environmental problems, opposing those who deny this fact. Wilson sets out two opposing views, labeling one, *exemptionalism* and the other, *environmentalism:*

Exemptionalism holds that since humankind is transcendent in intelligence and spirit, so must our species have been

released from the iron laws of ecology that bind all other species. No matter how serious the problem, civilized human beings, by ingenuity, force of will and—who knows—divine inspiration, will find a solution.

Environmentalism . . . sees humanity as a biological species tightly dependent on the natural world. . . . At the heart of the environmentalist world view is the conviction that human physical and spiritual health depends on sustaining the planet in a relatively unaltered state. Earth is our home in the full, genetic sense where humanity and its ancestors existed for all the millions of years of their evolution. Natural ecosystems—forests, coral reefs, marine blue waters—maintain the world exactly as we would wish it to be maintained. When we debase the global environment and extinguish the variety of life, we are dismantling a support system that is too complex to understand, let alone replace, in the foreseeable future.[2]

One exemptionalist is the economist Julian Simon, who defends the view that the supply of natural resources is infinite. Given this view, it is intelligible that Simon holds that "almost equally beyond any doubt, however, an additional person is a boon."[3] After all, he says, each will pay taxes "and make efforts to beautify the environment."[4]

Were it true that resources are infinite, it would considerably lessen worries about our burgeoning population and the sustainability of current patterns of consumption. Were it true, the question of fair distribution or equity might loom as the one important moral issue. There is, admittedly, no doubt that we will continue to discover ways of substituting one material for another as one becomes scarce and costly; for example, the use of fiber optic cables in place of copper wire. The belief that this substitution will *always* occur without enormous cost to humans or others seems firmly anchored in wish fulfillment and is largely an article of faith. In contrast, some prospects—for example, for developing virtually unlimited supplies of energy—are supportable by good evidence. We need not generalize about all resources, and we need not succumb to the psychologically seductive voices that say, "Don't worry; be happy, and there will be a technological fix in due time."

Wilson takes the view that some resources are finite and increasing population puts a strain on these resources: "Because Earth is finite in many resources that determine the quality of life—including arable soil, nutrients, fresh water and space for natural ecosystems—doubling of consumption at constant time intervals can bring disaster with shocking suddenness."[5] Wilson notes, "In Nigeria, to cite one of our more fecund nations, the population is expected to double from its 1988 level to 216 million by the year 2010. If the same rate of growth were to continue to 2110 its population would exceed that of the entire present population of the world."[6] Yes, the math is correct.

Despite Wilson's acknowledgment of a serious population problem, he says that favorable demographic signs provide reason for optimism. He also cites as reason for optimism the United Nations Conference on Environment and Development, held in Rio de Janeiro in June, 1992, which " . . . helped move environmental issues closer to the political center stage."[7] All this may be well and good. However, there are also reasons to believe that the population problem is more complicated than Wilson's discussion of it suggests. Interestingly, Wilson fails to mention that the Earth Summit managed not to include any discussion of human population issues on its official agenda. From the outset, 77 developing countries wanted to focus on issues other than population increases, for obvious reasons. Without question, a major cause of pollution, the using up of "sources" (fresh water, clean air, a third of the world's forests, other fossil fuels, and so on) and the elimination of "sinks" (places to put waste), is the leap from 1 billion humans in 1850 to almost 6 billion today.

However, the heavy human hand on the nonhuman environment is also a function of the degree of resource consumption *per person*. In the United States and many other "first-world" or industrialized nations, the population is highly stable. It is not unusual for such industrialized nations to view with alarm the rate of population growth in certain less-industrialized nations. It is tempting to lay blame here and to conclude that the heaviest impact on the planet's environment is generated by the increased numbers of humans in such countries. It is not just the numbers that matter, but the *ecological impact per person*. The environmental impact of one American on the available sources and sinks is 50 times that of one citizen of Bangladesh.[8] The amount of carbon emitted into the environment by the activity of the average American is five times the global average.[9] The environmental impact of the average person in other developed countries such as Japan, France, or Canada is very large. Political crosscurrents related to the dual emphasis on population size (and rate of growth) and consumption per person led to an impasse at the Earth Summit. The final outcome of the negotiations in Brazil is described by one observer in this fashion:

> When, in the final negotiating session, the United States moved to delete all references to consumption in the North, the G-77 retaliated by deleting references to the urgency of slowing population growth. That opened the way for extremely effective lobbying by the Holy See. The fate of the population language was sealed, ironically, by representatives of women. Feminist health groups, along with some women's groups in developing

countries and representatives of minority women in the United States have long been antagonistic to population control because they believe it jeopardizes women's health, is disguised genocide or places blame on women. . . ."[10]

The expression "population control" is one, of course, of which we should be wary; it can be used to refer to coercive methods of a more or less extreme sort, ranging from Hitler's "population control" of the Jews and Gypsies, to the massacres of Croats by the Serbs, or to policies of mandatory abortion or mandatory pregnancy. In India in the 1970s, thousands of women and men were coercively sterilized.[11] The plight of women in many countries is that of day laborers for the family; they are uneducated and do not understand the nature and function of contraception or are not given access to contraceptive devices and information. Often, they are oppressed by men who disallow their comparatively powerless wives from learning about or using contraception. In many cultures, including our own, a great deal of shame and guilt has been induced over *talking* about, not to mention *using*, contraceptives; often, Roman Catholic leaders tell those who wish to do so that they are "closing themselves off from God," perhaps dooming themselves to eternal suffering as a result. Dissuading people from using contraceptives, or preventing access to them, is, of course, viewed as a moral victory by such "leaders."

In India, one-fourth of the women are so badly off that they die by the time that they are 15 years of age. The low status of those that survive makes it difficult for them to have a voice, to get an education, to gain some autonomy, and to exercise deliberate choice over their own reproductive capacities. In India, some families have to chose between spending money on their daughter's education and spending it on her dowry. If the husband's family believes the wife's dowry is too small, family members sometimes engage in the notorious practice of bride-burning, although it is illegal. Under such enormous pressures (and frequently taught by her mother to acquiesce to the wishes of her husband for the sake of a "peaceful" or "happy" marriage), such a woman lives as a passive, powerless, laboring baby producer—with little hope and with little control.

When many children die young, the parents often decide that it is necessary to have many children ("gifts of God"), since it is not certain that many will live. The ideology that male babies are more valuable than females affects the attitudes of men and women: mothers are often deeply troubled if they have produced only females. The overwhelming majority of abortions in India are of female babies, a form of what some have called "gendercide." Thus, a nasty mixture of poverty, entrenched patriarchal attitudes, ignorance, passivity, prejudice, shame, and institutionalized barriers (sometimes expressive of cultural and religious ideologies), is at the root of the population excess in many poor nations; population control, abstractly speaking, is desirable, but it must address these difficulties and do so in a just manner.[12]

Perhaps Wilson's major contribution in the article reprinted here is his answer, *as a biologist*, to the question of why ". . . exemptionalism fails definitively."[13] Although entrepreneurial genius or political agreements can solve some crises—such as restoring the ozone layer by eliminating CFCs (chlorofluorocarbons) used for refrigeration and some aerosol products—Wilson explains how a similar kind of manipulation does not apply to the natural ecosystems and the millions of species they contain.

Environmental threats such as pollution and our trash problem are among our less serious environmental problems, according to Wilson's classification. Nevertheless, some forms of pollution are very visible and compelling. In December, 1992, a 28-foot sperm whale beached itself on the North Carolina coast, starving because of garbage clogging its digestive system. "We found a couple of plastic bottles, a chunk of rubber the size of a football and a Styrofoam float—the ones as big as basketballs—with 30 feet of rope attached,"[14] said David Webster, a professor of marine biology at the University of North Carolina at Wilmington.

Although Wilson is concerned about overconsumption, he does not here consider the relationship between overconsumption and pollution. People who overconsume throw too much away. This, according to Paul Connett, constitutes our trash crisis.[15] One seemingly easy answer to the problem of full landfills is trash incinerators. Why bother with dreary recycling when we can just burn the trash? Here's the catch. "For every three tons of trash that is burned, one ton of ash is produced."[16] The ash, it turns out, is toxic—hazardous waste. As Connett says,

> It doesn't make economic or environmental sense to convert three tons of trash into one ton of toxic ash. Ash landfills are proving as difficult to site as raw-waste landfills. People don't want the ash in their backyard any more than they wanted the trash. Nor will future generations thank us for these acres of toxic ash. We have to question the ethics of leaving future generations with the problems of containing, guarding, and monitoring our permanent toxics for eternity.[17]

Acknowledging that no one wants the trash in their backyard, the topic of "environmental racism" turns our attention to where the trash often is going and has gone. There has been, says Benjamin F. Chavis, Jr., a "deliberate targeting of people of color communities for toxic waste facilities" and an "official sanctioning of the life-threatening presence of poisons and pollutants in our communities."[18] " . . . [M]inorities bear a greater burden from lead poisoning, airborne toxins and contaminated drinking water . . . ," says Deeohn Ferris, an attorney for the National Wildlife Federation. "The condition is called 'environmental racism.'"[19] One environmental researcher says, "Small dirty industries have a tendency to locate in minority communities for two reasons: One, cheap labor. And two, their relative lack of knowledge about environmental concerns."[20]

Several studies indicate a discriminatory pattern of pollution:

- In a study of blacks and whites making less than $15,000 a year, twice as many blacks had dangerous levels of lead in their bloodstreams, according to the Centers for Disease Control.

- A National Law Journal study [in 1992] of 1,177 Superfund waste dumps found that the EPA [Environmental Protection Agency] began cleanups 20 percent quicker in white neighborhoods than in black neighborhoods. The same study found that EPA penalties against polluters averaged $335,566 in white neighborhoods compared to $55,318 in black areas.

- An estimated 300,000 farm workers— 90 percent of whom are minorities— suffer each year from pesticide-related illnesses, according to the EPA.[21]

Karl Grossman, in his essay, "Environmental Racism," analyzes the pattern of placing hazardous facilities in black and Native American communities in the U.S.; he also makes the connection between this phenomenon and the dumping of hazardous wastes in less industrialized countries.[22] One striking example of this can be found in an internal memo written by Lawrence Summers, chief economist of the World Bank. Leaked to the press, the December 12, 1991 memo begins, "Just between you and me, shouldn't the World Bank be encouraging *more* migration of the dirty industries to the LDCs [less developed countries]?"[23]

Environmental problems are many and it is difficult to say which ones matter the most. Edward O. Wilson and Norman Myers put biodiversity at the top of the list. Deep ecologists, as we shall see, give precedence to the preservation of wildlife and of open spaces. Urban advocates, such as Karl Grossman, focus on " . . . incinerators, . . . factories polluting the air, devastating occupational exposure."[24] What matters most, however, is that we acquire an understanding of the range and depth of human activities that are destructive to the earth and its ecosystems so that our construction of an environmental ethic is empirically and scientifically informed.

NOTES

1. Norman Myers, "Tropical Forests and Their Species: Going, Going . . . ?" in Donald VanDeVeer and Christine Pierce, *The Environmental Ethics and Policy Book: Philosophy, Ecology, Economics*, Belmont, CA: Wadsworth Publishing Company, 1994, p. 532.

2. Edward O. Wilson, "Is Humanity Suicidal?" *The New York Times Magazine*, May 30, 1993, p. 27.

3. Julian Simon, *The Ultimate Resource*, Princeton: Princeton University Press, 1981, p. 4.

4. Ibid.

5. Wilson, "Is Humanity Suicidal?" pp. 26–27.

6. Ibid., p. 26.

7. Ibid., p. 27.

8. Paul and Anne Ehrlich, *Healing the Planet*, Reading, MA: Addison-Wesley Publishing, 1991, p. 8.

9. Jonathan Weiner, *The Next One Hundred Years*, New York: Bantam Books, 1991, p. 41.

10. Jessica Matthews, "Rift Is Hampering Real Work on Population Issue," *The News and Observer*, Raleigh, NC, April 15, 1990, p. 13A.

11. Some were offered inducements, but the promised benefits were often not delivered.

12. A powerful film called *The People Bomb*, one which has influenced this paragraph, is available from the television network CNN.

13. Wilson, "Is Humanity Suicidal?" p. 29.

14. "Whale Starved Because Garbage Clogged Stomach," *The News and Observer*, Raleigh, NC, December 13, 1992, p. 10C.

15. Paul Connett, "The Disposable Society," in *Ecology, Economics, Ethics: The Broken Circle*, ed. F. Herbert Bormann and Stephen R. Kellert, New Haven: Yale University Press, 1991.

16. Ibid., p. 104.

17. Ibid., p. 105.

18. Benjamin F. Chavis, Jr., quoted in William Rees, "Black and Green," *The New Republic*, March 2, 1991, p. 15.

19. "Some See Racism in Waste Decisions," *The News and Observer*, Raleigh, NC, November 12, 1992, p. 1A.

20. Ibid., p. 12A.

21. Ibid.

22. Karl Grossman, "Environmental Racism," *The Crisis* 98, no. 4 (April 1991), p. 17.

23. "Let Them Eat Pollution," *The Economist*, February 8, 1992, p. 66.

24. Peggy Shepard, quoted in Karl Grossman, "Environmental Racism," p. 31.

Tropical Forests and Their Species: Going, Going . . . ?

Norman Myers

There is strong evidence that we are into the opening stages of an extinction spasm. That is, we are witnessing a mass extinction episode, in the sense of a sudden and pronounced decline worldwide in the abundance and diversity of ecologically disparate groups of organisms.

Of course extinction has been a fact of life since the emergence of species almost 4 billion years ago. Of all species that have ever existed, possibly half a billion or more, there now remain only a few million. But the natural background rate of extinction during the past 600 million years, the period of major life, has been on the order of only one species every year or so (Raup and Sepkoski, 1984). Today the rate is surely hundreds of times higher, possibly thousands of times higher (Ehrlich and Ehrlich, 1981; Myers, 1986; Raven, 1987; Soulé, 1986; Western and Pearl, in press; Wilson, 1987). Moreover, whereas past extinctions have occurred by virtue of natural processes, today the virtually exclusive cause is *Homo sapiens,* who eliminates entire habitats and complete communities of species in super-short order. It is all happening in the twinkling of an evolutionary eye.

To help us get a handle on the situation, let us take a lengthy look at tropical forests. These forests cover only 7% of Earth's land surface, yet they are estimated to contain at least 50% of all species (conceivably a much higher proportion). Equally important, they are being depleted faster than any other ecological zone.

Tropical Forests

There is general agreement that remaining primary forests cover rather less than 9 million square kilometers, out of the 15 million or so that may once have existed according to bioclimatic data. There is also general agreement that between 76,000 and 92,000 square kilometers are eliminated outright each year, and that at least a further 100,000 square kilometers are grossly disrupted each year (FAO and UNEP, 1982; Hadley and Lanley, 1983; Melillo et al., 1985; Molofsky et al., 1986; Myers, 1980, 1984). These figures for deforestation rates derive from a data base of the late 1970s; the rates have increased somewhat since then. This means, roughly speaking, that 1% of the biome is being deforested each year and that more than another 1% is being significantly degraded.

The main source of information lies with remote-sensing surveys, which constitute a thoroughly objective and systematic mode of inquiry. By 1980 there were remote-sensing data for approximately 65% of the biome, a figure that has risen today to 82%. In all countries where remote-sensing information has been available in only the past few years—notably Indonesia, Burma, India, Nigeria, Cameroon, Guatemala, Honduras, and Peru—we find there is greater deforestation than had been supposed by government agencies in question.

Tropical deforestation is by no means an even process. Some areas are being affected harder than others; some will survive longer than others. By the end of the century or shortly thereafter, there could be little left of the biome in primary status with a full complement of species, except for two large remnant blocs, one in the Zaire basin and the other in the western half of Brazilian Amazonia, plus two much smaller blocs, in Papua New Guinea and in the Guyana Shield of northern South America. These relict sectors of the biome may well endure for several decades further, but they are little likely to last beyond the middle of next century, if only because of sheer expansion in the numbers of small-scale cultivators.

Rapid population growth among communities of small-scale cultivators occurs mainly through immigration rather than natural increase, i.e., through the phenomenon of the shifted cultivator. As a measure of what ultrarapid growth rates can already impose on tropical forests, consider the situation in Rondonia, a state in the southern sector of Brazilian Amazonia. Between 1975 and 1986, the population grew from 111,000 to well over I million, i.e., a 10-times increase in little more than 10 years. In 1975, almost 1,250 square kilometers of forest were cleared. By 1982, this amount had grown to more than 10,000 square kilometers, and by late 1985, to around 17,000 square kilometers (Fearnside, 1986).

It is this broad-scale clearing and degradation of forest habitats that is far and away the main cause of species extinctions. Regrettably, we have no way to know the actual current rate of extinction, nor can we even come close with accurate estimates. But we can make substantive assessments by looking at species numbers before deforestation and then applying the analytic techniques of island biogeography. To help us gain an insight into the scope and scale of present extinctions, let us briefly consider three particular areas: the forested tracts of western Ecuador, Atlantic-coast Brazil, and Madagascar. Each of these areas features, or rather featured, exceptional concentrations of species with high levels of endemism. Western Ecuador is reputed to have once contained between 8,000 and 10,000 plant species with an endemism rate somewhere between 40 and 60% (Gentry, 1986). If we suppose, as we reasonably can by drawing on detailed inventories in sample plots, that there are at least 10 to 30 animal species for every one plant species, the species complement in western Ecuador must have amounted to 200,000 or more in all. Since 1960, at least 95% of the forest cover has been destroyed to make way for banana plantations, oil exploiters, and human settlements of various sorts. According to the theory of island biogeography, which is supported by abundant and diversified evidence, we can realistically expect that when a habitat has lost 90% of its extent, it will eventually lose half its species. Precisely how many species have actually been eliminated, or are on the point of extinction, in western Ecuador is impossible to say. But ultimate accuracy is surely irrelevant, insofar as the number must total tens of thousands at least, conceivably 50,000—all eliminated or at least doomed in the space of just 25 years.

Very similar baseline figures for species totals and endemism levels, and a similar story of forest depletion (albeit for different reasons and over a longer time period), apply to the Atlantic-coastal forest of Brazil, where the original 1 million square kilometers of forest cover have been reduced to less than 50,000 square kilometers (Mori et al., 1981). Parallel data apply also to Madagascar, where only 5% of the island's primary vegetation remains undisturbed—and where the endemism levels are rather higher (Rauh, 1979).

So in these three tropical forest areas alone, with their roughly 600,000 species, the recent past must have witnessed a sizeable fallout of species. Some may not have disappeared as yet, due to the time lag in equilibration, i.e., delayed fallout effects stemming from habitat depletion. But whereas the ultimate total of extinctions in these areas in the wake of deforestation to date will presumably amount to some 150,000 species, we may realistically assume that already half, some 75,000 species, have been eliminated or doomed.

Deforestation in Brazil's Atlantic-coastal forest and Madagascar has been going on for several centuries, but the main damage has occurred during this century, especially since 1950, i.e., since the spread of broad-scale industrialization and plantation agriculture in Brazil and since the onset of rapid population growth in Madagascar. This all means that as many as 50,000 species have been eliminated or doomed in these areas alone during the last 35 years. This works out to a crude average

of almost 1,500 species per year—a figure consistent with the independent assessment of Wilson (1987), who postulates an extinction rate in all tropical forests of perhaps 10,000 species per year. Of course many reservations attend these calculations. More species than postulated may remain until a new equilibrium is established and causes their disappearance. Conversely, more species will presumably have disappeared during the later stages of the 35-year period than during the opening stage. Whatever the details of the outcome, we can judiciously use the figures and conclusions to form a working appraisal of the extent that an extinction spasm is already under way.

Extinction Rates: Future

The outlook for the future seems all the more adverse, though its detailed dimensions are even less clear than those of the present. Let us look again at tropical forests. We have seen what is happening to three critical areas. We can identify a good number of other sectors of the biome that feature exceptional concentrations of species with exceptional levels of endemism and that face exceptional threat of depletion, whether quantitative or qualitative. They include the Choco forest of Colombia; the Napo center of diversity in Peruvian Amazonia, plus seven other centers (out of 20-plus centers of diversity in Amazonia) that lie around the fringes of the basin and hence are unusually threatened by settlement programs and various other forms of development; the Tai Forest of Ivory Coast; the montane forests of East Africa; the relict wet forest of Sri Lanka; the monsoon forests of the Himalayan foothills; northwestern Borneo; certain lowland areas of the Philippines; and several islands of the South Pacific (New Caledonia, for instance, is 16,100 square kilometers, almost the size of New Jersey, and contains 3,000 plant species, 80% of them endemic).

These various sectors of the tropical forest biome amount to roughly 1 million square kilometers (2.5 times the size of California), or slightly more than one-tenth of the remaining undisturbed forests. As far as we can best judge from their documented numbers of plant species, and by making substantiated assumptions about the numbers of associated animal species, we can estimate that these areas surely harbor 1 million species (could be many more)—and in many of the areas, there is marked endemism. If present land-use patterns and exploitation trends persist (and they show every sign of accelerating), there will be little left of these forest tracts, except in the form of degraded remnants, by the end of this century or shortly thereafter. Thus forest depletion in these areas alone could well eliminate large numbers of species, surely hundreds of thousands, within the next 25 years at most.

Looking at the situation another way, we can estimate, on the basis of what we know about plant numbers and distribution together with what we can surmise about their associated animal communities, that almost 20% of all species occur in forests of Latin America outside of Amazonia and that another 20% are present in forests of Asia and Africa outside the Zaire basin (Raven, 1987). That is, these forests contain some 1 million species altogether, even if we estimate that the planetary total is only 5 million. All the primary forests in which these species occur may well disappear by the end of this century or early in the next. If only half the species in these forests disappear, this will amount to several hundred thousand species.

What is the prognosis for the longer-term future? Could we eventually lose at least one-quarter, possibly one-third, or conceivably an even larger share of all extant species? Let us take a quick look at Amazonia (Simberloff, 1986). If deforestation continues at present rates until the year 2000, but then comes to a complete halt, we could anticipate an ultimate loss of about 15% of the plant species and a similar percentage of animal species. If Amazonia's forest cover were to be ultimately reduced to those areas now set aside as parks and reserves, we could anticipate that 66% of the plant species will eventually disappear together with almost 69% of bird species and similar proportions of all other major categories of species.

Of course we may learn how to manipulate habitats to enhance survival prospects. We may learn how to propagate threatened species in captivity. We may be able to apply other emergent conservation techniques, all of which could help to relieve the adverse repercussions of broad-scale deforestation. But in the main, the damage will have been done. For reasons of island biogeography and equilibration, some extinctions in Amazonia will not occur until well into the twenty-second century, or even further into the future. So a major extinction spasm in Amazonia is entirely possible, indeed plausible if not probable.

Tropical Forest and Climatic Change

Protected areas are not likely to provide a sufficient answer for reasons that reflect climatic factors. In Amazonia, for instance, it is becoming apparent that if as much as half the forest were to be safeguarded in some way or another (e.g., through multiple-use conservation units as well as protected areas), but the other half of the forest were to be developed out of existence, there could soon be at work a hydrological feedback mechanism that would allow a good part of Amazonia's moisture to be lost to the ecosystem (Salati and Vose, 1984). The remaining forest would likely be subjected to a steady desiccatory process, until the moist forest became more like a dry forest, even a woodland—with all that would mean for the species communities that are adapted to moist forest habitats. Even with a set of forest safeguards of exemplary type and scope, Amazonia's biotas would be more threatened than ever.

Still more widespread climatic changes with yet more marked impact are likely to occur within the foreseeable future. By the first quarter of the next century, we may well be experiencing the climatic dislocations of a planetary warming, stemming from a buildup of carbon dioxide and other so-called greenhouse gases in the global atmosphere (Bolin and Doos, 1986; DoE, 1985). The consequences for protected areas will be pervasive and profound. The present network of protected areas, grossly inadequate as it is, has been established in accord with present-day needs. Yet its ultimate viability will be severely threatened in the wake of a greenhouse effect as vegetation zones start to migrate away from the equator with all manner of disruptive repercussions for natural environments (Peters and Darling, 1985).

These, then, are some dimensions of the extinction spasm that we can reasonably assume will overtake the planet's biotas within the next few decades (unless of course we do a massively better job of conservation). In effect we are conducting an irreversible experiment on a global scale with Earth's stock of species.

Repercussions for the Future of Evolution

The foreseeable fallout of species, together with their subunits, is far from the entire story. A longer-term and ultimately more serious repercussion could lie in a disruption of the course of evolution, insofar as speciation processes will have to work with a greatly reduced pool of species and their genetic materials. We are probably being optimistic when we call it a disruption; a more likely outcome is that certain evolutionary processes will be suspended or even terminated. In the graphic phrasing of Soulé and Wilcox (1980), "Death is one thing; an end to birth is something else."

From what little we can discern from the geologic record, a normal recovery time may require millions of years. After the dinosaur crash, for instance, between 50,000 and 100,000 years elapsed before there started to emerge a set of diversified and specialized biotas, and another 5 to 10 million years went by before there were bats in the skies and whales in the seas (Jablonski, 1986). Following the crash during the late Permian Period, when marine invertebrates lost about half their families, as many as 20 million years elapsed before the survivors could establish even half as many families as they had lost (Raup, 1986).

The evolutionary outcome this time around could prove even more drastic. The critical factor lies with the likely loss of key environments. Not only do we appear ready to lose most if not virtually all tropical forests, but there is also progressive depletion of coral reefs, wetlands, estuaries, and other biotopes with exceptional biodiversity. These environments have served in the past as preeminent powerhouses of evolution, in that they have supported the emergence of more species than have other environments. Virtually every major group of vertebrates and many other large categories of animals have originated in spacious zones with warm, equable climates, notably tropical forests. In addition, the rate of evolutionary diversification— whether through proliferation of species or through the emergence of major new adaptations—has been greatest in the tropics, again most notably in tropical forests.

Of course tropical forests have been severely depleted in the past. During drier phases of the recent Ice Ages (Pleistocene Epoch), they have been repeatedly reduced to only a small fraction, occasionally as little as one-tenth, of their former expanse. Moreover, tropical biotas seem to have been unduly prone to extinction. But the remnant forest refugia usually contained sufficient stocks of surviving species to recolonize suitable territories when moister conditions returned (Prance, 1982). Within the foreseeable future, by contrast, it seems all too possible that most tropical forests will be reduced to much less than one-tenth of their former expanse, and their pockets of holdout species will be much less stocked with potential colonizers.

Furthermore, the species depletion will surely apply across most if not all major categories of species. This is almost axiomatic, if extensive environments are eliminated wholesale. The result will contrast sharply with the end of the Cretaceous Period, when not only placental mammals survived (leading to the adaptive radiation of mammals, eventually including humans), but also birds, amphibians, and crocodiles, among other nondinosaurian reptiles. In addition, the present extinction spasm looks likely to eliminate a sizeable share of terrestrial plant species, at least one-fifth within the next half century and a good many more within the following half century. By contrast, during most mass-extinction episodes of the prehistoric past, terrestrial plants have survived with relatively few losses (Knoll, 1984). They have thus supplied a resource base on which evolutionary processes could start to generate replacement animal species forthwith. If this biotic substrate is markedly depleted within the foreseeable future, the restorative capacities of evolution will be all the more reduced.

In sum, the evolutionary impoverishment of the impending extinction spasm, plus the numbers of species involved and the telescoped time scale of the phenomenon, may result in the greatest single setback to life's abundance and diversity since the first flickerings of life almost 4 billion years ago.

References

Bolin, B., and B. R. Doos, eds. 1986. The Greenhouse Effect: Climatic Change and Ecosystems. Wiley, New York. 541 pp.

DoE (U.S. Department of Energy). 1985. Direct Effects of Increasing Carbon Dioxide on Vegetation. U.S. Department of Energy, Washington, D.C.

Ehrlich, P. R., and A. H. Ehrlich. 1981. Extinction: The Causes and Consequences of the Disappearance of Species. Random House, New York. 305 pp.

FAO and UNEP (Food and Agriculture Organization and United Nations Environment Programme). 1982. Tropical Forest Resources. Food and Agriculture Organization of the United Nations, Rome, Italy, and United Nations Environment Programme, Nairobi, Kenya. 106 pp.

Fearnside, P. M, 1986. Human Carrying Capacity of the Brazilian Rain Forest. Columbia University Press, New York. 293 pp.

Gentry, A. H. 1986. Endemism in tropical versus temperate plant communities. Pp. 153–181 in M. E. Soul, ed. Conservation Biology: The Science of Scarcity and Diversity. Sinauer Associates, Sunderland, Mass. 584 pp.

Hadley, M., and J. P. Lanley. 1983. Tropical forest ecosystems: Identifying differences, seeing similarities. Nat. Resour. 19:2–19.

Jablonski, D. 1986. Causes and consequences of mass extinction: A comparative approach. Pp. 183–230 in D. K. Elliott, ed. Dynamics of Extinction. Wiley Interscience, New York.

Knoll, A. H. 1984. Patterns of extinction in the fossil record of vascular plants. Pp. 21–68 in M. H. Nitecki, ed. Extinctions. University of Chicago Press, Chicago.

Melillo, J. M., C. A. Palm, R. A. Houghton, G. M. Woodwell, and N. Myers. 1985. A comparison of recent estimates of disturbance in tropical forests. Environ. Conserv. 12(1):37–40.

Molofsky, J., C. A. S. Hall, and N. Myers. 1986. A Comparison of Tropical Forest Surveys. U.S. Department of Energy, Washington, D.C.

Mori, S. A., B. M. Boom, and G. T. Prance. 1981. Distribution patterns and conservation of eastern Brazilian coastal forest tree species. Brittonia 33(2):233–245.

Myers, N. 1980. Conservation of Tropical Moist Forests. A report prepared for the Committee on Research Priorities in Tropical Biology of the National Research Council. National Academy of Sciences, Washington, D.C. 205 pp.

Myers, N. 1984. The Primary Source: Tropical Forests and Our Future. W. W. Norton, New York. 399 pp.

Myers, N. 1986. Tackling Mass Extinction of Species: A Great Creative Challenge. Albright Lecture, University of California, Berkeley. 40 pp.

Peters, R. L., and J. D. S. Darling. 1985. The greenhouse effect and nature reserves. BioScience 35(11):707–717.

Prance, G. T., ed. 1982. Biological Diversification in the Tropics. Proceedings of the Fifth International Symposium of the Association for Tropical Biology, held at Macuto Beach, Caracas, Venezuela, February 8–13, 1979. Columbia University Press, New York. 714 pp.

Rauh, W. 1979. Problems of biological conservation in Madagascar. Pp. 405–421 in D. Bramwell, ed. Plants and Islands. Academic Press, London, U.K.

Raup, D. M. 1986. Biological extinction in earth history. Science 231:1528–1533.

Raup, D. M., and J. J. Sepkoski. 1984. Periodicity of extinction in the geologic past. Proc. Natl. Acad. Sci. USA 81:801–805.

Raven, P. H. 1987. We're Killing Our World. Keynote Paper Presented to Annual Conference of the American Association for the Advancement of Science, Chicago, February 1987. Missouri Botanical Garden, St. Louis.

Salati, E., and P. B. Vose. 1984. Amazon basin: A system in equilibrium. Science 225:129–138.

Simberloff, D. 1986. Are we on the verge of a mass extinction in tropical rain forests? Pp. 165–180 in D. K. Elliott, ed. Dynamics of Extinction. Wiley, New York.

Soulé, M. E. 1986. Conservation Biology, The Science of Scarcity and Diversity. Sinauer Associates, Sunderland, Mass.

Soulé, M. E., and B. A. Wilcox, eds. 1980. Conservation Biology: An Evolutionary-Ecological Perspective. Sinauer Associates, Sunderland, Mass. 395 pp.

Western, D., and M. Pearl, eds. In press. Conservation 2100. Proceedings of International Conference on Threatened Wildlife and Species, Manhattan, October 1986, organized by the New York Zoological Society. Oxford University Press, New York.

Wilson, E. 0. 1987. Biological diversity as a scientific and ethical issue. Pp. 29–48 in Papers Read at a Joint Meeting of the Royal Society and the American Philosophical Society. Volume 1. Meeting held April 24, 1986, in Philadelphia. American Philosophical Society, Philadelphia.

Is Humanity Suicidal?

Edward O. Wilson

Imagine that on an icy moon of Jupiter—say, Ganymede—the space station of an alien civilization is concealed. For millions of years its scientists have closely watched the earth. Because their law prevents settlement on a living planet, they have tracked the surface by means of satellites equipped with sophisticated sensors, mapping the spread of large assemblages of organisms, from forests, grasslands and tundras to coral reefs and the vast planktonic meadows of the sea. They have recorded millennial cycles in the climate, interrupted by the advance and retreat of glaciers and scattershot volcanic eruptions.

The watchers have been waiting for what might be called the Moment. When it comes, occupying only a few centuries and thus a mere tick in geological time, the forests shrink back to less than half their original cover. Atmospheric carbon dioxide rises to the highest level in 100,000 years. The ozone layer of the stratosphere thins, and holes open at the poles. Plumes of nitrous oxide and other toxins rise from fires in South America and Africa, settle in the upper troposphere and drift eastward across the oceans. At night the land surface brightens with millions of pinpoints of light, which coalesce into blazing swaths across Europe, Japan and eastern North America. A semicircle of fire spreads from gas flares around the Persian Gulf.

It was all but inevitable, the watchers might tell us if we met them, that from the great diversity of large animals, one species or another would eventually gain intelligent control of Earth. That role has fallen to Homo sapiens, a primate risen in Africa from a lineage that split away from the chimpanzee line five to eight million years ago. Unlike any creature that lived before, we have become a geophysical force, swiftly changing the atmosphere and climate as well as the composition of the world's fauna and flora. Now in the midst of a population explosion, the human species has doubled to 5.5 billion during the past 50 years. It is scheduled to double again in the next 50 years. No other single species in evolutionary history has even remotely approached the sheer mass in protoplasm generated by humanity.

Darwin's dice have rolled badly for Earth. It was a misfortune for the living world in particular, many scientists believe, that a carnivorous primate and not some more benign form of animal made the breakthrough. Our species retains hereditary traits that add greatly to our destructive impact. We are tribal and aggressively territorial, intent on private space beyond minimal requirements and oriented by selfish sexual and reproductive drives. Cooperation beyond the family and tribal levels comes hard.

Worse, our liking for meat causes us to use the sun's energy at low efficiency. It is a general rule of ecology that (very roughly) only about 10 percent of the sun's energy captured by photosynthesis to produce plant tissue is converted into energy in the tissue of herbivores, the animals that eat the plants. Of that amount, 10 percent reaches the tissue of the carnivores feeding on the herbivores. Similarly, only 10 percent is transferred to carnivores that eat carnivores. And so on for another step or two. In a wetlands chain that runs from marsh grass to grasshopper to warbler to hawk, the energy captured during green production shrinks a thousandfold.

In other words, it takes a great deal of grass to support a hawk. Human beings, like hawks, are top carnivores, at the end of the food chain whenever they eat meat, two or more links removed from the plants; if chicken, for example, two links, and if tuna, four links. Even with most societies confined today to a mostly vegetarian diet, humanity is gobbling up a large part of the rest of the living world. We appropriate between 20 and 40 percent of the sun's energy that would otherwise be fixed into the tissue of natural vegetation, principally by our consumption of crops and timber, construction of buildings and roadways and the creation of wastelands. In the relentless search for more food, we have reduced animal life in lakes, rivers and now, increasingly, the open ocean. And everywhere we pollute the air and water, lower water tables and extinguish species.

The human species is, in a word, an environmental abnormality. It is possible that intelligence in the wrong kind of species was foreordained to be a fatal combination for the biosphere. Perhaps a law of evolution is that intelligence usually extinguishes itself.

This admittedly dour scenario is based on what can be termed the juggernaut theory of human nature, which holds that people are programmed by their genetic heritage to be so selfish that a sense of global responsibility will come too late. Individuals place themselves first, family second, tribe third and the rest of the world a distant fourth. Their genes also predispose them to plan ahead for one or two generations at most. They fret over the petty problems and conflicts of their daily lives and respond swiftly and often ferociously to slight challenges to their status and tribal security. But oddly, as psychologists have discovered, people also tend to underestimate both the likelihood and impact of such natural disasters as major earthquakes and great storms.

The reason for this myopic fog, evolutionary biologists contend, is that it was actually advantageous during all but the last few millennia of the two millon years of existence of the genus Homo. The brain evolved into its present form during this long stretch of evolutionary time, during which people existed in small, preliterate hunter-gatherer bands. Life was precarious and short. A premium was placed on close attention to the near future and early reproduction, and little else. Disasters of a magnitude that occur only once every few centuries were forgotten or transmuted into myth. So today the mind still works comfortably backward and forward for only a few years, spanning a period not exceeding one or two generations. Those in past ages whose genes inclined them to short-term thinking lived longer and had more children than those who did not. Prophets never enjoyed a Darwinian edge.

The rules have recently changed, however. Global crises are rising in the life span of the generation now coming of age, a foreshortening that may explain why young people express more concern about the environment than do their elders. The time scale has contracted because of the exponential growth in both the human population and technologies impacting the environment. Exponential growth is basically the same as the increase of wealth by compound interest. The larger the population, the faster the growth; the faster the growth, the sooner the population becomes still larger. In Nigeria, to cite one of our more fecund nations, the population is expected to double from its 1988 level to 216 million by the year 2010. If the same rate of growth were to continue to 2110, its population would exceed that of the entire present population of the world.

With people everywhere seeking a better quality of life, the search for resources is expanding even faster than the population. The demand is being met by an increase in scientific knowledge, which doubles every 10 to 15 years. It is accelerated further by a parallel rise in environment-devouring technology. Because Earth is finite in many resources that determine the quality of life—including arable soil, nutrients, fresh water and space for natural ecosystems—doubling of consumption at constant time intervals can bring disaster with shocking suddenness. Even when a nonrenewable resource has been only half used, it is still only one interval away from the end. Ecologists like to make this point with the French riddle of the lily pond. At first there is only one lily pad in the pond, but the next day it doubles, and thereafter each of its descendants doubles. The pond completely fills with lily pads in 30 days. When is the pond exactly half full? Answer: on the 29th day.

Yet, mathematical exercises aside, who can safely measure the human capacity to overcome the perceived limits of Earth? The question of central interest is this: Are we racing to the brink of an abyss, or are we just gathering speed for a takeoff to a wonderful future? The crystal ball is clouded; the human condition baffles all the more because it is both unprecedented and bizarre, almost beyond understanding.

In the midst of uncertainty, opinions on the human prospect have tended to fall loosely into two schools. The first, exemptionalism, holds that since humankind is transcendent in intelligence and spirit, so must our species have been released from the iron laws of ecology that bind all other species. No matter how serious the problem, civilized human beings, by ingenuity, force of will and—who knows—divine dispensation, will find a solution.

Population growth? Good for the economy, claim some of the exemptionalists, and in any case a basic human right, so let it run. Land shortages? Try fusion energy to power the desalting of sea water, then reclaim the world's deserts. (The process might be assisted by towing icebergs to coastal pipelines.) Species going extinct? Not to worry. That is nature's way. Think of humankind as only the latest in a long line of exterminating agents in geological time. In any case, because our species has pulled free of old-style, mindless Nature, we have begun a different order of life. Evolution should now be allowed to proceed along this new trajectory. Finally, resources? The planet has more than enough resources to last indefinitely, if human genius is allowed to address each new problem in turn, without alarmist and unreasonable restrictions imposed on economic development. So hold the course, and touch the brakes lightly.

The opposing idea of reality is environmentalism, which sees humanity as a biological species tightly dependent on the natural world. As formidable as our intellect may be and as fierce our spirit, the argument goes, those qualities are not enough to free us from the constraints of the natural environment in which our human ancestors evolved. We cannot draw confidence from successful solutions to the smaller problems of the past. Many of Earth's vital resources are about to be exhausted, its atmospheric chemistry is deteriorating and human populations have already grown dangerously large. Natural ecosystems, the wellsprings of a healthful environment, are being irreversibly degraded.

At the heart of the environmentalist world view is the conviction that human physical and spiritual health depends on sustaining the planet in a relatively unaltered state. Earth is our home in the full, genetic sense, where humanity and its ancestors existed for all the millions of years of their evolution. Natural ecosystems—forests, coral reefs, marine blue waters—maintain the world exactly as we would wish it to be maintained. When we debase the global environment and extinguish the variety of life, we are dismantling a support system that is too complex to understand, let alone replace, in the foreseeable future. Space scientists theorize the existence of a virtually unlimited array of other planetary environments, almost all of which are uncongenial to human life. Our own Mother Earth, lately called Gaia, is a specialized conglomerate of organisms and the physical environment they create on a day-to-day basis, which can be destabilized and turned lethal by careless activity. We run the risk, conclude the environmentalists, of beaching ourselves upon alien shores like a great confused pod of pilot whales.

If I have not done so enough already by tone of voice, I will now place myself solidly in the environmentalist school, but not so radical as to wish a turning back of the clock, not given to driving spikes into Douglas firs to prevent logging and distinctly uneasy with such hybrid movements as ecofeminism, which holds that Mother Earth is a nurturing home for all life and should be revered and loved as in premodern (paleolithic and archaic) societies and that ecosystematic abuse is rooted in androcentric—that is to say, male-dominated—concepts, values and institutions.

Still, however soaked in androcentric culture, I am radical enough to take seriously the question heard with increasing frequency: Is humanity suicidal? Is the drive to environmental conquest and self-propagation embedded so deeply in our genes as to be unstoppable?

My short answer—opinion if you wish—is that humanity is not suicidal, at least not in the sense just stated. We are smart enough and have time enough to avoid an environmental catastrophe of civilization-threatening dimensions. But the technical problems are sufficiently formidable to require a redirection of much of science and technology, and the ethical issues are so basic as to force a reconsideration of our self-image as a species.

There are reasons for optimism, reasons to believe that we have entered what might someday be generously called the Century of the Environment. The United Nations Conference on Environment and Development, held in Rio de Janeiro in June 1992, attracted more than 120 heads of government, the largest number ever assembled, and helped move environmental issues closer to the political center stage; on Nov. 18, 1992, more than 1,500 senior scientists from 69 countries issued a "Warning to Humanity," stating that overpopulation and environmental deterioration put the very future of life at risk. The greening of religion has become a global trend, with theologians and religious leaders addressing environmental problems as a moral issue. In May 1992, leaders of most of the major American denominations met with scientists as guests of members of the United States Senate to formulate a "Joint Appeal by Religion and Science for the Environment." Conservation of biodiversity is increasingly seen by both national governments and major landowners as important to their country's future. Indonesia, home to a large part of the native Asian plant and animal species, has begun to shift to land-management practices that conserve and sustainably develop the remaining rain forests. Costa Rica has created a National Institute of Biodiversity. A pan-African institute for biodiversity research and management has been founded, with headquarters in Zimbabwe.

Finally, there are favorable demographic signs. The rate of population increase is declining on all continents, although it is still well above zero almost everywhere and remains especially high in sub-Saharan Africa. Despite entrenched traditions and religious beliefs, the desire to use contraceptives in family planning is spreading. Demographers estimate that if the demand were fully met, this action alone would reduce the eventual stabilized population by more than two billion.

In summary, the will is there. Yet the awful truth remains that a large part of humanity will suffer no matter what is done. The number of people living in absolute poverty has risen during the past 20 years to nearly one billion and is expected to increase another 100 million by the end of the decade. Whatever progress has been made in the developing countries, and that includes an overall improvement in the average standard of living, is threatened by a continuance of rapid population growth and the deterioration of forests and arable soil.

Our hopes must be chastened further still, and this is in my opinion the central issue, by a key and seldom-recognized distinction between the nonliving and living environments. Science and the political process can be adapted to manage the nonliving, physical environment. The human hand is now upon the physical homeostat. The ozone layer can be mostly restored to the upper atmosphere by elimination of CFC's, with these substances peaking at six times the present level and then subsiding during the next half century. Also, with procedures that will prove far more difficult and initially expensive, carbon dioxide and other greenhouse gases can be pulled back to concentrations that slow global warming.

The human hand, however, is not upon the biological homeostat. There is no way in sight to micromanage the natural ecosystems and the millions of species they contain. That feat might be accomplished by generations to come, but then it will be too late for the ecosystems—and perhaps for us. Despite the seemingly bottomless nature of creation, humankind has been chipping away at its diversity, and Earth is destined to become an impoverished planet within a century if present trends continue. Mass extinctions are being reported with increasing frequency in every part of the world. They include half the freshwater fishes of peninsular Malaysia, 10 birds native to Cebu in the Philippines, half the 41 tree snails of Oahu, 44 of the 68 shallow-water mussels of the Tennessee River shoals, as many as 90 plant species growing on the Centinela Ridge in Ecuador, and in the United States as a whole, about 200 plant species, with another 680 species and races now classified as in danger of extinction. The main cause is the destruction of natural habitats, especially tropical forests. Close behind, especially on the Hawaiian archipelago and other islands, is the introduction of rats, pigs, beard grass, lantana and other exotic organisms that outbreed and extirpate native species.

The few thousand biologists worldwide who specialize in diversity are aware that they can witness and report no more than a very small percentage of the extinctions actually occurring. The reason is that they have facilities to keep track of only a tiny fraction of the millions of species and a sliver of the planet's surface on a yearly basis. They have devised a rule of thumb to characterize the situation: that whenever careful studies are made of habitats before and after disturbance, extinctions almost always come to light. The corollary: the great majority of extinctions are never observed. Vast numbers of species are apparently vanishing before they can be discovered and named.

There is a way, nonetheless, to estimate the rate of loss indirectly. Independent studies around the world and in fresh and marine waters have revealed a robust connection between the size of a habitat and the amount of biodiversity it contains. Even a small loss in area reduces the number of species. The relation is such that when the area of the habitat is cut to a tenth of its original cover, the number of species eventually drops by roughly one-half. Tropical rain forests, thought to harbor a majority of Earth's species (the reason conservationists get so exercised about rain forests), are being reduced by nearly that magnitude. At the present time they occupy about the same area as that of the 48 conterminous United States, representing a little less than half their original, prehistoric cover, and they are shrinking each year by about 2 percent, an amount equal to the state of Florida. If the typical value (that is, 90 percent area loss causes 50 percent eventual extinction) is applied, the projected loss of species due to rain forest destruction worldwide is half a percent across the board for all kinds of plants, animals and microorganisms.

When area reduction and all the other extinction agents are considered together, it is reasonable to project a reduction by 20 percent or more of the rain forest species by the year 2020, climbing to 50 percent or more by midcentury, if nothing is done to change current practice. Comparable erosion is likely in other environments now under assault, including many coral reefs and Mediterranean-type heathlands of Western Australia, South Africa and California.

The ongoing loss will not be replaced by evolution in any period of time that has meaning for humanity. Extinction is now proceeding thousands of times faster than the production of new species. The average life span of a species and its descendants in past geological eras varied according to group (like mollusks or echinoderms or flowering plants) from about 1 to 10 million years. During the past 500 million years, there have been five great extinction spasms comparable to the one now being inaugurated by human expansion. The latest, evidently caused by the strike of an asteroid, ended the Age of Reptiles 66 million years ago. In each case it took more than 10 million years for evolution to completely replenish the biodiversity lost. And that was in an otherwise undisturbed natural environment. Humanity is now destroying most of the habitats where evolution can occur.

The surviving biosphere remains the great unknown of Earth in many respects. On the practical side, it is hard even to imagine what other species have to offer in the way of new pharmaceuticals, crops, fibers, petroleum substitutes and other products. We have only a poor grasp of the ecosystem services by which other organisms cleanse the water, turn soil into a fertile living cover and manufacture the very air we breathe. We sense but do not fully understand what the highly diverse natural world means to our esthetic pleasure and mental well-being.

Scientists are unprepared to manage a declining biosphere. To illustrate, consider the following mission they might be given. The last remnant of a rain forest is about to be cut over. Environmentalists are stymied. The contracts have been signed, and local landowners and politicians are intransigent. In a final desperate move, a team of biologists is scrambled in an attempt to preserve the biodiversity by extraordinary means. Their assignment is the following: collect samples of all the species of organisms quickly, before the cutting starts; maintain the species in zoos, gardens and laboratory cultures or else deep-freeze samples of the tissues in liquid nitrogen, and finally, establish the procedure by which the entire community can be reassembled on empty ground at a later date, when social and economic conditions have improved.

The biologists cannot accomplish this task, not if thousands of them came with a billion-dollar budget. They cannot even imagine how to do it. In the forest patch live legions of species: perhaps 300 birds, 500 butterflies, 200 ants, 50,000 beetles, 1,000 trees, 5,000 fungi, tens of thousands of bacteria and so on down a long roster of major groups. Each species occupies a precise niche, demanding a certain place, an exact microclimate, particular nutrients and temperature and humidity cycles with specified timing to trigger phases of the life cycle. Many, perhaps most, of the species are locked in symbioses with other species; they cannot survive and reproduce unless arrayed with their partners in the correct idiosyncratic configurations.

Even if the biologists pulled off the taxonomic equivalent of the Manhattan Project, sorting and preserving cultures of all the species, they could not then put the community back together again. It would be like unscrambling an egg with a pair of spoons. The biology of the microorganisms needed to reanimate the soil would be mostly unknown. The pollinators of most of the flowers and the correct timing of their appearance could only be guessed. The "assembly rules," the sequence in which species must be allowed to colonize in order to coexist indefinitely, would remain in the realm of theory.

In its neglect of the rest of life, exemptionalism fails definitively. To move ahead as though scientific and entrepreneurial genius will solve each crisis that arises implies that the declining biosphere can be similarly manipulated. But the world is too complicated to be turned into a garden. There is no biological homeostat that can be worked by humanity; to believe otherwise is to risk reducing a large part of Earth to a wasteland.

The environmentalist vision, prudential and less exuberant than exemptionalism, is closer to reality. It sees humanity entering a bottleneck unique in history, constricted by population and economic pressures. In order to pass through to the other side, within perhaps 50 to 100 years, more science and entrepreneurship will have to be devoted to stabilizing the global environment. That can be accomplished, according to expert consensus, only by halting population growth and devising a wiser use of resources than has been accomplished to date. And wise use for the living world in particular means preserving the surviving ecosystems, micromanaging them only enough to save the biodiversity they contain, until such time as they can be understood and employed in the fullest sense for human benefit.

Environmental Racism

Karl Grossman

"We're sitting in a center of a donut surrounded by a hazardous waste incinerator that gives off PCB's, seven landfills that are constantly growing—they look like mountains," Hazel Johnson was saying. "There are chemical plants, a paint factory, two steel mills which give off odors, and lagoons filled with all kinds of contaminants that emit 30,000 tons of poison into the air each year. And there's a water reclamation district where they dry sludge out in the open. The smell is horrible, like bodies decomposing."

Mrs. Johnson was describing Atgeld Gardens, a housing project in which 10,000 people, nearly all African-Americans, reside on the Southeast Side of Chicago, surrounded on every side by sources of pollution.

The result: environmental diseases and death.

"We have lots of cancer, respiratory problems, birth deformities," Mrs. Johnson went on. "Just the other day, there were three cancer deaths. Then more. We've been having babies born with brain tumors. One baby was born with her brain protruding from her head. She's two now, blind and she can't walk. My daughter was five months pregnant. She took ultra-sound and the doctors found the baby had no behind, no head," said Mrs. Johnson, the mother of seven. "The baby had to be aborted."

Mrs. Johnson has no doubt that "the terrible health problems we have in our community are related to the pollution," the product of trying to live amid one of the most concentrated areas of environmental contamination in the U.S.

And she is clear about why her area gets dumped on because it is largely inhabited by African-Americans and Hispanics. "In Chicago, everything is mostly dumped out in this area where we are. They figure that we're not going to come out and protest and disagree." But Mrs. Johnson has, for 10 years now, as the head of People for Community Recovery, been fighting back.

"Atgeld Gardens symbolizes environmental racism," the Rev. Benjamin Chavis, Jr., the noted civil rights leader and executive director of the United Church of Christ's Commission for Racial Justice, declared. "The community is surrounded on all four sides by pollution and has one of the highest cancer rates in the nation. The public officials in Chicago are well aware of the circumstances that these people are forced to live in, yet, because of their race, the city has no priority in stopping this type of environmental injustice."

Rev. Chavis was the first to use the term "environmental racism" in 1987 with the release of what has become a landmark study by the commission, "Toxic Wastes and Race In The United States." It has taken several years for the import of the report, notes Rev. Chavis, to take hold.

But now that has well begun. There have been a series of important events, including a week long tour by the Rev. Jesse Jackson, shortly before Earth Day 1990 of low-income minority communities struck by pollution. He stressed the "relationship between environment and empowerment" and declared it "a new day and a new way. No longer will corporations be allowed to use job blackmail to poison poor people be they black, brown, yellow, red, or white. We are demanding that all corporate poisoners sign agreements to stop the poisoning of our communities."

Rev. Jackson was accompanied by Dennis Hayes, a principal organizer of both the original Earth Day, in 1970, and last year's event, and John O'Connor, executive director of the National Toxics Campaign who emphasized that "for the environmental movement to be successful in saving the planet, it must include all races, ethnic groups, rich and poor, black and white, and young and old. When our movement to clean up the nation is truly a reflection of all people in the country, it is at that point that we will succeed in stopping the poisoning of America."

Issuing a report in 1990, at a National Minority Health Conference in Washington on environmental contamination, describing how "a marriage of the movement for social justice with environmentalism" was taking place was the Panos Institute. "Organizing for environmental justice among people of color has grown from a small group of activists in the 1970s to a movement involving thousands of people in neighborhoods throughout the U.S.," said Dana A. Alston, director of the Environment, Community Development and Race Project of Panos, an international group that works for "sustainable development." She added in the report, "We Speak For Ourselves: Social Justice, Race and Environment," that "communities of color have often taken a more holistic approach than the mainstream environmental movement, integrating 'environmental' concerns into a broader agenda that emphasizes social, racial, and economic justice."

In Atlanta in 1990, at a conference on environmental problems in minority areas sponsored by the federal Agency for Toxic Substances and Disease Registry and others, attended by 300 community leaders, doctors and governmental officials, Dr. Aubrey F. Manley, deputy assistant secretary of the Department of Health and Human Services, stated, "Poor and minority organizations charged eight major national environmental groups with racism in their hiring practices and demanded that they substantially increase the number of people of color on their staffs. The environmental groups acknowledged the problem—"The truth is that environmental groups have done a miserable job of reaching

out to minorities," said Frederick D. Krupp, executive director of the Environmental Defense Fund—and set up an Environmental Consortium for Minority Outreach.

And last year, too, the Commission for Racial Justice organized a workshop on racism and the environment for the Congressional Black Caucus whose members, unbeknownst to many, are rated as having among the best pro environmental voting records in Congress by the League of Conservation Voters which scores Congressional representatives on their environmental records.

A key event to be held this year will be the first National Minority Environmental Leadership Summit in Washington, D.C. in October. "We want to bring together leaders of community groups, environmental groups, civil rights organizations and academic, scientific, governmental and corporate organizations to participate in this three-day corporate meeting," says Charles Lee, research director of the Commission for Racial Justice, which is organizing the gathering. "The purpose of this summit is to develop a comprehensive and tangible national agenda of action that will help reshape and redirect environmental policy-making in the United States to fully embrace the concerns of minority Americans."

People of color have been the worst victim of environmental pollution for a long time. Lee tells of the building of the Gauley Bridge in West Virginia in the 1930's: "Hundreds of African-Americans workers from the Deep South were brought in by the New Kunawha Power Company, a subsidiary of the Union Carbide Corporation, to dig the Hawks Nest tunnel. Over a two year period, approximately 500 workers died and 1,500 were disabled from silicosis, a lung disease similar to Black Lung. Men literally dropped on their feet breathing air so thick with microscopic silica that they could not see more than a yard in front of them. Those who came out for air were beaten back into the tunnel with ax handles. At subsequent Congressional hearings, New Kanawha's contractor revealed, "I knew I was going to kill these niggers, but I didn't know it was going to be this soon."

Lee relates how "an undertaker was hired to bury dead workers in unmarked graves" and of his agreeing "to perform the service for an extremely low rate because the company assured him there would be a large number of deaths."

But it was not until recent years that this and other horror stories of environmental racism started to be examined in their systematic context.

It was in 1982 that residents of predominantly African-American Warren County, North Carolina asked the Commission for Racial Justice for help in their protests against the sitting of a dump for PCB's—the acronym for polychlorinated biphenyls, a carcinogen. In a campaign of civil disobedience that ensued, there were more than 500 arrests, including the commission's Rev. Chavis, Dr. Joseph Lowery of the Southern Christian Leadership Conference, and Congressman Walter Fauntroy of Washington.

It was during that effort that Rev. Chavis began considering the connection between the dumping in Warren County and the federal government's Savannah River nuclear facility, long a source of radioactive leaks and located in a heavily African-American area of South Carolina, and the "largest landfill in the nation" in the mainly black community of Emelle, Alabama. "We began to see evidence of a systematic pattern which led us to a national study," recounted Rev. Chavis.

That study—"Toxic Wastes and Race In The United States"—clearly shows what Rev. Chavis suspected: communities of color are where most of America's places of poison are located. In detail, the analysis looked at a cross-section of the thousands of U.S. commercial hazardous water facilities" (defined by the U.S. Environmental Protection Agency as places licensed for "treating, storing or disposing of hazardous wastes") and "uncontrolled toxic waste sites" (defined by EPA as closed and abandoned sites), and correlated them with the ethnicity of the communities in which they are located.

Some of the study's major findings:

- "Race proved to be the most influential among variables tested in association with the location of commercial hazardous waste facilities. This represented a consistent national pattern."
- "Communities with the greatest number of commercial hazardous wastes facilities had the highest composition of ethnic residents."
- "Although socio-economic status appeared to play an important role in the location of commercial hazardous waste facilities, race still proved to be more significant."

- "Three out of every five black and Hispanic Americans lived in communities with uncontrolled toxic waste sites."
- "Blacks were heavily over-represented in the populations of metropolitan areas with the largest number of uncontrolled toxic waste sites."—Memphis, St. Louis, Houston, Cleveland, Chicago, and Atlanta.
- "Approximately half of all Asian/Pacific Islanders and American Indians lived in communities with uncontrolled toxic waste sites."

The analysis called for change. "This report firmly concludes that hazardous wastes in black, Hispanic and other racial and ethnic communities should be made a priority issue at all levels of government. This issue is not currently at the forefront of the nation's attention. Therefore, concerned citizens and policymakers, who are cognizant of this growing national problem, must make this a priority concern."

It called for: the U.S. president "to issue an executive order mandating federal agencies to consider the impact of current policies and regulations on racial and ethnic communities;" state governments "to evaluate and make appropriate revisions in their criteria for the siting of new hazardous waste facilities to adequately take into account the racial and socio-economic characteristics of potential host communities;" the U.S. Conference of Mayors, the National Conference of Black Mayors and the National League of Cities "to convene a national conference to address these issues from a municipal perspective;" and civil rights and political organizations to gear up voter registration campaigns as a means to further empower racial and ethnic communities to effectively respond to hazardous wastes in racial and ethnic communities at the top of state and national legislative agendas."

Environmentalist Barry Commoner commented that the report showed the "functional relationship between poverty, racism and powerlessness and the chemical industry's assault on the environment."

It was in 1978 that sociologist Robert Bullard first began exploring environmental racism. He was asked by Linda McKeever Bullard, his wife, to conduct a study on the siting of municipal landfills and incinerators in Houston for a class-action lawsuit challenging a plan to site a new landfill in the "solid middle class" mostly African-American Houston neighborhood of Northwood Manor, notes Bullard. Just out of graduate school, a new professor at Texas Southern University, he found that from the 1920s to that time, all five of Houston's landfills and six out of eight of its incinerators were sited in black neighborhoods. That led to wider studies by Dr. Bullard on how "black communities, because of their economic and political vulnerability, have been routinely targeted for the siting of noxious facilities, locally unwanted land uses and environmental hazards."

He wrote several papers and, last year, his book, *Dumping in Dixie: Race, Class, and Environmental Quality*, came out. Black communities are consistently the ones getting dumped on "because of racism, plain and simple," says Dr. Bullard, now a professor at the University of California at Riverside.

Often it is a promise of "jobs, jobs, and jobs that are held out as a savior" for these communities although, in fact, "these are not labor-intensive industries." The companies involved, meanwhile, figure they can "minimize their investment" by avoiding the sort of lawsuit more likely to be brought by a white community faced with having a toxic dump, an incinerator, a paper mill, a slaughterhouse, a lead smelter, a pesticide plant, "you name it," said Dr. Bullard. Also, with planning and zoning boards commonly having "excluded people of color," the skids are further greased. And to top it off, "because of housing patterns and limited mobility, middle-income and lower-income blacks," unlike whites, often cannot "vote with their feet" and move out when a polluting facility arrives. "Targeting certain communities for poison is another form of discrimination," charged Dr. Bullard.

He tells in *Dumping in Dixie* of how African-Americans in Houston and Dallas; in Alsen, Louisiana; Institute, West Virginia; and Emelle, Alabama "have taken on corporate giants who would turn their areas into toxic wastelands." He is enthused by the existence of how "literally hundreds of environmental justice groups are made up of people of color."

One of the many organizations is the Gulf Coast Tenants Association. "We have not only the dumping here, but we get the upfront stuff; this is where much of the petrochemical industry is centered, and where they produce a lot of the stuff,"

says Darryl Malek-Wiley, the New Orleans-based group's director of research. "Cancer Alley is the nickname for this area," speaking of the 75-mile swath along the Mississippi from Baton Rouge to New Orleans. The group offers courses in environmental education and assists people to fight environmental hazards in their communities and block the siting of new ones. The placement of hazardous facilities in black communities in the South follows a pattern of subjugation going back "hundreds of years," notes Malek, with "the industrial age" giving this a new translation. And, he says, it should be viewed in connection with the dumping of hazardous waste in Third World countries.

Up North, in the middle of America's biggest city, New York—Peggy Shepard has been challenging environmental racism as a leader of West Harlem Environmental Action (WHE ACT). Obnoxious, "exploitive" facilities placed in our area in recent years, she notes, have included a huge sewage treatment plant, a "marine transfer station" for garbage, and yet another bus storage depot. "We organized around a series of issues in our community that turned out to be all environmental [in] nature." WHE ACT has been "networking with organizations around" New York City and found that what had happened to West Harlem is typical of what has occurred to other African-American and Hispanic neighborhoods. "We get so used to the stereotype that what environmentalism means is wildlife and the preservation of open space. There had not been sufficient movement on urban environmental problems: incinerators, sewage treatment plants, factories polluting the air, devastating occupational exposure."

Sulalman Mahdi is southeast regional director of the Center for Environment, Commerce and Energy in Atlanta. "Our work involves educating the African-American community around the whole question of the environment. I am particularly interested in bridging the civil rights movement and the environmental justice movement," says Mahdi.

He became involved in the "green" movement while working in the campaign for reparations in land for African-Americans for the injustices committed against them. Living in southern Georgia, near Brunswick, "a papermill town and smelling the sulfur all the time" from the papermill lands, he concluded as he choked on the putrid air, that "we need to fight for environmental protection or the land we seek might not be of any real value once it's returned."

He takes the African-American perspective on nature right back to Africa, and indeed is writing a book on African ecology. The African approach to nature "is very similar to that of the Native Americans," says Mahdi. He speaks of the "founder of agriculture, the founder of botany" both ancient Egyptians. He sees a solid "relationship between our freedom struggle" and battling the environmental abuse subjected on African-Americans, what he terms "environmental genocide."

Genocide is also the word used by Lance Hughes of Native Americans for a Clean Environment. "As states and various municipalities have been closing down a lot of dumps because of public opposition, the companies have been descending on the reservations across the country," says Hughes. Indian reservations are seen as good dump sites by their firms because they are considered sovereign entities not subject to local or state environmental restrictions.

The group of which he is director was formed six years ago because of radioactive contamination caused by a twin set of nuclear production facilities run by Kerr-McGee in northeast Oklahoma amid a large concentration of Native Americans. One produces nuclear fuel for weaponry, the other for nuclear power plants. Further, some of the nuclear waste generated at them is put in fertilizer throughout the state, and also by Kerr-McGee on 10,000 acres surrounding the nuclear facilities.

"The hay and cattle from that land is sold on the open market," says Hughes. The Native Americans who live in the area have many "unusual cancers" and a high rate of birth defects from "genetic mutation. It gets pretty sad," says Hughes, "with babies born without eyes, babies born with brain cancers."

Wildlife is also born deformed. "We found a nine-legged frog and a two-headed fish. And there was a four-legged chicken. Hughes emphasizes that the subjugation of Naive Americans "is still going on. The name of the game has been changed, but I would call it the same—genocide, because that is exactly what the result is."

The Southwest Organizing Project (SWOP) is a multi-ethnic, multi-issue organization which began a decade ago in a predominantly Chicano area of Albuquerque, New Mexico. "We have a municipal landfill, the largest pig farm in the city of Albuquerque, a dogfood plant, Texaco, Chevron, General Electric, a sewage plant," says Richard Moore, SWOP co-director. This, he said, is typical of Hispanic and African-American communities in the Southwest.

"Wherever you find working class, ethnic communities you find environmental injustice," says Moore, whose group has grown to fight environmental racism throughout New Mexico. "We have been organizing door-to-door, building strong organizations, going up against pretty major organizations." Non-partisan voter registration has been a key tool. The group was also the founding organization of the Southwest Network of Environmental and Economic Justice, which Moore co-chairs, that brings together people in seven Southwest states also on a multi-ethnic, multi-issue basis.

Moore was one of the signatories of the letter sent to eight major environmental organizations protesting their lack of minority representation (example: of the 315 staff members of the Audubon Society, only three were black).

Importantly, not scored in that letter were three prominent national environmental groups: Greenpeace, the National Toxics Campaign, and Earth Island Institute. In a breakthrough, in contradiction to the pattern elsewhere, the president of Earth Island Institute is an African-American.

Carl Anthony is not only president of Earth Island Institute, headquartered in San Francisco, but director of its Urban Habitat program. "We're very interested in issues at two ends of the spectrum: global warming, the ozone layer, depletion of global resources—and the negative environmental impacts on communities of poor people and people of color. In order to bring these two concerns together," says Anthony, "we have to develop a new kind of thrust and a new kind of leadership in communities of color to address the needs of our communities and also the larger urban community in making a transaction to more sustainable urban patterns." Urban Habitat is "basically a clearinghouse for a lot of people all over the country who want to work on these issues. And it helps alert people from our community to the issues that concern them: toxics, energy issues, air quality, water quality."

Anthony, an architect, says he has "always been aware of environmental issues" is a designer of buildings and is a professor of architecture at the University of California at Berkeley where he is now teaching a new course for the school, Race, Poverty, and the Environment. He speaks with great pleasure of his involvement with Earth Island Institute, but is dubious about whether some of the other national environmental groups will become fully multi-ethnic. They have long taken an "elitist perspective. I doubt that Audubon, for instance, will ever make a big push in this direction."

Chicago's Hazel Johnson has worked closely with Greenpeace, the national environmental group most committed to direct action. "I have a very good working relationship with Greenpeace. It is more than an action group. I have gone with Greenpeace to many places and they have come out to assist us." She spoke of one recent demonstration carried on by her People for Community Recovery against yet one more incinerator planned for her community in which, with Greenpeace, "we chained ourselves to trucks."

"Unequivocally," says Lee, of the Commission for Racial Justice, "minority communities are the communities most at risk to environmental pollution." He paints in words the panorama of pollution. There is the heavy exposure to pesticides of Hispanic farmworkers, including those in Delano, California, where "there is an estimated 300,000 pesticide-related cancers among farm workers each year."

There are the effects of radioactive contamination on Native Americans, especially the Navajos, the nation's primary work force in the mining of uranium—who have extreme cancer rates as a result. "There is lead poisoning of children in urban areas—with an estimated 55 percent of the victims being African-Americans," says Lee. There is the mess in Puerto Rico, "one of the most heavily polluted areas in the world," with U.S. petrochemical and pharmaceutical companies long having discharged toxics on a massive scale. All the people in the island's town of La Cuidad Cristiana were forced to be relocated due to mercury poisoning. The terrible stories go on and on. Says Lee: "We still

have a long way to go in truly addressing this issue."

"To understand the causes of these injustices, it is important to view them in a historical context," he notes. "Two threads of history help to explain the disproportionate impact of toxic pollution on racial and ethnic communities. The first is the long history of oppression and exploitation of African-Americans, Hispanic Americans, Asian-Americans, Pacific Islanders, and Native Americans. This has taken the form of genocide, chattel slavery, indentured servitude, and racial discrimination in employment, housing and practically all aspects of life in the United States. We suffer today from the remnant of this sordid history, as well as from new and institutionalized forms of racism. The other thread of history is the massive expansion of the petrochemical industry since World War II."

"Environmental racism is racial discrimination in environmental policy-making," says Rev. Chavis. "Wherever you find non-white people, that's where they want to dump stuff. And it's spreading all over the world. A lot of toxic chemicals have been going for dumping in the Pacific Islands, and Africa; it recently was revealed that Kenya has been allowing us to dump nuclear wastes." (The Organization of African Unity has denounced the dumping by the U.S. and European countries of hazardous waste in Africa as "toxic terrorism" and "a crime against Africa and the African people.")

"I think when we define the freedom movement, it now includes the environmental issues," says Rev. Chavis. "We now understand the insidious nature of racism. Fighting it does not just involve getting civil rights laws on the books. It goes beyond that. Racism has so permeated all facets of American society. We see the struggle against environmental racism as being an ongoing part of the civil rights and freedom movement in this country, something we are going to make part of our agenda, not a side issue but a primary issue. We must be just as vigilant in attacking environmental racism as racism in health care, housing, and schools."

II

THE OTHER ANIMALS

The famous German philosopher, Immanuel Kant, (1732–1804) thought that there is a very special dignity that human beings possess and that, because of this, they should never be treated as a mere means. In contrast, in his view it is permissible to so act toward nonhumans, the notable exception probably being any divine being.[1] Other nonhuman entities could be, as we pose the point today, of great instrumental value, and we may have serious duties *regarding* them (e.g., one's indirect duty not to destroy a sculpture of Rodin) but not duties *to* them. Are all nonhuman animals like that—of only instrumental value? Are they only of value if and when there is some human around who desires them for some reason or another? Or is it only a very deep-seated prejudice that we learn as children that we only have duties toward members of one of millions of species on the entire planet? And what would we think of such a claim if the word "species" were replaced with the word "race" or "sex"? What is the great gulf, the trait or set of traits that could reasonably be regarded as the morally relevant difference between humans and other animals—especially between humans and those closest to us in terms of intelligence and psychological capacities? By virtue of possessing what trait or traits does one have that special status of being owed a certain respect or owed certain duties of nonharm? Surely, these are among the most basic questions an environmental ethic must address.

A later selection is from James Rachels' 1990 book, *Created from Animals: The Moral Implications of Darwinism*. If one had to name the people whose ideas have had the most profound and revolutionary effect on our understanding of the world, they would include Charles Darwin, along with Isaac Newton, Sigmund Freud, and a few others. Darwin was born in 1809 in England. His father, Robert Darwin, thought his son unpromising and believed that he (Charles) would never amount to anything—a phrase familiar to many sons of overbearing fathers. One philosopher wrote that, judging by the numbers of them, God shows an "inordinate fondness for beetles"; Charles showed a similar interest as a teenager, along with a curiosity about a wide variety of living creatures. In spite of these natural tendencies, Charles was sent off to the University of Edinburgh to become a physician, but the desired result never came to pass. The next assigned destiny for him was to attend Cambridge University in England and become a clergyman. Charles went, graduated tenth in his class, but, upon graduating, accepted an offer to become a captain's mate on the H.M.S. *Beagle* on a trip to South America and the Galapagos Islands in 1831. On this trip, Darwin's understanding of the world was to become radically altered—as would the understanding of the entire literate population eventually. When the century began he, like most everyone else, understood the world to be only several thousand years old, to have been created by God at the outset, and to have always looked largely as it was at that early nineteenth-century time; i.e., mostly unchanged.

With the new geology of James Hutton and Charles Lyell, and the anatomical evidence Georges Cuvier uncovered, reasons accumulated in favor of the view that the earth was much, much older than anyone was imagining, that the forms of life on the planet were very different in the early nineteenth century than they had been in earlier times, and that certain dynamic natural processes at work in the nineteenth century may be part of the explanation for the alteration of forms of life over long periods. Darwin was becoming more aware of these matters as he set out on his momentous voyage.

The upshot was that Darwin ultimately concluded, as was manifest in *The Origin of Species*, published in 1859, that all life on earth has evolved over an extremely long period of time—has, indeed, evolved by a process of incredibly small changes (most not noteworthy, taken individually)—and that humans are simply among the comparative latecomers on the planet as a result of this quite natural process.[2]

Although Darwin was entirely ignorant of the genetic basis of evolutionary change, he observed that in the breeding of animals, the offspring exhibit diverse traits—often minor variations—from the traits shown by their parents. Furthermore, some of these traits might convey to the possessor certain advantages in the competition to survive in a world of scarce resources. The circumstance of scarcity is certain, given the capacity of most animals and plants to produce so many offspring that the resources of the planet cannot support their collective survival.

This was the point made by clergyman Thomas Malthus in the 1790s, in his now famous monograph, *On Population*. Hence, plants and animals with certain traits would be more likely to survive, on average, than others lacking those traits (other things being equal). Thus moths, for example, of darker shades of color would tend to be visible in a snowy climate and thus be more vulnerable to predators; hence over a possibly very long period of time such moths would tend to disappear (not surviving to reproduce) and those with the competitive advantage of being very light in color would tend to survive—and pass on such traits to future generations. So natural selection is not some mysterious force, but simply the tendency for some creatures to have an advantage under competitive circumstances, and thus be more likely to survive and reproduce—and to pass on their advanta-

geous traits (be they an advantageous color, a longer neck, a bigger brain, a proto-eye, a capacity for a faster pace or to survive a long time without food, and so on).

Judging from their capacity to survive under a wide variety of circumstances, among the most successful adapters are the roaches; they may outlive us. Indeed, in Darwin's view, *later in the evolutionary scheme (most recently evolved) is not necessarily better*—popular misconstruals of evolutionary theory to the contrary. Recall talk of human beings existing at the peak of the evolutionary ladder, etc. It is worth observing that, from the standpoint of being successful at surviving (for whatever that's worth), the dinosaurs lived for hundreds of millions of years, that human-like beings lived only several million, and that we modern humans (*Homo sapiens*) have been around only about 200,000 years.

What is the upshot of all this? What does the now canonical view of our biological history imply with respect to the notion that humans are unique in all the world, that human life is of infinite value, or that there is a "human dignity" possessed by all members of our species, or that it is the welfare of our species alone which is of value in all the universe? Rachels proposes an answer to this question.

Our next selection is "Animal Liberation," a well-known 1973 essay by Australian philosopher Peter Singer (his later book has the same title), in which he sketches the utilitarian-based case for the view that we have duties at least to all *sentient* creatures and we are, therefore, unjust in much of our treatment of animals, especially in our imposition of pain (as opposed to death) on them in scientific experiments and in the practice of factory farming. The facts about what is done to animals in these contexts are striking and crucial; no one should leave home, to do philosophy, without them.

Singer has little to say (and did not intend to say much) in that essay about how we should think about ecosystems or questions of preserving biodiversity. From the standpoint of some advocates of an environmental ethic, there is an important distinction to be made between domestic and wild animals. For example, J. Baird Callicott says that "From the perspective of the land ethic a herd of cattle, sheep, or pigs is as much or more a ruinous blight on the landscape as a fleet of four-wheel drive off-road vehicles." The wild/domestic distinction is not regarded as having any particular significance in the position of Singer, or in that of Tom Regan. Readers may wish to remember this point for further reflection.

In a discussion drawn from his 1983 book, *The Case for Animal Rights,* Tom Regan sets out a case for the view that we must radically alter our treatment of animals and that the appropriate view of things is one in which we recognize that (many) animals have rights, namely those that he characterizes as being "subjects of a life." To be a subject of a life, in his view, is roughly to be sentient and self-aware. Regan rejects the assumption that the utilitarian theory provides an acceptable approach to deciding how we ought to treat animals. He criticizes such a view as treating animals as mere "utility receptacles." In spite of this disagreement, there are, so it appears, many respects in which a rights theorist and a utilitarian may agree on practical policy questions, even if they disagree about the appropriate reasons for arriving at them. He calls for a complete halt to scientific experimentation on animals; since Singer allows that it is permissible to kill animals under any conditions in which doing so would maximize utility, his view is probably less in tension with conventional views than is Regan's.

Donald VanDeVeer's 1979 essay, "Interspecific Justice," does not endorse utilitarianism and does not conceptualize human-animal conflicts in terms of a conflict of rights; rather, the central difficulty is conceived in terms of resolution of conflicts of interests. He articulates the deeply entrenched intuition (for better or for worse) that the interests of beings that possess moral standing must be regarded as of diverse moral significance and, further, that even the most basic interests of different beings (say, the interest in the continued life of a mouse and the same interest of a human) may *not* deserve equal moral weight in decisions about how to treat them or how to resolve conflicts of interest between them.[3]

VanDeVeer starts sorting out cases of conflicts of interests by distinguishing between the *basic* and *nonbasic* interests of a being. An animal's or a human's interest in avoiding serious suffering, and in having basic nutritional needs satisfied, are basic interests. Normally a human's interest in not getting drenched during a storm is nonbasic. A human's interests in owning an exotic bird, in having ivory piano keys, in watching a nuclear explosion, in wearing musk perfume, or in shooting a wolf for pleasure are nonbasic; in fact, they are normally peripheral. One can sort human-animal conflicts into categories, the two most important of which are (1) those between basic human and basic animal (or plant) interests, and (2) those between nonbasic human and basic animal (or plant) interests.

VanDeVeer formulates several principles that we might use to guide our decision making and defends the one he calls "Two-Factor Egalitarianism," a principle he claims is not speciesist but that also avoids the extreme egalitarianism that is characteristic of some philosophical outlooks.[4] The principle gives weight to the comparative importance of the interest(s) at stake (to its possessor) as well as the psychological complexity of the beings whose interests are in conflict.

No doubt we believe that the life of an oyster is less rich than the life of most politicians. Does it follow that humans have a right to subordinate or somehow exploit the oyster, or another being with a less rich psychological existence? If one answers affirmatively, is one thereby committed to the view that it is all right for the normal person to subordinate the seriously retarded person, other things being equal? Does bright make right? Do traits that we may think fail to justify *intraspecific* differential treatment ("discrimination" in one sense) justify *interspecific* differential treatment? VanDeVeer insists on not ignoring differences in the psychological capacities of the beings in question. Is having lesser psychological capacity a sufficient, or only a necessary, condition of being justifiably given the short end of the stick (if relevant at all)?[5] Alternatively, is any view credible that implies that under some circumstances, the life of an oyster should be valued on a par with that of a normal human? What about a chimpanzee and a human? What about a chimpanzee and an anencephalic human baby?[6]

Among many examples of human/animal conflicts of interest, consider a recent instance.[7] In 1993, in *Church of the Lukumi Babalu Aye, Inc. and Ernest Picardo, Petitioners* v. *City of Hialeah*, the U.S. Supreme Court addressed a case in which a Hialeah, Florida, priest of the Santeria religion and his congregation claimed the right to exercise their religious beliefs, which called for the sacrifice of thousands of animals, including chickens, goats, turtles, and doves. These practices were, of course, common in the era of the Hebrew scriptures (the "Old Testament" among Christians), and we also note in passing the idea of Jesus as the "sacrificial lamb" whose death was thought necessary to placate a god who required such sacrifices. This is one of many cases in which basic animal interests are at stake, and we leave it open as to how basic the human ones are; of course, if one says that it is a basic interest to carry out any or all of one's religious beliefs, and that such an interest should always be fostered, then it is not clear why the door is not opened to *human* sacrifice as well, since some religions require it. In its decision, the Court maintained that "A law burdening religious practice that is not neutral or not of general application must undergo the most rigorous of scrutiny."[8] In general, the Court denied that the governmental interests at stake were sufficiently compelling to justify restrictions on religious practice. Since the statutes were not aimed at preventing cruelty to animals, it appears that the Court took this to be a good reason not to give serious consideration to the interests of the animals in their deliberations.

In a 1987 essay (reprinted here), "Animal Liberation or Animal Rights?" Peter Singer undertakes to respond to some of the objections that had been made to his views since the publication of his essay, "Animal Liberation," in 1975. Here Singer explicitly observes that although he occasionally used the language "animal rights" in his earlier publication, he does so only as shorthand for speaking of the way in which "the needs and desires of animals give rise to moral obligations on our part." Although he is not convinced that animals have rights in any other sense, he maintains that if there are any rights that all humans have, then "those rights are also possessed by nonhuman animals." If all humans possess rights, he reasons, it cannot be because of membership in *Homo sapiens* (an irrelevant trait), and it cannot be because of traits like autonomy, rationality, etc., since such traits, *even if relevant,* are not possessed by all humans; e.g., they are not possessed by all infants and not possessed by some of the congenitally disabled.

Alternatively, one can, Singer maintains, ground a moral theory on a duty to respect or promote interests, as does utilitarianism. If so, he claims at least all sentient animals "enter the sphere of moral concern" and ". . . their interests are to be given the same consideration as the like interests of any other being" (the *"principle of equal consideration of interests"*). It is worth paying attention to two points here; one concerns the range of things to which Singer is granting, in our terminology, *moral standing.* Second, note the crucial expression *"like* interests." What counts as such is no small matter. Singer maintains, in spite of the temptation to think otherwise, that the principle of equal consideration of interests, does not entail that "we must treat nonhuman animals in the same way that we treat human beings." What does follow is a matter of considerable interest and importance: How is Singer proposing that we resolve those conflicts of interests? Are all interests relevant? Are they to be given diverse weights? We leave these matters for the reader's reflection and scrutiny.

Part of Singer's essay aims, further, to rebut the charges brought by Tom Regan and perhaps other theorists of animal rights, that the utilitarian approach to things denies that some animals are subjects of a life, that they have intrinsic value, or that they are to be treated as mere "receptacles of valuable experiences" (or "mere utility-containers," as Robert Nozick, the original proponent of this criticism, argued).[5] The discussion of these matters actually probes, therefore, some deep points of controversy regarding the adequacy of utilitarianism as an ethical theory and the often-made claim that only some sort of rights theory can embody the view that, say, sentient creatures are to be valued not merely on the basis of the fact that they have valuable experiences (or to the extent and only to the extent that they do so). Such controversy has ramifications quite outside of environmental ethics, but also is surely at the base of some important divergence of outlooks concerning environmental policy. Singer's critique of the container or receptacle metaphor as misleading is not to be overlooked.

In the course of his discussion, Singer distinguishes his own brand of utilitarianism ("preference utilitarianism") from the classical view. In the latter, what is to be maximized is *pleasant experiences*—a certain type of mental state. However, in the preference utilitarian view, what is to be maximized is the *fulfillment of preferences.* To explain, often one experiences pleasure upon having one's preferences fulfilled, but one may have his or her preferences fulfilled (note the ambiguity of the word "satisfied") without the occurrence of pleasure. For example, a child may find a career that is satisfying, as the parent wished, but the parent

may not have lived to see the day. Conversely, one's wants may not be fulfilled but one may not experience dissatisfaction; e.g., one is betrayed by one's mate but never learns of it. The relevance of this distinction comes when one assesses the morality of painless killing (say, of animals) which, we observe, may involve no dissatisfaction to the one killed but may thwart the desire to continue to exist in the future if the being is capable of having such a desire. Those who are so capable are the kind of beings Singer and many other philosophers label "persons." Note Singer's acknowledgment of a relevant difference among sentient beings. In brief, the difference between classic and preference utilitarianism bears on the morality of killing and hence has implications for policy questions (killing animals for food, during scientific experiments, destruction of habitat, "culling" of herds, or elimination of "alien" or non-native species).

All the interesting environmental disputes involve some sort of conflict between preserving values (or preserving what is thought to have value) of one sort or another. Typically we must choose between these lives and those lives or between giving these benefits to these creatures at the price of causing those harms to those creatures. How to resolve these conflicts is a vital and sometimes a terrible question. When utilitarians defend doing whatever will maximize utility, the condoned policies often involve serious sacrifices or costs to some; at this point, their critics, rights theorists or not, often insist that such choices involve treating certain beings as a mere means and thus violate Kant's tempting dictum (in his view, it applied only to rational beings). Singer defends his view against such a charge. Indeed, he seems on the right side of the fence. Just because a theory condones harming an innocent party under certain circumstances does not entail that no weight has been given to the well-being of the party in the process of decision making. After all, choosing lots to see who might get the only available kidney machine in effect condemns some to death, but it is not obvious that they are treated as a mere means if they have a had fair chance at a scarce benefit, other things being morally equal. Unlike some discussions, Singer's theoretically rich contribution tries to state in detail reasons of a specific, principled nature for deciding policy one way or the other; thus, he advances the dialogue.

Much discussion of how we ought to treat animals speaks as if they are all at great distance from us psychologically, and perhaps physically, but this, Mary Midgley reminds us, is simply not fair to the facts. As she notes, "all human communities have involved animals." Indeed many of us have formed deep bonds of loyalty and affection with certain animals. Perhaps we are reluctant to say so out loud, but many of us are often not deeply moved at the death of selected human relatives although we are emotionally distraught for days or weeks or longer over the death of a nonhuman companion ("pet" seems too demeaning)—often a dog or a cat from whom we have often felt virtually unqualified, unconditional affection. What shall we make of the importance of this extraordinarily important experience that many of us feel in relation to certain animals? Why is it so often ignored or denied? Are not many of our families populated by mixed species? Do we have duties, however, toward (and perhaps only toward) those creatures with whom we have formed bonds of affection? Or is that only sufficient (but not necessary) for the existence of certain duties? At the least, some of our confrontations with conflicts of interests cases involve animals that are very much a part of our most intimate communities.

In discussing the question of what sorts of entities have moral standing and in inquiring how animals should be treated, the selections in this section focus on *individuals*. However, some think that the real locus of value is in *ecosystems*, or networks of life, and that, at the very least, the focus on individuals is misplaced and wrong-headed. The view of "hol-

ists" on this matter does not seem entirely clear, but one possible position (call it extreme holism) is that the value of individuals is derivative and dependent on their function in some larger network. Thus, individuals seem replaceable and perhaps of only instrumental value. Another possible form of holism (call it moderate holism) would hold that both the relevant individuals *and* the relevant system possess moral standing; in this latter view, the value of the individuals would not be merely derivative. These last remarks look ahead since such nonindividualist views receive discussion in Section III and later.

NOTES

1. Strictly, Kant speaks of persons (never treat a person as a mere means) and the value of rationality, but it is not obvious that he thought that any humans lacked this special dignity of which he speaks—or that he thought that any nonhuman possessed it.

2. Much of Darwin's view about human beings became clearer with the publication of *The Descent of Man, and Selection in Relation to Sex* in 1871.

3. Paul Taylor claims that we need not give much or any weight to our pretheoretical moral intuitions in deciding on the acceptability of a theory; see his essay in Section III. Whether one should accept a theory, no matter how counterintuitive it is, we leave for the reader to consider.

    We have spoken here of conflicts of interest. We have not, however, assumed that any being has a right to whatever is in its interest. After all, it might be in your interest (for now, conducive to your well-being) if all your friends committed themselves to form a Be Nice to _____ (fill in your name here) Club and donated 10 to 20 percent of their annual incomes to promoting your well-being. But it is doubtful that you have a right to such or should complain of a rights violation if they fail to do so. Still, rights and interests no doubt have some important relation to one another. We flag the question here.

4. How VanDeVeer's rather individualist orientation in that essay would be modified to take into account the powerful presumptive value of biodiversity and healthy ecosystems remains an open question.

5. Another perspective is worth noting here. One might think that the most stringent duties of all are directly owed to persons (in the psychological as

opposed to the biological interpretation), and yet other entities, say, the merely sentient ones, also possess moral standing. Thus, one might think that there is a sort of moral hierarchy of entities; for example, all and only sentient creatures have moral standing, but among those with such standing, the well-being or lives of some morally count more heavily than others. Thus, although there is a presumption against destroying or causing pain to any sentient creature, in certain conflicts of interest between persons and the merely sentient it is all right (or obligatory) to sacrifice the interest of the latter.

6. What if we could save the life of a rare white tiger from Siberia by transplanting an organ from a rightfully convicted mass murderer in an operation that would kill the mass murderer? This example brings up the question of the weight to be given to innocence or the lack of it on the part of one party involved in a conflict of interest. Robert Nozick (see the next reference) distinguishes between innocent and noninnocent attackers. A genuinely psychotic human or a rabid dog may serve as an example of the former. We often think it permissible to use vio-

lence, perhaps lethal, on a noninnocent aggressor who attacks us. Virtually all animals lack the capacity for functioning as moral agents and, hence, are not morally responsible for harms they cause; hence, they are not to blame for attacks they make and, thus, are innocent. Whether a being (innocent or not) has initiated an attack and whether that being is innocent seem to be morally relevant considerations in deciding how one ought to resolve a conflict of interest between the being and another. We note, then, a consideration about the moral relevance of prior acts, a consideration about the history or genesis of the conflict of interest. If we take away or destroy someone's food, say, a farmer's crops, we have attacked him or her; analogously, humans are often the initiators of aggression toward animals, e.g., by destroying their habitats or food sources.

7. *Church of the Lukumi Babalu Aye, Inc. and Ernest Picardo, Petitioners* v. *the City of Hialeah*, June 11, 1993, *The United States Law Week*, Vol. 61, no. 91–948 (June 8, 1993), 4587.

8. See Robert Nozick, *Anarchy, State, and Utopia* (New York: Basic Books, 1974).

Animal Liberation[1] _____

Peter Singer

I

We are familiar with Black Liberation, Gay Liberation, and a variety of other movements. With Women's Liberation some thought we had come to the end of the road. Discrimination on the basis of sex, it has been said, is the last form of discrimination that is universally accepted and practiced without pretense, even in those liberal circles which have long prided themselves on their freedom from racial discrimination. But one should always be wary of talking of "the last remaining form of discrimination." If we have learned anything from the liberation movements, we should have learned how difficult it is to be aware of the ways in which we discriminate until they are forcefully pointed out to us. A liberation movement demands an expansion of our moral horizons, so that practices that were previously regarded as natural and inevitable are now seen as intolerable.

Animals, Men and Morals is a manifesto for an Animal Liberation movement. The contributors to the book may not all see the issue this way. They are a varied group. Philosophers, ranging from professors to graduate students, make up the largest contingent. There are five of them, including the three editors, and there is also an extract from the unjustly neglected German philosopher with an English name, Leonard Nelson, who died in 1927. There are essays by two novelist/critics, Brigid Brophy and Maureen Duffy, and another by Muriel the Lady Dowding, widow of Dowding of Battle of Britain fame and the founder of "Beauty without Cruelty," a movement that campaigns against the use of animals for furs and cosmetics. The other pieces are by a psychologist, a botanist, a sociologist, and Ruth Harrison, who is probably best described as a professional campaigner for animal welfare.

Whether or not these people, as individuals, would all agree that they are launching a liberation movement for animals, the book as a whole amounts to no less. It is a demand for a complete change in our attitudes to nonhumans. It is a demand that we cease to regard the exploitation of other species as natural and inevitable, and that, instead, we see it as a continuing moral outrage. Patrick Corbett, Professor of Philosophy at Sussex University, captures the spirit of the book in his closing words:

> . . . we require now to extend the great principles of liberty, equality and fraternity over the lives of animals. Let animal slavery join human slavery in the graveyard of the past.

The reader is likely to be skeptical. "Animal Liberation" sounds more like a parody of liberation movements than a serious objective. The reader may think: We support the claims of blacks and women for equality because blacks and women really are equal to whites and males—equal in intelligence and in abilities, capacity for leadership, rationality, and so on. Humans and nonhumans obviously are not equal in these respects. Since justice demands only that we treat equals equally, unequal treatment of humans and nonhumans cannot be an injustice.

This is a tempting reply, but a dangerous one. It commits the non-racist and non-sexist to a dogmatic belief that blacks and women really are just as intelligent, able, etc., as whites and males—and no more. Quite possibly this happens to be the case. Certainly attempts to prove that racial or sexual differences in these respects have a genetic origin have not been conclusive. But do we really want to stake our demand for equality on the assumption that there are no genetic differences of this kind between the different races or sexes? Surely the appropriate response to those who claim to have found evidence for such genetic differences is not to stick to the belief that there are no differences, whatever the evidence to the contrary; rather one should be clear that the claim to equality does not depend on IQ. Moral equality is distinct from factual equality. Otherwise it would be nonsense to talk of the equality of human beings, since humans, as individuals, obviously differ in intelligence and almost any ability one cares to name. If possessing greater intelligence does not entitle one human to exploit another, why should it entitle humans to exploit nonhumans?

Jeremy Bentham expressed the essential basis of equality in his famous formula: "Each to count for one and none for more than one." In other words, the interests of every being that has interests are to be taken into account and treated equally with the like interests of any other being. Other moral philosophers, before and after Bentham, have made the same point in different ways. Our concern for others must not depend on whether they possess certain characteristics, though just what that concern involves may, of course, vary according to such characteristics.

Bentham, incidentally, was well aware that the logic of the demand for racial equality did not stop at the equality of humans. He wrote:

> The day *may* come when the rest of the animal creation may acquire those rights which never could have been withholden from them but by the hand of tyranny. The French have already discovered that the blackness of the skin is no reason why a human being should be abandoned without redress to the caprice of a tormentor. It may one day come to be recognized that the number of the legs, the villosity of the skin, or the termination of the *os sacrum*, are reasons equally insufficient for abandoning a sensitive being to the same fate. What else is it that should trace the insuperable line? Is it the faculty of reason, or perhaps the faculty of discourse? But a full-grown horse or dog is beyond comparison a more rational, as well as a more conversable animal, than an infant of a day, or a week, or even a month old. But suppose they were otherwise, what would it avail? The question is not, Can they *reason?* nor Can they *talk?* but, Can they *suffer?*[2]

Surely Bentham was right. If a being suffers, there can be no moral justification for refusing to take that suffering into consideration, and, indeed, to count it equally with the like suffering (if rough comparisons can be made) of any other being.

So the only question is: do animals other than man suffer? Most people agree unhesitatingly that animals like cats and dogs can and do suffer, and this seems also to be assumed by those laws that prohibit wanton cruelty to such animals. Personally, I have no doubt at all about this and find it hard to take seriously the doubts that a few people apparently do have. The editors and contributors of *Animals, Men and Morals* seem to feel the same way, for although the question is raised more than once, doubts are quickly dismissed each time. Nevertheless, because this is such a fundamental point, it is worth asking what grounds we have for attributing suffering to other animals.

It is best to begin by asking what grounds any individual human has for supposing that other humans feel pain. Since pain is a state of consciousness, a "mental event," it can never be directly observed. No observations, whether behavioral signs such as writhing or screaming or physiological or neurological recordings, are observations of pain itself. Pain is something one feels, and one can only infer that others are feeling it from various external indications. The fact that only philosophers are ever skeptical about whether other humans feel pain shows that we regard such inference as justifiable in the case of humans.

Is there any reason why the same inference should be unjustifiable for other animals? Nearly all the external signs which lead us to infer pain in other humans can be seen in other species, especially "higher" animals such as mammals and birds. Behavioral signs—writhing, yelping, or other forms of calling, attempts to avoid the source of pain, and many others—are present. We know, too, that these animals are biologically similar in the relevant respects, having nervous systems like ours which can be observed to function as ours do.

So the grounds for inferring that these animals can feel pain are nearly as good as the grounds for inferring other humans do. Only nearly, for there is one behavioral sign that humans have but nonhumans, with the exception of one or two specially raised chimpanzees, do not have. This, of course, is a developed language. As the quotation from Bentham indicates, this has long been regarded as an important distinction between man and other animals. Other animals may communicate with each other, but not in the way we do. Following Chomsky, many people now mark this distinction by say-

ing that only humans communicate in a form that is governed by rules of syntax. (For the purposes of this argument, linguists allow those chimpanzees who have learned a syntactic sign language to rank as honorary humans.) Nevertheless, as Bentham pointed out, this distinction is not relevant to the question of how animals ought to be treated, unless it can be linked to the issue of whether animals suffer.

This link may be attempted in two ways. First, there is a hazy line of philosophical thought, stemming perhaps from some doctrines associated with Wittgenstein, which maintains that we cannot meaningfully attribute states of consciousness to beings without language. I have not seen this argument made explicit in print, though I have come across it in conversation. This position seems to me very implausible, and I doubt that it would be held at all if it were not thought to be a consequence of a broader view of the significance of language. It may be that the use of a public, rule-governed language is a precondition of conceptual thought. It may even be, although personally I doubt it, that we cannot meaningfully speak of a creature having an intention unless that creature can use a language. But states like pain, surely, are more primitive than either of these, and seem to have nothing to do with language.

Indeed, as Jane Goodall points out in her study of chimpanzees, when it comes to the expression of feelings and emotions, humans tend to fall back on nonlinguistic modes of communication which are often found among apes, such as a cheering pat on the back, an exuberant embrace, a clasp of hands, and so on.[3] Michael Peters makes a similar point in his contribution to *Animals, Men and Morals* when he notes that the basic signals we use to convey pain, fear, sexual arousal, and so on are not specific to our species. So there seems to be no reason at all to believe that a creature without language cannot suffer.

The second, and more easily appreciated way of linking language and the existence of pain is to say that the best evidence that we can have that another creature is in pain is when he tells us that he is. This is a distinct line of argument, for it is not being denied that a non-language-user conceivably could suffer, but only that we could know that he is suffering. Still, this line of argument seems to me to fail, and for reasons similar to those just given. "I am in pain" is not the best possible evidence that the speaker is in pain (he might be lying) and it is certainly not the only possible evidence. Behavioral signs and knowledge of the animals' biological similarity to ourselves together provide adequate evidence that animals do suffer. After all, we would not accept linguistic evidence if it contradicted the rest of the evidence. If a man was severely burned, and behaved as if he were in pain, writhing, groaning, being very careful not to let his burned skin touch anything, and so on, but later said he had not been in pain at all, we would be more likely to conclude that he was lying or suffering from amnesia than that he had not been in pain.

Even if there were stronger grounds for refusing to attribute pain to those who do not have a language, the consequences of this refusal might lead us to examine these grounds unusually critically. Human infants, as well as some adults, are unable to use language. Are we to deny that a year-old infant can suffer? If not, how can language be crucial? Of course, most parents can understand the responses of even very young infants better than they understand the responses of other animals, and sometimes infant responses can be understood in the light of later development.

This, however, is just a fact about the relative knowledge we have of our own species and other species, and most of this knowledge is simply derived from closer contact. Those who have studied the behavior of other animals soon learn to understand their responses at least as well as we understand those of an infant. (I am not just referring to Jane Goodall's and other well-known studies of apes. Consider, for example, the degree of understanding achieved by Tinbergen from watching herring gulls.)[4] Just as we can understand infant human behavior in the light of adult human behavior, so we can understand the behavior of other species in the light of our own behavior (and sometimes we can understand our own behavior better in the light of the behavior of other species).

The grounds we have for believing that other mammals and birds suffer are, then, closely analogous to the grounds we have for believing that other humans suffer. It remains to consider how far down the evolutionary scale this analogy holds. Obviously it becomes poorer when we get further away from man. To be more precise would require a detailed examination of all that we know about other forms of life. With fish, reptiles, and other vertebrates the analogy still seems strong, with molluscs like oysters it is much weaker. Insects are more difficult, and it may be that in our present state of knowledge we must be agnostic about whether they are capable of suffering.

If there is no moral justification for ignoring suffering when it occurs, and it does occur in other species, what are we to say of our attitudes toward these other species? Richard Ryder, one of the contributors to *Animals, Men and Morals*, uses the term "speciesism" to describe the belief that we are entitled to treat members of other species in a way in which it would be wrong to treat members of our own species. The term is not euphonious, but it neatly makes the analogy with racism. The nonracist would do well to bear the analogy in mind when he is inclined to defend human behavior toward nonhumans. "Shouldn't we worry about improving the lot of our own species before we concern ourselves with other species?" he may ask. If we substitute "race" for "species" we shall see that the question is better not asked. "Is a vegetarian diet nutritionally adequate?" resembles the slave-owner's claim that he and the whole economy of the South would be ruined without slave labor. There is even a parallel with skeptical doubts about whether animals suffer, for some defenders of slavery professed to doubt whether blacks really suffer in the way that whites do.

I do not want to give the impression, however, that the case for Animal Liberation is based on the analogy with racism and no more. On the contrary, *Animals, Men and Morals* describes the various ways in which humans exploit nonhumans, and several contributors consider the defenses that have been offered, including the defense of meat-eating mentioned in the last paragraph. Sometimes the rebuttals are scornfully dismissive, rather than carefully designed to convince the detached critic. This may be a fault, but it is a fault that is inevitable, given the kind of book this is. The issue is not one on which one can remain detached. As the editors state in their Introduction:

> Once the full force of moral assessment has been made explicit there can be no rational excuse left for killing animals, be they killed for food, science, or sheer personal indulgence. We have not assembled this book to provide the reader with yet another manual on how to make brutali-

ties less brutal. Compromise, in the traditional sense of the term, is simple unthinking weakness when one considers the actual reasons for our crude relationships with the other animals.

The point is that on this issue there are few critics who are genuinely detached. People who eat pieces of slaughtered nonhumans every day find it hard to believe that they are doing wrong; and they also find it hard to imagine what else they could eat. So for those who do not place nonhumans beyond the pale of morality, there comes a stage when further argument seems pointless, a stage at which one can only accuse one's opponent of hypocrisy and reach for the sort of sociological account of our practices and the way we defend them that is attempted by David Wood in his contribution to this book. On the other hand, to those unconvinced by the arguments, and unable to accept that they are rationalizing their dietary preferences and their fear of being thought peculiar, such sociological explanations can only seem insultingly arrogant.

II

The logic of speciesism is most apparent in the practice of experimenting on nonhumans in order to benefit humans. This is because the issue is rarely obscured by allegations that nonhumans are so different from humans that we cannot know anything about whether they suffer. The defender of vivisection cannot use this argument because he needs to stress the similarities between man and other animals in order to justify the usefulness to the former of experiments on the latter. The researcher who makes rats choose between starvation and electric shocks to see if they develop ulcers (they do) does so because he knows that the rat has a nervous system very similar to man's, and presumably feels an electric shock in a similar way.

Richard Ryder's restrained account of experiments on animals made me angrier with my fellow men than anything else in this book. Ryder, a clinical psychologist by profession, himself experimented on animals before he came to hold the view he puts forward in his essay. Experimenting on animals is now a large industry, both academic and commercial. In 1969, more than 5 million experiments were performed in Britain, the vast majority without anesthetic (though how many of these involved pain is not known). There are no accurate US figures, since there is no federal law on the subject, and in many cases no state law either. Estimates vary from 20 million to 200 million. Ryder suggests that 80 million may be the best guess. We tend to think that this is all for vital medical research, but of course it is not. Huge numbers of animals are used in university departments from Forestry to Psychology, and even more are used for commercial purposes, to test whether cosmetics can cause skin damage, or shampoos eye damage, or to test food additives or laxatives or sleeping pills or anything else.

A standard test for foodstuffs is the "LD50." The object of this test is to find the dosage level at which 50 percent of the test animals will die. This means that nearly all of them will become very sick before finally succumbing or surviving. When the substance is a harmless one, it may be necessary to force huge doses down the animals, until in some cases sheer volume or concentration causes death.

Ryder gives a selection of experiments, taken from recent scientific journals. I will quote two, not for the sake of indulging in gory details, but in order to give an idea of what normal researchers think they may legitimately do to other species. The point is not that the individual researchers are cruel men, but that they are behaving in a way that is allowed by our speciesist attitudes. As Ryder points out, even if only 1 percent of the experiments involve severe pain, that is 50,000 experiments in Britain each year, or nearly 150 every day (and about fifteen times as many in the United States, if Ryder's guess is right). Here then are two experiments:

> O. S. Ray and R. J. Barrett of Pittsburgh gave electric shocks to the feet of 1,042 mice. They then caused convulsions by giving more intense shocks through cup-shaped electrodes applied to the animals' eyes or through pressure spring clips attached to their ears. Unfortunately some of the mice who "successfully completed Day One training were found sick or dead prior to testing on Day Two." [*Journal of Comparative and Physiological Psychology,* 1969, Vol. 67, pp. 110–116]
>
> At the National Institute for Medical Research, Mill Hill, London, W. Feldberg

and S. L. Sherwood injected chemicals into the brains of cats—"with a number of widely different substances, recurrent patterns of reaction were obtained. Retching, vomiting, defaecation, increased salivation and greatly accelerated respiration leading to panting were common features.". . .

The injection into the brain of a large dose of Tubocuraine caused the cat to jump "from the table to the floor and then straight into its cage, where it started calling more and more noisily whilst moving about restlessly and jerkily . . . finally the cat fell with legs and neck flexed, jerking in rapid clonic movements, the condition being that of a major [epileptic] convulsion . . . within a few seconds the cat got up, ran for a few yards at high speed and fell in another fit. The whole process was repeated several times within the next ten minutes, during which the cat lost faeces and foamed at the mouth."

This animal finally died thirty-five minutes after the brain injection. [*Journal of Physiology,* 1954, Vol. 123, pp. 148–167]

There is nothing secret about these experiments. One has only to open any recent volume of a learned journal, such as the *Journal of Comparative and Physiological Psychology,* to find full descriptions of experiments of this sort, together with the results obtained—results that are frequently trivial and obvious. The experiments are often supported by public funds.

It is a significant indication of the level of acceptability of these practices that, although these experiments are taking place at this moment on university campuses throughout the country, there has, so far as I know, not been the slightest protest from the student movement. Students have been rightly concerned that their universities should not discriminate on grounds of race or sex, and that they should not serve the purposes of the military or big business. Speciesism continues undisturbed, and many students participate in it. There may be a few qualms at first, but since everyone regards it as normal, and it may even be a required part of a course, the student soon becomes hardened and, dismissing his earlier feelings as "mere sentiment," comes to regard animals as statistics rather than sentient beings with interests that warrant consideration.

Argument about vivisection has often missed the point because it has been put in absolutist terms: would the abolitionist be prepared to let thousands die if they could be saved by experimenting on a single animal? The way to reply to this purely hypothetical question is to pose another: Would the experimenter be prepared to experiment on a human orphan under six months old, if it were the only way to save many lives? (I say "orphan" to avoid the complication of parental feelings, although in doing so I am being overfair to the experimenter, since the nonhuman subjects of experiments are not orphans.) A negative answer to this question indicates that the experimenter's readiness to use nonhumans is simple discrimination, for adult apes, cats, mice, and other mammals are more conscious of what is happening to them, more self-directing, and, so far as we can tell, just as sensitive to pain as a human infant. There is no characteristic that human infants possess that adult mammals do not have to the same or a higher degree.

(It might be possible to hold that what makes it wrong to experiment on a human infant is that the infant will in time develop into more than the nonhuman, but one would then, to be consistent, have to oppose abortion, and perhaps contraception, too, for the fetus and the egg and sperm have the same potential as the infant. Moreover, one would still have no reason for experimenting on a nonhuman rather than a human with brain damage severe enough to make it impossible for him to rise above infant level.)

The experimenter, then, shows a bias for his own species whenever he carries out an experiment on a nonhuman for a purpose that he would not think justified him in using a human being at an equal or lower level of sentience, awareness, ability to be self-directing, etc. No one familiar with the kind of results yielded by these experiments can have the slightest doubt that if this bias were eliminated the number of experiments performed would be zero or very close to it.

III

If it is vivisection that shows the logic of speciesism most clearly, it is the use of other species for food that is at the heart of our attitudes toward them. Most of *Animals, Men and Morals* is an attack on meat-eating—an attack which is based solely on concern for nonhumans, without reference to arguments derived from considerations of ecology, macrobiotics, health, or religion.

The idea that nonhumans are utilities, means to our ends, pervades our thought. Even conservationists who are concerned about the slaughter of wild fowl but not about the vastly greater slaughter of chickens for our tables are thinking in this way—they are worried about what we would lose if there were less wildlife. Stanley Godlovitch, pursuing the Marxist idea that our thinking is formed by the activities we undertake in satisfying our needs, suggests that man's first classification of his environment was into Edibles and Inedibles. Most animals came into the first category, and there they have remained.

Man may always have killed other species for food, but he has never exploited them so ruthlessly as he does today. Farming has succumbed to business methods, the objective being to get the highest possible ratio of output (meat, eggs, milk) to input (fodder, labor costs, etc.). Ruth Harrison's essay "On Factory Farming" gives an account of some aspects of modern methods, and of the unsuccessful British campaign for effective controls, a campaign which was sparked off by her *Animal Machines* (Stuart: London, 1964).

Her article is in no way a substitute for her earlier book. This is a pity since, as she says, "Farm produce is still associated with mental pictures of animals browsing in the fields, . . . of hens having a last forage before going to roost. . . ." Yet neither in her article nor elsewhere in *Animals, Men and Morals* is this false image replaced by a clear idea of the nature and extent of factory farming. We learn of this only indirectly, when we hear of the code of reform proposed by an advisory committee set up by the British government.

Among the proposals, which the government refused to implement on the grounds that they were too idealistic, were: *"Any animal should at least have room to turn around freely."*

Factory farm animals need liberation in the most literal sense. Veal calves are kept in stalls five feet by two feet. They are usually slaughtered when about four months old, and have been too big to turn in their stalls for at least a month. Intensive beef herds, kept in stalls only proportionately larger for much longer periods, account for a growing percentage of beef production. Sows are often similarly confined when pregnant, which, because of artificial methods of increasing fertility, can be most of the time. Animals confined in this way do not waste food by exercising, nor do they develop unpalatable muscle.

"A dry bedded area should be provided for all stock." Intensively kept animals usually have to stand and sleep on slatted floors without straw, because this makes cleaning easier.

"Palatable roughage must be readily available to all calves after one week of age." In order to produce the pale veal housewives are said to prefer, calves are fed on an all-liquid diet until slaughter, even though they are long past the age at which they would normally eat grass. They develop a craving for roughage, evidenced by attempts to gnaw wood from their stalls. (For the same reason, their diet is deficient in iron.)

"Battery cages for poultry should be large enough for a bird to be able to stretch one wing at a time." Under current British practice, a cage for four or five laying hens has a floor area of twenty inches by eighteen inches, scarcely larger than a double page of the *New York Review of Books*. In this space, on a sloping wire floor (sloping so the eggs roll down, wire so the dung drops through) the birds live for a year or eighteen months while artificial lighting and temperature conditions combine with drugs in their food to squeeze the maximum number of eggs out of them. Table birds are also sometimes kept in cages. More often they are reared in sheds, no less crowded. Under these conditions all the birds' natural activities are frustrated, and they develop "vices" such as pecking each other to death. To prevent this, beaks are often cut off and the sheds kept dark.

How many of those who support factory farming by buying its produce know anything about the way it is produced? How many have heard something about it, but are reluctant to check up for fear that it will make them uncomfortable? To nonspeciesists, the typical consumer's mixture of ignorance, reluctance to find out the truth, and vague belief that nothing really bad could be allowed seems analogous to the attitudes of "decent Germans" to the death camps.

There are, of course, some defenders of factory farming. Their arguments are considered, though again rather sketchily, by John Harris. Among the most common: "Since they have never known anything else, they don't suffer." This argument will not be put by anyone who knows anything about animal behavior, since he will know that not all behavior has to be learned. Chickens attempt to stretch wings, walk around, scratch, and even dust-bathe or build a nest, even though they have never lived under conditions that allowed these activities. Calves can suffer from maternal deprivation no matter at what age they were taken from their mothers. "We need these intensive methods to provide protein for a growing population." As ecologists and famine relief organizations know, we can produce far more protein per acre if we grow the right vegetable crop, soy beans for instance, than if we use the land to grow crops to be converted into protein by animals who use nearly 90 percent of the protein themselves, even when unable to exercise.

There will be many readers of this book who will agree that factory farming involves an unjustifiable degree of exploitation of sentient creatures, and yet will want to say that there is nothing wrong with rearing animals for food, provided it is done "humanely." These people are saying, in effect, that although we should not cause animals to suffer, there is nothing wrong with killing them.

There are two possible replies to this view. One is to attempt to show that this combination of attitudes is absurd. Roslind Godlovitch takes this course in her essay, which is an examination of some common attitudes to animals. She argues that from the combination of "animal suffering is to be avoided" and "there is nothing wrong with killing animals" it follows that all animal life ought to be exterminated (since all sentient creatures will suffer to some degree at some point in their lives). Euthanasia is a contentious issue only because we place some value on living. If we did not, the least amount of suffering would justify it. Accordingly, if we deny that we have a duty to exterminate all animal life, we must concede that we are placing some value on animal life.

This argument seems to me valid, although one could still reply that the value of animal life is to be derived from the pleasures that life can have for them, so that, provided their lives have a balance of pleasure over pain, we are justified in rearing them. But this would imply that we ought to produce animals and let them live as pleasantly as possible, without suffering.

At this point, one can make the second of the two possible replies to the view that rearing and killing animals for food is all right so long as it is done humanely. This second reply is that so long as we think that a nonhuman may be killed simply so that a human can satisfy his taste for meat, we are still thinking of nonhumans as means rather than as ends in themselves. The factory farm is nothing more than the application of technology to this concept. Even traditional methods involve castration, the separation of mothers and their young, the breaking up of herds, branding or ear-punching, and of course transportation to the abattoirs and the final moments of terror when the animal smells blood and senses danger. If we were to try rearing animals so that they lived and died without suffering, we should find that to do so on anything like the scale of today's meat industry would be a sheer impossibility. Meat would become the prerogative of the rich.

I have been able to discuss only some of the contributions to this book, saying nothing about, for instance, the essays on killing for furs and for sport. Nor have I considered all the detailed questions that need to be asked once we start thinking about other species in the radically different way presented by this book. What, for instance, are we to do about genuine conflicts of interest like rats biting slum children? I am not sure of the answer, but the essential point is just that we *do* see this as a conflict of interests, that we recognize that rats have interests too. Then we may begin to think about other ways of resolving the conflict—perhaps by leaving out rat baits that sterilize the rats instead of killing them.

I have not discussed such problems because they are side issues compared with the exploitation of other species for food and for experimental purposes. On these central matters, I hope that I have said enough to show that this book, despite its flaws, is a challenge to every human to recognize his attitudes to nonhumans as a form of prejudice no less objectionable than racism or sexism. It is a challenge that demands not just a change of attitudes, but a change in our way of life, for it requires us to become vegetarians.

Can a purely moral demand of this kind succeed? The odds are certainly against it. The book holds out no inducements. It does not tell us that we will become healthier, or enjoy life more, if we cease exploiting animals. Animal Liberation will require greater altruism on the part of mankind than any other liberation movement, since animals are incapable of demanding it for themselves, or of protesting against their exploitation by votes, demonstrations, or bombs. Is man capable of such genuine altruism? Who knows? If this book does have a significant effect, however, it will be a vindication of all those who have believed that man has within himself the potential for more than cruelty and selfishness.

Notes

1. This article originally appeared as a book review of *Animals, Men and Morals,* edited by Stanley and Roslind Godlovitch and John Harris.

2. *The Principles of Morals and Legislation,* Ch. XVII, Sec. 1, footnote to paragraph 4. (Italics in original.)

3. Jane van Lawick-Goodall, *In the Shadow of Man* (Houghton Mifflin, 1971), p. 225.

4. N. Tinbergen, *The Herring Gull's World* (Basic Books, 1961).

Created from Animals

James Rachels

Charles Darwin and Karl Marx, the two great revolutionaries of nineteenth-century thought, were almost exact contemporaries. Their deaths in 1882 and 1883 were separated by only a few months. For more than three decades, while writing their most important works, they lived sixteen miles apart, Marx in London and Darwin at his home in the Kentish village of Downe. But they never met, which is not surprising, considering how different were their lives and personalities. Marx spent much of his life in abject poverty, unable at times to feed his family. Because of his political activities, he was chased from country to country. Above all Marx was preoccupied with the great public events of his time: with industrialization, with political revolution, and with the vast changes he saw taking place in society. Darwin, by contrast, was oblivious to such matters. Born into a life of privilege, he would have a tranquil existence, rooted in one place, surrounded by servants and a loving family: the very picture of a nineteenth-century English gentleman. His revolution would be of a different sort.

Darwin's Early Life

When Darwin was born, on 12 February 1809, his family had high hopes. It was, after all, a noteworthy clan. Charles's father, Robert Waring Darwin II, a prosperous doctor in Shrewsbury, was himself the son of a distinguished father, the speculative evolutionist, Erasmus Darwin. His mother, Susannah Wedgwood, who died when Charles was eight, was the daughter of Josiah Wedgwood, founder of the famous pottery. But Robert Darwin soon despaired that his son would ever amount to anything: "You care for nothing but shooting, dogs, and rat-catching, and you will be a disgrace to yourself and all your family," the elder Darwin is said to have remarked. In this *Autobiography,* written privately for his family in 1876, Darwin himself remembered his youth as unpromising. His biographers have generally accepted this estimate. Ronald W. Clark says flatly: "Darwin had a youth unmarked by the slightest trace of genius."

This judgement, however, seems altogether too harsh. Even as a boy, Darwin was unusual in his love of nature. Collecting and studying insects, especially beetles, was an all-absorbing passion. "One day," he wrote in the *Autobiography,* "on tearing off some old bark, I saw two rare beetles and seized one in each hand; then I saw a third and new kind, which I could not bear to lose, so that I popped the one which I held in my right hand into my mouth. Alas it ejected some intensely acrid

© James Rachels 1990. Reprinted from *Created from Animals: The Moral Implications of Darwinism* by James Rachels (1990) by permission of Oxford University Press.

fluid, which burnt my tongue so that I was forced to spit the beetle out, which was lost, as well as the third one." He was an enthusiastic observer who recorded what he saw in great detail. The spirit of this youthful work may be judged from an entry in his diary for 1826:

> Caught a sea-mouse, Aphrodita Aculeata of Linnaeus; length about three or four inches; when its mouth was touched it tried to coil itself in a ball but was very inert; Turton states it has only two feelers. Does not Linnaeus say 4? I thought I perceived them. Found also 3 Palleta Vulgaris and Solen Siliquor.

There are many other entries of this kind. Clearly, he was ambitious to make *discoveries*—was Turton right, or Linnaeus?—and in the judgement of some of his elders he succeeded. In 1827 he appeared before the Plinian Society, an organization devoted to natural history, and its minutes for 27 March record that:

> Mr Darwin communicated to the Society two discoveries which he had made. 1. That the ova of the Flustra possess organs of motion. 2. That the small black globular body hitherto mistaken for the young Fucus lorius is in reality the ovum of the Pontobdella muricata.

At this time Darwin was 18 years old. This may not be evidence of "genius," but I venture that most families would find such a son remarkable. In some American universities tenure has been awarded for less.

Perhaps Robert Darwin's attitude was influenced by the fact that in those days natural history was so often carried on by amateurs. He might not have considered it a substantial enough pursuit to be chosen by a gentleman for his life's work—it was more the sort of thing to be pursued as a diverting and scholarly hobby. At any rate, Charles was sent at age 16 to study at Edinburgh, in the hope that he would become a physician like his father. This did not work out well, partly because Charles was too squeamish to bear the sight of operations performed without anaesthetic, which was yet to become available. Moreover, as he later confessed, Charles realized that he would never want for money, and this was "sufficient to check any stren-

uous effort to learn medicine." So, to his father's disappointment, he left Edinburgh after two terms.

Lacking other alternatives, and still thinking his son an unpromising youth, Robert Darwin now proposed that Charles enter the Church. After giving the matter some thought, the boy agreed. A quiet life as a country parson would leave him ample time to pursue natural history; and moreover, as he was later to reflect, there was nothing in his beliefs to rule out such a vocation: "I did not then in the least doubt the strict and literal truth of every word in the Bible."

So he went to Cambridge in 1827, and three-and-a-half years later took a degree, still intending to become a clergyman. Although he graduated tenth in his class, he was not known as an outstanding student. By his own account, his time 'was sadly wasted there and worse than wasted':

> From my passion for shooting and for hunting and, when this failed, for riding across country I got into a sporting set, including some dissipated low-minded young men. We used often to dine together in the evening, though these dinners often included men of a higher stamp, and we sometimes drank too much, with jolly singing and playing at cards afterwards.

Perhaps this sort of behaviour also contributed to Robert Darwin's despair about his son's future. Recalling these times in his *Autobiography*, however, Charles himself had mixed feelings: "I know that I ought to feel ashamed of days and evenings thus spent, but as some of my friends were very pleasant and we were all in the highest spirits, I cannot help looking back to these times with much pleasure."

But Darwin's days at Cambridge were not entirely misspent. He continued to pursue natural history, and became friends with two professors who encouraged him—Adam Sedgwick, the professor of geology, and John Henslow, who according to Darwin 'knew every branch of science'. Both took him on long walking tours studying the countryside. "I was called by some of the dons 'the man who walks with Henslow,'" Darwin said. Henslow's friendship turned out to be especially important, for it eventually resulted in Darwin's invitation to join the crew of HMS *Beagle* as naturalist.

The invitation came just after Darwin had returned home to Shrewsbury. Having completed his formal education, and without any specific prospects, it was not clear what he would do next. A letter from Henslow reported that Captain Robert FitzRoy, who had recently returned from a hydrographic survey of South America, had requested the services of a naturalist for his second voyage, and Darwin had been recommended for the job. The *Beagle* was to circumnavigate the globe, and do a detailed survey of the coasts of Brazil, Argentina, Chile, Peru, and "some islands in the Pacific." The journey would last five years. Unlike two other naturalists, who had already been offered the job and turned it down, Darwin jumped at it. His father at first refused permission, but with the help of an uncle, Charles persuaded him to relent.

The voyage of the *Beagle* was to be the great event in Darwin's life. It would transform him from an aimless, would-be parson into a full-fledged man of science. But why was he chosen for this assignment? It would be nice, but incorrect, to think that he earned the job solely by his reputation as an up-and-coming naturalist. Scientific ability, as it turned out, was only one of the requirements—perhaps it was not even the main requirement—for the job. Captain FitzRoy was looking for a companion. He could not, as Captain, socialize with his men, and naturally he did not want to face five years at sea with no one to talk to. The letter from Henslow put it plainly: "Capt. F. wants a man (I understand) more as a companion than a mere collector and would not take any one however good a Naturalist who was not recommended to him likewise as a *gentleman*." So Darwin was taken on to be Captain FitzRoy's dinner-partner, with "collecting" duties on the side. There was also one other qualification that Darwin possessed: money. The post carried no salary, and indeed, the ship's naturalist would have to pay a large part of his own expenses. It has been estimated that the voyage eventually cost Darwin between £1,500 and £2,000 from his own pocket, a large sum in those days. For comparison, Darwin's lifetime income from all his books—books that sold briskly—was £10,000.

The voyage was costly in other ways as well. For some time Darwin had been in love with Fanny Owen, the daughter of a friend of his father's. When the *Beagle* set sail on 27 December 1831, Charles left hoping that she would wait for him. He was then 22 years old. While in South America, he received word from his sister that Fanny had married someone else.

How the World Looked in 1831

As Darwin set out on his voyage of discovery, what was the state of the science he was to pursue? How did the world look to a young naturalist in 1831? In one way, 1831 was not so long ago. A man born in that year could easily have grandchildren alive today. But when we consider the world of science, 1831 seems part of another age altogether.

It was generally believed that the earth was only a few thousand years old. And why not? Until shortly before Darwin's birth, there was little reason to think otherwise. Nothing that was known about the heavens or the earth required any longer history. Today we know—or at least we think we know—that the universe began about 15 billion years ago in a "big bang," and that the earth was formed from some of the debris about 4.6 billion years ago. But in 1831 no one could have suspected such an incredible thing. The most widely accepted date for the beginning of creation was 4004 BC, a date which had been calculated from the biblical genealogies by James Ussher, Archbishop of Armagh, and printed in the Authorized Version of the Bible from 1701 on. Some scientists, as we shall see, had already done the work that was to discredit this history. But their views were yet to be generally accepted.

Moreover, it was agreed by most educated people that the earth had been created pretty much as it is now—again, there was little reason to think otherwise. As far as the large-scale history of the earth is concerned, things had remained the same for as long as humans had been keeping records: there had always been the same continents, the same oceans, and the same plants and animals inhabiting them. The scriptural account of creation therefore accorded with common experience.

But the scriptural account did more than just furnish a history. It also provided an explanation of *why* things are as they are. The world is full of wonders—plants and animals of the most complicated design, each one exquisitely adapted to its own special place in the natural order. No one was more aware of this than students of nature such as Darwin. But how could this be? How could the world come to contain such wonders? There seemed only two possible explanations. The first, that it all came about by chance, was too far-fetched to accept. The second and only reasonable explanation was that some guiding hand had brought it all about. When Darwin was at Cambridge, William Paley's *Evidences of the Existence and Attributes of the Deity* was required reading for all students. Paley's work, first published in 1802, was the classic presentation of the 'design' argument. In it he declared, "The marks of *design* are too strong to be gotten over. Design must have had a designer. That designer must have been a person. That person is God." Only a short time before setting out on the *Beagle*, Darwin had studied this reasoning and had decided that it was irrefutable.

This combination of ideas—that the earth was created by God in the relatively recent past, in pretty much the same state in which we now find it, inhabited by species with permanently fixed natures—is today known as "creationism." Creationism now has a bad name. In the hands of Christian fundamentalists, it has degenerated into a dismal pseudo-science, comparable to the shabbiest parapsychology or UFO-ology. But as late as the early nineteenth century, it was still a perfectly reasonable view, accepted by a majority of educated people, and supported, more or less, by such facts as were known. Darwin himself, at age 22, might fairly be described, with some qualifications, as a creationist.

Scientific opinion, however, had begun to change, and by the time the *Beagle* left England, a great shift of thought was underway. At first only a few pioneering scientists were willing to question the old ways of thinking. One of these was James Hutton, a Scottish physician who had taken up geology as a hobby. In his book *Theory of the Earth*, published fourteen years before Darwin's birth, Hutton argued that the prominent features of the earth's surface were produced by such ordinary forces as wind, water, and weather acting slowly and uniformly over a long period of time. (This general approach became known as "uniformitarianism.") River canyons are an obvious example. We can see the process of erosion occurring, as natural forces wear away the earth. When we examine the geological evidence of river canyons, they appear to have been formed in just this way. But, Hutton noted, in order for there to have been time enough

for this to have happened, the earth would have to be not thousands but millions of years old.

Hutton's argument might have been ignored except for the fact that it helped to explain something else that biologists were worrying about—the fossils. These little rocklike things, which at first had been dismissed as mere curiosities, had structures amazingly similar to the structures of living organisms. But how could rocks mimic living forms? Some biologists suggested that they were the remains of creatures destroyed by Noah's flood—they were the ones that did not make it into the ark. But why should they have turned to stone? The fate of dead organisms is not to turn to stone, but to rot. If Hutton's view was correct, an explanation was possible. As the dead creatures rotted, their natural substance might have been slowly replaced by the stony material in the soil around them. But that would mean that the fossils were the remains of creatures who lived millions of years ago—disturbing idea, to say the least.

The Industrial Revolution also played a part in our story. In the early nineteenth century, as part of the increasing industrialization, canals were being constructed all over England. In these excavations the strata were clearly exposed, and attracted the attention of many sharp-eyed observers. One particularly keen observer, William Smith—who became known as "Strata" Smith—noted that each stratum had its own characteristic pattern of rocks *and its own characteristic types of fossil.* To demonstrate the uniform correlation of strata and fossil content, Smith learned to identify different strata by looking at nothing but the associated fossils— shown the fossils, he could tell you from which stratum they had been extracted.

As a result of all this, a new picture of life on earth was emerging. The earth could be seen as millions of years old, and as having been inhabited in the past by creatures now vanished, whose remains are preserved in the fossil record. Moreover, the order in which these creatures lived could be determined by their positions in the strata: those in the lower strata lived earlier than those in the higher strata.

There was more to come. The French anatomist Georges Leopold Cuvier, whose life ended one year after the *Beagle* set sail, made two fundamental contributions. First, he studied the anatomy of different creatures, patiently comparing similarities and differences. (He is therefore credited with founding the science of comparative anatomy.) These studies eventually gave him such knowledge of anatomical relationships that he was able to reconstruct entire animals from only a few bones. This skill was to be invaluable in dealing with the fossils. Often only bits of animals would be found in the strata. Now, based on Cuvier's studies, it would be possible to infer from those bits an intelligent estimate of what the whole animal was like.

Cuvier's second contribution was equally important. Like most biologists of his day, he was intensely interested in systems of biological classification. Drawing on his anatomical studies, Cuvier developed a new and improved scheme, the most sophisticated yet devised. The system was developed, of course, to classify living organisms. But Cuvier discovered that it applied equally well to the fossils. (Thus he is also credited as the founder of palaeontology.) The long-dead animals could be now seen as members of the same families as living animals—as their relatives. Moreover, the way was now open to noticing, systematically and scientifically, the astounding fact that there was an apparent progression in the strata from simpler to more complex forms of life. Roughly speaking, only fossils of invertebrates were found in the lowest strata, while higher up came the remains of fish and sea animals; next birds and reptiles; and finally, in the highest strata, the remains of mammals.

Considering all this, the conclusion fairly leaps out: life has evolved. Species are not immutable. They change. The conclusion leaps out at *us*, because of what we know—everything seems obvious in retrospect—but for people in 1831 things were still not so clear. . . .

Are Humans Morally Special?

Darwin's earliest readers realized that an evolutionary outlook might undermine the traditional doctrine of human dignity, a doctrine which is at the core of Western morals. Darwin himself seems to suggest this when he says that the conception of man as "created from animals" contradicts the arrogant notion that we are a "great work." It is a disturbing idea, and Darwin's friends as well as his enemies were troubled by it. In explaining his initial reluctance to accept Darwin's theory, Lyell, for example, wrote:

You may well believe that it cost me a struggle to renounce my old creed. One of Darwin's reviewers put the alternative strongly by asking 'whether we are to believe that man is modified mud or modified monkey.' The mud is a great comedown from the 'archangel ruined.'

Surprisingly, philosophers have not taken this thought very seriously. I shall argue, however, that discrediting "human dignity" is one of the most important implications of Darwinism, and that it has consequences that people have barely begun to appreciate.

An Early Assessment of Our Problem

Huxley's lecture to the working men. In 1860 Thomas Henry Huxley delivered a series of lectures 'for working men only', to explain to them the shocking new idea that humans are descended from apelike ancestors. . . .

Most of the 1860 lectures were devoted to expounding the anatomical evidence for this kinship. The structural differences between man and the gorilla, Huxley argued, are much smaller than the differences between the gorilla and the monkey; thus, if we admit kinship between the gorilla and the monkey, how can we deny kinship between man and the gorilla? To buttress this argument he cites detail after detail concerning the anatomy of hands, feet, teeth, jaw, and brain.

Towards the end of the lectures, however, Huxley turns to the question that must have been on all their minds: If we are only advanced apes, what of the dignity and worth of man? We think ourselves not only different from, but superior to, the other creatures that inhabit the earth. All our ethics and religion tell us this. Are we now to understand that we are no better than mere apes? Huxley himself puts it this way:

On all sides I shall hear the cry—'We are men and women, not a mere better sort of apes, a little longer in the leg, more compact in the foot, and bigger in the brain than your brutal Chimpanzees and Gorillas. The power of knowledge—the conscience of good and evil—the pitiful tenderness of human affections, raise us out of all real fellowship with the brutes, however closely they may seem to approximate us.'

Huxley, however, thought this worry is based on a misunderstanding, easily corrected. He asks, "Could not a sensible child confute, by obvious arguments, the shallow rhetoricians who would force this conclusion upon us?" He was eager to reassure his audience that Darwinism has no adverse implications for the idea of human dignity. Even if we accept the idea that we are kin to the apes, he said, we can go right on thinking of ourselves as superior to, and somehow set apart from, the rest of creation. Although we may resemble the apes, we are of a different order. Huxley continued,

> I have endeavoured to show that no absolute structural line of demarcation, wider than that between the animals which immediately succeed us in the scale, can be drawn between the animal world and ourselves; and I may add the expression of my belief that the attempt to draw a psychical distinction is equally futile, and that even the highest faculties of feeling and of intellect begin to germinate in lower forms of life. At the same time, no one is more strongly convinced than I am of the vastness of the gulf between civilized man and the brutes; or is more certain that whether *from* them or not, he is assuredly not *of* them. No one is less disposed to think lightly of the present dignity, or despairingly of the future hopes, of the only consciously intelligent denizen of this world.

This is reassuring, but what reasoning lies behind it? Huxley tells us that "there is no absolute structural line of demarcation" that separates us from the other animals, and he adds that this is true not only regarding our physical characteristics, but our "highest faculties of feeling and intellect" as well. If this is so, where is our superiority? His answer is an old familiar one, that has appealed to philosophers in all ages: we can talk, while other animals cannot.

> Our reverence for the nobility of manhood will not be lessened by the knowledge that Man is, in substance and structure, one with the brutes; for, he alone possesses the marvelous endowment of intelligible and rational speech, whereby, in the secular period of his existence, he has slowly accumulated and organised the experience which is almost wholly lost with the cessation of every individual life in other animals; so that, now, he stands raised upon it as on a mountain top, far above the level of his humble fellows, and transfigured from his grosser nature by reflecting, here and there, a ray from the infinite source of truth.

Thus, Huxley's message was clear: we are kin to the apes, but we need not worry. It makes no difference to our exalted view of ourselves, or to our dismissive view of them. We are still men, noble and fit for reverence; and the brutes are still the brutes, without the 'marvelous endowment' that makes us special.

For Huxley, the idea that evolutionary thinking undermines human dignity was just another club that might be used by Darwin's enemies to discredit the new theory. It was nothing but a potential objection to Darwinism, to be disarmed as quickly as possible. Huxley was a polymath who would go on to write many books, including lengthy works about philosophy and ethics, but it never seems to have occurred to him that challenging the traditional idea of human dignity might be a positive contribution the new outlook could make. . . .

The Idea of Human Dignity

What, exactly, is the traditional idea of human dignity? I do not mean to be asking about some esoteric doctrine advanced by a philosopher; instead, like Huxley, I am interested in the basic idea that forms the core of Western morals, and that is expressed, not only in philosophical writing, but in literature, religion, and in the common moral consciousness. This core idea has two parts, and involves a sharp contrast between human life and non-human life. The first part is that human life is regarded as sacred, or at least as having a special importance; and so, it is said, the central concern of our morality must be the protection and care of human beings. The second part says that non-human life does not have the same degree of moral protection. Indeed, on some traditional ways of thinking, non-human animals have no moral standing at all. Therefore, we may use them as we see fit.

This idea has a long history, and much of that history is intertwined with the history of religion. The great religions provide large-scale explanations of the nature of the world, its cause, and its purpose. Those explanations are almost always flattering to humans, assigning them a privileged place in the scheme of things. The idea that human beings have a special place in creation is so prominent, in so many religious traditions, that religion itself has sometimes been explained as an expression of man's desire to affirm his own worth.

The Western religious tradition, a blend of Judaism and Christianity, is a case in point. Man, it is said, was made in the image of God, with the world intended to be his habitation, and everything else in it given for his enjoyment and use. This makes man, apart from God himself, the leading character in the whole cosmic drama. But that is only the beginning of the story. Other details reinforce the initial thought. Throughout human history, God has continued to watch over and interact with man, communicating with him through the saints and prophets. One of the things he has communicated is a set of instructions telling us how we are to live; and almost all those instructions concern how we must treat other humans. Our fellow humans are not to be killed, lied to, or otherwise mistreated. Their lives are sacred. Their needs are always to be taken into account, their rights always respected. The concern we are to show one another is, however, only a dim reflection of the love that God himself has for mankind: so great is God's love that he even became a man, and died sacrificially to redeem sinful mankind. And finally, we are told that after we die, we may be united with God to live forever. What is said about the other animals is strikingly different. They were given by God for man's use, to be worked, killed, and eaten at man's pleasure. Like the rest of creation, they exist for man's benefit.

The central idea of our moral tradition springs directly from this remarkable story. The story embodies a doctrine of the specialness of man and a matching ethical precept. Man is special because he alone is made in the image of God, and above all other creatures he is the object of God's love and attention; the other creatures, which were not made in God's image, were given for man's use. We might call this the "image of God thesis." The matching moral idea, which following tradition we will call

"human dignity," is that human life is sacred, and the central concern of our morality must be the protection and care of human beings, whereas we may use the other creatures as we see fit.

Of course, many people do not believe the religious story, and consider their own thoughts about ethics to be independent of it. Yet a religious tradition can influence the whole shape of a culture, and even determine the form that secular thought takes within it. Only a little reflection is needed to see that secular moral thought within the Western tradition follows the pattern set by these religious teachings.

Few Western moralists have been satisfied to leave the idea of man's specialness stated in an overtly theological way. If we are made in the image of God, they reasoned, it should be possible to identify the divine element in our make-up. In what way, exactly, do we resemble the Almighty? The favoured answer, throughout Western history, has been that man alone is rational. Aristotle, expressing the Greek view of the matter, had said that man is the rational animal, and differs in this respect from all other creatures. This thought was put to use by the doctors of the Church: the divine element in man, they said, is his rationality. This we might call the "rationality thesis": man is special because he alone is rational. Non-human animals are not rational, and so are not to be compared, in this regard, with humans.

In this way the doctrine of man's specialness was secularized, and cast into a form palatable even to those who are sceptical of the story behind the religious version of the idea. St Thomas Aquinas summarized all this—the rationality thesis, its relation to the image of God thesis, and their importance for the idea of human dignity—when he wrote that:

> Of all parts of the universe, intellectual creatures hold the highest place, because they approach nearest to the divine likeness. Therefore the divine providence provides for the intellectual nature for its own sake, and for all others for its sake.

The idea of a unique human mental capacity—a capacity unlike anything to be found elsewhere in nature—may therefore be viewed as the secular equivalent of the idea that man was created in the image of God. It does the same work in our moral system, namely, it buttresses the idea that, from a moral point of view, humans are special. This means that, even if the image of God thesis is rejected, the matching moral idea need not be abandoned. Secular thinkers who reject religion can continue to believe in human dignity, and can justify doing so by pointing to man's unique rationality.

Some Practical Implications of the Idea of Human Dignity

The idea of human dignity has numerous practical consequences, both for the treatment of human beings and for the treatment of non-human animals. Often, the idea has taken an extreme form, with human life taken to be inviolable while non-human life is held to be utterly inconsequential.

The sanctity of innocent human life. More precisely, in our moral tradition *innocent* human life is taken to be inviolable. Guilty persons—criminals, aggressors, and soldiers fighting unjust wars—are not given this protection, and in some circumstances they may justly be killed. The innocent, however, are surrounded by a wall of protection that cannot be breached for any reason whatever. Such practices as suicide, euthanasia, and infanticide are violations of innocent life, and so they are not permitted. The moral rule governing such actions is simple: they are absolutely forbidden.

Suicide will serve as a convenient example (although euthanasia or infanticide would do just as well). One might think that, since the suicide takes only his or her *own* life, the prohibition upon it would not be so strict as the prohibition upon killing others. Prior to the coming of Christianity, the philosophers of Greece and Rome took this attitude. Although they condemned cowardly suicides, they thought it could be permissible in special circumstances. The Christians, however, took a sterner view. St Augustine, whose thought shaped much of our tradition, argued that 'Christians have no authority for committing suicide in any circumstances whatever.' His argument was based mainly on an appeal to authority. The sixth commandment says "Thou shalt not kill." Augustine pointed out that the commandment does not say "Thou shalt not kill *thy neighbour*"; it says only "Thou shalt not kill," period. Thus, he argued, the rule applies with equal force to killing oneself.

Augustine held that man's reason is "the essence of his soul," and in this he laid the founda-

tion for later thought on the subject. A rational being, later thinkers would insist, can never justify doing away with himself, for he must realize that his own value is too great to be destroyed. St Thomas Aquinas, who held that man's rationality is central to his nature, argued that suicide is absolutely opposed to that nature. Suicide, he said, is "contrary to that charity whereby every man should love himself."

If Augustine and Aquinas were the towering figures of the Middle Ages, then the greatest of the modern philosophers, many would say, was Immanuel Kant. If we turn to Kant on suicide, we find that his views are almost indistinguishable from those of Augustine and Aquinas. Kant placed even more weight on the thesis of man's unique rationality than did Aquinas; his whole moral system was based on it. According to his famous formula, the ultimate moral principle is that we should treat human beings as "ends in themselves." Humans, he said, have "an intrinsic worth, i.e., *dignity*," which makes their value "above all price."

If human life has such extraordinary worth, then it is only to be expected that a man can never justify killing himself. Kant draws this conclusion. Like Augustine and Aquinas, he believed that suicide is never morally permissible. His argument relies heavily on comparisons of human life with animal life. People may offer various reasons to justify self-murder, he says, but these attempted justifications overlook the crucial point that "Humanity is worthy of esteem." To kill oneself is to regard one's life as something of such little value that it can be obliterated merely in order to escape troubles. In the case of mere animals, this might be true—we kill animals to put them out of misery, and that is permissible. However, we should not think that the same may be done for a man, because the value of a man's life is so much greater: "If [a man] disposes over himself," Kant says, "he treats his value as that of a beast." Again, "The rule of morality does not admit of [suicide] under any condition because it degrades human nature below the level of animal nature and so destroys it."

All this follows, Kant thought, from taking the idea of man as a rational being (and therefore, as an exalted being) seriously. One might think, then, that there is no need to invoke religious notions to clinch the argument—the secular version of man's specialness should do the job alone, unaided by religious conceptions. However, Kant saw the secular argument and the religious story as working hand in hand. To secure the conclusion, he added:

> But as soon as we examine suicide from the standpoint of religion we immediately see it in its true light. We have been placed in this world under certain conditions and for specific purposes. But a suicide opposes the purpose of his Creator; he arrives in the other world as one who has deserted his post; he must be looked upon as a rebel against God.

It is clear, then, that in Kant's mind—as in the minds of many others—the idea of man as a rational being was still closely linked to the idea of man as made in God's image.

The lesser status of non-human animals. The doctrine of man's specialness serves to exalt man at the expense of the other creatures that inhabit the earth: we are morally special, and they are not. Because we have a different nature, we have a moral standing that they lack. Once again, virtually all the important figures in our tradition agree on this. Aquinas was careful to point out that, although man's rationality gives him a special status, other animals have a very different place in the natural order. "Other creatures," he said, "are for the sake of the intellectual creatures." Therefore, "It is not wrong for man to make use of them, either by killing or in any other way whatever." But shouldn't we be kind to them out of simple charity? No, Aquinas says, because they are not rational:

> The love of charity extends to none but God and our neighbour. But the word neighbour cannot be extended to irrational creatures, since they have no fellowship with man in the rational life. Therefore charity does not extend to irrational creatures.

Kant, again, says much the same thing. Lacking the all-important quality of rationality, non-human animals are entirely excluded from the sphere of moral concern. It is man who is an "end in himself." Other entities have value only as means, to serve that end. Thus for Kant, animals have the status of mere things, and we have no duties to them whatsoever: "But so far as animals are concerned," he says, "we have no direct duties. Animals . . . are there merely as means to an end. That end is man." By a "direct duty" Kant meant a duty based on a concern for the animal's own welfare. We may indeed have duties that *involve* animals, but the reason behind these duties will always refer to a human interest, rather than to the animals' own interests. Kant adds that we should not torture animals pointlessly, but the reason, he insists, is only that "He who is cruel to animals becomes hard also in his dealings with men." We are not, morally speaking, required to do (or refrain from doing) anything at all for the animals' own sakes.

It may seem that, in citing Aquinas and Kant, I have chosen extreme examples. Surely, one might say, our tradition is more complicated than this, and includes thinkers whose views are less unsympathetic to the animals. There is some justice in this complaint. In the biblical sources we find not only the idea that man has dominion over nature but also the contrasting notion that all of creation is to be revered as God's handiwork. On this latter conception, man's duty is to be a good steward of nature, not its exploiter. Someone who wanted to oppose the cruel exploitation of animals might cite this idea for support. Moreover, St Francis, not St Thomas, could be taken as one's model. St Francis, who is said to have preached to the birds, is remembered principally for proclaiming that all living creatures were his brothers and sisters, and for his gentle wonder at all of nature.

Yet there can be little doubt which of these two approaches has dominated Western culture. St Francis is a striking figure precisely because the legends about him contrast so dramatically with more orthodox ways of thinking. But real dissenters are harder to find than one might think; even St Francis appears to be less of a maverick when we examine his views more closely. When he talked to the animals, he heard them replying: "Every creature proclaims: 'God made me for your sake, O man!'" He regarded the animals as his brothers and sisters, but he took the same attitude towards the sun, the moon, wind, and fire. All were part of a creation to be revered, but equally they were all intended for man's use. Moreover, his kindness to the animals apparently did not extend to refraining from eating them—he did not recommend vegetarianism to his followers. On balance, then, it seems that St Francis accepted most of what I have called the doctrine of human dignity, and the religious cosmology that supported it, even though he combined it with a more reverent attitude than most other Christian thinkers. And in any case, as the historian John Passmore remarks, "Francis had little or no influence."

How Darwinism might Undermine the Idea of Human Dignity

The foregoing exposition is familiar enough; yet philosophers are apt to be impatient with it because of a point we have already discussed. The image of God thesis and the rationality thesis are, speaking loosely, matters of (purported) fact. The matching moral idea is a normative view. What, exactly, is supposed to be the relation between them? It cannot be that the latter follows logically from the former, because, as Hume observed, normative conclusions cannot legitimately be derived from factual premises. It would seem that the fragment of traditional morality we have been discussing is based on just this error—or at least, that my reconstruction commits the error. First we "proceed in the ordinary way of reasoning" and "establish the being of a God," that God made us in his own image, that we are uniquely rational creatures, and so forth. These are matters of what (allegedly) *is* the case. But then we go on to conclude from this that the protection of human life *ought* to be the purpose of our morality—and here the mistake creeps in, for factual statements can never by themselves logically entail evaluations. Hume considers this point to be of the very last importance. "This small attention," he says, "would subvert all the vulgar systems of morality." There is no doubt that Hume thought the ideas we have been considering form one such "vulgar system."

Max Black refers to the general logical point, that facts do not entail evaluations, as "Hume's Guillotine." Hume's Guillotine might also come into our discussion in another way—it seems to provide a quick and easy answer to the worry of Huxley's working men. If we accept a Darwinian view of human origins, must we therefore abandon the idea of human dignity? No, for the facts of evolution do not, by themselves, entail any moral conclusions. Darwin's theory, if it is correct, only tells us what *is* the case with respect to the evolution of species; and so, strictly speaking, no conclusion follows from it regarding any matter of value. It does not follow, merely because we are descended from apelike ancestors, that our lives are less important. When Huxley asked, "Could not a sensible child confute, by obvious arguments, the shallow rhetoricians who would force this conclusion upon us?" he might well have had this sort of "obvious argument" in mind.

The majority of twentieth-century moral philosophers would agree. Moral philosophers have been largely indifferent to Darwin, and fear of Hume's Guillotine has been largely responsible for that indifference. "The facts of evolution do not entail any normative conclusions": most philosophers have assumed that, once this simple observation has been made, there is little more to be said.

Nevertheless, the nagging thought remains that Darwinism does have unsettling consequences. The philosopher's reassurance that there will be no problem if we only remember to distinguish "ought" from "is" seems altogether too quick and easy. I believe this feeling of discomfort is justified. Matters are more complicated than a simple reliance on Hume's Guillotine would suggest.

Matters are more complicated, first, because our beliefs are often tied together by connections other than strict logical entailment. One belief may provide *evidence* or *support* for another, without actually entailing it. As evidence accumulates, one's confidence in the belief may increase; and as evidence is called into question, one's confidence may diminish. This is a common pattern.

I want to highlight a part of this process that we may call *undermining* a belief. The basic idea is that a belief is undermined by new information when the new information *takes away the support* of the belief. Suppose, for example, you believe that "Hound Dog" was written by the great songwriting team of Jerry Lieber and Mike Stoller. You believe this because you read it in a copy of the *Elvis Newsletter*. But then you learn that the *Elvis Newsletter* is unreliable; it is produced by a careless fan who gets his facts wrong as often as right. So you come to doubt whether the newsletter can be trusted, and as a result, your confidence that Lieber and Stoller wrote "Hound Dog" is weakened. You may even come to have no belief at all about the authorship of that song.

Notice what has happened. Your original reason for believing Lieber and Stoller wrote "Hound Dog" was that the newsletter said so. But the fact that the newsletter said this does not *entail* that they wrote the song. Moreover, although you may stop believing they wrote it when you learn the newsletter is unreliable, the fact that the newsletter is unreliable does not entail that they did not write it. We are not dealing with a series of logical entailments. Rather, we are dealing with a situation in which one believes something based on available evidence, and in which one modifies one's beliefs as new evidence appears.

We should be careful to distinguish between undermining a belief and merely decreasing someone's confidence in the belief. The latter is a psychological effect that can be brought about in any number of ways, including non-rational ways. The former, however, is a rational process. After you learn that the *Elvis Newsletter* is unreliable, it is *reasonable* for you to have less confidence that Lieber and Stoller wrote "Hound Dog." It is a matter of adjusting belief to evidence.

We should also emphasize the difference between undermining a belief and proving the belief to be false. Your new evidence does not prove that Lieber and Stoller did not write "Hound Dog." It merely takes away your reason for thinking that they did. The original belief could still be true—and in fact, "Hound Dog" was written by Lieber and Stoller (not for Elvis but for Big Mama Thornton)—but, before it will be rational for you to believe it, you need another reason.

The situation is no different when evaluative judgements are involved. Suppose you are a member of the Songwriters Association and you say that Lieber and Stoller ought to be given the Association's Lifetime Achievement Award. You may legitimately be asked why, because any judgement about what ought to be done must have reasons in its support if it is to be taken seriously; otherwise, it can be dismissed as arbitrary or unfounded. So you say: Lieber and Stoller ought to be given this award because they wrote such classics as "Stardust" and "Hong Kong Blues."

Is there anything wrong with your reasoning? That Lieber and Stoller wrote these songs is (if true) a matter of fact. That they ought to be given the Lifetime Achievement Award is an evaluation. Therefore, according to Hume's Guillotine, one

does not "follow from" the other. But what is the logical importance of this? Is it, as Hume said, "of the last consequence"? Suppose someone who opposed a special award for Lieber and Stoller remembered Hume and objected that there is no logical entailment here. That would be true but irrelevant. In providing reasons, one need not be claiming that the facts logically entail the "ought" judgement. Rather, one need only claim that they provide *good reasons* for accepting the judgement. That is a weaker, but still significant, claim.

This person might, of course, dispute your reasons in other ways. He might argue that "Stardust" and "Hong Kong Blues" are not good songs (although he would have little chance of winning *that* argument). Or, more simply, he could point out that in fact Lieber and Stoller did not write those songs; they were written by Hoagy Carmichael. This undermines your judgement by taking away its support. You do not, of course, have to abandon the idea that Lieber and Stoller should be honoured; but if you are to continue to maintain it, you must come up with some other reason in its support. Luckily, this is easy to do. Even though they did not write the two songs you mentioned, they did write any number of other classics: not only "Hound Dog," but "Love Potion No. 9," "Kansas City," "Yakety Yak," and many others.

Philosophers love artificial examples, such as the Lieber-and-Stoller example I have been using, because artificial examples are easily controlled. They can be kept simple and manageable and so can be used to illustrate logical points in an uncomplicated way. Examples drawn from real life are, in contrast, messy and confusing. They abound with inconvenient details that don't fit neatly into one's preconceived framework. Nevertheless, the process of undermining beliefs is an important part of reasoning in the real world as well as in philosophers' fantasies.

Consider, for example, the seventeenth-century debate about embryological origins. In the seventeenth century many scientists believed in a view known as "preformationism"—as the name suggests, they believed that each organism starts off with all its parts already formed. The development of the organism therefore consists merely in its growing bigger and bigger. As one writer put it, the embryo's development consists in "a stretching or growth of parts." Observations by scientists such as

Marcello Malpighi (1628–94), who introduced the microscope into embryology, seemed to support preformationism. Peering through his primitive instrument, Malpighi thought he saw the "rudiments" of the chicken already present in the hen's egg. Applied to human reproduction, preformationism became the theory of *"emboîtement,"* which held that all future generations of humans were already present in Eve's ovaries—the emergence of new people being like the opening of an endless series of Chinese boxes.

Preformationists were also encouraged by another development in embryology, the theory of "ovism"—the idea that all organisms develop from eggs. William Harvey (1578–1657), who, in addition to discovering the circulation of blood, was one of the first great embryologists, declared that "An egg is the common origin of all animals." "Ovism" was a great advance over the received view that different types of creatures are generated in different ways—e.g. that plants and animals reproduce differently, that insects are generated spontaneously in rotten meat, and so on. It was a first attempt to provide a unified theory of generation. Ovism seemed to support preformationism, in that it permitted Malpighi's results to be generalized. If all organisms have a common origin (in eggs), and we can observe the "rudiments" of chicks in chicken-eggs, then we might reasonably expect that similar rudiments will be present in other types of eggs.

Ovism, however, was a short-lived theory. In 1677 Leeuwenhoek first observed spermatozoa, and concluded that the female ovum alone could not be the sole source of the human embryo. Other evidence quickly mounted. A Swedish doctor, Niklaas Hartsoeker (1656–1725) calculated that if *emboîtement* were true, then the original egg in Eve's ovaries (in 4004 BC) would have to be larger than its present-day descendant by a factor of $10^{30,000}$—and that did not even allow for future generations. Ovism was therefore abandoned, and preformationism was deprived of an important bit of support.

But the abandonment of ovism did not lead straightaway to the rejection of preformationism. On the contrary, ovism was replaced by a new view, "animaculism," which was interpreted in such a way as to support preformationism. Animaculism was a kind of reverse-image of ovism; it held that the egg is nothing but food for the developing organism, which is entirely contained in the male sperm. Despite his earlier calculation, Hartsoeker himself became an enthusiast for the new theory, and published a drawing of a fully formed infant curled up inside a spermatozoon. The demise of ovism was a setback for preformationists, but it was not until later that their view was finally discredited. What finally killed preformationism was, among other things, the simple realization that organisms inherit characteristics from both parents.

The story of the rise and fall of preformationism is not the story of scientist-logicians patiently drawing out the strict entailments of various discoveries. Malpighi's observations did not entail the truth of preformationism, nor did ovism: they were, however, evidence in its favour. They made preformationism plausible. Similarly, Hartsoeker's calculation was evidence against ovism, although it did not demonstrate incontrovertibly that ovism must be false. But by casting doubt on the truth of ovism, Leeuwenhoek's and Hartsoeker's results took away an important bit of support for preformationism. After ovism was rejected, it was reasonable to have less confidence in preformationism. It was a matter of adjusting belief to evidence. The original belief could still have been true—and in fact, it was defended by some scientists for many more years.

The debate over preformationism was also connected with moral matters in an instructive way. As we have seen, preformationism, with its accompanying doctrine of *emboîtement,* said that all the generations of humans were already present in Eve's ovaries, like dolls within dolls. This idea led the Christian Church to adopt a stricter view of abortion than it had previously accepted. St Thomas had held that the foetus does not become fully human until several weeks after conception, when it takes on a recognizably human form. Therefore abortion in the early weeks of pregnancy had been tolerated. But *emboîtement* suggested that the foetus already has a human form—no matter how tiny it is—from the very beginning, and so abortion at any point was the killing of a real human being. The Church's moral stance was tightened accordingly, and abortion came to be condemned as morally wrong.

The Church had taken a moral position, and had given a reason in its support: if *emboîtement* is correct, then abortion is the killing of a tiny, perfectly formed human being. This is a matter of (alleged) fact. Now suppose a defender of abortion, remembering Hume, objected that the fact does not logically entail the evaluation. Again, that would be true but irrelevant. Any judgement about what ought to be done must have reasons in its support if it is to be taken seriously; otherwise, it can be dismissed as arbitrary or unfounded. But in providing reasons, one need not be claiming that the facts logically entail the moral judgement. One need only claim that they provide good reasons for accepting the judgement.

Eventually, of course, the theory of *emboîtement* was shown to be false, and now it is just a historical curiosity. Today we know that, in fact, foetuses develop from fertilized ova which are single cells and are nothing like fully formed humans, except that they contain human genetic material. This new information undermined the Church's position, by removing its support. Therefore, one might have anticipated that, after *emboîtement* was discredited, the Church would have returned to its earlier, more permissive attitude towards abortion. But it did not, and there was no reason why it had to, because the new information did not entail the falsity of the moral position. That position could still be maintained, if other grounds could be found for it. And that is what happened: the Church found other arguments against abortion, and the stricter moral view was retained.

We can therefore see that Hume was both right and wrong. His point about the logical difference between factual and evaluative judgements may have been correct. But he was surely mistaken to think the point "subverts all the vulgar systems of morality"—among which he included the moral system based on traditional religious ideas. Traditional morality is not subverted because in fact it never depended on taking the matching moral idea as a strict logical deduction from the image of God thesis or the rationality thesis.

What, then, is the relation between the image of God thesis (or the rationality thesis) and the matching moral idea? It is not that the former is supposed to entail the latter. Rather, it is that the former is supposed to provide good reason for accepting the latter. In traditional morality, the doctrine of human dignity is not an arbitrary principle that hangs in logical space with no support. It is grounded in certain (alleged) facts about human nature; those facts are what (allegedly) make it reasonable to believe in the moral doctrine. The claim implicit in traditional morality is that humans are morally special *because* they are made in the image

of God, or because they are uniquely rational beings.

We are now in a position to explain how Darwinism might undermine traditional morality. The claim that Darwinism undermines traditional morality is not the claim that it entails that the doctrine of human dignity is false. It is, instead, the claim that Darwinism provides reason for doubting the truth of the considerations that support the doctrine. From a Darwinian perspective, both the image of God thesis and the rationality thesis are suspect. Moreover, there are good Darwinian reasons for thinking it unlikely that any other support for human dignity can be found. Thus, Darwinism furnishes the "new information" that undermines human dignity by taking away its support.

References

Aquinas, St. Thomas, *Basic Writings of St. Thomas Aquinas*, ed. Anton C. Pegis (2 vols.; New York: Random House, 1945).

——— *Summa Contra Gentiles*, trans. English Dominican Fathers (New York: Benziger Brothers, 1928).

——— *Summa Theologica*, trans. English Dominican Fathers (New York: Benziger Brothers, 1918).

Augustine, St., *The City of God*, ed. Vernon J. Bourke (Garden City, NY: Doubleday Image Books, 1958).

Black, Max, "The Gap between 'Is' and 'Should,'" *Philosophical Review*, 73 (1964). Reprinted in *The Is-Ought Question*, ed. W. D. Hudson (London: Macmillan, 1969).

Clark, Ronald W., *The Survival of Charles Darwin: A Biography of a Man and an Idea* (New York: Random House, 1984).

Darwin, Charles, *The Autobiography of Charles Darwin*, ed. Nora Barlow (New York: W. W. Norton, 1969).

——— *The Life and Letters of Charles Darwin*, ed. Francis Darwin (2 vols.; London: John Murray, 1888). Also published in a three-volume edition.

——— and Henslow, John Stevens, *Darwin and Henslow: Letters 1831–1860*, ed. Nora Barlow (Berkeley: University of California Press, 1967).

Hofstadter, Richard, *Social Darwinism in American Thought*, rev. edn. (Boston: Beacon Press, 1955).

Hume, David, *A Treatise of Human Nature*, ed. L. A. Selby-Bigge (Oxford: Oxford University Press, 1888).

Huxley, T. H., *Evidence as to Man's Place in Nature* (London: Williams and Norgate, 1863). Reprinted by the University of Michigan Press, Ann Arbor, 1959).

Kant, Immanuel, *Foundations of the Metaphysics of Morals,* trans. Lewis White Beck (Indianapolis: Bobbs-Merrill, 1959).

———— *Lectures on Ethics,* trans. Louis Infield (New York: Harper and Row, 1963).

Passmore, John, *Man's Responsibility for Nature* (New York: Charles Scribner's Sons, 1974).

Singer, Peter, *Animal Liberation* (New York: New York Review of Books, 1975).

Spencer, Herbert, *The Data of Ethics* (New York: Thomas Y. Crowell & Company, 1879).

Westfall, Richard S., *The Construction of Modern Science: Mechanisms and Mechanics* (Cambridge: Cambridge University Press, 1971).

The Case for Animal Rights

Tom Regan

I regard myself as an advocate of animal rights—as a part of the animal rights movement. That movement, as I conceive it, is committed to a number of goals, including:

1. the total abolition of the use of animals in science

2. the total dissolution of commercial animal agriculture

3. and the total elimination of commercial sport hunting and trapping.

There are, I know, people who profess to believe in animal rights who do not avow these goals. Factory farming, they say, is wrong—violates animals' rights—but traditional animal agriculture is all right. Toxicity tests of cosmetics on animals violates their rights; but not important medical research—cancer research, for example. The clubbing of baby seals is abhorrent; but not the harvesting of adult seals. I used to think I understood this reasoning. Not any more. You don't change unjust institutions by tidying them up.

What's wrong—what's fundamentally wrong—with the way animals are treated isn't the details that vary from case to case. It's the whole system. The forlornness of the veal calf is pathetic—heart wrenching; the pulsing pain of the chimp with electrodes planted deep in her brain is repulsive; the slow, torturous death of the raccoon caught in the leg hold trap, agonizing. But what is fundamentally wrong isn't the pain, isn't the suffering, isn't the deprivation. These compound what's wrong.

Sometimes—often—they make it much worse. But they are not the fundamental wrong.

The fundamental wrong is the system that allows us to view animals as *our resources,* here for us—to be eaten, or surgically manipulated, or put in our cross hairs for sport or money. Once we accept this view of animals—as our resources—the rest is as predictable as it is regrettable. Why worry about their loneliness, their pain, their death? Since animals exist for us, here to benefit us in one way or another, what harms them really doesn't matter—or matters only if it starts to bother us, makes us feel a trifle uneasy when we eat our veal scampi, for example. So, yes, let us get veal calves out of solitary confinement, give them more space, a little straw, a few companions. But let us keep our veal scampi.

But a little straw, more space, and a few companions don't eliminate—don't even touch—the fundamental wrong, the wrong that attaches to our viewing and treating these animals as our resources. A veal calf killed to be eaten after living in close confinement is viewed and treated in this way: but so, too, is another who is raised (as they say) "more humanely." To right the fundamental wrong of our treatment of farm animals requires more than making rearing methods "more human"—requires something quite different—requires the total dissolution of commercial animal agriculture.

How we do this—whether we do this, or as in the case of animals in science, whether and how we abolish their use—these are to a large extent politi-

In Defense of Animals, edited by Peter Singer (Oxford: Basil Blackwell, Inc., 1985), pp. 13–26. Reprinted by permission.

cal questions. People must change their beliefs before they change their habits. Enough people, especially those elected to public office, must believe in change—must want it—before we will have laws that protect the rights of animals. This process of change is very complicated, very demanding, very exhausting, calling for the efforts of many hands—in education, publicity, political organization and activity, down to the licking of envelopes and stamps. As a trained and practicing philosopher the sort of contribution I can make is limited, but, I like to think, important. The currency of philosophy is ideas—their meaning and rational foundation—not the nuts and bolts of the legislative process, say, or the mechanics of community organization. That's what I have been exploring over the past ten years or so in my essays and talks and, more recently, in my book, *The Case for Animal Rights*.[1] I believe the major conclusions I reach in that book are true because they are supported by the weight of the best arguments. I believe the idea of animal rights has reason, not just emotion, on its side.

In the space I have at my disposal here I can only sketch, in the barest outlines, some of the main features of the book. Its main themes—and we should not be surprised by this—involve asking and answering deep foundational moral questions, questions about what morality is, how it should be understood, what is the best moral theory all considered. I hope I can convey something of the shape I think this theory is. The attempt to do this will be—to use a word a friendly critic once used to describe my work—cerebral. In fact I was told by this person that my work is "too cerebral." But this is misleading. My feelings about how animals sometimes are treated are just as deep and just as strong as those of my more volatile compatriots. Philosophers do—to use the jargon of the day—have a right side to their brains. If it's the left side we contribute—or mainly should—that's because what talents we have reside there.

How to proceed? We begin by asking how the moral status of animals has been understood by thinkers who deny that animals have rights. Then we test the mettle of their ideas by seeing how well they stand up under the heat of fair criticism. If we start our thinking in this way we soon find that some people believe that we have no duties directly to animals—that we owe nothing *to them*—that we

can do nothing that *wrongs them*. Rather, we can do wrong acts that involve animals, and so we have duties regarding them, though none to them. Such views may be called indirect duty views. By way of illustration:

Suppose your neighbor kicks your dog. Then your neighbor has done something wrong. But not to your dog. The wrong that has been done is a wrong to you. After all, it is wrong to upset people, and your neighbor's kicking your dog upsets you. So you are the one who is wronged, not your dog. Or again: by kicking your dog your neighbor damages your property. And since it is wrong to damage another person's property, your neighbor has done something wrong—to you, of course, not to your dog. Your neighbor no more wrongs your dog than your car would be wronged if the windshield were smashed. Your neighbor's duties involving your dog are indirect duties to you. More generally, all of our duties regarding animals are indirect duties to one another—to humanity.

How could someone try to justify such a view? One could say that your dog doesn't feel anything and so isn't hurt by your neighbor's kick, doesn't care about the pain since none is felt, is as unaware of anything as your windshield. Someone could say this but no rational person will since, among other considerations, such a view will commit one who holds it to the position that no human being feels pain either—that human beings also don't care about what happens to them. A second possibility is that though both humans and your dog are hurt when kicked, it is only human pain that matters. But, again, no rational person can believe this. Pain is pain wheresoever it occurs. If your neighbor's causing you pain is wrong because of the pain that is caused, we cannot rationally ignore or dismiss the moral relevance of the pain your dog feels.

Philosophers who hold indirect duty views—and many still do—have come to understand that they must avoid the two defects just noted—avoid, that is, both the view that animals don't feel anything as well as the idea that only human pain can be morally relevant. Among such thinkers the sort of view now favored is one or another form of what is called *contractarianism*.

Here, very crudely, is the root idea: morality consists of a set of rules that individuals voluntarily agree to abide by—as we do when we sign a contract (hence the name: contractarianism). Those who understand and accept the terms of the contract are covered directly—have rights created by, and recognized and protected in, the contract. And these contractors can also have protection spelled out for others who, though they lack the ability to understand morality and so cannot sign the contract themselves, are loved or cherished by those who can. Thus young children, for example, are unable to sign and lack rights. But they are protected by the contract nonetheless because of the sentimental interests of others, most notably their parents. So we have, then, duties involving these children, duties regarding them, but no duties to them. Our duties in their case are indirect duties to other human beings, usually their parents.

As for animals, since they cannot understand the contract, they obviously cannot sign; and since they cannot sign, they have no rights. Like children, however, some animals are the objects of the sentimental interest of others. You, for example, love your dog . . . or cat. So these animals—those enough people care about: companion animals, whales, baby seals, the American bald eagle—these animals, though they lack rights themselves, will be protected because of the sentimental interests of people. I have, then, according to contractarianism, no duty directly to your dog or any other animal, not even the duty not to cause them pain or suffering; my duty not to hurt them is a duty I have to those people who care about what happens to them. As for other animals, where no or little sentimental interest is present—farm animals, for example, or laboratory rats—what duties we have grow weaker and weaker, perhaps to the vanishing point. The pain and death they endure, though real, are not wrong if no one cares about them.

Contractarianism could be a hard view to refute when it comes to the moral status of animals if it was an adequate theoretical approach to the moral status of human beings. It is not adequate in this latter respect, however, which makes the question of its adequacy in the former—regarding animals—utterly moot. For consider: morality, according to the (crude) contractarian position before us, consists of rules people agree to abide by. What people? Well, enough to make a difference—enough, that is, so that collectively they have the power to enforce the rules that are drawn up in the contract. That is very well and good for the signatories—but not so good for anyone who is not asked to sign. And there is nothing in contractarianism of

the sort we are discussing that guarantees or requires that everyone will have a chance to participate equitably in framing the rules of morality. The result is that this approach to ethics could sanction the most blatant forms of social, economic, moral, and political injustice, ranging from a repressive caste system to systematic racial or sexual discrimination. Might, on this theory, does make right. Let those who are the victims of injustice suffer as they will. It matters not so long as no one else—no contractor, or too few of them—cares about it. Such a theory takes one's moral breath away . . . as if, for example, there is nothing wrong with apartheid in South Africa if too few white South Africans are upset by it. A theory with so little to recommend it at the level of the ethics of our treatment of our fellow humans cannot have anything more to recommend it when it comes to the ethics of how we treat our fellow animals.

The version of contractarianism just examined is, as I have noted, a crude variety, and in fairness to those of a contractarian persuasion it must be noted that much more refined, subtle, and ingenious varieties are possible. For example, John Rawls, in his *A Theory of Justice*, sets forth a version of contractarianism that forces the contractors to ignore the accidental features of being a human being—for example, whether one is white or black, male or female, a genius or of modest intellect. Only by ignoring such features, Rawls believes, can we insure that the principles of justice contractors would agree upon are not based on bias or prejudice. Despite the improvement a view such as Rawls's shows over the cruder forms of contractarianism, it remains deficient: it systematically denies that we have direct duties to those human beings who do not have a sense of justice—young children, for instance, and many mentally retarded humans. And yet it seems reasonably certain that, were we to torture a young child or a retarded elder, we would be doing something that wrongs them, not something that is wrong if (and only if) other humans with a sense of justice are upset. And since this is true in the case of these humans, we cannot rationally deny the same in the case of animals.

Indirect duty views, then, including the best among them, fail to command our rational assent. Whatever ethical theory we rationally should accept, therefore, it must at least recognize that we have some duties directly to animals, just as we have some duties directly to each other. The next two theories I'll sketch attempt to meet this requirement.

The first I call the cruelty-kindness view. Simply stated, this view says that we have a direct duty to be kind to animals and a direct duty not to be cruel to them. Despite the familiar, reassuring ring of these ideas, I do not believe this view offers an adequate theory. To make this clearer, consider kindness. A kind person acts from a certain kind of motive—compassion or concern, for example. And that is a virtue. But there is no guarantee that a kind act is a right act. If I am a generous racist, for example, I will be inclined to act kindly toward members of my own race, favoring their interests above others. My kindness would be real and, so far as it goes, good. But I trust it is too obvious to require comment that my kind acts may not be above moral reproach—may, in fact, be positively wrong because rooted in injustice. So kindness, not withstanding its status as a virtue to be encouraged, simply will not cancel the weight of a theory of right action.

Cruelty fares no better. People or their acts are cruel if they display either a lack of sympathy for or, worse, the presence of enjoyment in, seeing another suffer. Cruelty in all its guises *is* a bad thing—is a tragic human failing. But just as a person's being motivated by kindness does not guarantee that they do what is right, so the absence of cruelty does not assure that they avoid doing what is wrong. Many people who perform abortions, for example, are not cruel, sadistic people. But that fact about their character and motivation does not settle the terribly difficult question about the morality of abortion. The case is no different when we examine the ethics of our treatment of animals. So, yes, let us be for kindness and against cruelty. But let us not suppose that being for the one and against the other answers questions about moral right and wrong.

Some people think the theory we are looking for is utilitarianism. A utilitarian accepts two moral principles. The first is a principle of equality: everyone's interests count, and similar interests must be counted as having similar weight or importance. White or black, male or female, American or Iranian, human or animal: everyone's pain or frustration matter and matter equally with the like pain or frustration of anyone else. The second principle a utilitarian accepts is the principle of utility: do that act that will bring about the best balance of satisfaction over frustration for everyone affected by the outcome.

As a utilitarian, then, here is how I am to approach the task of deciding what I morally ought to do: I must ask who will be affected if I choose to do one thing rather than another, how much each individual will be affected, and where the best results are most likely to lie—which option, in other words, is most likely to bring about the best results, the best balance of satisfaction over frustration. That option, whatever it may be, is the one I ought to choose.That is where my moral duty lies.

The great appeal of utilitarianism rests with its uncompromising *egalitarianism:* everyone's interests count and count equally with the like interests of everyone else. The kind of odious discrimination some forms of contractarianism can justify—discrimination based on race or sex, for example—seems disallowed in principle by utilitarianism, as is speciesism—systematic discrimination based on species membership.

The sort of equality we find in utilitarianism, however, is not the sort an advocate of animal or human rights should have in mind. Utilitarianism has no room for the equal moral rights of different individuals because it has no room for their equal inherent value or worth. What has value for the utilitarian is the satisfaction of an individual's interests, not the individual whose interests they are. A universe in which you satisfy your desire for water, food, and warmth, is, other things being equal, better than a universe in which these desires are frustrated. And the same is true in the case of an animal with similar desires. But neither you nor the animal have any value in your own right. Only your feelings do.

Here is an analogy to help make the philosophical point clearer: a cup contains different liquids—sometimes sweet, sometimes bitter, sometimes a mix of the two. What has value are the liquids: the sweeter the better, the bitter the worse. The cup—the container— has no value. It's what goes into it, not what they go into, that has value. For the utilitarian, you and I are like the cup; we have no value as individuals and thus no equal value. What has value is what goes into us, what we serve as receptacles for; our feelings of satisfaction have positive value, our feelings of frustration have negative value.

Serious problems arise for utilitarianism when we remind ourselves that it enjoins us to bring about the best consequences. What does this mean? It doesn't mean the best consequences for me alone, or for my family or friends, or any other person taken individually. No, what we must do is, roughly, as follows: we must add up—somehow!— the separate satisfactions and frustrations of everyone likely to be affected by our choice, the satisfactions in one column, the frustrations in the other. We must total each column for each of the options before us. That is what it means to say the theory is aggregative. And then we must choose that option which is most likely to bring about the best balance of totaled satisfactions over totaled frustrations. Whatever act would lead to this outcome is the one we morally ought to perform—is where our moral duty lies. And that act quite clearly might not be the same one that would bring about the best results for me personally, or my family or friends, or a lab animal. The best aggregated consequences for everyone concerned are not necessarily the best for each individual.

That utilitarianism is an aggregative theory— that different individual's satisfactions or frustrations are added, or summed, or totaled—is the key objection to this theory. My Aunt Bea is old, inactive, a cranky, sour person, though not physically ill. She prefers to go on living. She is also rather rich. I could make a fortune if I could get my hands on her money, money she intends to give me in any event, after she dies, but which she refuses to give me now. In order to avoid a huge tax bite, I plan to donate a handsome sum of my profits to a local children's hospital. Many, many children will benefit from my generosity, and much joy will be brought to their parents, relatives, and friends. If I don't get the money rather soon, all ambitions will come to naught. The once-in-a-life-time-opportunity to make a real killing will be gone. Why, then, not really kill my Aunt Bea? Oh, of course I *might* get caught. But I'm no fool and, besides, her doctor can be counted on to cooperate (he has an eye for the same investment and I happen to know a good deal about his shady past). The deed can be done . . . professionally, shall we say. There is *very* little chance of getting caught. And as for my conscience being guilt ridden, I am a resourceful sort of fellow and will take more than sufficient comfort—as I lie on the beach at Acapulco—in contemplating the joy and health I have brought to so many others.

Suppose Aunt Bea is killed and the rest of the story comes out as told. Would I have done anything wrong? Anything immoral? One would have thought that I had. But not according to utilitarianism. Since what I did brought about the best balance of totaled satisfaction over frustration for all those affected by the outcome, what I did was not wrong. Indeed, in killing Aunt Bea the physician and I did what duty required.

This same kind of argument can be repeated in all sorts of cases, illustrating, time after time, how the utilitarian's position leads to results that impartial people find morally callous. It *is* wrong to kill my Aunt Bea in the name of bringing about the best results for others. A good end does not justify an evil means. Any adequate moral theory will have to explain why this is so. Utilitarianism fails in this respect and so cannot be the theory we seek.

What to do? Where to begin anew? The place to begin, I think, is with the utilitarian's view of the value of the individual—or, rather, lack of value. In its place suppose we consider that you and I, for example, do have value as individuals— what we'll call *inherent value.* To say we have such value is to say that we are something more than, something different from, mere receptacles. Moreover, to insure that we do not pave the way for such injustices as slavery or sexual discrimination, we must believe that all who have inherent value have it equally, regardless of their sex, race, religion, birthplace, and so on. Similarly to be discarded as irrelevant are one's talents or skills, intelligence and wealth, personality or pathology, whether one is loved and admired—or despised and loathed. The genius and the retarded child, the prince and the pauper, the brain surgeon and the fruit vendor, Mother Theresa and the most unscrupulous used car salesman—all have inherent value, all possess it equally, and all have an equal right to be treated with respect, to be treated in ways that do not reduce them to the status of things, as if they exist as resources for others. My value as an individual is independent of my usefulness to you. Yours is not dependent on your usefulness to me. For either of us to treat the other in ways that fail to show respect for the other's independent value is to act immorally—is to violate the individual's rights.

Some of the rational virtues of this view—what I call the rights view—should be evident. Unlike (crude) contractarianism, for example, the rights view *in principle* denies the moral tolerability of any and all forms of racial, sexual, or social discrimination; and unlike utilitarianism, this view *in principle* denies that we can justify good results by using evil means that violate an individual's rights—denies, for example, that it could be moral to kill my Aunt Bea to harvest beneficial consequences for others. That would be to sanction the disrespectful treatment of the individual in the name of the social good, something the rights view will not—categorically will not—ever allow.

The rights view—or so I believe—is rationally the most satisfactory moral theory. It surpasses all other theories in the degree to which it illuminates and explains the foundation of our duties to one another—the domain of human morality. On this score, it has the best reasons, the best arguments, on its side. Of course, if it were possible to show that only human beings are included within its scope, then a person like myself, who believes in animal rights, would be obliged to look elsewhere than to the rights view.

But attempts to limit its scope to humans only can be shown to be rationally defective. Animals, it is true, lack many of the abilities humans possess. They can't read, do higher mathematics, build a bookcase, or make *baba ghanoush*. Neither can many human beings, however, and yet we don't say—and shouldn't say—that they (these humans) therefore have less inherent value, less of a right to be treated with respect, than do others. It is the *similarities* between those human beings who most clearly, most noncontroversially have such value—the people reading this, for example—it is our similarities, not our differences, that matter most. And the really crucial, the basic similarity is simply this; we are each of us the experiencing subject of a life, each of us a conscious creature having an individual welfare that has importance to us whatever our usefulness to others. We want and prefer things; believe and feel things; recall and expect things. And all these dimensions of our life, including our pleasure and pain, our enjoyment and suffering, our satisfaction and frustration, our continued existence or our untimely death—all make a difference to the quality of our life as lived, as experienced by us as individuals. As the same is true of those animals who concern us (those who are eaten and trapped, for example), they, too, must be viewed as the experiencing subjects of a life with inherent value of their own.

There are some who resist the idea that animals have inherent value. "Only humans have such value," they profess. How might this narrow view be defended? Shall we say that only humans have the requisite intelligence, or autonomy, or reason? But there are many, many humans who will fail to meet these standards and yet who are reasonably viewed as having value above and beyond their usefulness to others. Shall we claim that only humans belong to the right species—the species Homo sapiens? But this is blatant speciesism. Will it be said, then, that all—and only—humans have immortal souls? Then our opponents more than have their work cut out for them. I am myself not ill-disposed to there being immortal souls. Personally, I profoundly hope I have one. But I would not want to rest my position on a controversial ethical issue on the even more controversial question about who or what has an immortal soul. That is to dig one's hole deeper, not climb out. Rationally, it is better to resolve moral issues without making more controversial assumptions than are needed. The question of who has inherent value is such a question, one that is more rationally resolved without the introduction of the idea of immortal souls than by its use.

Well, perhaps some will say that animals have some inherent value, only *less* than we do. Once again, however, attempts to defend this view can be shown to lack rational justification. What could be the basis of our having more inherent value than animals? Will it be their lack of reason, or autonomy, or intellect? Only if we are willing to make the same judgement in the case of humans who are similarly deficient. But it is not true that such humans—the retarded child, for example, or the mentally deranged—have less inherent value than you or I. Neither, then, can we rationally sustain the view that animals like them in being the experiencing subjects of a life have less inherent value. All who have inherent value have it *equally,* whether they be human animals or not.

Inherent value, then, belongs equally to those who are the experiencing subjects of a life. Whether it belongs to others—to rocks and rivers, trees and glaciers, for example—we do not know. And may never know. But neither do we need to know, if we are to make the case for animal rights. We do not need to know how many people, for example, are eligible to vote in the next presidential election before we can know whether I am. Similarly, we do not need to know *how many* individuals have inherent value before we can know that some do. When it comes to the case for animal rights, then what we need to know is whether the animals who, in our culture are routinely eaten, hunted, and used in our laboratories, for example, are like us in being subjects of a life. And we *do* know this. We do *know* that many—literally, billions and billions—of these animals are the subjects of a life in the sense explained and so have inherent value if we do. And since, in order to have the best theory of our duties to one another, we must recognize our equal inherent value, as individuals, reason—not sentiment, not emotion—reason compels us to recognize the equal inherent value of these animals. And, with this, their equal right to be treated with respect.

That, *very* roughly, is the shape and feel of the case for animal rights. Most of the details of the supporting argument are missing. They are to be found in the book I alluded to earlier. Here, the details go begging and I must in closing limit myself to four final points.

The first is how the theory that underlies the case for animal rights shows that the animal rights movement is a part of, not antagonistic to, the human rights movement. The theory that rationally grounds the rights of animals also grounds the rights of humans. Thus are those involved in the animal rights movement partners in the struggle to secure respect for human rights—the rights of women, for example, or minorities and workers. The animal rights movement is cut from the same moral cloth as these.

Second, having set out the broad outlines of the rights view, I can now say why its implications for farming and science, for example, are both clear and uncompromising. In the case of using animals in science, the rights view is categorically abolitionist. Lab animals are not our tasters; we are not their kings. Because these animals are treated—routinely, systematically—as if their value is reducible to their usefulness to others, they are routinely, systematically treated with a lack of respect, and thus are their rights routinely, systematically violated. This is just as true when they are used in trivial, duplicative, unnecessary or unwise research as it is when they are used in studies that hold out real promise

of human benefits. We can't justify harming or killing a human being (my Aunt Bea, for example) just for these sorts of reasons. Neither can we do so even in the case of so lowly a creature as a laboratory rat. It is not just refinement or reduction that are called for, not just larger, cleaner cages, not just more generous use of anaesthetic or the elimination of multiple surgery, not just tidying up the system. It is replacement—completely. The best we can do when it comes to using animals in science is—not to use them. That is where our duty lies, according to the rights view.

As for commercial animal agriculture, the rights view takes a similar abolitionist position. The fundamental moral wrong here is not that animals are kept in stressful close confinement, or in isolation, or that they have their pain and suffering, their needs and preferences ignored or discounted. *All* these *are* wrong, of course, but they are not the fundamental wrong. They are symptoms and effects of the deeper, systematic wrong that allows these animals to be viewed and treated as lacking independent value, as resources for us—as, indeed, a renewable resource. Giving farm animals more space, more natural environments, more companions does not right the fundamental wrong, any more than giving lab animals more anaesthesia or bigger, cleaner cages would right the fundamental wrong in their case. Nothing less than the total dissolution of commercial animal agriculture will do this, just as, for similar reasons I won't develop at length here, morality requires nothing less than the total elimination of commercial sport hunting and trapping. The rights view's implications, then, as I have said, are clear—and are uncompromising.

My last two points are about philosophy—my profession. It is most obviously, no substitute for political action. The words I have written here and in other places by themselves don't change a thing. It is what we do with the thoughts the words express—our acts, our deeds—that change things. All that philosophy can do, and all I have attempted, is to offer a vision of what our deeds could aim at. And the why. But not the how.

Finally, I am reminded of my thoughtful critic, the one I mentioned earlier, who chastised me for being "too cerebral." Well, cerebral I have been: indirect duty views, utilitarianism, contractarianism—hardly the stuff deep passions are made of. I am also reminded, however, of the image another friend once set before me—the image of the ballerina as expressive of disciplined passion. Long hours of sweat and toil, of loneliness and practice, of doubt and fatigue; that is the discipline of her craft. But the passion is there, too; the fierce drive to excel, to speak through her body, to do it right, to pierce our minds. That is the image of philosophy I would leave with you; not "too cerebral," but *disciplined passion*. Of the discipline, enough has been seen. As for the passion:

There are times and these are not infrequent, when tears come to my eyes when I see, or read, or hear of the wretched plight of animals in the hands of humans. Their pain, their suffering, their loneliness, their innocence, their death. Anger. Rage. Pity. Sorrow. Disgust. The whole creation groans under the weight of the evil we humans visit upon these mute, powerless creatures. It *is* our heart, not just our head, that calls for an end, that demands of us that we overcome, for them, the habits and forces behind their systematic oppression. All great movements, it is written, go through three stages: ridicule, discussion, adoption. It is the realization of this third stage—adoption—that demands both our passion and our discipline, our heart and our head. The fate of animals is in our hands. God grant we are equal to the task.

Note

1. Tom Regan, *The Case for Animal Rights* (Berkeley: University of California Press, 1983).

Animal Liberation or Animal Rights?

Peter Singer

I

Attributing rights to animals is not, of course, the only way of changing their moral status. One can also ground the case for change on the fact that animals have interests. Interests are central to many moral theories. Utilitarian theories, in particular, tend to be based on interests or something closely related to interests, such as preferences, or the experience of pleasure and pain. Not all interest-based theories, however, are utilitarian. It is possible to combine a concern with interests and a non-utilitarian principle of distribution, for instance Rawls's maximin principle. Thus one does not have to be a utilitarian to take interests as the basis upon which moral judgments are to be made.

Given a moral theory based on interests, it is easy enough to argue that we are not justified in ignoring or discounting the interests of any human being on the grounds that he or she is not a member of the race or sex to which we belong. This principle of equal consideration of interests is widely accepted in so far as it applies to human beings. Once so accepted, however, it is very difficult to find any logical basis for resisting its extension to *all* beings with interests. This means that nonhuman animals, or at least all nonhuman animals capable of conscious experiences such as pain or pleasure, enter the sphere of moral concern. Moreover they enter it with a fundamentally equal moral status: their interests are to be given the same consideration as the like interests of any other being.[1]

Once nonhuman animals are recognized as coming within the sphere of equal consideration of interests, it is immediately clear that we must stop treating hens as machines for turning grain into eggs, rats as living toxicology testing kits, and whales as floating reservoirs of oil and blubber. All these practices—and the list could be continued for a long time—are based on treating animals as things to be used for our advantage, without any thought being given to the interests of the animals themselves. The inclusion of animals within the sphere of equal consideration could not leave such practices intact.

Other aspects of our treatment of animals require more detailed discussion. Since the interests of nonhuman animals are not always the same as those of normal non-infant human beings, it does not follow from the principle of equal consideration of interests that we must treat nonhuman animals in the same way as we treat humans. Would it, for instance, be morally acceptable to rear animals in conditions which satisfied all their needs, and then kill them painlessly for food? Are *any* experiments on animals justified? These are not easy questions and they do not have simple answers. I shall not attempt to answer them here, beyond saying that one obviously relevant issue is whether nonhuman animals have the same interest in continued life as normal humans do.[2] The point is that we must try in each case to work out what will be best for all those involved. In this way a view based on interests includes nonhuman animals within the moral sphere, on the basis of full equality of consideration. It also remains sensitive to the particular circumstances of the question at issue.

II

So what reason can there be for asserting that animals are entitled, not merely to equal consideration of their interests, but to moral *rights?* For an answer we can look at Regan's *The Case for Animal Rights.* Since this is easily the most careful and thorough defence of the claim that animals have rights, we can be sure that in considering its arguments, we are taking the case for rights in its strongest form.

Regan begins by assembling evidence for the belief that some nonhuman animals—in particular, mammals beyond the stage of infancy—are what he calls "subjects-of-a-life." By this expression Regan means that these animals are individuals with beliefs, desires, perception, memory, a sense of the future, an emotional life, preferences, the ability to initiate action in pursuit of goals, psychophysical identity over time, and an individual welfare in the sense that things can go well or badly for them. Regan then asserts that all subjects-of-a-life have inherent value.

To this point there is nothing with which a utilitarian need disagree. Whether nonhuman animals do in fact have beliefs, desires, preferences and so on is, of course, a factual question, not a moral one. Without pursuing the complex philosophical issues it raises, or going into the finer details of the kind of beliefs which creatures without language may have, I shall simply say that I think Regan is, on the whole, right about this factual question.

Moreover the utilitarian can also accept the substantive moral claim that subjects-of-a-life have inherent value. The meaning a utilitarian would give to this claim is as follows. Subjects-of-a-life are not *things.* They are not like lumps of coal, which have instrumental value because they keep us warm, but have no intrinsic value of their own. On the contrary, subjects-of-a-life have inherent value in precisely the same way as we do. They have preferences, and they have a welfare. Their welfare matters, and no defensible moral judgments can ignore or discount their interests.

Utilitarianism, therefore, does recognize the inherent value of those beings which Regan calls subjects-of-a-life. But Regan does not think that this recognition goes far enough. Let us look at what he says proper recognition would require:

> . . . we may say that we fail to treat individuals who have inherent value with the respect they are due, as a matter of strict justice, whenever we treat them *as if they lacked* inherent value, and we treat them in this way whenever we treat them *as if they were mere receptacles* of valuable experiences (e.g., pleasure or preference satisfaction) or *as if their value depended upon their utility* relative to the interests of others. In particular, therefore, we fail to display proper respect for those who have inherent value whenever we harm them so that we may bring about the best aggregate consequences for everyone affected by the outcome of such treatment.[3]

This passage needs to be dissected with some care, for it lumps together, under the heading of "treating individuals as if they lacked inherent value," three quite separate forms of treatment. These three forms of treatment are:

i. Treating individuals as if they were mere receptacles of valuable experiences;

ii. Treating individuals as if their value depended upon their utility relative to the interests of others; and

iii. Harming individuals so that we may bring about the best aggregate consequences for everyone affected by the outcome of such treatment.

It is obvious that the first two are not equivalent. Nor is it apparent how, as Regan's words suggest, the third can in some way be a particular application of the first two. We must therefore ask separately in each case whether the form of treatment described is genuinely a case of treating individuals as if they lacked inherent value.

Let us begin with (ii), since this is the least controversial. It is, in fact, a description of treating individuals as if they possessed only instrumental value. To use my earlier example, it is the way we treat lumps of coal, and Regan is clearly right to say that it is incompatible with a recognition of the inherent value of the individuals so treated. As we have already seen, no utilitarian would accept such treatment of subjects-of-a-life.

What about (i)? This is more difficult. It may seem that to treat individuals as "mere receptacles" must fail to recognize their inherent value. After all, when we think of receptacles such as boxes or bottles—considering them *qua* receptacle, and not as objects of artistic or commercial value in their own right—we think of their instrumental value in holding something else, and it is the contents which really matter. So, if utilitarians think of pigs, for instance, as valuable only because of the capacity of pigs to experience pleasure or preference satisfaction, aren't they necessarily denying inherent value to pigs?

The analogy is misleading. Sentient creatures are not receptacles for valuable experiences in the way that bottles, for instance, are receptacles for wine. If I have a bottle of wine in my hand, I can pour the wine out of the bottle; but there is no way in which I can separate the valuable experiences of pigs from the pigs themselves. We cannot even make sense of the idea of an experience—whether of pleasure, or preference satisfaction, or anything else—floating around detached from all sentient creatures. Hence the distinction between treating individuals as if they possessed inherent value, and treating them as if their experiences possessed inherent value, is much more problematic than we might at first glance suspect.

I can think of only two ways in which such a distinction might make sense. First, one might distinguish between those who hold that individuals possess inherent value only as long as they are capable of having certain experiences, and those who hold that individuals possess inherent value as long as they are alive. On the first view, an individual who falls into a total and irreversible coma

ceases to have inherent value; on the second view such an individual continues to have inherent value. Utilitarians would take the first view. It might be said that this shows that they treat individuals as if they were mere receptacles of valuable experiences, for as soon as individuals cease to be capable of having these experiences, utilitarians cease to value them. But I do not think this could be what Regan means when he refers to treating individuals as if they were mere receptacles of valuable experiences. After all, individuals in total and irreversible comas have ceased to be subjects-of-a-life, and so presumably Regan would agree with the utilitarian that they have lost the inherent value they once possessed.

The key to the second way in which one might distinguish between recognizing the inherent value of individuals, and recognizing the inherent value of their experiences, lies in our attitude to the continued existence of particular individuals over time. Suppose that we have a group of individuals enjoying pleasurable experiences, and we are faced with two options: the same group of individuals will continue to enjoy pleasurable experiences; or, they will all be painlessly killed, and replaced with another group of individuals enjoying equally pleasurable experiences. Utilitarians appear to be committed to saying that, other things being equal, there is no difference between these options. This may be taken as proof that they treat the individuals in question as lacking inherent value.

There are two points to be made about this example. First, it is essential to appreciate that the example does not allow us to drive a wedge between the inherent value of the individuals and the inherent value of their experiences, *while the individuals are having those experiences*. Even if utilitarians are committed to saying that there is no difference between the options, they will still hold that the individuals have inherent value during every instant of their existence. Thus the example has application only to the specific point of whether we attribute inherent value to the *continued*—rather than the moment-by-moment—existence of particular individuals.

Second not all utilitarians are committed to treating subjects-of-a-life as if they were replaceable in this manner. Hedonistic utilitarians may be, but preference utilitarians are not. In *Practical Ethics* I wrote:

Rational, self-conscious beings are individuals, leading lives of their own, not mere receptacles for containing a certain quantity of happiness. Beings that are conscious, but not self-conscious, on the other hand, can properly be regarded as receptacles for experiences of pleasure and pain, rather than as individuals leading lives of their own.[4]

With the benefit of hindsight, I can see that the use of the term "receptacles" was liable to mislead; but I still hold that a preference utilitarian must take into account the preferences for continued life which some individuals have. This means that preference utilitarians will not be indifferent to the choice between the two options described above, except in those cases in which the individuals have no preferences for continued existence. Note, incidentally, that at least so far as my own version of preference utilitarianism is concerned, Regan is wrong to describe "preference satisfaction" as some kind of "experience." What the preference utilitarian seeks to maximize is not an experience of satisfaction, but the bringing about of what is preferred, whether or not this produces "satisfaction" in the individual who has the preference. That is why killing an individual who prefers to go on living is not justified by creating a new individual with a preference to go on living. Even if the preference of this new individual will be satisfied, the negative aspect of the unsatisfied preference of the previous individual has not been made up by the creation of the new preference plus its satisfaction.[5]

Apart from individuals whose lives are so miserable that they do not wish to continue living, the only individuals likely to have no preferences for continued life will be those incapable of having such preferences because they are not self-conscious and hence are incapable of conceiving of their own life as either continuing or coming to an end. Since Regan includes memory and a sense of the future, including one's own future, in his list of the characteristics which subjects-of-a-life must possess, it is clear that the individuals which a preference utilitarian may regard as replaceable are not subjects-of-a-life.

We have been considering the suggestion that utilitarians fail to recognize the inherent value of individuals when they treat them as if they were mere receptacles of valuable experiences. We have now seen that utilitarians do not regard sentient creatures as "mere receptacles," if by this is meant that they value the experiences of these creatures and not the creatures themselves. Considered on an instant-by-instant basis, this distinction cannot intelligibly be drawn. If, on the other hand, we transform the question into one which hinges on whether utilitarians attribute value to the *continued* existence of particular individuals, we find that preference utilitarians, at least, *will* attribute value to the continued existence of all those beings whom Regan calls subjects-of-a-life. So even if we allow the issue to be re-stated in this manner, we still find that preference utilitarians deny inherent value only to beings who are not subjects-of-a-life. Since Regan attributes inherent value only to beings who are subjects-of-a-life, on this point he and the preference utilitarians do not disagree.

We come now to the third and most crucial of the ways in which Regan seeks to characterize treating individuals as if they lacked inherent value: harming individuals so that we may bring about the best aggregate consequences for everyone affected by the outcome of such treatment. We have seen that Regan writes as if the assertion that such treatment indicates a lack of proper respect for inherent value has somehow been deduced from the more general descriptions of treatment which preceded it. Even if we had unquestioningly accepted that the forms of treatment I have labelled (i) and (ii) were indicative of lack of respect for inherent value, however, it isn't easy to see how we could validly infer that this was also true of (iii). Regan gives a hint as to what he has in mind in the following passage:

> The grounds for claiming that such treatment is disrespectful and unjust should be apparent. It can hardly be just or respectful to harm individuals who have inherent value merely in order to secure the best aggregate consequences for everyone affected by the outcome. This cannot be respectful of inherent value because it is to view the individual who is harmed *merely* as a receptacle of what has value (e.g. pleasure), so that the losses of such value credited to the harmed individual can be made up for, or

more than compensated, by the sum of the gains in such values by others, *without any wrong having been done to the loser.* Individuals who have inherent value, however, have a kind of value that is distinct from, is not reducible to, and is incommensurate with such values as pleasure or preference satisfaction, either their own or those of others. To harm such individuals *merely* in order to produce the best consequences for all involved *is* to do what is wrong—*is* to treat them unjustly—because it fails to respect their inherent value. To borrow part of a phrase from Kant, individuals who have inherent value must never be treated *merely as means* to securing the best aggregate consequences.[6]

The first part of this passage attempts to link (iii) with (i) by claiming that (iii) involves treating individuals as if they were *merely* receptacles for valuable experiences. We have already seen that such references to receptacles can be misleading, and that to treat individuals as valuable only because of their capacity for certain experiences is not to deny them inherent value. So even if (iii) could be linked with (i), this would not show that (iii) involved a denial of inherent value. But this is by no means the only gap in the argument. It is simply not true that to harm an individual in order to secure the best aggregate consequences for everyone "is to view the individual who is harmed *merely* as a receptacle of what has value. . . ." After all, utilitarians and others who are prepared to harm individuals for this end will view those they are harming, along with those they are benefitting, as equally possessing inherent value. They differ with Regan only in that they prefer to maximize benefits to individuals, rather than to restrict such benefits by a requirement that no individual may be harmed.

Those who incline towards Regan's view of this matter might consider the following. Suppose you had to choose to live in one of two societies, call them R and S. All you know is that in R, no individual is ever harmed to secure the best aggregate consequences for everyone, while in S individuals are harmed if careful scrutiny shows beyond any doubt that such harm is the only possible way to secure

the best aggregate outcome for everyone. (Such harm is, of course, kept to the minimum necessary to secure the beneficial outcome, and the harm is included in the calculation as to whether the consequences really are the best aggregate outcome for everyone.) Assume that there are no differences between R and S, other than those traceable to this difference of moral principle. Let us also assume that the worst off in R and the worst off in S are at the same level; though there might, of course, be different reasons in the two societies for why they were at this level. Remember that you have no way of knowing whether, if you choose S, you will yourself be harmed; but you know from the description already given that, if there is any difference in the overall welfare of the two societies, it must favour S. How would you choose? I would certainly choose S, and so would anyone seeking to maximize her or his expected welfare. Is it plausible to say that a moral principle which would be chosen under such conditions is a principle which views those harmed merely as receptacles? Since we do not know if we will be harmed, to say this would imply that people who are rationally seeking to maximize their own welfare must view *themselves* merely as receptacles. This strikes me as absurd; and at the very least, it makes it clear that to maintain such a view is to empty all the critical impact from the charge of viewing individuals as receptacles.

We have now considered the first part of the passage in which Regan offers reasons for his view that (iii) involves a denial of the inherent value of individuals. In this first part, Regan attempted to link (iii) with (i). This attempt fails. Regan goes on, however, to make two additional claims about (iii), claims which go beyond (i) and (ii) and could thus be seen as giving support to (iii) as an independent assertion.

The first of these additional claims is that "individuals who have inherent value . . . have a kind of value that is distinct from, is not reducible to, and is incommensurate with such values as pleasure or preference satisfaction, either their own or those of others." The second claim is the Kantian assertion that "Individuals who have inherent value must never be treated *merely as means* to securing the best aggregate consequences."

The first claim looks like the point about receptacles again, but it adds to that a point about incommensurability. The difficulty of weighing up incommensurable values is a familiar one in normative ethics. Regan's invocation of incommensurability, however, is unusual in that he is not referring to the incommensurability of, say, justice and welfare, or knowledge and beauty. The incommensurability to which he refers is that between the inherent value of individuals, and values such as pleasure or preference satisfaction. For reasons already given in our discussion of receptacles, it is not easy to see how the individuals and the valued experiences are to be separated; but in any case, more crucial to the present discussion is the absence of any explanation why (iii) requires that these values be commensurable. Suppose, for example, that we inflict a specified harm on one individual in order to prevent ten other individuals from suffering exactly the same harm. Here there is no problem of comparing incommensurable values. All that is needed is the recognition that ten harms are worse than one harm, when all the harms to be considered are exactly the same. If, therefore, harming one person in order to secure the best aggregate consequences for everyone involves denying inherent value, this cannot be shown by reference to incommensurability.[7]

What of the second claim? Taken literally, the second claim is merely a re-statement of (ii). It amounts to a rejection of treating beings with inherent value as if they possessed only instrumental value. It is obvious that to harm an individual in order to produce the best aggregate outcome for everyone is not necessarily to treat that individual *merely as a means*. It is compatible with giving as much consideration to the interests of that individual as one gives to any other individual, including oneself.

Perhaps Regan means to assert more than this; Kant, no doubt, did mean much more. But there are notorious difficulties in Kant's own attempt to defend his categorical imperative. Moreover, as Regan himself acknowledges, he is borrowing only "part of a phrase" from Kant. To borrow Kant's argument in full, and apply it to all subjects-of-a-life, Regan would have to find an alternative to Kant's reliance on rationality and autonomy. It is not obvious what this would be. Regan certainly offers no further account.

We have now completed our discussion of the three ways of treating individuals which Regan says indicate a lack of respect for their inherent value. We have found that only the second is a clear-cut case, and this, of course, is the one that utilitarians reject as emphatically as Regan does. The third is not indicative of treating individuals as if they lacked inherent value; and the first is also not indicative of such treatment, unless we consider the attitude to continued, rather than instant-by-instant, existence. Even then, preference utilitarians will value the continued existence of subjects-of-a-life who wish to go on living, just as Regan will. We can conclude that respect for the inherent value of subjects-of-a-life is not a reason for embracing the rights view rather than the utilitarian view. The principle of equal consideration of interests, which is the foundation of utilitarianism as well as of many other ethical views, fully satisfies the demand that we recognize the inherent value of subjects-of-a-life.

III

It is not my aim, in this essay, to indicate all the difficulties which face defenders of rights. I have elsewhere indicated some of the problems Regan has in applying his moral views to two apparently similar situations: the experimental use of animals, and his own hypothetical case of the dog in the overcrowded lifeboat.[8] These problems are characteristic of the difficulties faced by all adherents of rights-based ethical theories, because such theories are too inflexible to respond to the various real and imaginary circumstances in which we want to make moral judgments. That is, however, another issue. My aim here has been to show how a position based on equal consideration of interests recognizes the inherent value of individuals, including nonhuman animals. The most impressive case for animal rights published so far is unable to provide adequate grounds for moving beyond the equal consideration stance, to a view based on rights. In the absence of any such grounds, there is no case for attributing rights, rather than equal consideration, to animals.

Notes

1. For a more detailed exposition of this point, see the first chapter of my *Animal Liberation* (New York, 1975).

2. See my *Practical Ethics* (Cambridge, 1979) chs. 4 and 5.

3. T. Regan, *The Case for Animal Rights* (Berkeley, CA: University of California Press, 1983) pp. 248–49; italics in original.

4. *Practical Ethics*, p. 102.

5. For further details see *Practical Ethics*, ch. 4; and also my reply to H. L. A. Hart's review of that book, in *The New York Review of Books* (August 14, 1980), pp. 53–54. I develop these ideas further in "Life's Uncertain Voyage," forthcoming in P. Pettit and R. Sylvan (eds) *Mind, Morality and Metaphysics: Essays in Honour of J. J. C. Smart* (Blackwell, Oxford, 1987).

6. *The Case for Animal Rights*, p. 249; italics in original.

7. Frank Jackson has pointed out to me that Regan's assertion of the incommensurability of the inherent value of the individuals, and values such as pleasure or preference satisfaction, should in any case be rejected because it has absurd consequences. Consider, for instance, what taking such a view seriously would do to perfectly ordinary projects, like your next car trip to the movies. There is a finite, though very slight, probability that you will hit and kill a pedestrian. Are you nevertheless justified in making the trip? We all agree that the death of a pedestrian is a *very* much greater evil than your enjoyment of the movie is a good; but the risk of killing a pedestrian is so extremely slight that we think it outweighed by a strong probability of achieving the lesser value. What if, however, the value of the pedestrian's life and of your enjoyment of the movie are truly *incommensurable?* If this means anything, it must mean that *no* finite probability of your causing the death of the pedestrian could be outweighed by *any* amount of enjoyment. You would never be justified in furthering your own, or anyone else's, pleasure or preference satisfaction by any activity which carried any finite risk of causing an individual's death. So long, movies—and most other recreational activities as well.

8. See my comments in "Ten Years of Animal Liberation," *The New York Review of Books* (January 17, 1985), pp. 46–52; and Regan's response, with my rejoinder, in "The Dog in the Lifeboat: An Exchange," *New York Review of Books* (April 25, 1985), pp. 57–58.

Interspecific Justice

Donald VanDeVeer

I have never committed an axe-murder, bludgeoned fellow-humans to death, nor eaten any of their babies. Even though I would not think of setting fire to cats (though I am not at all fond of them), I have most of my adult life paid people to axe-murder and bludgeon to death a considerable variety of creatures, some of whom were babies, so that I might eat them; they were, in fact, tasty. That this description applied to my actions or that there were moral questions about these practices is something to which I was largely oblivious until reading Peter Singer's essay "Animal Liberation" several years ago.[1]

The effect of Singer's early essay was sometimes—and in my case—to shake one from his "dogmatic slumbers." However, before the uptake could secure itself, Singer lost some hard-won credibility near the end of his essay by stating:

> What, for instance, are we to do about genuine conflicts of interest like rats biting slum children? I am not sure of the answer, but the essential point is just that we *do* see this as a conflict of interests, that we recognize that rats have interests too.[2]

To be fair, Singer does *not* say or suggest that the interests of rats ought to be weighed equally, but his willingness to consider that there might be a serious moral question here no doubt struck some readers as a *reductio* of his position. A further factor in such a reaction may be that there is naturally a powerful *desire* to believe that one is not party to morally outrageous practices and that arguments which suggest as much "must" be fallacious. This less than reflective reaction may have occurred, I speculate, with many initial encounters with Singer's essay.

In that essay and more explicitly in Singer's book by the same title, there is a simple, tempting argument in favor of the view that humans have some duties toward animals; one possible reconstruction is this:

Inquiry, Vol. 22, Nos. 1–2 (Summer 1979), pp. 55–70. Reprinted by permission.

1. All or virtually all human beings are sentient creatures.

2. Many animals are sentient creatures.

3. Moral agents have a duty not to cause suffering to sentient creatures.

4. So, moral agents have a duty to refrain from causing suffering to (sentient) humans and (sentient) animals.

5. The interests of *all* sentient creatures (in not suffering) must be given equal consideration.

6. So, the imposition of suffering on animals (an overriding of the duty mentioned in (4)) would have to be justified by grounds of the same moral weight as those which would be necessary to justify the imposition of suffering on humans.[3]

The argument seems plausible, and some of its premises are incontrovertible. Singer's strong and specific admonitions (e.g. to become a vegetarian) in his radical critique of almost universal current practices affecting animals appeal to this argument and to further assumptions about (a) the actual effects of existing practices on animals (e.g. experimentation, raising animals for food and other products), (b) judgments about the painfulness or disability of these practices for the animals involved, and (c) the falsity of the claim that certain human satisfactions are obtainable only by harming or killing animals. The first four claims of my reconstruction of Singer's argument are reasonable. What is meant, in (5), by giving the interests of all sentient creatures "equal consideration" is less clear. Does it mean 'taking into account' all such interests? Does this mean giving *equal* moral *weight* to like interests? If not, will (6) follow? Further, since killing may be performed painlessly the constraint on causing animals suffering (even if [6] is conceded) cannot yield an adequate basis for deciding on the legitimacy of killing animals if it is done painlessly. It is not my purpose to dwell on Singer's argument in any direct way, although I shall survey some principles which proffer answers to some of the above questions. Of the views to be considered, one emerges which is reasonable and in some important ways stands in agreement with *Animal Liberation*. At points, however, it delineates a competing view on the question of how we may legitimately treat animals. While I shall allude on occasion to the views of those who have taken a stand on these matters in recent literature, e.g. Peter Singer and Tom Regan, I conceive my task as a more constructive than critical one, and I shall try to sketch some of the features which I think must be incorporated in an adequate theory. Since I will focus on conflicts of interests between humans and animals and the question of a just resolution of competing morally relevant claims, one might describe what is needed as a theory of interspecific justice.[4] Questions about the treatment of animals, like questions about non-paradigm humans (e.g. Homo sapiens fetuses) are hard cases, and even if the suggestions posed here are correct, they will fall short of a fully adequate account. Indeed, it seems to me that the formulation of an adequate theoretical basis for the legitimate treatment of animals is no simple task and cannot be done simply by extending, in any straightforward way, principles widely accepted or thought to be uncontroversial. It is not surprising that some of the recalcitrant problems confronting the formulation of an adequate theory of justice with regard to humans have parallels in attempts to formulate an adequate theory of interspecific justice.

I. Interests and Conflicts of Interests

Of those animals capable of suffering we may assume that they have at least one interest, namely, in not suffering. By this assumption I do not mean that they are interested in not suffering (though they may be) but, roughly, that it is *in their interest* not to suffer. This last claim means that it is not conducive to an animal's well-being to suffer— whether or not the animal is capable of "consciously" wanting not to suffer. Further, the claim that it is not in the interest of an animal to suffer is, I think, a strong presumptive one. While pain *per se* is undesirable, it may be in the interest of animals to suffer *on balance* for the sake of a certain beneficial result—as in the painful removal of a gangrenous leg by surgery—as it is also for human beings. While the concept of an action's being in the interest of a creature is not transparently clear, it is contingently and commonly in the interest of a being not to suffer, although there are exceptions when it is in its over-all interest to do so. Since it is possible to cause death painlessly, an animal in whose interest it is not to suffer *may* not be such that it is in its interest not to die. However, I shall simply assume that *generally* when it is in some creature's interest not to suffer it is also in its interest not to die (and, hence, not to be killed). Let us assume, then—somewhat more strongly than our earlier (3)—that moral agents have a duty, *ceteris paribus,* not to cause suffering to those animals which can suffer and a duty, *ceteris paribus,* not to cause animals to die. On this view there are many common practices which are not in the interests of many animals, and there is a presumptive duty not to engage in certain practices, namely, any which cause suffering or death to *those* animals in whose interest it is not to suffer or not to die. The troublesome and difficult question which arises, once one is convinced that both human beings (or many) and animals (or many) have at least some morally relevant interests, concerns how to *weigh* their respective interests in general and how to adjudicate *conflicts of interest* which arise between humans and animals. What we crucially need, to advance the current reconsideration of our treatment of animals, is an identification and assessment of principles which provide a basis for comparatively weighing such interests. We may be guided here by the standard method of testing principles by checking their implications against our deepest and strongest pre-theoretical convictions about specific cases ("intuitions" in one sense of the term), and also by how well such principles cohere with other defensible principles, in particular, how well principles advocating interspecific discriminations (weightings of respective interests) seem to be consistent with parallel and defensible intraspecific discriminations.[5]

II. Principles of Adjudicating Conflicts of Interests

Singer characterizes views which advocate a certain preferential weighing of human interests over that of animals as "speciesist."[6] He claims:

> If a being suffers there can be no moral justification for refusing to take that suffering into consideration. No matter what the nature of the being, the principle of equality requires that its suffering be counted equally with the like suffering—

in so far as rough comparisons can be made—of any other being.

***

The racist violates the principle of equality by giving greater weight to the interests of members of his own race when there is a clash between their interests and the interests of those of another race. The sexist violates the principle of equality by favoring the interests of his own sex. Similarly the speciesist allows the interests of his own species to override the greater interests of members of other species. The pattern is identical in each case.[7]

The quoted passage does not distinguish some relevantly different principles which may be aptly classified as speciesist views and not all of which are equally tempting. I shall identify three forms of speciesism and two non-speciesist views which I shall dub Two Factor Egalitarianism and Species Egalitarianism respectively; the first three principles may be entitled "speciesist" because they all advocate a heavier weighting of human interests over that of animals or do not concede that animals have any interests at all. The fourth principle also weights human interests more heavily but only when certain contingent conditions are satisfied; for reasons mentioned later, it would be misleading to label it a speciesist view. I list the names of the principles here, and consider each in turn:

1. Radical Speciesism
2. Extreme Speciesism
3. Interest Sensitive Speciesism
4. Two Factor Egalitarianism
5. Species Egalitarianism

In turning to Radical Speciesism we consider the only one of the five principles to be identified which in fact is incompatible with the premises of the mentioned argument appealing to animal suffering.

Radical Speciesism

Radical Speciesism is the view that:

It is morally permissible, *ceteris paribus,* to treat animals in any fashion one chooses.

One ground for this claim is the view that there is no *intrinsic* feature of any animal per se in virtue of which there is any moral constraint on how it may be treated. I speak of "intrinsic feature" because the radical speciesist may allow that a given animal ought not to be harmed because of its relational trait, e.g. it is Smith's pet. This view is similar to the by now familiar view of Descartes's that animals were mere automata, extended things which neither think nor are sentient. With the further assumption that only thinking or sentient things are such that something may be in their interests, it follows that animals have no interests. So, it could not be the case that the interest of any animal outweighs that of any human being. There seem to be no premises which are both strong enough to entail Radical Speciesism (RS) and plausible. The Cartesian assumption is a strong one but not at all tempting. I shall not explore it. That many animals can and do suffer intensely is quite obvious. The anti-Cartesian arguments may be found elsewhere; in general, they are the arguments against extreme scepticism about Other Minds. Since many animals can suffer, the Cartesian assumption is evidently an untenable view. I include it for purposes of contrast and completeness. The reader may wish to examine the more patient discussions in Singer's book.[8]

What are the moral implications of Radical Speciesism? On RS there is no presumption at all, based on the effects *on the animal,* against putting live puppies in one's oven, and heating them in order to watch them squirm or convulse or fall over; the reader can imagine other 'perverse' experiments. The important issue here is simply put. Can animals (some) suffer? If so, it is, in general, in their interest not to suffer and moral agents have a presumptive duty to avoid causing such suffering. Hence, we must judge, if we acknowledge that animals suffer, that RS is mistaken or that the *ceteris paribus* clause is rarely satisfied.

It may be noted that Singer characterizes the "speciesist" as allowing "the interests of his own species to override the greater interests of members of other species" (see earlier quotation). While such unequal weighting of interests seems to be an objectionable feature of other principles which I have dubbed speciesist, it is worth observing that the Cartesian elaboration which may be associated with Radical Speciesism (as part of the ground for the latter) is not speciesist on Singer's criterion, for RS in its Cartesian elaboration does not weigh interests *unequally;* it simply concedes no interests at all to animals.

Those forms of speciesism which allow that animals have interests and which are compatible with the statements constituting the Suffering Argument are those remaining to be considered. They may all be regarded as principles purporting to guide action in cases of *conflicts of interests.* In examining such cases it is desirable to focus, when possible, on cases where the existence of animals is no threat to humans (e.g. not on cases of animals attacking humans) and, when possible, on "normal" before extreme or bizarre situations.

Extreme Speciesism

To distinguish two further forms of speciesism we must suppose that there is a difference between the basic and peripheral interests of a being. It would be difficult to elaborate such a distinction in a precise manner or offer a full-fledged defense of it. It is clear, however, that in the absence of certain sorts of goods many creatures cannot function in ways common to their species; they do not function in a "minimally adequate" way, for example, in the absence of food, water, oxygen or the presence of prolonged, intense pain. We may say that it is in a creature's *basic* interest to have (not have) such things. In contrast there are goods such that in their absence it is true only that the creature does not thrive and which are, then, not in its basic interest (e.g. toys for my dog). This distinction is admittedly vague but it is not empty. Its application must, in part, depend on contextual matters. Given such a distinction, Extreme Speciesism is the view that:

> When there is a conflict of interests between an animal and a human being, it is morally permissible, *ceteris paribus,* so to act that a basic interest of the animal is subordinated for the sake of promoting even a peripheral interest of a human being.

Extreme Speciesism (ES) proffers a different theoretical basis for actions affecting animals from Radical Speciesism when RS is linked to Cartesian assumptions, but, as stated, RS and ES will, in practice, sanction the same policies when there is, in fact, a requisite conflict of interests. When there is not, ES allows (is compatible with) acting to promote an animal interest, e.g. the interest in not suffering. As stated, however, ES would not prohibit puppy cooking and cat torturing as long as such acts promote some peripheral (or basic) human interest. In the end, perhaps, much may depend on *how* peripheral the human interest one is considering is or further discriminations of that sort. Nevertheless, unless we wish to defend the moral permissibility of recreational puppy cooking and like acts, ES must be rejected as well as RS. On ES the kind or level of animal interest involved in a conflict of interests is, in effect, unimportant and need not be considered; this is not true of the next form of speciesism to be considered.

Interest Sensitive Speciesism

Interest Sensitive Speciesism (ISS) is the view that:

> When there is a conflict of interests between an animal and a human being, it is morally permissible, *ceteris paribus*, so to act that an interest of the animal is subordinated for the sake of promoting a *like* interest of a human being (or a more basic one) but one may not subordinate a basic interest of an animal for the sake of promoting a *peripheral* human interest.

On this principle what is permissible depends importantly on whether or not the conflicting interests are basic or not; it is, thus, "interest sensitive." This principle sanctions a wide range of treatment preferential to human beings. For example, in a life raft case where the raft is overloaded and about to go under and either I or my dog will die (not both) before rescue, ISS permits me to sacrifice my dog if I so choose. In cases of conflict of *like* interests it is permissible, *ceteris paribus,* to subordinate that of the animal. Anti-speciesist principles which do *not* yield this result are hard to defend. Unlike RS and ES, which also yield this result, ISS does *not* permit puppy cooking or cat torturing for the pleasure of watching them squirm. This fact immediately makes ISS a more viable contender for the appellation, "justifiable form of speciesism."

While ISS clearly permits an evident discrimination in favor of human interests while not, in effect, assigning infinite weight to the latter, it will strike many as giving *insufficient* weight to human interests. For, on ISS, if it is in a bird's interest not to

be incarcerated (as in a cage) and this interest is more basic than a hedonistic interest of a human owner in keeping it there, then such acts are impermissible since they would subordinate a basic animal interest in order to promote a peripheral human one. Suppose that having musk perfume, leather wearing apparel or luggage, fur rugs, ivory piano keys, or animal derived glue are not necessary to promote basic human interests. If so, then ISS would entail that killing animals for these purposes would (supposing that doing so violates a basic interest of these animals in continuing to live), *ceteris paribus*, be impermissible. Given the mentioned suppositions some would judge ISS as "too strong" even though it plausibly prohibits cat torturing to promote sadistic pleasure. I leave the question of whether ISS is "too strong" or "too weak" open here. There is a more basic objection to ISS, namely, that it omits consideration of another factor which is morally relevant in adjudicating conflicts of interests.

The objection calls attention, in part, to the enormous diversity *among* animals whose basic interest may conflict with some human interest. In this regard, the use of the expression "speciesism" tends to suggest, perhaps, that we are only dealing with two groups and, hence, encourages formulating principles which suggest the permissibility of some sort of subordination of the interests of members of one group to the interests of members of the other.[9] This perspective reflects our tendency, Jonathan Swift to the contrary, to divide the animal world into the human and non-human or, analogously, into the inedible and the edible.[10] We ought not to forget that there are estimated to be about 1.5 million species and about 10,000 new ones discovered each year.[11] Significant differences *among* non-human species may become ignored with Interest Sensitive Speciesism. If it is in the interest of both an oyster and a chimpanzee not to be killed, ISS only requires that one consider the fact that the interest is in each case a basic and not a peripheral one. However, it is most tempting to think that while both interests are basic, the interest of the chimpanzee is of greater moral weight than that of the oyster, a judgment analogous to the one about the same-level or "like" interests of my dog and myself in my life raft case. If so, then a principle purporting to be a reasonable guide to weighting the interests of members of different species must take account of something other than whether the interests in question are "like" or "unlike." Such a consideration provides a basis for another principle, one to which we may now turn.

Two Factor Egalitarianism

It is necessary, to formulate our next principle, to recognize interests that are not basic in the sense suggested earlier yet not frivolous. I shall call such interests "serious interests." A rough criterion for serious interests would be that something is in a being's serious interest if and only if, though it can survive without it, it is difficult or costly (to its well-being) to do so. Hence, it may in the serious interest of a lonely child to have a pet or in the serious interest of an eagle to be able to fly. Serious interests are not as peripheral as Jones's interest in watching cockfights. It would be less messy if interests did not exhibit degrees of importance to their possessors; unfortunately, they do. This is also true of the other factor considered by the next principle, the factor of psychological capacities.

Two Factor Egalitarianism can now be formulated; it holds that:

> When there is an interspecies conflict of interests between two beings, A and B, it is morally permissible, *ceteris paribus*:
>
> (1) to sacrifice the interest of A to promote a like interest of B if A lacks significant psychological capacities possessed by B,
>
> (2) to sacrifice a basic interest of A to promote a serious interest of B if A substantially lacks significant psychological capacities possessed by B,
>
> (3) to sacrifice the peripheral interest to promote the more basic interest if the beings are similar with respect to psychological capacity (regardless of who possesses the interests).[12]

On TFE the subordination of basic animal interests (say, in living or not suffering) may be subordinated if the animal is (significantly) psychologically "inferior" to the human in question. "Psychological" is intended to include the "mental." Let us conjecture about the implications of TFE; I leave certain assumptions tacit. On TFE killing oysters or (most kinds of) fish for food for human survival would be permissible; killing them only for the human pleasure of doing so would not be. On this view *certain* forms of hunting (recreational killing) would seem to be immoral. Similarly certain rodeo activities and bull-fighting would not be justified. The killing of seals for food by an Eskimo would be justified; the killing (and radical deprivation and suffering) of veal calves by people in agriculturally affluent areas may be wrong.[13] TFE allows the sacrifice of my dog in our life raft case. Many of these implications are plausible. In general, TFE permits scientific experiments on animals where the promised utility for humans and/or animals is very considerable but not otherwise; recent criticisms suggest that a small proportion of the millions of experiments regularly performed can be so categorized.[14] It appears, then, on TFE as well as with some other speciesist principles, that fairly *simple* generalizations about the morality of hunting, killing animals for food, and experiments on animals are unreasonable. This feature of course parallels the difficulties with familiar simple generalizations about when it is permissible to kill or experiment on humans; this consideration is not unfavorable to TFE.

So far I have neglected what will strike the traditionally minded as an unfortunate and "radical" implication of TFE. On TFE if there is a conflict of interests between a human permanently and (seriously) psychologically incapacitated by illness, injury, or senility and, on the other hand, an animal with similar or superior psychological capacities (self-awareness, capacity for purposive action, diverse emotions, affection, devotion, and so on), then the more peripheral interest must be subordinated, and the peripheral interest *may* be that of the human being. If the animal is sufficiently developed psychologically, then even a serious interest of a no more capacitated human should not take precedence over the basic interests of the animal. An example where an "under-capacity" human is involved might be this. Suppose, contrary to fact, that an infant with Tay-Sachs disease could be saved from imminent death by a kidney transplant from a healthy chimpanzee at the expense of the chimpanzee's life; TFE prohibits this way of adjudicating the conflict of interests.[15] This case would be, at best, a statistically unusual one, and is mentioned in the attempt to get clearer about principles which have implications concerning other almost universal practices, e.g. raising and killing animals for certain human purposes. An important general characteristic of TFE is that not *any* interest of *any* human morally outweighs *any* interest of *any* animal, such a consideration seems a desideratum of any acceptable principle. TFE attempts to take into account both the kind of interests at stake and also psychological traits of the beings in question.

If the core of speciesism is the belief that it is permissible to give preferential treatment to humans over animals *just because* the former are human beings, then TFE is not a speciesist view. Being a member of Homo sapiens *per se* is not assumed to justify preferential treatment of humans over animals. It is a matter of fact as to whether a given human being will match or exceed a given animal in terms of psychological capacity; usually humans will. However, TFE allows that if there were, for example, beings physiologically like apes except for large brains and more complicated central nervous systems who had intellectual and emotional lives more developed than mature humans, then in a conflict of *like* interests the interests of these ape-looking persons should take precedence.[16]

We shall return (in Section IV) to further examination of TFE. First, I shall describe a final principle purporting to adjudicate interspecific conflicts of interest. Then I shall turn to the challenge posed by those who are sharply opposed to much of our preferential treatment of humans, with the larger aim of seeing whether any principle proposed here meets the challenge and provides a satisfactory basis for justifying certain preferential treatment of humans over animals.

Species Egalitarianism

In contrast to principles which permit the subordination of animal interests in *a priori* fashion (Radical Speciesism) or do so in practice even when like interests are being considered (Extreme Speciesism), is a view which is distinctly antispeciesist, one I label Species Egalitarianism.

> When there is a conflict of interests between an animal and a human being it is morally permissible, *ceteris paribus*, to subordinate the more peripheral to the more basic interest and not otherwise; facts not relevant to how basic the interests are, are not morally relevant to resolving this conflict.

SE is a one factor (level of interests) principle in contrast to TFE. Like TFE it plausibly denies that any interest of any human outweighs any interest of any animal. In fact it suggests, in a radical way, that species identification of the possessors of the interests is irrelevant except in so far as this might bear on a non-evaluative description of the interests in question.

It is tempting to call this view "radical egalitarianism" because it allows, like Interest Sensitive Speciesism, no weight to the many impressive and (seemingly) morally relevant psychological differences among species. On this view it is not "where you are on the evolutionary scale" or what psychological capacities you have but only how fundamental your interest is which counts. This view is unacceptable. That we should, for example, equally weigh the interest in not being killed of an oyster, earthworm, or fruitfly with that of a like interest of a human being, is an implication in virtue of which we can summarily judge, I submit, that SE indeed reduces to an absurdity. While Radical and Extreme Speciesism both give undue weight to human interests over that of animals, Species Egalitarianism swings to the opposite error of giving too little. Part of the attraction of the former views may in fact derive from the blatant ignoring of relevant differences which occurs with SE and the assumption that there are no plausible alterative positions. In view of reasons discussed to this point the least counter-intuitive principle appears to be Two Factor Egalitarianism, or possibly some variant of it. Before elaborating on such a view and considering objections to it, it will be useful to consider more thoroughly the challenge posed by those who are critical of current policies toward radically differential treatment of animals and humans. After doing so we will be in a better position to determine whether TFE is acceptable as it is, whether it requires revision, or whether it should be relegated to the wasteland of tempting but, in the end, irrational proposals.

III. The Challenge of the Critics

It has been argued by Tom Regan that the radically differential treatment that we extend toward animals as opposed to human beings cannot be justified unless "we are given some morally relevant difference that characterizes all humans, but no animals"—one that would, in other words, justify the different sorts of duties and/or rights which we commonly assume we have toward the two groups, or attribute to the two groups, respectively.[17] It is tempting to believe (as Regan allows), however, that not all animals have interests, e.g. protozoa. While protozoa, I shall assume, are not *sentient*, perhaps we should allow, to the contrary, that even for protozoa something may be in their interest, e.g. conducive to their well-being. If so, possession of some (at least one) interest will not serve as a difference, possibly a morally relevant one, between all human beings on the one hand and all animals on the other. A feature that *is* possessed by humans but not, however, by all animals is sentience. This feature, since it *is* possessed by many animals, will not, however, satisfy Regan's requirement that we be given 'some morally relevant difference that characterizes *all* humans, but *no* animals' (my italics). Such a feature will not, then, serve as a justification, or part of a justification, for radically differential treatment of all humans on the one hand and *all* animals on the other. The presence or absence of sentience is, however, a morally relevant trait, and it *will* serve to justify, or as part of a justification of, differential treatment of sentient creatures on the one hand and non-sentient creatures on the other, e.g. the subordination of certain animals (non-sentient ones) for the sake of the well-being of others (sentient humans and sentient non-humans). Hence, *some* differential treatment of humans on the one hand and *some* animals on the other is, *ceteris paribus,* justifiable, I believe, without satisfying the stringent requirement that there is "some morally relevant difference that characterizes all humans, but no animals." This conclusion serves to undermine certain arguments prohibiting radically differential treatment of non-sentient animals. The conclusion is, however, a very weak one. For most differential treatment of humans and animals which is controversial involves differential treatment *within* the class of sentient creatures. The challenge posed by critics of established practices toward animals, such as Tom Regan and, possibly, Peter Singer, is more reasonably posed in the following way: to justify radically differential treatment of creatures *all of whom are sentient* it is necessary to identify a morally relevant difference between those who receive preferential treatment and those who do not. Further, any such morally relevant difference must be sufficiently significant to justify the specific differential treatment in question.[18] Of the views previously considered the only one not subject to decisive objections (considered to this point) which also proposes a basis for subordinating the interests of animals when there is a conflict of like interests between humans and sentient animals, is Two Factor Egalitarianism. It, thus, *purports* to provide the requisite morally relevant difference which would serve to justify some, at least, of the radically differential treatment of humans and animals, treatment which is not merely the kind involved in extending preferential treatment to humans over *non-sentient* animals. TFE is, then, of special interest and, in view of current disputes, not uncontroversial. Let us examine it in more detail.

IV. Two Factor Egalitarianism Explored

Two Factor Egalitarianism assumes the relevance of two matters: (1) level or importance of interests to each being in a conflict of interests, and (2) the psychological capacities of the parties whose interests conflict. It is worth considering further the rationale for assuming their relevance. First, consider the importance of the respective interests. In familiar infelicitous situations where a conflict of interests can be resolved only by sacrificing the interest of one party, a plausible principle would seem to be that there is a *presumption* in favor of maximizing utility or at least choosing an alternative which will minimize net disutility.[19] Given our initial crude distinction between basic and peripheral interests we can classify four basic types of conflicts of interests between, to oversimplify, a human and an animal:

	human interest	*animal interest*
1	basic	basic
2	basic	peripheral
3	peripheral	basic
4	peripheral	peripheral

The following examples illustrate (roughly) the above conflicts, e.g. (1) my life versus my dog's in the life raft case, (2) giving up my career to move to a climate where my dog will be happier, (3) my obtaining a new flyswatter by killing a Wildebeest (for its tail), (4) my spending for a new wallet for myself or spending for a toy for my dog. If we suppose that the non-satisfaction of a basic interest yields a greater disutility than the non-satisfaction of a peripheral interest and if the conflict of interests in (2) and (3) is resolved by sacrificing the basic to the peripheral interest, it is tempting to suppose that there is a net loss of aggregate utility. Giving the interests of the animal no weight in calculating utilities in (2) or (3) is speciesism with a vengeance. That tack is an obvious target of current critics of many standard ways in which animals are treated and ways in which their interests are evaluated (if indeed recognized at all). For an example of the latter, to the criticism that DDT usage damages penguins, one writer states

> My criteria are oriented to people, not
> penguins. Damage to penguins . . . is . . .
> simply irrelevant . . . Penguins are impor-
> tant because people enjoy seeing them
> walk about rocks . . . I have no interest in
> preserving penguins for their own
> sake . . . it is the only tenable starting
> place for analysis . . . First, no other posi-
> tion corresponds to the way most people
> really think and act . . . [20]

On the principle that utility ought to be maximized in adjudicating conflicts of interests, peripheral interests ought to be subordinated to basic ones. Such a principle seems to underlie Interest Sensitive Speciesism. For reasons mentioned earlier such a view is problematic, e.g. if it is in any animal's basic interest to live then killing cockroaches for the sake of a certain convenience to humans would be prohibited. On the assumption that satisfaction (or non-satisfaction) of like interests involves promotion (or non-attainment) of like utilities and the assumption that we should maximize aggregate utility, it is not clear how to resolve conflicts of types (1) and (4). Recall the case of my dog and myself in the overloaded life raft. The conflict is between basic interests; one has to go overboard (assume drowning is then inevitable) so that the other may live. If promoting my dog's interest will promote the same utility as promoting my own, the principle of maximizing utility will fail to require what, intuitively, seems permissible, namely, that I sadly do away with my canine friend.[21]

It is reasonable to believe, however, that in the life raft example the disutilities of my dying and my dog's dying are not really equal, even though the case seems correctly describable as one where a basic interest of mine is in conflict with an *equally basic* interest of my dog. But would not the assignment of different utilities to *like interests* be arbitrary—a giving of greater *weight* to interests of my own species over like interests of members of other species—and, hence, in some sense, "speciesist"? The more important question, labels aside, is whether a case can be made for giving *greater weight* to my own interest in such a case as opposed to my dog's.[22] In general, is there a justification for weighting human interests more heavily than *comparable* or *like* interests of animals in cases of conflicts of interests and, thus, justifying the extension of differential treatment toward animals in certain cases where it would not be justified if extended to (most) other humans (e.g. it may be worth comparing a life raft case like the one discussed except that the conflict is between the reader and myself)?[23] Two Factor Egalitarianism assumes an affirmative answer to this question. The basis for doing so is *not* simply that human interests are, after all, *human* interests and necessarily deserving of more weight than comparable or like interests of animals. The ground is rather that the interests of beings with more complex psychological capacities deserve greater weight than those with lesser capacities—up to a point. Let us call this the Weighting Principle.[24] What may be said in defense of the Weighting Principle? I am not sure that an adequate defense can be proposed, but let us consider some possible attempts. It might be proposed that humans are typically subject to certain kinds of suffering that animals are not. For example, humans are typically capable of suffering from the dread of impending disaster (e.g. death from terminal cancer) in a way that animals are not (e.g. a turkey will not be wary of impending Thanksgiving events). This fact, however, may only show that a given type of act (e.g. death sentence) may cause unequal disutilities to an animal and a human. However, the *same amount* of suffering may be imposed on a human and an animal on a given occasion. Would there be any reason for assigning different disutilities to the two acts respectively? There may be if we take into account not just the comparative amounts of suffering on *that* occasion but consequent suffering over time, a factor affected by life span and the capacity to remember. Suppose it were true that the pain experienced by a steer upon being castrated and the pain experienced by a woman who was raped were of the "same amount."[25] The steer would not suffer from the memory of such an experience in the way that women continue to suffer from the trauma of rape, e.g. "reliving" of the experience in dreams, and so on. What such an example suggests is that in cases where a basic interest (e.g. an interest in not being subjected to serious bodily harm) is violated, the different disutilities to the animal and human may be obscured by focusing on the fact that a "basic interest" was violated in *both* cases. The long term disutilities of each individual may be radically different, and whether this is so is very much a function of the psychological capacities of the beings involved. That the *interests* of a human and an animal are "like or comparable" seems no sure guide to the comparative amounts of harm done in such cases. Hence, in conflicts of *like* interests between humans and animals (basic-basic, or peripheral-peripheral) it may be important to focus on the less obvious and long term disutilities which may accrue in not promoting the interest; focusing on "levels of interest" may fail to take into account matters of importance.

Another and, I believe, overlooked consideration which may be used in defense of the Weighting Principle concerns the economist's notion of "opportunity cost." Generally, in employing one's capital or one's efforts in achieving one goal, the cost of doing so can be thought of as the opportunities thereby forgone, goods and satisfactions that may not be obtained but which could have been if one's capital or efforts were employed in other ways. Most of my examples have focused on cases of inflicting pain or deprivation rather than death. The notion of opportunity cost is a useful one in trying to assign some weight to the imposition of death upon a human or an animal—as well as to weighting the imposition of pain or deprivation upon an animal or a human. Suppose that a group of rabbits is used in testing possibly toxic drugs and that the test is of the LD-50 type, where it is built into the experimental design that the experiment is complete only when fifty percent of the rabbits die (thus, Lethal Dosage—fifty percent).[26] Imagine a comparable test on a group of retarded human beings. Why are we inclined to think that if either experiment (but not both) is justified it must be the one involving rabbits? It need not be, I believe, because we think the suffering of rabbits has no weight. Neither must it be because we would deny that like interests are involved in the two cases. The psychological capabilities of even retarded human

beings, such as those suffering from Downs Syndrome, are, however, far greater than those of rabbits. Even with the predictable shorter than normal life span for Downs Syndrome persons, the opportunities for a satisfying life for the retarded which would be forgone in the event of death are enormously greater than those of rabbits—or even, to take a "less favorable" case—those of typical non-human primates. Generally, though not necessarily nor in every case, the prospects of satisfaction are qualitatively and quantitatively greater for human beings than for animals. And this fact, this morally relevant fact, is a function of the psychological complexity of the beings in question. Further, it is clear that membership in the species Homo sapiens is no *a priori* guarantee of the existence of greater psychological capacity to experience satisfaction than that which may be possessed by beings of other species. The more basic point is that, generally, the opportunity cost of dying for humans and for animals at comparable ages, barring abnormalities, is vastly greater for the former. The harm, then, of killing in the former case is much greater than in the latter. From the fact, *if it were a fact,* that nothing could be more important to a given human than preservation of his life and that nothing could be more important to a given animal than preservation of its life, it does not follow that the disvalue of the loss of life in the two cases is equal.[27] For reasons mentioned, the discounting of the value of the preservation of the lives of many animals seems reasonable. A principle such as Two Factor Egalitarianism, based in part, then, on the Weighting Principle, is not unreasonable, and need not appeal to species membership *per se* as a basis for assigning unequal weights to like interests of animals and humans respectively.

The extent of discounting the interests of a being, or more generally—weighting its interests—will, on this view, depend on the psychological complexities of the being in question. There is no reason, except to have practical presumptions, to make, a priori, generalizations about the capacities of all humans, all animals, all primates, or all chimpanzees. Non-trivial variations in capacity occur in any such group.

The importance of forgone satisfactions, as I have observed in passing, is a function not only of psychological capacity but of life span. The fact that the merciful letting die of quite aged humans with terminal diseases seems more acceptable than failure to extend analogous life preserving treatment to young adult humans, may reflect an implicit acceptance of the view that the opportunity cost of death is morally relevant and, in fact, a relevant difference in the two cases just mentioned.[28] In that respect, more familiar judgments about the comparative value of preserving human lives suggest that the emphasis here on opportunity cost accords with reflective moral judgments that are made with regard to differential treatment among human beings. Similarly, the general acceptance of allowing seriously defective infants to expire may assume the plausibility of attending to psychological capacity as part of the determination of the value of promoting or sacrificing a basic interest—such as the interest in the preservation of life.

If Two Factor Egalitarianism is correct, and for the reasons mentioned, it will *sometimes* be permissible to do what Singer regards as an arbitrary prejudice, namely, for the speciesist (or any human) to "allow the interests of his own species to override the greater interests of members of other species." The unfortunate implication of Singer's claim that this is impermissible is that it prohibits killing a minimally sentient non-human creature for the sake of a "lesser human interest" in cases where the human's psychological capacities are distinctly more complex. TFE is not anthropocentric in the way that a view is if it regards species membership in Homo sapiens as relevant *per se*. The latter assumption is what Singer takes to be invidious and arbitrary about views he labels speciesist. On this point Singer is right. If Singer, or others, were to claim that TFE is also invidious and arbitrary in its "psychocentric" emphasis, reasons need to be stated other than that it takes species membership *per se* as relevant; for it does not.

V. Some Persistent Difficulties

To this point I have argued that among the widely divergent proposals considered (Radical Speciesism, etc.), Two Factor Egalitarianism best accords with both matters of fact and considered and not unreasonable pre-theoretical convictions about how we ought to resolve conflicts of interests between humans and animals. Thus, it seems the most plausible among the five positions considered. I have further suggested an answer (or part of one) to the basic challenge posed by critics of our treatment of animals (as I would pose it): to justify radi-

cally differential treatment of creatures all of whom are sentient it is necessary to identify a morally relevant difference between those who receive preferential treatment and those who do not. The difference proposed is psychological complexity in so far as that bears on the capacity of the entity to live a satisfying life; further, to the extent that the entity lacks capacities necessary for such, it is reasonable to discount its interests. The thorny question of what counts as a reasonable discounting I have not tried to settle. I have further argued that TFE avoids the counter-intuitive implications of Singer's principle of equality which requires (of *any* being) "that its suffering be counted equally with the like suffering—in so far as rough comparisons can be made—of any other being." As I understand the principle it focuses on actual suffering and not also on forgone satisfactions. Further, TFE avoids the charge of taking species membership *per se* as a morally relevant difference serving to justify interspecific differential treatment. If the argument so far is correct (perhaps even, approximately correct), TFE stands as the most reasonable approach.

Nevertheless, TFE is subject to a number of objections not yet considered, some of which are obvious and some of which are not. Most evident, the principle is vague. There is no precise way of determining which interests are basic, which serious, and which are more peripheral or how to rank interests precisely. Similarly, no adequate account has been offered of how to determine levels of psychological complexity. I will not dwell on these problems. If they are relevant (I believe they are) we must do the best we can; perhaps these difficulties are *no more* difficult than those faced in analogous problems of intraspecies conflicts of interests. These difficulties do not strike me as *decisive* ones; in any case I do not pursue them here.

TFE is, I believe, more troubling in another respect. In regarding level of psychological complexity as morally important (rather than, say, possession or lack of fur, feathers, a tail, or claws) it may require or allow that the interests of human beings need not be assigned equal weight where it is the case that there are significant empirical differences among humans in terms of psychological capacity. If an implication exists that the interests of dull, psychologically less complicated humans (the retarded? the senile? the brain damaged?) need not be counted as much as that of other humans (in the process of coming to some all-things-considered moral judgment about acts affecting them and perhaps others), it will be tempting to judge that accepting TFE would commit one to sanctioning intraspecific injustices—perhaps on the conviction that "all human beings are of equal intrinsic worth" or convictions which appear to demand that the like interests of all human beings must be assigned equal moral weight initially regardless of final specific moral judgments. The worry is, generally, that a tempting basis for making *interspecific discrimination* entails possibly counter-intuitive results with regard to intraspecific discriminations.

Is there any way of reasonably weighting interests based on the psychological capacities of interest holders which will not commit one who does so to policies of intraspecific (human) discrimination of an objectionable sort. A simple principle—give greater weight to the interests of a being with greater psychological capacity than one with less, proportionately—may indeed lead to objectionable discrimination. But a plausible weighting principle need not look like this. We may well regard it as an arbitrary and unjustified extension of differential treatment to offer, other things being equal, to finance the college education of one of our children with an I.Q. of 140 but to refuse to do so for another with an I.Q. of 120. Possession of a capacity beyond a certain degree may not count as a morally relevant difference. Beyond a certain threshold point it may. It might not be unjustified to refuse such support for a Downs Syndrome child. Suppose we adopt a bright chimpanzee and a quite retarded Downs Syndrome child. Would it be permissible to torture either? Intuitively: no. Would it be permissible to extend differential treatment to them regarding the provision of educational opportunities? Intuitively, one would think so. My more general point is that differences in psychological capacity may, up to a point, not justify differential treatment. Beyond a certain point they may, and whether they do may depend in part on the kind of differential treatment we are considering and what difference it might make to the prospective satisfactions or dissatisfactions of the beings considered. For example, virtually all human beings are capable of understanding promises and forming expectations of their being kept. Wide variations in psychological capacity exist alongside this particular capacity. These variations may provide no reason for justifying differing presumptions about the importance of promise keeping for these humans. It is not evident

that any non-human is capable of understanding promises, although some certainly seem to form expectations.[29]

To clarify, a weighting principle may recognize threshold points. Possession of certain capacities (e.g. intelligence) above a certain point may preclude certain forms of differential treatment. Below a certain point it may not. These assumptions may justify certain forms of interspecific discrimination. They also may serve to justify *certain* forms of intraspecific discrimination (among humans), e.g. treating differently an anencephalic infant, a Downs Syndrome infant, and a normal infant.[30] Because of the recognition of the importance of threshold considerations it is not obvious that a weighting principle, if applied, would lead to *objectionable* forms of intraspecific discrimination. So, the genuine worry about such a consequence does not evidently disqualify TFE (or some variant on it), which presupposes a weighting principle, from consideration. If so, more needs to be said, but I shall make no attempt to say it here (at least partly because it is beyond *my* capacity).

For the reasons discussed TFE seems more adequate than other proposals about how we ought to treat animals—in spite of its deficiencies. Some of its deficiencies may be remedied by a more specific, determinate statement of a variant on TFE. Further, supplementary principles are needed to elaborate and defend distinctions among levels of interests, as well as an elaboration of which psychological capacities are relevant or which sets of such capacities are relevant (and relevant to different forms of proposed differential treatment). That such supplementary assumptions are necessary complicates what may be called, appropriately, a theory of interspecific justice. That such a theory would be complicated may be disappointing; most of us hope for and value simplicity in a theory. TFE is not itself complicated, from one standpoint. It explicitly recognizes only two considerations as morally relevant in adjudicating interspecific conflicts of interests (levels of interests and psychological complexity of the beings). As noted, however, these considerations need more complicated elaboration and defense. Given the difficulties commonly acknowledged today in formulating and defending principles of justice for human interaction, it should not be surprising that plausible principles for just interspecific interactions turn out to be not readily or easily formulated.

In testing the proposed principles I have depended considerably on what I take to be thoughtful pre-theoretic convictions about how specific conflicts ought to be or may permissibly be resolved. Some may claim that this approach is wrong-headed at the outset, but I will leave it to others to say why. More likely, some will claim that the convictions invoked are a by-product of prejudice or are uniquely mine. I do not find this obvious, and I have tried to show that distinctions among levels of interests are supposed by those who take a somewhat different view of these matters, e.g. Peter Singer. I have also indicated how some limited weighting of interests is presupposed in what appears to be reasonable albeit differential treatment of human beings. If the admittedly incomplete account presented here is approximately correct, then certain general criteria are available for assessing which sorts of subordination of animal interests are justifiable and which are not. That some subordination of animal interests is, in general, acceptable and that some is not is evident. The important and more practical task of ascertaining which is which remains. In general, the implications of the position defended here will, I think, neither sanction many common dealings with animals nor lend support to some of the sweeping condemnations of preferential treatment set out by recent critics. But a more moderate position on the proper treatment of animals must, I think, side with recent critics in judging much of the prevailing wholesale disregard of the basic interests of higher animals as unconscionable.[31]

Notes

1. Peter Singer's essay "Animal Liberation" appeared in *The New York Review of Books* (April 5, 1973), pp. 10–15.

2. Ibid., p. 15.

3. Later references will be to Singer's book, *Animal Liberation*, Avon Books, New York 1977. In that book Singer emphasizes that his primary moral assumption is "the principle of equality" which does not require identical treatment of but "equal consideration" of beings with interests (pp. 3, 6). Further, beings with interests are only those with a capacity for suffering and enjoyment (p. 8). Recognizing complexities about killing, as opposed to the imposition of pain, he claims that "the conclusions that are argued for in this book flow from the principle

of minimizing suffering alone" (p. 22). Given this last emphasis and Singer's rejection of any necessity to couch his position in terms of animal rights (see Peter Singer, "The Fable of the Fox and the Unliberated Animals," *Ethics*, Vol. 88, No. 2 [January 1978], p. 122), I have chosen to reconstruct his argument as above.

4. The parallel with current theories of justice "for" human beings, theories which attempt to adjudicate conflicting interests, is evident.

5. Of course, the radical subordination of certain *human* interests (those of "natural slaves") seemed intuitively innocent and natural to Aristotle, and, as J. S. Mill noted in *The Subjection of Women*, it is a standard mark of a deeply held prejudice that it seem perfectly *natural* to the one who holds it. There is always the danger of accepting only those principles which are compatible with our prejudices.

6. For aesthetic reasons I would prefer use of "specieism," but to avoid multiplication of variants I adhere to the current use of "speciesism."

7. Singer, op. cit., pp. 8–9.

8. Ibid., pp. 9–15.

9. It is worth noting a dissimilarity between racism or sexism on the one hand and speciesism on the other, namely, that in the former cases those whose interests are subordinated are biologically "homogeneous" with their subordinators but not in the latter case.

10. See Stanley Godlovitch, "Utilities" in *Animals, Men, and Morals*, Taplinger Publishing Company, New York 1972, p. 181.

11. A. J. Cain, *Animal Species and Their Evolution*, Harper & Row, New York 1960.

12. It would be plausible to add: (4) to use a fair (e.g. random) procedure to decide whose interest should be sacrificed if the beings are psychologically similar and the interests are like. But see the (here unincorporated) consideration in Note 19.

13. See Singer, op. cit., pp. 122–8.

14. Ibid., Ch. 2.

15. The Tay-Sachs infant will die "soon" anyway, typically by the age of five or six years and will suffer in the interim. Its interest in continuing to exist may, then, be less basic than that of the healthy chimpanzee in continuing to live. The capacities of the infant may not exceed those of the chimpanzee at the time supposed.

16. See the intriguing fictionalized thought-experiment in Desmond Stewart's "The Limits of Trooghaft" in Tom Regan and Peter Singer (Eds.), *Animal Rights and Human Obligations*, Prentice Hall, Englewood Cliffs, New Jersey 1976, pp. 238–45.

17. Tom Regan, "The Moral Basis of Vegetarianism," *Canadian Journal of Philosophy*, Vol. 5, No. 2 (October 1975), pp. 181–214.

18. Without this qualification (sufficiently . . .), someone might argue that since there is a morally relevant difference between those who commit traffic violations and those who do not, it is justified to extend capital punishment to the former but not the latter.

19. I have so far deliberately ignored a complicating factor which seems relevant, namely, how a conflict of interest arises. A fuller account of things should consider this; I make no such attempt here. To elaborate, however, conflicts of interests sometimes arise only because one party *wants* what another has, and resolution of such a conflict *may not* be a matter of balancing legitimate claims. There may be a conflict of interests between my neighbor and myself since I want his new car, or between a rapist and his victim. Many of the conflicts of interests between humans and animals are generated by human desires to do what is harmful to animals; we eat them more than they eat us.

20. William F. Baxter, *People or Penguins: The Case for Optimal Pollution*, Columbia University Press, New York 1974, p. 5.

21. Considering utilities or disutilities to others would likely weight the case in favor of my preservation—solely on grounds of maximizing aggregate utility. But we can imagine cases where this would not be so; in any case I exclude such considerations above by assumption.

22. The relation between having rights and having interests is not clear. It is doubtful that having interests is sufficient for having rights (on this see the discussions by myself and James Rachels in Tom Regan and Peter Singer's anthology, *Animal Rights and Human Obligations*, Prentice Hall, Englewood Cliffs, New Jersey 1976, pp. 205–32. More plausible is the claim that any entity having rights must also have interests. If so, at least many entities having interests also have rights. If the interests of rightholders are regarded as very important, according those interests may be thought to be sufficiently important to override the *interests* of others—or, and this seems not insignificant—the *rights* of others (who have not only interests but rights). For example, Lawrence Haworth, who defends the view that some non-humans have rights, maintains that when the latter rights conflict with "worthy human interests . . . then it is in general reasonable to give preference to these human concerns and violate . . . the rights of nonhumans." See Lawrence Haworth, "Rights, Wrongs, and Animals," *Ethics*, Vol. 88, No. 2 (January 1978), p. 100.

23. Again, I simplify. Assume that neither of us owns the boat, has a special duty to sacrifice for the other, consents to die, or agrees to "draw straws."

24. The notion of psychological complexity needs further elaboration. I do have in mind complexity bearing on capacity to experience satisfaction and dissatisfaction. After all there might be a type of psychological complexity *not* conducive to a greater capacity to experience satisfaction. Suppose a microcomputer could be implanted in a turkey so that it became an excellent chess player but in other respects remained turkey-like, e.g. still did not worry about the prospect of Thanksgiving rituals.

25. I am, of course, by-passing all sorts of difficulties about the possibility of having a cardinal measure of utility and making "interbeing" comparisons of utilities.

26. On this type of test, see Peter Singer, op. cit., p. 48.

27. While the death of an animal or a human results in its forgoing *all* the potential satisfactions either could have, still the quantity of such satisfactions would typically be different for each. Hence it is reasonable to conclude that the disvalue of the death of a normal animal is less than the disvalue of the death of a normal human (at similar stages in typical life spans) even though the death of each involves a total loss of their respective potential satisfactions. The difference in disvalues is partly a function of whatever differences there are in respective psychological capacities.

28. Compare the absence of capacities in aged humans due to their waning, their absence in defective humans, and their absence in young normal animals. Absence of capacities may be a result of natural decline, injury, disease, or one's genetic lot.

29. Who would not feel some sense of betrayal when an aged dog eagerly gets in the car for a ride but does not know that it is being taken to be put to death (commonly: "to sleep")? Further, it will not surprise me if communications with non-human primates, in Ameslan, provides evidence of a capacity for understanding promises or, indeed, a sense of regret or remorse.

30. It does not seem to me that one should shrink from the view that *some* weighting of human interests

and, hence, *some* differential treatment of humans is justified. There is great danger that I shall be misunderstood here—as approving in some degree the sorts of unequal consideration intrinsic to repulsive doctrines commonly labeled racist, sexist, or Nazi-like. Respect for persons requires respecting their interests but not, I think, giving equal weight to them.

31. With regard to various facets of this essay I have benefited from discussions with my colleagues, W. R. Carter, Robert Hoffman, Harold Levin, Tom Regan, and Alan Sparer—as well as the writings of both Tom Regan and Peter Singer. Any or all are, of course, entitled to complain that I did not benefit enough.

The Mixed Community

Mary Midgley

1 The Well-filled Stage

All human communities have involved animals. Those present in them always include, for a start, some dogs, with whom our association seems to be an incredibly ancient one, amounting to symbiosis. But besides them an enormous variety of other creatures, ranging from reindeer to weasels and from elephants to shags, has for ages also been domesticated. Of course they were largely there for use—for draught and riding, for meat, milk, wool and hides, for feathers and eggs, as vermin-catchers or as aids to fishing and hunting. In principle, it might seem reasonable to expect that these forms of exploitation would have produced no personal or emotional involvement at all. From a position of ignorance, we might have expected that people would view their animals simply as machines. If we impose the sharp Kantian dichotomy between *persons* and *things*, subjects and objects, and insist that everything must be considered as simply one or the other, we might have expected that they would be viewed unambiguously as things. But in fact, if people had viewed them like this, the domestication could probably never have worked. The animals, with the best will in the world, could not have reacted like machines. They became tame, not just through the fear of violence, but because they were able to form individual bonds with those who tamed them by coming to understand the social signals addressed to them. They learned to obey human beings personally. They were able to do this, not only because the people taming them were social beings, but because they themselves were so as well.

All creatures which have been successfully domesticated are ones which were originally social. They have transferred to human beings the trust and docility which, in a wild state, they would have developed towards their parents, and in adult life towards the leaders of their pack or herd. There are other, and perhaps equally intelligent, creatures which it is quite impossible to tame, because they simply do not have the innate capacity to respond to social signals in their own species, and therefore cannot reach those which come from outside. The various kinds of wild cat are an impressive example. Even their youngest kittens are quite untamable. Egyptian cats, from which all our domestic moggies are descended, are unique among the small-cat group in their sociability. It is interesting that they do not seem to have been domesticated in Egypt before about 1600 BC, and after that time they quickly became extremely popular.[1] Unless they were only discovered then—which would be odd—it seems that there may have been an actual mutation at that point producing a more responsive constitution.

Cats, however, are notoriously still not sociable or docile in quite the same way as dogs. Circus people do not usually waste their time trying to train cats. Similarly, there are important differences between the social natures, as well as the physiques, of horses, mules, donkeys, camels and the like. Both as species and as individuals they react variously to training; they cannot be treated just as standard-issue physical machines. People who succeed well with them do not do so just by some abstract, magical human superiority, but by

Animals And Why They Matter, by Mary Midgley. (Athens: University of Georgia Press, 1983), pp. 112–119. Reprinted by permission. © 1983 by Mary Midgley.

interacting socially with them—by attending to them and coming to understand how various things appear from each animal's point of view. To ignore or disbelieve in the existence of that point of view would be fatal to the attempt. The traditional assumption behind the domestication of animals has been that, as Thomas Nagel has put it, there is something which it is to be a bat,[2] and similarly there is something which it is to be a horse or donkey, and to be this horse or donkey. There is not, by contrast, any such experience as *being* a stone, or a model-T Ford, or even a jet-plane. There is no being which could have that experience, so mechanics do not have to attend to it.

2 Exploitation Requires Sympathy

I am saying that this has been the traditional assumption. Modern Behaviourists who think it a false one can of course argue against it. My present point is simply that their opinion is a recent and sophisticated one. It is not the view which has been taken for granted during the long centuries in which animals have been domesticated. If we ask an Indian farmer whether he supposes that the ox which he is beating can feel, he is likely to answer "Certainly it can, otherwise why would I bother?" A skilled horseman needs to respond to his horse as an individual, to follow the workings of its feelings, to use his imagination in understanding how things are likely to affect it, what frightens it and what attracts it, as much as someone who wants to control human beings needs to do the same thing. Horses and dogs are addressed by name, and are expected to understand what is said to them. Nobody tries this with stones or hammers or jet-planes. The treatment of domestic animals has never been impersonal. We can say that they are not "persons," because (apart from the Trinity) that word does generally signify *Homo sapiens*. But they are certainly not viewed just as things. They are animals, a category which, for purposes of having a point of view belongs, not with things, but with people.

This point is important because it shows what may seem rather surprising—a direct capacity in man for attending to, and to some extent understanding, the moods and reactions of other species.

No doubt this capacity is limited. Human callousness makes some of its limitations obvious. But then, similar callousness is also often found in our dealings with other human beings. The question whether somebody knows what suffering he is causing may be a hard one to answer in either case. The callous person may not positively *know,* because he does not want to; he does not attend. But he could know if he chose to scan the evidence. This seems to be equally true in either case. The reason for overworking an ox or horse is usually much the same as that for overworking a human slave— not that one does not believe that they mind it, or supposes that they cannot even notice it, but that one is putting one's own interest first. The treatment of domestic animals resembles that of slaves in being extremely patchy and variable. There is not normally a steady, unvarying disregard, such as should follow if one genuinely supposed that the creature was not sentient at all, or if one was quite unable to guess what its feelings might be. Disregard is varied by partial spasmodic kindness, and also by spasmodic cruelty. And cruelty is something which could have no point for a person who really did not believe the victim to have definite feelings. (There is very little comfort in working off ill-temper on a cushion.) Family pigs are often treated with real pride and affection during their lives, they may even be genuinely mourned—only this will not protect them from being eaten. Horses, bell-wethers, Lapp reindeer and the cattle of the Masai can similarly receive real regard, can be treated as dear companions and personally cherished, can form part of human households in a different way from any machine or inanimate treasure[3]—only they will still on suitable occasions be killed or otherwise ill-treated if human purposes demand it. But we should notice too a similar arbitrariness often appearing in the treatment of human dependents, so that we can scarcely argue that there is no real capacity for sympathy towards the animals. In the treatment of other people, of course, our natural caprice is constantly disciplined by the deliberate interference of morality. We know that we must not eat our grandmothers or our children merely because they annoy us. Over animals this restraint is usually much less active; caprice has much freer play. That does not mean that they are taken not to be conscious. Belief in their sentience is essential even for exploiting them successfully.

3 The Implausibility of Scepticism

This point matters because it tells strongly against the Behaviourist idea that the subjective feelings of animals are all, equally, quite hidden from us, cannot concern us and may well not even exist. This idea is often expressed by saying that belief in them is illicitly *anthropomorphic*. The notion of anthropomorphism is a very interesting one; we must look at it shortly. But straight away I want to point out how odd it would be if those who, over many centuries, have depended on working with animals, turned out to have been relying on a sentimental and pointless error in doing so, an error which could be corrected at a stroke by metaphysicians who may never have encountered those animals at all. For instance—working elephants can still only be successfully handled by mahouts who live in close and life-long one-to-one relations with them. Each mahout treats his elephant, not like a tractor, but like a basically benevolent if often tiresome uncle, whose moods must be understood and handled very much like those of a human colleague. If there were any less expensive and time-consuming way of getting work out of elephants, the Sri Lankan timber trade would by now certainly have discovered it. Obviously the mahout may have many beliefs about the elephants which are false because they are "anthropomorphic"—that is, they misinterpret some outlying aspects of elephant behaviour by relying on a human pattern which is inappropriate. But if they were doing this about the basic everyday feelings—about whether their elephant is pleased, annoyed, frightened, excited, tired, sore, suspicious or angry—they would not only be out of business, they would often simply be dead. And to describe and understand such moods, they use the same general vocabulary which is used for describing humans.

Nearer home, here is an example from the memoirs of a blind woman being taught to walk with a guide-dog. The dog-trainer says,

> Don't stop talking, or Emma'll think you've fallen asleep . . . You've got to keep her interest. She's a dog, and there are lots of nice, interesting smells all round, and things passing which you can't see. So unless you talk to her, she'll get distracted, and stop to sniff a lamp-post.[4]

This is a particularly good example, because it makes so clear the point that there is no question of illicitly attributing human sensibility. The trainer—whose interest is of course purely practical—is at pains to point out just what is distinctive about the dog's own sensibilities, simply because they must be allowed for if it is to do its work. But to make this point, he necessarily and properly uses the same words (interest, distract, she'll think you've fallen asleep) which would be used in a comparable human case. The wide difference between the two species does not affect the correctness of this language at all.

This is not, of course, the only context where a Behaviourist approach runs into difficulties. It encounters grave problems about the possibility of attributing subjective feelings to other humans, as well as to animals. I do not think that this problem will turn out very different for animals, certainly not in cases where either the feeling is very strong or the species is very familiar. The charge of "anthropomorphism" as a general objection to attributing *any* feelings to animals, rather than to attributing the wrong feelings, is probably a red herring.

4 What Are Pets?

Before we come to this larger point, however, we need to go into an aspect of the matter which might seem still more remarkable and unexpected to an observer who was totally ignorant of human affairs. This is the real individual affection, rather than exploitation, which can arise between animals and people. Since pet-keeping is sometimes denounced as a gratuitous perversion produced by modern affluence, I take a respectably ancient example from the prophet Nathan:

> The poor man had nothing save one little ewe lamb, which he had bought and nourished up; and it grew up together with him, and with his children; it did eat of his own morsel, and drank of his own cup, and lay in his bosom, and was to him as a daughter.[5]

Several things should be noticed here.

1. The man is *poor*. We are not dealing with the follies of the idle rich.

2. He is not childless; his children share the lamb's company with him.

3. The relation is regarded as a perfectly natural one.

Nathan chooses this story confidently to enlist King David's sympathy for the lamb-keeper. When he goes on to tell how the rich man killed this lamb for a feast, David breaks out in horror, "As the Lord liveth, the man that has done this is worthy to die." This makes it possible for Nathan to say "Thou art the man!" and to apply the fable to David's treatment of Uriah the Hittite. But what would Nathan have said if David had replied that of course poor men can expect that sort of thing to happen if they will go in for sentimental pet-keeping instead of adopting human orphans? Clearly no such answer was on the cards. David knows as well as Nathan does what the lamb meant to the poor man, and both understand clearly how this strong individual relation was possible, even in a society where lambs were being killed all the time. This paradoxical ambivalence of pastoral and hunting peoples comes out very often in the metaphors of Christ. The good shepherd lays down his life for his sheep, he searches out every single lost sheep and cherishes it—yet the Passover Lamb is eaten at the last supper, and in general this must be the destiny of nearly all Hebrew sheep. It is, to an economic eye, the main reason why they are kept at all.

5   The Flexibility of Parent-Child Behaviour

It is hopeless trying to understand this situation if we keep pressing the crude Kantian question "but are lambs people or things?" If we want to grasp it, we must wake up to a much wider range of possibilities. Our conceptual map needs revising. In extending it, our first guiding light should be the thought that the poor man's lamb "was to him as a daughter." His love for it was the kind of love suited to a child. He loved it in this way, *not* because he had no children and was so undiscriminating that he was ready to deceive himself and cuddle a cushion, but because the lamb really was a live creature needing love, and it was able to respond to parental cherishing. This is not fetishism, but a per-

fectly normal feeling. The appeal of small and helpless creatures is not limited by species. Animals in the wild certainly do not normally notice young outside their own kind, but if they are thrown together with them, as they are in captivity, they often respond in a remarkable way: they can adopt. Full-scale adoption is sometimes possible, even in the wild.[6] And it is striking how domestic animals will put up with rough treatment from small children, which they would certainly not tolerate from adults. How, we ask, does the cat know that a baby much larger than itself is a child—is, in effect, a kitten? What the signals are does not matter much—some of them may well be chemical. But if we ourselves were presented with a baby elephant, and had a chance to watch and take in its playful behaviour, we would be able to grasp the same point.

Play-signals penetrate species-barriers with perfect ease.[7] What is even more interesting is the startling set of emotional and practical consequences which the adult animal draws from the signals. The cat shows a mood of tolerance, playfulness and positive affection which would astonish us if we did not ourselves so readily share it. Of course it would be no use trying this kind of appeal on a codfish. Infantile signals work only with species which cherish their own young. And even there, the gap must not be too large if the message is to get across. Birds would in general be unlikely to decipher human infantile signals; if the ravens fed Elijah, it seems that he must have gaped like a young cuckoo. But where the message does get across, its power in producing fellowship is astonishing. It affects not only adults, but other young as well, releasing in them the hope of play. The human baby makes a bee-line for the cat. The cat, if it is a kitten, returns the compliment with particular fervour. Both are inquisitive and playful. This attraction seems, again, to be common to all those relatively intelligent species which are capable of play. In wild conditions, it normally will not overcome the stronger tendency to species-imprinting unless playmates of one's own species are uncommonly scarce, as in the case which Jane Goodall describes. But in a mixed human community it can very well do so. None of the creatures present is getting a really exclusive imprinting. Accordingly, the species-barrier there, imposing though it may look, is rather like one of those tall wire fences whose impressiveness is confined to their upper reaches.

To an adult in formal dress, engaged on his official statesmanly interactions, the fence is an insuperable barrier. Down below, where it is full of holes, it presents no obstacle at all. The young of *Homo sapiens*, like those of the other species present, scurry through it all the time. Since all human beings start life as children, this has the quite important consequence that hardly any of us, at heart, sees the social world as an exclusively human one.

6 The Child's Quest for Variety

To spell this out: The point is not just that most human beings have in fact been acquainted with other creatures early in life, and have therefore received some non-human imprinting. It is also that children who are not offered this experience often actively seek it. Animals, like song and dance, are an innate taste. Even those whose homes have contained none often seek them out and find them irresistible. The fact seems too obvious to need mentioning and does not usually attract much criticism. Even people who believe that there is something perverse and wrong about adults taking an interest in animals are often quite content that children should do so. Like some other interests which appeal to children it may, however, be considered as something which one ought to grow out of. Prolonged interest in it may seem a sign of emotional immaturity. Behind this thought lies the more general idea that animals are suitable only as practice material for the immature, because they are in effect nothing but simplified models of human beings. On this pattern, those who graduate past them to real human relationships are not expected to have any further interest in them, any more than a real golfer does in clock-golf in the park.

This way of thinking has a certain point, but beyond the crudest level it can be very misleading. No animal is just a simplified human being, nor do children take them to be so. However friendly they may be, their life is radically foreign, and it is just that foreignness which attracts a child. The point

about them is that they are different. As for immaturity, it is of course true that we must all come to terms first and foremost with our own species. Those unwilling to do this can indeed seek refuge with animals, as they can in other activities. But the mere fact of taking an interest in animals does not show that kind of motive, any more than taking an interest in machines or music does. Experience of animals is not essentially a substitute for experience of people, but a supplement to it—something more which is needed for a full human life. The ewe lamb did not come between the poor man and his children. Instead it formed an extra delight which he could share with them, and so strengthened the family bond. (That, surely, is why Nathan mentions the children.) One sort of love does not need to block another, because love, like compassion, is not a rare fluid to be economized, but a capacity which grows by use. And if we ask (again impersonating an ignorant observer) whether the limits of its natural use in human beings coincide with the species-barrier, we see plainly that they do not. In early childhood that barrier scarcely operates. And even in later life it seldom becomes absolute.

Notes

1. Muriel Beadle, *The Cat, its History, Biology and Behaviour* (Collins and Harvill Press, 1977), p. 66.

2. Thomas Nagel, *Mortal Questions* (Cambridge, 1979), essay 12, on 'What Is It Like to Be a Bat?'.

3. See the very touching account of Polyphemus and his ram, *Odyssey IX*, 447–60. Polyphemus, it should be noticed, was not an outstandingly sentimental person.

4. Sheila Hocken, *Emma and I* (Sphere Books, 1978), p. 33.

5. II Samuel xii:3.

6. For adoption by elephants, see Daphne Sheldrick, *The Tsavo Story* (Collins and Harvill Press, 1973).

7. See 'Play-Behaviour in Higher Primates, a Review' by Caroline Loizos, in *Primate Ethology*, ed. Desmond Morris (Weidenfeld & Nicolson, 1967).

SIDELIGHT: Do What's Natural, You Say? _____

We live in an age in which some marketing specialists exploit a certain revulsion against the plastic, i.e., what is quintessentially artificial, a matter of artifice, or human-made. Correlatively there is

a certain desire to live more naturally. "Natural" fibers and "all-natural" food are increasingly in demand. Indeed, the term "natural" seems honorific; conversely, the term "unnatural" is frequently used pejoratively, i.e., implying that the thing so labeled is bad or wrong. Is there any rational basis for associating the natural with the right and the unnatural with the wrong? In particular, should we scan the processes of nature to find normative models, i.e., types of behavior that we should emulate? There are indeed subtleties to this topic, but we shall make an initial assault on the matter here.

There is a broad sense of "natural" in which anything that happens is part of the nature of the world as we know it. In this sense any action is natural; so, none is unnatural. Thus, Jeffrey Dahmer's cannibalizing of humans is natural, as is the mass destruction of Jews and Gypsies by the Nazis, or the mass killing of hundreds of thousands of Japanese by the American bombing of Hiroshima and Nagasaki.

Typically, however, we mark out certain actions or events from the set of all that occur by using labels such as "natural" or "unnatural"; that is, we are drawing a contrast between some events and others when we say only of some that they are natural or of others that they are unnatural. Thus, by "natural" we do not normally mean "whatever happens." Although we humans are without question a part of nature, by "natural" we often mean that which occurs without deliberate human intervention or a by-product of such. Hence, the mass extinction of 65 million years ago, the glaciations of the last Ice Age, the tides, the ocean currents, the revolution of the earth about the sun, volcanic eruptions, typhoons, the occurrence of photosynthesis, or even the striking of the earth by a meteor are, or would be, natural occurrences. Some of these events may be tragic, but there is no obvious connection between the fact that they are natural and their assessment as good or bad. Natural processes are extremely wasteful of life and potential life: In the ejaculation of a male human, enough sperm are produced to inseminate several hundred million eggs; of the offspring produced by a single member of some species, only a tiny fraction can survive. Not what one would expect of a world guided by the Protestant God of "waste not, want not."[1]

Among "unnatural" events, i.e., those resulting from human action, are a wildly diverse lot: the expected leaking of plutonium into arctic waters above Norway from a deteriorating, sunken Russian submarine (not to worry: it will cease to be radioactive by the year 26,000), the selling of children into prostitution, destruction of 70 percent of the world's forests, the rescue of millions of people from the ravages of disease and injury, the heroic resistance against Nazi and fascist movements, the music of Mozart, the paintings of Seurat, Matisse, or van Gogh, and so on. All such behavior is unnatural if by the term one means involving human action or the result of such.

May we turn to animal behavior for inspiration as to how on earth to live (as if we are not animals and as if we are not part of nature)? Let us consider some interesting examples revealed by recent studies of animal behavior (some not to be read just before meals perhaps). Among nonhuman animals, there are many examples of wonderfully cooperative behavior. We find the analogue of monogamy among geese, swans, angelfish, beavers, and soldier beetles. Among owl monkeys, males rear the offspring and females search for food.[2]

Now let us focus elsewhere. Burying beetle couples prepare the corpses of small animals for their young to eat. When the young are born, the parents eat the numbers down to a size that the food supply can support (perhaps they have read Garrett Hardin on "carrying capacity"); thus, cannibalism gives the surviving youngsters a "head start," so to speak.

Or would you rather be a shark? Specifically a sand tiger shark. Out of the 100 eggs formed by the shark after mating, the first one to reach the uterus survives by eating all the other embryos and unfertilized eggs as they are released.[3] So among sharks, it is perfectly natural to kill off one's "unborn siblings." Are all mothers nourishing? Not among the emu; they abandon their offspring at the slightest sign of danger.[4]

Two woodpeckers often share a nest, but when one lays an egg another destroys it (perhaps to destroy the advantage the first one has). This continues until both lay an egg at the same time. A female of the praying mantis may start chewing off her partner's head while he is still mating. Among Australian red-back spiders, the male, halfway through the mating process, will jump into the female's jaws and allow itself to be eaten a bit; when he is done mating he surrenders the last time to her waiting fangs. For the red-back Australian spider, this is doing what comes naturally. A final gory example: The female Ormia fly has the capacity to detect a male cricket's sounds, drop down on it, and deposit a squirming maggot on it that bores into the cricket and eats it. Anxious mother flies may have an extra incentive to succeed, since if they fail the hungry maggots begin to devour the mother from the inside out.

So, perhaps nature won't do as a guide to family values. Sometimes, it seems, we *ought* to be unnatural. We note in passing that in the Roman Catholic religion it is routinely maintained that homosexuality, masturbation, and heterosexual sex without the possibility of procreation is unnatural, and, it is implied, is, hence, morally wrong (recall the discussion of natural law in the General Introduction. In this regard, various instances of homosexual behavior can be found among nonhuman creatures; it has been found in bulls, cows, cats, rams, goats, pigs, apes, lions, etc.[5] Further, homosexual pair bonding has been found among western gulls.[6] A comment by Alfred Kinsey and his co-workers is of interest: ". . . the sexual acts which are demonstrably part of the phylogenetic heritage of any species cannot be classified as acts contrary to nature, biologically unnatural, abnormal or perverse."[7]

We encounter appeals to the assumption that what is natural is right or the claim that what is unnatural is wrong with regard to questions of sexual behavior, who should be dominant, the accept-

ability of biotechnology, debates over vegetarianism, and so on. Perhaps enough has been said to discourage ready acceptance of the key normative, and often tacit, assumptions noted.

Notes

1. The apt expression is from David Hull in his introduction to Lamarck's Philosophy.

2. Facts about monogamy are derived from a column entitled "The Kinsey Report" by June Reinisch in the *News and Observer* (September 10, 1987) Raleigh, North Carolina.

3. In this discussion we have drawn on an article in the *New York Times*, "In Some Species, Eating Your Own Is Good Sense" (September 29, 1992) by Carol Kaesuk Yoon. We have also relied on a brief piece in *Science*, which reference has evaporated.

4. See the review by Rona Cherry of *Females of the Species* by Bettyann Kevles (Cambridge: Harvard University Press) found in the October 5, 1986 issue of the *New York Times Book Review*.

5. See the reference to the Kinsey studies in the useful article by James Weinrich, "Is Homosexuality Biologically Natural?" in *Homosexuality: Social, Psychological, and Biological Issues* (Beverly Hills: Sage Publications, 1982), p. 198.

6. Ibid., p. 200.

7. See Weinrich, *Homosexuality*, p. 204.

III

CONSTRUCTING AN ENVIRONMENTAL ETHIC

A. THE EXPANDING CIRCLE

The main focus of many "animal liberationists" is on sentient animals. In IIIA we begin to expand our inquiries into the broader, biotic community. Edward O. Wilson explains why it is useful to think about the little, probably nonsentient, creatures that we so often ignore, ones that, in fact, have at least an enormously instrumental value to the ongoing dynamic of life on earth. Should we think of them as beyond the moral pale—in the sense that they should be judged as lacking moral standing—even if they have enormous value as parts of ecosystems? What should be our view of, and our attitude toward, the land? Can we relate to land in ways other than the domination of it? Anthony Weston addresses this issue nicely when he says, "We need to think of the earth itself in a different way: not as an infinite waste sink, and not as a collection of resources fortuitously provided for our use, but as a complex system with its own integrity and dynamics, far more intricate than we understand or perhaps *can* understand, but still the system within which we live and on which we necessarily and utterly depend. We must learn a new kind of respect."[1]

If being more mindful and attentive to the way we interact with and depend on nature is, as Weston claims it is, a minimum required by an environmental ethic, what else is required? For answers here, we turn to an exploration of the insights of the "land ethic," deep ecology, social ecology, and ecofeminism, to name a few. We begin this larger discussion in Part IIIA with legal theorist Christopher Stone, philosopher Paul Taylor, and originator of the "land ethic" Aldo Leopold. They raise questions such as the following: Is sentience the correct standard for determining who or what has moral standing or inherent value? Do trees have rights? Do wildflowers have inherent value? Are ecosystems, rather than the individuals that make up such systems, the real source of inherent value? Even though Aldo Leopold is chronologically earlier than Stone and Taylor, some think his ideas are a more radical departure from traditional humanistic ethics than those of Stone and Taylor.[2] So our classification here is based on a logical progression of ideas rather than historical order. J. Baird Callicott, who follows Leopold, interprets and defends important aspects of the land ethic of Aldo Leopold.

Before pursuing these philosophical questions, we provide some background regarding nineteenth-century environmental movements in the United States called *conservationism* and *preservationism*. These movements influenced environmental thinkers such as Aldo Leopold, as well as contemporary philosophers such as J. Baird Callicott, Bryan G. Norton, and Anthony Weston.

HISTORICAL MOVEMENTS

The conservation movement had scientific roots. Some of its leaders, like Gifford Pinchot (1865–1914), came from fields such as forestry. The typical emphasis of the movement was wise management of resources for human welfare over the long run.

Pinchot favored commercial development of the U.S. forest reserves for present and future American citizens. In his book, *The Fight For Conservation*, he maintained:

The first great fact about conservation is that it stands for development. There has been a fundamental misconception that conservation means nothing but the husbanding of resources for future generations. There could be no more serious mistake. Conservation does mean provision for the future, but it means also and first of all the recognition of the right of the present generation to the fullest necessary use of all the resources with which this country is so abundantly blessed. Conservation demands the welfare of this generation first, and afterward the welfare of the generations to follow. The first principle of conservation is development, the use of the natural resources now existing on this continent for the benefit of the people who live here now.[3]

Pinchot further emphasized that forest resources should not fall into the hands of the powerful few—corporations, for example—but should be used to make homes for the plain American citizen. Pinchot, who in 1905 became head of the newly established U.S. Forest Service, once told the Society of American Foresters, "The object of our forest policy is not to preserve the forests because they are beautiful . . . or because they are refuges for the wild creatures of the wilderness . . . but . . . the making of prosperous homes."[4] As a spokesperson for the conservationist movement and a supporter of Theodore Roosevelt's policies, he said, "If we succeed, there will exist upon this continent a sane, strong people, living through the centuries in a land subdued and controlled for the service of the people, its rightful masters, owned by the many and not by the few."[5]

Pinchot was opposed by the preservationist movement, headed by John Muir

(1838–1914), founder of the Sierra Club. Muir wanted to preserve wilderness for aesthetic and spiritual reasons:

Watch the sunbeams over the forest awakening the flowers, feeding them every one, warming, reviving the myriads of the air, setting countless wings in motion—making diamonds of dewdrops, lakes, painting the spray of falls in rainbow colors. Enjoy the great night like a day, hinting the eternal and imperishable in nature amid the transient and material.[6]

For Muir, nature provided an experience of the sacred or holy. The experience was not simply one of inspiration, but one of recognition of the divine in nature. As Muir once reported his experience of a stroll in the woods, "How beautiful and fresh and Godful the world began to appear."[7]

One famous example of the opposition between the conservationists and the preservationists is the controversy over the Hetch Hetchy Valley in California. Muir and his followers fought for the protection of the Hetch Hetchy Valley in the Yosemite National Park. The city of San Francisco wanted to dam the area, thus flooding the park, and construct a reservoir. Pinchot, whose colleagues contemptuously referred to the preservationists as "nature lovers," threw his support behind James R. Garfield, Secretary of the Interior, who approved the city's request to build a dam. Both Pinchot and Muir brought pressure to bear on President Theodore Roosevelt who, in the end, supported Pinchot.

Despite their differences, it can be argued that both traditions, conservationism and preservationism, were anthropocentric or human-centered. That is, whether Hetch Hetchy Valley is used as a water supply for human beings or as a source of peak experiences for humans, its value lies in human use.[8] Nonetheless, one can find in the writings of

John Muir the idea that nature has value independent of human beings: "Rocks have a kind of life not so different from ours as we imagine. Anyhow their material beauty is only a veil covering spiritual beauty—a divine incarnation—instonation."[9] Although this independent value may not be independent of a pantheistic view of nature, it is nevertheless independent of human beings.[10] Muir and his followers influenced Aldo Leopold and later advocates of the land ethic, such as J. Baird Callicott, and advocates of the rights of trees, such as Christopher Stone. Callicott claims that nature has value in itself or for its own sake; that we should value nature in much the same way as parents value their children. Stone argues that trees and streams should be able to sue in court (or have guardians sue on their behalf) for their own injuries. One of the tasks of this section is to investigate the various grounds for attempting to establish the independent value of nature.

THE CONTEMPORARY DISCUSSION

Christopher Stone, a law professor at the University of Southern California, has written an important treatise entitled, *Should Trees Have Standing?* Stone sees the history of moral development as an extension of the scope of our moral concern to more and more beings and entities as we progressively are able to identify or empathize with them. Originally, according to Stone, "each man had regard only for himself and those of a very narrow circle around him."[11] As we have seen, the circle that Aristotle drew was very narrow indeed. What we have done, says Stone, is to view many beings and entities in the world as less than persons, and indeed as objects or things in the world that exist only for the use of persons. Our law increasingly has reflected a shift from this view by "making persons of children ... prisoners, aliens, women (espe-

cially of the married variety), the insane, Blacks, foetuses, and Indians."[12] Many authors in this volume argue against the notion that nature exists solely for the use of human beings. Some believe that such a denial points the way to expanding the circle of right-holders to include environmental objects such as trees and streams.

Stone suggests that as we become more sensitive we add more and more previously rightless entities to the list of persons. His remarks on sensitivity and empathy raise questions about the role of rational argument in ethics. On what basis is the law "making persons"? In Stone's view, it is only when we perceive nature as like us that we will be able to generate the love and empathy for the environment that in turn will enable us to attribute rights to it. Does such a thesis imply that rights should be attributed to all things cute and cuddly? Suppose we identify with human fetuses. Do they have rights on that account? Must E.T. be rightless if we do not empathize with him (it)? Is there anything in the universe we will not add to the list of persons, assuming we can empathize with it? Should our capacities for empathy be a determining factor in ascertaining what sorts of things possess rights? Suppose some cannot identify with Jews, gay people, or people of another color?

Justice Douglas, in the U.S. Supreme Court case, *Sierra v. Morton*, 1972, cited Stone's book in support of his dissenting opinion that "contemporary public concern for protecting nature's ecological equilibrium should lead to the conferral of standing upon environmental objects to sue for their own preservation."[13] In this landmark case, the Sierra Club tried to prevent Walt Disney Enterprises, Inc., from building a ski resort in the Mineral King Valley adjacent to Sequoia National Park. The case was not decided on the relative merits of ski resorts versus natural beauty. Rather, it was decided on the issue of the standing to sue. "Whether a party has a sufficient stake in an otherwise justiciable controversy to obtain judicial resolution of that controversy is what traditionally has been referred to as the question of standing to sue."[14] The law requires that the party seeking review must itself have suffered an injury or itself have been adversely affected. The Court decided in favor of Disney and against the Sierra Club. After all, it is hard to say that the Sierra Club members suffered an injury simply because others like to ski. Mineral King Valley might have received legal consideration if trees and streams had standing to sue for their own preservation and/or injury. Much of Stone's essay is a plea for a liberalized domain of *legal* standing. Since trees cannot initiate proceedings on their own behalf, Stone recommends a *guardianship* approach similar to the one we use now with respect to incompetent human beings (the profoundly retarded, young children, etc.). Incompetent humans have legal rights, even if they are unable to claim them for themselves; for example, rights to proper medical treatment.

It is interesting to note that as recently as June 12, 1992, in *Lujan* v. *Defenders of Wildlife*, the U.S. Supreme Court decided an important environmental case on the basis of the standing-to-sue doctrine articulated in *Sierra* v. *Morton*, 1972. As a result, the Court did not address substantive environmental issues such as alleged violations of the Endangered Species Act of 1973 by U.S.-funded agency projects in foreign countries and whether the Endangered Species Act applies only within the borders of the United States.

In 1978, the Carter administration issued a regulation saying that the Endangered Species Act did apply to American projects abroad. In 1983, Ronald Reagan's Secretary of the Interior, James Watt, reversed that policy. Several environmental groups sought to challenge the current policy continued by George Bush's Secretary of the Interior, Manuel Lujan. Two members of the Defenders of Wildlife, Joyce Kelly and Amy Skilbred, submitted affidavits claiming that certain federally supported projects threatened an endangered Egyptian crocodile and the Asian elephant and leopard in Sri Lanka. The information in the affidavits was based on Kelly and Skilbred's professional interest in the areas and their visits to the sites of the federal projects.

The Court said, "We shall assume for the sake of argument that these affidavits contain facts showing that certain agency-funded projects threatened listed species. . . . They plainly contain no facts, however, showing how damage to the species will produce 'imminent' injury to Mss. Kelly and Skilbred."[15] In making their case that Kelly and Skilbred were not injured, the Court weighed heavily the fact that the environmentalists were unable to say exactly when they would return to the areas. Despite the fact that a civil war was going on in Sri Lanka, thus hampering one plaintiff's ability to be precise about her future plans to return to the area, the Court demanded detail on future conduct.

In *Lujan*, the Court admitted that ". . . when the plaintiff is not himself the object of the government action or inaction he challenges, standing is not precluded, but it is ordinarily 'substantially more difficult' to establish."[16] In Stone's view, it is the crocodiles, elephants, and leopards who should have been the plaintiffs in this case, but, of course, they do not have standing to sue. In our efforts to ascertain ways of achieving better environmental policies in the United States, we need to consider whether changing the standing-to-sue doctrine will bring about significant gains.

In a move similar to Peter Singer's claim that species membership as such is irrelevant to moral standing, Paul Taylor rejects sentience as the criterion that must be met in order for a being (or entity) to count for something morally speaking. Singer believes that the species one happens to be, like the race or the sex one happens to be, is an arbitrary characteristic that has no moral significance. What matters, in his view, is whether a being can suffer. But Taylor, like the deep ecologists, thinks that seeing sentience as all-important is as arbitrary as claiming the same for membership in *Homo sapiens*. Philosopher Kenneth Goodpaster, in his influential article in 1978, "On Being Morally Considerable," says, "Nothing short of the condition of *being alive* seems to me to be a plausible and nonarbitrary criterion [of moral considerability]."[17] He adds, " . . . this criterion, if taken seriously, could admit of application to . . . the biosystem itself."[18] In making this claim, Goodpaster seems to be moving in the direction of what is called *ethical holism.*

Roughly speaking, *holism* is the view that the biosphere as an interconnected whole has moral standing. Such a view is often attributed to Aldo Leopold and is explicitly endorsed by his intellectual descendant, J. Baird Callicott. Paul Taylor's views must be distinguished from those of the holists. Taylor describes his view as *biocentric egalitarianism.* According to Taylor, all living beings have equal inherent worth in that each living being is a goal-directed system pursuing its own good.[19] Respect for nature is respect for these pursuits. However, Taylor's biocentric ethic, in contrast to Callicott, is individualistic and not holistic. In Taylor's view, according to reviewer T. L. S. Sprigge, "Total eco-systems only matter because individuals find their good within them; there is no over-all value of the whole, since the whole (it is claimed) is pursuing no good of its own."[20]

Taylor, as Sprigge points out, is prepared to push his individualistic biocentrism rather far. For example, it is just as important that nonconscious individuals such as plants achieve their goal as it is that a conscious individual should.[21] Plants do not have to be conscious in order to be valued for their own sake or in order to be as valuable as human beings. Taylor says, "[t]he killing of a wildflower, then, when taken in and of itself, is just as wrong, other-things-being-equal, as the killing of a human."[22]

Aldo Leopold (1887–1948) is a major figure in the emergence of contemporary ecological/environmental ethics. His ethical views, often referred to as the land ethic, are found mainly in his book, *A Sand County Almanac.* In this influential work, Leopold tells the story of Odysseus, who, after returning from the wars of Troy, hanged a dozen female slaves whom he suspected of misconduct. Because Odysseus thought of slaves as mere property, his concept of ethical obligation did not extend to them. He felt that he could dispose of them as he wished. Leopold draws an analogy between the former status of slaves and the current status of land. Land, Leopold argues, should not be viewed as property. His land ethic extends moral concern to "soils, waters, plants, and animals, or collectively: the land."[23] Land in Leopold's view is not a commodity that belongs to us, but a community to which we belong.[24] Elsewhere, Leopold refers to the land as an "organism." As might be expected, some expositors of Leopold have emphasized the "community" model and others the "organism" model. Callicott defends the metaphor of community in part on the grounds that it better represents the importance of individuals within a holistic framework that is committed to the importance of the whole.

A study of Leopold's work raises a host of important questions. Leopold advocated a harmonious relationship with the land. The land ethic, he said, "changes the role of *Homo sapiens* from conqueror of the land-community to plain member and citizen of it. It implies respect for his fellow-members, and also respect for the community as such."[25] But what does this respect entail? Respect for land, in his view, does not mean leaving it alone, since Leopold believed that we can alter it for the better. "The swampy forests of Caesar's Gaul were utterly changed by human use—for the better. Moses' land of milk and honey was utterly changed—for the worse."[26] In Leopold's view, a harmonious, as opposed to an exploitative, relationship with nature does not imply that humans will refrain from killing animals. As John Rodman characterizes Leopold's view, "it would be pretentious to talk of a land ethic until we have . . . shot a wolf (once) and looked into its eyes as it died."[27]

Callicott, in his essay, "The Conceptual Foundations of the Land Ethic," reads Leopold as intending to extend moral standing to things that are not themselves individual humans or animals. This, according to Callicott, is what is new and radical about Leopold's land ethic. "[The] standard modern model of ethical theory provides no possibility whatever for the moral consideration of wholes—of threatened *populations* of animals and plants, or of endemic, rare, or endangered *species,* or of biotic *communities,* or most expansively, of the *biosphere* in its totality. . . ."[28] Callicott emphasizes Leopold's call for "respect for the community as such" in the famous characterization of the land ethic (quoted above), where human beings are said to be plain members and citizens of the earth.

Not everyone agrees with Callicott that Leopold intended to attribute moral standing to the biosphere as a whole. Bryan Norton, for example, says the following: "That Leopold saw new and grave responsibilities limiting human activities in the modern world of bulldozers and concrete is without question. But whether he saw these obligations as deriving from sources outside of, and independent of, human affairs seems to me doubtful."[29] Although both Callicott and Norton characterize Leopold's view as "holistic," the two could not be further apart on the issue of whether the biosphere as a whole has moral standing or intrinsic value and whether Leopold claimed that it does. The difference is this: Norton means by "holism," ". . . the interests of the human species interpenetrate those of the living Earth. . . ."[30]

It might be helpful here to contrast Norton's view of holism with our earlier charac-

terization. Earlier, we said that holism is the view that the biosphere as an interconnected whole has moral standing. For Norton, holism is the view that the biosphere is an interconnected whole. As individuals, we are part of a larger system and we should value the system, but we value the system from the viewpoint of individuals rather than claiming that the system is the source of independent value.[31] Norton rejects the following dilemma: ". . . either nature is saved for future consumptive purposes or it is saved for itself . . . this reasoning ignores human, nonconsumptive motives for protecting natural ecosystems."[32]

Calling Leopold an "uncompromising preservationist," Norton goes on to claim that preservationism is characterized by ". . . the exclusion of disruptive human activities from specified areas"[33] for the purpose of preventing overexploitation and in turn ecological breakdown. "On the grandest scale, [preservationists] pursue . . . the setting aside of large, pristine tracts where the struggle to survive can continue untrammelled by human interference, or as nearly so as possible."[34] In Norton's view, whether preservationists are motivated by anthropocentrism or nonanthropocentrism matters little. Nonanthropocentrism, Norton says, ". . . is sufficient, but not necessary, to support preservationism. The preservationist perspective requires no more than a concern for long-term effects of pervasive management on biological diversity."[35]

The disagreement between integrator of perspectives, Bryan Norton, on the one hand, and Callicott and his followers on the other, runs deep. Norton is something of a pragmatist and would probably agree with the following assessment of Leopold's work by Anthony Weston. Leopold is ". . . not offering an ethical *theory,* [but] only a provisional statement of *some* of the values that ought to find their place in an ecologically intelligent land-use policy."[36] The values to which Weston refers are integrity, stability, and beauty—the ones expressed in Leopold's famous maxim: "A thing is right when it tends to preserve the integrity, stability, and beauty of the biotic community. It is wrong when it tends otherwise."[37] Callicott characterizes Leopold's maxim as the "'summary moral maxim' of the land ethic."[38] For Callicott, Leopold is not simply suggesting some intelligent land-use values; he is asserting a fundamental, if not ultimate, ethical principle that is part of a larger ethical theory called the "land ethic."

Callicott's approach to the land ethic has developed over a long period of time. In 1980, he wrote his provocative "Animal Liberation: A Triangular Affair" in which he argued that animal liberation, with its emphasis on the importance of individuals, and environmental ethics, with its holistic emphasis, are based on incompatible philosophies. Callicott now repudiates many of the views he expressed in this article. His essay, "Animal Liberation and Environmental Ethics: Back Together Again,"[39] is his major effort at reconciliation; however, some such effort can be seen in "The Conceptual Foundations of the Land Ethic," an essay reprinted in this section. We, as editors, have placed the pages from "The Conceptual Foundations of the Land Ethic" that address the issue of reconciliation in IIIC, the section that deals with the compatibility of animal liberation and environmental ethics.

NOTES

1. Anthony Weston, *Toward Better Problems: New Perspectives on Abortion, Animal Rights, the Environment, and Justice* (Philadelphia: Temple University Press, 1992), p. 105.

2. J. Baird Callicott, in correspondence.

3. Gifford Pinchot, *The Fight for Conservation* (Seattle: University of Washington Press, 1910), pp. 42–43.

4. Samuel P. Hays, *Conservation and the Gospel of Efficiency: The Progressive Conservation Movement, 1890–1920* (Cambridge: Harvard University Press, 1959), pp. 41–42.

5. Gifford Pinchot, *The Fight for Conservation*, p. 27.

6. John Muir, *To Yosemite and Beyond, Writings from the Years 1863 to 1875*, ed. Robert Engberg and Donald Wesling (Madison: University of Wisconsin Press, 1980), p. 113.

7. Ibid., p. 27.

8. Samuel Hays makes a similar point when he says that the crux of the controversy was over two public uses of the area: water supply and recreation. *Conservation and the Gospel of Efficiency*, p. 193.

9. Muir, *To Yosemite and Beyond*, p. 113.

10. John Rodman suggests this in "Four Forms of Ecological Consciousness Reconsidered," *Ethics and the Environment*, ed. Donald Scherer and Thomas Attig (Englewood Cliffs, NJ: Prentice-Hall, 1983), p. 85.

11. Christopher Stone, *Should Trees Have Standing? Toward Legal Rights for Natural Objects* (Los Altos, CA: William Kaufmann, Inc., 1974), p. 3.

12. Ibid., p. 4.

13. *Sierra v. Morton*, 70–34, April 19, 1972.

14. *Sierra v. Morton*, quoted in Stone, p. 62.

15. *Manuel Lujan, Jr., Secretary of the Interior, Petitioner* v. *Defenders of Wildlife, et al.*, June 12, 1992, *The United States Law Week*, Vol. 60, no. 48, June 9, 1992, p. 4498.

16. *Lujan*, p. 4497.

17. Kenneth E. Goodpaster, "On Being Morally Considerable," *Ethics and the Environment*, ed. Donald Scherer and Thomas Attig (Englewood Cliffs, NJ: Prentice-Hall, 1983), p. 31.

18. Ibid.

19. Tom Regan challenges Taylor's species egalitarianism by arguing that Taylor has made an improper inference from the "equal *independence* of the good of individual living beings" to the "equal *inherent* worth" of such beings. Tom Regan, "Less Is More: Some Remarks on Paul Taylor's *Respect for Nature*," unpublished paper presented at Brooklyn College, 1987, p. 13.

20. T. L. S. Sprigge, "Some Recent Positions in Environmental Ethics Examined," *Inquiry* 34, no. 1 (March 1991), p. 117.

21. This remark is a paraphrase of a point made by Sprigge, "Some Recent Positions in Environmental Ethics Examined," p. 116.

22. Paul Taylor, "In Defense of Biocentrism," *Environmental Ethics* 5 (1983), p. 242, quoted in Sprigge, p. 116.

23. Aldo Leopold, *A Sand County Almanac* (New York: Ballantine Books, 1970), p. 239.

24. Ibid., p. xviii.

25. Ibid., p. 240.

26. Aldo Leopold, "The Conservation Ethic," *Journal of Forestry* 31 (1933), p. 636.

27. John Rodman, "The Liberation of Nature," *Inquiry* 20 (1977), p. 110.

28. J. Baird Callicott, "The Conceptual Foundations of the Land Ethic," *Companion to A Sand County Almanac: Interpretive and Critical Essays*, ed. J. Baird

Callicott (Madison: University of Wisconsin Press, 1987) pp. 197–198.

29. Bryan G. Norton, *Toward Unity Among Environmentalists* (New York: Oxford University Press, 1991), p. 57.

30. Bryan G. Norton, "Conservation and Preservation: A Conceptual Rehabilitation," *Environmental Ethics* 8 (Fall 1986), p. 220.

31. This point is a paraphrase of a remark made by Norton in a review of J. Baird Callicott's *In Defense of the Land Ethic: Essays in Environmental Philosophy*, *Environmental Ethics* 13, no. 2 (Summer 1991), p. 182.

32. Norton, "Conservation and Preservation," p. 208.

33. Ibid., p. 201.

34. Ibid., p. 218.

35. Ibid., p. 214.

36. Weston, *Toward Better Problems*, p. 121.

37. Leopold, *A Sand County Almanac*, p. 262.

38. Callicott, "Conceptual Foundations of the Land Ethic," p. 196.

39. J. Baird Callicott, *In Defense of the Land Ethic: Essays in Environmental Philosophy* (Albany: State University of New York Press, 1989).

Should Trees Have Standing?
—Toward Legal Rights for Natural Objects

Christopher D. Stone

Introduction:
The Unthinkable

In *Descent of Man*, Darwin observes that the history of man's moral development has been a continual extension in the objects of his "social instincts and sympathies." Originally each man had regard only for himself and those of a very narrow circle about him; later, he came to regard more and more "not only the welfare, but the happiness of all his fellow-men"; then "his sympathies became more tender and widely diffused, extending to men of all races, to the imbecile, maimed, and other useless members of society, and finally to the lower animals. . . ."[1]

The history of the law suggests a parallel development. Perhaps there never was a pure Hobbesian state of nature, in which no "rights" existed except in the vacant sense of each man's "right to self-defense." But it is not unlikely that so far as the earliest "families" (including extended kinship groups and clans) were concerned, everyone outside the family was suspect, alien, rightless.[2] And even within the family, persons we presently regard as the natural holders of at least some rights had none. Take, for example, children. We know something of the early rights-status of children from the widespread practice of infanticide—espe-

cially of the deformed and female.[3] (Senicide,[4] as among the North American Indians, was the corresponding rightlessness of the aged.)[5] Maine tells us that as late as the Patria Potestas of the Romans, the father had *jus vitae necisque*—the power of life and death—over his children. A fortiori, Maine writes, he had power of "uncontrolled corporal chastisement; he can modify their personal condition at pleasure; he can give a wife to his son; he can give his daughter in marriage; he can divorce his children of either sex; he can transfer them to another family by adoption; and he can sell them." The child was less than a person: an object, a thing.[6]

The legal rights of children have long since been recognized in principle, and are still expanding in practice. Witness, just within recent time, *In re Gault*,[7] guaranteeing basic constitutional protections to juvenile defendants, and the Voting Rights Act of 1970.[8] We have been making persons of children although they were not, in law, always so. And we have done the same, albeit imperfectly some would say, with prisoners,[9] aliens, women (especially of the married variety), the insane,[10] Blacks, foetuses,[11] and Indians.

Nor is it only matter in human form that has come to be recognized as the possessor of rights. The world of the lawyer is peopled with inanimate

Should Trees Have Standing? Toward Legal Rights for Natural Objects, by Christopher D. Stone (Portola Valley, CA: Tioga Publishing Company, 1974), pp. 3–18, 24, 27–33, 45–46, 48–54. Reprinted by permission.

right-holders: trusts, corporations, joint ventures, municipalities, Subchapter R partnerships,[12] and nation-states, to mention just a few. Ships, still referred to by courts in the feminine gender, have long had an independent jural life, often with striking consequences.[13] We have become so accustomed to the idea of a corporation having "its" own rights, and being a "person" and "citizen" for so many statutory and constitutional purposes, that we forget how jarring the notion was to early jurists. "That invisible, intangible and artificial being, that mere legal entity" Chief Justice Marshall wrote of the corporation in *Bank of the United States v. Deveaux*[14]—could a suit be brought in *its* name? Ten years later, in the *Dartmouth College* case,[15] he was still refusing to let pass unnoticed the wonder of an entity "existing only in contemplation of law."[16] Yet, long before Marshall worried over the personifying of the modern corporation, the best medieval legal scholars had spent hundreds of years struggling with the notion of the legal nature of those great public "corporate bodies," the Church and the State. How could they exist in law, as entities transcending the living Pope and King? It was clear how a king could bind *himself*—on his honor—by a treaty. But when the king died, what was it that was burdened with the obligations of, and claimed the rights under, the treaty *his* tangible hand had signed? The medieval mind saw (what we have lost our capacity to see)[17] how *unthinkable* it was, and worked out the most elaborate conceits and fallacies to serve as anthropomorphic flesh for the Universal Church and the Universal Empire.[18]

It is this note of the *unthinkable* that I want to dwell upon for a moment. Throughout legal history, each successive extension of rights to some new entity has been, theretofore, a bit unthinkable. We are inclined to suppose the rightlessness of rightless "things" to be a decree of Nature, not a legal convention acting in support of some status quo. It is thus that we defer considering the choices involved in all their moral, social, and economic dimensions. And so the United States Supreme Court could straight-facedly tell us in *Dred Scott* that Blacks had been denied the rights of citizenship "as a subordinate and inferior class of beings, who had been subjugated by the dominant race. . . ."[19] In the nineteenth century, the highest court in California explained that Chinese had not the right to testify against white men in criminal matters because they were "a race of people whom nature has marked as inferior, and who are incapable of progress or intellectual development beyond a certain point . . . between whom and ourselves nature has placed an impassable difference."[20] The popular conception of the Jew in the 13th Century contributed to a law which treated them as "men *ferae naturae*, protected by a quasi-forest law. Like the roe and the deer, they form an order apart."[21] Recall, too, that it was not so long ago that the foetus was "like the roe and the deer." In an early suit attempting to establish a wrongful death action on behalf of a negligently killed foetus (now widely accepted practice), Holmes, then on the Massachusetts Supreme Court, seems to have thought it simply inconceivable "that a man might owe a civil duty and incur a conditional prospective liability in tort to one not yet in being."[22] The first woman in Wisconsin who thought she might have a right to practice law was told that she did not, in the following terms:

> The law of nature destines and qualifies the female sex for the bearing and nurture of the children of our race and for the custody of the homes of the world. . . . [A]ll life-long callings of women, inconsistent with these radical and sacred duties of their sex, as is the profession of the law, are departures from the order of nature; and when voluntary, treason against it. . . . The peculiar qualities of womanhood, its gentle graces, its quick sensibility, its tender susceptibility, its purity, its delicacy, its emotional impulses, its subordination of hard reason to sympathetic feeling, are surely not qualifications for forensic strife. Nature has tempered woman as little for the juridical conflicts of the court room, as for the physical conflicts of the battle field. . . .[23]

The fact is, that each time there is a movement to confer rights onto some new "entity," the proposal is bound to sound odd or frightening or laughable. This is partly because until the rightless thing receives its rights, we cannot see it as anything but a *thing* for the use of "us"—those who are holding rights at the time.[24] In this vein, what is striking about the Wisconsin case above is that the court, for all its talk about women, so clearly was never able to see women as they are (and might become). All it could see was the popular "idealized" version of *an object it needed*. Such is the way the slave South looked upon the Black.[25] There is something of a seamless web involved: there will be resistance to giving the thing "rights" until it can be seen and valued for itself; yet, it is hard to see it and value it for itself until we can bring ourselves to give it "rights"—which is almost inevitably going to sound inconceivable to a large group of people.

The reason for this little discourse on the unthinkable, the reader must know by now, if only from the title of the paper. I am quite seriously proposing that we give legal rights to forests, oceans, rivers and other so-called "natural objects" in the environment—indeed, to the natural environment as a whole.

As strange as such a notion may sound, it is neither fanciful nor devoid of operational content. In fact, I do not think it would be a misdescription of recent developments in the law to say that we are already on the verge of assigning some such rights, although we have not faced up to what we are doing in those particular terms.[26] We should do so now, and begin to explore the implications such a notion would hold.

Toward Rights for the Environment

Now, to say that the natural environment should have rights is not to say anything as silly as that no one should be allowed to cut down a tree. We say human beings have rights, but—at least as of the time of this writing—they can be executed. Corporations have rights, but they cannot plead the fifth amendment; *In re Gault* gave 15-year-olds certain rights in juvenile proceedings, but it did not give them the right to vote. Thus, to say that the environment should have rights is not to say that it should have every right we can imagine, or even the same body of rights as human beings have. Nor is it to say that everything in the environment should have the same rights as every other thing in the environment.

What the granting of rights does involve has two sides to it. The first involves what might be called the legal-operational aspects; the second, the psychic and socio-psychic aspects. I shall deal with these aspects in turn.

The Legal-Operational Aspects
What It Means to Be a Holder of Legal Rights

There is, so far as I know, no generally accepted standard for how one ought to use the term "legal rights." Let me indicate how I shall be using it in this piece.

First and most obviously, if the term is to have any content at all, an entity cannot be said to hold a legal right unless and until *some public authoritative body* is prepared to give *some amount of review* to actions that are colorably inconsistent with that "right." For example, if a student can be expelled from a university and cannot get any public official, even a judge or administrative agent at the lowest level, either (i) to require the university to justify its actions (if only to the extent of filling out an affidavit alleging that the expulsion "was not wholly arbitrary and capricious") or (ii) to compel the university to accord the student some procedural safeguards (a hearing, right to counsel, right to have notice of charges), then the minimum requirements for saying that the student has a legal right to his education do not exist.[27]

But for a thing to be *a holder of legal rights*, something more is needed than that some authoritative body will review the actions and processes of those who threaten it. As I shall use the term, "holder of legal rights," each of three additional criteria must be satisfied. All three, one will observe, go towards making a thing *count* jurally—to have a legally recognized worth and dignity in its own right, and not merely to serve as a means to benefit "us" (whoever the contemporary group of rights-holders may be). They are, first, that the thing can institute legal actions *at its behest*; second, that in determining the granting of legal relief, the court must take *injury to it* into account; and, third, that relief must run to the *benefit of it*. . . .

The Rightlessness of Natural Objects at Common Law

Consider, for example, the common law's posture toward the pollution of a stream. True, courts have always been able, in some circumstances, to issue orders that will stop the pollution. . . . But the stream itself is fundamentally rightless, with implications that deserve careful reconsideration.

The first sense in which the stream is not a rights-holder has to do with standing. The stream itself has none. So far as the common law is concerned, there is in general no way to challenge the polluter's actions save at the behest of a lower riparian—another human being—able to show an invasion of *his* rights. This conception of the riparian as the holder of the right to bring suit has more than theoretical interest. The lower riparians may simply not care about the pollution. They themselves may be polluting, and not wish to stir up legal waters. They may be economically dependent on their polluting neighbor. And, of course, when they discount the value of winning by the costs of bringing suit and the chances of success, the action may not seem worth undertaking. Consider, for example, that while the polluter might be injuring 100 downstream riparians $10,000 a year *in the aggregate*, each riparian separately might be suffering injury only to the extent of $100—possibly not enough for any one of them to want to press suit by himself, or even to go to the trouble and cost of securing co-plaintiffs to make it worth everyone's while. This hesitance will be especially likely when the potential plaintiffs consider the burdens the law puts in their way:[28] proving, *e.g.*, specific damages, the "unreasonableness" of defendant's use of the water, the fact that practicable means of abatement exist, and overcoming difficulties raised by issues such as joint causality, right to pollute by prescription, and so forth. Even in states which, like California, sought to overcome these difficulties by empowering the attorney-general to sue for abatement of pollution in limited instances, the power has been sparingly invoked and, when invoked, narrowly construed by the courts.[29]

The second sense in which the common law denies "rights" to natural objects has to do with the way in which the merits are decided in those cases in which someone is competent and willing to establish standing. At its more primitive levels, the system protected the "rights" of the property owning human with minimal weighing of any values: *"Cujus est solum, ejus est usque ad coelum et ad infernos."*[30] Today we have come more and more to make balances—but only such as will adjust the economic best interests of identifiable humans. For example, continuing with the case of streams, there are commentators who speak of a "general rule" that "a riparian owner is legally entitled to have the stream flow by his land with its quality unimpaired" and observe that "an upper owner has prima facie, no right to pollute the water."[31] Such a

doctrine, if strictly invoked, would protect the stream absolutely whenever a suit was brought; but obviously, to look around us, the law does not work that way. Almost everywhere there are doctrinal qualifications on riparian "rights" to an unpolluted stream.[32] Although these rules vary from jurisdiction to jurisdiction, and upon whether one is suing for an equitable injunction or for damages, what they all have in common is some sort of balancing. Whether under language of "reasonable use," "reasonable methods of use," "balance of convenience" or "the public interest doctrine," what the courts are balancing, with varying degrees of directness, are the economic hardships on the upper riparian (or dependent community) of abating the pollution vis-à-vis the economic hardships of continued pollution on the lower riparians. What does not weigh in the balance is the damage to the stream, its fish and turtles and "lower" life. So long as the natural environment itself is rightless, these are not matters for judicial cognizance. Thus, we find the highest court of Pennsylvania refusing to stop a coal company from discharging polluted mine water into a tributary of the Lackawana River because a plaintiff's "grievance is for a mere personal inconvenience; and . . . mere private personal inconveniences . . . must yield to the necessities of a great public industry, which although in the hands of a private corporation, subserves a great public interest."[33] The stream itself is lost sight of in "a quantitative compromise between *two* conflicting interests."[34]

The third way in which the common law makes natural objects rightless has to do with who is regarded as the beneficiary of a favorable judgment. Here, too, it makes a considerable difference that it is not the natural object that counts in its own right. To illustrate this point, let me begin by observing that it makes perfectly good sense to speak of, and ascertain, the legal damage to a natural object, if only in the sense of "making it whole" with respect to the most obvious factors. The costs of making a forest whole, for example, would include the costs of reseeding, repairing watersheds, restocking wildlife—the sorts of costs the Forest Service undergoes after a fire. Making a polluted stream whole would include the costs of restocking with fish, water-fowl, and other animal and vegetable life, dredging, washing out impurities, establishing natural and/or artificial aerating agents, and so forth. Now, what is important to note is that, under our present system, even if a plaintiff riparian wins a water pollution suit for damages, no money goes to the benefit of the stream itself to repair *its* damages. This omission has the further effect that, at most, the law confronts a polluter with what it takes to make the plaintiff riparians whole; this may be far less than the damages to the stream, but not so much as to force the polluter to desist. For example, it is easy to imagine a polluter whose activities damage a stream to the extent of $10,000 annually, although the aggregate damage to all the riparian plaintiffs who come into the suit is only $3000. If $3000 is less than the cost to the polluter of shutting down, or making the requisite technological changes, he might prefer to pay off the damages (*i.e.,* the legally cognizable damages) and continue to pollute the stream. Similarly, even if the jurisdiction issues an injunction at the plaintiffs' behest (rather than to order payment of damages), there is nothing to stop the plaintiffs from "selling out" the stream, *i.e.,* agreeing to dissolve or not enforce the injunction at some price (in the example above, somewhere between plaintiffs' damages—$3000—and defendant's next best economic alternative). Indeed, I take it this is exactly what Learned Hand had in mind in an opinion in which, after issuing an anti-pollution injunction, he suggests that the defendant "make its peace with the plaintiff as best it can."[35] What is meant is a peace between *them,* and not amongst them and the river.

I ought to make clear at this point that the common law as it affects streams and rivers, which I have been using as an example so far, is not exactly the same as the law affecting other environmental objects. Indeed, one would be hard pressed to say that there was a "typical" environmental object, so far as its treatment at the hands of the law is concerned. There are some differences in the law applicable to all the various resources that are held in common: rivers, lakes, oceans, dunes, air, streams (surface and subterranean), beaches, and so forth. And there is an even greater difference as between these traditional communal resources on the one hand, and natural objects on traditionally private land, *e.g.,* the pond on the farmer's field, or the stand of trees on the suburbanite's lawn.

On the other hand, although there be these differences which would make it fatuous to generalize about a law of the natural environment, most of these differences simply underscore the points made in the instance of rivers and streams. None of the natural objects, whether held in common or situated on private land, has any of the three criteria of a rights-holder. They have no standing in their own right; their unique damages do not count in determining outcome; and they are not the beneficiaries of awards. In such fashion, these objects have traditionally been regarded by the common law, and even by all but the most recent legislation, as objects for man to conquer and master and use— in such a way as the law once looked upon "man's" relationships to African Negroes. Even where special measures have been taken to conserve them, as by seasons on game and limits on timber cutting, the dominant motive has been to conserve them *for us*—for the greatest good of the greatest number of human beings. Conservationists, so far as I am aware, are generally reluctant to maintain otherwise.[36] As the name implies, they want to conserve and guarantee *our* consumption and *our* enjoyment of these other living things. In their own right, natural objects have counted for little, in law as in popular movements.

As I mentioned at the outset, however, the rightlessness of the natural environment can and should change; it already shows some signs of doing so.

Toward Having Standing in Its Own Right

It is not inevitable, nor is it wise, that natural objects should have no rights to seek redress in their own behalf. It is no answer to say that streams and forests cannot have standing because streams and forest cannot speak. Corporations cannot speak either; nor can states, estates; infants, incompetents, municipalities or universities. Lawyers speak for them, as they customarily do for the ordinary citizen with legal problems. One ought, I think, to handle the legal problems of natural objects as one does the problems of legal incompetents—human beings who have become vegetable. If a human being shows signs of becoming senile and has affairs that he is de jure incompetent to manage, those concerned with his well being make such a showing to the court, and someone is designated by the court with the authority to manage the incompetent's affairs. The guardian (or "conservator" or "committee"—the terminology varies) then represents the incompetent in his legal affairs. Courts make similar appointments when a corporation has become "incompetent"—they appoint a trustee in bankruptcy or reorganization to oversee its affairs and speak for it in court when that becomes necessary.

On a parity of reasoning, we should have a system in which, when a friend of a natural object perceives it to be endangered, he can apply to a court for the creation of a guardianship. Perhaps we already have the machinery to do so. California law, for example, defines an incompetent as "any person, whether insane or not, who by reason of old age, disease, weakness of mind, or other cause, is unable, unassisted, properly to manage and take care of himself or his property, and by reason thereof is likely to be deceived or imposed upon by artful or designing persons."[37] Of course, to urge a court that an endangered river is "a person" under this provision will call for lawyers as bold and imaginative as those who convinced the Supreme Court that a railroad corporation was a "person" under the fourteenth amendment, a constitutional provision theretofore generally thought of as designed to secure the rights of freedmen.[38]. . .

The guardianship approach, however, is apt to raise . . . [the following objection]: a committee or guardian could not judge the needs of the river or forest in its charge; indeed, the very concept of "needs," it might be said, could be used here only in the most metaphorical way. . . .

. . . Natural objects *can* communicate their wants (needs) to us, and in ways that are not terribly ambiguous. I am sure I can judge with more certainty and meaningfulness whether and when my lawn wants (needs) water, than the Attorney General can judge whether and when the United States wants (needs) to take an appeal from an adverse judgment by a lower court. The lawn tells me that it wants water by a certain dryness of the blades and soil—immediately obvious to the touch—the appearance of bald spots, yellowing, and a lack of springiness after being walked on; how does "the United States" communicate to the Attorney General? For similar reasons, the guardian-attorney for a smog-endangered stand of pines could venture with more confidence that his client wants the smog stopped, than the directors of a corporation can assert that "the corporation" wants dividends declared. We make decisions on behalf of, and in the purported interests of, others every day; these "others" are often creatures whose wants are far less verifiable, and even far more metaphysical in

conception, than the wants of rivers, trees, and land. . . .

The argument for "personifying" the environment, from the point of damage calculations, can best be demonstrated from the welfare economics position. Every well-working legal-economic system should be so structured as to confront each of us with the full costs that our activities are imposing on society. Ideally, a paper-mill, in deciding what to produce—and where, and by what methods—ought to be forced to take into account not only the lumber, acid and labor that its production "takes" from other uses in the society, but also what costs alternative production plans will impose on society through pollution. The legal system, through the law of contracts and the criminal law, for example, makes the mill confront the costs of the first group of demands. When, for example, the company's purchasing agent orders 1000 drums of acid from the Z Company, the Z Company can bind the mill to pay for them, and thereby reimburse the society for what the mill is removing from alternative uses.

Unfortunately, so far as the pollution costs are concerned, the allocative ideal begins to break down, because the traditional legal institutions have a more difficult time "catching" and confronting us with the full social costs of our activities. In the lakeside mill example, major riparian interests might bring an action, forcing a court to weigh *their* aggregate losses against the costs to the mill of installing the anti-pollution device. But many other interests—and I am speaking for the moment of recognized homocentric interests—are too fragmented and perhaps "too remote" causally to warrant securing representation and pressing for recovery: the people who own summer homes and motels, the man who sells fishing tackle and bait, the man who rents rowboats. There is no reason not to allow the lake to prove damages to them as the prima facie measure of damages to it. *By doing so, we in effect make the natural object, through its guardian, a jural entity competent to gather up these fragmented and otherwise unrepresented damage claims, and press them before the court even where, for legal or practical reasons, they are not going to be pressed by traditional class action plaintiffs.* Indeed, one way—the homocentric way—to view what I am proposing so far, is to view the guardian of the natural object as the guardian of unborn generations, as well as of the otherwise unrepresented, but distantly injured, contemporary humans.[39] By making the lake itself the focus of these damages, and "incorporating" it so to speak, the legal system can effectively take proof upon, and confront the mill with, a larger and more representative measure of the damages its pollution causes.

So far, I do not suppose that my economist friends (unremitting human chauvinists, every one of them!) will have any large quarrel in principle with the concept. Many will view it as a *trompe l'oeil* that comes down, at best, to effectuate the goals of the paragon class action, or the paragon water pollution control district. Where we are apt to part company is here—I propose going beyond gathering up the loose ends of what most people would presently recognize as economically valid damages. The guardian would urge before the court injuries not presently cognizable—the death of eagles and inedible crabs, the suffering of sea lions, the loss from the face of the earth of species of commercially valueless birds, the disappearance of a wilderness area. One might, of course, speak of the damages involved as "damages" to us humans, and indeed, the widespread growth of environmental groups shows that human beings do feel these losses. But they are not, at present, economically measurable losses: how can they have a monetary value for the guardian to prove in court?

The answer for me is simple. Wherever it carves out "property" rights, the legal system is engaged in the process of *creating* monetary worth. One's literary works would have minimal monetary value if anyone could copy them at will. Their economic value to the author is a product of the law of copyright; the person who copies a copyrighted book has to bear a cost to the copyright-holder because the law says he must. Similarly, it is through the law of torts that we have made a "right" of—and guaranteed an economically meaningful value to—privacy. (The value we place on gold—a yellow inanimate dirt—is not simply a function of supply and demand—wilderness areas are scarce and pretty to—, but results from the actions of the legal systems of the world, which have institutionalized that value; they have even done a remarkable job of stabilizing the price.) I am proposing we do the same with eagles and wilderness areas as we do with copyrighted works, patented inventions, and privacy: *make* the viola-

tion of rights in them to be a cost by declaring the "pirating" of them to be the invasion of a property interest.[40] If we do so, the net social costs the polluter would be confronted with would include not only the extended homocentric costs of his pollution (explained above) but also costs to the environment *per se*.

How, though, would these costs be calculated? When we protect an invention, we can at least speak of a fair market value for it, by reference to which damages can be computed. But the lost environmental "values" of which we are now speaking are by definition over and above those that the market is prepared to bid for: they are priceless.

One possible measure of damages, suggested earlier, would be the cost of making the environment whole, just as, when a man is injured in an automobile accident, we impose upon the responsible party the injured man's medical expenses. Comparable expenses to a polluted river would be the costs of dredging, restocking with fish, and so forth. It is on the basis of such costs as these, I assume, that we get the figure of $1 billion as the cost of saving Lake Erie.[41] As an ideal, I think this is a good guide applicable in many environmental situations. It is by no means free from difficulties, however.

One problem with computing damages on the basis of making the environment whole is that, if understood most literally, it is tantamount to asking for a "freeze" on environmental quality, even at the costs (and there will be costs) of preserving "useless" objects. Such a "freeze" is not inconceivable to me as a general goal, especially considering that, even by the most immediately discernible homocentric interests, in so many areas we ought to be cleaning up and not merely preserving the environmental status quo. In fact, there is presently strong sentiment in the Congress for a total elimination of all river pollutants by 1985,[42] notwithstanding that such a decision would impose quite large direct and indirect costs on us all. Here one is inclined to recall the instructions of Judge Hays, in remanding Consolidated Edison's Storm King application to the Federal Power Commission in *Scenic Hudson*:

> The Commission's renewed proceedings must include as a basic concern the preservation of natural beauty and of natural historic shrines, keeping in mind that, in our affluent society, the cost of a

project is only one of several factors to be considered.[43]

Nevertheless, whatever the merits of such a goal in principle, there are many cases in which the social price tag of putting it into effect are going to seem too high to accept. Consider, for example, an oceanside nuclear generator that could produce low cost electricity for a million homes at a savings of $1 a year per home, spare us the air pollution that comes of burning fossil fuels, but which through a slight heating effect threatened to kill off a rare species of temperature-sensitive sea urchins; suppose further that technological improvements adequate to reduce the temperature to present environmental quality would expend the entire one million dollars in anticipated fuel savings. Are we prepared to tax ourselves $1,000,000 a year on behalf of the sea urchins? In comparable problems under the present law of damages, we work out practicable compromises by abandoning restoration costs and calling upon fair market value. For example, if an automobile is so severely damaged that the cost of bringing the car to its original state by repair is greater than the fair market value, we would allow the responsible tortfeasor to pay the fair market value only. Or if a human being suffers the loss of an arm (as we might conceive of the ocean having irreparably lost the sea urchins), we can fall back on the capitalization of reduced earning power (and pain and suffering) to measure the damages. But what is the fair market value of sea urchins? How can we capitalize their loss to the ocean, independent of any commercial value they may have to someone else?

One answer is that the problem can sometimes be sidestepped quite satisfactorily. In the sea urchin example, one compromise solution would be to impose on the nuclear generator the costs of making the ocean whole somewhere else, in some other way, *e.g.*, reestablishing a sea urchin colony elsewhere, or making a somehow comparable contribution.[44] In the debate over the laying of the trans-Alaskan pipeline, the builders are apparently prepared to meet conservationists' objections halfway by re-establishing wildlife away from the pipeline, so far as is feasible.[45]

But even if damage calculations have to be made, one ought to recognize that the measurement of damages is rarely a simple report of economic facts about "the market," whether we are valuing the loss of a foot, a foetus, or a work of fine art. Decisions of this sort are always hard, but not impossible. We have increasingly taken (human) pain and suffering into account in reckoning damages, not because we think we can ascertain them as objective "facts" about the universe, but because, even in view of all the room for disagreement, we come up with a better society by making rude estimates of them than by ignoring them.[46] We can make such estimates in regard to environmental losses fully aware that what we are really doing is making implicit normative judgments (as with pain and suffering)—laying down rules as to what the society is going to "value" rather than reporting market evaluations. In making such normative estimates decision-makers would not go wrong if they estimated on the "high side," putting the burden of trimming the figure down on the immediate human interests present. All burdens of proof should reflect common experience; our experience in environmental matters has been a continual discovery that our acts have caused more long-range damage than we were able to appreciate at the outset.

To what extent the decision-maker should factor in costs such as the pain and suffering of animals and other sentient natural objects, I cannot say; although I am prepared to do so in principle.[47] Given the conjectural nature of the "estimates" in all events, and the roughness of the "balance of conveniences" procedure where that is involved, the practice would be of more interest from the socio-psychic point of view, discussed below, than from the legal-operational. . . .

The Psychic and Socio-psychic Aspects

The strongest case can be made from the perspective of human advantage for conferring rights on the environment. Scientists have been warning of the crises the earth and all humans on it face if we do not change our ways—radically—and these crises make the lost "recreational use" of rivers seem absolutely trivial. The earth's very atmosphere is threatened with frightening possibilities: absorption of sunlight, upon which the entire life cycle depends, may be diminished; the oceans may warm (increasing the "greenhouse effect" of the atmosphere), melting the polar ice caps, and destroying our great coastal cities; the portion of the atmosphere that shields us from dangerous radiation may be destroyed. Testifying before Congress, sea explorer Jacques Cousteau predicted that the oceans (to which we dreamily look to feed our booming populations) are headed toward their own death: "The cycle of life is intricately tied up with the cycle of water . . . the water system has to remain alive if we are to remain alive on earth."[48] We are depleting our energy and our food sources at a rate that takes little account of the needs even of humans now living.

These problems will not be solved easily; they very likely can be solved, if at all, only through a willingness to suspend the rate of increase in the standard of living (by present values) of the earth's "advanced" nations, and by stabilizing the total human population. For some of us this will involve forfeiting material comforts; for others it will involve abandoning the hope someday to obtain comforts long envied. For all of us it will involve giving up the right to have as many offspring as we might wish. Such a program is not impossible of realization, however. Many of our so-called "material comforts" are not only in excess of, but are probably in opposition to, basic biological needs. Further, the "costs" to the advanced nations is not as large as would appear from Gross National Product figures. G.N.P. reflects social gain (of a sort) without discounting for the social *cost* of that gain, *e.g.*, the losses through depletion of resources, pollution, and so forth. As has well been shown, as societies become more and more "advanced," their real marginal gains become less and less for each additional dollar of G.N.P.[49] Thus, to give up "human progress" would not be as costly as might appear on first blush.

Nonetheless, such far-reaching social changes are going to involve us in a serious reconsideration of our consciousness towards the environment. . . .

A radical new conception of man's relationship to the rest of nature would not only be a step towards solving the material planetary problems; there are strong reasons for such a changed consciousness from the point of making us far better humans. If we only stop for a moment and look at the underlying human qualities that our present attitudes toward property and nature draw upon and reinforce, we have to be struck by how stultify-

ing of our own personal growth and satisfaction they can become when they take rein of us. Hegel, in "justifying" private property, unwittingly reflects the tone and quality of some of the needs that are played upon:

> A person has as his substantive end the right of putting his will into any and every thing and thereby making it his, because it has no such end in itself and derives its destiny and soul from his will. This is the absolute right of appropriation which man has over all "things."[50]

What is it within us that gives us this need not just to satisfy basic biological wants, but to extend our wills over things, to object-ify them, to make them ours, to manipulate them, to keep them at a psychic distance? Can it all be explained on "rational" bases? Should we not be suspect of such needs within us, cautious as to why we wish to gratify them? When I first read that passage of Hegel, I immediately thought not only of the emotional contrast with Spinoza, but of the passage in Carson McCullers' *A Tree, A Rock, A Cloud,* in which an old derelict has collared a twelve year old boy in a streetcar cafe. The old man asks whether the boy knows "how love should be begun?"

The old man leaned closer and whispered:

> "A tree. A rock. A cloud."
>
> . . .
>
> "The weather was like this in Portland," he said. "At the time my science was begun. I meditated and I started very cautious. I would pick up something from the street and take it home with me. I bought a goldfish and I concentrated on the goldfish and I loved it. I graduated from one thing to another. Day by day I was getting this technique. . . .
>
> . . .
>
> . . . "For six years now I have gone around by myself and built up my science. And now I am a master. Son. I can love anything. No longer do I have to think about it even. I see a street full of people and a beautiful light comes in me.

I watch a bird in the sky. Or I meet a traveler on the road. Everything, Son. And anybody. All stranger and all loved! Do you realize what a science like mine can mean?"[51]

To be able to get away from the view that Nature is a collection of useful senseless objects is, as McCullers' "madman" suggests, deeply involved in the development of our abilities to love—or, if that is putting it too strongly, to be able to reach a heightened awareness of our own, and others' capacities in their mutual interplay. To do so, we have to give up some psychic investment in our sense of separateness and specialness in the universe. And this, in turn, is hard giving indeed, because it involves us in a flight backwards, into earlier stages of civilization and childhood in which we had to trust (and perhaps fear) our environment, for we had not then the power to master it. Yet, in doing so, we—as persons—gradually free ourselves of needs for supportive illusions. Is not this one of the triumphs for "us" of our giving legal rights to (or acknowledging the legal rights of) the Blacks and women?. . .

. . . A few years ago the pollution of streams was thought of only as a problem of smelly, unsightly, unpotable water, *i.e.*, to us. Now we are beginning to discover that pollution is a process that destroys wondrously subtle balances of life within the water, and as between the water and its banks. This heightened awareness enlarges our sense of the dangers to us. But it also enlarges our empathy. We are not only developing the scientific capacity, but we are cultivating the personal capacities *within us* to recognize more and more the ways in which nature—like the woman, the Black, the Indian and the Alien—is like us (and we will also become more able realistically to define, confront, live with and admire the ways in which we are all different).

The time may be on hand when these sentiments, and the early stirrings of the law, can be coalesced into a radical new theory or myth—felt as well as intellectualized—of man's relationships to the rest of nature. I do not mean "myth" in a demeaning sense of the term, but in the sense in which, at different times in history, our social "facts" and relationships have been comprehended and integrated by reference to the "myths" that we are co-signers of a social contract, that the Pope is God's agent, and that all men are created equal. Pantheism, Shinto and Tao all have myths to offer. But they are all, each in its own fashion, quaint, primitive and archaic. What is needed is a myth that can fit our growing body of knowledge of geophysics, biology and the cosmos. In this vein, I do not think it too remote that we may come to regard the Earth, as some have suggested, as one organism, of which Mankind is a functional part—the mind, perhaps: different from the rest of nature, but different as a man's brain is from his lungs. . . .

. . . As I see it, the Earth is only one organized "field" of activities—and so is the *human person*—but these activities take place at various levels, in different "spheres" of being and realms of consciousness. The lithosphere is not the biosphere, and the latter not the . . . ionosphere. The Earth is not *only* a material mass. Consciousness is not only "human"; it exists at animal and vegetable levels, and most likely must be latent, or operating in some form, in the molecule and the atom; and all these diverse and in a sense hierarchical modes of activity and consciousness should be seen integrated in and perhaps transcended by an all-encompassing and "eonic" planetary Consciousness.

. . .

Mankind's function within the Earth-organism is to extract from the activities of all other operative systems within this organism the type of consciousness which we call "reflective" or "self"-consciousness—or, we may also say to *mentalize* and give meaning, value, and "name" to all that takes place anywhere within the Earth-field. . . .[52]

As radical as such a consciousness may sound today, all the dominant changes we see about us point in its direction. Consider just the impact of space travel, of world-wide mass media, of increasing scientific discoveries about the interrelatedness of all life processes. Is it any wonder that the term "spaceship earth" has so captured the popular imagination? The problems we have to confront are increasingly the world-wide crises of a global organism: not pollution of a stream, but pollution of the atmosphere and of the ocean. Increasingly, the death that occupies each human's imagination is not his own, but that of the entire life cycle of the planet earth, to which each of us is as but a cell to a body.

To shift from such a lofty fancy as the planetarization of consciousness to the operation of our municipal legal system is to come down to earth hard. Before the forces that are at work, our highest court is but a frail and feeble—a distinctly human—institution. Yet, the Court may be at its best not in its work of handing down decrees, but at the very task that is called for: of summoning up from the human spirit the kindest and most generous and worthy ideas that abound there, giving them shape and reality and legitimacy. Witness the School Desegregation Cases which, more importantly than to integrate the schools (assuming they did), awakened us to moral needs which, when made visible, could not be denied. And so here, too, in the case of the environment, the Supreme Court may find itself in a position to award "rights" in a way that will contribute to a change in popular consciousness. It would be a modest move, to be sure, but one in furtherance of a large goal: the future of the planet as we know it.

How far we are from such a state of affairs, where the law treats "environmental objects" as holders of legal rights, I cannot say. But there is certainly intriguing language in one of Justice Black's last dissents, regarding the Texas Highway Department's plan to run a six-lane expressway through a San Antonio Park.[53] Complaining of the Court's refusal to stay the plan, Black observed that "after today's decision, the people of San Antonio and the birds and animals that make their home in the park will share their quiet retreat with an ugly, smelly stream of traffic. . . . Trees, shrubs, and flowers will be mowed down."[54] Elsewhere he speaks of the "burial of public parks," of segments of a highway which "devour parkland," and of the park's heartland.[55] Was he, at the end of his great career, on the verge of saying—just saying—that "nature has 'rights' on its own account"? Would it be so hard to do?

Notes

1. C. Darwin, Descent of Man 119, 120–21 (2d ed. 1874). *See also* R. Waelder, Progress and Revolution 39 *et seq.* (1967).

2. *See* Darwin, *supra* note 1, at 113–14. . . .

3. *See* Darwin, *supra* note 1, at 113. *See also* E. Westermarck, 1 The Origin and Development of the Moral Ideas 406–12 (1912). . . .

4. There does not appear to be a word "gericide" or "geronticide" to designate the killing of the aged. "Senicide" is as close as the Oxford English Dictionary comes, although, as it indicates, the word is rare. 9 Oxford English Dictionary 454 (1933).

5. *See* Darwin, *supra* note 1, at 386–93. Westermarck, *supra* note 3, at 387–89, observes that where the killing of the aged and infirm is practiced, it is often supported by humanitarian justification; this, however, is a far cry from saying that the killing is *requested* by the victim as his right.

6. H. Maine, Ancient Law 153 (Pollock ed. 1930).

7. 387 U.S. 1 (1967).

8. 42 U.S.C. §§ 1973 *et seq.* (1970).

9. *See* Landman v. Royster, 40 U.S.L.W. 2256 (E.D. Va., Oct. 30, 1971). . . .

10. *But see* T. Szasz, Law, Liberty and Psychiatry (1963).

11. *See* note 22. The trend toward liberalized abortion can be seen either as a legislative tendency back in the direction of rightlessness for the foetus—or toward increasing rights of women. This inconsistency is not unique in the law of course; it is simply support for Hohfeld's scheme that the "jural opposite" of someone's right is someone else's "no-right." W. Hohfeld, Fundamental Legal Conceptions (1923). . . .

12. Int. Rev. Code of 1954, § 1361 (repealed by Pub. L. No. 89-389, effective Jan. 1, 1969).

13. For example, *see* United States v. Cargo of the Brig Melek Adhel, 43 U.S. (2 How.) 210 (1844). There, a ship had been seized and used by pirates. All this was done without the knowledge or consent of the owners of the ship. After the ship had been captured, the United States condemned and sold the "offending vessel." The owners objected. In denying release to the owners, Justice Story cited Chief Justice Marshall from an earlier case: "This is not a proceeding against the owner; it is a proceeding against the vessel for an offense committed by the vessel; which is not the less an offense . . . because it was committed without the authority and against the will of the owner." 43 U.S. at 234, quoting from United States v. Schooner Little Charles, 26 F. Cas. 979 (No. 15,612) (C.C.D. Va. 1818).

14. 9 U.S. (5 Cranch) 61, 86 (1809).

15. Trustees of Darmouth College v. Woodward, 17 U.S. (4 Wheat.) 518 (1819).

16. *Id.* at 636.

17. Consider, for example, that the claim of the United States to the naval station at Guantanamo Bay, at

$2000-a-year rental, is based upon a treaty signed in 1903 by José Montes for the President of Cuba and a minister representing Theodore Roosevelt; it was subsequently ratified by two-thirds of a Senate no member of which is living today. Lease [from Cuba] of Certain Areas for Naval or Coaling Stations, July 2, 1903, T.S. No. 426; C. Bevans, 6 Treaties and Other International Agreements of the United States 1776–1949, at 1120 (U.S. Dep't of State Pub. 8549, 1971).

18. O. Gierke, Political Theories of the Middle Age (Maitland transl. 1927), especially at 22–30. . . .

19. Dred Scott v. Sandford, 60 U.S. (19 How.) 396, 404–05 (1856). . . .

20. People v. Hall, 4 Cal. 399, 405 (1854). . . .

21. Schechter, *The Rightlessness of Mediaeval English Jewry*, 45 Jewish Q. Rev. 121. 135 (1954) quoting from M. Bateson, *Medieval England* 139 (1904). . . .

22. Dietrich v. Inhabitants of Northampton, 138 Mass. 14, 16 (1884).

23. *In re* Goddell, 39 Wisc. 232, 245 (1875). The court continued with the following "clincher":

   And when counsel was arguing for this lady that the word, person, in sec. 32, ch. 119 [respecting those qualified to practice law], necessarily includes females, her presence made it impossible to suggest to him as *reductio ad absurdum* of his position, that the same construction of the same word . . . would subject woman to prosecution for the paternity of a bastard, and . . . prosecution for rape. *Id.* at 246.

   The relationship between our attitudes toward woman, on the one hand, and, on the other, the more central concern of this article—land—is captured in an unguarded aside of our colleague, Curt Berger: ". . . after all, land, like woman, was meant to be possessed. . . ." Land Ownership and Use 139 (1968).

24. Thus it was that the Founding Fathers could speak of the inalienable rights of all men, and yet maintain a society that was, by modern standards, without the most basic rights for Blacks, Indians, children and women. There was no hypocrisy; emotionally, no one *felt* that these other things were men.

25. The second thought streaming from . . . the older South [is] the sincere and passionate belief that somewhere between men and cattle, God created a *tertium quid*, and called it a Negro—a clownish, simple creature, at times even lovable within its limitations, but straitly foreordained to walk within the Veil. W. E. B. DuBois, The Souls of Black Folk 89 (1924).

26. The statement in text is not quite true; *cf.* Murphy, *Has Nature Any Right to Life?*, 22 Hast. L. J. 467 (1971). An Irish court, passing upon the validity of a testamentary trust to the benefit of someone's dogs, observed in dictum that "'lives' means lives of human beings, not of animals or trees in California." Kelly v. Dillon, 1932 Ir. R. 255, 261. (The intended gift over on the death of the last surviving dog was held void for remoteness, the court refusing "to enter into the question of a dog's expectation of life," although prepared to observe that "in point of fact neighbor's [sic] dogs and cats are unpleasantly long-lived. . . ." *Id.* at 260–61).

27. *See* Dixon v. Alabama State Bd. of Educ., 294 F.2d 150 (5th Cir.), *cert. denied*, 368 U.S. 930 (1961).

28. The law in a suit for injunctive relief is commonly easier on the plaintiff than in a suit for damages. *See* J. Gould, Law of Waters § 206 (1883).

29. However, in 1970 California amended its Water Quality Act to make it easier for the Attorney General to obtain relief, *e.g.*, one must no longer allege irreparable injury in a suit for an injunction. Cal. Water Code § 13350(b) (West 1971).

30. To whomsoever the soil belongs, he owns also to the sky and to the depths. *See* W. Blackstone, 2 Commentaries *18.

31. *See* Note, *Statutory Treatment of Industrial Stream Pollution*, 24 Geo. Wash. L. Rev. 302, 306 (1955); H. Farnham, 2 Law of Waters and Water Rights § 461 (1904); Gould, *supra* note 32, at § 204.

32. For example, courts have upheld a right to pollute by prescription, Mississippi Mills Co. v. Smith, 69 Miss. 299, 11 So. 26 (1882), and by easement, Luama v. Bunker Hill & Sullivan Mining & Concentrating Co., 41 F.2d 358 (9th Cir. 1930).

33. Pennsylvania Coal Co. v. Sanderson, 113 Pa. 126, 149, 6 A. 453, 459 (1886).

34. Hand, J. in Smith v. Staso Milling Co., 18 F.2d 736, 738 (2d Cir. 1927) (emphasis added). *See also* Harrisonville v. Dickey Clay Co., 289 U.S. 334 (1933) (Brandeis, J.).

35. Smith v. Staso, 18 F.2d 736, 738 (2d Cir. 1927).

36. By contrast, for example, with humane societies.

37. Cal. Prob. Code § 1460 (West Supp. 1971). . . .

38. Santa Clara County v. Southern Pac. R.R., 118 U.S. 394 (1886). . . .

39. *Cf.* Golding, *Ethical Issues in Biological Engineering*, 15 U.C.L.A L. Rev. 443, 451–63 (1968).

40. Of course, in the instance of copyright and patent protection, the creation of the "property right" can be more directly justified on homocentric grounds.

41. *See* Schrag, *Life on a Dying Lake,* in The Politics of Neglect 167, at 173 (R. Meek & J. Straayer eds. 1971).

42. On November 2, 1971, the Senate, by a vote of 86–0, passed and sent to the House the proposed Federal Water Pollution Control Act Amendments of 1971, 117 Cong. Rec. S17464 (daily ed. Nov. 2, 1971). Sections 101(a) and (a)(1) of the bill declare it to be "national policy that, consistent with the provisions of this Act—(1) the discharge of pollutants into the navigable waters be eliminated by 1985." S.2770, 92d Cong., 1st Sess., 117 Cong. Rec. S17464 (daily ed. Nov. 2, 1971).

43. 334 F.2d 608, 624 (2d Cir. 1965).

44. Again, there is a problem involving what we conceive to be the injured entity.

45. N.Y. Times, Jan. 14, 1971, § 1, col. 2, and at 74, col. 7.

46. Courts have not been reluctant to award damages for the destruction of heirlooms, literary manuscripts or other property having no ascertainable market value. In Willard v. Valley Gas Fuel Co., 171 Cal. 9, 151 Pac. 286 (1915), it was held that the measure of damages for the negligent destruction of a rare old book written by one of plaintiff's ancestors was the amount which would compensate the owner for all detriment including sentimental loss proximately caused by such destruction. . . .

47. It is not easy to dismiss the idea of "lower" life having consciousness and feeling pain, especially since it is so difficult to know what these terms mean even as applied to humans. *See* Austin, *Other Minds,* in *Logic and Language* 342 (S. Flew ed. 1965); Schopenhauer, *On the Will in Nature,* in Two Essays by Arthur Schopenhauer 193, 281–304 (1889). Some experiments on plant sensitivity—of varying degrees of extravagance in their claims— include Lawrence, *Plants Have Feelings, Too. . . ,* Organic Gardening & Farming 64 (April 1971); Woodlief, Royster & Huang, *Effect of Random Noise on Plant Growth,* 46 J. Acoustical Soc. Am. 481 (1969); Backster, *Evidence of a Primary Perception in Plant Life,* 10 Int'l J. Parapsychology 250 (1968).

48. Cousteau, *The Oceans: No Time to Lose,* L.A. Times, Oct. 24, 1971, § (opinion), at 1, col. 4.

49. *See* J. Harte & R. Socolow, Patient Earth (1971).

50. G. Hegel, Hegel's Philosophy of Right 41 (T. Knox transl. 1945).

51. C. McCullers, The Ballad of the Sad Cafe and Other Stories 150–51 (1958).

52. D. Rudhyar, Directives for New Life 21–23 (1971).

53. 136. San Antonio Conservation Soc'y v. Texas Highway Dep't, *cert. denied,* 400 U.S. 968 (1970) (Black, J. dissenting to denial of certiorari).

54. *Id.* at 969.

55. *Id.* at 971.

The Ethics of Respect for Nature

Paul W. Taylor

I. Human-centered and Life-centered Systems of Environmental Ethics

In this paper I show how the taking of a certain ultimate moral attitude toward nature, which I call "respect for nature," has a central place in the foundations of a life-centered system of environmental ethics. I hold that a set of moral norms (both standards of character and rules of conduct) governing human treatment of the natural world is a rationally grounded set if and only if, first, commitment to those norms is a practical entailment of adopting the attitude of respect for nature as an ultimate moral attitude, and second, the adopting of that attitude on the part of all rational agents can itself be justified. When the basic characteristics of the attitude of respect for nature are made clear, it will be seen that a life-centered system of environmental ethics need not be holistic or organicist in its conception of the kinds of entities that are deemed the appropriate objects of moral concern and consideration. Nor does such a system require that the concepts of ecological homeostasis, equilibrium, and integrity provide us with normative principles from which could be derived (with the addition of factual knowledge) our obligations with regard to natural ecosystems. The "balance of nature" is not itself a moral norm, however important may be the role it plays in our general outlook on the natural

Environmental Ethics, Vol. 3 (Fall 1981), pp. 197–218. Reprinted by permission.

world that underlies the attitude of respect for nature. I argue that finally it is the good (well-being, welfare) of individual organisms, considered as entities having inherent worth, that determines our moral relations with the Earth's wild communities of life.

In designating the theory to be set forth as life-centered, I intend to contrast it with all anthropocentric views. According to the latter, human actions affecting the natural environment and its nonhuman inhabitants are right (or wrong) by either of two criteria: they have consequences which are favorable (or unfavorable) to human well-being, or they are consistent (or inconsistent) with the system of norms that protect and implement human rights. From this human-centered standpoint it is to humans and only to humans that all duties are ultimately owed. We may have responsibilities *with regard to* the natural ecosystems and biotic communities of our planet, but these responsibilities are in every case based on the contingent fact that our treatment of those ecosystems and communities of life can further the realization of human values and/or human rights. We have no obligation to promote or protect the good of nonhuman living things, independently of this contingent fact.

A life-centered system of environmental ethics is opposed to human-centered ones precisely on this point. From the perspective of a life-centered theory, we have prima facie moral obligations that are owed to wild plants and animals themselves as members of the Earth's biotic community. We are morally bound (other things being equal) to protect or promote their good for *their* sake. Our duties to respect the integrity of natural ecosystems, to preserve endangered species, and to avoid environmental pollution stem from the fact that these are ways in which we can help make it possible for wild species populations to achieve and maintain a healthy existence in a natural state. Such obligations are due those living things out of recognition of their inherent worth. They are entirely additional to and independent of the obligations we owe to our fellow humans. Although many of the actions that fulfill one set of obligations will also fulfill the other, two different grounds of obligation are involved. Their well-being, as well as human well-being, is something to be realized *as an end in itself.*

If we were to accept a life-centered theory of environmental ethics, a profound reordering of our

moral universe would take place. We would begin to look at the whole of the Earth's biosphere in a new light. Our duties with respect to the "world" of nature would be seen as making prima facie claims upon us to be balanced against our duties with respect to the "world" of human civilization. We could no longer simply take the human point of view and consider the effects of our actions exclusively from the perspective of our own good.

II. The Good of a Being and the Concept of Inherent Worth

What would justify acceptance of a life-centered system of ethical principles? In order to answer this it is first necessary to make clear the fundamental moral attitude that underlies and makes intelligible the commitment to live by such a system. It is then necessary to examine the considerations that would justify any rational agent's adopting that moral attitude.

Two concepts are essential to the taking of a moral attitude of the sort in question. A being which does not "have" these concepts, that is, which is unable to grasp their meaning and conditions of applicability, cannot be said to have the attitude as part of its moral outlook. These concepts are, first, that of the good (well-being, welfare) of a living thing, and second, the idea of an entity possessing inherent worth. I examine each concept in turn.

1. Every organism, species population, and community of life has a good of its own which moral agents can intentionally further or damage by their actions. To say that an entity has a good of its own is simply to say that, without reference to any *other* entity, it can be benefited or harmed. One can act in its overall interest or contrary to its overall interest, and environmental conditions can be good for it (advantageous to it) or bad for it (disadvantageous to it). What is good for an entity is what "does it good" in the sense of enhancing or preserving its life and well-being. What is bad for an entity is something that is detrimental to its life and well-being.[1]

We can think of the good of an individual nonhuman organism as consisting in the full development of its biological powers. Its good is realized to the extent that it is strong and healthy. It possesses whatever capacities it needs for successfully coping with its environment and so preserving its existence throughout the various stages of the normal life cycle of its species. The good of a population or community of such individuals consists in the population or community maintaining itself from generation to generation as a coherent system of genetically and ecologically related organisms whose average good is at an optimum level for the given environment. (Here *average good* means that the degree of realization of the good of *individual organisms* in the population or community is, on average, greater than would be the case under any other ecologically functioning order of interrelations among those species populations in the given ecosystem.)

The idea of a being having a good of its own, as I understand it, does not entail that the being must have interests or take an interest in what affects its life for better or for worse. We can act in a being's interest or contrary to its interest without its being interested in what we are doing to it in the sense of wanting or not wanting us to do it. It may, indeed, be wholly unaware that favorable and unfavorable events are taking place in its life. I take it that trees, for example, have no knowledge or desires or feelings. Yet it is undoubtedly the case that trees can be harmed or benefited by our actions. We can crush their roots by running a bulldozer too close to them. We can see to it that they get adequate nourishment and moisture by fertilizing and watering the soil around them. Thus we can help or hinder them in the realization of their good. It is the good of trees themselves that is thereby affected. We can similarly act so as to further the good of an entire tree population of a certain species (say, all the redwood trees in a California valley) or the good of a whole community of plant life in a given wilderness area, just as we can do harm to such a population or community.

When construed in this way, the concept of a being's good is not coextensive with sentience or the capacity for feeling pain. William Frankena has argued for a general theory of environmental ethics in which the ground of a creature's being worthy of moral consideration is its sentience. I have offered some criticisms of this view elsewhere, but the full refutation of such a position, it seems to me, finally depends on the positive reasons for accepting a life-centered theory of the kind I am defending in this essay.[2]

It should be noted further that I am leaving open the question of whether machines—in particular, those which are not only goal-directed, but also self-regulating—can properly be said to have a good of their own.[3] Since I am concerned only with human treatment of wild organisms, species populations, and communities of life as they occur in our planet's natural ecosystems, it is to those entities alone that the concept "having a good of its own" will here be applied. I am not denying that other living things, whose genetic origin and environmental conditions have been produced, controlled, and manipulated by humans for human ends, do have a good of their own in the same sense as do wild plants and animals. It is not my purpose in this essay, however, to set out or defend the principles that should guide our conduct with regard to their good. It is only insofar as their production and use by humans have good or ill effects upon natural ecosystems and their wild inhabitants that the ethics of respect for nature comes into play.

2. The second concept essential to the moral attitude of respect for nature is the idea of inherent worth. We take that attitude toward wild living things (individuals, species populations, or whole biotic communities) when and only when we regard them as entities possessing inherent worth. Indeed, it is only because they are conceived in this way that moral agents can think of themselves as having validly binding duties, obligations, and responsibilities that are *owed* to them as their *due*. I am not at this juncture arguing why they *should* be so regarded; I consider it at length below. But so regarding them is a presupposition of our taking the attitude of respect toward them and accordingly understanding ourselves as bearing certain moral relations to them. This can be shown as follows:

What does it mean to regard an entity that has a good of its own as possessing inherent worth? Two general principles are involved: the principle of moral consideration and the principle of intrinsic value.

According to the principle of moral consideration, wild living things are deserving of the concern and consideration of all moral agents simply in virtue of their being members of the Earth's community of life. From the moral point of view their good must be taken into account whenever it is affected for better or worse by the conduct of rational agents. This holds no matter what species the creature belongs to. The good of each is to be accorded some value and so acknowledged as having some weight in the deliberations of all rational agents. Of course, it may be necessary for such agents to act in ways contrary to the good of this or that particular organism or group of organisms in order to further the good of others, including the good of humans. But the principle of moral consideration prescribes that, with respect to each being an entity having its own good, every individual is deserving of consideration.

The principle of intrinsic value states that, regardless of what kind of entity it is in other respects, if it is a member of the Earth's community of life, the realization of its good is something *intrinsically* valuable. This means that its good is prima facie worthy of being preserved or promoted as an end in itself and for the sake of the entity whose good it is. Insofar as we regard any organism, species population, or life community as an entity having inherent worth, we believe that it must never be treated as if it were a mere object or thing whose entire value lies in being instrumental to the good of some other entity. The well-being of each is judged to have value in and of itself.

Combining these two principles, we can now define what it means for a living thing or group of living things to possess inherent worth. To say that it possesses inherent worth is to say that its good is deserving of the concern and consideration of all moral agents, and that the realization of its good has intrinsic value, to be pursued as an end in itself and for the sake of the entity whose good it is.

The duties owed to wild organisms, species populations, and communities of life in the Earth's natural ecosystems are grounded on their inherent worth. When rational, autonomous agents regard such entities as possessing inherent worth, they place intrinsic value on the realization of their good and so hold themselves responsible for performing actions that will have this effect and for refraining from actions having the contrary effect.

III. The Attitude of Respect for Nature

Why should moral agents regard wild living things in the natural world as possessing inherent worth? To answer this question we must first take into account the fact that, when rational, autonomous agents subscribe to the principles of moral consideration and intrinsic value and so conceive of wild living things as having that kind of

worth, such agents are *adopting a certain ultimate moral attitude toward the natural world*. This is the attitude I call "respect for nature." It parallels the attitude of respect for persons in human ethics. When we adopt the attitude of respect for persons as the proper (fitting, appropriate) attitude to take toward all persons as persons, we consider the fulfillment of the basic interests of each individual to have intrinsic value. We thereby make a moral commitment to live a certain kind of life in relation to other persons. We place ourselves under the direction of a system of standards and rules that we consider validly binding on all moral agents as such.[4]

Similarly, when we adopt the attitude of respect for nature as an ultimate moral attitude we make a commitment to live by certain normative principles. These principles constitute the rules of conduct and standards of character that are to govern our treatment of the natural world. This is, first, an *ultimate* commitment because it is not derived from any higher norm. The attitude of respect for nature is not grounded on some other, more general, or more fundamental attitude. It sets the total framework for our responsibilities toward the natural world. It can be justified, as I show below, but its justification cannot consist in referring to a more general attitude or a more basic normative principle.

Second, the commitment is a *moral* one because it is understood to be a disinterested matter of principle. It is this feature that distinguishes the attitude of respect for nature from the set of feelings and dispositions that comprise the love of nature. The latter stems from one's personal interest in and response to the natural world. Like the affectionate feelings we have toward certain individual human beings, one's love of nature is nothing more than the particular way one feels about the natural environment and its wild inhabitants. And just as our love for an individual person differs from our respect for all persons as such (whether we happen to love them or not), so love of nature differs from respect for nature. Respect for nature is an attitude we believe all moral agents ought to have simply as moral agents, regardless of whether or not they also love nature. Indeed, we have not truly taken the attitude of respect for nature ourselves unless we believe this. To put it in a Kantian way, to adopt the attitude of respect for nature is to take a stance that one wills it to be a universal law for all rational beings. It is to hold that stance categorically, as being validly applicable to every moral agent without exception, irrespective of whatever personal feelings toward nature such an agent might have or might lack.

Although the attitude of respect for nature is in this sense a disinterested and universalizable attitude, anyone who does adopt it has certain steady, more or less permanent dispositions. These dispositions, which are themselves to be considered disinterested and universalizable, comprise three interlocking sets: dispositions to seek certain ends, dispositions to carry on one's practical reasoning and deliberation in a certain way, and dispositions to have certain feelings. We may accordingly analyze the attitude of respect for nature into the following components. (a) The disposition to aim at, and to take steps to bring about, as final and disinterested ends, the promoting and protecting of the good of organisms, species populations, and life communities in natural ecosystems. (These ends are "final" in not being pursued as means to further ends. They are "disinterested" in being independent of the self-interest of the agent.) (b) The disposition to consider actions that tend to realize those ends to be prima facie obligatory *because* they have that tendency. (c) The disposition to experience positive and negative feelings toward states of affairs in the world *because* they are favorable or unfavorable to the good of organisms, species populations, and life communities in natural ecosystems.

The logical connection between the attitude of respect for nature and the duties of a life-centered system of environmental ethics can now be made clear. Insofar as one sincerely takes that attitude and so has the three sets of dispositions, one will at the same time be disposed to comply with certain rules of duty (such as nonmaleficence and noninterference) and with standards of character (such as fairness and benevolence) that determine the obligations and virtues of moral agents with regard to the Earth's wild living things. We can say that the actions one performs and the character traits one develops in fulfilling these moral requirements are the way one *expresses* or *embodies* the attitude in one's conduct and character. In his famous essay, "Justice as Fairness," John Rawls describes the rules of the duties of human morality (such as fidelity, gratitude, honesty, and justice) as "forms of conduct in which recognition of others as persons is manifested."[5] I hold that the rules of duty governing our treatment of the natural world and its inhabitants are forms of conduct in which the attitude of respect for nature is manifested.

IV. The Justifiability of the Attitude of Respect for Nature

I return to the question posed earlier, which has not yet been answered: why *should* moral agents regard wild living things as possessing inherent worth? I now argue that the only way we can answer this question is by showing how adopting the attitude of respect for nature is justified for all moral agents. Let us suppose that we were able to establish that there are good reasons for adopting the attitude, reasons which are intersubjectively valid for every rational agent. If there are such reasons, they would justify anyone's having the three sets of dispositions mentioned above as constituting what it means to have the attitude. Since these include the disposition to promote or protect the good of wild living things as a disinterested and ultimate end, as well as the disposition to perform actions for the reason that they tend to realize that end, we see that such dispositions commit a person to the principles of moral consideration and intrinsic value. To be disposed to further, as an end in itself, the good of any entity in nature just because it is that kind of entity, is to be disposed to give consideration to *every* such entity and to place intrinsic value on the realization of its good. Insofar as we subscribe to these two principles we regard living things as possessing inherent worth. Subscribing to the principle is what it *means* to so regard them. To justify the attitude of respect for nature, then, is to justify commitment to these principles and thereby to justify regarding wild creatures as possessing inherent worth.

We must keep in mind that inherent worth is not some mysterious sort of objective property belonging to living things that can be discovered by empirical observation or scientific investigation. To ascribe inherent worth to an entity is not to describe it by citing some feature discernible by sense perception or inferable by inductive reasoning. Nor is there a logically necessary connection between the concept of a being having a good of its own and the concept of inherent worth. We do not contradict ourselves by asserting that an entity that has a good of its own lacks inherent worth. In order to show that such an entity "has" inherent worth we must give good reasons for ascribing that kind of value to it (placing that kind of value upon it, conceiving of it to be valuable in that way). Although it is humans (persons, valuers) who must do the valuing, for the ethics of respect for nature, the value so ascribed is not a human value. That is to say, it is not a value derived from considerations regarding human well-being or human rights. It is a value that is ascribed to nonhuman animals and plants themselves, independently of their relationship to what humans judge to be conducive to their own good.

Whatever reasons, then, justify our taking the attitude of respect for nature as defined above are also reasons that show why we *should* regard the living things of the natural world as possessing inherent worth. We saw earlier that, since the attitude is an ultimate one, it cannot be derived from a more fundamental attitude nor shown to be a special case of a more general one. On what sort of grounds, then, can it be established?

The attitude we take toward living things in the natural world depends on the way we look at them, on what kind of beings we conceive them to be, and on how we understand the relations we bear to them. Underlying and supporting our attitude is a certain *belief system* that constitutes a particular world view or outlook on nature and the place of human life in it. To give good reasons for adopting the attitude of respect for nature, then, we must first articulate the belief system which underlies and supports that attitude. If it appears that the belief system is internally coherent and well-ordered, and if, as far as we can now tell, it is consistent with all known scientific truths relevant to our knowledge of the object of the attitude (which in this case includes the whole set of the Earth's natural ecosystems and their communities of life), then there remains the task of indicating why scientifically informed and rational thinkers with a developed capacity of reality awareness can find it acceptable as a way of conceiving of the natural world and our place in it. To the extent we can do this we provide at least a reasonable argument for accepting the belief system and the ultimate moral attitude it supports.

I do not hold that such a belief system can be *proven* to be true, either inductively or deductively. As we shall see, not all of its components can be

stated in the form of empirically verifiable propositions. Nor is its internal order governed by purely logical relationships. But the system as a whole, I contend, constitutes a coherent, unified, and rationally acceptable "picture" or "map" of a total world. By examining each of its main components and seeing how they fit together, we obtain a scientifically informed and well-ordered conception of nature and the place of humans in it.

This belief system underlying the attitude of respect for nature I call (for want of a better name) "the biocentric outlook on nature." Since it is not wholly analyzable into empirically confirmable assertions, it should not be thought of as simply a compendium of the biological sciences concerning our planet's ecosystems. It might best be described as a philosophical world view, to distinguish it from a scientific theory or explanatory system. However, one of its major tenets is the great lesson we have learned from the science of ecology: the interdependence of all living things in an organically unified order whose balance and stability are necessary conditions for the realization of the good of its constituent biotic communities.

Before turning to an account of the main components of biocentric outlook, it is convenient here to set forth the overall structure of my theory of environmental ethics as it has now emerged. The ethics of respect for nature is made up of three basic elements: a belief system, ultimate moral attitude, and a set of rules of duty and standards of character. These elements are connected with each other in the following manner. The belief system provides a certain outlook on nature which supports and makes intelligible an autonomous agent's adopting, as an ultimate moral attitude, the attitude of respect for nature. It supports and makes intelligible the attitude in the sense that, when an autonomous agent understands its moral relations to the natural world in terms of this outlook, it recognizes the attitude of respect to be the only *suitable* or *fitting* attitude to take toward all wild forms of life in the Earth's biosphere. Living things are now viewed as *the appropriate objects of the attitude of respect* and are accordingly regarded as entities possessing inherent worth. One then places intrinsic value on the promotion and protection of their good. As a consequence of this, one makes a moral commitment to abide by a set of rules of duty and to fulfill (as far as one can by one's own efforts) certain standards of good character. Given one's adoption of the attitude of respect, one makes that moral commitment because one considers those rules and standards to be validly binding on all moral agents. They are seen as embodying forms of conduct and character structures in which the attitude of respect for nature is manifested.

This three-part complex which internally orders the ethics of respect for nature is symmetrical with a theory of human ethics grounded on respect for persons. Such a theory includes, first, a conception of oneself and others as persons, that is, as centers of autonomous choice. Second, there is the attitude of respect for persons as persons. When this is adopted as an ultimate moral attitude it involves the disposition to treat every person as having inherent worth or "human dignity." Every human being, just in virtue of her or his humanity, is understood to be worthy of moral consideration, and intrinsic value is placed on the autonomy and well-being of each. This is what Kant meant by conceiving of persons as ends in themselves. Third, there is an ethical system of duties which are acknowledged to be owned by everyone to everyone. These duties are forms of conduct in which public recognition is given to each individual's inherent worth as a person.

This structural framework for a theory of human ethics is meant to leave open the issue of consequentialism (utilitarianism) versus nonconsequentialism (deontology). That issue concerns the particular kind of system of rules defining the duties of moral agents toward persons. Similarly, I am leaving open in this paper the question of what particular kind of system of rules defines our duties with respect to the natural world.

V. The Biocentric Outlook on Nature

The biocentric outlook on nature has four main components. (1) Humans are thought of as members of the Earth's community of life, holding that membership on the same terms as apply to all the nonhuman members. (2) The Earth's natural ecosystems as a totality are seen as a complex web of interconnected elements, with the sound biological functioning of each being dependent on the sound biological functioning of the others. (This is the component referred to above as the great lesson

that the science of ecology has taught us.) (3) Each individual organism is conceived of as a teleological center of life, pursuing its own good in its own way. (4) Whether we are concerned with standards of merit or with the concept of inherent worth, the claim that humans by their very nature are superior to other species is a groundless claim and, in the light of elements (1), (2), and (3) above, must be rejected as nothing more than an irrational bias in our own favor.

The conjunction of these four ideas constitutes the biocentric outlook on nature. In the remainder of this paper I give a brief account of the first three components, followed by a more detailed analysis of the fourth. I then conclude by indicating how this outlook provides a way of justifying the attitude of respect for nature.

VI. Humans as Members of the Earth's Community of Life

We share with other species a common relationship to the Earth. In accepting the biocentric outlook we take the fact of our being an animal species to be a fundamental feature of our existence. We consider it an essential aspect of "the human condition." We do not deny the differences between ourselves and other species, but we keep in the forefront of our consciousness the fact that in relation to our planet's natural ecosystems we are but one species population among many. Thus we acknowledge our origin in the very same evolutionary process that gave rise to all other species and we recognize ourselves to be confronted with similar environmental challenges to those that confront them. The laws of genetics, of natural selection, and of adaptation apply equally to all of us as biological creatures. In this light we consider ourselves as one with them, not set apart from them. We, as well as they, must face certain basic conditions of existence that impose requirements on us for our survival and well-being. Each animal and plant is like us in having a good of its own. Although our human good (what is of true value in human life, including the exercise of individual autonomy in choosing our own particular value systems) is not like the good of a nonhuman animal or plant, it can no more be realized than their good can without the biological necessities for survival and physical health.

When we look at ourselves from the evolutionary point of view, we see that not only are we very recent arrivals on Earth, but that our emergence as a new species on the planet was originally an event of no particular importance to the entire scheme of things. The Earth was teeming with life long before we appeared. Putting the point metaphorically, we are relative newcomers, entering a home that has been the residence of others for hundreds of millions of years, a home that must now be shared by all of us together.

The comparative brevity of human life on Earth may be vividly depicted by imagining the geological time scale in spatial terms. Suppose we start with algae, which have been around for at least 600 million years. (The earliest protozoa actually predated this by several *billion* years.) If the time that algae have been here were represented by the length of a football field (300 feet), then the period during which sharks have been swimming in the world's oceans and spiders have been spinning their webs would occupy three quarters of the length of the field; reptiles would show up at about the center of the field; mammals would cover the last third of the field; hominids (mammals of the family *Hominidae*) the last two feet; and the species *Homo sapiens* the last six inches.

Whether this newcomer is able to survive as long as other species remains to be seen. But there is surely something presumptuous about the way humans look down on the "lower" animals, especially those that have become extinct. We consider the dinosaurs, for example, to be biological failures, though they existed on our planet for 65 million years. One writer has made the point with beautiful simplicity:

> We sometimes speak of the dinosaurs
> as failures; there will be time enough for
> that judgment when we have lasted even
> for one tenth as long. . . .[6]

The possibility of the extinction of the human species, a possibility which starkly confronts us in the contemporary world, makes us aware of another respect in which we should not consider ourselves privileged beings in relation to other species. This is the fact that the well-being of humans is dependent upon the ecological soundness and health of many plant and animal communities, while their soundness and health does not in the least depend upon human well-being. Indeed, from their standpoint the very existence of humans is quite unnecessary. Every last man, woman, and child could disappear from the face of the Earth without any significant detrimental consequence for the good of wild animals and plants. On the contrary, many of them would be greatly benefited. The destruction of their habitats by human "developments" would cease. The poisoning and polluting of their environment would come to an end. The Earth's land, air, and water would no longer be subject to the degradation they are now undergoing as the result of large-scale technology and uncontrolled population growth. Life communities in natural ecosystems would gradually return to their former healthy state. Tropical forests, for example, would again be able to make their full contribution to a life-sustaining atmosphere for the whole planet. The rivers, lakes, and oceans of the world would (perhaps) eventually become clean again. Spilled oil, plastic trash, and even radioactive waste might finally, after many centuries, cease doing their terrible work. Ecosystems would return to their proper balance, suffering only the disruptions of natural events such as volcanic eruptions and glaciation. From these the community of life could recover, as it has so often done in the past. But the ecological disasters now perpetrated on it by humans—disasters from which it might never recover—these it would no longer have to endure.

If, then, the total, final, absolute extermination of our species (by our own hands?) should take place and if we should not carry all the others with us into oblivion, not only would the Earth's community of life continue to exist, but in all probability its well-being would be enhanced. Our presence, in short, is not needed. If we were to take the standpoint of the community and give voice to its true interest, the ending of our six-inch epoch would most likely be greeted with a hearty "Good riddance!"

VII. The Natural World as an Organic System

To accept the biocentric outlook and regard ourselves and our place in the world from its perspective is to see the whole natural order of the Earth's biosphere as a complex but unified web of interconnected organisms, objects, and events. The ecological relationships between any community of living things and their environment form an organic whole of functionally interdependent parts. Each ecosystem is a small universe itself in which the interactions of its various species populations comprise an intricately woven network of cause-effect relations. Such dynamic but at the same time relatively stable structures as food chains, predator-prey relations, and plant succession in a forest are self-regulating, energy-recycling mechanisms that preserve the equilibrium of the whole.

As far as the well-being of wild animals and plants is concerned, this ecological equilibrium must not be destroyed. The same holds true of the well-being of humans. When one views the realm of nature from the perspective of the biocentric outlook, one never forgets that in the long run the integrity of the entire biosphere of our planet is essential to the realization of the good of its constituent communities of life, both human and nonhuman.

Although the importance of this idea cannot be overemphasized, it is by now so familiar and so widely acknowledged that I shall not further elaborate on it here. However, I do wish to point out that this "holistic" view of the Earth's ecological systems does not itself constitute a moral norm. It is a factual aspect of biological reality, to be understood as a set of causal connections in ordinary empirical terms. Its significance for humans is the same as its significance for nonhumans, namely, in setting basic conditions for the realization of the good of living things. Its ethical implications for our treatment of the natural environment lie entirely in the fact that our *knowledge* of these causal connections is an essential *means* to fulfilling the aims we set for ourselves in adopting the attitude of respect for nature. In addition, its theoretical implications for the ethics of respect for nature lie in the fact that it (along with the other elements of the biocentric outlook) makes the adopting of that attitude a rational and intelligible thing to do.

VIII. Individual Organisms as Teleological Centers of Life

As our knowledge of living things increases, as we come to a deeper understanding of their life cycles, their interactions with other organisms, and the manifold ways in which they adjust to the environment, we become more fully aware of how each of them is carrying out its biological functions according to the laws of its species-specific nature.

But besides this, our increasing knowledge and understanding also develop in us a sharpened awareness of the uniqueness of each individual organism. Scientists who have made careful studies of particular plants and animals, whether in the field or in laboratories, have often acquired a knowledge of their subjects as identifiable individuals. Close observation over extended periods of time has led them to an appreciation of the unique "personalities" of their subjects. Sometimes a scientist may come to take a special interest in a particular animal or plant, all the while remaining strictly objective in the gathering and recording of data. Nonscientists may likewise experience this development of interest when, as amateur naturalists, they make accurate observations over sustained periods of close acquaintance with an individual organism. As one becomes more and more familiar with the organism and its behavior, one becomes fully sensitive to the particular way it is living out its life cycle. One may become fascinated by it and even experience some involvement with its good and bad fortunes (that is, with the occurrence of environmental conditions favorable or unfavorable to the realization of its good). The organism comes to mean something to one as a unique, irreplaceable individual. The final culmination of this process is the achievement of a genuine understanding of its point of view and, with that understanding, an ability to "take" that point of view. *Conceiving of it as a center of life, one is able to look at the world from its perspective.*

This development from objective knowledge to the recognition of individuality, and from the recognition of individuality to full awareness of an organism's standpoint, is a process of heightening our consciousness of what it means to be an individual living thing. We grasp the particularity of the organism as a teleological center of life, striving to preserve itself and to realize its own good in its own unique way.

It is to be noted that we need not be falsely anthropomorphizing when we conceive of individual plants and animals in this manner. Understanding them as teleological centers of life does not necessitate "reading into" them human characteristics. We need not, for example, consider them to have consciousness. Some of them may be aware of the world around them and others may not. Nor need we deny that different kinds and levels of awareness are exemplified when consciousness in some form is present. But conscious or not, all are equally teleological centers of life in the sense that each is a unified system of goal-oriented activities directed toward their preservation and well-being.

When considered from an ethical point of view, a teleological center of life is an entity whose "world" can be viewed from the perspective of *its* life. In looking at the world from that perspective we recognize objects and events occurring in its life as being beneficent, maleficent, or indifferent. The first are occurrences which increase its powers to preserve its existence and realize its good. The second decrease or destroy those powers. The third have neither of these effects on the entity. With regard to our human role as moral agents, we can conceive of a teleological center of life as a being whose standpoint we can take in making judgments about what events in the world are good or evil, desirable or undesirable. In making those judgments it is what promotes or protects the being's own good, not what benefits moral agents themselves, that sets the standard of evaluation. Such judgments can be made about anything that happens to the entity which is favorable or unfavorable in relation to its good. As was pointed out earlier, the entity itself need not have any (conscious) *interest* in what is happening to it for such judgments to be meaningful and true.

It is precisely judgments of this sort that we are disposed to make when we take the attitude of respect for nature. In adopting that attitude those judgments are given weight as reasons for action in our practical deliberation. They become morally relevant facts in the guidance of our conduct.

IX. The Denial of Human Superiority

This fourth component of the biocentric outlook on nature is the single most important idea in establishing the justifiability of the attitude of respect for nature. Its central role is due to the special relationship it bears to the first three components of the outlook. This relationship will be brought out after the concept of human superiority is examined and analyzed.[7]

In what sense are humans alleged to be superior to other animals? We are different from them in having certain capacities that they lack. But why should these capacities be a mark of superiority? From what point of view are they judged to be signs of superiority and what sense of superiority is meant? After all, various nonhuman species have capacities that humans lack. There is the speed of a cheetah, the vision of an eagle, the agility of a monkey. Why should not these be taken as signs of *their* superiority over humans?

One answer that comes immediately to mind is that these capacities are not as *valuable* as the human capacities that are claimed to make us superior. Such uniquely human characteristics as rational thought, aesthetic creativity, autonomy and self-determination, and moral freedom, it might be held, have a higher value than the capacities found in other species. Yet we must ask: valuable to whom, and on what grounds?

The human characteristics mentioned are all valuable to humans. They are essential to the preservation and enrichment of our civilization and culture. Clearly it is from the human standpoint that they are being judged to be desirable and good. It is not difficult here to recognize a begging of the question. Humans are claiming human superiority from a strictly human point of view, that is, from a point of view in which the good of humans is taken as the standard of judgment. All we need to do is to look at the capacities of nonhuman animals (or plants, for that matter) from the standpoint of *their* good to find a contrary judgment of superiority. The speed of the cheetah, for example, is a sign of its superiority to humans when considered from the standpoint of the good of its species. If it were as slow a runner as a human, it would not be able to survive. And so for all the other abilities of nonhumans which further their good but which are lacking in humans. In each case the claim to human superiority would be rejected from a nonhuman standpoint.

When superiority assertions are interpreted in this way, they are based on judgments of *merit*. To judge the merits of a person or an organism one must apply grading or ranking standards to it. (As I show below, this distinguishes judgments of merit from judgments of inherent worth.) Empirical investigation then determines whether it has the "good-making properties" (merits) in virtue of which it fulfills the standards being applied. In the case of humans, merits may be either moral or nonmoral. We can judge one person to be better than (superior to) another from the moral point of view by applying certain standards to their character and conduct. Similarly, we can appeal to nonmoral criteria in judging someone to be an excellent piano player, a fair cook, a poor tennis player, and so on. Different social purposes and roles are implicit in the making of such judgments, providing the frame of reference for the choice of standards by which the nonmoral merits of people are determined. Ultimately such purposes and roles stem from a society's way of life as a whole. Now a society's way of life may be thought of as the cultural form given to the realization of human values. Whether moral or nonmoral standards are being applied, then, all judgments of people's merits finally depend on human values. All are made from an exclusively human standpoint.

The question that naturally arises at this juncture is: why should standards that are based on human values be assumed to be the only valid criteria of merit and hence the only true signs of superiority? This question is especially pressing when humans are being judged superior in merit to nonhumans. It is true that a human being may be a better mathematician than a monkey, but the monkey may be a better tree climber than a human being. If we humans value mathematics more than tree climbing, that is because our conception of civilized life makes the development of mathematical ability more desirable than the ability to climb trees. But is it not unreasonable to judge nonhumans by the values of human civilization, rather than by values connected with what it is for a member of *that* species to live a good life? If all living things have a good of their own, it at least makes sense to judge the merits of nonhumans by standards derived from *their* good. To use only standards based on human values is already to commit oneself to holding that humans are superior to nonhumans, which is the point in question.

A further logical flaw arises in connection with the widely held conviction that humans are *morally* superior beings because they possess, while others lack, the capacities of a moral agent (free will, accountability, deliberation, judgment, practical reason). This view rests on a conceptual confusion. As far as moral standards are concerned, only beings that have the capacities of a moral agent can properly be judged to be *either* moral (morally good) *or* immoral (morally deficient). Moral standards are simply not applicable to beings that lack such capacities. Animals and plants cannot therefore be said to be morally inferior in merit to humans. Since the only beings that can have moral merits *or be deficient in such merits* are moral agents, it is conceptually incoherent to judge humans as superior to nonhumans on the ground that humans have moral capacities while nonhumans don't.

Up to this point I have been interpreting the claim that humans are superior to other living things as a grading or ranking judgment regarding their comparative merits. There is, however, another way of understanding the idea of human superiority. According to this interpretation, humans are superior to nonhumans not as regards their merits but as regards their inherent worth. Thus the claim of human superiority is to be understood as asserting that all humans, simply in virtue of their humanity, have *a greater inherent worth* than other living things.

The inherent worth of an entity does not depend on its merits.[8] To consider something as possessing inherent worth, we have seen, is to place intrinsic value on the realization of its good. This is done regardless of whatever particular merits it might have or might lack, as judged by a set of grading or ranking standards. In human affairs, we are all familiar with the principle that one's worth as a person does not vary with one's merits or lack of merits. The same can hold true of animals and plants. To regard such entities as possessing inherent worth entails disregarding their merits and deficiencies, whether they are being judged from a human standpoint or from the standpoint of their own species.

The idea of one entity having more merit than another, and so being superior to it in merit, makes perfectly good sense. Merit is a grading or ranking concept, and judgments of comparative merit are based on the different degrees to which things satisfy a given standard. But what can it mean to talk about one thing being superior to another in inherent worth? In order to get at what is being asserted in such a claim it is helpful first to look at the social origin of the concept of degrees of inherent worth.

The idea that humans can possess different degrees of inherent worth originated in societies having rigid class structures. Before the rise of modern democracies with their egalitarian outlook, one's membership in a hereditary class determined one's social status. People in the upper classes were looked up to, while those in the lower classes were looked down upon. In such a society one's social superiors and social inferiors were clearly defined and easily recognized.

Two aspects of these class-structured societies are especially relevant to the idea of degrees of inherent worth. First, those born into the upper classes were deemed more worthy of respect than those born into the lower orders. Second, the superior worth of upper class people had nothing to do with their merits nor did the inferior worth of those in the lower classes rest on their lack of merits. One's superiority or inferiority entirely derived from a social position one was born into. The modern concept of a meritocracy simply did not apply. One could not advance into a higher class by any sort of moral or nonmoral achievement. Similarly, an aristocrat held his title and all the privileges that went with it just because he was the eldest son of a titled nobleman. Unlike the bestowing of knighthood in contemporary Great Britain, one did not earn membership in the nobility by meritorious conduct.

We who live in modern democracies no longer believe in such hereditary social distinctions. Indeed, we would wholeheartedly condemn them on moral grounds as being fundamentally unjust. We have come to think of class systems as a paradigm of social injustice, it being a central principle of the democratic way of life that among humans there are no superiors and no inferiors. Thus we have rejected the whole conceptual framework in which people are judged to have different degrees of inherent worth. That idea is incompatible with our notion of human equality based on the doctrine that all humans, simply in virtue of their humanity, have the same inherent worth. (The belief in universal human rights is one form that this egalitarianism takes.)

The vast majority of people in modern democracies, however, do not maintain an egalitarian outlook when it comes to comparing human beings with other living things. Most people consider our own species to be superior to all other species and this superiority is understood to be a matter of inherent worth, not merit. There may exist thoroughly vicious and depraved humans who lack all merit. Yet because they are human they are thought to belong to a higher class of entities than any plant or animal. That one is born into the species *Homo sapiens* entitles one to have lordship over those who are one's inferiors, namely, those born into other species. The parallel with hereditary social classes is very close. Implicit in this view is a hierarchical conception of nature according to which an organism has a position of superiority or inferiority in the Earth's community of life simply on the basis of its genetic background. The "lower" orders of life are looked down upon and it is considered perfectly proper that they serve the interests of those belonging to the highest order, namely humans. The intrinsic value we place on the well-being of our fellow humans reflects our recognition of their rightful position as our equals. No such intrinsic value is to be placed on the good of other animals, unless we choose to do so out of fondness or affection for them. But their well-being imposes no moral requirement on us. In this respect there is an absolute difference in moral status between ourselves and them.

This is the structure of concepts and beliefs that people are committed to insofar as they regard humans to be superior in inherent worth to all other species. I now wish to argue that this structure of concepts and beliefs is completely groundless. If we accept the first three components of the biocentric outlook and from that perspective look at the major philosophical traditions which have supported that structure, we find it to be at bottom nothing more than the expression of an irrational bias in our own favor. The philosophical traditions themselves rest on very questionable assumptions or else simply beg the question. I briefly consider three of the main traditions to substantiate the point. These are classical Greek humanism, Cartesian dualism, and the Judeo-Christian concept of the Great Chain of Being.

The inherent superiority of humans over other species was implicit in the Greek definition of man as a rational animal. Our animal nature was identified with "brute" desires that need the order and restraint of reason to rule them (just as reason is the special virtue of those who rule in the ideal state). Rationality was then seen to be the key to our superiority over animals. It enables us to live on a higher plane and endows us with a nobility and worth that other creatures lack. This familiar way of comparing humans with other species is deeply ingrained in our Western philosophical outlook. The point to consider here is that this view does not actually provide an argument *for* human superiority but rather makes explicit the framework of thought that is implicitly used by those who think of humans as inherently superior to nonhumans. The Greeks who held that humans, in virtue of their rational capacities, have a kind of worth greater than that of any nonrational being, never looked at rationality as but one capacity of living things among many others. But when we consider rationality from the standpoint of the first three elements of the ecological outlook, we see that its value lies in its importance for *human* life. Other creatures achieve their species-specific good without the need of rationality, although they often make use of capacities that humans lack. So the humanistic outlook of classical Greek thought does not give us a neutral (nonquestion-begging) ground on which to construct a scale of degrees of inherent worth possessed by different species of living things.

The second tradition, centering on the Cartesian dualism of soul and body, also fails to justify the claim to human superiority. That superiority is supposed to derive from the fact that we have souls while animals do not. Animals are mere automata and lack the divine element that makes us spiritual beings. I won't go into the now familiar criticisms of this two-substance view. I only add the point that, even if humans are composed of an immaterial, unextended soul and a material, extended body, this in itself is not a reason to deem them of greater worth than entities that are only bodies. Why is a soul substance a thing that adds value to its possessor? Unless some theological reasoning is offered here (which many, including myself, would find unacceptable on epistemological grounds), no logical connection is evident. An immaterial something which thinks is better than a material something which does not think only if thinking itself has value, either intrinsically or instrumentally. Now it is intrinsically valuable to humans alone, who value it as an end in itself, and it is instrumentally valuable to those who benefit from it, namely humans.

For animals that neither enjoy thinking for its own sake nor need it for living the kind of life for which they are best adapted, it has no value. Even if "thinking" is broadened to include all forms of consciousness, there are still many living things that can do without it and yet live what is for their species a good life. The anthropocentricity underlying the claim to human superiority runs throughout Cartesian dualism.

A third major source of the idea of human superiority is the Judeo-Christian concept of the Great Chain of Being. Humans are superior to animals and plants because their Creator has given them a higher place on the chain. It begins with God at the top, and then moves to the angels, who are lower than God but higher than humans, then to humans, positioned between the angels and the beasts (partaking of the nature of both), and then on down to the lower levels occupied by nonhuman animals, plants, and finally inanimate objects. Humans, being "made in God's image," are inherently superior to animals and plants by virtue of their being closer (in their essential nature) to God.

The metaphysical and epistemological difficulties with this conception of a hierarchy of entities are, in my mind, insuperable. Without entering into this matter here, I only point out that if we are unwilling to accept the metaphysics of traditional Judaism and Christianity, we are again left without good reasons for holding to the claim of inherent human superiority.

The foregoing considerations (and others like them) leave us with but one ground for the assertion that a human being, regardless of merit, is a higher kind of entity than any other living thing. This is the mere fact of the genetic makeup of the species *Homo sapiens*. But this is surely irrational and arbitrary. Why should the arrangement of genes of a certain type be a mark of superior value, especially when this fact about an organism is taken by itself, unrelated to any other aspect of its life? We might just as well refer to any other genetic makeup as a ground of superior value. Clearly we are confronted here with a wholly arbitrary claim that can only be explained as an irrational bias in our own favor.

That the claim is nothing more than a deep-seated prejudice is brought home to us when we look at our relation to other species in the light of the first three elements of the biocentric outlook. Those elements taken conjointly give us a certain overall view of the natural world and of the place of humans in it. When we take this view we come to understand other living things, their environmental conditions, and their ecological relationships in such a way as to awake in us a deep sense of our kinship with them as fellow members of the Earth's community of life. Humans and nonhumans alike are viewed together as integral parts of one unified whole in which all living things are functionally interrelated. Finally, when our awareness focuses on the individual lives of plants and animals, each is seen to share with us the characteristic of being a teleological center of life striving to realize its own good in its own unique way.

As this entire belief system becomes part of the conceptual framework through which we understand and perceive the world, we come to see ourselves as bearing a certain moral relation to nonhuman forms of life. Our ethical role in nature takes on a new significance. We begin to look at other species as we look at ourselves, seeing them as beings which have a good they are striving to realize just as we have a good we are striving to realize. We accordingly develop the disposition to view the world from the standpoint of their good as well as from the standpoint of our own good. Now if the groundlessness of the claim that humans are inherently superior to other species were brought clearly before our minds, we would not remain intellectually neutral toward that claim but would reject it as being fundamentally at variance with our total world outlook. In the absence of any good reasons for holding it, the assertion of human superiority would then appear simply as the expression of an irrational and self-serving prejudice that favors one particular species over several million others.

Rejecting the notion of human superiority entails its positive counterpart: the doctrine of species impartiality. One who accepts that doctrine regards all living things as possessing inherent worth—the *same* inherent worth, since no one species has been shown to be either "higher" or "lower" than any other. Now we saw earlier that, insofar as one thinks of a living thing as possessing inherent worth, one considers it to be the appropriate object of the attitude of respect and believes that attitude to be the only fitting or suitable one for all moral agents to take toward it.

Here, then, is the key to understanding how the attitude of respect is rooted in the biocentric outlook on nature. The basic connection is made through the denial of human superiority. Once we reject the claim that humans are superior either in merit or in worth to other living things, we are ready to adopt the attitude of respect. The denial of human superiority is itself the result of taking the perspective on nature built into the first three elements of the biocentric outlook.

Now the first three elements of the biocentric outlook, it seems clear, would be found acceptable to any rational and scientifically informed thinker who is fully "open" to the reality of the lives of nonhuman organisms. Without denying our distinctively human characteristics, such a thinker can acknowledge the fundamental respects in which we are members of the Earth's community of life and in which the biological conditions necessary for the realization of our human values are inextricably linked with the whole system of nature. In addition, the conception of individual living things as teleological centers of life simply articulates how a scientifically informed thinker comes to understand them as the result of increasingly careful and detailed observations. Thus, the biocentric outlook recommends itself as an acceptable system of concepts and beliefs to anyone who is clear-minded, unbiased, and factually enlightened, and who has a developed capacity of reality awareness with regard to the lives of individual organisms. This, I submit, is as good a reason for making the moral commitment involved in adopting the attitude of respect for nature as any theory of environmental ethics could possibly have.

X. Moral Rights and the Matter of Competing Claims

I have not asserted anywhere in the foregoing account that animals or plants have moral rights. This omission was deliberate. I do not think that the reference class of the concept, bearer of moral rights, should be extended to include nonhuman living things. My reasons for taking this position, however, go beyond the scope of this paper. I believe I have been able to accomplish many of the same ends which those who ascribe rights to animals or plants wish to accomplish. There is no reason, moreover, why plants and animals, including whole species populations and life communities, cannot be accorded *legal* rights under my theory. To grant them legal protection could be interpreted as giving them legal entitlement to be protected, and this, in fact, would be a means by which a society that subscribed to the ethics of respect for nature could give public recognition to their inherent worth.

There remains the problem of competing claims, even when wild plants and animals are not thought of as bearers of moral rights. If we accept the biocentric outlook and accordingly adopt the attitude of respect for nature as our ultimate moral attitude, how do we resolve conflicts that arise from our respect for persons in the domain of human ethics and our respect for nature in the domain of environmental ethics? This is a question that cannot adequately be dealt with here. My main purpose in this paper has been to try to establish a base point from which we can start working toward a solution to the problem. I have shown why we cannot just begin with an initial presumption in favor of the interests of our own species. It is after all within our power as moral beings to place limits on human population and technology with the deliberate intention of sharing the Earth's bounty with other species. That such sharing is an ideal difficult to realize even in an approximate way does not take away its claim to our deepest moral commitment.

Notes

1. The conceptual links between an entity *having* a good, something being good *for* it, and events doing good *to* it are examined by G. H. Von Wright in *The Varieties of Goodness* (New York: Humanities Press, 1963), chaps. 3 and 5.

2. See W. K. Frankena, "Ethics and the Environment," in K. E. Goodpaster and K. M. Sayre, eds., *Ethics and Problems of the 21st Century* (Notre Dame, University of Notre Dame Press, 1979), pp. 3–20. I critically examine Frankena's views in "Frankena on Environmental Ethics," *Monist*, forthcoming.

3. In the light of considerations set forth in Daniel Dennett's *Brainstorms: Philosophical Essays on Mind and Psychology* (Montgomery, Vermont: Bradford Books, 1978), it is advisable to leave this question unsettled at this time. When machines are developed that function in the way our brains do, we may well come to deem them proper subjects of moral consideration.

4. I have analyzed the nature of this commitment of human ethics in "On Taking the Moral Point of View," *Midwest Studies in Philosophy*, vol. 3, *Studies in Ethical Theory* (1978), pp. 35–61.

5. John Rawls, "Justice As Fairness," *Philosophical Review* 67 (1958): 183.

6. Stephen R. L. Clark, *The Moral Status of Animals* (Oxford: Clarendon Press, 1977), p. 112.

7. My criticisms of the dogma of human superiority gain independent support from a carefully reasoned essay by R. and V. Routley showing the many logical weaknesses in arguments for human-centered theories of environmental ethics. R. and V. Routley, "Against the Inevitability of Human Chauvinism," in K. E. Goodpaster and K. M. Sayre, eds., *Ethics and Problems of the 21st Century* (Notre Dame: University of Notre Dame Press, 1979), pp. 36–59.

8. For this way of distinguishing between merit and inherent worth, I am indebted to Gregory Vlastos, "Justice and Equality," in R. Brandt, ed., *Social Justice* (Englewood Cliffs, N.J.: Prentice-Hall, 1962), pp. 31–72.

The Little Things That Run the World*

Edward O. Wilson

On the occasion of the opening of the remarkable new invertebrate exhibit of the National Zoological Park, let me say a word on behalf of these little things that run the world. To start, there are vastly more kinds of invertebrates than of vertebrates. At the present time, on the basis of the tabulation that I have just completed (from the literature and with the help of specialists), I estimate that a total of 42,580 vertebrate species have been described, of which 6,300 are reptiles, 9,040 are birds, and 4,000 are mammals. In contrast, 990,000 species of invertebrates have been described, of which 290,000 alone are beetles—seven times the number of all the invertebrates together. Recent estimates have placed the number of invertebrates on the earth as

* Address given at the opening of the invertebrate exhibit, National Zoological Park, Washington, D.C., on May 7, 1987.

high as 30 million, again mostly beetles—although many other taxonomically comparable groups of insects and other invertebrates also greatly outnumber vertebrates.

We don't know with certainty why invertebrates are so diverse, but a commonly held opinion is that the key trait is their small size. Their niches are correspondingly small, and they can therefore divide up the environment into many more little domains where specialists can coexist. One of my favorite examples of such specialists living in microniches are the mites that live on the bodies of army ants: one kind is found only on the mandibles of the soldier caste, where it sits and feeds from the mouth of its host; another kind is found only on the hind foot of the soldier caste, where it sucks blood for a living; and so on through various bizarre configurations.

Another possible cause of invertebrate diversity is the greater antiquity of these little animals, giving them more time to explore and fill the environment. The first invertebrates appeared well back into Precambrian times, at least 600 million years ago. Most invertebrate phyla were flourishing before the vertebrates arrived on the scene, some 500 million years ago.

Invertebrates also rule the earth by virtue of sheer body mass. For example, in tropical rain forest near Manaus, in the Brazilian Amazon, each hectare (or 2.5 acres) contains a few dozen birds and mammals but well over one billion invertebrates, of which the vast majority are not beetles this time but mites and springtails. There are about 200 kilograms dry weight of animal tissue in a hectare, of which 93 percent consists of invertebrates. The ants and termites alone compose one third of this biomass. So when you walk through a tropical forest, or most other terrestrial habitats for that matter, or snorkel above a coral reef or some other marine or aquatic environment, vertebrates may catch your eye most of the time—biologists would say that your search image is for large animals—but you are visiting a primarily invertebrate world.

It is a common misconception that vertebrates are the movers and shakers of the world, tearing the vegetation down, cutting paths through the forest, and consuming most of the energy. That may be true in a few ecosystems such as the grasslands of Africa with their great herds of herbivorous mammals. It has certainly become true in the last few centuries in the case of our own species, which now

appropriates in one form or other as much as 40 percent of the solar energy captured by plants. That circumstance is what makes us so dangerous to the fragile environment of the world. But it is otherwise more nearly true in most parts of the world of the invertebrates rather than the nonhuman vertebrates. The leafcutter ants, for example, rather than deer, or rodents, or birds, are the principal consumers of vegetation in Central and South America. A single colony contains over two million workers. It sends out columns of foragers a hundred meters or more in all directions to cut forest leaves, flower parts, and succulent stems. Each day a typical mature colony collects about 50 kilograms of this fresh vegetation, more than the average cow. Inside the nest, the ants shape the material into intricate sponge-like bodies on which they grow a symbiotic fungus. The fungus thrives as it breaks down and consumes the cellulose, while the ants thrive by eating the fungus.

The leafcutting ants excavate vertical galleries and living chambers as deep as 5 meters into the soil. They and other kinds of ants, as well as bacteria, fungi, termites, and mites, process most of the dead vegetation and return its nutrients to the plants to keep the great tropical forests alive.

Much the same situation exists in other parts of the world. The coral reefs are built out of the bodies of coelenterates. The most abundant animals of the open are copepods, tiny crustaceans forming part of the plankton. The mud of the deep sea is home to a vast array of mollusks, crustaceans, and other small creatures that subsist on the fragments of wood and dead animals that drift down from the lighted areas above, and on each other.

The truth is that we need invertebrates but they don't need us. If human beings were to disappear tomorrow, the world would go on with little change. Gaia, the totality of life on Earth, would set about healing itself and return to the rich environmental states of a few thousand years ago. But if invertebrates were to disappear, I doubt that the human species could last more than a few months. Most of the fishes, amphibians, birds, and mammals would crash to extinction about the same time. Next would go the bulk of the flowering plants and with them the physical structure of the majority of the forests and other terrestrial habitats of the world. The earth would rot. As dead vegetation piled up and dried out, narrowing and closing the channels of the nutrient cycles, other complex forms of vegetation would die off, and with them the last remnants of the vertebrates. The remaining fungi, after enjoying a population explosion of stupendous proportions, would also perish. Within a few decades the world would return to the state of a billion years ago, composed primarily of bacteria, algae, and a few other very simple multicellular plants.

If humanity depends so completely on these little creatures that run the earth, they also provide us with an endless source of scientific exploration and naturalistic wonder. When you scoop up a double handful of earth almost anywhere except the most barren deserts, you will find thousands of invertebrate animals, ranging in size from clearly visible to microscopic, from ants and springtails to tardigrades and rotifers. The biology of most of the species you hold is unknown: we have only the vaguest idea of what they eat, what eats them, and the details of their life cycle, and probably nothing at all about their biochemistry and genetics. Some of the species might even lack scientific names. We have little concept of how important any of them are to our existence. Their study would certainly teach us new principles of science to the benefit of humanity. Each one is fascinating in its own right. If human beings were not so impressed by size alone, they would consider an ant more wonderful than a rhinoceros.

New emphasis should be placed on the conservation of invertebrates. Their staggering abundance and diversity should not lead us to think that they are indestructible. On the contrary, their species are just as subject to extinction due to human interference as are those of birds and mammals. When a valley in Peru or an island in the Pacific is stripped of the last of its native vegetation, the result is likely to be the extinction of several kinds of birds and some dozen of plant species. Of that tragedy we are painfully aware, but what is not perceived is that hundreds of invertebrate species will also vanish.

The conservation movement is at last beginning to take recognition of the potential loss of invertebrate diversity. The International Union for the Conservation of Nature has an ongoing invertebrate program that has already published a Red Data Book of threatened and endangered species—although this catalog is obviously still woefully incomplete. The Xerces Society, named after an extinct California butterfly, was created in 1971 to further the protection of butterflies and other inver-

tebrates. These two programs are designed to complement the much larger organized efforts of other organizations on behalf of vertebrates and plants. They will help to expand programs to encompass entire ecosystems instead of just selected star species. The new invertebrate exhibition of the National Zoological Park is one of the most promising means for raising public appreciation of invertebrates, and I hope such exhibits will come routinely to include rare and endangered species identified prominently as such.

Several themes can be profitably pursued in the new field of invertebrate conservation:

- It needs to be repeatedly stressed that invertebrates as a whole are even more important in the maintenance of ecosystems than are vertebrates.

- Reserves for invertebrate conservation are practicable and relatively inexpensive. Many species can be maintained in large, breeding populations in areas too small to sustain viable populations of vertebrates. A 10-ha plot is likely to be enough to sustain a butterfly or crustacean species indefinitely. The same is true for at least some plant species. Consequently, even if just a tiny remnant of natural habitat exists, and its native vertebrates have vanished, it is still worth setting aside for the plants and invertebrates it will save.

- The *ex situ* preservation of invertebrate species is also very cost-effective. A single pair of rare mammals typically costs hundreds or thousands of dollars yearly to maintain in a zoo (and worth every penny!). At the same time, large numbers of beautiful tree snails, butterflies, and other endangered invertebrates can be cultured in the laboratory, often in conjunction with public exhibits and educational programs, for the same price.

- It will be useful to concentrate biological research and public education on star species when these are available in threatened habitats, in the manner that has proved so successful in vertebrate conservation. Examples of such species include the tree snails of Moorea, Hawaii, and the Florida Keys; the Prairie sphinx moth of the Central States; the birdwing butterflies of New Guinea; and the metallic blue and golden ants of Cuba.

- We need to launch a major effort to measure biodiversity, to create a complete inventory of all the species of organisms on Earth, and to assess their importance for the environment and humanity. Our museums, zoological parks, and arboreta deserve far more support than they are getting—for the future of our children.

A hundred years ago few people thought of saving any kind of animal or plant. The circle of concern has expanded steadily since, and it is just now beginning to encompass the invertebrates. For reasons that have to do with almost every facet of human welfare, we should welcome this new development.

Kneeling at the pipes

Marge Piercy

Princely cockroach, inheritor,
I used to stain the kitchen wall with your
    brothers,
flood you right down the basin.
I squashed you underfoot, making faces.
I repent.
I am relieved to hear somebody
will survive our noises.
Thoughtlessly I judged you dirty
while dropping poisons and freeways
    and bombs

on the melted landscape.
I want to bribe you
to memorize certain poems.
My generation too craves posterity.
Accept this dish of well aged meat.
In the warrens of our rotting cities
where those small eggs
round as earth wait,
spread the Word.

The Land Ethic

Aldo Leopold

When god-like Odysseus returned from the wars in Troy, he hanged all on one rope a dozen slave-girls of his household whom he suspected of misbehavior during his absence.

This hanging involved no question of propriety. The girls were property. The disposal of property was then, as now, a matter of expediency, not of right and wrong.

Concepts of right and wrong were not lacking from Odysseus' Greece: witness the fidelity of his wife through the long years before at last his black-prowed galleys clove the wine-dark seas for home. The ethical structure of that day covered wives, but had not yet been extended to human chattels. Dur-

ing the three thousand years which have since elapsed, ethical criteria have been extended to many fields of conduct, with corresponding shrinkages in those judged by expediency only.

The Ethical Sequence

This extension of ethics, so far studied only by philosophers, is actually a process in ecological evolution. Its sequences may be described in ecological as well as in philosophical terms. An ethic, ecologically, is a limitation on freedom of action in the struggle for existence. An ethic, philosophically, is a differentiation of social from anti-social conduct.

These are two definitions of one thing. The thing has its origin in the tendency of interdependent individuals or groups to evolve modes of co-operation. The ecologist calls these symbioses. Politics and economics are advanced symbioses in which the original free-for-all competition has been replaced, in part, by cooperative mechanisms with an ethical content.

The complexity of cooperative mechanisms has increased with population density, and with the efficiency of tools. It was simpler, for example, to define the anti-social uses of sticks and stones in the days of the mastodons than of bullets and billboards in the age of motors.

The first ethics dealt with the relation between individuals; the Mosaic Decalogue is an example. Later accretions dealt with the relation between the individual and society. The Golden Rule tries to integrate the individual to society; democracy to integrate social organization to the individual.

There is as yet no ethic dealing with man's relation to land and to the animals and plants which grow upon it. Land, like Odysseus' slave girls, is still property. The land-relation is still strictly economic, entailing privileges but not obligations.

The extension of ethics to this third element in human environment is, if I read the evidence correctly, an evolutionary possibility and an ecological necessity. It is the third step in a sequence. The first two have already been taken. Individual thinkers since the days of Ezekiel and Isaiah have asserted that the despoliation of land is not only inexpedient but wrong. Society, however, has not yet affirmed their belief. I regard the present conservation movement as the embryo of such an affirmation.

An ethic may be regarded as a mode of guidance for meeting ecological situations so new or intricate, or involving such deferred reactions, that the path of social expediency is not discernible to the average individual. Animal instincts are modes of guidance for the individual in meeting such situations. Ethics are possibly a kind of community instinct in-the-making.

The Community Concept

All ethics so far evolved rest upon a single premise: that the individual is a member of a community of interdependent parts. His instincts prompt him to compete for his place in the community, but his ethics prompt him also to co-operate (perhaps in order that there may be a place to compete for).

The land ethic simply enlarges the boundaries of the community to include soils, waters, plants, and animals, or collectively: the land.

This sounds simple: do we not already sing our love for and obligation to the land of the free and the home of the brave? Yes, but just what and whom do we love? Certainly not the soil, which we are sending helter-skelter down river. Certainly not the waters, which we assume have no function except to turn turbines, float barges, and carry off sewage. Certainly not the plants, of which we exterminate whole communities without batting an eye. Certainly not the animals, of which we have already extirpated many of the largest and most beautiful species. A land ethic of course cannot prevent the alteration, management, and use of these "resources," but it does affirm their right to continued existence, and, at least in spots, their continued existence in a natural state.

In short, a land ethic changes the role of *Homo sapiens* from conqueror of the land-community to plain member and citizen of it. It implies respect for his fellow-members, and also respect for the community as such.

In human history, we have learned (I hope) that the conqueror role is eventually self-defeating. Why? Because it is implicit in such a role that the conqueror knows, *ex cathedra,* just what makes the community clock tick, and just what and who is valuable, and what and who is worthless, in community life. It always turns out that he knows neither, and this is why his conquests eventually defeat themselves.

In the biotic community, a parallel situation exists. Abraham knew exactly what the land was for: it was to drip milk and honey into Abraham's mouth. At the present moment, the assurance with which we regard this assumption is inverse to the degree of our education.

The ordinary citizen today assumes that science knows what makes the community clock tick; the scientist is equally sure that he does not. He knows that the biotic mechanism is so complex that its workings may never be fully understood.

That man is, in fact, only a member of a biotic team is shown by an ecological interpretation of history. Many historical events, hitherto explained solely in terms of human enterprise, were actually biotic interactions between people and land. The characteristics of the land determined the facts quite as potently as the characteristics of the men who lived on it.

Consider, for example, the settlement of the Mississippi valley. In the years following the Revolution, three groups were contending for its control: the native Indian, the French and English traders, and the American settlers. Historians wonder what would have happened if the English at Detroit had thrown a little more weight into the Indian side of those tipsy scales which decided the outcome of the colonial migration into the cane-lands of Kentucky. It is time now to ponder the fact that the cane-lands, when subjected to the particular mixture of forces represented by the cow, plow, fire, and axe of the pioneer, became bluegrass. What if the plant succession inherent in this dark and bloody ground had, under the impact of these forces, given us some worthless sedge, shrub, or weed? Would Boone and Kenton have held out? Would there have been any overflow into Ohio, Indiana, Illinois, and Missouri? Any Louisiana Purchase? Any transcontinental union of new states? Any Civil War?

Kentucky was one sentence in the drama of history. We are commonly told what the human actors in this drama tried to do, but we are seldom told that their success, or the lack of it, hung in large degree on the reaction of particular soils to the impact of the particular forces exerted by their occupancy. In the case of Kentucky, we do not even know where the bluegrass came from—whether it is a native species, or a stowaway from Europe.

Contrast the cane-lands with what hindsight tells us about the Southwest, where the pioneers were equally brave, resourceful, and persevering. The impact of occupancy here brought no bluegrass, or other plant fitted to withstand the bumps and buffetings of hard use. This region, when grazed by livestock, reverted through a series of more and more worthless grasses, shrubs, and weeds to a condition of unstable equilibrium. Each recession of plant types bred erosion; each increment to erosion bred a further recession of plants. The result today is a progressive and mutual deterioration, not only of plants and soils, but of the animal community subsisting thereon. The early settlers did not expect this: on the ciénegas of New Mexico some even cut ditches to hasten it. So subtle has been its progress that few residents of the region are aware of it. It is quite invisible to the tourist who finds this wrecked landscape colorful and charming (as indeed it is, but it bears scant resemblance to what it was in 1848).

This same landscape was 'developed' once before, but with quite different results. The Pueblo Indians settled the Southwest in pre-Columbian times, but they happened *not* to be equipped with range livestock. Their civilization expired, but not because their land expired.

In India, regions devoid of any sod-forming grass have been settled, apparently without wrecking the land, by the simple expedient of carrying the grass to the cow, rather than vice versa. (Was this the result of some deep wisdom, or was it just good luck? I do not know.)

In short, the plant succession steered the course of history; the pioneer simply demonstrated, for good or ill, what successions inhered in the land. Is history taught in this spirit? It will be, once the concept of land as a community really penetrates our intellectual life.

The Ecological Conscience

Conservation is a state of harmony between men and land. Despite nearly a century of propaganda, conservation still proceeds at a snail's pace; progress still consists largely of letterhead pieties and convention oratory. On the back forty we still slip two steps backward for each forward stride.

The usual answer to this dilemma is "more conservation education." No one will debate this, but is it certain that only the *volume* of education needs stepping up? Is something lacking in the *content* as well?

It is difficult to give a fair summary of its content in brief form, but, as I understand it, the content is substantially this: obey the law, vote right, join some organizations, and practice what conservation is profitable on your own land; the government will do the rest.

Is not this formula too easy to accomplish anything worth-while? It defines no right or wrong, assigns no obligation, calls for no sacrifice, implies no change in the current philosophy of values. In respect of land-use, it urges only enlightened self-interest. Just how far will such education take us? An example will perhaps yield a partial answer.

By 1930 it had become clear to all except the ecologically blind that southwestern Wisconsin's topsoil was slipping seaward. In 1933 the farmers were told that if they would adopt certain remedial practices for five years, the public would donate CCC labor to install them, plus the necessary machinery and materials. The offer was widely accepted, but the practices were widely forgotten when the five-year contract period was up. The farmers continued only those practices that yielded an immediate and visible economic gain for themselves.

This led to the idea that maybe farmers would learn more quickly if they themselves wrote the rules. Accordingly the Wisconsin Legislature in 1937 passed the Soil Conservation District Law. This said to farmers, in effect: *We, the public, will furnish you free technical service and loan you specialized machinery, if you will write your own rules for land-use. Each county may write its own rules, and these will have the force of law.* Nearly all the counties promptly organized to accept the proffered help, but after a decade of operation, *no county has yet written a single rule.* There has been visible progress in such practices as strip-cropping, pasture renovation, and soil liming, but none in fencing woodlots against grazing, and none in excluding plow and cow from steep slopes. The farmers, in short, have selected those remedial practices which were profitable anyhow, and ignored those which were profitable to the community, but not clearly profitable to themselves.

When one asks why no rules have been written, one is told that the community is not yet ready to support them; education must precede rules. But the education actually in progress makes no mention of obligations to land over and above those dictated by self-interest. The net result is that we have more education but less soil, fewer healthy woods, and as many floods as in 1937.

The puzzling aspect of such situations is that the existence of obligations over and above self-interest is taken for granted in such rural community enterprises as the betterment of roads, schools, churches, and baseball teams. Their existence is not taken for granted, nor as yet seriously discussed, in bettering the behavior of the water that falls on the land, or in the preserving of the beauty or diversity of the farm landscape, Land-use ethics are still governed wholly by economic self-interest, just as social ethics were a century ago.

To sum up: we asked the farmer to do what he conveniently could to save his soil, and he has done just that, and only that. The farmer who clears the woods off a 75 per cent slope, turns his cows into the clearing, and dumps its rainfall, rocks, and soil into the community creek, is still (if otherwise decent) a respected member of society. If he puts lime on his fields and plants his crops on contour, he is still entitled to all the privileges and emoluments of his Soil Conservation District. The District is a beautiful piece of social machinery, but it is coughing along on two cylinders because we have been too timid, and too anxious for quick success, to tell the farmer the true magnitude of his obligations. Obligations have no meaning without conscience, and the problem we face is the extension of the social conscience from people to land.

No important change in ethics was ever accomplished without an internal change in our intellectual emphasis, loyalties, affections, and convictions. The proof that conservation has not yet touched these foundations of conduct lies in the fact that philosophy and religion have not yet heard of it. In our attempt to make conservation easy, we have made it trivial.

Substitutes for a Land Ethic

When the logic of history hungers for bread and we hand out a stone, we are at pains to explain how much the stone resembles bread. I now describe some of the stones which serve in lieu of a land ethic.

One basic weakness in a conservation system based wholly on economic motives is that most members of the land community have no economic value. Wildflowers and songbirds are examples. Of the 22,000 higher plants and animals native to Wisconsin, it is doubtful whether more than 5 per cent can be sold, fed, eaten, or otherwise put to economic use. Yet these creatures are members of the biotic community, and if (as I believe) its stability depends on its integrity, they are entitled to continuance.

When one of these non-economic categories is threatened, and if we happen to love it, we invent subterfuges to give it economic importance. At the beginning of the century songbirds were supposed to be disappearing. Ornithologists jumped to the rescue with some distinctly shaky evidence to the effect that insects would eat us up if birds failed to control them. The evidence had to be economic in order to be valid.

It is painful to read these circumlocutions today. We have no land ethic yet, but we have at least drawn nearer the point of admitting that birds should continue as a matter of biotic right, regardless of the presence or absence of economic advantage to us.

A parallel situation exists in respect of predatory mammals, raptorial birds, and fish-eating birds. Time was when biologists somewhat overworked the evidence that these creatures preserve the health of game by killing weaklings, or that they control rodents for the farmer, or that they prey only on "worthless" species. Here again, the evidence had to be economic in order to be valid. It is only in recent years that we hear the more honest argument that predators are members of the community, and that no special interest has the right to exterminate them for the sake of a benefit, real or fancied, to itself. Unfortunately this enlightened view is still in the talk stage. In the field the extermination of predators goes merrily on: witness the impending erasure of the timber wolf by fiat of Congress, the Conservation Bureaus, and many state legislatures.

Some species of trees have been "read out of the party" by economics-minded foresters because they grow too slowly, or have too low a sale value to pay as timber crops: white cedar, tamarack, cypress, beech, and hemlock are examples. In Europe, where forestry is ecologically more advanced, the non-commercial tree species are recognized as members of the native forest community, to be preserved as such, within reason. Moreover some (like beech) have been found to have a valuable function in building up soil fertility. The interdependence of the forest and its constituent tree species, ground flora, and fauna is taken for granted.

Lack of economic value is sometimes a character not only of species or groups, but of entire biotic communities: marshes, bogs, dunes, and "deserts" are examples. Our formula in such cases is to relegate their conservation to government as refuges, monuments, or parks. The difficulty is that these communities are usually interspersed with more valuable private lands; the government cannot possibly own or control such scattered parcels. The net effect is that we have relegated some of them to ultimate extinction over large areas. If the private owner were ecologically minded, he would be proud to be the custodian of a reasonable proportion of such areas, which add diversity and beauty to his farm and to his community.

In some instances, the assumed lack of profit in these "waste" areas has proved to be wrong, but only after most of them had been done away with. The present scramble to reflood muskrat marshes is a case in point.

There is a clear tendency in American conservation to relegate to government all necessary jobs that private landowners fail to perform. Government ownership, operation, subsidy, or regulation is now widely prevalent in forestry, range management, soil and watershed management, park and wilderness conservation, fisheries management, and migratory bird management, with more to come. Most of this growth in governmental conservation is proper and logical, some of it is inevitable. That I imply no disapproval of it is implicit in the fact that I have spent most of my life working for it. Nevertheless the question arises: What is the ultimate magnitude of the enterprise? Will the tax base carry its eventual ramifications? At what point will governmental conservation, like the mastodon, become handicapped by its own dimensions? The answer, if there is any, seems to be in a land ethic, or some other force which assigns more obligation to the private landowner.

Industrial landowners and users, especially lumbermen and stockmen, are inclined to wail long and loudly about the extension of government ownership and regulation to land, but (with notable exceptions) they show little disposition to develop the only visible alterative: the voluntary practice of conservation on their own lands.

When the private landowner is asked to perform some unprofitable act for the good of the community, he today assents only with outstretched palm. If the act costs him cash this is fair and proper, but when it costs only forethought, open-mindedness, or time, the issue is at least debatable. The overwhelming growth of land-use subsidies in recent years must be ascribed, in large part, to the government's own agencies for conservation education: the land bureaus, the agricultural colleges, and the extension services. As far as I can detect, no ethical obligation toward land is taught in these institutions.

To sum up: a system of conservation based solely on economic self-interest is hopelessly lopsided. It tends to ignore, and thus eventually to eliminate, many elements in the land community that lack commercial value, but that are (as far as we know) essential to its healthy functioning. It assumes, falsely, I think, that the economic parts of the biotic clock will function without the uneconomic parts. It tends to relegate to government many functions eventually too large, too complex, or too widely dispersed to be performed by government.

An ethical obligation on the part of the private owner is the only visible remedy for these situations.

The Land Pyramid

An ethic to supplement and guide the economic relation to land presupposes the existence of some mental image of land as a biotic mechanism. We can be ethical only in relation to something we can see, feel, understand, love, or otherwise have faith in.

The image commonly employed in conservation education is "the balance of nature." For reasons too lengthy to detail here, this figure of speech fails to describe accurately what little we know about the land mechanism. A much truer image is the one employed in ecology: the biotic pyramid. I shall first sketch the pyramid as a symbol of land, and later develop some of its implications in terms of land-use.

Plants absorb energy from the sun. This energy flows through a circuit called the biota, which may be represented by a pyramid consisting of layers. The bottom layer is the soil. A plant layer rests on the soil, an insect layer on the plants, a bird and rodent layer on the insects, and so on up through various animal groups to the apex layer, which consists of the larger carnivores.

The species of a layer are alike not in where they came from, or in what they look like, but rather in what they eat. Each successive layer depends on those below it for food and often for other services, and each in turn furnishes food and services to those above. Proceeding upward, each successive layer decreases in numerical abundance. Thus, for every carnivore there are hundreds of his prey, thousands of their prey, millions of insects, uncountable plants. The pyramidal form of the system reflects this numerical progression from apex to base. Man shares an intermediate layer with the bears, raccoons, and squirrels which eat both meat and vegetables.

The lines of dependency for food and other services are called food chains. Thus soil-oak-deer-Indian is a chain that has now been largely converted to soil-corn-cow-farmer. Each species, including ourselves, is a link in many chains. The deer eats a hundred plants other than oak, and the cow a hundred plants other than corn. Both, then, are links in a hundred chains. The pyramid is a tangle of chains so complex as to seem disorderly, yet the stability of the system proves it to be a highly organized structure. Its functioning depends on the cooperation and competition of its diverse parts.

In the beginning, the pyramid of life was low and squat; the food chains short and simple. Evolution has added layer after layer, link after link. Man is one of thousands of accretions to the height and complexity of the pyramid. Science has given us many doubts, but it has given us at least one certainty: the trend of evolution is to elaborate and diversify the biota.

Land, then, is not merely soil; it is a fountain of energy flowing through a circuit of soils, plants, and animals. Food chains are the living channels which conduct energy upward; death and decay return it to the soil. The circuit is not closed; some energy is dissipated in decay, some is added by absorption from the air, some is stored in soils, peats, and long-lived forests; but it is a sustained circuit, like a slowly augmented revolving fund of life. There is always a net loss by downhill wash, but this is normally small and offset by the decay of rocks. It is deposited in the ocean and, in the course of geological time, raised to form new lands and new pyramids.

The velocity and character of the upward flow of energy depend on the complex structure of the plant and animal community, much as the upward flow of sap in a tree depends on its complex cellular organization. Without this complexity, normal circulation would presumably not occur. Structure means the characteristic numbers, as well as the characteristic kinds and functions, of the component species. This interdependence between the complex structure of the land and its smooth functioning as an energy unit is one of its basic attributes.

When a change occurs in one part of the circuit, many other parts must adjust themselves to it. Change does not necessarily obstruct or divert the flow of energy; evolution is a long series of self-induced changes, the net result of which has been to elaborate the flow mechanism and to lengthen the circuit. Evolutionary changes, however, are usually slow and local. Man's invention of tools has enabled him to make changes of unprecedented violence, rapidity, and scope.

One change is in the composition of floras and faunas. The larger predators are lopped off the apex of the pyramid; food chains, for the first time in history, become shorter rather than longer. Domesticated species from other lands are substituted for wild ones, and wild ones are moved to new habitats. In this worldwide pooling of faunas and floras, some species get out of bounds as pests and diseases, others are extinguished. Such effects are seldom intended or foreseen; they represent unpredicted and often untraceable readjustments in the structure. Agricultural science is largely a race between the emergence of new pests and the emergence of new techniques for their control.

Another change touches the flow of energy through plants and animals and its return to the soil. Fertility is the ability of soil to receive, store, and release energy. Agriculture, by overdrafts on the soil, or by too radical a substitution of domestic for native species in the superstructure, may derange the channels of flow or deplete storage. Soils depleted of their storage, or of the organic matter which anchors it, wash away faster than they form. This is erosion.

Waters, like soil, are part of the energy circuit. Industry, by polluting waters or obstructing them with dams, may exclude the plants and animals necessary to keep energy in circulation.

Transportation brings about another basic change: the plants or animals grown in one region are now consumed and returned to the soil in another. Transportation taps the energy stored in rocks, and in the air, and uses it elsewhere; thus we fertilize the garden with nitrogen gleaned by the guano birds from the fishes of seas on the other side of the Equator. Thus the formerly localized and self-contained circuits are pooled on a world-wide scale.

The process of altering the pyramid for human occupation releases stored energy, and this often gives rise, during the pioneering period, to a deceptive exuberance of plant and animal life, both wild and tame. These releases of biotic capital tend to becloud or postpone the penalties of violence.

This thumbnail sketch of land as an energy circuit conveys three basic ideas:

1. That land is not merely soil.
2. That the native plant and animals kept the energy circuit open; others may or may not.
3. That man-made changes are of a different order than evolutionary changes, and have effects more comprehensive than is intended or foreseen.

These ideas, collectively, raise two basic issues: Can the land adjust itself to the new order? Can the desired alterations be accomplished with less violence?

Biotas seem to differ in their capacity to sustain violent conversion. Western Europe, for example, carries a far different pyramid than Caesar found there. Some large animals are lost; swampy forests have become meadows or plowland; many new plants and animals are introduced, some of which escape as pests; the remaining natives are greatly changed in distribution and abundance. Yet the soil is still there and, with the help of imported nutrients, still fertile; the waters flow normally; the new structure seems to function and to persist. There is no visible stoppage or derangement of the circuit.

Western Europe, then, has a resistant biota. Its inner processes are tough, elastic, resistant to strain. No matter how violent the alterations, the pyramid, so far, has developed some new *modus vivendi* which preserves its habitability for man, and for most of the other natives.

Japan seems to present another instance of radical conversion without disorganization.

Most other civilized regions, and some as yet barely touched by civilization, display various stages of disorganization, varying from initial symptoms to advanced wastage. In Asia Minor and North Africa diagnosis is confused by climatic changes, which may have been either the cause or the effect of advanced wastage. In the United States the degree of disorganization varies locally; it is worst in the Southwest, the Ozarks, and parts of the South, and least in New England and the Northwest. Better land-uses may still arrest it in the less advanced regions. In parts of Mexico, South America, South Africa, and Australia a violent and accelerating wastage is in progress, but I cannot assess the prospects.

This almost world-wide display of disorganization in the land seems to be similar to disease in an animal, except that it never culminates in complete disorganization or death. The land recovers, but at some reduced level of complexity, and with a reduced carrying capacity for people, plants, and animals. Many biotas currently regarded as 'lands of opportunity' are in fact already subsisting on exploitative agriculture, i.e. they have already exceeded their sustained carrying capacity. Most of South America is overpopulated in this sense.

In arid regions we attempt to offset the process of wastage by reclamation, but it is only too evident that the prospective longevity of reclamation projects is often short. In our own West, the best of them may not last a century.

The combined evidence of history and ecology seems to support one general deduction: the less violent the man-made changes, the greater the probability of successful readjustment in the pyramid. Violence, in turn, varies with human population density; a dense population requires a more violent conversion. In this respect, North America has a better chance for permanence than Europe, if she can contrive to limit her density.

This deduction runs counter to our current philosophy, which assumes that because a small increase in density enriched human life, that an indefinite increase will enrich it indefinitely. Ecology knows of no density relationship that holds for indefinitely wide limits. All gains from density are subject to a law of diminishing returns.

Whatever may be the equation for men and land, it is improbable that we as yet know all its terms. Recent discoveries in mineral and vitamin nutrition reveal unsuspected dependencies in the up-circuit: incredibly minute quantities of certain substances determine the value of soils to plants, of plants to animals. What of the down-circuit? What of the vanishing species, the preservation of which we now regard as an aesthetic luxury? They helped build the soil; in what unsuspected ways may they be essential to its maintenance? Professor Weaver proposes that we use prairie flowers to reflocculate the wasting soils of the dust bowl; who knows for what purpose cranes and condors, otters and grizzlies may some day be used?

Land Health
and the A-B Cleavage

A land ethic, then, reflects the existence of an ecological conscience, and this in turn reflects a con-

viction of individual responsibility for the health of the land. Health is the capacity of the land for self-renewal. Conservation is our effort to understand and preserve this capacity.

Conservationists are notorious for their dissensions. Superficially these seem to add up to mere confusion, but a more careful scrutiny reveals a single plane of cleavage common to many specialized fields. In each field one group (A) regards the land as soil, and its function as commodity-production; another group (B) regards the land as a biota, and its function as something broader. How much broader is admittedly in a state of doubt and confusion.

In my own field, forestry, group A is quite content to grow trees like cabbages, with cellulose as the basic forest commodity. It feels no inhibition against violence; its ideology is agronomic. Group B, on the other hand, sees forestry as fundamentally different from agronomy because it employs natural species, and manages a natural environment rather than creating an artificial one. Group B prefers natural reproduction on principle. It worries on biotic as well as economic grounds about the loss of species like chestnut, and the threatened loss of the white pines. It worries about a whole series of secondary forest functions: wildlife, recreation, watersheds, wilderness areas. To my mind, Group B feels the stirrings of an ecological conscience.

In the wildlife field, a parallel cleavage exists. For Group A the basic commodities are sport and meat; the yardsticks of production are ciphers of take in pheasants and trout. Artificial propagation is acceptable as a permanent as well as a temporary recourse—if its unit costs permit. Group B, on the other hand, worries about a whole series of biotic side issues. What is the cost in predators of producing a game crop? Should we have further recourse to exotics? How can management restore the shrinking species, like prairie grouse, already hopeless as shootable game? How can management restore the threatened rarities, like trumpeter swan and whooping crane? Can management principles be extended to wildflowers? Here again it is clear to me that we have the same A-B cleavage as in forestry.

In the larger field of agriculture I am less competent to speak, but there seem to be somewhat parallel cleavages. Scientific agriculture was actively developing before ecology was born, hence a slower penetration of ecological concepts might be expected. Moreover the farmer, by the very nature of his techniques, must modify the biota more radically than the forester or the wildlife manager. Nevertheless, there are many discontents in agriculture which seem to add up to a new vision of 'biotic farming.'

Perhaps the most important of these is the new evidence that poundage or tonnage is no measure of the food-value of farm crops; the products of fertile soil may be qualitatively as well as quantitatively superior. We can bolster poundage from depleted soils by pouring on imported fertility, but we are not necessarily bolstering food-value. The possible ultimate ramifications of this idea are so immense that I must leave their exposition to abler pens.

The discontent that labels itself 'organic farming,' while bearing some of the earmarks of a cult, is nevertheless biotic in its direction, particularly in its insistence on the importance of soil flora and fauna.

The ecological fundamentals of agriculture are just as poorly known to the public as in other fields of land-use. For example, few educated people realize that the marvelous advances in technique made during recent decades are improvements in the pump, rather than the well. Acre for acre, they have barely sufficed to offset the sinking level of fertility.

In all of these cleavages, we see repeated the same basic paradoxes: man the conqueror *versus* man the biotic citizen; science the sharpener of his sword *versus* science the searchlight on his universe; land the slave and servant *versus* land the collective organism. Robinson's injunction to Tristram may well be applied, at this juncture, to *Homo sapiens* as a species in geological time:

> Whether you will or not
> You are a King, Tristram, for you are one
> Of the time-tested few that leave the world,
> When they are gone, not the same place it was.
> Mark what you leave.

The Outlook

It is inconceivable to me that an ethical relation to land can exist without love, respect, and admiration for land, and a high regard for its value. By value, I of course mean something far broader than mere economic value; I mean value in the philosophical sense.

Perhaps the most serious obstacle impeding the evolution of a land ethic is the fact that our educational and economic system is headed away from, rather than toward, an intense consciousness of land. Your true modern is separated from the land by many middlemen, and by innumerable physical gadgets. He has no vital relation to it; to him it is the space between cities on which crops grow. Turn him loose for a day on the land, and if the spot does not happen to be a golf links or a "scenic" area, he is bored stiff. If crops could be raised by hydroponics instead of farming, it would suit him very well. Synthetic substitutes for wood, leather, wool, and other natural land products suit him better than the originals. In short, land is something he has "outgrown."

Almost equally serious as an obstacle to a land ethic is the attitude of the farmer for whom the land is still an adversary, or a taskmaster that keeps him in slavery. Theoretically, the mechanization of farming ought to cut the farmer's chains, but whether it really does is debatable.

One of the requisites for an ecological comprehension of land is an understanding of ecology, and this is by no means co-extensive with "education"; in fact, much higher education seems deliberately to avoid ecological concepts. An understanding of ecology does not necessarily originate in courses bearing ecological labels; it is quite as likely to be labeled geography, botany, agronomy, history, or economics. This is as it should be, but whatever the label, ecological training is scarce.

The case for a land ethic would appear hopeless but for the minority which is in obvious revolt against these "modern" trends.

The "key-log" which must be moved to release the evolutionary process for an ethic is simply this: quit thinking about decent land-use as solely an economic problem. Examine each question in terms of what is ethically and esthetically right, as well as what is economically expedient. A thing is right when it tends to preserve the integrity, stability, and beauty of the biotic community. It is wrong when it tends otherwise.

It of course goes without saying that economic feasibility limits the tether of what can or cannot be done for land. It always has and it always will. The fallacy the economic determinists have tied around our collective neck, and which we now need to cast off, is the belief that economics determines *all* land-use. This is simply not true. An innumerable host of actions and attitudes, comprising perhaps the bulk of all land relations, is determined by the land-users' tastes and predilections, rather than by his purse. The bulk of all land relations hinges on investments of time, forethought, skill, and faith rather than on investments of cash. As a land-user thinketh, so is he.

I have purposely presented the land ethic as a product of social evolution because nothing so important as an ethic is ever "written." Only the most superficial student of history supposes that Moses "wrote" the Decalogue; it evolved in the minds of a thinking community, and Moses wrote a tentative summary of it for a "seminar." I say tentative because evolution never stops.

The evolution of a land ethic is an intellectual as well as emotional process. Conservation is paved with good intentions which prove to be futile, or even dangerous, because they are devoid of critical understanding either of the land, or of economic land-use. I think it is a truism that as the ethical frontier advances from the individual to the community, its intellectual content increases.

The mechanism of operation is the same for any ethic: social approbation for right actions: social disapproval for wrong actions.

By and large, our present problem is one of attitudes and implements. We are remodeling the Alhambra with a steam-shovel, and we are proud of our yardage. We shall hardly relinquish the shovel, which after all has many good points, but we are in need of gentler and more objective criteria for its successful use.

The Conceptual Foundations of the Land Ethic

J. Baird Callicott

As Wallace Stegner observes, *A Sand County Almanac* is considered "almost a holy book in conservation circles," and Aldo Leopold a prophet, "an American Isaiah." And as Curt Meine points out, "The Land Ethic" is the climactic essay of *Sand County*, "the upshot of 'The Upshot.'"[1] One might, therefore, fairly say that the recommendation and justification of moral obligations on the part of people to nature is what the prophetic *A Sand County Almanac* is all about. . . .

Here I first examine and elaborate the compactly expressed abstract elements of the land ethic and expose the "logic" which binds them into a proper, but revolutionary, moral theory. I then discuss the controversial features of the land ethic and defend them against actual and potential criticism. I hope to show that the land ethic cannot be ignored as merely the groundless emotive exhortations of a moonstruck conservationist or dismissed as entailing wildly untoward practical consequences. It poses, rather, a serious intellectual challenge to business-as-usual moral philosophy.

"The Land Ethic" opens with a charming and poetic evocation of Homer's Greece, the point of which is to suggest that today land is just as routinely and remorsely enslaved as human beings then were. A panoramic glance backward to our most distant cultural origins, Leopold suggests, reveals a slow but steady moral development over three millennia. More of our relationships and activities ("fields of conduct") have fallen under the aegis of moral principles ("ethical criteria") as civilization has grown and matured. If moral growth and development continue, as not only a synoptic review of history, but recent past experience suggest that it will, future generations will censure today's casual and universal environmental bondage as today we censure the casual and universal human bondage of three thousand years ago.

A cynically inclined critic might scoff at Leopold's sanguine portrayal of human history. Slavery survived as an institution in the "civilized" West, more particularly in the morally self-congratulatory United States, until a mere genera-

Companion to A Sand County Almanac: Interpretive and Critical Essays, edited by J. Baird Callicott. Madison: University of Wisconsin Press, 1987, pp. 186–214. Reprinted by permission.

tion before Leopold's own birth. And Western history from imperial Athens and Rome to the Spanish Inquisition and the Third Reich has been a disgraceful series of wars, persecutions, tyrannies, pogroms, and other atrocities.

The history of moral practice, however, is not identical with the history of moral consciousness. Morality is not descriptive; it is prescriptive or normative. In light of this distinction, it is clear that today, despite rising rates of violent crime in the United States and institutional abuses of human rights in Iran, Chile, Ethiopia, Guatemala, South Africa, and many other places, and despite persistent organized social injustice and oppression in still others, moral consciousness is expanding more rapidly now than ever before. Civil rights, human rights, women's liberation, children's liberation, animal liberation, etc., all indicate, as expressions of newly emergent moral ideals, that ethical consciousness (as distinct from practice) has if anything recently accelerated—thus confirming Leopold's historical observation.

Leopold next points out that "this extension of ethics, so far studied only by philosophers"—and therefore, the implication is clear, not very satisfactorily studied—"is actually a process in ecological evolution" (202).* What Leopold is saying here, simply, is that we may understand the history of ethics, fancifully alluded to by means of the Odysseus vignette, in biological as well as philosophical terms. From a biological point of view, an ethic is "a limitation on freedom of action in the struggle for existence" (202).

I had this passage in mind when I remarked that Leopold manages to convey a whole network of ideas in a couple of phrases. The phrase "struggle for existence" unmistakably calls to mind Darwinian evolution as the conceptual context in which a biological account of the origin and development of ethics must ultimately be located. And at once it points up a paradox: Given the unremitting competitive "struggle for existence" how could

"limitations on freedom of action" ever have been conserved and spread through a population of *Homo sapiens* or their evolutionary progenitors?

For a biological account of ethics, as Harvard social entomologist Edward O. Wilson has recently written, "the central theoretical problem . . . [is] how can altruism [elaborately articulated as morality or ethics in the human species], which by definition reduces personal fitness, possibly evolve by natural selection?"[2] According to modern sociobiology, the answer lies in kinship. But according to Darwin—who had tackled this problem himself "exclusively from the side of natural history" in *The Descent of Man*—the answer lies in society.[3] And it was Darwin's classical account (and its divers variations), from the side of natural history, which informed Leopold's thinking in the late 1940s.

Let me put the problem in perspective. How, we are asking, did ethics originate and, once in existence, grow in scope and complexity?

The oldest answer in living human memory is theological. God (or the gods) imposes morality on people. And God (or the gods) sanctions it. . . .

Western philosophy, on the other hand, is almost unanimous in the opinion that the origin of ethics in human experience has somehow to do with human reason. . . .

An evolutionary natural historian, however, cannot be satisfied with either of these general accounts of the origin and development of ethics. The idea that God gave morals to man is ruled out in principle—as any supernatural explanation of a natural phenomenon is ruled out in principle in natural science. And while morality might *in principle* be a function of human reason (as, say, mathematical calculation clearly is), to suppose that it is so *in fact* would be to put the cart before the horse. Reason appears to be a delicate, variable, and recently emerged faculty. It cannot, under any circumstances, be supposed to have evolved in the absence of complex linguistic capabilities which depend, in turn, for their evolution upon a highly developed social matrix. But we cannot have become social beings unless we assumed limitations on freedom of action in the struggle for existence. Hence we must have become ethical before we became rational.

Darwin, probably in consequence of reflections somewhat like these, turned to a minority tradition of modern philosophy for a moral psychology con-

* Page references are to Aldo Leopold's *A Sand County Almanac with Sketches Here and There* (New York: Oxford University Press, 1949).

sistent with and useful to a general evolutionary account of ethical phenomena. A century earlier, Scottish philosophers David Hume and Adam Smith had argued that ethics rest upon feelings or "sentiments"—which, to be sure, may be both amplified and informed by reason.[4] And since in the animal kingdom feelings or sentiments are arguably far more common or widespread than reason, they would be a far more likely starting point for an evolutionary account of the origin and growth of ethics.

Darwin's account, to which Leopold unmistakably (if elliptically) alludes in "The Land Ethic," begins with the parental and filial affections common, perhaps, to all mammals.[5] Bonds of affection and sympathy between parents and offspring permitted the formation of small, closely kin social groups, Darwin argued. Should the parental and filial affections bonding family members chance to extend to less closely related individuals, that would permit an enlargement of the family group. And should the newly extended community more successfully defend itself and/or more efficiently provision itself, the inclusive fitness of its members severally would be increased, Darwin reasoned. Thus, the more diffuse familial affections, which Darwin (echoing Hume and Smith) calls the "social sentiments," would be spread throughout a population.[6]

Morality, properly speaking—i.e., morality as opposed to mere altruistic instinct—requires, in Darwin's terms, "intellectual powers" sufficient to recall the past and imagine the future, "the power of language" sufficient to express "common opinion," and "habituation" to patterns of behavior deemed, by common opinion, to be socially acceptable and beneficial.[7] Even so, ethics proper, in Darwin's account, remains firmly rooted in moral feelings or social sentiments which were—no less than physical faculties, he expressly avers—naturally selected, by the advantages for survival and especially for successful reproduction, afforded by society.[8]

The protosociobiological perspective on ethical phenomena, to which Leopold as a natural historian was heir, leads him to a generalization which is remarkably explicit in his condensed and often merely resonant rendering of Darwin's more deliberate and extended paradigm: Since "the thing [ethics] has its origin in the tendency of interdependent individuals or groups to evolve modes of cooperation, . . . all ethics so far evolved rest upon a single premise: that the individual is a member of a community of interdependent parts" (202–3).

Hence, we may expect to find that the scope and specific content of ethics will reflect both the perceived boundaries and actual structure or organization of a cooperative community or society. *Ethics and society or community are correlative.* This single, simple principle constitutes a powerful tool for the analysis of moral natural history, for the anticipation of future moral development (including, ultimately, the land ethic), and for systematically deriving the specific precepts, the prescriptions and proscriptions, of an emergent and culturally unprecedented ethic like a land or environmental ethic.

Anthropological studies of ethics reveal that in fact the boundaries of the moral community are generally coextensive with the perceived boundaries of society.[9] And the peculiar (and, from the urbane point of view, sometimes inverted) representation of virtue and vice in tribal society—the virtue, for example, of sharing to the point of personal destitution and the vice of privacy and private property—reflects and fosters the life way of tribal peoples.[10] Darwin, in his leisurely, anecdotal discussion, paints a vivid picture of the intensity, peculiarity, and sharp circumscription of "savage" mores: "A savage will risk his life to save that of a member of the same community, but will be wholly indifferent about a stranger."[11] As Darwin portrays them, tribespeople are at once paragons of virtue "within the limits of the same tribe" and enthusiastic thieves, manslaughterers, and torturers without.[12]

For purposes of more effective defense against common enemies, or because of increased population density, or in response to innovations in subsistence methods and technologies, or for some mix of these or other forces, human societies have grown in extent or scope and changed in form or structure. Nations—like the Iroquois nation or the Sioux nation—came into being upon the merger of previously separate an mutually hostile tribes. Animals and plants were domesticated and erstwhile hunter-gatherers became herders and farmers. Permanent habitations were established. Trade, craft, and (later) industry flourished. With each change in society came corresponding and correlative changes in ethics. The moral community expanded to become coextensive with the newly drawn boundaries of societies and the representation of virtue and vice, right and wrong, good and evil, changed to accommodate, foster, and preserve the economic and institutional organization of emergent social orders. . . .

Most educated people today pay lip service at least to the ethical precept that all members of the human species, regardless of race, creed, or national origin, are endowed with certain fundamental rights which it is wrong not to respect. According to the evolutionary scenario set out by Darwin, the contemporary moral ideal of human rights is a response to a perception—however vague and indefinite—that mankind worldwide is united into one society, one community—however indeterminate or yet institutionally unorganized. As Darwin presciently wrote:

> As man advances in civilization, and small tribes are united into larger communities, the simplest reason would tell each individual that he ought to extend his social instincts and sympathies to all the members of the same nation, though personally unknown to him. This point being once reached, there is only an artificial barrier to prevent his sympathies extending to the men of all nations and races. If, indeed, such men are separated from him by great differences of appearance or habits, experience unfortunately shows us how long it is, before we look at them as our fellow-creatures.[13]

According to Leopold, the next step in this sequence beyond the still incomplete ethic of universal humanity, a step that is clearly discernible on the horizon, is the land ethic. The "community concept" has, so far, propelled the development of ethics from the savage clan to the family of man. "The land ethic simply enlarges the boundary of the community to include soils, waters, plants, and animals, or collectively: the land" (204).

As the foreword to *Sand County* makes plain, the overarching thematic principle of the book is the inculcation of the idea—through narrative description, discursive exposition, abstractive generalization, and occasional preachment—"that land is a community" (viii). The community concept is "the basic concept of ecology" (viii). Once land is popularly perceived as a biotic community—as it

is professionally perceived in ecology—a correlative land ethic will emerge in the collective cultural consciousness.

Although anticipated as far back as the mid-eighteenth century—in the notion of an "economy of nature"—the concept of the biotic community was more fully and deliberately developed as a working model or paradigm for ecology by Charles Elton in the 1920s.[14] The natural world is organized as an intricate corporate society in which plants and animals occupy "niches," or as Elton alternatively called them "roles" or "professions," in the economy of nature.[15] As in a feudal community, little or no socioeconomic mobility (upward or otherwise) exists in the biotic community. One is born to one's trade.

Human society, Leopold argues, is founded, in large part, upon mutual security and economic interdependency and preserved only by limitations on freedom of action in the struggle for existence—that is, by ethical constraints. Since the biotic community exhibits, as modern ecology reveals, an analogous structure, it too can be preserved, given the newly amplified impact of "mechanized man," only by analogous limitations on freedom of action—that is, by a land ethic (viii). A land ethic, furthermore, is not only "an ecological necessity," but an "evolutionary possibility" because a moral response to the natural environment—Darwin's social sympathies, sentiments, and instincts translated and codified into a body of principles and precepts—would be automatically triggered in human beings by ecology's social representation of nature (203).

Therefore, the key to the emergence of a land ethic is, simply, universal ecological literacy.

The land ethic rests upon three scientific cornerstones: (1) evolutionary and (2) ecological biology set in a background of (3) Copernican astronomy. Evolutionary theory provides the conceptual link between ethics and social organization and development. It provides a sense of "kinship with fellow-creatures" as well, "fellow-voyagers" with us in the "odyssey of evolution" (109). It establishes a diachronic link between people and nonhuman nature.

Ecological theory provides a synchronic link—the community concept—a sense of social integration of human and nonhuman nature. Human beings, plants, animals, soils, and waters are "all interlocked in one humming community of cooperations and competitions, one biota."[16] The simplest reason, to paraphrase Darwin, should, therefore, tell each individual that he or she ought to extend his or her social instincts and sympathies to all the members of the biotic community though different from him or her in appearance or habits.

And although Leopold never directly mentions it in *A Sand County Almanac*, the Copernican perspective, the perception of the Earth as "a small planet" in an immense and utterly hostile universe beyond, contributes, perhaps subconsciously, but nevertheless very powerfully, to our sense of kinship, community, and interdependence with fellow denizens of the Earth household. It scales the Earth down to something like a cozy island paradise in a desert ocean.

Here in outline, then, are the conceptual and logical foundations of the land ethic: Its conceptual elements are a Copernican cosmology, a Darwinian protosociobiological natural history of ethics, Darwinian ties of kinship among all forms of life on Earth, and an Eltonian model of the structure of biocenoses all overlaid on a Humean-Smithian moral psychology. Its logic is that natural selection has endowed human beings with an affective moral response to perceived bonds of kinship and community membership and identity; that today the natural environment, the land, is represented as a community, the biotic community; and that, therefore, an environmental or land ethic is both possible—the biopsychological and cognitive conditions are in place—and necessary, since human beings collectively have acquired the power to destroy the integrity, diversity, and stability of the environing and supporting economy of nature. In the remainder of this essay I discuss special features and problems of the land ethic germane to moral philosophy.

The most salient feature of Leopold's land ethic is its provision of what Kenneth Goodpaster has carefully called "moral considerability" for the biotic community per se, not just for fellow members of the biotic community:[17]

> In short, a land ethic changes the role of *Homo sapiens* from conqueror of the land-community to plain member and citizen of it. It implies respect for his fellow-

members, *and also respect for the community as such.* (204, emphasis added)

The land ethic, thus, has a holistic as well as an individualistic cast.

Indeed, as "The Land Ethic" develops, the focus of moral concern shifts gradually away from plants, animals, soils, and waters severally to the biotic community collectively. Toward the middle, in the subsection called Substitutes for a Land Ethic, Leopold invokes the "biotic rights" of *species*—as the context indicates—of wildflowers, songbirds, and predators. In The Outlook, the climactic section of "The Land Ethic," nonhuman natural entities, first appearing as fellow members, then considered in profile as species, are not so much as mentioned in what might be called the "summary moral maxim" of the land ethic: "A thing is right when it tends to preserve the integrity, stability, and beauty of the biotic community. It is wrong when it tends otherwise" (224–25).

By this measure of right and wrong, not only would it be wrong for a farmer, in the interest of higher profits, to clear the woods off a 75 percent slope, turn his cows into the clearing, and dump its rainfall, rocks, and soil into the community creek, it would also be wrong for the federal fish and wildlife agency, in the interest of individual animal welfare, to permit populations of deer, rabbits, feral burros, or whatever to increase unchecked and thus to threaten the integrity, stability, and beauty of the biotic communities of which they are members. The land ethic not only provides moral considerability for the biotic community per se, but ethical consideration of its individual members is preempted by concern for the preservation of the integrity, stability, and beauty of the biotic community. The land ethic, thus, not only has a holistic aspect; it is holistic with a vengeance.

The holism of the land ethic, more than any other feature, sets it apart from the predominant paradigm of modern moral philosophy. It is, therefore, the feature of the land ethic which requires the most patient theoretical analysis and the most sensitive practical interpretation.

As Kenneth Goodpaster pointed out, mainstream modern ethical philosophy has taken egoism as its point of departure and reached a wider circle of moral entitlement by a process of generalization:[18] I am sure that *I*, the enveloped ego, am intrinsically or inherently valuable and thus that *my* interests ought to be considered, taken into account, by "others" when their actions may substantively affect *me*. My own claim to moral consideration, according to the conventional wisdom, ultimately rests upon a psychological capacity—rationality or sentiency were the classical candidates of Kant and Bentham, respectively—which is arguably valuable in itself and which thus qualifies *me* for moral standing.[19] However, then I am forced grudgingly to grant the same moral consideration I demand from others, on this basis, to those others who can also claim to possess the same general psychological characteristic.

A *criterion* of moral value and consideration is thus identified. Goodpaster convincingly argues that mainstream modern moral theory is based, when all the learned dust has settled, on this simple paradigm of ethical justification and logic exemplified by the Benthamic and Kantian prototypes.[20] If the criterion of moral values and consideration is pitched low enough—as it is in Bentham's criterion of sentiency—a wide variety of animals are admitted to moral entitlement.[21] If the criterion of moral value and consideration is pushed lower still—as it is in Albert Schweitzer's reverence-for-life ethic—all minimally conative things (plants as well as animals) would be extended moral considerability.[22] The contemporary animal liberation/rights, and reverence-for-life/life-principle ethics are, at bottom, simply direct applications of the modern classical paradigm of moral argument. But this standard modern model of ethical theory provides no possibility whatever for the moral consideration of wholes—of threatened *populations* of animals and plants, or of endemic, rare, or endangered *species*, or of biotic *communities*, or most expansively, of the *biosphere* in its totality—since wholes per se have no psychological experience of any kind.[23] Because mainstream modern moral theory has been "psychocentric," it has been radically and intractably individualistic or "atomistic" in its fundamental theoretical orientation.

Hume, Smith, and Darwin diverged from the prevailing theoretical model by recognizing that altruism is as fundamental and autochthonous in human nature as is egoism. According to their analysis, moral value is not identified with a nat-

ural quality objectively present in morally considerable beings—as reason and/or sentiency is objectively present in people and/or animals—it is, as it were, projected by valuing subjects.[24]

Hume and Darwin, furthermore, recognize inborn moral sentiments which have society as such as their natural object. Hume insists that "we must renounce the theory which accounts for every moral sentiment by the principle of self-love. We must adopt a more *public affection* and allow that the *interests of society* are not, *even on their own account*, entirely indifferent to us."[25] And Darwin, somewhat ironically (since "Darwinian evolution" very often means natural selection operating exclusively with respect to individuals), sometimes writes as if morality had no other object than the commonweal, the welfare of the community as a corporate entity:

> We have now seen that actions are regarded by savages, and were probably so regarded by primeval man, as good or bad, solely as they obviously affect the welfare of the tribe,—not that of the species, nor that of the individual member of the tribe. This conclusion agrees well with the belief that the so-called moral sense is aboriginally derived from social instincts, for both relate at first exclusively to the community.[26]

Theoretically then, the biotic community owns what Leopold, in the lead paragraph of The Outlook, calls "value in the philosophical sense"—i.e., direct moral considerability—because it is a newly discovered proper object of a specially evolved "public affection" or "moral sense" which all psychologically normal human beings have inherited from a long line of ancestral social primates (223). . . .[27]

[T]he conceptual foundations of the land ethic provide a well-formed, self-consistent theoretical basis for including both fellow members of the biotic community and the biotic community itself (considered as a corporate entity) within the purview of morals. The preemptive emphasis, however, on the welfare of the community as a whole, in Leopold's articulation of the land ethic, while certainly *consistent* with its Humean-Darwinian theoretical foundations, is not *determined* by them alone. The overriding holism of the land ethic results, rather, more from the way our moral sensibilities are informed by ecology.

Ecological thought, historically, has tended to be holistic in outlook.[28] Ecology is the study of the *relationships* of organisms to one another and to the elemental environment. These relationships bind the *relata*—plants, animals, soils, and waters—into a seamless fabric. The ontological primacy of objects and the ontological subordination of relationships, characteristic of classical Western science, is, in fact, reversed in ecology.[29] Ecological relationships determine the nature of organisms rather than the other way around. A species is what it is because it has adapted to a niche in the ecosystem. The whole, the system itself, thus, literally and quite straightforwardly shapes and forms its component parts.

Antedating Charles Elton's community model of ecology was F. E. Clements' and S. A. Forbes' organism model.[30] Plants and animals, soils and waters, according to this paradigm, are integrated into one superorganism. Species are, as it were, its organs; specimens its cells. Although Elton's community paradigm (later modified, as we shall see, by Arthur Tansley's ecosystem idea) is the principal and morally fertile ecological concept of "The Land Ethic," the more radically holistic superorganism paradigm of Clements and Forbes resonates in "The Land Ethic" as an audible overtone. In the peroration of Land Health and the A-B Cleavage, for example, which immediately precedes The Outlook, Leopold insists that

> in all of these cleavages, we see repeated the same basic paradoxes: man the conqueror *versus* man the biotic citizen; science the sharpener of his sword *versus* science the searchlight on his universe; land the slave and servant *versus* land the collective organism. (223)

And on more than one occasion Leopold, in the latter quarter of "The Land Ethic," talks about the "health" and "disease" of the land—terms which are at once descriptive and normative and which, taken literally, characterize only organisms proper.

In an early essay, "Some Fundamentals of Conservation in the Southwest," Leopold speculatively flirted with the intensely holistic superorganism model of the environment as a paradigm pregnant with moral implications:

> It is at least not impossible to regard the earth's parts—soil, mountains, rivers, atmosphere, etc.—as organs or parts of organs, of *a coordinated whole*, each part with a definite function. And if we could see *this whole, as a whole*, through a great period of time, we might perceive not only organs with coordinated functions, but possibly also that process of consumption and replacement which in biology we call metabolism, or growth. In such a case we would have all the visible attributes of a living thing, which we do not realize to be such because it is too big, and its life processes too slow. And there would also follow that invisible attribute —a soul or consciousness—which . . . many philosophers of all ages ascribe to all living things and aggregates thereof, including the "dead" earth.
>
> Possibly in our intuitive perceptions, which may be truer than our science and less impeded by words than our philosophies, we realize the indivisibility of the earth—its soil, mountains, rivers, forests, climate, plants, and animals—and *respect it collectively* not only as a useful servant but as a living being, vastly less alive than ourselves, but vastly greater than ourselves in time and space. . . . Philosophy, then, suggests one reason why we cannot destroy the earth with moral impunity; namely, that the "dead" earth is an organism possessing a certain kind and degree of life, which we intuitively respect as such.[31]

Had Leopold retained this overall theoretical approach in "The Land Ethic," the land ethic would doubtless have enjoyed more critical attention from philosophers. The moral foundations of a land or, as he might then have called it, "earth" ethic, would rest upon the hypothesis that the Earth is alive and ensouled—possessing inherent psychological characteristics, logically parallel to reason and sentiency. This notion of a conative whole Earth could plausibly have served as a general criterion of intrinsic worth and moral considerability, in the familiar format of mainstream moral thought.

Part of the reason, therefore, that "The Land Ethic" emphasizes more and more the integrity, stability, and beauty of the environment as a whole, and less and less the "biotic right" of individual plants and animals to life, liberty, and the pursuit of happiness, is that the superorganism ecological paradigm invites one, much more than does the community paradigm, to hypostatize, to reify the whole, and to subordinate its individual members.

In any case, as we see, rereading "The Land Ethic" in light of "Some Fundamentals," the whole Earth organism image of nature is vestigially present in Leopold's later thinking. Leopold may have abandoned the "earth ethic" because ecology had abandoned the organism analogy, in favor of the community analogy, as a working theoretical paradigm. And the community model was more suitably given moral implications by the social/sentimental ethical natural history of Hume and Darwin. . . .

The Land Pyramid is the pivotal section of "The Land Ethic"—the section which effects a complete transition from concern for "fellow-members" to the "community as such." It is also its longest and most technical section. A description of the "ecosystem" ([1935 British ecologist Arthur] Tansley's deliberately nonmetaphorical term) begins with the sun. Solar energy "flows through a circuit called the biota" (215). It enters the biota through the leaves of green plants and courses through plant-eating animals, and then on to omnivores and carnivores. At last the tiny fraction of solar energy converted to biomass by green plants remaining in the corpse of a predator, animal feces, plant detritus, or other dead organic material is garnered by decomposers—worms, fungi, and bacteria. They recycle the participating elements and degrade into entropic equilibrium any remaining energy. According to this paradigm

land, then, is not merely soil; it is a fountain of energy flowing through a circuit of

soils, plants, and animals. Food chains are the living channels which conduct energy upward; death and decay return it to the soil. The circuit is not closed; . . . but it is a sustained circuit, like a slowly augmented revolving fund of life. (216)

In this exceedingly abstract (albeit poetically expressed) model of nature, process precedes substance and energy is more fundamental than matter. Individual plants and animals become less autonomous beings than ephemeral structures in a patterned flux of energy. . . . The maintenance of "the complex structure of the land and its smooth functioning as an energy unit" emerges in The Land Pyramid as the *summum bonum* of the land ethic (216).

From this good Leopold derives several practical principles slightly less general, and therefore more substantive, than the summary moral maxim of the land ethic distilled in The Outlook. "The trend of evolution [not its "goal," since evolution is ateleological] is to elaborate and diversify the biota" (216). Hence, among our cardinal duties is the duty to preserve what species we can, especially those at the apex of the pyramid—the top carnivores. "In the beginning, the pyramid of life was low and squat; the food chains short and simple. Evolution has added layer after layer, link after link" (215–16). Human activities today, especially those, like systematic deforestation in the tropics, resulting in abrupt massive extinctions of species, are in effect "devolutionary"; they flatten the biotic pyramid; they choke off some of the channels and gorge others (those which terminate in our own species).[32]

The land ethic does not enshrine the ecological status quo and devalue the dynamic dimension of nature. Leopold explains that "evolution is a long series of self-induced changes, the net result of which has been to elaborate the flow mechanism and to lengthen the circuit. Evolutionary changes, however, are usually slow and local. Man's invention of tools has enabled him to make changes of unprecedented violence, rapidity, and scope" (216–17). "Natural" species extinction, i.e., species extinction in the normal course of evolution, occurs when a species is replaced by competitive exclusion or evolves into another form.[33] Normally speciation outpaces extinction. Mankind inherited a richer, more diverse world than had ever existed before in the 3.5 billion-year odyssey of life on Earth.[34] What is wrong with anthropogenic species extirpation and extinction is the *rate* at which it is occurring and the *result:* biological impoverishment instead of enrichment.

Leopold goes on here to condemn, in terms of its impact on the ecosystem, "the world-wide pooling of faunas and floras," i.e., the indiscriminate introduction of exotic and domestic species and the dislocation of native and endemic species; mining the soil for its stored biotic energy, leading ultimately to diminished fertility and to erosion; and polluting and damming water courses (217).

According to the land ethic, therefore: Thou shalt not extirpate or render species extinct; thou shalt exercise great caution in introducing exotic and domestic species into local ecosystems, in extracting energy from the soil and releasing it into the biota, and in damming or polluting water courses; and thou shalt be especially solicitous of predatory birds and mammals. Here in brief are the express moral precepts of the land ethic. They are all explicitly informed—not to say derived—from the energy circuit model of the environment.

The living channels—"food chains"—through which energy courses are composed of individual plants and animals. A central, stark fact lies at the heart of ecological processes: Energy, the currency of the economy nature, passes from one organism to another, not from hand to hand, like coined money, but, so to speak, from stomach to stomach. Eating *and being eaten,* living *and dying* are what make the biotic community hum.

The precepts of the land ethic, like those of all previous accretions, reflect and reinforce the structure of the community to which it is correlative. Trophic asymmetries constitute the kernel of the biotic community. It seems unjust, unfair. But that is how the economy of nature is organized (and has been for thousands of millions of years). The land ethic, thus, affirms as good, and strives to preserve, the very inequities in nature whose social counterparts in human communities are condemned as bad and would be eradicated by familiar social ethics, especially by the more recent Christian and secular egalitarian exemplars. A "right to life" for individual members is not consistent with the structure of the biotic community and hence is not mandated by the land ethic. This disparity between the land ethic and its more familiar social precedents contributes to the apparent devaluation of individual *members* of the biotic community and augments and reinforces the tendency of the land ethic, driven by the systemic vision of ecology, toward a more holistic or community-per-se orientation. . . .

Today, two processes internal to civilization are bringing us to a recognition that our renunciation of our biotic citizenship was a mistaken self-deception. Evolutionary science and ecological science, which certainly are products of modern civilization now supplanting the anthropomorphic and anthropocentric myths of earlier civilized generations, have rediscovered our integration with the biotic community. And the negative feedback received from modern civilization's technological impact upon nature—pollution, biological impoverishment, etc.—forcefully reminds us that mankind never really has, despite past assumptions to the contrary, existed apart from the environing biotic community.

This reminder of our recent rediscovery of our biotic citizenship brings us face to face with the paradox posed by Peter Fritzell:[35] Either we are plain members and citizens of the biotic community, on a par with other creatures, or we are not. If we are, then we have no moral obligations to our fellow members or to the community per se because, as understood from a modern scientific perspective, nature and natural phenomena are amoral. Wolves and alligators do no wrong in killing and eating deer and dogs (respectively). Elephants cannot be blamed for bulldozing acacia trees and generally wreaking havoc in their natural habitats. If human beings are natural beings, then human behavior, however destructive, is natural behavior and is as blameless, from a natural point of view, as any other behavioral phenomenon exhibited by other natural beings. On the other hand, we are moral beings, the implication seems clear, precisely to the extent that we are civilized, that we have removed ourselves from nature. We are more than natural beings; we arc metanatural—not to say, "supernatural"—beings. But then our moral community is limited to only those beings who share our transcendence of nature, i.e., to human beings (and perhaps to pets who have joined our civilized community as surrogate persons) and to the human community. Hence, have it either way—we are members of the biotic community or we are not—a land or environmental ethic is aborted by either choice.

But nature is *not* amoral. The tacit assumption that we are deliberating, choice-making ethical beings only to the extent that we are metanatural, civilized beings, generates this dilemma. The biosocial analysis of human moral behavior, in which the land ethic is grounded, is designed precisely to show that in fact intelligent moral behavior *is* natural behavior. Hence, we are moral beings not in spite of, but in accordance with, nature. To the extent that nature has produced at least one ethical species, *Homo sapiens*, nature is not amoral.

Alligators, wolves, and elephants are not subject to reciprocal interspecies duties or land ethical obligations themselves because they are incapable of conceiving and/or assuming them. Alligators, as mostly solitary, entrepreneurial reptiles, have no apparent moral sentiments or social instincts whatever. And while wolves and elephants certainly do have social instincts and at least protomoral sentiments, as their social behavior amply indicates, their conception or imagination of community appears to be less culturally plastic than ours and less amenable to cognitive information. Thus, while we might regard them as ethical beings, they are not able, as we are, to form the concept of a universal biotic community, and hence conceive an all-inclusive, holistic land ethic.

The paradox of the land ethic, elaborately noticed by Fritzell, may be cast more generally still in more conventional philosophical terms: Is the land ethic prudential or deontological? Is the land ethic, in other words, a matter of enlightened (collective, human) self-interest, or does it genuinely admit nonhuman natural entities and nature as a whole to true moral standing?

The conceptual foundations of the land ethic, as I have here set them out, and much of Leopold's hortatory rhetoric, would certainly indicate that the land ethic is deontological (or duty oriented) rather than prudential. In the section significantly titled The Ecological Conscience, Leopold complains that the then-current conservation philosophy is inadequate because "it defines no right or wrong, assigns no obligation, calls for no sacrifice, implies no change in the current philosophy of values. In

respect of land-use, it urges *only* enlightened self-interest" (207–8, emphasis added). Clearly, Leopold himself thinks that the land ethic goes beyond prudence. In this section he disparages mere "self-interest" two more times, and concludes that "obligations have no meaning without conscience, and the problem we face is the extension of the social conscience from people to land" (209).

In the next section, Substitutes for a Land Ethic, he mentions rights twice—the "biotic right" of birds to continuance and the absence of a right on the part of human special interest to exterminate predators.

Finally, the first sentences of The Outlook read: "It is inconceivable to me that an ethical relation to land can exist without love, respect, and admiration for land, and a high regard for its value. By value, I of course mean something far broader than mere economic value; I mean value in the philosophical sense" (223). By "value in the philosophical sense," Leopold can only mean what philosophers more technically call "intrinsic value" or "inherent worth."[36] Something that has intrinsic value or inherent worth is valuable in and of itself, not because of what it can do for us. "Obligation," "sacrifice," "conscience," "respect," the ascription of rights, and intrinsic value—all of these are consistently opposed to self-interest and seem to indicate decisively that the land ethic is of the deontological type.

Some philosophers, however, have seen it differently. Scott Lehmann, for example, writes,

> Although Leopold claims for communities of plants and animals a "right to continued existence," his argument is homocentric, appealing to the human stake in preservation. Basically it is an argument from enlightened self-interest, where the self in question is not an individual human being but humanity—present and future—as a whole. . . . [37]

Lehmann's claim has some merits, even though it flies in the face of Leopold's express commitments. Leopold does frequently lapse into the language of (collective, long-range, human) self-interest. Early on, for example, he remarks, "in human history, we have learned (I hope) that the conqueror role is eventually *self*-defeating" (204, emphasis added). And later, of the 95 percent of Wisconsin's species which cannot be "sold, fed, eaten, or otherwise put to economic use," Leopold reminds us that "these creatures are members of the biotic community, and if (as I believe) its stability depends on its integrity, they are entitled to continuance" (210). The implication is clear: the economic 5 percent cannot survive if a significant portion of the uneconomic 95 percent are extirpated; nor may *we*, it goes without saying, survive without these "resources."

Leopold, in fact, seems to be consciously aware of this moral paradox. Consistent with the biosocial foundations of his theory, he expresses it in sociobiological terms:

> An ethic may be regarded as a mode of guidance for meeting ecological situations so new or intricate, or involving such deferred reactions, that the path of social expediency is not discernible to the average individual. Animal instincts are modes of guidance for the individual in meeting such situations. Ethics are possibly a kind of community instinct-in-the-making. (203)

From an objective, descriptive sociobiological point of view, ethics evolve because they contribute to the inclusive fitness of their carriers (or, more reductively still, to the multiplication of their carriers' genes); they are expedient. However, the path to self-interest (or to the self-interest of the selfish gene) is not discernible to the participating individuals (nor, certainly, to their genes). Hence, ethics are grounded in instinctive feeling—love, sympathy, respect—not in self-conscious calculating intelligence. Somewhat like the paradox of hedonism—the notion that one cannot achieve happiness if one directly pursues happiness per se and not other things—one can only secure self-interest by putting the interests of others on a par with one's own (in this case long-range collective human self-interest and the interest of other forms of life and of the biotic community per se).

So, is the land ethic deontological or prudential, after all? It is both—self-consistently both—depending upon point of view. From the inside, from the lived, felt point of view of the community member with evolved moral sensibilities, it is deontological. It involves an affective-cognitive posture of genuine love, respect, admiration, obligation, self-sacrifice, conscience, duty, and the ascription of intrinsic value and biotic rights. From the outside, from the objective and analytic scientific point of view, it is prudential. "There is no other way for land to survive the impact of mechanized man," nor, therefore, for mechanized man to survive his own impact upon the land (viii).

Notes

1. Wallace Stegner, "The Legacy of Aldo Leopold"; Curt Meine, "Building 'The Land Ethic.'" The oft-repeated characterization of Leopold as a prophet appears traceable to Roberts Mann, "Aldo Leopold: Priest and Prophet," *American Forests* 60, no. 8 (August 1954): 23, 42–43; it was picked up, apparently, by Ernest Swift, "Aldo Leopold: Wisconsin's Conservationist Prophet," *Wisconsin Tales and Trails* 2, no. 2 (September 1961): 2–5; Roderick Nash institutionalized it in his chapter, "Aldo Leopold: Prophet," in *Wilderness and the American Mind* (New Haven: Yale University Press, 1967; revised edition, 1982).

2. Edward O. Wilson, *Sociobiology: The New Synthesis* (Cambridge: Harvard University Press, 1975), 3. See also W. D. Hamilton, "The Genetical Theory of Social Behavior," *Journal of Theoretical Biology* 7 (1964): 1–52.

3. Charles R. Darwin, *The Descent of Man and Selection in Relation to Sex* (New York: J. A. Hill and Company, 1904). The quoted phrase occurs on p. 97.

4. See Adam Smith, *Theory of the Moral Sentiments* (London and Edinburgh: A Millar, A. Kinkaid, and J. Bell, 1759) and David Hume, *An Enquiry Concerning the Principles of Morals* (Oxford: The Clarendon Press, 1777; first published in 1751). Darwin cites both works in the key fourth chapter of *Descent* (pp. 106 and 109, respectively).

5. Darwin, *Descent*, 98ff.

6. Ibid., 105f.

7. Ibid., 113ff.

8. Ibid., 105.

9. See, for example, Elman R. Service, *Primitive Social Organization: An Evolutionary Perspective* (New York: Random House, 1962).

10. See Marshall Sahlins, *Stone Age Economics* (Chicago: Aldine Atherton, 1972).

11. Darwin, *Descent*, 111.

12. Ibid., 117ff. The quoted phrase occurs on p. 118.

13. Ibid., 124.

14. See Donald Worster, *Nature's Economy: The Roots of Ecology* (San Francisco: Sierra Club Books, 1977).

15. Charles Elton, *Animal Ecology* (New York: Macmillan, 1927).

16. Aldo Leopold, *Round River* (New York: Oxford University Press, 1953), 148.

17. Kenneth Goodpaster, "On Being Morally Considerable," *Journal of Philosophy* 22 (1978): 308–25. Goodpaster wisely avoids the term *rights*, defined so strictly albeit so variously by philosophers, and used so loosely by nonphilosophers.

18. Kenneth Goodpaster, "From Egoism to Environmentalism" in *Ethics and Problems of the 21st Century*, ed. K. E. Goodpaster and K. M. Sayre (Notre Dame, Ind.: University of Notre Dame Press, 1979), 21–35.

19. See Immanuel Kant, *Foundations of the Metaphysics of Morals* (New York: Bobbs-Merrill, 1959; first published in 1785); and Jeremy Bentham, *An Introduction to the Principles of Morals and Legislation*, new edition (Oxford: The Clarendon Press, 1823).

20. Goodpaster, "Egoism to Environmentalism." Actually Goodpaster regards *Hume* and Kant as the cofountainheads of this sort of moral philosophy. But Hume does not reason in this way. For Hume, the other-oriented sentiments are as primitive as self-love.

21. See Peter Singer, *Animal Liberation: A New Ethics for Our Treatment of Animals* (New York: Avon Books, 1975) for animal liberation; and see Tom Regan, *All That Dwell Therein: Animal Rights and Environmental Ethics* (Berkeley: University of California Press, 1982) for animal rights.

22. See Albert Schweitzer, *Philosophy of Civilization: Civilization and Ethics*, trans. John Naish (London: A. & C. Black, 1923). For a fuller discussion see J. Baird Callicott, "On the Intrinsic Value of Nonhuman Species," in *The Preservation of Species*, ed. Bryan Norton (Princeton: Princeton University Press, 1986), 138–72.

23. Peter Singer and Tom Regan are both proud of this circumstance and consider it a virtue. See Peter Singer, "Not for Humans Only: The Place of Nonhumans in Environmental Issues" in *Ethics and Problems of the 21st Century*, 191–206; and Tom Regan, "Ethical Vegetarianism and Commercial Animal Farming" in *Contemporary Moral Problems*, ed. James E. White (St. Paul, Minn.: West Publishing Co., 1985), 279–94.

24. See J. Baird Callicott, "Hume's Is/Ought Dichotomy and the Relation of Ecology to Leopold's Land Ethic," *Environmental Ethics* 4 (1982): 163–74, and "Non-anthropocentric Value Theory and Environmental Ethics," *American Philosophical Quarterly* 21 (1984): 299–309, for an elaboration.

25. Hume, *Enquiry*, 219.

26. Darwin, *Descent*, 120.

27. I have elsewhere argued that "value in the philosophical sense" means "intrinsic" or "inherent" value. See J. Baird Callicott, "The Philosophical Value of Wildlife," in *Valuing of Wildlife: Economic and Social Values of Wildlife*, ed. Daniel J. Decker and Gary Goff (Boulder, Col.: Westview Press, 1986), 214–221.

28. See Worster, *Nature's Economy*.

29. See J. Baird Callicott, "The Metaphysical Implications of Ecology," *Environmental Ethics* 8 (1986): 300–315, for an elaboration of this point.

30. Robert P. McIntosh, *The Background of Ecology: Concept and Theory* (Cambridge: Cambridge University Press, 1985).

31. Aldo Leopold, "Some Fundamentals of Conservation in the Southwest," *Environmental Ethics* 1 (1979): 139–40, emphasis added.

32. I borrow the term "devolution" from Austin Meredith, "Devolution," *Journal of Theoretical Biology* 96 (1982): 49–65.

33. Holmes Rolston, III, "Duties to Endangered Species," *Bioscience* 35 (1985): 718–26. See also Geerat Vermeij, "The Biology of Human-Caused Extinction," in Norton, *Preservation of Species*, 28–49.

34. See D. M. Raup and J. J. Sepkoski, Jr., "Mass Extinctions in the Marine Fossil Record," *Science* 215 (1982): 1501–3.

35. Peter Fritzell, "The Conflicts of Ecological Conscience," in *Companion to A Sand County Almanac*, edited by J. Baird Callicott (Madison: University of Wisconsin Press, 1987).

36. See Worster, *Nature's Economy*.

37. Scott Lehmann, "Do Wildernesses Have Rights?" *Environmental Ethics* 3 (1981): 131.

B. COMPETING VISIONS ———————————————

E. B. White's *Charlotte's Web*, says Mark Sagoff, "... serves as an environmental parable for our time."[1]

> As we reflect on our relationship with nature, we might consider the three ways in which Wilbur the pig was valued in White's story. His instrumental value cashes out in ham hocks and sausage. His aesthetic value earns him a ribbon at the county fair. His moral value is the value he has in and of himself, and Charlotte the spider loves him for it. We can value nature the way Charlotte valued Wilbur, or we can, as the farmer Zuckerman did at first, see the natural world only in terms of the pork chops it provides.[2]

In a variety of policy contexts, Sagoff argues that the best environmental solutions to problems such as pollution and rain forest depletion stem from understanding the *intrinsic* value of nature rather than the *instrumental* value of nature, by which is meant "... valu[ing] the object itself rather than just the benefits it confers on us."[3] According to Sagoff, there are two forms of intrinsic value: aesthetic and moral.

It is Sagoff's thesis that we face, over and over again, Zuckerman's dilemma with respect to environmental questions. "What reasons have we to preserve biodiversity, protect rain forests, and maintain the quality of lakes, rivers, and estuaries? ... As we come to depend on nature less and less for instrumental reasons, we may recognize more and more the intrinsic reasons for preserving it."[4] For example, whales have lost their instrumental value, i.e., we no longer need them for whale oil to light oil lamps. Why, then, asks Sagoff, do so many people care about saving whales? "Are they concerned about maintaining a strategic reserve of blubber? ... No; as whales have lost their instrumental value, their aesthetic and moral worth has become all the more evident."[5]

In his discussion of pollution, Sagoff points to the ways in which arguments based on instrumental value can have surprising consequences. Biotechnology, for example, has developed fish that can withstand pollution as well as fish that do not migrate to polluted areas. Sagoff asserts: "It may not be efficient to regulate pollution to accommodate species. It may be cheaper to regulate species to accommodate pollution."[6] To opt here for inefficiency is in some sense to value nature for its own sake.

Biotechnologists have also developed stupid fish. This grand discovery allows human beings who pay to fish in some areas to go home happy with baskets of fish and a desire to return.[7] We can in many ways construct the world to serve the interests and preferences of human beings. Some see this as anthropocentrism of the worst sort. There are different forms of anthropocentrism, and it is important to sort them out. Bryan G. Norton does this in the second selection, "Environmental Ethics and Weak Anthropocentrism."

Norton proposes that there are two kinds of anthropocentrism: weak and strong. Strong anthropocentrism, which Norton opposes, is the view that only humans matter. William Baxter's "People or Penguins" in Part IVA is a good example of strong anthropocentrism and could have been included here to represent this theoretical position.[8] Baxter says, "Damage to penguins, or sugar pines, or geological marvels is ... simply irrelevant. ... Penguins are important because people enjoy seeing them walk about rocks. ..."[9] Assertions like this one tempt many to think that attributing intrinsic value to nature is the only way to construct an adequate environmental ethic. Norton identifies another alternative, which he calls weak anthropocentrism. Weak anthropocentrism, he argues, "... provides a basis for criticizing individual, consumptive needs and ... provid[es] an adequate basis for environmental ethics without the questionable ontological commitments made by nonanthropocentrists in attributing intrinsic value to nature."[10]

Part of Norton's objection to "ontological commitments" is not to ontology (the philosophical inquiry into the nature of being) per se, but to the focus of some philosophers who devote their attention to producing volumes about the correct theory of intrinsic value while species vanish, forests disappear, and pollution spreads. A similar plea for reordering priorities is seen in Anthony Weston's "Enabling Environmental Practice," in Part V, where he argues that a focus on environmental practice should take precedence over theory construction.

We turn now to *deep ecology*, which some would label as a striking example of a nonanthropocentric position. Others, such as social ecologist critic Murray Bookchin, as we shall see later, claim that deep ecology is misanthropic, i.e., shows a hatred of, or disregard for, human beings.

The term "deep ecology" was coined by the Norwegian philosopher Arne Naess in his "The Shallow and the Deep, Long-Range Ecology Movement. A Summary."[11] Deep ecology, in what Warwick Fox calls the "formal" sense, refers to a level of questioning that is fundamental. In an interview with Bill Devall and George Sessions, Naess states, "The essence of deep ecology is to ask deeper questions. The adjective 'deep' stresses that we ask why and how, where others do not."[12] Again, he maintains, " . . . the deep ecological movement tries to clarify the fundamental presuppositions underlying our economic approach in terms of value priorities, philosophy, religion. In the shallow movement, argument comes to halt long before this."[13] The deep/shallow distinction has come under fire as " . . . pejorative . . . smug, self-congratulatory, self-righteous, or holier-than-thou . . . [and] patronizing. . . . "[14] Nevertheless, neither Naess nor his followers (for the most part) have abandoned the phrase.

Presumably Fox labels this construal of deep ecology—asking deeper questions—as "formal" because it refers only to a depth of questioning and not to the content of any answers to these questions. However, deep ecology must mean more than this if only because those who call themselves deep ecologists typically do have substantive views that can be characterized as nonanthropocentric or ecocentric. For example, according to Devall and Sessions, deep ecology subscribes to two fundamental or ultimate norms: *biocentric egalitarianism* and *self-realization*. Fox singles out the idea of self-realization as central to his views and renames his development of the idea "transpersonal ecology."

Biocentric egalitarianism is the claim that all living things are of equal moral worth or equal intrinsic value. It is important to recognize that the word "life" is being used here in a very broad sense to include, for example, " . . . rivers (watersheds), landscapes, ecosystems."[15] A central idea here is that humans are in nature. Humans are not " . . . above or outside of nature."[16] Deep ecology challenges the human-centeredness of the dominant Western world view.

Arne Naess has the following to say about biospherical egalitarianism:

> The ecological field-worker acquires a deep-seated respect . . . for ways and forms of life. He reaches . . . a kind of understanding that others reserve for fellow men and for a narrow section of ways and forms of life. To the ecological field-worker, *the equal right to live and blossom* is an intuitively clear and obvious value axiom. Its restriction to humans is an anthropocentrism with detrimental effects upon the life quality of humans themselves. This quality depends in part upon the deep pleasure and satisfaction we receive from close partnership with other forms of life. The attempt to ignore our dependence and to establish a master-

slave role has contributed to the alien-ation of man from himself.[17]

Carolyn Merchant, in her discussion of deep ecology, suggests that there is a connection between our world view and our attitude toward the earth. Of the deep ecologists, she says, "Modesty and humility and an awe of evolution take precedence over an assertion of power over the biosphere."[18] Changing our attitude toward nature, according to some, is mainly what deep ecology is about. For example, Eric Katz says, "Deep Ecology, its advocates argue, is not an attempt to discover 'intrinsic value' or to develop universal moral rules, but a re-shaping and re-direction of human consciousness."[19] In a review of Devall and Sessions' *Deep Ecology: Living as if Nature Mattered*, Evelyn M. Hurwich expresses pleasure at the prospect that concepts like biocentric equality and self-realization "... may serve to develop ecological consciousness ... an experiential and uniquely personal process of discovery," but she is frustrated because these phrases and concepts do "... not help move us forward as a global society faced by critical issues that require choices made between varying and often conflicting ... values."[20] Hurwich continues: "Until an ecological basis is articulated by which competing vital interests can be weighed and evaluated, it cannot be expected that any meaningful decision-making process will evolve out of the deep ecology movement."[21] It may be true that deep ecologists do not formulate specific trade-off principles of the type Hurwich (and others) desire; nonetheless, in fairness to Naess, he does address questions about conflict.

In "Self-realization in Mixed Communities of Humans, Bears, Sheep, and Wolves," Naess says, "the interaction between the members of the community is not systematically codified."[22] He calls his approach *a posteriori*.[23] *A posteriori* is a Latin phrase used especially by philosophers when they refer to knowledge obtained by experience rather than by reasoning alone. So, Naess means here that the way to achieve the well-being of the members of the community is not by applying previously adopted rules established by reason, but by experiencing the problems and character of individual bears. In listening to Arne Naess talk about bears, it seems like the bears are "Fred" and "Esther"—folks we know:

> Bears and humans live in overlapping territories in southern Norway. Conflicts arise because some bears develop a habit of killing sheep. No sheep-owner thinks that all bears in his area should be killed. The cultural pattern is such that bears are considered to have a right to live and flourish. They are considered to have a value in themselves. The problem is one of co-existence with humans and with sheep.
>
> When sheep are killed in southern Norway and a bear seems to have been responsible, an expert is called in. He investigates closely the way the sheep has been killed and notes all the signs of the presence of the bear. Knowing the various habits of practically all the bears of the area—even if he has not actually seen them—he is generally able to tell not only whether a bear has been there, but also which bear.
>
> The sheep-owner is paid an indemnity if the expert arrives at the conclusion that a bear is responsible. If that bear has been guilty of similar "crimes," a verdict may be reached that it has forfeited its right to existence. An expert bear-hunter is given license to kill it, but if he does not succeed, a whole team of hunters is mobilized. (Somewhat inexplicably, bears are able under such circumstances to hide for years, which is deeply embarrassing as well as mystifying for the hunters.) Many factors are considered before a bear is condemned to death. What is his or her total record of misdeeds? How many sheep have been killed? Does he or she

mainly kill to eat, or does he or she maim or hurt sheep without eating? Is particular cruelty shown? Is it a bear mother who will probably influence her cubs in a bad way? Did the sheep enter the heart of the bear area or did the bear stray far into established sheep territory?[24]

Whatever guidelines are used by Naess emerge from the situation in which bears, wolves, sheep, and people find themselves. For a more abstract principled or rule-oriented approach to conflict resolution by a biocentric egalitarian, the reader may examine the views of Paul Taylor in IIIA.

Self-realization is the remaining ultimate norm of deep ecology to be considered. "We underestimate ourselves," says Naess, if we " . . . confuse [self] with the narrow ego."[25] In a fairly sophisticated summary of the notion, Naess says, self-realization "in its absolute maximum is . . . the mature experience of oneness in diversity. . . . The minimum is the self-realization by more or less consistent egoism—by the narrowest experience of what constitutes one's self and a maximum of alienation. As empirical beings we dwell somewhere in between, but increased maturity involves increase of the wideness of the self."[26] We develop a wider self, according to Naess, by a process of identification. Sometimes Naess talks as though identification is a psychological process something like empathy or solidarity by which we establish connection with other life forms. For example, he says, "Identification is a spontaneous, nonrational, but not irrational, process which *the interest or interests of another being are reacted to as our own interest or interests.*"[27]

At other times, when speaking of identification, he seems to be talking about what is real (metaphysics or ontology) or what we can know (epistemology). For example, Naess says, "In the shallow ecological movement, intense and wide identification is described and explained psychologically. In the deep

movement [mysticism] is at least taken seriously: reality consists of wholes which we cut down rather than of isolated items which we put together,"[28] Eric Katz maintains that in " . . . the most complete expression of the philosophy of deep ecology, [Naess] makes clear that deep ecology is much less a theory of ethics than a theory of ontology and epistemology."[29]

Naess leans heavily on Hindu metaphysics. Note that in the selection reprinted here he says, "As a student and admirer since 1930 of Gandhi's nonviolent direct action, I am inevitably influenced by his metaphysics. . . . "[30] However, it is also true that Naess's view has implications for ethics even if his deep ecology (ecosophy, as he would prefer) is not, in his view, properly called ethics.

Both the concept of self-realization and its ethical implications are analyzed by Val Plumwood in her essay, "Nature, Self, and Gender: Feminism, Environmental Philosophy, and the Critique of Rationalism," in this section. Here we note one ethical implication of the self-realization doctrine. As Plumwood explains, "The motivation for the expansion of self is to allow the self to operate on the fuel of self-interest. . . . This is apparent from [Fox's] claim that 'in this light . . . ecological resistance is simply another name for self-defense.'"[31] This consequence for ethics is also apparent in the following remark by Naess: " . . . *if* your *self* in the wide sense embraces another being, you need no moral exhortation to show care. You care for yourself without feeling any moral pressure to do it—unless you have succumbed to a neurosis of some kind, developed self-destructive tendencies, or hate yourself."[32] Another commentator's remarks are also illustrative here:

> Indeed, I consider that this shift [to an emphasis on our "capacity to identify with the larger collective of all beings"] is essential to our survival at this point in

history precisely because it can serve in lieu of morality and because moralizing is so ineffective. . . . It would not occur to me, for example, to exhort you to refrain from cutting off your leg. That wouldn't occur to me or to you, because your leg is part of you. Well, so are the trees in the Amazon Basin; they are our external lungs. We are gradually discovering that we are our world.[33]

" . . . [I]n environmental affairs," Naess says, "we should primarily try to influence people toward beautiful acts by finding ways to work on their inclinations rather than their morals."[34] Naess borrows the phrase, "beautiful action" from the philosopher Immanuel Kant. Naess notes in the selection reprinted here that for Kant, a moral act is one done out of duty, not inclination. Indeed, acts done from inclination, according to Kant, are suspect from a moral point of view even if we do the right thing. Doing the right thing from inclination Naess calls—and claims that Kant does, too—a beautiful action. Naess wants to dispense with moral actions in favor of beautiful ones. Recall what he said above about "no moral exhortation," no "moral pressure." Bill Devall talks about not "imposing environmental ethics"; instead, " . . . we will naturally respect, love, honor and protect that which is our self."[35] Still, it is worth observing how many people are "naturally" self-destructive! Elsewhere Arne Naess has said, "The history of cruelty [inflicted] in the name of morals has convinced me that increase in identification might achieve what moralizing cannot: beautiful actions."[36]

We turn now to ecofeminism. Ecological feminism, says Karen J. Warren, "is the position that there are important connections—historical, symbolic, theoretical—between the domination of women and the domination of nonhuman nature."[37] Warren argues that " . . . the conceptual connections between the dual dominations of women and nature are located in an oppressive patriarchal concep-

tual framework characterized by a logic of domination."[38] What is implied by the claim that there is a logic of domination that extends to both women and nature is that there is a need for feminism to become ecological feminism and for environmental ethics to become distinctively feminist. Warren concludes: "A *re-conceiving* and *re-visioning* of both feminism and environmental ethics is, I think, the power and the promise of ecofeminism."[39]

Crucial to the logic of domination is the assumption that in situations of diversity, differences (real or alleged) such as those between humans and rocks or men and women are interpreted as moral hierarchies. For example, it is thought that humans are better than rocks and that men are better than women in some moral sense of the term "better." This assumption, plus the further assumption that moral superiority justifies subordination, transforms talk about diversity—or, for that matter, superiority or hierarchies—into a logic of domination. As Warren puts it, " . . . without a logic of domination, a description of similarities and differences would be just that—a description of similarities and differences."[40] In an important qualifying observation, she says, "Contrary to what many feminists and ecofeminists have said or suggested, there may be nothing *inherently* problematic about 'hierarchical thinking' or even 'value hierarchical thinking' in contexts other than contexts of oppression."[41]

Warren's view that the oppressions of women and nature are connected is shared by Val Plumwood. Plumwood sees rationalism as " . . . the key to the connected oppressions . . . in the West."[42] She begins with a critique of rationalism and universalistic ethics as found in Paul Taylor and Tom Regan. This view of morality, says Plumwood, is " . . . oppositional to the personal, the particular, and the emotional. . . . Special relationships . . . are treated by universalistic positions as at best morally irrelevant and at worst a positive hindrance to the moral life. . . . "[43]

In her essay, Plumwood develops a " . . . relational account of self, which clearly recognizes the distinctiveness of nature but also our relationship and continuity with it."[44] Her position is opposed to both rationalism and deep ecology. She takes the view that the rationalism that brought us the human/nature dualism in the first place is in no position to provide an account of a decent relationship between humans and nature. Deep ecology, however, has tried to heal the human/nature bifurcation. Listen to Robert Sessions explain what he believes is at the core of deep ecology:

> Modern humans have lost touch with nature and thus with their own natures— we no longer feel the rhythms of nature within ourselves, we have split ourselves from the world (dualism), and we live at a distance (alienation) from what is natural, leaving us fearful (insecure) and able to deal with the world only on our own terms (control). . . . the basic strategy deep ecologists recommend for ending the domination of nature is to somehow reverse this dualism, to join together what humans have split asunder.[45]

Plumwood's quarrel is not with the goal of deep ecology, but with the accounts of self given by particular deep ecologists such as Arne Naess, John Seed, and Warwick Fox. All of these accounts, according to Plumwood, come up short. She labels them (1) the indistinguishability account, (2) the expanded self, and (3) the transpersonal self.

Let us focus on one very important point of difference between Plumwood's notion of "self-in-relationship" and the deep ecology ideas of "self as other" (the indistinguishability account) and the expanded self. These deep ecology ideas do not recognize the distinctness and independence of the other (in this case, the earth). On the indistinguishability

account, self and nature are completely merged; there are no boundaries between them. Here Plumwood quotes Seed: "'I am protecting the rainforest' develops to 'I am part of the rainforest protecting myself. I am that part of the rainforest recently emerged into thinking.'"[46] The self as expanded is not so much a self identical with the other, but a self that widens its interests or concerns. Plumwood's overriding concern in this whole discussion is that " . . . the widening of interest is obtained at the expense of failure to recognize unambiguously the distinctness and independence of the other."[47] Again, " . . . we need to recognize not only our continuity with the natural world but also its distinctness and independence from us and the distinctness of the needs of things in nature from ours."[48] In espousing this view, Plumwood is rejecting the idea that good relationships (between humans and/or between humans and the earth) are of the type where the self completely merges with the other. She is arguing against relationships of fusion, which entail the loss of boundaries of the self and have rightly been characterized by Plumwood and others as exemplifying "a feminine ideal."[49]

Plumwood's account of "self-in-relationship," which is critical of both masculine "separation" and feminine "merger" views of the self,[50] is in harmony with other feminist critiques of gender roles such as those developed by Victoria Davion[51] and Christine Cuomo.[52] Davion, for example, argues that " . . . a truly feminist perspective cannot embrace either the feminine or the masculine uncritically, as a truly feminist perspective requires a critique of gender roles, and this critique must include masculinity *and* femininity."[53] Davion renames as "ecofeminine" a number of purported ecofeminist views that critique masculinity, but fail to do the same in the case of femininity. To push the point, ecofeminine views see the problem as the devaluation of the feminine role, whereas

Davion says that feminists should be highly critical and suspicious of the feminine role in part because the feminine role is both inextricable from, and senseless without, its counterpart, the masculine role. So, it would be unlikely that the one role would have damaging effects for those who play it, but the other role would not. Moreover, says Davion, "A vital tradition in feminist critique has long argued that gender roles cannot exist without domination and subordination."[54] According to Davion, then, feminists see gender roles as the problem, not the undervaluing of the feminine role.

Ecological feminism is not the only environmental theoretical view to be critical of oppressive social hierarchies. Murray Bookchin, social ecology's best-known representative says:

> We are not simply talking about ending class exploitation . . . as important as that is. We are talking about uprooting *all* forms of hierarchy and domination, in all spheres of social life. Of course, the immediate source of the ecological crisis is capitalism, but, to this, social ecologists add a deeper problem at the heart of our civilization—the existence of hierarchies and of a hierarchial mentality or culture that preceded the emergence of economic classes and exploitation. The early radical feminists in the 1970s who first raised the issue of patriarchy clearly understood this. . . . We must look into the cultural forms of domination that exist in the family, between generations, sexes, racial and ethnic groups, in all institutions of political, economic, and social management, and very significantly in the way we experience reality as a whole, including nature and non-human life forms.[55]

Bookchin's appreciation of feminist analysis, evident throughout his writings, does not extend to the spiritual, goddess-worshiping aspects of feminism and ecofeminism. Social ecology is thoroughly humanistic. As Bookchin puts it, "Humanism from its inception has meant a shift in vision from the skies to the earth, from superstition to reason, from deities to people—who are no less products of natural evolution than grizzly bears and whales."[56]

In answer to the question, "What is Social Ecology?," Bookchin has given the following overview:

> *Philosophically,* social ecology stems from a solid organismic tradition in Western philosophy, beginning with Heraclitus, the near-evolutionary dialectic of Aristotle and Hegel, and the critical approach of the famous Frankfurt school—particularly its devastating critique of logical positivism (which surfaces in Naess repeatedly) and the primitivistic mysticism of Heidegger (which pops up all over the place in deep ecology's literature).
>
> *Socially,* it is revolutionary, not merely "radical." It critically unmasks the entire evolution of hierarchy in all its forms. . . . It is rooted in the profound ecoanarchistic analyses of Peter Kropotkin, the radical economic insights of Karl Marx, the emancipatory promise of revolutionary Enlightenment as articulated by . . . Denis Diderot . . . the revolutionary feminist ideals of Louise Michel and Emma Goldman, the communitarian visions of Paul Goodman and E. A. Gutkind, and the various ecorevolutionary manifestoes of the early 1960s.
>
> *Politically,* it is *green*—radically green. It takes its stand with the left-wing tendencies in the German Greens and the extraparlimentary street movements of European cities; with the American radical ecofeminist movement; with the demands for a new politics based on citizens' initiatives, neighborhood assemblies, and New England's tradition of town meetings; with non-aligned anti-imperialist movements at home and abroad; with the

struggle by people of color for complete
freedom from the domination of privileged whites and from the superpowers.
  Morally, it is *humanistic*.[57]

Human beings, Bookchin argues, in the
piece reprinted here, are products of natural
evolution; they are also unique as thinking
beings. Bookchin rejects both strong anthropocentrism, that " . . . confers on the privileged few the right to plunder the world of
life, including human life . . . "[58] and biocentricity, which " . . . denies or degrades the
uniqueness of human beings, human subjec-
tivity, rationality, aesthetic sensibility, and the
ethical potentiality of humanity. . . . "[59]

When Bookchin speaks of "biocentricity,"
he is talking about the views of deep ecologists. A severe and irreverent critic of deep
ecology, Bookchin once said that deep ecology
" . . . parachuted into our midst . . . from the
sunbelt's bizarre mix of Hollywood and Disneyland. . . . "[60] This, of course, is untrue, insofar as deep ecology comes from Norway. In a
serious vein, Bookchin has for many years
asserted that deep ecologists care only about
wilderness preservation and little or nothing
about social justice. He has been particularly
critical of Dave Foreman, who represents the
activist wing of deep ecology. Founder of
Earth First!, a radical environmental group,
Foreman is often associated with tactics called
"monkeywrenching."

Monkeywrenching, or ecological sabotage
(alternatively called "ecotage" or "night
work"), is a name, as Foreman explains, "for
the destruction of machines or property that
are used to destroy the natural world."[61] It
includes wrecking heavy equipment, spiking
trees (driving nails into trees in order to damage saw blades), and sinking holes in whaling
ships as the Sea Shepherds do. Foreman is perhaps best known for his 1987 book, *Ecodefense:
A Field Guide to Monkeywrenching*. A how-to-

do-it book, it contains, as Rik Scarce nicely
summarizes, "detailed instructions for destroying just about anything used to ruin wild
places, including heavy equipment, power
and seismographic lines, and snowmobiles.
Jamming locks, making smoke bombs, engaging in sabotage in the urban environment, and
protecting oneself against discovery are
among the topics exhaustively discussed."[62]

No longer associated with Earth First!,
Foreman has joined environmentalists who
support the North American Wilderness
Recovery Project, alternatively known as the
Wildlands Project. Its supporters are calling
for the return of millions of acres throughout
North America to wilderness. Corridors that
link existing wildlife refuges would have to be
created in order to have an area large enough
to support wolves, bears, and puma. Oregon
conservation biologist Reed F. Noss says
"[c]onnecting the Greater Yellowstone Ecosystem with a nearby region known as the Northern Continental Divide Ecosystem and with
the Canadian Rockies could create such a system."[63] As Foreman and other founders of the
Wildlands Project put it, "Our vision is simple:
we live for the day when Grizzlies in Chi-
huahua have an unbroken connection to Grizzlies in Alaska; when Gray Wolf populations
are continuous from New Mexico to Green-
land; when vast unbroken forests and flowing
plains again thrive and support pre-
Columbian populations of plants and animals."[64] Noss recommends " . . . the establishment of 'core' reserves off limits to all people
and stripped of all human artifacts."[65] He suggests that " . . . at least half of the land area of
the 48 conterminous states should be encompassed in core reserves and inner corridors."[66]

In 1989, Murray Bookchin and Dave Foreman shared a public forum in an effort to find
common ground. What is of particular interest
in the dialogue is that Bookchin talks about
the importance of wilderness and Foreman
talks about the irresponsibility of corpora-

tions—just the reverse of positions they are known to defend. For those who would like to pursue these issues further, the account of this first-ever face-to-face meeting is available in published form.[67]

NOTES

1. Mark Sagoff, Abstract, "Zuckerman's Dilemma: A Plea for Environmental Ethics," *Hastings Center Report,* September-October 1991, p. 32.

2. Ibid.

3. Mark Sagoff, "Zuckerman's Dilemma: A Plea for Environmental Ethics," *Hastings Center Report,* September-October 1991, p. 33.

4. Ibid., p. 34.

5. Ibid., p. 33.

6. Ibid., p. 35.

7. Mark Sagoff, "On Making Nature Safe for Biotechnology," in *Assessing Ecological Risks of Biotechnology,* ed. Lev R. Ginzburg (Boston: Butterworth-Heinemann, 1991), pp. 350–51.

8. Kathie Jennie, University of Redlands, made this suggestion.

9. William Baxter, *People or Penguins: The Case for Optimal Pollution* (New York: Columbia University Press, 1974), p. 5.

10. Bryan G. Norton, Abstract, "Environmental Ethics and Weak Anthropocentrism, "*Environmental Ethics* 6, no. 2 (Summer 1984) p. 131.

11. Arne Naess, "The Shallow and the Deep, Long-Range Ecology Movement. A Summary," *Inquiry* 16, no. 1 (Spring 1973). This piece is a summary of an introductory lecture at the 3rd World Future Research Conference, Bucharest, September 3–10, 1972.

12. Arne Naess, "Interview With Naess," in Bill Devall and George Sessions, *Deep Ecology: Living as if Nature Mattered* (Salt Lake City: Utah, Peregrine Smith, 1985), p. 74.

13. Arne Naess, "The Deep Ecological Movement: Some Philosophical Aspects," *Philosophical Inquiry* 8, nos. 1–2 (1986), p. 22.

14. Warwick Fox, *Toward a Transpersonal Ecology* (Boston: Shambhala Publications, Inc., 1990), pp. 112–23.

15. Devall and Sessions, *Deep Ecology,* p. 71.

16. Bill Devall, "The Deep Ecology Movement," *Natural Resources Journal* 20, no. 2 (April 1980), p. 303.

17. Naess, "The Shallow and the Deep," pp. 95–96.

18. Carolyn Merchant, *Radical Ecology: The Search for a Livable World* (New York: Routledge, 1992), p. 87.

19. Eric Katz, "Ethics and Philosophy of the Environment: A Brief Review of the Major Literature," *Environmental History Review* 15, no. 2 (1991), p. 84.

20. Evelyn M. Hurwich, review of *Deep Ecology: Living as if Nature Mattered* (Bill Devall and George Sessions) in *Ecology Law Quarterly* 13 (1986), pp. 770–71.

21. Ibid. See also Bryan G. Norton's discussion of deep ecology in his book, *Toward Unity Among Environmentalists* (New York: Oxford University Press, 1991).

22. Arne Naess, "Self-realization in Mixed Communities of Humans, Bears, Sheep, and Wolves," *Inquiry* 22, nos. 1–2 (Summer 1979), p. 238.

23. Ibid.

24. Ibid., p. 237.

25. Arne Naess, "*Self* Realization: An Ecological Approach to Being in the World," in *Thinking Like a Mountain: Towards a Council of All Beings,* ed. John Seed, Joanna Macy, Pat Fleming, and Arne Naess (Philadelphia: New Society Publishers, 1988), p. 19.

26. Arne Naess, "Identification as a Source of Deep Ecological Attitudes," in *Radical Environmentalism: Philosophy and Tactics,* ed. Peter C. List (Belmont, CA: Wadsworth Publishing Company, 1993), p. 28.

27. Ibid., p. 29.

28. Ibid., p. 30.

29. Katz, "Ethics and Philosophy of the Environment," p. 85. Katz means by "most complete expression" Naess's *Ecology, Community and Lifestyle* (New York: Cambridge University Press, 1989).

30. Naess, "*Self* Realization: An Ecological Approach," p. 24.

31. Val Plumwood, "Nature, Self, and Gender: Feminism, Environmental Philosophy, and the Critique of Rationalism," *Hypatia* 6, no. 1 (Spring 1991), p. 14. Warwick Fox, "Approaching Deep Ecology: A Response to Richard Sylvan's Critique of Deep Ecology," *Environmental Studies Occasional Paper 20* (Hobart: University of Tasmania Centre for Environmental Studies, 1986), p. 60. See also *Green Rage,* where the following position is attributed to Arne Naess, Bill Devall, and other deep ecologists: "If our selves belong to a larger self that encompasses the whole biological community in which we dwell, then an attack on the trees, the wolves, the rivers, is an attack upon all of us. Defense of place becomes a form of self-defense, which in most ethical and legal

systems would be ample grounds for spiking a tree or ruining a tire." Christopher Manes, *Green Rage: Radical Environmentalism and the Unmaking of Civilization* (Boston: Little, Brown and Company, 1990), p. 177.

32. Naess, "*Self* Realization: An Ecological Approach," pp. 26–27.

33. Joanna Macy in Fox, *Toward a Transpersonal Ecology,* p. 229.

34. Naess, "*Self* Realization: An Ecological Approach," p. 28.

35. Bill Devall, *Simple in Means, Rich in Ends: Practicing Deep Ecology* (Salt Lake City: Peregrine Smith Books, 1988), p. 43.

36. Naess, "Identification," p. 32.

37. Karen J. Warren, "Abstract," "The Power and the Promise of Ecological Feminism," *Environmental Ethics* 12, no. 2 (Summer 1990), p. 125.

38. Warren, "Abstract," p. 125.

39. Warren, "The Power and the Promise of Ecological Feminism," p. 125.

40. Ibid., p. 129.

41. Ibid., p. 128.

42. Val Plumwood, Abstract, "Nature, Self, and Gender: Feminism, Environmental Philosophy, and the Critique of Rationalism," *Hypatia* 6, no. 1 (Spring 1991), p. 3.

43. Plumwood, "Nature, Self, and Gender," p. 6, 7.

44. Ibid., p. 20.

45. Robert Sessions, "Deep Ecology versus Ecofeminism: Healthy Differences or Incompatible Philosophies?" *Hypatia* 6, no.1 (Spring 1991), pp. 95, 96.

46. Plumwood, "Nature, Self, and Gender," p. 12. John Seed, "Beyond Anthropocentrism," in Seed, et al., *Thinking Like a Mountain,* p. 36.

47. Plumwood, "Nature, Self, Gender," p. 15.

48. Ibid., p. 13.

49. Ibid.

50. Ibid., p. 20.

51. Victoria Davion, "How Feminist Is Ecofeminism?" in *The Environmental Ethics and Policy Book: Philosophy, Ecology, and Economics,* ed. Donald VanDeVeer and Christine Pierce (Belmont, CA: Wadsworth Publishing Company, 1994).

52. Christine J. Cuomo, "Unravelling the Problems in Ecofeminism," *Environmental Ethics* 14, no. 4 (Winter 1992).

53. Davion, "How Feminist Is Ecofeminism?" p. 288.

54. Ibid., p. 292.

55. Murray Bookchin, *Defending the Earth: A Dialogue Between Murray Bookchin and Dave Foreman,* ed. Steve Chase (Boston: South End Press, 1991), pp. 57–58.

56. Murray Bookchin, "Social Ecology and Deep Ecology," *Socialist Review* 88, no. 3 (1988), p. 27.

57. Ibid., p. 27.

58. Ibid.

59. Ibid.

60. Ibid., p. 13.

61. Dave Foreman, *Confessions of an Eco-Warrior* (New York: Harmony Books, 1991), p. 118.

62. Rik Scarce, *Eco-Warriors: Understanding the Radical Environmental Movement* (Chicago: The Noble Press, Inc., 1990), p. 74.

63. Reed F. Noss, quoted in Elizabeth Pennisi, "Conservation's Ecocentrics," *Science News* 144, no. 11 (September 11, 1993), p. 169.

64. The Wildlands Project Mission Statement, written by Dave Foreman, John Davis, David Johns, Reed Noss, and Michael Soulé in "The Wildlands Project," special issue of *Wild Earth,* Canton, NY, 1992, p. 3.

65. Pennisi, "Conservation's Ecocentrics," p. 169.

66. Ibid.

67. Bookchin, "Defending the Earth," pp. 57–58.

Zuckerman's Dilemma: A Plea for Environmental Ethics _____

Mark Sagoff

Many of us recall from childhood—or from reading to our own children—E. B. White's story of the spider Charlotte and her campaign to save Wilbur, a barnyard pig.[1] Charlotte wove webs above Wilbur's sty proclaiming the pig's virtues in words—"TERRIFIC," "RADIANT," and "HUMBLE"—she copied from newspaper advertisements salvaged by a helpful rat. Wilbur won a special prize at the county fair. Moved by these events, Zuckerman, the farmer who owned Wilbur, spared

Hastings Center Report, Vol. 21, No. 5 (Sept.-Oct. 1991), 32–40. Reprinted by permission.

him from being sent to market. Charlotte saved Wilbur's life.

"Why did you do all this for me?" the pig asks at the end of *Charlotte's Web*. "I don't deserve it. I've never done anything for you."

"You have been my friend," Charlotte replied. "That in itself is a tremendous thing. I wove my webs for you because I liked you. After all, what's a life, anyway? We're born, we live a little while, we die. A spider's life can't help being something of a mess, what with all this trapping and eating flies. By helping you, perhaps I was trying to lift up my life a little. Heaven knows, anyone's life can stand a little of that" (p. 164).

The Varieties of Goodness

Charlotte's Web illustrates three ways we value nature. First, nature benefits us. Nature is useful: it serves a purpose, satisfies a preference, or meets a need. This is the *instrumental* good. Traders have this kind of value in mind when they bid on pork belly futures. Price is the usual measure of the instrumental good.

Second, we may value nature as an object of knowledge and perception. This is the *aesthetic* good.[2] While the basis of instrumental value lies in our wants and inclinations, the basis of aesthetic value lies in the object itself—in qualities that demand an appreciative response from informed and discriminating observers. The judges who awarded Wilbur a prize recognized in him superb qualities—qualities that made him a pig to be appreciated rather than a pig to be consumed.

Third, we may regard an object (as Charlotte did Wilbur) with love or affection. Charlotte's love for Wilbur included feelings of altruism, as we would expect, since anyone who loves a living object (we might include biological systems and communities) will take an interest in its well-being or welfare. Love might also attach to objects that exemplify ideals, aspirations, and commitments that "lift up" one's life by presenting goals that go beyond one's own welfare. We might speak of "love of country" in this context. Objects of our love and affection have a *moral* good, and, if they are living, *a good of their own*.

Aesthetic value depends on qualities that make an object admirable of its kind; when these qualities change, the aesthetic value of the object may change with them. With love, it is different. Shakespeare wrote that love alters not where it alteration finds, and even if this is not strictly true, love still tolerates better than aesthetic appreciation changes that may occur in its object.

Although love is other-regarding in that it promotes the well-being of its object, it does not require actions to be entirely altruistic. Only saints are completely selfless, and it is hardly obvious that we should try to be like them.[3] Nevertheless, anyone's life can stand some dollop of idealistic or altruistic behavior, as Charlotte says.

When we regard an object with appreciation or with love, we say it has *intrinsic* value, by which we mean that we value the object itself rather than just the benefits it confers on us. This essay concerns the intrinsic value of nature in its relation to environmental policy. The two forms of intrinsic value—aesthetic and moral—differ in important ways, as one would expect, since moral value arises in the context of action, while aesthetic value has to do with perception. I shall touch on these differences, but I do not have space to explicate them here.

The Value of Nature

Those of us who wish to protect estuaries, forests, species, and other aspects of nature may give any of three kinds of arguments—instrumental, aesthetic, or moral—to support our conviction. We might argue on instrumental grounds, for example, that we should save species for their possible medicinal applications, or rain forests because they add to global oxygen budgets. An aesthetic argument, in contrast, would point to the magnificent qualities a ten-thousand-year-old forest or estuary may possess. In nature we find perhaps for the last time in history objects commensurate with our capacity to wonder.

A moral argument describes obligations we have toward objects of nature insofar as we regard them with reverence, affection, and respect. Such an argument may contend that humanity confronts a great responsibility in learning to share the world with other species. Love of or respect for the natural world increases our stature as moral beings, and it may teach us to be critical of and to change our preferences and desires. By taking an interest in the welfare of some creature beside herself, Charlotte too found there is more to life than "all this trapping and eating flies."

Within the next decade or two, we shall decide the fate of many estuaries, forests, species, and other wonderful aspects of the natural world. How can we justify efforts to protect them? Will instrumental or prudential arguments do the trick? If not, how will we justify the sacrifices we must make to save our evolutionary and ecological heritage?

Why Save the Whales?   Consider, as a real-world example, whales. Two centuries ago, whale oil fetched a high price because people used it in lamps. Whales had instrumental value. Electric lights are better and cheaper than oil lamps; accordingly, there is little or no market for whale oil today.

Why, then, do so many people care about saving whales? Is it for instrumental reasons? Are they concerned about maintaining a strategic reserve of blubber? Do they worry that the seas might fill up with krill? No; as whales have lost their instrumental value, their aesthetic and moral worth has become all the more evident.

Whale oil has substitutes in a way that whales do not. We get along easily without whale oil because electricity lights our lamps. The extinction of whales, in contrast, represents an aesthetic and moral loss—something like the destruction of a great painting or the death of a friend. Life goes on, of course, but we mourn such a loss and, if we caused it, we should feel guilty or ashamed of it. No one cares about the supply of whale oil, but we do care about the abundance of whales. Aesthetic and moral value attaches to those animals themselves rather than to any function they serve or benefit they confer on us. When they perish, all that was valuable about them will perish with them.

Fungibility as the Mark of the Instrumental. Insofar as we care about an object for instrumental reasons, we would accept a substitute—for example, ball point pens in place of quills—if it performs the same function at a lower cost. The market price of any object should in theory not exceed that of the cheapest substitute.

With intrinsic value, it is different. When we see, for example, a Jacques Cousteau film about the ability of humpback whales to communicate with each other over hundreds of miles, we are properly moved to admire this impressive species. That we can fax junk mail faster and farther is irrelevant. We admire the ability of these whales to do what they do. It is *this* species we admire; *its* qualities demand admiration and attention.

Similarly, love is not transferable but attaches to the individuals one happens to love. At one time, people had children, in part, because they needed them as farm hands. Today, we think the relation between parents and children should be primarily moral rather than instrumental. One can purchase the services of farmhands and even of sexual partners, but our relationship to hired labor or sex is nothing like our relationship to children or spouses. We would not think of trading a child, for example, for a good tractor.

Technology, though still in its infancy, promises to do for many aspects of nature what it has done for whales and for children, namely, to make us economically less dependent on them. This need not concern us. That we no longer require whales for oil or children for tending bobbins does not imply that we cease to value them. The less we depend on nature economically, the more we may find that the reasons to value species, forests, estuaries, and other aspects of nature are not instrumental but aesthetic and moral.

Why Protect the Natural Environment?   We undertake many environmental programs primarily to protect the well-being of nature, even if we defend them as necessary to promote the welfare of human beings. Why, for example, did the Environmental Protection Agency ban DDT in the 1970s? The pesticide killed pelicans and other wildlife; that was the reason to prohibit its use. EPA banned it, however, as a human carcinogen—which it is not.[4] Today we should make no such pretense.[5] The new Clean Air Act undertakes an expensive program to control acid rain. The law does not pretend that acid rain causes cancer. It answers directly to moral and aesthetic concerns about what coal-burning power plants are doing to trees and fish.

We environmentalists often appeal to instrumental arguments for instrumental reasons, i.e., not because we believe them, but because we think that they work. I submit, however, that advances in technology will continue to undermine these arguments. The new biotechnologies, for example, seem poised to replace nature as the source of many agricultural commodities. As one environmentalist observes: "In the years to come, an increasing number of agricultural activities are going to be taken indoors and enclosed in vats and caldrons, sealed off from the outside world."[6]

When machinery replaced child labor in mills and mines, people did not stop raising children. Society found it possible to treat children as objects of love rather than as factors of production. As biotechnology industrializes agriculture, we may protect farmland for its aesthetic and symbolic value rather than for its products. We may measure wealth not in terms of what we can consume but in terms of what we can do without—what we treasure for its own sake.

Poverty is one of today's greatest environmental and ecological problems. This is because people who do not share in the wealth technology creates must live off nature; in their need to exploit the natural commons, they may destroy it. Analogously, in an urban context, poor people have had to send their children to work in sweat shops—to survive. The problem, of course, is not that poor people have the wrong values. Extreme and deplorable inequalities in the distribution of wealth lead to the mistreatment of children and to the destruction of the environment.

Accordingly, I question the adequacy of the argument environmentalists often make that we must protect nature to provide for the welfare of human beings. I think it is also true that we must provide for the welfare of human beings if we are to protect the natural environment.

Zuckerman's Dilemma

Zuckerman faced a dilemma. He had to choose whether to butcher Wilbur (the slaughterhouse would have paid for the pig) or on moral and aesthetic grounds to spare his life.

What reasons have we to preserve biodiversity, protect rain forests, and maintain the quality of lakes, rivers, and estuaries? I should like to suggest that we confront Zuckerman's dilemma with respect to many of the most wonderful aspects of nature. As we come to depend on nature less and less for instrumental reasons, we may recognize more and more the intrinsic reasons for preserving it.

Water Pollution. Consider, as an example, the problem of water pollution. The question I wish to ask here is whether instrumental arguments would justify the expenditure of the roughly $200 billion Americans invested between 1970 and 1984 in controlling water pollution.[7] Did this investment pay off in terms of our health, safety, or welfare? Could we conclude that, in this instance, instrumental as well as intrinsic values justify the protection of the environment?

I think it fair to say that the large public investment in water pollution control cannot be justified on instrumental grounds alone. The same money put into public clinics, education, or antismoking campaigns might have led to greater improvements in public safety and health. This is true in part because the major uses of water—commercial, industrial, agricultural, and municipal—are not very sensitive to water quality. Drinking water can be treated very cheaply and thus can tolerate many common pollutants. "Much of what has been said about the need for high quality water supplies," two experts write, "is more a product of emotion than logic . . . [A] plant at Düsseldorf, Germany, withdraws water from the Rhine River, which is of far lower quality than the Delaware, the Hudson, or the Missouri, treats it . . . and produces quite potable drinking water."[8]

The Value of an Estuary. In the Chesapeake Bay, as in other prominent aquatic ecosystems, pollution must concern us deeply for moral and aesthetic reasons. It is not clear, however, that the harm pollution does to nature translates into damage to human health, safety, or welfare. Indeed, more pollution might be better from a strictly instrumental point of view.

The reason is that the major uses of the Bay are fairly insensitive to water quality. The Chesapeake possesses instrumental value as a liquid highway (Baltimore is a major port), as a sewer (tributaries drain several major cities), and as a site for a huge naval base (Norfolk). These uses affect but are not greatly affected by water quality or, for that matter, by the biological health, integrity, richness, or diversity of the Chesapeake ecosystem.

How does pollution affect the health of commercial and recreational fisheries in estuaries? Consider rockfish (striped bass). Environmentalists for many years deplored the pollution of the Hudson off Manhattan; they pronounced that portion of the estuary— one of the most degraded in the world— biologically dead. Developers of the Westway Project, who wished to fill the offshore waters to build condos, hired scientists who confirmed that rockfish did not and probably could not visit the polluted lower Hudson.

Environmentalists were able to stop the project, however, by arguing in the nick of time that even though the "interpier" area may be the most polluted ecosystem in the world, it functions as perhaps the most important, healthy, and thriving hatchery for rockfish on the Atlantic coast. The well-being of fish populations—at least as we view it—can have more to do with politics than with pollution.[9]

In the Chesapeake, rockfish populations rebounded after a moratorium on fishing. One might surmise, then, that while fisheries have been hurt by overharvesting, the effects of pollution are harder to prove. Bluefish, crabs, and other "scavengers" abound in polluted waters, including the Chesapeake. And organic pollutants, primarily compounds of nitrogen and phosphorus, could support oysters and other filter feeders if their populations (depleted by overfishing and natural disease) returned to the Bay.

Maryland's former director of tidal fisheries, recognizing the benefits of genetic engineering, argued that the Chesapeake Bay "should be run more like a farm than a wilderness."[10] He believed that the state should subsidize efforts to fabricate fish the way Frank Perdue manufactures chickens. Many experts agree that industrial mariculture, by pushing fish populations far beyond the carrying capacity of ecosystems, will render capture fisheries obsolete.[11]

Pollution at present levels hardly bothers boaters, which is why there are so many "stinkpots" out there. Even in a "sick" estuary, a 347 Evinrude outboard gives people what they apparently want: plenty of noise and plenty of wake. Many recreational fish remain plentiful, and biotechnologists are engineering others to withstand pollutants to which they now succumb. They have perfected a nonmigrating rockfish that need not transit the anoxic stem of the Bay. (They have also perfected an acid-tolerant trout that does well in acidified lakes.) It may not be efficient to regulate pollution to accommodate species. It may be cheaper to regulate species to accommodate pollution.

Since a nasty jellyfish occurring naturally in the Bay makes swimming too painful, recreational interest in the Chesapeake is limited in any case. Most vacationers experience the Bay from bridges, where they sit in terrific traffic jams on their way to resorts on the Atlantic shore. They seem willing to pay a lot to visit the Ho Jos, discos, go gos, peep shows, and condos that stretch from Atlantic City to Virginia Beach. If you are looking for recreational benefits people are willing to pay for, look for them there.

Why Not Pollute?   We may find acts of environmental destruction to be aesthetically and morally outrageous even if they do no damage to human health, safety, or welfare. News reports tell us that Prince William Sound, now "sparkling with sea life and renewed health," has produced a record salmon catch a little more than a year after the tragic Valdez spill.[12] From a strictly instrumental point of view, that spill was not nearly so detrimental as many environmentalists thought. The immediate victims, more than 36,000 waterfowl, at least 1,016 sea otters, and 144 bald eagles, have no commercial value. Populations of wildlife will be detrimentally affected probably forever. Theses animals have enormous aesthetic and moral—but little instrumental—worth.

I do not mean to suggest that water pollution, especially when it is illegal or careless, is anything but morally and aesthetically outrageous. I do not mean to minimize the harm it does. I am arguing only that pollution may represent a failure in aesthetic appreciation and moral responsibility without representing a market failure, that is, without impairing any of the uses we make of an estuary. The Chesapeake will perform its major economic tasks: to function as a sewer, a liquid highway, and a place for boating. If it were only the beneficial use rather than the intrinsic value of the Bay that concerned us, controlling pollution further might not be worth the cost.

The Problem of Scale

"What's wrong with this argument," a reader might object, "is that it leaves out the question of scale. We can get away with polluting an estuary here and there if elsewhere healthy ecosystems support the global processes essential to life. At a local scale, an instrumental calculus may argue for industrializing a particular environment. The problem, though, is that when we apply the same calculus to every ecosystem, we end up by destroying the crucial services nature provides."

This argument has weight with respect to activities that affect the atmosphere. Scientists have shown a connection between the use of CFCs and changes in stratospheric ozone. Likewise, the excessive combustion of coal and oil threatens to change the world's climate. That we should follow policies that prudence recommends, I have no doubt. The Montreal Protocol concerning CFCs represents an important first step. Prudence also recommends that we reach similar international agreements to decrease the amount of fuel we burn and, perhaps, to increase our reliance on those forms of energy that do not involve combustion.

While it is urgent that we limit atmospheric pollution, this does not give us a reason to protect intrinsically valuable species or ecosystems. The pollution, degradation, and exploitation of the Chesapeake Bay, for example, has no cognizable effect on global biochemical processes. One may argue, indeed, that the more eutrophic the Bay becomes, the more carbon it will store, thus helping to counter the "greenhouse" effect. By solving the problems of the Chesapeake, we do little to solve the problems of the atmosphere. The two sets of problems arise from different causes, involve different sorts of values, and require different solutions.

Rain Forests. Consider the rain forests, which seem doomed by economic progress. One can argue persuasively that humanity has no more important ethical or aesthetic task than to keep these magnificent ecosystems from being turned into particle boards and disposable diapers. Popular arguments to the effect that rain forests store net carbon or add to global oxygen budgets, however, may not be convincing.

Since rain forests are climax ecosystems, they absorb through the cold burning of decay as much oxygen as they release through respiration; thus the popular belief that these forests add to global oxygen budgets betrays a naivete about how climax ecosystems work.[13] One way to get a rain forest to store net carbon may be to chop it down and plant instead of trees fast-growing crops genetically designed to do very nicely in the relevant soil and climatic conditions. (The biologist Dan Janzen has described this dreadful possibility.)[14] The trees

could be used to make disposable diapers which, after use, would go to landfills where they would store carbon nearly forever.

Biodiversity. Anyone with any moral or aesthetic sense must agree that another of humanity's greatest responsibilities today is to arrest shameful and horrendous rates of extinction. Yet one is hard pressed to find credible instrumental arguments for protecting endangered species in their habitats. The reason that we produce Thanksgiving turkeys by the millions while letting the black-footed boobie become extinct is that one bird has instrumental value while the other has not. The boobie had no ecological function; it was epiphenomenal even in its own habitat. Its demise in no way contributed, for example, to the loss of stratospheric ozone or to the "greenhouse" effect.

Environmentalists, to justify their efforts to protect biological diversity, sometimes speculate that exotic species might prove useful for medical purposes, for instance. No public health professional, as far as I know, has vouched for this proposition. Pharmaceutical companies are not known for contributing to the Nature Conservancy or for otherwise encouraging efforts to preserve biodiversity. They are interested in learning from folk medicine, but they cannot even think of tracking down, capturing, and analyzing the contents of millions of species (many of them unidentified) each of which may contain thousands of compounds.

If pharmaceutical companies wanted to mine exotic species, they would not preserve them in their habitats. They might trap and freeze them or sequence their genes for later reconstruction. Seed companies would likewise store germ tissue in banks, not leave it in the wild. Capturing and freezing specimens, not preserving habitats, would be the way to go, to make biodiversity benefit us.

Even a single endangered species enlists our respect and admiration, since (as one observer has said) it would require another heaven and earth to produce such a being. The grand diversity of life, particularly the existence of rare and exotic species, presents a profound moral obligation for civilization, which is to share the earth peaceably with other species. This obligation exists whether or not we can defend the preservation of species on grounds of self-interest rather than morality. The destruction of biodiversity may be immoral, even sinful, without being irrational or imprudent.

A Plea for Environmental Ethics

In an old movie, a character played by W. C. Fields, having, it appears, negligently killed a baby, confronts its hysterical mother. Eyeing her youthful figure, he says: "No matter, madam; I would be happy to get you with another."

What we find chilling in this scene is Fields's appeal wholly to instrumental value. He sees nothing wrong with killing a baby as long has he can "get" its mother with another child who, one day, will be equally capable of supporting her in her old age. To Fields, objects have only instrumental value; we can evaluate all our actions in terms of costs and benefits. They have no other meaning.

Moral Value—a Benefit or Cost? The scene in the movie might remind us of the way the EXXON Corporation dealt with public outrage over the recent unpleasantness in Prince William Sound. The corporation assured everyone that the salmon fishery would bounce back. If anyone was out of pocket, EXXON would lavishly compensate them. EXXON said to the outraged public: "No matter, madam; we will be happy to make you at least as well off."

From the point of view of instrumental value alone, both Fields and EXXON were correct. They could replace whatever was lost with equally beneficial or useful substitutes. Another baby could grow up to plow land or tend bobbins as well as the first. The mother's income in old age would not decrease. EXXON too would make up lost income. Isn't it irrational, then, for people to complain when children are killed or wildlife is destroyed? From the point of view of instrumental value, they aren't worth much. They may have meaning, but they confer few benefits on us. They make demands on us. They are mostly costs.

Indeed, raising children, preserving nature, cherishing art, and practicing the virtues of civil life are all costs—the costs of being the people we are. Why do we pay these costs? We can answer only that these costs are benefits; these actions justify themselves; these virtues are their own reward.

I wonder, therefore, whether we environmentalist do well to argue for environmental protection primarily on instrumental rather than on moral and aesthetic grounds. Are the possible medicinal or agricultural uses of rare and endangered species really what we care about? We might as well argue

that we should protect whales for the sake of their oil or sea otters to harvest their teeth. I think the destruction and extinction of wildlife would horrify us even if we knew sea otter, murres, and eagles would never benefit us. How do we differ from Charlotte, then, who saved Wilbur even though he did nothing for her?

Preference versus Judgment. "The distinction between instrumental and intrinsic value," someone may object, "lies beside the point of environmental policy, since a cost-benefit analysis, based in willingness-to-pay estimates, can take both sorts of preferences into account. Whether people are willing to pay to protect wildlife for moral, aesthetic, or self-interested reasons (hunting, for example) is their business; all the policy maker needs to know is what their preferences are and how much they are willing to pay to satisfy them."

This objection misses the crucial importance of the way we choose to make decisions. Consider, for example, how we determine whether a person is innocent or guilty of a crime. We might do this by sending questionnaires to a random sample of citizens to check off whether they prefer a guilty or innocent verdict and, perhaps, how much they are willing to pay for each. This method of reaching a verdict would be "rational" in the sense that it aggregates "given" preferences (data) to mathematical principles laid down in advance. The method is also "neutral" in that it translates a data set into a social choice without itself entering, influencing, or affecting the outcome.

On the other hand, we may trust the finding of innocence or guilt to a jury who are steeped in the evidence, who hear the arguments, and then, by deliberation, reach a collective judgment. This procedure, since it involves discussion and even persuasion, would not proceed from "given" preferences according to rules laid down in advance. The process or method itself is *supposed* to affect the result.

Which model would be most appropriate for environmental policy? Consider erosion. Public officials must assess instrumental reasons for protecting soil: they must determine how much arable land we need for crops, how much we are losing, and how best to conserve what we have. They also weigh intrinsic values, for example, what soil and its protection expresses about us or means to us as a community. Our policy, presumably, should be based not on the revealed or expressed preferences of a random sample of people, no matter how rigorous our techniques of sampling and aggregating may be, but on the judgment of responsible authorities after appropriate public consideration and debate.

Similarly, policies for civil rights, education, the arts, child labor, and the environment depend on judgment—often moral and aesthetic judgment—concerning facts about the world and about ourselves, that is, about our goals and intentions as a community. People who believe we ought to save the whales, for example, do not tell us simply what they prefer; rather, they call for the reasoned agreement or disagreement of others. That is why public policy is always argued in public terms—in terms of what *we* ought to do, not what *I* happen to want.

With respect to aesthetic experience, anyone can tell you what he or she likes, but not everyone can tell you what is worth appreciating. A person judges aesthetically not for himself or herself only but on the basis of reasons, arguments, or ideas that he or she believes would lead others to the same conclusion. Knowledge, experience, sensitivity, discernment—these distinguish judgments of taste from expressions of preference.

To be sure, we enjoy objects we appreciate, but we do not value these objects because we enjoy them. Rather, we enjoy them because we find them valuable or, more precisely, enjoyment is one way of perceiving their value. To enjoy ecological communities aesthetically or to value them morally is to find directly in them or in their qualities the reasons that justify their protection. This is not a matter of personal preference. It is a matter of judgment and perception, which one might believe correct or mistaken, and thus argue for or against, within an open political process.

The contrast I have drawn between instrumental and intrinsic value borrows a great deal, of course, from Kant, who summed up the distinction as follows. "That which is related to general human inclination and needs has a *market price* . . . But that which constitutes . . . an end in itself does not have a mere relative worth, i.e., a price, but an intrinsic worth, i.e., a *dignity*."[15] Kant believed that dignity attaches to objects because of what they are and, therefore, how we judge them. The discovery of what things are—whether it is their moral, aesthetic, or scientific properties—has to do with knowledge. Like any form of knowledge it is inter-

subjective: it represents not the preference of individuals but the will, the perception, or the considered opinion of a community.

Are Values Relative? While many Americans may share an environmental ideology—the United States has been described as Nature's Nation[16]—this does not apply everywhere. Even if the love of nature belongs to most cultures, moreover, it might express itself in different ways. The Japanese may not experience whales as we do; *Moby Dick* is one of our classics. Italians, who treasure their artistic heritage, might as soon eat as listen to a song bird. How can we expect other cultures to respond to nature in the ways we do?

This kind of question may lead environmentalists to suppose that instrumental arguments for protecting nature have a universality that intrinsic arguments do not. Yet instrumental arguments depend on interpretations of fact—models of climate change, for example—that invite all kinds of disagreement. And ethical issues arise, moreover, even when instrumental concerns are paramount, such as when determining how much industrialized and developing nations should cut back combustion to counter global warming. It may be easier to persuade, attract, or cajole other nations to cooperate (if not agree) with our moral and aesthetic concerns than with our reading of prudence or self-interest. The process of reaching agreement is the same, however, whether instrumental or intrinsic values are at stake.

Living with Nature. I have argued that we ought to preserve nature for its sake and not simply our benefit. How far, however, should we go? The Chesapeake Bay commends itself to us for intrinsic but also for instrumental reasons. How can we balance our need to use with our desire to protect this ecosystem?

We confront this kind of question, I believe, also in relation to people whom we love and whose freedom and spontaneity we respect but with whom we have to live. Children are examples. We could treat our children—as we might treat nature—completely as means to our own ends. We would then simply use them to take out the empties, perform sexual favors, tend bobbins, or whatever it is that benefits us. This would be despicable as well as criminal. We know that morality requires that we treat our children as ends in themselves and not merely as means to our own ends.

At the same time, we have to live with our kids, and this allows us to make certain demands on them, like not to wake us up too early in the morning, no matter how much we love them for their own sake. While we insist on protecting our children's innate character, independence, and integrity, we have to socialize the little devils or they will destroy us and themselves. I think this is true of nature: we can respect the integrity of ecosystems even if we change them in ways that allow us all to share the same planet.

No clear rules determine how far one should go in disciplining one's children or in modifying their behavior; socialization may have fairly broad limits. But there are limits; we recognize child abuse when we see it. Have we such a conception of the abuse of nature? I think we need one. At least we should regard as signs of environmental abuse the typical results of egregious assaults on ecosystems, such as eutrophication, pandemic extinctions, and so on. We might then limit changes we make in nature by keeping this notion of ecological health— or disease—in mind.

Zuckerman's Response

William Reilly, administrator of the Environmental Protection Agency, recently wrote: "Natural ecosystems . . . have intrinsic values independent of human use that are worthy of protection." He cited an advisory scientific report that urged the agency to attach as much importance to intrinsic ecological values as to risks to human health and welfare. Mr. Reilly added:

> Whether it is Long Island Sound or Puget Sound, San Francisco Bay or the Chesapeake, the Gulf of Mexico or the Arctic tundra, it is time to get serious about protecting what we love. Clearly we do love our great water bodies: . . . They are part of our heritage, part of our consciousness. Let us vow not to let their glory pass from this good Earth.[17]

In 1991 the State of Maryland offered anyone registering an automobile the option of paying $20 (which would go to an environmental fund) to receive a special license plate bearing the motto:

"Treasure the Chesapeake." A surprising number of registrants bought the plate. How many of us would have ponied up the $20 for a plate that read: "Use the Chesapeake Efficiently" or "The Chesapeake: It Satisfies Your Revealed and Expressed Preferences"?

To treasure the Chesapeake is to see that it has a good of its own—and therefore a "health" or "integrity"—that we should protect even when to do so does not benefit us. "Why did you do all this for me?" Wilbur asked. "I've never done anything for you." Even when nature does not do anything for us—one might think, for example, of the eagles and otters destroyed in Prince William Sound—we owe it protection for moral and aesthetic reasons. Otherwise our civilization and our lives will amount to little more than the satisfaction of private preferences: what Charlotte described as "all this trapping and eating flies."

In this essay, I have proposed that we may lift up our lives a little by seeing nature as Charlotte did, not just as an assortment of resources to be managed and consumed, but also as a setting for collective moral and aesthetic judgment. I have also suggested that our evolutionary heritage—the diversity of species, the miracle of life—confronts us with the choice Zuckerman had to make: whether to butcher nature for the market or to protect it as an object of moral attention and aesthetic appreciation.

If Zuckerman had not learned to appreciate Wilbur for his own sake, he would have converted the pig to bacon and chops. Likewise, if we do not value nature for ethical and aesthetic reasons, then we might well pollute and degrade it for instrumental ones. If a spider could treat a pig as a friend, however, then we should be able to treat a forest, an estuary, or any other living system in the same way.

References

1. E. B. White, *Charlotte's Web* (New York: Harper & Row, 1952).

2. In defining the instrumental and aesthetic good, I follow the analysis of Georg Henrik von Wright, *The Varieties of Goodness* (London: Routledge & Kegan Paul, 1963), pp. 19–40. Von Wright, however, uses the term *technical good* where I use the term *aesthetic good*.

3. See Susan Wolf, "Moral Saints," *Journal of Philosophy* 79 (1982): 419–39.

4. During the early 1970s an enormous investment in research led to completely inconclusive findings based on animal studies, although one prominent pharmacologist summed up the available evidence by saying that at then-current levels DDT was not a human carcinogen. For documentation, see Thomas R. Dunlap, *DDT: Scientists, Citizens, and Public Policy* (Princeton: Princeton University Press, 1981), esp. pp. 214–17. Oddly, there have been few epidemiological studies during the 1980s, but those that were done show no clear link between DDT exposure and cancer risk. For a review with citations, see Harold M. Schmeck, Jr., "Study Finds No Link Between Cancer Risk and DDT Exposure," *New York Times*, 14 February 1989, reporting a decade-long study of nearly 1,000 people with higher than average exposure to DDT; it found no statistically significant link between the amount of DDT in their bodies and the risk of death by cancer.

5. Scholars argue correctly, I believe, that "in the 1970s, the prevention of cancer risks was accepted as a proxy for all environmental damage." A. Dan Tarlock, "Earth and Other Ethics: The Institutional Issues," *Tennessee Law Review* 56, no. 1 (1988): 63 (citing the DDT controversy as an example). See also, *Regulating Pesticides*, National Academy of Sciences (Washington, D.C.: NAS Press, National Research Council, 1980), pp. 18–28.

6. Jeremy Rifkin, *Biosphere Politics: A New Consciousness for a New Century* (New York: Crown, 1991), p. 69.

7. Office of Policy Analysis, EPA, *The Cost of Clean Air and Water*, Executive Summary (1984), p. 3. For an overview of the disappointing results of water quality protection, see William Pedersen, "Turning the Tide on Water Quality," *Ecology Law Quarterly* 15 (1988): 69–73.

8. A. Kneese and B. Bower, *Managing Water Quality: Economics, Technology, Institutions* (Baltimore: John Hopkins Press, Resources for the Future, 1968), p. 125.

9. For details about the Westway Project, see *The Westway Project: A Study of Failure of Federal/State Relations*, Sixty-Sixth Report by the Committee on Government Operations, 98th Cong. 2d Sess., HR 98–1166, Washington, D.C., U.S.G.P.O., 1984. See also *Action for a Rational Transit v. West Side Highway Project*, 536 F. Supp. 1225 (S.D.N.Y. 1982); *Sierra Club v. U.S. Army Corps of Engineers*, 541 F.Supp. 1327 (S.D.N.Y 1982) and 701 F.2d 1011 (2d Cir. 1983). For another case history exemplifying the same point farther up the Hudson, see L. W. Barnhouse et al., "Population Biology in the Courtroom: The Hudson River Controversy," *BioScience* 34, no. 1 (1984): 14–19.

10. George Krantz is quoted in the *Washington Post*, 26 September 1984.

11. See, for example, Harold Webber, "Aquabusiness," in *Biotechnology and the Marine Sciences*, ed. R. Colwell, A. Sinskey, and E. Pariser (New York: Wiley, 1984), pp. 115–16. Webber believes we depend on traditional fisheries only because the "results of recent research and development in the biotechnological sciences have not yet been integrated into the broader context of large scale, vertically integrated, high technology, centrally controlled, aquabusiness food production systems." He calls the substitution of industrial for "natural" methods of fish production in aquatic environments "Vertically Integrated Aquaculture (VIA)."

12. Jay Mathews, "In Alaska, Oil Spill Has Lost Its Sheen," *Washington Post*, 9 February 1991.

13. For discussion, see T. C. Whitmore, "The Conservation of Tropical Rain Forests," in *Conservation Biology: An Evolutionary Perspective*, ed. M. Soulé and B. A. Wilcox (Sunderland, Mass.: Sinauer, 1980), p. 313: "The suggestion, sometimes made, that atmospheric oxygen levels would be lowered by the removal of tropical rain forests rests on a mistaken view of climax ecosystems."

14. See William Allen, "Penn Prof Views Biotechnology as Potential Threat to Tropical Forests," *Genetic Engineering News* 7, no. 10 (1987): 10. The article quotes a letter by Janzen: "Tropical wildlands and most of the earth's contemporary species still exist because humanity has not had organisms capable of converting all tropical land surfaces to profitable agriculture and animal husbandry. Within one to three decades, organisms modified through genetic engineering will be capable of making agriculture or animal husbandry, or both, profitable on virtually any land surface. Agricultural inviability, the single greatest tropical conservation force, will be gone."

    Some commentators have speculated that transpiration from rain forests may play some role in the atmosphere. Since more than 85 percent of water absorbed into the atmosphere comes from the oceans, however, the marginal difference—if any—in transpiration between natural and biotech species in rain forests is unlikely to be consequential.

15. Immanuel Kant, *Foundations of the Metaphysics of Morals*, ed. R. P. Wolff, trans. L. W. Beck (Indianapolis: Bobbs-Merrill, 1959), p. 53. Emphasis in original.

16. Perry Miller, *Nature's Nation* (Cambridge, Mass.: Harvard University Press, 1967).

17. William K. Reilly, "A Strategy to Save the Great Water Bodies," *EPA Journal* 16, no. 6 (1990): 4.

Environmental Ethics and Weak Anthropocentrism _____

*Bryan G. Norton**

I. Introduction

[I]n the present paper . . . I address the question of whether there must be a distinctively environmental ethic.

Discussions of this question in the literature have equated a negative answer with the belief that the standard categories of rights, interests, and duties of individual human beings are adequate to furnish ethical guidance in environmental decision making. A positive answer is equated with the suggestion that nature has, in some sense, intrinsic value. In other words, the question of whether environmental ethics is distinctive is taken as equivalent to the question of whether an environmental ethic must reject anthropocentrism, the view that only humans are loci of fundamental value.[1] Environmental ethics is seen as distinctive vis-à-vis standard ethics if and only if environmental ethics can be founded upon principles which assert or presuppose that nonhuman natural entities have value independent of human value.

I argue that this equivalence is mistaken by showing that the anthropocentrism/nonanthropocentrism debate is far less important than is usually assumed. Once an ambiguity is noted in its central terms, it becomes clear that nonanthropocentrism is not the only adequate basis for a truly environmental ethic.[2] I then argue that another dichotomy, that of individualism versus nonindividualism, should be seen as crucial to the distinctiveness of environmental ethics and that a successful environmental ethic cannot be individualistic in the way that standard contemporary ethical systems are. Finally, I examine the consequences of these conclusions for the nature and shape of an environmental ethic.

Before beginning these arguments, I need to clarify how I propose to test an adequate environmental ethic. I begin by assuming that all environmentally sensitive individuals believe that there is a set of human behaviors which do or would damage the environment. Further, I assume that there is considerable agreement among such individuals about what behaviors are included in that set. Most would decry, for example, careless storage of toxic wastes, grossly overpopulating the world with humans, wanton destruction of other species, air and water pollution, and so forth. There are other behaviors which would be more controversial, but I take the initial task of constructing an adequate environmental ethic to be the statement of some set of principles from which rules can be derived proscribing the behaviors included in the set which virtually all environmentally sensitive individuals agree are environmentally destructive. The further task of refining an environmental ethic then involves moving back and forth between the basic principles and the more or less controversial behaviors, adjusting principles and/or rejecting intuitions until the best possible fit between principles and sets of proscribed behaviors is obtained for the whole environmental community. In the present paper I address the prior question of basic principles. I am here only seeking to clarify which principles do (and which do not) support the large set of relatively uncontroversial cases of behaviors damaging to the environment. An ethic will be adequate, on this approach, if its principles are sufficient to entail rules proscribing the behaviors involved in the noncontroversial set. My arguments, then, are not directed at determining which principles are *true*, but which are *adequate* to uphold certain shared intuitions. Questions concerning the truth of such principles must be left for another occasion.

* Work on the present paper was completed under a National Endowment for the Humanities Summer Stipend on Ecological Theory and Ethics and under a National Science Foundation grant. Valuable comments and criticisms of earlier drafts of this paper were received from J. Baird Callicott, Robert Fullinwider, Holmes Rolston, III, Mark Sagoff, and Richard A. Watson.

Environmental Ethics, Vol. 6, No. 2 (Summer 1984), 131–136, 138–148. Reprinted by permission.

II. Anthropocentrism and Nonanthropocentrism

I suggest that the distinction between anthropocentrism and nonanthropocentrism has been given more importance in discussions of the foundations of environmental ethics than it warrants because a crucial ambiguity in the term *anthropocentrism* has gone unnoticed.[3] Writers on both sides of the controversy apply this term to positions which treat humans as the only loci of intrinsic value.[4] Anthropocentrists are therefore taken to believe that every instance of value originates in a contribution to human values and that all elements of nature can, at most, have value instrumental to the satisfaction of human interests.[5] Note that anthropocentrism is defined by reference to the position taken on *loci* of value. Some nonanthropocentrists say that human beings are the *source* of all values, but that they can designate nonhuman objects as loci of fundamental value.[6]

It has also become common to explain and test views on this point by reference to "last man examples" which are formulated as follows.[7] Assume that a human being, *S*, is the last living member of *Homo sapiens* and that *S* faces imminent death. Would *S* do wrong to wantonly destroy some object *X*? A positive answer to this question with regard to any nonhuman *X* is taken to entail nonanthropocentrism. If the variable *X* refers to some natural object, a species, an ecosystem, a geological formation, etc., then it is thought that positions on such questions determine whether a person is an anthropocentrist or not, because the action in question cannot conceivably harm any human individual. If it is wrong to destroy *X*, the wrongness must derive from harm to *X* or to some other natural object. But one can harm something only if it is a good in its own right in the sense of being a locus of fundamental value.

Or so the story goes. I am unconvinced because not nearly enough has been said about what counts as a human interest. In order to explore this difficult area, I introduce two useful definitions. A *felt preference* is any desire or need of a human individual that can at least temporarily be sated by some specifiable experience of that individual. A *considered preference* is any desire or need that a human individual would express after careful deliberation, including a judgment that the desire or need is consistent with a rationally adopted world view—a world view which includes fully supported scientific theories and a metaphysical framework interpreting those theories, as well as a set of rationally supported aesthetic and moral ideals.

When interests are assumed to be constructed merely from felt preferences, they are thereby insulated from any criticism or objection. Economic approaches to decision making often adopt this approach because it eschews "value judgments"— decision makers need only ask people what they want, perhaps correct these preferences for intensity, compute the preferences satisfied by the various possible courses of action, and let the resulting ordinal ranking imply a decision.

A considered preference, on the other hand, is an idealization in the sense that it can only be adopted after a person has rationally accepted an entire world view and, further, has succeeded in altering his felt preferences so that they are consonant with that world view. Since this is a process no one has ever completed, references to considered preferences are hypothetical—they refer to preferences the individual would have if certain contrary-to-fact conditions were fulfilled. Nonetheless, references to considered preferences remain useful because it is possible to distinguish felt preferences from considered preferences when there are convincing arguments that felt preferences are not consistent with some element of a world view that appears worthy of rational support.

It is now possible to define two forms of anthropocentrism. A value theory is *strongly anthropocentric* if all value countenanced by it is explained by reference to satisfactions of felt preferences of human individuals. A value theory is *weakly anthropocentric* if all value countenanced by it is explained by reference to satisfaction of some felt preference of a human individual or by reference to its bearing upon the ideals which exist as elements in a world view essential to determinations of considered preferences.

Strong anthropocentrism, as here defined, takes unquestioned felt preferences of human individuals as determining value. Consequently, if humans have a strongly consumptive value system, then their "interests" (which are taken merely to be their felt preferences) dictate that nature will be used in an exploitative manner. Since there is no check upon the felt preferences of individuals in the value system of strong anthropocentrism, there exists no means to criticize the behavior of individuals who use nature merely as a storehouse of raw materials to be extracted and used for products serving human preferences.

Weak anthropocentrism, on the other hand, recognizes that felt preferences can be either rational or not (in the sense that they can be judged not consonant with a rational world view). Hence, weak anthropocentrism provides a basis for criticism of value systems which are purely exploitative of nature. In this way, weak anthropocentrism makes available two ethical resources of crucial importance to environmentalists. First, to the extent that environmental ethicists can make a case for a world view that emphasizes the close relationship between the human species and other living species, they can also make a case for ideals of human behavior extolling harmony with nature. These ideals are then available as a basis for criticizing preferences that merely exploit nature.

Second, weak anthropocentrism as here defined also places value on human experiences that provide the basis for value formation. Because weak anthropocentrism places value not only on felt preferences, but also on the process of value formation embodied in the criticism and replacement of felt preferences with more rational ones, it makes possible appeals to the value of experiences of natural objects and undisturbed places in human value formation. To the extent that environmentalists can show that values are formed and informed by contact with nature, nature takes on value as a teacher of human values. Nature need no longer be seen as a mere satisfier of fixed and often consumptive values—it also becomes an important source of inspiration in value formation.[8]

In the final section of this paper I develop these two sources of value in nature more fully. Even there my goal is not to defend these two bases for environmental protection as embodying true claims about the value of nature—that, as I said at the outset is a larger and later task. My point is only that, within the limits set by weak anthropocentrism as

here defined, there exists a framework for developing powerful reasons for protecting nature. Further, these reasons do not resemble the extractive and exploitative reasons normally associated with strong anthropocentrism.

And they do not differ from strongly anthropocentric reasons in merely theoretical ways. Weakly anthropocentric reasoning can affect behavior as can be seen by applying it to last man situations. Suppose that human beings choose, for rational or religious reasons, to live according to an ideal of maximum harmony with nature. Suppose also that this ideal is taken seriously and that anyone who impairs that harmony (by destroying another species, by polluting air and water, etc.) would be judged harshly. But such an ideal need not attribute intrinsic value to natural objects, nor need the prohibitions implied by it be justified with nonanthropocentric reasoning attributing intrinsic value to nonhuman natural objects. Rather, they can be justified as being implied by the ideal of harmony with nature. This ideal, in turn, can be justified either on religious grounds referring to human spiritual development or as being a fitting part of a rationally defensible world view.

Indeed, there exist examples of well developed world views that exhibit these characteristics. The Hindus and Jains, in proscribing the killing of insects, etc., show concern for their own spiritual development rather than for the actual lives of those insects. Likewise, Henry David Thoreau is careful not to attribute independent, intrinsic value to nature. Rather he believes that nature expresses a deeper spiritual reality and that humans can learn spiritual values from it.[9] Nor should it be inferred that only spiritually oriented positions can uphold weakly anthropocentric reasons. In a post-Darwinian world, one could give rational and scientific support for a world view that includes ideals of living in harmony with nature, but which involve no attributions of intrinsic value to nature.

Views such as those just described are weakly anthropocentric because they refer only to human values, but they are not strongly so because human behavior is limited by concerns other than those derivable from prohibitions against interfering with the satisfaction of human felt preferences. And practically speaking, the difference in behavior between strong anthropocentrists and weak anthropocentrists of the sort just described and exemplified is very great. In particular, the reaction of these weak anthropocentrists to last man situations is undoubtedly more similar to that of nonanthropocentrists than to that of strong anthropocentrists. Ideals such as that of living in harmony with nature imply rules proscribing the wanton destruction of other species or ecosystems even if the human species faces imminent extinction. . . .

Nor need weak anthropocentrism collapse into strong anthropocentrism. It would do so if the dichotomy between preferences and ideals were indefensible. If all values can, ultimately, be interpreted as satisfactions of preferences, then ideals are simply human preferences. The controversy here is reminiscent of that discussed by early utilitarians. John Stuart Mill, for example, argued that because higher pleasures ultimately can be seen to provide greater satisfactions, there is thus only a single scale of values—preference satisfaction.[10] It is true that weak anthropocentrists must deny that preference satisfaction is the only measure of human value. They must take human ideals seriously enough so that they can be set against preference satisfactions as a limit upon them. It is therefore no surprise that weak anthropocentrists reject the reductionistic position popular among utilitarians. Indeed, it is precisely the rejection of that reductionism that allows them to steer their way between strong anthropocentrism and nonanthropocentrism. The rejection of this reduction is, of course, a commitment that weak anthropocentrists share with nonanthropocentrists. Both believe there are values distinct from human preference satisfaction, rejecting the reduction of ideals to preferences. They differ not on this point, but on whether the justification of those ideals must appeal to the intrinsic value of nonhuman objects.

Weak anthropocentrism is, therefore, an attractive position for environmentalists. It requires no radical, difficult-to-justify claims about the intrinsic value of nonhuman objects and, at the same time, it provides a framework for stating obligations that goes beyond concern for satisfying human preferences. It, rather, allows the development of arguments to the effect that current, largely consumptive attitudes toward nature are indefensible, because they do not fit into a world view that is rationally defensible in terms not implying intrinsic value for nonhumans. It can also emphasize the value of nature in forming, rather than in satisfying human preferences, as preferences can be modified in the process of striving toward a consistent and rationally defensible world view.

III. Individualism and Nonindividualism

The distinctions and arguments presented above convince me that, while the development of a nonanthropocentric axiology committed to intrinsic value for nonhuman natural entities remains an interesting philosophical enterprise, the dichotomy on which it is based has less importance for the nature of environmental ethics than is usually thought. In particular, I see no reason to think that, if environmental ethics is distinctive, its distinctiveness derives from the necessity of appeals to the intrinsic value of nonhuman natural objects. Once two forms of anthropocentrism are distinguished, it appears that from one, weak anthropocentrism, an adequate environmental ethic can be derived. If that is true, authors who equate the question of the distinctiveness of an adequate environmental ethic with the claim that nature or natural objects have intrinsic value are mistaken.

There is, nevertheless, reason to believe that an adequate environmental ethic is distinctive. In this section, I argue that no successful environmental ethic can be derived from an individualistic basis, whether the individuals in question are human or nonhuman. Since most contemporary ethical systems are essentially individualistic, an adequate environmental ethic is distinctive, not by being necessarily nonanthropocentric as many environmental ethicists have argued or assumed, but, rather, by being nonindividualistic.

Standard contemporary ethical theories, at least in the United States and Western Europe are essentially individualistic. By this I mean that the behavioral prohibitions embodied in them derive from the principle that actions ought not to harm other individuals unjustifiably. Utilitarians derive ethical rules from the general principle that all actions should promote the greatest possible happiness for the greatest possible number of individuals. This means that actions (or rules) are judged to be legitimate or not according to whether more good (and less harm) for individuals will result from the action than from any alternative. On this view, the satisfaction of each individual interest is afforded an initial prima facie value. Some such interests are not to be satisfied because the information available indicates that if they are, some greater interest or sets of interests of some individuals cannot be satisfied concurrently with them. The utilitarian principle, supplemented by empirical predictions about the consequences of actions for individuals, filters happiness-maximizing actions from others that do not maximize happiness. For present purposes, the important point is that the satisfaction of individual interests are the basic unit of value for utilitarians, and in this sense, utilitarianism (either of the act or rule variety) is essentially individualistic.[11]

Contemporary deontologists derive ethical prohibitions from individual rights and obligations to protect those rights.[12] Individuals make claims, and when these claims conflict with claims made by other individuals, they are judged to be legitimate or illegitimate according to a set of ethical rules designed to make such decisions. Although these rules, in essence, are the embodiment of a system of justice and fairness, the rules adjudicate between claims of individuals, and consequently modern deontology is essentially individualistic.[13] Therefore, both utilitarianism and modern deontology are essentially individualistic in the sense that the basic units of ethical concern are interests or claims of individuals.

It is characteristic of the rules of environmental ethics that they must prohibit current behaviors that have effects upon the long-range future as well as the present. For example, storage of radioactive wastes with a half-life of thousands of years in containers that will deteriorate in a few centuries must be prohibited by an adequate environmental ethic, even if such actions, on the whole, provide the most benefits and no harms to currently living individuals. Likewise, human demographic growth, if subsequent generations continue that policy, will create severe overpopulation, a behavior negatively affecting the future of the environment, and hence human reproductive behavior must be governed by an adequate environmental ethic. An adequate environmental ethic must therefore prohibit current activities generally agreed to have negative effects on the environment of the future.

I have argued at length elsewhere that a paradox, due to Derek Parfit, effectively precludes systems of ethics which are individualistic in the sense defined above from governing current decisions by reference to their effects on future individuals.[14] To summarize that argument briefly, it exploits the insight that no system of ethics built exclusively upon adjudications of interests of present and future individuals can govern current decisions and their effects on future individuals because current environmental decisions determine what individuals will exist in the future. Parfit's argument notes that current decisions regarding consumption determine how many individuals and which individuals will be born in the future. On a policy of fast demographic growth and high consumption, different individuals will exist a century from now than would exist if the current generation adopts a policy of low growth and moderate consumption. Assume, as most environmentalists do, that a policy of high growth and immoderate consumption will leave the future with a lower quality of life than more moderate growth policies would. The individuals who are, in fact, born as a result of the immoderate growth policies cannot complain that they would have been better off had the policies been different—for they would not even have existed had moderate policies been adopted. That is, Parfit's paradox shows that current policy cannot be governed by reference to harms to the interests of future individuals, because those policies determine who those individuals will be and what interests they will have. Attempts to govern behaviors affecting the distant future cannot, therefore, be governed by appeal to individual interests of future persons, since the very existence of such individuals hangs in the balance until all relevant decisions are made.

Since the ethical intuitions shared by all environmentally sensitive individuals include prohibitions against behaviors which may have negative effects only in the long-term future (and not in the present), the rules of environmental ethics cannot be derived from the usual, individualistic systems of ethics currently in vogue. Note, also, that my argument concerning individualism makes no assumption that only human individuals make claims or have interests and rights. Future nonhuman individuals are, likewise, affected by human policies regarding consumption and reproduction. Consequently, expansion of the loss of individual rights holders, or preference havers to include nonhumans in no way affects the argument. No ethical system which is essentially individualistic, regardless of how broadly the reference category of individuals is construed, can offer ethical guidance concerning current environmental policy in all cases.

IV. A Proposal for an Adequate Anthropocentric Environmental Ethic

The arguments of the last section are surprisingly simple and general, but if they are sound, they explain the fairly general intuition that environmental ethics must be distinctive in some sense, although not in the sense usually assumed. So far my conclusions have all been negative—I have argued that an adequate environmental ethic *need not* be nonanthropocentric and that an adequate environmental ethic *must not* be limited to considerations of individual interests. From these conclusions a new direction for environmental ethics emerges which is weakly anthropocentric—it finds all value in human loci—and which is also nonindividualistic in the sense that value is not restricted to satisfactions of felt preferences of human individuals. In other words, the arguments of the first two sections of the paper (1) positively define a space by establishing the possibility of a weakly, but not strongly, anthropocentric environmental ethic and (2) negatively constrain that ethic by eliminating the possibility that it be purely individualistic.

My purpose now is not to demonstrate that the ethical principles I have set out are definitely correct or that they are the only adequate principles available. My goal, rather, is to present a valid alternative for environmental ethics that is adequate in a manner that no purely individualistic, strongly anthropocentric ethic can be, while avoiding difficult-to-defend references to the intrinsic value of nonhuman natural objects.

I begin my explication with an analogy. Suppose an extremely wealthy individual, through a will, sets up a very large trust fund "to be managed for the economic well-being of my descendants." Over the years, descendants will be born and die, and the class of beneficiaries will change through time. Suppose, also, that the family drifts apart emotionally and becomes highly contentious. I suggest that two sorts of controversies, each with its own distinctive logic, could arise concerning the fund. First, there may be issues about the *fair distribution* of proceeds of the trust. Some descendants

might claim that other descendants are not entitled to full shares, because they are, or are descended from, an illegitimate offspring of a member of the family. Or it might be disputed whether adopted children of descendants are included in the terms of the will.

Second, there may well be disputes about the *management* of the trust. Here, there may be questions concerning what sorts of investments are "good investments." Should all investments be safe ones, thereby insuring a continued, although smaller income? Might the principle of the trust be invaded in years where the income from investments is unusually low? Might one generation simply spend the principle, dividing it fairly among themselves, showing no concern for future descendants?

To apply this analogy in obvious ways, ethical questions about the environment can be divided into ones concerning distributional fairness within generations and others concerning longer-term, cross-generational issues. If the arguments in the third section are correct, then the latter are not reducible to the former; nor do they have the same logic. It can be assumed that many environmental concerns, as well as nonenvironmental ones, can be resolved as issues of distributional fairness. If a property owner pollutes a stream running through his property, this action raises a question of fairness between him and his downstream neighbor.[15] These moral issues are, presumably, as amenable to resolution using the categories and rules of standard, individualistic ethics as are nonenvironmental ones.

But there are also many questions in environmental ethics that are analogous to questions of management of a trust across time. Soil, water, forests, coal, oil, etc. are analogous to the principle of the trust. If they are used up, destroyed, or degraded, they no longer provide benefits. The income from the trust provides an analogy for renewable resources. As long as the productive resource (analogous to the principle of the trust) is intact, one can expect a steady flow of benefits.

One feature that makes environmental ethics distinctive is concern for protection of the resource base through indefinite time. Parfit's paradox shows that these concerns cannot be accounted for by reference to concerns for individuals and to the obligation not to harm other individuals unjustifiably. The obligations are analogous to those accepted by an individual who is appointed executor of the trust fund. Although decisions made by the executor affect individuals and their well-being, the obligation is to the integrity of the trust, not to those individuals. While one might be tempted to say that the obligation of the executor is to future individuals who will be born, but who are at this time unknown, this conceptualization also involves a failure to perceive the profundity of Parfit's paradox. Suppose all of the members of a given generation of the family in question sign an agreement not to have offspring and thereby convince the executor to disburse the principle of the trust equally among current beneficiaries. Perhaps this is consistent with the terms of the trust, but it shows that the current choices of the executor cannot be guided by abstract conceptions of "future individuals." When current decisions about management are interlocked with not-yet-decided questions affecting the future existence of individuals, it is impossible to refer to those individuals as the basis of guidance in making current management decisions.

Suppose a generation of the entire human species freely decided to sterilize itself, thereby freeing itself to consume without fear of harming future individuals. Would they do wrong? Yes.[16] The perpetuation of the human species is a good thing because a universe containing human consciousness is preferable to one without it.[17] This value claim implies that current generations must show concern for future generations. They must take steps to avoid the extinction of the species and they must provide a reasonably stable resource base so that future generations will not suffer great deprivation. These are the bases of rules of management analogous to the rules for administering a trust fund. They do not have individuals or individual interests as their reference point, but they do govern behavior that will affect future individuals.

It is now possible to outline a weakly anthropocentric, nonindividualistic environmental ethic. Such an ethic has two levels. The distributional level has as its principle that one ought not to harm other human individuals unjustifiably. This principle rests upon the assumption that felt preferences, desires that occur within individual human consciousness, have equal prima facie value. Rules for the fair treatment of individuals are derived from the principle of no harm and prescribe fair treatment of individuals, whether regarding benefits derived from the environment or from other

sources. Since there is nothing distinctive about the environmental prescriptions and proscriptions that occur on this level—they do not differ in nature from other issues of individual fairness—I do not discuss them further.

Decisions on the second level of environmental ethics, which I call the level of "allocation," cannot, however, be based upon individual considerations. The central value placed on human consciousness is not a result of aggregating the value of individual consciousnesses, because the value of ongoing consciousness cannot be derived from the value of individual consciousnesses—they cannot be identified or counted prior to the making of decisions on resource allocation.[18] Therefore, obligations on this level are owed to no individual and can be called "generalized obligations." They are obligations of the current generation to maintain a stable flow of resources into the indefinite future and, consequently, they are stated vis-à-vis resources necessary for ongoing human life, not vis-à-vis individual requirements. Resources represent the means for supporting life looked at from a nonindividual perspective. The individual perspective determines needs and wants and then seeks means to fulfill them. Concern for the continued flow of resources insures that sources of goods and services such as ecosystems, soil, forests, etc. remain "healthy" and are not deteriorating. In this way, options are held open and reasonable needs of individuals for whatever goods and services can be fulfilled with reasonable labor, technology, and ingenuity. The emphasis of this concern, however, is not individualistic since it is not focused on the fulfillment of specifiable needs, but rather on the integrity and health of ongoing ecosystems as holistic entities.

While the long-term nature of the concern implies that the stability of the resource base must be protected, this stability is not the same thing as ecological stability. It is an open (and controversial) question as to what the stability of ecosystems means. Further, there are controversies concerning the extent to which there are scientifically supportable generalizations about what is necessary to protect ecological stability. For example, it is highly controversial whether diversity, in general, promotes and/or is necessary for ecological stability.[19] These controversies are too complex to enter into here, but they are relevant. To the extent that scientists know what is necessary to protect the resource base, there is an obligation to act upon it. Even if there are few sweeping generalizations such as those concerning diversity and stability, there are a wide variety of less general rules that are well supported and are being systematically ignored in environmental policy. Ecologists and resource managers know that clear-cutting tropical forests on steep slopes causes disastrous erosion, that intensely tilling monocultures causes loss of topsoil, and that overexploitation of fisheries can cause new and far less productive species compositions. Further, there is an obligation, where knowledge is lacking, to seek that knowledge in order to avoid unintentional destruction.

An ethic of resource allocation should apply to nonrenewable resources as well as to renewable ones and should also imply a population policy. The general injunction to maintain the stability of the resource base across generations follows from the value of human consciousness. It implies that, with respect to renewable, or interest-bearing resources, present generations should not harvest more than the maximum sustainable yield of the resource. But what does stability imply with respect to nonrenewable resources? Although at first glance it would seem to suggest that a stable supply can only be sustained if no utilization takes place, this reasoning is based on a confusion—it is not the case that there is an obligation to have a certain, fixed amount of goods in supply, but rather there is an obligation to maintain a stable level of goods *available for use*. The ethical principle, in other words, is directed at maintaining the possibility of human consciousness which requires resource use. What is required, then, is a constant supply of resources available for utilization by succeeding generations. Once the problem is framed in this manner, human technology and the phenomenon of substitutability of products become relevant. Present humans may use up nonrenewable resources, provided they take steps to provide suitable substitutes. If, for example, the present generation uses up a major portion of the accumulated fossil fuels available, they will have done nothing wrong if they leave the next generation with a technology capable of deriving energy from renewable sources such as the sun, wind, or ocean current.[20] There are significant trade-offs available back and forth between renewable and nonrenewable resources.

Note also that this system implies a population principle—the level of population in any given generation should be determined by the requirements for the stability of the resource flow. Such a determination would be based on an assessment of (a) how many people are consistent with the maximal sustainable yield of renewable resources and (b) how many people are consistent with a level of use for nonrenewable resources which does not outstrip the ability of the existing technology to produce suitable substitutes. A population principle follows, in turn, from this stability principle. One need not identify future individuals or worry about utilities of possible individuals on this approach. The obligation is to maintain maximum sustainable yield consistent with the stability of the resource flow. The population principle sets a population policy for a generation as a whole based on the carrying capacity of the environment. Questions about who, in a given generation, should have children and how many each individual can have, may be treated as questions of interpersonal equity among the existing individuals of any given generation.

The ethical obligations constituting an ethic of allocation are quite simple as they derive from a single value—that of ongoing human consciousness. In general form, however, they do not state specifically what to do; they only require actions necessary to retain a stable resource base through indefinite time. Scientific knowledge can, in principle, nevertheless, indicate specific actions necessary in order to fulfill that obligation. Scientific evidence is sufficient to imply that many currently widespread practices violate those obligations either directly or cumulatively and are, in terms of this system, immoral. There are also areas where scientific knowledge is insufficient to decide whether and how certain practices are destructive. Here, the obligation is to be cautious and to proceed to obtain the information necessary.

While science plays a crucial role in this system, the system is not naturalistic. It does not derive moral obligations from purely scientific statements. Central to all obligations of present individuals to the future is an obligation to perpetuate the value of human consciousness. Science elucidates and makes concrete the specific obligations flowing from that central obligation but does not support it.

V. Relating the Two Levels

The ethic proposed has two levels—one has the prima facie equality of felt preferences of individual humans as its central value principle; the other has the value of ongoing human life and consciousness as its central value principle. Rules and behaviors justified on these two levels can, of course, conflict. If felt preferences are overly consumptive, then the future of human life may be threatened. Conversely, one can imagine situations where concern for the future of the human species might lead to draconian measures threatening the life or livelihood of current individuals by limiting the satisfaction of felt preferences. Weak anthropocentrism, nevertheless, because it recognizes the important difference between felt and considered preferences, can adjudicate these disputes.

The most common conflict, the one many environmentalists fear we now face, exists when overly consumptive felt preferences cause serious over-exploitation of nature and thereby threaten the resource base necessary for continued human life. This conflict can be resolved by taking human ideals into consideration. If, for example, one's total world view contains as an ideal the continuation of human life and consciousness, then the felt preferences in question are irrational—they are inconsistent with an important ethical ideal. Similarly, if a rational world view recognizing that the human species evolved from other life forms includes an ideal calling for harmony with nature, this ideal, likewise, can function to criticize and alter felt preferences. By building ecological principles and ideals regarding the proper human treatment of nature into a rationally supported world view, weak anthropocentrists can develop vast resources for criticizing felt preferences of human individuals which threaten environmental stability and harmony.

It can be argued that experiences of nature are essential in constructing a rational world view. Likewise, scientific understanding of nature seems essential for the construction of such a world view. Nor would it be very surprising if it turned out that analogies, symbols, and metaphors drawn from nature provided an essential source of guidance in choosing ethical and aesthetic ideals as well.[21] Other species and unspoiled places would thereby have great value to humans not only for the way in which they satisfy human felt preferences but also for the way they serve to enlighten those preferences. Once one recognizes the distinction between felt preferences and considered preferences, nature assumes a crucial role in informing values by con-

tributing to the formation of a rational world view, the criterion by which felt preferences are criticized.

VI. Environmental Ethics and Intrinsic Value

The conflicts that exist between the levels of distributive fairness and allocation require thoughtful discussion and debate, but that discussion and debate can take place without appeal to the intrinsic value of nonhuman natural objects. The value of ongoing human consciousness and the rules it implies for resource allocation can serve as a basis for criticism of consumptive and exploitative felt preferences. Further, ideas such as that of human harmony with nature and the human species' evolutionary affinity to other species, can serve to strengthen and add flesh to the world view available for the critique of current environmentally destructive behaviors.

When I refer to an environmental ethic, then, I refer, first of all, to the rules of distributive fairness guiding behaviors affecting other human beings' use of the environment. Second, I refer to the rules of allocation affecting the long-term health of the biosphere as a functioning, organic unit. An environmental ethic, nevertheless, is more than these rules: it also encompasses the ideals, values, and principles that constitute a rational world view regarding the human species' relationship to nature. In these sources are bases for evaluating the rules of right action and for criticizing currently felt preferences. Aesthetic experience of nature is an essential part of the process of forming and applying these ideals and, hence, is also a central part of the environmental ethic here described.

Some nonanthropocentrists, such as J. Baird Callicott, have developed in more detail such ideas as the human affinity to other species and have concluded that it is rational for humans to "attribute" intrinsic value to other species on the basis of affective feelings toward them,[22] but if, as I have argued, a sense of harmony with nature can, once it becomes an entrenched part of our world view, serve to correct felt preferences, then it can also serve to bring felt preferences more in line with the requirements of resource allocation without any talk about intrinsic value. Of course, since human beings, as highly evolved animals, share many needs for clean air, clean water, ecosystem services, etc., in the long term with other species it would not be surprising that *speaking as if* nature has intrinsic value could provide useful guidance in adjusting human felt preferences. And since these preferences are now far too exploitative and too consumptive for the good of our own species, showing concern for other species that share our long-term needs for survival might be one useful tool in a very large kit.

The point of this essay, however, has been to show that one need not make the questionable ontological commitments involved in attributing intrinsic value to nature, since weak anthropocentrism provides a framework adequate to criticize current destructive practices to incorporate concepts of human affinity to nature, and to account for the distinctive nature of environmental ethics. All of these are essential elements in an ethic that recognizes the distinction between felt and considered preferences and includes important aesthetic and ethical ideals. These ideals, which can be derived from spiritual sources or from a rationally constructed world view, can be based on and find their locus in human values. And yet they are sufficient to provide the basis of criticism of currently overconsumptive felt preferences. As such they adjudicate between ethical concerns for distributional fairness in the present and concerns of allocation which have reference to the long-term future. Essential to this adjudication is the development of principles of conduct that respect the ongoing integrity of functioning ecosystems seen as wholes. In this way they transcend concern for individualistically expressed felt preferences and focus attention on the stable functioning of ongoing systems. If all of this is true, Occam's razor surely provides a basis for favoring weak anthropocentrism over nonanthropocentrism.

Notes

1. See, for example, Richard Routley, "Is There a Need for a New, an Environmental Ethic?" *Proceedings of the XV World Congress of Philosophy*, vol. 1 (1973), pp. 205–10; Holmes Rolston, III, "Is There an Ecological Ethic?" *Ethics* 85 (1975): 93–109; Tom Regan, "The Nature and Possibility of an Environmental Ethic," *Environmental Ethics* 3 (1981): 19–34; and Evelyn B. Pluhar, "The Justification of an Environmental Ethic," *Environmental Ethics* 4 (1982): 319–37.

2. See Regan, "The Nature and Possibility of an Environmental Ethic," who distinguishes "an ethic of the environment" from "an ethic for the use of the environment" (p. 20), where the former, but not the latter, recognizes the intrinsic (inherent) value of nonhuman elements of nature. If the arguments of this paper are persuasive, Regan's distinction will lose interest.

3. My thoughts on this subject have been deeply affected by discussions of the work of Donald Regan and J. Baird Callicott. See, Donald Regan, "Duties of Preservation," and J. Baird Callicott, "On the Intrinsic Value of Nonhuman Species," in *The Preservation of Species*, edited by Bryan G. Norton (in preparation).

4. I borrow this phrase from Donald Scherer, "Anthropocentrism, Atomism, and Environmental Ethics," *Environmental Ethics* 4 (1982): 115–23.

5. I take anthropocentrism to be interchangeable with homocentrism. See R. and V. Routley, "Against the Inevitability of Human Chauvinism," in *Ethics and Problems of the 21st Century*, edited by K. E. Goodpaster and K. M. Sayre (Notre Dame, Ind.: University of Notre Dame Press, 1979), pp. 56–7. Routley and Routley show that "human chauvinism" (anthropocentrism, homocentrism) are equivalent to the thesis of man's "dominion," which they describe as "the view that the earth and all its nonhuman contents exist or are available for man's benefit and to serve his interests."

6. See J. Baird Callicott, "On the Intrinsic Value of Nonhuman Species," in Norton, *The Preservation of Species* (in preparation), and Pluhar, "The Justification of an Environmental Ethic."

7. See, for example, Richard Routley, "Is There a Need for a New, an Environmental, Ethic?" p. 207; Routley and Routley, "Human Chauvinism and Environmental Ethics," in *Environmental Philosophy*, edited by D. S. Mannison, M. A. McRobbie and R. Routley (Canberra: Australian National University, Department of Philosophy, 1980), p. 121; and Donald Regan, "Duties of Preservation," in Norton, *The Preservation of Species*.

8. For fuller discussions of this point, see Mark Sagoff, "On Preserving the Natural Environment," *Yale Law Journal* 84 (1974): 205–67; Holmes Rolston, III, "Can and Ought We to Follow Nature?" *Environmental Ethics* 1 (1979): 7–21; and Bryan G. Norton, *The Spice of Life* (in preparation).

9. See Henry David Thoreau, *Walden* (New York: Harper and Row, 1958). Note page 64, for example, where Thoreau writes: "One value of even the smallest well is, that when you look into it you see that earth is not continent but insular. This is as important as that it keeps butter cool."

10. John Stuart Mill, *Utilitarianism*, chap. 2.

11. I do not intend to imply here that utilitarians are limited to treating human interests as felt preferences. Utilitarians adopt varied interpretations of interests in relation to happiness. My point is only that human individual interests, however determined, are the basis of their moral calculus.

12. I qualify the position here discussed as "contemporary" deontology because there is a strain of thought in Kant which emphasizes that the imperatives are abstract principles. Modern neo-Kantians such as Rawls, however, emphasize the more individualistic strains in Kant, placing him more in the contractarian tradition. Contractarian deontologists—those that fit clearly into the liberal tradition—are my concern here. (I am indebted to Douglas Berggren for clarifying this point.)

13. For a clear explanation of how rights function to adjudicate individual claims, see Joel Feinberg, "The Nature and Value of Rights," *Journal of Value Inquiry* 4 (1970): 243–57. While not all writers agree that rights originate in claims, the disputes are immaterial here. For example, McCloskey's linkage of rights to "entitlements" is not inconsistent with my point. H. J. McCloskey, "Rights," *Philosophical Quarterly* 15 (1965): 115–27.

14. See, "Energy and the Further Future," in *Energy and the Future*, edited by Douglas MacLean and Peter G. Brown (Totowa, N.J.: Rowman and Littlefield, 1983). I apply Parfit's "paradox" to environmental ethics in "Environmental Ethics and the Rights of Future Generations," *Environmental Ethics* 4 (1982): 321. See that essay for a more detailed discussion.

15. This is not to suggest, of course, that such action could not also have more long-term effects raising issues of the second sort as well.

16. This answer implies a disanalogy with the trust fund situation, provided one accepts the judgment that no wrong would be committed if a generation of the family chose not to reproduce. I think there is a disanalogy here, as different reproductive obligations would arise if the future of the human species were at stake. Suppose one answers this question negatively regarding the future of human kind and then considers the possibility that the last human individual might wantonly destroy other species, natural places, etc. I would still reject such wanton acts as inconsistent with good human behavior, relying upon weakly anthropocentric arguments as described above.

17. I willingly accept the implication of this value claim that, in a situation of severely contracting human population, some or all individuals would have an obligation to reproduce, but I will not defend this central claim here. Although I believe it can be defended, I am more interested in integrating it into a coherent ethical system than in defending it.

18. On a closely related point, see Brian Barry, "Circumstances of Justice and Future Generations," in Sikora and Barry, eds. *Obligations to Future Generations* (Philadelphia: Temple University Press, 1978).

19. See Norton, *The Spice of Life*.

20. I am, for the sake of the example, ignoring other long-term effects of the use of fossil fuels. Problems due to the greenhouse effect would, of course, also have to be solved.

21. See references in note 8 above.

22. Callicott, "On the Intrinsic Value of Nonhuman Species." Also see Pluhar, "The Justification of an Environmental Ethic" for a somewhat different approach to attribution of intrinsic value.

Self Realization: An Ecological Approach to Being in the World ____

Arne Naess

For at least 2500 years, humankind has struggled with basic questions about who we are, what we are heading for, what kind of reality we are part of. Two thousand five hundred years is a short period in the lifetime of a species, and still less in the lifetime of the Earth, on whose surface we belong as mobile parts.

What I am going to say more or less in my own way, may roughly be condensed into the following six points:

Thinking Like a Mountain: Towards a Council of All Beings, by John Seed, Joanna Macy, Pat Fleming, Arne Naess (Philadelphia: New Society Publishers, 1988), pp. 19–30. Reprinted by permission.

1. We underestimate ourselves. I emphasize *self*. We tend to confuse it with the narrow ego.

2. Human nature is such that with sufficient all-sided maturity we cannot avoid "identifying" ourselves with all living beings, beautiful or ugly, big or small, sentient or not. I will elucidate my concept of identifying later.

3. Traditionally the *maturity of the self* develops through three stages—from ego to social self, and from social self to metaphysical self. In this conception of the process nature—our home, our immediate environment, where we belong as children, and our identification with living human beings—is largely ignored. I therefore tentatively introduce the concept of an *ecological self*. We may be in, of and for nature from our very beginning. Society and human relations are important, but our self is richer in its constitutive relations. These relations are not only relations we have with humans and the human community, but with the larger community of all living beings.

4. The joy and meaning of life is enhanced through increased self-realization, through the fulfillment of each being's potential. Whatever the differences between beings, increased self-realization implies broadening and deepening of the *self*.

5. Because of an inescapable process of identification with others, with growing maturity, the self is widened and deepened. We "see ourself in others." Self-realization is hindered if the self-realization of others, with whom we identify, is hindered. Love of ourself will labor to overcome this obstacle by assisting in the self-realization of others according to the formula "live and let live." Thus, all that can be achieved by altruism—the dutiful, *moral* consideration of others—can be achieved—and much more—through widening and deepening ourself. Following Immanuel Kant's critique, we then act *beautifully* but neither morally nor immorally.

6. The challenge of today is to save the planet from further devastation which violates both the enlightened self-interest of humans and nonhumans, and decreases the potential of joyful existence for all.

The simplest answer to who or what I am is to point to my body, using my finger. But clearly I cannot identify my self or even my ego with my body. For example, compare:

I know Mr. Smith.	*with*	My body knows Mr. Smith.
I like poetry.		My body likes poetry.
The only difference		The only difference
between us is that		between our bodies is that
you are a Presbyterian		your body is Presbyterian
and I am a Baptist.		whereas mine is Baptist.

In the above sentences we cannot substitute "my body" for "I" nor can we substitute "my mind" or "my mind and body" for "I." But this of course does not tell us what the ego or self is.

Several thousand years of philosophical, psychological and social-psychological discourse has not brought us any stable conception of the "I," ego, or the self. In modern psychotherapy these notions play an indispensable role, but the practical goal of therapy does not necessitate philosophical clarification of the terms. For our purposes, it is important to remind ourselves what strange and marvelous phenomena we are dealing with. They are extremely close to each of us. Perhaps the very nearness of these objects of reflection and discourse adds to our difficulties. I shall only offer a single sentence resembling a definition of the ecological self. The ecological self of a person is that with which this person identifies.

This key sentence (rather than definition) about the self, shifts the burden of clarification from the term *self* to that of *identification* or more accurately, the *process of identification*.

What would be a paradigmatic situation of identification? It is a situation in which identification elicits intense empathy. My standard example has to do with a nonhuman being I met forty years ago. I looked through an old-fashioned microscope at the dramatic meeting of two drops of different chemicals. A flea jumped from a lemming strolling along the table and landed in the middle of the acid chemicals. To save it was impossible. It took many minutes for the flea to die. Its movements were dreadfully expressive. What I felt was, naturally, a painful compassion and empathy. But the empathy was *not* basic. What *was* basic was the process of identification, that "I see myself in the flea." If I was alienated from the flea, not seeing intuitively anything resembling myself, the death struggle would have left me indifferent. So there must be identification in order for there to be compassion and, among humans, solidarity.

One of the authors contributing admirably to clarification of the study of self is Erich Fromm:

> The doctrine that love for oneself is identical with *selfishness* and an alternative to love for others has pervaded theology, philosophy, and popular thought; the same doctrine has been rationalized in scientific language in Freud's theory of narcissism. Freud's concept presupposes a fixed amount of libido. In the infant, all of the libido has the child's own person as its objective, the stage of *primary narcissism* as Freud calls it. During the individual's development, the libido is shifted from one's own person toward other objects. If a person is blocked in his *object-relationships* the libido is withdrawn from the objects and returned to his or her own person; this is called *secondary narcissism*. According to Freud, the more love I turn toward the outside world the less love is left for myself, and vice versa. He thus describes the phenomenon of love as an impoverishment of one's self-love because all libido is turned to an object outside oneself.[1]

Fromm, however, disagrees with Freud's analysis. He concerned himself solely with love of humans, but as "ecosophers" we find the notions of "care, respect, responsibility, knowledge" applicable to living beings in the wide sense.

> Love of others and love of ourselves are not alternatives. On the contrary, an attitude of love toward themselves will be found in all those who are capable of loving others. Love, in principle, is indivisible as far as the connection between *objects* and one's own self is concerned. Genuine love is an expression of productiveness and implies care, respect, responsibility, and knowledge. It is not an *effect* in the sense of being effected by somebody, but an active striving for the growth

and happiness of the loved person, rooted in one's own capacity to love.[2]

Fromm is very instructive about unselfishness—diametrically opposite to selfishness, but still based upon alienation and a narrow perception of self. What he says applies also to persons experiencing sacrifice of themselves.

The nature of unselfishness becomes particularly apparent in its effect on others and most frequently, in our culture, in the effect the "unselfish" mother has on her children. She believes that by her unselfishness her children will experience what it means to be loved and in turn to learn what it means to love. The effect of her unselfishness, however, does not at all correspond to her expectations. The children do not show the happiness of persons who are convinced that they are loved; they are anxious, tense, afraid of the mother's disapproval, and anxious to live up to her expectations. Usually, they are affected by their mother's hidden hostility against life, which they sense rather than recognize, and eventually become imbued with it themselves:

> If one has a chance to study the effect of a mother with genuine self-love, one can see that there is nothing more conducive to giving a child the experience of what love, joy, and happiness are than being loved by a mother who loves herself.[3]

From the viewpoint of ecophilosophy, the point is this: We need environmental ethics, but when people feel they unselfishly give up, even sacrifice, their interest in order to show love for nature, this is probably in the long run a treacherous basis for ecology. Through broader identification, they may come to see their own interest served by environmental protection, through genuine self-love, love of a widened and deepened self.

As a student and admirer since 1930 of Gandhi's nonviolent direct action, I am inevitably influenced by his metaphysics which furnished him tremendously powerful motivation to keep on going until his death. His supreme aim, as he saw it, was not only India's *political* liberation. He led crusades against extreme poverty, caste suppression, and against terror in the name of religion. These crusades were necessary, but the liberation of the individual human being was his highest end. Hearing Gandhi's description of his ultimate goal may sound strange to many of us.

> What I want to achieve—what I have been striving and pining to achieve these thirty years—is self-realization, to see God face to face, to attain *Moksha* (Liberation). I live and move and have my being in pursuit of that goal. All that I do by way of speaking and writing, and all my ventures in the political field, are directed to this same end.[4]

This sounds individualistic to the Western mind, a common misunderstanding. If the self Gandhi is speaking about were the ego or the "narrow" self (*jiva*) of egocentric interest, of narrow ego gratifications, why then work for the poor? For him it is the supreme or universal Self—the *atman*—that is to be realized. Paradoxically, it seems, he tries to reach self-realization through *selfless action,* that is, through reduction of the dominance of the narrow self or ego. Through the wider Self every living being is connected intimately, and from this intimacy follows the capacity of *identification* and as its natural consequences, the practice of nonviolence. No moralizing is necessary, just as we do not require moralizing to make us breathe. We need to cultivate our insight, to quote Gandhi again "The rockbottom foundation of the technique for achieving the power of nonviolence is belief in the essential oneness of all life."

Historically we have seen how ecological preservation is nonviolent at its very core. Gandhi notes:

> I believe in *advaita* (non-duality), I believe in the essential unity of man and, for that matter, of all that lives. Therefore I believe that if one man gains spirituality, the whole world gains with him and, if one man fails, the whole world fails to that extent.[5]

Some people might consider Gandhi extreme in his personal consideration for the self-realization of liv-

ing beings other than humans. He traveled with a goat to satisfy his need for milk. This was part of a nonviolent witness against certain cruel features in the Hindu way of milking cows. Furthermore, some European companions who lived with Gandhi in his ashram were taken aback that he let snakes, scorpions and spiders move unhindered into their bedrooms—animals fulfilling their lives. He even prohibited people from having a stock of medicines against poisonous bites. He believed in the possibility of satisfactory coexistence and he proved right. There were no accidents. Ashram people would naturally look into their shoes for scorpions before putting them on. Even when moving over the floor in darkness one could easily avoid trampling on one's fellow beings. Thus, Gandhi recognized a basic, common right to live and blossom, to self-realization applicable to any being having interests or needs. Gandhi made manifest the internal relation between self-realization, nonviolence and what is sometimes called biospherical egalitarianism.

In the environment in which I grew up, I heard that what is important in life is to *be* somebody—usually implying to outdo others, to be victorious in comparison of abilities. This conception of the meaning and goal of life is especially dangerous today in the context of vast international economic competition. The law of supply and demand of separate, isolatable "goods and services" independent of real needs, must not be made to reign over increasing areas of our lives. The ability to cooperate, to work with people, to make them feel good *pays* of course in a fiercely individualist society, and high positions may require it. These virtues are often subordinated to the career, to the basic norms of narrow ego fulfillment, not to a self-realization worth the name. To identify self-realization with ego indicates a vast underestimation of the human self.

According to a usual translation of Pali or Sanskrit, Buddha taught his disciples that the human *mind* should embrace all living things as a mother cares for her son, her only son. For some it is not meaningful or possible for a human *self* to embrace all living things, then the usual translation can remain. We ask only that your *mind* embrace all living beings, and that you maintain an intention to care, feel and act with compassion.

If the Sanskrit word *atman* is translated into English, it is instructive to note that this term has the basic meaning of *self* rather than *mind* or *spirit*, as you see in translations. The superiority of the translation using the word *self* stems from the consideration that *if* your *self* in the wide sense embraces another being, you need no moral exhortation to show care. You care for yourself without feeling any moral pressure to do it—unless you have succumbed to a neurosis of some kind, developed self-destructive tendencies, or hate yourself.

The Australian ecological feminist Patsy Hallen uses a formula close to that of Buddha: "we are here to embrace rather than conquer the world." Notice that the term *world* is used here rather than *living beings*. I suspect that our thinking need not proceed from the notion of living being to that of the world. If we can conceive of reality or the world we live in as alive in a wide, not easily defined sense then there will be no non-living beings to care for!

If "self-realization" today is associated with life-long narrow ego gratification, isn't it inaccurate to use this term for self-realization in the widely different sense of Gandhi, or less religiously loaded, as a term for the widening and deepening of the self so it embraces all life forms? Perhaps it is. But I think the very popularity of the term makes people listen for a moment and feel safe. In that moment the notion of a greater Self can be introduced, contending that if people equate self-realization with narrow ego fulfillment, they seriously *underestimate* themselves. We are much greater, deeper, more generous and capable of dignity and joy than we think! A wealth of non-competitive joys is open to us!

I have another important reason for inviting people to think in terms of deepening and widening their selves, starting with narrow ego gratification as the crudest, but inescapable starting point. It has to do with the notion usually placed as the opposite of egoism, namely the notion of *altruism*. The Latin term *ego* has as its opposite the *alter*. Altruism implies that ego sacrifices its interest in favour of the other, the *alter*. The motivation is primarily that of duty; it is said that we *ought* to love others as strongly as we love ourself.

What humankind is capable of loving from mere duty or more generally from moral exhortation is, unfortunately, very limited. From the Renaissance to the Second World War about four hundred cruel wars have been fought by Christian nations, usually for the flimsiest of reasons. It seems to me that in the future more emphasis has to be given to the conditions which naturally widen and

deepen our self. With a sufficiently wide and deep sense of self, ego and alter as opposites are eliminated stage by stage as the distinctions are transcended.

Early in life, the social *self* is sufficiently developed so that we do not prefer to eat a big cake alone. We share the cake with our family and friends. We identify with these people sufficiently to see our joy in their joy, and to see our disappointment in theirs. Now is the time to share with all life on our maltreated earth by deepening our identification with all life-forms, with the ecosystems, and with Gaia, this fabulous, old planet of ours.

The philosopher Immanuel Kant introduced a pair of contrasting concepts which deserve extensive use in our effort to live harmoniously in, for and of nature: the concept of *moral* act and that of *beautiful* act. Moral acts are acts motivated by the intention to follow moral laws, at whatever cost, that is, to do our moral duty solely out of respect for that duty. Therefore, the supreme indication of our success in performing a pure, moral act is that we do it completely against our inclination, that we hate to do it, but are compelled by our respect for moral law. Kant was deeply awed by two phenomena, "the heaven with its stars above me and the moral law within me."

If we do something we should because of a moral law, but do it out of inclination and with pleasure—what then? If we do what is right because of positive inclination, then, according to Kant, we perform a *beautiful* act. My point is that in environmental affairs we should primarily try to influence people toward beautiful acts by finding ways to work on their inclinations rather than their morals. Unhappily, the extensive moralizing within the ecological movement has given the public the false impression that they are primarily asked to sacrifice, to show more responsibility, more concern, and better morals. As I see it we need the immense variety of sources of joy opened through increased sensitivity toward the richness and diversity of life, through the profound cherishing of free natural landscapes. We all can contribute to this individually, and it is also a question of politics, local and global. Part of the joy stems from the consciousness of our intimate relation to something bigger than our own ego, something which has endured for millions of years and is worth continued life for millions of years. The requisite care flows naturally if the self is widened and deepened so that protection of free nature is felt and conceived of as protection of our very selves.

What I am suggesting is the supremacy of ecological ontology and a higher realism over environmental ethics as a means of invigorating the ecology movement in the years to come. If reality is experienced by the ecological Self, our behavior *naturally* and beautifully follows norms of strict environmental ethics. We certainly need to hear about our ethical shortcomings from time to time, but we change more easily through encouragement and a deepened perception of reality and our own *self*, that is, through a deepened realism. How that is to be brought about is too large a question for me to deal with here. But it will clearly be more a question of community therapy than community science: we must find and develop therapies which

heal our relations with the widest community, that of all living beings.

Notes

1. Erich Fromm, "Selfishness, Self-love, and Self-interest," in *The Self: Explorations in Personal Growth*, edited by Clark E. Moustakas (New York, NY: Harper, 1956), page 58.

2. Ibid., page 59.

3. Gandhi quotations are taken from Arne Naess, *Gandhi and Group Conflict* (Oslo, Norway: Universitetsforlaget, 1974), page 35 where the metaphysics of self-realization are treated more thoroughly in that work.

4. Ibid.

5. Ibid.

Nature, Self, and Gender: Feminism, Environmental Philosophy, and the Critique of Rationalism

Val Plumwood

Environmental philosophy has recently been criticized on a number of counts by feminist philosophers. I want to develop further some of this critique and to suggest that much of the issue turns on the failure of environmental philosophy to engage properly with the rationalist tradition, which has been inimical to both women and nature. Damaging assumptions from this tradition have been employed in attempting to formulate a new environmental philosophy that often makes use of or embeds itself within rationalist philosophical frameworks that are not only biased from a gender perspective, but have claimed a negative role for nature as well.

In sections I. through IV. I argue that current mainstream brands of environmental philosophy, both those based in ethics and those based in deep ecology, suffer from this problem, that neither has an adequate historical analysis, and that both continue to rely implicitly upon rationalist-inspired accounts of the self that have been a large part of the problem. In sections V. and VI. I show how the critique of rationalism offers an understanding of a range of key broader issues that environmental philosophy

has tended to neglect or treat in too narrow a way. Among these issues are those connected with concepts of the human self and with instrumentalism.

I. Rationalism and the Ethical Approach

The ethical approach aims to center a new view of nature in ethics, especially universalizing ethics or in some extension of human ethics. This approach has been criticized from a feminist perspective by a number of recent authors (especially Cheney 1987, 1989). I partly agree with and partly disagree with these criticisms; that is, I think that the emphasis on ethics as the central part (or even the whole) of the problem is misplaced, and that although ethics (and especially the ethics of non-instrumental value) has a role, the particular ethical approaches that have been adopted are problematic and unsuitable. I shall illustrate this claim by a brief discussion of two recent books: Paul Taylor's *Respect for Nature* (1986) and Tom Regan's *The Case for Animal Rights* (1986). Both works are significant,

Hypatia vol. 6, no. 1 (Spring 1991), pp. 3–27. Reprinted by permission of the author.

and indeed impressive, contributions to their respective areas.

Paul Taylor's book is a detailed working out of an ethical position that rejects the standard and widespread Western treatment of nature as instrumental to human interests and instead takes living things, as teleological centers of life, to be worthy of respect in their own right. Taylor aims to defend a biocentric (life-centered) ethical theory in which a person's true human self includes his or her biological nature (Taylor 1986, 44), but he attempts to embed this within a Kantian ethical framework that makes strong use of the reason/emotion dichotomy, thus we are assured that the attitude of respect is a moral one because it is universalizing and disinterested, "that is, each moral agent who sincerely has the attitude advocates its universal adoption by all other agents, regardless of whether they are so inclined and regardless of their fondness or lack of fondness for particular individuals" (41). The essential features of morality having been established as distance from emotion and "particular fondness," morality is then seen as the domain of reason and its touchstone, belief. Having carefully distinguished the "valuational, conative, practical and affective dimensions of the attitude of respect," Taylor goes on to pick out the essentially cognitive "valuational" aspect as central and basic to all the others: "It is *because* moral agents look at animals and plants in this way that they are disposed to pursue the aforementioned ends and purposes" (82) and, similarly, to have the relevant emotions and affective attitudes. The latter must be held at an appropriate distance and not allowed to get the upper hand at any point. Taylor claims that actions do not express moral respect unless they are done as a matter of moral principle conceived as ethically obligatory and pursued disinterestedly and not through inclination, solely or even primarily:

> If one seeks that end solely or primarily from inclination, the attitude being expressed is not moral respect but personal affection or love. . . . It is not that respect for nature *precludes* feelings of care and concern for living things. One may, as a matter of simple kindness, not want to harm them. But the fact that one is so motivated does not itself indicate the presence of a moral attitude of respect. Having the desire to preserve or protect

> the good of wild animals and plants for their sake is neither contrary to, nor evidence of, respect for nature. It is only if the person who has the desire understands that the actions fulfilling it would be obligatory even in the absence of the desire, that the person has genuine respect for nature. (85–86)

There is good reason to reject as self-indulgent the "kindness" approach that reduces respect and morality in the protection of animals to the satisfaction of the carer's own feelings. Respect for others involves treating them as worthy of consideration for their own sake and not just as an instrument for the carer's satisfaction, and there is a sense in which such "kindness" is not genuine care or respect for the other. But Taylor is doing much more than this—he is treating care, viewed as "inclination" or "desire," as irrelevant to morality. Respect for nature on this account becomes an essentially *cognitive* matter (that of a person believing something to have "inherent worth" and then acting from an understanding of ethical principles as universal).

The account draws on the familiar view of reason and emotion as sharply separated and opposed, and of "desire," caring, and love as merely "personal" and "particular" as opposed to the universality and impartiality of understanding and of "feminine" emotions as essentially unreliable, untrustworthy, and morally irrelevant, an inferior domain to be dominated by a superior, disinterested (and of course masculine) reason. This sort of rationalist account of the place of emotions has come in for a great deal of well-deserved criticism recently, both for its implicit gender bias and its philosophical inadequacy, especially its dualism and its construal of public reason as sharply differentiated from and controlling private emotion (see, for example, Benhabib 1987; Blum 1980; Gilligan 1982, 1987; Lloyd 1983a and 1983b).

A further major problem in its use in this context is the inconsistency of employing, in the service of constructing an allegedly biocentric ethical theory, a framework that has itself played such a major role in creating a dualistic account of the genuine human self as essentially rational and as sharply discontinuous from the merely emotional, the merely bodily, and the merely animal elements. For emotions and the private sphere with which they are associated have been treated as sharply differentiated and inferior as part of a pattern in which they are seen as linked to the sphere of nature, not the realm of reason.

And it is not only women but also the earth's wild living things that have been denied possession of a reason thus construed along masculine and oppositional lines and which contrasts not only with the "feminine" emotions but also with the physical and the animal. Much of the problem (both for women and nature) lies in rationalist or rationalist-derived conceptions of the self and of what is essential and valuable in the human makeup. It is in the name of such a reason that these other things—the feminine, the emotional, the merely bodily or the merely animal, and the natural world itself—have most often been denied their virtue and been accorded an inferior and merely instrumental position. Thomas Aquinas states this problematic positions succinctly: "the intellectual nature is alone requisite for its own sake in the universe, and all others for its sake" (Thomas Aquinas 1976, 56). And it is precisely reason so construed that is usually taken to characterize the authentically human and to create the supposedly sharp separation, cleavage, or discontinuity between all humans and the nonhuman world, and the similar cleavage within the human self. The supremacy accorded an oppositionally construed reason is the key to the anthropocentrism of the Western tradition. The Kantian-rationalist framework, then, is hardly the area in which to search for a solution. Its use, in a way that perpetuates the supremacy of reason and its opposition to contrast areas, in the service of constructing a supposedly biocentric ethic is a matter for astonishment.

Ethical universalization and abstraction are both closely associated with accounts of the self in terms of rational egoism. Universalization is explicitly seen in both the Kantian and the Rawlsian framework as needed to hold in check natural self-interest; it is the moral complement to the account of the self as "disembodied and disembedded," as the autonomous self of liberal theory, the rational egoist of market theory, the falsely differentiated self of object-relations theory (Benhabib 1987; Poole 1984, 1985). In the same vein, the broadening of the scope of moral concern along with the according of rights to the natural world has been seen by influential environmental philosophers (Leopold 1949, 201–2) as the final step in a process of increasing moral abstraction and generalization, part of the

move away from the merely particular—my self, my family, my tribe—the discarding of the merely personal and, by implication, the merely selfish. This is viewed as moral progress, increasingly civilized as it moves further away from primitive selfishness. Nature is the last area to be included in this march away from the unbridled natural egoism of the particular and its close ally, the emotional. Moral progress is marked by increasing adherence to moral rules and a movement away from the supposedly natural (in human nature), and the completion of its empire is, paradoxically, the extension of its domain of adherence to abstract moral rules to nature itself.

On such a view, the particular and the emotional are seen as the enemy of the rational, as corrupting, capricious, and self-interested. And if the "moral emotions" are set aside as irrelevant or suspect, as merely subjective or personal, we can only base morality on the rules of abstract reason, on the justice and rights of the impersonal public sphere.

This view of morality as based on a concept of reason as oppositional to the personal, the particular, and the emotional has been assumed in the framework of much recent environmental ethics. But as a number of feminist critics of the masculine model of moral life and of moral abstraction have pointed out (Blum 1980, Nicholson 1983), this increasing abstraction is not necessarily an improvement. The opposition between the care and concern for particular others and generalized moral concern is associated with a sharp division between public (masculine) and private (feminine) realms. Thus it is part of the set of dualistic contrasts in which the problem of the Western treatment of nature is rooted. And the opposition between care for particular others and general moral concern is a false one. There *can* be opposition between particularity and generality of concern, as when concern for particular others is accompanied by *exclusion* of others from care or chauvinistic attitudes toward them (Blum 1980, 80), but this does not automatically happen, and emphasis on oppositional cases obscures the frequent cases where they work together—and in which care for particular others is essential to a more generalized morality. Special relationships, which are treated by universalizing positions as at best morally irrelevant and at worst a positive hindrance to the moral life, are thus mistreated. For as Blum (1980, 78–83) stresses, special relationships form the basis for much of our moral life and concern, and it could hardly be otherwise. With nature, as with the human sphere, the capacity to care, to experience sympathy, understanding, and sensitivity to the situation and fate of particular others, and to take responsibility for others is an index of our moral being. Special relationship with, care for, or empathy with particular aspects of nature as experiences rather than with nature as abstraction are essential to provide a depth and type of concern that is not otherwise possible. Care and responsibility for particular animals, trees, and rivers that are known well, loved, and appropriately connected to the self are an important basis for acquiring a wider, more generalized concern. (As we shall see, this failure to deal adequately with particularity is a problem for deep ecology as well.)

Concern for nature, then, should not be viewed as the completion of a process of (masculine) universalization, moral abstraction, and disconnection, discarding the self, emotions, and special ties (all, of course, associated with the private sphere and femininity). Environmental ethics has for the most part placed itself uncritically in such a framework, although it is one that is extended with particular difficulty to the natural world. Perhaps the kindest thing that can be said about the framework of ethical universalization is that it is seriously incomplete and fails to capture the most important elements of respect, which are not reducible to or based on duty or obligation any more than the most important elements of friendship are, but which are rather an expression of a certain kind of selfhood and a certain kind of relation between self and other.

II. Rationalism, Rights, and Ethics

An extension to nature of the standard concepts of morality is also the aim of Tom Regan's *The Case for Animal Rights* (1986). This is the most impressive, thorough, and solidly argued book in the area of animal ethics, with excellent chapters on topics such as animal intentionality. But the key concept upon which this account of moral concern for animals is based is that of rights, which requires strong individual separation of rights-holders and is set in a framework of human community and legality. Its extension to the natural world raises a host of problems (Midgley 1983, 61–64). Even in the

case of individual higher animals for which Regan uses this concept of rights, the approach is problematic. His concept of rights is based on Mill's notion that, if a being has a right to something not only should he or she (or it) have that thing but others are obliged to intervene to secure it. The application of this concept of rights to individual wild living animals appears to give humans almost limitless obligations to intervene massively in all sorts of far reaching and conflicting ways in natural cycles to secure the rights of a bewildering variety of beings. In the case of the wolf and the sheep, an example discussed by Regan, it is unclear whether humans should intervene to protect the sheep's rights or to avoid doing so in order not to violate the wolf's right to its natural food.

Regan attempts to meet this objection by claiming that since the wolf is not itself a moral agent (although it is a moral patient), it cannot violate the sheep's rights not to suffer a painful and violent death (Regan 1986, 285). But the defense is unconvincing, because even if we concede that the wolf is not a moral agent, it still does not follow that on a rights view we are not obliged to intervene. From the fact that the wolf is not a moral agent it only follows that it is not *responsible* for violating the sheep's rights, not that they are not violated or that others do not have an obligation (according to the rights view) to intervene. If the wolf were attacking a human baby, it would hardly do as a defense in that case to claim that one did not have a duty to intervene because the wolf was not a moral agent. But on Regan's view the baby and the sheep do have something like the same rights. So we do have a duty, it seems, (on the rights view) to intervene to protect the sheep—leaving us where with the wolf?

The concept of rights seems to produce absurd consequences and is impossible to apply in the context of predators in a natural ecosystem, as opposed to a particular human social context in which claimants are part of a reciprocal social community and conflict cases either few or settleable according to some agreed-on principles. All this seems to me to tell against the concept of rights as the correct one for the general task of dealing with animals in the natural environment (as opposed, of course, to domestic animals in a basically humanized environment).[1]

Rights seem to have acquired an exaggerated importance as part of the prestige of the public sphere and the masculine, and the emphasis on separation and autonomy, on reason and abstraction. A more promising approach for an ethics of nature, and also one much more in line with the current directions in feminism, would be to remove rights from the center of the moral stage and pay more attention to some other, less dualistic, moral concepts such as respect, sympathy, care, concern, compassion, gratitude, friendship, and responsibility (Cook 1977, 118–9). These concepts, because of their dualistic construal as feminine and their consignment to the private sphere as subjective and emotional, have been treated as peripheral and given far less importance than they deserve for several reasons. First, rationalism and the prestige of reason and the public sphere have influenced not only the concept of what morality is (as Taylor explicates it, for example, as essentially a rational and cognitive act of understanding that certain actions are ethically obligatory) but of what is *central* to it or what count as moral concepts. Second, concepts such as respect, care, concern, and so on are resistant to analysis along lines of a dualistic reason/emotion dichotomy, and their construal along these lines has involved confusion and distortion (Blum 1980). They *are* moral "feelings" but they involve reason, behavior and emotion in ways that do not seem separable. Rationalist-inspired ethical concepts are highly ethnocentric and cannot account adequately for the views of many indigenous peoples, and the attempted application of these rationalist concepts to their positions tends to lead to the view that they lack a real ethical framework (Plumwood 1990). These alternative concepts seem better able to apply to the views of such peoples, whose ethic of respect, care and responsibility for land is often based on special relationships with particular areas of land via links to kin (Neidjie, 1985, 1989). Finally these concepts, which allow for particularity and mostly do not require reciprocity, are precisely the sorts of concepts feminist philosophers have argued should have a more significant place in ethics at the expense of abstract, malestream concepts from the public sphere such as rights and justice (Gilligan 1982, 1987, Benhabib 1987). The ethic of care and responsibility they have articulated seems to extend much less problematically to the nonhuman world than do the impersonal concepts which are currently seen as central, and it also seems capable of providing an excellent basis for the noninstrumental treatment of nature many environmental philosophers have now called for. Such an approach treats ethical relations as an expression of self-in-relationship (Gilligan 1987, 24) rather than as the discarding, containment, or generalization of a self viewed as self-interested and non-relational, as in the conventional ethics of universalization.[2] As I argue later, there are important connections between this relational account of the self and the rejection of instrumentalism.

It is not that we need to abandon ethics or dispense with the universalized ethical approach entirely, although we do need to reassess the centrality of ethics in environmental philosophy.[3] What is needed is not so much the abandonment of ethics as a different and richer understanding of it (and, as I argue later, a richer understanding of environmental philosophy generally than is provided by ethics), one that gives an important place to ethical concepts owing to emotionality and particularity and that abandons the exclusive focus on the universal and the abstract associated with the nonrelational self and the dualistic and oppositional accounts of the reason/emotion and universal/particular contrasts as given in rationalist accounts of ethics.

III. The Discontinuity Problem

The problem is not just one of restriction *in* ethics but also of restriction *to* ethics. Most mainstream environmental philosophers continue to view environmental philosophy as mainly concerned with ethics. For example, instrumentalism is generally viewed by mainstream environmental philosophers as a problem in ethics, and its solution is seen as setting up some sort of theory of intrinsic value. This neglects a key aspect of the overall problem that is concerned with the definition of the human self as separate from nature, the connection between this and the instrumental view of nature, and broader *political* aspects of the critique of instrumentalism.

One key aspect of the Western view of nature, which the ethical stance neglects completely, is the view of nature as sharply discontinuous or ontologically divided from the human sphere. This leads to a view of humans as apart from or "outside of" nature, usually as masters or external controllers of it. Attempts to reject this view often speak alternatively of humans as "part of nature" but rarely distinguish this position from the obvious claim that human fate is interconnected with that of the biosphere, that humans are subject to natural laws. But on the divided-self theory it is the essentially or authentically human part of the self, and in that sense the human realm proper, that is outside nature, not the human as a physical phenomenon. The view of humans as outside of and alien to nature seems to be especially strongly a Western one, although not confined to the West. There are many other cultures which do not hold it, which stress what connects us to nature as genuinely human virtues, which emphasize continuity and not dissimilarity.[4]

As ecofeminism points out, Western thought has given us a strong human/nature dualism that is part of the set of interrelated dualisms of mind/body, reason/nature, reason/emotion, masculine/feminine and has important interconnected features with these other dualisms.[5] This dualism has been especially stressed in the rationalist tradition. In this dualism what is characteristically and authentically human is defined against or in opposition to what is taken to be natural, nature, or the physical or biological realm. This takes various forms. For example, the characterization of the genuinely, properly, characteristically, or authentically human, or of human virtue, in polarized terms to exclude what is taken to be characteristic of the natural is what John Rodman (1980) has called "the Differential Imperative" in which what is virtuous in the human is taken to be what maximizes distance from the merely natural. The maintenance of sharp dichotomy and polarization is achieved by the rejection and denial of what links humans to the animal. What is taken to be authentically and characteristically human, defining of the human, as well as the ideal for which humans should strive is *not* to be found in what is shared with the natural and animal (e.g., the body, sexuality, reproduction, emotionality, the senses, agency) but in what is thought to separate and distinguish them—especially reason and its offshoots. Hence humanity is defined not as part of nature (perhaps a special part) but as separate from and in opposition to it. Thus the relation of humans to nature is treated as an oppositional and value dualism.

The process closely parallels the formation of other dualisms, such as masculine/feminine, reason/emotion, and spirit/body criticized in feminist thought (see, for example, Ruether 1975, Griffin 1978, Griscom 1981, King 1981, Lloyd 1983, Jaggar 1983) but this parallel logic is not the only connection between human/nature dualism and masculine/feminine dualism. Moreover, this exclusion of the natural from the concept of the properly human is not the only dualism involved, because what is involved in the construction of this dualistic conception of the human is the rejection of those parts of the human character identified as feminine—also identified as less than fully human—giving the masculine conception of what it is to be human. Masculinity can be linked to this exclusionary and polarized conception of the human, via the desire to exclude and distance from the feminine and the nonhuman. The features that are taken as characteristic of humankind and as where its special virtues lie, are those such as rationality, freedom, and transcendence of nature (all traditionally viewed as masculine), which are viewed as not shared with nature. Humanity is defined oppositionally to both nature and the feminine.

The upshot is a deeply entrenched view of the genuine or ideal human self as not including features shared with nature, and as defined *against* or in *opposition* to the nonhuman realm, so that the human sphere and that of nature cannot significantly overlap. Nature is sharply divided off from the human, is alien and usually hostile and inferior. Furthermore, this kind of human self can only have certain kinds of accidental or contingent connections to the realm of nature. I shall call this the discontinuity problem or thesis and I argue later that it plays a key role with respect to other elements of the problem.

IV. Rationalism and Deep Ecology

Although the discontinuity problem is generally neglected by the ethical stance, a significant exception to its neglect within environmental philosophy seems to be found in deep ecology, which is also critical of the location of the problem within ethics.[6] Furthermore, deep ecology also seems initially to be more likely to be compatible with a feminist philosophical framework, emphasizing as it does connections with the self, connectedness, and merger. Nevertheless, there are severe tensions between deep ecology and a feminist perspective.

Deep ecology has not satisfactorily identified the key elements in the traditional framework or observed their connections to rationalism. As a result, it fails to reject adequately rationalist assumptions and indeed often seems to provide its own versions of universalization, the discarding of particular connections, and rationalist accounts of self.

Deep ecology locates the key problem area in human-nature relations in the separation of humans and nature, and it provides a solution for this in terms of the "identification" of self with nature. "Identification" is usually left deliberately vague, and corresponding accounts of self are various and shifting and not always compatible.[7] There seem to be at least three different accounts of self involved—indistinguishability, expansion of self, and transcendence of self—and practitioners appear to feel free to move among them at will. As I shall show, all are unsatisfactory from both a feminist perspective and from that of obtaining a satisfactory environmental philosophy, and the appeal of deep ecology rests largely on the failure to distinguish them.

A. The Indistinguishability Account

The indistinguishability account rejects boundaries between self and nature. Humans are said to be just one strand in the biotic web, not the source and ground of all value and the discontinuity thesis is, it seems, firmly rejected. Warwick Fox describes the central intuition of deep ecology as follows: "We can make no firm ontological divide in the field of existence . . . there is no bifurcation in reality between the human and nonhuman realms. . . . to the extent that we perceive boundaries, we fall short of deep ecological consciousness" (Fox 1984, 7). But much more is involved here than the rejection of discontinuity, for deep ecology goes on to replace the human-in-environment image by a holistic or gestalt view that "dissolves not only the human-in-environment concept, but every compact-thing-in-milieu concept"—except when talking at a superficial level of communication (Fox 1984, 1). Deep ecology involves a cosmology of "unbroken wholeness which denies the classical idea of the analyzability of the world into separately and independently existing parts."[8] It is strongly attracted to a variety of mystical traditions and to the Perennial Philosophy, in which the self is merged with the other—"the other is none other than yourself." As John Seed puts it: "I am protect-ing the rain forest" develops into "I am part of the rain forest protecting myself. I am that part of the rain forest recently emerged into thinking" (Seed et al. 1988, 36).

There are severe problems with these claims, arising not so much from the orientation to the concept of self (which seems to me important and correct) or from the mystical character of the insights themselves as from the indistinguishability metaphysics which is proposed as their basis. It is not merely that the identification process of which deep ecologists speak seems to stand in need of much more clarification, but that it does the wrong thing. The problem, in the sort of account I have given, is the discontinuity between humans and nature that emerges as part of the overall set of Western dualisms. Deep ecology proposes to heal this division by a "unifying process," a metaphysics that insists that everything is really part of and indistinguishable from everything else. This is not only to employ overly powerful tools but ones that do the wrong job, for the origins of the particular opposition involved in the human/nature dualism remain unaddressed and unanalyzed. The real basis of the discontinuity lies in the concept of an authentic human being, in what is taken to be valuable in human character, society, and culture, as what is distinct from what is taken to be natural. The sources of and remedies for this remain unaddressed in deep ecology. Deep ecology has confused dualism and atomism and then mistakenly taken indistinguishability to follow from the rejection of atomism. The confusion is clear in Fox, who proceeds immediately from the ambiguous claim that there is no "bifurcation in reality between the human and nonhuman realms" (which could be taken as a rejection of human discontinuity from nature) to the conclusion that what is needed is that we embrace an indistinguishability metaphysics of unbroken wholeness in the whole of reality. But the problem must be addressed in terms of this specific dualism and its connections. Instead deep ecology proposes the obliteration of all distinction.

Thus deep ecology's solution to removing this discontinuity by obliterating *all* division is far too powerful. In its overgenerality it fails to provide a genuine basis for an environmental ethics of the kind sought, for the view of humans as metaphysically unified with the cosmic whole will be equally true whatever relation humans stand in with nature—the situation of exploitation of nature exemplifies such unity equally as well as a con-server situation and the human self is just as indis-tinguishable from the bulldozer and Coca-Cola bot-tle as the rocks or the rain forest. What John Seed seems to have in mind here is that once one has realized that one is indistinguishable from the rain forest, its needs would become one's own. But there is nothing to guarantee this—one could equally well take one's own needs for its.

This points to a further problem with the indistinguishability thesis, that we need to recog-nize not only our human continuity with the nat-ural world but also its distinctness and indepen-dence from us and the distinctness of the needs of things in nature from ours. The indistinguishability account does not allow for this, although it is a very important part of respect for nature and of conservation strategy.

The dangers of accounts of the self that involve self-merger appear in feminist contexts as well, where they are sometimes appealed to as the alter-native to masculine-defined autonomy as discon-nection from others. As Jean Grimshaw writes of the related thesis of the indistinctness of persons (the acceptance of the loss of self-boundaries as a feminine ideal): "It is important not merely because certain forms of symbiosis or 'connection' with oth-ers can lead to damaging failures of personal devel-opment, but because care for others, understanding of them, are only possible if one can adequately dis-tinguish oneself *from* others. If I see myself as 'indis-tinct' from you, or you as not having your own being that is not merged with mine, then I cannot preserve a real sense of your well-being as opposed to mine. Care and understanding require the sort of distance that is needed in order not to see the other as a projection of self, or self as a continuation of the other" (Grimshaw 1986, 182–3).

These points seem to me to apply to caring for other species and for the natural world as much as they do to caring for our own species. But just as dualism is confused with atomism, so holistic self-merger is taken to be the only alternative to egoisti-cal accounts of the self as without essential connec-tion to others or to nature. Fortunately, this is a false choice;[9] as I argue below, nonholistic but relational accounts of the self, as developed in some feminist and social philosophy, enable a rejection of dualism, including human/nature dualism, without deny-ing the independence or distinguishability of the

other. To the extent that deep ecology is identified with the indistinguishability thesis, it does not pro-vide an adequate basis for a philosophy of nature.

B. The Expanded Self

In fairness to deep ecology it should be noted that it tends to vacillate between mystical indistin-guishability and the other accounts of self, between the holistic self and the expanded self. Vacillation occurs often by way of slipperiness as to what is meant by identification of self with the other, a key notion in deep ecology. This slipperiness reflects the confusion of dualism and atomism previously noted but also seems to reflect a desire to retain the mystical appeal of indistinguishability while avoid-ing its many difficulties. Where "identification" means not "identity" but something more like "empathy," identification with other beings can lead to an expanded self. According to Arne Naess, "The self is as comprehensive as the totality of our identifications. . . . Our Self is that with which we identify."[10] This larger self (or Self, to deep ecolo-gists) is something for which we should strive "insofar as it is in our power to do so" (Fox 1986, 13–19), and according to Fox we should also strive to make it as large as possible. But this expanded self is not the result of a critique of egoism; rather, it is an enlargement and an extension of egoism.[11] It does not question the structures of possessive ego-ism and self-interest; rather, it tries to allow for a wider set of interests by an expansion of self. The motivation for the expansion of self is to allow for a wider set of concerns while continuing to allow the self to operate on the fuel of self-interest (or Self-interest). This is apparent from the claim that "in this light . . . ecological resistance is simply another name for self defense" (Fox 1986, 60). Fox quotes with approval John Livingstone's statement: "When I say that the fate of the sea turtle or the tiger or the gibbon is mine, I mean it. All that is in my universe is not merely mine; it is *me*. And I shall defend myself. I shall defend myself not only against overt aggression but also against gratuitous insult" (Fox 1986, 60).

Deep ecology does not question the structures of rational egoism and continues to subscribe to two of the main tenets of the egoist framework—that human nature is egoistic and that the alternative to egoism is self-sacrifice.[12] Given these assumptions about egoism, the obvious way to obtain some sort of human interest in defending nature is through the expanded Self operating in the interests of nature but also along the familiar lines of self-interest.[13] The expanded-self strategy might initially seem to be just another pretentious and obscure way of saying that humans empathize with nature. But the strategy of transfering the structures of egoism is highly problematic, for the widening of interest is obtained at the expense of failing to recognise unambiguously the distinctness and independence of the other.[14] Others are recognized morally only to the extent that they are incorporated into the self, and their difference denied (Warren 1990). And the failure to critique egoism and the disembedded, nonrelational self means a failure to draw connections with other contemporary critiques.

C. The Transcended or Transpersonal Self

To the extent that the expanded Self requires that we detach from the particular concerns of the self (a relinquishment that despite its natural difficulty we should struggle to attain), expansion of self to Self also tends to lead into the third position, the transcendence or overcoming of self. Thus Fox urges us to strive for *impartial* identification with *all* particulars, the cosmos, discarding our identifications with our own particular concerns, personal emotions, and attachments (Fox 1990, 12). Fox presents here the deep ecology version of universalization, with the familiar emphasis on the personal and the particular as corrupting and self-interested—"the cause of possessiveness, war and ecological destruction" (1990, 12).

This treatment of particularity, the devaluation of an identity tied to particular parts of the natural world as opposed to an abstractly conceived whole, the cosmos, reflects the rationalistic preoccupation with the universal and its account of ethical life as oppositional to the particular. The analogy in human terms of impersonal love of the cosmos is the view of morality as based on universal principles or the impersonal and abstract "love of man." Thus Fox (1990, 12) reiterates (as if it were unproblematic) the view of particular attachments as ethically suspect and as oppositional to genuine, impartial "identification," which necessarily falls short with all particulars.

Because this "transpersonal" identification is so indiscriminate and intent on denying particular meanings, it cannot allow for the deep and highly particularistic attachment to place that has motivated both the passion of many modern conservationists and the love of many indigenous peoples for their land (which deep ecology inconsistently tries to treat as a model). This is based not on a vague, bloodless, and abstract cosmological concern but on the formation of identity, social and personal, in relation to particular areas of land, yielding ties often as special and powerful as those to kin, and which are equally expressed in very specific and local responsibilities of care.[15] This emerges clearly in the statements of many indigenous peoples, such as in the moving words of Cecilia Blacktooth explaining why her people would not surrender their land:

> You ask us to think what place we like next best to this place where we always lived. You see the graveyard there? There are our fathers and our grandfathers. You see that Eagle-nest mountain and that Rabbit-hole mountain? When God made them, He gave us this place. We have always been here. We do not care for any other place. . . . We have always lived here. We would rather die here. Our fathers did. We cannot leave them. Our children were born here—how can we go away? If you give us the best place in the world, it is not so good as this. . . . This is our home. . . . We cannot live any where else. We were born here and our fathers are buried here. . . . We want this place and no other. . . . (McLuhan 1979, 28)

In inferiorizing such particular, emotional, and kinship-based attachments, deep ecology gives us another variant on the superiority of reason and the inferiority of its contrasts, failing to grasp yet again the role of reason and incompletely critiquing its influence. To obtain a more adequate account than that offered by mainstream ethics and deep ecology it seems that we must move toward the sort of ethics feminist theory has suggested, which can allow for both continuity and difference and for ties to nature which are expressive of the rich, caring relationships of kinship and friendship rather than increasing abstraction and detachment from rela-tionship.[16]

V. The Problem in Terms of the Critique of Rationalism

I now show how the problem of the inferioriza-tion of nature appears if it is viewed from the per-spective of the critique of rationalism and seen as part of the general problem of revaluing and reinte-grating what rationalist culture has split apart, denied, and devalued. Such an account shifts the focus away from the preoccupations of both main-stream ethical approaches and deep ecology, and although it does retain an emphasis on the account of the self as central, it gives a different account from that offered by deep ecology. In section VI. I conclude by arguing that one of the effects of this shift in focus is to make connections with other cri-tiques, especially feminism, central rather than peripheral or accidental, as they are currently viewed by deep ecologists in particular.

First, what is missing from the accounts of both the ethical philosophers and the deep ecologists is an understanding of the problem of discontinuity as created by a dualism linked to a network of related dualisms. Here I believe a good deal can be learned from the critique of dualism feminist phi-losophy has developed and from the understand-ing of the mechanisms of dualisms ecofeminists have produced. A dualistically construed dichot-omy typically polarizes difference and minimizes shared characteristics, construes difference along lines of superiority/inferiority, and views the infe-rior side as a means to the higher ends of the supe-rior side (the instrumental thesis). Because its nature is defined oppositionally, the task of the superior side, that in which it realizes itself and expresses its true nature, is to separate from, domi-nate, and control the lower side. This has happened both with the human/nature division and with other related dualisms such as masculine/femi-nine, reason/body, and reason/emotion. Challeng-ing these dualisms involves not just a reevaluation of superiority/inferiority and a higher status for the underside of the dualisms (in this case nature) but also a reexamination and reconceptualizing of the dualistically construed categories themselves. So in the case of the human/nature dualism it is not just

a question of improving the status of nature, moral or otherwise, while everything else remains the same, but of reexamining and reconceptualizing the concept of the human, and also the concept of the contrasting class of nature. For the concept of the human, of what it is to be fully and authenti-cally human, and of what is genuinely human in the set of characteristics typical humans possess, has been defined oppositionally, by *exclusion* of what is associated with the inferior natural sphere in very much the way that Lloyd (1983), for exam-ple, has shown in the case of the categories of mas-culine and feminine, and of reason and its contrasts. Humans have both biological and mental character-istics, but the mental rather than the biological have been taken to be characteristic of the human and to give what is "fully and authentically" human. The term "human" is, of course, not merely descriptive here but very much an evaluative term setting out an ideal: it is what is essential or worthwhile in the human that excludes the natural. It is not necessar-ily denied that humans have some material or ani-mal component—rather, it is seen in this framework as alien or inessential to them, not part of their fully or truly human nature. The human essence is often seen as lying in maximizing control over the natural sphere (both within and without) and in qualities such as rationality, freedom, and transcendence of the material sphere. These qualities are also identi-fied as masculine, and hence the *oppositional* model of the human coincides or converges with a mascu-line model, in which the characteristics attributed are those of the masculine ideal.

Part of a strategy for challenging this human/ nature dualism, then, would involve recognition of these excluded qualities—split off, denied, or con-strued as alien, or comprehended as the sphere of supposedly *inferior* humans such as women and blacks—as equally and fully human. This would provide a basis for the recognition of *continuities* with the natural world. Thus reproductivity, sensu-ality, emotionality would be taken to be as fully and authentically human qualities as the capacity for abstract planning and calculation. This proceeds from the assumption that one basis for discontinu-ity and alienation from nature is alienation from those qualities which provide continuity with nature in ourselves.

This connection between the rationalist ac-count of nature within and nature without has powerful repercussions. So part of what is involved is a challenge to the centrality and dominance of the rational in the account of the human self. Such a challenge would have far-reaching implications for what is valuable in human society and culture, and it connects with the challenge to the cultural legacy of rationalism made by other critiques of rationalism such as feminism, and by critiques of technocracy, bureaucracy, and instrumentalism.

What is involved here is a reconceptualization of the human side of the human/nature dualism, to free it from the legacy of rationalism. Also in need of reconceptualization is the underside of this dualism, the concept of nature, which is construed in polarized terms as bereft of qualities appropriated to the human side, as passive and lacking in agency and teleology, as pure materiality, pure body, or pure mechanism. So what is called for here is the development of alternatives to mechanistic ways of viewing the world, which are also part of the legacy of rationalism.

VI. Instrumentalism and the Self

There are two parts to the restructuring of the human self in relation to nature—reconceptualizing the human and reconceptualizing the self, and especially its possibilities of relating to nature in other than instrumental ways. Here the critique of the egoistic self of liberal individualism by both feminist and social philosophers, as well as the critique of instrumental reason, offers a rich set of connections and insights on which to draw. In the case of both of these parts what is involved is the rejection of basically masculine models, that is, of humanity and of the self.

Instrumentalism has been identified as a major problem by the ethical approach in environmental philosophy but treated in a rather impoverished way, as simply the problem of establishing the inherent worth of nature.[17] Connection has not been made to the broader account that draws on the critique of instrumental reason. This broader account reveals both its links with the discontinuity problem and its connection with the account of the self. A closer look at this further critique gives an indication of how we might develop an account that enables us to stress continuity without drowning in a sea of indistinguishability.

We might notice first the strong connections between discontinuity (the polarization condition of dualism) and instrumentalism—the view that the excluded sphere is appropriately treated as a means to the ends of the higher sphere or group, that its value lies in its usefulness to the privileged group that is, in contrast, worthwhile or significant in itself. Second, it is important to maintain a strong distinction and maximize distance between the sphere of means and that of ends to avoid breaking down the sharp boundaries required by hierarchy. Third, it helps if the sphere treated instrumentally is seen as lacking ends of its own (as in views of nature and women as passive), for then others can be imposed upon it without problem. There are also major connections that come through the account of the self which accompanies both views.

The self that complements the instrumental treatment of the other is one that stresses sharply defined ego boundaries, distinctness, autonomy, and separation from others—that is defined *against* others, and lacks essential connections to them. This corresponds to object/relations account of the masculine self associated with the work of Nancy Chodorow (1979, 1985) and also to the self-interested individual presupposed in market theory (Poole 1985, 1990).[18] This self uses both other humans and the world generally as a means to its egoistic satisfaction, which is assumed to be the satisfaction of interests in which others play no essential role. If we try to specify these interests they would make no essential reference to the welfare of others, except to the extent that these are useful to serve predetermined ends. Others as means are interchangeable if they produce equivalent satisfactions—anything which conduces to that end is as valuable, other things being equal, as anything else which equally conduces to that end. The interests of such an individual, that of the individual of market theory and of the masculine self as theorized by Chodorow, are defined as essentially independent of or disconnected from those of other people, and his or her transactions with the world at large consist of various attempts to get satisfaction for these predetermined private interests. Others are a "resource," and the interests of others connect with the interests of such autonomous selves only accidentally or contingently. They are not valued for themselves but for their effects in producing gratification. This kind of instrumental picture, so obviously a misdescription in the case of relations to other humans, is precisely still the normal Western model of what our relations to nature should be.

Now this kind of instrumental, disembedded account of the relation of self to others has been extensively criticized in the area of political theory from a variety of quarters, including feminist theory, in the critique of liberalism, and in environmental philosophy (Benhabib 1987; Benhabib and Cornell 1987; Benjamin 1985; Chodorow 1985; Gilligan 1982, 1987; Grimshaw 1986; Jagger 1983; Miller 1978; Plumwood 1980; Poole 1984, 1985, 1990; Warren 1990). It has been objected that this account does not give an accurate picture of the human self—that humans are social and connected in a way such an account does not recognize. People do have interests that make *essential* and not merely accidental or contingent reference to those of others, for example, when a mother wishes for her child's recovery, the child's flourishing is an essential *part* of her flourishing, and similarly with close others and indeed for others more widely ("social others"). But, the objection continues, this gives a misleading picture of the world, one that omits or impoverishes a whole significant dimension of human experience, a dimension which provides important insight into gender difference, without which we cannot give an adequate picture of what it is to be human. Instead we must see human beings and their interests as *essentially* related and interdependent. As Karen Warren notes "Relationships are not something extrinsic to who we are, not an 'add on' feature of human nature; they play an essential role in shaping what it is to be human" (Warren 1990, 143). That people's interests are relational does not imply a holistic view of them—that they are merged or indistinguishable. Although some of the mother's interests entail satisfaction of the child's interests, they are not identical or even necessarily similar. There is overlap, but the relation is one of intentional inclusion (her interest is *that* the child should thrive, that certain of the child's key interests are satisfied) rather than accidental overlap.

This view of self-in-relationship is, I think, a good candidate for the richer account of self deep ecologists have sought and for which they have mistaken holistic accounts. It is an account that avoids atomism but that enables a recognition of interdependence and relationship without falling into the problems of indistinguishability, that acknowledges both continuity and difference, and that breaks the culturally posed false dichotomy of egoism and altruism of interests;[19] it bypasses both masculine "separation" and traditional-feminine "merger" accounts of the self. It can also provide an appropriate foundation for an ethic of connectedness and caring for others, as argued by Gilligan (1982, 1987) and Miller (1978).

Thus it is unnecessary to adopt any of the stratagems of deep ecology—the indistinguishable self, the expanded self, or the transpersonal self—in order to provide an alternative to anthropocentrism or human self-interest. This can be better done through the relational account of self, which clearly recognizes the distinctness of nature but also our relationship and continuity with it. On this relational account, respect for the other results neither from the containment of self nor from a transcendence of self, but is an *expression* of self in relationship, not egoistic self as merged with the other but self as embedded in a network of essential relationships with distinct others.

The relational account of self can usefully be applied to the case of human relations with nature and to place. The standard Western view of the relation of the self to the nonhuman is that it is always *accidentally* related, and hence the nonhuman can be used as a means to the self-contained ends of human beings. Pieces of land are real estate, readily interchangeable as equivalent means to the end of human satisfaction; no place is more than "a stage along life's way, a launching pad for higher flights and wider orbits than your own" (Berman 1982, 327). But, of course, we do not all think this way, and instances of contrary behavior would no doubt be more common if their possibility were not denied and distorted by both theoretical and social construction. But other cultures have recognized such essential connection of self to country clearly enough, and many indigenous voices from the past and present speak of the grief and pain in loss of their land, to which they are as essentially connected as to any human other. When Aboriginal people, for example, speak of the land as part of them, "like brother and mother" (Neidjie 1985, 51; 1989, 4, 146), this is, I think, one of their meanings. If instrumentalism is impoverishing and distorting as an account of our relations to other human beings, it is equally so as a guiding principle in our relations to nature and to place.[20]

But to show that the self can be essentially related to nature is by no means to show that it normally would be, especially in modern Western culture. What is culturally viewed as alien and inferior, as not worthy of respect or respectful knowledge, is not something to which such essential connection can easily be made. Here are three parts of the problem—the conception of the human, the conception of the self, and the conception of nature—connect again. And normally such essential relation would involve particularity, through connection to and friendship for *particular* places, forests, animals, to which one is particularly strongly related or attached and toward which one has specific and meaningful, not merely abstract, responsibilities of care.

One of the effects of viewing the problem as arising especially in the context of rationalism is to provide a rich set of connections with other critiques; it makes the connection between the critique of anthropocentrism and various other critiques that also engage critically with rationalism, such as feminism and critical theory, much more important—indeed essential—to the understanding of each. The problem of the Western account of the human/nature relation is seen in the context of the other related sets of dualisms; they are linked through their definitions as the underside of the various contrasts of reason. Since much of the strength and persistence of these dualisms derives from their connections and their ability to mirror, confirm, and support one another, critiques of anthropocentrism that fail to take account of these connections have missed an essential and not merely additional feature.

Anthropocentrism and androcentrism in particular are linked by the rationalist conception of the human self as masculine and by the account of authentically human characteristics as centered around rationality and the exclusion of its contrasts (especially characteristics regarded as feminine, animal, or natural) as less human. This provides a different and richer account of the notion of anthropocentrism, now conceived by deep ecology (Fox 1990, 5) in terms of the notion of equality, which is both excessively narrow and difficult to articulate in any precise or convincing way in a context where needs are so different. The perception of the connection as at best accidental is a feature of some recent critiques of ecofeminism, for example the discussion of Fox (1990) and Eckersley (1989) on the rela-

tion of feminism and environmental philosophy. Fox misses entirely the main thrust of the ecofeminist account of environmental philosophy and the critique of deep ecology which results or which is advanced in the ecofeminist literature, which is that it has failed to observe the way in which anthropocentrism and androcentrism are linked.[21] It is a consequence of my arguments here that this critique needs broadening—deep ecology has failed to observe (and often even goes out of its way to deny) connections with a number of other critiques, not just feminism, for example, but also socialism, especially in the forms that mount a critique of rationalism and of modernity. The failure to observe such connections is the result of an inadequate historical analysis and understanding of the way in which the inferiorization of both women and nature is grounded in rationalism, and the connections of both to the inferiorizing of the body, hierarchical concepts of labor, and disembedded and individualist accounts of the self.

Instead of addressing the real concerns of ecofeminism in terms of connection, Fox takes ecofeminism as aiming to replace concern with anthropocentrism by concern with androcentrism.[22] This would have the effect of making ecofeminism a reductionist position which takes women's oppression as the basic form and attempts to reduce all other forms to it. This position is a straw woman;[23] the effect of ecofeminism is not to absorb or sacrifice the critique of anthropocentrism, but to deepen and enrich it.

Notes

An earlier version of this paper, was read at the Women in Philosophy Conference in Canberra, July, 1989. The author would like to thank Jim Cheney and Karen Warren for comments on an earlier draft.

1. Regan, of course, as part of the animal rights movement, is mainly concerned not with wild animals but with domestic animals as they appear in the context and support of human society and culture, although he does not indicate any qualification in moral treatment. Nevertheless, there may be an important moral boundary here, for natural ecosystems cannot be organized along the lines of justice, fairness and rights, and it would be absurd to try to impose such a social order upon them via intervention in these systems. This does not mean, of course, that humans can do anything in such a situation, just that certain kinds of intervention are not in

order. But these kinds of intervention may be in order in the case of human social systems and in the case of animals that have already been brought into these social systems through human intervention, and the concept of rights and of social responsibility may have far more application here. This would mean that the domestic/wild distinction would demarcate an important moral boundary in terms of duties of intervention, although neither Regan (1986) nor Taylor (1986) comes to grips with this problem. In the case of Taylor's "wild living things" rights seem less important than respect for independence and autonomy, and the prima facie obligation may be nonintervention.

2. If the Kantian universalizing perspective is based on self-containment, its major contemporary alternative, that of John Rawls, is based on a "definitional identity" in which the "other" can be considered to the extent that it is not recognized as truly different, as genuinely other (Benhabib 1987, 165).

3. Contra Cheney, who appears to advocate the abandonment of all general ethical concepts and the adoption of a "contextual" ethics based in pure particularity and emotionality. We do need both to reintegrate the personal and particular and reevaluate more positively its role, but overcoming moral dualism will not simply amount to an affirmation of the personal in the moral sphere. To embrace pure particularity and emotionality is implicitly to accept the dualistic construction of these as oppositional to a rationalist ethics and to attempt to reverse value. In general this reactive response is an inadequate way to deal with such dualisms. And rules themselves, as Grimshaw (1986, 209) points out, are not incompatible with recognition of special relationships and responsibility to particular others. Rules themselves are not the problem, and hence it is not necessary to move to a ruleless ethics; rather it is rules that demand the discarding of the personal, the emotional, and the particular and which aim at self-containment.

4. For example, Bill Neidjie's words "This ground and this earth / like brother and mother" (Neidjie 1985, 46) may be interpreted as an affirmation of such kinship or continuity. (See also Neidjie 1985, 53, 61, 62, 77, 81, 82, 88).

5. The logic of dualism and the masculinity of the concept of humanity are discussed in Plumwood (1986, 1988) and Warren (1987, 1989).

6. Nonetheless, deep ecology's approach to ethics is, like much else, doubtfully consistent, variable and shifting. Thus although Arne Naess (1974, 1984, 1988) calls for recognition of the intrinsic value of nature, he also tends to treat "the maxim of self-realization" as *substituting for* and obviating an ethi-

cal account of care and respect for nature (Naess 1988, 20, 86), placing the entire emphasis on phenomenology. In more recent work, however, the emphasis seems to have quietly shifted back again from holistic intuition to a broad and extremely vague "biocentric egalitarianism" which places the center once again in ethics and enjoins an ethic of maximum expansion of Self (Fox 1990).

7. Other critics of deep ecology, such as Sylvan (1985) and Cheney (1987) have also suggested that it shifts between different and incompatible versions. Ecofeminist critics of deep ecology have included Salleh (1984), Kheel (1985), Biehl (1987), and Warren (1990).

8. Arne Naess, quoted in Fox (1982, 3, 10).

9. This is argued in Plumwood (1980), where a relational account of self developed in the context of an anarchist theory is applied to relations with nature. Part of the problem lies in the terminology of "holism" itself, which is used in highly variable and ambiguous ways, sometimes carrying commitment to indistinguishability and sometimes meaning only "nonatomistic."

10. Arne Naess, quoted in Fox (1986, 54).

11. As noted by Cheney (1989, 293–325).

12. Thus John Seed says: "Naess wrote that when most people think about conservation, they think about sacrifice. This is a treacherous basis for conservation, because most people aren't capable of working for anything except their own self-interest. . . . Naess argued that we need to find ways to extend our identity into nature. Once that happens, being out in front of bulldozers or whatever becomes no more of a sacrifice than moving your foot if you notice that someone's just about to strike it with an axe" (Seed 1989).

13. This denial of the alterity of the other is also the route taken by J. Baird Callicott, who indeed asserts that "The principle of axiological complementarity posits an essential unity between self and world and establishes the problematic intrinsic value of nature in relation to the axiologically privileged value of self" (1985, 275). Given the impoverishment of Humean theory in the area of relations (and hence its inability to conceive a self-in-relationship whose connections to others are not merely contingent but essential), Callicott has little alternative to this direction of development.

14. Grimshaw (1986, 182). See also the excellent discussion in Warren (1990, 136–38) of the importance of recognition and respect for the other's difference; Blum (1980, 75); and Benhabib (1987, 166).

15. This traditional model of land relationship is closely linked to that of bioregionalism, whose strategy is to

engage people in greater knowledge and care for the local areas that have meaning for them and where they can most easily evolve a caring and responsible life-style. The feat of "impartial identification with all particulars" is, beyond the seeking of individual enlightenment, strategically empty. Because it cares "impartially" for everything it can, in practice, care for nothing.

16. Thus some ecofeminists, such as Cheney (1987, 1989) and Warren (1990), have been led to the development of alternative accounts of ethics and ethical theory building and the development of distinctively ecofeminist ethics.

17. Although the emphasis of early work in this area (for example, Plumwood 1975) was mainly directed toward showing that a respectful, noninstrumental view of nature was logically viable since that was widely disputed, it is certainly well past time to move beyond that. Although there is now wider support for a respectful, noninstrumental position, it remains controversial; see, for example, Thompson (1990) and Plumwood (1991).

18. Poole (1984) has also shown how this kind of self is presupposed in the Kantian moral picture, where desire or inclination is essentially self-directed and is held in check by reason (acting in the interests of universality).

19. In the sense of altruism in which one's own interests are neglected in favor of another's, essentially relational interests are neither egoistic nor altruistic.

20. On rationalism and place see Edward Relph (1976, 1981).

21. Fox (1990, 12), in claiming gender neutrality for cosmologically based identification and treating issues of gender as irrelevant to the issue, ignores the historical scholarship linking conceptions of gender and conceptions of morality via the division between public and private spheres (for example, Lloyd [1984] and Nicholson [1983]). To the extent that the ecofeminist thesis is not an essentialist one linking *sex* to emotionality and particularity or to nature but one linking social and historical conceptions of *gender* to conceptions of morality and rationality, it is not refuted by examples of women who buy a universalizing view or who drive bulldozers, or by Mrs. Thatcher. Fox's argument here involves a sex/gender confusion. On the sex/gender distinction see Plumwood (1989, 2–11).

22. Thus Fox (1990) throughout his discussion, like Zimmerman (1987, 37), takes "the ecofeminist charge against deep ecology" to be that "androcentrism is 'the real root' of ecological destruction" (1990, 14), so that "there is no need to worry about any form of human domination other than androcentrism"

(1990, 18). Warren (1990, 144) tellingly discusses Fox's claim that "feminist" is redundant as an addition to a deep ecological ethic.

23. This reductionist position has a few representatives in the literature (perhaps Andrée Collard [1988], and Sally Miller Gearhart [1982]), but cannot be taken as representative of the main body of ecofeminist work. Fox, I believe, is right to resist such a reduction and to insist on the noneliminability of the form of oppression the critique of anthropocentrism is concerned with, but the conclusion that the critiques are unrelated does not follow. Critiques and the different kinds of oppression they correspond to can be distinguishable but, like individuals themselves, still related in essential and not merely accidental ways. The choice between merger (reductive elimination) and disconnection (isolation) of critiques is the same false dichotomy that inspires the false contrasts of holism and atomism, and of self as merged, lacking boundaries, versus self as isolated atom, lacking essential connection to others.

References

Benhabib, Seyla. 1987. The generalised and the concrete other. In *Women and moral theory*, 154–77. E. Kittay and D. Meyers, eds. Totowa, N.J.: Rowman and Allenheld.

Benhabib, Seyla and Drucilla Cornell, eds. 1987. *Feminism as critique.* Minneapolis: University of Minnesota Press; Cambridge: Polity Press.

Benjamin, Jessica. 1985. The bonds of love: Rational violence and erotic domination. In *The future of difference.* H. Eisenstein and A. Jardine, eds. New Brunswick: Rutgers University Press.

Berman, Marshall. 1982. *All that is solid melts into air: The experience of modernity.* New York: Simon & Schuster; London: Penguin.

Biehl, Janet. 1987. It's deep, but is it broad? An ecofeminist looks at deep ecology. *Kick It Over* special supplement (Winter).

Blum, Lawrence A. 1980. *Friendship, altruism and morality.* Boston and London: Routledge & Kegan Paul.

Callicott, J. Baird. 1985. Intrinsic value, quantum theory, and environmental ethics. *Environmental Ethics* 7: 261–62.

Cheney, Jim. 1987. Ecofeminism and deep ecology. *Environmental Ethics* 9: 115–145.

———. 1989. The neo-stoicism of radical environmentalism. *Environmental Ethics* 11: 293–325.

Chodorow, Nancy. 1979. *The reproduction of mothering.* Berkeley: University of California Press.

———. 1985. Gender, relation and difference in psychoanalytic perspective. In *The future of difference*, 3–19.

H. Eisenstein and A. Jardine, eds. New Brunswick: Rutgers University Press.

Collard, Andrée. 1988. *Rape of the wild: Man's violence against animals and the earth*. Bloomington: Indiana University Press; London: The Woman's Press.

Cook, Francis. 1977. *Hua-Yen Buddhism: The jewel net of Indra*. Pennsylvania: Pennsylvania State University Press. 118–119.

Eckersley, Robyn. 1989. Divining evolution: The ecological ethics of Murray Bookchin. *Environmental Ethics* 11: 99–116.

Fox, Warwick. 1982. The intuition of deep ecology. Paper presented at Environment, Ethics and Ecology Conference, Canberra. Also published under the title Deep ecology: A new philosophy of our time? *The Ecologist* 14 (1984): 194–200.

———. 1986. Approaching deep ecology: A response to Richard Sylvan's critique of deep ecology. Environmental Studies Occasional Paper 20. Hobart: University of Tasmania Centre for Environmental Studies.

———. 1989. The deep ecology-ecofeminism debate and its parallels. *Environmental Ethics* 11: 5–25.

———. 1990. *Towards a transpersonal ecology: Developing new foundations for environmentalism*. Boston: Shambala.

Gearhart, Sally Miller. 1982. The Future—if there is one—is female. In *Reweaving the web of life*, 266–285. P. McAllister, ed. Philadelphia and Santa Cruz: New Society Publishers.

Gilligan, Carol. 1982. *In a different voice*. Cambridge: Harvard University Press.

———. 1987. Moral orientation and moral development. In *Women and moral theory*, 19–33. E. Kittay and D. Meyers, eds. Totowa, N.J.: Rowman and Allenheld.

Griffin, Susan. 1978. *Woman and nature: The roaring inside her*. New York: Harper and Row.

Grimshaw, Jean. 1986. *Philosophy and feminist thinking*. Minneapolis: University of Minnesota Press. Also published as *Feminist philosophers*. Brighton: Wheatsheaf.

Griscom, Joan L. 1981. On healing the nature/history split in feminist thought. *Heresies* 4(1): 4–9.

Jaggar, Alison. 1983. *Feminist politics and human nature*. Totowa, N.J.: Rowman & Allenheld; Brighton: Harvester.

Kheel, Marti. 1985. The liberation of nature: A circular affair. *Environmental Ethics* 7: 135–49.

King, Ynestra. 1981. Feminism and revolt. *Heresies* 4(1): 12–16.

———. 1989. The ecology of feminism and the feminism of ecology. In *Healing the wounds*. J. Plant, ed., Philadelphia and Santa Cruz: New Society Publishers.

Leopold, Aldo. 1949. *A sand county almanac*, 201–2. Oxford and New York: Oxford University Press.

Lloyd, Genevieve. 1983a. Public reason and private passion. *Metaphilosophy* 14: 308–26.

———. 1983b. Reason, gender and morality in the history of philosophy. *Social Research* 50(3): 490–513.

———. 1984. *The man of reason*. London: Methuen.

McLuhan T. C., ed. 1973. *Touch the earth*. London: Abacus.

Miller, Jean Baker. 1976, 1978. *Toward a new psychology of women*. Boston: Beacon Press; London: Pelican.

Midgley, Mary. 1983. *Animals and why they matter*. Athens: University of Georgia Press; London: Penguin.

Naess, Arne. 1973. The shallow and the deep, long-range ecology movement: A summary. *Inquiry* 16: 95–100.

———. 1986. Intrinsic value: Will the defenders of nature please rise. In *Conservation biology*. M. Soulé, ed. Sunderland, MA: Sinauer Associates.

———. 1988. *Ecology, community and lifestyle*. Cambridge: Cambridge University Press.

Neidjie, Bill. 1985. *Kakadu man*. With S. Davis and A. Fox. Canberra: Mybrood P/L.

Neidjie, Bill and Keith Taylor, eds. 1989. *Story about feeling*. Wyndham: Magabala Books.

Nicholson, Linda J. 1983. Women, morality and history. *Social Research* 50(3): 514–36.

Plumwood, Val. 1975. Critical notice of Passmore's *Man's responsibility for nature*. *Australasian Journal of Philosophy* 53(2): 171–85.

———. 1980. Social theories, self-management and environmental problems. In *Environmental Philosophy*, 217–332. D. Mannison, M. McRobbie, and R. Routley eds. Canberra: ANU Department of Philosophy Monograph Series RSSS.

———. 1986. Ecofeminism: an overview and discussion of positions and arguments. In *Women and philosophy*, Supplement to vol. 64 *Australasian Journal of Philosophy* (June 1986): 120–38.

———. 1988, 1990. Women, humanity and nature. *Radical Philosophy* 48: 6–24. Reprinted in *Feminism, socialism and philosophy: A radical philosophy reader*. S. Sayers, ed. London: Routledge.

———. 1989. Do we need a sex/gender distinction? *Radical Philosophy* 51: 2–11.

———. 1990. Plato and the bush. *Meanjin* 49(3): 524–36.

———. 1991. Ethics and instrumentalism: A response to Janna Thompson. *Environmental Ethics*. Forthcoming.

Poole, Ross. 1984. Reason, self-interest and "commercial society": The social content of Kantian morality. *Critical Philosophy* 1: 24–46.

————. 1985. Morality, masculinity and the market. *Radical Philosophy* 39: 16–23.

————. 1990. Modernity, rationality and "the masculine." In *Femininity/Masculinity and representation*. T. Threadgold and A. Cranny-Francis, eds. Sydney: George Allen and Unwin, 1990.

Regan, Tom. 1986. *The case for animal rights*. Berkeley: University of California Press.

Relph, Edward. 1976. *Place and placelessness*. London: Pion.

————. 1981. *Rational lanscapes and humanistic geography*. London: Croom Helm.

Rodman, John. 1980. Paradigm change in political science. *American Behavioural Scientist* 24(1): 54–55.

Ruether, Rosemary Radford. 1975. *New woman new earth*. Minneapolis: Seabury Press.

Salleh, Ariel. 1984. deeper than deep ecology. *Environmental Ethics* 6: 339–45.

Seed, John. 1989. Interviewed by Pat Stone. *Mother Earth News* (May/June).

Seed, John, Joanna Macy, Pat Fleming, and Arne Naess.

1988. *Thinking like a mountain: Towards a council of all beings* Philadelphia and Santa Cruz: New Society Publishers.

Sylvan, Richard. 1985. A critique of deep ecology. *Radical Philosophy* 40 and 41.

Taylor, Paul. 1986. *Respect for nature*. Princeton: Princeton University Press.

Thomas Aquinas. 1976. *Summa contra Gentiles*. Bk. 3, Pt. 2, chap. 62. Quoted in *Animal rights and human obligations*, 56. T. Regan and P. Singer, eds. Englewood Cliffs, N.J.: Prentice Hall.

Thompson, Janna. 1990. A refutation of environmental ethics. *Environmental Ethics* 12(2): 147–60.

Warren, Karen J. 1987. Feminism and ecology: Making connections. *Environmental Ethics* 9: 17–18.

————. 1990. The power and promise of ecological feminism. *Environmental Ethics* 12(2): 121–46.

Zimmerman, Michael E. 1987. Feminism, deep ecology, and environmental ethics. *Environmental Ethics* 9.

The Power and the Promise of Ecological Feminism

Karen J. Warren

Introduction

Ecological feminism (ecofeminism) has begun to receive a fair amount of attention lately as an alternative feminism and environmental ethic.[1] Since Francoise d'Eaubonne introduced the term *ecofeminism* in 1974 to bring attention to women's potential for bringing about an ecological revolution,[2] the term has been used in a variety of ways. As I use the term in this paper, ecological feminism is the position that there are important connections—historical, experiential, symbolic, theoretical—between the domination of women and the domination of nature, an understanding of which is crucial to both feminism and environmental ethics. I argue that the promise and power of ecological feminism is that *it provides a distinctive framework both for reconceiving feminism and for developing an environmental ethic which takes seriously connections between the domination of women and the domination of*

nature. I do so by discussing the nature of a feminist ethic and the ways in which ecofeminism provides a feminist and environmental ethic. I conclude that any feminist theory *and* any environmental ethic which fails to take seriously the twin and interconnected dominations of women and nature is at best incomplete and at worst simply inadequate.

Feminism, Ecological Feminism, and Conceptual Frameworks

Whatever else it is, feminism is at least the movement to end sexist oppression. It involves the elimination of any and all factors that contribute to the continued and systematic domination or subordination of women. While feminists disagree about the nature of and solutions to the subordination of women, all feminists agree that sexist oppression exists, is wrong, and must be abolished.

Environmental Ethics, Vol. 12, No. 2 (Summer 1990), pp. 125–146. Reprinted by permission.

A "feminist issue" is any issue that contributes in some way to understanding the oppression of women. Equal rights, comparable pay for comparable work, and food production are feminist issues wherever and whenever an understanding of them contributes to an understanding of the continued exploitation or subjugation of women. Carrying water and searching for firewood are feminist issues wherever and whenever women's primary responsibility for these tasks contributes to their lack of full participation in decision making, income producing, or high status positions engaged in by men. What counts as a feminist issue, then, depends largely on context, particularly the historical and material conditions of women's lives.

Environmental degradation and exploitation are feminist issues because an understanding of them contributes to an understanding of the oppression of women. In India, for example, both deforestation and reforestation through the introduction of a monoculture species tree (e.g., eucalyptus) intended for commercial production are feminist issues because the loss of indigenous forests and multiple species of trees has drastically affected rural Indian women's ability to maintain a subsistence household. Indigenous forests provide a variety of trees for food, fuel, fodder, household utensils, dyes, medicines, and income-generating uses, while monoculture-species forests do not.[3] Although I do not argue for this claim here, a look at the global impact of environmental degradation on women's lives suggests important respects in which environmental degradation is a feminist issue.

Feminist philosophers claim that some of the most important feminist issues are *conceptual* ones: these issues concern how one conceptualizes such mainstay philosophical notions as reason and rationality, ethics, and what it is to be human. Ecofeminists extend this feminist philosophical concern to nature. They argue that, ultimately, some of the most important connections between the domination of women and the domination of nature are conceptual. To see this, consider the nature of conceptual frameworks.

A *conceptual framework* is a set of *basic* beliefs, values, attitudes, and assumptions which shape and reflect how one views oneself and one's world. It is a socially constructed lens through which we perceive ourselves and others. It is affected by such factors as gender, race, class, age, affectional orientation, nationality, and religious background.

Some conceptual frameworks are oppressive. An *oppressive conceptual framework* is one that explains, justifies, and maintains relationships of domination and subordination. When an oppressive conceptual framework is *patriarchal,* it explains, justifies, and maintains the subordination of women by men.

I have argued elsewhere that there are three significant features of oppressive conceptual frameworks: (1) value-hierarchical thinking, i.e., "up-down" thinking which places higher value, status, or prestige on what is "up" rather than on what is "down"; (2) value dualisms, i.e., disjunctive pairs in which the disjuncts are seen as oppositional (rather than as complementary) and exclusive (rather than as inclusive), and which place higher value (status, prestige) on one disjunct rather than the other (e.g., dualisms which give higher value or status to that which has historically been identified as "mind," "reason," and "male" than to that which has historically been identified as "body," "emotion," and "female"); and (3) logic of domination, i.e., a structure of argumentation which leads to a justification of subordination.[4]

The third feature of oppressive conceptual frameworks is the most significant. A logic of domination is not *just* a logical structure. It also involves a substantive value system, since an ethical premise is needed to permit or sanction the "just" subordination of that which is subordinate. This justification typically is given on grounds of some alleged characteristic (e.g., rationality) which the dominant (e.g., men) have and the subordinate (e.g., women) lack.

Contrary to what many feminists and ecofeminists have said or suggested, there may be nothing *inherently* problematic about "hierarchical thinking" or even "value-hierarchical thinking" in contexts other than contexts of oppression. Hierarchical thinking is important in daily living for classifying data, comparing information, and organizing material. Taxonomies (e.g., plant taxonomies) and biological nomenclature seem to require *some* form of "hierarchical thinking." Even "value-hierarchical thinking" may be quite acceptable in certain contexts. (The same may be said of "value dualisms" in non-oppressive contexts.) For example, suppose it is true that what is unique about humans is our conscious capacity to radically reshape our social environments (or "societies"), as Murray Bookchin suggests.[5] Then one could truthfully say that humans are better equipped to radically reshape their environments than are rocks or plants—a "value-hierarchical" way of speaking.

The problem is not simply *that* value-hierarchical thinking and value dualisms are used, but *the way* in which each has been used *in oppressive conceptual frameworks* to establish inferiority and to justify subordination.[6] It is the logic of domination, *coupled with* value-hierarchical thinking and value dualisms, which "justifies" subordination. What is explanatorily basic, then, about the nature of oppressive conceptual frameworks is the logic of domination.

For ecofeminism, that a logic of domination is explanatorily basic is important for at least three reasons. First, without a logic of domination, a description of similarities and differences would be just that—a description of similarities and differences. Consider the claim, "Humans are different from plants and rocks in that humans can (and plants and rocks cannot) consciously and radically reshape the communities in which they live; humans are similar to plants and rocks in that they are both members of an ecological community." Even if humans are "better" than plants and rocks with respect to the conscious ability of humans to radically transform communities, one does not *thereby* get any *morally* relevant distinction between humans and nonhumans, or an argument for the domination of plants and rocks by humans. To get *those* conclusions one needs to add at least two powerful assumptions, viz., (A2) and (A4) in argument A below:

> (A1) Humans do, and plants and rocks do not, have the capacity to consciously and radically change the community in which they live.
>
> (A2) Whatever has the capacity to consciously and radically change the community in which it lives is morally superior to whatever lacks this capacity.
>
> (A3) Thus, humans are morally superior to plants and rocks.
>
> (A4) For any X and Y, if X is morally superior to Y, then X is morally justified in subordinating Y.
>
> (A5) Thus, humans are morally justified in subordinating plants and rocks.

Without the two assumptions that *humans are morally superior* to (at least some) nonhumans, (A2), and that *superiority justifies subordination*, (A4), all one has is some difference between humans and some nonhumans. This is true *even if* that difference is given in terms of superiority. Thus, it is the logic of domination, (A4), which is the bottom line in ecofeminist discussions of oppression.

Second, ecofeminists argue that, at least in Western societies, the oppressive conceptual framework which sanctions the twin dominations of women and nature is a patriarchal one characterized by all three features of an oppressive conceptual framework. Many ecofeminists claim that, historically, within at least the dominant Western culture, a patriarchal conceptual framework has sanctioned the following argument B:

> (B1) Women are identified with nature and the realm of the physical; men are identified with the "human" and the realm of the mental.
>
> (B2) Whatever is identified with nature and the realm of the physical is inferior to ("below") whatever is identified with the "human" and the realm of the mental; or, conversely, the latter is superior to ("above") the former.
>
> (B3) Thus, women are inferior to ("below") men; or, conversely, men are superior to ("above") women.
>
> (B4) For any X and Y, if X is superior to Y, then X is justified in subordinating Y.
>
> (B5) Thus, men are justified in subordinating women.

If sound, argument B establishes *patriarchy*, i.e., the conclusion given at (B5) that the systematic domination of women by men is justified. But according to ecofeminists, (B5) is justified by just those three features of an oppressive conceptual framework identified earlier: value-hierarchical thinking, the assumption at (B2); value dualisms, the assumed dualism of the mental and the physical at (B1) and the assumed inferiority of the physical vis-à-vis the mental at (B2); and a logic of domination, the assumption at (B4), the same as the previous premise (A4). Hence, according to ecofeminists, insofar as an oppressive patriarchal conceptual framework has functioned historically (within at least dominant Western culture) to sanction the twin dominations of women and nature (argument B), both argument B and the patriarchal conceptual framework, from whence it comes, ought to be rejected.

Of course, the preceeding does not identify which premises of B are false. What is the status of premises (B1) and (B2)? Most, if not all, feminists claim that (B1), and many ecofeminists claim that (B2), have been assumed or asserted within the dominant Western philosophical and intellectual tradition.[7] As such, these feminists assert, as a matter of historical fact, that the dominant Western philosophical tradition has assumed the truth of (B1) and (B2). Ecofeminists, however, either deny (B2) or do not affirm (B2). Furthermore, because some ecofeminists are anxious to deny any historical identification of women with nature, some ecofeminists deny (B1) when (B1) is used to support anything other than a strictly historical claim about what has been asserted or assumed to be true within patriarchal culture—e.g., when (B1) is used to assert that women properly are identified with the realm of nature and the physical.[8] Thus, from a ecofeminist perspective, (B1) and (B2) are properly viewed as problematic though historically sanctioned claims: they are problematic precisely because of the way they have functioned historically in a patriarchal conceptual framework and culture to sanction the dominations of women and nature.

What *all* ecofeminists agree about, then, is the way in which *the logic of domination* has functioned historically within patriarchy to sustain and justify the twin dominations of women and nature.[9] Since *all* feminists (and not just ecofeminists) oppose patriarchy, the conclusion given at (B5), all feminists (including ecofeminists) must oppose at least the logic of domination, premise (B4), on which argument B rests—whatever the truth-value status of (B1) and (B2) *outside of* a patriarchal context.

That *all* feminists must oppose the logic of domination shows the breadth and depth of the ecofeminist critique of B: it is a critique not only of the three assumptions on which this argument for the domination of women and nature rests, viz., the assumptions at (B1), (B2), and (B4); it is also a critique of patriarchal conceptual frameworks generally, i.e., of those oppressive conceptual frameworks which put men "up" and women "down," allege some way in which women are morally inferior to men, and use that alleged difference to justify the subordination of women by men. Therefore,

ecofeminism is necessary to *any* feminist critique of patriarchy, and, hence, necessary to feminism (a point I discuss again later).

Third, ecofeminism clarifies why the logic of domination, and any conceptual framework which gives rise to it, must be abolished in order both to make possible a meaningful notion of difference which does not breed domination and to prevent feminism from becoming a "support" movement based primarily on shared experiences. In contemporary society, there is no one "woman's voice," no *woman* (or *human*) *simpliciter*: every woman (or human) is a woman (or human) of some race, class, age, affectional orientation, marital status, regional or national background, and so forth. Because there are no "monolithic experiences" that all women share, feminism must be a "solidarity movement" based on shared beliefs and interests rather than a "unity in sameness" movement based on shared experiences and shared victimization.[10] In the words of Maria Lugones, "Unity—not to be confused with solidarity—is understood as conceptually tied to domination."[11]

Ecofeminists insist that the sort of logic of domination used to justify the domination of humans by gender, racial or ethnic, or class status is also used to justify the domination of nature. Because eliminating a logic of domination is part of a feminist critique—whether a critique of patriarchy, white supremacist culture, or imperialism—ecofeminists insist that *naturism* is properly viewed as an integral part of any feminist solidarity movement to end sexist oppression and the logic of domination which conceptually grounds it.

Ecofeminism Reconceives Feminism

The discussion so far has focused on some of the oppressive conceptual features of patriarchy. As I use the phrase, the "logic of traditional feminism" refers to the location of the conceptual roots of sexist oppression, at least in Western societies, in an oppressive patriarchal conceptual framework characterized by a logic of domination. Insofar as other systems of oppression (e.g., racism, classism, ageism, heterosexism) are also conceptually maintained by a logic of domination, appeal to the logic of traditional feminism ultimately locates the basic conceptual interconnections among *all* systems of oppression in the logic of domination. It thereby explains at a *conceptual* level why the eradication of sexist oppression requires the eradication of the other forms of oppression.[12] It is by clarifying this conceptual connection between systems of oppression that a movement to end sexist oppression—traditionally the special turf of feminist theory and practice—leads to a reconceiving of feminism as *a movement to end all forms of oppression.*

Suppose one agrees that the logic of traditional feminism requires the expansion of feminism to include other social systems of domination (e.g., racism and classism). What warrants the inclusion of nature in these "social systems of domination"? Why must the logic of traditional feminism include the abolition of "naturism" (i.e., the domination or oppression of nonhuman nature) among the "isms" feminism must confront? The conceptual justification for expanding feminism to include ecofeminism is twofold. One basis has already been suggested: by showing that the conceptual connections between the dual dominations of women and nature are located in an oppressive and, at least in Western societies, patriarchal conceptual framework characterized by a logic of domination, ecofeminism explains how and why feminism, conceived as a movement to end sexist oppression, must be expanded and reconceived as also a movement to end naturism. This is made explicit by the following argument C:

(C1) Feminism is a movement to end sexism.

(C2) But Sexism is conceptually linked with naturism (through an oppressive conceptual framework characterized by a logic of domination).

(C3) Thus, Feminism is (also) a movement to end naturism.

Because, ultimately, these connections between sexism and naturism are conceptual—embedded in an oppressive conceptual framework—the logic of traditional feminism leads to the embracement of ecological feminism.[13]

The other justification for reconceiving feminism to include ecofeminism has to do with the concepts of gender and nature. Just as conceptions of gender are socially constructed, so are conceptions of nature. Of course, the claim that women and nature are social constructions does not require anyone to deny that there are actual humans and actual trees, rivers, and plants. It simply implies that *how* women and nature are conceived is a matter of historical and social reality. These conceptions vary cross-culturally and by historical time period. As a result, any discussion of the "oppression or domination of nature" involves reference to historically specific forms of social domination of nonhuman nature by humans, just as discussion of the "domination of women" refers to historically specific forms of social domination of women by men. Although I do not argue for it here, an ecofeminist defense of the historical connections between the dominations of women and of nature, claims (B1) and (B2) in argument B, involves showing that within patriarchy the feminization of nature and the naturalization of women have been crucial to the historically successful subordinations of both.[14]

If ecofeminism promises to reconceive traditional feminism in ways which include naturism as a legitimate feminist issue, does ecofeminism also promise to reconceive environmental ethics in ways which are feminist? I think so. This is the subject of the remainder of the paper.

Climbing from Ecofeminism to Environmental Ethics

Many feminists and some environmental ethicists have begun to explore the use of first-person narrative as a way of raising philosophically germane issues in ethics often lost or underplayed in mainstream philosophical ethics. Why is this so? What is it about narrative which makes it a significant resource for theory and practice in feminism and environmental ethics? Even if appeal to first-person narrative is a helpful literary device for describing ineffable experience or a legitimate social science methodology for documenting personal and social history, how is first-person narrative a valuable vehicle of argumentation for ethical decision making and theory building? One fruitful way to begin answering these questions is to ask them of a particular first-person narrative.

Consider the following first-person narrative about rock climbing:

For my very first rock climbing experience, I chose a somewhat private spot, away from other climbers and on-lookers. After studying "the chimney," I focused all my energy on making it to the top. I climbed with intense determination, using whatever strength and skills I had to accomplish this challenging feat. By midway I was exhausted and anxious. I couldn't see what to do next—where to put my hands or feet. Growing increasingly more weary as I clung somewhat desperately to the rock, I made a move. It didn't work. I fell. There I was, dangling midair above the rocky ground below, frightened but terribly relieved that the belay rope had held me. I knew I was safe. I took a look up at the climb that remained. I was determined to make it to the top. With renewed confidence and concentration, I finished the climb to the top.

On my second day of climbing, I rappelled down about 200 feet from the top of the Palisades at Lake Superior to just a few feet above the water level. I could see no one—not my belayer, not the other climbers, no one. I unhooked slowly from the rappel rope and took a deep cleansing breath. I looked all around me—really looked—and listened. I heard a cacophony of voices—birds, trickles of water on the rock before me, waves lapping against the rocks below. I closed my eyes and began to feel the rock with my hands—the cracks and crannies, the raised lichen and mosses, the almost imperceptible nubs that might provide a resting place for my fingers and toes when I began to climb. At that moment I was bathed in serenity. I began to talk to the rock in an almost inaudible, child-like way, as if the rock were my friend. I felt an overwhelming sense of gratitude for what it offered me—a chance to know myself and the rock differently, to appreciate unforeseen miracles like the tiny flowers growing in the even tinier cracks in the rock's surface, and to come to know a sense of *being in relationship* with the natural environment. It felt as if the rock and I were silent conversational partners in a longstanding friendship. I realized then that I had come to care about this cliff which was so different from me, so unmovable and invinci-

ble, independent and seemingly indifferent to my presence. I wanted to be with the rock as I climbed. Gone was the determination to conquer the rock, to forcefully impose my will on it; I wanted simply to work respectfully with the rock as I climbed. And as I climbed, that is what I felt. I felt myself *caring* for this rock and feeling thankful that climbing provided the opportunity for me to know it and myself in this new way.

There are at least four reasons why use of such a first-person narrative is important to feminism and environmental ethics. First, such a narrative gives voice to a felt sensitivity often lacking in traditional analytical ethical discourse, viz., a sensitivity to conceiving of oneself as fundamentally "in relationship with" others, including the nonhuman environment. It is a modality which *takes relationships themselves seriously.* It thereby stands in contrast to a strictly reductionist modality that takes relationships seriously only or primarily because of the nature of the *relators* or parties to those relationships (e.g., relators conceived as moral agents, right holders, interest carriers, or sentient beings). In the rock-climbing narrative above, it is the climber's relationship with the rock she climbs which takes on special significance—which is itself a locus of value—in addition to whatever moral status or moral considerability she or the rock or any other parties to the relationship may also have.[15]

Second, such a first-person narrative gives expression to a variety of ethical attitudes and behaviors often overlooked or underplayed in mainstream Western ethics, e.g., the difference in attitudes and behaviors toward a rock when one is "making it to the top" and when one thinks of oneself as "friends with" or "caring about" the rock one climbs.[16] These different attitudes and behaviors suggest an ethically germane contrast between two different types of relationship humans or climbers may have toward a rock: an imposed conqueror-type relationship, and an emergent caring-type relationship. This contrast grows out of, and is faithful to, felt, lived experience.

The difference between conquering and caring attitudes and behaviors in relation to the natural environment provides a third reason why the use of first-person narrative is important to feminism and environmental ethics: it provides a way of conceiving of ethics and ethical meaning *as emerging out of* particular situations moral agents find themselves in, rather than as being *imposed on* those situations (e.g., as a derivation or instantiation of some predetermined abstract principle or rule). This emergent feature of narrative centralizes the importance of *voice*. When a multiplicity of cross-cultural *voices* are centralized, narrative is able to give expression to a range of attitudes, values, beliefs, and behaviors which may be overlooked or silenced by imposed ethical meaning and theory. As a reflection of and on felt, lived experiences, the use of narrative in ethics provides a stance from which ethical discourse can be held accountable to the historical, material, and social realities in which moral subjects find themselves.

Lastly, and for our purposes perhaps most importantly, the use of narrative has argumentative significance. Jim Cheney calls attention to this feature of narrative when he claims, "To contextualize ethical deliberation is, in some sense, to provide a narrative or story, from which the solution to the ethical dilemma emerges as the fitting conclusion."[17] Narrative has argumentative force by suggesting *what counts* as an appropriate conclusion to an ethical situation. One ethical conclusion suggested by the climbing narrative is that what counts as a proper ethical attitude toward mountains and rocks is an attitude of respect and care (whatever that turns out to be or involve), not one of domination and conquest.

In an essay entitled "In and Out of Harm's Way: Arrogance and Love," feminist philosopher Marilyn Frye distinguishes between "arrogant" and "loving" perception as one way of getting at this difference in the ethical attitudes of care and conquest.[18] Frye writes:

> The loving eye is a contrary of the arrogant eye.
> The loving eye knows the independence of the other. It is the eye of a seer who knows that nature is indifferent. It is the eye of one who knows that to know the seen, one must consult something other than one's own will and interests and fears and imagination. One must look at the thing. One must look and listen and check and question.

> The loving eye is one that pays a certain sort of attention. This attention can require a discipline but *not* a self-denial. The discipline is one of self-knowledge, knowledge of the scope and boundary of the self. . . . In particular, it is a matter of being able to tell one's own interests from those of others and of knowing where one's self leaves off and another begins. . . .
> The loving eye does not make the object of perception into something edible, does not try to assimilate it, does not reduce it to the size of the seer's desire, fear and imagination, and hence does not have to simplify. It knows the complexity of the other as something which will forever present new things to be known. The science of the loving eye would favor The Complexity Theory of Truth [in contrast to The Simplicity Theory of Truth] and presuppose The Endless Interestingness of the Universe.[19]

According to Frye, the loving eye is not an invasive, coercive eye which annexes others to itself, but one which "knows the complexity of the other as something which will forever present new things to be known."

When one climbs a rock as a conqueror, one climbs with an arrogant eye. When one climbs with a loving eye, one constantly "must look and listen and check and question." One recognizes the rock as something very different, something perhaps totally indifferent to one's own presence, and finds in that difference joyous occasion for celebration. One knows "the boundary of the self," where the self—the "I," the climber—leaves off and the rock begins. There is no fusion of two into one, but a complement of two entities *acknowledged* as separate, different, independent, yet *in relationship*; they are in relationship *if only* because the loving eye is perceiving it, responding to it, noticing it, attending to it.

An ecofeminist perspective about both women and nature involves this shift in attitude from "arrogant perception" to "loving perception" of the nonhuman world. Arrogant perception of nonhumans by humans presupposes and maintains *sameness* in such a way that it expands the moral community to those beings who are thought to resemble (be like, similar to, or the same as) humans in some morally significant way. Any environmental movement or ethic based on arrogant perception builds a moral hierarchy of beings and assumes some common denominator of moral considerability in virtue of which like beings deserve similar treatment or moral consideration and unlike beings do not. Such environmental ethics are or generate a "unity in sameness." In contrast, "loving perception" presupposes and maintains *difference*—a distinction between the self and other, between human and at least some nonhumans—in such a way that perception of the other as other *is* an expression of love for one who/which is recognized at the outset as independent, dissimilar, different. As Maria Lugones says, in loving perception, "Love is seen not as fusion and erasure of difference but as incompatible with them."[20] "Unity in sameness" alone is an *erasure of difference.*

"Loving perception" of the nonhuman natural world is an attempt to understand what it means *for humans* to care about the nonhuman world, a world *acknowledged* as being independent, different, perhaps even indifferent to humans. Humans *are* different from rocks in important ways, even if they are also both members of some ecological community. A moral community based on loving perception of oneself *in relationship with* a rock, or with the natural environment as a whole, is one which acknowledges and respects difference, whatever "sameness" also exists.[21] The limits of loving perception are determined only by the limits of one's (e.g., a person's, a community's) ability to respond lovingly (or with appropriate care, trust, or friendship)—whether it is to other humans or to the nonhuman world and elements of it.[22]

If what I have said so far is correct, then there are very different ways to climb a mountain and *how* one climbs it and *how* one narrates the experience of climbing it matter ethically. If one climbs with "arrogant perception," with an attitude of "conquer and control," one keeps intact the very sorts of thinking that characterize a logic of domination and an oppressive conceptual framework. Since the oppressive conceptual framework which sanctions the domination of nature is a patriarchal one, one also thereby keeps intact, even if unwittingly, a patriarchal conceptual framework. Because the dismantling of patriarchal conceptual frame-

works is a feminist issue, *how* one climbs a mountain and *how* one narrates—or tells the story—about the experience of climbing also are *feminist issues*. In this way, ecofeminism makes visible why, at a conceptual level, environmental ethics is a feminist issue. I turn now to a consideration of ecofeminism as a distinctively feminist and environmental ethic.

Ecofeminism as a Feminist and Environmental Ethic

A feminist ethic involves a twofold commitment to critique male bias in ethics wherever it occurs, and to develop ethics which are not male-biased. Sometimes this involves articulation of values (e.g., values of care, appropriate trust, kinship, friendship) often lost or underplayed in mainstream ethics.[23] Sometimes it involves engaging in theory building by pioneering in new directions or by revamping old theories in gender sensitive ways. What makes the critiques of old theories or conceptualizations of new ones "feminist" is that they emerge out of sex-gender analyses and reflect whatever those analyses reveal about gendered experience and gendered social reality.

As I conceive feminist ethics in the pre-feminist present, it rejects attempts to conceive of ethical theory in terms of necessary and sufficient conditions, because it assumes that there is no essence (in the sense of some transhistorical, universal, absolute abstraction) of feminist ethics. While attempts to formulate joint necessary and sufficient conditions of a feminist ethic are unfruitful, nonetheless, there are some necessary conditions, what I prefer to call "boundary conditions," of a feminist ethic. These boundary conditions clarify some of the minimal conditions of a feminist ethic without suggesting that feminist ethics has some ahistorical essence. They are like the boundaries of a quilt or collage. They delimit the territory of the piece without dictating what the interior, the design, the actual pattern of the piece looks like. Because the actual design of the quilt emerges from the multiplicity of voices of women in a cross-cultural context, the design will change over time. It is not something static.

What are some of the boundary conditions of a feminist ethic? First, nothing can become part of a feminist ethic—can be part of the quilt—that promotes sexism, racism, classism, or any other "isms" of social domination. Of course, people may disagree about what counts as a sexist act, racist attitude, classist behavior. What counts as sexism, racism, or classism may vary cross-culturally. Still, because a feminist ethic aims at eliminating sexism and sexist bias, and (as I have already shown) sexism is intimately connected in conceptualization and in practice to racism, classism, and naturism, a feminist ethic must be anti-sexist, anti-racist, anti-classist, anti-naturist and opposed to any "ism" which presupposes or advances a logic of domination.

Second, a feminist ethic is a *contextualist* ethic. A contextualist ethic is one which sees ethical discourse and practice as emerging from the voices of people located in different historical circumstances. A contextualist ethic is properly viewed as a *collage* or *mosaic*, a *tapestry* of voices that emerges out of felt experiences. Like any collage or mosaic, the point is not to have *one picture* based on a unity of voices, but a *pattern* which emerges out of the very different voices of people located in different circumstances. When a contextualist ethic is *feminist*, it gives central place to the voices of women.

Third, since a feminist ethic gives central significance to the diversity of women's voices, a feminist ethic must be structurally pluralistic rather than unitary or reductionistic. It rejects the assumption that there is "one voice" in terms of which ethical values, beliefs, attitudes, and conduct can be assessed.

Fourth, a feminist ethic reconceives ethical theory as theory in process which will change over time. Like all theory, a feminist ethic is based on some generalizations.[24] Nevertheless, the generalizations associated with it are themselves a pattern of voices within which the different voices emerging out of concrete and alterative descriptions of ethical situations have meaning. The coherence of a feminist theory so conceived is given within a historical and conceptual context, i.e., within a set of historical, socioeconomic circumstances (including circumstances of race, class, age, and affectional orientation) and within a set of basic beliefs, values, attitudes, and assumptions about the world.

Fifth, because a feminist ethic is contextualist, structurally pluralistic, and "in-process," one way to evaluate the claims of a feminist ethic is in terms of their *inclusiveness:* those claims (voices, patterns of voices) are morally and epistemologically favored (preferred, better, less partial, less biased) which are more inclusive of the felt experiences and perspectives of oppressed persons. The condition of inclusiveness requires and ensures that the diverse voices of women (as oppressed persons) will be given legitimacy in ethical theory building. It thereby helps to minimize empirical bias, e.g., bias rising from faulty or false generalizations based on stereotyping, too small a sample size, or a skewed sample. It does so by ensuring that any generalizations which are made about ethics and ethical decision making include—indeed cohere with—the patterned voices of women.[25]

Sixth, a feminist ethic makes no attempt to provide an "objective" point of view, since it assumes that in contemporary culture there really is no such point of view. As such, it does not claim to be "unbiased" in the sense of "value-neutral" or "objective." However, it does assume that whatever bias it has as an ethic centralizing the voices of oppressed persons is a *better bias*—"better" because it is more inclusive and therefore less partial—than those which exclude those voices.[26]

Seventh, a feminist ethic provides a central place for values typically unnoticed, underplayed, or misrepresented in traditional ethics, e.g., values of care, love, friendship, and appropriate trust.[27] Again, it need not do this at the exclusion of considerations of rights, rules, or utility. There may be many contexts in which talk of rights or of utility is useful or appropriate. For instance, in contracts or property relationships, talk of rights may be useful and appropriate. In deciding what is cost-effective or advantageous to the most people, talk of utility may be useful and appropriate. In a feminist *qua* contextualist ethic, whether or not such talk is useful or appropriate depends on the context; *other values* (e.g., values of care, trust, friendship) are *not* viewed as reducible to or captured solely in terms of such talk.[28]

Eighth, a feminist ethic also involves a reconception of what it is to be human and what it is for humans to engage in ethical decision making, since it rejects as either meaningless or currently untenable any gender-free or gender-neutral description of humans, ethics, and ethical decision making. It thereby rejects what Alison Jaggar calls "abstract individualism," i.e., the position that it is possible to identify a human essence or human nature that exists independently of any particular historical context.[29] Humans and human moral conduct are properly understood essentially (and not merely accidentally) in terms of networks or webs of historical and concrete relationships.

All the props are now in place for seeing how ecofeminism provides the framework for a distinctively feminist and environmental ethic. It is a feminism that critiques male bias wherever it occurs in ethics (including environmental ethics) and aims at providing an ethic (including an environmental ethic) which is not male biased—and it does so in a way that satisfies the preliminary boundary conditions of a feminist ethic.

First, ecofeminism is quintessentially anti-naturist. Its anti-naturism consists in the rejection of any way of thinking about or acting toward nonhuman nature that reflects a logic, values, or attitude of domination. Its anti-naturist, anti-sexist, anti-racist, anti-classist (and so forth, for all other "isms" of social domination) stance forms the outer boundary of the quilt: nothing gets on the quilt which is naturist, sexist, racist, classist, and so forth.

Second, ecofeminism is a contextualist ethic. It involves a shift *from* a conception of ethics as primarily a matter of rights, rules, or principles predetermined and applied in specific cases to entities viewed as competitors in the contest of moral standing, *to* a conception of ethics as growing out of what Jim Cheney calls "defining relationships," i.e., relationships conceived in some sense as defining who one is.[30] As a contextualist ethic, it is not that rights, or rules, or principles are *not* relevant or important. Clearly they are in certain contexts and for certain purposes.[31] It is just that what *makes* them relevant or important is that those to whom they apply are entities *in relationship with* others.

Ecofeminism also involves an ethical shift *from* granting moral consideration to nonhumans *exclusively* on the grounds of some similarity they share with humans (e.g., rationality, interests, moral agency, sentiency, right-holder status) *to* "a highly contextual account to see clearly what a human being is and what the nonhuman world might be, morally speaking, *for* human beings."[32] For an ecofeminist, *how* a moral agent is in relationship to another becomes of central significance, not simply *that* a moral agent is a moral agent or is bound by rights, duties, virtue, or utility to act in a certain way.

Third, ecofeminism is structurally pluralistic in that it presupposes and maintains difference—difference among humans as well as between humans and at least some elements of nonhuman nature. Thus, while ecofeminism denies the "nature/culture" split, it affirms that humans are both members of an ecological community (in some respects) and different from it (in other respects). Ecofeminism's attention to relationships and community is not, therefore, an erasure of difference but a respectful acknowledgement of it.

Fourth, ecofeminism reconceives theory as theory in process. It focuses on patterns of meaning which emerge, for instance, from the storytelling and first-person narratives of women (and others) who deplore the twin dominations of women and nature. The use of narrative is one way to ensure that the content of the ethic—the pattern of the quilt—may/will change over time, as the historical and material realities of women's lives change and as more is learned about women-nature connections and the destruction of the nonhuman world.[33]

Fifth, ecofeminism is inclusivist. It emerges from the voices of women who experience the harmful domination of nature and the way that domination is tied to their domination as women. It emerges from listening to the voices of indigenous peoples such as Native Americans who have been dislocated from their land and have witnessed the attendant undermining of such values as appropriate reciprocity, sharing, and kinship that characterize traditional Indian culture. It emerges from listening to voices of those who, like Nathan Hare, critique traditional approaches to environmental ethics as white and bourgeois, and as failing to address issues of "black ecology" and the "ecology" of the inner city and urban spaces.[34] It also emerges out of the voices of Chipko women who see the destruction of "earth, soil, and water" as intimately connected with their own inability to survive economically.[35] With its emphasis on inclusivity and difference, ecofeminism provides a framework for recognizing that what counts as ecology and what counts as appropriate conduct toward both human and nonhuman environments is largely a matter of context.

Sixth, as a feminism, ecofeminism makes no attempt to provide an "objective" point of view. It is a social ecology. It recognizes the twin dominations of women and nature as social problems rooted both in very concrete, historical, socioeconomic circumstances and in oppressive patriarchal conceptual frameworks which maintain and sanction these circumstances.

Seventh, ecofeminism makes a central place for values of care, love, friendship, trust, and appropriate reciprocity—values that presuppose that our relationships to others are central to our understanding of who we are.[36] It thereby gives voice to the sensitivity that in climbing a mountain, one is doing something in relationship with an "other," an "other" whom one can come to care about and treat respectfully.

Lastly, an ecofeminist ethic involves a reconception of what it means to be human, and in what human ethical behavior consists. Ecofeminism denies abstract individualism. Humans are who we are in large part by virtue of the historical and social contexts and the relationships we are in, including our relationships with nonhuman nature. Relationships are not something extrinsic to who we are, not an "add on" feature of human nature; they play an essential role in shaping what it is to be human. Relationships of humans to the nonhuman environment are, in part, constitutive of what it is to be a human.

By making visible the interconnections among the dominations of women and nature, ecofeminism shows that both are feminist issues and that explicit acknowledgement of both is vital to any responsible environmental ethic. Feminism *must* embrace ecological feminism if it is to end the domination of women because the domination of women is tied conceptually and historically to the domination of nature.

A responsible environmental ethic also *must* embrace feminism. Otherwise, even the seemingly most revolutionary, liberational, and holistic ecological ethic will fail to take seriously the interconnected dominations of nature and women that are so much a part of the historical legacy and conceptual framework that sanctions the exploitation of nonhuman nature. Failure to make visible these interconnected, twin dominations results in an inaccurate account of how it is that nature has been and continues to be dominated and exploited and produces an environmental ethic that lacks the depth necessary to be truly *inclusive* of the realities of persons who at least in dominant Western culture have been intimately tied with that exploitation, viz.,

women. Whatever else can be said in favor of such holistic ethics, a failure to make visible ecofeminist insights into the common denominators of the twin oppressions of women and nature is to perpetuate, rather than overcome, the source of that oppression.

This last point deserves further attention. It may be objected that as long as the end result is "the same"—the development of an environmental ethic which does not emerge out of or reinforce an oppressive conceptual framework—it does not matter whether that ethic (or the ethic endorsed in getting there) is feminist or not. Hence, it simply is *not* the case that any adequate environmental ethic must be feminist. My argument, in contrast, has been that it *does* matter, and for three important reasons. First, there is the scholarly issue of accurately representing historical reality, and that, ecofeminists claim, requires acknowledging the historical feminization of nature and naturalization of women as part of the exploitation of nature. Second, I have shown that the conceptual connections between the domination of women and the domination of nature are located in an oppressive and, at least in Western societies, patriarchal conceptual framework characterized by a logic cf domination. Thus, I have shown that failure to notice the nature of this connection leaves at best an incomplete, inaccurate, and partial account of what is required of a conceptually adequate environmental ethic. An ethic which *does not* acknowledge this is simply *not* the same as one that does, whatever else the similarities between them. Third, the claim that, in contemporary culture, one can have an adequate environmental ethic which is *not* feminist assumes that, in contemporary culture, the label *feminist* does not add anything crucial to the nature or description of environmental ethics. I have shown that at least in contemporary culture this is false, for the word *feminist* currently helps to clarify just *how* the domination of nature is conceptually linked to patriarchy and, hence, how the liberation of nature, is conceptually linked to the termination of patriarchy. Thus, because it has critical bite in contemporary culture, it serves as an important reminder that in contemporary sex-gendered, raced, classed, and naturist culture, an unlabeled position functions as a privileged and "unmarked" position. That is, without the addition of the word *feminist*, one presents environmental ethics as if it has no bias, including male-gender bias, which is just what ecofeminists deny: failure to notice the connections between the twin oppressions of women and nature *is* male-gender bias.

One of the goals of feminism is the eradication of all oppressive sex-gender (and related race, class, age, affectional preference) categories and the creation of a world in which *difference does not breed domination*—say, the world of 4001. If in 4001 an "adequate environmental ethic" is a "feminist environmental ethic," the word *feminist* may then be redundant and unnecessary. However, this is *not* 4001, and in terms of the current historical and conceptual reality the dominations of nature and of women are intimately connected. Failure to notice or make visible that connection in 1990 perpetuates the mistaken (and privileged) view that "environmental ethics" is *not* a feminist issue, and that *feminist* adds nothing to environmental ethics.[37]

Conclusion

I have argued in this paper that ecofeminism provides a framework for a distinctively feminist and environmental ethic. Ecofeminism grows out of the felt and theorized about connections between the domination of women and the domination of nature. As a contextualist ethic, ecofeminism refocuses environmental ethics on what nature might mean, morally speaking, *for* humans, and on how the relational attitudes of humans to others—humans as well as nonhumans—sculpt both what it is to be human and the nature and ground of human possibilities to the nonhuman environment. Part of what this refocusing does is to take seriously the voices of women and other oppressed persons in the construction of that ethic.

A Sioux elder once told me a story about his son. He sent his seven-year-old son to live with the child's grandparents on a Sioux reservation so that he could "learn the Indian ways." Part of what the grandparents taught the son was how to hunt the four leggeds of the forest. As I heard the story, the boy was taught, "to shoot your four-legged brother in his hind area, slowing it down but not killing it. Then, take the four legged's head in your hands, and look into his eyes. The eyes are where all the suffering is. Look into your brother's eyes and feel his pain. Then, take your knife and cut the four-legged under his chin, here, on his neck, so that he dies quickly. And as you do, ask your brother, the four-legged, for forgiveness for what

you do. Offer also a prayer of thanks to your four-legged kin for offering his body to you just now, when you need food to eat and clothing to wear. And promise the four-legged that you will put yourself back into the earth when you die, to become nourishment for the earth, and for the sister flowers, and for the brother deer. It is appropriate that you should offer this blessing for the four-legged and, in due time, reciprocate in turn with your body in this way, as the four-legged gives life to you for your survival." As I reflect upon that story, I am struck by the power of the environmental ethic that grows out of and takes seriously narrative, context, and such values and relational attitudes as care, loving perception, and appropriate reciprocity, and doing what is appropriate in a given situation—however that notion of appropriateness eventually gets filled out. I am also struck by what one is able to see, once one begins to explore some of the historical and conceptual connections between the dominations of women and of nature. A *re-conceiving* and *re-visioning* of both feminism and environmental ethics, is, I think, the power and promise of ecofeminism.

Notes

1. Explicit ecological feminist literature includes works from a variety of scholarly perspectives and sources. Some of these works are Leonie Caldecott and Stephanie Leland, eds., *Reclaim the Earth: Women Speak Out for Life on Earth* (London: The Women's Press, 1983); Jim Cheney, "Eco-Feminism and Deep Ecology," *Environmental Ethics* 9 (1987): 115–45; Andrée Collard with Joyce Contrucci, *Rape of the Wild: Man's Violence against Animals and the Earth* (Bloomington: Indiana University Press, 1988); Katherine Davies, "Historical Associations: Women and the Natural World," *Women & Environments* 9, no. 2 (Spring 1987): 4–6; Sharon Doubiago, "Deeper than Deep Ecology: Men Must Become Feminists," in *The New Catalyst Quarterly*, no. 10 (Winter 1987/88): 10–11; Brian Easlea, *Science and Sexual Oppression: Patriarchy's Confrontation with Women and Nature* (London: Weidenfeld & Nicholson, 1981); Elizabeth Dodson Gray, *Green Paradise Lost* (Wellesley, Mass.: Roundtable Press, 1979); Susan Griffin, *Women and Nature: The Roaring Inside Her* (San Francisco: Harper and Row, 1978); Joan L. Griscom, "On Healing the Nature/History Split in Feminist Thought," in *Heresies #13: Feminism and Ecology* 4, no. 1 (1981): 4–9; Ynestra King, "The Ecology of

Feminism and the Feminism of Ecology," in *Healing Our Wounds: The Power of Ecological Feminism*, ed. Judith Plant (Boston: New Society Publishers, 1989), pp. 18–28; "The Eco-feminist Imperative," in *Reclaim the Earth*, ed. Caldecott and Leland (London: The Women's Press, 1983), pp. 12–16, "Feminism and the Revolt of Nature," in *Heresies #13: Feminism and Ecology* 4, no. 1 (1981): 12–16, and "What is Ecofeminism?" *The Nation*, 12 December 1987; Marti Kheel, "Animal Liberation Is A Feminist Issue," *The New Catalyst Quarterly*, no. 10 (Winter 1987–88): 8–9; Carolyn Merchant, *The Death of Nature: Women, Ecology and the Scientific Revolution* (San Francisco, Harper and Row, 1980); Patrick Murphy, ed., "Feminism, Ecology, and the Future of the Humanities," special issue of *Studies in the Humanities* 15, no. 2 (December 1988); Abby Peterson and Carolyn Merchant, "'Peace with the Earth': Women and the Environmental Movement in Sweden," *Women's Studies International Forum* 9, no. 5–6. (1986): 465–79; Judith Plant, "Searching for Common Ground: Ecofeminism and Bioregionalism," in *The New Catalyst Quarterly*, no. 10 (Winter 1987/88): 6–7; Judith Plant, ed., *Healing Our Wounds: The Power of Ecological Feminism* (Boston: New Society Publishers, 1989); Val Plumwood, "Ecofeminism: An Overview and Discussion of Positions and Arguments," *Australasian Journal of Philosophy*, Supplement to vol. 64 (June 1986): 120–37; Rosemary Radford Ruether, *New Woman/New Earth: Sexist Ideologies & Human Liberation* (New York: Seabury Press, 1975); Kirkpatrick Sale, "Ecofeminism—A New Perspective," *The Nation*, 26 September 1987): 302–05; Ariel Kay Salleh, "Deeper than Deep Ecology: The Eco-Feminist Connection," *Environmental Ethics* 6 (1984): 339–45, and "Epistemology and the Metaphors of Production: An Eco-Feminist Reading of Critical Theory," in *Studies in the Humanities* 15 (1988): 130–39; Vandana Shiva, *Staying Alive: Women, Ecology and Development* (London: Zed Books, 1988); Charlene Spretnak, "Ecofeminism: Our Roots and Flowering," *The Elmswood Newsletter*, Winter Solstice 1988; Karen J. Warren, "Feminism and Ecology: Making Connections," *Environmental Ethics* 9 (1987): 3–21; "Toward an Ecofeminist Ethic," *Studies in the Humanities* 15 (1988): 140–156; Miriam Wyman, "Explorations of Ecofeminism," *Women & Environments* (Spring 1987): 6–7; Iris Young, "'Feminism and Ecology' and 'Women and Life on Earth: Eco-Feminism in the 80's'," *Environmental Ethics* 5 (1983): 173–80; Michael Zimmerman, "Feminism, Deep Ecology, and Environmental Ethics," *Environmental Ethics* 9 (1987): 21–44.

2. Francoise d'Eaubonne, *Le Feminisme ou la Mort* (Paris: Pierre Horay, 1974), pp. 213–52.

3. I discuss this in my paper, "Toward An Ecofeminist Ethic."

4. The account offered here is a revision of the account given earlier in my paper "Feminism and Ecology: Making Connections." I have changed the account to be about "oppressive" rather than strictly "patriarchal" conceptual frameworks in order to leave open the possibility that there may be some patriarchal conceptual frameworks (e.g., in non-Western cultures) which are *not* properly characterized as based on value dualisms.

5. Murray Bookchin, "Social Ecology versus 'Deep Ecology'," in *Green Perspectives: Newsletter of the Green Program Project*, no. 4–5 (Summer 1987): 9.

6. It may be that in contemporary Western society, which is so thoroughly structured by categories of gender, race, class, age, and affectional orientation, that there simply is no meaningful notion of "value-hierarchical thinking" which does not function in an oppressive context. For purposes of this paper, I leave that question open.

7. Many feminists who argue for the historical point that claims (B1) and (B2) have been asserted or assumed to be true within the dominant Western philosophical tradition do so by discussion of that tradition's conceptions of reason, rationality, and science. For a sampling of the sorts of claims made within that context, see "Reason, Rationality, and Gender," ed. Nancy Tuana and Karen J. Warren, a special issue of the American Philosophical Association's *Newsletter on Feminism and Philosophy* 88, no. 2 (March 1989): 17–71. Ecofeminists who claim that (B2) has been assumed to be true within the dominant Western philosophical tradition include: Gray, *Green Paradise Lost*; Griffin, *Woman and Nature: The Roaring Inside Her*; Merchant, *The Death of Nature*; Ruether, *New Woman/New Earth*. For a discussion of some of these ecofeminist historical accounts, see Plumwood, "Ecofeminism." While I agree that the historical connections between the domination of women and the domination of nature is a crucial one, I do not argue for that claim here.

8. Ecofeminists who deny (B1) when (B1) is offered as anything other than a true, descriptive, historical claim about patriarchal culture often do so on grounds that an objectionable sort of biological determinism, or at least harmful female sex-gender stereotypes, underlie (B1). For a discussion of this "split" among those ecofeminists ("nature feminists") who assert and those ecofeminists ("social feminists") who deny (B1) as anything other than a true historical claim about how women are described in patriarchal culture, see Griscom, "On Healing the Nature/History Split."

9. I make no attempt here to defend the historically sanctioned truth of these premises.

10. See, e.g., bell hooks, *Feminist Theory: From Margin to Center* (Boston: South End Press, 1984), pp. 51–52.

11. Maria Lugones, "Playfulness, 'World-Travelling,' and Loving Perception," *Hypatia* 2, no. 2 (Summer 1987): 3.

12. At an *experiential* level, some women are "women of color," poor, old, lesbian, Jewish, and physically challenged. Thus, if feminism is going to liberate these women, it also needs to end the racism, classism, heterosexism, anti-Semitism, and discrimination against the handicapped that is constitutive of their oppression as black, or Latina, or poor, or older, or lesbian, or Jewish, or physically challenged women.

13. This same sort of reasoning shows that feminism is also a movement to end racism, classism, ageism, heterosexism and other "isms," which are based in oppressive conceptual frameworks characterized by a logic of domination. However, there is an important caveat: ecofeminism is *not* compatible with all feminisms and all environmentalisms. For a discussion of this point, see my article, "Feminism and Ecology: Making Connections." What it *is* compatible with is the minimal condition characterization of feminism as a movement to end sexism that is accepted by all contemporary feminisms (liberal, traditional Marxist, radical, socialist, Blacks and non-Western).

14. See, e.g., Gray, *Green Paradise Lost*; Griffin, *Women and Nature*; Merchant, *The Death of Nature*; and Ruether, *New Woman/New Earth*.

15. Suppose, as I think is the case, that a necessary condition for the existence of a moral relationship is that at least one party to the relationship is a moral being (leaving open for our purposes what counts as a "moral being"). If this is so, then the Mona Lisa cannot properly be said to have or stand in a moral relationship with the wall on which she hangs, and a wolf cannot have or properly be said to have or stand in a moral relationship with a moose. Such a necessary-condition account leaves open the question whether *both* parties to the relationship must be moral beings. My point here is simply that however one resolves *that* question, recognition of the relationships themselves as a locus of value is a recognition of a source of value that is different from and not reducible to the values of the "moral beings" in those relationships.

16. It is interesting to note that the image of being friends with the Earth is one which cytogeneticist Barbara McClintock uses when she describes the importance of having "a feeling for the organism," "listening to the material [in this case the corn plant]," in one's work as a scientist. See Evelyn Fox Keller, "Women, Science, and Popular Mythology," in *Machina Ex Dea: Feminist Perspectives on Technology*, ed. Joan Rothschild (New York: Pergamon Press, 1983), and Evelyn Fox Keller, *A Feeling For the Organism: The Life and Work of Barbara McClintock* (San Francisco: W. H. Freeman, 1983).

17. Cheney, "Eco-Feminism and Deep Ecology," 144.

18. Marilyn Frye, "In and Out of Harm's Way: Arrogance and Love," *The Politics of Reality* (Trumansburg, New York: The Crossing Press, 1983), pp. 66–72.

19. Ibid., pp. 75–76.

20. Maria Lugones, "Playfulness," p. 3.

21. Cheney makes a similar point in "Eco-Feminism and Deep Ecology," p. 140.

22. Ibid., p. 138.

23. This account of a feminist ethic draws on my paper "Toward an Ecofeminist Ethic."

24. Marilyn Frye makes this point in her illuminating paper, "The Possibility of Feminist Theory," read at the American Philosophical Association Central Division Meetings in Chicago, 29 April–1 May 1986. My discussion of feminist theory is inspired largely by that paper and by Kathryn Addelson's paper "Moral Revolution," in *Women and Values: Reading in Recent Feminist Philosophy*, ed. Marilyn Pearsall (Belmont, Calif.: Wadsworth Publishing Co., 1986) pp. 291–309.

25. Notice that the standard of inclusiveness does not exclude the voices of men. It is just that those voices must cohere with the voices of women.

26. For a more in-depth discussion of the notions of impartiality and bias, see my paper, "Critical Thinking and Feminism," *Informal Logic* 10, no. 1 (Winter 1988): 31–44.

27. The burgeoning literature on these values is noteworthy. See, e.g., Carol Gilligan, *In a Different Voice: Psychological Theories and Women's Development* (Cambridge: Harvard University Press, 1982); *Mapping the Moral Domain: A Contribution of Women's Thinking to Psychological Theory and Education*, ed. Carol Gilligan, Janie Victoria Ward, and Jill McLean Taylor, with Betty Bardige (Cambridge: Harvard University Press, 1988); Nel Noddings, *Caring: A Feminine Approach to Ethics and Moral Education* (Berkeley: University of California Press, 1984); Maria Lugones and Elizabeth V. Spelman, "Have We Got a Theory for You! Feminist Theory, Cultural Imperialism, and the Women's Voice," *Women's Studies International Forum* 6 (1983); 573–81; Maria Lugones, "Playfulness"; Annette C. Baier, "What Do

Women Want In A Moral Theory?" *Nous* 19 (1985): 53–63.

28. Jim Cheney would claim that our fundamental relationships to one another as moral agents are not as moral agents to rights holders, and that whatever rights a person properly may be said to have are relationally defined rights, not rights possessed by atomistic individuals conceived as Robinson Crusoes who do not exist essentially in relation to others. On this view, even rights talk itself is properly conceived as growing out of a relational ethic, not vice versa.

29. Alison Jaggar, *Feminist Politics and Human Nature* (Totowa, N.J.: Rowman and Allanheld, 1980) pp. 42–44.

30. Henry West has pointed out that the expression "defining relations" is ambiguous. According to West, "the "defining" as Cheney uses it is an adjective, not a principle—it is not that ethics defines relationships; it is that ethics grows out of conceiving of the relationships that one is in as defining what the individual is.

31. For example, in relationships involving contracts or promises, those relationships might be correctly described as that of moral agent to rights holders. In relationships involving mere property, those relationships might be correctly described as that of moral agent to objects having only instrumental value, "relationships of instrumentality." In comments on an earlier draft of this paper, West suggested that possessive individualism, for instance, might be recast in such a way that an individual is defined by his or her property relationships.

32. Cheney, "Eco-Feminism and Deep Ecology," p. 144.

33. One might object that such permission for change opens the door for environmental exploitation. This is not the case. An ecofeminist ethic is anti-naturist. Hence, the unjust domination and exploitation of nature is a "boundary condition" of the ethic; no

such actions are sanctioned or justified on ecofeminist grounds. What it *does* leave open is some leeway about what counts as domination and exploitation. This, I think, is a strength of the ethic, not a weakness, since it acknowledges that *that* issue cannot be resolved in any practical way in the abstract, independent of a historical and social context.

34. Nathan Hare, "Black Ecology," in *Environmental Ethics*, ed. K. S. Shrader-Frechette (Pacific Grove, Calif.: Boxwood Press, 1981), pp. 229–36.

35. For an ecofeminist discussion of the Chipko movement, see my "Toward an Ecofeminist Ethic," and Shiva's *Staying Alive*.

36. See Cheney, "Eco-Feminism and Deep Ecology," p. 122.

37. I offer the same sort of reply to critics of ecofeminism such as Warwick Fox who suggest that for the sort of ecofeminism I defend, the word *feminist* does not add anything significant to environmental ethics and, consequently, that an ecofeminist like myself might as well call herself a deep ecologist. He asks: "Why doesn't she just call it [i.e., Warren's vision of a transformative feminism] deep ecology? Why specifically attach the label *feminist* to it . . . ?" (Warwick Fox, "The Deep Ecology-Ecofeminism Debate and Its Parallels," *Environmental Ethics* 11, no. 1 [1989]: 14, n. 22). Whatever the important similarities between deep ecology and ecofeminism (or, specifically, my version of ecofeminism)—and, indeed, there are many—it is precisely my point here that the word *feminist* does add something significant to the conception of environmental ethics, and that any enviornmental ethic (including deep ecology) that fails to make explicit the different kinds of interconnections among the domination of nature and the domination of women will be, from a feminist (and ecofeminist) perspective such as mine, inadequate.

Remaking Society: Pathways to a Green Future _____

Murray Bookchin

Early in June, 1987, I was privileged to be a feature speaker in a six-day National Gathering of American Greens in Amherst, Massachusetts. The event received a surprising amount of national press coverage—and rightly so. About two thousand people from at least forty-two states came to Amherst to

debate the theoretical and practical problems of a Green movement in the United States. This was the biggest gathering of independent American radicals in many years. Largely anti-capitalist and activist, these Greens were deeply involved in their neighborhoods, communities, and workplaces.

Remaking Society: Pathways to a Green Future, by Murray Bookchin. (Boston: South End Press, 1990), pp. 7–13, 22–24, 30, 32–33, 35–36, 38–39. Reprinted by permission.

They reflected a wide spectrum of radicalism in America—giving expression to its promise and its problems, its hopes and limitations. . . .

Something fairly new surfaced in these debates. A number of tendencies, indeed, ways of thinking, appeared that may seem uniquely American, but which I think have already emerged or will emerge in Green movements, and perhaps radical movements generally, outside the United States.

I can best describe at least one of these tendencies by giving an account of the incident that troubled me. It occurred in an after-dinner conversation when people relaxed in small groups on the broad lawn of our meeting place to discuss the events of the day. A young, tall, rather robust man from California began to talk in a vague way about the need to "obey" the "laws of nature," to "humbly subjugate ourselves" (if I recall his words correctly) "to nature's commands." Rhetorical as his words seemed at first utterance, I began to find his increasingly strident monologue very disturbing.

His use of words like "obey," "laws of nature," "subjugate," and "commands" reminded me of the very same language l have heard from anti-ecological people who believe that nature must "obey" our commands and *its* "laws" must be used to "subjugate" the natural world itself. Whether I was thinking of the young California Green who was bombarding me with his seemingly "ecological" verbiage, or of modern acolytes of the cold deities of science who believe that "man" must ruthlessly control nature in "his" own interest, it was clear to me that these two seemingly opposed views had a basic thing in common. They jointly shared the vocabulary of domination and subjugation. Just as my California Green believes that human beings should be dominated by nature, so the acolytes of scientism believe that nature should be dominated by "man."

My California Green, in effect, had merely reversed this unsavoury relationship between human beings and nature by turning people into objects of domination, just as his scientist opponents (usually big industrialists, financiers, and entrepreneurs in our modern corporate society) turn the world of life, including human beings, into objects of domination. The fact that humanity, together with nature, were being locked into a common destiny based on domination by a hierarchical mentality and society, seemed to elude my Califor-

nia Green with his simplistic message of "surrendering" to nature and its "laws."

Already deeply disturbed by the fact that a self-professed Green could think so much like his ecological opponents, I decided to ask him a blunt question: "What do you think is the cause of the present ecological crisis?" His answer was very emphatic: "Human beings! *People* are responsible for the ecological crisis!"

"Do you mean that people such as blacks, women, and the oppressed are causing ecological imbalances—not corporations, agribusiness, ruling elites, and the State?" I asked with complete astonishment.

"Yes, people!" he answered even more heatedly. "*Everyone!* They overpopulate the earth, they pollute the planet, they devour its resources, they are greedy. That's why corporations exist—to give people the things they want."

I suspect our discussion would have become explosive if my California Green had not been distracted by a nearby game of volley-ball and leaped up to join it.

I could not forget this conversation. Indeed, it haunts me to the present day because of the extent, as I have since learned, to which it reflects the thinking of many environmentalists, some of whom would militantly call themselves "radicals."

The most striking feature of such a way of thinking is not only that it closely parallels the way of thinking that is found in the corporate world. What is more serious is that it serves to deflect our attention from the role society plays in producing ecological breakdown. If "people" as a *species* are responsible for environmental dislocations, these dislocations cease to be the result of *social* dislocations. A mythic "Humanity" is created—irrespective of whether we are talking about oppressed ethnic minorities, women, Third World people, or people in the First World—in which everyone is brought into complicity with powerful corporate elites in producing environmental dislocations. In this way, the social roots of ecological problems are shrewdly obscured. A new kind of biological "original sin" is created in which a vague group of animals called "Humanity" is turned into a destructive force that threatens the survival of the living world.

Reduced to a mere species, human beings can now be treated as a simple zoological phenomenon subject to the "biological laws" that presumably determine the "struggle for existence" in the natural world. If there is a famine, for example, it can be "explained" by simple biological notions like a "shortage of food," presumably caused by "excess population." If there is a war, it can be explained by the "stresses" produced by "overcrowding" or the need for "living space."

In a like manner, we can dismiss or explain away hunger, misery, or illness as "natural checks" that are imposed on human beings to retain the "balance of nature." We can comfortably forget that much of the poverty and hunger that afflicts the world has its origin in the corporate exploitation of human beings and nature—in agribusiness and social oppression. Human beings, you see, are merely a species like rabbits, lemmings, and the like, who are inexorably subject to relentless "natural laws."

If one views the human condition this way, such that all life-forms are "biocentrically" interchangeable despite their unique qualities, people, too, become interchangeable with locusts or, for that matter, viruses—as has been seriously suggested in a debate by advocates of this viewpoint—and are equally expendable in the interplay of so-called natural laws.[1]

The young Californian who presented these views expressed only the crudest notions that make up this growing ideology. He may very well have been one of those people I have recently encountered in the United States who believes that African children—presumably like other "animals"—should be permitted to starve because they are "overpopulating" the continent and burdening the biological "carrying capacity" of their respective countries. Or, what is equally vicious, that the AIDS epidemic should be welcomed as a means of reducing "excessive" population. Or, more chauvinistically, that "immigrants" to the United States from Latin America (often Indians whose ancestors came to the Americas thousands of years ago) should be kept out because they threaten "our" resources.

Presented in so crude and racist a form, with the use of words like "our" to designate an America whose resources are actually owned by a handful of giant corporations, this viewpoint is likely to be repugnant to most Americans. Nevertheless, as simple-minded, purely zoological answers to highly complex social questions, the viewpoint tends to gain a growing following, particularly among the more macho, authoritarian, and reactionary types who have always used "nature" and "natural laws" as substitutes for a study of real social issues and concerns.

The temptation to equate human beings who live in complex, highly institutionalized, and bitterly divided societies with ordinary animals, is finding its voice in seemingly sophisticated arguments that often parade under the guise of "radical" ecological philosophies. The resurgence of a new Malthusianism that contends that growth rates in population tend to exceed growth rates in food production is the most sinister ideological development of all.

The myth that population increases in places [like] the Sudan, for example, result in famine (not the notorious fact that the Sudanese could easily feed themselves if they were not forced by the American-controlled World Bank and International Monetary Fund to grow cotton instead of grains) typically represents the kind of arguments that are gaining popularity among many environmentalists. "Nature," we are arrogantly told by privileged Euro-Americans who parade as "natural law" theorists, "must be permitted to take its course"—as though the profits of corporations, banks, and agribusiness have anything to do with the "course" of nature.

What renders this new "biocentrism," with its antihumanistic image of human beings as interchangeable with rodents or ants, so insidious is that it now forms the premise of a growing movement called "deep ecology."[2] "Deep ecology" was spawned among well-to-do people who have been raised on a spiritual diet of Eastern cults mixed with Hollywood and Disneyland fantasies. The American mind is formless enough without burdening it with "biocentric" myths of a Buddhist and Taoist belief in a universal "oneness" so cosmic that human beings with all their distinctiveness dissolve into an all-encompassing form of "biocentric equality." Reduced to merely one life-form among many, the poor and the impoverished either become fair game for outright extermination if they are socially expendable, or they become objects of brutal exploitation if they can be used to aggrandize the corporate world. Accordingly, terms like "oneness" and a "biocentric democracy" go hand-in-hand with a pious formula for human oppression, misery, and even extermination.

Finally, ecological thinking is not enriched by recklessly blending such disparate religions as Buddhism and Taoism with Christianity, much less philosophers like the Jewish thinker Spinoza with a Nazi apologist like Heidegger. To declare, as Arne Naess, the pontiff of "deep ecology," has done, that the "basic principles of the deep ecology movement lie in religion or philosophy," is to make a conclusion notable for its absence of reference to social theory.[3]

There is enough in this mix of "biocentrism," antihumanism, mysticism, and religion with its "natural law" ethos to feed extremely reactionary and atavistic tendencies, all well-meaning references in deep ecology about "decentralization" and "nonhierarchy" aside. This raises the question of still another exotic tendency that is percolating through the ecology movements. I refer to the paradoxical need for a new theistic ecological "spirituality." That the word "spirituality" may often mean a decent, indeed, a wholesome sensitivity to nature and its subtle interconnections, is a very substantial reason to guard ourselves against its degeneration into an atavistic, simple-minded form of nature religion peopled by gods, goddesses, and eventually a new hierarchy of priests and priestesses. Mystical versions of feminism, as well as the ecology movement as a whole, alas, have sometimes proved themselves to be all too vulnerable to this tendency. The clear-sighted *naturalism* to which ecology so vividly lends itself is now in danger of being supplanted by a *super*natural outlook that is inherently alien to nature's own fecundity and self-creativity.

May we not reasonably ask why the natural world has to be peopled with earth gods and goddesses when natural evolution exhibits a marvelous power of its own to generate such a rich and wondrous variety of living beings? Is this alone not enough to fill the human mind with admiration and respect? Is it not the crudest form of "anthropocentrism" (to use a word for the projection of the human into the natural that evokes so much disdain in ecology movements) to introduce deified forms created by the human imagination into the natural world in the name of ecological "spirituality?"

To worship or revere *any* being, natural or supernatural, will always be a form of self-subjugation and servitude that ultimately yields social domination, be it in the name of nature, society, gender, or religion. More than one civilization was riddled by "nature deities" that were cynically used by ruling elites to support the most rigid, oppressive, and dehumanizing of social hierarchies. The moment human beings fall to their knees before *any* thing that is "higher" than themselves, hierarchy will have made its first triumph over freedom, and human backs will be exposed to all the burdens that can be inflicted on them by social domination.

I have raised some of the problems posed by the misanthropic, antihuman tendencies in the ecology movement not to defame the movement as a whole. Quite to the contrary: my purpose in surveying these tendencies is to peel away the fungus that has accumulated around the movement and look at the promising fruit ecology can yield for the future. . . .

Admittedly, few antihumanists, "biocentrists," and misanthropes, who theorize about the human condition, are prepared to follow the logic of their premises to . . . an absurd point. What is vitally important about this medley of moods and unfinished ideas is that the various forms, institutions, and relationships that make up what we should call "society" are largely ignored. Instead, just as we use vague words like "humanity" or zoological terms like *homo sapiens* that conceal vast differences, often bitter antagonisms, that exist between privileged whites and people of colour, men and women, rich and poor, oppressor and oppressed; so do we, by the same token, use vague words like "society" or "civilization" that conceal vast differences between free, nonhierarchical, class, and stateless societies on the one hand, and others that are, in varying degrees, hierarchical, class-ridden, statist, and authoritarian. Zoology, in effect, replaces socially oriented ecology. Sweeping "natural laws" based on population swings among animals replace conflicting economic and social interests among people. . . .

Of course, we are not any less animals than other mammals, but we are more than herds that browse on the African plains. The way in which we are more—namely, the *kinds* of societies that we form and how we are divided against each other into hierarchies and classes—profoundly affects our behavior and our effects on the natural world.

. . . [B]y so radically separating humanity and society from nature or naïvely reducing them to mere zoological entities, we can no longer see how human nature is *derived* from nonhuman nature and social evolution from natural evolution. Humanity becomes estranged or alienated not only from itself in our "age of alienation," but from the natural world in which it has always been rooted as a complex and thinking life-form.

Accordingly, we are fed a steady diet of reproaches by liberal and misanthropic environmentalists alike about how "we" as a species are responsible for the breakdown of the environment. One does not have to go to enclaves of mystics and gurus in San Francisco to find this species-centred, asocial view of ecological problems and their sources. New York City will do just as well. I shall not easily forget an "environmental" presentation staged by the New York Museum of Natural History in the seventies in which the public was exposed to a long series of exhibits, each depicting examples of pollution and ecological disruption. The exhibit which closed the presentation carried a startling sign, "The Most Dangerous Animal on Earth," and it consisted simply of a huge mirror which reflected back the human viewer who stood before it. I clearly recall a black child standing before the mirror while a white school teacher tried to explain the message which this arrogant exhibit tried to convey. There were no exhibits of corporate boards or directors planning to deforest a mountainside or government officials acting in collusion with them. The exhibit primarily conveyed one, basically misanthropic, message: people *as such*, not a rapacious society and its wealthy beneficiaries, are responsible for environmental dislocations—the poor no less than the personally wealthy, people of colour no less than privileged whites, women no less than men, the oppressed no less than the oppressor. A mythical human "species" had replaced classes; individuals had replaced hierarchies; personal tastes (many of which are shaped by a predatory media) had replaced social relationships; and the disempowered who live meagre, isolated lives had replaced giant corporations, self-serving bureaucracies, and the violent paraphernalia of the State. . . .

Perhaps one of social ecology's most important contributions to the current ecological discussion is the view that the basic problems which pit society against nature emerge from *within* social development itself—not *between* society and nature. That is to say, the divisions between society and nature have their deepest roots in divisions within the social realm, namely, deep-seated conflicts between human and human that are often obscured by our broad use of the word "humanity."

This crucial view cuts across the grain of nearly all current ecological thinking and even social theorizing. One of the most fixed notions that present-day ecological thinking shares with liberalism, Marxism, and conservatism is the historic belief that the "domination of nature" requires the domination of human by human. This is most obvious in social theory. Nearly all of our contemporary social ideologies have placed the notion of human domination at the centre of their theorizing. It remains one of the most widely accepted notions, from classical times to the present, that human freedom from the "domination of man by nature" entails the domination of human by human as the earliest means of production and the use of human beings as instruments for harnessing the natural world. Hence, in order to harness the natural world, it has been argued for ages, it is necessary to harness human beings as well, in the form of slaves, serfs, and workers.

That this instrumental notion pervades the ideology of nearly all ruling elites and has provided both liberal and conservative movements with a justification for their accommodation to the status quo, requires little, if any, elaboration. The myth of a "stingy" nature has always been used to justify the "stinginess" of exploiters in their harsh treatment of the exploited—and it has provided the excuse for the political opportunism of liberal, as well as conservative, causes. To "work within the system" has always implied an acceptance of domination as a way of "organizing" social life and, in the best of cases, a way of freeing humans from their presumed domination by nature.

What is perhaps less known, however, is that Marx, too, justified the emergence of class society and the State as stepping stones toward the domination of nature and, presumably, the liberation of humanity. It was on the strength of this historical vision that Marx formulated his materialist conception of history and his belief in the need for class society as a stepping stone in the historic road to communism.

Ironically, much that now passes for antihumanistic, mystical ecology involves exactly the same kind of thinking—but in an inverted form.

Like their instrumental opponents, these ecologists, too, assume that humanity is dominated by nature, be it in the form of "natural laws" or an ineffable "earth wisdom" that must guide human behavior. But while their instrumental opponents argue the need to achieve nature's "surrender" to a "conquering" active-aggressive humanity, anti-humanist and mystical ecologists argue the case for achieving humanity's passive-receptive "surrender" to an "all-conquering" nature. However much the two views may differ in their verbiage and pieties, *domination* remains the underlying notion of both: a natural world conceived as a taskmaster—either to be controlled or obeyed.

Social ecology springs this trap dramatically by re-examining the entire concept of domination, be it in nature and society or in the form of "natural law" and "social law." What we normally call domination in nature is a human projection of highly organized systems of *social* command and obedience onto highly idiosyncratic, individual, and asymmetrical forms of often mildly coercive behaviour in animal communities. Put simply, animals do not "dominate" each other in the same way that a human elite dominates, and often exploits, an oppressed social group. Nor do they "rule" through institutional forms of systematic violence as social elites do. Among apes, for example, there is little or no coercion, but only erratic forms of dominant behavior. Gibbons and orangutans are notable for their peaceable behaviour toward members of their own kind. Gorillas are often equally pacific, although one can single out "high status," mature, and physically strong males among "lower status," younger and physically weaker ones. . . .

None of these remarks are meant to metaphysically oppose nature to society or society to nature. On the contrary, they are meant to argue that what unites society with nature in a graded evolutionary continuum is the remarkable extent to which human beings, living in a rational, ecologically oriented society, could *embody* the *creativity* of nature—this, as distinguished from a purely *adaptive* criterion of evolutionary success. The great achievements of human thought, art, science, and technology serve not only to monumentalize culture, *they serve also to monumentalize natural evolution itself.* They provide heroic evidence that the human species is a warm-blooded, excitingly versatile, and keenly intelligent life-form—not a cold-blooded, genetically programmed, and mindless insect—that expresses *nature's* greatest powers of creativity.

Life-forms that create and consciously alter their environment, hopefully in ways that make it more rational and ecological, represent a vast and indefinite extension of nature into fascinating, perhaps unbounded, lines of evolution which no branch of insects could ever achieve—notably, the evolution of a fully *self-conscious* nature. If this be humanism—more precisely, ecological humanism—the current crop of antihumanists and misanthropes are welcome to make the most of it.

Nature, in turn, is not a scenic view we admire through a picture window—a view that is frozen into a landscape or a static panorama. Such "landscape" images of nature may be spiritually elevating but they are ecologically deceptive. Fixed in time and place, this imagery makes it easy for us to forget that nature is not a static vision of the natural world but the long, indeed cumulative, *history* of natural development. This history involves the evolution of the inorganic, as well as the organic, realms of phenomena. Wherever we stand in an open field, forest, or on a mountain top, our feet rest on ages of development, be they geological strata, fossils of long-extinct life-forms, the decaying remains of the newly dead, or the quiet stirring of newly emerging life. Nature is not a "person," a "caring Mother," or, in the crude materialist language of the last century, "matter and motion." Nor is it a mere "process" that involves repetitive cycles like seasonal changes and the building-up and breaking-down process of metabolic activity—some "process philosophies" to the contrary notwithstanding. Rather, natural history is a *cumulative* evolution toward ever more varied, differentiated, and complex forms and relationships. . . .

The issue, then, is not whether social evolution stands opposed to natural evolution. The issue is *how* social evolution can be situated *in* natural evolution and *why* it has been thrown—needlessly, as I will argue—against natural evolution to the detriment of life as a whole. The capacity to be rational and free does not assure us that this capacity will be realized. If social evolution is seen as the potentiality for expanding the horizon of natural evolution along unprecedented creative lines, and human beings are seen as the potentiality for nature to become self-conscious and free, the issue we face is *why* these potentialities have been warped and *how* they can be realized.

It is part of social ecology's commitment to natural evolution that these potentialities are indeed real and that they can be fulfilled. This commitment stands flatly at odds with a "scenic" image of nature as a static view to awe mountain men or a romantic view for conjuring up mystical images of a personified deity that is so much in vogue today. The splits between natural and social evolution, nonhuman and human life, an intractable "stingy" nature and a grasping, devouring humanity, have all been specious and misleading when they are seen as inevitabilities. No less specious and misleading have been reductionist attempts to absorb social into natural evolution, to collapse culture into nature in an orgy of irrationalism, theism, and mysticism, to equate the human with mere animality, or to impose a contrived "natural law" on an obedient human society.

Whatever has turned human beings into "aliens" in nature are social changes that have made many human beings "aliens" in their own social world: the domination of the young by the old, of women by men, and of men by men. Today, as for many centuries in the past, there are still oppressive human beings who literally own society and others who are owned by it. Until society can be reclaimed by an undivided humanity that will use its collective wisdom, cultural achievements, technological innovations, scientific knowledge, and innate creativity for its own benefit and for that of the natural world, all ecological problems will have their roots in social problems.

Notes

1. I have not penned this reference to viruses light-mindedly. The "unimpeachable right" of pathogenic viruses to exist is seriously discussed in David Ehrenfeld's *The Arrogance of Humanism,* (New York: Oxford University Press, 1978), 208–210.

2. See Bill Devall and George Sessions, *Deep Ecology,* (Salt Lake City: Peregrine Smith Books, 1985) for a comprehensive book-length account of the views expressed by the "deep ecology" movement. Much of the language used by "deep ecologists"—such as"biocentric equality"—will be found in this work.

3. *Ibid.,* 225.

C. ANIMAL LIBERATION AND ENVIRONMENTAL ETHICS

Most of the theoretical focus of the animal liberation or animal rights movement has been to defend the position that we owe duties to a large array of individual animals and not merely to human beings. In the view of various commentators, many included in prior sections of this volume, we human beings have not only failed to recognize this moral fact, we have consequently been culpable of a vast variety of serious wrongs toward individual animals. We have either imposed serious pain on them, caused them premature death, or so constrained them otherwise that they have not been, and commonly are not, allowed to live natural lives for their kind. Chimpanzees are torn away from their parents for purposes of medical experimentation; buffalo have been virtually wiped out and condors forced to the brink of extinction; the giant panda and the Siberian tiger have precious little habitat left.

However, we will not dwell much on wild animals here, for most of the concern of the animal liberation movement has been on domesticated animals, e.g., the plight of veal calves, the manner in which chickens are raised on factory farms (see the earlier essay by Peter Singer, "Animal Liberation"), the way in which dogs from pounds are sometimes sold for purposes of medical experimentation, the artificial marginal lives of many zoo animals (especially those in old-fashioned zoos that tend to imprison animals in small cages until death). If eagles experience any joy, it is not from an activity that is allowed them in zoos; it is as if we were to take away the piano from an individual whose only joy is playing the piano.

The focus has generally been not on all animals but on a subset—on sentient creatures, in the utilitarian view of Singer and others; and on self-conscious animals, surely a subset of those which are sentient, in the view of an animal rights advocate such as Tom Regan. As we have observed in prior sections, in the writings of Aldo Leopold, Paul Taylor, and others, there is a moral case to be made that it is not merely sentient creatures that possess moral standing, but others as well. Furthermore, there is a case to be made that we should be concerned with the viability of ecosystems, the sustainability of natural processes, and thus those conditions that have and do make life on earth as we know it possible. In the event of conflicts in which we must choose between the alternatives of fostering the welfare of individual animals, especially sentient ones, and fostering certain ecological virtues such as sustainability, biodiversity, and ecological balance, many environmental ethicists claim that we should choose the latter at the expense of the welfare of individual animals—perhaps especially domesticated ones such as cows, which have been referred to by some as "hoofed locusts" (that is, as a serious threat to the preservation of natural environments). In short there is a tension, or the appearance of some unavoidable incompatibility, between the views of "animal liberationists" and so-called "environmental ethicists."

This tension was described by American philosopher J. Baird Callicott in his provocative 1980 essay, "Animal Liberation: A Triangular Affair." As he notes, environmentalists may cheer on the predators while animal liberationists may advocate rescue from predation. The former are concerned about wholes or collectivities and the latter are concerned about individuals. These two camps may find themselves not only at odds with each other, but with those whom we have called anthropocentrists (those Callicott labels, perhaps misleadingly, "ethical humanists") who refuse to acknowledge that any living but nonhuman

organism possesses moral standing or is directly owed any duties.[1] Hence certain ongoing debates between three groups may bear the marks of a "triangular affair."

Can the views of animal liberationists and environmental ethicists be reconciled? Recall Leopold's maxim that what is right is what promotes the integrity, stability, and beauty of the biotic community. Callicott refers to the maxim as " . . . the categorical imperative or principle precept of the land ethic."[2] It expresses the idea that the good of the biotic community is the ultimate measure of the moral value, the rightness or wrongness of actions.[3] Callicott interpreted Leopold's maxim as prescribing that the biotic system should take precedence over the welfare of individual animals. He says, "The land ethic manifestly does not accord equal moral worth to each and every member of the biotic community; the moral worth of individuals (including, N.B., human individuals) is relative, to be assessed in accordance with the particular relation of the collective entity which Leopold called 'land.'"[4]

Claims like the above seem to imply that individual animals may be sacrificed for ecological reasons, or that humans might be killed for obstructing a sustainable future. They prompted Tom Regan to accuse holistic-minded advocates of the land ethic of environmental fascism—a charge that Callicott alludes to in "The Conceptual Foundations of the Land ethic" (partly reprinted in Section IIIA). Explicitly, Regan claims,

> The implications of (Leopold's maxim) include the clear prospect that the individual may be sacrificed for the greater biotic good. . . . It is difficult to see how the notion of rights of the individual could find a home within a view that . . . might be fairly dubbed "environmental fascism." . . . The rights view cannot abide this position . . . because it denies the propriety of deciding what should be done to individuals who have rights by appeal to

aggregative considerations, including therefore, computations about what will or will not maximally contribute to the integrity, stability, and beauty of the biotic community. Individual rights are not to be outweighed by such considerations. . . . Environmental fascism and the rights view are like oil and water: they don't mix.[5]

As we observed in the Preview to IIIA, Callicott recently repudiated some of the views he held in "Animal Liberation: A Triangular Affair." In an excerpt from his essay, "The Conceptual Foundations of the Land Ethic," which we have reprinted in this section under the (editorially chosen) title "Second Thoughts on 'A Triangular Affair'" he, agreeing with British philosopher Mary Midgley, talks approvingly of ever-widening circles of kinship that eventually embrace the land. However, " . . . the land ethic . . . neither replaces nor overrides . . . inner social circles to which we belong. . . . "[6] In fact, ". . . as a general rule, the duties correlative to the inner social circles to which we belong eclipse those correlative to the rings farther from the heartwood when conflicts arise."[7] One's duties as a citizen do not supplant one's duties as a family member, for example. Being a member of the biotic community does not, Callicott maintains, supplant one's duties as a member of the human community. Thus Callicott aims at allowing a place for legitimate concern for the well-being of individual animals and humans *as well as* an assignment of some weight for "the land," or what we may dub more holistic considerations. Once we allow that not only humans (or most humans) have moral standing, but also that many nonhuman animals, plants, rivers, trees (and so on) do so as well, then the issue of how to settle conflicts of interests between and among such beings becomes both difficult and urgent.[8] Satisfactory solutions to these problems are not obviously at hand. Callicott suggests that we might find some clues by looking at the models of Native American communities. Let us think further about the seeming disparity of viewpoints between animal liberationists and environmental ethicists.

In some respects animal liberationists seem (although the point needs qualification) to reason from the bottom up (concern for the welfare of individual animals) and their environmental ethicists opponents from the top down (in the sense of defending the comparatively greater importance of holistic virtues such as ecological balance, sustainability of practices over generations, and so on). Disagreements over particular practices can spring up in various contexts, but a familiar one is the permissibility of hunting. It is not unusual for defenders of animal rights to condemn hunting as cruel and unnecessary. Hunting is often defended on various grounds, one being that it keeps certain animal populations in check, which, in the absence of the practice, would grow to disastrous size. However, hunting can occur in wildly different contexts and be carried out for very diverse sorts of reasons. Gary Varner has done important analytic work on this matter in the essay we have printed here, "Can Animal Rights Activists Be Environmentalists?" As his title suggests, his concern is not merely with the issue of hunting, but with the deeper question of whether the theoretical and principled commitments of animal rights theorists logically preclude their adoption of a reasonable view about our duties with respect to the larger environment. The attempt to trace these connections is too often left implied and undone, i.e., the arguments are not spelled out. His essay provides an opportunity to explore the relevant details.

Varner explicates the widely held assumption that environmental ethics and animals rights theories are incompatible. He attributes such a view to Mark Sagoff, Eric Katz, (the earlier views of) J. Baird Callicott, and Bryan Norton. What he labels "the consensus claim" that environmental ethics is incompatible with anthropocentric and animal rights views is, he asserts, "multiply confused." He rightly notes that there is no need to identify environmental ethics with holist views, since the latter do not encompass certain positions that surely fall within the province of "environmental ethics" if one does not exclude them by arbitrary definitional fiat.[9] Varner holds the view that both an enlightened form of anthropocentrism (recall Norton's essay in IIIB) and an animal rights ethic can be the basis of, or at least compatible with, the right environmental ethic. In his essay, he defends the latter point.

Although it has received modest attention in the literature, the hunting issue springs readily to mind when one begins to reflect on the morality of what we as a society commonly do to animals. Frequently those who have been hunters, or are, have a great fondness for their practice and are startled that some find it immoral. Indeed the reaction may be outrage, and a counterchallenge about the eating habits of the critics and questions to the effect "do you know where your evening meal comes from?" City-dwellers, we crudely speculate, will tend to bring a very different set of attitudes to these issues than will rural-raised, experienced, hunters-at-one-time. A good deal of the more well known literature of the animal rights sort has, however, focused more on factory farming techniques and the circumstances or the hardships (we put the matter too mildly) of certain animals that are subjects of scientific experimentation.[10] So it is useful for Varner to analyze the hunting issue. What becomes clear, as one begins to reflect critically on the matter, is that there is a great deal of crude generalization that goes on in popular discussions of hunting. For starters, the *reasons* people hunt vary enormously; if that is of moral relevance, we need to sort out the relevantly different kinds of hunting. Similarly, the *consequences* of hunting vary enormously with the different kinds of hunting done in different circumstances—as do the consequences of not hunting. Varner addresses these issues.

It is tempting to think that the morality of hunting is a narrower question than it actually is. To investigate it, however, requires one to consider not only the dispute over moral standing, but the question of the appropriate basis for deciding what constitutes a permissible sacrifice of animal interests for the sake of human interests (or conversely). This is a deep matter and is one of the root sources of difficulty in resolving environmental policy disputes. In some respects, then, the dispute over hunting is quite representative of the type and the complexity of a wide variety of environmental disputes.

The fact that one may choose to have one's child inoculated against disease, and thus deliberately subjected to some degree of discomfort or pain, does not *necessarily* entail that one is indifferent to the welfare of one's child. The fact that a military leader, a prime minister, or a president may send troops into battle knowing that the certain result is the death of some of them does not necessarily show that he or she is indifferent to their welfare. Analogously the choice to hunt does not necessarily mean that one is indifferent to the welfare of the animals involved. Hunters need not be indifferent to the welfare of animals; they may believe that their prey animals have rights—as might a conscientious jury bringing in a verdict of capital punishment. Why, then, cannot environmentalists, who may endorse culling of certain herds, and animal liberationists, who tend to oppose such acts, both agree that the welfare of individual animals has some weight in coming to an all-morally-relevant-things-considered decision about what should be done? Such agreement, of course, would only be a modest step forward.

NOTES

1. Unfortunately, the term "ethical humanist" has been adopted by some philosophers, and others, to designate those who hold an anthropocentric view (understood here to mean the view that all and only

humans have moral standing). The term, we believe, has not commonly implied anthropocentrism; it has stood for decent treatment of all humans (hence, "humane" treatment), but has not necessarily implied that there are not serious duties toward nonhumans—even though it is almost certain that most humanists have been anthropocentrists.

2. J. Baird Callicott, "Animal Liberation: A Triangular Affair," in *People, Penguins, and Plastic Trees*, ed. Donald VanDeVeer and Christine Pierce (Belmont, Ca: Wadsworth Publishing Company, 1986), p. 188.

3. Ibid.

4. Ibid., p. 192.

5. Tom Regan, *The Case for Animal Rights* (Berkeley: University of California Press, 1983), pp. 361–62.

6. J. Baird Callicott, "The Conceptual Foundations of the Land Ethic," *Companion to Sand County Almanac: Interpretive and Critical Essays*, ed. J. Baird Callicott (Madison: University of Wisconsin Press, 1987), pp. 207–8.

7. Ibid., p. 208.

8. On the matter of resolving conflicts of interests, see the section "Approaches to Conflict Resolution" in Donald VanDeVeer and Christine Pierce, *The Environmental Ethics and Policy Book* (Belmont, CA: Wadsworth Publishing Company, 1994), pp. 171–210.

9. Varner observes that such a move is not atypical of some philosophers who try to exclude, by definition, "applied ethics" from the field of "ethics" or "ethical theory." By way of editorial concurrence, it is of interest to note that traditional ethical theory has almost invariably finessed (that is, ignored) a most fundamental question for any ethical theory—and frequently continues to do so. The question is simply: What sorts of beings or entities possess moral standing? The rarely noted, questioned, or defended presupposition of traditional ethics has been that all and only members of *Homo sapiens* have moral standing. It has mainly been work in so-called "applied ethics," in the last quarter of a century, on abortion, the treatment of incompetents, infanticide, and nonhuman beings, that has identified and addressed this question in a serious manner. Ironically, then, it is frequently practitioners of "merely applied ethics" who have been doing some basic theoretical work left unattended by certain self-described "theoreticians" whose view of things seems clouded at the lofty heights they inhabit.

10. We urge the importance of readers' becoming knowledgeable about actual practices. On these matters, see Peter Singer, *Animal Liberation;* and Dale Jamieson and Tom Regan, "On the Ethics of the Use Of Animals In Science," in *And Justice For All*, ed. Tom Regan and Donald VanDeVeer (Totowa, NJ: Rowman and Littlefield, 1982), pp. 169–96.

Animal Liberation: A Triangular Affair*

J. Baird Callicott

Environmental Ethics and Animal Liberation

Partly because it is so new to Western philosophy (or at least heretofore only scarcely represented) *environmental ethics* has no precisely fixed conventional definition in glossaries of philosophical terminology. Aldo Leopold, however, is universally recognized as the father or founding genius of recent environmental ethics. His "land ethic" has

become a modern classic and may be treated as the standard example, the paradigm case, as it were, of what an environmental ethic is. *Environmental ethics* then can be defined ostensively by using Leopold's land ethic as the exemplary type. I do not mean to suggest that all environmental ethics should necessarily conform to Leopold's paradigm, but the extent to which an ethical system resembles Leopold's land ethic might be used, for want of anything better, as a criterion to measure the extent to which it is or is not of the environmental sort.

It is Leopold's opinion, and certainly an overall review of the prevailing traditions of Western ethics, both popular and philosophical, generally confirms it, that traditional Western systems of

* The author expresses his appreciation to Richard A. Watson for helpful comments on the final version of this paper.
Environmental Ethics Vol. 2, No. 4 (Winter 1980), pp. 311–38. Reprinted by permission.

ethics have not accorded moral standing to nonhuman beings.[1] Animals and plants, soils and waters, which Leopold includes in his community of ethical beneficiaries, have traditionally enjoyed no moral standing, no rights, no respect, in sharp contrast to human persons whose rights and interests ideally must be fairly and equally considered if our actions are to be considered "ethical" or "moral." One fundamental and novel feature of the Leopold land ethic, therefore, is the extension of *direct* ethical considerability from people to nonhuman natural entities.

At first glance, the recent ethical movement usually labeled "animal liberation" or "animal rights" seems to be squarely and centrally a kind of environmental ethics.[2] The more uncompromising among the animal liberationists have demanded equal moral consideration on behalf of cows, pigs, chickens, and other apparently enslaved and oppressed nonhuman animals.[3] The theoreticians of this new hyper-egalitarianism have coined such terms as *speciesism* (on analogy with *racism* and *sexism*) and *human chauvinism* (on analogy with *male chauvinism)*, and have made animal liberation seem, perhaps not improperly, the next and most daring development of political liberalism.[4] Aldo Leopold also draws upon metaphors of political liberalism when he tells us that his land ethic "changes the role of *Homo sapiens* from conqueror of the land community to plain member and citizen of it."[5] For animal liberationists it is as if the ideological battles for equal rights and equal consideration for women and for racial minorities have been all but won, and the next and greatest challenge is to purchase equality, first theoretically and then practically, for all (actually only *some*) animals, regardless of species. This more rhetorically implied than fully articulated historical progression of moral rights from fewer to greater numbers of "persons" (allowing that animals may also be persons) as advocated by animal liberationists, also parallels Leopold's scenario in "The Land Ethic" of the historical extension of "ethical criteria" to more and more "fields of conduct" and to larger and larger groups of people during the past three thousand or so years.[6] As Leopold develops it, the land ethic is a cultural "evolutionary possibility," the next "step in a sequence."[7] For Leopold, however, the next step is much more sweeping, much more inclusive than the animal liberationists envision, since it "enlarges the boundaries of the [moral] community to include soils, waters, [and] plants . . ." as well as animals.[8] Thus, the animal liberation movement *could* be construed as partitioning Leopold's perhaps undigestable and totally inclusive environmental ethic into a series of more assimilable stages: today animal rights, tomorrow equal rights for plants, and after that full moral standing for rocks, soil, and other earthy compounds, and perhaps sometime in the still more remote future, liberty and equality for water and other elementary bodies.

Put just this way, however, there is something jarring about such a graduated progression in the exfoliation of a more inclusive environmental ethic, something that seems absurd. A more or less reasonable case might be made for rights for some animals, but when we come to plants, soils, and waters, the frontier between plausibility and absurdity appears to have been crossed. Yet, there is no doubt that Leopold sincerely proposes that *land* (in his inclusive sense) be ethically regarded. The beech and chestnut, for example, have in his view as much "biotic right" to life as the wolf and the deer, and the effects of human actions on mountains and streams for Leopold is an ethical concern as genuine and serious as the comfort and longevity of brood hens.[9] In fact, Leopold to all appearances never considered the treatment of brood hens on a factory farm or steers in a feed lot to be a pressing moral issue. He seems much more concerned about the integrity of the farm *wood lot* and the effects of clear-cutting steep slopes on neighboring *streams*.

Animal liberationists put their ethic into practice (and display their devotion to it) by becoming vegetarians, and the moral complexities of vegetarianism have been thoroughly debated in the recent literature as an adjunct issue to animal rights.[10] (No one however has yet expressed, as among Butler's Erewhonians, qualms about eating plants, though such sentiments might be expected to be latently present, if the rights of plants are next to be defended.) Aldo Leopold, by contrast did not even condemn hunting animals, let alone eating them, nor did he personally abandon hunting, for which he had had an enthusiasm since boyhood, upon becoming convinced that his ethical responsibilities extended beyond the human sphere.[11] There are several interpretations for this behavioral peculiarity. One is that Leopold did not see that his land ethic actually ought to prohibit hunting, cruelly killing, and eating animals. A corollary of this interpretation is that Leopold was so unperspicacious as deservedly to be thought stupid—a conclusion hardly comporting with the intellectual subtlety he usually evinces in most other respects. If not stupid, then perhaps Leopold was hypocritical. But if a hypocrite, we should expect him to conceal his proclivity for blood sports and flesh eating and to treat them as shameful vices to be indulged secretively. As it is, bound together between the same covers with "The Land Ethic" are his unabashed reminiscences of killing and consuming *game*.[12] This term (like *stock*) when used of animals, moreover, appears to be morally equivalent to referring to a sexually appealing young woman as a "piece" or to a strong, young black man as a "buck"—if animal rights, that is, are to be considered as on a par with women's rights and the rights of formerly enslaved races. A third interpretation of Leopold's approbation of regulated and disciplined sport hunting (and *a fortiori* meat eating) is that it is a form of human/animal behavior not inconsistent with the land ethic as he conceived it. A corollary of this interpretation is that Leopold's land ethic and the environmental ethic of the animal liberation movement rest upon very different theoretical foundations, and that they are thus two very different forms of environmental ethics.

The urgent concern of animal liberationists for the suffering of *domestic* animals, toward which Leopold manifests an attitude which can only be described as indifference, and the urgent concern of Leopold, on the other hand, for the disappearance of *species* of plants as well as animals and for soil erosion and stream pollution, appear to be symptoms not only of very different ethical perspectives, but profoundly different cosmic visions as well. The neat similarities, noted at the beginning of this discussion, between the environmental ethic of the animal liberation movement and the classical Leopoldian land ethic appear in light of these observations to be rather superficial and to conceal substrata of thought and value which are not at all similar. The theoretical foundations of the animal liberation movement and those of the Leopoldian land ethic may even turn out not to be companionable, complementary, or mutually consistent. The animal liberationists may thus find themselves not only engaged in controversy with the many conservative philosophers upholding *apartheid* between

man and "beast," but also faced with an unexpected dissent from another, very different, system of environmental ethics.[13] Animal liberation and animal rights may well prove to be a triangular rather than, as it has so far been represented in the philosophical community, a polar controversy.

Ethical Humanism and Humane Moralism

The orthodox response of "ethical humanism" (as this philosophical perspective may be styled) to the suggestion that nonhuman animals should be accorded moral standing is that such animals are not worthy of this high perquisite. Only human beings are rational, or capable of having interests, or possess *self*-awareness, or have linguistic abilities, or can represent the future, it is variously argued.[14] These essential attributes taken singly or in various combinations make people somehow exclusively deserving of moral consideration. The so-called "lower animals," it is insisted, lack the crucial qualification for ethical considerability and so may be treated (albeit humanely, according to some, so as not to brutalize man) as things or means, not as persons or as ends.[15]

The theoreticians of the animal liberation movement ("humane moralists" as they may be called) typically reply as follows.[16] Not all human beings qualify as worthy of moral regard, according to the various criteria specified. Therefore, by parity of reasoning, human persons who do not so qualify as moral patients may be treated, as animals often are, as mere things or means (e.g., used in vivisection experiments, disposed of if their existence is inconvenient, eaten, hunted, etc., etc.). But the ethical humanists would be morally outraged if irrational and inarticulate infants, for example, were used in painful or lethal medical experiments, or if severely retarded people were hunted for pleasure. Thus, the double-dealing, the hypocrisy, of ethical humanism appears to be exposed.[17] Ethical humanism, though claiming to discriminate between worthy and unworthy ethical patients on the basis of objective criteria impartially applied, turns out after all, it seems, to be *speciesism*, a philosophically indefensible prejudice (analogous to racial prejudice) against animals. The tails side of this argument is that some animals, usually the "higher" lower animals (cetaceans, other primates, etc.), as ethological studies seem to indicate, may meet the criteria specified for moral worth, although the ethical humanists, even so, are not prepared to grant them full dignity and the rights of persons. In short, the ethical humanists' various criteria for moral standing do not include all or only human beings, humane moralists argue, although in practice ethical humanism wishes to make the class of morally considerable beings coextensive with the class of human beings.

The humane moralists, for their part, insist upon *sentience* (*sensibility* would have been a more precise word choice) as the only relevant capacity a being need possess to enjoy full moral standing. If animals, they argue, are conscious entities who, though deprived of reason, speech, forethought or even *self*-awareness (however that may be judged), are capable of suffering, then their suffering should be as much a matter of ethical concern as that of our fellow human beings, or strictly speaking, as our very own. What, after all, has rationality or any of the other allegedly uniquely human capacities to do with ethical standing? Why, in other words, should beings who reason or use speech (etc.) qualify for moral status, and those who do not fail to qualify?[18] Isn't this just like saying that only persons with white skin should be free, or that only persons who beget and not those who bear should own property? The criterion seems utterly unrelated to the benefit for which it selects. On the other hand, the capacity to suffer is, it seems, a more relevant criterion for moral standing because—as Bentham and Mill, notable among modern philosophers, and Epicurus, among the ancients, aver—pain is evil, and its opposite, pleasure and freedom from pain, good. As moral agents (and this seems axiomatic), we have a duty to behave in such a way that the effect of our actions is to promote and procure good, so far as possible, and to reduce and minimize evil. That would amount to an obligation to produce pleasure and reduce pain. Now pain is pain wherever and by whomever it is suffered. As a *moral* agent, I should not consider my pleasure and pain to be of greater consequence in determining a course of action than that of other persons. Thus, by the same token, if animals suffer pain—and among philosophers only strict Cartesians would deny that they do—then we are morally obliged to consider their suffering as much an evil to be minimized by conscientious moral agents as human suffering.[19] Certainly actions of ours which contribute to the suffering of animals, such as hunting them, butchering and eating them, experimenting on them, etc., are on these assumptions morally reprehensible. Hence, a person who regards himself or herself as not aiming in life to live most selfishly, conveniently, or profitably, but rightly and in accord with practical principle, if convinced by these arguments, should, among other things, cease to eat the flesh of animals, to hunt them, to wear fur and leather clothing and bone ornaments and other articles made from the bodies of animals, to eat eggs and drink milk, if the animal producers of these commodities are retained under inhumane circumstances, and to patronize zoos (as sources of psychological if not physical torment of animals). On the other hand, since certain very simple animals are almost certainly insensible to pleasure and pain, they may and indeed should be treated as morally inconsequential. Nor is there any *moral* reason why trees should be respected or rivers or mountains or anything which is, though living or tributary to life processes, unconscious. The humane moralists, like the moral humanists, draw a firm distinction between those beings worthy of moral consideration and those not. They simply insist upon a different but quite definite cut-off point on the spectrum of natural entities, and accompany their criterion with arguments to show that it is more ethically defensible (granting certain assumptions) and more consistently applicable than that of the moral humanists.[20]

The First Principle of the Land Ethic

The fundamental principle of humane moralism, as we see, is Benthamic. Good is equivalent to pleasure and, more pertinently, evil is equivalent to pain. The presently booming controversy between moral humanists and humane moralists appears, when all the learned dust has settled, to be essentially internecine; at least, the lines of battle are drawn along familiar watersheds of the conceptual terrain.[21] A classical ethical theory, Bentham's, has been refitted and pressed into service to meet relatively new and unprecedented ethically relevant situations—the problems raised especially by factory farming and ever more exotic and frequently ill-conceived scientific research employing animal subjects. Then, those with Thomist, Kantian, Lockean, Moorean (etc.) ethical affiliation have heard the bugle and have risen to arms. It is no wonder that so many academic philosophers have been drawn into the fray. The issues have an apparent newness about them; moreover, they are socially and politically *avant garde*. But there is no serious challenge to cherished first principles.[22] Hence, without having to undertake any creative ethical reflection or exploration, or any reexamination of historical ethical theory, a fresh debate has been stirred up. The familiar historical positions have simply been retrenched, applied, and exercised.

But what about the third (and certainly minority) party to the animal liberation debate? What sort of reasonable and coherent moral theory would at once urge that animals (and plants and soils and waters) be included in the same class with people as beings to whom ethical consideration is owed and yet not object to some of them being slaughtered (whether painlessly or not) and eaten, others hunted, trapped, and in various other ways seemingly cruelly used? Aldo Leopold provides a concise statement of what might be called the categorical imperative or principal precept of the land ethic: "A thing is right when it tends to preserve the integrity, stability, and beauty of the biotic community. It is wrong when it tends otherwise."[23] What is especially note-worthy, and that to which attention should be directed in this proposition, is the idea that the good of the biotic *community* is the ultimate measure of the moral value, the rightness or wrongness, of actions. Thus, to hunt and kill a white-tailed deer in certain districts may not only be ethically permissible, it might actually be a moral requirement, necessary to protect the local environment, taken as a whole, from the disintegrating effects of a cervid population explosion. On the other hand, rare and endangered animals like the lynx should be especially nurtured and preserved. The lynx, cougar, and other wild feline predators, from the neo-Benthamite perspective (if consistently and evenhandedly applied) should be regarded as merciless, wanton, and incorrigible murderers of their fellow creatures, who not only kill, it should be added, but cruelly toy with their victims, thus increasing the measure of pain in the world. From the perspective of the land ethic, predators generally should be nurtured and preserved as critically important members of the biotic communities to which they are native. Certain plants, similarly, may be overwhelmingly important to the stability,

integrity, and beauty of biotic communities, while some animals, such as domestic sheep (allowed perhaps by egalitarian and humane herdspersons to graze freely and to reproduce themselves without being harvested for lamb and mutton) could be a pestilential threat to the natural floral community of a given locale. Thus, the land ethic is logically coherent in demanding at once that moral consideration be given to plants as well as to animals and yet in permitting animals to be killed, trees felled, and so on. In every case the effect upon ecological systems is the decisive factor in the determination of the ethical quality of actions. . . .

The Land Ethic and the Ecological Point of View

. . . Since ecology focuses upon the relationships between and among things, it inclines its students toward a more holistic vision of the world. Before the rather recent emergence of ecology as a science the landscape appeared to be, one might say, a collection of objects, some of them alive, some conscious, but all the same, an aggregate, a plurality of separate individuals. With this "atomistic" representation of things it is no wonder that moral issues might be understood as competing and mutually contradictory clashes of the "rights" of separate individuals, each separately pursuing its "interests." Ecology has made it possible to apprehend the same landscape as an articulate unity (without the least hint of mysticism or ineffability). Ordinary organic bodies have articulated and discernible parts (limbs, various organs, myriad cells); yet, because of the character of the network of relations among those parts, they form in a perfectly familiar sense a second-order whole. Ecology makes it possible to see land, similarly, as a unified system of integrally related parts, as, so to speak, a third-order organic whole.[24]

Another analogy that has helped ecologists to convey the particular holism which their science brings to reflective attention is that land is integrated as a human community is integrated. The various parts of the "biotic community" (individual animals and plants) depend upon one another *economically* so that the system as such acquires distinct characteristics of its own. Just as it is possible to characterize and define collectively peasant societies, agrarian communities, industrial complexes, capitalist, communist, and socialist economic systems, and so on, ecology characterizes and defines various biomes as desert, savanna, wetland, tundra, wood land, etc., communities, each with its particular "professions," "roles," or "niches."

Now we may think that among the duties we as moral agents have toward ourselves is the duty of self-preservation, which may be interpreted as a duty to maintain our own organic integrity. It is not uncommon in historical moral theory, further, to find that in addition to those peculiar responsibilities we have in relation both to ourselves and to other persons severally, we also have a duty to behave in ways that do not harm the fabric of society *per se*. The land ethic, in similar fashion, calls our attention to the recently discovered integrity—in other words, the unity—of the biota and posits duties binding upon moral agents in relation to that whole. Whatever the strictly formal logical connections between the concept of a social community and moral responsibility, there appears to be a strong psychological bond between that idea and conscience. Hence, the representation of the natural environment as, in Leopold's terms, "one humming community" (or, less consistently in his discussion, a third-order organic being) brings into play, whether rationally or not, those stirrings of conscience which we feel in relation to delicately complex, functioning social and organic systems.[25]

The neo-Benthamite humane moralists have, to be sure, digested one of the metaphysical implications of modern biology. They insist that human beings must be understood continuously with the rest of organic nature. People are (and are only) animals, and much of the rhetorical energy of the animal liberation movement is spent in fighting a rear guard action for this aspect of Darwinism against those philosophers who still cling to the dream of a special metaphysical status for people in the order of "creation." To this extent the animal liberation movement is biologically enlightened and argues from the taxonomical and evolutionary continuity of man and beast to moral standing for some nonhuman animals. Indeed, pain, in their view the very substance of evil, is something that is conspicuously common to people and other sensitive animals, something that we as people experience not in virtue of our metasimian cerebral capabilities, but because of our participation in a more generally animal, limbic-based consciousness. *If* it is pain and suffering that is the ultimate evil besetting human life, and this not in virtue of our humanity but in virtue of our animality, then it seems only fair to promote freedom from pain for those animals who share with us in this mode of experience and to grant them rights similar to ours as a means to this end.

Recent ethological studies of other primates, ceteceans, and so on, are not infrequently cited to drive the point home, but the biological information of the animal liberation movement seems to extend no further than this—the continuity of human with other animal life forms. The more recent ecological perspective especially seems to be ignored by humane moralists. The holistic outlook of ecology and the associated value premium conferred upon the biotic community, its beauty, integrity, and stability may simply not have penetrated the thinking of the animal liberationists, or it could be that to include it would involve an intolerable contradiction with the Benthamite foundations of their ethical theory. Bentham's view of the "interests of the community" was bluntly reductive. With his characteristic bluster, Bentham wrote, "The community is a fictitious *body* composed of the individual persons who are considered as constituting as it were its *members*. The interest of the community then is, what?—the sum of the interests of the several members who compose it."[26] Bentham's very simile—the community is like a body composed of members—gives the lie to his reduction of its interests to the sum of its parts taken severally. The interests of a person are not those of his or her cells summed up and averaged out. Our organic health and well-being, for example, require vigorous exercise and metabolic stimulation which cause stress and often pain to various parts of the body and a more rapid turnover in the life cycle of our individual cells. For the sake of the person taken as whole, some parts may be, as it were, unfairly sacrificed. On the level of social organization, the interests of society may not always coincide with the sum of the interests of its parts. Discipline, sacrifice, and individual restraint are often necessary in the social sphere to maintain social integrity as within the bodily organism. A society, indeed, is particularly vulnerable to disintegration when its members become preoccupied totally with their own particular interest, and ignore those distinct and independent interests of the community as a whole. One example, unfortunately, our own society, is altogether too close at hand to be examined with strict academic detachment. The United States seems to pursue uncritically a social policy of reductive utilitarianism, aimed at promoting the happiness of all its members severally. Each special interest accordingly clamors more loudly to be satisfied while the community as a whole becomes noticeably more and more infirm economically, environmentally, and politically.

The humane moralists, whether or not they are consciously and deliberately following Bentham on this particular, nevertheless, in point of fact, are committed to the welfare of certain kinds of animals distributively or reductively in applying their moral concern for nonhuman beings.[27] They lament the treatment of animals, most frequently farm and laboratory animals, and plead the special interests of these beings. We might ask, from the perspective of the land ethic, what the effect upon the natural environment taken as whole would be if domestic animals were actually liberated? There is, almost certainly, very little real danger that this might actually happen, but it would be instructive to speculate on the ecological consequences.

Ethical Holism

Before we take up this question, however, some points of interest remain to be considered on the matter of a holistic versus a reductive environmental ethic. To pit the one against the other as I have done without further qualification would be mistaken. A society is constituted by its members, an organic body by its cells, and the ecosystem by the plants, animals, minerals, fluids, and gases which compose it. One cannot affect a system as a whole without affecting at least some of its components. An environmental ethic which takes as its *summum bonum* the integrity, stability, and beauty of the biotic community is not conferring moral standing on something *else* besides plants, animals, soils, and waters. Rather, the former, the good of the community as a whole, serves as a standard for the assessment of the relative value and relative ordering of its constitutive parts and therefore provides a means of adjudicating the often mutually contradictory demands of the parts considered separately for *equal* consideration. If diversity does indeed contribute to stability (a classical "law" of ecology), then *specimens* of rare and endangered species, for example, have a *prima facie* claim to preferential consideration from the perspective of the land

ethic. Animals of those species, which, like the honey bee, function in ways critically important to the economy of nature, moreover, would be granted a greater claim to moral attention than psychologically more complex and sensitive ones, say, rabbits and moles, which seem to be plentiful, globally distributed, reproductively efficient, and only routinely integrated into the natural economy. Animals and plants, mountains, rivers, seas, the atmosphere are the *immediate* practical beneficiaries of the land ethic. The well-being of the biotic community, the biosphere as a whole, cannot be logically separated from their survival and welfare.

Some suspicion may arise at this point that the land ethic is ultimately grounded in *human* interests, not in those of nonhuman natural entities. Just as we might prefer a sound and attractive house to one in the opposite condition so the "goodness" of a whole, stable, and beautiful environment seems rather to be of the instrumental, not the autochthonous, variety. The question of ultimate value is a very sticky one for environmental as well as for all ethics and cannot be fully addressed here. It is my view that there can be no value apart from an evaluator, that all value is as it were in the eye of the beholder. The value that is attributed to the ecosystem, therefore, is humanly dependent or (allowing that other living things may take a certain delight in the well-being of the whole of things, or that the gods may) at least dependent upon some variety of morally and aesthetically sensitive consciousness. Granting this, however, there is a further, very crucial distinction to be drawn. It is possible that while things may only have value because we (or someone) values them, they may nonetheless be valued for themselves as well as for the contribution they might make to the realization of our (or someone's) interests. Children are valued for themselves by most parents. Money, on the other hand, has only an instrumental or indirect value. Which sort of value has the health of the biotic community and its members severally for Leopold and the land ethic? It is especially difficult to separate these two general sorts of value, the one of moral significance, the other merely selfish, when something that may be valued in *both ways at once* is the subject of consideration. Are pets, for example, well-treated, like children, for the sake of themselves, or, like mechanical appliances, because of the sort of services they provide their owners? Is a healthy biotic community something we value because we are so utterly and (to the biologically well-informed) so obviously dependent upon it not only for our happiness but for our very survival, or may we also perceive it disinterestedly as having an independent worth? Leopold insists upon a noninstrumental value for the biotic community and *mutatis mutandis* for its constituents. According to Leopold, collective enlightened self-interest on the part of human beings does not go far enough; the land ethic in his opinion (and no doubt this reflects his own moral intuitions) requires "love, respect, and admiration for land, and a high regard for its value." The land ethic, in Leopold's view, creates "obligations over and above self-interest." And, "obligations have no meaning without conscience, and the problem we face is the extension of the social conscience from people to land."[28] If, in other words, any genuine ethic is possible, if it is possible to value *people* for the sake of themselves, then it is equally possible to value *land* in the same way.

Some indication of the genuinely biocentric value orientation of ethical environmentalism is indicated in what otherwise might appear to be gratuitous misanthropy. The biospheric perspective does not exempt *Homo sapiens* from moral evaluation in relation to the well-being of the community of nature taken as a whole. The preciousness of individual deer, as of any other specimen, is inversely proportional to the population of the species. Environmentalists, however reluctantly and painfully, do not omit to apply the same logic to their own kind. As omnivores, the population of human beings should, perhaps, be roughly twice that of bears, allowing for differences of size. A global population of more than four billion persons and showing no signs of an orderly decline presents an alarming prospect to humanists, but it is at present a global disaster (the more *per capita* prosperity, indeed, the more disastrous it appears) for the biotic community. If the land ethic were only a means of managing nature for the sake of man, misleadingly phrased in moral terminology, then man would be considered as having an ultimate value essentially different from that of his "resources." The extent of misanthropy in modern environmentalism thus may be taken as a measure of the degree to which it is biocentric. Edward Abbey in his enormously popular *Desert Solitaire* bluntly states that he would sooner shoot a man than a snake.[29] Abbey may not be simply depraved; this is perhaps only

his way of dramatically making the point that the human population has become so disproportionate from the biological point of view that if one had to choose between a specimen of *Homo sapiens* and a specimen of a rare even if unattractive species, the choice would be moot. Among academicians, Garret Hardin, a human ecologist by discipline who has written extensively on ethics, environmental and otherwise, has shocked philosophers schooled in the preciousness of human life with his "lifeboat" and "survival" ethics and his "wilderness economics." In context of the latter, Hardin recommends limiting access to wilderness by criteria of hardiness and woodcraft and would permit no emergency roads or airborne rescue vehicles to violate the pristine purity of wilderness areas. If a wilderness adventurer should have a serious accident, Hardin recommends that he or she get out on his or her own or die in the attempt. Danger, from the strictly human-centered, psychological perspective, is part of the wilderness experience, Hardin argues, but in all probability his more important concern is to protect from mechanization the remnants of wild country that remain even if the price paid is the incidental loss of human life which, from the perspective once more of the biologist, is a commodity altogether too common in relation to wildlife and to wild landscapes.[30] . . .

. . . Modern systems of ethics have, it must be admitted, considered the principle of the equality of persons to be inviolable. This is true, for example, of both major schools of modern ethics, the utilitarian school going back to Bentham and Mill, and the deontological, originating with Kant. The land ethic manifestly does not accord equal moral worth to each and every member of the biotic community; the moral worth of individuals (including, n.b., human individuals) is relative, to be assessed in accordance with the particular relation of each to the collective entity which Leopold called "land."

There is, however, a classical Western ethic, with the best philosophical credentials, which assumes a similar holistic posture (with respect to the social moral sphere). I have in mind Plato's moral and social philosophy. Indeed, two of the same analogies figuring in the conceptual foundations of the Leopold land ethic appear in Plato's value theory.[31] From the ecological perspective, according to Leopold as I have pointed out, land is like an organic body or like a human society.

According to Plato, body, soul, and society have similar structures and corresponding virtues.[32] The goodness of each is a function of its structure or organization and the relative value of the parts or constituents of each is calculated according to the contribution made to the integrity, stability, and beauty of each whole.[33] In the *Republic,* Plato, in the very name of virtue and justice, is notorious for, among other things, requiring infanticide for a child whose only offense was being born without the sanction of the state, making presents to the enemy of guardians who allow themselves to be captured alive in combat, and radically restricting the practice of medicine to the dressing of wounds and the curing of seasonal maladies on the principle that the infirm and chronically ill not only lead miserable lives but contribute nothing to the good of the polity.[34] Plato, indeed, seems to regard individual human life and certainly human pain and suffering with complete indifference. On the other hand, he shrinks from nothing so long as it seems to him to be in the interest of the community. Among the apparently inhuman recommendations that he makes to better the community are a program of eugenics involving a phony lottery (so that those whose natural desires are frustrated, while breeding proceeds from the best stock as in a kennel or stable, will blame chance, not the design of the rulers), the destruction of the pair bond and nuclear family (in the interests of greater military and bureaucratic efficiency and group solidarity), and the utter abolition of private property.[35]

When challenged with the complaint that he is ignoring individual human happiness (and the happiness of those belonging to the most privileged class at that), he replies that it is the well-being of the community as a whole, not that of any person or special class at which his legislation aims.[36] This principle is readily accepted, first of all, in our attitude toward the body, he reminds us—the separate interests of the parts of which we acknowledge to be subordinate to the health and well-being of the whole—and secondly, assuming that we accept his faculty psychology, in our attitude toward the soul—whose multitude of desires must be disciplined, restrained, and, in the case of some, altogether repressed in the interest of personal virtue and a well-ordered and morally responsible life.

Given these formal similarities to Plato's moral philosophy, we may conclude that the land ethic— with its holistic good and its assignment of differential values to the several parts of the environment irrespective of their intelligence, sensibility, degree of complexity, or any other characteristic discernible in the parts considered separately—is somewhat foreign to modern systems of ethical philosophy, but perfectly familiar in the broader context of classical Western ethical philosophy. If, therefore, Plato's system of public and private justice is properly an "ethical" system, then so is the land ethic in relation to environmental virtue and excellence.[37]

Reappraising Domesticity

Among the last philosophical remarks penned by Aldo Leopold before his untimely death in 1948 is the following: "Perhaps such a shift of values [as implied by the attempt to weld together the concepts of ethics and ecology] can be achieved by reappraising things unnatural, tame, and confined in terms of things natural, wild, and free."[38] John Muir, in a similar spirit of reappraisal, had noted earlier the difference between the wild mountain sheep of the Sierra and the ubiquitous domestic variety. The latter, which Muir described as "hooved locusts," were only, in his estimation, "half alive" in comparison with their natural and autonomous counterparts.[39] One of the more distressing aspects of the animal liberation movement is the failure of almost all its exponents to draw a sharp distinction between the very different plights (and rights) of wild and domestic animals.[40] But this distinction lies at the very center of the land ethic. Domestic animals are creations of man. They are living artifacts, but artifacts nevertheless, and they constitute yet another mode of extension of the works of man into the ecosystem. From the perspective of the land ethic a herd of cattle, sheep, or pigs is as much or more a ruinous blight on the landscape as a fleet of four-wheel drive off-road vehicles. There is thus something profoundly incoherent (and insensitive as well) in the complaint of some animal liberationists that the "natural behavior" of chickens and bobby calves is cruelly frustrated on factory farms. It would make almost as much sense to speak of the natural behavior of tables and chairs.

Here a serious disanalogy (which no one to my knowledge has yet pointed out) becomes clearly evident between the liberation of blacks from slavery (and more recently, from civil inequality) and the liberation of animals from a similar sort of subordination and servitude. Black slaves remained, as it were, metaphysically autonomous: they were by nature if not by convention free beings quite capable of living on their own. They could not be enslaved for more than a historical interlude, for the strength of the force of their freedom was too great. They could, in other words, be retained only by a continuous counterforce, and only temporarily. This is equally true of caged wild animals. African cheetas in American and European zoos are captive, not indentured, beings. But this is not true of cows, pigs, sheep, and chickens. They have been bred to docility, tractability, stupidity, and dependency. It is literally meaningless to suggest that they be liberated. It is, to speak in hyperbole, a logical impossibility.

Certainly it is a practical impossibility. Imagine what would happen if the people of the world became morally persuaded that domestic animals were to be regarded as oppressed and enslaved persons and accordingly *set free*. In one scenario we might imagine that like former American black slaves they would receive the equivalent of forty acres and a mule and be turned out to survive on their own. Feral cattle and sheep would hang around farm outbuildings waiting forlornly to be sheltered and fed, or would graze aimlessly through their abandoned and deteriorating pastures. Most would starve or freeze as soon as winter settled in. Reproduction which had been assisted over many countless generations by their former owners might be altogether impossible in the feral state for some varieties, and the care of infants would be an art not so much lost as never acquired. And so in a very short time, after much suffering and agony, these species would become abruptly extinct. Or, in another scenario beginning with the same simple emancipation from human association, survivors of the first massive die-off of untended livestock might begin to recover some of their remote wild ancentral genetic traits and become smaller, leaner, heartier, and smarter versions of their former selves. An actual contemporary example is afforded by the feral mustangs ranging over parts of the American West. In time such animals as these would become (just as the mustangs are now) competitors both with their former human masters and (with perhaps more tragic

consequences) indigenous wildlife for food and living space.

Foreseeing these and other untoward consequences of immediate and unplanned liberation of livestock, a human population grown morally more perfect than at present might decide that they had a duty, accumulated over thousands of years, to continue to house and feed as before their former animal slaves (whom they had rendered genetically unfit to care for themselves), but not to butcher them or make other ill use of them, including frustrating their "natural" behavior, their right to copulate freely, reproduce, and enjoy the delights of being parents. People, no longer having meat to eat, would require more vegetables, cereals, and other plant foods, but the institutionalized animal incompetents would still consume all the hay and grains (and more since they would no longer be slaughtered) than they did formerly. This would require clearing more land and bringing it into agricultural production with further loss of wildlife habitat and ecological destruction. Another possible scenario might be a decision on the part of people not literally to liberate domestic animals but simply to cease to breed and raise them. When the last livestock have been killed and eaten (or permitted to die "natural" deaths), people would become vegetarians and domestic livestock species would thus be rendered deliberately extinct (just as they had been deliberately created). But there is surely some irony in an outcome in which the beneficiaries of a humane extension of conscience are destroyed in the process of being saved.[41]

The land ethic, it should be emphasized, as Leopold has sketched it, provides for the *rights* of nonhuman natural beings to a share in the life processes of the biotic community. The conceptual foundation of such rights, however, is less conventional than natural, based upon, as one might say, evolutionary and ecological entitlement. Wild animals and native plants have a particular place in nature, according to the land ethic, which domestic animals (because they are products of human art and represent an extended presence of human beings in the natural world) do not have. The land ethic, in sum, is as much opposed, though on different grounds, to commercial traffic in wildlife, zoos, the slaughter of whales and other marine mammals, etc., as is the humane ethic. Concern for animal (and plant) rights and well-being is as fundamental to the land ethic as to the humane ethic, but the difference between naturally evolved and humanly bred species is an essential consideration for the one, though not for the other.

The "shift of values" which results from our "reappraising things unnatural, tame, and confined in terms of things natural, wild, and free" is especially dramatic when we reflect upon the definitions of *good* and *evil* espoused by Bentham and Mill and uncritically accepted by their contemporary followers. Pain and pleasure seem to have nothing at all to do with good and evil if our appraisal is taken from the vantage point of ecological biology. Pain in particular is primarily information. In animals, it informs the central nervous system of stress, irritation, or trauma in outlying regions of the organism. A certain level of pain under optimal organic circumstances is indeed desirable as an indicator of exertion—of the degree of exertion needed to maintain fitness, to stay "in shape," and of a level of exertion beyond which it would be dangerous to go. An arctic wolf in pursuit of a caribou may experience pain in her feet or chest because of the rigors of the chase. There is nothing bad or wrong in that. Or, consider a case of injury. Suppose that a person in the course of a wilderness excursion sprains an ankle. Pain informs him or her of the injury and by its intensity the amount of further stress the ankle may endure in the course of getting to safety. Would it be better if pain were not experienced upon injury or, taking advantage of recent technology, anaesthetized? Pleasure appears to be, for the most part (unfortunately it is not always so) a reward accompanying those activities which contribute to organic maintenance, such as the pleasures associated with eating, drinking, grooming, and so on, or those which contribute to social solidarity like the pleasures of dancing, conversation, teasing, etc., or those which contribute to the continuation of the species, such as the pleasures of sexual activity and of being parents. The doctrine that life is the happier the freer it is from pain and that the happiest life conceivable is one in which there is continuous pleasure uninterrupted by pain is biologically preposterous. A living mammal which experienced no pain would be one which had a lethal dysfunction of the nervous system. The idea that pain is evil and ought to be minimized or eliminated is as primitive a notion as that of a tyrant who puts to death messengers bearing bad news on the supposition that thus his well-being and security is improved.[42]

More seriously still, the value commitments of the humane movement seem at bottom to betray a world-denying or rather a life-loathing philosophy. The natural world as actually constituted is one in which one being lives at the expense of others.[43] Each organism, in Darwin's metaphor, struggles to maintain its own organic integrity. The more complex animals seem to experience (judging from our own case, and reasoning from analogy) appropriate and adaptive psychological accompaniments to organic existence. There is a palpable passion for self-preservation. There are desire, pleasure in the satisfaction of desires, acute agony attending injury, frustration, and chronic dread of death. But these experiences are the psychological substance of living. To live *is* to be anxious about life, to feel pain and pleasure in a fitting mixture, and sooner or later to die. That is the way the system works. If nature as a whole is good, then pain and death are also good. Environmental ethics in general require people to play fair in the natural system. The neoBenthamites have in a sense taken the uncourageous approach. People have attempted to exempt themselves from the life/death reciprocities of natural processes and from ecological limitations in the name of a prophylactic ethic of maximizing rewards (pleasure) and minimizing unwelcome information (pain). To be fair, the humane moralists seem to suggest that we should attempt to project the same values into the nonhuman animal world and to widen the charmed circle—no matter that it would be biologically unrealistic to do so or biologically ruinous if, per impossible, such an environmental ethic were implemented.

There is another approach. Rather than imposing our alienation from nature and natural processes and cycles of life on other animals, we human beings could reaffirm our participation in nature by accepting life as it is given without a sugar coating. Instead of imposing artificial legalities, rights, and so on on nature, we might take the opposite course and accept and affirm natural biological laws, principles, and limitations in the human personal and social spheres. Such appears to have been the posture toward life of tribal peoples in the past. The chase was relished with its dangers, rigors, and hardships as well as its rewards: animal flesh was respectfully consumed; a tolerance for pain was cultivated; virtue and magnanimity were prized; lithic, floral, and faunal spirits were worshipped; population was routinely optimized by sexual continency, abortion, infanticide, and stylized warfare; and other life forms, although certainly appropriated, were respected as fellow players in a magnificent and awesome, if not altogether idyllic, drama of life. It is impossible today to return to the symbiotic relationship of Stone Age man to the natural environment, but the ethos of this by far the longest era of human existence could be abstracted and integrated with a future human culture seeking a viable and mutually beneficial relationship with nature. Personal, social, and environmental *health* would, accordingly, receive a premium value rather than comfort, self-indulgent pleasure, and anaesthetic insulation from pain. Sickness would be regarded as a worse evil than death. The pursuit of health or wellness at the personal, social, and environmental levels would require self-discipline in the form of simple diet, vigorous exercise, conservation, and social responsibility.

Leopold's prescription for the realization and implementation of the land ethic—the reappraisal of things unnatural, tame, and confined in terms of things natural, wild, and free—does not stop, in other words, with a reappraisal of nonhuman domestic animals in terms of their wild (or willed) counterparts; the human ones should be similarly reappraised. This means, among other things, the reappraisal of the comparatively recent values and concerns of "civilized" *Homo sapiens* in terms of those of our "savage" ancestors.[44] Civilization has insulated and alienated us from the rigors and challenges of the natural environment. The hidden agenda of the humane ethic is the imposition of the anti-natural prophylactic ethos of comfort and soft pleasure on an even wider scale. The land ethic, on the other hand, requires a shrinkage, if at all possible, of the domestic sphere; it rejoices in a recrudescence of wilderness and a renaissance of tribal cultural experience.

The converse of those goods and evils, axiomatic to the humane ethic, may be illustrated and focused by the consideration of a single issue raised by the humane morality: a vegetarian diet. Savage people seem to have had, if the attitudes and values of surviving tribal cultures are representative, something like an intuitive grasp of ecological relationships and certainly a morally charged appreciation of eating. There is nothing more intimate than eating, more symbolic of the connectedness of life, and more mysterious. What we eat and how we eat is by no means an insignificant ethical concern.

From the ecological point of view, for human beings universally to become vegetarians is tantamount to a shift of trophic niche from omnivore with carnivorous preferences to herbivore. The shift is a downward one on the trophic pyramid, which in effect shortens those food chains terminating with man. It represents an increase in the efficiency of the conversion of solar energy from plant to human biomass, and thus, by bypassing animal intermediates, increases available food resources for human beings. The human population would probably, as past trends overwhelmingly suggest, expand in accordance with the potential thus afforded. The net result would be fewer nonhuman beings and more human beings, who, of course, have requirements of life far more elaborate than even those of domestic animals, requirements which would tax other "natural resources" (trees for shelter, minerals mined at the expense of topsoil and its vegetation, etc.) more than under present circumstances. A vegetarian human population is therefore *probably* ecologically catastrophic.

Meat eating as implied by the foregoing remarks may be more *ecologically* responsible than a wholly vegetable diet. Meat, however, purchased at the supermarket, externally packaged and internally laced with petrochemicals, fattened in feed lots, slaughtered impersonally, and, in general, mechanically processed from artificial insemination to microwave roaster, is an affront not only to physical metabolism and bodily health but to conscience as well. From the perspective of the land ethic, the immoral aspect of the factory farm has to do far less with the suffering and killing of nonhuman animals than with the monstrous transformation of living things from an organic to a mechanical mode of being. Animals, beginning with the Neolithic Revolution, have been debased through selective breeding, but they have nevertheless remained animals. With the Industrial Revolution an even more profound and terrifying transformation has overwhelmed them. They have become, in Ruth Harrison's most apt description, "animal machines." The very presence of animals, so emblematic of delicate, complex organic tissue, surrounded by machines, connected to machines, penetrated by machines in research laboratories or crowded together in space-age "production facilities" is surely the more real and visceral source of our outrage at vivisection and factory farming than the contemplation of the quantity of pain that these unfortunate beings experience. I wish to denounce as loudly as the neo-Benthamites this ghastly abuse of animal life, but also to stress that the pain and suffering of research and agribusiness animals is not greater than that endured by free-living wildlife as a consequence of predation, disease, starvation, and cold—indicating that there is something immoral about vivisection and factory farming which is not an ingredient in the natural lives and deaths of wild beings. That immoral something is the transmogrification of organic to mechanical processes.

Ethical vegetarianism to all appearances insists upon the human consumption of plants (in a paradoxical moral gesture toward those animals whose very existence is dependent upon human carnivorousness), even when the tomatoes are grown hydroponically, the lettuce generously coated with chlorinated hydrocarbons, the potatoes pumped up with chemical fertilizers, and the cereals stored with the help of chemical preservatives. The land ethic takes as much exception to the transmogrification of plants by mechanicochemical means as to that of animals. The important thing, I would think, is not to eat vegetables as opposed to animal flesh, but to resist factory farming in all its manifestations, including especially its liberal application of pesticides, herbicides, and chemical fertilizers to maximize the production of *vegetable* crops.

The land ethic, with its ecological perspective, helps us to recognize and affirm the organic integrity of self and the untenability of a firm distinction between self and environment. On the ethical question of what to eat, it answers, not vegetables instead of animals, but organically as opposed to mechanicochemically produced food. Purists like Leopold prefer, in his expression, to get their "meat from God," i.e., to hunt and consume wildlife and to gather wild plant foods, and thus to live within the parameters of the aboriginal human ecological niche.[45] Second best is eating from one's own orchard, garden, henhouse, pigpen, and barnyard. Third best is buying or bartering organic foods from one's neighbors and friends.

Conclusion

Philosophical controversy concerning animal liberation/rights has been most frequently represented as a polar dispute between traditional moral humanists and seemingly *avant garde* humane moralists. Further, animal liberation has been assumed to be closely allied with environmental ethics, possibly because in Leopold's classical formulation moral standing and indeed rights (of some unspecified sort) is accorded nonhuman beings, among them animals. The purpose of this discussion has been to distinguish sharply environmental ethics from the animal liberation/rights movement both in theory and practical application and to suggest, thereupon, that there is an underrepresented, but very important, point of view respecting the problem of the moral status of nonhuman animals. The debate over animal liberation, in short, should be conceived as triangular, not polar, with land ethics or environmental ethics, the third and, in my judgement, the most creative, interesting, and practicable alternative. Indeed, from this third point of view moral humanism and humane moralism appear to have much more in common with one another than either have with environmental or land ethics. On reflection one might even be led to suspect that the noisy debate between these parties has served to drown out the much deeper challenge to "business-as-usual" ethical philosophy represented by Leopold and his exponents, and to keep ethical philosophy firmly anchored to familiar modern paradigms.

Moral humanism and humane moralism, to restate succinctly the most salient conclusions of this essay, are *atomistic* or distributive in their theory of moral value, while environmental ethics (again, at least, as set out in Leopold's outline) is *holistic* or collective. Modern ethical theory, in other words, has consistently located moral value in individuals and set out certain metaphysical reasons for including some individuals and excluding others. Humane moralism remains firmly within this modern convention and centers its attention on the competing criteria for moral standing and rights holding, while environmental ethics locates ultimate value in the "biotic community" and assigns differential moral value to the constitutive individuals relatively to that standard. This is perhaps the most fundamental theoretical difference between environmental ethics and the ethics of animal liberation.

Allied to this difference are many others. One of the more conspicuous is that in environmental ethics, plants are included within the parameters of the ethical theory as well as animals. Indeed, inanimate entities such as oceans and lakes, mountains, forests, and wetlands are assigned a greater value than individual animals and in a way quite different from systems which accord them moral considerability through a further multiplication of competing individual loci of value and holders of rights.

There are intractable practical differences between environmental ethics and the animal liberation movement. Very different moral obligations follow in respect, most importantly, to domestic animals, the principal beneficiaries of the humane ethic. Environmental ethics sets a very low priority on domestic animals as they very frequently contribute to the erosion of the integrity, stability, and beauty of the biotic communities into which they have been insinuated. On the other hand, animal liberation, if pursued at the practical as well as rhetorical level, would have ruinous consequences on plants, soils, and waters, consequences which could not be directly reckoned according to humane moral theory. As this last remark suggests, the animal liberation/animal rights movement is in the final analysis utterly unpracticable. An imagined society in which all animals capable of sensibility received equal consideration or held rights to equal consideration would be so ludicrous that it might be more appropriately and effectively treated in satire than in philosophical discussion. The land ethic, by contrast, even though its ethical purview is very much wider, is nevertheless eminently practicable, since, by reference to a single good, competing individual claims may be adjudicated and relative values and priorities assigned to the myriad components of the biotic community. This is not to suggest that the implementation of environmental ethics as social policy would be easy. Implementation of the land ethic would require discipline, sacrifice, retrenchment, and massive economic reform, tantamount to a virtual revolution in prevailing attitudes and life styles. Nevertheless, it provides a unified and coherent practical principle and thus a decision procedure at the practical level which a distributive or atomistic ethic may achieve only artificially and so imprecisely as to be practically indeterminate.

Notes

1. Aldo Leopold, *A Sand County Almanac* (New York: Oxford University Press, 1949), pp. 202–3. Some traditional Western systems of ethics, however, have accorded moral standing to nonhuman beings. The Pythagorean tradition did, followed by Empedocles of Acragas; Saint Francis of Assisi apparently believed in the animal soul; in modern ethics Jeremy Bentham's hedonic utilitarian system is also an exception to the usual rule. John Passmore ("The Treatment of Animals," *Journal of the History of Ideas* 36 [1975]: 196–218) provides a well-researched and eye-opening study of historical ideas about the moral status of animals in Western thought. Though exceptions to the prevailing attitudes have existed, they are exceptions indeed and represent but a small minority of Western religious and philosophical points of view.

2. The tag "animal-liberation" for this moral movement originates with Peter Singer whose book *Animal Liberation* (New York: New York Review, 1975) has been widely influential. "Animal rights" have been most persistently and unequivocally championed by Tom Regan in various articles, among them: "The Moral Basis of Vegetarianism," *Canadian Journal of Philosophy* 5 (1975): 181–214; "Exploring the Idea of Animal Rights" in *Animal Rights: A Symposium*, eds. D. Patterson and R. Ryder (London: Centaur, 1979); "Animal Rights, Human Wrongs," *Environmental Ethics* 2 (1980): 99–120. A more complex and qualified position respecting animal rights has been propounded by Joel Feinberg, "The Rights of Animals and Unborn Generations," in *Philosophy and Environmental Crisis*, ed. William T. Blackstone (Athens: University of Georgia Press, 1974), pp. 43–68, and "Human Duties and Animal Rights," in *On the Fifth Day*, eds. R. K. Morris and M. W. Fox (Washington: Acropolis Books, 1978), pp. 45–69. Lawrence Haworth ("Rights, Wrongs and Animals," *Ethics* 88 [1978]: 95–105), in the context of the contemporary debate, claims limited rights on behalf of animals. S. R. L. Clark's *The Moral Status of Animals* (Oxford: Clarendon Press, 1975) has set out arguments which differ in some particulars from those of Singer, Regan, and Feinberg with regard to the moral considerability of some nonhuman animals. In this discussion, as a tribute to Singer, I use the term *animal liberation* generically to cover the several philosophical rationales for a humane ethic. Singer has laid particular emphasis on the inhumane usage of animals in agribusiness and scientific research. Two thorough professional studies from the humane perspective of these institutions are Ruth Harrison's *Animal Machines* (London: Stuart, 1964) and Richard Ryder's *Victims of Science* (London: Davis-Poynter, 1975), respectively.

3. Peter Singer and Tom Regan especially insist upon *equal* moral *consideration* for nonhuman animals. Equal moral *consideration* does not necessarily imply

equal *treatment*, however, as Singer insists. Cf. Singer, *Animal Liberation*, pp. 3, 17–24, and Singer, "The Fable of the Fox and the Unliberated Animals," *Ethics* 88 (1978): 119–20. Regan provides an especially clear summary of both his position and Singer's in "Animal Rights, Human Wrongs," pp. 108–12.

4.   We have Richard Ryder to thank for coining the term *speciesism*. See his *Speciesism: The Ethics of Vivisection* (Edinburgh: Scottish Society for the Prevention of Vivisection, 1974). Richard Routley introduced the term *human chauvinism* in "Is There a Need for a New, an Environmental Ethic?" *Proceedings of the Fifteenth World Congress of Philosophy 1* (1973): 205–10. Peter Singer ("All Animals Are Equal," in *Animal Rights and Human Obligations*, eds. Tom Regan and Peter Singer [Englewood Cliffs, N.J.: Prentice-Hall, 1976], pp. 148–62) developed the egalitarian comparison of speciesism with racism and sexism in detail. To extend the political comparison further, animal liberation is also a reformist and activist movement. We are urged to act, to become vegetarians, to boycott animal products, etc. The concluding paragraph of Regan's "Animal Rights, Human Wrongs," (p. 120) is especially zealously hortatory.

5.   Leopold, *Sand County Almanac*, p. 204.

6.   Ibid., pp. 201–3. A more articulate historical representation of the parallel expansion of legal rights appears in C. D. Stone's *Should Trees Have Standing?* (Los Altos: William Kaufman, 1972), pp. 3–10, however without specific application to animal liberation.

7.   Leopold, *Sand County Almanac*, p. 203.

8.   Ibid., p. 204.

9.   Ibid., p. 221 (trees); pp. 129–133 (mountains); p. 209 (streams).

10.   John Benson ("Duty and the Beast," *Philosophy* 53 [1978]: 547–48) confesses that in the course of considering issues raised by Singer et al he was "obliged to change my own diet as a result." An elaborate critical discussion is Philip E. Devine's "The Moral Basis of Vegetarianism" (*Philosophy* 53 [1978]: 481–505).

11.   For a biography of Leopold including particular reference to Leopold's career as a "sportsman," see Susan L. Flader, *Thinking Like a Mountain* (Columbia: University of Missouri Press, 1974).

12.   See especially, Leopold, *Sand County Almanac*, pp. 54–58; 62–66; 120–22; 149–54; 177–87.

13.   A most thorough and fully argued dissent is provided by John Rodman in "The Liberation of Nature," *Inquiry* 20 (1977): 83–131. It is surprising that Singer, whose book is the subject of Rodman's extensive critical review, or some of Singer's philosophical allies, has not replied to these very penetrating and provocative criticisms. Another less specifically targeted dissent is Paul Shepard's "Animal Rights and Human Rites" (*North American Review* [Winter, 1974]: 35–41). More recently Kenneth Goodpaster ("From Egoism to Environmentalism" in *Ethics and Problems of the 21st Century*, eds. K. Goodpaster and K. Sayre [Notre Dame: Notre Dame University Press, 1979], pp. 21–35) has expressed complaints about the animal liberation and animal rights movement in the name of environmental ethics. "The last thing we need," writes Goodpaster, "is simply another 'liberation movement'" (p. 29).

14.   Singer, "All Animals Are Equal" (p. 159), uses the term *humanist* to convey a speciesist connotation. Rationality and future-conceiving capacities as criteria for rights holding have been newly revived by Michael E. Levin with specific reference to Singer in "Animal Rights Evaluated," *The Humanist* (July/August, 1977): 12; 14–15. John Passmore, in *Man's Responsibility for Nature* (New York: Charles Scribner's Sons, 1974), cf., p. 116, has recently insisted upon having interests as a criterion for having rights and denied that nonhuman beings have interests. L. P. Francis and R. Norman ("Some Animals Are More Equal than Others," *Philosophy* 53 [1978]: 507–27) have argued, again with specific reference to animal liberationists, that linguistic abilities are requisite for moral status. H. J. McCloskey ("The Right to Life," *Mind* 84 [1975]: 410–13, and "Moral Rights and Animals," *Inquiry* 22 [1979]: 23–54), adapting an idea of Kant's, defends *autonomy* as the main ingredient of human nature which entitles human beings to rights. Michael Fox ("Animal Liberation: A Critique," *Ethics* 88 [1978]: 106–18) defends, among other exclusively human qualifications for rights holding, *self*-awareness. Richard A. Watson ("Self-Consciousness and the Rights of Nonhuman Animals and Nature," *Environmental Ethics* 1 [1979]: 99–129) also defends self-consciousness as a criterion for rights holding, but allows that some nonhuman animals also possess it.

15.   In addition to the historical figures, who are nicely summarized and anthologized in *Animal Rights and Human Obligations*, John Passmore has recently defended the reactionary notion that cruelty towards animals is morally reprehensible for reasons independent of any obligation or duties people have to animals as such (*Man's Responsibility*, cf., p. 117).

16.   "Humane moralists" is perhaps a more historically accurate designation than "animal liberationists."

John Rodman, "The Liberation of Nature" (pp. 88–89), has recently explored in a programmatic way the connection between the contemporary animal liberation/rights movements and the historical humane societies movement.

17. Tom Regan styles more precise formulations of this argument, "the argument from marginal cases," in "An Examination and Defense of One Argument Concerning Animal Rights," *Inquiry* 22 (1979): 190. Regan directs our attention to Andrew Linzey, *Animal Rights* (London: SCM Press, 1976) as well as to Singer, *Animal Liberation,* for paradigmatic employment of this argument on behalf of moral standing for animals (p. 144).

18. A particularly lucid advocacy of this notion may be found in Feinberg, "Human Duties and Animal Rights," especially p. 53ff.

19. Again, Feinberg in "Human Duties and Animal Rights" (pp. 57–59) expresses this point especially forcefully.

20. John Rodman's comment in "The Liberation of Nature" (p. 91) is worth repeating here since it has to all appearances received so little attention elsewhere: "If it would seem arbitrary . . . to find one species claiming a monopoly on intrinsic value by virtue of its allegedly exclusive possession of reason, free will, soul, or some other occult quality, would it not seem almost as arbitrary to find that same species claiming a monopoly of intrinsic value for itself and those species most resembling it (e.g. in type of nervous system and behavior) by virtue of their common and allegedly exclusive possession of sentience [i.e., sensibility]?" Goodpaster ("From Egoism to Environmentalism," p. 29) remarks that in modern moral philosophy "a fixation on egoism and a consequent loyalty to a model of moral sentiment or reason which in essence generalizes or universalizes that egoism . . . makes it particularly inhospitable to our recent felt need for an environmental ethic. . . . For such an ethic does not readily admit of being reduced to 'humanism'—nor does it sit well with any class or generalization model of moral concern."

21. John Rodman, "The Liberation of Nature" (p. 95), comments: "Why do our 'new ethics' seem so old? . . . Because the attempt to produce a 'new ethics' by the process of 'extension' perpetuates the basic assumptions of the conventional modern paradigm, however much it fiddles with the boundaries." When the assumptions remain conventional, the boundaries are, in my view, scalar, but triangular when both positions are considered in opposition to the land ethic. The scalar relation is especially clear when two other positions, not specifically discussed in the text, the reverence-for-life ethic and pan-moralism, are considered. The reverence-for-life

ethic (as I am calling it in deference to Albert Schweitzer) seems to be the next step on the scale after the humane ethic. William Frankena considers it so in "Ethics and the Environment," *Ethics and Problems of the 21st Century,* pp. 3–20. W. Murry Hunt ("Are *Mere Things* Morally Considerable," *Environmental Ethics* 2 [1980]: 59–65) has gone a step past Schweitzer, and made the bold suggestion that *everything* should be accorded moral standing, pan-moralism. Hunt's discussion shows clearly that there is a similar logic ("slippery slope" logic) involved in taking each downward step, and thus a certain commonality of underlying assumptions among all the ethical types to which the land ethic stands in opposition. Hunt is not unaware that his suggestion may be interpreted as a *reductio ad absurdum* of the whole matter, but insists that that is not his intent. The land ethic is not part of this linear series of steps and hence may be represented as a point off the scale. The principal difference, as I explain below, is that the land ethic is collective or "holistic" while the others are distributive or "atomistic." Another relevant difference is that moral humanism, humane moralism, reverence-for-life ethics, and the limiting case, pan-moralism, either openly or implicitly espouse a pecking-order model of nature. The land ethic, founded upon an ecological model of nature emphasizing the contributing roles played by various species in the economy of nature, abandons the "higher"/"lower" ontological and axiological schema, in favor of a functional system of value. The land ethic, in other words, is inclined to establish value distinctions not on the basis of higher and lower orders of being, but on the basis of the importance of organisms, minerals, and so on to the biotic community. Some bacteria, for example, may be of greater value to the health or economy of nature than dogs, and thus command more respect.

22. Rodman, "The Liberation of Nature" (p. 86), says in reference to Singer's humane ethic that "the weakness . . . lies in the limitation of its horizon to the late eighteenth and early nineteenth century Utilitarian humane movement [and] its failure to live up to its own noble declaration that 'philosophy ought to question the basic assumptions of the age'. . . ."

23. Leopold, *Sand County Almanac,* pp. 224–25.

24. By "first," "second," and "third" order wholes I intend paradigmatically single cell organisms, multicell organisms, and biocoenoses, respectively.

25. "Some Fundamentals of Conservation in the Southwest," composed in the 1920s but unpublished until it appeared last year (*Environmental Ethics* 1 [1979]: 131–41), shows that the organic analogy, conceptually representing the nature of the whole resulting from ecological relationships, antedates the community

analogy in Leopold's thinking, so far at least as its moral implications are concerned. "The Land Ethic" of *Sand County Almanac* employs almost exclusively the community analogy but a rereading of "The Land Ethic" in the light of "Some Fundamentals" reveals that Leopold did not entirely abandon the organic analogy in favor of the community analogy. For example, toward the end of "The Land Ethic" Leopold talks about "land health" and "land the collective organism" (p. 258). William Morton Wheeler, *Essays in Philosophical Biology* (New York: Russell and Russell, 1939), and Lewis Thomas, *Lives of a Cell* (New York: Viking Press, 1974), provide extended discussions of holistic approaches to social, ethical, and environmental problems. Kenneth Goodpaster, almost alone among academic philosophers, has explored the possibility of a holistic environmental ethical system in "From Egoism to Environmentalism."

26. *An Introduction to the Principles of Morals and Legislation* (Oxford: Oxford University Press, 1823), chap. 1, sec. 4.

27. This has been noticed and lamented by Alistair S. Gunn ("Why Should We Care About Rare Species?" *Environmental Ethics* 2 [1980]: 36) who comments, "Environmentalism seems incompatible with the 'Western' obsession with individualism, which leads us to resolve questions about our treatment of animals by appealing to the essentially atomistic, competitive notion of rights. . . ." John Rodman, "The Liberation of Nature" (p. 89), says practically the same thing: "The moral atomism that focuses on individual animals and their subjective experiences does not seem well adapted to coping with ecological systems." Peter Singer has in fact actually stressed the individual focus of his humane ethic in "Not for Humans Only: The Place of Nonhumans in Environmental Issues" (*Ethics and Problems of the 21st Century*, pp. 191–206) as if it were a virtue! More revealingly, the only grounds that he can discover for moral concern over species, since species are *per se* not sensible entities (and that is the extent of his notion of an ethically relevant consideration), are anthropocentric grounds, human aesthetics, environmental integrity for humans, etc.

28. Leopold, *Sand County Almanac*, pp. 223 and 209.

29. Edward Abbey, *Desert Solitaire* (New York: Balantine Books, 1968), p. 20.

30. Garrett Hardin, "The Economics of Wilderness," *Natural History* 78 [1969]: 173–77. Hardin is blunt: "Making great and spectacular efforts to save the life of an individual makes sense only when there is a shortage of people. I have not lately heard that there is a shortage of people" (p. 176).

31. In *Republic* 5 Plato directly says that "the best governed state most nearly resembles an organism" (462D) and that there is no "greater evil for a state than the thing that distracts it and makes it many instead of one, or a greater good than that which binds it together and makes it one" (462A). Goodpaster in "From Egoism to Environmentalism" (p. 30) has in a general way anticipated this connection: "The oft-repeated plea by some ecologists and environmentalists that our thinking needs to be less atomistic and more 'holistic' translates in the present context into a plea for a more embracing object of moral consideration. In a sense it represents a plea to return to the richer Greek conception of man by nature social and not intelligibly removable from his social and political context though it goes beyond the Greek conception in emphasizing that societies too need to be understood in a context, an ecological context, and that it is this larger whole that is the 'bearer of value.'"

32. See especially *Republic* 4.444A–E.

33. For a particularly clear statement by Plato of the idea that the goodness of anything is a matter of the fitting order of the parts in relation to respective wholes see *Gorgias* 503D–507A.

34. Cf., *Republic* 5.461C (infanticide); 468A (disposition of captives); *Republic* 3.405D–406E (medicine).

35. Cf., *Republic* 5.459A–460E (eugenics, nonfamily life and child rearing), *Republic* 3.416D–417B (private property).

36. Cf., *Republic* 4.419A–421C and *Republic* 7.419D–521B.

37. After so much strident complaint has been registered here about the lack of freshness in self-proclaimed "new" environmental ethics (which turn out to be "old" ethics retreaded) there is surely an irony in comparing the (apparently brand new) Leopoldian land ethic to Plato's ethical philosophy. There is, however, an important difference. The humane moralists have simply revived and elaborated Bentham's historical application of hedonism to questions regarding the treatment of animals with the capacity of sensibility. There is nothing new but the revival and elaboration. Plato, on the other hand, never develops anything faintly resembling an *environmental* ethic. Plato never reached an ecological view of living nature. The wholes of his universe are body, soul, society, and cosmos. Plato is largely, if not exclusively, concerned with moral problems involving individual human beings in a political context and he has the temerity to insist that the good of the whole transcends individual claims. (Even in the *Crito* Plato is sympathetic to the city's claim to put *Socrates* to death however unjust the verdict against him.) Plato thus espouses a holistic ethic which is valuable as a (very different) paradigm to which the Leopoldian *land* ethic, which is

also holistic but in relation to a very different whole, may be compared. It is interesting further that some (but not all) of the analogies which Plato finds useful to convey his holistic social values are also useful to Leopold in his effort to set out a land ethic.

38. Leopold, *Sand County Almanac*, p. ix.

39. See John Muir, "The Wild Sheep of California," *Overland Monthly* 12 (1874): 359.

40. Roderick Nash (*Wilderness and the American Mind* rev. ed. [New Haven and London: Yale University Press, 1973], p. 2) suggests that the English word *wild* is ultimately derived from *will*. A wild being is thus a willed one—"self-willed, willful, or uncontrollable." The humane moralists' indifference to this distinction is rather dramatically represented in Regan's "Animal Rights, Human Wrongs" (pp. 99–104) which begins with a bid for the reader's sympathy through a vivid description of four concrete episodes of human cruelty toward animals. I suspect that Regan's intent is to give examples of four principal categories of animal abuse at the hands of man: whaling, traffic in zoo captives, questionable scientific experimentation involving unquestionable torture, and intensive meat production. But his illustration, divided according to precepts central to land ethics, concern two episodes of wanton slaughter of *wild* animals, a blue whale and a gibbon, aggravated by the consideration that both are specimens of disappearing species, and two episodes of routine cruelty toward *domestic* animals, a "bobby calf" (destined to become veal) and a laboratory rabbit. The misery of the calf and the agony of the rabbit are, to be sure, reprehensible, from the perspective of the land ethic, for reasons I explain shortly, but it is, I think, a trivialization of the deeper environmental and ecological issues involved in modern whaling and wildlife traffic to discuss the exploitation and destruction of blue whales and gibbon apes as if they are wrong for the same reasons that the treatment of laboratory rabbits and male dairy calves is wrong. The inhumane treatment of penned domestics should not be, I suggest, even discussed in the same context as whaling and wildlife traffic; it is a disservice to do so.

41. John Rodman, "The Liberation of Nature" (p. 101), castigates Singer for failing to consider what the consequences of wholesale animal liberation might be. With tongue in cheek he congratulates Singer for taking a step toward the elimination of a more subtle evil, the genetic debasement of other animal beings, i.e., domestication *per se*.

42. A particularly strong statement of the ultimate value commitment of the neo-Benthamites is found in Feinberg's "Human Duties and Animal Rights" (p. 57): "We regard pain and suffering as an intrinsic evil . . . simply because they are pain and suffering. . . . The question 'What's wrong with pain anyway?' is never allowed to arise." I shall raise it. I herewith declare in all soberness that I see nothing wrong with pain. It is a marvelous method, honed by the evolutionary process, of conveying important organic information. I think it was the late Alan Watts who somewhere remarks that upon being asked if he did not think there was too much pain in the world replied, "No, I think there's just enough."

43. Paul Shepard, "Animal Rights and Human Rites" (p. 37), comments that "the humanitarian's projection onto nature of illegal murder and the rights of civilized people to safety not only misses the point but is exactly contrary to fundamental ecological reality: the structure of nature is a sequence of killings."

44. This matter has been ably and fully explored by Paul Shepard, *The Tender Carnivore and the Sacred Game* (New York: Scribner's Sons, 1973). A more empirical study has been carried out by Marshall Sahlins, *Stone Age Economics* (Chicago: Aldine/Atherton, 1972).

45. The expression "our meat from God" is found in Leopold, *Sand County Almanac*, p. viii. Leopold mentions "organic farming" as something intimately connected with the land ethic; in the same context he also speaks of "biotic farming" (p. 222).

Can Animal Rights Activists Be Environmentalists? _____

Gary E. Varner

Introduction

I have never thought of myself as an activist. I occasionally write letters to the editor and to my legislators, but to date, I have only once held a protest sign, and that had nothing to do with the environment or animals.[1] Nevertheless, I began to study and write on questions in environmental ethics and animal rights because I cared about

Previously unpublished manuscript. Reprinted by permission of Gary E. Varner.

animals and the environment and I believed that philosophical work on these questions would ultimately make a difference in practice. I recall thinking, as early as eighth grade, that humans had commandeered too much of the earth's surface and that we often mistreated animals because we thought that only human beings mattered, morally speaking. I hadn't yet heard the word "anthropocentric," and I was unaware of philosophy as a discipline, but I believed that part of the problem was a question of moral theory.

After coming to Texas A&M in the fall of 1990, I began consciously to distance myself from self-professed activists, especially animal rights activists. For I learned that, to many of the people I was interacting with (animal scientists studying production agriculture and veterinary and medical scientists who use animals in their research, but also older forestry and rangeland people), "activists" were by definition dangerous, unscientific lunatics acting irrationally in the grip of their emotions. I found that, as soon as I was introduced as a philosopher who studies environmental ethics and animal rights, people jumped to a host of conclusions about me. Many of those conclusions turned out to be true (I vote democratic, I eat tofu, and I ride my bicycle to the office), but as soon as I raised the topic of animal rights, many in the audience would assume that I was against all hunting, all use of animals for food or fiber, and all experimentation, which I am not. I have therefore spent a great deal of time lately emphasizing the ways a critical, more philosophical approach to the animal rights issue yields different conclusions than those endorsed by many self-professed animal rights activists.

Among environmental philosophers there is a parallel tendency to equate "animal rights" and "environmental ethics" with specific views in ethical theory and/or specific accounts of what those views imply. Notoriously, it was J. Baird Callicott who, in his early paper "Animal Liberation: A Triangular Affair," appeared to delight in driving a very deep wedge between environmentalism and animal rights.[2] But the one point on which environmental philosophers reached a general consensus during the field's first decade was that both the theoretical foundations and practical implications of animal rights views were inconsis-

tent with those of environmentalism. Because so many environmental philosophers believed that "the ecological crisis" could be averted only by adopting a non-anthropocentric value theory, there was some hope early on that animal rights philosophies would be of some use understanding environmental ethics. Tom Regan's early essay "The Nature and Possibility of an Environmental Ethic"[3] is an example. However, there very quickly emerged a broad-based consensus that animal rights views were no more compatible with sound environmental ethics and sound environmental policy than were anthropocentric views.

To appreciate how hegemonic this view of the animal rights/environmental ethics split has become, consider the following quotations. Under a 1984 title extending Callicott's amorous metaphor (the essay was called "Animal Liberation and Environmental Ethics: Bad Marriage, Quick Divorce") Mark Sagoff wrote:

> Environmentalists cannot be animal liberationists. Animal liberationists cannot be environmentalists. . . . moral obligations to nature cannot be enlightened or explained—one cannot even take the first step—by appealing to the rights of animals . . .[4]

More recently, Eric Katz relied on the now familiar dichotomy in advising businesses engaged in animal research on how to blunt the criticisms of animal rights activists:

> I suggest that the adoption by business of a more conscious environmentalism can serve as a defense against the animal liberation movement. This strategy may seem paradoxical: how can business defend its use of animals by advocating the protection of the environment? But the paradox disappears once we see that animal liberation and environmentalism are incompatible practical moral doctrines.[5]

I myself may have been guilty of perpetuating the perception of dichotomy. In an essay on captive breeding I wrote, very simplistically:

From the perspective of individual sentient creatures involved in a program, captive breeding [of endangered species] is a moral atrocity.[6]

Although Callicott subsequently regretted the fulminatory rhetoric of his "Triangular Affair" piece,[7] he continues to think of animal rights and environmental ethics as incompatible. For instance, he argues for moral monism on the grounds that a pluralism embracing both animal rights and environmental ethics would be inconsistent, because

animal rights would prohibit controlling the populations of sentient animals by means of hunting, while environmental ethics would permit it.[8]

Even Bryan Norton, whose overarching concern in his latest book, *Toward Unity Among Environmentalists,* is to find points of agreement at the level of practice amid disagreement at the level of moral principle, writes as if animal rights and environmental ethics can never be reconciled. During a discussion of deep ecologists' profession of biocentric egalitarianism—the view that all organisms are equal (ostensively very similar to animal rights theorists' claim of animal [or at least vertebrate] equality)—Norton states that

As academics, spokespersons for deep ecology have been able to avoid adopting policies on difficult, real-world cases such as elk destroying their wolf-free ranges, feral goats destroying indigenous vegetation on fragile lands, or park facilities overwhelmed by human visitors.[9]

Norton goes on to explain that equal rights for non-human animals is environmentally unsound because

It can never be "fair" by human standards to kill 10 percent of an elk population because it exceeds the capacity of its range.[10]

That even a consensus-seeking pragmatist like Norton writes as if animal rights views are systematically environmentally unsound suggests just how deeply rooted is the perceived dichotomy between "environmental ethics" and "animal rights."

So the consensus claim among environmental philosophers is that environmental ethics is incompatible, both theoretically and practically, with both anthropocentric and animal rights views. This claim strikes me as multiply confused. First, to identify "environmental ethics" with specifically holistic theories, as the consensus view does, is to deny that thinkers like John Passmore, Bryan Norton, Richard Watson, and Paul Taylor are doing environmental ethics. Yet this strikes me as every bit as arbitrary as denying that environmental ethicists are "doing philosophy." Environmental ethicists should have learned not to define the opposition out of the discipline—for too long, "pure" philosophers succeeded in doing this with "applied" ethicists in general, and with environmental ethicists in particular.

Second, even if we identified *"environmental ethics"* with holistic views, I do not think that either anthropocentric or animal rights views necessarily have environmentally hazardous implications. I think that a sufficiently enlightened anthropocentrism can ground aggressive environmental regulation. In particular, anthropocentrism can be enlightened by an ecologically informed concept of harm of others. On such a concept, no one owns, but everyone has the right to use, ecological processes which (like the hydrologic cycle, or the breeding cycle of migratory waterfowl) necessarily extend beyond the boundaries of private real property. On this view, governments may prohibit uses of land which, when broadly practiced, significantly interfere with such processes, and they may do so without compensating landowners whose activities (e.g. filling wetlands) are prohibited, on the theory that the right to use one's land in a way that harms others was never part of the bundle of rights which the landowner received in the first place. I've argued this at length in a forthcoming paper.[11] Here I want to focus instead on the other claim, that animal rights views are incompatible with environmental ethics.

Self-professed animal rights activists have, I think, contributed to the perception that animal rights views have environmentally unsound implications by truncating and radicalizing their views. Animal rights activists have very little interest in or need for being clear about what their philosophical views are and what those views do and don't imply. In political debates, it is often impossible to describe one's position fully or ineffective to do so even if one has time. "Animals are not ours to eat, wear, or experiment on" is a politically expedient slogan for someone who believes that radical reform is called for, even if that person actually believes that *some* uses are acceptable under *some* conditions. The necessity of producing sound-bite sized quotations for the news media contributes to the truncation of peoples' position statements, but also a general principle of negotiation is to begin with a position which demands more than one is ultimately willing to settle for. So animal rights activists have good reasons for their commonly espoused impatience with philosophical subtlety. The political utility of radicalization and activists' tendency to ignore philosophical subtleties are well documented in Jaspers' and Nelkin's *The Animal Rights Crusade: The Growth of a Moral Protest*.[12]

But there *is* a difference between a philosophy and a bumper sticker, and once we move beyond the political posturing and sloganeering, to a careful examination of the philosophical bases of the animal rights movement, we see that convergence is possible at the level of policy between animal rights views and the views of environmentalists. As Norton put it with regard to convergence between anthropocentrism and holism:

> Long-sighted anthropocentrists and ecocentrists tend to adopt more and more similar policies as scientific evidence is gathered, because both value systems— *and several others as well*—point toward the common-denominator objective of protecting ecological contexts.[13]

Our question, practically speaking, is whether or not an animal rights perspective is one of those "several other" value systems which can agree with ecocentrism on broad, long-range policy goals. Given his insistence that "long-sighted anthropocentrists" can agree with ecocentrists about the importance of protecting ecological contexts," it is surprising that Norton never asks whether the goals of "long-sighted animal rights activists" might also converge with those of the ecocentrists.

The Issues

As I understand it, environmental philosophers' antagonism to animal rights views grows out of their perception that the practical implications of such views would be anti-environmental in two basic ways.

1. With regard to wildlife population control the concerns are that:
   a. *hunting* would be prohibited, even when it is required to preserve the integrity of an ecosystem, and
   b. humans would have an obligation to prevent natural *predation* (including not restoring locally extinct predators).

2. With regard to preserving biodiversity the concerns are that:
   a. it would be impermissible to kill destructive *exotics*, and
   b. it would be impermissible to breed members of *endangered species* in captivity.

In what follows, I am going to begin with, and spend the most time on, hunting. Admittedly, this is the easiest case in which to reconcile the views of animal rights activists and environmentalists, but a careful treatment of this issue sets the stage for a careful treatment of the others.

What I say about hunting will, I think, be met with skepticism by many self-professed animal rights activists. Some will suspect me of being an apologist for the wildlife managers, a philosophical hired gun. And some of what I say (more briefly) about the other three issues will be rejected out of hand by many animal activists. But everything I have to say about these issues is at least *consistent with* a full-blown animal rights philosophy, and that shows, I maintain, that the gulf between animal rights and environmental ethics has been unnecessarily exaggerated.

Therapeutic Hunting of Obligatory Management Species

When teaching the hunting issue, I find it useful to distinguish among three types of hunting in terms of the purposes hunting is taken to serve. By *therapeutic hunting* I mean hunting motivated by and designed to secure the aggregate welfare of the target species and/or the integrity of its ecosystem (I'll discuss later the question of whether the two are separable). By *subsistence* hunting I mean hunting aimed at securing food for human beings. By *sport* hunting I mean hunting aimed at maintaining religious or cultural traditions, reenacting national or evolutionary history, honing certain skills, or just securing a trophy. Many would prefer to recognize a distinction within this third category between hunting for sport and hunting as a ritual. Although there may be some important differences, I class them together because both activities serve human needs (which is what distinguishes both sport and subsistence hunting from therapeutic hunting), but needs which are less fundamental (in the sense of universal) than nutrition (which is what distinguishes subsistence hunting from both ritual and sport hunting).

Obviously these are abstract archetypes. Wildlife managers designing a hunt and hunters going into the field almost always have some composite of these three goals in mind. Inuits taking a whale are engaged in subsistence hunting, but so is a Hill Country Texan who cherishes venison. And both are engaged in sport hunting as I conceive of it: the Inuits' communal life is structured around hunting—it has great social and religious significance—but so is the Texan's insofar as he views hunting as an expression of his cultural and/or evolutionary history.

Although my typology is an abstraction, sorting out the ends hunting is supposed to serve does help us to say where the prospects for convergence lie. Significantly, the defense hunters and environmentalists most often offer in the face of criticism by animal rights activists—that it is necessary to prevent overpopulation and/or environmental degradation—clearly is a defense of *therapeutic* hunting specifically, not sport or subsistence hunting. The thesis I wish to defend here is that environmentalists and animal rights activists can agree on the moral necessity of therapeutic hunting of *obligatory management species*.

I owe the term "obligatory management species" to Ron Howard of the Texas Agricultural Extension Service, who distinguishes among "obligatory" and "permissive" management species in the following way. An *obligatory management species* is one that has a fairly regular tendency to overshoot the carrying capacity of its range, to the detriment of future generations of it and other species. A *permissive management species* is one that does not normally exhibit this tendency. Examples of obligatory management species would be ungulates

(hooved mammals like white-tailed and mule deer, elk, and bison) and elephants. Examples of permissive management species would be mourning doves, cottontail rabbits, gray squirrels, bobwhite, and blue quail.[14] It is not that permissive management species do not become overpopulated. They do every year, in the straightforward sense of producing more young than their habitat can feed through the winter. But they usually do not degrade their habitat in ways that threaten future generations of their own or other species. This is what makes their management environmentally optional, or "merely *permissible*" in Ron Howard's terminology. By contrast, management of ungulates (and some other species) is environmentally necessary, or "*obligatory*" in Howard's terms.[15]

Environmental groups have taken great pains in recent years to distance themselves from animal rights groups, fearing that the widespread perception of animal rights activists as anti-scientific romantics would rub off on them, and much of the distancing has had to do with the hunting issue. In 1990, *Audubon* magazine published an article with the scathing title "Animal Rights: Ignorance About Nature."[16] Also in 1990, the Wisconsin Greens adopted a resolution condemning Madison's Alliance for Animals for disrupting hunts in Blue Mound State Park.[17] And in 1991 a Sierra Club fundraiser said in a phone conversation that the Club was not "doing more to expose the enormous environmental damage caused by factory farming because they wanted to keep their membership as large as possible."[18]

Still, environmentalists do not uniformly support hunting. Audubon and the Sierra Club both oppose hunting in the national parks, and the Texas chapters of both clubs recently opposed a bill which opened the state's parks to recreational hunting. Texas law already allowed hunting in state parks on an *ad hoc* basis, "as sound biological management practices warrant,"[19] e.g. to deal with ungulate population irruptions. But S.B. 179, which was signed into law May 18, 1993, amended the state's Parks and Recreation Code to allow classification of state parks as "game management areas" in addition to as "recreational areas, natural areas, or historical areas."[20] According to its *State Capitol Report*, "The Sierra Club opposes any bill that will shift the burden of proof from no hunting in state parks unless 'biologically necessary', to hunting is allowed unless proven harmful to the area's resources."[21] That's not well written, but the sense is clear enough: the Sierra Club opposes allowing sport hunting on a regular basis in state parks, but it will support sport hunting in the state parks on an *ad hoc* basis, when "biologically necessary."

Sierra's and Audubon's position on hunting in national and state parks shows that the only hunting environmentalists feel *compelled* to support is "biologically necessary" hunting, that is, *therapeutic* hunting, and therapeutic hunting normally is necessary only where obligatory management species are concerned. Officially, both organizations are noncommittal on sport hunting outside of the national and Texas state parks. This mirrors a difference of opinion within the environmental community. Many environmentalists would prefer that sport hunting which is not also therapeutic be stopped, and many would prefer that natural predators be restored to levels at which human hunting is less often biologically necessary. But many environmentalists are also avid hunters who attach great ritual significance to their hunting.

So the only hunting that environmentalists feel *compelled* to support is therapeutic hunting of obligatory management species. However, the received interpretation of the animal rights/environmental ethics split would have it that animal rights activists must oppose hunting even when it is biologically necessary. When we look behind the sound-bite sized quotations and political slogans of self-professed animal rights *activists,* and examine carefully formulated animal rights *philosophies,* we see that it is *not* necessary for animal rightists to oppose environmentally sound hunting. Animal rightists can support exactly the same policy in regard to hunting which environmental groups like Audubon and the Sierra Club support in regard to the national and state parks. The easiest way to bring this out is by making the now familiar and basic philosophical distinction between an animal liberation or animal welfare view and a true animal rights view, and by beginning with the former's application to the hunting question.

Animal *Liberation* and Therapeutic Hunting

Peter Singer's 1975 book *Animal Liberation*[22] has become the Bible of the "animal rights move-

ment." Singer wrote that book for popular consumption and in it he spoke loosely of animals having "moral rights." But all that he intended by this was that animals (or at least "higher animals," like vertebrates) have some basic moral standing and that there are right and wrong ways of treating them. In later, more philosophically rigorous work (summarized in his *Practical Ethics,* which has just been reissued[23]), he explicitly eschews the term "rights," noting that, as a utilitarian ethical theorist, not only does he deny that animals have moral rights, but in his view, neither do human beings. In *Animal Liberation* Singer was writing in the vernacular in order to make his arguments appeal to the widest variety of audiences—he did not want to tie his critiques of agriculture and animal research to his specific moral philosophy.

When ethical philosophers speak of an individual "having moral rights," they mean something much more specific than that the individual has some basic moral standing and that there are right and wrong ways of treating him or her (or it). Although there is much controversy as to the specifics, there is general agreement on this: to attribute moral rights to an individual is to assert that the individual has some kind of special moral dignity, the cash value of which is that there are certain things which cannot justifiably be done to him or her (or it) for the sake of benefit to others. For this reason, moral rights have been characterized as "trump cards" against utilitarian arguments. Utilitarian arguments are arguments based on aggregate benefits and aggregate harms. Utilitarianism is usually defined as the view that right actions maximize aggregate happiness. In principle, nothing is inherently or intrinsically wrong, according to a utilitarian; any action could be justified under some possible circumstances. One way of characterizing rights views in ethics, by contrast, is that there are some things which, regardless of the consequences, it is simply wrong to do to individuals, and that moral rights single out these things.

Although a technical and stipulative definition of the term, this philosophical usage reflects a familiar concept. One familiar way in which appeals to individuals' rights are used in day-to-day discussions is to assert, in effect, that there is a limit to what individuals can be forced to do, or to the harm that may be inflicted upon them, for the benefit of others. So the philosophical usage of rights talk reflects the common-sense view that there are limits to what we can justifiably do to an individual for the benefit of society.

To defend the moral rights of animals would be to claim that certain ways of treating animals cannot be justified on utilitarian grounds. In the professional philosophical writings cited earlier, Peter Singer explicitly rejects rights views and adopts a utilitarian stance for dealing with our treatment of nonhuman animals. So the author of the Bible of the animal rights movement is not an animal *rights* theorist at all.

When the views of animal rights activists are understood this way, in Singer's theoretical terms, animal rights advocates opposed to hunting actually have a lot in common with wildlife managers and hunters who defend hunting as a means to minimizing suffering in wildlife populations. Both factions are appealing to the utilitarian tradition in ethics; both believe that it is permissible (at least where nonhuman animals are concerned) to sacrifice (even involuntarily) the life of one individual for the benefit of others, at least where the aggregated benefits to others clearly outweigh the costs to that individual.

Relatedly, the specific conception of happiness which defenders of therapeutic hunting apply to animals is one which Singer himself uses, at least in regard to many or most animals. Since utilitarianism is the view that right actions maximize aggregate *happiness,* it is important for utilitarians to be clear about what happiness consists in. *Hedonistic utilitarians* define happiness in terms of the presence of pleasure and the absence of pain, where both "pleasure" and "pain" are broadly construed to include not only physical pleasures and pains (e.g. those accompanying orgasms and third degree burns), but various kinds of pleasant and unpleasant psychological states (e.g. tension and nervousness, and glee and exhilaration). *Preference utilitarians* define happiness in terms of the satisfaction of preferences (conscious aims, desires, plans, projects), which can, but need not, be accompanied by pleasure.

In *Animal Liberation* Singer employed a strongly hedonistic conception of happiness. He admitted that, "to avoid speciesism," we need *not* hold that

> it is as wrong to kill a dog as it is to kill a normal human being . . . [Without being

> guilty of speciesism] we could still hold that, for instance, it is worse to kill a normal adult human, [or any other being] with a capacity for self-awareness, and the ability to plan for the future and have meaningful relations with others, than it is to kill a mouse, which presumably does not share all of these characteristics . . .[24]

For this reason he said that "The wrongness of killing a being is more complicated" than the wrongness of inflicting pain. Nevertheless, he there kept the question of killing "in the background," because

> in the present state of human tyranny over other species the more simple, straightforward principle of equal consideration of pain or pleasure is a sufficient basis for identifying and protesting against all the major abuses of animals that human beings practice.[25]

In *Practical Ethics,* by contrast, he devotes four chapters (almost 140 pages) to the "more complicated" question. There he stresses that, with regard to "self-conscious individuals, leading their own lives and wanting to go on living,"[26] it is implausible to say that the death of one happy individual is made up for by the birth of an equally happy individual. That is, when dealing with self-conscious beings, preference utilitarianism is more appropriate than hedonistic utilitarianism.

An easy way to clarify Singer's point is with the following example. Suppose I sneak into your bedroom tonight and, without ever disturbing your sleep, kill you (by silently releasing an odorless gas, for instance). Since you led a happy life (hopefully) and died painlessly, on a hedonistic conception of happiness, the only sense we can make of the harm I have done you is in terms of lost future opportunities for pleasure. In the case of human beings, who have complicated desires, intentions, plans, and projects,[27] this seems an inadequate accounting of the harm I've done you. For humans (and any similarly cognitively sophisticated animals) a desire-based conception of harm seems more appropriate. But, Singer argues, self-conscious beings are not replaceable. When a being with future-oriented desires dies, those desires remain unsatisfied even if another being is brought into existence and has similar desires satisfied.

Singer cites research which he says clearly shows that the great apes (chimpanzees, gorillas, and orangutans) have projects,[28] and, without saying what specific research leads him to these conclusions, that fish and chickens do not have projects,[29] but that

> A case can be made, though with varying degrees of confidence, on behalf of whales, dolphins, monkeys, dogs, cats, pigs, seals, bears, cattle, sheep and so on, perhaps even to the point at which it may include all mammals . . .[30]

Elsewhere I have characterized carefully the evidence I think shows that all mammals and birds have desires but fish do not.[31] However, I doubt that either birds or the "lower" mammals (by which I here mean mammals other than primates and cetaceans) have projects of the kind Singer is interested in, that is, desires that significantly transcend the present. Certainly the desire to go on living (which Singer mentions repeatedly as a sort of *sine qua non* of self-consciousness) constitutes a very sophisticated project. Dogs and cats almost certainly have desires that transcend the present. When a lion flushes a wildebeest in the direction of a hidden pridemate[32] (or, more prosaically, when my cat comes from the back room to where I am sitting and, having gotten my attention by jumping in my lap, leads me to the back door to be let out) it undoubtedly has a desire for something in the future. But it is a very near future about which cats and dogs are concerned. The desire to catch a prey animal here now, or even the desire to get a human being from the other room to come open the door to the outside, is not on a par with aspiring to longer life. Having the desire to go on living involves not only being self-conscious, but having concepts of life and death, and of self.

So I doubt that self-consciousness, as Singer conceives it, extends as far down "the phylogenetic scale" as Singer believes. But for present purposes, I will not try to settle this issue, for two reasons. First, the switch from hedonistic utilitarianism to preference utilitarianism would not in and of itself rule out hunting. As Singer put it, blocking the replaceability argument's application to many mammals

> raised a very large question mark over the justifiability of a great deal of killing of animals carried out by humans, even

> when this killing takes place painlessly and without causing suffering to other members of the animal community.[33]

But to "raise a very large question mark" is to increase the burden of proof on a justification of killing on preference utilitarian grounds; it is not to rule it out.

Second, in the following section, I will consider the application of a much stronger view—Tom Regan's rights view—to the hunting question, and there I will assume (with Regan) that all mammals have moral rights as he construes them. Since all of the obligatory management species listed above are mammals, this puts a very heavy burden of proof on the defender of therapeutic hunting. My point is that if even Regan's rights view can be used to defend therapeutic hunting of obligatory management species, then certainly a preference utilitarian could defend it as well.

For present purposes, then, let us consider therapeutic hunting from a hedonistic utilitarian perspective. The defense is obvious. Consider the following argument:

> 1) We have a moral obligation to minimize pain.
>
> 2) In the case of obligatory management species, more pain would be caused by letting nature take its course than by conducting carefully regulated therapeutic hunts.
>
> 3) Therefore, we are morally obligated to conduct carefully regulated therapeutic hunts of obligatory management species rather than let nature take its course.

Since premise (1) is just a (partial) restatement[34] of the hedonistic utilitarian principle, and the argument is valid, premise (2) is the obvious point of controversy. But premise (2) states an empirical claim. Thus Singer's disagreement with the hunters and wildlife managers is purely empirical. They agree at the level of moral principle; they disagree only about that principle's application in practice.

Specifically, Singer appears to believe that non-lethal means of population control are (or at least could be made) available, and that using them would minimize suffering *vis à vis* therapeutic hunting. Singer has very little to say about hunting specifically. However, in *Practical Ethics* he at one point clearly indicates that a hedonistic utilitarian could endorse hunting under some circumstances.

> [The replaceability argument is severely] limited in its application. It cannot justify factory farming, where animals do not have pleasant lives. Nor does it *normally* justify the killing of wild animals. A duck shot by a hunter . . . has probably had a pleasant life, but the shooting of a duck does not lead to its replacement by another. *Unless the duck population is at the maximum that can be sustained by the available food supply,* the killing of a duck ends a pleasant life without starting another, and is for that reason wrong on straightforward utilitarian grounds.[35]

Here Singer admits that the replaceability argument could be used to justify, not just therapeutic hunting of obligatory management species, but sport hunting of permissive management species. Ducks are not obligatory management species. Ducks do not, in the normal course of events, overshoot the carrying capacity of their habitat in ways that degrade that habitat for future generations of their own and other species. Their management is therefore environmentally permissible, but not environmentally obligatory. Nevertheless, a hedonistic utilitarian could endorse sport hunting of permissive management species when, as Singer indicates here, their populations are at or above the carrying capacity of their ranges. As noted above, permissive management species regularly overshoot the carrying capacity of their range, producing more young than their habitat can support. Where this is clearly the case, a painlessly killed individual is, in effect, replaced by an individual who survives as a result. So long as the average death ducks suffer at the hands of hunters involves as little or less pain than the average death surplus ducks would have suffered in nature, pain is minimized.

However, in *Animal Liberation* Singer writes:

> If it is true that in special circumstances their population grows to such an extent that they damage their own environment and the prospects of their own survival, or that of other animals who share their habitat, then it may be right for humans

to take some supervisory action; but obviously if we consider the interests of the animals, this action will not be to allow hunters to kill some animals, inevitably wounding others in the process, but rather to reduce the fertility of the animals.[36]

Here Singer is admitting that therapeutic hunting of obligatory management species is better than letting nature take its course, but he is arguing that there is yet a better option. Singer appears to be substituting into the above argument a different empirical premise:

> 2') By using non-lethal means of controlling populations of obligatory management species we would minimize suffering *vis à vis* both letting nature take its course and performing carefully regulated therapeutic hunts.

To reach a different conclusion:

> 3') We are morally obligated to use non-lethal means to control populations of obligatory management species.

When all of the learned dust has settled, the disagreement between the Peter Singers of the world and the self-professed advocates of animal welfare among hunters and wildlife managers boils down to an empirical controversy over the effectiveness of non-lethal wildlife population control measures. Both factions agree at the level of moral principle; they disagree over the facts.

My sense is that, at least in the current state of nonlethal wildlife population control, the defenders of hunting have it right. In a retrospective essay written for the centennial of Aldo Leopold's birth, Dale McCullough (the A. Starker Leopold Professor of Wildlife Management at Berkeley) recounted the controversy over deer management on Angel Island in the San Francisco Bay. Under pressure from the San Francisco Society for the Prevention of Cruelty to Animals, the state of California tried both relocating deer and birth control implants. In a follow-up study, McCullough found that 85% of the relocated deer had died within one year of relocation, and the birth control program was abandoned after the Society was unable to trap and implant enough females to prevent continued population growth (it was estimated that about 60 would need to be implanted). McCullough concluded that "the alternatives to shooting for control of deer populations are expensive, ineffective, and not particularly humane."[37]

For present purposes, however (for assessing convergence of environmentalists' and animal rightists' views on hunting), the point is moot, for two reasons. First, in cases where overpopulation already exists, it is not safe to let all the animals live out their natural lives. If the result of this year's breeding season is a herd already significantly over the carrying capacity of its range, then all the fertility control in the world will not prevent the kind of habitat degradation which Singer admits would justify culling some individuals.

Singer's intention, presumably, is to use fertility control to stabilize populations at sustainable levels. But even with regard to such preemptive population control, for present purposes the choice between therapeutic hunting and nonlethal means is moot. For if, as the defenders of hunting maintain, hunting is in fact the only effective method of preemptive control, then both environmentalists and the Peter Singers of the world are compelled to support therapeutic hunting. If, on the other hand, effective non-lethal means were currently available, then the Peter Singers of the world would be compelled to support the use of those means rather than therapeutic hunting. Notice, however, that in the latter case an environmentalist would have the same choice open to her. For as we noted earlier, the only hunting environmentalists feel compelled to support is "biologically necessary" hunting. But if nonlethal population control were equally effective, *hunting* would not be biologically necessary, only the disjunctive choice: hunting *or* equivalent nonlethal means. That is, an environmentalist would reach conclusion 3":

3") We are morally obligated to use *either* (a) therapeutic hunting *or* (b) biologically equivalent non-lethal means to control populations of obligatory management species.

Just as environmentalists are of two minds with regard to sport hunting which is not also therapeutic, they would be of two minds with regard to the choice between therapeutic hunting and equally effective nonlethal means.

My sense is that the contemporary situation with respect to nonlethal means of deer population management is analogous to the use of hunting as a management tool in Leopold's days. Leopold was skeptical of wildlife managers' ability to control wildlife populations through hunting. He characterized hunting as

a crude, slow, and inaccurate tool, which needs to be supplemented by a precision instrument. The natural aggregation of lions and other predators on an overstocked range, and their natural dispersion from an understocked one, is the only precision instrument known to deer management.[38]

I think that Leopold's skepticism of game management was overblown as a result of his having witnessed the Kaibab irruption in the 1920's and similar population problems in Wisconsin during the 1940's. Decades later, during the 1970's and 1980's, the state of Wisconsin used better censusing techniques and a zone-sensitive permit system[39] to sustain harvests of still wolfless deer in numbers far exceeding the highest yields ever achieved during Leopold's lifetime.[40] Certainly other factors were involved—there was less edge habitat in Wisconsin in the 1940's—but Leopold's dim view of game management probably resulted in large measure from his living during the early days of scientific wildlife management. Nonlethal population control is still slow and crude, and needs to be supplemented with a precision instrument (therapeutic hunting and/or natural predation).

Recognizing that effective nonlethal population control is not currently available, animal rights activists might nevertheless choose to go on opposing therapeutic hunting for political purposes. In doing so, they would be practicing brinkmanship: they would be risking disaster (from the perspective of the individual animals involved) in order to force the development of more precise nonlethal techniques of population control. There is no precise way to determine when such brinkmanship is justified, anymore than there is any precise way to determine when civil disobedience or ecosabotage is justified.[41] In both cases, a rough utilitarian calculation is relied upon: in the case of civil disobedience and sabotage, the adverse effects on public order are weighed against the likely benefit of the law breaking; in the case of brinkmanship, the risk of a disastrous outcome is weighed against the probability of a breakthrough. However, part of the classic defense of civil disobedience and sabotage is that the conscientious lawbreaker has exhausted available legal means to achieve her goal, and in the case of therapeutic hunting, I don't think that activists can plausibly claim to have done this. Just as they have successfully forced private companies (like Mary Kay Cosmetics) and government agencies (like the NIH) to investigate alternatives to animal models in scientific research and product safety testing, activists could force agencies to put more money into investigations of nonlethal population control methods. So my conclusion is that we should not practice brinkmanship in this case. Therapeutic hunting is a precision tool already available, and as advocates of animal welfare, we should push for more research into nonlethal means of population control while supplementing nonlethal means with hunting.

I do, however, think that eventually precision methods of nonlethal wildlife population control will be developed. Recently, extensive experiments with animals have validated the technique of using genetically engineered viruses to spread infertility among wild animals. By inserting part of the protein sheath from the species' sperm into a virus which spreads easily in the population and then distributing food laced with the virus, Australian researchers hope to eradicate the rabbit, an exotic which has devastated their country. Trials of a similar technique to induce *temporary* infertility in other species are now underway.[42] The public in general and animal rights activists in particular are apprehensive of biotechnologies, but I think this method should, with appropriate caution, be embraced by the animal rights movement as a very promising approach to nonlethal control of wildlife populations.

The earlier discussion of environmentalists' ambivalent attitudes towards hunting suggests that if and when effective nonlethal alternatives to therapeutic hunting become available, environmentalists will be split. For some, the availability of nonlethal alternatives will strengthen their opposition to hunting; others will regard the choice between hunting and equally effective nonlethal means as morally moot. For present purposes what is important is this: animal rights activists operating from a hedonistic utilitarian stance will be compelled to support therapeutic hunting of obligatory management species in the absence of precision, nonlethal methods of wildlife population control. Only when such methods are available must such animal rights activists oppose therapeutic hunting, and then they will oppose it only in order to embrace a more humane alternative *with the same environmental effect.*

Animal *Rights* and Therapeutic Hunting

Although Peter Singer's *Animal Liberation* has become the Bible of the animal rights movement, Tom Regan's *The Case for Animal Rights* is the best defense available to date of a true animal rights position. It is impossible to do justice to the argument of a 400 page book in a few paragraphs. In what follows I will simply summarize the conclusions Regan reaches, without trying to reproduce his arguments in detail, and without critically assessing them apart from their application to the hunting controversy. It is my view that without resolving the theoretical question of which individuals (if any) have moral rights, we can still hope to make some progress on the practical question of which hunting policy to adopt. Specifically, I argue that in the absence of effective nonlethal means of population control, therapeutic hunting of obligatory management species *can* be defended from a true animal rights perspective.

According to Regan, there is basically one moral right—the right not to be harmed on the grounds that doing so benefits others—and at least all normal mammals of a year or more have this basic moral right. In the preface to his most recent anthology, Gene Hargrove characterizes Regan's position as

> more narrowly focused [than Singer's,] on protecting the rights of those nonhuman entities with inherent value—those capable of being the subject of a life—which turn out to be mammals and no other forms of life.[43]

This is misleading. Regan does not deny that any non-mammalian animals have rights. Although he does explicitly restrict the reference of "animal" to "mentally normal mammals of a year or more," Regan does this to avoid the controversy over "line drawing," that is, trying to say precisely where in the phylogenetic scale and where in their ontogeny animals' mental capacities become so impoverished as to make them incapable of being subjects of a life. And Regan clearly says that he chooses mammals in order to make sure that his arguments "refer [to] individuals *well beyond* the point where anyone could reasonably 'draw the line' separating those who have the mental abilities in question from those who lack them."[44] In thus restricting the reference of "animal" he is only acknowledging that the analogical reasoning which would establish that any non-human animal has moral rights is strongest in the case of mentally normal adult mammals and becomes progressively weaker as we consider birds and then reptiles, amphibians, and vertebrate fish.

Regan defends two principles to use in deciding whom to harm where it is impossible not to harm someone who has moral rights: the miniride and worse-off principles. The *worse-off principle* applies where *non-comparable* harms are involved and it requires us to avoid harming the worse-off individual. Regan adopts the kind of desire-based conception of harm discussed earlier in relation to preference utilitarianism. Regan measures harm in terms of the degree to which an individual's capacity to form and satisfy desires has been restricted. The degree of restriction is measured in absolute, rather than relative terms. For if harm were measured relative to the individual's original capacity to form and satisfy desires, rather than in absolute terms, then death would be death wherever it occurs, but Regan reasons that although death is always the greatest harm which any individual can suffer (because it forecloses all opportunity for desire formation and satisfaction), death to a normal human being in the prime of her life is non-comparably worse than death to any non-human animal in the prime of its life, because a normal human being's capacity to form and satisfy desires is so much greater. To illustrate the use of the worse-off principle, Regan imagines that five individuals, four humans and a dog, are in a lifeboat that can support only four of them. Since death to any of the human beings would be non-comparably worse than death to the dog, the worse-off principle applies, and it requires us to avoid harming the human beings, who stand to lose the most.[45]

The *miniride* principle applies to cases where *comparable* harms are involved, and it requires us to harm the few rather than the many. Regan admits that, where it applies, this principle implies the same conclusions as the principle of utility, but he emphasizes that the reasoning is non-utilitarian: the focus is on individuals rather than the aggregate; what the miniride principle instructs us to do is to minimize the overriding of individuals' rights, rather than to maximize aggregate happiness. He says that the rights view (as Regan calls his position) advocates harming the few (at least where *comparable* harms are involved), because it respects all individuals equally. To illustrate the miniride principle's application, Regan imagines that a runaway mine train must be sent down one of two shafts, and that fifty miners would be killed by sending it down the first shaft but only one by sending it down the second. Since the harms that the various individuals in the example would suffer are comparable, the miniride principle applies, and we are obligated to send the runaway train down the second shaft.

Regan argues that the rights view calls for the total abolition of scientific research on animals, of commercial animal agriculture, and of hunting and trapping.[46] He contrasts his views to Singer's in this regard, stressing that, because he is reasoning from a rights-based theory, his conclusions are not contingent upon the facts in the same way as those of a utilitarian like Singer.

At first glance, the prospects for convergence are slim when a true animal rights position like Regan's is opposed to the position of environmentalists. For if having moral rights means that there are certain things that cannot be done to an individual for the sake of the group, and a true animal rights position extends moral rights to animals, then the basic rationale for therapeutic hunting—killing some in order that others may live—appears to be lost. As Regan puts it:

> Put affirmatively, the goal of wildlife managers should be to defend wild animals in the possession of their rights, providing them with the opportunity to live their own life, by their own lights, as best they can, spared that human predation that goes by the name of "sport." . . . If, in reply, we are told that [this] will not minimize the total amount of suffering wild

animals will suffer over time, our reply should be that this cannot be the over-arching goal of wildlife management, once we take the rights of animals seriously.[47]

Regan appears to be opposed even to therapeutic hunting, and his opposition appears to follow from the attribution of moral rights to the animals.

However, Regan never considers the applicability of the miniride principle to hunting. Note that in the passage quoted above, he focuses on the reasoning presented in defense of therapeutic hunting by wildlife managers. They offer an aggregative, utilitarian argument, and as a rights theorist, Regan rejects utilitarian justifications for overriding individual rights. But Regan never considers what the implications would be of applying the miniride principle to the hunting question. Given Regan's conception of harm, death harms all normal individuals of the same species equally. So if it is true that fewer animals will die if therapeutic hunting is used to regulate a wildlife population than if natural attrition is allowed to take its course, then Regan's view implies that therapeutic hunting is not only permissible but a morally mandatory expression of respect for animals' rights.

Similar conclusions could, I think, be reached about certain kinds of medical research using the worse-off principle. Consider AIDS research, for example. Given Regan's conception of harm, the harm that death from AIDS is to a normal human being is non-comparably worse than the harm that death from AIDS is to a mouse or even a chimpanzee. So the worse-off principle would, if applicable, imply that non-human lives may be sacrificed to save human beings from preventable death. Here again, however, Regan does not apply his principle.

With regard to medical research, Regan bases his abolitionist conclusion primarily on the "special consideration" that *"Risks are not morally transferable to those who do not voluntarily choose to take them,"* which, he claims, blocks the application of the worse-off principle.[48] Returning to the hunting question, Regan might similarly cite a "special consideration" which blocks the application of the miniride principle. He might claim that a violation of an individual's moral rights occurs only when a moral agent is responsible for the harm in question, and that while hunters would be responsible for the

deaths of the animals they kill in a therapeutic hunt, no one would be responsible for deaths due to natural attrition. Regan and Singer both give the following reason for thinking that natural predators do no wrong when they kill. They point out that only the actions of moral agents can be evaluated as right or wrong, and that presumably only human beings are moral agents (only human beings are capable of recognizing moral principles and altering their behavior accordingly).

But when a responsible agent knowingly allows nature to take its course, is he or she not responsible by omission for the foreseeable deaths which result? Regan's answer would presumably be no, but this does not seem to me to be a plausible position. In a recent article, Dale Jamieson presents a relevant counterexample. Suppose that a boulder is rolling down a hill toward a hiker and that you can save the hiker by calling out to her. Jamieson asks, does it make the slightest difference whether the boulder was dislodged by the wind rather than by a would-be murderer? If we are not responsible for allowing nature to take its course, then although you violate the hiker's rights by failing to warn her in the latter case, in the former case you would do her no wrong. But this seems implausible.[49]

There *would*, I think, be a good reason for not culling overpopulated humans: it is possible for any normal adult human to both understand the gravity of the situation and alter his or her behavior accordingly. A human being can recognize and act on the obligation of individuals to avoid contributing to overpopulation; a deer, an elephant, or a water buffalo cannot. This gives us a reason for being more reticent about involuntarily culling human beings in a situation of overpopulation. However, I would maintain that this is only a reason for *waiting longer* before engaging in involuntary culling, for *letting the situation get significantly worse* before one resorts to such drastic means. Even with regard to humans, it is, I submit, implausible to maintain that the numbers never count. At some point (admittedly unspecifiable in advance), some number of innocent human beings ought to be killed to prevent the foreseeable deaths of some larger number (although again, the minimum required ratio of saved to culled cannot be specified in advance).

Regan claims that the rights view calls for the total abolition of animal research and hunting, and that because he is reasoning from a rights-based theory, his conclusions are not contingent upon the facts in the same way as those of a utilitarian like Singer.[50] But the discussion in this section has suggested that a rights view cannot plausibly be insulated from the facts, and that, therefore, a true animal rights view need not rule out hunting or research *simpliciter.* Where therapeutic hunting is the only means available to prevent a large number of foreseeable deaths, a full-blown animal rights position *can* support therapeutic hunting. And where nonlethal means *are* available, the case against brinkmanship is stronger from Regan's perspective than it is from Singer's. For as I suggested earlier, the defense of brinkmanship would parallel the classic defense of conscientious lawbreaking, and that defense is in terms of a utilitarian balancing of the magnitude and likelihood of the benefits of law breaking (or brinkmanship) against the magnitude and likelihood of the harms of law breaking (or brinkmanship). Although I agree with Jamieson that "Regan's theory has serious problems" and that the remedies "would be less clearly in conflict with consequentialist morality,"[51] I think the case against brinkmanship would remain stronger with Regan. Respect for individuals' rights would seem to require greater aversion to brinkmanship than would treating individuals as receptacles for hedonic utility.

Scrambling Positions on Hunting

A critical look at the philosophical foundations of the animal rights movement shows that an individual genuinely concerned with animal welfare, and even one who attributes moral rights to non-human animals, can support the only kind of hunting environmentalists feel compelled to support, namely therapeutic hunting of obligatory management species.

A critical look at the hunting issue also scrambles the soundbyte-sized positions portrayed in the media. Animal rights activists tend to condemn hunters for being unsportsmanlike, and they tend to condemn management aimed at achieving maximum sustainable yield (MSY) and/or trophy bucks. However, when it comes to designing an actual therapeutic hunt, some animal welfare and animal rights views ought, arguably, to endorse the same management principles that are appropriate to tro-

phy hunting and/or MSY, and the ideal therapeutic hunt would be anything but sportsmanlike. On the latter point, consider that various unsportsmanlike practices would be conducive to killing specific categories of animals as quickly and painlessly as possible. In the ideal therapeutic hunt, deer would be lured to bait stations near blinds from which sharpshooters with high caliber, automatic weapons would be able to kill them selectively and quickly. This is hardly a paradigm of sportsmanlike hunting, but it is, arguably, the ideal which serious animal welfarists should advocate.

The former point, about management principles, cannot be made without a brief discussion of wildlife management principles. For ecologists, the carrying capacity of a deer range is the maximum number of deer the habitat will support on a sustained basis. Wildlife managers, in contrast, have tended to think of carrying capacity in terms of MSY (maximum sustainable yield). To avoid confusion, Dale McCullough advocates calling the former the *K carrying capacity* of the range, the latter its *I carrying capacity.*[52] Deer respond to higher population densities by producing fewer fawns (reabsorption of fetuses becomes more common and twins less common), and denser populations are more susceptible to disease and malnutrition. Consequently, maximum yearly recruitment (addition of new adults) occurs well short of K carrying capacity. Management for MSY therefore requires maintenance of deer populations substantially below K-carrying capacity, where recruitment rates are highest.

The significance is this. Average individual welfare arguably is higher in populations at I carrying capacity than in populations at K carrying capacity, as evidenced both by more fawns surviving and in higher average weights and reduced parasitism and malnutrition among adults. Only a version of utilitarianism which placed preeminent emphasis on the sheer number of animals in the field would find management at K carrying capacity attractive. But McCullough's model suggests that MSY is achieved short of K carrying capacity, where individual welfare is higher. The ironic result that when hunters are harvesting the maximum number of animals, they see fewer afield and expend more effort per kill, has occasioned tension between wildlife managers and hunters.[53] Here is an opportunity for further convergence between pro- and anti-hunting forces. The policy positions of sport hunters educated to accept management at I carrying capacity for the sake of MSY will converge with those of animal welfare advocates educated to see that MSY management maximizes average individual welfare.

Perhaps more surprising is the fact that management practices which produce the best trophy bucks are arguably more consistent with Regan's rights view than is either management for MSY or K carrying capacity. The largest racks occur on older (4 to 6 years), heavier bucks, and heavier animals have to eat more to maintain themselves. So managing a deer herd to produce the best trophy bucks means sustaining fewer total deer and having fewer "hunting opportunities." As one how-to manual for East Texas deer managers puts it:

> On heavily hunted deer ranges, 90 percent of all the bucks are harvested before they reach four years old. Under these conditions deer do not live long enough to become trophy animals. . . . When managing for maximum quality [read: a preferred trophy], the forked-antlered buck harvest must be at least 30–50 percent less than when managing for maximum harvest.[54]

That is, to produce the best trophy bucks on a range, the population must be maintained below MSY, and this must be accomplished by killing more does and spike bucks[55] and fewer fork-antlered bucks.[56] Although the sex ratio of animals killed changes, by maintaining the population below I carrying capacity and MSY, fewer animals are killed yearly. Here is an opportunity for convergence between the views of trophy hunters and animal rights activists who think like Tom Regan. The miniride principle implies that it is better to manage herds in ways that minimize killing. The trophy management principles just described do just this, by emphasizing the taking of does and maintenance of the population below MSY. But enlightened trophy hunters will accept this—the manual just cited is designed to get hunters to stop thinking that good trophy management means buck-only hunting.

It would also be possible to endorse the trophy improvement strategy over MSY management from a hedonistic utilitarian perspective. Assuming that on average death is death in hedonistic terms, however it occurs (whether from starvation or human or natural predation), the trophy improvement strategy would minimize pain *vis à vis* the other two management strategies. (Although managing a population at K carrying capacity would involve less hunting than at I carrying capacity, at K carrying capacity total mortality is greatest.)[57]

One further point needs to be emphasized. I defined an obligatory management species as one with "a fairly regular tendency to overshoot the carrying capacity of its range," but this does not mean that obligatory management species *always* need to be hunted. If that were so, then it would not make sense to limit hunting in parks to situations in which hunting becomes "biologically necessary." As McCullough points out:

> Most wildlife biologists and managers can point to situations where deer populations have not been hunted yet do not fluctuate greatly or cause damage to vegetation. Certainly deer reach overpopulation status in some park situations, but the surprising thing is how many parks containing deer populations have no problem.[58]

From an animal welfare or animal rights perspective, the presumption is against hunting. With regard to obligatory management species, it is not unusual for this presumption to be met, although this is not always the case. Ungulates are the classic example of obligatory management species, but even among them there are important variations. In climax-adapted ungulates (like bison, bighorn sheep, mountain goats, muskox, and caribou) the magnifying effects of time lags in vegetation damage are less severe than in subclimax ungulates (like deer, pronghorn antelope, and moose).[59] So the burden of proof necessary to justify therapeutic hunting is more likely to be met with some ungulates (e.g. deer and moose) than others (e.g. mountain goats or bighorn sheep). The parallel point with regard to permissive management species is that although they do not degrade their habitats on anything like a regular basis, they *can* under certain circumstances, and in those circumstances animal rights views can support hunting of them.

Endangered Species, Exotics, and Natural Predators

I said that I would spend most of my time on the hunting issue because a careful treatment of it sets the stage for my treatment of the other issues mentioned earlier: captive breeding of endangered species, removal of exotics, and natural predation. The received view has it that animal rights philosophies have environmentally unsound implications on each of these issues. Environmentalists recognize prima facie duties to remove exotics, to reintroduce locally extinct predators to their former ranges, and to captive breed critically endangered species. My thesis in this section is that a more critical understanding of animal rights philosophies shows how an animal rights activist could recognize each of these prima facie duties on one or the other of two closely related grounds: duties to future generations of animals and/or duties to future generations of human beings.

Let me begin with the latter ground. Singer and Regan both emphasize the formal moral equality of human and (some) non-human animals. Yet, as I had occasion to point out in previous sections, both think hierarchically in the last analysis. For that reason, scientists and agriculturalists who say that, "For an animal rightist, human and animal lives are strictly equal," or "According to animal rights philosophies, 'a rat is a pig is a dog is a boy'," are committing the same intellectual sin they so love to charge animal rights activists with. For they are attacking animal rights philosophies without having troubled to read any of the relevant professional literature (or, if they have read anything it is only *Animal Liberation,* and they have not read it with careful attention to the philosophical arguments). This is every bit as intellectually irresponsible as a follower of Peter Singer refusing to inform himself about the empirical realities of scientific experimentation or animal agriculture. Singer *clearly* states that it is *not* speciesist to hold that killing a normal adult human is as morally serious as killing a mouse,[60] and Regan *clearly* says that death is a greater harm to a normal adult human than it is to any non-human animal. No fair reading

of Singer's *Animal Liberation* (let alone his *Practical Ethics*) or Regan's *The Case for Animal Rights* could yield scientists' common, fundamental misunderstanding of their views.

Although fair-minded scientists and agriculturalists will find this inegalitarian aspect of Singer's and Regan's views comforting, no doubt many animal rights activists will reject it. But this is not a point about which animal rights activists need be apologetic. Any workable ethics will recognize *some* hierarchies. Albert Schweitzer is renowned for assiduously refusing to prioritize forms of life and their various interests, maintaining that

> Whenever I in any way sacrifice or injure life, I am not within the sphere of the ethical, but I become guilty, whether it be egoistically guilty for the sake of maintaining my own existence or welfare, or unegoistically guilty for the sake of maintaining a greater number of other existences or their welfare.[61]

Here Schweitzer clearly says that even killing in self preservation incurs guilt. Yet he also admits that "The necessity to destroy and to injure life is imposed upon me" at every step,[62] implying that we cannot help but incur guilt all the time. Elsewhere he appears to contradict himself, saying that "Whenever I injure life of any sort, I must be quite clear whether it is necessary. Beyond the unavoidable, I must never go,"[63] suggesting that "unavoidable" or "necessary" injuries are permissible. It may be that Schweitzer's point was one with which I agree, namely that any adverse impact on the interests of any organism (even a disease microbe) introduces some evil into the world. If this were the meaning of the former passage, then it would be consistent with the latter passage, because (as any utilitarian will admit) the production of some evil can be justified by the preservation or production of good. Speaking in terms of unavoidable guilt is a confusing way of making this point, however. Probably Schweitzer's overarching aim was to urge people, in very dramatic terms, to take more seriously decisions involving injury or death to living things of any species. With that laudable goal I agree. But Schweitzer's own talk about the necessity of injury and death[64] gives the lie to any practically useful ethics entirely free of hierarchies. Any workable ethics must recognize some hierarchy of interests, and from this a hierarchy of life forms follows, if it turns out (as I think it does[65]) that only some forms of life have the favored kinds of interests.

The point of this digression on moral hierarchies is this: if

1. we have a general duty to preserve the integrity of ecosystems as the necessary context in which future generations of humans can pursue their most important interests,

2. these interests are of overriding moral importance, and

3. safeguarding future generations' pursuit of these interests requires us to remove exotics, breed endangered species, and reintroduce predators,

then long-sighted anthropocentrists and animal rights activists can agree that these things should be done (or at least that there is a presumptive, prima facie duty to do these things).

Bryan Norton has offered an anthropocentric defense of the duty to preserve natural variety which leads fairly naturally to the three prima facie duties in question. Norton's argument

> recognizes the crucial role of creative, self-organizing systems in supporting human economic, recreational, aesthetic, and spiritual values. Because self-organizing systems maintain a degree of stable functioning across time, they provide a sufficiently stable context to which human individuals and cultures can adapt their practices.[66]

Norton doubts that adequate indicators of ecosystemic health are currently available, because of the "centrality and intransigence of scaling problems,"[67] but he stresses the general importance of total diversity—a combination of within-habitat diversity and cross-habitat diversity[68]—and the preservation of normal rates of change in environmental systems.[69] He therefore unpacks the duty to preserve natural variety in terms of preserving (or,

where necessary, restoring) the integrity of ecosystems. He says that

> An ecosystem has maintained its integrity . . . if it retains (1) the total diversity of the system—the sum total of the species and associations that have held sway historically—and (2) the systematic organization which maintains that diversity, including, especially, the system's multiple layers of complexity through time.[70]

Preserving "the sum total of the species and associations that have held sway historically" will sometimes require captive breeding of critically endangered species, sometimes it will require us to remove exotics, and sometimes it will require us to reintroduce locally extinct predators.

If future generations of human beings can only fulfill their most important interests against a background of relatively intact ecosystems, then relatively intact ecosystems we must preserve. And if, as environmentalists claim, preserving relatively intact ecosystems necessarily involves (some) breeding of endangered species, (some) removal of exotics, and allowing (some) natural predation, then animal rights activists who acknowledge the primacy of humans' most important interests can agree with both long-sighted anthropocentrists and environmentalists that we have prima facie duties to do these things.

I said that animal rights activists could also recognize prima facie duties to breed critically endangered species, remove exotics, and reintroduce predators as duties to future generations of *animals* and I will end by very briefly outlining how this is so. If human flourishing requires a relatively stable ecological context, then so too, presumably, does the flourishing of the nonhuman animals with which Singer and Regan are concerned. Norton's point about ecological integrity is not (or not just) that intact ecosystems are storehouses of resources useful to future generations of humans. If they were only that, then nontechnological creatures like deer and owls would not need intact ecosystems. But Norton's point is that total diversity is crucial to the dynamic stability of ecosystems through time. Certainly some species (e.g. coyotes and raccoons) are opportunistic and can thrive in newly disturbed ecosystems. Others (e.g. beaver) must disturb ecosystems to survive at all. But only if a patchwork of habitats in various stages of succession is maintained in every region will the needs of such species be met, for cross-habitat diversity provides the species on which these animals' lives depend. Although any one species may require a specific habitat to survive, in the long haul, all species depend on an ecological background of cross-habitat diversity. So without invoking the interests of future generations of humans, an animal rights activist could defend captive breeding, removal of exotics, and reintroduction of predators where these are necessary to preserve the ecological background conditions on which future generations of animals will depend.

Notes

1. It was a demonstration in response to Texas A&M's decision, in early 1991, to remove "sexual orientation" from the list of protected categories in its official anti-discrimination policy. The sign said: "Straight but not narrow." (I wish I could say I made it up, but someone handed it to me!)

2. J. Baird Callicott, "Animal Liberation: A Triangular Affair," *Environmental Ethics* 2 (1980), pp. 311–38; reprinted in Callicott, *In Defense of the Land Ethic* (Albany: SUNY Press, 1989).

3. Tom Regan, "The Nature and Possibility of an Environmental Ethic," *Environmental Ethics* 3 (1981), pp. 19–34.

4. Mark Sagoff, "Animal Liberation and Environmental Ethics: Bad Marriage, Quick Divorce," *Osgood Hall Law Journal* 22 (1984), pp. 297–307, at pp. 304, 306.

5. Eric Katz, "Defending the Use of Animals by Business: Animal Liberation and Environmental Ethics," in W. Michael Hoffman, Robert Frederick, and Edward S. Petry, Jr., eds., *Business, Ethics, and the Environment: The Public Policy Debate* (New York: Quorum Books, 1990), pp. 223–32, at p. 224.

6. Gary E. Varner and Martha C. Monroe, "Ethical Perspectives on Captive Breeding: Is it For the Birds?" *Endangered Species UPDATE* vol. 8, no. 1 (November 1990), pp. 27–29, at p. 28.

7. J. Baird Callicott, "Animal Liberation and Environmental Ethics: Back Together Again," in *In Defense of the Land Ethic* (SUNY Press, 1989), pp. 49–59.

8. Abstract of "Moral Monism in Environmental Ethics Defended," presented to the Central Division Meeting of the American Philosophical Association,

April 24, 1993. *Proceedings and Addresses of the American Philosophical Association,* Vol. 66 (1993), No. 6, p. 69.

9. Bryan Norton, *Toward Unity Among Environmentalists* (Oxford University Press, 1991), p. 222.

10. Ibid., p. 223.

11. Gary E. Varner, "Environmental Law and the Eclipse of Land as Private Property," forthcoming in Frederick Ferré and Peter Hartel, eds., *Ethics and Environmental Policy: Theory Meets Practice* (forthcoming in 1994 from the University of Georgia Press).

12. James M. Jasper and Dorothy Nelkin, *The Animal Rights Crusade: The Growth of a Moral Protest* (New York: Free Press, 1992).

13. Norton, *Toward Unity Among Environmentalists,* p. 246, emphasis added.

14. Ron Howard, personal communication dated 18 June 1992.

15. It might be preferable to speak in terms of "necessary" and "optional" rather than "obligatory" and "permissible," because Howard's labels are intended to be descriptive, rather than normative. Also, note the qualification, in the penultimate section of this paper, that even among obligatory management species, hunting is not *always* necessary to prevent environmental damage.

16. "Animal Rights: Ignorance About Nature," *Audubon,* November 1990.

17. Julie A. Smith, "Wisconsin Greens Support Hunting—The Alliance Wonders Why?" *The Alliance News,* Vol. 8, No. 1 (February, 1991), pp. 1, 7.

18. Marian Bean, "Environmental Groups and Animal Rights," *The Alliance News,* Vol. 8, No. 1 (February, 1991), p. 6.

19. Title 5 (Hunting and Fishing), §62.062(a).

20. S.B. 179, Section 1; Texas Code, Title 2 (Parks and Recreational Areas), §13.001(b).

21. Lone Star Chapter of the Sierra Club, *State Capitol Report,* Vol. 10, No. 5 (May 1, 1993), p. 2.

22. Peter Singer, *Animal Liberation,* second edition (New York: Avon, 1990).

23. Peter Singer, *Practical Ethics,* second edition (Cambridge University Press, 1993).

24. *Animal Liberation,* pp. 18–19.

25. Ibid., p. 17.

26. Ibid., p. 125.

27. There are subtle but important differences among these terms. See Michael R. Bratman's treatment in his *Intentions, Plans, and Practical Reason* (Harvard University Press, 1987).

28. *Practical Ethics,* pp. 111–16, 118, and 132.

29. Ibid., pp. 95, 133.

30. Ibid., p. 132.

31. Gary Varner, "Localizing Desire," chapter two of *In Nature's Interests? Interests, Animal Rights, and Environmental Ethics*, in manuscript.

32. See the anecdote reported by Donald Griffin, *Animal Minds* (University of Chicago Press, 1992), pp. 64–65.

33. *Practical Ethics*, p. 132.

34. Sans the (possibly incoherent) obligation to maximize simultaneously two variables (minimize pain *and* maximize pleasure).

35. *Practical Ethics*, pp. 133–34, emphasis added.

36. *Animal Liberation*, p. 234. Two points about this argument. First, with regard to obligatory management species, it is not just "in special circumstances" that a population of animals "grows to such an extent that they damage their own environment and the prospects of their own survival, or that of other animals who share their habitat." The regularity with which this happens with obligatory management species is what separates them from permissive management species. Second, the choice is not simply between "allow[ing] hunters to kill some animals, inevitably wounding others in the process" and "reduc[ing] the fertility of the animals" by non-lethal means. Hunting regulations could be radically changed to minimize the wounding of animals. For instance, hunting could (in principle) be confined to bait stations with nearby blinds, from which hunters with high calibre, automatic weapons and telescopic sights would kill habituated animals in a selective way (e.g. only does and sicker animals).

37. Dale McCullough, "North American Deer Ecology: Fifty Years Later," in Thomas Tanner, ed., *Aldo Leopold: The Man and His Legacy* (Ankeny, Iowa: Soil Conservation Society of America, 1987), pp. 115–22, at p. 121.

38. "Report to American Wildlife Institute on the Utah and Oregon Wildlife Units," quoted in Susan Flader, *Thinking Like a Mountain: Aldo Leopold and the Evolution of an Ecological Attitude toward Deer, Wolves, and Forests* (Lincoln: University of Nebraska Press, 1978), p. 176.

39. Described in William Creed, *et al.*, "Harvest Management: The Wisconsin Experience," in Lowell K. Halls, ed., *White-Tailed Deer: Ecology and Management* (Harrisburg, Pennsylvania: Stackpole Books, 1984), pp. 211–42.

40. In Leopold's time, it was unusual to harvest over 40,000 animals a year. By the middle 1980's, by contrast, Wisconsin was consistently harvesting over a quarter of a million deer annually. Wisconsin Department of Natural Resources, *Wisconsin Game and Fur Harvest Summary, 1930–1986* (Madison, Wisconsin, 1987), pp. 3–4.

41. Here I am employing Michael Martin's analysis of conscientious law breaking, in "Ecosabotage and Civil Disobedience," *Environmental Ethics* 12 (1990), pp. 291–310, and adapting it to the case of brinkmanship.

42. Malcolm W. Browne, "New Animal Vaccines Spread Like Diseases," *New York Times*, 11 November 1991, pp. B5, B7.

43. Eugene C. Hargrove, "Preface," *The Animal Rights/Environmental Ethics Debate: The Environmental Perspective*, p. x. See also Callicott's review of Regan's book, *Environmental Ethics* 7 (1985), pp. 365–72.

44. Tom Regan, *The Case For Animal Rights* (University of California Press, 1983), p. 78 (emphasis in original).

45. Ibid., pp. 285–86.

46. The phrase "*commercial* animal agriculture" is Regan's. It is not obvious why the qualification "commercial" is included.

47. Regan, *Case for Animal Rights*, p. 357.

48. Regan, *Case for Animal Rights*, pp. 322 and 377, emphasis in original.

49. Dale Jamieson, "Rights, Justice, and Duties to Provide Assistance," *Ethics* 100 (1990), pp. 349–62, at pp. 351ff.

50. Regan, *Case for Animal Rights*, section 6.4.

51. Jamieson, "Rights, Justice, and Duties to Provide Assistance," pp. 349, 362

52. Dale McCullough, *The George Reserve Deer Herd: Population Ecology of a K-Selected Species* (Ann Arbor: University of Michigan Press, 1979).

53. McCullough, "Lessons from the George Reserve," pp. 219–22.

54. Gary E. Spencer, *Piney Woods Deer Management*, Texas Parks & Wildlife Department bulletin #7000–88 (February 1983), pp. 29, 32.

55. In bad years or on an already overstocked range, spike bucks (bucks 18 months or older with unforked antlers) are the result of poor nutrition rather than genetic "inferiority." But under good conditions such as those obtaining at or below I carrying capacity, bucks who produce spikes as yearlings will never achieve the same degree of antler development as fork-antlered yearlings.

56. McCullough argues that management for MSY simultaneously maximized trophy buck production

in the George Reserve. While agreeing that average rack size is correlated with average weight, McCullough denies that heavier bucks must be older: "Record bucks were produced not at high densities, which have the oldest individuals, but rather at the lowest densities . . . having the youngest age structure in both the population and the kill" ("Lessons from the George Reserve," p. 234). But this makes it unclear why he says, earlier in the same article, that "It is ironic that those opposing hunting are most incensed by trophy hunting . . . a practice that assures that the fewest deer will die from gunshots" (p. 230). By his own account, maintaining the population at I carrying capacity involves the *most* animals dying from gunshots.

57. Notice, however, that a single-minded emphasis on eliminating pain would seem to imply that hunting a population of sentient creatures to extinction would be a good thing, since this would prevent an infinite amount of pain. Arthur Schopenhauer, the German pessimist philosopher who placed a premium on the elimination of suffering, advocated extinction of the human race on this ground. Although the hedonistic utilitarian principle as usually formulated involves potentially inconsistent goals (minimizing pain *and* maximizing pleasure), it is therefore preferable to a negative utilitarian principle of minimize pain, simpliciter.

58. McCullough, "Lessons from the George Reserve," pp. 239–40.

59. McCullough, *The George Reserve Deer Herd*, pp. 160 and 172.

60. *Animal Liberation*, p. 17–18, quoted above. See also *Practical Ethics*, chapter three.

61. Albert Schweitzer, *The Philosophy of Civilization* (New York: MacMillan, 1955), p. 325.

62. Ibid., p. 316.

63. Ibid., p. 318.

64. Unanalyzed, the notion of "necessity" is of very little help, however. See Susan Finsen, "On Moderation," in Marc Bekoff and Dale Jamieson, eds., *Interpretation and Explanation in the Study of Animal Behavior*, vol. 2 (Boulder: University of Colorado Press, 1990), pp. 394–419.

65. See generally, my *In Nature's Interests? Interests, Animal Rights, and Environmental Ethics*, in manuscript.

66. Bryan Norton, "A New Paradigm for Environmental Management," in Robert Costanza and Bryan Norton, eds., *Ecosystem Health: New Goals for Environmental Management* (Island Press, 1992), pp. 23–41, at p. 24.

67. Ibid., p. 34.

68. Bryan Norton, *Why Preserve Natural Variety?* (Princeton University Press, 1987).

69. Norton, *Toward Unity Among Environmentalists*.

70. "A New Paradigm for Environmental Management," p. 26.

Second Thoughts on "A Triangular Affair"

J. Baird Callicott

Of the few moral philosophers who have given the land ethic a moment's serious thought, most have regarded it with horror because of its emphasis on the good of the community and its deemphasis on the welfare of individual members of the community. Not only are other sentient creatures members of the biotic community and subordinate to its integrity, beauty, and stability; so are *we*. Thus, according to Tom Regan, the land ethic is a clear case of "environmental fascism."[1]

Of course Leopold never intended the land ethic to have either inhumane or antihumanitarian implications or consequences. But whether he intended them or not, a logically consistent deduction from the theoretical premises of the land ethic might force such untoward conclusions. And give their magnitude and monstrosity, these derivations would constitute a *reductio ad absurdum* of the whole land ethic enterprise and entrench and reinforce our current human chauvinism and moral alienation from nature. If this is what membership in the biotic community entails, then all but the most radical misanthropes would surely want to opt out.

"The Conceptual Foundations of the Land Ethic," in *Companion to a Sand County Almanac: Interpretive and Critical Essays*, edited by J. Baird Callicott. Madison: University of Wisconsin Press, 1987, pp. 186–214. Reprinted by permission.

The land ethic, happily, implies neither inhumane nor inhuman consequences. That some philosophers think it must follows more from their own theoretical presuppositions than from the theoretical elements of the land ethic itself. Conventional modern ethical theory rests moral entitlement, as I earlier pointed out, on a criterion or qualification. If a candidate meets the criterion—rationality or sentiency are the most commonly posited—he, she, or it is entitled to equal moral standing with others who possess the same qualification in equal degree. Hence, reasoning in this philosophically orthodox way, and forcing Leopold's theory to conform: if human beings are, with other animals, plants, soils, and waters, equally members of the biotic community, and if community membership is the criterion of equal moral consideration, then not only do animals, plants, soils, and waters have equal (highly attenuated) "rights," but human beings are equally subject to the same subordination of individual welfare and rights in respect to the good of the community as a whole.

But the land ethic, as I have been at pains to point out, is heir to a line of moral analysis different from that institutionalized in contemporary moral philosophy. From the biosocial evolutionary analysis of ethics upon which Leopold builds the land ethic, it (the land ethic) neither replaces nor overrides previous accretions. Prior moral sensibilities and obligations attendant upon and correlative to prior strata of social involvement remain operative and preemptive.

Being citizens of the United States, or the United Kingdom, or the Soviet Union, or Venezuela, or some other nation-state, and therefore having national obligations and patriotic duties, does not mean that we are not also members of smaller communities or social groups—cities or townships, neighborhoods, and families—or that we are relieved of the peculiar moral responsibilities attendant upon and correlative to these memberships as well. Similarly, our recognition of the biotic community and our immersion in it does not imply that we do not also remain members of the human community—the "family of man" or "global village"—or that we are relieved of the attendant and correlative moral responsibilities of that membership, among them to respect universal human rights and uphold the principles of individual human worth and dignity. The biosocial development of morality does not grow in extent like an expanding balloon, leaving no trace of its previous boundaries, so much as like the circumference of a tree.[2] Each emergent, and larger, social unit is layered over the more primitive, and intimate, ones.

Moreover, as a general rule, the duties correlative to the inner social circles to which we belong eclipse those correlative to the rings farther from the heartwood when conflicts arise. Consider our moral revulsion when zealous ideological nationalists encourage children to turn their parents in to the authorities if their parents should dissent from the political or economic doctrines of the ruling party. A zealous environmentalist who advocated visiting war, famine, or pestilence on human populations (those existing somewhere else, of course) in the name of the integrity, beauty, and stability of the biotic community would be similarly perverse. Family obligations in general come before nationalistic duties and humanitarian obligations in general come before environmental duties. The land ethic, therefore, is not draconian or fascist. It does not cancel human morality. The land ethic may, however, as with any new accretion, demand choices which affect, in turn, the demands of the more interior social-ethical circles. Taxes and the military draft may conflict with family-level obligations. While the land ethic, certainly, does not cancel human morality, neither does it leave it unaffected.

Nor is the land ethic inhumane. Nonhuman fellow members of the biotic community have no "human rights," because they are not, by definition, members of the human community. As fellow members of the biotic community, however, they deserve respect.

How exactly to express or manifest respect, while at the same time abandoning our fellow members of the biotic community to their several fates or even actively consuming them for our own needs (and wants), or deliberately making them casualties of wildlife management for ecological integrity, is a difficult and delicate question.

Fortunately, American Indian and other traditional patterns of human-nature interaction provide rich and detailed models. Algonkian woodland peoples, for instance, represented animals, plants, birds, waters, and minerals as other-than-human persons engaged in reciprocal, mutually beneficial socioeconomic intercourse with human beings.[3]

Tokens of payment, together with expressions of apology, were routinely offered to the beings whom it was necessary for these Indians to exploit. Care not to waste the usable parts, and care in the disposal of unusable animal and plant remains, were also an aspect of the respectful, albeit necessarily consumptive, Algonkian relationship with fellow members of the land community. As I have more fully argued elsewhere, the Algonkian portrayal of human-nature relationships is, indeed, although certainly different in specifics, identical in abstract form to that recommended by Leopold in the land ethic. . . .[4]

Notes

1. Tom Regan, *The Case for Animal Rights* (Berkeley: University of California Press, 1983) 262, and "Ethical Vegetarianism," 291. See also Eliott Sober, "Philo-sophical Problems for Environmentalism," in Norton, *Preservation of Species*, see 173–94.

2. I owe the tree-ring analogy to Richard and Val Routley (now Sylvan and Plumwood, respectively), "Human Chauvinism and Environmental Ethics," in *Environmental Philosophy*, ed. D. Mannison, M. McRobbie, and R. Routley (Canberra: Department of Philosophy, Research School of the Social Sciences, Australian National University, 1980), 96–189. A good illustration of the balloon analogy may be found in Peter Singer, *The Expanding Circle: Ethics and Sociobiology* (New York: Farrar, Straus and Giroux, 1983).

3. For an elaboration see Thomas W. Overholt and J. Baird Callicott, *Clothed-in-Fur and Other Tales: An Introduction to an Ojibwa World View* (Washington, D.C.: University Press of America, 1982).

4. J. Baird Callicott, "Traditional American Indian and Western European Attitudes Toward Nature: An Overview," *Environmental Ethics* 4 (1982): 163–74.

D. THE VALUE OF INDIVIDUALS, SPECIES, AND ECOSYSTEMS

Let us think about whether intrinsic value of some sort can be assigned either to ecosystems as such, or to individual beings that are not even sentient. We tend to assign value to objects, or states of affairs that make possible, or foster, the development of certain processes in nature; or make possible the development of certain capacities or activities in the lives of individual animals, plants, or communities of such. To be less abstract, we may judge that a particular meadow has good soil and good water and a good climate *because* it enables certain plants to grow there—for example, a red oak tree. But if the oak were "deformed," twisted, and tiny (for a red oak)—that is, not "good of its kind"—we might withhold our judgment that the soil is good or that the climate is good, and so on. Thus we tend to judge that soil, water, climate, etc., are good when they are causally sufficient (other things being equal) for the growth and development of living things—and the development of the latter in a certain way—not, e.g., in ways that

we describe as "stunted" or "deformed." So, arguably, we judge certain stages of, and arrangements of, plants, animals, and energy flows as good, as normal, or as mature, because they allow, or have fostered, the development of living things in ways that strike us as normal or desirable. Matters are, of course, more complex. If the meadow grew healthy oaks and little else, we would not judge it a healthy meadow. More likely, we will judge the meadow healthy if and only if there is a certain variety of living creatures there and able to function a way we classify as "thriving" or at least "normal." Cautiously then, we may judge an ecosystem healthy if it is constituted as a network of relations between living things, the things exhibiting certain patterns of diversity and the things generally being rather healthy instances of their kind.

We are indirectly approaching two questions of considerable importance here. Is there some reasonably clear basis for saying that an *individual* plant or animal is healthy or is a good one of its kind? The other large question is whether there is some stage or state of affairs that we can objectively classify as mature or stable (and hence desirable) in the dynamic development of an *ecosystem.*

Before we pursue these matters further, let us ask why any of these matters are significant. The answer seems to be this. Many of us have some, however inarticulate, conception of what is involved in the planet's being healthy, or an ecosystem's being healthy. We tend to assume that the existence of a healthy planet and the existence of healthy ecosystems are good states of affairs—and thus worth promoting even if at some considerable cost. We may, as suggested, assume that a healthy ecosystem is one that fosters thriving individual plants and animals in ways that are perhaps sustainable indefinitely over time. We may believe, then, that under desirable conditions ecosystems develop in ways that are desirable, and that at a certain stage they are stable, biodiverse, and mature. "Invasion" by "exotic" plants and animals we may regard as "disruptive," "subversive of what is natural," and so on. In short, we have some conception of how ecosystems naturally develop or will under favorable conditions. This occurrence is good and its prevention is bad—so we commonly think. As hinted, we may believe that a good ecosystem is good *because* it is one that fosters the healthy development or thriving of individual plants and animals—or at least ones of a certain kind.[1] In this view, a good ecosystem is one that produces a biodiverse array of living things that generally get to reach their natural potential.

But is there, indeed, some natural potential that each living thing has? Can we speak of a "good of its kind" for our red oak, an amoeba, a giant panda, and a member of *Homo sapiens*? To raise these questions calls to mind earlier considerations. With regard to the vast majority of humans, we can speak of their lives being better or worse depending, in part, on whether they have been able to achieve a number of their consciously chosen projects—whether they have been able to fulfill many of their considered desires and all things they consider as goals. Many sentient beings are conscious to some degree, but are not able to consciously reflect upon the merits of different alternatives and adopt goals. Of these beings, we can still say that their lives go well or badly in the sense that how things go matters to them, i.e., consciously matters to them in that they are not indifferent to what occurs. Some states of affairs, to emphasize a point, *please* such beings and others do not, or even cause them discomfort or pain. But what can be said about the vast majority of living beings that are neither self-aware—conscious formulators and revisers of purposes and goals—nor are sentient? They lack conscious desires, but are they lacking in goals (or morally relevant interests)? What sense can we make of the notion that their lives are good or bad for them, that their condition is a healthy one, or that their interests are fulfilled or thwarted? Do they have a good of their own?

The belief that they do not is no doubt what has led many philosophers and others to conclude that it is only beings that are sentient, or those that are even more psychologically complex, that possess moral standing. From here it is a short leap to infer that if any other beings have value, it is only instrumental in nature. The question of what things or states of affairs have a good of their own is commonly linked, rightly or wrongly, to the questions of whether there are certain ends or goals, the fulfillment of which constitute a "good of its own" for the entity in question. We have noted that in one view, *ecosystems* have a certain natural end or goal that they move toward (although not as a matter of conscious choice)—an end describable as a state of maturity or stability. The criterion for the existence of this state or normal movement toward this state might be the existence and development of healthy living things (or perhaps efficient energy usage, or . . .). The criterion for what constitutes healthy *individuals,* in the case of those that are neither self-aware nor sentient, might be that they fulfill natural ends or get to exercise natural capacities.

There are serious difficulties with this line of thinking. First it may be claimed that there are no natural ends an organism tends to achieve. There is only cause and effect; under some conditions the plant grows this way, and under other conditions it grows that way. If we say that it realizes its natural capacities under favorable conditions, that may only be members of *Homo sapiens* projecting their own valuations onto nature (nonhuman nature). From this standpoint, if we say that the tomato is healthy, it is only because it suits our needs or desires; likewise for prime rib, or grade A tobacco. Is there, then, no objective basis for speaking of the interests of organisms that are not sentient?[2] If there is not, then we may have no reasonable basis for saying that the development of ecosystems in certain directions is a process of maturation or that one state is better than another, e.g., is healthy or is degraded. If there is no basis for thinking along such lines, one cannot defend certain environmental policy proposals on the ground that they will foster healthier ecosystems; the only basis for supporting one policy over another may be that one fosters the well-being of those beings who *do* have a good of their own—perhaps only sentient creatures, but this skeptical view is certainly contrary to a basic supposition of many environmental thinkers. It is contrary to those who believe that some ecosystem states are intrinsically better than others, and contrary to those who believe that the lives of even nonsentient creatures have a value of their own, and of those who believe that species or communities of beings have a good of their own not identifiable with, or reducible to, the good of individual sentient and/or self-aware creatures.

Our first selection, by historian Donald Worster, reviews some changes in the thinking of ecologists in the last half century. Prior to World War II a dominant view was Frederic Clement's "dynamic ecology," which saw ecosystems as developing through different stages, from pioneer organisms to the system's succession to a final "climax" stage. As Worster describes Clement's view, at that stage the "superorganism" achieves "the close integration and self-organizing capability of a single animal or plant" and exercises "some control over the nonliving world around it."[3] After World War II, Clement's view was elaborated by Eugene Odum, who saw the whole earth as an interlocking series of ecosystems, each of which share a kind of "strategy of development" aimed at achieving a large and diverse organic structure.[4] In short, ecosystems have a natural endpoint, one that involves stability and diversity. Nature is not chaotic. In this view, there are *desirable* natural states of affairs and humans can either live compatibly with them or they can subvert them.

For further reflection, it is worth flagging here, is the question of the relation of normative and empirical judgments. The empirical question concerns *how* nature works: Do we, in fact, find the kind of development and order in the short or long run suggested by Clements and Odum? Second, is the ostensibly balanced, complex, diverse "end-state" a *desirable* one? Can a case be made for the desirability of such states, even if there is nothing inevitable or even likely about their coming to exist?

As the reader may have surmised, there are post-Odum chapters to this story. In the last quarter of a century, many ecologists have adopted the view that *there is only change, not necessarily progress and order* "out there." We leave the details to Worster's discussion. He conjectures that the acceptance of the view that there is no natural order may be ideologically comfortable to those who fear that environmentalists or others may advocate authoritarian methods to prevent human disruptions of the development of natural communities, e.g., forcing farms to be eliminated and allowing the land to return to a more natural state.

Whatever we conclude about the empirical question, we observe that we cannot avoid deciding how we humans *should* choose to influence the course of environmental developments. We have, do, and will exercise a profound effect—arguably the most profound effect on the planet exercised collectively by any single species on earth since the inception of life about 3.5 billion years ago.

As noted earlier, the question arises as to whether we can find "purposiveness," in some sense of that elusive word (cf. "function," "end," "goal," and "outcome"), not only (if at all) in the changes of ecosystems over time, but in those beings *incapable* of sentience or conscious choice (who can adopt goals for reasons, have purposes, etc.). If many plants and animals lack conscious goals, why should we speak of their interests? Can we speak of what is good or bad for them? Are their lives better or worse, without reference to human desires or values? To put an edge on our inquiry, is it the case that clams, paramecia, burying beetles, or HIV viruses *have* interests, and, if so, are these interests *morally significant* (and if so, *how* significant)? If such nonconscious beings do have interests, we may have a basis for concluding that a certain ecosystem state is desirable, e.g., one that fosters the joint realization of such interests. So this inquiry is relevant to questions noted in connection with Worster's essay.

Gary Varner, in the essay reprinted here, "Biological Functions and Biological Interests," argues against accepting a "conative" conception of interests that requires that to have interests, a being must have *conscious* wishes or desires. As we have observed earlier, anyone who attributes moral standing to all living things (Paul Taylor, Aldo Leopold, and the deep ecologists, among others), will reject the conative conception or hold a view incompatible with it. But what are the alternatives? If, for example, plants have needs (few

dispute this point), can a nonarbitrary criterion be specified that will indicate what is and what is not in a plant's interest? Further, if so, why think such interests are morally relevant? Varner takes on the tasks of defending affirmative answers to these questions. As he notes, his effort is a partial defense of "biocentric individualism," the view "that all and only living organisms have interests."[5] In the end, he argues that an organism's *biological interests* depend on the etiology of its species and the fact that the possession of certain functions is *adaptive* for that species. Suffice it to say, these matters turn out to be difficult, and some of the arguments are rooted in recent discussions of "teleological explanations" in the philosophy of biology. In Varner's view, what is in the interest of a plant is an objective, nonarbitrary matter, and not a function of human purposes or desires with respect to that organism. If this is correct and these interests are morally nontrivial ones, then they are important factors in determining the direction of environmental policy decisions.

Those who recognize morally relevant interests in all or most living individuals may or may not recognize interests or some sort of intrinsic value in more complex entities such as species or ecosystems. Worster's essay suggests a tendency in recent ecology to deny the existence of natural end-states in ecosystems, states that some have thought especially valuable. Still, a significant amount of environmental thinking (Aldo Leopold, John Rodman, Bryan Norton, J. Baird Callicott, earlier Holmes Rolston, James Heffernan, Laura Westra, Lawrence E. Johnson,[6] and the deep ecologists) tends to assume that we go seriously astray if we focus only on individuals and affirms that we must think "ecologically," e.g., in terms of complex dynamic systems: holistic webs of changing relations between mutually dependent beings.

Varner also claims that "no sober ecologist today believes that ecosystems are in any literal sense organisms."[7] If they are not, it is tempting to think that they cannot have interests. Sympathetic to this point of view is Harley Cahen in his essay (reprinted here), "Against the Moral Considerabilty of Ecosystems." Cahen emphasizes that we must distinguish between an ecosystem's *by-products* and any *goals* that it might have, i.e., the effects of the behavior of the parts of the ecosystem. Like Varner, Cahen explores the resistant-to-analysis concept of *goal-directedness* and allows that it can be attributed to individual organisms unproblematically (no need to postulate "vitalism" in nature, no spooky metaphysics, etc.) but denies that it can be reasonably attributed to ecosystems. Arguably, there are only by-products of ecosystems, no goals, and if no goals, no interests that might be of moral significance. Indeed, this is Cahen's view. In his essay he also argues that the best understanding we have today of the process of natural selection is that it operates only at the level of individual organisms. All things considered we cannot, in his view, attribute interests to ecosystems in spite of their appearance of striving toward stability, etc. Whether Cahen's view, if correct, drives us toward certain forms of biocentric individualism is another matter. What place it leaves for holistic considerations in an adequate environmental ethic is also a further question.

We do not wish to suggest that questions about species and questions about ecosystems can be handled in one fell swoop, or that there are no relevant differences; this is an editorial invitation to caution when reading Rolston, who discusses both issues in the excerpt we have reprinted here that we have entitled "Duties to Endangered Species."[8] When a common individual pigeon dies, only an individual dies; when the last passenger pigeon died, a whole species ceased to be. A unique genetic line going back millions of years was extinguished forever on planet earth. Whatever constitutes a species, it is tempting to think that a species is not simply identical with the set of individuals that happen to instantiate it at a given moment. As Rolston notes, when a wolf is destroying an individual

elk, an individual member of the species of elk is being harmed, but in fact the species may not be in danger; indeed, it may well be in the process of being improved (e.g., the genetically less well-endowed is being sloughed off) by the wolf's predation.

Do we have duties to certain or all species? Do we have duties to preserve certain or all species? If so, are they duties *with respect to* the species but not duties owed *to* the species themselves? Analogously, one might have a duty not to destroy one's neighbor's car but it is a duty *owed to* the neighbor, not the car. Rolston claims that the elimination of a species is a kind of superkilling; a killing beyond the killing of individuals. Further, in many cases it is we humans who are the superkillers; he says of us, "One form of life has never endangered so many others." However, in line with our earlier discussion, are species bearers of interests? What do we mean (or could we mean) when we speak of "the good of the species?" Must we deviate here from "individualism"? In order to answer, we may need more clarity about what we mean by an "individualist view."

Rolston argues for the value of the species that exist on the planet. He asks " . . . ought not *Homo sapiens* value this host of species as something with a claim to their care in its own right? A reverence for life seems called for." Rolston's "in its own right" qualification suggests that he does *not* view a duty to preserve species as a duty owed to, say, future generations of humans and thus a duty merely *with respect to* species. Can we owe duties directly to an entity that is not an individual living thing? Perhaps something, therefore, that does not itself possess interests? Does it matter *to whom* the duty is owed? Is not the more important question *whether* we have such duties and, if so, how stringent such duties are? But if so, can we decide that matter *without* knowing to whom we owe duties?[9]

The tension between individualist positions and holistic, or nonindividualist, views is evident. There are challenging questions here, the answers to which may affect our attitudes about what deserves preservation and, hence, ultimately how we should decide questions of environmental policy—public matters as well as questions about how we decide to live our "private" lives.[10] What may be clearest of all is that some states of affairs on this planet are morally preferable to others and that some possible futures for the earth are better than others, even if we are less clear about the exact basis of our duties to bring them about. At the least, we must consider the numbers of living beings that possess moral standing, their interaction, the phenomenon of mutual interdependence, the facts of natural selection, and the extraordinary, unparalleled, enduring influence of human activity during our recent moment is the course of life on earth.

NOTES

1. Various qualifications may be in order; some might insist that an ecosystem should not be judged a good one if it fosters the thriving of the smallpox virus. What to say about this we leave open.

2. If there is an objective basis for speaking of the interests of organisms that are not sentient, we may still insist that the question of whether those interests (their fulfillment) is morally significant and, if so, how significant.

3. Donald Worster, "The Ecology of Order and Chaos," *Environmental History Review* 14, Nos. 1–2, p. 4.

4. Ibid., p. 5.

5. Strictly he defends the view that *virtually* all living things have interests.

6. See especially Lawrence E. Johnson's essay, "Toward the Moral Considerability of Species and Ecosystems," reprinted In Donald VanDeVeer and Christine Pierce, *The Environmental Ethics and Policy Book: Ethics, Ecology, Economics* (Belmont, Cal.: Wadsworth Publishing Co., 1994), pp. 493–501. It appeared originally in *Environmental Ethics* 14, no. 2 (Summer 1992), pp. 145–57.

7. See the last page of Varner's essay.

8. Our selection is from Rolston's important book, *Environmental Ethics: Duties to and Values in the Natural World* (Philadelphia: Temple University Press, 1988), pp. 126–49. We have edited out only a paragraph or so from what is Chapter 4 in his book.

9. We remind readers of Bryan Norton's position in his essay reprinted in IIIB, in which he calls attention to the *indeterminacy* of any members of future generations to which it is often said we have serious duties, e.g., to pass on a fair share of what is of value—"stock" of one sort or another. To emphasize one matter, Norton's argument poses a difficulty for the view that we have duties *only* to existing individuals (one form of "individualism").

10. It is worth observing here that of so-called "private choices," virtually all have public consequences—if by "public" we mean "environmental" ones, e.g., the kind of car one buys, the choice to fly, the type of toilet one purchases, etc.

The Ecology of Order and Chaos

Donald Worster

The science of ecology has had a popular impact unlike that of any other academic field of research. Consider the extraordinary ubiquity of the word itself: it has appeared in the most everyday places and the most astonishing, on day-glo T-shirts, in corporate advertising, and on bridge abutments. It has changed the language of politics and philosophy—springing up in a number of countries are political groups that are self-identified as "Ecology Parties." Yet who ever proposed forming a political party named after comparative linguistics or advanced paleontology? On several continents we have a philosophical movement termed "Deep Ecology," but nowhere has anyone announced a movement for "Deep Entomology" or "Deep Polish Literature." Why has this funny little word, ecol-

Environmental History Review, Vol. 14, Nos. 1–2 (Spring/Summer 1990), pp. 1, 3–16. Reprinted by permission.

ogy, coined by an obscure 19th-century German scientist, acquired so powerful a cultural resonance, so widespread a following?

Behind the persistent enthusiasm for ecology, I believe, lies the hope that this science can offer a great deal more than a pile of data. It is supposed to offer a pathway to a kind of moral enlightenment that we can call, for the purposes of simplicity, "conservation." The expectation did not originate with the public but first appeared among eminent scientists within the field. For instance, in his 1935 book *Deserts on the March,* the noted University of Oklahoma, and later Yale, botanist Paul Sears urged Americans to take ecology seriously, promoting it in their universities and making it part of their governing process. . . .

At the time *Deserts on the March* appeared in print, and through the time of its second and even third edition, the dominant name in the field of American ecology was that of Frederic L. Clements, who more than any other individual introduced scientific ecology into our national academic life. He called his approach "dynamic ecology," meaning it was concerned with change and evolution in the landscape. At its heart Clements's ecology dealt with the process of vegetational succession—the sequence of plant communities that appear on a piece of soil, newly made or disturbed, beginning with the first pioneer communities that invade and get a foothold.[1] Here is how I have defined the essence of the Clementsian paradigm:

> Change upon change became the inescapable principle of Clements's science. Yet he also insisted stubbornly and vigorously on the notion that the natural landscape must eventually reach a vaguely final climax stage. Nature's course, he contended, is not an aimless wandering to and fro but a steady flow toward stability that can be exactly plotted by the scientist.[2]

Most interestingly, Clements referred to that final climax stage as a "superorganism," implying that the assemblage of plants had achieved the close integration of parts, the self-organizing capability, of a single animal or plant. In some unique sense, it had become a live, coherent thing, not a mere collection of atomistic individuals, and exercised some control over the nonliving world around it, as organisms do.

Until well after World War II Clements's climax theory dominated ecological thought in this country.[3] Pick up almost any textbook in the field written forty, or even thirty, years ago, and you will likely find mention of the climax. It was this theory that Paul Sears had studied and took to be the core lesson of ecology that his county ecologists should teach their fellow citizens: that nature tends toward a climax state and that, as far as practicable, they should learn to respect and preserve it. Sears wrote that the chief work of the scientist ought to be to show "the unbalance which man has produced on this continent" and to lead people back to some approximation of nature's original health and stability.[4]

But then, beginning in the 1940s, while Clements and his ideas were still in the ascendent, a few scientists began trying to speak a new vocabulary. Words like "energy flow," "trophic levels," and "ecosystem" appeared in the leading journals, and they indicated a view of nature shaped more by physics than botany. Within another decade or two nature came to be widely seen as a flow of energy and nutrients through a physical or thermodynamic system. The early figures prominent in shaping this new view included C. Juday, Raymond Lindeman, and G. Evelyn Hutchinson. But perhaps its most influential exponent was Eugene P. Odum, hailing from North Carolina and Georgia, discovering in his southern saltwater marshes, tidal estuaries, and abandoned cotton fields the animating, pulsating force of the sun, the global flux of energy. In 1953 Odum published the first edition of his famous textbook, *The Fundamentals of Ecology.*[5] In 1966 he became president of the Ecological Society of America.

By now anyone in the United States who regularly reads a newspaper or magazine has come to know at least a few of Odum's ideas, for they furnish the main themes in our popular understanding of ecology, beginning with the sovereign idea of the ecosystem. Odum defined the ecosystem as "any unit that includes all of the organisms (i.e., the 'community') in a given area interacting with the physical environment so that a flow of energy leads to clearly defined trophic structure, biotic diversity, and material cycles (i.e., exchange of materials between living and nonliving parts) within the system."[6] The whole earth, he argued, is organized into an interlocking series of such "ecosystems," ranging in size from a small pond to so vast an expanse as the Brazilian rainforest.

What all those ecosystems have in common is a "strategy of development," a kind of game plan that gives nature an overall direction. That strategy is, in Odum's words, "directed toward achieving as large and diverse an organic structure as is possible within the limits set by the available energy input and the prevailing physical conditions of existence."[7] Every single ecosystem, he believed, is either moving toward or has already achieved that goal. It is a clear, coherent, and easily observable strategy; and it ends in the happy state of order.

Nature's strategy, Odum added, leads finally to a world of mutualism and cooperation among the organisms inhabiting an area. From an early stage of competing against one another, they evolve toward a more symbiotic relationship. They learn, as it were, to work together to control their surrounding environment, making it more and more suitable as a habitat, until at last they have the power to protect themselves from its stressful cycles of drought and flood, winter and summer, cold and heat. Odum called that point "homeostasis." To achieve it, the living components of an ecosystem must evolve a structure of interrelatedness and cooperation that can, to some extent, manage the physical world—manage it for maximum efficiency and mutual benefit.

I have described this set of ideas as a break from the past, but that is misleading. Odum may have used different terms than Clements, may even have had a radically different vision of nature at times; but he did not repudiate Clements's notion that nature moves toward order and harmony. In the place of the theory of the "climax" stage he put the theory of the "mature ecosystem." His nature may have appeared more as an automated factory than as a Clementsian super-organism, but like its predecessor it tends toward order.

The theory of the ecosystem presented a very clear set of standards as to what constituted order and disorder, which Odum set forth in the form of a "tabular model of ecological succession." When the ecosystem reaches its end point of homeostasis, his table shows, it expends less energy on increasing production and more on furnishing protection from external vicissitudes: that is, the biomass in an area reaches a steady level, neither increasing nor decreasing, and the emphasis in the system is on keeping it that way—on maintaining a kind of no-growth economy. Then the little, aggressive, weedy organisms common at an early stage in development (the r-selected species) give way to larger, steadier creatures (K-selected species), who may have less potential for fast growth and explosive reproduction but also better talents at surviving in dense settlements and keeping the place on an even keel.[8] At that point there is supposed to be more diversity in the community—i.e., a greater array of species. And there is less loss of nutrients to the outside; nitrogen, phosphorous, and calcium all stay in circulation within the ecosystem rather than leaking out. Those are some of the key indicators of ecological order, all of them susceptible to precise measurement. The suggestion was implicit but clear that if one interfered too much with nature's strategy of development, the effects might be costly: a serious loss of nutrients, a decline in species diversity, an end to biomass stability. In short, the ecosystem would be damaged.

The most likely source of that damage was no mystery to Odum: it was human beings trying to force up the production of useful commodities and stupidly risking the destruction of their life support system.

> Man has generally been preoccupied
> with obtaining as much "production"
> from the landscape as possible, by developing and maintaining early successional
> types of ecosystems, usually monocultures. But, of course, man does not live by
> food and fiber alone; he also needs a balanced CO_2–O_2 atmosphere, the climatic
> buffer provided by oceans and masses of
> vegetation, and clean (that is, unproductive) water for cultural and industrial
> uses. Many essential life-cycle resources,
> not to mention recreational and esthetic
> needs, are best provided man by the less
> "productive" landscapes. In other words,
> the landscape is not just a supply depot
> but is also the *oikos*—the home—in which
> we must live.[9]

Odum's view of nature as a series of balanced ecosystems, achieved or in the making, led him to take a strong stand in favor of preserving the landscape in as nearly natural a condition as possible. He suggested the need for substantial restraint on human activity—for environmental planning "on a rational and scientific basis." For him as for Paul Sears, ecology must be taught to the public and made the foundation of education, economics, and politics; America and other countries must be "ecologized."

Of course not every one who adopted the ecosystem approach to ecology ended up where Odum did. Quite the contrary, many found the ecosystem idea a wonderful instrument for promoting global technocracy. Experts familiar with the ecosystem and skilled in its manipulation, it was hoped in some quarters, could manage the entire planet for improved efficiency. "Governing" all of nature with the aid of rational science was the dream of these ecosystem technocrats.[10] But technocratic management was not the chief lesson, I believe, the public learned in Professor Odum's classroom; most came away devoted, as he was, to preserving large parts of nature in an unmanaged state and sure that they had been given a strong scientific rationale, as well as knowledge base, to do it. We must defend the world's endangered ecosystems, they insisted. We must safeguard the integrity of the Greater Yellowstone ecosystem, the Chesapeake Bay ecosystem, the Serengeti ecosystem. We must protect species diversity, biomass stability, and calcium recycling. We must make the world safe for K-species.[11]

That was the rallying cry of environmentalists and ecologists alike in the 1960s and early 1970s, when it seemed that the great coming struggle would be between what was left of the great pristine nature, delicately balanced in Odum's beautifully rational ecosystems, and a human race bent on mindless, greedy destruction. A decade or two later the situation changed considerably. There are still environmental threats around, to be sure, and they are more dangerous than ever. The newspapers inform us of continuing disasters like the massive 1989 oil spill in Alaska's Prince William Sound, and reporters persist in using words like "ecosystem" and "balance" and "fragility" to describe such disasters. So do many scientists, who continue to acknowledge their theoretical indebtedness to Odum. For instance, in a recent British poll, 447 ecologists out of 645 questioned ranked the "eco-system" one of the most important concepts their discipline has contributed to our understanding of the natural world; indeed, "ecosystem" ranked first on their list, drawing more votes than nineteen other leading concepts.[12] But all the same, and despite the persistence of environmental problems, Odum's ecosystem is no longer the main theme in research or teaching in the science. A survey of recent ecology textbooks shows that the concept is not even mentioned in one leading work and has a much diminished place in the others.[13]

Ecology is not the same as it was. A rather drastic change has been going on in this science of late—a radical shifting away from the thinking of Eugene Odum's generation, away from its assumptions of order and predictability, a shifting toward what we might call a new *ecology of chaos.*

In July 1973, the *Journal of the Arnold Arboretum* published an article by two scientists associated with the Massachusetts Audubon Society, William Drury and Ian Nisbet, and it challenged Odum's ecology fundamentally. The title of the article was simply "Succession," indicating that old subject of observed sequences in plant and animal associations. With both Frederic Clements and Eugene Odum, succession had been taken to be the straight and narrow road to equilibrium. Drury and Nisbet disagreed completely with that assumption. Their observations, drawn particularly from northeastern temperate forests, strongly suggested that the process of ecological succession does not lead anywhere. Change is without any determinable direction and goes on forever, never reaching a point of stability. They found no evidence of any progressive development in nature: no progressive increase over time in biomass stabilization, no progressive diversification of species, no progressive movement toward a greater cohesiveness in plant and animal communities, nor toward a greater success in regulating the environment. Indeed, they found none of the criteria Odum had posited for mature ecosystems. The forest, they insisted, no matter what its age, is nothing but an erratic, shifting mosaic of trees and other plants. In their words, "most of the phenomena of succession should be understood as resulting from the differential growth, differential survival, and perhaps differential dispersal of species adapted to grow at different points on stress gradients."[14] In other words, they could see lots of individual species, each doing its thing, but they could locate no emergent collectivity, nor any strategy to achieve one.

Prominent among their authorities supporting this view was the nearly forgotten name of Henry A. Gleason, a taxonomist who, in 1926, had challenged Frederic Clements and his organismic theory of the climax in an article entitled, "The Individualistic Concept of the Plant Association." Gleason had argued that we live in a world of constant flux and impermanence, not one tending toward Clements's climaxes. There is no such thing, he argued, as balance or equilibrium or steady-state. Each and every plant association is nothing but a temporary gathering of strangers, a clustering of species unrelated to one another, here for a brief while today, on their way somewhere else tomorrow. "Each . . . species of plant is a law unto itself" he wrote.[15] We look for cooperation in nature and we find only competition. We look for organized wholes, and we can discover only loose atoms and fragments. We hope for order and discern only a mishmash of conjoining species, all seeking their own advantage in utter disregard of others.

Thanks in part to Drury and Nisbet, this "individualistic" view was reborn in the mid-1970s and, during the past decade, it became the core idea of what some scientists hailed as a new, revolutionary paradigm in ecology. To promote it, they attacked the traditional notion of succession; for to reject that notion was to reject the larger idea that organic nature tends toward order. In 1977 two more biologists, Joseph Connell and Ralph Slatyer, continued the attack, denying the old claim that an invading community of pioneering species, the first stage in Clements's sequence, works to prepare the ground for its successors, like a group of Daniel Boones blazing the trail for civilization. The first comers, Connell and Slatyer maintained, manage in most cases to stake out their claims and successfully defend them; they do not give way to a later, superior group of colonists. Only when the pioneers die or are damaged by natural disturbances, thus releasing the resources they have monopolized, can latecomers find a foothold and get established.[16]

As this assault on the old thinking gathered momentum, the word "disturbance" began to appear more frequently in the scientific literature and be taken far more seriously. "Disturbance" was not a common subject in Odum's heyday, and it almost never appeared in combination with the adjective "natural." Now, however, it was as though scientists were out looking strenuously for signs of disturbance in nature—especially signs of disturbance that were not caused by humans—and they were finding it everywhere. . . .

One of the most provocative and impressive expressions of the new post-Odum ecology is a book of essays edited by S. T. A. Pickett and P. S. White, *The Ecology of Natural Disturbance and Patch Dynamics* (published in 1985). . . . The message in all these papers is consistent: The climax notion is dead, the ecosystem has receded in usefulness, and in their place we have the idea of the lowly "patch." Nature should be regarded as a landscape of patches, big and little, patches of all textures and colors, a patchwork quilt of living things, changing continually through time and space, responding to an unceasing barrage of perturbations. The stitches in that quilt never hold for long.

Now, of course, scientists have known about gophers and winds, the Ice Age and droughts for a considerable time. Yet heretofore they have not let those disruptions spoil their theories of balanced plant and animal associations, and we must ask why that was so. Why did Clements and Odum tend to dismiss such forces as climatic change, at least of the less catastrophic sort, as threats to the order of nature? Why have their successors, on the other hand, tended to put so much emphasis on those same changes, to the point that they often see nothing but instability in the landscape?

One clue comes from the fact that many of these disturbance boosters are not and have never been ecosystem scientists; they received their training in the subfield of population biology and reflect the growing confidence, methodological maturity, and influence of that subfield.[17] When they look at a forest, the population ecologists see only the trees. See them and count them—so many white pines, so many hemlocks, so many maples and birches. They insist that if we know all there is to know about individual species that constitute a forest, and can measure their lives in precise, quantitative terms, we will know all there is to know about that forest. . . .

There is another reason for the paradigmatic shift I have been describing, though I suggest it quite tentatively and can offer only sketchy evidence for it. For some scientists, a nature characterized by highly individualistic associations, constant disturbance, and incessant change may be more ideologically satisfying than Odum's ecosystem, with its stress on cooperation, social organization, and environmentalism. A case in point is the very successful popularizer of contemporary ecology, Paul Colinvaux, author of *Why Big Fierce Animals Are Rare* (1978). His chapter on succession begins with these lines: "If the planners really get hold of us so that they can stamp out all individual liberty and do what they like with our land, they might decide that whole counties full of inferior farms should be put back into forest." Clearly, he is not enthusiastic about land-use planning or forest restoration. And he ends that same chapter with these remarkably revealing and self-assured words:

> We can now . . . explain all the intriguing, predictable events of plant successions in simple, matter of fact, Darwinian ways. Everything that happens in successions comes about because all the different species go about earning their livings as best they may, each in its own individual manner. What look like community properties are in fact the summed results of all these bits of private enterprise.[18]

Apparently, if this example is any indication, the social Darwinists are back on the scene, and at least some of them are ecologists, and at least some of their opposition to Odum's science may have to do with a revulsion toward its political implications, including its attractiveness for environmentalists. Colinvaux is very clear about the need to get some distance between himself and groups like the Sierra Club. . . .

I wish, however, that the emergence of the new post-Odum ecology could be explained so simply in those two ways: as a triumph of reductive population dynamics over holistic consciousness, or as a triumph of social Darwinist or entrepreneurial ideology over a commitment to environmental preservation. There is, it seems, more going on than that, and it is going on all through the natural sciences— biology, astronomy, physics—perhaps going on through all modern technological societies. It is nothing less than the discovery of chaos. Nature, many have begun to believe, is *fundamentally* erratic, discontinuous, and unpredictable. It is full

of seemingly random events that elude our models of how things are supposed to work. As a result, the unexpected keeps hitting us in the face. Clouds collect and disperse, rain falls or doesn't fall, disregarding our careful weather predictions, and we cannot explain why. Cars suddenly bunch up on the freeway, and the traffic controllers fly into a frenzy. A man's heart beats regularly year after year, then abruptly begins to skip a beat now and then. A ping pong ball bounces off the table in an unexpected direction. Each little snowflake falling out of the sky turns out to be completely unlike any other. Those are ways in which nature seems, in contrast to all our previous theories and methods, to be chaotic. If the ultimate test of any body of scientific knowledge is its ability to predict events, then all the sciences and pseudo-sciences—physics, chemistry, climatology, economics, ecology—fail the test regularly. They all have been announcing laws, designing models, predicting what an individual atom or person is supposed to do; and now, increasingly, they are beginning to confess that the world never quite behaves the way it is supposed to do.

Making sense of this situation is the task of an altogether new kind of inquiry calling itself the science of chaos. Some say it portends a revolution in thinking equivalent to quantum mechanics or relativity. Like those other 20th-century revolutions, the science of chaos rejects tenets going back as far as the days of Sir Isaac Newton. In fact, what is occurring may be not two or three separate revolutions but a single revolution against all the principles, laws, models, and applications of classical science, the science ushered in by the great Scientific Revolution of the 17th century.[19] For centuries we have assumed that nature, despite a few appearances to the contrary, is a perfectly predictable system of linear, rational order. Give us an adequate number of facts, scientists have said, and we can describe that order in complete detail—can plot the lines along which everything moves and the speed of that movement and the collisions that will occur. Even Darwin's theory of evolution, which in the last century challenged much of the Newtonian worldview, left intact many people's confidence that order would prevail at last in the evolution of life; that out of the tangled history of competitive struggle would come progress, harmony, and stability. Now that traditional assumption may have broken down irretrievably. For whatever reason, whether because empirical data suggests it or because extra-scientific cultural trends do—the experience of so much rapid social change in our daily lives—scientists are beginning to focus on what they had long managed to avoid seeing. The world is more complex than we imagined, they say, and indeed, some would add, ever can imagine.[20] . . .

The entire study of chaos began in 1961, with efforts to simulate weather and climate patterns on a computer at MIT. There, meteorologist Edward Lorenz came up with his now famous "Butterfly Effect," the notion that a butterfly stirring the air today in a Beijing park can transform storm systems next month in New York City. Scientists call this phenomenon "sensitive dependence on initial conditions." What it means is that tiny differences in input can quickly become substantial differences in output. A corollary is that we cannot know, even with all our artificial intelligence apparatus, every one of the tiny differences that have occurred or are occurring at any place or point in time; nor can we know which tiny differences will produce which substantial differences in output. Beyond a short range, say, of two or three days from now, our predictions are not worth the paper they are written on.

The implications of this "Butterfly Effect" for ecology are profound. If a single flap of an insect's wings in China can lead to a torrential downpour in New York, then what might it do to the Greater Yellowstone Ecosystem? What can ecologists possibly know about all the forces impinging on, or about to impinge on, any piece of land? What can they safely ignore and what must they pay attention to? What distant, invisible, minuscule events may even now be happening that will change the organization of plant and animal life in our back yards? This is the predicament, and the challenge, presented by the science of chaos, and it is altering the imagination of ecologists dramatically.

John Muir once declared, "When we try to pick out anything by itself, we find it hitched to everything else in the universe."[21] For him, that was a manifestation of an infinitely wise plan in which everything functioned with perfect harmony. The new ecology of chaos, though impressed like Muir with interdependency, does not share his view of "an infinitely wise plan" that controls and shapes everything into order. There is no plan, today's scientists say, no harmony apparent in the events of

nature. If there is order in the universe—and there will no longer be any science if all faith in order vanishes—it is going to be much more difficult to locate and describe than we thought.

For Muir, the clear lesson of cosmic complexity was that humans ought to love and preserve nature just as it is. The lessons of the new ecology, in contrast, are not at all clear. Does it promote, in Ilya Prigogine and Isabelle Stenger's words, "a renewal of nature," a less hierarchical view of life, and a set of "new relations between man and nature and between man and man"?[22] Or does it increase our alienation from the world, our withdrawal into post-modernist doubt and self-consciousness? What is there to love or preserve in a universe of chaos? How are people supposed to behave in such a universe? If such is the kind of place we inhabit, why not go ahead with all our private ambitions, free of any fear that we may be doing special damage? What, after all, does the phrase "environmental damage" mean in a world of so much natural chaos? Does the tradition of environmentalism to which Muir belonged, along with so many other nature writers and ecologists of the past—people like Paul Sears, Eugene Odum, Aldo Leopold, and Rachel Carson—make sense any longer? I have no space here to attempt to answer those questions or to make predictions but only issue a warning that they are too important to be left for scientist alone to answer. Ecology today, no more than in the past, can be assumed to be all-knowing or all-wise or eternally true.

Whether they are true or false, permanent or passingly fashionable, it does seem entirely possible that these changes in scientific thinking toward an emphasis on chaos will not produce any easing of the environmentalist's concern. Though words like ecosystem or climax may fade away and some new vocabulary take their place, the fear of risk and danger will likely become greater than ever. Most of us are intuitively aware, whether we can put our fears into mathematical formulae or not, that the technological power we have accumulated is *destructively* chaotic; not irrationally, we fear it and fear what it can to do us as well as the rest of nature.[23] It may be that we moderns, after absorbing the lessons of today's science, find we cannot love nature quite so easily as Muir did; but it may also be that we have discovered more reason than ever to respect it—to respect its baffling complexity, its inherent unpredictability, its daily turbulence. And to flap our own wings in it a little more gently.

Notes

1. This is the theme in particular of Clements's book *Plant Succession* (Washington: Carnegie Institution, 1916).

2. Donald Worster, *Nature's Economy: A History of Ecological Ideas* (New York: Cambridge University Press, 1977).

3. Clements's major rival for influence in the United States was Henry Chandler Cowles of the University of Chicago, whose first paper on ecological succession appeared in 1899. The best study of Cowles's ideas is J. Ronald Engel, *Sacred Sands: The Struggle for Community in the Indiana Dunes* (Middletown, CT: Wesleyan University Press, 1983), pp. 137–59. Engel describes him as having a less deterministic, more pluralistic notion of succession, one that "opened the way to a more creative role for human beings in nature's evolutionary adventure." (p. 150). See also Ronald C. Tobey, *Saving the Prairies: The Life Cycle of the Founding School of American Plant Ecology, 1895–1955* (Berkeley: University of California, 1981).

4. Paul Sears, *Deserts on the March*, 3rd ed. (Norman: University of Oklahoma Press, 1959), p. 162.

5. This book was co-authored with his brother Howard T. Odum, and it went through two more editions, the last appearing in 1971.

6. Eugene P. Odum, *Fundamentals of Ecology* (Philadelphia: W. B. Saunders, 1971), p. 8.

7. Odum, "The Strategy of Ecosystem Development," *Science*, 164 (18 April 1969): 266.

8. The terms "K-selection" and "r-selection" came from Robert MacArthur and Edward O. Wilson, *Theory of Island Biogeography* (Princeton: Princeton University Press, 1967). Along with Odum, MacArthur was the leading spokesman during the 1950s and 60s for the view of nature as a series of thermodynamically balanced ecosystems.

9. Odum, "Strategy of Ecosystem Development," p. 266. See also Odum, "Trends Expected in Stressed Ecosystems," *BioScience*, 35 (July/August 1985): 419–422.

10. A book of that title was published by Earl F. Murphy, *Governing Nature* (Chicago: Quadrangle Books, 1967). From time to time, Eugene Odum himself seems to have caught that ambition or leant his support to it, and it was certainly central to the work of his brother, Howard T. Odum. On this theme see

Peter J. Taylor, "Technocratic Optimism, H. T. Odum, and the Partial Transformation of Ecological Metaphor after World War II," *Journal of the History of Biology*, 21 (Summer 1988): 213–44.

11. A very influential popularization of Odum's view of nature (though he is never actually referred to in it) is Barry Commoner's *The Closing Circle: Nature, Man, and Technology* (New York: Alfred A. Knopf, 1971). See in particular the discussion of the four "laws" of ecology, pp. 33–46.

12. Communication from Malcolm Cherrett, *Ecology*, 70 (March 1989): 41–42.

13. See Michael Begon, John L. Harper, and Colin R. Townsend, *Ecology: Individuals, Populations, and Communities* (Sunderland, Mass.: Sinauer, 1986). In another textbook, Odum's views are presented critically as the traditional approach: R. J. Putnam and S. D. Wratten, *Principles of Ecology* (Berkeley: University of California Press, 1984). More loyal to the ecosystem model are Paul Ehrlich and Jonathan Roughgarden, *The Science of Ecology* (New York: Macmillan, 1987); and Robert Leo Smith, *Elements of Ecology*, 2nd ed. (New York: Harper & Row, 1986), though the latter admits that he has shifted from an "ecosystem approach" to more of an "evolutionary approach" (p. xiii).

14. William H. Drury and Ian C. T. Nisbet, "Succession," *Journal of the Arnold Arboretum*, 54 (July 1973): 360.

15. H. A. Gleason, "The Individualistic Concept of the Plant Association," *Bulletin of the Torrey Botanical Club*, 53 (1926): 25. A later version of the same article appeared in *American Midland Naturalist*, 21 (1939): 92–110.

16. Joseph H. Connell and Ralph O. Slatyer, "Mechanisms of Succession in Natural Communities and Their Role in Community Stability and Organization," *The American Naturalist*, 111 (November-December 1977): 1119–1144.

17. For the rise of population ecology see Sharon E. Kingsland, *Modeling Nature: Episodes in the History of Population Ecology* (Chicago: University of Chicago Press, 1985).

18. Paul Colinvaux, *Why Big Fierce Animals Are Rare: An Ecologist's Perspective* (Princeton: Princeton University Press, 1978), pp. 117, 135.

19. This argument is made with great intellectual force by Ilya Prigogine and Isabelle Stengers, *Order Out of Chaos: Man's New Dialogue with Nature* (Boulder: Shambala/New Science Library, 1984). Prigogine won the Nobel Prize in 1977 for his work on the thermodynamics of nonequilibrium systems.

20. An excellent account of the change in thinking is James Gleick, *Chaos: The Making of a New Science* (New York: Viking, 1987). I have drawn on his explanation extensively here. What Gleick does not explore are the striking intellectual parallels between chaotic theory in science and post-modern discourse in literature and philosophy. Post-Modernism is a sensibility that has abandoned the historic search for unity and order in nature, taking an ironic view of existence and debunking all established faiths. According to Todd Gitlin, "Post-Modernism reflects the fact that a new moral structure has not yet been built and our culture has not yet found a language for articulating the new understandings we are trying, haltingly, to live with. It objects to all principles, all commitments, all crusades—in the name of an unconscientious evasion." On the other hand, and more positively, the new sensibility leads to emphasis on democratic coexistence: "a new 'moral ecology'—that in the preserva-

tion of the other is a condition for the preservation of the self." Gitlin, "Post-Modernism: The Stenography of Surfaces," *New Perspectives Quarterly*, 6 (Spring 1989): 57, 59.

21. John Muir, *My First Summer in the Sierra* (1911; Boston: Houghton Mifflin, 1944), p. 157.

22. Prigogine and Stengers, pp. 312–13.

23. Much of the alarm that Sears and Odum, among others, expressed has shifted to a global perspective, and the older equilibrium thinking has been taken up by scientists concerned about the geo- and biochemical condition of the planet as a whole and about human threats, particularly from the burning of fossil fuels, to its stability. One of the most influential texts in this new development is James Lovelock's *Gaia: A New Look at Life on Earth* (Oxford: Oxford University Press, 1979). See also Edward Goldsmith, "Gaia: Some Implications for Theoretical Ecology," *The Ecologist*, 18, nos. 2/3 (1988): 64–74.

Biological Functions and Biological Interests

Gary E. Varner

I. Feinberg's Dictum

In a widely cited article, Kenneth Goodpaster makes the following point about the "intelligibility" of attributing interests to plants:

> There is no absurdity in imagining the representation of the needs of a tree for sun and water in the face of a proposal to cut it down or pave its immediate radius for a parking lot. We might of course, on reflection, decide to go ahead and cut it down or do the paving, but there is hardly an intelligibility problem about representing the tree's interest in our deciding not to.

And immediately thereafter, he writes:

> In the face of their obvious tendencies to maintain and heal themselves, it is very difficult to reject the idea of interests on the part of trees (and plants generally) in remaining alive.[1]

I agree that there is no problem making *intelligible* a proposal to attribute interests to plants because

they have such tendencies, but from this it does not follow that there is no *absurdity* in it. For if we are going to attribute interests to plants on the grounds that they exhibit goal-directed behavior, then by the same token we will have to assign an interest in regulating temperature to a home heating system, and to do so would constitute a *reductio ad absurdum* of the proposal.

Goodpaster's remarks dramatize the challenges which face a defender of the claim that plants have interests. Since simple artifacts clearly have needs in certain senses of the word, two things will have to be established before we can understand how the fact that plants have needs suffices to show that they have interests. The first is an empirical claim:

> *The empirical claim:* plants have needs in some sense in which artifacts do not.

The second is a normative claim:

> *The normative claim:* this difference qualifies plants, but not artifacts, for direct moral consideration.[2]

Southern Journal of Philosophy, Vol. XXVIII, No. 2 (1990), 251–270. Reprinted by permission.

Goodpaster's remarks dramatize these twin challenges. But there is another challenge implicit in establishing the empirical claim, a problem that may have been in the back of Joel Feinberg's mind when he wrote a puzzling section of his seminal essay on "The Rights of Animals and Unborn Generations." Early in the essay Feinberg appears to endorse a disjunctive criterion for the possession of interests. He says that a being can have interests only if it has conations, but under the concept of "conative life" he includes both "*conscious* wishes, desires, and hopes; or urges and impulses" and "*unconscious* drives, aims, and goals; or latent tendencies, direction[s] of growth, and natural fulfillments."[3] In the section on plants, however, Feinberg insists that only *conscious* conations can define interests. Feinberg's insistence on drawing up the wagons around sentience has puzzled several commentators.[4] He gives very little by way of argument for abandoning the second disjunct of his earlier criterion. I suspect that a particular epistemological problem was troubling Feinberg when he wrote the section, and that this, more so than any argument he explicitly gives, explains his insistence on a sentience criterion for the possession of interests.

This interpretation explains what is otherwise a very puzzling remark in the "Vegetables" section of Feinberg's essay. Early in the section, Feinberg admits that

> Plants . . . are not "mere things"; they are vital objects with inherited biological propensities determining their natural growth . . . They grow and develop according to the laws of their own nature.[5]

Later in the section, however, he insists that "Plants may need things in order to discharge their functions, but their functions are assigned by human interests, not their own."[6] Given that in the same paragraph he defines a thing's needs, in a morally neutral sense, as whatever is "necessary to the achievement of [its] goals, or to the performance of [its] functions,"[7] this is a very puzzling remark to make. If plants are "vital objects with inherited biological propensities," then why can it not be said that they have needs, at least in this morally neutral sense, quite independently of human interests in them?

Feinberg's puzzling remark, which I refer to as "Feinberg's dictum," has drawn a response from every author writing in defense of the claim that plants have interests. Yet I think that most of that ink has been wasted, because most of these responses ignore the epistemological problem. What Feinberg may have meant to say, I am suggesting, is not that plants *have* no functions aside from those which humans assign to them, but rather that plants' functions cannot be *specified* on any other basis, and that therefore any attempt to identify plants' interests with the fulfillment of their functions is doomed. The problem, in sum, is this:

> *The epistemological problem:* even if plants *have* needs in some sense that artifacts do not, is it possible to specify, in a non-arbitrary way, what these needs are?

If we interpret Feinberg's dictum this way, then it becomes evident why certain responses commentators have made to his dictum fall very short of the mark.

In section II, I first look at several of these responses and evaluate them simultaneously as responses to Feinberg's dictum and as responses to the epistemological problem. In the process, I identify and develop a response to Feinberg's dictum that simultaneously solves the epistemological problem and supports the empirical claim. However, this will not by itself establish the claim that plants have interests. After I argue that plants have needs in a sense in which artifacts do not and that a non-arbitrary criterion of what is and is not in a plant's interests can be given by appealing to what does and does not fulfill these needs, I will then show why the "interests" so described are morally significant.

My arguments provide a partial and tentative defense of biocentric individualism, by which I mean the view that all and only living organisms have interests. The defense is partial because, in a few special cases, some living organisms will not have interests on the view I advance. However, I argue, these cases are rare in a way that renders them insignificant. The defense is tentative because I cannot establish the normative claim with deductive certainty. I show only that it would be plausible to respond to a problem with some views that restrict interests to sentient creatures in a way that commits us to recognizing that all (or, in light of the above qualification, *very nearly all*) living organisms have interests. This is, logically, a significant weakness of my argument. However, my primary goal is to show that an individual who expresses concern for the interests of plants and "lower" animals[8] need not be guilty of maudlin sentimentalism and need not be committing a variant of what Ralph Barton Perry called "the pathetic fallacy."[9] My tentative defense of the normative claim, coupled with my defense of the empirical claim and my response to the epistemological problem, suffices to show this.

Before proceeding, I offer two general clarifying remarks. First, since the burden of this paper is to explain how non-conscious beings such as plants can have interests, and since our paradigm of an interest involves the endeavors of *conscious* beings, it is useful to introduce a terminological distinction between those interests that do involve consciousness in some way and those that do not. Tom Regan marks this difference by distinguishing between conscious "preference interests" on the one hand, and "welfare interests" on the other.[10] Although I use Regan's term for the former, I instead call the latter *biological interests*. My reason is that "welfare" suggests too strongly something like the integrated satisfaction of all an individual's interests, and when I say that "*A* has a biological interest in *X*" I mean only that *X* is in *one* of *A*'s interests, that *X* would be good for *A* in some respect or other, rather than that *X* would be best for *A*, all things considered.

Second, I leave for another paper all questions of how morally significant preference interests may be in comparison to biological interests, or plants' interests in comparison to those of "higher" animals such as human beings. Here I seek only to establish that plants are morally considerable, not that their interests qualify them for any particular level of moral significance.[11]

II. Responding to Feinberg's Dictum

In a paper with the provocative title, "Animal Chauvinism, Plant-Regarding Ethics and the Torture of Trees," the aptly-named J. L. Arbor says the following in response to Feinberg's dictum:

it is clearly an error to put trees into the class of objects which have their ends

determined outside themselves by conscious beings. Trees, like animals and other plants, but unlike machines, have end-states which are not decided by human beings. Given the right conditions and barring interference they will in the course of natural events reach this state. There is nothing mysterious or improper about insisting that whatever helps trees achieve their natural end-state is in their interest.[12]

Arbor agrees with Feinberg that the "end-states" of artifacts are "decided by human beings," while insisting that plants have "natural end-states."

There is an initial air of plausibility to this claim. The view that there is one course of development that is "natural" for each species of organism (including all plants), in the sense that individuals of that species will inevitably develop along that course unless "external" factors "interfere," *is* a feature of popular consciousness. If shown two mature chestnut trees, for instance, a thin, gangly one living in a crowded woodlot, and a massive, spreading specimen in an open field, we have a strong tendency to say that the latter is the "natural" state of a chestnut tree, and we expect a botanist to be able to explain why the gangly one has "failed" to develop "naturally."

However, Arbor's move fails as a response to Feinberg's dictum because it rests on an essentialist view of organic species which, as Elliott Sober has detailed, is thoroughly discredited in modern biology. The essentialist treats variations within a species as deviations from "natural tendencies" caused by "interfering forces." The problem for the biological essentialist is that, in light of modern biological theory, it is impossible to draw a non-arbitrary distinction between "natural tendencies" on the one hand and "interfering forces" on the other.

The natural tendencies of a species cannot be defined in terms of a specific genotype, because the genetic variability found among members of any given species—specially species that reproduce sexually—is staggering. But neither can the distinction be drawn in terms of the phenotypes that develop given a specific genotype. The problem, as Sober puts it, is that

when one looks to genetic theory for a conception of the relation between genotype and phenotype, one finds no such distinction between natural states and states which are the results of interference. One finds, instead, the *norm of reaction,* which graphs the different phenotypic results that a genotype can have in different environments. . . . Each of the [phenotypes] indicated in the norm of reaction is as "natural" as any other . . .[13]

That is why a botanist's explanation of the chestnut trees' different "forms," that is their different phenotypes, would (perhaps to our disappointment) advert to something like the effect root constriction has on the size and shape of these trees' canopies, rather than to "interference" with a "natural" course of development.

An importantly different response to Feinberg's dictum is offered by Paul Taylor in his recent book on environmental ethics. Taylor writes:

> Though [many] machines are understandable as teleological systems . . . [t]he ends they are programmed to accomplish are not purposes of their own, independent of the human purposes for which they were made . . . [and] it is precisely this fact that separates them from living things. . . . The ends and purposes of machines are built into them by their human creators. It is the original purposes of humans that determine the structures and hence the teleological functions of those machines. . . . [A living thing] seeks its own ends in a way that is not true of any teleologically structured mechanism. It is in terms of *its* goals that we can give teleological explanations of why it does what it does. We cannot do the same for machines, since any such explanation must ultimately refer to the goals their human producers had in mind when they made the machines.[14]

Taylor claims that while both plants and artifacts exhibit goal-directed behavior, the goals of artifacts cannot be identified without reference to the intentions of their human designers, whereas plants' goals can be identified without reference to any human purpose, and that in this sense plants' goals are their own in a way that artifacts' are not.

While not biologically naive like Arbor's response to Feinberg, Taylor's response is no more convincing. For on any viable analysis of what goal-directed behavior is, Taylor's claim about the goals of artifacts is going to turn out to be false. Certain artifacts are clearly goal-directed, and their goals can be objectively specified quite independently of reference to any human purpose. Consider, for instance, Ernest Nagel's paradigmatic analysis in *The Structure of Science.* Nagel argues that

> [the] characteristic feature of such systems is that they continue to manifest a certain state or property G (or that they exhibit a persistence of development "in the direction" of attaining G) in the face of a relatively extensive class of changes in their external environments or in some of their internal parts—changes which, if not compensated for by internal modification in the system, would result in the disappearance of G (or in an altered direction of development of the systems).[15]

Although Nagel does not argue the point specifically, on his analysis, not only is it true that "the distinctive features of goal-directed systems can be formulated without invoking purposes and goals as dynamic agents,"[16] it is also true that the goals of goal-directed artifacts can be identified without having ultimately to refer to the goals of their human producers or users.

For example, suppose that a team of alien scientists reach earth after a nuclear holocaust and discover a supply of functional Stinger missiles in a Middle Eastern cave. With a little experimental ingenuity, they will soon discover that the missiles seek heat. Not wanting to put a fine point on it, the scientist assigned to investigate the missiles will tell the head scientist that "The missiles follow any available heat source," or "The missiles turn in order to follow any available heat source." Such explanations of the missiles' flight paths will be teleological, and the relevant goal will have been accurately identified, but without the scientists ever understanding a thing about contemporary aerial warfare.

Moreover, it is not always the case that "The ends and purposes of machines are built into them by their human creators," as Taylor claims. If the Pentagon revealed that the inventor of the Stinger missile intended to build a ballistic missile for gathering weather data, that would not affect the accuracy of the foregoing explanation of its flight path, so long as the finished product in fact follows any available heat source.

Goodpaster's own response to Feinberg's dictum is similar to Taylor's, but, significantly, he speaks of "tasks" rather than "goals":

> As if it were human interests that assigned to trees the tasks of growth or maintenance! The interests at stake are clearly those of the living things themselves, not simply those of the owners or users or other human persons involved.[17]

The significance is this: insofar as Goodpaster is talking about biological functions rather than goals or end-states, it *is* possible to draw a sharp distinction between all artifacts, on the one hand, and all living organisms on the other. None of Feinberg's critics carefully distinguishes between ends, or goals, on the one hand, and *functions* on the other. The reason may be simply that Feinberg fails to draw the distinction in his essay. Yet philosophers of biology have emphasized that a distinction must be drawn, and once the distinction is made, a more promising approach to the empirical claim becomes obvious.

Although there is general agreement that functional claims in biology are grounded somehow in reproductive success, it is clear that the functions of a given organism's organs or subsystems[18] cannot be unpacked in terms of behavior directed to this goal. For if they were, then statements like "The function of a mule's eyes is to enable it to see" would all be false. Mules are sterile. So if functional claims about individual organisms' organs were based on the reproductive fitness of the individual in question, mules' organs would have no functions.

Larry Wright has proposed a plausible analysis which avoids this problem. Wright claims that attributions of biological function are best understood by looking at attributions of functions to artifacts. On Wright's view, for both biological and artificial functions, "The function of S is X" is true if and only if

a) X is a consequence of S's being there, and

b) S is there because it results in X.

In short, on Wright's analysis, the function of a subsystem is "that particular consequence of its being where it is which explains why it is there."[19]

For artifacts, in filling in the "because" in clause (b) we advert to conscious selection. The consequence of a floor mounted headlight dimmer switch being where it is and having the form it has (being connected in certain ways to the car's electrical system), which explains why it is there, is that it allows the headlights to be switched between high-beam and low-beam. The designer consciously chose to put it there because its being there would have this consequence.[20]

Wright's claim is that attributions of biological function began as useful, but purely metaphorical attributions of analogous intentions to organisms, the metaphorical overtones of which were dropped once the theory of natural selection provided us with an alternative and nonmetaphorical way of filling in the "because" in clause (b). The consequence of woodpeckers' toes being where they are (in opposing pairs, rather than in a 3/1 opposition as in perching birds), which explains why they are where they are, is that their being so arranged helps woodpeckers cling to the trunks of trees. Although no designer consciously chose to arrange them this way, this arrangement evolved because it was adaptive for creatures filling the woodpeckers' ecological niche.

On Wright's analysis, functional explanations concern the etiology of the system in question. Thus they are backward-looking, and this is why his analysis neatly overcomes the problem involving sterile organisms. Sight has been selected for in horses and in donkeys, and this is what explains the presence of eyeballs in the mule whether or not they contribute to the reproductive fitness of the mule.

For present purposes, what is most important about Wright's analysis is that it provides us with a clear response to Feinberg's dictum *and* a clear answer to the epistemological problem. I propose the following criterion for the identification of biological interests:

> An organism A has a welfare interest in X if and only if X is the biological function of some organ or subsystem S of A, where X is the biological function of S in A if and only if

a) *X* is a consequence of *A*'s having *S*, and

b) *A* has *S* because achieving *X* was adaptive for *A*'s ancestors.

This view provides us with a clear answer to the epistemological problem because on it, what interests a given plant has depends entirely on its species' etiology. Admittedly a great deal of evolutionary research would have to go into giving a detailed and accurate answer to the question, "Exactly what is and is not in the interests of this plant?" But on the view defended here, the answer to this question is objective, non-arbitrary, and—at least in principle—fairly precise and specific. The proposed view also provides us with an answer to Feinberg's dictum and support for the empirical claim, because all and only living organisms are subject to natural selection. We can say that plants have needs in a sense in which artifacts do not, because plants' subsystems have biological functions, but artifacts' subsystems do not.

Selective breeding of domesticated organisms might appear to constitute a difficult case for the view I am defending. For here, it might seem, what once were biological functions, determined by natural selection, are replaced by, or transformed into, artificial functions determined by human interests. This sort of worry begins to fade, however, as soon as we look at concrete examples.

In most cases, selective breeding does not alter the biological functions of any subsystem of the organism. Consider, for example, what selective breeding has done to the dairy cow. Today's heifers give much more milk on much less feed, but the selective breeding has not made it false that the (or at least a) biological function of the cows' mammary glands is to nourish their calves. The etiology of the species is still the same at the relevant point. Cows do not have mammary glands because milk fetches a profit for farmers; they have mammary glands because mammary glands produce the milk that sustains their calves.

In most cases selective breeding operates in this way: it alters some norm of reaction without thereby altering or eliminating any biological function. But now suppose that a strain of domestic turkey is produced with breast muscles so large that they cannot fly, like a powerlifter so muscle bound that he can no longer comb his hair. In such a case, I admit, these turkeys' breast muscles have lost their original biological function due to selective breeding. The capacity for flight is no longer a consequence of the turkeys' having breast muscles, and therefore condition (a) in Wright's criterion is no longer met.[21] So selective breeding can affect the biological functions of an organism's subsystems. Moreover, in such a case it is true that the breast muscles have in the process acquired an artificial function. Farmers' getting more profit out of each turkey is a consequence of the turkeys' having the larger breast muscles, and the larger breast muscles are there because farmers wanted more profitable turkeys.

In such a case, I admit, selective breeding has quite literally replaced the biological function of the breast muscles with an artificial function. But this is a very limited sort of case, and even here the organisms still have many subsystems with biological functions. It is still true, for instance, that they have gizzards, stomachs, and intestines, because these organs result in their being nourished. Suppose, however, that in producing breast muscles so large that the turkeys can no longer fly, we have also made it impossible for them to breed except via artificial insemination. In such a case, it might seem plausible to argue, "natural" selection is no longer operative at all, and, since all further evolution of the birds is contingent upon the conscious choices of human beings, such thoroughly domesticated animals are, as Baird Callicott has claimed, "living artifacts." In a contentious passage of his essay, "Animal Liberation: A Triangular Affair," Callicott writes:

> Domestic animals are creations of man. They are living artifacts. . . . There is thus something profoundly incoherent . . . in the complaint of some animal liberationists that the "natural behavior" of chickens and bobby calves is cruelly frustrated on factory farms. It would make almost as much sense to speak of the natural behavior of tables and chairs.[22]

The example of the turkeys who cannot breed is more dramatic than, but not relevantly different from, the case of some wild animals like the California condor, and once we recognize and account for this similarity, the turkey example loses its force. The entire population of California condors is now in a captive breeding program designed to maintain maximum genetic diversity within the species. These birds breed when and only when the conservation biologists in charge of the program decide that they should. But do we want to say that here "natural selection" is no longer occurring? I think not, and the reason, apparently, is that the "natural" in "natural selection" does not mean "unaffected by *human* organisms." "Natural selection" refers to the way biological organisms evolve via random genetic mutation under selective pressure from their environment, whether the environment is under human control or not. (This explains, by the way, the propriety of referring to the functions identified by Wright's criterion as *"biological* functions" rather than *"natural* functions.")

It is therefore a mistake to conclude, in the case of the turkeys, that selective breeding has *replaced* all biological functions with artificial ones. Rather, what has happened is that some artificial functions have been added onto the original biological functions of the birds' various organs and subsystems. The turkey example, therefore, in no way threatens my response to Feinberg's dictum. So long as all and only living organisms evolve via random genetic mutation under reproductive pressure from their environments, all and only living organisms will have subsystems with biological functions.

When the claim is restated in this way it becomes apparent that only in one very limited kind of case will a living organism fail to have any biological functions. On Wright's criterion first mutations are accidents, which acquire biological functions only via subsequent selective pressure.[23] This leads Christopher Boorse to object that if a species "simply sprang into existence by an unparalleled saltation" then, on Wright's view, its organs would have no functions.[24] However, for this to be literally true of an organism, it would have to have no ancestors, or at least share no non-vestigial organs or subsystems with its ancestors. Although it is *possible* that researchers will one day create a complete complement of DNA *ex nihilo*, all currently foreseeable DNA research either modifies one small portion of a given species' DNA or "splices" in genetic material from another organism, and in either case many biological functions are left unaffected.

Neither selective breeding nor currently foreseeable genetic research constitutes a significant challenge to the claim that all and only living

organisms have biological interests, where these interests are identified with the fulfillment of the biological functions of their component subsystems, and where these functions are in turn identified using Wright's criterion. Using Wright's criterion, then, I have (a) developed a response to Feinberg's dictum that (b) supports the empirical claim while (c) solving the epistemological problem. I have (a) explained a sense in which plants have functions that are not assigned to them by human interests, I have (b) shown that plants have "needs" in a sense in which artifacts do not, namely what they need to fulfill the biological functions of their component subsystems, and I have (c) shown that a non-arbitrary account of what is and is not in a plant's interests can be given when a plant is said to have biological interests in the fulfillment of the biological functions of its subsystems. It remains to be shown, however, that these "biological interests" are interests in a morally relevant sense. Why should we think that the biological functions of a plant's subsystems define interests?

III. Supporting the Normative Claim

After responding to Feinberg's dictum in the first section of "The Good of Trees," Robin Attfield asks us to imagine that the last sentient organism on Earth is a man who "hew[s] down with an axe the last tree of its kind, a hitherto healthy elm . . . which could propagate its kind if left unassaulted." He concludes that

> Most people who face the question would . . . conclude that the world would be the poorer for this act of the 'last man' and that it would be wrong . . . And if, without being swayed by the interests of sentient creatures, we share in these conclusions and reactions, [then] we must also conclude that the interests of trees are of moral significance.[25]

A specific problem with Attfield's thought experiment is that it is not clear why we must attribute *interests* to the tree in order to explain this intuition. The flourishing of trees can be of moral significance without the trees having interests. Lilly-Marlene

Russow has convincingly argued that specimens of some endangered species have high aesthetic value.[26] Would "most people" still think it was wrong of the last man to chop down the tree if it were not "the last . . . of its kind"? To the extent that peoples' intuitions change when the question is rephrased in this way, the explanation may be that they think the tree in question is a thing of beauty, and that this gives it some moral significance, albeit of a different (and probably weaker) kind than it would have if it had interests. (Notice that Attfield himself says that "the world would be the poorer for this act of the 'last man'," not that the tree itself would be harmed.)

Apart from the specifics of Attfield's thought experiment, however, I have general misgivings about using appeals to intuitions about such cases. I admit that widely shared intuitions about "normal" cases—cases involving human beings—can serve as fixed points against which to check our moral theories, but I think that the more "marginal" the case in question, the more a theorist should feel called upon to follow theory, rather than intuition. Since the progression from non-human animals to plants provides an example of what I mean by increasingly "marginal" subjects of moral judgments, I maintain that a theorist can always feel justified in following a theory in the face of contrary intuitions about the interests of plants and "lower" animals.

This problem can be avoided, however, by arguing that the biological functions of a *human being's* body define morally significant interests of that individual, quite independently of his or her (or anyone else's) conscious mental states. J. L. Arbor appears to be taking such a tack when she or he asks us to imagine a society in which certain children are systematically mutilated in ways that normally would be quite painful, but only after brain surgery has left them incapable of feeling the pain and unhappiness which would otherwise attend these operations and mutilations. Arbor concludes that to unpack the "wrong" done to these children as a violation of an indirect duty to other, normal children and adults, would be "an artificial and awkward way of responding to a straightforward ethical intuition."[27]

While Arbor's approach is more promising than Attfield's, it does not provide the strongest possible defense of the normative claim. The reason is that perfectly good sense can be made of the claim that direct duties to the children are being violated in this case, without abandoning a sentience criterion of moral considerability. The sentientist need only appeal to the *loss* of potential, positive experiences of pleasure and/or desire satisfaction in order to claim that the children have been harmed. The sentientist can say that these children have been made drastically less well off than they would otherwise have been, and that they have in that sense been seriously harmed. The strongest possible defense of the normative claim would be one that questions the adequacy of a mental state theory of benefit and harm in relation to human beings.

I therefore believe that Kenneth Goodpaster is on the right track when he suggests that allegiance to a hedonistic theory of individual welfare is responsible for Western philosophers' general reluctance to recognize the moral considerability of non-sentient organisms. Since only creatures capable of being benefitted and harmed can be the objects of direct duties of beneficence and non-maleficence, Western authors' general allegiance to a hedonistic conception of individual welfare would explain their reluctance to recognize the moral considerability of non-sentient creatures.[28] However, there are two problems with Goodpaster's argument, problems that seriously weaken it as a defense of the normative claim.

The first problem is that Goodpaster offers no specific argument *against* the adequacy of a hedonistic conception of welfare and in favor of a non-sentientist conception.[29] Without such an argument, the normative claim is very weakly supported, because no argument has been offered for thinking that the alternative, non-sentientist conception of welfare is superior to the hedonistic conception.

The second problem is that in characterizing as "hedonistic" the dominant theory of individual welfare, Goodpaster has cast his net too narrowly. A common conception of individual welfare runs through Henry Sidgwick's *The Methods of Ethics,* John Rawls' *A Theory of Justice,* and Richard A. Brandt's *A Theory of the Good and the Right,* a conception that is sentientist without being narrowly hedonistic. On it, to say that "X is in A's interest" or that "X would be good for A" can mean either

1) *A* now desires (or prefers) *X*,

or

2) *A* would desire (or prefer) *X*, if *A* were

a) adequately informed, and

b) sufficiently impartial across phases of his or her life.

Where clause (1) is satisfied, *X* is said to be good for *A* in a qualified sense, good in some respect or other. Where clause (2) is satisfied, *X* is said to be best for *A*, or good for *A*, all things considered. Harms are in turn conceived as whatever prevents the fulfillment of some actual desire (this is harm in a qualified, conditional sense) or whatever prevents the fulfillment of one's enlightened (clause (2)) desires (this is harm in an unqualified, unconditional sense, and since, presumably, one's enlightened desires form an integrated set, harms of this sort vary greatly in degree).[30] I call this *the mental state theory of welfare*.

Since it would be more plausible to say that this, rather than a narrowly hedonistic conception of welfare, is the dominant conception in contemporary Western philosophy, the strongest defense of the normative claim would be one that called it into question, rather than the hedonistic conception, and that (in light of my earlier remarks) did so without appealing to intuitions about plants. In the remainder of this section, I advance such an argument. My argument consists in showing how this mental state theory of welfare is inferior in two ways to an account of welfare that incorporates the view proffered in the preceding section. I argue that the best account of individual welfare would be one that recognizes the existence of *two* kinds of interests, *preference* interests on the one hand and *biological* interests on the other, where the latter are defined in terms of the account proffered in the preceding section and the former are defined in terms of one's actual and/or enlightened desires (for present purposes it does not matter which).

On this alternative conception of welfare, which I call *the biological theory of welfare*, to say that "*X* is in *A*'s interest" or that "*X* would be good for *A*" can mean either

1) *A* has a biological interest in *X*, meaning that *X* would fulfill a biological func-

tion of one or more of *A*'s organs or subsystems,

or

2) *A* has a preference interest in *X*, meaning that either

a) *A* now desires (or prefers) *X*, or

b) *A* would desire (or prefer) *X*, if *A* were

i) adequately informed, and

ii) sufficiently impartial across phases of his or her or its life.

Here I ignore the issues of how morally significant biological interests are *vis à vis* preference interests and of what constitutes an individual's good on the whole. My criticism of the mental state theory of welfare is independent of these issues, discussion of which I leave to another occasion.[31]

Consider the case of Maude, an unusually intelligent, acutely rational, and generally farsighted young adult, with a strong desire to smoke. Concerned for her welfare, we bring to her attention the fact that the best available evidence indicates that this smoking will shorten her life by a certain number of years. Suppose that Maude really takes this fact to heart, that (in Sidgwick's words) "the consequences [of her conduct are] accurately foreseen and adequately realized in [her] imagination at the present point in time,"[32] but that she nevertheless goes right on smoking.

On the mental state theory of harm, no sense whatsoever can be made of the claim that Maude's smoking is bad for her. For she does not now desire to stop smoking, and on the mental state theory of harm this implies that continuing to smoke is only bad for her if her enlightened preference would be to stop smoking. But by hypothesis, Maude is both adequately informed and sufficiently impartial across phases of her life. Therefore, her actual preference *is* her enlightened preference, and therefore, on the mental state theory of harm, Maude's smoking is in no way bad for her.

This criticism of the mental state theory of welfare does not imply that the biological theory of welfare is true. All it implies is that we must accept *some* alternative to the mental state theory of welfare, and a conjunction of the proffered account of biological interests with an account of preference interests is just one candidate. But such a view would provide a clear and concise account of the sense in which Maude's smoking is bad for her: regardless of her preferences, smoking is always bad for an individual insofar as it impairs effective oxygenation of one's blood by one's lungs, and this is at least one biological function of one's lungs.

Another virtue of the biological theory of welfare is that it illuminates an important distinction among our interests which the mental state theory of welfare does not capture. It would seem that, in talking about some of our interests—particularly those we label "needs"—substitution of coreferential expressions preserves truth value.[33] For instance, if it is in my interest to ingest at least 10 milligrams of vitamin C each day (the amount needed to prevent scurvy) then it is also in my interest to ingest at least 10 milligrams of ascorbic acid each day. But desire contexts are referentially opaque. Where A desires X and $X = Y$, it can still be false that A desires Y. Nineteenth-century mariners desired to avoid scurvy, and they desired citrus fruit to that end. Ingesting ascorbic acid in crystalline form would have accomplished the same end, but they had no desire for ascorbic acid. So what sense can be made of the claim that 19th-century mariners needed to ingest 10 milligrams of ascorbic acid each day? On the mental state theory of welfare, it would have to be claimed that *if they had known* that it was the ascorbic acid in citrus fruit that prevented scurvy, then the sailors would have formed a desire for it specifically. But would they? When offered ascorbic acid in crystalline form, the most rational of sailors is unlikely to form a desire for it, unless and until citrus fruit becomes unavailable. And this means, on the mental state theory of welfare, that a sailor would first come to need ascorbic acid when the fruit runs out. By contrast, on the biological theory of welfare we can say that getting 10 milligrams of ascorbic acid each day is a biological interest of every sailor, whether or not he desires it, because of the role the vitamin plays in the functioning of his various organs and subsystems. The biological theory of welfare allows us to draw a clear distinction between a class of interests which are referentially opaque (preference interests) and a class of those which are not (biological interests).[34]

My defense of the proffered view is indeed tentative. I have argued only that some alternative to the mental state theory of welfare must be accepted, and that my account of welfare interests has some points to recommend it in this regard. I have argued that the conjunction of a desire-based account of *preference* interests with the proffered account of *biological* interests provides a theory of individual welfare which is in certain ways superior to that provided by the mental state theory of welfare, but I have not argued that this conjunction is the *only* way to remedy the identified faults of the mental state theory. However, most of the "tinkering" which has been done with the mental state theory of welfare has focussed on the second clause, rather than on the first (that is, on the notion of what is *best*, all things considered), whereas my criticism of the mental state theory of welfare focussed on a shortcoming of its first clause. I am therefore skeptical that any alternative will overcome the specific problem I have been focussing on, and it is in relation to this specific problem that I have recommended the biological theory.

IV. Concluding Remarks

In this paper I have defended an account of biological interests which both is consistent with contemporary views of teleological and functional explanations and allows us to attribute interests to a living organism as such—i.e., independently of its being a *conscious* living organism—without at the same time attributing interests to simple artifacts. I conclude with some observations on the larger significance of this inquiry.

Although the view defended here is what Tom Regan would recognize as a truly *environmental* ethic, because it extends moral consideration well beyond the sentient realm,[35] I doubt that an *adequate* environmental ethic[36] can be teased out of an interest-based approach to ethics. The reason is that sound environmental policy seems always to be focussed on systems or wholes, rather than on individuals, whereas only individual organisms can plausibly be said to have interests.[37] It has been proposed, of course, that an individual ecosystem and/or the earth's ecosphere in its entirety is a living organism,[38] but no sober ecologist today believes that ecosystems are in any literal sense organisms.[39] Even if this were so, however, an ecosystem could not have any biological interests, inasmuch as its component subsystems could not have acquired any biological functions via natural selection. There is general agreement among evolutionary biologists that group selection occurs, but only among "species made of many very discrete, socially cohesive groups in direct competition with each other,"[40] like colonies of social insects. Thus the various "organs" of an ant or bee colony (the *individual* queen, the worker *class*, and so on) may have biological functions which define biological interests of the colony, but unless or until evolutionary biology abandons the individualistic stance it inherited from Darwin, the view defended here will not imply that any more inclusive entity has biological interests.[41]

However, as I said earlier, my primary goal in this paper was to show that an individual who expresses concern for the interests of plants and "lower" animals need not be guilty of maudlin sentimentalism and need not be committing a variant of "the pathetic fallacy." And on the view defended here, we *can* say, quite literally and without anthropomorphizing, that a forest fire sets back the interests of the trees it burns and that a child who tears the wings off of a fly is setting back the interests of that fly.[42]

Notes

1. Kenneth Goodpaster, "On Being Morally Considerable," *Journal of Philosophy* 75 (1978), p. 319.

2. I take it that to say that an entity has interests is to say that it warrants direct moral consideration because its needs, desires, etc. (whatever we take to define its interests) ought, other things being equal, to be fulfilled or satisfied, and that for their own sake. To say that a thing has interests is to say that it has a good of its own, a good which moral agents have direct, *prima facie* duties to protect (a duty of non-maleficence) and further (a duty of beneficence).

3. Joel Feinberg, "The Rights of Animals and Unborn Generations," in William T. Blackstone, ed., *Philosophy and Environmental Crisis* (Athens: University of Georgia Press, 1974), pp. 49–50, emphasis added.

4. See, for instance, Goodpaster, "On Being Morally Considerable," p. 320; Robin Attfield, *The Ethics of Environmental Concern* (New York: Columbia University Press, 1983), pp. 144–45, and Attfield, "The Good of Trees," *Journal of Value Inquiry* 15 (1981), pp. 39–40.

5. Feinberg, pp. 51–52.

6. *Ibid.*, p. 54.

7. *Ibid.*, p. 53.

8. Although, for simplicity's sake, I will usually speak simply of "plants," the arguments I advance are intended to hold for all non-conscious organisms.

9. Ralph Barton Perry, *General Theory of Value* (New York: Longman's, Green and Company, 1926), p. 56.

10. Tom Regan, *The Case for Animal Rights* (Berkeley: University of California Press, 1983), pp. 87–88.

11. Goodpaster develops this distinction in "On Being Morally Considerable," pp. 311–12. See also note #31 below.

12. J. L. Arbor, "Animal Chauvinism, Plant-Regarding Ethics and the Torture of Trees," *Australasian Journal of Philosophy* 64 (1986), p. 337.

13. Elliott Sober, "Evolution, Population Thinking, and Essentialism," *Philosophy* 47 (1980), p. 374.

14. Paul Taylor, *Respect for Nature: A Theory of Environmental Ethics* (Princeton: Princeton University Press, 1986), pp. 123–24.

15. Ernest Nagel, *The Structure of Science: Problems in the Logic of Scientific Explanation* (London: Routledge & Kegan Paul, 1961), p. 411.

16. *Ibid.*, p. 418.

17. Goodpaster, "On Being Morally Considerable," p. 319.

18. Biological functions do not always (or even usually) attach to organs like the heart or lungs, but rather to the *systems* (circulatory or respiratory) of which these organs form a part. In single celled organisms, biological functions attach to *organelles* or subsystems.

19. Larry Wright, *Teleological Explanations* (Berkeley: University of California Press, 1976), p. 81.

20. The example is Wright's. See *Teleological Explanations*, pp. 77 and 79–80 (notes 3 and 4).

21. This is how Wright treats all vestigal organs. See *Teleological Functions*, pp. 89 and 91.

22. J. Baird Callicott, "Animal Liberation: A Triangular Affair," *Environmental Ethics* 2 (1980), p. 330.

23. Wright, *Teleological Explanations*, p. 114.

24. Christopher Boorse, "Wright on Functions," reprinted in Elliott Sober, ed., *Conceptual Issues in Evolutionary Biology* (Cambridge: MIT Press, 1984), p. 373.

25. Attfield, "The Good of Trees," p. 51.

26. Lilly-Marlene Russow, "Why Do Species Matter?" *Environmental Ethics* 3 (1981), pp. 101–12.

27. Arbor, "Animal Chauvinism," p. 338.

28. Goodpaster, "On Being Morally Considerable," section five, pp. 320–22.

29. Goodpaster appears to presume that by offering support for the empirical claim he is simultaneously offering support for the normative claim, but, as we have seen, a complete defense of the thesis that plants have morally significant interests requires logically separate defenses of each of these claims.

30. For examples of this view in action, see Henry Sidgwick, *The Methods of Ethics*, 7th edition (London: Macmillan, 1907), pp. 111–12; John Rawls, *A Theory of Justice* (Cambridge: Harvard University Press, 1971), chapter 7, "Goodness as Rationality," especially pp. 407–16; and Richard Brandt, *A Theory of the Good and the Right* (Oxford: Clarendon Press, 1979), chapter 3, "The Cognitive Theory of Action."

31. My own view is that a variant of Ralph Barton Perry's "Principle of Inclusiveness" (*General Theory of Value* [New York: Longman's, Green & Co., 1926], p. 648) can be used to show both (1) that while any human desire, even the most trivial or malicious, trumps any interest of a plant, we also have a general duty to rid ourselves of such desires, and (2) that the fulfillment of a person's "ground projects" or "categorical desires" (terminology adopted from Bernard Williams, "Persons, Character, and Morality," in his *Moral Luck* [Cambridge: Cambridge University Press, 1981], pp. 1–19) are the primary components of a person's good on the whole. See my "Perry's Principle of Inclusiveness and Establishing Priorities Among Interests," in preparation.

32. Sidgwick, *loc. cit.*

33. Garrett Thomson makes a similar claim in *Needs* (London: Routledge and Kegan Paul, 1987), p. 101.

34. Thomson argues that a person's "fundamental needs" are defined in part by his or her biology, but he offers no criteria for determining how and when this is so.

35. Tom Regan, "The Nature and Possibility of an Environmental Ethic," *Environmental Ethics* 3 (1981), pp. 19–20.

36. On the notion of an "adequate" environmental ethic, see J. Baird Callicott, "The Search for an Environmental Ethics," in Tom Regan, ed., *Matters of Life and Death*, 2nd ed. (New York: Random House, 1986), p. 383.

37. This oft-repeated claim was first defended in Bryan Norton's essay, "Environmental Ethics and Nonhuman Rights," *Environmental Ethics* 4 (1982), pp. 17–36.

38. On the former claim, see Donald Worster's account of the Chicago Organicists in chapter 15 of his *Nature's Economy* (Cambridge: Cambridge University Press, 1985); on the latter claim, see James Lovelock and Sidney Epton, "The Quest for Gaia," *New Scientist* 65 (1975), pp. 304–06.

39. See R. V. O'Neill et al., *A Hierarchical Concept of Ecosystems* (Princeton: Princeton University Press, 1986), chapters one and two, for a brief overview of the relevant theoretical issues; and see Worster, *loc. cit.*, for a popular account of the meteoric rise (and fall) of organicism among professional ecologists.

40. Stephen Jay Gould, "Caring Groups and Selfish Genes," reprinted in Elliott Sober, ed., *Conceptual Issues in Evolutionary Biology* (Cambridge: MIT Press, 1984), p. 122.

41. In a recent article, Harley Cahen argues that what appears to be goal directed behavior in ecosystems is actually a byproduct of the goal directed behavior of individual organisms. Harley Cahen, "Against the Moral Considerability of Ecosystems," *Environmental Ethics* 10 (1988), pp. 195–216. Although Cahen offers no explicit defense of either the empirical claim or the normative claim, and although he does not notice the special significance of function attributions which I emphasize in section two of this paper, his is the most lucid article to date in the literature of biocentric individualism.

42. I am increasingly convinced that the intuitions of the environmental movement are best unpacked in terms of an ethical commitment to the preservation of aesthetic value. See Eugene C. Hargrove, *Foundations of Environmental Ethics* (Englewood Cliffs, New Jersey: Prentice Hall, 1989). As an individual who is intuitively and politically committed to the more idealistic goals of the environmental movement, however, I worry that these goals cannot be harmonized with the equally intuitive principle that the protection of interests takes precedence over the preservation of beauty. But that is a topic for another paper.

Against the Moral Considerability of Ecosystems

Harley Cahen*

I

If natural areas had no value at all for human beings, would we still have a duty to preserve them? Some preservationists think that we would. Aldo Leopold, for instance, argues brilliantly for the cultural and psychological value of wilderness; yet he insists that even "enlightened" self-interest is not enough.[1] According to Leopold, an "ecological conscience" recognizes "obligations to land."[2] The ecological conscience sees that preservation is a good thing in itself—something we have a prima facie duty to promote—apart from any contribution it makes to human welfare. For convenience, let us call this conviction the *preservationist intuition.*[3]

I share this intuition. Can we justify it? I see at least four plausible strategies. We might, first, appeal to the intrinsic value of natural ecosystems.[4] A second strategy relies on the interests of the individual creatures that are inevitably harmed when we disturb an ecosystem.[5] A third possibility is a virtue-based approach. Perhaps what offends us—as preservationists—is that anyone who would damage an ecosystem for inadequate reasons falls short of our "ideals of human excellence."[6] Each of these three strategies has something to recommend it. But none captures the element of the preservationist intuition that involves a feeling of obligation *to* "land." This suggests a fourth strategy, the appeal to what Kenneth Goodpaster calls *moral considerability.* This strategy represents an ecosystem as something that has interests of its own, and thus can directly be victimized or benefited by our actions.[7] If ecosystems do have interests of their own, perhaps we owe it to them to consider those

interests in our moral deliberations. This fourth strategy is the one that I wish to call into question.

There is a fifth strategy—an appeal to the moral right of a natural ecosystem to be left alone. This strategy is similar to the fourth one but may be distinct. Rights, some would say, automatically "trump" other kinds of moral claim.[8] If so, an appeal to ecosystem rights would be much stronger than an appeal to moral considerability. (Too strong, I suspect: I find it best to regard talk of the rights of nonhumans as an enthusiastic way of asserting moral considerability.[9]) We can leave this question open, though, for if they are trumps, moral rights have at least this much in common with moral considerability: they both presuppose interests.

I contend that ecosystems cannot be morally considerable because they do not have interests—not even in the broad sense in which we commonly say that plants and other nonsentient organisms "have interests." The best we can do on behalf of plant interests, I believe, is the argument from *goal-directedness.* Nonsentient organisms—those not capable of consciously taking an interest in anything—have interests (and thus are candidates for moral considerability) in achieving their biological goals. Should ecosystems, too, turn out to be goal directed, they would be candidates for moral considerability.[10]

Although the argument from goal-directedness fails, we should not dismiss the argument too hastily. Some ecosystems are strikingly stable and resilient. They definitely have a goal-directed look. Yet there are reasons to doubt whether this apparent goal-directedness is genuine. The key is to distinguish the goals of a system's behavior from other outcomes that are merely behavioral *byproducts.* Armed with this distinction, we can see that the conditions for genuine goal-directedness are tougher than environmental ethicists typically realize. Ecosystems seem unlikely to qualify.

In sections two and three of this paper I define *moral considerability* and distinguish it from other ways that something can matter morally. In section

* Cahen thanks Elizabeth Meer, Barry Ingber, John Herring, Diane Wray-Cahen, the anonymous referees from *Environmental Ethics,* and Holmes Rolston, III (who, though disagreeing with the thrust of this manuscript, commented on it with his characteristic generosity). Research for this paper was partially supported by a fellowship from the National Science Foundation.

Environmental Ethics, Vol. 10, No. 3 (Fall 1988), 195–216. Reprinted by permission.

four I establish that goal-directedness plays a key role in arguments for the considerability of plants and other nonsentient organisms. In sections five and six I argue that this appeal to goal-directedness is plausible as long as we keep the goal/byproduct distinction in mind. In sections seven through nine, I argue that ecology and evolutionary biology cast serious doubt on the possibility that ecosystems are genuinely goal-directed.

II

The literature of environmental ethics is full of appeals to the interests of ecosystems. Consider Aldo Leopold's famous remark: "A thing is right when it tends to preserve the integrity, stability, and beauty of the biotic community. It is wrong when it tends otherwise."[11] Is Leopold suggesting that the biotic community has an interest in its own integrity and stability? Some commentators interpret his remark this way. James Heffernan, for instance, defends Leopold by insisting that "even ecosystems . . . are things that have interests and hence, may be benefited or harmed."[12] Holmes Rolston, III likewise would found an "ecological ethic" upon the obligation to promote "ecosystemic interests."[13]

More often the appeal to ecosystem interests is implicit. Consider John Rodman, criticizing animal liberationists such as Peter Singer for drawing the moral considerability boundary to include only sentient beings. Rodman complains: "The moral atomism that focuses on individual animals . . . does not seem well adapted to coping with ecological systems."[14] Why is "atomism" inadequate? Because, Rodman explains, an ecological community as a whole has a good of its own, a "welfare":

> I need only to stand in the midst of clear-cut forest, a strip-mined hillside, a defoliated jungle, or a dammed canyon to feel uneasy with assumptions that could yield the conclusion that no human action can make any difference to the welfare of anything but sentient animals.[15]

Of course, Rodman believes that individual plants and nonsentient animals are morally considerable, too. That is reason enough for him to feel uneasy with Singer's assumptions. It cannot be his only reason, however, for it would leave him as guilty of moral atomism as Singer. Whose *welfare* could Rodman have in mind? The welfare, I take it, of the communities themselves.[16]

III

Moral considerability is a potentially confusing term. Let me clarify and defend my use of it. I take moral considerability to be the moral status x has if, and only if (a) x has interests (a good of its own), (b) it would be prima facie wrong to frustrate x's interests (to harm x), and (c) the wrongness of frustrating x's interests is direct—that is, does not depend on how the interests of any other being are affected. It is the concern with interests that distinguishes moral considerability from the other varieties of moral status upon which the preservationist intuition might possibly be based.

Goodpaster plainly means to restrict moral considerability to beings with *interests.* In his first paper on moral considerability he explains that life is the "key" to moral considerability because living things have interests; this, he points out, is what makes them "capable of being beneficiaries."[17] Goodpaster makes a point of agreeing with Joel Feinberg about what Feinberg calls "mere things." "Mere things," Goodpaster says, are not candidates for moral considerability because they are "incapable of being benefited or harmed—they have no 'well-being' to be sought or acknowledged."[18] That is why he insists that "x's being a living being" is not only sufficient for moral considerability but is also *necessary.*[19]

In Goodpaster's subsequent work, he characterizes the entire biosphere as a "bearer of value."[20] Yet he does not appear to have changed his understanding of the requirements for moral considerability. "The biosystem as a whole" is considerable, he says. Why? Because it is, in effect, an "organism"—"an integrated, self-sustaining unity which puts solar energy to work in the service of growth and maintenance."[21] Goodpaster's focus remains on interests and he expresses his confidence that the "biosystem as a whole" has them.[22]

Some philosophers speak of moral considerability but do not associate it with interests at all. Andrew Brennan, for instance, asserts that natural objects such as ecosystems, mountains, deserts, the air, rocky crests, and rivers may have this moral status though they have no interests and thus can be harmed only metaphorically." This is no longer moral considerability as I understand it.[23]

Other philosophers equate moral considerability with intrinsic value, holding that both equally presuppose interests. Robin Attfield, for instance, writes, "I follow Goodpaster in holding that things which lack a good of their own cannot be morally considerable . . . or have intrinsic value."[24] J. Baird Callicott attributes to Goodpaster the view that because "life is intrinsically valuable . . . all living beings should be granted moral considerability."[25] As Callicott sums up his own view:

> If the self is intrinsically valuable, then nature is intrinsically valuable. If it is rational for me to act in my own best interest, and I and nature are one, then it is rational for me to act in the best interests of nature.[26]

The association of intrinsic value with interests seems odd to me. Many readers will suppose that "mere things"—things which have no interests, no good of their own—might conceivably be intrinsically valuable. As Eric Katz puts it, "many natural entities worth preserving [i.e., valuable in their own right] are not clearly the possessors of interests."[27]

Is this just a quibble about words? I think not. We have more than one paradigm of moral relevance, and it makes a difference which one we adopt as the model for our ethical thinking about ecosystems. If we aim to justify preservation by appeal to the intrinsic value of natural ecosystems, our arguments must build on the way ecosystems resemble other things that we preserve for their intrinsic *value.* Moral considerability is another matter. To ground the preservationist intuition upon the *interests* of ecosystems, we have to look for an analogy between ecosystems and beings that clearly have interests. Given that ecosystems are not sentient, the most promising models are plants and other nonsentient organisms.[28]

IV

Some ethicists would object that we cannot even get this argument for ecosystems off the ground—it is absurd, they would say, to think that plants could be morally considerable. Such a dismissal of plants, however, is too quick, for it ignores goal-directedness. Peter Singer, for instance, regards *rocks* as representative of all nonsentient beings. "A stone," he says, "does not have interests because it cannot suffer. Nothing that we can do to it could possibly make any difference to its welfare." He therefore boldly concludes: "If a being is not capable of suffering, or of experiencing enjoyment or happiness, there is nothing to be taken into account."[29]

Although sentience may turn out, after all, to be necessary for moral considerability, this just cannot be as obvious as Singer assumes. There is a world of difference between plants and rocks. Surely there might be something to "take into account" even in the absence of sentience. All we need, as Bryan Norton observes, is something appropriately analogous to sentience. Norton rejects the possibility of ecosystem "rights" because "collectives such as mountain ranges, species, and ecosystems have no significant analogues to human sentience on which to base assignments of interests." Since collectives lack any analogue to sentience, he reasons, "the whole enterprise of assigning interests [to them] becomes virtually arbitrary."[30] Norton reaches this conclusion too quickly, as I argue below, but he makes two crucial points. First, we can plausibly attribute moral considerability to x only when we have a nonarbitrary way of identifying x's interests. Second, this project does not require actual sentience. It is plain enough that plants, for instance, have interests in a straightforward sense, though they feel nothing.[31] Paul Taylor puts it this way:

> Trees have no knowledge or feelings. Yet it is undoubtedly the case that trees can be harmed or benefited by our actions. We can crush their roots by running a bulldozer too close to them. We can see to it that they get adequate nourishment and moisture. . . . It is the good of trees themselves that is thereby affected.[32]

In general, Taylor explains, "the good of an individual nonhuman organism [consists in] the full development of its biological powers." Every organism is "a being whose standpoint we can take in making judgments about what events in the world are good or evil."[33]

Let us grant, in spite of Singer and his allies, that there is something about trees that we might intelligibly "take into account" for moral purposes. Can we be more specific? What is it that plants have and rocks do not? The obvious, but unilluminating answer is "life." Just what is it about being alive that makes plants candidates for moral considerability?

Goal-directedness is the key. Taylor, for instance, describes organisms as "teleological centers of life."[34] Goodpaster points to plants' "tendencies [to] maintain and heal themselves" and locates the "core of moral concern" in "respect for self-sustaining organization and integration."[35] Attfield writes of a tree's "latent tendencies, direction of growth and natural fulfillment."[36] Jay Kantor bases his defense of plant interests on their "self-regulating and homeostatic functions."[37] Rodman condemns actions that impose our will upon "natural entities that have their own internal structures, needs, and potentialities," potentialities that are actively "striving to actualize themselves."[38] Finally, James K. Mish'alani points to each living thing's *self-ameliorative competence:* "that is, a power for coordinated movement towards favorable states, a capacity to adjust to its circumstances in a manner to enhance its survival and natural growth."[39]

The goal-directedness of living things gives us a plausible and nonarbitrary standard upon which to "base assignments of interests." If ecosystems, though not sentient, are goal-directed, then we may (without absurdity) attribute interests to them, too. Goodpaster is right: there is no *a priori* reason to think that "the universe of moral considerability [must] map neatly onto our medium-sized framework of organisms."[40] Of course, we must not get carried away with this line of thinking. Goal-directedness is certainly not sufficient for moral considerability. One problem is that some machines are goal-directed—e.g., guided missiles, thermostatic heating systems, chess-playing computers, and "The Terminator."[41] The defender of moral considerability for plants must distinguish plants, morally, from goal-directed but inanimate objects.[42] Still, the possession of goals is what makes the notion of a plant's "standpoint" intelligible. Can we locate an ecosystem's standpoint by understanding its goals? Not if it doesn't have any goals.

V

We often know goal-directedness when we see it. The analysis of goal-directedness is, however, a terribly unsettled subject in the philosophy of science.[43] In light of this unsettledness, one must be cautious. Here are three claims. First, the attribution of goal-directedness to organisms can be scientifically and philosophically respectable—even when the organisms in question are nonsentient. Teleology talk need not be vitalistic, anthropomorphic, or rooted in obsolete Aristotelian biology or physics. It does not imply "backward causation." Nor need it run afoul of the "missing goal-object" problem.[44]

Second, some of these respectable accounts of goal-directedness are useful for the environmental ethicist. They enable us to resist crude versions of the common slippery-slope argument against the moral considerability of plants and other nonsentient living things. Once we admit nonsentient beings into the moral considerability club, how can we bar the door to ordinary inanimate objects? Porches, paintings, automobiles, garbage dumps, buildings, and other ordinary objects are allegedly lurking just outside, waiting for us to admit plants.[45] Goal-directedness can keep them out.

Third, we ought to recognize a distinction between goals and behavioral byproducts. A defensible conception of goal-directedness must distinguish true goals from outcomes that a system achieves incidentally. Ecosystem resilience and stability look like goals, but this appearance may deceive us. An ecosystem property such as stability might turn out to be just a byproduct, the incidental result of individual activities aimed exclusively at the individuals' own goals.

I shall discuss two of the main approaches to understanding goal-directedness. The approaches differ in important ways. I favor the second, but either will do for my purposes. The first approach is propounded by Ernest Nagel (among many others). Nagel holds that a system is goal-directed when it can reach (or remain in) some particular state by means of behavior that is sufficiently *persistent and plastic.*[46] Persistence refers to the system's ability to "compensate" for interfering factors that would otherwise take the system away from its goal.[47]

Plasticity refers to the system's ability to reach the same outcome in a variety of ways.[48]

Nagel assumes that this approach will count all living things as goal-directed. It seems to.[49] There are problems, to be sure. Chief among these is the danger that it will include some behavior that plainly is not goal-directed—the movement of a pendulum, for instance, or the behavior of a buffered chemical solution.[50] Nagel, however, shows that with some plausible tinkering—mainly, by adding a third condition that he calls "orthogonality"—we can deal with these counterexamples.[51]

The second approach, pioneered by Charles Taylor, insists that goal-directed behavior "[really does] occur 'for the sake of' the state of affairs which follows."[52] Subsequent philosophers have developed this basic insight in various ways.

An especially influential exponent of Taylor's approach is Larry Wright. Taylor's considered formulation of his insight requires that the behavior in question be both necessary and sufficient for the goal. Wright finds this unsatisfactory—too generous in some ways and too strict in others.[53] He suggests what he calls an "etiological" account, one that focuses on the causal background of the behavior in question. A system is goal-directed, Wright contends, only if it behaves as it does just because that is the type of behavior that tends to bring about that type of goal. Formally, behavior B occurs for the sake of goal-state G if "(i) B tends to bring about G," and "(ii) B occurs because (i.e. is brought about by the fact that) it tends to bring about G."[54] The key condition is (ii). Some machines, say guided missiles, meet it, for a machine may B because it is designed to B, and it may be designed to B, in turn, because B tends to bring about some G desired by the designer. Organisms meet it, too, because of the way that natural selection operates. The fitness of an organism usually depends on how appropriate its behavior is—that is, the extent to which it does the sort of thing (say, B) that tends to help that kind of organism survive and reproduce. If the disposition to B is heritable, organisms whose tendency to B helps make them fit will leave descendants that tend to B. Those descendants are disposed to B, then, in part because B is an appropriate type of behavior.[55]

Some people emphatically do not find Wright's approach respectable. He has, for example, recently been accused of "misrepresenting" natural selection as a teleological process in the old-fashioned

(and discredited) sense according to which nature selects with certain outcomes in mind.[56] This charge, however, misses the mark, for there is nothing wrong with Wright's understanding of natural selection.[57] In addition, Wright has also dealt effectively with other, better-founded criticisms that need not be discussed here.[58]

Wright's development of Taylor's insight is the best approach for my purposes because alternative versions of Taylor's approach are not as good for sustaining attributions of goal-directedness to plants and lower animals.[59] With regard specifically to the slippery slope and the alleged "needs" of paintings and porches, Nagel's approach seems good enough, for these objects do not act persistently or plastically toward any result that we could seriously be tempted to call a goal. With Wright's criteria, however, we sidestep questions of degree that can plague Nagel. Consider my car, which responds to the upstate New York environment by rusting. The car rusts in spite of my efforts to stop it, and it would rust even if I tried much harder. Eventually it will fall apart. Does this unpleasantly persistent behavior count as goal-directed? A dedicated slippery-sloper might suggest that the car has the goal of rusting, a "need" to rust. Both Nagel and Wright can resist this suggestion, but Nagel would have a tougher time due to the vagueness of his persistence and plasticity conditions. Wright would simply check the behavior's etiology. My car, we may safely say, does not rust because rusting tends to cause cars to fall apart. It rusts because rust is just what happens when steel meets moisture and road salt. The car's behavior fails Wright's condition (ii).

We can imagine an etiology that would make my car's rusting genuinely goal-directed. Assume that car designers know how to make sturdy rust-free cars. Suppose, however, that they greedily conspire to build cars that are susceptible to rust in order to force people to buy new cars more frequently. We would then be unable fully to understand my car's rusting as a purely chemical process, for—on the conspiracy theory of rust—my car would be rusting (in part) because rusting tends to cause cars to fall apart.

Now, what about ecosystems? I concede that the heralded stability and resilience of some ecological systems make them prima facie goal-directed. When such an ecosystem is perturbed in any one of various ways, it bounces back. The members of the ecosystem do just what is necessary (within limits) to restore the system to equilibrium.[60] But are they cooperating in order to restore equilibrium? That is surely imaginable. On the other hand, each creature might instead be "doing its own thing," with the fortunate but incidental result that the ecosystem remains stable. If this is correct, then we are dealing with a behavioral byproduct, not a systemic goal.

The goal/byproduct distinction is well entrenched in the literature on natural selection and biological adaptation. Let me illustrate this distinction with an example from George Williams. Williams asks us to consider the behavior of a panic-stricken crowd rushing from a burning theater. A biologist newly arrived from Mars, he suggests, might be impressed by

> [the group's] rapid 'response' to the stimulus of fire. It went rapidly from a widely dispersed distribution to the formation of dense aggregates that very effectively sealed off the exits.[61]

If the crowd clogs the exits in spite of strenuous crowd-control efforts, would our Martian be entitled to report that he had observed a crowd that was goal-directed toward self-destruction via the sealing off of the exits? Of course not. We know that the clogging of the exits is just incidental. The people are trying to get out. The crowd clogs the exits in spite of the dreadful consequences.

Any theory of goal-directedness ought to be able to avoid the Martian's conclusion. Wright's theory does that easily via condition (ii): G can be a goal of behavior B only if B occurs *because* it tends to bring about G. If G plays no explanatory role it cannot be a genuine goal.[62]

Nagel's account also permits us to distinguish goal from byproduct. The persistence condition does the work here. There is no reason to think that the theater crowd's behavior is truly persistent toward clogging the exits. If there were more exits, or larger exits, the people would have escaped smoothly. We may be sure that the crowd would not compensate for greater ease of exit by modifying its behavior in order to achieve clogging.

VI

If the idea that organisms have morally considerable "interests" seems plausible, it must, I think,

be because organisms are genuinely goal-directed. When Taylor, for instance, characterizes a tree's good as "the full realization of its biological powers," we know what he means. We naturally assume that *powers* does not refer to everything that can happen to a tree—disease, say, or stunting from lack of nutrients. The tree's powers are the capabilities that the tree exercises in the service of its goals of growth, survival, and reproduction. We certify that those are the tree's goals, in turn, by employing criteria such as Wright's or Nagel's.

Should we find moral significance in an organism's goals? Perhaps not. We may coherently admit that plants have goals, yet deny that we have duties to them. Still, there is a tempting analogy between the goal-directed behavior of organisms and the intentional behavior of humans. Recall the rhetorical role that the notion of natural "striving" plays in Paul Taylor's argument for an ethic of respect for nature.[63] Recall Katz's choice of the term *autonomy* to characterize an organism's capacity for independent pursuit of its own interests.[64] Indeed the word *interests* itself conveys the flavor of intention.[65] This flavor lends persuasiveness to arguments such as Taylor's.

Let us, in any event, grant that to have natural goals is to have morally considerable interests. Where does this leave behavioral byproducts? It leaves them where they were—morally irrelevant. We need a nonarbitrary standard for deciding which states of affairs are good ones from the organism's own "standpoint." Sentience gives us such a standard by way of the organism's own preferences (which we are capable of discovering in various ways). By analogy, a nonsentient organism's biological goal—its "preferred" states—can do the same thing. But is there any reason at all for supposing that either mere natural tendencies or behavioral byproducts give rise to interests? I think not. Why, from a given system's "standpoint," should it matter whether some natural tendency, unconnected (except incidentally) to the system's goals, plays itself out?

Consider John Rodman's account of why it is wrong to dam a wild river. Rodman emphasizes that the river "struggles" against the dam "like an instinct struggles against inhibition."[66] One might be tempted to say that this way of talking is unnecessary, that every natural tendency is morally privileged. Such a claim, however, is implausible. What leads Rodman to talk of instinct and struggle is, I take it, the notion that the river actually has goals and would be frustrated, by the dam, in its pursuit of them.

I do not expect this example to be convincing. To see clearly that mere tendencies are in themselves morally irrelevant, we should consider something really drastic—like *death*. Usually, death is something that just happens—by accident, by disease, or simply when the body wears out. Organisms tend to die, but they do not ordinarily aim to die. As Jonathan Bennett puts it: "Every animal is tremendously plastic in respect of becoming dead: throw up what obstacles you may, and death will still be achieved. Yet animals seldom have their deaths as a goal."[67]

Consider a salmon of a species whose members routinely die after spawning. Even here death seems unlikely to be the organism's goal. The salmon dies because the arduous upstream journey has worn it out. If it could spawn without dying, it would do so. Once in a while that actually happens. When it does, do we say (without further evidence) that the salmon has been frustrated in its efforts to die after spawning? No. We would say that the salmon has managed to spawn without having had the misfortune to die.

Behavioral byproducts, like mere tendencies, seem not to generate anything we can comfortably call "interests." The salmon example illustrates this, if we interpret the death of the adult as a byproduct of its spawning. Williams' theater example illustrates it, too. It would be truly bizarre to suggest that the panicky crowd has an interest in being trapped and incinerated.

Although there is much more that needs to be said about whether the argument from goal-directedness can establish the moral considerability of plants, let us go ahead and accept plant moral considerability. But does ecosystem moral considerability follow? No, an obstacle remains: the goal/byproduct distinction. We still need to determine whether stability (or any other property) of an ecosystem is a genuine goal of the whole system rather than merely a byproduct of self-serving individual behavior.

VII

Donald Worster has written in his history of ecological ideas that "More often than not, the eco-

logical text [holistic environmentalists] know and cite is either of their own writing or a pastiche from older, superseded models. Few appreciate that the science they are eagerly pursuing took another fork back yonder up the road."[68] Orthodox ecology, Worster says, has abandoned the "organismic" view of ecosystems and adopted a fundamentally individualistic one.[69] Robert M. May represents this individualistic orthodoxy. Of course, says May, there are "patterns at the level of ecological systems." He insists that these patterns do not represent goals. They are entirely explicable in terms of "the interplay of biological relations that act to confer specific advantages or disadvantages on individual organisms."[70]

What then are we to make of ecosystem stability and resilience? If May is right, the tendency of an ecosystem to bounce back after a disturbance is merely the net result of self-serving responses by individual organisms. We need not view stability as a system "goal." We may not even be entitled to do so. As Robert Ricklefs explains:

> The ability of the community to resist change [is] the sum of the individual properties of component populations. . . . Relationships between predators and prey, and between competitors, can affect the inherent stability of the community, but trophic structure does not evolve to enhance community stability.[71]

Certain forms of trophic structure typically enhance community stability, Ricklefs agrees, but trophic structure does not take on particular form because that form enhances stability.[72]

Someone might be tempted to conclude that my own argument undermines the moral considerability of organisms. Organisms, after all, consist of cells. The cells have goals of their own. Does my individualism require us to regard the behavior of organisms as merely a byproduct of the selfish behavior of cells? It does not. Cells do have their own goals, but these goals are largely subordinated to the organism's goals, because natural selection selects *bodies*, not cells. If the cells do not cooperate for the body's sake, the body dies and the cells die, too. That, very roughly, is how natural selection coordinates the body's activities.[73] Selection tends to eliminate individuals that are not good at the survival "game" (taking kin selection into account). Eventually this process leaves us with organisms that are good at it, and these organisms are goal-directed toward those states of affairs that have in the past made them winners.

So much for organisms. A familiar process—ordinary, individualistic natural selection—ensures that they are goal-directed. Is there a process that could account for goal-directedness in ecosystems? The only candidate I know of for this job is group selection operating at the community level.[74]

VIII

Does group selection have a part to play in the full explanation of the behavior of species populations or ecosystems? I hold that the answer is no. Now this may seem hard to believe. "Ecosystem behavior," you might counter, "is just too well coordinated for stability to be an accident." To undermine this intuition, let us consider a description of a simple situation in which there is a result that we could construe as "good for the group," but which is strictly speaking a byproduct of self-serving individual action, and then a second situation, a more complicated one, in which an extremely stable group property is, again, a byproduct.[75]

Consider any single-species population. Suppose that some individuals (call them the A-individuals) run into a stretch of bad luck and consequently fail to reproduce. Their failure to reproduce reduces the intensity of competition. This (other things being equal) permits other members of the population (the B-individuals) to reproduce more effectively than they otherwise would have. Should we regard this population as a goal-directed whole, answering a threat to its survival by redirecting its reproductive effort? Of course not. Williams explains the general difficulty in this way:

> Certainly species survival is one result of reproduction. This fact, however, does not constitute evidence that species survival is a function of reproduction. If reproduction is entirely explainable on the basis of adaptation for individual genetic survival, species survival would have to be considered merely an incidental effect.[76]

There is no reason to think of the B-individuals' increased reproductive success as "compensating" for the failure of the A-individuals. If fact, each of the B-individuals has simply taken advantage of the A-individuals' failure. The net result is survival of the group, to be sure, but a postulated goal of group survival has no explanatory role to play.

Let us now consider a more difficult and controversial example, the clutch size in birds, long a bone of contention between group selectionists and Neo-Darwinians. Clutch size in some species of birds is remarkably constant; certain species of plover, for instance, almost always lay four eggs. If an egg is removed from the plover's nest, the bird lays a replacement, bringing the number back up to four. That is not so strange, in itself; yet it shows that the plover is physiologically able to lay more than four eggs. Why should it lay only four to start with?

Perhaps this is a sign of group selection at work, favoring a population of birds in which individual birds restrain themselves for the good of their group. V. C. Wynne-Edwards, the dean of group selectionism, would say so. Consider what Wynne-Edwards says about "reproductive rate":

> If intraspecific selection was all in favor of the individual, there would be an overwhelming premium on higher and ever higher individual fecundity, provided it resulted in a greater posterity than one's fellows. Manifestly this does not happen in practice; in fact, the reproductive rate in many species . . . is varied according to the current needs of the population.[77]

If this group-selectionist account is correct, then the plover population's behavior is goal-directed, even by Wright's criteria, for the individual birds are laying exactly four fertilized eggs just because of the consequences this activity has—that is, just because their self-restraint meets the "current needs of the population"—and we are entitled to speak of the group's goal of maintaining a certain specified average clutch size.

There is, however, an alternative account, an individualistic Neo-Darwinian explanation. Each individual bird seeks to maximize its own inclusive fitness. If laying more than four eggs were a sound strategy for the individual, then that is the strategy it would pursue. Chances are, however, that if a pair of plovers divide their parental energy and attention among five offspring instead of four, fewer of the offspring will survive than if the parents had been conservative. "Exactly four eggs" is a sound strategy from the standpoint of each individual. Seen in this way, it does not represent individual self-restraint for the good of the group. There is no group goal.[78]

Evolutionary biologists are by and large skeptical about group selection. For one thing, the argument for group selection in nature is essentially negative: as Wynne-Edwards puts it, group selection simply *must* occur, since normal natural selection would not be "at all effective" in generating "the kind of social adaptations . . . in which the interests of the individual are actually submerged or subordinated to those of the community as a whole."[79] This negative argument for group selection is undermined when we discover plausible individualistic explanations—when, as in the clutch size case, we find that the interests of the individual are not "submerged" at all. Williams and others, including Richard Dawkins, have shown that we do not need group selection to explain any of the phenomena upon which Wynne-Edwards builds his case.[80]

Worster is correct about which fork ecology has taken. To be sure, a number of theorists have shown how something they label "group selection" could occur under the right circumstances.[81] These particular theories, however, insofar as they are extensions of kin selection, are fundamentally "individualistic," and are not much like the theories that earlier advocates of group selection had hoped for.[82] We have little or no reason to believe that evolution by group selection, as traditionally conceived, is significant in nature.[83]

IX

When we turn from group selection operating on single-species populations to community selection, the result is much the same. According to Robert May, for instance:

> Natural selection acts almost invariably on individuals or on groups of related individuals. Populations, much less communities of interacting populations, cannot be regarded as units subject to Darwinian evolution.[84]

This view has been seconded by Elliott Sober. "Darwinism," Sober asserts, "is a profoundly individualistic doctrine":

> [It] rejects the idea that species, communities, and ecosystems have adaptations that exist for their own benefit. These higher-level entities are not conceptualized as goal-directed systems; what properties of organization they possess are viewed as artifacts of processes operating at lower levels of organization.[85]

To be fair, I should report Robert McIntosh's recent lament that "organismic ecology is alive and well." McIntosh worries that parts of the ecosystem-as-organism view survive in "systems" ecology.[86] John L. Harper shares this worry and he warns against "one of the dangers of the systems approach to community productivity"—namely, the temptation to "treat the behavior that [one] discovers as something that can be interpreted *as if* community function is organized." Harper insists that we must resist this temptation: "What we see as the organized behavior of systems is the result of the fate of individuals. Evolution is about individuals and their descendants."[87]

Some systems ecologists contend that ecosystems have some "organismic" features while conceding that "natural selection operates only on a community's constituent populations, not on the community as a whole."[88] These sources, as I read them, hold small comfort for the advocate of ecosystem interests. They support at best an analogy that is too weakly organismic to generate ecosystem goals.[89]

Obviously there is room for rebuttal here. Still, this testimony suggests the scorn with which ecologists and evolutionary biologists typically regard group selection.[90] Could anything else cause individuals to cooperate for the sake of ecosystem goals? I know of no plausible candidates. If the verdict against group selection stands up, I see no way to justify ecosystem moral considerability with the argument from goal-directedness.

X

Earlier I mentioned several distinct strategies for justifying what I call the "preservationist intuition"—intrinsic value, the good of individual plants and animals, and ideals of human excellence. Any of these might be enough. Still, we may find ourselves tempted to believe that whole ecosystems have interests and are therefore morally considerable. This avenue, however, is not promising. Genuine goal-directedness is a step—an essential step—toward moral considerability. It makes sense (as I have argued) to claim that plants and other nonsentient organisms are morally considerable— but only because those beings' own biological goals provide a nonarbitrary standard for our judgments about their welfare. Were ecosystems genuinely goal-directed, we could try for the next step.[91]

Some ecosystems do indeed appear to have goals—stability, for example. There is a complication, however. Mere behavioral byproducts, which are outcomes of no moral significance, can look deceptively like goals. Moreover, on what I take to be our best current ecological and evolutionary understanding, the goal-directed appearance of ecosystems is in fact deceptive. Stability and other ecosystem properties are byproducts, not goals. Ecosystem interests are, I conclude, a shaky foundation for the preservationist intuition.

Notes

1. Aldo Leopold, *A Sand County Almanac: With Essays on Conservation from Round River* (New York: Ballantine, 1966) p. 244. He characterizes economic arguments for preservation as "subterfuges," invented to justify what we know we should do on other grounds (p. 247). He also describes "despoliation of land" as "not only inexpedient but wrong" (p. 239).

2. Ibid., p. 245.

3. Eric Katz expresses the preservationist intuition clearly in "Utilitarianism and Preservation," *Environmental Ethics* 1 (1979): 357–64. The "danger" posed by an ethic based exclusively on human interests, Katz says, is that it "can support a policy of preservation only on a contingent basis" (p. 362).

4. See, e.g., Holmes Rolston, III, "Are Values in Nature Subjective or Objective?" *Environmental Ethics* 4 (1982): 125–51 and Peter Miller, "Value as Richness: Toward a Value Theory for the Expanded Naturalism in Environmental Ethics," *Environmental Ethics* 4 (1982): 101–14. Bryan Norton worries, properly, that there are "questionable ontological commitments involved in attributing intrinsic value to nature." "Environmental Ethics and Weak Anthropocentrism," *Environmental Ethics* 6 (1984): 147–48. Some who argue for the "intrinsic value" of nature might be happy with something less worrisome ontologi-

cally—namely, what C. I. Lewis calls "inherent value." See Lewis, *An Analysis of Knowledge and Valuation* (La Salle, Ill.: Open Court, 1946), pp. 382–92. The problem with this strategy is that aesthetic and other kinds of inherent value, though objective, are fundamentally anthropocentric. See Rolston, "Are Values in Nature Subjective or Objective?" p. 151, and Robin Attfield, *The Ethics of Environmental Concern* (New York: Columbia University Press, 1983), pp. 151–52. These waters are very muddy, and J. Baird Callicott has lately stirred them up some more by defining inherent value in a way that is explicitly at odds with Lewis's conception. "Intrinsic Value, Quantum Theory, and Environmental Ethics," *Environmental Ethics* 7 (1985): 262.

5. See Paul W. Taylor, *Respect for Nature: A Theory of Environmental Ethics* (Princeton: Princeton University Press, 1986), pp. 70–71. Taylor makes it clear that when he speaks of the "good of a whole biotic community," he does not imagine that the community—as a whole—has a good of its own. The community's good is, he says, a "statistical concept" compounded out of the interests of the individual creatures that comprise the community.

6. See Thomas E. Hill, Jr., "Ideals of Human Excellence and Preserving Natural Environments," *Environmental Ethics* 5 (1983): 211–24. See also Bryan G. Norton, "Environmental Ethics and Weak Anthropocentrism," *Environmental Ethics* 6 (1984): 131–48. If the "excellence" in question is the ability to recognize intrinsic (or even inherent) value when one encounters it, then this strategy turns out to be a variant of the first one.

7. Goodpaster coined the term *moral considerability* in "On Being Morally Considerable," *Journal of Philosophy* 75 (1978): 308–25. When I speak of an organism's interests I do not mean to imply anything about its state of mind—or even that it has a mind. Throughout this paper I use the terms *interests* and *good of one's own* interchangeably. I recognize that there are good reasons not to equate these terms (see Taylor, *Respect for Nature*, pp. 62–68), but even Taylor concedes that it is "convenient" (pp. 270–71) to speak of whatever furthers a being's good as also promoting its interests. I find it convenient too.

8. See, for example, Ronald Dworkin, *Taking Rights Seriously* (Cambridge, Mass.: Harvard University Press, 1978).

9. According to Joel Feinberg, rights talk is merely a way of referring to *valid claims*. On this view, having rights is equivalent to being morally considerable. See Feinberg, "The Nature and Value of Rights," *Journal of Value Inquiry* 4 (1971): 263–77 and "The Rights of Animals and Unborn Generations," in *Philosophy and Environmental Crisis*, ed. William T.

Blackstone (Athens: University of Georgia Press, 1974).

10.   I classify all beings that have interests as "candidates" for moral considerability. If my analysis of organismic interests is correct, then having interests is only the first step to moral considerability.

11.   Leopold, *Sand County Almanac*, p. 262.

12.   James D. Heffernan, "The Land Ethic: A Critical Appraisal," *Environmental Ethics* 4 (1982): 242. On balance I think Heffernan is right: Leopold is asserting moral considerability for ecosystems. In that case, Heffernan's point is well-taken: an ecosystem must be seen as the sort of entity that we can not only damage (i.e., put in a state of diminished value or impaired usefulness), but also *harm* (i.e., make worse off from the standpoint of its own interests).

13.   Holmes Rolston, III, "Is There an Ecological Ethic?" *Ethics* 85 (1975): 106. Rolston no longer speaks in these terms, though his talk of "projects" suggests that something like an appeal to goal-directedness is still at work. See "Are Values in Nature Subjective or Objective?" pp. 146–47, where Rolston speaks of achievements that "do not have wills or interests," but do have "headings, trajectories, traits, successions, which give them a tectonic integrity." More recently still, even while conceding that "ecologists . . . have doubted whether ecosystems exist as anything over their component parts," and agreeing that in ecosystems there are "no policy makers, no social wills, no goals," Rolston is still drawn to speak, tentatively, of "the good of the system" and to claim that "a spontaneous ecosystem is typically healthy." "Valuing Wildlands," *Environmental Ethics* 7 (1985): 26, 30.

14.   John Rodman, "The Liberation of Nature?" *Inquiry* 20 (1977): 89.

15.   Ibid. See also Rodman's description of a river as a "victim" of a dam (pp. 114–15). A hillside (or even a river) is not likely to be a complete ecosystem, of course. My arguments apply equally, I think, to ecosystems and to ecological communities.

16.   Here are two more examples of the sort of language that raises my suspicions. (1) "Deep ecologists" Bill Devall and George Sessions, in "The Development of Natural Resources and the Integrity of Nature," assert that when "humans have distressed an ecosystem," we are obliged to make "reparations" (*Environmental Ethics* 6 [1984]: 305, 312). (2) J. Baird Callicott denies that he wishes to extend "moral considerability" to "inanimate entities such as oceans, lakes, mountains, forests, and wetlands"; yet he refers to the "well-being of the biotic community, the biosphere as a whole," and employs "the good of the community as a whole" as a standard for the

assessment of the relative value . . . of its constitutive parts" ("Animal Liberation: A Triangular Affair," *Environmental Ethics* 2 [1980]: 337, 324–25).

17.   Goodpaster, "On Being Morally Considerable," pp. 323, 319.

18.   Ibid., p. 318. Feinberg's remarks on "mere things" are in "The Rights of Animals and Unborn Generations," pp. 49–50.

19.   Goodpaster, "On Being Morally Considerable," p. 313.

20.   Kenneth E. Goodpaster, "From Egoism to Environmentalism," in *Ethics and Problems of the 21st Century*, ed. Goodpaster and Sayre (Notre Dame: Notre Dame University Press, 1979), p. 30.

21.   Ibid., pp. 32, 35, n. 25. Here he picks up a suggestion that he had already made in "On Being Morally Considerable," pp. 310, 323.

22.   Goodpaster now rejects "generalizations of egoism" that extend moral concern to a class of beneficiaries that includes "forests, lakes, rivers, air and land" ("From Egoism to Environmentalism," p. 28). Moral considerability for ecosystems is in the same "egoistic" spirit, I suppose. Goodpaster prefers to speak of "bearers of value," a term that de-emphasizes the possession of interests. Yet this talk is misleading. It can only obscure Goodpaster's assumptions about what makes the biosphere considerable—including its capacity for "successful self-protection" (p. 32).

23.   Andrew Brennan, "The Moral Standing of Natural Objects," *Environmental Ethics* 6 (1984): 53, 49, 51. Brennan uses the term *moral standing*, which he introduces as a synonym for moral considerability (p. 37). I am not attacking the substance of Brennan's view here; I am objecting to his claim to be explicating Goodpaster's concept (p. 35). Brennan has severed moral considerability completely from the notion that Goodpaster finds crucial—that of being a potential beneficiary. I believe that Goodpaster would not recognize the concept after this surgery.

24.   Attfield, *The Ethics of Environmental Concern*, p. 149. See also p. 159.

25.   Callicott, "Intrinsic Value, Quantum Theory," p. 258.

26.   Ibid., p. 275.

27.   Eric Katz, "Organism, Community, and the 'Substitution Problem,'" *Environmental Ethics* 7 (1985): 243. Oddly, Katz goes on to associate intrinsic value with "autonomy," which he in turn locates (p. 246) in the fact that "natural individuals . . . pursue their own *interests* while serving roles in the community."

28.   Leaving aside Callicott's argument for nature as one's "extended self."

29. Peter Singer, *Animal Liberation* (New York: Avon Books, 1975), p. 8. Singer repeats this section verbatim in *Practical Ethics* (Cambridge: Cambridge University Press, 1979), p. 50. The leap is surprisingly common. See, e.g., William Frankena, "Ethics and the Environment," in *Ethics and Problems of the 21st Century*, p. 11, and G. J. Warnock, *The Object of Morality* (London: Methuen & Co., 1971), p. 151. Scott Lehmann judges this to be "the standard view among moral philosophers" and rests his case against the "rights" of wilderness areas on the premise that "only subjects of experience can be harmed or benefited" ("Do Wildernesses Have Rights?" *Environmental Ethics* 3 [1981]: 136–38).

30. Norton, "Environmental Ethics and Nonhuman Rights," p. 35.

31. Devastating critiques of claims to have demonstrated plant sentience include Arthur Galston "The Unscientific Method," *Natural History*, March 1974, and Arthur W. Galston and Clifford L. Slayman, "The Not-So-Secret Life of Plants," *American Scientist* 67 (1979): 337–44.

32. Paul Taylor, "The Ethics of Respect for Nature," *Environmental Ethics* 3 (1981): 200. Taylor has reiterated this in *Respect for Nature*.

33. Ibid., p. 199.

34. Ibid., pp. 210–11.

35. Goodpaster, "On Being Morally Considerable," pp. 319, 323.

36. Robin Attfield, "The Good of Trees," *Journal of Value Inquiry* 15 (1981): 37. See also Attfield, *The Ethics of Environmental Concern*, pp. 140–65.

37. Jay Kantor, "The 'Interests' of Natural Objects," *Environmental Ethics* 2 (1980): 169.

38. Rodman, "The Liberation of Nature?" pp. 100, 117.

39. James K. Mish'alani, "The Limits of Moral Community and the Limits of Moral Thought," *Journal of Value Inquiry* 16 (1982): 138.

40. Goodpaster, "On Being Morally Considerable," p. 323.

41. Goodpaster correctly describes the idea that a house's porch has interests as "simply incoherent" ("On Stopping at Everything: A Reply to W. M. Hunt," *Environmental Ethics* 2 [1980]: 282). We cannot dismiss the machines in my list so easily.

42. Mish'alani and Taylor recognize this, but I find their solutions unpersuasive. They seem to imply (implausibly) that if we humans should turn out to be the artifacts of a Creator, we should cease to regard ourselves as morally considerable. Taylor, *Respect for Nature*, p. 124 and Mish'alani, "Limits of Moral Community," p. 139.

43. Even so, it is surprising that environmental ethicists have not looked more often to the philosophy of science literature. Brennan is an exception. See "Moral Standing of Natural Objects," pp. 41–44. (Taylor mentions, in passing, that a philosophical literature about goal-directedness exists, but he does not make much use of it. [*Respect for Nature*, p. 122, n. 8].)

44. The problem of the "missing goal-object" is that behavior may be directed at a goal that happens to be unattainable or even nonexistent. This fact seems fatal for accounts of goal-directedness in terms of feedback. See Israel Scheffler, *The Anatomy of Inquiry*, (New York: Alfred A. Knopf, 1963), pp. 112–16. These worries, nevertheless, still trouble many. It is for this reason that William C. Wimsatt insists, defensively, that "teleology, properly so-called, does have a respectable role in the scientific characterization of non-cognitive systems" ("Teleology and the Logical Structure of Function Statements," *Studies in the History and Philosophy of Science* 3 [1972]: 80). Wimsatt maintains that he is innocent of anthropomorphism (p. 65). See also Michael Ruse, *The Philosophy of Biology* (London: Hutchinson, 1973), pp. 174–76.

45. W. Murray Hunt claims that a porch's "needs" (e.g., to be painted) are as evident as a lawn's need to be watered ("Are Mere *Things* Morally Considerable?" *Environmental Ethics* 2 [1980]: 59–66). R. G. Frey asserts that a Rembrandt painting has interests in every sense in which a dog has them, in *Interests and Rights: The Case Against Animals* (Oxford: Clarendon Press, 1980), p. 79. Elliott Sober claims that he cannot see how the needs of plants can be plausibly distinguished from the needs of "automobiles, garbage dumps, and buildings." "Philosophical Problems of Environmentalism," in *The Preservation of Species*, ed. Bryan G. Norton (Princeton, New Jersey: Princeton University Press, 1986), p. 184.

46. Ernest Nagel, *The Structure of Science* (Indianapolis: Hackett, 1961), pp. 398–421 and "Teleology Revisited," in *Teleology Revisited and Other Essays in the Philosophy and History of Science* (New York: Columbia University Press, 1979). See also Richard Braithwaite, *Scientific Explanation* (Cambridge: Cambridge University Press, 1953), pp. 319–41 and Ruse, *Philosophy of Biology*, pp. 174–96.

47. Nagel says that persistence is "the continued maintenance of the system in its goal-directed behavior, by changes occurring in the system that compensate for any disturbances . . . which, were there no compensating changes . . . would prevent the realization of the goal" ("Teleology Revisited," p. 286).

48. In Nagel's words: "the goal . . . can generally be reached by the system following alternate paths or

starting from different initial positions" (Ibid). See also Braithwaite, *Scientific Explanation*, pp. 329–34. Braithwaite conducts his analysis entirely in terms of plasticity.

49. Nagel also seems to believe, though, that mechanistic accounts of behavior, when they become available, automatically drive out teleological accounts ("Teleology Revisited," pp. 289–90). He doesn't say whether he thinks we have successful mechanistic accounts of plant behavior yet.

50. For other problems, see Wimsatt, "Teleology," p. 26, David Hull, *Philosophy of Biological Science* (Englewood Cliffs, N.J.: Prentice-Hall, 1974), pp. 107–09, and Larry Wright, "The Case Against Teleological Reductionism," *British Journal for the Philosophy of Science* 19 (1968): 211–23.

51. Nagel, *Structure and Science*, pp. 418–21, and "Teleology Revisited," pp. 287–90.

52. Charles Taylor, *The Explanation of Behavior* (London: Routledge and Kegan Paul, 1964), p. 5.

53. Larry Wright, "Explanation and Teleology," *Philosophy of Science* 29 (1972): 204–18. One problem especially relevant to my thesis here is that, as Wright points out, Taylor's formulation admits "all sorts of bizarre accidents into the category of goal-directed activity" (p. 209).

54. Ibid., p. 211. This formulation obviously fails in the case of intentional but misguided action unless we understand "tends to bring about *G*" as "tends *under normal circumstances* to bring about *G*." If I submit a paper to a defunct journal, that may not tend to bring about the goal of having my paper published, but my behavior is clearly goal-directed. I have submitted the paper in order to have it published.

55. This "because" applies, as Wright acknowledges, in a rather "involuted" way. It applies, nevertheless. See "Explanation and Teleology," pp. 216–17.

56. Kristen Shrader-Frechette, "Organismic Biology and Ecosystems Ecology: Description or Explanation?" in *Current Issues in Teleology*, ed. Nicholas Rescher (Lanham, Md.: University Press of America, 1986), pp. 84–85, n. 28.

57. See Larry Wright, "Functions," *Philosophical Review* 82 (1973): 139–68, esp. 159–64.

58. See, for example, Andrew Woodfield, *Teleology* (Cambridge: Cambridge University Press, 1976), pp. 83–88, and Arthur Minton, "Wright and Taylor: Empiricist Teleology," *Philosophy of Science* 42 (1975): 299. Wright defends himself in "The Ins and Outs of Teleology: A Critical Examination of Woodfield," *Inquiry* 21 (1978): 233–45.

59. Jonathan Bennett, for instance, in *Linguistic Behavior* (Cambridge: Cambridge University Press, 1976), pp. 36–81. Bennett introduces the concept of "registra-

tion" and says that a system (*S*) is goal-directed toward *B* when it does *B* because it registers that it is in a situation where *B* will bring about *G*. This analysis does not immediately exclude plants. The question, as Bennett sees it (p. 79), is whether the behavior of plants has a "unitary" mechanistic explanation. Because phototropism in green plants is "controlled by one unitary mechanism," he refuses to count it as a goal-directed behavior.

60. For a sound discussion of ecosystem stability see John Lemons, "Cooperation and Stability as a Basis for Environmental Ethics," *Environmental Ethics* 3 (1981): 219–30.

61. George Williams, *Adaptation and Natural Selection: A Critique of Some Current Evolutionary Thought* (Princeton: Princeton University Press, 1966 , pp. 210–11. We can, by the way, imagine a system that is goal-directed toward self-destruction. Wimsatt describes a "suicide machine" in "Teleology," pp. 20–22.

62. Wright is keen on distinguishing goals from byproducts, though not in precisely those terms. "Teleological behavior is not simply appropriate behavior," he insists, "it is appropriate behavior with a certain etiology" ("Explanation and Teleology," p. 215). Byproducts result, after all, from behavior that is appropriate in a trivial sense—appropriate for producing those byproducts. Bennett, too, has a good discussion of "fraudulent" attributions of goal-directedness (*Linguistic Behavior*, pp. 75–77).

63. Taylor, "Respect for Nature," p. 210.

64. See note 27 above. See also Heffernan, "The Land Ethic," p. 242.

65. General treatments of teleology often point this out. In *Linguistic Behavior*, Jonathan Bennett treats human intention as a special case of goal-directedness. Andrew Woodfield reverses the analysis, claiming that attributions of goal-directedness to nonsentient things such as plants and machines are extensions of the "core concept" of having an "intentional" object of desire (*Teleology*, pp. 164–66, 201–02).

66. Rodman, "Liberation of Nature?" p. 115.

67. Bennett, *Linguistic Behavior*, p. 45.

68. Donald Worster, *Nature's Economy: A History of Ecological Ideas* (Cambridge: Cambridge University Press, 1985), pp. 332–33.

69. Here is an "organismic" characterization of ecosystems from an ecology text popular throughout the 1950s: "The community maintains a certain balance, establishes a biotic border, and has a certain unity paralleling the dynamic equilibrium and organization of other living systems. Natural selection operates upon the whole interspecies system, resulting in a slow evolution of adaptive integration and balance. Division of labor, integration and homeostasis

characterize the organism. . . . The interspecies system has also evolved these characteristics of the organism and may thus be called an ecological supraorganism." W. A. Allee et al., *Principles of Animal Ecology* (Philadelphia: W. B. Saunders, 1949), p. 728.

70. Robert M. May, "The Evolution of Ecological Systems," *Scientific American*, September 1987, p. 161. This sort of individualism by no means excludes altruism. Many individual organisms aim to some extent at the survival of their kin.

71. Robert E. Ricklefs, *The Economy of Nature* (Portland, Oreg.: Chiron Press, 1976), p. 355.

72. See also J. Engelberg and L. L. Boyarsky, "The Noncybernetic Nature of Ecosystems," *The American Naturalist* 114 (1979): 317–24. "That a system is stable, that it can resist perturbations, is not a sign that it is cybernetic." Engelberg and Boyarsky's main point is that ecosystems lack the "global information networks" that integrate the parts of goal-directed systems such as organisms.

73. See, for logic similar to mine, Elliott Sober's treatment of "selfish DNA" in *The Nature of Selection: Evolutionary Theory in Philosophical Focus* (Cambridge, Mass.: MIT Press, 1984), pp. 305–14.

74. I agree with William Wimsatt, who suggests that "*all* teleological phenomena are ultimately to be explained in terms of selection processes" (*Teleology*, p. 15). David Hull criticizes Wimsatt (unsuccessfully, I think) in *Philosophy of Biological Science*, p. 113.

75. Both of my examples concern single-species populations. I picked them for their simplicity. They make a point that seems to hold, a fortiori, for ecosystems and communities as well.

76. Williams, *Adaptation and Natural Selection*, p. 160. See also pp. 107–08. Jan Narveson also makes this point, observing that as long as some people have children for selfish reasons, then the race is "perpetuated willy-nilly" whether or not anyone has children *in order* to perpetuate the race. Narveson, "On the Survival of Humankind," in *Environmental Philosophy*, ed. Robert Elliot and Arran Gare (St. Lucia: University of Queensland Press, 1983), pp. 51–52.

77. V. C. Wynne-Edwards, *Animal Dispersion in Relation to Social Behavior* (New York: Hafner, 1962), p. 19. See pp. 484–90.

78. David Lack offers evidence that (other things being equal) larger-than-normal clutches typically reduce the number of surviving offspring per nest. David Lack, *The Natural Regulation of Animal Numbers* (Oxford: Clarendon Press, 1954), pp. 21–32, and *Population Studies of Birds* (Oxford: Clarendon Press, 1966), pp. 3–7 and throughout. Reducing the number of eggs does not sufficiently improve each off-

spring's chances to make that a worthwhile strategy, either. Michael Ruse claims (*The Philosophy of Biology*, pp. 179–81) that the tendency of a bird population toward laying clutches of a particular size *is* goal-directed behavior even though (he assumes) it isn't a result of group selection. He thinks he is using Nagel's conception of goal-directedness. The problem, I suspect, is that he does not subject the population's behavior to a robust version of the persistence test. It is not clear that Ruse can get the right answer even in the theater-crowd case.

79. Wynne-Edwards, *Animal Dispersion*, p. 18.

80. Richard Dawkins, *The Selfish Gene* (Oxford: Oxford University Press, 1976), esp. chaps. 5–7. See, for example, Dawkins' explanation of how sterile castes have evolved in the social insects. Compare Wynne-Edwards' view that it is *inconceivable* that sterile castes could have evolved except where "selection had promoted the interests of the social group, as an evolutionary unit in its own right" (*Animal Dispersion*, p. 19).

81. See, e.g., David Sloan Wilson, *The Natural Selection of Populations and Communities* (Menlo Park, Calif.: Benjamin/Cummings, 1980) and Michael Gilpin, *Group Selection in Predator-Prey Communities* (Princeton: Princeton University Press, 1975).

82. John Cassidy, "Philosophical Aspects of Group Selection," *Philosophy of Science* 45 (1978): 575–94. See also Sober, *The Nature of Selection*, pp. 255–66, 314–68.

83. Some parasites may be an exception. See Peter W. Price, *Evolutionary Biology of Parasites* (Princeton: Princeton University Press, 1980). I am not sure, either, exactly what to say about cases of exceedingly close symbiosis, as in lichens.

84. Robert M. May, "The Evolution of Ecological Systems," *Scientific American*, September 1978, p. 161.

85. Sober, "Philosophical Problems for Environmentalism," p. 185. The upshot? "An environmentalism based on the idea that the ecosystem is directed toward stability and diversity," he says, "must find its foundation elsewhere." Thus Sober has anticipated the central theme of my argument, though in my opinion he is much too quick to draw this conclusion.

86. Robert McIntosh, "The Background and Some Current Problems of Theoretical Ecology," in *Conceptual Issues in Ecology*, ed. Esa Saarinen (Dordrecht, Holland: D. Reidel, 1982), p. 10. The context makes it clear that McIntosh finds this survival lamentable.

87. John L. Harper, "Terrestrial Ecology," in *Changing Scenes in the Natural Sciences, 1776–1976* ed. Clyde E. Goulden (Philadelphia: Academy of Natural Sciences, 1977), pp. 148–49 (emphasis added).

88. See J. L. Richardson, "The Organismic Community: Resilience of an Embattled Ecological Concept," *Bioscience,* July 1980, pp. 465–71. See also R. V. O'Neill et al., *A Hierarchical Concept of Ecosystems* (Princeton: Princeton University Press, 1986), pp. 37–54.

89. See, e.g., Richardson's discussion of "keystone" species.

90. Could my dismissal of group selection be too hasty? A referee points out that group selection is "not a scientific joke like 'Creation Science'." True enough. One respected ecologist who assumes group selection at the community level is Eugene Odum. See *Fundamentals of Ecology,* 3rd ed. (Philadelphia: W. B. Saunders, 1971), pp. 251–75. See also M. J. Dunbar, "The Evolution of Stability in Marine Environments: Natural Selection at the Level of the Ecosystem,"

American Naturalist 94 (1960): 129–36. Nevertheless, Wynne-Edwards (whom the referee mentions favorably) has something in common with Creation scientists I have read—he carefully ignores the explanations that his opponents offer. See, for example, Lack's annoyed reply to Wynne-Edwards in *Population Studies,* pp. 299–312.

91. The next step—to ecosystem moral considerability—might not be as tempting as some have thought. It tends to devalue the individual, perhaps too much. See Katz's criticism of Callicott's ethical holism in "Organism, Community, and the 'Substitution Problem'." See also H. J. McCloskey's criticism of holistic political philosophies in "The State as an Organism, as a Person, and as an End in Itself," *Philosophical Review* 72 (1963): 306–26.

Duties to Endangered Species

Holmes Rolston III

Duties to Species

Humans value their environment and have duties to fellow humans. But these duties yield an ethic concerning the environment that, from an interspecific viewpoint, is submoral, although it is moral intraspecifically within *Homo sapiens.* Even those duties that we have been advancing to extend ethics into the nonhuman environment—duties to sentient animals and to plants and other organisms—are not duties to species. Can we make any sense of the idea of duties to species? Especially with regard to endangered species, such duties might supplement or challenge—even override—our duties to persons or to individual animals and plants.

Humans versus Endangered Species

Based on the claims of human superiority . . . the obligation to protect humans trumps the obligation to protect *individual* animals and plants, short of extenuating circumstances and even if critical animal and plant goods sometimes outweigh nonbasic humans goods. But it does not follow that the obligation to protect one or even a group of humans trumps the obligation to protect whole *species.* Further, our obligation to protect *existing* lives can be

greater than our obligation to bring into existence yet *unborn* lives, and this may offset the otherwise greater obligation to protect humans over animals and plants. It could be more important to protect one million existing species than to bring into existence an additional one million persons—a choice not as farfetched as it may first appear in view of the present pace of tropical deforestation.

The mountain gorilla (*Gorilla gorilla beringei*) survives in a population of about 240 animals, with most hope of survival in a group of 150 in the Pare des Volcans, a 30,000-acre national park in Rwanda. This small African country has the highest human population density in Africa, a population expected to double by the end of the century. About 95 percent of the people subsist on small farms that average 2.5 acres per family. The park has already been shrunk by 40 percent to bring land into cultivation; there are pressures to reduce it more. Elimination of the park could support perhaps 36,000 persons at a subsistence level, only 25 percent of one year's population growth. Most persons in Rwanda have little interest in wildlife. Some poach gorillas to make the skulls and hands into souvenirs for tourists or to use organs—testicles, tongues, ears—for their magical powers over enemies.[1] One gorilla, Digit, who had been seen by millions on a National Geo-

Environmental Ethics: Duties to and Values in the Natural World, by Holmes Rolston III (Philadelphia: Temple University Press, 1988), 137–159. Reprinted by permission.

graphic television feature, was speared and his head and hands sold for $20. Gorillas in the zoo trade sell for over $10,000. In captivity they reproduce poorly.

Do the human values here—land for an exploding population, souvenirs, magical charms, zoo sales—justify exterminating the gorilla? There would be many negative effects: clearing the high ground would bring erosion and reduced income from tourism; moreover, given the existing social institutions, the benefits of cattle grazing and zoo sales are unlikely to reach many of the poor. There is really no evidence that the Rwandans would, on average, be any better off a decade hence, since nothing would have been done about the real sources of poverty and injustice. Extinction of the gorilla would provide only momentary relief space for a fraction of an annually enlarging population of subsistence farmers. It would not solve any of the deeper problems.

Though humans are superior to gorillas, gorillas are a majestic life form. Often they are placed in family Pongidae, but many think they should be placed in family Hominidae, the same family as humans. (Recall the intelligence and affection shown by Koko.) Humans are an overpopulating species; mountain gorillas are on the verge of extinction due to human encroachments. The benefits to be gained by the humans doubtfully exceed the losses to be suffered, even from the human point of view; they are often doubtful benefits to existing humans (magical charms, income inequitably distributed, the short-term relief of moving onto new lands) and real but marginal benefits to a small group of not yet existing humans (a future generation of subsistence farmers who would live on the new land, perhaps only until erosion made it useless). For this is traded extinction for the gorillas—forever. Here it seems that if in fact they have anything to lose, humans ought, to lose.

A Florida panther, one of about thirty surviving in an endangered subspecies, was mangled when hit by a car. Named Big Guy, he was flown by helicopter to the state university veterinary medical school. Steel plates were inserted in both legs, and the right foot rebuilt. Is this appropriate treatment? Is it something humans ought to do out of justice or benevolence? Because of concern for the individual animal or for the subspecies? Big Guy's story mostly served to bring to focus a bigger issue. He cannot be released into the wild but is being bred

and his offspring will be used for experiments to protect his species.

Protecting the panther, Florida's state animal, could cost $112.5 million. The subspecies is peculiarly adapted to the Florida swamps, in contrast with the dry, mountainous areas inhabited by the West's cougars. The panther is nearly extinct because of dwindling habitat, and the last critical habitat—the Big Cypress Swamp, adjacent to the Everglades—is being cut in half by Interstate 75. Florida has argued for spending $27 million (about $1 million per panther) to build forty bridges that will allow the panthers to pass under the high-fenced interstate: both "animal crossings," bridges over dry land, and "extended bridges," bridges over water with spans over land at each end. Otherwise, as Big Guy illustrates, many will be killed by the fast, increasing traffic. Critics—including some federal authorities, who bear 90 percent of the costs—say this is too expensive and won't work. Wildlife biologists claim that it will (as the Alaska pipeline was redesigned to permit caribou migration); they have tracked radio-collared cats and located their routes. The ten-foot-high fence, combined with an outrigger and a drainage canal beside it, will discourage the cats from entering the highway. Most of the remaining costs are to compensate several dozen landowners for isolating their land and for the purchase of buffer zones. It will also be necessary to restrict deer hunters (deer are the panther's principal prey) and to curb 4,000 offroad vehicle recreationists who disturb the area.[2] Although federal authorities were unable to release any money for this project, the state of Florida is building thirty-seven of the bridges at state expense.

Again, though humans are superior to panthers, the human costs here (about $10 per Floridian, about fifty cents per U.S. citizen) hardly seem high enough to justify the extinction of a subspecies. The loss of limited recreation and sport hunting would be offset by renewed respect for life. Wildlands acquired or protected in an already overcrowded state are valuable with or without the panther. Corridors and crossings that connect otherwise isolated reserves are important for many mammals. The bridges may prove futile, but Americans regularly risk those amounts of money in lotteries. To be gained is the continued existence of an animal handsome enough to be chosen as the state symbol, highly evolved on the top trophic rung of a rare Everglades ecosystem, thought by many to be the most aesthetically exciting animal on the North American continent. In this case too, if in fact humans can be shown to lose, they ought to be the losers in favor of the cat.

Sentient Life versus Endangered Species

A concern for species is not just a way of protecting sentient lives or even individual organisms. The National Park Service allows hundreds of elk to starve in Yellowstone each year, but the starving of an equal number of grizzly bears, which would involve about the same loss in felt experience, would be of much greater concern. Only about 100 whooping cranes remain; to kill and eat them would result in jail sentences. But we kill and eat 100 turkeys without a thought. Something more is at stake ethically than a concern for individual lives. Humans have no duty to deny their ecology and thus do not interrupt spontaneous nature (assume no duty to feed the elk), and humans do sacrifice individual animals and plants to meet their needs. But humans have at least some duty not to cause ecological disruption, a duty not to waste species. If we can identify this concern more precisely, we can formulate our duties to species and complete this chapter in an environmental ethic.

On San Clemente Island, the U.S. Fish and Wildlife Service and the California Department of Fish and Game asked the Navy to shoot 2,000 feral goats to save three endangered plant species: *Malacothamnus clementinus, Castilleja grisea, Delphinium kinkiense*. That would mean killing several goats for each known surviving plant. Isolated from the mainland, the island had evolved a number of unique species. Goats, introduced in the early 1800s, thrived even after humans abandoned them but adversely affected the ecosystem. They have probably already eradicated several never-known species. Following renewed interest in endangered species, officials decided to eliminate the goats. By herding and trapping, 21,000 were removed, but the remaining goats were in inaccessible canyons, which required their being shot from helicopters.

The Fund for Animals filed suit to prevent this, and the court ordered all goats removed. After the shooting of 600 goats, the Fund put political pressure on the Department of the Navy to secure a moratorium on further shooting. Happily, workers

for the Fund rescued most of the goats with novel trapping techniques; unhappily, neither they nor others have been able to live-trap them all. The goats reproduce rapidly during any delay, and there are still more than 1,000 on the island.[3]

Despite the Fund's objections, the Park Service did kill hundreds of rabbits on Santa Barbara Island to protect a few plants of *Dudleya traskiae*, once thought extinct and curiously called the Santa Barbara live-forever. This island endemic was once common. But New Zealand red rabbits, introduced about 1900, fed on it; by 1970 no *Dudleya* could be found. With the discovery in 1975 of five plants, a decision was made to eradicate the rabbits.

Does protecting endangered species justify causing suffering and death? Does the fact that the animals were exotic make a difference? An ethic based on animal rights will come to one answer, but a more broadly based environmental ethic will prefer plant species, especially species in their ecosystems, over sentient animals that are exotic misfits.

Following the theory worked out . . . a goat does have more intrinsic value than a plant, although plants have more instrumental value in ecosystems than goats. So if the tradeoff were merely 1,000 goats for 100 plants, regardless of instrumental, ecosystemic, and species considerations, the goats would override the plants. But the picture is more complex. Out of place from their original ecosystems, goats are degrading the ecosystems in which they currently exist, producing the extinctions of species that are otherwise well fitted and of instrumental value in those ecosystems. At this point the well-being of plants outweighs the welfare of the goats. . . .

Speciation and Superkilling Species

A consideration of species is both revealing and challenging because it offers a biologically based counterexample to the focus on individuals—typically sentient and usually persons—so characteristic of Western ethics. In an evolutionary ecosystem it is not mere individuality that counts; the species is also significant because it is a dynamic life form maintained over time by an informed genetic flow. The individual represents (re-presents) a species in each new generation. It is a token of a type, and the type is more important than the token.

It is as logical to say that the individual is the species' way of propagating itself as to say that the embryo or egg is the individual's way of propagating itself. We can think of the cognitive processing as taking place not merely in the individual (either in the brain or in the genetic set) but in the populational gene pool. Genetically, though not neurally, a species over generations "learns" (discovers) pathways previously unknown. A form of life reforms itself, tracks its environment, and sometimes passes over to a new species. There is a specific groping for a valued *ought-to-be* beyond what now *is* in any individual. Though species are not moral agents, a biological identity—a kind of value—is here defended. The dignity resides in the dynamic form; the individual inherits this, exemplifies it, and passes it on. To borrow a metaphor from physics, life is both a particle (the individual) and a wave (the specific form).

Because a species lacks moral agency, reflective self-awareness, sentience, or organic individuality, we may be tempted to say that specific-level processes cannot count morally. But each ongoing species defends a form of life—on the whole, good things; prolife impulses that have achieved all the planetary richness of life. All ethicists say that in *Homo sapiens* one species has appeared that not only exists but ought to exist. But why say this exclusively of a latecoming, highly developed form? Why not extend this duty more broadly to the other species (though not with equal intensity over them all, in view of varied levels of development)? These kinds too defend their forms of life. We humans are the product of such defenses during long eons past. Only the human species contains moral agents, but perhaps conscience *ought not* be used to exempt every other form of life from consideration, with the resulting paradox that the sole moral species acts only in its collective self-interest toward all the rest.

The main thing wrong is that extinction shuts down the generative processes. The wrong that humans are doing, or allowing to happen through carelessness, is stopping the historical gene flow in which the vitality of life is laid and which, viewed at another level, is the same as the flow of natural kinds. The story at the microlevel (in the genes) is really the same story as that at the macrolevel (the phenotypes fitting into a biotic community); the molecular biology records and tracks the molar level. The ecosystem determines the biochemistry as much as the other way round. The shape that the microscopic genetic molecules take is controlled "from above" as information discovered about how

to make a way through the macroscopic, terrestrial-range world (or marine world) is stored in the molecules. In a species we cannot say which level is prior and which is subordinate; the story of life is told at multiple levels. One thing is obvious: the singular individual is neither the only level at which the flow of life is to be understood nor at which its stopping is cause for concern.

Every extinction is an incremental decay in this stopping of the flow of life, no small thing. Every extinction is a kind of superkilling. It kills forms (*species*), beyond individuals. It kills "essences" beyond "existences," the "soul" as well as the "body." It kills collectively, not just distributively. A duty to a species is more like being responsible to a cause than to a person. It is commitment to an *idea* (Greek, *idea*, "form," sometimes a synonym for the Latin *species*). This duty is a categorical imperative to living categories. It is not merely the loss of potential human information that we lament but the loss of biological information that is present independent of instrumental human uses of it. At stake is something vital, past something biological, and all this is something more than an anthropocentric concern. We are called on, again, objectively to evaluate (appraise the worth of) what we may or may not subjectively value (have a personal preference for).

Much is conserved in Earth's subroutines and cycles (matter, energy, materials); much can be recycled and renewed (water, energy, nutrients); there are many equilibria (food chains, species turnover, natural extinctions with respeciation). But in human-caused extinctions there is the loss of unique biological information, with no conservation by respeciation. A shutdown of the life stream is the most destructive event possible. "Ought species x to exist?" is a distributive increment in the collective question, "Ought life on Earth to exist?" Life on Earth cannot exist without its individuals either, but a lost individual is always reproducible; a lost species is never reproducible. The answer to the species question is not always the same as the answer to the collective question, but since life on Earth is an aggregate of many species, the two are sufficiently related that the burden of proof lies with those who wish deliberately to extinguish a species and simultaneously to care for life on Earth.

Every species is a "display" or "show" (also a meaning of the Latin *species*) in the natural history book. These stories are plural, diverse, erratic, but they are not wholly fragmented episodes. The pressures of natural selection pull them into roles into their communities, fit them into niches, give continuity to the stories, and make more unified ecosystemic stories of the many stories. Always, there are themes in their settings, characters moving through space and time, problems and their resolutions, the plotting of life paths. Exceeding the births and deaths of individual members, a specific form of life unfolds an intergenerational narrative. What humans are bound to respect in natural history is not one another's scientific, recreational, or reading material, not rivets in their Earthship, but the living drama, continuing with all its actors. To kill a species is to shut down a unique story, and although all specific stories must eventually end, we seldom want unnatural ends. Humans ought not to play the role of murderers. The duty to species can be overridden—for example, in the case of pests or disease organism—but a prima facie duty stands nevertheless.

One form of life has never endangered so many others. Never before has this level of question—superkilling by a superkiller—been deliberately faced. Humans have more understanding than ever of the natural world they inhabit and of the speciating processes, more predictive power to foresee the intended and unintended results of their actions, and more power to reverse the undesirable consequences. The duties that such power and vision generate no longer attach simply to individuals or persons but are emerging duties to specific forms of life. If, in this world of uncertain moral convictions, it makes any sense to claim that one ought not to kill individuals without justification, it makes more sense to claim that one ought not to superkill the species without superjustification.

Individuals and Species

Many will be uncomfortable with claims about duties to species because their ethical theory does not allow duty to a collection, only to individuals. Only individuals can inject preferences into the system. As Joel Feinberg writes, "A whole collection, as such, cannot have beliefs, expectations, wants, or desires. . . . Individual elephants can have interests, but the species elephant cannot."[4] That premise underlies Feinberg's conclusion, cited earlier, that duties cannot be to species but must be to future

humans, who will have beliefs, desires, and so on. Singer asserts, "Species as such are not conscious entities and so do not have interests above and beyond the interests of the individual animals that are members of the species." That premise supports Singer's conclusion that all our duties must be to sentient beings.[5]

Tom Regan defines the "rights view" as "a view about the moral rights of individuals. Species are not individuals, and the rights view does not recognize the moral rights of species to anything, including survival."[6] Nicholas Rescher says, "Moral obligation is thus always interest-oriented. But only individuals can be said to have interests; one only has moral obligations to particular individuals or particular groups thereof. Accordingly, the duty to save a species is not a matter of moral duty toward it, because moral duties are only oriented to individuals. A species as such is the wrong sort of target for a moral obligation."[7] But beliefs, desires, conscious awareness, rights, individuality, and so forth, are not the only relevant criteria in an emerging environmental ethic.

Individual Goods and the Good of the Species

Even those who recognize that organisms, nonsentient as well as sentient, can have goods, owing to their *telos*, may see the good of a species as the sum of, and reducible to, the goods of individuals. The species is well off when and because its members are; species well-being is just aggregated individual well-being. The "interest of a species" constitutes only a convenient device—something like a "center of gravity" in physics or a "mean" in statistics (neither of which actually exists in the real natural world)—for speaking of an aggregated focus of many contributing individual member units.

But duties to a species are not to a class or category, not to an aggregation or average of sentient interests, but to a life line. An ethic about species needs to see how the species *is* a bigger event than the individual interests or sentience. Making this clearer can support a conviction that a species *ought* to continue.

Events can be good for the well-being of the species, considered collectively, even though they are harmful if considered as distributed to individuals. This is one way to interpret what is often called genetic load, genes that somewhat reduce health, efficiency, or fertility in most individuals but introduce enough variation to permit improvement of the specific form.[8] Not all variation is load; much of it is harmless. And much load may never prove beneficial. But some load, carried detrimentally through generations, on later occasion proves to be beneficial. Less of this variation and better repetition in reproduction would, on average, benefit more individuals in any one next generation, since individuals would have less "load." But in the longer view, variation, including the load, can confer stability in a changing world. A greater experimenting with individuals, although this typically makes individuals less fit and is a disadvantage from that perspective, benefits rare and lucky individuals selected in each generation, with a resulting improvement in the species. Most individuals in any particular generation carry some (usually slightly) detrimental genes, but the variation is good for the species. Note that this does not imply species selection; selection perhaps operates only on individuals. But it does mean that we can distinguish between the goods of individuals and the larger good of the species.

Predation on individual elk conserves and improves the species *Cervus canadensis*.[9] The species survives by its individual elk being eaten! When a wolf is tearing up an elk, the individual elk is in distress, but the species is in no distress. The species is being improved, as is shown by the fact that wolves will subsequently find elk harder to catch. If the predators are removed and the carrying capacity is exceeded, wildlife managers may have to benefit a species by culling half its member individuals. A forest fire harms individual aspen trees, but it helps *Populus tremuloides* by restarting forest succession, without which the species would go extinct.

Even the individuals that escape external demise die of old age; and their deaths, always to the disadvantage of individuals, are a necessity for the species. A finite life span makes room for those replacements that enable development, allowing the population to improve in fitness or to adapt to a shifting environment. The surplus of young, with most born to perish prematurely, is disadvantageous to such individuals but advantageous to the species. Without the "flawed" reproduction that incorporates mutation and permits variation, without the surplus of young, without predation and

death, which all harm individuals, the species would soon go extinct in a changing environment, as all environments eventually are. The individual is a receptacle of the form, and the receptacles are broken while the form survives, but the form cannot otherwise survive.

When a biologist remarks that a breeding population of a rare species is at a dangerously low level, who or what is the danger to? To humans, in view of their impending loss? To individual members of the species? Rather, the remark seems to imply a specific-level, point-of-no-return threat to the continuing of that form of life. No individual crosses the extinction threshold; the species does. Reproduction is typically assumed to be a need of individuals, but since any particular individual can flourish somatically without reproducing at all, indeed may be put through duress and risk or spend much energy reproducing, by another logic we can interpret reproduction as the species keeping up its own kind by reenacting itself again and again, individual after individual. It stays in place by its replacements.

In this sense a female grizzly does not bear cubs to be healthy herself, any more than a woman needs children to be healthy. Rather, her cubs are *Ursus arctos*, threatened by nonbeing, recreating itself by continuous performance. A species in reproduction defends its own kind from other species, and this seems to be some form of "caring." The locus of the intrinsic value—the value that is really defended over generations—seems as much in the form of life, the species, as in the individuals, since the individuals are genetically impelled to sacrifice themselves in the interests of reproducing their kind.

Conservation biologists recommend that adjacent nature preserves should be designated in a triangular rather than a linear pattern, preferably with adequate corridors preserved between them. This increases crossbreeding between seedbed colonies, which benefits species even though it steps up the genetic experimentation and may sacrifice numerous individuals that serve as probes to produce still more healthy later individuals. Vitality is a property of the population as readily as of the individuals within it. An insistent individualist can claim that species-level phenomena (vitality in a population, danger to a species, reproduction of a life form, tracking a changing environment) are only epiphenomena, byproducts of aggregated individuals in their interrelationships, and that the phenomena really center on individual organisms. But our more comprehensive account, interpreting the species itself as a kind of individual, historic lineage over time, is just as plausible. We want individuality, too, but also at the species level. And we want individuality within community, the one as real as the other.

Biologists have often and understandably focused on individual organisms, and some recent trends interpret biological processes from the perspective of genes. A consideration of species reminds us that many events can be interpreted at this level too. As noted already, properly understood, the story at the microscopic genetic level reflects the story at the ecosystemic specific level, with the individual a macroscopic midlevel. The genome is a kind of map coding the species; the individual is an instance incarnating it.

The biological individual is certainly a cybernetic achievement. An individual organism maintains its negentropy by metabolic defenses. On the basis of genetic information it runs a telic course through the environment, taking in environmental materials, using these resourcefully, discharging wastes. But much of what we said . . . about individual organisms as nonmoral normative systems can now be resaid, *mutatis mutandis*, of species. The single, organismic directed course is part of a bigger picture in which a species too runs a telic course through the environment, using individuals resourcefully to maintain its course over much longer periods of time.

In this way of thinking, the life that the individual has is something passing through the individual as much as something it intrinsically possesses. The individual is subordinate to the species, not the other way around. The species too is a cybernetic achievement. The genetic set, in which is coded the *telos*, is as evidently the property of the species as of the individual through which it passes. Some will object that a species does not act on needs or with interests because there is no "it" to act. But the specific type, no less than individual tokens, is an "it." A specific form of life urges survival of "its" kind, defends "its" life form. The "it" is a historic process with vital individuality, though it is not a single organism. This helps us to see that the *telos* of a species is not a fixed end but rather one evolving

over the propagation of the gene linkage, an endless end, although some lines go extinct and others so transform that taxonomists recognize successive species.

Value at the Species Level

There is no value without an evaluator. So runs a well-entrenched dogma in value theory. Humans clearly evaluate their world; sentient animals may do so also. Less clearly, an organism "evaluates" its environment, as when an *Escherichia coli* bacterium prefers glucose over lactose (even though it is programmed to do this genetically). But (some say) no species—whatever "species" exactly is—can evaluate anything, and therefore nothing called "species" can be the holder of intrinsic value, although a collection may be of instrumental value to ("valuable," able to be valued by) bona fide evaluators. Hence, any duties that humans have cannot be to species (though they may concern them) but must be to those evaluators (normally other humans) in whom sooner or later values come to birth.

But we need to revise this logic. Biologists and linguists have learned to accept the concept of information without any subject who speaks or understands. Can environmental ethicists learn to accept value in, and duty to, an informed process in which centered individuality or sentience is absent? Here events can be of value at the specific level, an additional consideration to whether they are beneficial to individuals. The species-in-environment is an interactive complex, a selective system where individuals are pawns on a chessboard. When human conduct endangers these specific games of life, destroying the habitats in which they are played, duties may appear.

The older ethic will say that duties attach to singular lives, most evidently those with a self or some analogue to a self. In an individual organism the organs report to a center; the good of a whole is defended. But the members of a species report to no center. A species has no self. It is not a bounded singular. Each individual has its own centeredness, but the species has no specific analogue to the nervous hookups or circulatory flows that characterize the organism. Like the market in economics, however, an organized system does not have to have a controlling center to have identity. Perhaps singularity, centeredness, selfhood, individuality are not the only processes to which duty attaches.

Having a biological identity reasserted genetically over time is as true of the species as of the individual. In fact, taxonomists can often distinguish two species more readily than two individuals within a species. Uniqueness attaches to the dynamic historical lineage, even if the members also are, in their own ways, idiographic. Individual organisms come and go; the marks of the individual species collectively remain much longer. Biological identity need not attach to the centered organism; it can persist as a discrete, vital pattern over time.

A consideration of species strains any ethic fixed on individual organisms, much less on sentience or persons. But the result can be biologically sounder, though it revises what was formerly thought logically permissible or ethically binding. When ethics is informed by this kind of biology, it is appropriate to attach duty dynamically to the specific form of life. The species line is the more fundamental living system, the whole of which individual organisms are the essential parts. The species too has its integrity, its individuality, its "right to life" (if we must use the rhetoric of rights), and it is more important to protect this than to protect individual integrity. Again and again, processes of value found first in an organic individual reappear at the specific level: defending a particular form of life, pursuing a pathway through the world, resisting death (extinction), regeneration maintaining a normative identity over time, storied achievements, creative resilience learning survival skills. If, at the specific level, these processes are just as evident or even more so, what prevents duties from arising at that level? The appropriate survival unit is the appropriate level of moral concern.

Protecting Species versus Protecting Individual Organisms

Should sportsmen forgo shooting ducks at twilight, when it is difficult to distinguish common ducks from endangered species? Migratory game birds are hunted on national forest lands; regulations ordinarily permit shooting from a half-hour before sunrise to a half-hour after sunset. The Defenders of Wildlife sued the Department of the Interior and its secretary, Cecil Andrus, to prohibit shooting at dawn and dusk and thus reduce the accidental shooting of endangered species.[10] The court found that the impact of twilight shooting might be considerable, that the Interior Department had not sufficiently studied the question, that it must adjust hunting hours to keep the killing of endangered species at a minimum, consistent with the other responsibilities assigned by Congress to the department.

In this case there was little concern for individual ducks sacrificed in the hunt; sportsmen were asked to reduce their recreational pleasures (twilight shooting is prime time) in deference to endangered duck species. This seems to value a form of life over these hunters' recreational interests. One could weigh in the recreational pleasures of bird watchers, who enjoy seeing rare ducks, and perhaps argue that on overall balance humans lose nothing. And there is always the sense in which those who do the right thing never lose. Yet there remains in this decision some respect for species that overrides human preferences, a respect that operates at a different level from respect for individual ducks—in contrast, for instance, to the moral concern that seeks to prohibit the use of lead shot. . . .

Should fisherman suffer reduced fishing privileges to protect the endangered crocodile? Everglades National Park authorities have restricted fishing to protect the American crocodile, in jeopardy throughout southern Florida and the Caribbean. The crocodile, while nesting, is quite sensitive to human disturbances especially from motorboats. Commercial fishing, involving about $1.2 million annually, is to be prohibited entirely, and recreational fishing forbidden in 18,000 of the total 660,000 estuarine acres of the park. The Organized Fishermen of Florida sued the Department of the Interior (and Secretary Andrus again!) to relax the restriction. But the court found undisputed evidence that the stricter regulations would benefit the species.[11]

Here again, consideration for an endangered species, beyond the concern for individuals, seems to override the interests of the fishermen. In Louisiana, where the alligator is no longer threatened, there are no comparable restrictions, though the life of an individual alligator is presumably the approximate equal of the life of an individual crocodile. Many thousands of alligators are killed every year. . . .

Again too, one could introduce the recreational interests of crocodile watchers and say that humans on overall balance have nothing to lose. Yet meanwhile, we have an ethic, enforced by law, that restricts human preferences in favor of a crocodile species, without any particular regard to the welfare of individuals.

The legislation establishing Everglades National Park provides that "the said area or areas shall be permanently reserved as a wilderness, and no development of the project or plan for the entertainment of visitors shall be undertaken which will interfere with the preservation intact of the unique flora and fauna and the essential primitive natural conditions now prevailing in the area."[12] The tone of that legislation is oriented as much to ecosystem and to species ("unique flora and fauna") as to individuals. The principal intent of the Endangered Species Act is to protect species—with their individuals—but nothing in the act takes individuals as such to be the object of particular concern. . . .

Species and Ecosystem

A species is what it is inseparably from the environmental niche into which it fits. Although a creative response within it, the species has the form of the niche. Particular species may not be essential—in the sense that the ecosystem can survive the loss of individual species without adverse effect—but habitats are essential to species, and an endangered species typically means an endangered habitat. Species play lesser or greater roles in their habitats, which is not denied by noticing that often there are available substitutes. A specific identity is polar to a communal ecosystem, both in tandem balance.

The species stands off the world; at the same time it interacts with its environment, functions in the ecosystem, and is supported and shaped by it. Humans value a species for its contribution of richness to the system, but its richness exceeds its role effectiveness. Integrity in the species fits into integrity in the ecosystem. The species and the community are not identical goods but complementary goods in synthesis, parallel to but a level above the way the species and the individual have distinguishable but entwined goods. It is not preservation of *species* that we wish but the preservation of *species in the system*. It is not merely *what* they are but *where* they are that we must value correctly.

In Situ and *Ex Situ* Preservation

The species *can* only be preserved *in situ*; the species *ought* to be preserved *in situ*. Zoos and botanical gardens can lock up a collection of individuals, but they cannot begin to simulate the ongoing dynamism of gene flow over time under the selection pressures in a wild biome. They amputate the species from its habitat. The full integrity of the species must be integrated into the ecosystem. This species-environment complex ought to be preserved because it is the generative context of value. *Ex situ* preservation, while it may save resources and souvenirs, does not preserve the generative process intact. Besides missing half the beauty of what is taking place, it misses the burden of the human duties. Again, the appropriate survival unit is the appropriate level of moral concern.

Pere David's deer, extinct in the wild for 2,000–3,000 years, was preserved by Chinese royalty. In the last century Pere Armand David brought some deer to Europe from the Imperial Garden in Peking, and there are now about 800 in zoos throughout the world. The deer in China were killed during the Boxer Rebellion, but some have been returned to Chinese zoos. The original habitat of the deer is unknown and, so far as it can be guessed, is gone. The deer do well in captivity. Should they be preserved? By any duty to species, they need not be. In an important sense they cannot be, for the deer have already become domestic animals, no longer subject to natural selection. One has only the product, not the process. But they might be preserved as relics, souvenirs, entertainment for persons. Since the extinction was artificial, one might argue that if the natural habitat were known and available, they should be restored to the wild.

Anthropogenic versus Natural Extinctions

It might seem that ending the history of a species now and again is not far out of line with the routines of the universe. But artificial extinction, caused by human encroachments, is radically different from natural extinction. Relevant differences make the two as morally distinct as death by natural causes is from murder. Though harmful to a species, extinction in nature is no evil in the system; it is rather the key to tomorrow. The species is employed in but abandoned to the general currents of life much as the individual is employed in but abandoned to the specific currents of life. Such extinction is normal turnover in ongoing speciation.

But anthropogenic extinction has nothing to do with evolutionary speciation. Hundreds of thousands of species will perish because of culturally altered environments that are radically different from the spontaneous environments in which such species were naturally selected and in which they sometimes go extinct. In natural extinction, nature takes away life—when it has become unfit in habitat or when the habitat alters—and supplies other life in its place. Artificial extinction shuts down tomorrow because it shuts down speciation. Natural extinction typically occurs with transformation either of the extinct line or related or competing lines. Artificial extinction is without issue. One opens doors; the other closes them. In artificial extinctions, humans generate and regenerate nothing; they only dead-end these lines.

From this perspective, humans have no duty of benevolence to preserve rare species from natural extinction, although they may have a duty to other humans to save such species as resources or museum pieces. No species has a "right to life" apart from the continued existence of the ecosystem with which it cofits. But humans do have a duty of nonmaleficence to avoid artificial extinction, which superkills the species in the formative process in which it stands. This prima facie duty can on occasion be overridden: for example with the extinction (which we have almost achieved) of *Orthopoxvirus variola,* the smallpox virus or (could we ever achieve it) of *Plasmodium vivax,* a malaria parasite. But a prima facie duty stands nevertheless. Humans cannot and need not save the product without the process.

Through evolutionary time nature has provided new species at a higher rate than the extinction rate: hence the accumulated diversity. In one of the best-documented studies of the marine fossil record, D. W. Raup and J. J. Sepkoski find that in Cambrian times there were perhaps 100 marine families, in Pennsylvanian times 400, in Triassic times 700. . . .

There have been four or five catastrophic extinctions, anomalies in the record, each succeeded by a recovery of previous diversity. The late Permian and late Cretaceous extinctions are the most startling, with still more remarkable regenera-

tions. Although natural events, these extinctions so deviate from the trends that many paleontologists look for causes external to the evolutionary ecosystem. If caused by supernovae, collisions with asteroids, oscillations of the solar system above and below the plane of the galaxy, or other extraterrestrial upsets, such events are accidental to the evolutionary ecosystem. Thousands of species perished at the impingement of otherwise unrelated causal lines. The disasters were irrelevant to the kinds of ecosystems in which such species had been selected. If the causes were more terrestrial—cyclic changes in climates or continental drift—the biological processes that characterize Earth are still to be admired for their powers of recovery. Uninterrupted by accident, or even interrupted so, they steadily increase the numbers of species.

Raup and Sepkoski further find that the normal extinction rate declines over evolutionary time from 4.6 families per million years in the Early Cambrian to 2.0 families in recent times, even though the number of families (and species) enormously increases. The general increase in diversity results from increased speciation and decreased extinction rates. The reduced extinction rate from Early Cambrian to recent times means that approximately 710 family extinctions did not occur that would have if the Cambrian rate had been sustained. This seems to mean that optimization of fitness increases through evolutionary time.

An ethicist has to be circumspect. An argument might commit what logicians call the genetic fallacy to suppose that present value depends upon origins. Species judged today to have intrinsic value may have arisen anciently and anomalously from a valueless context, akin to the way in which life arose mysteriously from nonliving materials. But in an ecosystem, what a thing is differentiates poorly from the generating and sustaining matrix. In a historical story that sweeps over time, the individual and the species have what value they have to some extent inevitably in the context of the forces that beget them. . . .

There is something awesome about an Earth that begins with zero and runs up toward five to ten million species in several billion years, setbacks notwithstanding.

What is valuable about species is not merely to be located in them for what they are in themselves; rather, the dynamic account evaluates species set as process, product, and instrument in the larger drama, toward which humans have duties instanced in duties to species. R. H. Whittaker finds, despite "island" and other local saturations and equilibria, that on continental scales and for most groups "increase of species diversity . . . is a self-augmenting evolutionary process without any evident limit." There is a natural tendency toward increased "species packing."[13] Nature seems to produce as many species as it can, certainly not just enough to stabilize an ecosystem, much less only species that can directly or indirectly serve human needs. Humans ought not to inhibit this exuberant lust for kinds. That process, with its products, is about as near to ultimacy as humans come in their relationship with the natural world. The human limiting of this limitless process seems wrong intuitively, although we are straining to develop an ethic that clearly specifies why.

Several billion years' worth of creative toil, several million species of teeming life, have been handed over to the care of this latecoming species in which mind has flowered and morals have emerged. Ought not this sole moral species do something less self-interested than count all the products of an evolutionary ecosystem as rivets in their spaceship, resources in their larder, laboratory materials, recreation for their ride? Such an attitude hardly seems biologically informed, much less ethically adequate. It is too provincial for superior humanity. Or, in a biologist's term, it is ridiculously territorial. If true to their specific epithet, ought not Homo sapiens value this host of species as something with a claim to their care in its own right? A reverence for life seems "called for."

An Endangered Ethic?

When an ethicist compares this description of Earth's biological history with the threatened human disruption of Earth's adventure, human activities seem misfit in the system. Although humans are maximizing their own species interests, and in this respect behaving as does each of the other species, they do not have any adaptive fitness. They are not really fitting into the evolutionary processes of ongoing biological conservation and elaboration. They are not really dynamically stable in their ecosystems. Humans do not transcend their own interests to become moral overseers. . . . They do not follow nature, evaluating what is going on.

Yet contemporary ethical systems limp when they try to prescribe right conduct here. They too seem misfits in the roles most recently demanded of them.

The most common cause of extinction in spontaneous nature is for a species to fall into the ever deepening ruts of overspecialization. Homo sapiens has proved remarkably unspecialized and seems in no danger of extinction. Still, there is something overspecialized about an ethic, held by the dominant class of Homo sapiens, that regards the welfare of only one of several million species as an object and beneficiary of duty.

There is nothing wrong with humans exploiting their environment, resourcefully using it. Nature requires this of every species, humans not excepted. What is the case—that humans must consume their environment—ought to be so: humans ought to consume their environment. But humans have options about the extent to which they do so; they also have, or ought to have, a conscience about it. The consumption of individual animals and plants is one thing; it can be routinely justified. But the consumption of species is something else; it cannot be routinely justified. To the contrary, each species made extinct is forever slain, and each extinction incrementally erodes the regenerative powers on our planet.

If this requires a paradigm change about the sorts of things to which duty can attach, so much the worse for those humanistic ethics no longer functioning in, or suited to, their changing environment. The anthropocentrism associated with them was fiction anyway. There is something Newtonian, not yet Einsteinian, as well as something morally naive, about living in a reference frame where one species takes itself as absolute and values everything else relative to its utility. Such limited theories can become true only when they learn their limits.

Concluding a survey of paleontology, D. V. Ager writes, "The history of any one part of the earth, like the life of a soldier, consists of long periods of boredom and short periods of terror."[14] Boredom is not the most apt description of the long routines of evolutionary speciation, but the mass extinctions were certainly periods of terror. Of late, in the most recent chapter in the story, humankind is the great terror—but a terror with a conscience. Turned in on itself to value the human species alone, this conscience makes humankind only a greater terror. Turned outward to accept duties to species and to the ecosystemic Earth, this conscience could make humans the noblest species and give them a more inclusive environmental fitness.

Notes

1. Details from Richard C. Bishop, "Endangered Species: An Economic Perspective," in Kenneth Sabol, ed., *Transactions of the Forty-Fifth North American Wildlife and Natural Resources Conference* (Washington, D.C.: Wildlife Management Institute, 1980), pp. 208–18, esp. 215–16.

2. Juanita Greene, "Fast Growth of Civilization Threatens Panther Survival," and Mark Obmascik, "Protecting Panther Could Cost $112.5 Million," both in *Miami Herald* (International Edition), 12 November 1984, pp. 1A, 7A. Further details from Gary Evink, Florida Department of Transportation, Tallahassee, Florida. In another facet of this case, James E. Billie, chairman of the Seminole Indian tribe, shot, killed, and ate a panther, and was charged with violating the Endangered Species Act. But Billie claims he had a right to kill and eat the panther as part of a religious ritual, under Indian treaty rights and under freedom of religion rights from the First Amendment. See Philip Shabecoff, "Killing of a Panther: Indian Treaty Rights Vs. Law on Wildlife," *New York Times*, 15 April 1987, pp. Al, A24.

3. Details from Jan Larson, Natural Resources Manager, Naval Air Station, North Island, San Diego, California.

4. Joel Feinberg, "Rights of Animals and Unborn Generations," in W. T. Blackstone, ed., *Philosophy and Environmental Crisis* (Athens: University of Georgia Press, 1974), pp. 55–56.

5. Peter Singer, "Not for Humans Only: The Place of Nonhumans in Environmental Issues," in K. E. Goodpaster and K. M. Sayre, eds., *Ethics and Problems of the 21st Century* (Notre Dame, Ind.: University of Notre Dame Press, 1979), pp. 191–206, citation on p. 203.

6. Tom Regan, *The Case for Animal Rights* (Berkeley: University of California Press, 1983), p. 359.

7. Nicholas Rescher, "Why Save Endangered Species?" in *Unpopular Essays on Technological Progress* (Pittsburgh, Pa.: University of Pittsburgh Press, 1980), pp. 79–92, citation on p. 83. Rescher holds that there is an *ethical* (distinguished from *moral*) duty to conserve the value associated with species, but this is a responsibility not *to* species but *for* species, derived from a generalized duty to protect value.

8. G. R. Fraser, "Our Genetical 'Load': A Review of Some Aspects of Genetical Variation," *Annals of Human Genetics* 25 (1962): 387–415.

9. The American wapiti, *Cervus canadensis*, has been recently regrouped by some taxonomists with the red deer of Europe, *C. elaphus*.

10. Defenders of Wildlife vs. Andrus, 428 F. Suppl. 167 (D.D.C. 1977).

11. Organized Fisherman of Florida v. Andrus, 488 F. Suppl. 1351 (S.D. Fla. 1980).

12. 16 *United States Code*, sec. 410 (c) (1982, vol. 6, p. 251).

13. R. H. Whittaker, "Evolution and Measurement of Species Diversity," *Taxon* 21 (1972): 213–51, citation on p. 214.

14. D. V. Ager, *The Nature of the Stratigraphical Record* (New York: Wiley, 1973), p. 100.

E. LAND AND LANDSCAPE

Many important issues arise when we begin to think about the land and the relation of human beings to the land. Here, only a few of the significant inquiries are explored. We pose some key questions. What is property? Is the institution of property good or bad from an environmentally conscious point of view? Are property rights in any sense "absolute"? Do owners have a right to maximally profit from any and all uses of their property? What are some Native American views toward the land? How are Native American views different from the Anglo-American tradition of property? What are some third-world views toward first-world land policies?

We begin this section with Garrett Hardin's famous essay, "The Tragedy of the Commons." In Hardin's view, a great deal of environmental harm has occurred because much that is valuable in the natural world has been *held in common*, and, thus, not divided up according to some scheme of property rights. When resources are held in common, often there are few effective restraints (or no restraints) on use (tightly knit communities are often exceptions). Hardin believes that the

existence of commons may lead to exploitation or overuse because individuals have little
or no disincentive not to withdraw benefits
(consume, destroy, and so on) and pass on
costs to others. Consider what has happened
historically to what is thought of as "unowned" or sometimes "public" property, i.e.,
the air, many rivers, lakes, the oceans, and
outer space. A free good is likely to become an
overused good. Thus, the way to conserve or
preserve nature's goods, or perhaps to use
them in a more equitable and sustainable way,
is to privatize them.

Garrett Hardin points out some of the
drawbacks of not having property rights in
certain goods. Eugene Hargrove, on the other
hand, indicates some of the drawbacks of having such systems, or at least of the Lockean
system that is the Anglo-American heritage.
In his essay, Hargrove traces the Anglo-
American tradition of property rights from the
German and Saxon land use practices to the
writings of Thomas Jefferson and John Locke.

Locke (1632–1704) held the view that one
may make something unowned one's own
property by *mixing one's labor* with it. So, if one
tills land unowned by others and grows crops,
the fruit of one's labor belongs by right to that
person. Locke also added another condition
(often called "the Lockean proviso"): one must
"leave as much and as good for others."[1]

Locke's view has been criticized on many
fronts. For example, contemporary philosopher Robert Nozick, who takes seriously
much of Locke's view, finds the "mixing one's
labor" requirement for property rights problematic. Why, he asks,

> . . . does mixing one's labor with some-
> thing make one the owner of it? . . . why
> isn't mixing what I own with what I don't
> own a way of losing what I own rather
> than a way of gaining what I don't? If I
> own a can of tomato juice and spill it in
> the sea so that its molecules (made
> radioactive, so I can check this) mingle
> evenly throughout the sea, do I thereby

come to own the sea, or have I foolishly
dissipated my tomato juice?[2]

Nozick, however, retains the Lockean proviso. Intuitively, Locke has plausibly insisted
on a *fairness condition;* one cannot just take as
much as one wants. It is worth considering the
reasonableness of the "fairness rider," and
especially its implications for questions about
what we owe future generations. If we owe
them as much capital or environmental stock
as has been available to us, it would seem to
follow that we have serious duties not to
destroy access to clean air, not to kill lakes, not
to create a mass of toxic wastes (in short, not to
diminish the quality and quantity of the
sources and sinks that have benefited us), and
so on.

Two notes of caution are in order here.
First, Nozick manages to interpret "as much
and as good" in a niggardly way, however
much the famous phrase may prompt intuitions of fairness in some of us. Secondly, the
Lockean proviso only applies to resources not
already owned. When something is already
owned, as is most of the land today, different
standards for (re)possession apply.

Nozick says a chemical researcher who
discovers a drug to cure a fatal illness and sells
it for whatever he wishes, even though those
who cannot afford it will die, has not violated
the Lockean proviso. The researcher has left as
much and as good for others by leaving the
chemicals in the earth.[3] In effect, Nozick condones telling dying persons who cannot afford
the drug that they have enough and as good
because they can get a Ph.D. in chemistry and
figure out how to make the drug themselves
(even though said persons will die long before any of this could be done or even
approached).

Once something is owned, what makes its
transfer permissible is voluntariness. If someone steals my VCR, the VCR has been transferred from me to a new owner, but the transfer is not just because I was not a voluntary

party to the exchange. Thus, this view of Nozick's, which he got from Locke, at the least rules out transfers by theft, by force, and by fraud.

Philosopher David Lyons has written an interesting essay in which he analyzes the ethics of land distribution regarding what has come to be known as the United States.[4] The original acquisition by the Native Americans, Lyons maintains, was just because all of the relevant Lockean requirements were met. The Native Americans took land that was not already owned, mixed their labor with it, and were willing to leave as much and as good for others. However, massive unjust transfers took place insofar as the Europeans took much of the land from the Native Americans by force and by fraud. Lyons argues that, on Nozickian and Lockean principles, rectification of this injustice requires some redistribution of the land.

Locke's views are also criticized by Eugene Hargrove. Hargrove shows how Locke's theory of property was used by members of Congress in the late nineteenth century to oppose the preservation of Yellowstone as a national park. Moreover, he sees the Lockean tradition behind some of the amoral and asocial attitudes of contemporary landowners toward the land. Hargrove says, "[e]nvironmentalists in the United States are often confronted by rural landowners who feel that they have the right to do whatever they want with their land regardless of the consequences for other human beings or of the damage to the environment."[5] Hargrove does not explain how the same tradition of property rights in some respects seems to have had a lesser impact on England than the United States. For example, in England it is not uncommon to have laws against building structures on private land that block the view of others.[6]

Hargrove also asserts that " . . . whenever Locke's theory of property . . . surface[s] in county courts, at planning and zoning meetings . . . they still remain a formidable obstacle to constructive political action."[7] He fails to mention that zoning can destroy neighborhoods as well as protect them. Some environmentally-conscious architects and landscape architects see post–World War II restrictive zoning as preventing the possibility of genuine neighborhoods. Carol Faye Ashcraft explains:

> World War II, combined with the increasing romance with the car, marked the beginning of the suburbs and a rush to single-use zoning. . . . [M]ore restricted zoning . . . moved commercial areas to strip centers and offices to commercial areas. The neighborhood concept has vanished. "Zoning codes since World War II really have forced the segregation of uses," says Xavier Iglesias, an architect with the Duany/Plater-Zyberk of Miami, which espouses a return to more traditional neighborhoods.[8]

In a traditional neighborhood, one doesn't need a car to do everything. One can walk to get groceries, to the cleaners, even to the garage that fixes one's car. Current zoning restrictions that prevent mixed uses have the environmentally bad consequence of increasing our dependence on the car.

In "How Much of the Earth Is Sacred?" we see how Native American attitudes toward the land differ radically from how European traditions—both Lockean and Christian—view the land. Hughes and Swan explain why the meeting of the American Indians and the Europeans " . . . was foredoomed to tragedy."[9]

Sacred space, the authors contend, " . . . is a place where human beings . . . experience a sense of connection to the universe."[10] The Christian belief that human beings, like God, transcend nature does not lend itself to the idea of connection. In his famous 1967 essay, "The Historic Roots of our Ecologic Crisis," Lynn White, Jr. pursues some of these same themes. In antiquity, White reminds us, " . . . every tree, every spring, every stream, every hill had its own . . . guardian spirit."[11]

This belief is called *animism*. Christianity destroyed animism . . . and many forests. As White points out, "For nearly two millennia Christian missionaries have been chopping down sacred groves, which are idolatrous because they assume spirit in nature."[12] Spirit then, belongs to humans only.

It is not that Christians have no notion of sacred space; rather, they have not found sacred space in nature. Moreover, some Christians who have tried to reinterpret old doctrines have met with profound opposition. For example, Pope John Paul II has said that " . . . some Roman Catholic feminists threaten to 'undermine' Christianity by practicing 'forms of nature worship' that stray far afield from church teaching."[13] Helen Hull Hitchcock, executive director of Women for Faith and Family, further asserted that " . . . a form of spirituality that attempts to copy Native American rituals and 'adopts certain forms of paganism and gives it a Christian gloss' was spreading among Catholic feminists."[14] Sister Maureen Fiedler, co-coordinator of Catholics Speak Out, replied that feminists who draw on Native American religious traditions do so to create " . . . a sense of connectedness to all of creation." She adds, "I doubt the pope has gotten the full story on this sort of thing."[15]

By destroying pagan animism, Lynn White, Jr. asserts, " . . . Christianity made it possible to exploit nature in a mood of indifference to the feelings of natural objects."[16] Perhaps, however, the idea that the earth is a living being can be carried a bit too far. Hughes and Swan note that Native Americans perceived the earth as " . . . a living being, sacred in all her parts."[17] Amazingly, they conclude from this that "[w]hen tribal elders speak of Mother Earth, they are not using a metaphor."[18] Val Plumwood sees "Mother Earth" as not only a metaphor, but a bad one. Her remarks on the image of Gaia and the repopularization of the notion of Mother Nature apply equally well to Hughes and Swan on the words of Black Elk and Smohalla.

Admittedly, Lovelock's message is that we need to become aware of Gaia and to recognize what she does for us. But the approach remains that of enlightened instrumentalism rather than of recognition of the natural world as a being-for-itself with needs of its own, to be respected for its own sake. Using familiar concepts of motherhood may tempt us to uses of the Gaia concept which are even more problematic: it does not matter if we don't wash our dishes and throw our dirty linen on the floor because Gaia, a sort of super housekeeping goddess operating with whiter than white homeostatic detergent, will clean it all up for us. In this form the concept not only backgrounds the feminine/natural but denies the need for any reciprocal human responsibilities towards Gaia. Such a Gaia might have the trappings of a goddess but is really conceived of a sort of super servant.[19]

One final critical point. Hughes and Swan quote briefly from Chief Seattle without mentioning the controversy surrounding the origins of Chief Seattle's speech. We quote extensively from Eugene Hargrove's, "The Gospel of Chief Seattle Is a Hoax," to familiarize readers with the issue:

It has been informally known for several years that Chief Seattle's famous environmental speech—sometimes known as the "Fifth Gospel," and considered by many to be the best statement ever made on behalf of nature—is actually a work of fiction. . . . Chief Seattle really did make a speech in 1853, 1854, or 1855, in connection either with negotiations associated with the Port Elliott Treaty of 1855 or with the actual signing of the treaty. The chief spoke Duwamish and his words were translated into English by a Dr. Henry Smith, who happened to be on the scene. How accurate the translation is a matter of speculation. This speech, which has been given the title "The Indian's Night Promises to be

Dark," and laments the untimely decay and impending passing of the Red Man, can be found in W. C. Vanderwerth, ed., *Indian Oratory: Famous Speeches by Noted Indian Chieftains* (Norman: University of Oklahoma Press, 1971), pp. 118–22. There are various authentic versions of this speech, but all are derived from this one speech. Chief Seattle never wrote a letter to President Franklin Pierce. The famous environmental speech was written more than one hundred years later by Ted Perry, a screen writer, for a film called *Home,* produced by the Southern Baptist Convention, using a version of the original speech as a model. The words were written in the winter of 1971/72 and the film was shown on national television in 1972.[20]

Having quoted from the Vanderwerth volume, it appears that Hughes and Swan have cited a credible source. Nevertheless, there are numerous other uncontroversial sources available to substantiate their claims.

Even as the ideas of property rights and transcendent spirit are not universally held, so the American penchant for wilderness preservation—seen so clearly in the deep ecologists—does not apply globally. Ramachandra Guha makes clear that in exporting our valuing of wilderness preservation to third-world countries, as in our supporting tiger preserves, Americans fail to realize how culture-bound their values are. America, as a large and rich country, can afford to preserve wilderness. As Guha sees it, doing so is just one more consumer luxury, and one that third-world countries cannot afford. They must give higher priority to the "... integration of ecological concerns with livelihood and work."[21] Here and in his concern for equity and social justice, Guha is in agreement with Vandana Shiva. Guha would in all likelihood agree with Ian Barbour's statement that "[w]ilderness has molded [the United States] as a nation."[22] Barbour also claimed that "... wilderness can

teach us moral lessons; we can learn humility and gratitude, independence, and courage in facing the challenge of the wild."[23] Perhaps Guha would even agree that wilderness has taught Americans some virtues, but social justice and moderation in consumption have not been among them.

NOTES

1. Despite our gender-neutral language here, Locke's views on property are not free of gender bias. See the original texts. See also Lorenne M. G. Clark, "Women and Locke: Who Owns the Apples in the Garden of Eden?" *The Sexism of Social and Political Theory: Women and Reproduction from Plato to Nietzsche,* ed. Lorenne M. G. Clark and Lynda Lange (Toronto: University of Toronto Press, 1979).

2. Robert Nozick, *Anarchy, State, and Utopia* (NY: Basic Books, 1974) pp. 174–75.

3. Ibid., p. 181.

4. David Lyons, "The New Indian Land Claims and Original Rights to Land," *Social Theory and Practice* 4 (Fall 1977).

5. Eugene Hargrove, Abstract, "Anglo-American Land Use Attitudes," *Environmental Ethics* 2, no. 2 (Summer 1980) p. 121.

6. Alan E. Evans, "'Rabbit Hutches on Postage Stamps': Planning, Development, and Political Economy," *Urban Studies* 28, no. 6 (1991).

7. Eugene Hargrove, "Anglo-American Land Use Attitudes," *Environmental Ethics* 2, no. 2 (Summer 1980) p. 148.

8. Carol Faye Ashcraft, "When PUD (Planned Unit Developments) Walked the Earth," *The News and Observer,* Raleigh, NC, October 17, 1993.

9. J. Donald Hughes and Jim Swan, "How Much of the Earth Is Sacred Space?" *Environmental Review* 10, no. 4 (Winter 1986), p. 251.

10. Ibid., p. 247.

11. Lynn White, Jr., "The Historic Roots of our Ecologic Crisis," *Science* 155, no. 3767 (March 1967), p. 1205.

12. Ibid., p. 1206.

13. Gustav Niebuhr, "Pope Levels Criticism at Catholic Feminists," *The Washington Post,* July 4, 1993.

14. Ibid.

15. Ibid.

16. White, "Historic Roots," p. 1205.

17. Hughes and Swan, "Sacred Space," p. 247.

18. Ibid.

19. Val Plumwood, "Conversations With Gaia," in *APA Newsletters* 91, no. 1 (Spring 1992), p. 63.

20. Eugene C. Hargrove, "The Gospel of Chief Seattle Is a Hoax," *Environmental Ethics* 11, no. 3 (Fall 1989), p. 195. See also J. Baird Callicott, "American Indian Land Wisdom? Sorting Out the Issues," *Journal of Forest History* 33, no. 1 (January 1989).

21. Ramachandra Guha, "Radical American Environmentalism and Wilderness Preservation: A Third World Critique," *Environmental Ethics* 11, no. 1 (Spring 1989), p. 81.

22. Ian Barbour, *Technology, Environment, and Human Values* (New York: Praeger, 1980), p. 83.

23. Ibid.

The Tragedy of the Commons*

Garrett Hardin

At the end of a thoughtful article on the future of nuclear war, Wiesner and York[1] concluded that: "Both sides in the arms race are . . . confronted by the dilemma of steadily increasing military power and steadily decreasing national security. *It is our considered professional judgment that this dilemma has no technical solution.* If the great powers continue to look for solutions in the area of science and technology only, the result will be to worsen the situation."

I would like to focus your attention not on the subject of the article (national security in a nuclear world) but on the kind of conclusion they reached, namely that there is no technical solution to the problem. An implicit and almost universal assumption of discussions published in professional and semipopular scientific journals is that the problem under discussion has a technical solution. A technical solution may be defined as one that requires a change only in the techniques of the natural sciences, demanding little or nothing in the way of change in human values or ideas of morality.

In our day (though not in earlier times) technical solutions are always welcome. Because of previous failures in prophecy, it takes courage to assert that a desired technical solution is not possible. Wiesner and York exhibited this courage; publishing in a science journal, they insisted that the solu-tion to the problem was not to be found in the natural sciences. They cautiously qualified their statement with the phrase, "It is our considered professional judgment. . . . " Whether they were right or not is not the concern of the present article. Rather, the concern here is with the important concept of a class of human problems which can be called "no technical solution problems," and more specifically, with the identification and discussion of one of these.

It is easy to show that the class is not a null class. Recall the game of tick-tack-toe. Consider the problem, "How can I win the game of tick-tack-toe?" It is well known that I cannot, if I assume (in keeping with the conventions of game theory) that my opponent understands the game perfectly. Put another way, there is no "technical solution" to the problem. I can win only by giving a radical meaning to the word "win." I can hit my opponent on the head; or I can drug him; or I can falsify the records. Every way in which I "win" involves in some sense, an abandonment of the game, as we intuitively understand it. (I can also, of course, openly abandon the game—refuse to play it. This is what most adults do.)

The class of "no technical solution problems" has members. My thesis is that the "population problem," as conventionally conceived, is a member of this class. How it is conventionally conceived needs some comment. It is fair to say that most people who anguish over the population problem are trying to find a way to avoid the evils of overpopulation without relinquishing any of the privileges

* This article is based on a presidential address presented before the meeting of the Pacific Division of the American Association for the Advancement of Science at Utah State University, Logan, 25 June 1968.

they now enjoy. They think that farming the seas or developing new strains of wheat will solve the problem—technologically. I try to show here that the solution they seek cannot be found. The population problem cannot be solved in a technical way, any more than can the problem of winning the game of tick-tack-toe.

What Shall We Maximize?

Population, as Malthus said, naturally tends to grow "geometrically," or, as we would now say, exponentially. In a finite world this means that the per capita share of the world's goods must steadily decrease. Is ours a finite world?

A fair defense can be put forward for the view that the world is infinite; or that we do not know that it is not. But, in terms of the practical problems that we must face in the next few generations with the foreseeable technology, it is clear that we will greatly increase human misery if we do not, during the immediate future, assume that the world available to the terrestrial human population is finite. "Space" is no escape.[2]

A finite world can support only a finite population; therefore, population growth must eventually equal zero. (The case of perpetual wide fluctuations above and below zero is a trivial variant that need not be discussed.) When this condition is met, what will be the situation of mankind? Specifically, can Bentham's goal of "the greatest good for the greatest number" be realized?

No—for two reasons, each sufficient by itself. The first is a theoretical one. It is not mathematically possible to maximize for two (or more) variables at the same time. This was clearly stated by von Neumann and Morgenstern,[3] but the principle is implicit in the theory of partial differential equations, dating back at least to D'Alembert (1717–1783).

The second reason springs directly from biological facts. To live, any organism must have a source of energy (for example, food). This energy is utilized for two purposes: mere maintenance and work. For man, maintenance of life requires about 1600 kilocalories a day ("maintenance calories"). Anything that he does over and above merely staying alive, will be defined as work, and is supported by "work calories" which he takes in. Work calories are used not only for what we call work in common

speech; they are also required for all forms of enjoyment, from swimming and automobile racing to music and writing poetry. If our goal is to maximize population it is obvious what we must do: We must make the work calories per person approach as close to zero as possible. No gourmet meals, no vacations, no sports, no music, no literature, no art. . . . I think that everyone will grant, without argument or proof, that maximizing population does not maximize goods. Bentham's goal is impossible.

In reaching this conclusion, I have made the usual assumption that it is the acquisition of energy that is the problem. The appearance of atomic energy has led some to question this assumption. However, given an infinite source of energy, population growth still produces an inescapable problem. The problem of the acquisition of energy is replaced by the problem of its dissipation, as J. H. Fremlin has so wittily shown.[4] The arithmetic signs in the analysis are, as it were, reversed; but Bentham's goal is still unobtainable.

The optimum population is, then, less than the maximum. The difficulty of defining the optimum is enormous; so far as I know, no one has seriously tackled this problem. Reaching an acceptable and stable solution will surely require more than one generation of hard analytical work—and much persuasion.

We want the maximum good per person; but what is good? To one person it is wilderness, to another it is ski lodges for thousands. To one it is estuaries to nourish ducks for hunters to shoot; to another it is factory land. Comparing one good with another is, we usually say, impossible because goods are incommensurable. Incommensurables cannot be compared.

Theoretically this may be true; but in real life incommensurables *are* commensurable. Only a criterion of judgment and a system of weighting are needed. In nature the criterion is survival. Is it better for a species to be small and hideable, or large and powerful? Natural selection commensurates the incommensurables. The compromise achieved depends on a natural weighting of the values of the variables.

Man must imitate this process. There is no doubt that in fact he already does, but unconsciously. It is when the hidden decisions are made explicit that the arguments begin. The problem for the years ahead is to work out an acceptable theory of weighting. Synergistic effects, nonlinear variation, and difficulties in discounting the future make the intellectual problem difficult, but not (in principle) insoluble.

Has any cultural group solved this practical problem at the present time, even on an intuitive level? One simple fact proves that none has: there is no prosperous population in the world today that has, and has had for some time, a growth rate of zero. Any people that has intuitively identified its optimum point will soon reach it, after which its growth rate becomes and remains zero.

Of course, a positive growth rate might be taken as evidence that a population is below its optimum. However, by any reasonable standards, the most rapidly growing populations on earth today are (in general) the most miserable. This association (which need not be invariable) casts doubt on the optimistic assumption that the positive growth rate of a population is evidence that it has yet to reach its optimum.

We can make little progress in working toward optimum population size until we explicitly exorcize the spirit of Adam Smith in the field of practical demography. In economic affairs, *The Wealth of Nations* (1776) popularized the "invisible hand," the idea that an individual who "intends only his own gain," is, as it were, "led by an invisible hand to promote . . . the public interest."[5] Adam Smith did not assert that this was invariably true, and perhaps neither did any of his followers. But he contributed to a dominant tendency of thought that has ever since interfered with positive action based on rational analysis, namely, the tendency to assume that decisions reached individually will, in fact, be the best decisions for an entire society. If this assumption is correct, it justifies the continuance of our present policy of laissez-faire in reproduction. If it is correct, we can assume that men will control their individual fecundity so as to produce the optimum population. If the assumption is not correct, we need to reexamine our individual freedoms to see which ones are defensible.

Tragedy of Freedom in a Commons

The rebuttal to the invisible hand in population control is to be found in a scenario first sketched in a little-known pamphlet[6] in 1833 by a mathematical amateur named William Forster Lloyd (1794–1852). We may well call it "the tragedy of the commons," using the word "tragedy" as the philosopher Whitehead used it[7]: "The essence of dramatic tragedy is not unhappiness. It resides in the solemnity of the remorseless working of things." He then goes on to say, "This inevitableness of destiny can only be illustrated in terms of human life by incidents which in fact involve unhappiness. For it is only by them that the futility of escape can be made evident in the drama."

The tragedy of the commons develops in this way. Picture a pasture open to all. It is to be expected that each herdsman will try to keep as many cattle as possible on the commons. Such an arrangement may work reasonably satisfactorily for centuries because tribal wars, poaching, and disease keep the numbers of both man and beast well below the carrying capacity of the land. Finally, however, comes the day of reckoning, that is, the day when the long-desired goal of social stability becomes a reality. At this point, the inherent logic of the commons remorselessly generates tragedy.

As a rational being, each herdsman seeks to maximize his gain. Explicitly or implicitly, more or less consciously, he asks, "What is the utility *to me* of adding one more animal to my herd?" This utility has one negative and one positive component.

1. The positive component is a function of the increment of one animal. Since the herdsman receives all the proceeds from the sale of the additional animal, the positive utility is nearly +1.

2. The negative component is a function of the additional overgrazing created by one more animal. Since, however, the effects of overgrazing are shared by all the herdsmen, the negative utility for any particular decision-making herdsman is only a fraction of –1.

Adding together the component partial utilities, the rational herdsman concludes that the only sensible course for him to pursue is to add another animal to his herd. And another; and another. . . . But this is the conclusion reached by each and every rational herdsman sharing a commons. Therein is the tragedy. Each man is locked into a system that compels him to increase his herd without limit—in a world that is limited. Ruin is the destination toward which all men rush, each pursuing his own best interest in a society that believes in the freedom of the commons. Freedom in a commons brings ruin to all.

Some would say that this is a platitude. Would that it were! In a sense, it was learned thousands of years ago, but natural selection favors the forces of psychological denial.[8] The individual benefits as an individual from his ability to deny the truth even though society as a whole, of which he is a part, suffers.

Education can counteract the natural tendency to do the wrong thing, but the inexorable succession of generations requires that the basis for this knowledge be constantly refreshed.

A simple incident that occurred a few years ago in Leominster, Massachusetts, shows how perishable the knowledge is. During the Christmas shopping season the parking meters downtown were covered with plastic bags that bore tags reading: "Do not open until after Christmas. Free parking courtesy of the mayor and city council." In other words, facing the prospect of an increased demand for already scarce space, the city fathers reinstituted the system of the commons. (Cynically, we suspect that they gained more votes than they lost by this retrogressive act.)

In an approximate way, the logic of the commons has been understood for a long time, perhaps since the discovery of agriculture or the invention of private property in real estate. But it is understood mostly only in special cases which are not sufficiently generalized. Even at this late date, cattlemen leasing national land on the western ranges demonstrate no more than an ambivalent understanding, in constantly pressuring federal authorities to increase the head count to the point where overgrazing produces erosion and weed dominance. Likewise, the oceans of the world continue to suffer from the survival of the philosophy of the commons. Maritime nations still respond automatically to the shibboleth of the "freedom of the seas." Professing to believe in the "inexhaustible resources of the oceans" they bring species after species of fish and whales closer to extinction.[9]

The National Parks present another instance of the working out of the tragedy of the commons. At present they are open to all, without limit. The parks themselves are limited in extent—there is only one Yosemite Valley—whereas population seems to grow without limit. The values that visitors seek in the parks are steadily eroded. Plainly, we must soon cease to treat the parks as commons or they will be of no value to anyone.

What shall we do? We have several options. We might sell them off as private property. We might keep them as public property, but allocate the right to enter them. The allocation might be on the basis of wealth, by the use of an auction system. It might be on the basis of merit, as defined by some agreed upon standards. It might be by lottery. Or it might be on a first-come, first-served basis, administered to long queues. These, I think, are all the reasonable possibilities. They are all objectionable. But we must choose—or acquiesce in the destruction of the commons that we call our National Parks.

Pollution

In a reverse way, the tragedy of the commons reappears in problems of pollution. Here it is not a question of taking something out of the commons, but of putting something in—sewage, or chemical, radioactive, and heat wastes into water; noxious and dangerous fumes into the air; and distracting and unpleasant advertising signs into the line of sight. The calculations of utility are much the same as before. The rational man finds that his share of the cost of the wastes he discharges into the commons is less than the cost of purifying his wastes before releasing them. Since this is true for everyone, we are locked into a system of "fouling our own nest," so long as we behave only as independent, rational, free-enterprisers.

The tragedy of the commons as a food basket is averted by private property, or something formally like it. But the air and waters surrounding us cannot readily be fenced, and so the tragedy of the commons as a cesspool must be prevented by different means, by coercive laws or taxing devices that make it cheaper for the polluter to treat his pollutants than to discharge them untreated. We have not progressed as far with the solution of this problem as we have with the first. Indeed, our particular concept of private property, which deters us from exhausting the positive resources of the earth, favors pollution. The owner of a factory on the bank of a stream—whose property extends to the middle of the stream—often has difficulty seeing why it is not his natural right to muddy the waters flowing past his door. The law, always behind the times, requires elaborate stitching and fitting to adapt it to this newly perceived aspect of the commons.

The pollution problem is a consequence of population. It did not much matter how a lonely American frontiersman disposed of his waste. "Flowing water purifies itself every 10 miles" my grandfather used to say, and the myth was near enough to the truth when he was a boy, for there were not too many people. But as population became denser, the natural chemical and biological recycling processes became overloaded, calling for a redefinition of property rights.

How to Legislate Temperance?

Analysis of the pollution problem as a function of population density uncovers a not generally recognized principle of morality, namely: *the morality of an act is a function of the state of the system at the time it is performed.*[10] Using the commons as a cesspool does not harm the general public under frontier conditions, because there is no public; the same behavior in a metropolis is unbearable. A hundred and fifty years ago a plainsman could kill an American bison, cut out only the tongue for his dinner, and discard the rest of the animal. He was not in any important sense being wasteful. Today, with only a few thousand bison left, we would be appalled at such behavior.

In passing, it is worth noting that the morality of an act cannot be determined from a photograph. One does not know whether a man killing an elephant or setting fire to the grassland is harming others until one knows the total system in which his act appears. "One picture is worth a thousand words," said an ancient Chinese; but it may take 10,000 words to validate it. It is as tempting to ecologist as it is to reformers in general to try to persuade others by way of the photographic shortcut. But the essence of an argument cannot be photographed: it must be presented rationally in words.

That morality is system-sensitive escaped the attention of most codifiers of ethics in the past. "Thou shalt not . . . " is the form of traditional ethical directives which make no allowance for particular circumstances. The laws of our society follow

the pattern of ancient ethics, and therefore are poorly suited to governing a complex, crowded, changeable world. Our epicyclic solution is to augment statutory law with administrative law. Since it is practically impossible to spell out all the conditions under which it is safe to burn trash in the backyard or to run an automobile without smog-control, by law we delegate the details to bureaus. The result is administrative law, which is rightly feared for an ancient reason—*Quis custodiet ipsos custodes?*—"Who shall watch the watchers themselves?" John Adams said that we must have "a government of laws and not men." Bureau administrators, trying to evaluate the morality of acts in the total system, are singularly liable to corruption, producing a government by men, not laws.

Prohibition is easy to legislate (though not necessarily to enforce); but how do we legislate temperance? Experience indicates that it can be accomplished best through the mediation of administrative law. We limit possibilities unnecessarily if we suppose that the sentiment of *Quis custodiet* denies us the use of administrative law. We should rather retain the phrase as a perpetual reminder of fearful dangers we cannot avoid. The great challenge facing us now is to invent the corrective feedbacks that are needed to keep custodians honest. We must find ways to legitimate needed authority of both the custodians and corrective feedbacks.

Freedom to Breed Is Intolerable

The tragedy of the commons is involved in population problems in another way. In a world governed solely by the principle of "dog eat dog"—if indeed there ever was such a world—how many children a family had would not be a matter of public concern. Parents who bred too exuberantly would leave fewer descendants, not more, because they would be unable to care adequately for their children. David Lack and others have found that such a negative feedback demonstrably controls the fecundity of birds.[11] But men are not birds, and have not acted like them for millenniums, at least.

If each human family were dependent only on its own resources; *if* the children of improvident parents starved to death; *if*, thus, overbreeding brought its own "punishment" to the germ line— *then* there would be no public interest in controlling the breeding of families. But our society is deeply committed to the welfare state,[12] and, hence, is confronted with another aspect of the tragedy of the commons.

In a welfare state, how shall we deal with the family, the religion, the race, or the class (or indeed any distinguishable and cohesive group) that adopts overbreeding as a policy to secure its own aggrandizement?[13] To couple the concept of freedom to breed with the belief that everyone born has equal right to the commons is to lock the world into a tragic course of action.

Unfortunately this is just the course of action that is being pursued by the United Nations. In late 1967, some 30 nations agreed to the following:[14]

> The Universal Declaration of Human Rights describes the family as the natural and fundamental unit of society. It follows that any choice and decision with regard to the size of the family must irrevocably rest with the family itself, and cannot be made by anyone else.

It is painful to have to deny categorically the validity of this right; denying it, one feels as uncomfortable as a resident of Salem, Massachusetts, who denied the reality of witches in the 17th century. At the present time, in liberal quarters, something like a taboo acts to inhibit criticism of the United Nations. There is a feeling that the United Nations is "our last and best hope," that we shouldn't find fault with it; we shouldn't play into the hands of the archconservatives. However, let us not forget what Robert Louis Stevenson said: "The truth that is suppressed by friends is the readiest weapon of the enemy." If we love the truth we must openly deny the validity of the Universal Declaration of Human Rights, even though it is promoted by the United Nations. We should also join with Kingsley Davis[15] in attempting to get Planned Parenthood-World Population to see the error of its ways in embracing the same tragic ideal.

Conscience Is Self-Eliminating

It is a mistake to think that we can control the breeding of mankind in the long run by an appeal to conscience. Charles Galton Darwin made this point when he spoke on the centennial of the publication of his grandfather's great book. The argument is straightforward and Darwinian.

People vary. Confronted with appeals to limit breeding, some people will undoubtedly respond to the plea more than others. Those who have more children will produce a larger fraction of the next generation than those with more susceptible consciences. The difference will be accentuated, generation by generation.

In C. G. Darwin's words: "It may well be that it would take hundreds of generations for the progenitive instinct to develop in this way, but if it should do so, nature would have taken her revenge, and the variety *Homo contracipiens* would become extinct and would be replaced by the variety *Homo progenitivus*."[16]

The argument assumes that conscience or the desire for children (no matter which) is hereditary—but hereditary only in the most general formal sense. The result will be the same whether the attitude is transmitted through germ cells, or exosomatically, to use A. J. Lotka's term. (If one denies the latter possibility as well as the former, then what's the point of education?) The argument has here been stated in the context of the population problem, but it applies equally well to any instance in which society appeals to an individual exploiting a commons to restrain himself for the general good—by means of his conscience. To make such an appeal is to set up a selective system that works toward the elimination of conscience from the race.

Pathogenic Effects of Conscience

The long-term disadvantage of an appeal to conscience should be enough to condemn it; but [it] has serious short-term disadvantages as well. If we ask a man who is exploiting a commons to desist "in the name of conscience," what are we saying to him? What does he hear?—not only at the moment but also in the wee small hours of the night when, half asleep, he remembers not merely the words we used but also the nonverbal communication cues we gave him unawares? Sooner or later, consciously or subconsciously, he senses that he has received two communications, and that they are contradictory: (i) (intended communication) "If you don't do as we ask, we will openly condemn you for not acting like a responsible citizen"; (ii) (the unintended communication) "If you *do* behave as we ask, we will secretly condemn you for a simpleton who can be shamed into standing aside while the rest of us exploit the commons."

Everyman then is caught in what Bateson has called a "double bind." Bateson and his co-workers have made a plausible case for viewing the double bind as an important causative factor in the genesis of schizophrenia.[17] The double bind may not always be so damaging, but it always endangers the mental health of anyone to whom it is applied. "A bad conscience," said Nietzsche, "is a kind of illness."

To conjure up a conscience in others is tempting to anyone who wishes to extend his control beyond the legal limits. Leaders at the highest level succumb to this temptation. Has any President during the past generation failed to call on labor unions to moderate voluntarily their demands for higher wages, or to steel companies to honor voluntary guidelines on prices? I can recall none. The rhetoric used on such occasions is designed to produce feelings of guilt in noncooperators.

For centuries it was assumed without proof that guilt was a valuable, perhaps even an indispensable, ingredient of the civilized life. Now, in this post-Freudian world, we doubt it.

Paul Goodman speaks from the modern point of view when he says: "No good has ever come from feeling guilty, neither intelligence, policy, nor compassion. The guilty do not pay attention to the object but only to themselves, and not even to their own interests, which might make sense, but to their anxieties."[18]

One does not have to be a professional psychiatrist to see the consequences of anxiety. We in the Western world are just emerging from a dreadful two-centuries-long Dark Ages of Eros that was sustained partly by prohibition laws, but perhaps more effectively by the anxiety-generating mechanisms of education. Alex Comfort has told the story well in *The Anxiety Makers*[19]; it is not a pretty one.

Since proof is difficult, we may even concede that the results of anxiety may sometimes, from certain points of view, be desirable. The larger question we should ask is whether, as a matter of policy, we should ever encourage the use of a technique the tendency (if not the intention) of which is psychologically pathogenic. We hear much talk these days of responsible parenthood; the coupled words are incorporated into the titles of some organizations devoted to birth control. Some people have proposed massive propaganda campaigns to instill

responsibility into the nation's (or the world's) breeders. But what is the meaning of the word *responsibility* in this context? Is it not merely a synonym for the word conscience? When we use the word responsibility in the absence of substantial sanctions, are we not trying to browbeat a free man in a commons into acting against his own interest? Responsibility is a verbal counterfeit for a substantial *quid pro quo*. It is an attempt to get something for nothing.

If the word *responsibility* is to be used at all, I suggest that it be in the sense Charles Frankel uses it.[20] "Responsibility," says this philosopher, "is the product of definite social arrangements." Notice that Frankel calls for social arrangements—not propaganda.

Mutual Coercion Mutually Agreed Upon

The social arrangements that produce responsibility are arrangements that create coercion, of some sort. Consider bank-robbing. The man who takes money from a bank acts as if the bank were a commons. How do we prevent such action? Certainly not by trying to control his behavior solely by a verbal appeal to his sense of responsibility. Rather than rely on propaganda, we follow Frankel's lead and insist that a bank is not a commons; we seek the definite social arrangements that will keep it from becoming a commons. That we thereby infringe on the freedom of would-be robbers we neither deny nor regret.

The morality of bank-robbing is particularly easy to understand because we accept complete prohibition of this activity. We are willing to say, "Thou shalt not rob banks," without providing for exceptions. But temperance also can be created by coercion. Taxing is a good coercive device. To keep downtown shoppers temperate in their use of parking space, we introduce parking meters for short periods, and traffic fines for longer ones. We need not actually forbid a citizen to park as long as he wants to; we need merely make it increasingly expensive for him to do so. Not prohibition, but carefully biased options are what we offer him. A Madison Avenue man might call this persuasion; I prefer the greater candor of the word coercion.

Coercion is a dirty word to most liberals now, but it need not forever be so. As with the four-letter words, its dirtiness can be cleansed away by exposure to the light, by saying it over and over without apology or embarrassment. To many, the word coercion implies arbitrary decisions of distant and irresponsible bureaucrats; but this is not a necessary part of its meaning. The only kind of coercion I recommend is mutual coercion, mutually agreed upon by the majority of the people affected.

To say that we mutually agree to coercion is not to say that we are required to enjoy it, or even to pretend we enjoy it. Who enjoys taxes? We all grumble about them. But we accept compulsory taxes because we recognize that voluntary taxes would favor the conscienceless. We institute and (grumblingly) support taxes and other coercive devices to escape the horror of the commons.

An alternative to the commons need not be perfectly just to be preferable. With real estate and other material goods, the alternative we have chosen is the institution of private property coupled with legal inheritance. Is this system perfectly just? As a genetically trained biologist I deny that it is. It seems to me that, if there are to be differences in individual inheritance, legal possession should be perfectly correlated with biological inheritance—that those who are biologically more fit to be the custodians of property and power should legally inherit more. But genetic recombination continually makes a mockery of the doctrine of "like father, like son" implicit in our laws of legal inheritance. An idiot can inherit millions, and a trust fund can keep his estate intact. We must admit that our legal system of private property plus inheritance is unjust—but we put up with it because we are not convinced, at the moment, that anyone has invented a better system. The alternative of the commons is too horrifying to contemplate. Injustice is preferable to total ruin.

It is one of the peculiarities of the warfare between reform and the status quo that it is thoughtlessly governed by a double standard. Whenever a reform measure is proposed it is often defeated when its opponents triumphantly discover a flaw in it. As Kingsley Davis has pointed out,[21] worshippers of the status quo sometimes imply that no reform is possible without unanimous agreement, an implication contrary to histori-cal fact. As nearly as I can make out, automatic rejection of proposed reforms is based on one of two unconscious assumptions: (i) that the status quo is perfect; or (ii) that the choice we face is between reform and no action; if the proposed reform is imperfect, we presumably should take no action at all, while we wait for a perfect proposal.

But we can never do nothing. That which we have done for thousands of years is also action. It also produces evils. Once we are aware that the status quo is action, we can then compare its discoverable advantages and disadvantages with the predicted advantages and disadvantages of the proposed reform, discounting as best we can for our lack of experience. On the basis of such a comparison, we can make a rational decision which will not involve the unworkable assumption that only perfect systems are tolerable.

Recognition of Necessity

Perhaps the simplest summary of this analysis of man's population problems is this: the commons, if justifiable at all, is justifiable only under conditions of low-population density. As the human population has increased, the commons has had to be abandoned in one aspect after another.

First we abandoned the commons in food gathering, enclosing farm land and restricting pastures and hunting and fishing areas. These restrictions are still not complete throughout the world.

Somewhat later we saw that the commons as a place for waste disposal would also have to be abandoned. Restrictions on the disposal of domestic sewage are widely accepted in the Western world; we are still struggling to close the commons to pollution by automobiles, factories, insecticide sprayers, fertilizing operations, and atomic energy installations.

In a still more embryonic state is our recognition of the evils of the commons in matters of pleasure. There is almost no restriction on the propagation of sound waves in the public medium. The shopping public is assaulted with mindless music, without its consent. Our government is paying out billions of dollars to create a supersonic transport which will disturb 50,000 people for every one person who is whisked from coast to coast three hours faster. Advertisers muddy the airwaves of radio and television and pollute the view of travelers. We are a long way from outlawing the commons in matters of pleasure. Is this because our Puritan inheritance makes us view pleasure as something of a sin, and pain (that is, the pollution of advertising) as the sign of virtue?

Every new enclosure of the commons involves the infringement of somebody's personal liberty. Infringements made in the distant past are accepted because no contemporary complains of a loss. It is the newly proposed infringements that we vigorously oppose; cries of "rights" and "freedom" fill the air. But what does "freedom" mean? When men mutually agreed to pass laws against robbing, mankind became more free, not less so. Individuals locked into the logic of the commons are free only to bring on universal ruin; once they see the necessity of mutual coercion, they become free to pursue other goals. I believe it was Hegel who said, "Freedom is the recognition of necessity."

The most important aspect of necessity that we must now recognize is the necessity of abandoning the commons in breeding. No technical solution can rescue us from the misery of overpopulation. Freedom to breed will bring ruin to all. At the moment, to avoid hard decisions many of us are tempted to propagandize for conscience and responsible parenthood. The temptation must be resisted, because an appeal to independently acting consciences selects for the disappearance of all conscience in the long run, and an increase in anxiety in the short.

The only way we can preserve and nurture other and more previous freedoms is by relinquishing the freedom to breed, and that very soon. "Freedom is the recognition of necessity"—and it is the role of education to reveal to all the necessity of abandoning the freedom to breed. Only so, can we put an end to this aspect of the tragedy of the commons.

References

1. J. B. Wiesner and H. F. York, *Sci. Amer.* 211 (No. 4), 27 (1964).

2. G. Hardin, *J. Hered.* 50, 68 (1959); S. von Hoernor, *Science* 137, 18 (1962).

3. J. von Neumann and O. Morgenstern, *Theory of Games and Economic Behavior* (Princeton Univ. Press, Princeton, N.J., 1947), p. 11.

4. J. H. Fremlin, *New Sci.*, No. 415 (1964), p. 285.

5. A. Smith, *The Wealth of Nations* (Modern Library, New York, 1937), p. 423.

6. W. F. Lloyd, *Two Lectures on the Checks to Population* (Oxford Univ. Press, Oxford, England, 1833), reprinted (in part) in *Population, Evolution and Birth Control*, G. Hardin, Ed. (Freeman, San Francisco, 1964), p. 37.

7. A. N. Whitehead, *Science and The Modern World* (Mentor, New York, 1948), p. 17.

8. G. Hardin, Ed. *Population, Evolution and Birth Control* (Freeman, San Francisco, 1964), p. 56.

9. S. McVay, *Sci. Amer.* 216 (No. 8), 13 (1966).

10. J. Fletcher, *Situation Ethics* (Westminster, Philadelphia, 1966).

11. D. Lack, *The Natural Regulation of Animal Numbers* (Clarendon Press, Oxford, 1954).

12. H. Girvetz, *From Wealth to Welfare* (Stanford Univ. Press, Stanford, Calif., 1950).

13. G. Hardin, *Perspec. Biol. Med.* 6, 366 (1963).

14. U. Thant, *Int. Planned Parenthood News*, No. 168 (February 1968), p. 3.

15. K. Davis, *Science* 158, 730 (1967).

16. S. Tax, Ed., *Evolution after Darwin* (Univ. of Chicago Press, Chicago, 1960), vol. 2, p. 469.

17. G. Bateson, D. D. Jackson, J. Haley, J. Weakland, *Behav. Sci.* 1, 251 (1956).

18. P. Goodman, *New York Rev. Books* 10(8), 22 (23 May 1968).

19. A. Comfort, *The Anxiety Makers* (Nelson, London, 1967).

20. C. Frankel, *The Case for Modern Man* (Harper, New York, 1955), p. 203.

21. J. D. Roslansky, *Genetics and the Future of Man* (Appleton-Century-Crofts, New York, 1966), p. 177.

Anglo-American Land Use Attitudes*

Eugene C. Hargrove

Introduction

Such protected areas as Yosemite, Yellowstone, and the Grand Canyon are often cited as great successes of the environmental movement in nature preservation and conservation. Yet, not all natural objects and areas worthy of special protection or management are of such national significance and these must be dealt with at state, regional, or local levels. In such cases, environmentalists almost always plead their cause before a county court, a local administrative political body, usually consisting of three judges elected by the rural community, who may or may not have legal backgrounds.

Here the environmentalists are probably in for a great shock. Inevitably, some rural landowner will defend his special property rights to the land in question. He will ask the court rhetorically, "What right do these outsiders, these so-called environmentalists, have to come in here and try to tell me what to do with my land?" and answering his own question, he will continue, "They don't have any right. I worked that land; it's my property, and no one has the right to tell me what to do with it!" The environmentalists may be surprised that the farmer does not bother to reply to any of their carefully made points, but the real shock comes at the end when the county court dismisses the environmental issues, ruling in the favor of the landowner.

While the environmentalists may suspect corruption (and such dealings are not unlikely), usu-ally both the judges and the landowner are honestly convinced that they have all acted properly. The property rights argument recited by the rural landowner is a very powerful defense, particularly when presented at this level of government. The argument is grounded in a political philosophy almost three centuries old as well as in land use practices which go back at least to Saxon and perhaps even to Celtic times in Europe and England. When the argument is presented to county court judges who share these beliefs and land use traditions, the outcome of the court decision is rarely in doubt. On the other hand, the tradition that natural objects and areas of special beauty or interest ought to be protected from landowners claiming special property rights, and from the practice of landowning in general, is of very recent origin, and without comparable historical and emotional foundations.

For several decades in the late nineteenth century, the rural landowner's theory of property and land use rights was the primary basis for arguments opposing the preservation of Yellowstone as a national park. During the floor debate on the Yellowstone bill in 1872, for example, Senator Cole of California stated:

> The geysers will remain no matter where the ownership of the land may be, and I do not know why settlers should be excluded from a tract of land forty miles square, as I understand this to be in the Rocky Mountains or any other place. . . . There are some places, perhaps this is one, where persons can and would go and settle and improve and cultivate the grounds, if there be ground fit for cultivation.

When Senator Edmunds of Vermont reminded Cole that, according to reports, the land could not be cultivated, Cole replied, "The Senator is probably mistaken in that. Ground of a greater height than that has been cultivated and occupied," and he continued:

* This paper is based on research undertaken by the author as a Rockefeller Foundation Fellow in Environmental Affairs. The author wishes to thank the Rockefeller Foundation and the John Muir Institute for Environmental Studies for their support during the fellowship period. An earlier version of part of this paper was presented at the 1977 National Speleological Society Convention under the title "Man's Relation to the Land: John Locke and the Private Landowner" (*Proceedings of the 1977 NSS Annual Convention*, pp. 13–17). The author expresses his appreciation to Richard A. Watson for extensive criticism and editing.

Environmental Ethics, Vol. 2, No. 2 (Summer 1980), 121–123, 125–126, 129–131, 133–148. Reprinted by permission.

But if it cannot be occupied and culti-vated, why should we make a public park of it? If it cannot be occupied by men, why protect it from occupation: I see no reason in that. If nature has excluded men from its occupation, why set it apart and exclude persons from it? If there is any sound reason for the passage of the bill, of course, I would not oppose it; but really I do not see any myself.[1]

Similarly, during the floor debate in 1883 in which the Senate considered for the first time whether Congress ought to appropriate money for maintaining the roads of the park and for the salary of the superintendent, until then an unpaid posi-tion, Senator Ingalls of Kansas rose to inform his colleagues that "the best thing that the Government could do with Yellowstone National Park is to sur-vey it and sell it as other public lands are sold." . . .

To environmentalists, the attitudes of Cole, [and] Ingalls . . . seem as unenlightened as those of the rural landowner in the county court today, but at the time of the Yellowstone National Park bill, a mere ten years after the passage of the immensely popular Homestead Act, they were probably a more accurate representation of public attitudes towards western lands than those of the supporters of either park. Most people in those days believed that western lands should be distributed free, and freely, to unpropertied Americans willing to work and improve the land over a short period of time. . . .

My present purpose is to examine traditional land use attitudes. First, I examine the ancient land use practices which gave rise to these attitudes, sec-ond, the political activities and views of Thomas Jefferson which secured a place for them in Ameri-can political and legal thought, and, finally, the political philosophy of John Locke which provided them with a philosophical foundation.

Landholding Among Early German and Saxon Freeman

About two thousand years ago most of Europe was occupied by tribes of peoples known collec-tively today as the Celts. At about that time, these peoples came under considerable pressure from the

Romans moving up from the south and from Ger-manic tribes entering central Europe from the east. Five hundred years later, the Celts had either been subjugated by the German and Roman invaders or pushed back into Ireland and fringe areas of England. The Roman Empire, too, after asserting its presence as far north as England, was in decay. Roman influence would continue in the south, but in northern and central Europe as well as in most of England German influence would prevail.

The Germanic tribes which displaced the Celts and defeated the Romans were composed of four classes: a few nobles or earls, a very large class of freemen, a smaller class of slaves, and a very small class of semifree men or serfs. Freemen were the most common people in early German society. They recognized no religious or political authority over their own activities, except to a very limited degree. As *free* men, they could, if they desired, settle their accounts with their neighbors and move to another geographical location. Each freeman occupied a large amount of land, his freehold farmstead, on which he grazed animals and, with the help of his slaves, grew crops. When necessary, he joined together with other freemen for defense or, more often, for the conquest of new territories.[2] . . .

Strictly speaking, a freeman did not own his land. The idea of landownership in the modern sense was still many centuries away. In England, for example, landowning did not become a political and legal reality until 1660 when feudal dues were finally abolished once and for all. Freemen, how-ever, lived in prefeudal times. They usually made a yearly offering to the local noble or earl, but techni-cally this offering was a gift rather than a feudal payment and had nothing to do with their right to their land. As the term *freehold* suggests, a freeman held his land freely without any forced obligations to an overlord or to his neighbors.

Today, when a landowner demands to know what right the court or anyone has to tell him what to do with his own land he is referring to the origi-nal limitations set on the authority of the county court, and is appealing to the rights which he has informally inherited from his political ancestors, Saxon or German freemen—specifically, the right to do as he pleases without considering any interests except his own.

A modern landowner's argument that he has the right to do as he wishes is normally composed of a set series of claims given in a specific order. First, he points out that he or his father or grandfather worked the land in question. Second, he asserts that his ownership of the land is based on the work or labor put into it. Finally, he proclaims the right of uncontrolled use as a result of his ownership claim. Not all of this argument is derived directly from the freemen's world view. As mentioned above, the modern concept of ownership was unknown to freemen who were engaged in landholding rather than landowning. In other respects, however, there are strong similarities between the views of modern landowners and those of the freemen.

Landholding among German freemen was based on work. A freeman, like the nineteenth-century American homesteader, took possession of a tract of land by clearing it, building a house and barns, and dividing the land into fields for the grazing of animals and for the growing of crops. In this way, his initial work established his claim to continued use.

This emphasis on work as the basis for landholding is especially clear in connection with inheritance. When plenty of vacant land was available, landholdings were never divided among the sons, but, as described above, the sons moved to unoccupied land nearby and started their own freehold farmsteads. Thus, inheritance in those early times was not the acquisition of land itself but rather the transferal of the right to acquire land through work. This distinction is reflected in the early German word for inheritance, *Arbi* in Gothic and *Erbi* in Old High German, both of which have the same root as the modern High German word, *Arbeit*, meaning work.[3]

Thus freemen were interested in land use rather than landownership. The right to land was determined by their social status as freemen and not by the fact that they or their fathers had occupied or possessed a particular piece of ground. The specific landholdings, thus, were not of major importance to the early freemen. Conceivably, they might move several times to new landholdings abandoning the old without the size of their landholdings being affected in any way. As mentioned above, it was their ability to use their holdings, the number of grazing animals, and slave workers they owned, not some form of ownership, which determined the size of their landholdings at any particular time in their lives.

Of course, once unoccupied land ceased to be readily available, freemen started paying much more attention to their land as property, encouraging the development of the idea of landownership in the modern sense. When the inheritance of sons became only the right to work a portion of their father's holdings, the transition from landholding to landowning was well on its way.

Until the time when there were no more unoccupied lands to move to, there was really no reason for freemen to be concerned with proper use or management of their land or for them to worry about possible long-term problems for themselves or their neighbors resulting from misuse and abuse of particular pieces of land. When a freeman lost his mobility, however, he did start trying to take somewhat better care of his land, occasionally practicing crop rotation and planting trees to replace those he cut down, but apparently these new necessities had little influence on his general conviction that as a freeman he had the right to use and even abuse his land as he saw fit.

Today's rural landowner finds himself in a situation not unlike that of freemen in the days when inheritance became the division of land rather than the multiplication of it. In the late eighteenth century and during most of the nineteenth, American rural landowners led a way of life much like that of prefeudal German freemen; now modern landowners face the same limitations their freeman ancestors did as feudal conditions began to develop. Although willing to take some steps toward good land management, especially those which provide obvious short-term benefit, when faced with broader issues involving the welfare of their neighbors and the local community and the protection and the preservation of the environment as a whole, they claim ancient rights which have come down to them from German freemen, and take advantage of their special influence with the local county court, a political institution as eager to please them today as it was more than a thousand years ago.

Thomas Jefferson and the Allodial Rights of American Farmers

When British colonists arrived in North America, they brought with them the land laws and land practices that were current in England at that time. These included entail,* primogeniture,** and most other aspects of the feudal tenure system which had taken hold in England after the Norman Conquest. The American Revolution called into question the right of the king of England to lands in North America which in turn led to attempts to bring about major land reform—specifically, efforts to remove all elements of the feudal system from American law and practice and replace them with the older Saxon freehold tenure system. At the forefront of this movement was a young Virginian lawyer named Thomas Jefferson. . . .

From the first moment that Jefferson began airing his land tenure opinions, he made it completely clear that they were based entirely on Saxon, and not on Norman, common law. Thus, he consistently spoke of allodial rights—*allodial* being the adjectival form of the Old English word *allodium* which refers to an estate held in absolute dominion without obligation to a superior—i.e., the early Germany and Saxon freehold farmstead. . . .

Noting the right of a Saxon freeman to settle his accounts and move to another realm at his own pleasure without obligation to the lord of his previous domain, Jefferson argues that this is also the case with the British citizens who moved to North America. According to this analogy, England has no more claim over residents of America than Germany has over residents of England. In accordance with Saxon tradition, the lands of North America belong to the people living there and not to the king of England.[4] . . .

It is not the king, Jefferson declares, but the individual members of a society collectively or their legislature that determine the legal status of land, and, if they fail to act, then in accordance with the traditions of Saxon freemen, "each individual of the society may appropriate to himself such lands as he finds vacant, and occupancy will give him title."[5] . . .

Jefferson, of course, did not succeed in refuting the claim of the king of England to all land in British America, but by arguing in terms of this old dispute, he gives his position a legal basis which

would have strong appeal among Englishmen with Saxon backgrounds, assuring some political support of the American cause in England.

In 1776, Jefferson got the opportunity to try to turn his theory into practice. Although Jefferson is most famous for writing the *Declaration of Independence,* most of his time that year was spent working on his draft of the Virginia constitution and on the reform of various Virginia laws including the land reform laws. In his draft constitution, Jefferson included a provision which gave every person of full age the right to fifty acres of land "in full and absolute dominion." In addition, lands previously "holden of the crown in feesimple" and all other lands appropriated in the future were to be "holden in full and absolute dominion, of no superior whatever."[6] Although these provisions were deleted, and similar bills submitted to the legislature failed to pass, Jefferson, nevertheless, did succeed in getting the legislature to abolish the feudal inheritance laws, entail and primogeniture.

In a series of letters exchanged with Edmund Pendleton, the speaker of the House of Delegate, during the summer of 1776, Jefferson expresses his desire to reestablish ancient Saxon law in Virginia. In one letter, after insisting that unoccupied land should neither be rented nor given away in return for military service, Jefferson continues:

> Has it not been the practice of all other nations to hold their lands as their personal estate in absolute dominion? Are we not the better for what we have hitherto abolished of the feudal system? Has not every restitution of the antient Saxon laws had happy effects? Is it not now better that we return at once to that happy system of our ancestors, the wisest and most perfect ever yet devised by the wit of man, as it stood before the 8th century?

As for the government selling the land, Jefferson was completely opposed. "I am against selling the land at all," he writes to Pendleton, "By selling the lands to them, you will disgust them, and cause an avulsion of them from the common union. They will settle the lands in spite of every body." This prediction proved to be remarkably correct as evidenced by the fact that the next eighty years of American history was cluttered with squatters illegally occupying government land and then de-

---

* Inheritance along selected family lines.

** A common form of entail, according to which the eldest son inherited everything and the others little or nothing.

manding compensation for their "improvements" through special preemption laws.[7]

In 1784, when he was appointed to head the land committee in the Congress of the Confederacy, Jefferson had a second opportunity to reestablish the Saxon landholding system. Whether Jefferson tried to take advantage of this opportunity is not known because the report of the committee, called the Ordinance of 1784, contains nothing about allodial rights to land. In addition, it even contains recommendations for the selling of western lands as a source of revenue for the government. It should be noted, however, that in one respect at least the document still has a very definite Saxon ring to it. Jefferson managed to include in his report a recommendation that settlers be permitted to organize themselves into new states on an equal footing with the original colonies. This recommendation, which was retained in the Ordinance of 1787, a revised version of the earlier ordinance, not only created the political structure necessary to turn the thirteen colonies into a much larger union of states, but also provided future generations of Americans with an independence and mobility similar to that enjoyed by the early Saxon and German freemen. In his *Summary View* of 1774, as mentioned above, Jefferson had argued that just as the Saxons invading England had had the right to set up an independent government, so British Americans had the right to an independent government in North America. The Ordinances of 1784 and 1787 extended this right to movement and self-determination of American settlers leaving the jurisdiction of established states and moving into the interior of the continent. In large measure, it is thanks to this provision that Americans today are able to move from state to state without any governmental control in the form of visas, passports, immigration quotas, or the like as unhassled by such details as were early German freemen.

The absence of any provisions specifically granting landowners absolute dominion over their land, however, does not mean that Jefferson abandoned this conception of landholding or ownership. Privately and in his unpublished writings he continued to champion the right of Americans to small freehold farmsteads. The only major change seems to be that Jefferson stopped trying to justify his position in terms of historical precedents and instead began speaking in moral terms claiming that small independent landholders were the most virtuous citizens any state could ever hope to have. In a letter to John Jay in 1785, Jefferson writes:

> Cultivators of the earth are the most valuable citizens. They are the most vigorous, the most independent, the most virtuous, and they are tied to their country and wedded to it's liberty and interests by the most lasting bands.[8]

In a letter to James Madison in the same year, he adds:

> Whenever there is in any country, uncultivated lands and unemployed poor, it is clear that the laws of property have been so far extended as to violate natural right. The earth is given as a common stock for man to labour and live on. If, for the encouragement of industry we allow it to be appropriated, we must take care that other employment be furnished to those excluded from that appropriation. If we do not the fundamental right to labour the earth returns to the unemployed. It is too soon yet in our country to say that every man who cannot find employment but who can find uncultivated land, shall be at liberty to cultivate it, paying a moderate rent. But it is not too soon to provide by every possible means that as few as possible shall be without a little portion of land. The small landholders are the most precious part of the state.[9]

In *Notes on the State of Virginia* published in 1787 Jefferson continues in much the same vein:

> Those who labour in the earth are the chosen people of God, if ever he had a chosen people, whose breasts he has made his peculiar deposit for substantial and genuine virtue. It is the focus in which he keeps alive that sacred fire, which otherwise might escape from the face of the earth. . . . While we have land to labour then, let us never wish to see our citizens occupied at a work-bench, or twirling a distaff.[10]

It is in the context of these remarks that Senator Cole and Senator Ingalls felt the need to convince their colleagues in Congress of the necessity of surveying Yellowstone into lots and opening it to settlement. From their point of view, the moral character of the American people as a whole was at stake. These remarks are probably also the basis for the position of rural landowners today when faced with environmental issues. They are defending the American moral virtues which they have always been told their style of life and independence represents.

Had Jefferson been alive in the late nineteenth century when his views were being cited in opposition to the preservation of Yellowstone or were he alive today to see his Saxon freemen busily sabotaging county planning and zoning, he might have become disillusioned with his faith in the virtues of independent rural landowners. Jefferson, after all, as a result of his purchase of the Natural Bridge, perhaps the first major act of nature preservation in North America, ranks as a very important figure in the history of the nature preservation movement. Unfortunately, however, Jefferson's homesteaders and their modern day descendants did not always retain his aesthetic interest in nature or his respect for sound agricultural management which he interwove with his Saxon land use attitudes to form a balanced land use philosophy.

In part, the callousness and indifference of most rural landowners to environmental matters reflects the insensitivity of ancient Saxon freemen who viewed land as something to be used for personal benefit and who, being semi-nomadic, were unconcerned about whether that use would result in irreparable damage to the particular piece of land that they held at any given point in their lives. In addition, however, it can also be traced back to the political philosophy and theory of property of John Locke, a seventeenth-century British philosopher, who had a major impact on the political views of Jefferson and most other American statesmen during the American Revolution and afterwards. This influence is the subject of the next section.

John Locke's Theory of Property

As noted above, German and Saxon freemen did not have a concept of landownership, but only of landholding. As long as there was plenty of land for everyone's use, they did not concern themselves with exact boundaries. Disputes arose only when two freemen wanted to use the same land at the

same time. By the end of the Middle Ages, however, with land in short supply, landholders began enclosing their landholdings to help ensure exclusive use. Enclosure kept the grazing animals of others away and also provided a sign of the landholder's presence and authority. Although enclosure was only a small step towards the concept of landownership, it, nonetheless, proved useful as a pseudo-property concept in early seventeenth-century New England where Puritans were able to justify their occupation of Indian lands on the grounds that the lack of enclosures demonstrated that the lands were vacant. Landownership became an official legal distinction in England after 1660 with the abolishment of feudal dues. The concept of landownership was introduced into British social and political philosophy thirty years later as part of John Locke's theory of property. This theory was presented in detail in Locke's *Two Treatises of Government*, a major work in political philosophy first published in 1690.[11]

Jefferson had immense respect and admiration for Locke and his philosophical writings. On one occasion, he wrote to a friend that Locke was one of the three greatest men that had ever lived—Bacon and Newton being the other two. Jefferson's justification of the American Revolution in "The Declaration of Independence" was borrowed directly from the *Second Treatise*. Many of Jefferson's statements in the document are almost identical to remarks made by Locke. For example, when Jefferson speaks of "life, liberty, and the pursuit of happiness," he is closely paraphrasing Locke's own views. His version differs from Locke's in only one minor respect: Jefferson substitutes for Locke's "enjoyment of property" the more general phrase "the pursuit of happiness," a slight change made to recognize other enjoyments in addition to those derived from the ownership of property. Years later, when Jefferson was accused by John Adams and others of having stolen most of his ideas from Locke's writings, he simply acknowledged his debt pointing out that he had been asked to write a defense of the American Revolution in 1776, not to create an entirely new and original political philosophy. He added that he had not referred to Locke's writings when writing "The Declaration of Independence" or consciously tried to paraphrase Locke's remarks. Locke's influence on him, however, had been so strong that without his being fully aware of it, bits and pieces of Locke's own words had found their way into the document.[12] . . .

In the *Second Treatise* Locke bases property rights on the labor of the individual:

> Though the Earth, and all inferior Creatures be common to all Men, yet, every Man has a *Property* in his own *Person*. This no Body has any Right to but himself. The *Labour* of his Body, and the *Work* of his Hands, we may say, are properly his. Whatsoever then he removes out of the State that Nature hath provided, and left in, he hath mixed his *Labour* with, and joyned to it something that is his own, and thereby makes it his *Property*.[13]

This theory of property served Locke's friends well since it made their property rights completely independent of all outside interest. According to Locke, property rights are established without reference to kings, governments, or even the collective rights of other people. If a man mixes his labour with a natural object, then the product is his.

The relevance of Locke's labor theory to the American homestead land use philosophy becomes especially clear when he turns to the subject of land as property:

> But the *chief matter of Property* being now not the Fruits of the Earth, and the Beasts that subsist on it, but the *Earth it self* as that which takes in and carries with it all the rest; I think it is plain, that *Property* in that too is acquired as the former. *As much land* as a Man Tills, Plants, Improves, Cultivates, and can use the Product of, so much is his *Property*. He by his Labour does, as it were, inclose it from the Common. . . . God, when He gave the World in common to all Mankind, commanded Man also to labour, and the penury of his Condition required it of him. God and his Reason commanded him to subdue the Earth, *i.e.* improve it for the benefit of Life, and therein lay out something upon it that was his own, his labour. He that in Obedience to this Command of God, subdued, tilled, sowed any part of it, thereby annexed to it something

that was his *Property*, which another had no Title to, nor could without injury take from him.[14]

In this passage, the right of use and ownership is determined by the farmer's labor. When he mixes his labor with the land, the results are *improvements*, the key term in homesteading days and even today in rural America where the presence of such improvements may qualify landowners for exemption from planning and zoning under a grandfather clause. Since property rights are established on an individual basis independent of a social context, Locke's theory of property also provides the foundation for the landowner's claim that society has little or no role in the management of his land, that nobody has the right to tell him what to do with his property.

Locke reenforces the property owner's independence from societal restraints with an account of the origins of society in which property rights are supposedly more fundamental than society itself. According to Locke, the right to the enjoyment of property is a presocietal *natural right*. It is a natural right because it is a right which a person would have in a state of nature. Locke claims that there was once, at some time in the distant past, a true state of nature in which people possessed property as a result of their labor, but, nevertheless, did not yet have societal relations with one another. This state of nature disappeared when these ancient people decided to form a society, thereby giving up some of their previous powers and rights. They did not, however, Locke emphatically insists, relinquish any of their natural rights to their own property, and the original social contract establishing the society did not give society any authority at all over personal property. In fact, the main reason that society was formed, according to Locke's account, was to make it possible for individuals to enjoy their own property rights more safely and securely. Thus, society's primary task was and allegedly still is to protect private property rights, not to infringe on them. A government which attempts to interfere with an individual's natural and uncontrolled right to the enjoyment of his property, moreover, deserves to be overthrown and the citizens of the society are free to do so at their pleasure. In effect, Locke is arguing along lines completely compatible with the early Saxon and Jeffersonian doctrine that a landowner holds his property in full and absolute dominion without any obligation to a superior.

The similarity of Locke's position to this doctrine invites the conclusion that Locke, like Jefferson, was drawing inspiration from Saxon common law and that Locke's social contract was actually the establishment of the shire or county court by Saxon freemen. Curiously, however, Locke makes no mention of the Saxons in these contexts and, even more curiously, no political philosopher ever seems to have considered the possibility that Locke might have been referring to this period of English history. In his chapter on conquest, nevertheless, Locke does demonstrate (1) that he knew what a freeman was, (2) that he was aware of the legal conflicts resulting from the Norman Conquest, and (3) that he sided with the Saxons in that controversy. In the one paragraph where he mentions the Saxons by name, he flippantly remarks that, even if they did lose their rights as freemen at the time of the conquest, as a result of the subsequent six centuries of intermarriage all Englishmen of Locke's day could claim freeman status through some Norman ancestor and it would "be very hard to prove the contrary."[15] Locke may have chosen not to mention the specifics of Saxon history fearing that if he did so, his political philosophy might have been treated as nothing more than just another call for a return to Saxon legal precedents. It is hard to imagine, nonetheless, that Locke's readers in the seventeenth century were not aware of these unstated connections considering the ease with which Jefferson saw them eighty years later in colonial North America. It is also possible, of course, that Locke may have been ignorant of the details of Saxon common law and may have simply relied on the popular land use attitudes of his day without being aware of their Saxon origin. At any rate, however, the ultimate result would be the same—a political philosophy which provides philosophical foundations for the ancient Saxon land use attitudes and traditions. . . .

Not everyone in the first half of the nineteenth century shared Jefferson's enthusiasm for land reform based on Saxon common law modified by Locke's theory of property, and for a time the idea of landholding independent of landowning continued to be influential in American political and legal thought. Early versions of the homestead bill before the beginning of the Civil War, for example, often contained inalienability and reversion clauses.

According to these, a homesteader had the right to use the land, but could not subdivide it, sell it, or pass it on to his children after his death. These limitations, however, were not compatible with the wishes of potential homesteaders who wanted to be landowners, not just landholders, and, as a result, they were not included in the Homestead Act of 1862. It is unlikely that homesteading based entirely on Saxon common law ever had much chance of passing Congress because early nineteenth-century settlers squatting illegally on Western lands and demanding the enactment of special preemption laws had always had landownership as their primary objective.[16]

Because it was probably Locke's theory of property as much as Saxon common law which encouraged American citizens and immigrants to move westward, both should be given a share of the credit for the rapid settlement of the American West which ultimately established a national claim to all the lands west of the Appalachians as far as the Pacific. This past benefit to the American people, nevertheless, should not be the only standard for evaluating this doctrine's continuing value. We must still ask just how well the position is suited to conditions in twentieth-century America.

Modern Difficulties with Locke's Position

One obvious problem with Locke's theory today is his claim that there is enough land for everyone.[17] This premise is of fundamental importance to Locke's argument because, if a present or future shortage of land can be established, then any appropriation of land past or present under the procedure Locke recommends, enclosure from the common through labor, is an injustice to those who must remain unpropertied. By Locke's own estimates there was twice as much land at the end of the seventeenth century as all the inhabitants of the Earth could use. To support these calculations Locke pointed to the "in-land, vacant places of America"—places which are now occupied.[18] Since Locke's argument depends on a premise which is now false, Locke would have great difficulty advancing and justifying his position today.

Another problem is Locke's general attitude towards uncultivated land. Locke places almost no value on such land before it is improved and after improvement he says the labor is still the chief factor in any value assessment:

> . . . when any one hath computed, he will then see, how much *labour makes the far greatest part of the value* of things we enjoy in this World: And the ground which produces the materials, is scarce to be reckon'd in, as any, or at most, but a very small part of it; So little, that even amongst us, Land that is left wholly to Nature, that hath no improvement of Pasturage, Tillage, or Planting, is called, as indeed it is, *waste* and we shall find the benefit of it amount to little more than nothing.

According to Locke's calculations, 99 to 99.9 percent of the value of land even after it is improved still results from the labor and not the land. Although these absurdly high figures helped strengthen Locke's claim that labor establishes property rights over land, by making it seem that it is primarily the individual's labor mixed with the land rather than the land itself which is owned, such estimates, if presented today, would be considered scientifically false and contrary to common sense.[19]

Locke's land-value attitudes reflect a general desire prevalent in Locke's time as well as today for maximum agricultural productivity. From Locke's point of view, it was inefficient to permit plants and animals to grow naturally on uncultivated land:

> . . . I ask whether in the wild woods and uncultivated waste of America left to Nature, without any improvement, tillage, or husbandry, a thousand acres will yield the needy and wretched inhabitants as many conveniences of life as ten acres of equally fertile land doe in Devonshire where they are well cultivated?[20]

The problem, however, is not just productivity and efficiency, but also a general contempt for the quality of the natural products of the Earth. Locke writes with great conviction that "*Bread* is more worth than *Acorns*, *Wine* than Water, and *Cloth* or *Silk* than Leaves, Skins or Moss."[21] Even though we might be inclined to agree with Locke's pronouncements in certain contexts, the last two hundred

years of the American experience have provided us with new attitudes incompatible with those of Locke and his contemporaries, and apparently completely unknown to them, which place high value on trees, water, animals, and even land itself in a wholly natural and unimproved condition. Unlike Locke, we do not always consider wilderness land or uncultivated land synonymous with waste.

At the very core of Locke's land-value attitudes is his belief that "the Earth, and all that is therein, is given to Men for the Support and Comfort of their being." In one sense, this view is very old, derived from the biblical and Aristotelian claims that the Earth exists for the benefit and use of human beings. At the same time, it is very modern because of Locke's twin emphasis on labor and consumption. Both of these activities are of central importance in communistic and capitalistic political systems, and they became so important precisely because the founders and ideologists of each system originally took their ideas about labor and consumption from Locke's philosophy. In accordance with these ideas, the Earth is nothing more than raw materials waiting to be transformed by labor into consumable products. The Greeks and Romans would have objected to this view on the grounds that labor and consumption are too low and demeaning to be regarded as primary human activities.[22] From a twentieth-century standpoint, given the current emphasis on consumption, the neglect of the aesthetic and scientific (ecological) value of nature seems to be a more fundamental and serious objection to this exploitative view.

The worst result of Locke's property theory is the amoral or asocial attitude which has evolved out of it. Locke's arguments have encouraged landowners to behave in an antisocial manner and to claim that they have no moral obligation to the land itself, or even to the other people in the community who may be affected by what they do with their land. This amoral attitude, which has been noted with dismay by Aldo Leopold, Garrett Hardin, and others, can be traced directly to Locke's political philosophy, even though Locke himself may not have intended to create this effect. The reasons why this moral apathy developed are complex.

First, the divine rights of kings had just been abolished. In accordance with this doctrine, the king had had *ultimate* and *absolute* property rights over all the land in his dominion. He could do whatever he wanted with this land—give it away, take it back, use it himself, or even destroy it as he saw fit. Locke's new theory of property stripped the king of this power and authority and transferred these *ultimate* and *absolute* rights to each and every ordinary property owner. This transfer has been a moral disaster in large part because the king's rights involved moral elements which did not carry over to the new rights of the private landowner. As God's agent on Earth, the king was morally obligated to adhere to the highest standards of right and wrong. Furthermore, the king, as the ruler of the land, had a moral and political obligation to consider the general welfare of his entire kingdom whenever he acted. Of course, kings did not always behave as they should have, but, nevertheless, there were standards recognized by these kings and their subjects as to what constituted proper and kingly moral behavior. Private landowners, however, did not inherit these sorts of obligations. Because they were not instruments of church or state, the idea that they should have moral obligations limiting their actions with regard to their own property does not seem to have come up. The standard which landowners adopted to guide their actions was a purely selfish and egotistical one. Because it involved nothing more than the economic interest of the individual, it was devoid of moral obligation or moral responsibility.

If Locke had been writing in a more politically stable period of English history, it is possible that he might not have developed these views. As mentioned above, one of the primary reasons that Locke developed his theory of property was to help protect personal property from arbitrary governmental interference. Locke had grown up during the reign of Charles I whose behavior had brought about a civil war and the establishment of the commonwealth under Cromwell. Afterwards, Locke had lived through much of the reigns of Charles II and James II in exile. Thus, with good reason for fearing the uncontrolled power of English kings, Locke sought to put as much power into the hands of the people as he could. The result was a weakening of governmental power without a comparable lessening of governmental responsibility.

This difficulty is revealed momentarily in the *First Treatise* where Locke argues that property

owners have the right to destroy their property if they can derive an advantage from doing so. Locke apparently feels compelled to acknowledge the right of property owners to destroy *in general* in order to justify the killing of animals for food but, obviously uneasy about the point he has just made, he adds that the government has the responsibility of making sure that this destruction does not adversely affect the property of others:

> Property, whose Original is the Right a Man has to use any of the Inferior Creatures, for Subsistence and Comfort of his life, is for the benefit and sole Advantage of the Proprietor, so that he may even destroy the thing, that he has Property in by his use of it, where need requires; but Government being for the Preservation of every Man's Right and Property, by preserving him from the Violence or Injury of others, is for the good of the Governed.[23]

Ironically, the very rights to property which the government is supposed to protect hinder or even prevent the government from carrying out this responsibility.

Theoretically, Locke's qualification of the right to destroy property is compatible with the American conception of checks and balances and it might have provided a *political* solution to the problem, though not a moral one. Unfortunately, however, it as not been carried over into our political and legal system as successfully as the right to destroy. A man certainly has a right in the United States to sue for damages in court after the fact, when the actions of others have clearly injured him or his property, but the right of the government to take preventive action before the damage is done has not been effectively established. It is this preventive action which private landowners are assailing when they assert their right to use and even destroy their land as they see fit without any outside interference. The success of landowners in this area is amply demonstrated by the great reluctance of most state legislatures to place waste management restrictions on small private *landowners* which have long governed the activities of rural land *developers*.

Government regulation of individual private landowners has been ineffective historically because, from the very beginnings of American government, representation at state and federal levels has nearly always been based on landownership, an approach which has usually assured rural control of the legislature even when most of the citizens in the state lived in urban population centers. Government leaders intent on acting primarily in the interests of landowners could hardly have been expected to play the preventive role which Locke recommends. The unwillingness of legislators to act in this way in the nineteenth century and most of the twentieth, moreover, further contributed to the amoral belief of rural landowners that they can do whatever they want without being concerned about the welfare or rights of others.

When Jefferson attempted to build American society on a Lockeian foundation of small landowners, he did so in large measure because he believed that small landowners would make the most virtuous citizens. He failed to foresee, however, that the independence provided by Locke's presocietal natural rights would discourage rather than encourage social responsibility, and, therefore, would contribute little to the development of moral character in American landowners. Since social responsibility is basic to our conception of morality today, the claim of landowners that their special rights relieve them of any obligation or responsibility to the community can be regarded only as both socially and morally reprehensible. The position of such rural landowners is analogous to that of a tyrannical king. Tyranny is always justified, when it is justified at all, by a claim that the tyrant has the *right* to do as he pleases regardless of the consequences. In practice, however, the impact of rural landowners more closely approaches anarchy than tyranny, but only because landowners, though sharing a common desire to preserve their special rights, do not always have common economic interests. As a result, landowners are usually more willing to promote the theoretical rights of their fellow property owners than their specific land use and development projects, which as members of society, they may find objectionable or even despicable—in spite of their Saxon and Lockeian heritage rather than because of it.

A landowner cannot justify his position morally except with the extravagant claim that his actions are completely independent and beyond any standard of right and wrong—a claim which Locke, Jefferson, and even Saxon freemen would probably have hesitated to make. Actually, there is only one precedent for such a claim. During the Middle Ages, church philosophers concluded that God was independent of all moral standards. They felt compelled to take this position because moral limitations on God's actions would have conflicted with His omnipotence. Therefore, they reasoned that God's actions created moral law—i.e., defined moral law—and that theoretically moral law could be radically changed at any moment. Descartes held this position in the seventeenth century, and in the nineteenth and twentieth centuries some atheistic existential philosophers have argued that because God is dead each man is now forced to create his own values through his individual actions. Although this position could be adopted as a defense of the landowner's extraordinary amoral rights, it would probably be distasteful to most landowners. Without it, this aspect of the rural landowners' position may be indefensible.[24]

Today, of course, whenever Locke's theory of property and the heritage of the ancient Saxon freeman surface in county courts, at planning and zoning meetings, and at state and federal hearings on conservation and land management, they still remain a formidable obstacle to constructive political action. As they are normally presented, however, they are certainly not an all-purpose answer to our environmental problems or even a marginally adequate reply to environmental criticism. When a landowner voices a Lockeian argument he is consciously or unconsciously trying to evade the land management issues at hand and to shift attention instead to the dogmatic recitation of his special rights as a property owner.

As I noted above, some of Locke's fundamental assumptions and attitudes are either demonstrably false or no longer generally held even among landowners. These difficulties need to be ironed out before the landowners can claim that they are really answering their environmental critics. Furthermore it is likely that, even if the position can be and is modernized, the moral issues will still be unresolved.

As it stands, the force of the rural landowners' arguments depends on their historical association—their Biblical trappings, the echoes of Locke's political philosophy, the Saxon common-law tradition, the feudal doctrine of the divine rights of kings, and the spirit of the nineteenth-century American land laws. Can they be modernized?

That remains to be seen. Until they are, however, landowners, environmentalists, politicians, and ordinary citizens should regard them with some suspicion.

Notes

1. U.S., Congress, Senate, *Congressional Globe*, 42nd Cong., 2d Sess., 1 (30 January 1872), p. 697.

2. The account given in this section is based most directly on Denman W. Ross, *The Early History of Land-Holding Among the Germans* (Boston: Soule and Bugbee, 1883), and Walter Phelps Hall, Robert Greenhalgh Albion, and Jennie Barnes Pope, *A History of England and the Empire-Commonwealth*, 4th ed. (Boston: Ginn and Company, 1961).

3. Ross, *Land-Holding*, p. 24.

4. Thomas Jefferson, "A Summary View of the Rights of British America," in *The Portable Thomas Jefferson*, ed. Merrill D. Peterson (New York: Viking Press, 1975), pp. 4–5.

5. Ibid., pp. 17–19.

6. Thomas Jefferson, "Draft Constitution for Virginia," in *Portable Jefferson*, p. 248.

7. Jefferson to Edmund Pendleton, 13 August 1776, in *Papers of Thomas Jefferson*, 1: 492.

8. Jefferson to John Jay, 23 August 1785, in *Portable Jefferson*, p. 384.

9. Jefferson to James Madison, 28 October 1785, in *Portable Jefferson*, p. 397.

10. Thomas Jefferson, *Notes on the State of Virginia*, in *Portable Jefferson*, p. 217.

11. John Locke, *Two Treatises of Government*, ed. Thomas I. Cook (New York and London: Hafner Press, 1947).

12. Jefferson to John Trumbull, 15 February 1789, in *Portable Jefferson*, pp. 434–35; Locke, *Second Treatise*, sec. 6; Carl Becker, *The Declaration of Independence: A Study in the History of Political Ideas* (New York: Alfred A. Knopf, 1960), pp. 24–28.

13. Locke, *Second Treatise*, sec. 27.

14. Ibid., sec. 32.

15. Ibid., sec. 177.

16. Paul W. Gates, *History of Public Land Law Development* (Washington, D.C.: Public Land Law Commission, 1968), pp. 390–93.

17. Locke, *Second Treatise*, sec. 33.

18. Ibid., sec. 36.

19. Ibid., secs. 42–43.

20. Ibid., sec. 37.

21. Ibid., sec. 42.

22. Ibid., sec. 26; for a full discussion of labor and consumption see Hannah Arendt, *The Human Condition* (Chicago and London: University of Chicago Press, 1958), chap. 3.

23. Locke, *First Treatise*, sec. 92; Locke also addresses this point to some degree in the *Second Treatise*, sec. 31, where he writes that "Nothing was made by God for Man to spoil or destroy." Here Locke emphasizes the abundance of the natural things supplied by God and states that human beings who set limits on themselves with their reason will not claim more than their fair share.

24. Jean-Paul Sartre, *Existentialism and Human Emotions*, (New York: Philosophical Library, 1957), pp. 13–18.

How Much of the Earth Is Sacred Space?

J. Donald Hughes and Jim Swan

One of the happiest events of recent years was the return of Blue Lake to the Taos Pueblo. This locality is a holy place for the Taos people, one of whom said, "We go there and talk to our Great Spirit in our own language, and talk to Nature and what is going to grow."[1] In giving back the lake and the forest surrounding it, Congress acknowledged, as it later did more explicitly in the American Indian Religious Freedom Act,[2] that Native American Indian tribes recognize certain places as sacred space, an attitude which is found in all tribes. The Lakota and others have a spiritual relationship to Mato Tipi (Bear Butte) in the Black Hills, and both the Navajo and Hopi regard the San Francisco Peaks near Flagstaff as sacred, although the courts have been remiss in protecting them from desecration.

Sacred space is a place where human beings find a manifestation of where they experience a sense of connectedness to the universe. There, in some special way, spirit is present to them. People in many parts of the world and in all times have

Environmental Review, Vol. 10, No. 4 (Winter 1986), 247–259. Reprinted by permission.

come to designate some places as sacred: in Japan, Mount Fuji is a *kami* or shrine; an island in Lake Titicaca is for the Aymara an altar to the Sun God, Inti; and the Bimin-Kukusmin of Papua New Guinea, revere the area around a spring of ritual oil.[3] Such examples could be multiplied.

But when one asks a traditional Indian, "How much of the earth is a sacred space?" the answer is unhesitating: "All." As Chief Seattle, a Suquamish of the Puget Sound area, told the governor of Washington, "Every part of this soil is sacred in the estimation of my people."[4] When tribal elders speak of Mother Earth, they are not using a metaphor. They perceive that earth is a living being, sacred in all her parts. Black Elk, a Lakota holy man, addressed her in these words: "Every step we take upon you should be done in a sacred manner; each step should be as a prayer."[5] For this reason Smohalla, a Wanapum shaman of the upper Columbia River country, required his followers to use the gentle digging instead of the plow, which tears Mother Earth's bosom like a knife. He also forbade them to mine, because that would be to dig under her skin for her bones.[6] Those venerable teachers knew that one could experience a sense of connectedness to the universe virtually anywhere, so there were no boundaries or places that were not sacred.

The last sentence does not contradict what was said before about sacred spaces. In the traditional Indian view, all of nature is sacred but in certain spots the spirit power manifests itself more clearly, readily. It is to those places that a person seeking a vision would make a quest. They were localities where the great events of tribal history and the era of creation took place. They were associated with particular beings whom one ought not even to name unless one were prepared to encounter the energy they wielded, which could either strengthen or destroy. So the Indian view of the universe is that of a sacred continuum that contains foci of power.

Again, this conception of the earth is widespread among traditional peoples around the world and through history. The ancient Chinese practice of *Feng Shui* (geomancy) treats the landscape as a network of potent spots connected by lines of energy.[7] One would be foolish, its practitioners believed, to ignore this sacred geography when locating house, road, or temple. The Greek philosopher Plato affirmed that the earth is a living organism, alive in every part, and also that there are particular locations where spiritual powers operate positively or negatively. In the *Laws*, he advised founders of cities to take careful account of these influences.[8]

But this is not the only approach that has been taken to sacred space. The Old World produced in ancient times another view that contrasts strongly with the North American Indian version, and which has had a pervasive influence in the history of western thought. That is the idea of sanctuary, an area marked off so as to be separated from the space around it, usually by a wall. The Greek word for such a place, *temenos*, is instructive because it derives from the verb *temnō*, meaning "I cut off." The Latin word *templum*, the root of the word "temple" also means "a part cut off" or "a space marked out." Once dedicated by the proper authorities, such a precinct was protected by all the sanctions of religious custom and local law.

The places chosen were almost always distinguished by some natural feature: an impressive grove of large old trees, a spring, a lake, a fissure in the earth, or a mountain peak. These were often landscapes of great natural beauty. In locating and marking a *temenos*, the seers took account of the lay of the land and the mountain forms visible from it. Within the boundary, all human use other than religious worship was forbidden. There was to be no cutting or removal of wood, no hunting, grazing, or cultivation. The only building permitted was a shelter for the statue of god or goddess. What we call a temple is such a structure, but for the ancients the enclosure itself, and everything within it, served as the temple. There the god lived and became manifest. And there a fugitive could seek sanctuary, a sick person could ask for healing, and anyone seeking wisdom—that is, to know the will of the gods—could sleep overnight in expectation of a meaningful dream. There were hundreds of those places in the ancient world.

Another type of sacred space that deserves mention is a tract of agricultural land dedicated to a god or goddess, the produce of which served as an offering. The Linear B tablets record such land use in ancient Crete. In Athens, the Council of the Areopagus had jurisdiction over groves of sacred olive trees, whose oil was reserved for sacrifices, prizes for the winners of the Panathenaic Games, and other purposes sacred to the goddess Athena. The institution of "God's Acre" had a long subsequent history in Europe.

Even within the great ancient cities, sacred spaces retained something of the natural. Babylonian ziggurats were crowned by groves of trees, Egyptian temples were graced with sacred lakes and gardens, and the Acropolis of Athens had its sacred caves, spring, and cypress trees. Those places had to be walled both for protection and to distinguish the sacred space within from the congested streets outside.

But the practice of setting physical boundaries for sacred spaces gives another answer, contrasting with that of the American Indians, to the question, "How much of the world is sacred?" That answer is: "As much as has been consecrated to the gods." Outside the limits, the gods no longer protected the earth, and people were free to use it as they saw fit. Inside the *temenos,* there might be glimpsed a holy light, but outside shone only the ordinary light of day. Thus an enormous step had been taken toward desacralizing nature, but it is also true that the boundaries themselves had been endowed with a numinous quality.

In order to understand how the concept of sacred space entered the medieval and modern mind, one must consider how the Hebrews transformed it. The psalmist proclaimed that all the earth, in a certain sense, is sacred: "The earth is the Lord's and the fullness thereof, the world and those who dwell therein."[9] The early Hebrews had their sacred places: Sinai, where God gave the commandments to Moses, and Bethel, where Jacob had wrestled with the angel. But the dominant view in Judaism held that God the Creator is not to be identified with His creation, even though it might serve as a marvelous sign of His power and benevolence. Since God is transcendent, He cannot be said to dwell in any spot on earth in an ontological sense. The Hebrews experienced a long struggle with the religions of the surrounding peoples, who worshipped in sacred groves and high places. God had commanded the destruction of those sanctuaries.

The designation of sacred spaces like those of the Canaanites might have suggested that God is present in the natural world in a more intimate way than Judaism was ready to affirm. Since all the world belongs to God, the designation of a particular locale as sacred space could be arbitrary. To avoid the confusion caused by having many sanc-tuaries, which might have implied to the common people that many gods were being worshipped, the religious authorities under King Josiah centralized the sacrificial worship of the one God in a single sacred space: the Temple of Jerusalem. Even though Mount Zion was undoubtedly a sacred place before it was reconsecrated for the Temple, the Judaic belief was that it was holy because it had been sanctified by God's people at God's command, not because of any special sacredness inherent in the spot. So while the Greeks may be said to have *recognized* sacred space in the landscape, the Hebrews *declared* the Temple space to be sacred.

Christianity took a further step. The early missionaries were anxious that their converts from paganism should not confuse the creation with the creator. Paul the Apostle taught that the natural world had fallen along with mankind and needed to be redeemed through the work of Christ. John urged the Christians not "to love the world or the things in the world."[10] By "world," John doubtlessly meant "non-Christian society," but the Church has insisted on taking the word to mean "the creation." "God who made the world . . . does not live in shrines made by mankind."[11]

It is true that the New Testament does not teach that nature is evil, but that even in its fallen state it exhibits the eternal power and deity of God. Within the first few centuries, however, many Christians were convinced that the natural world was the province of the devil, the adversary of God. Although that idea is not really orthodox, because the sacraments show natural creation as a vehicle of the grace of God, the conception of the world that has fallen into the power of darkness was an image that shaped the imagination of medieval European Christianity. Basil said Satan's "dominion extends over all the earth,"[12] and Synesius of Cyrene prayed to be released from "the demon of the earth, the demon of matter, . . . who stands athwart the ascending path."[13]

The Christians of that time, therefore, were not encouraged to look for sacred space within the world of nature. For them, the churches and monasteries were sacred space, with the enclosed cloisters and churchyards that adjoined them, filled with trees that sheltered the burial places of the sainted dead. They were oases of sanctity in a desert of evil. As outposts of heaven on a fallen earth, they could be established anywhere, though it was considered an act of merit to locate them on the former sites of pagan temples as signs of the victory of Christianity over the demonic gods.

But older attitudes of the pagan converts often surfaced, and some earlier practices continued in the new sacred spaces. From a distance, the appearance of the new sanctuaries was not unlike that of the old, with a sacred building standing within a grove of trees, surrounded by a wall. They still look so today. And within, the right of sanctuary was often given, and those suffering from various maladies were allowed to sleep there in the expectation that God would send them dreams as a means of healing. Once consecrated, they required a different behavior inside the walls, including cloister or churchyard, from that allowed outside. The threshold of the church divided two quite different kinds of space, and boundaries retained a religious sanction.

By the time the Europeans were ready to invade the homeland of the American Indians, the idea of sacred space as a distinct area consecrated by ecclesiastical authority was firmly established. In addition, the concept of a boundary as a sacrosanct limit, whether marked by a wall or an imaginary line, had the force of millennia of tradition. The meeting of the two peoples was foredoomed to tragedy, since the Indians had no way to grasp the alien concept; and because the program of the Europeans amounted to cultural genocide, they had little interest in Indian ideas of the sacred.

A further development, however, was taking place in Europe in regard to sacred space, and that was the final step in desacralizing nature. Nationalism placed the claims of the State above those of the Church, effectively denying that even Church land was sacred space. And rising capitalism defined land as a commodity, subject to division and sale, no more sacred than any other economic resource. The Church perforce acquiesced in both of those developments. But the old sense of the inviolability of boundaries persisted; now they were boundaries of nations or of private land rather than religious sanctuaries, but the new order believed in them as firmly as the old. Trespass, the violation of boundaries, was still as heinous a sin.

Indians encountered the strange desire of the Europeans to buy land almost as soon as the foreigners appeared on their coasts. It happened again and again, whether in the "sale" of Manhattan

Island or in William Penn's "treaty" in Pennsylvania. The Indians seem to have regarded such arrangements as permission for specific uses of the land, not as "conveyance in fee simple." Indians were incredulous at the idea that the earth could be divided by a line drawn on a map. How could Mother Earth be cut up in that way? In the opening years of the nineteenth century, Tecumseh said, "Sell a country? Why not sell the air, the clouds, and the great sea as well as the earth?"[14] He was protesting not against commercialism, but sacrilege.

For their part, Europeans were shocked at the failure of Indians to respect their boundaries. To Europeans, treaty lines embodied the integrity of the nation state and therefore were inviolable, even if they crossed territory that a European had not seen. Similarly, property lines demanded the same respect as the principle of private ownership itself, and the fact that Indians would return to the hunt on their traditional tribal lands after they had become royal, public, or private property was to Europeans an inexcusable trespass of the limits. For the Europeans to violate the boundaries in the other direction was not a similar trespass in their own minds, because they had convinced themselves that the Indians did not really "occupy" or "use" the land. Indian sacred space was not respected because Indian religions were regarded not as "real" religions, but "superstitions," and Indians were expected to accept the new order either by adopting European-American ways or by withdrawing beyond the frontiers.

The Indian reservation, as an area set aside within recognized boundaries, represents something of an anomaly within the context of the European-American view. Once the limits had been set, and Indians recognized as the proper occupants of the enclosed land, all the forces of legality and centuries of customary attitudes should have caused Americans to respect the reservations. That they did not, shows that the economic culture of late nineteenth-century and early twentieth-century America placed a higher value on the acquisition and exploitation of resources located on Indian lands than on the ideals of sacred property boundaries and whatever relict religious feelings might still have attached to them.

An engine for the destruction of reservations, the General Allotment Act of 1887, was a pious fraud imposing American law on Indian tradition.

The congressional advocates of the measure claimed that it would acculturate the Indians by giving them property, but after its enactment, the administrators of allotment managed to alienate two-thirds of all Indian land within fifty years. That process showed no concern for the preservation of Indian sacred sites. Indeed, Indian religions were specifically denied the protection of the First Amendment to the United States Constitution during the same period, and an effort was made to stamp them out through proscription of the religions themselves and the reeducation of Indian children.

At the same time, a similar desire to exploit natural resources was altering the American landscape and destroying the character of the Indians' sacred places. "Wilderness" is a western idea, but it is clear that Indian holy places tended to be unspoiled areas, so that the exploitation of wilder country infringed upon many if not most of them. But also during the late nineteenth and early twentieth centuries, what might be regarded as a resurgence of the idea of demarcating sacred spaces appeared in America. That was the movement to preserve natural areas as national parks, forests, and wilderness areas. While it might not seem at first glance that those reservations are sacred in the sense used here, many of the most vocal exponents of the new conservation were motivated in large part by a concern for the sacred. True, that concern was not an expression of ecclesiastical religion, but of what has been called civil religion because it involved secular governmental action for conservation. But "civil religion" as a term does not quite capture the way in which they had recovered the perception of sacred space. Deeply religious, the conservationists were highly orthodox. They found their temples in the wilderness, not in churches. And they did regard wild nature as sacred.

John Muir, whose role in the creation and protection of national parks was enormous, believed that what he was doing was saving sacred spaces. He spoke of mountains and meadows as places of healing, renewal, and worship. What better statement, if the sacred is a feeling of connectedness with the all, than Muir's words, "The clearest way into the Universe is through a forest wilderness."[15] Mircea Eliade connects the sacred with the times and places of creation; Muir found Eden in the wild places, saying, "I have discovered that I also live in 'creation's dawn.'"[16] "In God's wildness," he added, "lies the hope of the world."[17] And when Hetch Hetchy—a miniature valley like the more famous Yosemite, located in the same national park and one of the places he honored most—was threatened with flooding for a reservoir to supply the city of San Francisco, he stated the principle of its sacredness unequivocally:

> These temple destroyers, devotees of ravaging commercialism, seem to have a perfect contempt for Nature, and, instead of lifting their eyes to the God of the mountains, lift them to the Almighty Dollar. Dam Hetch Hetchy! As well dam for water-tanks the people's cathedrals and churches, for no holier temple has ever been consecrated by the heart of man.[18]

Why did the conservation movement in America go so far in its perception of the sacred beyond its precedents in the Old World? George Catlin, Henry Thoreau, Muir, John Wesley Powell, and others among its leaders knew American Indians well and reflected upon Indian ideas in their writings. Catlin, the artist whose work did so much to rescue the culture of Indians in the 1830s from oblivion, was the person who first suggested that a national park be set aside to preserve not just the landscape and wildlife, but also the way of life of the Plains Indians.[19] Thoreau spent months in wild country with the Algonquian Indian guide, Joe Polis. Muir stayed for a while among the Tlingits of Alaska, found their ideas of nature and wild animals very much like his own, and was adopted into the tribe.[20] Powell was fluent in Paiute and published perceptive translations of Indian poetry.[21] Those lovers of nature were putting down spiritual roots in the land, and encountering the fact that Indian tribes had already established a relationship with the earth through thousands of years of tradition.

But when national parks and forests were created, unfortunately little provision was made for the Indian people who lived in them. In actual practice, the Park and Forest Services worked out a method of issuing special use permits for Indians who lived in or used the areas, although there were a few cases of attempted eviction like the repeated endeavors to remove the Havasupai settlement from Grand Canyon Village. Especially important is the fact that the outstanding natural features that caused the parks to be created were usually themselves sacred places in tribal traditions.

Indians generally understood that the parks and forests had been established to protect the land, animals, and plants within them. From the Indian standpoint, it was good to have the areas protected because their integrity as sacred space required that forest and park lands be maintained in the natural state. But the natives were frustrated by the way the laws were administered to interfere with their religions, as well as their traditional hunting and fishing rights. As a member of the Crow tribe stated:

> The Laws that protect birds, animals, plants and our Mother Earth from people who have no respect for these things serve to inhibit the free exercise of religion . . . and free access to religious sites when these American Indians pose no threat to them.[22]

For most of this century, no consistent policy granted Indians access to their sacred spaces, and developments such as roads, spraying and removal of trees, ski areas, other recreational facilities, and river channelization and dams, often committed desecrations in Indian eyes.

In recent years, a more considerate attitude has been reflected in congressional action, although it still remains to be put into practice fully. The American Indian Religious Freedom Act of 1978 (AIRFA) guarantees the right to "believe, express, and exercise the traditional religions of the American Indian, Eskimo, Aleut, and Native Hawaiian."[23] The law charges all United States governmental agencies to consult traditional religious leaders in order to preserve Native American religious rights and practices, and to inventory all sacred places on federal lands and come up with proposed policies of management that will preserve the traditional religious values and practices associated with them. The law, it seemed, came none too soon, because the surviving American Indian sacred spaces have never been so threatened with desecration or outright destruction as they now are. The law recognizes that all communities are equally entitled to protection of their freedom of religion, and that in applying this principle to Native Americans, the government must acknowledge the special role of sacred spaces.

But court cases brought under AIRFA to protect sacred sites have failed, with one or two notable exceptions. Among the unsuccessful cases were attempts to protect Navajo rights of worship at Rainbow Bridge, Utah; to save Cherokee sites threatened with flooding by the Tellico Dam in Tennessee; to prevent intrusion of a ski resort into San Francisco Peaks, Arizona, an area sacred to both Hopis and Navajos; and to allow undisturbed ceremonies by Lakota and Cheyenne people at Bear Butte, South Dakota.[24] In these cases, use by the general public in the form of reservoirs or recreational facilities took precedence over Native American religious rights. Even in a case that succeeded, where the Yurok, Karok, and Tolowa tribes of northern California managed to block construction of a road near their traditional mountain prayer sites, their First Amendment rights, not AIRFA, were held to be decisive.[25] One case where AIRFA appears to have helped was in the denial of a license for Northern Lights, Inc., to build a water project that would have destroyed Kootenai Falls, Idaho, a sacred place for the Kootenai tribe.[26]

The weaknesses of AIRFA are that it is only an advisory resolution of Congress directed at federal agencies, which means it can be ignored with impunity; that it has no enforcement provisions; and that it offers to help in weighing American Indian religious rights against other rights and interests. A federal agency may comply with AIRFA by considering Indian rights; it does not have to decide that they take precedence over skiing, dirt-biking, or electrical power generation. American Indian religious freedom in regard to sacred places can only be guaranteed by a new, stronger, and more carefully drafted law.

But underlying the ineffectiveness of AIRFA is a failure to recognize the difference between the American Indian and European concepts of sacred space. In the successful Yurok-Karok-Tolowa case, usually called the "G-O Road Case," the court defined sacred space in terms of the federal land survey, in a decision quoted here in part:

> It is hereby ordered that the defendants are permanently enjoined from constructing the Chimney Rock Section of the G-O Road and/or any alternative route . . . which would traverse the high country, which constitutes [specified] sections in

Six Rivers Forest. . . . It is further hereby ordered that the defendants are permanently enjoined from engaging in commercial timber harvesting.[27]

The decision also requires preparation of Environmental Impact Statements for other future plans in the general area. The provisions resemble those that have been used in demarcating sacred land in the European tradition. The modern officials, without realizing it, are acting like ancient Greeks delimiting a *temenos*. Unlike the Greeks and in accord with modern secular thought, they are doing so without really believing that there is anything inherently sacred inside the lines they are drawing.

Traditional Indians, on the other hand, are faced with difficult alternatives. They can accept the decisions of land managers and/or bring cases to court like the G-O Road Case, thus contenting themselves with saving a few shattered fragments of their heritage and leaving unchallenged the non-Indian idea that sacred space is as much as has been set aside, and no more. This course has the advantage of using federal law to achieve a measure of justice. But another alternative would be to insist on the ancient Indian conception that all the earth is sacred. Taken seriously, this second course could open a dialogue and raise the national consciousness of Indian values. Some tribal elders have already begun to do the latter, as Robert S. Michaelsen indicates in an important recent article:

Some traditionalists have claimed that in keeping with their religion, *all* land on which the tribe has lived, celebrated, and worshipped in the past is sacred and hence essential to tribal free exercise of religion. Such a claim was made before the Federal agencies Task Force by the combined nineteen Pueblo representatives and in Senate testimony on the [AIRFA] resolution by Yakima representatives. It has also been made in court by the Sioux, the Hopi, and the Navajo.[28]

It has been reported that Hopi spokesmen lay claim, in spirit, to the entire North American continent. In the Ghost Dance, Indians of many tribes prayed for the renewal of the whole land, and the spirit of that prayer did not die at the first Wounded Knee.

The federal law, of course, lacks the same vision. Without realizing it, Congress promised far more than can be delivered. It has recognized that the Indian consensus—that certain lands are sacred—can be respected and protected as long as it does not seriously interfere with the rights and interests of others. But Congress and the courts have not even begun to deal with the basic traditional tribal principle that Mother Earth, as a holistic entity, is sacred.

Another fact has to be considered. There are a large, vocal, and increasingly influential number of people in America today who are recovering the ancient idea of the sacredness of the earth. They hold, not as a fad or pose, but as a deep conviction, that wilderness is sacred ground, and that visits to places of power enhance wisdom and health. They advocate that we should learn to know the earth, and the plants and animals that inhabit it, in the places where we live. They feel, as Indians long have felt, that human beings are not the lords of creation but fellow creatures with the bears, the ravens, and the running streams.

Who are these people? They have as yet no name and no church, and perhaps they never will. Gary Snyder is one of them, and Paul Winter is another. It is interesting that the first who come to mind are a poet and a musician. Another, the writer Wendell Berry, speaks characteristically of agricultural land and inhabited place. The idea that holiness inheres in the place where one lives is alien to the European tradition, for in that tradition sacred space is sundered, set aside, a place one goes only to worship. But to live in what one regards as sacred space is the most forceful affirmation of the sacredness of the whole earth. Snyder has made a deep and sympathetic study of Indian traditions, and both Winter and Berry acknowledge the closeness of their ideas to Indian insights.[29]

We are now at the point where those people can talk with traditional Native American elders. The Indian sacred places that remain, the places of power within the sacred continuum, must be preserved. A conversation on how to amend and strengthen AIRFA offers at least a place to start. A better law would give leverage to people who believe in the sacredness of those places. It is encouraging that, as in the G-O Road Case, environmental groups and Indian tribes have joined together. That cooperation has happened because both Indians and environmentalists wish to keep the sacred space in its natural condition. And their motives for wanting to do so, while not identical, are not incompatible either.

The situation should encourage the two groups to engage in a wider dialogue, one in which non-Indians may learn something about the Indian conception of sacred space, while Indians can hear other Americans who feel that many of the same spaces are sacred. Some of the sites, by their nature, must be kept secret and closed to outsiders, a need envisioned by AIRFA and honored in some court cases. In the Kootenai case, for example, tribal elders were allowed to give "limited distribution" testimony that presumably located sites and documented their sacred character; the testimony did not become part of the published court record, however, and its secrecy was preserved. But many of the places that need protection are great shrines that should be held open for most of the year as places where all people may seek wisdom and health. Of course, this must be done in a way that would prevent gross intrusions, vandalism, and theft of holy objects by visitors who did not honor sacred space.

The dialogue has begun. All those who participate in it should be willing to learn. Recent developments in science have shown some support for the Indian view of sacred space. By understanding ecology, we learn the intimate way that all parts of the biosphere are interconnected. Life on earth, as ecologists see it, forms a net in which there are important foci of energy. We cannot allow the net to be broken in too many places without destroying the most basic processes that sustain us. The atmospheric chemist James Lovelock and the biologist Lynn Margulis have advanced a theory called the Gaia hypothesis.[30] This postulates that the living systems of the earth—the animals and plants collectively called the biosphere—regulate physical systems such as temperature and the balance of gases and acidity in the atmosphere so as to protect and support life.

If we grant the truth of the Gaia hypothesis for a moment, it seems that we humans are likely to act to keep the planetary system functioning only if we recognize that every part of it is sacred in the sense of being connected to the whole. Whether we are Indians or others, we can agree with the words of John Muir, "we all dwell in a house of one room— the world with the firmament for its roof—and we are sailing the celestial spaces without leaving any

track."[31] We will know that all decisions affecting any part of the natural environment are decisions about sacred space. Thus the visions of the tribal elders can combine with the most daring new conceptions of ecological scientists to show us how to see wholeness—the holiness—of the earth, and how we must act while we live together here.

Notes

1. John Collier, *On the Gleaming Way* (Denver, 1962), 124.

2. Public Law 95–341, Senate Joint Resolution 102, 42 U.S.C. par. 1996, August 11, 1978.

3. Fitz John Porter Poole, "Erosion of a Sacred Landscape," in Michael Tobias, ed., *Mountain Peoples: Profiles of Twentieth Century Adaptation* (Norman, forthcoming from University of Oklahoma Press).

4. W. C. Vanderwerth, ed,, *Indian Oratory: Famous Speeches by Noted Indian Chieftains* (Norman, 1971), 120–21.

5. Black Elk, as quoted in Joseph Epes Brown, *The Sacred Pipe* (Norman, 1953), 12–13.

6. James Mooney, "The Ghost-dance Religion," *Fourteenth Annual Report of the Bureau of Ethnology* (Washington, DC, 1896), 724.

7. Ernest John Eitel, *Feng-Shui: or, the Rudiments of Natural Science in China* (London, 1873).

8. Plato, *The Laws*, 5.747 D-E.

9. Psalm 24:1.

10. I John 2:15.

11. Acts 17:24.

12. J. P. Migne, ed., *Patrologiae Cursus Completus*, Greek Series, vol. 31 (Rome, 1800), 352A.

13. Synesius of Cyrene, *The Essays and Hyms of Synesius of Cyrene*, trans. A. Fitzgerald, vol. 1 (Oxford, 1930), Hymn IV, pp. 240 ff.

14. Glenn Tucker, *Tecumseh: Vision of Glory* (Indianapolis, 1956), 163.

15. Edwin Way Teale, ed., *The Wilderness World of John Muir* (Boston, 1954), 312.

16. Ibid., 311.

17. Ibid., 315.

18. Ibid., 320.

19. George Catlin, *Letters and Notes on the Manners, Customs, and Condition of the North American Indians*, vol. 1 (1841; reprint, Minneapolis, 1965), 261–62.

20. John Muir, *The Writings of John Muir*, manuscript ed., vol. 3 (Boston, 1916), 208–11.

21. John Wesley Powell, *First Annual Report of the Bureau of American Ethnology* (Washington, DC, 1881), 23.

22. Hearings, Senate Committee on Indian Affairs, Joint Resolution 102, February 24, 1978, quoted in *American Indian Religious Freedom Act Report*, P. L. 95–341, Federal Agencies Task Force, Chairman, Cecil D. Andrus, Secretary of the Interior (Washington, DC, 1979), Appendix A, 1.

23. See note 2.

24. *Badoni* v. *Higginson*, 638 F.2d 172 (10th Cir. 1980), *cert. denied*, 452 U.S. 954 (1981), regarding Navajo rights at Rainbow Bridge, Utah; *Sequoyah* v. *Tennessee Valley Authority*, 620 F.2d 1159 (6th Cir. 1980), *cert. denied*, 449 U.S. 953 (1980), regarding Cherokee rights in the Little Tennessee Valley; *Wilson* v. *Block*, 708 F.2d 735 (D.C. Cir. 1983), regarding Hopi and Navajo rights in the San Francisco Peaks, Arizona; and *Frank Fools Crow* v. *Gullet*, 706 F.2d 856 (8th Cir. 1983), regarding Lakota Sioux and Cheyenne rights at Bear Butte, South Dakota.

25. *Northwest Indian Cemetery Protective Association* v. *Peterson*, 565 F.Supp. 586 (N.D. California 1983).

26. Northern Lights, Inc., Project No. 2752–000, 27 Federal Energy Regulatory Commission, par. 63,024, April 23, 1984.

27. See note 25.

28. Robert S. Michaelson, "The Significance of the American Indian Religious Freedom Act of 1978," *Journal of the American Academy of Religion* 52 (no. 1, 1984), 93–115, quotation pp. 108–9.

29. Gary Snyder, "Good, Wild, Sacred," *The CoEvolution Quarterly* (Fall 1983), 8–17; Paul Winter, *Missa Gaia: Earth Mass* (Litchfield, CT: Living Music records, 1982), see notes in 33-rpm disk version; Wendell Berry, *The Gift of Good Land* (San Francisco, 1981), 267–81, and Berry, "The Body and the Earth," in *The Unsettling of America: Culture and Agriculture* (New York, 1978), 97–140.

30. James E. Lovelock, *Gaia: A New Look at Life on Earth* (Oxford, 1979).

31. Teale, *Wilderness World of John Muir*, 310.

Radical American Environmentalism and Wilderness Preservation: A Third World Critique

*Ramachandra Guha**

I. Introduction

The respected radical journalist Kirkpatrick Sale recently celebrated "the passion of a new and growing movement that has become disenchanted with the environmental establishment and has in recent years mounted a serious and sweeping attack on it—style, substance, systems, sensibilities and all."[1] The vision of those whom Sale calls the "New Ecologists"—and what I refer to in this article as deep ecology—is a compelling one. Decrying the narrowly economic goals of mainstream envi-

ronmentalism, this new movement aims at nothing less than a philosophical and cultural revolution in human attitudes toward nature. In contrast to the conventional lobbying efforts of environmental professionals based in Washington, it proposes a militant defence of "Mother Earth," an unflinching opposition to human attacks on undisturbed wilderness. With their goals ranging from the spiritual to the political, the adherents of deep ecology span a wide spectrum of the American environmental movement. As Sale correctly notes, this emerging strand has in a matter of a few years made its presence felt in a number of fields: from academic philosophy (as in the journal *Environmental Ethics*) to popular environmentalism (for example, the group Earth First!).

In this article I develop a critique of deep ecology from the perspective of a sympathetic outsider. I critique deep ecology not as a general (or even a foot soldier) in the continuing struggle between the ghosts of Gifford Pinchot and John Muir over con-

* Centre for Ecological Sciences, Indian Institute of Science, Bangalore 560 012, India. This essay was written while the author was a visiting lecturer at the Yale School of Forestry and Environmental Studies. He is grateful to Mike Bell, Tom Birch, Bill Burch, Bill Cronon, Diane Mayerfeld, David Rothenberg, Kirkpatrick Sale, Joel Seton, Tim Weiskel, and Don Worster for helpful comments.

Environmental Ethics, Vol. 11, No. 1 (Spring 1989), pp. 71–83. Reprinted by permission.

trol of the U.S. environmental movement, but as an outsider to these battles. I speak admittedly as a partisan, but of the environmental movement in India, a country with an ecological diversity comparable to the U.S., but with a radically dissimilar cultural and social history.

My treatment of deep ecology is primarily historical and sociological, rather than philosophical, in nature. Specifically, I examine the cultural rootedness of a philosophy that likes to present itself in universalistic terms. I make two main arguments: first, that deep ecology is uniquely American, and despite superficial similarities in rhetorical style, the social and political goals of radical environmentalism in other cultural contexts (e.g., West Germany and India) are quite different; second, that the social consequences of putting deep ecology into practice on a worldwide basis (what its practitioners are aiming for) are very grave indeed.

II. The Tenets of Deep Ecology

While I am aware that the term *deep ecology* was coined by the Norwegian philosopher Arne Naess, this article refers specifically to the American variant.[2] Adherents of the deep ecological perspective in this country, while arguing intensely among themselves over its political and philosophical implications, share some fundamental premises about human-nature interactions. As I see it, the defining characteristics of deep ecology are fourfold:

First, deep ecology argues, that the environmental movement must shift from an "anthropocentric" to a "biocentric" perspective. In many respects, an acceptance of the primacy of this distinction constitutes the litmus test of deep ecology. A considerable effort is expended by deep ecologists in showing that the dominant motif in Western philosophy has been anthropocentric—i.e., the belief that man and his works are the center of the universe—and conversely, in identifying those lonely thinkers (Leopold, Thoreau, Muir, Aldous Huxley, Santayana, etc.) who, in assigning man a more humble place in the natural order, anticipated deep ecological thinking. In the political realm, meanwhile, establishment environmentalism (shallow ecology) is chided for casting its arguments in human-centered terms. Preserving nature, the deep ecologists say, has an intrinsic worth quite apart from any benefits preservation may convey to

future human generations. The anthropocentric-biocentric distinction is accepted as axiomatic by deep ecologists, it structures their discourse, and much of the present discussion remains mired within it.

The second characteristic of deep ecology is its focus on the preservation of unspoilt wilderness—and the restoration of degraded areas to a more pristine condition—to the relative (and sometimes absolute) neglect of other issues on the environmental agenda. I later identify the cultural roots and portentous consequences of this obsession with wilderness. For the moment, let me indicate three distinct sources from which it springs. Historically, it represents a playing out of the preservationist (read *radical*) and utilitarian (read *reformist*) dichotomy that has plagued American environmentalism since the turn of the century. Morally, it is an imperative that follows from the biocentric perspective; other species of plants and animals, and nature itself, have an intrinsic right to exist. And finally, the preservation of wilderness also turns on a scientific argument—viz., the value of biological diversity in stabilizing ecological regimes and in retaining a gene pool for future generations. Truly radical policy proposals have been put forward by deep ecologists on the basis of these arguments. The influential poet Gary Snyder, for example, would like to see a 90 percent reduction in human populations to allow a restoration of pristine environments, while others have argued forcefully that a large portion of the globe must be immediately cordoned off from human beings.[3]

Third, there is a widespread invocation of Eastern spiritual traditions as forerunners of deep ecology. Deep ecology, it is suggested, was practiced both by major religious traditions and at a more popular level by "primal" peoples in non-Western settings. This complements the search for an authentic lineage in Western thought. At one level, the task is to recover those dissenting voices within the Judeo-Christian tradition; at another, to suggest that religious traditions in other cultures are, in contrast, dominantly if not exclusively "biocentric" in their orientation. This coupling of (ancient) Eastern and (modern) ecological wisdom seemingly helps consolidate the claim that deep ecology is a philosophy of universal significance.

Fourth, deep ecologists, whatever their internal differences, share the belief that they are the "leading edge" of the environmental movement. As the polarity of the shallow/deep and anthropocentric/biocentric distinctions makes clear, they see themselves as the spiritual, philosophical, and political vanguard of American and world environmentalism.

III. Toward a Critique

Although I analyze each of these tenets independently, it is important to recognize, as deep ecologists are fond of remarking in reference to nature, the interconnectedness and unity of these individual themes.

(1) Insofar as it has begun to act as a check on man's arrogance and ecological hubris, the transition from an anthropocentric (human-centered) to a biocentric (humans as only one element in the ecosystem) view in both religious and scientific traditions is only to be welcomed.[4] What is unacceptable are the radical conclusions drawn by deep ecology, in particular, that intervention in nature should be guided primarily by the need to preserve biotic integrity rather than by the needs of humans. The latter for deep ecologists is anthropocentric, the former biocentric. This dichotomy is, however, of very little use in understanding the dynamics of environmental degradation. The two fundamental ecological problems facing the globe are (i) overconsumption by the industrialized world and by urban elites in the Third World and (ii) growing militarization, both in a short-term sense (i.e., ongoing regional wars) and in a long-term sense (i.e., the arms race and the prospect of nuclear annihilation). Neither of these problems has any tangible connection to the anthropocentric-biocentric distinction. Indeed, the agents of these processes would barely comprehend this philosophical dichotomy. The proximate causes of the ecologically wasteful characteristics of industrial society and of militarization are far more mundane: at an aggregate level, the dialectic of economic and political structures, and at a micro-level, the life style choices of individuals. These causes cannot be reduced, whatever the level of analysis, to a deeper anthropocentric attitude toward nature; on the contrary, by constituting a grave threat to human survival, the ecological degradation they cause does not even serve the best interests of human beings! If my identification of the major dangers to the integrity of the natural world is correct, invoking the bogy of anthropocentricism is at best irrelevant and at worst a dangerous obfuscation.

(2) If the above dichotomy is irrelevant, the emphasis on wilderness is positively harmful when applied to the Third World. If in the U.S. the preservationist/utilitarian division is seen as mirroring the conflict between "people" and "interests," in countries such as India the situation is very nearly the reverse. Because India is a long settled and densely populated country in which agrarian populations have a finely balanced relationship with nature, the setting aside of wilderness areas has resulted in a direct transfer of resources from the poor to the rich. Thus, Project Tiger, a network of parks hailed by the international conservation community as an outstanding success, sharply posits the interests of the tiger against those of poor peasants living in and around the reserve. The designation of tiger reserves was made possible only by the physical displacement of existing villages and their inhabitants; their management requires the continuing exclusion of peasants and livestock. The initial impetus for setting up parks for the tiger and other large mammals such as the rhinoceros and elephant came from two social groups, first, a class of ex-hunters turned conservationists belonging mostly to the declining Indian feudal elite and second, representatives of international agencies, such as the World Wildlife Fund (WWF) and the International Union for the Conservation of Nature and Natural Resources (IUCN), seeking to transplant the American system of national parks onto Indian soil. In no case have the needs of the local population been taken into account, and as in many parts of Africa, the designated wildlands are managed primarily for the benefit of rich tourists. Until very recently, wildlands preservation has been identified with environmentalism by the state and the conservation elite; in consequence, environmental problems that impinge far more directly on the lives of the poor—e.g., fuel, fodder, water shortages, soil erosion, and air and water pollution—have not been adequately addressed.[5]

Deep ecology provides, perhaps unwittingly, a justification for the continuation of such narrow and inequitable conservation practices under a newly acquired radical guise. Increasingly, the international conservation elite is using the philosophical, moral, and scientific arguments used by deep ecologists in advancing their wilderness crusade. A striking but by no means atypical example is the recent plea by a prominent American biologist for the takeover of large portions of the globe by the author and his scientific colleagues. Writing in a prestigious scientific forum, the *Annual Review of Ecology and Systematics,* Daniel Janzen argues that only biologists have the competence to decide how the tropical landscape should be used. As "the representatives of the natural world," biologists are "in charge of the future of tropical ecology," and only they have the expertise and mandate to "determine whether the tropical agroscape is to be populated only by humans, their mutualists, commensals, and parasites, or whether it will also contain some islands of the greater nature—the nature that spawned humans, yet has been vanquished by them." Janzen exhorts his colleagues to advance their territorial claims on the tropical world more forcefully, warning that the very existence of these areas is at stake: "if biologists want a tropics in which to biologize, they are going to have to buy it with care, energy, effort, strategy, tactics, time, and cash."[6]

This frankly imperialist manifesto highlights the multiple dangers of the preoccupation with wilderness preservation that is characteristic of deep ecology. As I have suggested, it seriously compounds the neglect by the American movement of far more pressing environmental problems within the Third World. But perhaps more importantly, and in a more insidious fashion, it also provides an impetus to the imperialist yearning of Western biologists and their financial sponsors, organizations such as the WWF and IUCN. The wholesale transfer of a movement culturally rooted in American conservation history can only result in the social uprooting of human populations in other parts of the globe.

(3) I come now to the persistent invocation of Eastern philosophies as antecedent in point of time but convergent in their structure with deep ecology. Complex and internally differentiated religious traditions—Hinduism, Buddhism, and Taoism—are lumped together as holding a view of nature believed to be quintessentially biocentric. Individual philosophers such as the Taoist Lao Tzu are identified as being forerunners of deep ecology. Even an intensely political, pragmatic, and Christian influenced thinker such as Gandhi has been accorded a wholly undeserved place in the deep ecological pantheon. Thus the Zen teacher Robert Aitken Roshi makes the strange claim that Gandhi's thought was not human-centered and that he practiced an embryonic form of deep ecology which is "traditionally Eastern and is found with differing emphasis in Hinduism, Taoism and in Theravada and Mahayana Buddhism."[7] Moving away from the realm of high philosophy and scriptural religion, deep ecologists make the further claim that at the level of material and spiritual practice "primal" peoples subordinated themselves to the integrity of the biotic universe they inhabited.

I have indicated that this appropriation of Eastern traditions is in part dictated by the need to construct an authentic lineage and in part a desire to present deep ecology as a universalistic philosophy. Indeed, in his substantial and quixotic biography of John Muir, Michael Cohen goes so far as to suggest that Muir was the "Taoist of the [American] West."[8] This reading of Eastern traditions is selective and does not bother to differentiate between alternate (and changing) religious and cultural traditions; as it stands, it does considerable violence to the historical record. Throughout most recorded history the characteristic form of human activity in the "East" has been a finely tuned but nonetheless conscious and dynamic manipulation of nature. Although mystics such as Lao Tzu did reflect on the spiritual essence of human relations with nature, it must be recognized that such ascetics and their reflections were supported by a society of cultivators whose relationship with nature was a far more *active* one. Many agricultural communities do have a sophisticated knowledge of the natural environment that may equal (and sometimes surpass) codified "scientific" knowledge; yet, the elaboration of such traditional ecological knowledge (in both material and spiritual contexts) can hardly be said to rest on a mystical affinity with nature of a deep ecological kind. Nor is such knowledge infallible; as the archaeological record powerfully suggests, modern Western man has no monopoly on ecological disasters.

In a brilliant article, the Chicago historian Ronald Inden points out that this romantic and essentially positive view of the East is a mirror image of the scientific and essentially pejorative view normally upheld by Western scholars of the Orient. In either case, the East constitutes the Other, a body wholly separate and alien from the West; it is defined by a uniquely spiritual and nonrational "essence," even if this essence is valorized quite differently by the two schools. Eastern man exhibits a spiritual dependence with respect to nature—on the one hand, this is symptomatic of his prescientific and backward self, on the other, of his ecological wisdom and deep ecological consciousness. Both views are monolithic, simplistic, and have the characteristic effect—intended in one case, perhaps unintended in the other—of denying agency and reason to the East and making it the privileged orbit of Western thinkers.

The two apparently opposed perspectives have then a common underlying structure of discourse in which the East merely serves as a vehicle for Western projections. Varying images of the East are raw material for political and cultural battles being played out in the West; they tell us far more about the Western commentator and his desires than about the "East." Inden's remarks apply not merely to Western scholarship on India, but to Orientalist constructions of China and Japan as well:

Although these two views appear to be strongly opposed, they often combine together. Both have a similar interest in sustaining the Otherness of India. The holders of the dominant view, best exemplified in the past in imperial administrative discourse (and today probably by that of 'development economics'), would place a traditional, superstition-ridden India in a position of perpetual tutelage to a modern, rational West. The adherents of the romantic view, best exemplified academically in the discourses of Christian liberalism and analytic psychology, concede the realm of the public and impersonal to the positivist. Taking their succour not from governments and big business, but from a plethora of religious foundations and self-help institutes, and from allies in the 'consciousness industry,' not to mention the important industry of tourism, the romantics insist that India embodies a private realm of the imagination and the religious which modern, western man lacks but needs. They, therefore, like the positivists, but for just the opposite rea-

son, have a vested interest in seeing that the Orientalist view of India as 'spiritual,' 'mysterious,' and 'exotic' is perpetuated.[9]

(4) How radical, finally, are the deep ecologists? Notwithstanding their self-image and strident rhetoric (in which the label "shallow ecology" has an opprobrium similar to that reserved for "social democratic" by Marxist-Leninists), even within the American context their radicalism is limited and it manifests itself quite differently elsewhere.

To my mind, deep ecology is best viewed as a radical trend within the wilderness preservation movement. Although advancing philosophical rather than aesthetic arguments and encouraging political militancy rather than negotiation, its practical emphasis—viz., preservation of unspoilt nature—is virtually identical. For the mainstream movement, the function of wilderness is to provide a temporary antidote to modern civilization. As a special institution within an industrialized society, the national park "provides an opportunity for respite, contrast, contemplation, and affirmation of values for those who live most of their lives in the workaday world."[10] Indeed, the rapid increase in visitations to the national parks in postwar America is a direct consequence of economic expansion. The emergence of a popular interest in wilderness sites, the historian Samuel Hays points out, was "not a throwback to the primitive, but an integral part of the modern standard of living as people sought to add new 'amenity' and 'aesthetic' goals and desires to their earlier preoccupation with necessities and conveniences."[11]

Here, the enjoyment of nature is an integral part of the consumer society. The private automobile (and the life style it has spawned) is in many respects the ultimate ecological villain, and an untouched wilderness the prototype of ecological harmony; yet, for most Americans it is perfectly consistent to drive a thousand miles to spend a holiday in a national park. They possess a vast, beautiful, and sparsely populated continent and are also able to draw upon the natural resources of large portions of the globe by virtue of their economic and political dominance. In consequence, America can simultaneously enjoy the material benefits of an expanding economy and the aesthetic benefits of unspoilt nature. The two poles of "wilderness" and "civilization" mutually coexist in an internally coherent whole, and philosophers of both poles are assigned a prominent place in this culture. Paradoxically as it may seem, it is no accident that Star Wars technology and deep ecology both find their fullest expression in that leading sector of Western civilization, California.

Deep ecology runs parallel to the consumer society without seriously questioning its ecological and socio-political basis. In its celebration of American wilderness, it also displays an uncomfortable convergence with the prevailing climate of nationalism in the American wilderness movement. For spokesmen such as the historian Roderick Nash, the national park system is America's distinctive cultural contribution to the world, reflective not merely of its economic but of its philosophical and ecological maturity as well. In what Walter Lippman called the American century, the "American invention of national parks" must be exported worldwide. Betraying an economic determinism that would make even a Marxist shudder, Nash believes that environmental preservation is a "full stomach" phenomenon that is confined to the rich, urban, and sophisticated. Nonetheless, he hopes that "the less developed nations may eventually evolve economically and intellectually to the point where nature preservation is more than a business."[12]

The error which Nash makes (and which deep ecology in some respects encourages) is to equate environmental protection with the protection of wilderness. This is a distinctively American notion, borne out of a unique social and environmental history. The archetypal concerns of radical environmentalists in other cultural contexts are in fact quite different. The German Greens, for example, have elaborated a devastating critique of industrial society which turns on the acceptance of environmental limits to growth. Pointing to the intimate links between industrialization, militarization, and conquest, the Greens argue that economic growth in the West has historically rested on the economic and ecological exploitation of the Third World. Rudolf Bahro is characteristically blunt:

> The working class here [in the West] is the richest lower class in the world. And if I look at the problem from the point of view of the whole of humanity, not just from that of Europe, then I must say that the metropolitan working class is the

worst exploiting class in history. . . . What made poverty bearable in eighteenth or nineteenth-century Europe was the prospect of escaping it through exploitation of the periphery. But this is no longer a possibility, and continued industrialism in the Third World will mean poverty for whole generations and hunger for millions.[13]

Here the roots of global ecological problems lie in the disproportionate share of resources consumed by the industrialized countries as a whole *and* the urban elite within the Third World. Since it is impossible to reproduce an industrial monoculture worldwide, the ecological movement in the West must begin by cleaning up its own act. The Greens advocate the creation of a "no growth" economy, to be achieved by scaling down current (and clearly unsustainable) consumption levels.[14] This radical shift in consumption and production patterns requires the creation of alternate economic and political structures—smaller in scale and more amenable to social participation—but it rests equally on a shift in cultural values. The expansionist character of modern Western man will have to give way to an ethic of renunciation and self-limitation, in which spiritual and communal values play an increasing role in sustaining social life. This revolution in cultural values, however, has as its point of departure an understanding of environmental processes quite different from deep ecology.

Many elements of the Green program find a strong resonance in countries such as India, where a history of Western colonialism and industrial development has benefited only a tiny elite while exacting tremendous social and environmental costs. The ecological battles presently being fought in India have as their epicenter the conflict over nature between the subsistence and largely rural sector and the vastly more powerful commercial-industrial sector. Perhaps the most celebrated of these battles concerns the Chipko (Hug the Tree) movement, a peasant movement against deforestation in the Himalayan foothills. Chipko is only one of several movements that have sharply questioned the nonsustainable demand being placed on the land and vegetative base by urban centers and industry. These include opposition to large dams by displaced peasants, the conflict between small artisan fishing and large-scale trawler fishing for export, the countrywide movements against commercial forest operations, and opposition to industrial pollution among downstream agricultural and fishing communities.[15]

Two features distinguish these environmental movements from their Western counterparts. First, for the sections of society most critically affected by environmental degradation—poor and landless peasants, women, and tribals—it is a question of sheer survival, not of enhancing the quality of life. Second, and as a consequence, the environmental solutions they articulate deeply involve questions of equity as well as economic and political redistribution. Highlighting these differences, a leading Indian environmentalist stresses that "environmental protection per se is of least concern to most of these groups. Their main concern is about the use of the environment and who should benefit from it."[16] They seek to wrest control of nature away from the state and the industrial sector and place it in the hands of rural communities who live within that environment but are increasingly denied access to it. These communities have far more basic needs, their demands on the environment are far less intense, and they can draw upon a reservoir of cooperative social institutions and local ecological knowledge in managing the "commons"—forests, grasslands, and the waters—on a sustainable basis. If colonial and capitalist expansion has both accentuated social inequalities and signaled a precipitous fall in ecological wisdom, an alternate ecology must rest on an alternate society and polity as well.

This brief overview of German and Indian environmentalism has some major implications for deep ecology. Both German and Indian environmental traditions allow for a greater integration of ecological concerns with livelihood and work. They also place a greater emphasis on equity and social justice (both within individual countries and on a global scale) on the grounds that in the absence of social regeneration environmental regeneration has very little chance of succeeding. Finally, and perhaps most significantly, they have escaped the preoccupation with wilderness perservation so characteristic of American cultural and environmental history.[17]

IV. A Homily

In 1958, the economist J. K. Galbraith referred to overconsumption as the unasked question of the American conservation movement. There is a marked selectivity, he wrote, "in the conservationist's approach to materials consumption. If we are concerned about our great appetite for materials, it is plausible to seek to increase the supply, to decrease waste, to make better use of the stocks available, and to develop substitutes. But what of the appetite itself. Surely this is the ultimate source of the problem. If it continues its geometric course, will it not one day have to be restrained? Yet in the literature of the resource problem this is the forbidden question. Over it hangs a nearly total silence."[18]

The consumer economy and society have expanded tremendously in the three decades since Galbraith penned these words; yet his criticisms are nearly as valid today. I have said "nearly," for there are some hopeful signs. Within the environmental movement several dispersed groups are working to develop ecologically benign technologies and to encourage less wasteful life styles. Moreover, outside the self-defined boundaries of American environmentalism, opposition to the permanent war economy is being carried on by a peace movement that has a distinguished history and impeccable moral and political credentials.

It is precisely these (to my mind, most hopeful) components of the American social scene that are missing from deep ecology. In their widely noticed book, Bill Devall and George Sessions make no mention of militarization or the movements for peace, while activists whose practical focus is on developing ecologically responsible life styles (e.g., Wendell Berry) are derided as "falling short of deep ecological awareness."[19] A truly radical ecology in the American context ought to work toward a synthesis of the appropriate technology, alternate life style, and peace movements.[20] By making the (largely spurious) anthropocentric-biocentric distinction central to the debate, deep ecologists may have appropriated the moral high ground, but they are at the same time doing a serious disservice to American and global environmentalism.[21]

Notes

1. Kirkpatrick Sale, "The Forest for the Trees: Can Today's Environmentalists Tell the Difference," *Mother Jones* 11, no. 8 (November 1986): 26.

2. One of the major criticisms I make in this essay concerns deep ecology's lack of concern with inequalities *within* human society. In the article in which he

coined the term *deep ecology*, Naess himself expresses concerns about inequalities between and within nations. However, his concern with social cleavages and their impact on resource utilization patterns and ecological destruction is not very visible in the later writings of deep ecologists. See Arne Naess, "The Shallow and the Deep, Long-Range Ecology Movement: A Summary," *Inquiry* 16 (1973): 96 (I am grateful to Tom Birch for this reference).

3. Gary Snyder, quoted in Sale, "The Forest for the Trees," p. 32. See also Dave Foreman, "A Modest Proposal for a Wilderness System," *Whole Earth Review*, no. 53 (Winter 1986–87): 42–45.

4. See, for example, Donald Worster, *Nature's Economy: The Roots of Ecology* (San Francisco, Sierra Club Books, 1977).

5. See Centre for Science and Environment, *India: The State of the Environment 1982: A Citizens Report* (New Delhi: Centre for Science and Environment, 1982); R. Sukumar, "Elephant-Man Conflict in Karnataka," in Cecil Saldanha, ed., *The State of Karnataka's Environment* (Bangalore: Centre for Taxonomic Studies, 1985). For Africa, see the brilliant analysis by Helge Kjekshus, *Ecology Control and Economic Development in East African History* (Berkeley: University of California Press, 1977).

6. Daniel Janzen, "The Future of Tropical Ecology," *Annual Review of Ecology and Systematics* 17 (1986): 305–06; emphasis added.

7. Robert Aitken Roshi, "Gandhi, Dogen, and Deep Ecology," reprinted as appendix C in Bill Devall and George Sessions, *Deep Ecology: Living as if Nature Mattered* (Salt Lake City: Peregrine Smith Books, 1985). For Gandhi's own views on social reconstruction, see the excellent three volume collection edited by Raghavan Iyer, *The Moral and Political Writings of Mahatma Gandhi* (Oxford: Clarendon Press, 1986–87).

8. Michael Cohen, *The Pathless Way* (Madison: University of Wisconsin Press, 1984), p. 120.

9. Ronald Inden, "Orientalist Constructions of India," *Modern Asian Studies* 20 (1986): 442. Inden draws inspiration from Edward Said's forceful polemic, *Orientalism* (New York: Basic Books, 1980). It must be noted, however, that there is a salient difference between Western perceptions of Middle Eastern and Far Eastern cultures respectively. Due perhaps to the long history of Christian conflict with Islam, Middle Eastern cultures (as Said documents) are consistently presented in pejorative terms. The juxtaposition of hostile and worshiping attitudes that Inden talks of applies only to Western attitudes toward Buddhist and Hindu societies.

10. Joseph Sax, *Mountains Without Handrails: Reflections on the National Parks* (Ann Arbor: University of Michigan Press, 1980), p. 42. Cf. also Peter Schmitt, *Back to Nature: The Arcadian Myth in Urban America* (New York: Oxford University Press, 1969), and Alfred Runte, *National Parks: The American Experience* (Lincoln: University of Nebraska Press, 1979).

11. Samuel Hays, "From Conservation to Environment: Environmental Politics in the United States since World War Two," *Environmental Review* 6 (1982): 21. See also the same author's book entitled *Beauty, Health and Permanence: Environmental Politics in the United States, 1955–85* (New York: Cambridge University Press, 1987).

12. Roderick Nash, *Wilderness and the American Mind*, 3rd ed. (New Haven: Yale University Press, 1982).

13. Rudolf Bahro, *From Red to Green* (London: Verso Books, 1984).

14. From time to time, American scholars have themselves criticized these imbalances in consumption patterns. In the 1950s, William Vogt made the charge that the United States, with one-sixteenth of the world's population, was utilizing one-third of the globe's resources. (Vogt, cited in E. F. Murphy, *Nature, Bureaucracy and the Rule of Property* [Amsterdam: North Holland, 1977, p. 29]). More recently, Zero Population Growth estimated that each American consumes thirty-nine times as many resources as an Indian. See *Christian Science Monitor,* 2 March 1987.

15. For an excellent review, see Anil Agarwal and Sunita Narain, eds., *India: The State of the Environment 1984–85: A Citizens Report* (New Delhi: Centre for Science and Environment, 1985). Cf. also Ramachandra Guha, *The Unquiet Woods: Ecological Change and Peasant Resistance in the Indian Himalaya* (Berkeley: University of California Press, forthcoming).

16. Anil Agarwal, "Human-Nature Interactions in a Third World Country," *The Environmentalist* 6, no. 3 (1986): 167.

17. One strand in radical American environmentalism, the bioregional movement, by emphasizing a greater involvement with the bioregion people inhabit, does indirectly challenge consumerism. However, as yet bioregionalism has hardly raised the questions of equity and social justice (international, intranational, and intergenerational) which I argue must be a central plank of radical environmentalism. Moreover, its stress on (individual) *experience* as the key to involvement with nature is also somewhat at odds with the integration of nature with livelihood and work that I talk of in this paper. Cf. Kirkpatrick Sale, *Dwellers in the Land:*

The Bioregional Vision (San Francisco: Sierra Club Books, 1985).

18. John Kenneth Galbraith, "How Much Should a Country Consume?" in Henry Jarrett, ed., *Perspectives on Conservation* (Baltimore: Johns Hopkins Press, 1958), pp. 91–92.

19. Devall and Sessions, *Deep Ecology*, p. 122. For Wendell Berry's own assessment of deep ecology, see his "Amplications: Preserving Wildness," *Wilderness* 50 (Spring 1987): 39–40, 50–54.

20. See the interesting recent contribution by one of the most influential spokesmen of appropriate technology—Barry Commoner, "A Reporter at Large: The Environment," *New Yorker,* 15 June 1987. While Commoner makes a forceful plea for the convergence of the environmental movement (viewed by him primarily as the opposition to air and water pollution and to the institutions that generate such pollution) and the peace movement, he significantly does not mention consumption patterns, implying that "limits to growth" do not exist.

21. In this sense, my critique of deep ecology, although that of an outsider, may facilitate the reassertion of those elements in the American environmental tradition for which there is a profound sympathy in other parts of the globe. A global perspective may also lead to a critical reassessment of figures such as Aldo Leopold and John Muir, the two patron saints of deep ecology. As Donald Worster has pointed out, the message of Muir (and, I would argue, of Leopold as well) makes sense only in an American context; he has very little to say to other cultures. See Worster's review of Stephen Fox's *John Muir and His Legacy,* in *Environmental Ethics* 5 (1983): 277–81.

IV

ECONOMICS, ETHICS, AND ECOLOGY

A. ENVIRONMENTAL POLICY AND WILLINGNESS TO PAY

MARKETS AND MORAL STANDING

Many people probably share the sentiments of two economists who, in commenting on the despoliation of our natural heritage and the poisoning of the environment with the use of pesticides, stated that "although, it is obvious that what we are doing is wrong, it is by no means obvious what would be right."[1] Indeed, the perplexities are deep. There is disagreement about whether certain practices are wrong, what proper policies would be, and, importantly, the *grounds* for deciding such matters. As noted in the introduction to this book, one source of dispute concerns what sorts of things have moral standing. Even if that difficult question were resolved, there are other sources of perplexity. One way of categorizing competing approaches to deciding an important range of environmental disputes is to divide them into (1) those that assume that the mechanism of the marketplace is the proper means of determining both the allocation of resources to different productive uses and the distribution of benefits and burdens across the relevant populations, and (2) those that assume that these matters should not be left much, or at all, to the contingencies of the marketplace (that is, certain matters should be decided politically and certain protections, or constraints on the market, must be politically enforced in order to avoid certain failures or abuses to which

unconstrained markets lead). We need to think about the effects of the market mechanism on the environment and assess the arguments for claiming that the environmental effects of the market mechanism are tolerable or desirable. Markets, of course, existed long before economists or ecologists did. A major source of defense of the desirability of the market mechanism comes, however, from economists.

Because economists, more than any other group of social scientists, have explored environmental issues in considerable detail, it is important to identify and examine some fundamental strands in economic theory and to see how economists tend to approach particular current problems, e.g., pollution, species extinction, or the question of whether we should save for the sake of future generations. Economic reasoning—indeed, the economic point of view—is extremely influential in policy making and, in some respects, inviting. Understanding this theoretical approach and the critique of it is demanding and the going will be slow at times (this is our highway warning sign to readers, i.e, "twisted, rocky road ahead"); in this preview, we explicate some technical concepts. The reader may prefer to read the selections first and then backtrack after encountering the concepts, in an extended, more partisan context, in the ensuing selections. We suggest that you read the preview once, then the selections, and backtrack when necessary or useful.

Shortly, we shall note a number of objections to orthodox economic theory; first, however, we should make it quite clear that economists deserve special praise for paying careful attention to consequences and to related trade-offs. In short, the economic approach is sensitive to empirical data, it is specific, and it suggests a method for resolving questions of trade-offs between competing and valued ends. The economic approach seems, then, practical, hard-nosed, and realistic, and its use of precise, formal modes of quantification and calculation is alluring.

In recent years there has developed a more concentrated effort to identify the points of agreement and disagreement between economic theory, ethical theory, and ecological perspectives. This effort (of which some essays in this volume are examples) promises to be an important and revealing one for developing an adequate view of our environment and a reasonable approach to setting policy on environmental matters.

On the one hand, markets seem terribly useful. They provide us (or many of us) with all sorts of goods, including decent shelter, nutrition, medical care, and transportation—items that few fail to value. In a decentralized fashion, without stereotypically maligned "government bureaucrats" deciding for the rest of us, the market allocates resources to myriad productive functions and provides a mode for distributing benefits (as well as the burdens of work, risk-taking, and so on). That the market mechanism produces all sorts of wonderful results is not subverted by the disdain we may rightly feel for certain insipid, tasteless, or defective products that it also generates. Sometimes, one person's junk is another's treasure; sometimes, it is just another person's junk as well.

The main defense of the market mechanism appeals to the value of efficiency; the defense proceeds as follows. In the best, idealized, case, two parties (for example) are mature, have settled preferences, are well-informed, and with no undue pressure or misrepresentation agree to exchange goods or services. Perhaps one agrees to paint the other's house in exchange for an old car. One values the car more than the labor-effort the other must make, and the other values having her house painted more than the car. After the exchange, both are better off. Other things being equal, the welfare of each is enhanced, and their respective utility levels are raised. Thus, the sum of (their) utilities is increased; alternatively, even if utilities cannot be summed (there is a dispute about this issue, and many economists since the 1930s "ordinalist" revolution deny the possibility), we may conclude that overall utility has increased if the judgment of all the affected parties is affirmative (and credible). The pretrade situation was one in which at least one of the two could be better off and no one worse off. It was, in the technical sense in which economists use the term, an inefficient situation. The posttrade situation is more efficient. Someone has become better off, and no one is worse off.

Why is efficiency valuable? The answer from orthodox economic theory is that moving toward more efficient arrangements is valuable because to do so is a means of increasing the total utility or welfare (to take a step toward maximization of total net expected utility, to put matters more carefully). Thus the main defense of the market appears to rest on the utilitarian assumption that we should arrange things so as to maximize (human) utility.[2] To understand the argument for adopting or perpetuating the use of the market mechanism, it is crucial to note these assumptions— ones that too often are in the background and that, hence, frequently escape scrutiny and moral appraisal.

To highlight some crucial assumptions and to emphasize which values or principles are being treated as basic, or alternatively, as derivative ones, it is useful to set out certain elements of economic reasoning more explicitly and systematically. Typically, what is implicit is the anthropocentric view that all and only humans morally count; thus, only benefits (utilities) or harms (disutilities) to humans have weight in evaluating actions or policies. For example, consider this representative remark by economist William Baxter, author of our first selection here: "To assert that there is a pollution problem or an environmental problem is to assert, at least implicitly, that one or more resources is not being used so as to maximize human satisfactions."[3] Thus, what is conceptually to count (for example) as pollution, directly or indirectly, must involve harm to humans; if penguins are poisoned by an industrial chemical but no humans (now or in the future) are affected, that is not "pollution" (or, at least, morally significant pollution). Representative of this view are these remarks by Baxter:

> My criteria are oriented to people, not penguins. Damage to penguins, or sugar pines, or geological marvels is, without more, simply irrelevant. One must . . . say: Penguins are important because people enjoy seeing them walk about rocks. . . .

> I reject the proposition that we ought to respect the "balance of nature" or to "preserve the environment" unless the reason for doing so, express or implied, is the benefit of man. Every man is entitled to his own definition of Walden Pond, but there is no definition that has any moral superiority over another, except by reference to the selfish needs of the human race.[4]

To make an important point briefly, *if the anthropocentric assumption embodied in orthodox economic theory is indefensible, then the theory as it stands is unacceptable*—as would be a theory that regarded only benefits and harms to white people as having moral significance. A theory that is not anthropocentric will be a more complex one. But simplicity is not the sole determinant of the rationality of a theory.

THE ALLEGED "VALUE-FREE" NATURE OF ECONOMIC THEORY

The modern economic approach also presupposes and accepts (however inexplicitly) a distribution of legally protected property rights. Often, there are further implicit assumptions. For example, human beings can be owners but cannot be owned. Any nonhuman can be owned. This view reflects the anthropocentric criterion of moral standing. Legal property in an object X is best understood as possession of a package of rights over what is owned, often a right to use X, to exclude others from doing so, to authorize others to use X, to be compensated for unauthorized uses, and, sometimes, to destroy X if one wishes. There is a moral question as to whether anyone should have a legal right to kill (or torture) his or her animals. The "it's my property to do with as I please" mentality implies an affirmative answer. The main point here, however, is just that orthodox economists typically assume the moral legitimacy of some set of well-defined property rights. (On these matters, recall Section IIIE.). Further, it is assumed that these rights will foster certain sorts of exchanges— for example, voluntary, nonfraudulent ones between competent persons. Thus, the core of the market mechanism, exchanges of goods or services (and rights to such), is understood to occur against the background of morally acceptable norms and institutions; the latter constitute "the rules of the game," as it were. Hence (this is no small matter), the recommendation to maximize efficiency or to produce and distribute goods in accord with people's willingness and ability to pay for them *presupposes, but does not supply, all the requisite moral norms.*

Many economists insist, however, that they engage in value-free inquiry; that they are impotent (as economists) to say whether the rules are good or right. Many deny that evaluative claims are rationally decidable or that they are any more than expressions of emotion. For example, Richard McKenzie and Gordon Tullock claim that "the approach of the economist is amoral" and that "as economists we cannot say what is 'just' or 'fair.'"[5] Paul Heyne and Thomas Johnson maintain that "we do not have any (means) of resolving ethical disagreements, they are ultimately judgments of value . . . and cannot finally be proved or disproved."[6] These stances are questionable (and have been explored systematically and in detail in the philosophical literature for years), but many economists seem oblivious to this fact, and to the fact that their own implicit or explicit commitment to the value of the market mechanism or to efficiency or to maximizing utility (or aggregate human want-satisfaction) suggests, to the contrary, that the discipline of economics (in so far as it purports not merely to explain or predict human behavior) rests, in part, on evaluative assumptions.[7] One who thought that only benefits or harms to penguins were significant would be making an important evaluative assumption. So also does one who says, "Aryans count; Jews do not" (or whites count but blacks do not; or blacks count but whites do not; or straights count but gays do not—or vice versa). The question, rather, would seem to be which view is rationally *superior;* we cannot simply avoid evaluations, but they need not be unreasoned.

In late 1993, a man named David Lee Thompson was reported to have taken a five-year-old girl from her home in Illinois and molested her several times during a 100-mile drive. Amazingly, the little girl told him that he could help himself by throwing away his pornographic magazines and that she had asked God to help him. Thompson cried on hearing this, but then he molested her again—and has since confessed to forcing children from four to eight years of age in five states into oral sex and other activities.[8]

Imagine, however unlikely, a dispute over the morality of such acts. Can we possibly avoid evaluating such acts? Is it conceivable that we would say of the two sides (one maintaining the impermissibility of the acts and the other maintaining the permissibility) that both views are equally reasonable? What should we make of a person who says that "*as* an economist" he or she must be morally neutral? More germane to mainstream economic theory, how can it be "value-free" when any defense of the market presupposes property rights?

EFFICIENCY AS A NORMATIVE GUIDE TO SOCIAL ARRANGEMENTS

The ideal of efficiency, and its assumed high value (or, possibly, overriding value), is so central in economic approaches to environmental matters that we should dissect it more thoroughly. To do so requires a bit of technical terminology; one would be helpless in trying to assess the economic approach without mastery of a few concepts.

In ordinary (nontechnical) talk, there is a strong tendency to use *efficient* as an honorific term; thus, if X is efficient, X is thought to be good (in a respect). Conversely, if X is inefficient, X is thought to be bad (in a respect). Given such usage, it seems perverse to question or oppose the efficient course, and unobjectionable or "nice" to urge efficient policies. All this can mislead us, however. The term *efficient* has a technical sense in economics; further, we should distinguish (1) what it means to say that some state of affairs is efficient, and (2) whether efficiency is a valuable goal that we ought to pursue. And, importantly, is efficiency valuable in itself or only as a means? First, we have noted that a standard implicit assumption is, not surprisingly, that efficiency is understood as efficiency for humans. Modern factory farms that raise veal calves may be quite efficient for humans, but hardly so, let us assume, for the calves.[9]

Let us return to considering question (1). The standard criterion of efficiency that is employed is called the Pareto criterion (after the early-twentieth-century economist-sociologist Vilfredo Pareto). If a situation in which parties possess various goods is such that at least one party could be better off (in that party's own estimation) without making anyone worse off, the situation is said to be inefficient (or not maximally efficient). A *Pareto improvement* could be made; that is, at least one party could be better off without worsening another's situation. In our earlier tale, in which one individual got another's car and the other got her house painted, a Pareto improvement was made. Voluntary exchanges are thought to generate Pareto improvements; that is, to increase efficiency. If a situation is one in which it is not possible for anyone to become better off without worsening another's circumstance, it is said to be *Pareto-optimal* (or maximally efficient).[10] As noted before, the core idea is that in a more efficient situation, the total welfare of the relevant parties is greater than in the less efficient one, even if one is not able to say by how much. Moving toward more efficient circumstances seems desirable, since it moves things closer to maximum utility. If, in fact, the sketched mechanism is the best means of maximizing welfare or achieving ever-increasing improvements, that fact seems to be a strong reason to employ it. Thus, the market is often defended on grounds that it best maximizes utility (quite apart from, or in addition to, appeals to implementation of, or respecting, some sort of human right to choose). Although we may give three cheers for markets as we commonly encounter them, critical reflection may make us wonder whether they deserve three, or even two. Much depends on how much we

should value utility maximization, or efficiency as a means of fostering it, whether voluntary exchanges invariably or usually increase efficiency, and to what extent exchanges really are voluntary when elements of misrepresentation are often present.[11]

It is easy to overlook some crucial points. We may have serious moral reservations about even maximally efficient situations. For example, suppose that X is a master and Y is X's slave. There may be no way to alter this arrangement so that one can be better off and no one worse off. That is, it may be Pareto-optimal or maximally efficient. The criterion focuses on a given situation and prospective departures from it, not on how it came about. As noted, a distribution of goods between master and slave may be Pareto-optimal or maximally efficient (in the Paretian sense), but morally indefensible. In short, it seems absurd to believe that whatever is efficient is right or permissible. *If so, then we must conclude that although efficiency is desirable, it only is desirable other things being equal.*[12]

In the exchange of an old car for the painting of a house, there was a gain from trade, both parties were better off, and aggregate welfare increased. In applying the Pareto criterion, economists typically assume that the proper way of determining whether the parties to the transaction are better off is to solicit the judgments of the parties themselves (usually posttrade). Several comments are relevant here, and all of them may reduce one's enthusiasm for thinking that the market is invariably the proper vehicle (or an effective one) to enhance social (human) welfare. First, in idealized models, the traders should possess complete information. In fact, actual traders are ignorant to a degree (sometimes victimized by self-interested, or profit-maximizing, individuals or corporations). We may believe, prior to trading, that acquiring a widget and foregoing some money may improve our lot. On getting the widget, the car, the meal, or the compact disc, we often regard ourselves as worse off. In fact, voluntary exchanges do not always yield a Pareto improvement over the preexchange situation, because one party is worse off postexchange. This point tends to be overlooked or denied by some ostensibly empirical scientists.

To avoid, so it would seem, this awkward result of observing what actually happens with some actual transactions, some economists seem to stipulatively define "voluntary exchange" as one an individual would engage in if and only if beneficial to that individual. Thus, with this conceptual sleight of hand, it becomes analytically true (roughly, true by definition) that "all voluntary exchanges benefit the parties who engage in them." But then this definition of "voluntary exchange" does not mean what most of us mean by the expression. Mark Sagoff develops this point in his critique of the essay (following) by Steven Edwards.[13]

And now, a comment on the *content* on our desires. We desire things *under-a-description* (at least often). Thus, in the Greek tragedy of Oedipus, the king, Oedipus, wanted to marry Jocasta. He got what he wanted. Was he better off? He did not want to marry his mother, but since (unbeknownst to him) Jocasta *was* his mother, he also got what, in one sense, he did not want. A common economic model of human psychology and choice seems too simple in not attending sufficiently to complexities that result from the existence of multiple true descriptions of what one wants, and further, of self-deception, ambivalence, weakness of will, subconscious motivation, and so on.[14]

Another feature of the market mechanism concerns who participates in market transactions, either small or large. It is worth observing that only those who are willing and able to pay have access to markets—that is, can participate in market transactions. It may not be far wrong to estimate that of the world's (almost) 6 billion members of *Homo sapiens,* at least a billion or so are unable to cast, or are radically hindered from casting, an effective vote in the economic marketplace, e.g., the extremely poor, the very young, the severely retarded, the seriously (mentally) disturbed. Nonhumans are not the only ones who have no say about the distribution of benefits and burdens generated by market transactions; a large number of existing humans are also voiceless in this way—not to mention future generations.

For the reasons mentioned, it is doubtful that voluntary, informed exchanges invariably benefit existing human participants in those exchanges. Even if they did, much of the world's population effectively is excluded from participation in market transactions. In spite of the incautious praise heaped upon capitalism by some ideologues, the proper assessment of markets (and especially commercial practices and environmental effects) must involve consideration of the alternatives to a given market system.

Basic questions of political philosophy and economics arise that cannot be explored here. However, there are two basic alternatives to a comparatively unconstrained market system. If a given system seems intolerable in some respect, it may be possible to add a new constraint to it in order to remedy the problem. This is the alternative of setting appropriate constraints on the market. Thus, if we judge that blood (or bodily parts, or babies) ought not to be bought and sold (to the highest bidder), we can legally prohibit the practice—and let the distribution be determined by nonmarket procedures. Similarly, if we judge that a corporation's self-interest in maintaining a good reputation is not an adequate safeguard to prevent it from selling defective products or polluting the environment, we can require governmental testing and set stringent liability rules that function as disincentives to corporate distribution of dangerous products or polluting. Defenders of the market are fond of pointing out (rightly) that it is not the baker's altruism, but his self-interest, that makes bread available for purchase. This is no doubt true, but this same motive can and does lead to industrial spying, theft of trade secrets, corporate bribery, and coverups of dangerous products. We do care about motives and not just consequences—a point made by Thomas Power and Paul Rauber in their essay in this section. A key question concerns how to harness and channel self-interest, but it is naive to think that we will always get "pie in the sky" if we "laissez-faire" it—i.e, let it alone.

We have noted some important criticisms of letting the market mechanism determine allocation and distribution questions. The alleged efficiency of the market process is thought to be a means to maximizing utility. However, utility maximization is hardly an uncontroversial goal. There are powerful philosophical arguments in favor of the view that maximizing utility allows, and may even *require*, unjust distributions of benefits and burdens. As we have noted, to assume the value of maximizing only *human* utility is to beg the question against anti-anthropocentric counterarguments. Further, even if those difficulties were not serious, there are reasons (as noted) to doubt that all voluntary participants in market exchanges are better off as a result. If they are not, there may be no net increase in efficiency or total utility. *Why should maximization of the sum of human utilities be the ultimate desideratum for decision making, anyway?* Further, we have observed also that much of the world's population is disenfranchised from casting an effective monetary vote in the market decision process.

THE PROBLEM OF "EXTERNALITIES"

In this brief survey of moral and other worries about the market, we have omitted a concern that economists rightly and increasingly have stressed in recent decades: that many parties who are not participants to voluntary, informed exchanges are made worse off as a result of the exchanges. These are what are called *negative externalities*. The focus here is on the generation of unconsented-to harms to some individuals; costs generated for which compensation is not paid. Thus, much pollution of the air or water is a prime example of negative externalities. Because only some of the costs to all parties are borne by the private parties, the social costs exceed the private costs. It is commonly held that if external costs only could be *internalized* (borne by those who seek to benefit from activities that generate them), there would be no problem (no moral complaint?). Thus, it is claimed that we ought to prevent or minimize externalities (some economists might be uncomfortable with this blatantly normative mode of speaking).

How can we do that? To oversimplify, three basic alternatives present themselves: (1) persuade people or corporations or nations not to generate externalities, that is, appeal to voluntary self-restraint; (2) coerce by attaching criminal penalties to violations of publicly set standards; or (3A) coerce by attaching taxes or charges to each additional unit of pollution emitted beyond a certain amount; or (3B) coerce by requiring possession of legal rights to pollute and possibly allowing trading in such rights. Many economists have a sufficiently low estimate of human nature so as to dismiss (1) rather quickly. This less-than-rosy estimate of human nature is surely correct, even if one regards the picture of people embodied in *Homo economicus* (roughly the assumption of psychological egoism and the earlier mentioned simplifications regarding motives) as a nontrivial misrepresentation of human nature.[15]

The current debate between defenders of (2) and (3) is important, intriguing, and embodies noteworthy psychological and moral assumptions. Once more, the focus on unconsented-to harm to others is viewed anthropocentrically. Only harms to humans count. The English hunter W. D. M. Bell is reported to have killed 1011 elephants in his lifetime. This slaughter, if involving no unconsented-to-harm to humans, fails to count as an externality needing any internalizing—according to the orthodox economic view. The term "social costs" is used to mean "costs to human society." An obvious question is whether a cost/benefit accounting can be thought complete when costs to nonhumans are either not recognized or recognized but treated as irrelevant. We will return to these matters.

It should not go unnoticed that many economists would object to labeling negative externalities as instances of market failure. Instead, they would maintain that unconsented-to harms (negative externalities, overexploitation of resources, pollution, and so on) result from the failure to *have* a market. As some have argued, the solution is to allow property rights in "resources." The "tragedy of the commons" is that goods that are unowned (except as they are owned by all) get misused in one fashion or another (recall Hardin's essay in IIIE). Since "chunks" of air or water rarely can be partitioned off so that particular individuals have a right to them, such persons may have little (self-interest) incentive to preserve, respect, or ration consumption of such things. According to the view being considered, it is better to allow the market to operate more broadly (by creating a more extensive distribution of property rights) than to restrict the market's scope of operation. We leave it to the reader to critically appraise this proposal—as well as the criticisms we have set forth.

NORMATIVE USES OF COST/BENEFIT ANALYSIS

Two Uses of Cost/Benefit Analysis

As noted earlier, it is widely agreed that markets as they exist are thought to fail in various respects. Unowned, or commonly held, resources are overused or exploited. Some

goods, such as fossil fuels, clean air, or water, are thought to be used up too quickly or in the wrong manner. Burdens are imposed on parties who do not consent to them (hence, negative externalities). It is often held that government intervention in certain cases is appropriate, e.g., prohibiting certain activities by regulation (and perhaps criminal penalties) or placing charges on certain activities (e.g., through licensing or effluent charges). In some cases a government agency decides whether to undertake a project such as building a dam. If the aggregate costs were to exceed the aggregate benefit, it would be foolish to proceed. It is reasonable to claim that (a) if a policy is adopted, then the costs must not exceed the benefits. We should distinguish this claim and the following two claims from one another: (b) if a policy, *P*, ought to be carried out for whatever are the relevant reasons, *P* should be carried out in the way that maximizes benefits-minus-costs, and (c) if a policy, *P*, maximizes benefits minus costs, then *P* ought to be carried out (call this the *maximization principle*). One major controversy surrounds (c). Specifically, those who argue for the adoption of a particular policy (such as flooding a valley and building a dam) may do so as follows:

1. We (or a governmental agency) ought to do whatever maximizes benefits-minus-costs.
2. Policy *P* maximizes benefits-minus-costs. Hence,
3. We ought to carry out *P*.

Two basic questions are, why should we do whatever maximizes benefits-minus-costs, and is it ever possible to know or reasonably believe of some (or any) policy that it maximizes benefits-minus-costs? Further, in a given case, is it reasonable to believe that a particular policy does so? Steven Kelman's essay explores these matters.[16]

Here we begin to lay out the Pandora's box of puzzles that arise when one sets out to identify and reassess what is presupposed by the sort of normative cost/benefit approach identified above (whose core is [c]: that the policy that maximizes benefits-minus-costs is right and, therefore, ought to be adopted). What seems at first only a simple truism like "don't be wasteful" is not so at all; rather, the presuppositions are many, hard to unearth, entrenched, and extremely influential.

The Concepts of Cost and Benefit

The concepts of cost and benefit are not as straightforward as is often implied. What is to count as a cost? A number of possibilities come to mind: premature death, injury, pain, (felt) frustration of preferences, or (unfelt) nonfulfillment of preferences. Such suggestions may focus only on costs to humans. We have noted reasons to reject such anthropocentrism. Should we not include what economists (and many others) almost invariably exclude, such as pain or premature death to animals, or destruction of a river or forest if there is no nontrivial loss to humans? Analogously, what is to count as a benefit? Is pure life prolongation of humans a benefit? Are all instances of human preference satisfaction to be weighed positively in a cost/benefit calculation? There is a tendency to equate "benefit," "good," "welfare," "satisfaction," "utility," and "preference fulfillment," but should we regard the fulfillment of "antisocial preferences" (such as sadistic, envious, jealous ones) as a benefit? Recall David Lee Thompson's desire for sex with five-year-olds. As noted earlier, should not preferences be "laundered"?

Orthodox economists, perhaps in an excess of antipaternalism, antimoralism, or uncritical acceptance of moral subjectivism (an instance of egalitarianism run amok), express the normative position that we ought not to pass judgment on existing preferences—and imply, therefore, that all preferences are equally deserving of fulfillment (again, consider a hunter's intense preference to maximize his or her kill of whales, a rapist's desire to rape, or a resentful soldier's desire to bash gay comrades. If one says that some preferences do not deserve satisfaction (or that their fulfillment has no positive moral weight), then evaluation enters at a fundamental level, and it is inappropriate to proclaim value neutrality for any such economic theory (even if it does not insist on cardinal measures of utility).[17] However, any theory advocating unqualified want-fulfillment seems morally problematic for the reasons discussed.

Similarly, in many cases little is said about the relationship between beliefs and preferences (as if preferences were like itches and unconnected with cognition). However, it is clear that one's preferences are heavily dependent (sometimes causally and sometimes conceptually) on one's beliefs. Compare preferences for and against slavery, polygamy, the use of DDT, the killing of whales, or Oedipus's preference for Jocasta when he believed, and when he did not believe, Jocasta to be his mother. If preferences (such as for destroying all Jews, keeping women barefoot and pregnant, "nuking" the latest enemy, always giving preference to women) are based on irrational beliefs (Jews are vermin; women rightly are property of males—God's designated "helpmates" for men; retaliation by the enemy would be minor; all women are innocent victims), it is not at all clear why satisfaction of such preferences is a benefit to be weighed positively in some cost/benefit calculations. Thus, aside from the fact that only effects on humans are given weight in the calculations, it seems doubtful that all instances of preference fulfillment should be conceptualized as benefits. If so, why maximize them? Further, it is not obvious that all harms to humans (costs) can be viewed as frustration of wants. When urban children suffer brain damage (and consequent retardation) from exposure to lead (from our use of leaded gasoline), what preference of the child is frustrated? Suppose the child is only a year old. If acid rain destroys many of our forests, is there no cost if and when people do not care, and we come to prefer plastic trees (as a result of indoctrination or not missing what we never experienced)?[18]

A different, competing analysis of welfare/illfare, benefit/cost, gain/loss is presented in terms of promoting or subverting the *interests* of a person or other organism—in terms of what is *in the interest of,* or subversive of, a being. When one takes into account children, the comatose, or the severely retarded—as philosophers and social theorists sometimes forget to do—it is especially clear that *what people want* and *what is in their interest* only overlap. Those who identify benefits with want satisfaction need to give reasons for rejecting a competing analysis of benefit. The person on the street probably believes that cost/benefit techniques are aimed at promoting welfare, but arguably want satisfaction and the promotion of welfare are not the same thing.

Even if it were unproblematic that benefit equals want satisfaction, it is questionable whether all benefits (so understood) can be identified and measured. There is no established market in some goods. Thus, economists infer by indirect means how much people (consumers) valued a good or a service ("value," in economics, often means "prefer" in English). There are two main approaches to determining value: (a) determine which packages of goods people are willing and able to pay for if there is a market for them, and (b) the contingent valuation method (CVM): ask people direct or indirect questions. The essay following by Edwards defends CVM, and it is attacked in the essay by Sagoff.

Consider (a) here. What people are *willing* to pay is, in part, a function of how much they are *able* to pay. If willingness to pay for safety devices in a car is the criterion, then one may believe that the rich value their lives more than the poor value theirs. Should we believe as much? Suppose Jones is out of work and starving on Monday and then takes a highly risky job on Tuesday (washing windows on the fifth floor). He may demand only a modest premium to compensate for the extra risk to his life (suppose he could have had the first-floor job for a slightly smaller salary). Should we infer that the value of Jones's life is small—that he does not value it much? According to another approach, the value (or "economic value"?) of a person's life is equivalent to his or her foregone earnings. Perhaps this is a suitable criterion for determining how much compensation should be made to a person's estate when that person is wrongfully killed. As a measure of the value of that person's life or the amount of money that should be spent to prevent premature death, a monetary measure seems dubious. Happenstance affects earnings (as do preferences for leisure time and moral convictions). Would Shaquille O'Neal's life be worth less if there were no market for basketball players? Is a ditchdigger's life at age 21 worth less than that of a clever 21-year-old software designer?[19]

THE MATTER OF CONSENT

In law and in common sense, whether another party (voluntarily and knowingly) consents to the imposition of a "harm" is thought morally significant in deciding on the permissibility or desirability of generating the harm. The surgeon and the mugger may make similar "incisions," perhaps with similar results, but we view the unconsented-to cutting as wrong, and the one to which there is consent as acceptable. It is striking that, in some discussions defending cost/benefit analysis, little attention is paid to whether those who are harmed, or subjected to risks, consent or not. It is clear that (more or less) voluntary smoking results in great harms (on average and in the aggregate) to smokers. A cost/benefit analysis of smoking (or alcohol usage) might suggest strongly that the practice fails to maximize benefits-minus-costs. It is natural to wonder, however, whether the burdens on the smokers (aside from associated indirect burdens on nonsmokers) should be counted as a cost in a cost/benefit calculation. At the least, we raise the question of whether *imposed* costs and *voluntarily absorbed* costs should be viewed similarly. As the issue is often discussed, this distinction tends to be ignored. Sometimes consent is simply and dubiously postulated, e.g., because a consumer lives in a wooden house he or she is said to tacitly consent to the stripping of old-growth timber from the national forests.

THE MAXIMIZATION PRINCIPLE

Although an analyst may purport to identify only costs and benefits (and, thus, remain untainted by ethical commitments) and not subscribe to the maximization principle (we ought to do whatever maximizes benefits-minus-costs), further questions arise for anyone who accepts the (normative) maximization principle. If the prior difficulties cannot be overcome, the principle may be inapplicable.[20] The main objection to be noted here concerns whether a policy of maximizing the balance of benefits over costs is defensible when it gives no direct weight to how those benefits and costs are *distributed* among the relevant population.[21]

Perhaps, however, a coupling (somehow) of cost/benefit analysis and principles of just distribution may be more attractive. If so, one may have to surrender the unqualified maximization principle. Further, one may have to drop the pervasive meta-ethical assumption seemingly made by some (perhaps earlier vintage) environmental economists that "the proper use of environmental resources is more a matter of economics than of morals."[22] This last assumption is plausible only if one accepts the maximization principle and the assumption that one can measure all the relevant benefits and costs. These claims cannot, however, be decided without careful inquiry.

Matters are not all this simple, of course. The claims that some environmentalists, philosophers, and scientists have proposed as guidelines for use in making environmental decisions (maxims such as "nature knows best," "a thing is right when it tends to preserve the integrity, stability, and beauty of the biotic community," "maximize utility" [again], "preserve endangered species," "everything has a right to exist") seem to be too vague and indeterminate to be analytic truisms, or otherwise objectionable. The essays that follow address the attractions of efficiency, market solutions, the contingent valuation method, and mainstream uses of cost/benefit calculations—as grounds for policy determination.

To speak at length of these matters is not to talk directly of rain forests, blue whales, acid rain, marshlands, or estuaries; rather, it is to explore grounds for choices that will determine the destiny of such entities as well as that of humans. If one is concerned with the fate of our planet, to ignore such matters is to choose to be a naive and ineffectual environmentalist.

THE ESSAYS

In the first selection that follows, economist William Baxter expresses, in no uncertain terms, an anthropocentric approach to environmental trade-offs. As Baxter states, "Damage to penguins, or sugar pines, or geological marvels is, without more, simply irrelevant." Baxter optimistically believes that what is good for people, often at least, is good for the environment. One might question whether "maximize human satisfaction" underlies Baxter's economic viewpoint and, if so, what assessment should be made.

Public policy analyst Steven Kelman, in "Cost-Benefit Analysis: An Ethical Critique," argues that, apart from considering questions about the anthropocentric nature of cost/benefit analysis, a policy might be right even if it does *not* maximize benefits-minus-costs. Further, he questions the attempt to assign monetary values to nonmarketed benefits and costs, i.e., the use of CVM.

Economist Steven Edwards, in his essay, "In Defense of Environmental Economics," argues that *economic* values and *market* values should not be equated. The use of CVM, roughly asking people (in the absence of actual markets for the good in question) what they would be willing to pay in order to preserve certain environmental conditions, e.g., the remnants of old-growth forests in the Appalachians, is the right way to determine environmental policy. He argues that objections to this method (e.g., they are biased) are surmountable. In his view, economic value should be maximized and the economic value of anything is determined entirely by that thing's "ability to yield personal utility." We thus appear to have a defense of the basic mainstream-utilitarian perspective as well as a defense of the contingent valuation method of determining economic value. Edwards denies that placing monetary values on environmental entities must cheapen them. He claims not to argue that the economists' model of "egoist man" is true, but he maintains that " . . . most critics of environmental economics are also presumptuous when they take normative positions on what preferences *should be* without also attending to what they actually *are.*" We suggest that the reader juxtapose Edwards's view and the counterpoint that critics are perfectly well aware of people's actual preferences, do unabashedly morally condemn some preferences (recall David Lee Thompson's), and maintain that one has an indefensible position if one does not. The important question is whether to assume that all (human) want or preference fulfillment is a good and is what ought to be promoted.[23] If this is correct, then what Edwards describes as "the difference between economists and ethicists" is not just "an empirical matter," as he maintains.

In his essay, "Some Problems with Environmental Economics," Mark Sagoff zeroes in on the equation of the concept of social welfare with preference satisfaction, and insists that it is important to appraise the *content* of the preference or desire. He claims that there is no necessary increase in social welfare when desires are fulfilled. Furthermore, when government bureaucrats use the contingent valuation method to determine what value to place on environmental preservation, they thereby give weight to purely hypothetical choices and not actual ones. The procedure, he claims, lends itself to highly centralized planning and undue paternalistic intervention; one might read Sagoff as defending the use of actual markets instead of governmental agencies to decide what happens to the environment. But given his rejection of the equation of want-satisfaction and welfare (or "economic value"), it is clear that he offers no endorsement of that view. In general he charges defenders of mainstream (micro)economics with treating normative issues about what we ought to do as questions to be decided by seeing which alternative will maximize satisfaction. He states "they assume that paying to protect whales and paying for psychic satisfaction come to the same thing." In his view, and, arguably, the view of most ethicists, moral commitments ought not to be thought of simply as individual preferences based on considerations of personal welfare.

Our final selection by Thomas Power and Paul Rauber, "The Price of Everything," focuses directly on free-market environmentalism, roughly the view that we should let the marketplace provide its own solutions to environmental difficulties. It is characterized by advocating expansion of property rights to new areas (reducing or eliminating "the commons"), and letting resources go to the highest bidders; the authors further advocate elimination of hidden governmental subsidies and thus a cessation of "distortion" of prices in the market—ones said to result in that *bete noir* of the market: inefficiency. Basically, the authors argue that we must settle our environmental goals *first* and only then employ market-type devices on a purely pragmatic, piecemeal, basis to reach those goals. Why this is so is, of course, developed in their down-to-earth essay.

There are numerous sources of dispute in current discussions, but their becoming more overt is a healthy sign, one suggesting that disciplinary isolation is breaking down and a joining of the issues is beginning to occur and not just on an intra-academic-field basis. In case no one has noticed, much of this volume testifies to the shaking of intellectual foundations when paradigms clash openly.

NOTES

1. Robert Dorfman and Nancy Dorfman, eds., *Economics of the Environment* (New York: W. W. Norton Company, 1972), p. xix.

2. In the ensuing selection by Mark Sagoff, he expresses doubt that the defense of efficiency rests on utilitarian assumptions. We also note here that it is worth keeping in mind that two versions of utilitarianism, classical and preference, should be considered in exploring the connections of mainstream economic theory to utilitarianism. Recall Singer's essay in Section II and the preview to that section.

3. William Baxter, *People or Penguins: The Case for Optimal Pollution* (New York: Columbia University Press, 1974), p. 17. His title partially inspired that of this volume.

4. Ibid., p. 5.

5. Richard B. McKenzie and Gordon Tullock, *The New World of Economics* (Homewood, IL: Richard D. Irwin, 1978), p. 7.

6. Paul Heyne and Thomas Johnson, *Toward Economic Understanding* (Chicago: Science Research Associates, 1976), p. 767.

7. Although we are critical of economists at points, moral philosophers and environmental ethicists can learn a great deal from economists as well. Much work has been done by economists in game theory, decision theory, and examination of slippery issues surrounding the notions of efficiency and utility—all matters relating to decision making. For example,

the idea of choosing from behind a veil of ignorance, one which has been put to such important use by philosopher John Rawls, could have been found in the work of economist John Harsanyi in the 1950s; we do not know whether Harsanyi's work influenced Rawls on this score.

8. See "Child Molester Tells of a Rampage in 5 States" in *The New York Times* (December 26, 1993), p. 9.

9. See Peter Singer, *Animal Liberation* (New York: A New York Review Book, distributed by Random House, 1975). See also the first essay by Singer, which we have included in this volume.

10. There may be many Pareto-optimal situations, and some may be, on the face of things, unjust and have been arrived at in an unjust manner.

11. Recently General Electric offered a light bulb advertised as one to replace 100-watt bulbs and one which would save money; a good deal one might conclude, but the fine print indicates that the bulb is a 90-watt bulb and is thus less light for less money. Should we have a free market that allows this sort of slimy behavior? One would think that Kant's dictum, "never treat a person as a mere means," might condemn such attempts to deceive.

12. The expression "other things being equal" in the sentence above means roughly "in the absence of morally relevant considerations to the contrary."

13. In his essay, Mark Sagoff plausibly suggests (putting it in our terms) that economists may be stipulatively defining terms like "better off" or "utility increase" as meaning "desire fulfillment" (and assuming that in every voluntary act one gets what he or she desires). If so, voluntary market transactions, by definition, result in an increase in utility. But then, by the same token, one might conclude that eating oysters has an aphrodisiac effect by stipulating that the term "oyster" means "an object whose consumption has an aphrodisiac effect." As someone said, to do so has all the advantages of theft over honest toil (argument).

14. We refer readers to the growing literature in philosophical psychology and the philosophy of mind; one might explore the *Encyclopedia of Philosophy,* the *Philosopher's Index* or the *Encyclopedia of Ethics* for bibliography.

15. "Psychological egoism" is the logically extreme thesis that every human action is motivated by self-interest. The thesis, we emphasize, is not about outcomes but about motivation. In this view, even people who endure torture rather than betray their friends, loved ones, or country do so out of self-interest. The denial of this view is *not* the view that everyone always acts unselfishly.

16. For a critique of the sort of view expressed by Kelman, see Herman B. Leonard and Richard J. Zeckhauser, "Cost-Benefit Analysis Defended" in Donald VanDeVeer and Christine Pierce, eds., *The Environmental Ethics and Policy Book* (Belmont, CA.: Wadsworth Publishing Company, 1994).

17. "Moral weight" is not some spooky, metaphysical kind of weight but simply positive weight in deciding what ought to be done.

18. One writer proposed that real trees on the Los Angeles freeways be replaced with plastic trees; if the only goal is to fulfill human wants and such plastic objects do the job, why not? See Martin Krieger, "What's Wrong with Plastic Trees?" 179 *Science* 446 (1973). Our title is partly inspired by Krieger's essay.

19. Years ago the Ford motor company did a cost/benefit analysis on the policy of adding certain devices to its cars in order to prevent the gas tanks from rupturing. One of the protective benefits was saving a certain number of lives. How valuable is one life? Can a life rationally be assigned a monetary value? Ford figured $200,000 (for 1971!) as the cost of a death. Presumably, this figure largely reflects costs to others; only $10,000 of the amount as designated as the cost (value?) of the victim's pain and suffering. Why not $50,000 or 100,000? Is the benefit of preserving a life equal to the cost of avoiding the death (which is assumed to be a function of wages forgone)? Of course, the figure that is assigned here directly affects the outcome of the cost/benefit calculation and the ultimate policy determination. We note here the obvious questions that arise about the reasonableness of assigning monetary values to certain goods and bads. There are important questions about the way "cost" and "benefit" are conceptualized, problems in attempting to identify all the costs and benefits, and difficulties in rationally assigning a monetary measure to many costs and benefits— even when one takes an anthropocentric approach. Avoiding complexities, however, can have a high price. Our cost/benefit calculations would be comparatively simpler if we did not count the well-being of children or the severely retarded.

20. The principle seems subject to the well-known difficulties with the principle of utility; in one construal, "maximize benefits-minus-costs" is just the principle of utility. (Except that the classic utilitarians, Jeremy Bentham and John Stuart Mill, were not anthropocentric in their conception of "cost" and "benefit." Both explicitly maintained that the suffering of animals must be given weight in deciding what to do.).

21. The policy that maximizes benefits-minus-costs may make some individuals worse off. Thus, adopting the policy may not be an efficient step in the sense of making a Pareto improvement (see the earlier discussion for an explanation). The gains to the winners, however, may outweigh the losses to the losers. If so, it would be *possible* in principle for the gainers to *compensate* the loser thus, making the latter nonlosers (no worse off). The costs of making the transfer (information costs, and so on) may make full compensation impossible. If, however, full compensation were made, a Pareto improvement would occur; there would be no losers on balance, and an injustice could not be claimed, namely, that some suffered an unconsented to, on balance, harm. (Note, however, that some might be relatively, if not absolutely, worse off—on one objective measure, at least.) Some economists, and others, however, believe a "potential compensation principle" (or potential Pareto criterion) is satisfactory. The results of a policy must make full compensation *possible,* but the compensation need not be paid. This view is puzzling. To accept the potential compensation principle is to set aside an intuitively attractive feature of the strict Pareto principle (that no one will lose), one that sidesteps important moral objections based on considerations of justice. If salesperson *A* "steals" salesperson *B*'s $5,000 car, and as a result earns an extra $50,000 a year, perhaps *A* could compensate *B* for his or her losses. If *A* does not, *B* has ground for serious moral complaint. We do not pursue the point here, but there may be ground for complaint *even if* compensation is made (assuming it can be).

    To maximize benefits-minus-costs without compensating losers looks suspiciously like merely maximizing total net utility. Uncompensated losses look like market failures or negative externalities. A supposed attraction of cost/benefit analysis is that it helps to eliminate or reduce such externalities. Pure maximization policies (regardless of what is to be maximized, e.g., GNP, utility, wealth, or benefits-minus-costs) seem to give no direct weight to concerns about how benefits and costs are distributed. This seems morally intolerable.

22. Dorfman and Dorfman, *Economics of the Environment*, p. xl.

23. It is one thing to *evaluate* another's preferences as being self-destructive, or as resulting in a wrong to others if acted upon (the urge to kill) and another to coercively *intervene* to prevent preferences from being acted upon. But we do both, e.g., halting an attempted murder, a conspiracy so to act, or halting some would-be suicides. The latter may be done for paternalistic reasons. For just when paternalistic intervention is permissible, see: Joel Feinberg, *Harm to Self;* John Kleinig, *Paternalism;* and Donald VanDeVeer, *Paternalistic Intervention.*

People or Penguins

William Baxter

I start with the modest proposition that, in dealing with pollution, or indeed with any problem, it is helpful to know what one is attempting to accomplish. Agreement on how and whether to pursue a particular objective, such as pollution control, is not possible unless some more general objective has been identified and stated with reasonable precision. We talk loosely of having clean air and clean water, of preserving our wilderness areas, and so forth. But none of these is a sufficiently general objective: each is more accurately viewed as a means rather than as an end.

With regard to clean air, for example, one may ask, "how clean?" and "what does clean mean?" It is even reasonable to ask, "why have clean air?" Each of these questions is an implicit demand that a more general community goal be stated—a goal sufficiently general in its scope and enjoying sufficiently general assent among the community of actors that such "why" questions no longer seem admissible with respect to that goal.

If, for example, one states as a goal the proposition that "every person should be free to do whatever he wishes in contexts where his actions do not interfere with the interests of other human beings," the speaker is unlikely to be met with a response of "why." The goal may be criticized as uncertain in its implications or difficult to implement, but it is so basic a tenet of our civilization—it reflects a cultural value so broadly shared, at least in the abstract—that the question "why" is seen as impertinent or imponderable or both.

I do not mean to suggest that everyone would agree with the "spheres of freedom" objective just stated. Still less do I mean to suggest that a society could subscribe to four or five such general objectives that would be adequate in their coverage to serve as testing criteria by which all other disagreements might be measured. One difficulty in the attempt to construct such a list is that each new goal added will conflict, in certain applications, with each prior goal listed; and thus each goal serves as a limited qualification on prior goals.

Without any expectation of obtaining unanimous consent to them, let me set forth four goals that I generally use as ultimate testing criteria in attempting to frame solutions to problems of human organization. My position regarding pollution stems from these four criteria. If the criteria appeal to you and any part of what appears hereafter does not, our disagreement will have a helpful focus: which of us is correct, analytically, in supposing that his position on pollution would better serve these general goals. If the criteria do not seem acceptable to you, then it is to be expected that our more particular judgments will differ, and the task will then be yours to identify the basic set of criteria upon which your particular judgments rest.

My criteria are as follows:

1. The spheres of freedom criterion stated above.

2. Waste is a bad thing. The dominant feature of human existence is scarcity—our available resources, our aggregate labors, and our skill in employing both have always been, and will continue for some time to be, inadequate to yield to every man all the tangible and intangible satisfactions he would like to have. Hence, none of those resources, or labors, or skills, should be wasted—that is, employed so as to yield less than they might yield in human satisfactions.

3. Every human being should be regarded as an end rather than as a means to be used for the betterment of another. Each should be afforded dignity and regarded as having an absolute claim to an evenhanded application of such rules as the community may adopt for its governance.

4. Both the incentive and the opportunity to improve his share of satisfactions should be preserved to every individual. Preservation of incentive is dictated by the "no waste" criterion and enjoins against the continuous, totally egalitarian redistribution of satisfac-

People or Penguins: The Case for Optimal Pollution, William F. Baxter, 1974, © Columbia University Press, New York. Reprinted with permission of the publisher.

tions, or wealth; but subject to that constraint, everyone should receive, by continuous redistribution if necessary, some minimal share of aggregate wealth so as to avoid a level of privation from which the opportunity to improve his situation becomes illusory.

The relationship of these highly general goals to the more specific environmental issues at hand may not be readily apparent, and I am not yet ready to demonstrate their pervasive implications. But let me give one indication of their implications. Recently scientists have informed us that use of DDT in food production is causing damage to the penguin population. For the present purposes let us accept that assertion as an indisputable scientific fact. The scientific fact is often asserted as if the correct implication—that we must stop agricultural use of DDT—followed from the mere statement of the fact of penguin damage. But plainly it does not follow if my criteria are employed.

My criteria are oriented to people, not penguins. Damage to penguins, or sugar pines, or geological marvels is, without more, simply irrelevant. One must go further, by my criteria, and say: Penguins are important because people enjoy seeing them walk about rocks; and furthermore, the well-being of people would be less impaired by halting use of DDT than by giving up penguins. In short, my observations about environmental problems will be people-oriented, as are my criteria. I have no interest in preserving penguins for their own sake.

It may be said by way of objection to this position, that it is very selfish of people to act as if each person represented one unit of importance and nothing else was of any importance. It is undeniably selfish. Nevertheless I think it is the only tenable starting place for analysis for several reasons. First, no other position corresponds to the way most people really think and act—i.e., corresponds to reality.

Second, this attitude does not portend any massive destruction of nonhuman flora and fauna, for people depend on them in many obvious ways, and they will be preserved because and to the degree that humans do depend on them.

Third, what is good for humans is, in many respects, good for penguins and pine trees—clean air for example. So that humans are, in these respects, surrogates for plant and animal life.

Fourth, I do not know how we could administer any other system. Our decisions are either private or collective. Insofar as Mr. Jones is free to act privately, he may give such preferences as he wishes to other forms of life: he may feed birds in winter and do with less himself, and he may even decline to resist an advancing polar bear on the ground that the bear's appetite is more important than those portions of himself that the bear may choose to eat. In short my basic premise does not rule out private altruism to competing life-forms. It does rule out, however, Mr. Jones' inclination to feed Mr. Smith to the bear, however hungry the bear, however despicable Mr. Smith.

Insofar as we act collectively on the other hand, only humans can be afforded an opportunity to participate in the collective decisions. Penguins cannot vote now and are unlikely subjects for the franchise—pine trees more unlikely still. Again each individual is free to cast his vote so as to benefit sugar pines if that is his inclination. But many of the more extreme assertions that one hears from some conservationists amount to tacit assertions that they are specially appointed representatives of sugar pines, and hence that their preferences should be weighted more heavily than the preferences of other humans who do not enjoy equal rapport with "nature." The simplistic assertion that agricultural use of DDT must stop at once because it is harmful to penguins is of that type.

Fifth, if polar bears or pine trees or penguins, like men, are to be regarded as ends rather than means, if they are to count in our calculus of social organization, someone must tell me how much each one counts, and someone must tell me how these life-forms are to be permitted to express their preferences, for I do not know either answer. If the answer is that certain people are to hold their proxies, then I want to know how those proxy-holders are to be selected: self-appointment does not seem workable to me.

Sixth, and by way of summary of all the foregoing, let me point out that the set of environmental issues under discussion—although they raise very complex technical questions of how to achieve any objective—ultimately raise a normative question: what *ought* we to do. Questions of *ought* are unique to the human mind and world—they are meaningless as applied to a nonhuman situation.

I reject the proposition that we *ought* to respect the "balance of nature" or to "preserve the environment" unless the reason for doing so, express or implied, is the benefit of man.

I reject the idea that there is a "right" or "morally correct" state of nature to which we should return. The word "nature" has no normative connotation. Was it "'right" or "wrong" for the earth's crust to heave in contortion and create mountains and seas? Was it "right" for the first amphibian to crawl up out of the primordial ooze? Was it "wrong" for plants to reproduce themselves and alter the atmospheric composition in favor of oxygen? For animals to alter the atmosphere in favor of carbon dioxide both by breathing oxygen and eating plants? No answers can be given to these questions because they are meaningless questions.

All this may seem obvious to the point of being tedious, but much of the present controversy over environment and pollution rests on tacit normative assumptions about just such nonnormative phenomena: that it is "wrong" to impair penguins with DDT, but not to slaughter cattle for prime rib roasts. That it is wrong to kill stands of sugar pines with industrial fumes, but not to cut sugar pines and build housing for the poor. Every man is entitled to his own preferred definition of Walden Pond, but there is no definition that has any moral superiority over another, except by reference to the selfish needs of the human race.

From the fact that there is no normative definition of the natural state, it follows that there is no normative definition of clean air or pure water—hence no definition of polluted air—or of pollution—except by reference to the needs of man. The "right" composition of the atmosphere is one which has some dust in it and some lead in it and some hydrogen sulfide in it—just those amounts that attend a sensibly organized society thoughtfully and knowledgeably pursuing the greatest possible satisfaction for its human members.

The first and most fundamental step toward solution of our environmental problems is a clear recognition that our objective is not pure air or water but rather some optimal state of pollution. That step immediately suggests the question: How do we define and attain the level of pollution that will yield the maximum possible amount of human satisfaction?

Low levels of pollution contribute to human satisfaction but so do food and shelter and education and music. To attain ever lower levels of pollution, we must pay the cost of having less of these other things. I contrast that view of the cost of pollution control with the more popular statement that pollution control will "cost" very large numbers of dollars. The popular statement is true in some senses, false in others; sorting out the true and false senses is of some importance. The first step in that sorting process is to achieve a clear understanding of the difference between dollars and resources. Resources are the wealth of our nation; dollars are merely claim checks upon those resources. Resources are of vital importance; dollars are comparatively trivial.

Four categories of resources are sufficient for our purposes: At any given time a nation, or a planet if you prefer, has a stock of labor, of technological skill, of capital goods, and of natural resources (such as mineral deposits, timber, water, land, etc.). These resources can be used in various combinations to yield goods and services of all kinds—in some limited quantity. The quantity will be larger if they are combined efficiently, smaller if combined inefficiently. But in either event the resource stock is limited, the goods and services that they can be made to yield are limited; even the most efficient use of them will yield less than our population, in the aggregate, would like to have.

If one considers building a new dam, it is appropriate to say that it will be costly in the sense that it will require x hours of labor, y tons of steel and concrete, and z amount of capital goods. If these resources are devoted to the dam, then they cannot be used to build hospitals, fishing rods, schools, or electric can openers. That is the meaningful sense in which the dam is costly.

Quite apart from the very important question of how wisely we can combine our resources to produce goods and services, is the very different question of how they get distributed—who gets how many goods? Dollars constitute the claim checks which are distributed among people and which control their share of national output. Dollars are nearly valueless pieces of paper except to the extent that they do represent claim checks to some fraction of the output of goods and services. Viewed as claim checks, all the dollars outstanding during any period of time are worth, in the aggregate, the goods and services that are available to be claimed with them during that period—neither more nor less.

It is far easier to increase the supply of dollars than to increase the production of goods and services—printing dollars is easy. But printing more dollars doesn't help because each dollar then simply becomes a claim to fewer goods, i.e., becomes worth less.

The point is this: many people fall into error upon hearing the statement that the decision to build a dam, or to clean up a river, will cost $X million. It is regrettably easy to say: "It's only money. This is a wealthy country, and we have lots of money." But you cannot build a dam or clean a river with $X million—unless you also have a match, you can't even make a fire. One builds a dam or cleans a river by diverting labor and steel and trucks and factories from making one kind of goods to making another. The cost in dollars is merely a shorthand way of describing the extent of the division necessary. If we build a dam for $X million, then we must recognize that we will have $X million less housing and food and medical care and electric can openers as a result.

Similarly, the costs of controlling pollution are best expressed in terms of the other goods we will have to give up to do the job. This is not to say the job should not be done. Badly as we need more housing, more medical care, and more can openers, and more symphony orchestras, we could do with somewhat less of them, in my judgment at least, in exchange for somewhat cleaner air and rivers. But that is the nature of the trade-off, and analysis of the problem is advanced if that unpleasant reality is kept in mind. Once the trade-off relationship is clearly perceived, it is possible to state in a very general way what the optimal level of pollution is. I would state it as follows:

People enjoy watching penguins. They enjoy relatively clean air and smog-free vistas. Their

health is improved by relatively clean water and air. Each of these benefits is a type of good or service. As a society we would be well advised to give up one washing machine if the resources that would have gone into that washing machine can yield greater human satisfaction when diverted into pollution control. We should give up one hospital if the resources thereby freed would yield more human satisfaction when devoted to elimination of noise in our cities. And so on, trade-off by trade-off, we should divert our productive capacities from the production of existing goods and services to the production of a cleaner, quieter, more pastoral nation up to—and no further than—the point at which we value more highly the next washing machine or hospital that we would have to do without than we value the next unit of environmental improvement that the diverted resources would create.

Now this proposition seems to me unassailable but so general and abstract as to be unhelpful—at least unadministerable in the form stated. It assumes we can measure in some way the incremental units of human satisfaction yielded by very different types of goods. The proposition must remain a pious abstraction until I can explain how this measurement process can occur. In subsequent chapters I will attempt to show that we can do this—in some contexts with great precision and in other contexts only by rough approximation. But I insist that the proposition stated describes the result for which we should be striving—and again, that it is always useful to know what your target is even if your weapons are too crude to score a bull's eye.

Cost-Benefit Analysis: An Ethical Critique

Steven Kelman

At the broadest and vaguest level, cost-benefit analysis may be regarded simply as systematic thinking about decision-making. Who can oppose, economists sometimes ask, efforts to think in a

systematic way about the consequences of different courses of action? The alternative, it would appear, is unexamined decision-making. But defining cost-benefit analysis so simply leaves it

Regulation (Jan., Feb. 1981), pp. 74–82. Reprinted by permission of the American Enterprise Institute for Public Policy Research, Washington, D.C.

with few implications for actual regulatory decision-making. Presumably, therefore, those who urge regulators to make greater use of the technique have a more extensive prescription in mind. I assume here that their prescription includes the following views:

1. Their exists a strong presumption that an act should not be undertaken unless its benefits outweigh its costs.

2. In order to determine whether benefits outweigh costs, it is desirable to attempt to express all benefits and costs in a common scale or denominator, so that they can be compared with each other, even when some benefits and costs are not traded on markets and hence have no established dollar values.

3. Getting decision-makers to make more use of cost-benefit techniques is important enough to warrant both the expense required to gather the data for improved cost-benefit estimation and the political efforts needed to give the activity higher priority compared to other activities, also valuable in and of themselves.

My focus is on cost-benefit analysis as applied to environmental, safety, and health regulation. In that context, I examine each of the above propositions from the perspective of formal ethical theory, that is, the study of what actions it is morally right to undertake. My conclusions are:

1. In areas of environmental, safety, and health regulation, there may be many instances where a certain decision might be right even though its benefits do not outweigh its costs.

2. There are good reasons to oppose efforts to put dollar values on non-marketed benefits and costs.

3. Given the relative frequency of occasions in the areas of environmental, safety, and health regulation where one would not wish to use a benefits-outweigh-costs test as a decision rule, and given the reasons to oppose the monetizing of nonmarketed benefits or costs that is a prerequisite for cost-benefit analysis, it is not justifiable to devote major resources to the generation of data for cost-benefit calculations or to undertake efforts to "spread the gospel" of cost-benefit analysis further.

I

How do we decide whether a given action is morally right or wrong and hence, assuming the desire to act morally, why it should be undertaken or refrained from? Like the Molière character who spoke prose without knowing it, economists who advocate use of cost-benefit analysis for public decisions are philosophers without knowing it: the answer given by cost-benefit analysis, that actions should be undertaken so as to maximize net benefits, represents one of the classic answers given by moral philosophers—that given by utilitarians. To determine whether an action is right or wrong, utilitarians tote up all the positive consequences of the action in terms of human satisfaction. The act that maximizes attainment of satisfaction under the circumstances is the right act. That the economists' answer is also the answer of one school of philosophers should not be surprising. Early on, economics was a branch of moral philosophy, and only lately did it become an independent discipline.

Before proceeding further, the subtlety of the utilitarian position should be noted. The positive and negative consequences of an act for satisfaction may go beyond the act's immediate consequences. A facile version of utilitarianism would give moral sanction to a lie, for instance, if the satisfaction of an individual attained by telling the lie was greater than the suffering imposed on the lie's victim. Few utilitarians would agree. Most of them would add to the list of negative consequences the effect of the one lie on the tendency of the person who lies to tell other lies, even in instances when the lying produced less satisfaction for him than dissatisfaction for others. They would also add the negative effects of the lie on the general level of social regard for truth-telling, which has many consequences for future utility. A further consequence may be added as well. It is sometimes said that we should include in a utilitarian calculation the feeling of dissatisfaction produced in the liar (and perhaps in others) because, by telling a lie, one has "done the wrong thing." Correspondingly, in this view, among the positive consequences to be weighed into a utilitarian calculation of truth-telling is satisfaction arising from "doing the right thing." This view, rests on an error, however, because it *assumes* what it is the purpose of the calculation to *determine*—that telling the truth in the instance in question is indeed the right thing to do. Economists are likely to object to this point, arguing that no feeling ought "arbitrarily" to be excluded from a complete cost-benefit calculation, including a feeling of dissatisfaction at doing the wrong thing. Indeed, the economists cost-benefit calculations would, at least ideally, include such feelings. Note the difference between the economist's and the philosopher's cost-benefit calculations, however. The economist may choose to include feelings of dissatisfaction in his cost-benefit calculation, but what happens if somebody asks the economist, "Why is it right to evaluate an action on the basis of a cost-benefit test?" If an answer is to be given to that question (which does not normally preoccupy economists but which does concern both philosophers and the rest of us who need to be persuaded that cost-benefit analysis is right), then the circularity problem reemerges. And there is also another difficulty with counting feelings of dissatisfaction at doing the wrong thing in a cost-benefit calculation. It leads to the perverse result that under certain circumstances a lie, for example, might be morally right if the individual contemplating the lie felt no compunction about lying and morally wrong only if the individual felt such a compunction!

This error is revealing, however, because it begins to suggest a critique of utilitarianism. Utilitarianism is an important and powerful moral doctrine. But it is probably a minority position among contemporary moral philosophers. It is amazing that economists can proceed in unanimous endorsement of cost-benefit analysis as if unaware that their conceptual framework is highly controversial in the discipline from which it arose—moral philosophy.

Let us explore the critique of utilitarianism. The logical error discussed before appears to suggest that we have a notion of certain things being right or wrong that *predates* our calculation of costs and benefits. Imagine the case of an old man in Nazi Germany who is hostile to the regime. He is wondering whether he should speak out against Hitler. If he speaks out, he will lose his pension. And his action will have done nothing to increase the chances that the Nazi regime will be overthrown: he is regarded as somewhat eccentric by those around him, and nobody has ever consulted his views on political questions. Recall that one cannot add to the benefits of speaking out any satisfaction from doing "the right thing," because the pur-

pose of the exercise is to determine whether speaking out *is* the right thing. How would the utilitarian calculation go? The benefits of the old man's speaking out would, as the example is presented, be nil, while the costs would be his loss of his pension. So the costs of the action would outweigh the benefits. By the utilitarians' cost-benefit calculation, it would be *morally wrong* for the man to speak out.

To those who believe that it would not be morally wrong for the old man to speak out in Nazi Germany, utilitarianism is insufficient as a moral view. We believe that some acts whose costs are greater than their benefits may be morally right and, contrariwise, some acts whose benefits are greater than their costs may be morally wrong.

This does not mean that the question whether benefits are greater than costs is morally irrelevant. Few would claim such. Indeed, for a broad range of individual and social decisions, whether an act's benefits outweigh its costs is a sufficient question to ask. But not for all such decisions. These may involve situations where certain duties—duties not to lie, break promises, or kill, for example—make an act wrong, even if it would result in an excess of benefits over costs. Or they may involve instances where people's rights are at stake. We would not permit rape even if it could be demonstrated that the rapist derived enormous happiness from his act, while the victim experienced only minor displeasure. We do not do cost-benefit analyses of freedom of speech or trial by jury. The Bill of Rights was not RARGed.[1] As the United Steelworkers noted in a comment on the Occupational Safety and Health Administration's economic analysis of its proposed rule to reduce worker exposure to carcinogenic coke-oven emissions, the Emancipation Proclamation was not subjected to an inflationary impact statement. The notion of human rights involves the idea that people may make certain claims to be allowed to act in certain ways or to be treated in certain ways, even if the sum of benefits achieved thereby does not outweigh the sum of costs. It is this view that underlies the statement that "workers have a right to a safe and healthy work place" and the expectation that OSHA's decisions will reflect that judgment.

In the most convincing versions of nonutilitarian ethics, various duties or rights are not absolute. But each has a *prima facie* moral validity so that, if duties or rights do not conflict, the morally right act is the act that reflects a duty or respects a right. If duties or rights do conflict, a moral judgment, based on conscious deliberation, must be made. Since one of the duties non-utilitarian philosophers enumerate is the duty of beneficence (the duty to maximize happiness), which in effect incorporates all of utilitarianism by reference, a non-utilitarian who is faced with conflicts between the results of cost-benefit analysis and non-utility-based considerations will need to undertake such deliberation. But in that deliberation, additional elements, which cannot be reduced to a question of whether benefits outweigh costs, have been introduced. Indeed, depending on the moral importance we attach to the right or duty involved, cost-benefit questions may, within wide ranges, become irrelevant to the outcome of the moral judgment.

In addition to questions involving duties and rights, there is a final sort of question where, in my view, the issue of whether benefits outweigh costs should not govern moral judgment. I noted earlier that, for the common run of questions facing individuals and societies, it is possible to begin and end our judgment simply by finding out if the benefits of the contemplated act outweigh the costs. This very fact means that one way to show the great importance, or value, attached to an area is to say that decisions involving the area should not be determined by cost-benefit calculations. This applies, I think, to the view many environmentalists have of decisions involving our natural environment. When officials are deciding what level of pollution will harm certain vulnerable people—such as asthmatics or the elderly—while not harming others, one issue involved may be the right of those people not to be sacrificed on the altar of somewhat higher living standards for the rest of us. But more broadly than this, many environmentalists fear that subjecting decisions about clean air or water to the cost-benefit tests that determine the general run of decisions removes those matters from the realm of specially valued things.

II

In order for cost-benefit calculations to be performed the way they are supposed to be, all costs and benefits must be expressed in a common measure, typically dollars, including things not normally bought and sold on markets, and to which

dollar prices are therefore not attached. The most dramatic example of such things is human life itself; but many of the other benefits achieved or preserved by environmental policy—such as peace and quiet, fresh-smelling air, swimmable rivers, spectacular vistas—are not traded on markets either.

Economists who do cost-benefit analysis regard the quest after dollar values for nonmarket things as a difficult challenge—but one to be met with relish. They have tried to develop methods for imputing a person's "willingness to pay," for such things, their approach generally involving a search for bundled goods that *are* traded on markets and that vary as to whether they include a feature that is, *by itself*, not marketed. Thus, fresh air is not marketed, but houses in different parts of Los Angeles that are similar except for the degree of smog are. Peace and quiet is not marketed, but similar houses inside and outside airport flight paths are. The risk of death is not marketed, but similar jobs that have different levels of risk are. Economists have produced many often ingenious efforts to impute dollar prices to nonmarketed things by observing the premiums accorded homes in clean air areas over similar homes in dirty areas or the premiums paid for risky jobs over similar nonrisky jobs.

These ingenious efforts are subject to criticism on a number of technical grounds. It may be difficult to control for all the dimensions of quality other than the presence or absence of the nonmarketed thing. More important, in a world where people have different preferences and are subject to different constraints as they make their choices, the dollar value imputed to the non-market things that most people would wish to avoid will be lower than otherwise, because people with unusually weak aversion to those things or unusually strong constraints on their choices will be willing to take the bundled good in question at less of a discount than the average person. Thus, to use the property value discount of homes near airports as a measure of people's willingness to pay for quiet means to accept as a proxy for the rest of us the behavior of those least sensitive to noise, of airport employees (who value the convenience of a near-airport location) or of others who are susceptible to an agent's assurances that "it's not so bad." To use the wage premiums accorded hazardous work as a measure of the value of life means to accept as proxies for the rest of us the choices of people who do not have many choices or who are exceptional risk-seekers.

A second problem is that the attempts of economists to measure people's willingness to pay for non-marketed things assume that there is no difference between the price a person would require for *giving up* something to which he has a preexisting right and the price he would pay to *gain* something to which he enjoys no right. Thus, the analysis assumes no difference between how much a homeowner would need to be paid in order to give up an unobstructed mountain view that he already enjoys and how much he would be willing to pay to get an obstruction moved once it is already in place. Available evidence suggests that most people would insist on being paid far more to assent to a worsening of their situation than they would be willing to pay to improve their situation. The difference arises from such factors as being accustomed to and psychologically attached to that which one believes one enjoys by right. But this creates a circularity problem for any attempt to use cost-benefit analysis to determine *whether* to assign to, say, the homeowner the right to an unobstructed mountain view. For willingness to pay will be different depending on whether the right is assigned initially or not. The value judgment about whether to assign the right must thus be made first. (In order to set an upper bound on the value of the benefit, one might hypothetically assign the right to the person and determine how much he would need to be paid to give it up.)

Third, the efforts of economists to impute willingness to pay invariably involve bundled goods exchanged in *private* transactions. Those who use figures garnered from such analysis to provide guidance for *public* decisions assume no difference between how people value certain things in private individual transactions and how they would wish those same things to be valued in public collective decisions. In making such assumptions, economists insidiously slip into their analysis an important and controversial value judgment, growing naturally out of the highly individualistic micro-economic tradition—namely, the view that there should be no difference between private behavior and the behavior we display in public social life. An alternate view—one that enjoys, I would suggest, wide resonance among citizens—would be that public, social decisions provide an opportunity

to give certain things a higher valuation than we choose, for one reason or another, to give them in our private activities.

Thus, opponents of stricter regulation of health risks often argue that we show by our daily risk-taking behavior that we do not value life infinitely, and therefore our public decisions should not reflect the high value of life that proponents of strict regulation propose. However, an alternative view is equally plausible. Precisely because we fail, for whatever reasons, to give life-saving the value in everyday personal decisions that we in some general terms believe we should give it, we may wish our social decisions to provide us the occasion to display the reverence for life that we espouse but do not always show. By this view, people do not have fixed unambiguous "preferences" to which they give expression through private activities and which therefore should be given expression in public decisions. Rather, they may have what they themselves regard as "higher" and "lower" preferences. The latter may come to the fore in private decisions, but people may want the former to come to the fore in public decisions. They may sometimes display racial prejudice, but support anti-discrimination laws. They may buy a certain product after seeing a seductive ad, but be skeptical enough of advertising to want the government to keep a close eye on it. In such cases, the use of private behavior to impute the values that should be entered for public decisions, as is done by using willingness to pay in private transactions, commits grievous offense against a view of the behavior of the citizen that is deeply engrained in our democratic tradition. It is a view that denudes politics of any independent role in society, reducing it to a mechanistic, mimicking recalculation based on private behavior.

Finally, one may oppose the effort to place prices on a non-market thing and hence in effect incorporate it into the market system out of a fear that the very act of doing so will reduce the thing's perceived value. To place a price on the benefit may, in other words, reduce the value of that benefit. Cost-benefit analysis thus may be like the thermometer that, when placed in a liquid to be measured, itself changes the liquid's temperature.

Examples of the perceived cheapening of a thing's value by the very act of buying and selling it abound in everyday life and language. The disgust that accompanies the idea of buying and selling human beings is based on the sense that this would dramatically diminish human worth. Epithets such as "he prostituted himself," applied as linguistic analogies to people who have sold something, reflect the view that certain things should not be sold because doing so diminishes their value. Praise that is bought is worth little, even to the person buying it. A true anecdote is told of an economist who retired to another university community and complained that he was having difficulty making friends. The laconic response of a critical colleague—"If you want a friend why don't you buy yourself one"—illustrates in a pithy way the intuition that, for some things, the very act of placing a price on them reduces their perceived value.

The first reason that pricing something decreases its perceived value is that, in many circumstances, non-market exchange is associated with the production of certain values not associated with market exchange. These may include spontaneity and various other feelings that come from personal relationships. If a good becomes less associated with the production of positively valued feelings because of market exchange, the perceived value of the good declines to the extent that those feelings are valued. This can be seen clearly in instances where a thing may be transferred both by market and by non-market mechanisms. The willingness to pay for sex bought from a prostitute is less than the perceived value of the sex consummating love. (Imagine the reaction if a practitioner of cost-benefit analysis computed the benefits of sex based on the price of prostitute services.)

Furthermore, if one values in a general sense the existence of a non-market sector because of its connection with the production of certain valued feelings, then one ascribes added value to any non-marketed good simply as a repository of values represented by the non-market sector one wishes to preserve. This seems certainly to be the case for things in nature, such as pristine streams or undisturbed forests: for many people who value them, part of their value comes from their position as repositories of values the non-market sector represents.

The second way in which placing a market price on a thing decreases its perceived value is by removing the possibility of proclaiming that the thing is "not for sale," since things on the market by definition are for sale. The very statement that something is not for sale affirms, enhances, and protects a thing's value in a number of ways. To begin with, the statement is a way of showing that a thing is valued for its own sake, whereas selling a thing for money demonstrates that it was valued only instrumentally. Furthermore, to say that something cannot be transferred in that way places it in the exceptional category—which requires the person interested in obtaining that thing to be able to offer something else that is exceptional, rather than allowing him the easier alternative of obtaining the thing for money that could have been obtained in an infinity of ways. This enhances its value. If I am willing to say "You're a really kind person" to whoever pays me to do so, my praise loses the value that attaches to it from being exchangeable only for an act of kindness.

In addition, if we have already decided we value something highly, one way of stamping it with a cachet affirming its high value is to announce that it is "not for sale." Such an announcement does more, however, than just reflect a preexisting high valuation. It signals a thing's distinctive value to others and helps us persuade them to value the thing more highly than they otherwise might. It also expresses our resolution to safeguard that distinctive value. To state that something is not for sale is thus also a source of value for that thing, since if a thing's value is easy to affirm or protect, it will be worth more than an otherwise similar thing without such attributes.

If we proclaim that something is not for sale, we make a once-and-for-all judgment of its special value. When something is priced, the issue of its perceived value is constantly coming up, as a standing invitation to reconsider that original judgment. Were people constantly faced with questions such as "how much money could get you to give up your freedom of speech?", or "how much would you sell your vote for if you could?", the perceived value of the freedom to speak or the right to vote would soon become devastated as, in moments of weakness, people started saying "maybe it's not worth *so much* after all." Better not to be faced with the constant questioning in the first place. Something similar did in fact occur when the slogan "better red than dead" was launched by some pacifists during the Cold War. Critics pointed out that the very posing of this stark choice—in effect, "would you *really* be willing to give up your life in exchange for not living under communism?"—reduced the value people attached to freedom and thus diminished resistance to attacks on freedom.

Finally, of some things valued very highly it is stated that they are "priceless" or that they have "infinite value." Such expressions are reserved for a subset of things not for sale, such as life or health. Economists tend to scoff at talk of pricelessness. For them, saying that something is priceless is to state a willingness to trade off an infinite quantity of all other goods for one unit of the priceless good, a situation that empirically appears highly unlikely. For most people, however, the word priceless is pregnant with meaning. Its value-affirming and value-protecting functions cannot be bestowed on expressions that merely denote a determinate, albeit high, valuation. John Kennedy in his inaugural address proclaimed that the nation was ready to "pay any price [and] bear any burden . . . to assure the survival and the success of liberty." Had he said instead that we were willing to "pay a high price" or "bear a large burden" for liberty, the statement would have rung hollow.

III

An objection that advocates of cost-benefit analysis might well make to the preceding argument should be considered. I noted earlier that, in cases where various non-utility-based duties or rights conflict with the maximization of utility, it is necessary to make a deliberative judgment about what act is finally right. I also argued earlier that the search for commensurability might not always be a desirable one, that the attempt to go beyond expressing benefits in terms of (say) lives saved and costs in terms of dollars is not something devoutly to be wished.

In situations involving things that are not expressed in a common measure, advocates of cost-benefit analysis argue that people making judgments "in effect" perform cost-benefit calculations anyway. If government regulators promulgate a regulation that saves 100 lives at a cost of $1 billion, they are "in effect" valuing a life at (a minimum of) $10 million, whether or not they say that they are willing to place a dollar value on a human life. Since, in this view, cost-benefit analysis "in effect" is inevitable, it might as well be made specific.

This argument misconstrues the real difference in the reasoning processes involved. In cost-benefit analysis, equivalencies are established *in advance* as one of the raw materials for the calculation. One determines costs and benefits, one determines equivalencies (to be able to put various costs and benefits into a common measure), and then one sets to toting things up—waiting, as it were, with bated breath for the results of the calculation to come out. The outcome is determined by the arithmetic; if the outcome is a close call or if one is not good at long division, one does not know how it will turn out until the calculation is finished. In the kind of deliberative judgment that is performed without a common measure, no establishment of equivalencies occurs in advance. Equivalencies are not aids to the decision process. In fact, the decision-maker might not even be aware of what the "in effect" equivalencies were, at least before they are revealed to him afterwards by someone pointing out what he had "in effect" done. The decision-maker would see himself as simply having made a deliberate judgment; the "in effect" equivalency number did not play a causal role in the decision but at most merely reflects it. Given this, the argument against making the process explicit is the one discussed earlier in the discussion of problems with putting specific values on things that are not normally quantified—that the very act of doing so may serve to reduce the value of those things.

My own judgment is that modest efforts to assess levels of benefits and costs are justified, although I do not believe that government agencies ought to sponsor efforts to put dollar prices on non-market things. I also do not believe that the cry for more cost-benefit analysis in regulation is, on the whole, justified. If regulatory officials were so insensitive about regulatory costs that they did not provide acceptable raw material for deliberative judgments (even if not of a strictly cost-benefit nature), my conclusion might be different. But a good deal of research into costs and benefits already occurs—actually, far more in the U.S. regulatory process than in that of any other industrial society. The danger now would seem to come more from the other side.

Note

1. The Regulatory Analysis Review Group (RARG) was created by President Carter to improve the cost-benefit analysis of regulatory policy. It was subsequently disbanded by President Reagan. (editor's note)

In Defense of Environmental Economics _____

*Steven Edwards**

I. Introduction

The monetization of environmental values is criticized widely for being imperialistic, reductionistic, illogical, irrelevant, and inappropriate.[1] While there has been a tendency by some economists to accept the symmetry between monetary valuations and rigorous definitions of economic value, most critics of economics conclude incorrectly that economic value is restricted necessarily to markets and consumption. This paper is written in part in defense of environmental economics in general and the contingent valuation method of valuing natural resources in particular. . . .

The introspection that leads to a defense of environmental economics also suggests situations when monetary valuations and economic valuations are asymmetric, however. This may occur when genuine commitments to the well-being of others motivate an individual's preferences. One who personifies some of the normative positions expressed in this journal is a possible example. Thus, the paper is also written to raise the implications of this asymmetry for economic valuations, and, hopefully in the process, to make a modest contribution to a constructive dialogue between economists and ethicists.

Section two presents the egoistic model of individual preferences that describes "economic man" and that serves as the basis for rigorous definitions of economic value. The main conclusion of this section is that markets and prices emerge from economic behavior and are not themselves requirements for economic value. With this foundation, section three emphasizes that neither consumption nor use is even a prerequisite for economic valuation. The contingent valuation method is defended

* Woods Hole Oceanographic Institution, Woods Hole, MA 02543. Edwards is a Social Scientist at the Marine Policy and Ocean Management Center of the Woods Hole Oceanographic Institution. His primary field of study is environmental and resource economics.

as an instrument for elucidating nonmarket and nonconsumptive values derived from the natural environment. Leaving the defense behind, section four considers the implications of nonegoistic ethics for contingent valuation research on natural resources. Building on insightful discussions by Rolston, Steven Kelman, Amartya Sen, and Lawrence Tribe,[2] this section explains why a genuinely altruistic commitment to the well-being of others would undermine the symmetry between statements of willingness-to-pay and theoretical notions of economic value. Section five concludes the paper.

II. The Purview of Economics

Kelman observes that "economists advocating the use of cost-benefit analysis for public decisions are philosophers without knowing it."[3] Indeed, neoclassical economists are intellectual decendents of Jeremy Bentham and other utilitarians, with cost-benefit analysis being a special case of utilitarianism. While practitioners of cost-benefit analysis were confined once to assessments of market values only, recent conceptual and methodological advances in environmental economics now facilitate the monetization of nonmarket values associated with the natural environment. However, this "imperialistic" expansion of economics's purview has been criticized severely by many environmental ethicists.

Critiques of cost-benefit analysis seem to take two levels. At the macro level one might reject utilitarianism as an improper method of amalgamating values across individuals. Many of the ethical positions described in this journal which combine the interests of present humans, wildlife, and future generations fit the macro level.[4] Economists have considered alternative systems of humanistic ethics (e.g., egalitarianism) also when assessing environmental policies that involve high risks and costs incurred by future generations.[5]

However, much of the disagreement between economists and environmental ethicists actually centers on the micro or individual level of analysis.

Environmental Ethics, Vol. 9, No. 1 (Spring 1987), 73–85. Reprinted by permission.

More and more, economists use willingness-to-pay surveys to elicit valuations of the natural environment. In contrast, many environmental ethicists reject monetization as an appropriate measure of instrumental value and debate each other about the possible rights or intrinsic values of individual wildlife and unborn humans.

This paper focuses on the micro level of the debate and individuals' preferences for environmental protection. From an objective point of view, the appropriateness of monetary valuations of natural resources depends on the motivations which underly preferences. Two individualistic preference structures for environmental protection are evaluated. One—indifference motivated by egoism—substantiates monetary valuation. The second—lexicalities motivated by an altruistic commitment to the well-being of others—challenges monetary valuation at a fundamental level. The reader should understand, however, that I am not advocating any particular ethic. Nor am I confirming any assumptions about motivations from observed or expressed behavior. Instead, I discuss some of the implications of egoism and altruism for economic analysis. I stress these points because I know that I am in danger of being misunderstood by ethicists and economists who are not comfortable with the views being raised here.

In the economic model of egoistic man, definitions of economic value are derived from a preference structure called indifference.[6] That is, economic man is indifferent between amounts and assortments of things that provide equal satisfaction, or utility.[7] Because choices are constrained by personal assets, economic behavior is characterized broadly by the allocation of income (and time in some cases) among things that provide personal utility.

It is crucial to understand the importance of indifference and the relationship between income and personal utility in order to understand definitions of economic value and why economic values are monetized. Clearly if economic man's income increases, so will personal utility, since more money is available to increase the amounts of things that provide personal satisfaction. Similarly, if income decreases, utility will decrease. Looked at another way, we ask, if something changes to reduce the availability, amount, or quality of something that provides instrumental value, what is the maximum

that the person is willing to pay to prevent the change? Notice that the change (e.g., price increase for a marketed commodity, reduction in ground water quality, reduction in the population size of the endangered blue whale) would lower utility for economic man, and that maximum willingness-to-pay is the reduction in income that prevents the change. That is, maximum willingness-to-pay is *the change in income that holds personal utility constant*. A similar process could be followed to define a willingness-to-be-compensated in terms of the minimum acceptable change in income that keeps personal utility constant when the conditions are allowed to change. These utility-held-constant or Hicksian values are the theoretical notions of economic value that economists presume to measure with assessments of willingness-to-pay.[8]

Four important points are implicit in this brief characterization of economic man and economic value. The first three concerning indifference, monetization, and the relationships among economic value, markets, and prices are elaborated in this section. The measurement of nonconsumptive and nonuse values with willingness-to-pay surveys is discussed in section three.

Indifference is the cornerstone of rigorous definitions of economic values. Something's economic value—whether it be a marked commodity, an unpriced environmental resource, or sympathy for future generations—is determined entirely by its ability to yield personal utility. Furthermore, the measure of something's instrumental value to economic man decreases as its level increases because the person moves toward satiation. That is, while something's total instrumental value manifest in total willingness-to-pay increases with its level, marginal willingness-to-pay for incremental units decreases. In this context, the cold truth is that there is nothing unique about an apple, a day of fishing, a scenic vista, a blue whale, or a bequest of clean ground water to future generations. Economic man trades these off at the margin to identify positions of equal personal satisfaction.

Nor is there anything special about the money metric. Monetization simply reflects economic man's allocation of income over things that yield personal utility. If choices were constrained by time or beads, economic value would be measured in minutes or numbers of beads. Dollars, or more accurately changes in income, are convenient and legitimate proxies for the change in commodities that leaves economic man indifferent between initial and final conditions.

This brings us to a third and crucial point: markets and prices are not necessary conditions for economic value. Rather, markets and prices emerge from collective economic behavior when people can be excluded from the use and benefits of things unless they pay for them.[9] Property rights protect owners' claims to things while prices facilitate an allocation of their claims. Without exclusivity, there is little reason for people other than a philanthropist to supply a commodity or an environmental resource, since without it they would not be compensated. Without exclusivity on the supply side and a sufficient interest or demand on the part of others to pay for something, markets and prices would not emerge.

Contrast things that are exchanged in markets with scenic vistas, clean ground water, national forests, and blue whales. Although the latter usually are not priced in traditional single-commodity markets, economic man still gets personal satisfaction from their existence. In fact, it seems difficult to argue that marketlike mechanisms, albeit nontraditional, do not allocate resources to protect environmental quality, wilderness, wildlife, and the likely interests of future generations when we pay taxes (and in many cases vote to raise taxes) for pollution control, ecosystem preservation, endangered species programs, and so on. In addition, conservation organizations are in effect voluntary, market-like systems for providing nonconsumptive recreation, species preservation, and environmental protection. Traditional markets and prices provide only one mechanism whereby these values are revealed. Limiting economics to the analysis of traditional markets is arbitrary.

This third point seems to be widely unknown to or ignored by critics of environmental economics. For example, Rolston implies that economic value and market-price value are synonymous and separate from other instrumental values:

> Only economic uses tend to consume wildlands. The question faced here is not whether the past economic reduction of the continent was justified, but whether it

is enough. How much more of the goods (value $_{ip,sg}$) we already amply have (fiber, timber, energy) can we obtain by consuming the surviving wildlands, and do we want these as economic benefits (value $_{mp}$) by trading away the nonconsumptive set of values? Although this seems to pit market value against some or all of values 2–12 [i.e., life support, recreational, scientific, genetic diversity, aesthetic, cultural symbolization, historical, character building, therapeutic, religious, intrinsic], for the wider public it only pits a little more extracted from the 2 percent wild (the 4 percent half wild) of what we have extracted already.[10]

Again, restricting economic value to market value/price, or as Taylor writes, commercial value, is arbitrary since economic value is determined by the allocation of personal assets over things that provide personal utility.[11]

There also seems to be general agreement with Kelman's view that monetizing environmental values somehow cheapens the resource, making the process inappropriate.[12] As examples of this curious assertion that markets/prices form preferences rather than vice versa, he cites praise that is bought, the sale of humans, and prostitution. While pitiable or reprehensible to others, the value to those who engage in these actions *voluntarily* is consistent with egoistic motives and preferences. That is, Kelman uses the preferences of others to reject the preferences of self a priori. In addition, Kelman presumes incorrectly that the instrumental value of superficially similar things will be equal—he compares apples with oranges, so to speak. Or, to use his example, it seems unlikely that "prostitute services" and "sex that consummates love" are identical for most people.[13] Clearly, these acts are quite different and should be expected to yield different levels of instrumental value. In the context of this paper, it would not be surprising for someone to value a commercialized campground and a domestic rabbit differently from a remote national forest and a wild rabbit, since the things themselves are different. Economic assessments of individual, instrumental values are indeed appropriate for economic man.

III. Measurement of Nonconsumptive and Nonuse Values

Recently Rolston criticized the monetization of nonmarket values as well as the use of willingness-to-pay surveys to measure instrumental values associated with the natural environmental.[14] He raises certain profound points regarding individual and social preferences that will be considered in the next section. However, most of the critique uses the unsubstantiated position that market values and other possible instrumental values like scenic value, recreational value, and economic notions of existence values are fundamentally different. Also, the evaluation is preoccupied with prices and consumption. This section is written primarily in response to Rolston's critique.

Rolston's references to consumption in the passage quoted above brings us to my final important point in defense of environmental economics—neither consumption nor use is necessary for economic value to be well-defined. In fact, empirical problems aside, anything that is valued instrumentally and in comparison to the instrumental value derived from other things can in principle be handled by economics, be it acts of friendship or love[15] or wilderness recreation, aesthetics, levels of species preservation, or bequests of natural resources to future generations. Although this might be disquieting, it is, nevertheless, true for economic man, since something's instrumental value is determined solely by the utility that it yields, and since changes in income standardize changes in market and nonmarket things.

This final point must be elaborated given its relationship to the contingent valuation method. Kevin Boyle and Richard Bishop distinguish among: (1) consumptive use values such as hunting whereby economic man derives personal satisfaction from harvesting natural resources; (2) nonconsumptive use values such as wildlife photography and nature walks whereby personal satisfaction is derived from using, but not consuming, wildlife and wilderness; (3) indirect use values where, for example, wildlife and the outdoors are enjoyed indirectly through television and literature; and (4) nonuse values whereby personal satisfaction is derived from preserving wildlife or the environment, but where use is not involved.[16] The unifying characteristic of these values and their definitions in the economics literature is that their assignment is based solely on personal utility and indifference. Rolston acquiesces somewhat on the recreational value of "wildlands."[17] However, he focuses on market prices involved with travel costs rather than on the individual's motivation to be willing to incur these costs.

The nonuse category is tantamount to the economist's notions of existence value.[18] Stated simply, preservation value is the personal satisfaction that one receives from preserving wildlife. It is defined rigorously in terms of maximum willingness-to-pay which is presumed to keep personal utility constant. Similarly, bequest value is defined as the personal satisfaction (also manifest in willingness-to-pay) from leaving natural resources for the possible use by future generations. Since future amounts of these things and/or one's future preferences may be uncertain, an additional component called option value call be defined loosely as the willingness-to-pay to eliminate supply uncertainty.[19] Each type of nonuse value (and use value) has an option value complement. Finally, and for the sake of completeness, option "price" is one's total willingness-to-pay against/for a change in the natural environment, including the expected value of relevant use and nonuse benefits plus the associated option values.[20]

While it is a relatively easy matter to define these values for economic man, their assessment awaited methodological advances. Economists responded to the need to internalize human impacts on the environment in policy decisions by developing an array of market-related and nonmarket methods which are consistent with utility theory. Of the methods that are now available, the contingent valuation method is required to assess the nonuse values, and it has distinct advantages when the so-called market-related approaches are faced with significant empirical problems.[21] It is being used increasingly to assess the economic value of recreation, scenic beauty, air quality, water quality, species preservation, and bequests to future generations.[22] In essence, people are presented with an expected change in the level of an environmental resource and usually asked for their maximum willingness-to-pay to prevent the change, if it is a reduction, or to promote the change, if it is an improvement.

To build his case against the contingent valuation method, Rolston details several familiar technical issues that can present empirical problems, but which do not themselves undermine the utility-theoretic foundation of the method. First, he argues that the inherent hypothetical nature of the contingent valuation and the alleged unfamiliarity of respondents with monetizing nonmarket values undermines the technique. The frequency of protest responses to contingent valuation surveys of up to fifty percent is cited as evidence. Economists, however, are quite familiar with the potential for hypothetical bias, as well as with several other sources of potential bias that are not mentioned in the critique. This bias is less of a problem than Rolston suggests, for the percentage of protest bids is usually considerably less, closer to ten percent. Also, people are familiar with paying for many natural resources through the public sector with taxes and increasingly through contributions to conservation organizations. In fact, information on payments to public programs improves willingness-to-pay responses.[23] Finally, recent experiments by Richard Bishop and others at the University of Wisconsin reveal a statistical similarity between willingness-to-pay that is elicited from contingent valuations of outdoor recreation and from actual experimental markets.[24]

Rolston does underscore a difficult problem: whether it is best to ask for willingness-to-pay or willingness-to-be-compensated. However, this can be appropriately viewed as a technical matter associated with perceptions of property rights; alone, it does not undermine the utility-theoretic foundation of the method.

He also raises problems with the plurality of values associated with the environment and the likely difficulty of separating them into components in empirical studies. It should be noted that the various use, nonuse, and option values do have separable utility-theoretic definitions. More importantly, though, it is usually unnecessary to isolate value components in economic analyses of environmental policies which require only information on total value (i.e., option price).[25]

Rolston mentions the familiar criticisms that economic analyses do not resolve social problems associated with inequitable distributions of wealth and intergenerational justice. However, economists do not pretend to resolve these problems, although we can measure the distribution of economic impacts of environmental policies on different individuals or groups.

Finally, Rolston asserts incorrectly that contingent valuation questions request valuations of social preferences and social good. On the contrary, valuations corresponding to individuals' preferences are requested clearly. However, it is fair to question whether respondents actually interpret the questions as intended or in terms of unselfish preferences for others. In section four I consider the implications of other-regarding preferences for economic analysis.

IV. Implications of Commitments to Others for Economic Analysis

Lest the reader think differently, I have not argued that economic man actually characterizes mankind. Nor have I argued that markets, prices, and people's willingness-to-pay for environmental resources necessarily proves the existence of economic man. This reasoning would be circular and illogical. Instead, my discussion focuses on the proposition that *if* man's preferences are selfish and structured by indifference, then economic value is well-defined and measured appropriately in monetary terms. This simple abstraction of man is powerful in the sense that it yields testable hypotheses about willingness-to-pay.

For much economic inquiry—positive (vis-à-vis normative) economics—it is sufficient to predict behavior from the model of economic man. The realistic detail of the model is irrelevant when one seeks only accurate predictions of behavior. For example, contingent valuation experiments facilitate tests of whether and how much people are willing-to-pay for environmental resources. Difficulty arises, however, when it is necessary to interpret the meaning of willingness-to-pay. Whether willingness-to-pay is a rigorous measure of economic value where personal utility is held constant depends entirely on the validity of the assumptions about motivations and preferences. On this subject, environmental ethicists describe points of view that compete with the model of economic man.

Discussions of moralistic and social preferences found in thoughtful papers by Daly, Kelman, Rolston, and Tribe cause one to consider the implications of alternative motivations and preference structures for economic valuations.[26] Indeed, ethical views that argue for the intrinsic value or rights of other humans, wildlife, and future generations could be personified by a genuine altruist with unselfish commitments to the well-being of others.[27] The question thus arises: does such a stereotype of altruistic man—the antithesis of economic man—have implications for interpreting expressions of willingness-to-pay?

As Amartya Sen, an economist, argues, attitudes and behavior that are motivated by genuine commitments to others have profound implications for economic valuation:

> [C]ommitment does involve, in a very real sense, counterpreferential choice, destroying the crucial assumption that a chosen alternative must be better than (or at least as good as) the others for the person choosing it, and this would certainly require that models be formulated in an essentially different way. . . . Commitment is, of course, closely related to one's morals. . . . it drives a wedge between personal choice and personal welfare, and much of traditional economic theory relies on the identity of the two.[28]

Although Sen discusses intragenerational commitments and an individual's so-called preferences, his rationale extends to moral principles that involve commitments to wildlife and future generations.[29] The "wedge between personal choice and personal welfare" requires a preference structure that differs radically from personal utility and indifference. A suitable candidate is a lexicographic ordering of preferences whereby changes in the population size of blue whales, in bequests of clean ground water to future generations, and so on are viewed as being morally right or wrong by the altruist.[30] Tribe touched on the possibility of lexicographic preferences for environmental protection, but did not delve into its technical implications for economic analysis.[31]

Elsewhere I examine some of the technical implications of altruistic choice which are revealed by a lexicographic preference structure.[32] While the details cannot be illustrated here, the implications of commitments to others are straightforward. Most importantly, indifference is undefined for the altruist, since no two states of the world involving trade-offs between the well-being of others and personal utility can have equal ranking. This is not to say, however, that willingness-to-pay and personal utility are undefined. For example, a person committed to stopping the killing of whales would always sacrifice income to prevent whaling and the accidental bicatch of whales in fisheries, since he always prefers more whales to fewer. The altruist's willingness-to-pay is defined, and in terms of it personal well-being obviously declines since disposable income decreases. However, this relationship is asymmetric, since willingness-to-pay is not based on changes in personal utility, and, therefore, does not match rigorous notions of economic values.

The upshot of this brief inspection of an altruist's preferences is that neither willingness-to-pay nor willingness-to-be-compensated approximates rigorous notions of economic values which hold personal utility constant (i.e., Hicksian values). This is true simply because self-interest is a secondary concern to the altruist. For example, a maximum willingness-to-pay of $x to Greenpeace, Inc. to help reduce the killing of whales worldwide from N to n whales cannot be interpreted as the amount of money that leaves the altruist indifferent between a situation with the loss of N whales and an income of $X (where $X is greater than $x) and a situation with a loss of n whales and an income of $(X−x).

V. Conclusions

After erecting a value taxonomy, Rolston asks rhetorically, "Can the preceding array of value levels and types be reduced, wholly or in part, to economic terms as a prerequisite for cost-benefit analysis?"[33] The answer is a qualified yes, although the word *reduced* has unnecessary connotations. Monetization of nonmarket, environmental values by individuals is relevant and appropriate when a person's preferences are based on self-interest and on indifference between amounts of things that provide equal satisfaction. There is no category mistake in these cases since all use and nonuse concepts for economic man are homologous.[34] Methodologies that are used to assess these values, including the contingent valuation method, are also relevant, being limited only by empirical problems in some applications. Whether cost-benefit analysis can be used to amalgamate these values across individuals is another matter for consideration at the macro level of analysis.[35]

The qualification involves empirical ignorance about underlying motivations and preference structures. I have argued that willingness-to-pay is not a proxy for utility-held-constant notions of economic value when choices are not motivated by self-interest and indifference is undefined. Ethicists challenge economists for presuming, a priori, that people attempt to think and behave like economic man, and that the "total" value of the natural environment can be measured in economic terms. However, most critics of environmental economics are also presumptuous when they take strongly normative positions on what preferences *should be* without also attending to what they actually *are*.

From an objective perspective, the disagreement between economists and ethicists on individual ethics is an empirical matter. Adam Smith's inductive reasoning and Richard Dawkin's discussion of the genetic basis for selfish behavior argue for the existence of economic man.[36] However, Stephen Kellert's studies of attitudes toward animals suggest a richer, pluralistic system of preferences within individuals and throughout society.[37] For example, of the ten attitudes that he identifies, the humanistic, moralistic, and utilitarian attitudes were dominant in 35%, 20%, and 20% of his sample, respectively. The issue is complicated further by the possibility of complex preference structures such as "preferences over preferences" whereby economic man and altruistic man might exist in one person.[38]

Notes

1. Herman E. Daly, "Alternative Strategies for Integrating Economics and Ecology," in A. M. Jansson, ed., *Integration of Economy and Ecology* (Stockholm: Stockholm University Press, 1984); Steven Kelman, "Cost-Benefit Analysis and Environmental, Safety and Health Regulation: Ethical and Philosophical Considerations," in D. Swartzman, R. A. Liroff and K. G. Croke, eds., *Cost-benefit Analysis and Environmental Regulation: Politics, Ethics and Methods* (Washington, D.C.: Conservation Foundation, 1982); Steven Kelman, *What Price Incentives? Economists and the Environment,* (Boston: Auburn House, 1981); Holmes Rolston, III, "Valuing Wildlands," *Environmental Ethics* 7 (1985): 23–48; Mark Sagoff, "At the Shrine of Our Lady of Fatima or Why Political Questions are

Not All Economic," *Arizona Law Review* 23, (1981): 1283–98.

2. Kelman, *What Price Incentives;* Rolston, "Valuing Wildlands"; Amartya Sen, "Rational Fools: A Critique of the Behavioral Foundations of Economic Theory," *Philosophy and Public Affairs* 6 (1977): 317–44; Lawrence H. Tribe, "Ways Not to Think About Plastic Trees," in L. H. Tribe, C. S. Schelling, and J. Voss, eds., *When Values Conflict: Essays on Environmental Analysis, Discourse, and Decision* (Cambridge, Mass.: Ballinger Publishing, 1976).

3. Kelman, "Cost-Benefit Analysis," p. 138.

4. E.g., biocentrism. P. W. Taylor, "Are Humans Superior to Animals?" *Environmental Ethics* 6 (1984): 149–60.

5. William D. Schulze and Allen V. Kneese, "Risk in Benefit-Cost Analysis," *Risk Analysis* 1 (1981): 81–88; William D. Schulze, D. S. Brookshire, D. S. and T. Sandler, "The Social Rate of Discount for Nuclear Waste Storage: Economics or Ethics," *Natural Resources Journal* 21 (1981): 811–32.

6. I assume that everyone agrees that profit is a well-defined notion of value in economics. Therefore, I will not discuss economic values associated with market supply. See Richard E. Just, Darrell Hueth and Andrew Schmitz, *Applied Welfare Economics and Public Policy* (Englewood Cliffs, N.J.: Prentice-Hall, 1982), for a discussion of economic profit, economic rent, and producer's surplus.

7. *Indifference does not imply a lack of interest* in any one thing or assortment of things. Indifference is a *relative* term for things that provide equal levels of personal utility. Also, my inelegant use of the word *thing* to refer generally to everything animate and inanimate is merely a matter of convenience and should not carry negative connotations.

8. This is not the place to teach microeconomics and welfare economics. Those interested in achieving a clear understanding of the relationships among price, marginal willingness-to-pay, total willingness-to-pay, utility, marginal utility, consumer's (Marshallian) surplus, and the four Hicksian surpluses might begin with Just, Hueth, and Schmitz's book, *Applied Welfare Economics.* This is recommended given the confusion that is apparent in critiques of economics.

9. See Alan Randall's characterization of environmental resources according to divisibility, exclusivity, and rivalry, *Resource Economics: An Economic Approach to Natural Resource and Environmental Policy* (New York: John Wiley and Sons, 1981).

10. Rolston, "Valuing Wildlands," p. 41.

11. Taylor, "Are Humans Superior to Animals."

12. Kelman, "Cost-Benefit Analysis" and *What Price Incentives.*

13. Kelman, *What Price Incentives,* p. 71.

14. Rolston, "Valuing Wildlands."

15. Kelman seems to agree that "in principle the analysis can be extended to valued feelings as well as valued material goods" (*What Price Incentives,* p. 21).

16. Kevin Boyle and Richard C. Bishop, "The Total Value of Wildlife Resources: Conceptual and Empirical Issues," presented at the Association of Environmental and Resource Economists' Workshop on Recreation and Demand Modeling, Boulder, Colo., 17–18 May 1985.

17. Rolston, "Valuing Wildlands."

18. Rolston, ("Valuing Wildlands") used a somewhat dated value typology from environmental economics. As discussed above, existence value subsumes preservation value and bequest value; it is not separate from bequest value. Furthermore, these concepts are not separable from option value in the sense used by Rolston. In fact, each use and nonuse value concept in economics has an option value component when demand or supply is uncertain. See Alan Randall and John R. Stoll, "Existence Value in a Total Valuation Framework," in R. D. Rowe and L. G. Chestnut, eds., *Managing Air Quality and Scenic Resources at National Parks and Wilderness Areas* (Boulder, Colo.: Westview Press, 1983), for a discussion of a complete value typology.

19. Sagoff might prefer inchoate to uncertain ("At the Shrine"). Either way, these notions of economic value are not undermined when a person's intent is to value the environment relative to the personal benefits that other things provide.

20. Terms like option *price* and *consumers* surplus are regrettable when one tries to overcome semantical as well as substantive barriers between disciplines. While economists are comfortable with unnecessary references to market concepts, critics may find false corroboration when the words price and consumption are used to discuss nonmarket and nonconsumptive valuations. I hope that the reader will look beyond a sometimes confusing and careless nomenclature and into the underlying meaning of the concepts.

21. See A. Myrick Freeman, *The Benefits of Environmental Improvement: Theory and Practice* (Washington, D.C.: Resources for the Future, 1979), for a discussion of the various methods in environmental economics and of their comparative advantages.

22. Rolston ("Valuing Wildlands") cited many of these studies in footnote 3. For additional studies see issues of *Land Economics* and the *Journal of Environmental Economics and Management.*

23. Boyle and Bishop, "Total Value."

24. Richard C. Bishop, Thomas A. Heberlein, and M. J. Kealy, "Contingent Valuation of Environmental Assets: Comparisons with a Simulated Market," *Natural Resources Journal* 23 (1983): 610–33; Boyle and Bishop, "Total Value"; Kevin J. Boyle, Richard C. Bishop, and Michael P. Welsh, "Starting Point Bias in Contingent Valuation Research," *Land Economics* 61 (1985): 182–87.

25. Boyle and Bishop, "Total Value."

26. Daly, "Alternative Strategies"; Kelman, *What Price Incentives;* Rolston, *Valuing Wildlands;* Sen, "Rational Fools"; Tribe, "Ways Not to Think About Plastic Trees."

27. Most environmental economists agree that some form of altruism motivates existence values. However, Boyle and Bishop ("Total Value"), Randall and Stoll ("Existence Value"), and others actually describe what D. A. Kennett, "Altruism and Economic Behavior: I. Developments in the Theory of Public and Private Redistribution," *American Journal of Economics and Sociology* 39 (1980): 183–98, would call *quasi-altruism,* whereby ostensibly altruistic acts or statements actually are motivated by self-interest. (ed. note: philosophers would probably reject *any* use of the term "altruism" for such acts.)

28. Sen, "Rational Fools," p. 328–89.

29. For similar viewpoints on the rights of wildlife and future generations see: Joel Feinberg, "The Rights of Animals and Future Generations," in W. T. Blackstone, ed., *Philosophy and Environmental Crisis* (Athens: University of Georgia Press, 1974); J. Ferejohn and T. R. Page, "On the Foundations of Intertemporal Choice," *American Journal of Agricultural Economics* 60 (1978): 269–75; Peter Singer, *Animal Liberation: A New Ethics for Our Treatment of Animals,* (New York: New York Review, 1975); Taylor, "Are Humans Superior to Animals?"; Tribe, "Ways Not to Think about Plastic Trees"; E. B. Weiss, "The Planetary Trust: Conservation and Intergenerational Equity," *Ecology Law Quarterly* 11 (1984): 495–581.

30. Just as words in a dictionary are ordered, lexicographical orderings over states of the world are ranked according to priorities. That is, more of a thing is always preferred to less regardless of what happens to other things that are ranked lower. This is in contrast to indifference whereby different things can be exchanged to identify positions of indifference.

31. Tribe, "Ways Not to Think about Plastic Trees."

32. Steven F. Edwards, "Environmental Ethics and the Assessment of Existence Values: Does the Neoclassical Fit?" *Northeastern Journal of Agricultural and Resource Economics,* forthcoming.

33. Rolston, "Valuing Wildlands," p. 38.

34. Sagoff criticizes economists for allegedly making category mistakes when monetizing the values of the natural environment ("At the Shrine"). However, no logical mistake is made when concepts are homologous. That is, market and nonmarket values for economic man are derived from personal utility and indifference, and, therefore, have a common derivative. This is in contrast to things that are similar, or as taxonomists in the biological sciences emphasize, analogous but which lack a common derivative.

35. It is interesting to note, however, that well defined economic values ascertained for individuals could be amalgamated in ways other than cost-benefit analysis. For example, they could be used in an egal-itarian framework to undertake policies that make individual welfare more equal. Alternatively, the individual assessments could be used within a libertarian framework to determine if a policy reduces the welfare of any one individual.

36. Richard Dawkins, *The Selfish Gene* (New York: Oxford University Press, 1976).

37. Stephen R. Kellert, "Contemporary Values of Wildlife in American Society," in W. W. Shaw and E. H. Zube, eds., *Wildlife Values,* Institutional Series Report No. 1, Center for Assessment of Noncommodity Natural Resource Values, Rocky Mountain Forest and Range Experiment Station, U.S. Forest Service, 1980); Kellert, "Assessing Wildlife and Environmental Values in Cost-Benefit Analysis," *Journal of Environmental Management* 18 (1984): 353–63.

38. R. C. Jeffrey, "Preferences Among Preferences," *Journal of Philosophy* 71 (1974): 377–91; H. Margolis, "A New Model of Rational Choice," *Ethics* 91 (1981): 265–79; Sen, "Rational Fools."

Some Problems with Environmental Economics

Mark Sagoff*

I. Introduction

In a paper appearing recently in this journal, Steven Edwards points out, correctly, that "[m]ore and more, economists use willingness-to-pay surveys to elicit valuations of the natural environment."[1] Economists have devised surveys, questionnaires, and other experimental instruments to determine how much individuals are willing to pay, for example, to preserve natural environments ("preservation" or "existence" value), to maintain the option of using natural, environments ("option" value); and to leave the environment unspoiled for future generations ("bequest" value). This "contingent valuation method," Edwards notes, "is being used increasingly to assess the economic value of recreation, scenic beauty, air quality, water quality, species preservation, and bequests to future generations" (p. 80). Edwards defends the contingent valuation method against its critics "as an instrument for elucidating nonmarket and nonconsumptive values derived from the natural environment" (p. 74).

Edwards offers three important arguments to back up his "defense of environmental economics in general and the contingent valuation method of valuing natural resources in particular" (p. 74). First, he describes "the utility-theoretic foundation of the method (p. 80), which asserts a relation between willingness to pay and personal utility. Edwards writes: "Maximum willingness-to-pay is *the change in income that holds personal utility constant*" (p. 76). This suggests that willingness-to-pay measures or at least varies with something valuable, namely, personal utility.

Edwards' second point begins with an important assumption. He assumes that the sort of economic theory he defends applies as a useful analysis of traditional markets. These are markets in

* Sagoff's research has been supported by grants from the National Science Foundation to the Center for Philosophy and Public Policy. The views expressed, however, are those of the author and not necessarily of any governmental agency. This paper draws on arguments Sagoff presents in a book, *The Economy of the Earth: Philosophy, Law, and the Environment,* published by Cambridge University Press.

Environmental Ethics, Vol. 10, No. 1 (Spring 1988), 55–74. Reprinted by permission.

which buyers and sellers transfer property voluntarily at prices they agree upon. Edwards argues that "limiting economics to the analysis of traditional markets is arbitrary" (p. 77). He notes that people derive personal utility from publicly owned assets, and they may be willing to pay for them, even though the absence of exclusive property rights in these assets prevents traditional markets from setting prices for them.

Third, Edwards defends the contingent valuation method (CVM) against the difficulty posed by the "frequency of protest responses . . . of up to fifty percent . . ." (pp. 80–81). He attributes this observed resistance or noncooperation to a kind of hypothetical and potential bias with which economists are familiar (p. 81).

In this paper, I reply to Edwards' presentation, and, in particular, to these three arguments. I argue, first, that the relation between willingness-to-pay and personal utility, as it occurs in Edwards' paper and environmental economics generally, is an analytic, not an empirical or contingent one. Willingness-to-pay does not measure, reflect, or vary with happiness, pleasure, contentment, or personal utility in any substantive sense, that is, any sense that allows us to understand why personal utility is valuable. The relation Edwards asserts is entirely stipulative: the term *personal utility* is simply a stand-in for "willingness-to-pay" and has no independent meaning or normative significance.

Second, I argue that the kind of economic analysis Edwards defends has no basis in or application to traditional markets in which buyers and sellers must agree upon prices. His willingness-to-pay approach, on the contrary, envisions a kind of universal bidding game in which resources go to those willing to pay the most for them, even if the owners refuse to sell their rights. Thus, Edwards is correct, but only in a trivial way, when he says that it is arbitrary to limit welfare economic analysis to traditional markets. It is actually "contingent" markets that constitute the paradigm for the kind of allocation-to-the-highest-bidder that Edwards favors. This kind of allocation has little relevance to traditional markets, which do not typically allocate resources to the highest bidder, since willingness to sell is just as important as willingness to pay.

Finally, I argue that Edwards is mistaken in his characterization of protest bids and other kinds of resistance by respondents to contingent valuation surveys. Apparently, Edwards attributes this sort of noncooperation to "strategic" bidding behavior, e.g., to bluffing. I argue, on the contrary, that respondents may enter protest bids because they believe the contingent valuation method conflicts with representative democracy, political deliberation, and the rule of law. In other words, respondents may believe that the property rights in question are not for sale—a concept entirely familiar in traditional markets, but unknown in Edwards' sort of analysis.

In this essay, I argue for each of these views in turn. I then apply these criticisms to a prominent example of the contingent valuation method.

II. Edwards' Defense of Environmental Economics

Edwards speaks of "income" and "personal utility" as if these concepts, as he employs them, were logically distinct. He writes, for example (p. 76):

> Clearly if economic man's income increases, so will personal utility, since more money is available to increase the amounts of things that provide personal satisfaction. Similarly, if income increases, utility will decrease.

If we assume that these sentences express an empirical judgment—roughly, that money buys happiness—then we must conclude that they are false. There is no evidence (and Edwards cites none) to show that people become happier, more satisfied, or better off in some substantive sense (after basic needs are met) when their income, and, therefore, the amount they can and will pay for things, increases. Rather, the extensive empirical evidence that exists runs strongly in the opposite direction.[2]

Economists have long followed ordinary wisdom in acknowledging that we become happier—our welfare increases in a substantive sense—not insofar as we satisfy our preferences on a willing-to-pay basis, but insofar as we improve those desires or overcome or outgrow them. A. O. Hirschman, for example, has argued that "acts of consumption . . . which are undertaken because they are expected to yield satisfaction, also yield disappointment and dissatisfaction."[3] And Frank Knight, following Mill and other classical utilitarians, observes that the education, not necessarily the satisfaction, of desire leads to happiness. "The chief thing which the common sense individual actually wants," Knight says, "is not the satisfaction of the wants he has, but more, and better wants. . . . [T]rue achievement is the refinement and elevation of the plane of desire, the refinement of taste."[4]

We may conclude, then, that Edwards does not mean to argue that economic value (in other words, willingness-to-pay) varies with or is determined by personal utility in an empirical or contingent sense, for this thesis flies in the face of ordinary wisdom and is obviously false.[5] Rather, Edwards might mean to point out, correctly, that resource economists often define "personal utility" as that which willingness-to-pay measures—in other words, he might mean that the concepts are equivalent. To contend that policies that satisfy preferences ranked by willingness-to-pay to that extent maximize personal utility, then, is to defend an empty and uninformative tautology. It is not to provide a "utility-theoretic foundation" for contingent market valuation.

Edwards writes that cost-benefit analysis is a special case of utilitarianism (p. 74), but this is not so, since welfare economics and the techniques of cost-benefit analysis it employs have no relation to substantive conceptions of the good, such as pleasure or happiness, of the kind that utilitarianism values. Welfare economists earlier in this century, imbued with a positivistic philosophy of science popular at the time, took pains to divorce their theory from any such substantive conception of utility, like happiness, since it could not be quantified, and insisted instead on defining utility in relation to measureable quantities, such as willingness-to-pay, even if these have no normative significance and no basis, therefore, in utilitarianism. Thus, sophisticated advocates of welfare economics, like Richard Posner, point out that the efficiency criterion is independent of utilitarian ethical theory. "The most important thing to bear in mind about the concept of value [in the economist's sense]," he writes, "is that it is based on what people are willing to pay for something rather than the happiness they would derive from having it."[6]

Let me now turn to Edwards' second point (p. 77), namely, that it is arbitrary to limit economic analysis to traditional markets. While this is true, it leads us to ask whether the kind of economic analysis that is relevant to the "contingent" valuation of resources applies to traditional markets in the first place. I believe, on the contrary, that it is arbitrary to *limit* it because it is arbitrary to *apply* this sort of analysis to traditional markets.

The big difference between traditional markets, in which property rights are well defined, and "contingent" markets, in which resources go, in principle, to the highest bidder, is this. In traditional markets people can and do refuse to sell their property even to those who will pay the highest price for it; rather than sell out to a trespasser at the highest price, an individual is likely to try to enjoin the trespass. Thus, if your neighbor starts operating a stamping mill, drowning you in noise, you may proceed against him, and a court will enjoin the nuisance, especially if the zoning ordinances are on your side. The rights in question here are not for sale to the highest bidder; the owner may defend them in court. The rights to exclude and not to transfer are the most common incidents of ownership; they cannot be overridden, even by theorists who believe, for some reason, that all resources should be put up for auction to the highest bidder.

It is a commonplace that traditional markets will not allocate resources to those willing to pay the most for them, because of market "failures" and for other reasons, one of which is that many owners will refuse on principle to "sell out," e.g., to polluters.[7] If resources are to be allocated efficiently, an agency of the government must transfer them to the highest bidders whether the original owners (including the public that owns "common" resources) consent to that transfer or not.

The economic analysis that Edwards defends applies to an auction in which every item is determined beforehand to be for sale to the highest bidder. Edwards may believe that "publicly" owned resources are essentially "unowned" and should be auctioned off; hence, economic analysis applies to them at least as well as it does to privately owned resources. An enormous structure of public law, like the Clean Air and Clean Water Acts, however, establishes that the public knows it owns environmental resources and has decided not to market them even to the highest bidder. The public has decided to prohibit or enjoin certain takings, as it were, rather than simply to accept them for a price. Likewise in traditional markets, an owner may refuse to sell to polluters rights to person and property even for a profit.

Let me put this point in technical terms. In traditional markets, property rights are backed by property rules. When such rules apply, victims of a trespass (for example, a nuisance such as noise pollution) can get injunctive relief in court. In the sort of "market" that the welfare economist envisions, however, property rights are backed at most by liability rules. When property rights are backed by liability rules, victims must endure pollution and other violations of those rights. There is no exclusivity. Instead a court awards the victim of a nuisance damages in the amount that it appraises the relevant property rights to be worth. The victim, in other words, must transfer the relevant rights to polluters willing to pay the price, that an agency of the state, usually a court, determines those rights are worth.[8]

As two legal scholars explain, "[A]n entitlement is protected by a property rule to the extent that someone who wishes to remove the entitlement from its holder must buy it from him in a voluntary transaction in which the value of the entitlement is agreed upon by the seller."[9] In the hypothetical "markets" that welfare economists imagine, in contrast, anyone can remove an entitlement from anyone else as long as he is willing to pay the highest price the entitlement might fetch in an auction. This is the amount a court might say the "damage" is objectively worth. "Whenever someone may destroy the initial entitlement if he is willing to pay an objectively determined value for it, an entitlement is protected by a liability rule."[10]

To see this distinction, imagine you are a farmer and your neighbor, a rancher, sends his sheep to graze on your corn. In a traditional market—one which backs up property rights with property rules—you can get an injunction to compel your neighbor to stop the trespass. This is true because traditional markets recognize the traditional incidents of property, including the right to exclude.

In the sort of "market" welfare economists envision, injunctive relief of this sort is unavailable; you have to bargain with your neighbor to reach an "efficient" allocation of the resource. If bargaining breaks down, a court determines what your corn is "objectively" worth and awards you damages in that amount. What matters is how much each of you is willing to pay; ownership determines at most the direction in which payment is made.

If a victim of some market "externality," such as pollution, refuses to sell the relevant rights and

seeks injunctive relief instead, this signifies, to the economic theorist, that the property owner is "uncooperative"; he or she is trying to "gouge" the tortfeasor by holding out for a higher price. The economic theorist, by interpreting the actions of property holders in this way, easily overrides their right not to sell, and has the state impose an "efficient" bargain, e.g., by awarding damages, instead.[11]

The nature, meaning, and extent of property rights depend entirely on the legal regime that backs them up. A legal regime that takes property rights seriously, and thus allows people (including the public as a whole) to refuse to sell out to polluters, is consistent with traditional markets in which actual consent is necessary for a transfer to take place. A regime that takes property rights seriously, then, will not allocate resources efficiently, i.e., to those willing to pay the most for them, because people—and the public—may prefer not to sell at any price.[12]

The kind of economic analysis Edwards proposes, in contrast, eliminates exclusivity in principle by allocating property rights to those willing to pay the most for them, even if the original owners, including the public that owns many resources, go on record (as the public has done in a variety of statutes) to insist that they do not wish to market, but rather to regulate the use of those resources. This kind of analysis thus applies to abstract bidding games among individuals who are abstractions created by the analysis itself, not to traditional or actual markets. It is perverse for Edwards to suggest that this sort of analysis has anything to do with property rights. It is little more than a studied refusal to acknowledge the ideals of exclusivity and consent that we associate with those rights.

Put more generally, Edwards' position illustrates an unwillingness to take liberty and consent seriously. Edwards acknowledges that many respondents refuse to cooperate with contingent valuation surveys, e.g., they refuse to stipulate amounts at which they are willing to buy or sell environmental goods and resources. These refusals are noteworthy because the famous Milgram experiments have demonstrated that in social science research settings people are so cowed by authority that they will do anything, even torture and murder, when asked to do so.[13] It seems that the only kinds of experiments that respondents reject in large numbers are contingent valuation surveys conducted by resource economists. Why is this?

I imagine the primary reason is that respondents believe that environmental policy—for example, the degree of pollution permitted in national parks—involves ethical, cultural, and aesthetic questions over which society must deliberate on the merits, and that this has nothing to do with pricing the satisfaction of preferences at the margin. Respondents may know that a representative democracy possesses excellent processes of public discussion and debate for settling issues fraught with moral and political significance; they may also be aware that there are statutes that regulate and refuse to market the use of many publicly owned environmental resources. Accordingly, these respondents may resist "backdoor" cost-benefit analyses that defy in principle the letter and the spirit of the legislation. They may also reject these surveys because they see through the circular definitions of utility on which the survey methodology is based.

Edwards, however, interprets this rejection differently. He ascribes it to sources of bias with which economists "are quite familiar" (p. 81). I assume Edwards refers to "strategic" bias, that is, the strategic misrepresentation of one's "bid" or "asked" price in order to influence the overall result to which one's own contribution would otherwise be small. Once refusals are construed as misrepresentations in this way, they can be excluded from the analysis. In this way, resource economists adjust to the "cognitive dissonance" that they encounter when citizens reject their surveys.

In doing so, however, resource economists refuse to acknowledge the possibility that citizens may believe that environmental resources should be allocated on normative, political, and cultural grounds, which citizens can understand, rather than on an efficiency principle, which may appeal to no one but the economists who invented it. By not recognizing refusals to sell for what they are, analysts show that they have no interest in property rights, in exclusivity, or in consent. They are concerned only to allocate resources in a way that maximizes some technical notion that they apparently understand, e.g., potential Pareto improvement, Kaldor-Hicks efficiency, consumer and factorial surplus, or some other arcane and academic concept that they learned as graduate students. When

citizens refuse to see the value and legitimacy of these notions, these resource economists attribute this rejection to strategic bias and unwillingness to bargain in good faith.

In order to weigh Edwards' defense against my criticisms, the reader may wish to consider an example of a contingent valuation of an environmental resource. In the following sections, I describe one such experimental survey and I consider the extent to which it provides a legitimate basis for social choice.

III. Tangible and Intangible Values

In 1975, the Environmental Protection Agency, enforcing the "Prevention of Significant Deterioration" (PSD) requirement of the Clean Air Act, directed states to amend their implementation plans to protect air quality in areas where it exceeds national health and safety minimums. The regulation, in other words, intends to keep clean air clean beyond health and safety requirements. While these PSD requirements may appeal to us on aesthetic and on ethical grounds, they may, nevertheless, impede economic growth and development: for example, they may conflict with plans to locate a network of power plants in the southwest, where coal and clean air are abundant. What to do? How do we enforce idealistic regulations when they blink at important economic facts?

In a recent article, "An Experiment on the Economic Value of Visibility," three economists from the University of Wyoming have tackled this problem. The authors attempt to interpret and to evaluate PSD requirements in economic terms. "Aesthetics," the authors say, "will play a major role. The PSD requirements amount to formal governmental admission that aesthetics, at least as embodied in atmospheric visibility, is a 'good' that might have a positive value."[14]

These writers point out that economists "generally have shied away from attempting to quantify aesthetic phenomena because they are usually defined as intangible."[15] This is correct. By and large, economists who engage in cost-benefit analysis assign prices only to goods and services of the sort that are typically traded in markets and thus that can easily be priced. These economists generally list other values as "intangibles" to bring them to the attention of the political authority. The "intangible" values involved in environmental, health, and safety policy may often be more important than "tangible" ones, of course, since they include social, moral, aesthetic, and cultural goals that have carried the day before Congress—hence, the PSD requirements of the Clean Air Act.

This is not to say that Congress gives regulators, for example, the Administrator of the EPA, a great deal of discretion in weighing "intangible" benefits against those markets price. On the contrary, legislation may instruct the Administrator to preserve and protect environmental quality without regard to the effect on consumer markets. The Clean Air Act, to continue the example, requires that "economic growth will occur in a manner consistent with the preservation of existing clean air resources."[16] The law sets the prevention of significant deterioration of air quality, then, as a normative constraint on economic growth and development, at least in certain areas, e.g., those in and around national parks.

The Wyoming economists, however, apparently interpret the law differently. Evidently, they believe that the law does not require that the Administrator protect air quality in and around national parks against the "intrusions" of industrial civilization. Instead, they apparently read the law as instructing the Administrator to strike an economically efficient balance between the costs and benefits likely to result, for example, from protecting visibility or from providing more electric power. They suggest that, if a way could be found to give "intangible" values an accurate "shadow" or surrogate market price, then this "balancing" might take place within the framework of cost-benefit analysis. Accordingly, the authors write:

> The perspective that aesthetic phenomena are unquantifiable employing economic analysis may be unduly pessimistic. Beauty, or aesthetic phenomena, given that some physical measure is available which is perceivable with human senses, should be measurable in economic terms. Further, PSD regulations indirectly necessitate quantification. How then, has the economist responded to the intangible which must of necessity become tangible?[17]

To solve this problem, the authors showed a variety of people photographs of scenes in the southwest. In some of these photographs the air quality was better or at least the visibility was greater than in others. The authors asked the participants how much they would be willing to pay on their monthly utility bills to preserve the visibility depicted in one photograph rather than to switch to that shown in the next. The economists attempted in this way to establish a surrogate market in which "intangible" aesthetic values could be priced.

Many statutes other than the Clean Air Act set strong normative constraints on commercial exploitation of the environment. The Endangered Species Act, for example, expresses this aspect of the national conscience.[18] It requires all federal agencies to "insure that actions authorized, funded, or carried out by them do not jeopardize the continued existence of such endangered species."[19] As Chief Justice Burger wrote for the Supreme Court: "One would be hard pressed to find a statutory provision whose terms were any plainer than those . . . of the Endangered Species Act. . . . The language admits of no exception."[20]

Because the plain language as well as the judicial interpretation of the Endangered Species Act explicitly prohibit an interest-balancing or cost-benefit test, the statute has worked rather well. Developers by and large have found mitigating strategies to protect species that their projects might otherwise eradicate. Conflicts have given way so quickly to deliberation and negotiation on a case-by-case basis, indeed, that a special Endangered Species Committee, set up to grant exemptions, has only met twice,[21] and very few cases have been litigated under the act.[22]

Some analysts, however, would take a different approach to endangered species policy. "The existence of such statutes as the Endangered Species Act," Judith Bentkover writes, "provides evidence that man values preservation of species and ecological diversity, although the art of converting those values into economic terms is relatively undeveloped."[23] Bentkover observes that economists have developed theoretical means for quantifying "intangible" benefits of this kind, but that "the application of these methodologies is fraught with difficulties."[24] In recent years, economists have dealt extensively with the methodological difficulties involved in assessing environmental benefits.[25]

They have attempted, in this way, to place endangered species and other forms of environmental policy on a rational and scientific basis.

The Wyoming researchers followed the economic literature in supposing that environmental preservation may have value in various ways to which consumer markets may not adequately respond. First, it may have recreational use value, and this may be estimated by reference to entrance fees, travel costs, and the like.[26] Second, a preserved environment may have "existence" value either because it gives a person an option to use the resource or because it provides him or her the ideological satisfaction of merely knowing it is there.[27] Hence, these economists write:

> Individuals and households who may never visit the Grand Canyon may still value visibility there simply because they wish to preserve a natural treasure. Individuals also may wish to know that the Grand Canyon retains its relatively pristine air quality even on days when they are not visiting the park. Concern about preserving air quality at the Grand Canyon may be just as intense in New York or in Chicago as in nearby states and communities.[28]

To speak more generally, the Wyoming economists treated visibility, e.g., in southwestern national parks, as a pure public good, that is, a good any person can enjoy without thereby lessening the amount that may be enjoyed by others.[29] They were concerned, in part, with determining the "preservation" or "existence" value of visibility, i.e., "the value assigned to the existence of a certain level of visibility aesthetics at a site even though one does not *ever* intend to participate in activity at the site."[30] The economists wrote another questionnaire to determine how much *users* of parks would pay in additional entrance fees to protect air quality or visibility. In this way, they devised bidding games or "contingent" or hypothetical markets in which to estimate, on a willingness-to-pay basis, the value of an amenity resource.

The attempt to "price" aesthetic or "existence" values, however it might serve to buttress arguments for environmental protection, invites a variety of objections. I have suggested one: the law directs the Administrator to keep clean air clean "in national parks, national wilderness areas, national monuments, national seashores, and other areas of special national or regional natural, recreational, scenic, or historic value." The PSD requirements as they stand (of course, they could be amended by Congress) do not just set goals but also make rules; they establish air quality as a normative constraint on economic development. Thus, the law does not indirectly or directly necessitate quantification of aesthetic "benefits." It does not ask us to make the intangible tangible. The Wyoming economists might lobby Congress to have the law changed, but until it is changed, it does not permit, much less require, a cost-benefit or "balancing" test.[31]

The Wyoming economists might plausibly reply that we cannot always take laws at their face value. Environmental legislation, in particular, sets lofty, noble, and aspirational national goals that we may not fully achieve without bringing the economy to a screeching halt. Any project that causes air pollution in the southwest, for example, could arguably affect air quality in a national park. Yet no one would insist, therefore, on forbidding all polluting activities in that area. The ideal of a perfectly unpolluted environment—like the ideal of a completely risk-free workplace—is a chimera. At some point, the Administrator of the EPA (and of the other regulatory agencies) has to recognize not only the law of the land, but also the law of diminishing returns. The question will then arise: how much safety, purity, or whatever are we willing to pay for? How much clean air—as opposed to other goods and services—is enough?

This reply makes an important point that everyone—even those who interpret environmental laws as strong normative constraints on economic development—must concede. We must acknowledge, however idealistic we may be, that clean air, workplace safety, etc., have a price, and that at some point the additional amount we may buy may be grossly disproportionate to the goods and services we must forgo in order to pay for it.[32] It hardly seems reasonable to ask industry to pay hundreds of millions of dollars, for example, to provide a tiny or insignificant improvement in workplace safety; yet, it is surely appropriate to require companies to pay even large sums to prevent significant risks. But how to determine what is appropriate from an ethical point of view? What counts as a "significant" risk or a "significant" deterioration of air quality? When should we apply the law of diminishing returns?

IV. Two Approaches to Rationality

In order to evaluate the economic approach to environmental policy, it is important to distinguish two senses in which social policy decisions might be described as "rational" and as "scientific."[33] In one sense, a decision is "rational" if it uses mathematical criteria and methodologies, laid down in advance, to infer policy recommendations from independent or exogenous preferences in the client society. This approach conforms to a philosophy of science that stresses notions like "value neutrality," "replicable experiments," and "correspondence to an independent reality."

A decision or policy might be described as "rational" or as "scientific" in another sense if it is based on good reasons—reasons that are open and yet stand up to criticism. The words *rational* and *scientific* in this second sense, as Richard Rorty writes, means something more like "sane" and "reasonable" than "methodical." The term *rationality*, on this second approach, "names a set of moral virtues: tolerance, respect for the opinions of others, willingness to listen, reliance on persuasion rather than force."[34]

In accordance with the first approach, economists study data that have to do with prices and with the preferences consumers reveal or express in actual and surrogate markets. Economic analysts can then answer questions like "how safe, clean, etc., is safe or clean enough?" in terms of data about preferences—data that therefore represent independent variables or exogenous states of the world. In doing so, they are able to balance the benefits of environmental protection, measured in this way, against the opportunity costs of economic development.

The second approach, in contrast, uses a juridical or deliberative model to weigh various normative constraints, established by statute, against these opportunity costs. In accordance with this approach, public officials must not only recognize both the legal and ethical force of these constraints, but at the same time take account of technical, economic, and other realities, since no one can pursue

a goal without adjusting to the obstacles that stand in the way of achieving it. Because there is no methodology for making this sort of judgment, public officials have only statutory language, judicial interpretation of that language, their general knowledge and experience, and the virtues of inquiry to rely upon. This is the reason why statutes generally require that officials respond to views presented at public hearings that they set policies that are reasonable and feasible, and that they create a record of their deliberations which can be reviewed by the courts.

The problem-solving approach of the Endangered Species Act, which sets up a committee to mitigate conflicts, illustrates this ethical and juridical approach to social regulation. This approach ties the rationality of the policy-making process to virtues, particularly, the virtues of deliberation, for example, intellectual honesty, civility, willingness to see a problem in a larger context, and openness of mind. It does not require decisions to conform to criteria, methodologies, or guidelines laid down in advance. Rather, it depends upon an open process in which decision makers respond on the record to the merits of arguments and proposals.

Economists, in measuring the value of "unpriced" social and environmental benefits, approach situations in a way that brings these two conceptions of science and rationality into serious conflict. This conflict becomes apparent when analysts must decide how much information to present to subjects and how much discussion, deliberation, and education to allow as part of a survey experiment. An analysis or assessment can be "scientific" in the sense of "gathering data on exogeneous variables" only if it allows no discussion, education, or deliberation to take place. An approach which is "scientific" and "neutral" in this way, however, cannot be "scientific" in the sense of being "reasonable," "civilized," or "intelligent."

V. The Wyoming Experiment

The Wyoming economists attempted to make their analyses "scientific" by basing them on quantitative methodologies and on independently existing data that can be verified through replicable experiments. Accordingly, these economists sought to develop quantified methodologies to identify exogenous preferences as data and to aggregate them in a way that permits the calculation of a social decision. In other words, they tried to make intangible values tangible. Can this be done?

Anyone trying to deal with these intangibles has to answer a lot of questions. How valuable is atmospheric visibility in parks, wilderness areas, and so on? How important is it for us to be able to stand on a mountaintop in Yosemite and contemplate an "integral vista" free of power plants, hotels, highways, or other signs of industrial civilization? What are the expressive or symbolic values of nature untouched by man and how much are these worth to us? How draconian should prohibitions on development be in order to keep the wilderness experience pristine?

Let us stick to the example of visibility in and near national parks. In measuring the value of visibility, we need to know, first, how a loss of atmospheric clarity or quality is caused. A mist or fog hanging on the mountains, for example, can be very beautiful, perhaps more beautiful than a clear view, as the Japanese show us in their paintings. A mist or fog, then, need not impair aesthetic value. Even a volcano which distributes ash over hundreds of miles may be viewed as an aesthetic marvel; people will come from as far just to see it. If soot and precipitates from a power plant impede visibility, however, the resulting loss of air quality, even if indistinguishable from that caused by a volcano, has a completely different meaning. We no longer think of it as natural or compare it with aspects of nature and its beauty; we may perceive it, rather, as an assault on nature and as destructive of its integrity.

The Wyoming economists faced something of a dilemma when they designed their experiment: they had to decide whether or not to explain to the participants how the visibility would be lost in the vistas presented in the photographs. If they let the participants assume that the cause would be natural, e.g., an approaching storm, then they might elicit a preference for *less* visibility, since oncoming storms in deserts can be considered beautiful. If the experimenters identified the cause as the belching smokestacks of Humongous Megawatt, a coal-fired utility, however, the respondents might not reveal aesthetic but political preferences. They might express opinions, for example, about the inadvisability of increasing supply as opposed to decreas-

ing demand for energy through conservation. They might even offer legal arguments based on the PSD provisions of the Clean Air Act.

In fact, this is what happened. The Wyoming team (appropriately, I believe) informed the respondents that the visibility would be obscured by pollution from a power plant. They described the amount of energy (in kilowatt hours) to be produced, the location of the facilities, the levels of emission of various pollutants, and so on. I do not know whether the economists gave the subjects of the experiment information about the PSD requirements of the Clean Air Act; the respondents, however, may have had that information. The economists asked the subjects, first, how much they would pay (the "equivalent" or "ES" measure of consumer surplus) to prevent the deterioration of the visibility caused by the power plant. They then asked for "compensating" or "CS" values, which is to say, the amounts that the respondents would accept to allow the power plant to emit that much pollution.

When the respondents were asked how much they would demand in compensation (the "CS" or "WTA" value) to permit the loss of visibility shown in the photographs, at least half of them used the question as an occasion to express a political opinion. The Wyoming experimenters report:

> The CS values . . . put the liability for maintaining visibility with the power companies and presupposes [sic] that the power companies will attempt to buy off consumers rather than cleanse the air. If respondents reject this concept of "being bought off to permit pollution" they might increase their compensation. Strategically, respondents may give large or infinite valuations as an indication that this concept is unacceptable. This is partially supported in that slightly over one-half of the sample required infinite compensation or refused to cooperate with the CS portion of the survey instrument.[35]

The experimenters found even in their own experiment that a majority of a sample of citizens rejected a cost-benefit or "consumer surplus" approach to trade-offs between health, safety, or environmental quality and economic growth, an approach which also seems to be precluded by the Clean Air Act, the Occupational Safety and Health Act, and by other legislation.[36] Attempting to make their approach practicable, if not legal, they ended up in an awkward position: they asked citizens participating in the experiment to accept the concept of trading dollars for pollution "rights," a concept that many citizens reject,[37] and most of the subjects responded by entering protest bids or by refusing to cooperate with the experiment.

VI. The Problem of Information

In an excellent paper on "Information Disclosure and Endangered Species Evaluation," a group of economists from Hawaii describe bidding games and surrogate markets, i.e., the contingent valuation method (CVM), they used to determine citizen willingness to pay to preserve endangered species. The Hawaii group observed that WTP values are deeply influenced by the information subjects receive in the survey or experiment. These authors write:

> . . . willingness to pay (WTP) to preserve a particular animal is significantly influenced by information provided about the animal's physical and behavioral characteristics, and about its endangered status. While this proposition may appear obvious, it bears important implications for the proper type and amount of information disclosed in preservation valuation studies.[38]

In the Hawaii experiment, subjects were asked how much they were willing to contribute to a fund for preserving humpback whales, an endangered species. Then an experimental group saw *The Singing Whale*, a Jean Cousteau film describing the humpback and the threats to its survival. A control group viewed a film unrelated to whales, *The Sixty Minute Spot: The Making of a Television Commercial*. All subjects were then asked to reevaluate or reconsider their bids. After seeing the films, one-third of the experimental group and one-fifth of the control group increased their bids. The authors note that

this "lends support to the view that preferences are learned during the interview process, even in the absence of new relevant information."[39]

The Hawaii economists point out that relevant information can influence preservation bids in many ways. An individual is likely to decrease his bid, for example, if he learns that the population of a particular species is so large that it will survive or so small that it will go extinct no matter how much he and others contribute. A reasonable individual, in other words, is likely to apply some principle of triage to deal with the number and characteristics of endangered species. The economists conclude that "information disclosure can influence perceived marginal efficiency investment in a preservation fund, and thereby result in changes in an individual's budget allocation strategy."[40]

The Hawaii experimenters recognized the importance of their results for the contingent valuation of preservation, amenity, and other benefits of environmental protection. They identified a methodological question about the extent to which respondents are given information or otherwise allowed to educate themselves, discuss, or deliberate over the issues. Should valuation be based on the immediate, untutored, *ex ante* preferences of the respondents or should valuation refer to their informed or educated judgment instead?

One alternative, the authors note, "is to accept the state of the respondents' ignorance about the resource as given, and provide only enough information about the resource to create a realistic market situation." This alternative has the advantage of keeping the response exogenous to or independent of the experiment. It has the disadvantage (as we saw in the Wyoming experiment), however, "that respondents may not readily accept operating in a hypothetical market situation with unknown payoffs and opportunity costs."[41]

At the other extreme, "the analyst could provide vast amounts of information to respondents about the resource being valued, along with complete information about its substitutes and complements." The respondents might discuss, in the visibility case, for example, various alternatives to constructing power plants near national parks, e.g., the possibility of energy conservation. They might try to size up or define the problem in terms which allow a different sort of solution. This kind of approach, the Hawaii economists point out, "could change the preference mappings of respondents and therefore make individual values endogenous to the valuation process."[42]

How should we choose between these alternatives? Should we accept the first alternative, insisting that the valuation of environmental benefits be "rational" in the sense of being methodical, derived from exogenous variables, and determined by criteria laid down in advance? Should we prefer the second alternative, emphasizing the virtues of deliberation rather than the methods of derivation, and hence a conception of "rationality" which is less akin to "methodological" than to "civilized," "reasonable," and "sane"?

An analogy may help us answer this question. Let us suppose that a person has been called to perform jury duty. The judge informs each that a Mr. Smith has been accused of robbing a liquor store. Then the judge asks each juror separately whether Mr. Smith is guilty. If the judge is methodologically sophisticated, indeed, he or she may ask how much each juror is willing to pay for the preferred verdict. The judge may then report the verdict in terms of the mean, the average, or some statistical transformation of the weighted average of the jurors' preferences.

If you were a juror, how would you respond to the judge? You might complain that the methodology is flawed—the judge should use the average rather than the mean bid to set the sentence. The judge may point, however, to a large literature which investigates all the ins and outs of the statistical methodologies—perhaps the software—used by the court. He or she may reply, moreover, that the verdict rests entirely on *ex ante* preferences which remain completely independent or exogenous to the decision-making process.

You might, on the other hand, ask the judge to let the jury hear the case—the evidence for and against—and to deliberate to reach a consensus in good faith. The judge could rule this out on the grounds that the verdict would then be biased by the means of obtaining it. What is more, he could point out that no quantified methodology exists for reaching a verdict through deliberation on the evidence. To be scientific, so the judge might reason, the verdict must be derived from exogenous variables by quantified criteria laid down in advance. Jurors might be permitted to make use of any hearsay evidence that they may have picked up

beforehand from the newspapers. No further inquiry, however, may bias or prejudice preference.

If you were faced with this situation, what would you think? You would think that the judge is *crazy*. You would probably refuse to cooperate with this sort of "valuation." You might protest, for example, or just vote to acquit Mr. Smith.

Economists often confront this kind of resistance to their surveys. Their subjects may reject cost-benefit balancing as an inappropriate and illegal framework for making social policy. Two resource economists observe:

> Bidding questions for changes in air quality are not always well received by respondents due to rejection of the hypothetical scenario, rejection of the implied property rights or liability rules presented in a situation, or rejection for moral and ethical reasons. . . . Rejection and protest bids have varied from 20 percent to 50 percent for specific applications of the bidding technique. *In these cases, respondents' true values remain unknown and unaccounted for.*[43]

I contend that just the reverse is true: it is only in this way—by lodging a protest—that respondents can begin to make their values known. These respondents may not perceive themselves as bundles of exogenous preferences, but rather as thinking beings capable of reaching informed judgments in the context of public inquiry and deliberation. They may regard themselves as a jury who might reach a considered judgment after discussion of all relevant views and information, including the relevant statutes. The contingent valuation method (CVM), however, insofar as it tries to make respondents express preferences rather than form judgments, denies their status both as thinking and political beings.[44] This is possibly the major reason that respondents so often enter protest bids or otherwise resist this sort of experiment.

Notes

1. Steven Edwards, "In Defense of Environmental Economics," *Environmental Ethics* 9 (1987): 74–85. Quotation at p. 75. Subsequent page references in the text are to this essay.

2. For a discussion of relevant surveys, see Nicholas Rescher, *Welfare: The Social Issues in Philosophical Perspective* (Pittsburgh: University of Pittsburgh Press, 1972), esp. chap. 3, and *Unpopular Essays on Technological Progress* (Pittsburgh: University of Pittsburgh Press, 1980), chap. 1. See also A. Campbell, P. E. Converse, and W. Rodgers, *The Quality of American Life: Perceptions, Evaluations, and Satisfactions* (New York: Russell Sage Foundation, 1976). Welfare in a substantive sense does increase with the satisfaction of basic needs, of course, but this is an argument for justice or equality, not necessarily for efficiency, in the allocation of resources.

3. Albert O. Hirschman, *Shifting Involvements: Private Interest and Public Action* (Princeton: Princeton University Press, 1982), p. 10.

4. F. H. Knight, *The Ethics of Competition and Other Essays* (New York: Harper and Brothers, 1935), pp. 22–23. Compare John Stuart Mill, "What Utilitarianism Is," in *The Utilitarians* (Garden City, N.Y.: Doubleday, 1961), p. 410, where he argues that it is better to be Socrates dissatisfied than a fool satisfied. As far as I know, no economist has offered any evidence to show that people are only willing to pay, in general, for what makes them better off in a substantive sense (consider tobacco). Economists who have studied this question have concluded, on the contrary, that willingness-to-pay has no non-stipulative or non-definitional relationship with personal welfare. For arguments to this effect, see: Tibor Scitivsky, *The Joyless Economy* (Oxford: Oxford University Press, 1976); Richard Easterlin, "Does Money Buy Happiness?" *Public Interest* 30 (1973): 3–10; and Fred Hirsch, *Social Limits to Growth* (Cambridge, Mass.: Harvard University Press, 1976).

5. I have argued at length in other places that by satisfying consumer preferences (in the sense of "meeting" or "filling" them) we do not as a rule produce satisfaction (in the sense of contentment or happiness). The assertion that the satisfaction of preferences produces consumer or any other kind of satisfaction is either false, tautological, or merely a bad pun. See, for example, "Values and Preferences," *Ethics* 96 (1986): 301–16.

6. Richard Posner, *The Economics of Justice* (Cambridge, Mass.: Harvard University Press, 1981), p. 60.

7. Many commentators recognize that cost-benefit analysis is an instrument of centralized government planning and that efficiency can be achieved only in an authoritarian system that substitutes bureaucratic control for free markets. The central authority, to justify its authoritarian allocation, need only say it is correcting a market failure. As Duncan Kennedy writes, it is rare that an analyst "lacks a handy externality to justify a particular . . . measure" (Duncan Kennedy, "Cost-Benefit Analysis of Entitlement Problems: A Critique," *Standard Law Review* 33 (1980): 419. I am urging an additional reason for the same conclusion, namely, that in traditional markets owners for ethical, cultural, or other reasons can refuse to sell, while in the hypothetical markets envisioned by economic analysis, resources essentially are auctioned off to the highest bidder. The point I am making here has nothing the do with the gap between "bid" and "asked" prices for property rights, which economists recognize. My point is that environmental law deals with resources that people in fact refuse to sell at all—and this includes publicly as well as privately owned resources.

8. A Kaldor-Hicks or "potential" Pareto improvement criterion for efficiency would permit the pollution as long as the polluter could compensate his victims at this "objective" price; compensation need not in fact be paid.

9. Guido Calabresi and A. Douglas Melamed, "Property Rules, Liability Rules, and Inalienability: One View of the Cathedral," *Harvard Law Review* 85 (1972): 1092. I have presented the argument I make here more extensively in "The Principles of Pollution Control Law," *Minnesota Law Review* 71 (1986): 19–95, esp. pp. 46–55.

10. Calabresi and Melamed, "Property Rules," p. 1092.

11. This is the reason that "libertarianism rejects in principle the use of cost-benefit analysis as a basis to justify pollution." Libertarians recognize that in traditional markets, where property rules are backed by property rights, "processes of production which involve pollution, so long as the harmful imposition upon others occurs, without the consent of the victims, . . . may not be carried out." Tibor R. Machan, "Pollution and Political Theory," in *Earthbound,* ed. Tom Regan (New York: Random House, 1984), p. 98. A society that takes property rights and consent seriously, such as ours, will then at least enact environmental laws that seek to minimize and eventually eliminate pollution. A planned or centralized economy, in contrast, may permit and may even require pollution and any other transfer of property rights, without the consent of the initial owners, as long as the transfer is efficient or the benefits exceed the costs.

12. Prosser observes that "the great majority of nuisance suits have been in equity and concerned primarily with the prevention of future damage." William Presser, *Handbook on the Law of Torts,* 4th ed. (St. Paul: West Publishing Company, 1971), par. 87,

p. 576. Environmental groups that routinely sue polluters seek to stop the pollution. Although they may assert economic injury to establish standing, they seek injunctive relief.

13. Stanley Milgram, *Obedience to Authority* (New York: Harper and Row, 1974).

14. R. Rowe, R. D'Arge, and D. Brookshire, "An Experiment on the Economic Value of Visibility," *Journal of Environmental Economics and Management* (1980): 1. For a similar study and useful bibliography, see John Balling and John Falk, "Development of Visual Preference for Natural Environments," *Environmental Behavior* 14 (1982): 5–28.

15. Rowe et al., "An Experiment," p. 2.

16. The Clean Air Act as amended August 1977 (Public Law 95–11), sec. 160(3).

17. Rowe et al., "An Experiment," p. 2.

18. The Sixth Circuit Court in *TVA* v. *Hill* described the statute as an expression of the "public conscience." 549 F.2d 1064, 1074 (6th Cir. 1976), *aff'd*, 437 U.S. 153 (1978).

19. 16 U.S.C. Section 1536 (1976).

20. 437 U.S. 153. 173 (1978).

21. The 1978 amendments to the Endangered Species Act created a high-level Endangered Species Committee to deal in a juridical way with "irresolvable conflicts." The committee unanimously voted to deny an exemption in the Tellico Dam case. It permitted the Grayrocks reservoir to continue after conditions were met to mitigate its effect on the habitat of the whooping crane.

22. I have discussed the legislative and judicial history of the Endangered Species Act in "On the Preservation of Species," *Columbia Journal of Environmental Law* 7 (1980): 33–67.

23. Judith Bentkover, "The Role of Benefits Assessment in Public Policy Development," in Judith Bentkover, Vincent Covello, and Jeryl Mumpower, *Benefits Assessments: The State of the Art* (Boston: D. Reidel, 1986), p. 10.

24. Ibid., p. 11.

25. For major surveys, discussions, and bibliographies, see Bentkover et al., *Benefits Assessments,* and George L. Peterson and Alan Randall, eds., *Valuation of Resource Benefits* (Boulder, Colo.: Westview, 1984).

26. For a sample of this literature, see Marion Clawson and Jack Knetsch, *Economics of Outdoor Recreation* (Baltimore: Resources for the Future, 1966).

27. For discussion of "existence value," see J. V. Krutilla, "Conservation Reconsidered," *American Economic Review* 57 (1967): 777–86. For discussion of "option

value," see Burton A. Weisbrod, "Collective-Consumption Services of Individual Consumption Goods," *Quarterly Journal of Economics* 78 (1964): 471–77.

28. William Schulze et al., "The Economic Benefits of Preserving Visibility in the National Parklands of the Southwest," *Natural Resources Journal* 23 (1983): 149–73; quotation at p. 154.

29. For a definition of public goods, see Paul Samuelson, *Economics,* 10th ed. (New York: McGraw-Hill, 1976), pp. 159–60.

30. Robert D. Rowe and Lauraine G. Chesnut, *The Value of Visibility: Economic Theory and Applications for Air Pollution Control* (Cambridge, Mass.: Abt Associates, 1982), p. 10.

31. Congress intended clean and safe air—not allocatory efficiency—to be the goal of the Clean Air Act. Thus, the statute precludes the kind of cost-benefit balancing envisioned by the Wyoming economists. See *American Textile Manufacturers Institute* v. *Donovan,* 452 U.S. 490, 510 (1981), which states: "When Congress has intended that an agency engage in cost-benefit analysis, it has clearly indicated such intent on the face of the statute." The D.C. Circuit, in permitting EPA to consider costs in regulating vinyl chloride emissions, distinguishes taking costs into account from cost-benefit analysis. See *NRDC* v. *USEPA,* 824 F. 2d 1146, 1160–1161, note 6 (D.C. Cir. 1987).

32. Thus, it seems to be EPA policy that, in the presence of scientific uncertainty concerning risk, the cost of regulations should not be "grossly disproportionate" to health benefits. See the *Vinyl Chloride* case cited above.

33. I have explained this distinction in more detail in "Where Ickes Went Right or Reason and Rationality in Environmental Law," *Ecology Law Quarterly* 14 (1987): 265–323.

34. Richard Rorty, "Science as Solidarity," unpublished manuscript, 1984, p. 3.

35. Rowe et al., "An Experiment," p. 9.

36. *American Textile Manufacturers* v. *Donovan* (*Cotton Dust*), 452 U.S. 490 (1981).

37. For discussion, see Steven Kelman, *What Price Incentives: Economists and the Environment* (Boston: Auburn House, 1981).

38. Karl Samples, John Dixon, and Marcia Gowen, "Information Disclosure and Endangered Species Evaluation," *Land Economics* 62 (1986): 306–12; quotation at 306.

39. Ibid., p. 310.

40. Ibid., p. 311.

41. Ibid., p. 312.

42. Ibid.

43. Rowe and Chestnut, *The Value of Visibility*, pp. 80–81 (citations omitted, italics added). These authors cite three studies that encountered a 50 percent protest or rejection rate.

44. I have argued elsewhere that resource economists commit a "category mistake" by asking of objective beliefs and judgments a question that is appropriate only to subjective preferences and wants. See "Economic Theory and Environmental Law," *Michigan Law Review* 79 (1981): 1393–419, esp. pp. 1410–18.

The Price of Everything

Thomas Michael Power and Paul Rauber

Maybe it has something to do with the approaching millennium: the lion will lie down with the lamb, and toxic polluters will drink herbal tea with environmental activists. The wonderful new development is lauded in the press and preached from scores of think tanks. No longer, we are told, do we have to rely on threats of fines or jail time in order to get industry to do the right thing. The business leaders of today, working together with enlightened environmentalists, have discovered in the magic of the marketplace a cheaper, more effective, and less contentious remedy to just about any environmental ailment.

The debate over environmental protection in the 1990s fills the ideological vacuum left by the end of the Cold War. It is now fashionable, for instance, to compare government regulation to the "command-and-control" economic arrangements of the former Soviet Union. As the Soviet system failed, the analogy suggests, so too will a regulatory system based on the *diktat* of federal bureaucrats telling industry how much pollution to reduce and how to reduce it. "Command and control" is said to cost U.S. businesses $140 billion a year, handicapping the economy, hobbling the recovery, and unfairly vilifying many environmentally concerned Americans who just happen to own polluting industries.

The alternative to this clumsy, old-fashioned, and vaguely unpatriotic-sounding system is "free-market environmentalism" (a.k.a. "new resource economics"), which promises to harness the vigor and inventiveness of capitalism to heal the earth. To do so, it proposes to vastly expand our present notion of private property, to sell that property to the highest bidder, and then to let the logic of the market sort things out.

Already a new property right has been created: the right to pollute. One section of the 1990 Clean Air Act allows plants that pollute below certain levels to sell pollution "credits" to dirtier concerns; innovative, clean industries profit from their cleanliness, while the dirty industries pay for their sins until they can get around to cleaning up their acts. A market in these "pollution credits" has been established at the Chicago Board of Trade, where rights to emit tons of sulfur dioxide are bought and sold like pork bellies or soybean futures.

Having set prices on pollution, free marketeers are also trying to figure out what those who enjoy environmental quality should be made to pay for it. What will the market bear for the use of a regional park? Hopefully the public will pay more for Sunday hikes than the local developer will for condos, because if not, farewell forest. And if people want wolves in Yellowstone National Park, free marketeers argue, they should be willing to pay for them, cash on the barrelhead. It's just a question of settling on the price.

Not all proponents of free-market environmentalism subscribe to all of its logical but occasionally wacky conclusions. Every ideology has its ideologues; in this case, they are the libertarian-minded think tanks and academics who have provided the theoretical spadework for the new discipline. More common, however, are those who seek to pick and choose at the free-market table, ignoring dishes that

Sierra, November/December 1993, 87–90, 92–96. Reprinted by permission.

don't coincide with their interests. Many businesses, for example, are enthusiastic about market solutions, but only when they result in a further giveaway of public resources. Contrarily, some environmentalists advocate market mechanisms in the name of efficiency, reasoning that making environmental responsibility cheaper will result in a corollary reduction of political opposition, the end result being the possibility of greater protection.

This, crudely put, is the position of the Environmental Defense Fund, the most market-oriented of the major environmental groups, as well as of some individuals within the Sierra Club. "We're finally getting past the debate about whose position is morally superior and moving on to a point where we will accomplish real reductions in pollution and resource use," says Dan Dudek, a senior economist at the EDF. His organization, which helped write the pollution-credit section in the Clean Air Act, looks forward to the establishment of national markets for nitrogen oxides, and perhaps even global markets for CFCs and carbon dioxide.

A big plus for free-market environmentalism has been its bipartisan support; neo-liberal Clintonian Democrats and anti-regulatory Bob Dole Republicans embrace it with equal enthusiasm. *Mandate for Change,* candidate Clinton's policy blueprint, contained a chapter ("The Greening of the Market") calling for a harnessing of the "daily self-interest" of firms and individuals to replace "command-and-control" regulations. During the campaign, Clinton himself said that we must "recognize that Adam Smith's invisible hand can have a green thumb," and called for a "market-based environmental-protection strategy."

This is a bitter draught for many environmental activists, weaned on regulatory triumphs like the National Environmental Policy Act and practiced in lobbying the government to toughen environmental laws, not abandon them. Most environmentalists are innately suspicious of economists anyway. They are the ones, after all, who tried to portray environmental quality as an expensive frivolity; who tell us that pollution controls hamper productivity and threaten private property; that zero levels of toxic releases are a naively impossible goal; and that protecting endangered species without regard for the economic consequences is irrational—as, perhaps, are many environmentalists.

(This suspicion of the dismal science is well warranted historically. From its beginning, the intellectual mission of Anglo-American economics has been to demonstrate the secret logic of allowing businesses to maximize profits, unfettered by social controls. That was, after all, Adam Smith's goal—to depict the selfish, even antisocial actions of private commerce as ultimately benefiting the public. No wonder the business community enthusiastically supported the intellectual venture that came to be known as economics.)

Yet these same wary environmentalists frequently endorse the use of economic instruments—perhaps without quite realizing it, and often to the profound distress of the affected industry. They insist, for example, that a price be put on empty beverage containers to create an economic incentive for recycling. (The deposit idea is now being considered for other, more dangerous solid wastes, such as automobile batteries, or refrigerators containing CFCs.) They argue that water "shortages" in arid regions result from the absence of incentives to conserve when the low price of government-subsidized irrigation reflects neither what the water costs to provide nor its value in alternate uses. They attack government subsidies for destructive programs such as the U.S. Forest Service's below-cost timber sales. Yet they remain queasy about extending this approach to all other environmental problems—with good reason, as it turns out.

This ambivalence reflects a healthy respect for the limitations of market "solutions." Economic instruments are tools, but using them does not require us to embrace a new ideology or to jettison all government regulation. It *does* require environmentalists to determine when such tools can be used productively, and which specific sort of tool is appropriate to a given situation or industry. It requires the adoption of an explicitly pragmatic approach to solving environment problems. Most importantly, it requires that political problems be faced first.

Whenever environmental policy is made, three crucial issues must be resolved:

- What level of environmental protection is desired in each particular location?

- Who is going to pay the direct costs of achieving the targeted level of protection?
- What policy tools will be used to achieve these levels and to impose the costs?

Since economic instruments are merely policy tools, it's no use talking about them until the first two far more contentious questions have been settled. Otherwise, market mechanisms will end up doing what they have always done, i.e., maximizing profits by ignoring pollution or shifting environmental costs elsewhere. Market measures, then, are appropriate in situations with firmly established pollution-control objectives, where conventional environmental regulation would result in pure economic waste. Say, for example, that we have decided to reduce the amount of solid waste going into a city's landfill. Instead of issuing a decree ordering such a reduction by every citizen and business, we change the way garbage fees are paid; instead of extracting them from property taxes, as is usually the case, we start charging by weight or volume, and institute curbside recycling at the same time. Recyclers get a break, and others pay in relation to the amount of garbage they produce. Here economic instruments have something to offer, but only *after* the basic political questions have been settled.

This was not entirely the case in the pollution-permit market created by the 1990 Clean Air Act and implemented earlier this year. This pet program of the free-market environmentalists was designed to ease the pain for industries required to halve their 1980 level of SO_2 emissions by 2000. While promising in theory, however, its actual implementation revealed a number of hidden problems.

Unaddressed, for instance, was the question of who had to live with continued high levels of pollution. When the geographic area over which pollution credits can be traded is very large—nationwide in the case of SO_2—the effect of the market can be to stick some people in dirty areas with the bill. In some parts of the country air quality dramatically improves; in others, serious pollution problems persist with the full blessings of the market and the law. (The geographic question is what got World Bank Chief Economist Lawrence Summers in such hot water last year when his memo about the "impeccable" logic of dumping toxic waste in the "underpolluted" Third World was leaked to

the press.) At its worst, trading pollution rights can legitimize continuing pollution. In one of the very first acid-rain trades under the new program, the Wisconsin Electric Power Company sold a Pennsylvania utility 20,000 tons of pollution credits. Under Wisconsin law, however, the company would not have been entitled to emit the pollution in the first place—yet federal law still allowed it to be peddled to Pennsylvania.

Meanwhile, East Coast utilities have been selling their SO_2 credits to midwestern power plants, allowing them to continue burning high-sulfur midwestern coal. But what goes around comes around: the midwestern emissions ultimately drift back through the Atlantic and New England states, where they fall as acid rain.

Since it was concern over acid rain in the Northeast that led to the Clean Air Act's SO_2 caps in the first place, New York is now trying to prevent its utilities from selling SO_2 permits to upwind states. In the Midwest, on the other hand, ratepayers pay higher bills in order to finance their utilities' SO_2 purchases, but don't see any reduction in local SO_2. Had their utilities been forced by regulation to reduce emissions, at least the higher bills would have been offset by cleaner air; now the public pays for "pollution control," but gets none.

Supporters of emission trading argue that New York's fears are overstated, and that the benefits of local utilities cleaning up enough to sell credits far exceed the relatively small excess SO_2 blown in from upwind. Indeed, the Sierra Club itself has intervened with Ohio's public utilities commission in support of an acid-rain-reduction plan consisting of emission trading, energy efficiency, and use of low-sulphur eastern coal. "By forcing the marketplace to the lowest-cost solution that really works," says Sierra Club Ohio Chapter Energy Chair Ned Ford, "environmentalists gain credibility and enhance the opportunity for further reduction."

Of course, a simpler market mechanism could have been employed by taxing emissions above a certain level. While this would have had the same effect of rewarding the clean and punishing the dirty, it is anathema to free-market ideologues, whose interest is the creation of new private-property rights—in this case, a right to pollute.

Ironically, some of the businesses pollution-trading systems are supposed to assist don't want to play ball. The Ohio Power Company would prefer simply installing a scrubber. In Southern California, two dozen major businesses are opposing an emission-trading scheme proposed by the South Coast Air Quality Management District, claiming that it would "substantially raise the costs" of pollution control, and pleading to be allowed to continue with "command and control."

Many environmentalists also attack pollution-credit trading as fundamentally flawed. That is not necessarily true. The real problem is that the program was established before all the basic questions were answered—in this case, what level of environmental quality should be assured for *all* areas covered by the trade. Those answers can only be reached through a political process, not bought at the market.

There is a fundamental conflict here that goes far beyond the use of economic instruments. Environmental protection necessarily involves the transfer of control over very valuable resources from one group of people to another. These resources are the wealth of the natural world, extractable and otherwise, and the limited capacity of the air, water, and land to assimilate the wastes associated with economic activity. Historically (and to a considerable extent today), this natural wealth has been the province of industry. The Forest Service sells the national forests for a song to giant timber companies; the Bureau of Land Management allows gentlemen ranchers to denude the public range for a pittance; the 1872 Mining Law gives away the public's mineral wealth to multinational corporations. Until very recently, the cost of waste disposal was however much it took to build a smokestack, or a drainpipe to the nearest river.

Taken for granted, these hidden subsidies—economists call them "externalities"—are not reflected in the price of commodities. Timber is cheap because the Forest Service gives it away; driving is cheap because drivers don't pay for air pollution. The real cost, of course, is paid in sick children, eroded farmlands, vanished fisheries, and extinction of species, and is shunted to the public, preferably the public of future generations.

Over the past several decades, the environmental movement has attempted to transfer control of these natural resources—worth, literally, trillions of dollars—from the commercial sector to the public. A transfer of wealth of this magnitude cannot take place without considerable conflict. In the past, such power shifts have required revolutions.

The continuing struggle over environmental policy, therefore, is hardly surprising. Economic instruments can make a modest contribution toward resolving it, to the extent that they can reduce the cost of environmental protection. But the fundamental conflict over who controls the use of our air, water, and landscapes cannot be decided merely through a change in the instrument of enforcement.

Business sometimes argues that it doesn't really matter *who* pays the direct costs of pollution control, since the costs will ultimately be borne by the general citizenry in the form of higher prices anyway. But in this case environmentalists have Econ 1-A on their side: it is elementary economic theory that markets can change behavior only if the full costs of an activity—the externalities—are incorporated into the immediate prices paid. If the price of gasoline included the direct costs of maintaining a permanent fleet (let alone fighting a war) in the Persian Gulf, our transportation system would reform itself in a hurry.

If the free marketeers based their program on charging the true environmental costs for all resources used, the environmental movement would sign up *en masse*. But ideological free-market environmentalists often seem more concerned with the market than with the environment; they tend to feel that equity—the distribution of access to scarce resources, or the right to a clean and healthful environment—is less important than economic efficiency and property rights.

This is exactly what is being demanded in the current attempt to expand the legal concept of "takings" to include environmental regulations. (See "Look Who's Taking," September/October.) By this theory, any environmental regulation that results in lost profits requires government compensation. This assumes, of course, that people have a "property right" to pollute or damage the environment in any way they wish, and that the public has to pay them if that right to damage the environment is changed or revoked. Oddly, free marketeers somehow always assign property rights to those doing the polluting rather than to those being damaged by the pollution.

This is one example of the huge ideological gulf that separates the vision of a good society shared by most environmentalists from that of the free-market enthusiasts. Environmentalists act collectively to preserve certain qualities associated with the natural and, often, social environments. In this sense, they are fundamentally conservative: they wish things to remain the same, or even to return to a previous preferred condition. It is ironic, then, that their suspicion of market instruments is sometimes taken as proof of their "watermelon" character: green on the outside but red on the inside.

Free marketeers, on the other hand, are enthusiastic about the constant change that a market economy encourages, and are suspicious of any efforts to guide the direction of the economy or society collectively. They see such attempts as authoritarian, economically destructive, and tantamount to socialism. The economy for them is an adventure of unknown destination. Columnist George Will, for instance, writes fondly of the "billions of daily decisions that propel a free society into an exhilaratingly unknown future." We should learn to enjoy the excitement and change, and trust that the overall result, whatever it may be, will be much better than anything we could collectively arrange.

Ideological free marketeers insist that we should not use individual market tools without buying the whole package. Advocates such as John Baden of the Foundation for Research on Economics and the Environment (FREE) object strenuously to the use of market instruments "simply as tools for the efficient delivery of environmental goals . . . [while] the goals themselves remain collectively determined." Again, environmentalists are plainly the conservatives to the radical free marketeers, who are willing to trust everything to their faith in the inevitably positive outcome of market forces.

It is not necessary for the environmental movement to respond to one type of extremism and ideological wishful thinking by adopting another. Incentives *do* matter, and market instruments can help us, collectively, to protect the environment. Consider, for example, the following possibilities:

• In western rural areas, streams often run dry during peak summer irrigation periods. Because irrigation water is usually provided at very low cost to farmers, it is often used inefficiently (growing rice in California's Central Valley, for example). One solution is to allow government fish-and-wildlife agencies, water-quality agencies, or private-sector environmental groups to purchase water rights from farmers and use them to protect streams and their associated fisheries. These rights could be purchased on the basis of a willing buyer and a willing seller, a straightforward market transaction. Another approach is simply to raise the price of the water to the farmers to more closely approximate its real cost, thus discouraging ecologically foolish uses.

• Many of the most serious urban environmental problems—congestion, air pollution, noise—are associated with the automobile. Driving is rewarded in many ways, such as when businesses provide free parking for employees. But what if employers paid employees the cash value of parking privileges in higher wages, and then charged full cost for the parking? Those who choose to use mass transit or car pools would have higher net incomes, but no one would be worse off. Resources might well be saved and environmental costs reduced. Similarly, public agencies could charge commuters the full costs—including environmental costs—of using private automobiles. Increasing rush-hour tolls for lone drivers while forgiving them to car poolers are steps in this direction.

• In the same vein, dramatically raising the price of gasoline to reflect its real costs—a ready military, poisoned ecosystems in Alaska, polluted low-income neighborhoods next to refineries—would shortly result in increased fuel efficiency and reduced automobile usage. Other auto-related costs, like collision insurance, could also be included in the gas price.

These examples are purposely speculative to give a feeling for the range of environmentally productive uses for economic instruments. Once environmentalists begin to think in this direction, they are likely to generate many more ideas. Call it "the magic of the marketplace."

Some free-market ideas, while undeniably creative, need careful scrutiny. A good example is the proposal to charge increased fees to recreational users of public lands. (See "What Price a Walk in the Woods?" May/June.) The idea is to provide a positive incentive for bureaucrats whose revenues are closely tied to the amount of economic activity they generate. The more timber they harvest, the more mines they permit, the more land they lease for grazing, the larger are their budgets. (Since the government does not factor externalities into the equation, these activities show up as pluses on bureaucratic balance sheets, even when the activity results in a net loss to the public.)

Because recreationists pay few if any fees, the argument goes, no revenue is associated with their interests and the land managers ignore them. Hence the notion to charge hikers, campers, and skiers whatever the market will bear, thus producing a cash flow that will impress the bureaucrats enough to preserve and enhance recreational values. This, we are told, will automatically provide protection for public lands, because recreational fees would bring in far more than the timber, forage, and mineral charges that now largely finance these agencies.

Recreation-fee advocate Randal O'Toole explicitly suggests that if public lands were in private hands, the widespread environmental damage we observe in the West would be much reduced. This is hard to believe for anyone who has ever flown over the Pacific Northwest and seen the checkerboard of clearcut private lands next to still-intact bits of public forests, or peered beyond the beauty strips in Maine.

There is no doubt that when an agency develops a financial stake in serving a particular clientele, it becomes a strong advocate for that clientele's interests. Consider the many state fish-and-game agencies. Funded primarily by the sale of fishing and hunting licenses, they are single-minded defenders of fishing and hunting interests. In Montana and Wyoming, fish-and-game agencies have resisted wolf reintroduction because they fear that wolves will reduce the number of ungulates available to hunters. The Montana agency has opposed listing of the grizzly bear as an endangered species because it would ban grizzly hunting, and has also refused to support the reintroduction of bighorn sheep in any area where they could not be hunted.

The moral is that when cash flow alone guides government agencies, some perversity almost always follows. In order to imagine how a recreational fee system might work, one need look no further than those national-forest areas that have been surrendered to intensive downhill-ski development. Nor does giving recreationists more influence in the management of wild areas necessarily guarantee a haven for backpackers and birdwatchers. The Bureau of Land Management could well find that more money could be made sponsoring off-road-vehicle rallies than from either backpackers *or* cattle. Perhaps currently roadless wildlands would produce a larger cash flow were they open to motorized tours: snowmobile trails, helicopter lifts into campsites, Going-to-the-Sun-type roads through all of the spectacular mountain country. Already the solitude of the Grand Canyon is marred by the noise of sightseeing aircraft; in the Wasatch Mountains of Utah, backcountry skiing has been almost completely displaced by heli-skiing.

There is an important distinction to be made here. When we are talking about relatively common commodities such as timber or forage or minerals, it is perfectly reasonable to expect market approaches to work. After all, we already trust the production and use of those commodities to commercial markets. But to most of us, the management of our public lands is not (or should not be) primarily about adjusting slightly upward or downward the quantity of 2×4s or sheep pasture or phosphate rock that make it onto the market. The issues at stake in the management of public lands—biodiversity, wilderness, sustainability—go far beyond the world of commodities and the language of economics.

The problem with this method of influencing public-land management is that many of the things we want public lands managed for do not and cannot have dollar values attached to them. There is no way for cash-flow analysis to put an accurate price tag on a spotted owl or a grizzly bear, nor to indicate what wilderness is worth. Rather, we seek to protect wilderness and grizzlies not as playgrounds and playthings for tourists and fee-payers, but because we wish at least some small part of our natural heritage to continue to exist apart from us and our cash registers. Wilderness is "valuable" to us precisely to the extent that it is *not* used by humans; consequently, "use" is meaningless as a measure for accurately valuing it.

Markets are not neutral, technological devices. They are social institutions whose use has profound consequences. All societies purposely limit the extent of the market in order to protect their basic values. We, for instance, do not allow the buying and selling of votes and judicial decisions; we do not allow the selling of the sexual services of children; we do not allow human beings to be sold into slavery.

Free-market enthusiasts assume that market-oriented, calculating, self-regarding (i.e., "greedy") behavior is all that is needed for a good, responsible society. Such behavior, they assert, should be encouraged, not constrained. But what kind of decent society can depend upon this type of motivation alone? Selling certain things, in fact, degrades them: selling praise, spiritual favors, intimacy, the privileges of citizenship, or the outcomes of athletic events does not enhance their value, but reduces or destroys it.

Even the commercial market is built on a basic morality that takes the larger society and its values into account. Well-functioning markets do not simply spring into being spontaneously. Rather, they are regulated by elaborate public and private social institutions like courts, contract law, industrial associations, and our stock, bond, and commodity exchanges. When the regulatory apparatus breaks down, so do the markets, as can be seen in the recent history of the savings-and-loan industry. Without social structures the pursuit of commercial gain degenerates into banditry, as is evident in the drug trade, in frontier societies (such as our own in the last century), or in countries like Somalia where those social institutions have collapsed. Unadorned market-oriented behavior leads to "gangster capitalism," not to the good society.

This raises a disturbing aspect of the use of economic instruments to solve environmental problems. A basic assumption of the free-market approach is that motives don't matter, only results. If bribing polluters out of polluting works, fine. If giving civil servants bonuses for obeying the law is effective, pay them. Assume the worst of all human beings and arrange incentives to harness the basest of human motives. This is the social logic of free-market environmentalism.

But to most of us, motives *do* matter. A lie is not the same as a mistake; murder is not the same as self-defense or manslaughter; prostitution is not the same as love. Oliver Wendell Holmes once said that even a dog distinguishes between being stumbled over and being kicked. Most of us have at least the sensibilities of that dog. We do care about the motives of our fellow citizens; it matters if someone seeks to protect the community and its land base because they actually care, as opposed to doing it only to protect their pocketbooks (or pick ours). Ethics and conscience matter, and markets can undermine both.

The basic operating principle behind a "free market society" is an anti-democratic one: that peoples' preferences, whatever they may be, should be accepted and given an importance in proportion to the dollars that back them up. But most of us—including those without a great deal of money—have moral and social values that lead us to be very critical of some preferences, the expression of which we seek to block regardless of their financial backing. Even when we do not support the use of legal restrictions to constrain their expression, most of us would be uncomfortable passively accepting all market outcomes as legitimate. Instead, we seek social and cultural means to discourage some and encourage others. That is what "manners" and "public opinion" and "community standards" are all about. One of the worrisome things about allowing the use of public lands to be determined entirely by the highest bidder is the implicit legitimization of those outcomes. Destructive behavior should not automatically become legitimate and acceptable simply because it is backed by the largest wad of cash.

Environmentalists should be concerned with the waste of *all* resources: natural, social, and political. Policies that are unnecessarily costly and that do not accomplish their objectives involve pure waste, and should be reexamined. Economic instruments for controlling pollution and managing public lands *can* offer more efficient ways to reach our objectives; at the very least, by reducing the cost of environmental control, they open up the possibility of attaining higher standards of quality. Many market plans begin by setting a goal, and then proceed to attain it in the least costly way. That is a positive approach. Finally, economic instruments can solve certain types of environmental conflicts to the mutual satisfaction of all involved— a rare and attractive option in an otherwise contentious struggle.

But this mutual satisfaction can never be achieved by the commercial market mentality alone. On the contrary, that mentality tends to gnaw away at the ethical underpinning of society, and can even undermine the foundations of markets themselves: witness the insider trading, market manipulation, and regulatory corruption scandals of the 1980s. The social and community values that environmentalists hold should not be abandoned to

an ideological fad. They are crucial to building a healthy society, and should form the basis for the pragmatic decisions that will get us there.

B. ECOLOGICAL SUSTAINABILITY

Mainstream economic theory has tended to proceed as if human societies constitute a uni-directional system that is open at both ends. At one end, there is an infinite supply of resources (at least if one allows for unending discoveries of adequate substitutes for certain materials that, it may be acknowledged, literally will run out, e.g., nonrenewable fossil fuels generated over the earth's 4.5 billion-year history). We have, in effect, already noted the evaluative dimension of "resource," since the question of moral standing determines in large part what we will classify as, for example, "food." Thus, cannibals may not run out of "resources" as quickly as others. At the other end of our envisioned system is an outlet to a sink, a place where you can get rid of the things that you do not want, that are harmful, or otherwise in the way. These things we tend to call wastes, toxic wastes, trash, garbage, or pollutants. These terms, we too seldom acknowledge, are quasi-evaluative terms; we apply them to certain entities only because of certain normative standards to which we adhere. In the right place, X is "fertilizer," and in the wrong place, X is just "merde," as the French would call it. With the emergence of significant amounts of oxygen on the planet in the distant past, anerobic organisms encountered a "poisonous gas." However, the point here is to note the tendency of most people and much economic theory, until quite recently, to assume that, or act as if, sinks are in virtually infinite supply also.

If resources are in infinite supply and sinks are in infinite supply, then the task of an efficient economy, some seem to think, is simply to optimize the rate of throughput in the process of producing items that satisfy human wants. The objects wanted range from mil-

lions of Malcolm X caps, Elvis dolls, and plastic replicas of Jesus to artificial limbs and life-saving drugs. The views of economists have been split. Many have considered wants as given and applaud a system that effectively supplies them, no matter what their content. There may be a certain reluctance here to embrace the view that we are ever in the position of knowing better than another person whether what he or she wants is, in fact, for his or her own good or whether we are even in a good position to question whether someone's wants are self-destructive or fail to reflect the person's all-things-considered judgment.[1] Some people hold the view that a want cannot be rationally appraised, since wants are like involuntary sensations: something that just happen to people, over which they have no voluntary control, and which are not cognitive in nature (unless they are desires to have things that are means to ends, in which case the wanter's beliefs may be subject to cognitive appraisal).

Some economists, and many philosophers, oppose the idea that *any* sort of want-fulfillment can, and should, be identified with the "intrinsic good," with "utility," or as something whose production should be thought of, in itself, as right-making (although not necessarily right-making on balance when all relevant matters are considered). In this latter view, preferences need to be "laundered." For example, the fulfillment of the torturer's desire to torture should not count one whit toward a moral justification of the act of torturing. Or recall serial killer Jeffrey Dahmer's desire to kill and dismember fellow humans. Thus, in trying to repair or revise utilitarianism, some wish to exclude from any positive counting in the utilitarian calculus what utilitarian-economist John Harsanyi has labeled the "fulfillment of antisocial preferences." How can one discriminate between antisocial and the other types of preferences? There is a deep problem here.[2]

Let us not lose sight of the forest for looking at the trees. What does all this have to do with the market and with sustainability? The market is a device that takes sources, produces objects or services to fulfill human wants, and discards most of the residue (some is recycled) into sinks. It is worth recalling that among the sinks are humans and most animals and plants, since we and they breathe the air that contains the lead and drink the water that contains the heavy metals. So this "production machine" (we do not question that it is in many respects enormously beneficial) often passes on costs to individuals other than those who benefit from their generation.

As a related matter, what is a sink, or an acceptable sink? If we regard various nonhumans, or for that matter all living things, as having inherent value or worth, then the dumping of certain wastes into animal habitats is morally problematic. To put the matter differently, what we view as (acceptable) sinks depends on our suppositions regarding what sorts of things have moral standing. What counts as a sink, then, is partly an evaluative matter and, popular academic pronouncements to the contrary, is not strictly an economic or strictly a scientific question. We have already observed that, for similar reasons, what counts as a (an acceptable) source is also partly an evaluative issue. It is fair to say that philosophers and economists by and large have not addressed these issues and have simply made tacit anthropocentric assumptions. Today, this practice is beginning to change with the emergence of green economic theory, ecological economics, and nonanthropocentric environmental philosophy.[3]

Indeed, as we scrutinize certain key concepts employed in our judgments about progress, improvement, and so on, it is becoming clearer that many are ambiguous, value-

laden in ways we have not previously recognized, and tend to grease the path to conceptual confusion and, hence, to problematic or disastrous policy conclusions. An urgent task, we believe, is to deepen our conceptual scrutiny and to sort out the relationships of the various associated evaluative assumptions. It may be that some principles of fairness mandate achieving ecological sustainability. We will return to this point later.

In the same vein, it is usually thought that growth, progress, development, wealth, productivity, and more rather than fewer choices are all good things. However, what do we mean by such terms? By what standards are they to be deemed good? Are they always good, for everyone, or just sometimes good? And if they are good, do we succeed in measuring them properly? Is a higher employment rate always better? We could push it up by legalizing drugs (and thus recognizing the occupations of drug dealers). We judge the health of our national economy by calculating increases in the Gross National Product or the Net National Product. There are reasons to be deeply skeptical about the assumption that our collective (human) well-being increases with all positive changes in the GNP. The following essays elaborate this point. Philosophers have done a fair amount of work investigating the notion of the good of (individual) persons (the relation of happiness to health, to rational choice, and to enhanced autonomy, for example). What they (we) have paid less attention to is the material or economic criteria for judging the well-being of a society, community, or nation, especially when those criteria should be ecologically enlightened and not lead us to false assurances about long-term human, nonhuman, or planetary well-being.[4]

We briefly comment further on some of these fundamental notions. People frequently say that they are pro-growth, and since growth tends to be a term of positive valuation, we seldom hear people say that they are "anti-growth."[5] But who is in favor of the growth of cancer, rape, racism, slavery, or torture? Growth, as such, is not necessarily a good. What of the growth of an individual's wealth? How it is obtained would seem to be a relevant question. Has it occurred by enslavement, by kidnapping and ransom, by blackmail? Or, more to the point of environmental ethics, has it occurred by passing on the risk of radioactive emissions of plutonium to however many generations might live over the next 24,000 years, or by profits from a steel mill that caused the acidification of a lake, or by dumping wastes along a North Carolina road at 1:30 A.M.? Some wealth is obtained by morally and legally wrongful means, and much by means that are legal but in a manner that is ecologically subversive, e.g., a manner that is not ecologically sustainable. The burning of the rain forests in Brazil comes to mind; farmers there clear the land in this manner to farm on poor soil, but they generate erosion, flooding, loss of species of ancient lineage, and a diminishment of the planet's capacity to recycle carbon emissions. Just what sort of growth or development is morally acceptable? Is there a type that does not result in "stagnation" (however that term is to be defined) and that does not involve our species selling the planet down the intergalactic river—not to mention future generations of people and other living things?

It is worth observing that "growth" and "development" are not used only in a technical sense. In ordinary conversation, their meanings do not stand in sharp contrast to one another, but some writers wish to contrast growth and development. One can stipulate that the terms have clearly contrasting meanings, but we should be aware that this is a deviation from ordinary usage and that other writers may use the terms in a nontechnical way or stipulate their meanings in a different manner. The more important question concerns what kind of social improvements can be achieved when society lives in an ecologically sustainable way, regardless of how we linguistically mark the distinction. If we can achieve this, we might call it "development without growth."

Some sources are renewable indefinitely, e.g., the energy from the sun. Some are finite, e.g., fossil fuels (such as oil or coal), clean water, and clean air (we note that normative standards are involved in the determination of what is "clean"). Some sinks are finite; our landfills can take only so much discarded material. Many lakes are dying; children in parts of Poland are taken into caves for part of each day to allow them to breathe clean air. Obviously, what is finite cannot be consumed forever. Our use of fossil fuels at a rate that exceeds their replenishment cannot be sustained in the long run; once we spend all the "capital," there will be no "income" off of which to live—no matter how high the GNP soars in the meantime. At that point, we can only ask the high priests of infinite resources (e.g., Herman Kahn or Julian Simon) to pray for another technological fix. Occasionally we get fixes, but even they seem to be finite or they are not available when we need them. For example, a technological patching of the hole in the ozone layer does not appear to be imminent, although we may be getting improvement and the remedy is within the scope of human achievement.[6] It is doubtful that anyone factored in the resulting increase in incidences of skin cancer in the Southern hemisphere as a part of the production costs of certain chlorofluorocarbons. The atmosphere, indeed the skin of millions of humans and nonhumans, is being treated as an acceptable sink.

It is not obvious how best to characterize the ideal of sustainability or even to define sustainability. We might consider the following, however, as a useful initial working definition:

> A practice is ecologically sustainable if its indefinite continuation would not diminish the stock of natural and capital resources now available.

Let us call the above the rough definition of ecological sustainability, or RES. For the

RES to be useful, we need to clarify what counts as a capital stock and what counts as a natural resource. Buildings and human-made tools are usually counted as capital, but what about the current arsenals of nuclear weapons and the frightening stocks of nerve gas the United States and other nations possess?[7] If we count these as capital, we may not wish to advocate ecological sustainability as it is defined in the RES. We note here only a few considerations relevant to revising our definition. Should fetal cell tissue count as a natural resource, or as capital? Is this tissue instrumentally valuable in helping people with Parkinson's disease or Alzheimer's? How are we to regard human body parts (e.g., hearts, lungs, livers, corneas)? Reflection on this matter suggests that there may be hidden normative assumptions in judgments about what we count as part of usable stock. An easier problem, perhaps, is that we may not wish to construe nondiminishment literally; for example, given the advent of substitutable materials such as fiberglass, we would be foolish to insist on no diminishment of the amount of existing copper wire. But why should we accept ecological sustainability (sensibly formulated) as an ideal? The answer depends on whether we have duties to future generations of humans, nonhumans, and/or the nested ecosystems that constitute the biosphere. In particular, is it not a matter (at least in part) of fairness that we do not use up all, or disproportionate parts of, the available sources and sinks? The value of ecological sustainability is derived in part (or wholly) from a moral principle that requires fair sharing of the earth's resources with others, where "others" does not refer only to humans or to existing beings. A complete and satisfactory environmental ethic would clarify this issue.

Indeed, one may wish to refine the RES further. Perhaps a more useful characterization would be in terms of nondiminishment of the capacities for future generations to live in a manner that is not inferior to that of the average person today. Although this revision has attractions, which we will not list, the reader should find its difficulties quickly. Some of them may be surmountable.

It is clear that if we humans are to live in an ecologically sustainable manner, we are going to have to redesign many of our institutions and practices and to alter our ways of thinking at a fundamental level. We are going to have to figure out what constraints on our ways of living are appropriate. We may find, however, that our lives improve even if our incomes do not rise, for many of our unsustainable practices already impose heavy costs on many of us. Perhaps we should begin our reconsideration at an even more fundamental level—namely, thinking in terms of sustaining *whatever is of value*. This may include ways of life, traditions, cultures, and communities; as well as clean air, clean water, renewable energy, and a biodiverse planet. Ecological sustainability is, however, even more basic since it is the *precondition* of good living for any randomly chosen generation.

In the first essay that follows, William Ruckelshaus, former head of the U.S. Environmental Protection Agency, focuses on the difficulty of bringing about political change to achieve the goal of allowing growth and development to take place. He compares the magnitude of change he believes is necessary to that of the agricultural revolution of the late Neolithic period and the Industrial Revolution of the past two centuries. Ruckelshaus defends the use of market-based incentives, in part, and governmental modifications of the market to reflect environmental costs in order to move toward a sustainable way of living.

In the next essay, "A Declaration of Sustainability," Paul Hawken, cofounder of Smith and Hawken, outlines a number of fundamental steps he believes we must take as a society to start functioning in a manner that is ecologically sustainable. A good deal of his focus is on how we must transform the system of commerce in order to achieve this end. Thus he urges that "in order to approximate a sustainable society, we need to describe a system of commerce and production in which each and every act is inherently sustainable and restorative." Practically, how can a company with a conscience, one such as Ben and Jerry's Homemade, Inc., act in an ecologically responsible manner on a planet in which 5.5. billion people " . . . breeding exponentially and fulfilling their wants and needs is stripping the earth of its biotic capacity to produce life . . . "? Hawken calls for a reconceptualization of our system of production and consumption. We must stop lusting after muscle cars, transoceanic flights without number, and status-conferring objects that do not decompose or are costly to recycle. We need to categorize products into consumables, durables, and nonsalable ones. We need to redesign them especially for decomposition, a process in which the demise of one thing becomes food for another generation of living things. We might call this a new, secular doctrine of reincarnation.

Corporations, contrary to the advice of Nobel–prize winning economist Milton Friedman, do have obligations beyond maximizing the profits of their corporate share holders; this is at least the clear implication of Hawken's view. He notes that the charter which society has with corporations makes it a privilege for the corporation to operate; it is not merely a right. Society can revoke that charter. Hawken insists that some activities, particularly those that involve the extraction of raw materials, need to be run more like utility companies and in a manner that is ecologically sustainable in the long run. Thus Hawken is suggesting some fundamental changes in the way that commerce is allowed to occur and, no doubt, is recommending voluntary receptiveness toward these modes of operation by ecologically sensitive corporations.

Further, the actual marketplace frequently gives us wrong information, Hawken claims. We are led to believe that discount jet flights are cheap, but in fact the long-run ecological cost is high; existing market prices simply fail to reflect the cost being imposed on others, on ecosystems, on future generations, and so on. The market price of pesticide-grown food is often less than that of organically grown food, but in fact the former is ecologically more costly. Defenders of the marketplace typically rest heavy weight on the argument that the market, unlike command economies, provides the "right signals" about the true costs of production. This, however, seems to be true at best under highly restricted conditions. Arguably, faith in the free market, and the belief that we are getting ecologically informed signals in existing market prices, is only greasing the path to more and more frequent, irreversible ecological disasters. Rethinking these matters is going to take more than a weekend—or a semester. Changing will not be painless. It may already be too late. Those of us who try to be ecologically responsible are discovering that many of our habits are not as ecologically pure as we once thought. Maybe we need not aspire to giving up Ben and Jerry's ice cream (the good news), but what about jetting off on another eco-tour (the bad news) or the purchase of that hard-to-recycle cappuccino machine? Avoiding ostentatious consumption (itself a goal widely rejected during the 1980s) is not enough (questions of more personal choice and habit receive some discussion in Section V).

In another essay, Vandana Shiva, theoretical physicist and director of a foundation for science and ecology in India, analyzes and makes explicit certain value commitments underlying a number of concepts important in Western economic thought: namely, development, productivity, and especially the notion of *poverty*. According to Shiva, Western development in "third-world" countries " . . . destroys wholesome and sustainable lifestyles and creates real material poverty, or misery, by the denial of survival needs themselves through the diversion of resources to resource intensive commodity production."[8] The point is that many of the resources needed to produce cash crops for a market economy (e.g., the export of wood for furniture or houses) are resources that are already being used by third-world people for purposes of sustenance. As Shiva says, "The needs of the Amazonian tribes are more than satisfied by the rich rainforest; their poverty begins with its destruction."[9] Thus there is in these remarks a serious challenge to the assumption that such indigenous people are "poor," and a challenge to the assumption that Western measures of economic well-being (or any sort of well-being) should be employed without scrutiny (a scrutiny that they seldom receive). Culturally perceived poverty is one thing; real material deprivation and suffering is another. Many, not all, "*impoverished* lifestyles," by Western standards, are ecologically rich ones in the sense of being ecologically virtuous, sustainable ways of living.

Although men as well as women suffer from the devastation of their environment, women are more the losers because they, as the primary gatherers or producers of food, water, and fuel, have lost their livelihood; their knowledge and practices have been undermined. Moreover, unsurprisingly, they have virtually no access, and certainly less access than do men, to land ownership, technology, employment for wages, and small business loans should they have any desire to adopt a more Western lifestyle. The frustration over the loss of forests can be heard in the voice of Hima Devi, a member of the woman-led Chipko ("tree-hugging") movement, when she says to her audiences:

> My sisters are busy harvesting the
> Kharif crop. They are busy in winnowing.
> I have come to you with their message.
> Stop cutting trees. There are no trees even
> for birds to perch on. Birds flock to our
> crops and eat them. What will we eat?
> The firewood is disappearing; how will
> we cook?[10]

Shiva calls Western-style development "mal-development" because it results in *real* poverty (the denial of survival needs) while, ironically, trying to eliminate conditions perceived as poverty by "first-world" cultures. By describing subsistence economies as situations of poverty, those who favor market economies can present themselves as rescuing "third-world" countries from poverty. The point is reflected in one of Shiva's subtitles: "Development as a new project of Western patriarchy." In characterizing subsistence economies as "situations of poverty," Shiva says, pro-development forces mask the need to argue the case that market economies are, in fact, superior to subsistence economies. Indeed, the Western view tends to deny that subsistence economies count as economies at all. The work done for the sake of sustenance is not counted as "productive." And if the work done by many women in the Western world is not considered productive, or worth anything from an economic point of view, it is easy to see how woman-based subsistence economies can be viewed as falling into that quintessential hell of capitalism: being "non-productive." Economists may take issue with many of these claims; the more important question is the acceptability of what industrialized or less industrialized nations and businesses are doing in their economic dealings with less-developed nations (be wary of what evaluations are implied by "developed").

Further, in contemplating the sustainability of our own ways of living *we* may need to learn how to be "poor"—poor in the right way; if we were all poor in the right way, perhaps the world would be a better, more just, more biodiverse, more vital, more fulfilled place. We might wind up richer in the right way as well. In short, we need to fundamentally re-think what it is to live responsibly, and what is essential to personal success—perhaps doing what is right and what one loves, and not necessarily what gets attention, applause, social status, parental endorsement, corporate recognition, and so on. Cannot one live a good life—in every sense of the expression—in a manner that is also ecologically good?

NOTES

1. In last decade or so, there has been a considerable amount of philosophical discussion of questions about whether, and when, it is permissible to interfere with another person (especially an adult) for his or her own good, i.e., questions about when paternalistic intervention toward competent adults is defensible and, if so, under what conditions. On this topic, see Donald VanDeVeer, *Paternalistic Intervention* (Princeton: Princeton University Press, 1986); Joel Feinberg, *Harm to Self* (New York: Oxford University Press, 1986); John Kleinig, *Paternalism* (Totowa, NJ: Rowman and Allanheld, 1983).

2. One serious problem concerns why we should regard want-fulfillment as such as an intrinsic good and why we should therefore be tempted by "preference utilitarianism," which substitutes want-fulfillment for (the mental state of) pleasure in the formula of classic utilitarianism.

3. There is now a journal entitled *Ecological Economics*.

4. In the last decade or so, there has been more recognition of the inadequacy of standard economic measure of well-being, e.g., use of the gross national product. On these matters, see the excellent piece by Robert Repetto, "Earth in the Balance Sheet," in *The Environmental Ethics and Policy Book* ed. Donald VanDeVeer and Christine Pierce (Belmont, CA: Wadsworth Publishing Co., 1994), pp. 362–69.

5. Analogously, critics of the "pro-life" position try to imply by their chosen name that their opponents are "anti-life."

6. In this respect, the ozone problem may contrast with the irreversible losses involved in the massive extinction of species.

7. A somewhat macabre stumper at the next party would be to ask the name of the nation with the third-largest nuclear arsenal in the world as of late 1993. The less-than-well-known answer: the Ukraine.

8. Vandana Shiva, "Development, Ecology and Women," in *Staying Alive: Women, Ecology and Development* (London: Zed Books Ltd., 1988), p. 10.

9. Ibid., p. 12.

10. Ibid., pp. 74–75.

Toward a Sustainable World

William D. Ruckelshaus

The difficulty of converting scientific findings into political action is a function of the uncertainty of the science and the pain generated by the action. Given the current uncertainties surrounding just one aspect of the global environmental crisis—the predicted rise in greenhouse gases—and the enormous technological and social effort that will be required to control that rise, it is fair to say that responding successfully to the multifaceted crisis will be a difficult political enterprise. It means trying to get a substantial proportion of the world's people to change their behavior in order to (possibly) avert threats that will otherwise (probably) affect a world most of them will not be alive to see.

The models that predict climatic change, for example, are subject to varying interpretations as to the timing, distribution and severity of the changes in store. Also, whereas models may convince scientists, who understand their assumptions and limitations, as a rule projections make poor politics. It is hard for people—hard even for the groups of people who constitute governments—to change in response to dangers that may not arise for a long time or that just might not happen at all.

How, then, can we make change happen? . . . [P]revious articles . . . have documented the reality of the global ecological crisis and have pointed to some specific ameliorative measures. This article is about how to shape the policies, launch the programs and harness the resources that will lead to the adoption of such measures—and that will actually convince ordinary people throughout the world to start doing things differently.

Insurance is the way people ordinarily deal with potentially serious contingencies, and it is appropriate here as well. People consider it prudent to pay insurance premiums so that if catastrophe strikes, they or their survivors will be better off than if there had been no insurance. The analogy is clear. Current resources foregone or spent to prevent the buildup of greenhouse gases are a kind of premium. Moreover, as long as we are going to pay premiums, we might as well pay them in ways that will yield dividends in the form of greater efficiency, improved human health or more widely distributed prosperity. If we turn out to be wrong on greenhouse warming or ozone depletion, we still retain the dividend benefits. In any case, no one complains to the insurance company when disaster does not strike.

That is the argument for some immediate, modest actions. We can hope that if shortages or problems arise, there will turn out to be a technological fix or set of fixes, or that technology and the normal workings of the market will combine to solve the problem by product substitution. Already, for example, new refrigerants that do not have the atmospheric effects of the chlorofluorocarbons are being introduced; perhaps a cheap and nonpolluting source of energy will be discovered.

It is comforting to imagine that we might arrive at a more secure tomorrow with little strain, to suppose with Dickens's Mr. Micawber that something will turn up. Imagining is harmless, but counting on such a rescue is not. We need to face up to the fact that something enormous may be happening to our world. Our species may be pushing up against some immovable limits on the combustion of fossil fuels and damage to ecosystems. We must at least consider the possibility that, besides those modest adjustments for the sake of prudence, we may have to prepare for far more dramatic changes, changes that will begin to shape a sustainable world economy and society.

Sustainability is the nascent doctrine that economic growth and development must take place, and be maintained over time, within the limits set by ecology in the broadest sense—by the interrelations of human beings and their works, the biosphere and the physical and chemical laws that govern it. . . . The doctrine of sustainability holds too that the spread of a reasonable level of prosperity and security to the less developed nations is essential to protecting ecological balance and hence essential to the continued prosperity of the wealthy nations. It follows that environmental protection and economic development are complementary rather than antagonistic processes.

Can we move nations and people in the direction of sustainability? Such a move would be a modification of society comparable in scale to only two other changes: the agricultural revolution of the late Neolithic and the Industrial Revolution of the past two centuries. Those revolutions were gradual, spontaneous and largely unconscious. This one will have to be a fully conscious operation, guided by the best foresight that science can provide—foresight pushed to its limit. If we actually do it, the undertaking will be absolutely unique in humanity's stay on the earth.

The shape of this undertaking cannot be clearly seen from where we now stand. The conventional image is that of a crossroads: a forced choice of one direction or another that determines the future for some appreciable period. But this does not at all capture the complexity of the current situation. A more appropriate image would be that of a canoeist shooting the rapids: survival depends on continually responding to information by correct steering. In this case the information is supplied by science and economic events; the steering is the work of policy, both governmental and private.

Taking control of the future therefore means tightening the connection between science and policy. We need to understand where the rocks are in time to steer around them. Yet we will not devote the appropriate level of resources to science or accept the policies mandated by science unless we do something else. We have to understand that we are all in the same canoe and that steering toward sustainability is necessary.

Sustainability was the original economy of our species. Preindustrial peoples lived sustainably because they had to; if they did not, if they expanded their populations beyond the available resource base, then sooner or later they starved or had to migrate. The sustainability of their way of life was maintained by a particular consciousness regarding nature: the people were spiritually connected to the animals and plants on which they subsisted; they were part of the landscape, or of nature, not set apart as masters.

The era of this "original sustainability" eventually came to an end. The development of cities and the maintenance of urban populations called for intensive agriculture yielding a surplus. As a population grows, it requires an expansion of production, either by conquest or colonization or improved technique. A different consciousness, also embodied in a structure of myth, sustains this mode of life. The earth and its creatures are considered the property of humankind, a gift from the supernatural. Man stands outside of nature, which is a passive playing field that he dominates, controls and manipulates. Eventually, with industrialization, even the past is colonized: the forests of the Carboniferous are mined to support ever-expanding populations. Advanced technology gives impetus to the basic assumption that there is essentially no limit to humanity's power over nature.

This consciousness, this condition of "transitional unsustainability," is dominant today. It has two forms. In the underdeveloped, industrializing world, it is represented by the drive to develop at any environmental cost. It includes the wholesale destruction of forests, the replacement of sustainable agriculture by cash crops, the attendant exploitation of vulnerable lands by people such cash cropping forces off good land and the creation of industrial centers that are also centers of environmental pollution.

In the industrialized world, unsustainable development has generated wealth and relative comfort for about one fifth of humankind, and among the populations of the industrialized nations the consciousness supporting the unsustainable economy is nearly universal. With a few important exceptions, the environmental-protection movement in those nations, despite its major achievements in passing legislation and mandating pollution-control measures, has not had a substantial effect on the lives of most people. Environmentalism has been ameliorative and corrective—not a restructuring force. It is encompassed within the consciousness of unsustainability.

Although we cannot return to the sustainable economy of our distant ancestors, in principle there is no reason why we cannot create a sustainability consciousness suitable to the modern era. Such a consciousness would include the following beliefs:

1. *The human species is part of nature. Its existence depends on its ability to draw sustenance from a finite natural world; its continuance depends on its ability to abstain from destroying the natural systems that regenerate this world.* This seems to be the major lesson of the current environmental situation as well as being a direct corollary of the second law of thermodynamics.

2. *Economic activity must account for the environmental costs of production.* Environmental regulation has made a start here, albeit a small one. The market has not even begun to be mobilized to preserve the environment; as a consequence an increasing amount of the "wealth" we create is in a sense stolen from our descendants.

3. *The maintenance of a livable global environment depends on the sustainable development of the entire human family.* If 80 percent of the members of our species are poor, we can not hope to live in a world at peace; if the poor nations attempt to improve their lot by the methods we rich have pioneered, the result will eventually be world ecological damage.

This consciousness will not be attained simply because the arguments for change are good or because the alternatives are unpleasant. Nor will exhortation suffice. The central lesson of realistic policy-making is that most individuals and organizations change when it is in their interest to change, either because they derive some benefit from changing or because they incur sanctions when they do not—and the shorter the time between change (or failure to change) and benefit (or sanction), the better. This is not mere cynicism. Although people will struggle and suffer for long periods to achieve a goal, it is not reasonable to expect people or organizations to work against their immediate interests for very long—particularly in a democratic system, where what they perceive to be their interests are so important in guiding the government.

To change interests, three things are required. First, a clear set of values consistent with the consciousness of sustainability must be articulated by leaders in both the public and the private sector. Next, motivations need to be established that will support the values. Finally, institutions must be developed that will effectively apply the motivations. The first is relatively easy, the second much harder and the third perhaps hardest of all.

Values similar to those I described above have indeed been articulated by political leaders throughout the world. In the past year the president and the secretary of state of the U.S., the leader of the Soviet Union, the prime minister of Great Britain and the presidents of France and Brazil have all made major environmental statements. In July the leaders of the Group of Seven major industrialized nations called for "the early adoption, worldwide, of policies based on sustainable development." Most industrialized nations have a structure of national environmental law that to at least some extent reflects such values, and there is even a small set of international conventions that begin to do the same thing.

Mere acceptance of a changed value structure, although it is a prerequisite, does not generate the required change in consciousness, nor does it change the environment. Although diplomats and lawyers may argue passionately over the form of words, talk is not action. In the U.S., which has a set of environmental statutes second to none in their stringency, and where for the past 15 years poll after poll has recorded the American people's desire for increased environmental protection, . . . the majority of the population participates in the industrialized world's most wasteful and most polluting style of life. The values are there; the appropriate motivations and institutions are patently inadequate or nonexistent.

The difficulties of moving from stated values to actual motivations and institutions stem from basic characteristics of the major industrialized nations—the nations that must, because of their economic strength, preeminence as polluters and dominant share of the world's resources, take the lead in any changing of the present order. These nations are market-system democracies. The difficulties, ironically, are inherent in the free-market economic system on the one hand and in democracy on the other.

The economic problem is the familiar one of externalities: the environmental cost of producing a good or service is not accounted for in the price paid for it. As the economist Kenneth E. Boulding has put it: "All of nature's systems are closed loops, while economic activities are linear and assume inexhaustible resources and 'sinks' in which to throw away our refuse." In willful ignorance, and in violation of the core principle of capitalism, we often refuse to treat environmental resources as capital. We spend them as income and are as befuddled as any profligate heir when our checks start to bounce.

Such "commons" as the atmosphere, the seas, fisheries and goods in public ownership are particularly vulnerable to being overspent in this way, treated as either inexhaustible resources or bottomless sinks. The reason is that the incremental benefit to each user accrues exclusively to that user, and in the short term it is a gain. The environmental degradation is spread out among all users and is apparent only in the long term, when the resource shows signs of severe stress or collapse. Some years ago the biologist Garrett Hardin called this the tragedy of the commons.

The way to avoid the tragedy of the commons—to make people pay the full cost of a resource use—is to close the loops in economic systems. The general failure to do this in the industrialized world is related to the second problem, the problem of action in a democracy. Modifying the market to reflect environmental costs is necessarily a function of government. Those adversely affected by such modifications, although they may be a tiny minority of the population, often have disproportionate influence on public policy. In general, the much injured minority proves to be a more formidable lobbyist than the slightly benefited majority.

The Clean Air Act of 1970 in the U.S., arguably the most expensive and far-reaching environmental legislation in the world, is a case in point. Parts of the act were designed not so much to cleanse the air as to protect the jobs of coal miners in high-sulfur coal regions. Utilities and other high-volume consumers were not allowed to substitute low-sulfur coal to meet regulatory requirements but instead had to install scrubbing devices.

Although the act expired seven years ago, Congress found it extraordinarily difficult to develop a revision, largely because of another set of contrary interests involving acid rain. The generalized national interest in reducing the environmental damage attributable to this long-range pollution had to overcome the resistance of both high-sulfur-coal mining interests and the Midwestern utilities that would incur major expenses if they were forced to control sulfur emissions. The problem of conflicting interests is exacerbated by the distance between major sources of acid rain and the regions that suffer the most damage. . . . It is accentuated when the pollution crosses state and national boundaries: elected representatives are less likely to countenance short-term adverse effects on their constituents when the immediate beneficiaries are nonconstituents.

The question, then, is whether the industrial democracies will be able to overcome political constraints on bending the market system toward long-term sustainability. History provides some cause for optimism: a number of contingencies have led nations to accept short-term burdens in order to meet a long-term goal.

War is the obvious example. Things considered politically or economically impossible can be accomplished in a remarkably short time, given the belief that national survival is at stake. World War II mobilized the U.S. population, changed work patterns, manipulated and controlled the price and supply of goods and reorganized the nation's industrial plant.

Another example is the Marshall Plan for reconstructing Europe after World War II. In 1947 the U.S. spent nearly 3 percent of its gross domestic product on this huge set of projects. Although the impetus for the plan came from fear that Soviet influence would expand into Western Europe, the plan did establish a precedent for massive investment in increasing the prosperity of foreign nations.

There are other examples. Feudalism was abandoned in Japan, as was slavery in the U.S., in the 19th century; this century has seen the retreat of imperialism and the creation of the European Economic Community. In each case important interests gave way to new national goals.

If it is possible to change, how do we begin to motivate change? Clearly, government policy must lead the way, since market prices of commodities typically do not reflect the environmental costs of extracting and replacing them, nor do the prices of energy from fossil fuels reflect the risks of climatic change. Pricing policy is the most direct means of ensuring that the full environmental cost of goods and services is accounted for. When government owns a resource, or supplies it directly, the price charged can be made to reflect the true cost of the product. The market will adjust to this as it does to true scarcity: by product substitution . . . and conservation.

Environmental regulation should be refocused to mobilize rather than suppress the ingenuity and creativity of industry. For example, additional gains in pollution control should be sought not simply by increasing the stringency or technical specificity of command-and-control regulation but also by implementing incentive-based systems. Such systems magnify public-sector decisions by tens of thousands of individual and corporate decisions. To be sure, incentive systems are not a panacea. For some environmental problems, such as the use of unacceptably dangerous chemicals, definitive regulatory measures will always be required. Effective policies will include a mixture of incentive-based and regulatory approaches.

Yet market-based approaches will be a necessary part of any attempt to reduce the greenhouse effect. Here the most attractive options involve the encouragement of energy efficiency. Improving efficiency meets the double-benefit standard of insurance: it is good in itself, and it combats global warming by reducing carbon dioxide emissions. If the world were to improve energy efficiency by 2 percent a year, the global average temperature could be kept within one degree Celsius of present levels. Many industrialized nations have maintained a rate of improvement close to that over the past 15 years.

Promoting energy efficiency is also relatively painless. The U.S. reduced the energy intensity of its domestic product by 23 percent between 1973 and 1985 without much notice. Substantial improvement in efficiency is available even with existing technology. Something as simple as bringing all U.S. buildings up to the best world standards could save enormous amounts of energy. Right now more energy passes through the windows of buildings in the U.S. than flows through the Alaska pipeline.

Efficiency gains may nevertheless have to be promoted by special market incentives, because energy prices tend to lag behind increases in income. A "climate protection" tax of $1 per million Btu's on coal and 60 cents per million Btu's on oil is an example of such an incentive. It would raise gasoline prices by 11 cents a gallon and the cost of electricity an average of 10 percent, and it would yield $53 billion annually.

Direct regulation by the setting of standards is cumbersome, but it may be necessary when implicit market signals are not effective. Examples are the mileage standards set in the U.S. for automobiles and the efficiency standards for appliances that were adopted in 1986. The appliance standards will save $28 billion in energy costs by the year 2000 and keep 342 million tons of carbon out of the atmosphere.

Over the long term it is likely that some form of emissions-trading program will be necessary—and on a much larger scale than has been the case heretofore. (Indeed, the President's new Clean Air Act proposal includes a strengthened system of tradeable permits.) In such a program all major emitters of pollutants would be issued permits specifying an allowable emission level. Firms that decide to reduce emissions below the specified level—for example, by investing in efficiency—could sell their excess "pollution rights" to other firms. Those that find it prohibitively costly to retrofit old plants or build new ones could buy such rights or could close down their least efficient plants and sell the unneeded rights.

Another kind of emissions trading might reduce the impact of carbon dioxide emissions. . . . Companies responsible for new greenhouse-gas emissions could be required to offset them by improving overall efficiency or closing down plants, or by planting or preserving forests that would help absorb the emissions. Once the system is established, progress toward further reduction of emissions would be achieved by progressively cranking down the total allowable levels of various pollutants, on both a national and a permit-by-permit basis.

The kinds of programs I have just described will need to be supported by research providing a scientific basis for new environmental-protection strategies. Research into safe, nonpolluting energy sources and more energy-efficient technologies would seem to be particularly good bets. An example: in the mid-1970's the U.S. Department of Energy developed a number of improved-efficiency technologies at a cost of $16 million; among them were a design for compact fluorescent lamps that could replace incandescent bulbs, and window coatings that save energy during both heating and cooling seasons. At current rates of implementation, the new technologies should generate $63 billion in energy savings by the year 2010.

The motivation of change toward sustainability will have to go far beyond the reduction of pol-

lution and waste in the developed countries, and it cannot be left entirely to the environmental agencies in those countries. The agencies whose goals are economic development, exploitation of resources and international trade—and indeed foreign policy in general—must also adopt sustainable development as a central goal. This is a formidable challenge, for it touches the heart of numerous special interests. Considerable political skill will be required to achieve for environmental protection the policy preeminence that only economic issues and national security (in the military sense) have commanded.

But it is in relations with the developing world that the industrialized nations will face their greatest challenge. . . . Aid is both an answer and a perpetual problem. Total official development assistance from the developed to the developing world stands at around $35 billion a year. This is not much money. The annual foreign-aid expenditure of the U.S. alone would be $127 billion if it spent the same proportion of its gross national product on foreign aid as it did during the peak years of the Marshall Plan.

There is no point, of course, in even thinking about the adequacy of aid to the undeveloped nations until the debt issue is resolved. The World Bank has reported that in 1988 the 17 most indebted countries paid the industrialized nations and multilateral agencies $31.1 billion more than they received in aid. This obviously cannot go on. Debt-for-nature swapping has taken place between such major lenders as Citicorp and a number of countries in South America: the bank forgives loans in exchange for the placing of land in conservation areas or parks. This is admirable, but it will not in itself solve the problem. Basic international trading relations will have to be redesigned in order to eliminate, among other things, the ill effects on the undeveloped world of agricultural subsidies and tariff barriers in the industrialized world.

A prosperous rural society based on sustainable agriculture must be the prelude to future development in much of the developing world, and government there will have to focus on what motivates people to live in an environmentally responsible manner. Farmers will not grow crops when governments subsidize urban populations by keeping prices to farmers low. People will not stop having too many children if the labor of children is the only economic asset they have. Farmers will not improve the land if they do not own it; it is clear that land-tenure reform will have to be instituted.

Negative sanctions against abusing the environment are also missing throughout much of the undeveloped world; to help remedy this situation, substantial amounts of foreign aid could be focused directly on improving the status of the environmental ministries in developing nations. These ministries are typically impoverished and ineffective, particularly in comparison with their countries' economic-development and military ministries. To cite one small example: the game wardens of Tanzania receive an annual salary equivalent to the price paid to poachers for two elephant tusks—one reason the nation has lost two thirds of its elephant population to the ivory trade in the past decade.

To articulate the values and devise the motivations favoring a sustainable world economy, existing institutions will need to change and new ones will have to be established. These will be difficult tasks, because institutions are powerful to the extent that they support powerful interests—which usually implies support of the status quo.

The important international institutions in today's world are those concerned with money, with trade and with national defense. Those who despair of environmental concerns ever reaching a comparable level of importance should remember that current institutions (for example, NATO, the World Bank, multinational corporations) have fairly short histories. They were formed out of pressing concerns about acquiring and expanding wealth and maintaining national sovereignty. If concern for the environment becomes comparably pressing, comparable institutions will be developed.

To further this goal, three things are wanted. The first is money. The annual budget of the United Nations Environment Program (UNEP) is $30 million, a derisory amount considering its responsibili-

ties. If nations are serious about sustainability, they will provide this central environmental organization with serious money, preferably money derived from an independent source in order to reduce its political vulnerability. A tax on certain uses of common world resources has been suggested as a means to this end.

The second thing wanted is information. We require strong international institutions to collect, analyze and report on environmental trends and risks. The Earthwatch program run by the UNEP is a beginning, but there is need for an authoritative source of scientific information and advice that is independent of national governments. There are many non-governmental or quasi-governmental organizations capable of filling this role; they need to be pulled together into a cooperative network. We need a global institution capable of answering questions of global importance.

The third thing wanted is integration of effort. The world cannot afford a multiplication of conflicting efforts to solve common problems. On the aid front in particular, this can be tragically absurd: Africa alone is currently served by 82 international donors and more than 1,700 private organizations. In 1980, in the tiny African nation Burkina Faso (population about eight million) 340 independent aid projects were under way. We need to form and strengthen coordinating institutions that combine the separate strengths of nongovernmental organizations, international bodies and industrial groups and to focus their efforts on specific problems.

Finally, in creating the consciousness of advanced sustainability, we shall have to redefine our concepts of political and economic feasibility. These concepts are, after all, simply human constructs; they were different in the past, and they will surely change in the future. But the earth is real, and we are obliged by the fact of our utter dependence on it to listen more closely than we have to its messages.

EDITOR'S NOTE: Ruckelshaus acknowledges the major contribution of Michael A. Gruber, a senior policy analyst at the E.P.A., in the preparation of this essay.

A Declaration of Sustainability

Paul Hawken

I recently performed a social audit for Ben and Jerry's Homemade Inc., America's premier socially responsible company. After poking and prodding around, asking tough questions, trying to provoke debate and generally making a nuisance of myself, I can attest that their status as the leading social pioneer in commerce is safe for at least another year. They are an outstanding company. Are there flaws? Of course. Welcome to planet Earth. But the people at Ben & Jerry's are relaxed and unflinching in their willingness to look at, discuss, and deal with problems.

In the meantime, the company continues to put ice cream shops in Harlem, pay outstanding benefits, keep a compensation ratio of seven to one from the top of the organization to the bottom, seek out vendors from disadvantaged groups, and donate generous scoops of their profits to others. And they are about to overtake their historic rival Häagen-Dazs, the ersatz Scandinavian originator of super-premium ice cream, as the market leader in their category. At present rates of growth, Ben & Jerry's will be a $1 billion company by the end of the century. They are publicly held, nationally recognized, and rapidly growing, in part because Ben wanted to show that a socially responsible company could make it in the normal world of business.

Ben and Jerry's is just one of a growing vanguard of companies attempting to redefine their social and ethical responsibilities. These companies no longer accept the maxim that the business of business is business. Their premise is simple: Corporations, because they are the dominant institution on the planet, must squarely face the social and environmental problems that afflict humankind. Organizations such as Business for Social Responsibility and the Social Venture Network, corporate "ethics" consultants, magazines such as *In Business* and *Business Ethics*, non-profits including the Council on Economic Priorities, investment funds such as Calvert and Covenant, newsletters like *Greenmoney*, and thousands of unaffiliated companies are drawing up new codes of conduct for corporate life that integrate social, ethical, and environmental principles.

Ben and Jerry's and the roughly 2,000 other committed companies in the social responsibility movement here and abroad have combined annual sales of approximately $2 billion, or one-hundredth of 1 percent of the $20 trillion sales garnered by the estimated 80 million to 100 million enterprises worldwide. The problems they are trying to address are vast and unremittingly complex: 5.5 billion people are breeding exponentially, and fulfilling their wants and needs is stripping the earth of its biotic capacity to produce life; a climactic burst of consumption by a single species is overwhelming the skies, earth, waters, and fauna.

As the Worldwatch Institute's Lester Brown patiently explains in his annual survey, *State of the World*, every living system on earth is in decline. Making matters worse, we are having a once-in-a-billion-year blowout sale of hydrocarbons, which are being combusted into the atmosphere, effectively double glazing the planet within the next 50 years with unknown climatic results. The cornucopia of resources that are being extracted, mined, and harvested is so poorly distributed that 20 percent of the earth's people are chronically hungry or starving, while the top 20 percent of the population, largely in the north, control and consume 80 percent of the world's wealth. Since business in its myriad forms is primarily responsible for this "taking," it is appropriate that a growing number of companies ask the question, How does one honorably conduct business in the latter days of industrialism and the beginning of an ecological age? The ethical dilemma that confronts business begins with the acknowledgment that a commercial system that functions well by its own definitions unavoidably defies the greater and more profound ethic of biology. Specifically, how does business face the prospect that creating a profitable, growing company requires an intolerable abuse of the natural world?

Despite their dedicated good work, if we examine all or any of the businesses that deservedly earn high marks for social and environmental responsibility, we are faced with a sobering irony: If

Utne Reader, September/October 1993, pp. 54–61. Reprinted by permission of the author.

every company on the planet were to adopt the environmental and social practices of the best companies—of, say, the Body Shop, Patagonia, and Ben and Jerry's—the world would still be moving toward environmental degradation and collapse. In other words, if we analyze environmental effects and create an input-output model of resources and energy, the results do not even approximate a tolerable or sustainable future. If a tiny fraction of the world's most intelligent companies cannot model a sustainable world, then that tells us that being socially responsible is only one part of an overall solution, and that what we have is not a management problem but a design problem.

At present, there is a contradiction inherent in the premise of a socially responsible corporation: to wit, that a company can make the world better, can grow, and can increase profits by meeting social and environmental needs. It is a have-your-cake-and-eat-it fantasy that cannot come true if the primary cause of environmental degradation is overconsumption. Although proponents of socially responsible business are making an outstanding effort at reforming the tired old ethics of commerce, they are unintentionally creating a new rationale for companies to produce, advertise, expand, grow, capitalize, and use up resources: the rationale that they are doing good. A jet flying across the country, a car rented at an airport, an air-conditioned hotel room, a truck full of goods, a worker commuting to his or her job—all cause the same amount of environmental degradation whether they're associated with the Body Shop, the Environmental Defense Fund, or R. J. Reynolds.

In order to approximate a sustainable society, we need to describe a system of commerce and production in which each and every act is inherently sustainable and restorative. Because of the way our system of commerce is designed, businesses will not be able to fulfill their social contract with the environment or society until the system in which they operate undergoes a fundamental change, a change that brings commerce and governance into alignment with the natural world from which we receive our life. There must be an integration of economic, biologic, and human systems in order to create a sustainable and interdependent method of commerce that supports and furthers our existence. As hard as we may strive to create sustainability on

a company level, we cannot fully succeed until the institutions surrounding commerce are redesigned. Just as every act of production and consumption in an industrial society leads to further environmental degradation, regardless of intention or ethos, we need to imagine—and then design—a system of commerce where the opposite is true, where doing good is like falling off a log, where the natural, everyday acts of work and life accumulate into a better world as a matter of course, not a matter of altruism. A system of sustainable commerce would involve these objectives:

1. It would reduce absolute consumption of energy and natural resources among developed nations by 80 percent within 40 to 60 years.

2. It would provide secure, stable, and meaningful employment for people everywhere.

3. It would be self-actuating as opposed to regulated, controlled, mandated, or moralistic.

4. It would honor human nature and market principles.

5. It would be perceived as more desirable than our present way of life.

6. It would exceed sustainability by restoring degraded habitats and ecosystems to their fullest biological capacity.

7. It would rely on current solar income.

8. It should be fun and engaging, and strive for an aesthetic outcome.

Strategies for Sustainability

At present, the environmental and social responsibility movements consist of many different initiatives connected primarily by values and beliefs rather than by design. What is needed is a conscious plan to create a sustainable future, including a set of design strategies for people to follow. For the record, I will suggest 12.

1. Take back the charter.

Although corporate charters may seem to have little to do with sustainability, they are critical to any long-term movement toward restoration of the planet. Read *Taking Care of Business; Citizenship and the Charter of Incorporation*, a 1992 pamphlet by Richard Grossman and Frank T. Adams (Charter

Ink, Box 806, Cambridge, MA 02140). In it you find a lost history of corporate power and citizen involvement that addresses a basic and crucial point: Corporations are chartered by, and exist at the behest of, citizens. Incorporation is not a right but a privilege granted by the state that includes certain considerations such as limited liability. Corporations are supposed to be under our ultimate authority, not the other way around. The charter of incorporation is a revocable dispensation that was supposed to ensure accountability of the corporation to society as a whole. When Rockwell criminally despoils a weapons facility at Rocky Flats, Colorado, with plutonium waste, or when any corporation continually harms, abuses, or violates the public trust, citizens should have the right to revoke its charter, causing the company to disband, sell off its enterprises to other companies, and effectively go out of business. The workers would have jobs with the new owners, but the executives, directors, and management would be out of jobs, with a permanent notice on their résumés that they mismanaged a corporation into a charter revocation. This is not merely a deterrent to corporate abuse but a critical element of an ecological society because it creates feedback loops that prompt accountability, citizen involvement, and learning. We should remember that the citizens of this country originally envisioned corporations to be part of a public-private partnership, which is why the relationship between the chartering authority of state legislatures and the corporation was kept alive and active. They had it right.

2. Adjust price to reflect cost.

The economy is environmentally and commercially dysfunctional because the market does not provide consumers with proper information. The "free market" economies that we love so much are excellent at setting prices but lousy when it comes to recognizing costs. In order for a sustainable society to exist, every purchase must reflect or at least approximate its actual cost, not only the direct cost of production but also the costs to the air, water, and soil; the cost to future generations; the cost to worker health; the cost of waste, pollution, and toxicity. Simply stated, the marketplace gives us the wrong information. It tells us that flying across the country on a discount airline ticket is cheap when it is not. It tells us that our food is inexpensive when

its method of production destroys aquifers and soil, the viability of ecosystems, and workers' lives. Whenever an organism gets wrong information, it is a form of toxicity. In fact, that is how pesticides work. A herbicide kills because it is a hormone that tells the plant to grow faster than its capacity to absorb nutrients allows. It literally grows itself to death. Sound familiar? Our daily doses of toxicity are the prices in the marketplace. They are telling us to do the wrong thing for our own survival. They are lulling us into cutting down old growth forests on the Olympic Peninsula for apple crates, into patterns of production and consumption that are not just unsustainable but profoundly short-sighted and destructive. It is surprising that "conservative" economists do not support or understand this idea, because it is they who insist that we pay as we go, have no debts, and take care of business. Let's do it.

3. Throw out and replace the entire tax system.

The present tax system sends the wrong messages to virtually everyone, encourages waste, discourages conservation, and rewards consumption. It taxes what we want to encourage—jobs, creativity, payrolls, and real income—and ignores the things we want to discourage—degradation, pollution, and depletion. The present U.S. tax system costs citizens $500 billion a year in record-keeping, filing, administrative, legal, and governmental costs—more than the actual amount we pay in personal income taxes. The only incentive in the present system is to cheat or hire a lawyer to cheat for us. The entire tax system must be incrementally replaced over a 20-year period by "Green fees," taxes that are added onto existing products, energy, services, and materials so that prices in the marketplace more closely approximate true costs. These taxes are not a means to raise revenue or bring down deficits, but must be absolutely revenue neutral so that people in the lower and middle classes experience no real change of income, only a shift in expenditures. Eventually, the cost of non-renewable resources, extractive energy, and industrial modes of production will be more expensive than renewable resources, such as solar energy, sustainable forestry, and biological methods of agriculture. Why should the upper middle class be able to afford to conserve while the lower income classes cannot? So far the environmental movement has only made the world better for upper middle class white people. The only kind of environmental movement that can succeed has to start from the bottom up. Under a Green fee system the incentives to save on taxes will create positive, constructive acts that are affordable for everyone. As energy prices go up to three to four times their existing levels (with commensurate tax reductions to offset the increase), the natural inclination to save money will result in carpooling, bicycling, telecommuting, public transport, and more efficient houses. As taxes on artificial fertilizers, pesticides, and fuel go up, again with offsetting reductions in income and payroll taxes, organic farmers will find that their produce and methods are the cheapest means of production (because they truly are), and customers will find that organically grown food is less expensive than its commercial cousin. Eventually, with the probable exception of taxes on the rich, we will find ourselves in a position where we pay no taxes, but spend our money with a practiced and constructive discernment. Under an enlightened and redesigned tax system, the cheapest product in the marketplace would be best for the customer, the worker, the environment, and the company. That is rarely the case today.

4. Allow resource companies to be utilities.

An energy utility is an interesting hybrid of public-private interests. A utility gains a market monopoly in exchange for public control of rates, open books, and a guaranteed rate of return. Because of this relationship and the pioneering work of Amory Lovins, we now have markets for "negawatts." It is the first time in the history of industrialism that a corporation has figured out how to make money by selling the absence of something. Negawatts are the opposite of energy: They represent the collaborative ability of a utility to harness efficiency instead of hydrocarbons. This conservation-based alternative saves ratepayers, shareholders, and the company money—savings that are passed along to everyone. All resource systems, including oil, gas, forests, and water, should be run by some form of utility. There should be markets in negabarrels, negatrees, and negacoal. Oil companies, for example, have no alternative at present other than to lobby for the absurd, like drilling in the Arctic National Wildlife Refuge. That

project, a $40 billion to $60 billion investment for a hoped-for supply of oil that would meet U.S. consumption for only six months, is the only way an oil company can make money under our current system of commerce. But what if the oil companies formed an oil utility and cut a deal with citizens and taxpayers that allowed them to "invest" in insulation, super-glazed windows, conservation rebates on new automobiles, and the scrapping of old cars? Through Green fees, we would pay them back a return on their conservation investment equal to what utilities receive, a rate of return that would be in accord with how many barrels of oil they save, rather than how many barrels they produce. Why should they care? Why should we? A $60 billion investment in conservation will yield, conservatively, four to ten times as much energy as drilling for oil. Given Lovins' principle of efficiency extraction, try to imagine a forest utility, a salmon utility, a copper utility, a Mississippi River utility, a grasslands utility. Imagine a system where the resource utility benefits from conservation, makes money from efficiency, thrives through restoration, and profits from sustainability. It is possible today.

5. Change linear systems to cyclical ones.

Our economy has many design flaws, but the most glaring one is that nature is cyclical and industrialism is linear. In nature, no linear systems exist, or they don't exist for long because they exhaust themselves into extinction. Linear industrial systems take resources, transform them into products or services, discard waste, and sell to consumers, who discard more waste when they have consumed the product. But of course we don't consume TVs, cars, or most of the other stuff we buy. Instead, Americans produce six times their body weight every week in hazardous and toxic waste water, incinerator fly ash, agricultural wastes, heavy metals, and waste chemicals, paper, wood, etc. This does not include CO_2, which if it were included would double the amount of waste. Cyclical means of production are designed to imitate natural systems in which waste equals food for other forms of life, nothing is thrown away, and symbiosis replaces competition. Bill McDonough, a New York architect who has pioneered environmental design principles, has designed a system to retrofit every window in a major American city. Although it still awaits final approval, the project is planned to go like this: The city and a major window manufacturer form a joint venture to produce energy-saving super-glazed windows in the town. This partnership company will come to your house or business, measure all windows and glass doors, and then replace them with windows with an R-8 to R-12 energy-efficiency rating within 72 hours. The windows will have the same casements, molding, and general appearance as the old ones. You will receive a $500 check upon installation, and you will pay for the new windows over a 10- to 15-year period in your utility or tax bill. The total bill is less than the cost of the energy the windows will save. In other words, the windows will cost the home or business owner nothing. The city will pay for them initially with industrial development bonds. The factory will train and employ 300 disadvantaged people. The old windows will be completely recycled and reused, the glass melted into glass, the wooden frames ground up and mixed with recycled resins that are extruded to make the casements. When the city is reglazed, the residents and businesses will pocket an extra $20 million to $30 million every year in money saved on utility bills. After the windows are paid for, the figure will go even higher. The factory, designed to be transportable, will move to another city; the first city will retain an equity interest in the venture. McDonough has designed a win-win-win-win-win system that optimizes a number of agendas. The ratepayers, the homeowners, the renters, the city, the environment, and the employed all thrive because they are "making" money from efficiency rather than exploitation. It's a little like running the industrial economy backwards.

6. Transform the making of things.

We have to institute the Intelligent Product System created by Michael Braungart of the EPEA (Environmental Protection Encouragement Agency) in Hamburg, Germany. The system recognizes three types of products. The first are *consumables*, products that are either eaten, or, when they're placed on the ground, turn into dirt without any bio-accumulative effects. In other words, they are products whose waste equals food for other living systems. At present, many of the products that should be "consumable," like clothing and shoes are not. Cotton cloth contains hundreds of different chemicals, plasticizers, defoliants, pesticides, and dyes; shoes are tanned with chromium and their soles contain lead; neckties and silk blouses contain zinc, tin, and toxic dye. Much of what we recycle today turns into toxic by-products, consuming more energy in the recycling process than is saved by recycling. We should be designing more things so that they can be thrown away—into the compost heap. Toothpaste tubes and other non-degradable packaging can be made out of natural polymers so that they break down and become fertilizer for plants. A package that turns into dirt is infinitely more useful, biologically speaking, than a package that turns into a plastic park bench. Heretical as it sounds, designing for decomposition, not recycling, is the way of the world around us.

The second category is *durables,* but in this case, they would not be sold, only licensed. Cars, TVs, VCRs, and refrigerators would always belong to the original manufacturer, so they would be made, used, and returned within a closed-loop system. This is already being instituted in Germany and to a lesser extent in Japan, where companies are beginning to design for disassembly. If a company knows that its products will come back someday, and that it cannot throw anything away when they do, it creates a very different approach to design and materials.

Last, there are *unsalables*—toxins, radiation, heavy metals, and chemicals. There is no living system for which these are food and thus they can never be thrown away. In Braungart's Intelligent Product System, unsalables must always belong to the original maker, safeguarded by public utilities called "parking lots" that store the toxins in glass lined barrels indefinitely, charging the original manufacturers rent for the service. The rent ceases when an independent scientific panel can confirm that there is a safe method to detoxify the substances in question. All toxic chemicals would have molecular marketers identifying them as belonging to their originator, so that if they are found in wells, rivers, soil, or fish, it is the responsibility of the company to retrieve them and clean up. This places the problem of toxicity with the makers, where it belongs, making them responsible for full-life-cycle effects.

7. Vote, don't buy.

Democracy has been effectively eliminated in America by the influence of money, lawyers, and a political system that is the outgrowth of the first two. While we can dream of restoring our democratic system, the fact remains that we live in a plutocracy—government by the wealthy. One way out is to vote with your dollars, to withhold purchases from companies that act or respond inappropriately. Don't just avoid buying a Mitsubishi automobile because of the company's participation in the destruction of primary forests in Malaysia, Indonesia, Ecuador, Brazil, Bolivia, Canada, Chile, . . . Siberia, and Papua New Guinea. Write and tell them why you won't. Engage in dialogue, send one postcard a week, talk, organize, meet, publish newsletters, boycott, patronize and communicate with companies like General Electric. Educate nonprofits, organizations, municipalities, and pension funds to act affirmatively, to support the ecological CERES (formerly *Valdez*) Principles for business, to invest intelligently, and to *think* with their money, not merely spend it. Demand the best from the companies you work for and buy from. You deserve it and your actions will help them change.

8. Restore the "guardian."

There can be no healthy business sector unless there is a healthy governing sector. In her book *Systems of Survival*, author Jane Jacobs describes two overarching moral syndromes that permeate our society: the commercial syndrome, which arose from trading cultures, and the governing, or guardian, syndrome that arose from territorial cultures. The guardian system is hierarchical, adheres to tradition, values loyalty, and shuns trading and inventiveness. The commercial system, on the other hand, is based on trading, so it values trust of outsiders, innovation, and future thinking. Each has qualities the other lacks. Whenever the guardian tries to be in business, as in Eastern Europe, business doesn't work. What is also true, but not so obvious to us, is that when business plays government, governance fails as well. Our guardian system has almost completely broken down because of the money, power, influence, and control exercised by business and, to a lesser degree, other institutions. Business and unions have to get out of government. We need more than campaign reform: We need a vision that allows us all to see that when Speaker of the House Tom Foley exempts the aluminum industry in his district from the proposed Btu tax, or when Philip Morris donates $200,000 to

the Jesse Helms Citizenship Center, citizenship is mocked and democracy is left gagging and twitching on the Capitol steps. The irony is that business thinks that its involvement in governance is good corporate citizenship or at least is advancing its own interests. The reality is that business is preventing the economy from evolving. Business loses, workers lose, the environment loses.

9. Shift from electronic literacy to biologic literacy.

That an average adult can recognize one thousand brand names and logos but fewer than ten local plants is not a good sign. We are moving not to an information age but to a biologic age, and unfortunately our technological education is equipping us for corporate markets, not the future. Sitting at home with virtual reality gloves, 3D video games, and interactive cable TV shopping is a barren and impoverished vision of the future. The computer revolution is not the totem of our future, only a tool. Don't get me wrong. Computers are great. But they are not an uplifting or compelling vision for culture or society. They do not move us toward a sustainable future any more than our obsession with cars and televisions provided us with newer definitions or richer meaning. We are moving into the age of living machines, not, as Corbusier noted, "machines for living in." The Thomas Edison of the future is not Bill Gates of Microsoft, but John and Nancy Todd, founders of the New Alchemy Institute, a Massachusetts design lab and think tank for sustainability. If the Todds' work seems less commercial, less successful, and less glamorous, it is because they are working on the real problem— how to live—and it is infinitely more complex than a microprocessor. Understanding biological processes is how we are going to create a new symbiosis with living systems (or perish). What we can learn on-line is how to model complex systems. It is computers that have allowed us to realize how the synapses in the common sea slug are more powerful than all of our parallel processors put together.

10. Take inventory.

We do not know how many species live on the planet within a factor of ten. We do not know how many are being extirpated. We do not know what is contained in the biological library inherited from the Cenozoic age. (Sociobiologist E. O. Wilson estimates that it would take 25,000 person-years to catalog most of the species, putting aside the fact that there are only 1,500 people with the taxonomic ability to undertake the task.) We do not know how complex systems interact—how the transpiration of the giant lily, *Victoria amazonica*, of Brazil's rainforests affects European rainfall and agriculture, for example. We do not know what happens to 20 percent of the CO_2 that is off-gassed every year (it disappears without a trace). We do not know how to calculate sustainable yields in fisheries and forest systems. We do not know why certain species, such as frogs, are dying out even in pristine habitats. We do not know the long-term effects of chlorinated hydrocarbons on human health, behavior, sexuality, and fertility. We do not know what a sustainable life is for existing inhabitants of the planet, and certainly not for future populations. (A Dutch study calculated that your fair share of air travel is one trip across the Atlantic in a lifetime.) We do not know how many people we can feed on a sustainable basis, or what our diet would look like. In short, we need to find out what's here, who has it, and what we can or can't do with it.

11. Take care of human health.

The environmental and socially responsible movements would gain additional credibility if they recognized that the greatest amount of human suffering and mortality is caused by environmental problems that are not being addressed by environmental organizations or companies. Contaminated water is killing a hundred times more people than all other forms of pollution combined. Millions of children are dying from preventable diseases and malnutrition.

The movement toward sustainability must address the clear and present dangers that people face worldwide, dangers that ironically increase population levels because of their perceived threat. People produce more children when they're afraid they'll lose them. Not until the majority of the people in the world, all of whom suffer in myriad preventable yet intolerable ways, understand that environmentalism means improving their lives directly will the ecology movement walk its talk. Americans will spend more money in the next 12 months on the movie and tchotchkes of *Jurassic Park*

than on foreign aid to prevent malnutrition or provide safe water.

12. Respect the human spirit.

If hope is to pass the sobriety test, then it has to walk a pretty straight line to reality. Nothing written, suggested, or proposed here is possible unless business is willing to integrate itself into the natural world. It is time for business to take the initiative in a genuinely open process of dialogue, collaboration, reflection, and redesign. "It is not enough," writes Jeremy Seabrook of the British Green party, "to declare, as many do, that we are living in an unsustainable way, using up resources, squandering the substance of the next generation however true this may be. People must feel subjectively the injustice and unsustainability before they will make a more sober assessment as to whether it is worth maintaining what is, or whether there might not be more equitable and satisfying ways that will not be won at the expense either of the necessities of the poor or of the wasting fabric of the planet."

Poet and naturalist W. S. Merwin (citing Robert Graves) reminds us that we have one story, and one story only, to tell in our lives. We are made to believe by our parents and businesses, by our culture and televisions, by our politicians and movie stars that it is the story of money, of finance, of wealth, of the stock portfolio, the partnership, the country house. These are small, impoverished tales and whispers that have made us restless and craven; they are not stories at all. As author and garlic grower Stanley Crawford puts it, "The financial statement must finally give way to the narrative, with all its exceptions, special cases, imponderables. It must finally give way to the story, which is perhaps the way we arm ourselves against the next and always unpredictable turn of the cycle in the quixotic dare that is life; across the rock and cold of lifelines, it is our seed, our clove, our filament cast toward the future." It is something deeper than anything commercial culture can plumb, and it is waiting for each of us.

Business must yield to the longings of the human spirit. The most important contribution of the socially responsible business movement has little to do with recycling, nuts from the rainforest, or employing the homeless. Their gift to us is that they are leading by trying to do something, to risk, take a chance, make a change—any change. They are not waiting for "the solution," but are acting without guarantees of success or proof of purchase. This is what all of us must do. Being visionary has always been given a bad rap by commerce. But without a positive vision for humankind we can have no meaning, no work, and no purpose.

Two Kinds of Poverty

Vandana Shiva

In a book entitled *Poverty: The Wealth of the People*[1] an African writer draws a distinction between poverty as subsistence, and misery as deprivation. It is useful to separate a cultural conception of subsistence living as poverty from the material experience of poverty that is a result of dispossession and deprivation. Culturally perceived poverty need not be real material poverty: subsistence economies which satisfy basic needs through self-provisioning are not poor in the sense of being deprived. Yet the ideology of development declares them so because they do not participate overwhelmingly in the market economy, and do not consume commodities produced for and distributed through the market *even though they might be satisfying those needs through self-provisioning mechanisms*. People are perceived as poor if they eat millets (grown by women) rather than commercially produced and distributed processed foods sold by global agribusiness. They are seen as poor if they live in self-built housing made from natural material like bamboo and mud rather than in cement houses. They are seen as poor if they wear handmade garments of natural fibre rather than synthetics. Subsistence, as culturally perceived poverty, does not necessarily imply a low physical quality of life. On the contrary, millets are nutritionally far superior to processed foods, houses built with local materials are far superior, being better adapted to the local climate and ecology, natural fibres are preferable to man-made fibres in most cases, and certainly more affordable. This cultural perception of prudent subsistence living as poverty has provided the legitimization for the development process as a poverty removal project. As a culturally biased project it destroys wholesome and sustainable lifestyles and creates real material poverty, or misery, by the denial of survival needs themselves, through the diversion of resources to resource intensive commodity production. Cash crop production and food processing take land and water resources away from sustenance needs, and exclude increasingly large numbers of people from their entitlements to food. "The inexorable processes of agriculture-industrialisation and internationalisation are probably responsible for more hungry people than either cruel or unusual whims of nature. There are several reasons why the high-technology-export-crop model increases hunger. Scarce land, credit, water and technology are preempted for the export market. Most hungry people are not affected by the market at all. . . . The profits flow to corporations that have no interest in feeding hungry people without money."[2]

The Ethiopian famine is in part an example of the creation of real poverty by development aimed at removing culturally perceived poverty. The displacement of nomadic Afars from their traditional pastureland in Awash Valley by commercial agriculture (financed by foreign companies) led to their struggle for survival in the fragile uplands which degraded the ecosystem and led to the starvation of cattle and the nomads.[3] The market economy conflicted with the survival economy in the Valley, thus creating a conflict between the survival economy and nature's economy in the uplands. At no point has the global marketing of agricultural commodities been assessed against the background of the new conditions of scarcity and poverty that it has induced. This new poverty moreover, is no longer cultural and relative: it is absolute, threatening the very survival of millions on this planet.

The economic system based on the patriarchal concept of productivity was created for the very

Staying Alive, by Vandana Shiva (London: Zed Books Ltd., 1988), pp. 10–13. Reprinted by permission.

specific historical and political phenomenon of colonialism. In it, the input for which efficiency of use had to be maximized in the production centres of Europe, was industrial labour. For colonial interest therefore, it was rational to improve the labor resource *even at the cost of wasteful use of nature's wealth*. This rationalisation has, however, been illegitimately universalized to all contexts and interest groups and, on the plea of increasing productivity, labour reducing technologies have been introduced in situations where labour is abundant and cheap, and resource demanding technologies have been introduced where resources are scarce and already fully utilised for the production of sustenance. Traditional economies with a stable ecology have shared with industrially advanced affluent economies the ability to use natural resources to satisfy basic vital needs. The former differ from the latter in two essential ways: first, the same needs are satisfied in industrial societies through longer technological chains requiring higher energy and resource inputs and excluding large numbers without purchasing power; and second, affluence generates new and artificial needs requiring the increased production of industrial goods and services. Traditional economies are not advanced in the matter of non-vital needs satisfaction, but as far as the satisfaction of basic and vital needs is concerned, they are often what Marshall Sahlins has called 'the original affluent society'. The needs of the Amazonian tribes are more than satisfied by the rich rainforest; their poverty begins with its destruction. The story is the same for the Gonds of Bastar in India or the Penans of Sarawak in Malaysia.

Thus are economies based on indigenous technologies viewed as 'backward' and 'unproductive'. Poverty, as the denial of basic needs, is not necessarily associated with the existence of traditional technologies, and its removal is not necessarily an outcome of the growth of modern ones. On the contrary, the destruction of ecologically sound traditional technologies, often created and used by women, along with the destruction of their material base is generally believed to be responsible for the 'feminization' of poverty in societies which have had to bear the costs of resource destruction.

The contemporary poverty of the Afar nomad is not rooted in the inadequacies of traditional nomadic life, but in the *diversion of the productive pastureland of the Awash Valley*. The erosion of the resource base for survival is increasingly being caused by the demand for resources by the market economy, dominated by global forces. The creation of inequality through economic activity which is ecologically disruptive arises in two ways: first, inequalities in the distribution of privileges make for unequal access to natural resources—these include privileges of both a political and economic nature. Second, resource intensive production processes have access to subsidized raw material on which a substantial number of people, especially from the less privileged economic groups, depend for their survival. The consumption of such industrial raw material is determined purely by market forces, and not by considerations of the social or ecological requirements placed on them. The costs of resource destruction are externalised and unequally divided among various economic groups in society, but are borne largely by women and those who satisfy their basic material needs directly from nature, simply because they have no purchasing power to register their demands on the goods and services provided by the modern production system. Gustavo Esteva has called development a permanent war waged by its promoters and suffered by its victims.[4]

The paradox and crisis of development arises from the mistaken identification of culturally perceived poverty with real material poverty, and the mistaken identification of the growth of commodity production as better satisfaction of basic needs. In actual fact, there is less water, less fertile soil, less genetic wealth as a result of the development process. Since these natural resources are the basis of nature's economy and women's survival economy, their scarcity is impoverishing women and marginalised peoples in an unprecedented manner. Their new impoverishment lies in the fact that resources which supported their survival were absorbed into the market economy while they themselves were excluded and displaced by it.

The old assumption that with the development process the availability of goods and services will automatically be increased and poverty will be removed, is now under serious challenge from women's ecology movements in the Third World, even while it continues to guide development thinking in centres of patriarchal power. Survival is based on the assumption of the sanctity of life;

maldevelopment is based on the assumption of the sacredness of 'development'. Gustavo Esteva asserts that the sacredness of development has to be refuted because, it threatens survival itself. "My people are tired of development," he says, "they just want to live."[5]

The recovery of the feminine principle allows a transcendence and transformation of these patriarchal foundations of maldevelopment. It allows a redefinition of growth and productivity as categories linked to the production, not the destruction, of life. It is thus simultaneously an ecological and a feminist political project which legitimizes the way of knowing and being that create wealth by enhancing life and diversity, and which delegitimises the knowledge and practise of a culture of death as the basis for capital accumulation.

Notes

1. R. Bahro, *From Red to Green*, London: Verso, 1984, p. 211.

2. R. J. Barnet, *The Lean Years*, London: Abacus, 1981, p. 171.

3. U. P. Koehn, "African Approaches to Environmental Stress: A Focus on Ethiopia and Nigeria" in R. N. Barrett (ed.), *International Dimensions of the Environmental Crisis*, Colorado: Westview, 1982, pp. 253–89.

4. Gustavo Esteva, 'Regenerating People's Space' in S. N. Mendlowitz and R. B. J. Walker, *Towards a Just World Peace: Perspectives from Social Movements*, London: Butterworths and Committee for a Just World Peace, 1987.

5. G. Esteva, Remarks made at a Conference of the Society for International Development, Rome, 1985.

PERSONAL CHOICES AND
THE ECOLOGICALLY GOOD LIFE

Many of us are struggling with ethical choices about how we relate to nonhumans and to the rest of the earth, from trying vegetarianism to recycling waste products to becoming conscious "green consumers." In this section, we focus on the power of those individual decisions, those day-to-day choices about what we eat and how we shape the spaces we live in, because those choices will ultimately determine the fate of the planet.

Scores of choices made by individuals inevitably add up to significant long-term consequences. Some of those choices lead to environmental destruction: the choice to eat beef, for example. Maintaining the world's enormous cattle population—"their combined weight exceeds that of the human population on earth"[1]—results in the destruction of ecosystems of the South American rain forests. Though few these days are unaware of the loss of acres of rain forest, many do not make the connection between this devastation and their choice of grabbing a hamburger for lunch. Other choices manifest an image of ourselves to the rest of the world. Tidy suburban lawns, for instance, seem nothing more than a statement of justifiable homeowner pride. But each of those lawns, kept artificially green with fertilizers and bug-free with pesticides, represent a piece of the original ecosystem vanquished and vanished.

Jeremy Rifkin asks us to consider the impact of our own culture's emphasis upon eating beef: "Every second, 200 Americans purchase one or more hamburgers at a fast-food outlet. . . ."[2] The hamburger, says Rifkin, author of *Beyond Beef: The Rise and Fall of the Cattle Culture*, is the " . . . quintessential symbol of the American dream and lifestyle. Today, people line up in Stockholm and Tokyo waiting to file under the 'golden arches' of McDonald's and become part of 'the American experience.'"[3] In an earlier article, Rifkin pointed out that Ray Kroc, one of the founders of the McDonald's hamburger chain, " . . . first sited his restaurants near churches, wanting to create a hamburger sanctuary: a place where pilgrims could rest and be refreshed, knowing that everything would be orderly and predictable, according to a secular catechism."[4] What Rifkin calls "the cattle culture" has shaped our world. In the selection reprinted here, we focus on the enormous cost—in particular, the environmental cost—of the American love affair with beef.

Millions of acres of ancient rain forests have been razed and burned to create pasture land for grazing cattle. As the forests are cleared at an alarming rate, the many species in the forests are simultaneously destroyed. A four-square-mile section of rain forest, according to the National Academy of Sciences, contains

> as many as 1500 species of flowering plants and as many as 750 species of trees; such a patch also contains 125 mammal species, 400 species of birds, 100 of reptiles, 60 of amphibians, and 150 of butterflies.[5]

Our hamburger habit is directly implicated in species extinction and the loss of biodiversity. "Each imported hamburger required the clearing of 6 square yards of jungle for pasture."[6] Other environmental costs stemming in part from the large numbers of cows are global warming, soil erosion, and desertification—the turning of fertile places into desert. "Today, the [United States] has lost nearly one-third of its prime top soil as a result of over-grazing, overcropping, and deforestation."[7] An inch of topsoil, Rifkin says, " . . . takes between 200 and 1000 years to form under natural conditions."[8] He concludes: "Every beef-eating American contributes personally to the process [of soil erosion]."[9]

The impact of cattle extends even to matters of personal health and issues of social justice. A beef-rich diet contributes to cancer, strokes, and heart disease. Also problematic is the process of beef inspection and the presence of tainted beef.[10] In addition, issues of social justice arise with the creation of "an artificial protein chain."[11] Maintaining a beef culture results in "[t]he anomaly of rich people dieting and poor people starving, of the human species increasingly separated into two branches, one atop the protein ladder, the other at the bottom. . . ."[12] Says Rifkin, it " . . . seems more than a bit macabre, even to modern sensibilities, which are often accustomed to naked self-interest and unabashed utilitarianism."[13]

Lawns are as much a part of American culture, says Sara Stein in her new book on ecology, as Rifkin claims eating beef to be. Symbolically, lawns have been encouraged by " . . . an esthetic based on class distinctions. . . . The great lawns from which our little ones descended proclaimed the extent of the landowner's holding."[14] However, says Stein:

> Lawns can no longer claim pastoral validity. They have outgrown it monstrously. Though now I understand why they need such care, I question why we give it. We spend $25 billion a year coddling this carpet that on a August day lies sprawled over 30 million acres of America, stupefied in the sun.
>
> How we love our lawns! How we take it with us wherever we go, plant and tend it even in the desert, can't get comfortable without it, must have it underfoot, are

moved to display it proudly as the very emblem of our civilization!

> And with what moral rectitude we mow.[15]

Certainly, Stein points out, suburban landscaping as it is now practiced did not arise from environmental concerns or any acquaintance with ecology.

> America's clean, spare landscaping and gardening tradition has devastated rural ecology. The relentless spread of suburbia's neat yards and gardens has caused local extinctions of such important predators as foxes, has dangerously reduced the habitat of many kinds of birds, and has threatened the total extinction of fragile species such as orchids that rely on a single pollinator, butterflies that require a specific host plant, songbirds that inhabit deep woods, and turtles whose routes to breeding sites are interrupted by roads or obliterated by drainage projects.[16]

In her book, *Noah's Garden: Restoring the Ecology of Our Own Backyards,* Stein argues for creating a new landscape, a new way of gardening—a return to native plants, wildflowers and meadows, and animal habitats destroyed by the construction and maintenance of tidy, uniform lawns. Her rueful awareness of the costs of our modern way of gardening is cogently captured when she says, "We didn't consider, when we cut down a stand of milkweed, how many butterflies it fed."[17] Wiping out animal species through practices that destroy their habitats is of particular concern to Stein. She notes: " . . . swamps . . . drained, meadows bulldozed, . . . and drives paved . . . have wrought in our time a calamity of habitat destruction unprecedented even during the previous three centuries of agricultural abuse."[18]

As noted earlier, Stein mentions the high maintenance costs of preserving lawns as yet another negative effect of artificial, i.e., non-native environments. Others have remarked about the great costs of maintaining manicured urban parks with fleets of lawn-mowers.[19] "When Frederick Law Olmsted designed Prospect Park in Brooklyn and Franklin Park in Boston, it was accepted that sheep would graze the large meadows in both parks. . . . Sheep can easily nibble the grass at the base of trees, but large lawnmowers find it much more difficult to negotiate tree trunks."[20]

Stein, whose purpose is to restore the original ecology to our yards, would perhaps appreciate the following definitions of lawns as cultural icons: Lawns drink " . . . from the national stream of images, lift our gaze from the real places we live and fix it on unreal places elsewhere. Lawns are a form of television."[21] The suburban lawn attempts to tell us we are eighteenth-century landowners in a pastoral world.

In the selection from *Noah's Garden* reprinted here, Stein makes reference to "what Mrs. Dana saw." Stein is referring to Mrs. William Starr Dana, author of the classic, *How to Know the Wild Flowers*, in 1893, and *According to Season* in 1894. It seems that Mrs. Dana saw meadow lilies, purple asters, intense red-purple ironweed, tall yellow sunflowers, and heard "the happy tinkle" of bobolinks.[22] Stein reports of the same New England area: "I've never seen a meadow lily or heard a bobolink. . . . [the] replacements of our native flowers are all alien species—and all weeds."[23]

Stein's book is about opening up new ways of living in our own backyards. We do not have to drain every wet area, mow great expanses, and pave over everything in sight. In this regard her work on a specific topic illustrates a more general thesis put forward by Anthony Weston: Forming environmental values in a deeply anthropocentric world comes about in part by being open to new possibilities. According to Weston:

A central part of the challenge is to create the social, psychological and phenomenological preconditions—the conceptual, experiential, or even quite literal "Space"—for new or stronger environmental values to evolve. This is what I call "enabling" such values; we may call the practical project *enabling environmental practice*.[24]

Weston, like Rifkin and Stein, emphasizes what individuals can do to bring about " . . . reciprocity *between* humans and the rest of nature."[25] How we as individuals can live our lives differently is the focus of this section.[26] We call attention here to Paul Hawken's "A Declaration of Sustainability" in IVB. His essay, which originally carried the subtitle, "12 steps society can take to save the whole enchilada," is about redesigning our commercial systems—for example, changing the way businesses do business. Thus his piece is in the spirit of this section insofar as it emphasizes practice, but its suggestions for change are not things that any individual can do.

Weston contends that environmental practice—at least at this point in time—should take precedence over the construction of a theoretical environmental ethic. Theories systematize values. Since environmental values, he says, are not settled (indeed, in many circles do not even exist), insisting on a "complete, unified, closed"[27] theory of environmental ethics right now is premature. "Rather than systematizing environmental values . . . the overall project at this stage must be to begin to *co-evolve* those values with practices and institutions that make them even *un*systematically possible."[28]

Weston entitled the essay we have reprinted here "Before Environmental Ethics." One goal of the preceding paragraph is to make clear the meaning of his title. As editors, we have chosen the title, "Enabling Environmental Practice." How to engage in environmental practice as individuals is the focus of this section. Enabling environmental practice is also what Weston thinks—as between theory and practice—should be our highest priority.

NOTES

1. Jeremy Rifkin, *Beyond Beef: The Rise and Fall of the Cattle Culture* (New York: Penguin Books USA, 1992), p. 1.

2. Ibid., p. 260.

3. Ibid.

4. Jeremy Rifkin, "Anatomy of a Cheeseburger, " *Granta* (Cambridge, England: Penguin Books, Ltd.), Winter 1991, p. 88.

5. Rifkin, *Beyond Beef*, p. 197.

6. Ibid., p. 192.

7. Ibid., p. 203.

8. Ibid., p. 202.

9. Ibid., p. 203.

10. See especially Rifkin, "Anatomy of a Cheeseburger." See also, the entry on "tainted beef" in *The 1994 Information Please Environmental Almanac* compiled by the World Resources Institute (New York: Houghton Mifflin Company, 1994).

11. Rifkin, *Beyond Beef*, p. 180.

12. Ibid., p. 179.

13. Ibid. "Utilitarianism" here is a negative term. To see it so used in the popular press is all the more reason to read carefully the work of Peter Singer and others who defend utilitarianism as the best ethical theory.

14. Sara Stein, *Noah's Garden: Restoring the Ecology of Our Own Backyards* (New York: Houghton Mifflin Company, 1993), p. 16.

15. Ibid., p. 151.

16. Ibid., pp. 9–10.

17. Ibid., p. 14.

18. Ibid., p. 37.

19. Anne Whiston Spirn, *The Granite Garden: Urban Nature and Human Design* (New York: Basic Books, 1984).

20. Ibid., p. 182.

21. Michael Pollen, *Second Nature* (New York: Atlantic Monthly Press, 1991), p. 63.

22. See chapter 3, "What Mrs. Dana Saw," of *Noah's Garden*.

23. Stein, *Noah's Garden*, p. 36.

24. Anthony Weston, "Before Environmental Ethics," in *Environmental Ethics: Divergence and Convergence*, ed. Susan J. Armstrong and Richard G. Botzler (New York: McGraw Hill, 1993), p. 100.

25. Ibid.

26. On this subject see also Anthony Weston, *Back to Earth: Tomorrow's Environmentalism* (Philadelphia: Temple University Press, 1994), especially chapter 6, "Coming to our Senses."

27. Ibid., p. 99.

28. Ibid., p. 100.

The Cattle Culture

Jeremy Rifkin

There are currently 1.28 billion cattle populating the earth.[1] They graze on nearly 24 percent of the landmass of the planet and consume enough grain to feed hundreds of millions of people.[2] Their combined weight exceeds that of the human population on earth.

The ever-increasing cattle population is wreaking havoc on the earth's ecosystems, destroying habitats on six continents. Cattle raising is a primary factor in the destruction of the world's remaining tropical rain forests. Millions of acres of ancient forest in Central and South America are being felled and cleared to make room for pastureland to graze cattle. Cattle herding is responsible for much of the spreading desertification in the sub-Sahara of Africa and the western rangeland of the United States and Australia. The overgrazing of semiarid and arid lands has left parched and barren deserts on four continents. Organic runoff from feedlots is now a major source of organic pollution in our nation's groundwater. Cattle are also a major cause of global warming. They emit methane, a potent global warming gas, blocking heat from escaping the earth's atmosphere.

Cattle and other livestock consume over 70 percent of all the grain produced in the United States. Today, about one-third of the world's total grain harvest is fed to cattle and other livestock while as many as a billion people suffer from chronic hunger and malnutrition.[3] In developing nations, millions of peasants are being forced off their ancestral lands to make room for the conversion of farmland from subsistence food grain production to commercial feed grain production.

While millions of human beings go hungry for lack of adequate grain, millions more in the industrial world die from diseases caused by an excess of grain-fed animal flesh, and especially beef, in their diets. Americans, Europeans, and increasingly the Japanese are gorging on grain-fed beef and dying from the "diseases of affluence"—heart attacks, strokes and cancer.

The devastating environmental, economic, and human toll of maintaining a worldwide cattle complex is little discussed in public policy circles. Most people are largely unaware of the wide-ranging effects cattle are having on the ecosystems of the planet and the fortunes of civilization. Yet, cattle production and beef consumption now rank among the gravest threats to the future well-being of the earth and its human population. . . .

In the United States, "beef is king." Some 100,000 cows are slaughtered every twenty-four hours in the United States.[4] In a given week, 91 percent of all United States households purchase beef.[5] People in the southern United States spend slightly more on beef than those in any other region of the country. People in the west spend the least amount. Households in the top 20 percent income bracket spend relatively more for beef than others.[6] Americans currently consume 23 percent of all the beef produced in the world.[7] Today, the average American consumes 65 pounds of beef per year.[8] . . .

While Americans are among the premier beef eaters of the world, the Australians are not far behind. Western Europeans consume half as much beef as Americans, while the Japanese consume only 10 percent as much beef.[9] These figures are likely to change dramatically in the next decade as more and more Japanese consumers join the world's exclusive beef club. Between 1965 and 1990, the Japanese demand for beef rose 3.5 times.[10] In 1989, more McDonald's hamburgers were sold in Tokyo than in New York City.[11] Although beef prices are four times higher in Japan than in the United States, Japanese trade officials expect to see a doubling in beef consumption over the next ten to fifteen years.[12] . . .

Since 1960 more than 25 percent of the forests of Central America have been cleared to create pastureland for grazing cattle.[13] By the late 1970s two-thirds of all the agricultural land in Central America was taken up by cattle and other livestock, most of it destined for export to North America.[14] While American consumers saved, on the average, close to a nickel on every hamburger imported from Central America, the cost to the native environment was overwhelming and irreversible. Each imported hamburger required the clearing of 6 square yards of jungle for pasture. . . .

The creation of a vast cattle complex in Central America has enriched the lives of a select few, pauperized much of the rural peasantry, and spawned widespread social unrest and political upheaval. Over half the rural families in Central America—35 million people—are now landless or own too little land to support themselves, while the landed aristocracy and transnational corporation continue to gobble up every available acre, using much of it for pastureland.[15] . . .

The pattern of forest clearing, land concentration, and displacement of peasant populations is being repeated throughout Latin America in a systematic effort to transform an entire continental landmass into a grazing land to support the rich beef diets of wealthy Latin Americans, Europeans, Americans, and Japanese. In Mexico, 37 million acres of forest have been destroyed since 1987 to provide additional grazing land for cattle. Mexican ecologist Gabriel Quadri summed up the feelings of many of his countrymen when he warned, "We are exporting the future of Mexico for the benefit of a few powerful cattle farmers."[16] . . .

The destructive impact of cattle extends well beyond the rain forests to include vast stretches of the world's rangeland. Cattle are now a major cause of desertification, which the United Nations Environmental Program defines as

impoverishment of arid, semiarid and subarid ecosystems by the impact of man's activities. This process leads to reduced productivity of desirable plants, alterations in the biomass and in the diversity of life forms, accelerated soil degradation, and increased hazards for human occupancy.[17]

Desertification is caused by the overgrazing of livestock; overcultivation of the land; deforestation; and improper irrigation techniques. Cattle production is a primary factor in all four causes of desertification. The United Nations estimates that 29 percent of the earth's landmass now suffers "slight, moderate or severe desertification."[18] . . . Some 850 million human beings live on land threatened by desertification.[19] Over 230 million people live on land so severely desertified that they are unable to sustain their existence and face the prospect of imminent starvation.[20] . . .

Today, the billion or more cattle on the planet are overgrazing and trampling native and artificial grasses, stripping much of the vegetative cover from the earth's remaining grasslands. Without flora to anchor the soil, absorb water, and recycle nutrients, the land becomes increasingly vulnerable to wind and water erosion. More than 60 percent of the world's rangeland has been damaged by overgrazing in the course of the last half century.[21] . . .

An inch of topsoil takes between 200 and 1,000 years to form under natural conditions.[22] With the human and cattle population growing at an unprecedented rate, it seems that virtually every available square mile of rangeland and cropland is being exploited, depleted, and eroded with little thought of tomorrow or the needs of future generations.

Soil erosion and spreading desertification have become a serious problem in the United States. Two hundred years ago, most cropland in the United States contained at least twenty-one inches of topsoil. Today, the country has lost nearly one-third of its prime top soil as a result of overgrazing, overcropping, and deforestation. In some regions of the country, less than six inches of soil remain.[23] Iowa, once considered the greatest agricultural land in world, has lost over half its topsoil in less than one century.[24] Each year, over 4 billion tons of soil are lost to rain erosion and 3 billion to wind erosion in the United States.[25] . . .

Cattle are destroying much of the American west. Between 2 and 3 million cattle are currently grazing on some 306 million acres of public land in the eleven far-western states. Their domain encompasses about 40 percent of the landmass of the American west and 12 percent of the total landmass of the lower forty-eight states.[26] While western beef cattle make up only a small percentage of the beef production in the United States, they are a primary cause of much of the ecological destruction of the western half of the United States.[27]

Let loose on public lands, each animal eats its way through 900 pounds of vegetation every month.[28] They strip the rangeland of its forage of grass and herbage and browse on shrubs and trees, even consuming cactus and tree bark. Their powerful cloven hoofs trample native plants and compact the soil with the pressure of 24 pounds per square inch.[29] The soil compaction reduces the air space between soil-particles, reducing the amount of water that can be absorbed.[30] The soil is less able to hold the water from the spring melting of snow and is more prone to erosion from flash floods that run along the surface. In western Colorado alone, grazed watershed areas produce up to 76 percent more sediment than ungrazed areas.[31]

The constant pounding of the soil by cattle hoofs has far more subtle but equally profound impacts on the microworld of life on the rangelands. Billions of organisms—bacteria, protozoa, fungi, algae, nematodes, insects, earthworms, and mites—live in the top two inches of soil, where they play a critical role in maintaining soil fertility and building new soil. The trampling of soil by cattle disrupts and destabilizes these mini-habitats, further weakening the already compromised soil base on the rangeland.[32]

The combination of overgrazing and the relentless pounding of the soil has destabilized the plain biome and devastated native flora and fauna. By eliminating the plant cover, the cattle have left the rest of the animal kingdom—insects, birds, mammals—without adequate food and shelter. By compacting the soil, the cattle have greatly diminished the capacity of the land to both retain water and rebuild soil, further undermining the already precarious vegetative cycle. No longer anchored by plant roots or shaded from the sun, and unable to absorb water, the topsoil is being blown away by wind and carried off by surface floods at an alarming rate. In some areas of the west, over half of the topsoil has already been eroded. . . .

Writing in the magazine *Audubon,* Philip Fradkin summed up the dimensions of the crisis on our western lands—a crisis that has, up to now, remained among the best-kept environmental secrets in the country.

The impact of countless hooves and mouths over the years has done more to alter the type of vegetation and land forms of the West than all the water projects, strip mines, power plants, freeways, and subdivision developments combined.[33] . . .

The grain-fed cattle complex is now a significant factor in the emission of three of the four global warming gases—methane, carbon dioxide, and nitrous oxides—and is likely to play an even larger role in the coming decades. . . .

A thick blanket of greenhouse gases has existed in the earth's atmosphere for as long as there has been life. The gases allow solar radiation to enter the earth's atmosphere. The earth's surface absorbs much of the solar energy, converting it to infrared energy, or heat. The heat then rises from the earth's surface and bombards the gaseous molecules in the atmosphere, forcing the molecules to vibrate. The gas molecules act as reflectors, sending some of the heat back toward the surface of the earth, creating a warming effect. The greenhouse phenomenon is an essential feature of the earth's atmosphere, providing a warm temperature band conducive to the emergence of life on the planet. The greenhouse cover has remained relatively constant over the long period of evolutionary history.

In the industrial age, massive amounts of coal, oil, and natural gas have been burned to propel the machine culture. The carbon dioxide released into the atmosphere has increased rapidly, blocking the release of heat from the planet. In 1750, the earth's atmosphere contained approximately 288 ppm (parts per million) of carbon dioxide. Today, the atmosphere contains over 350 ppm.[34] From the outset of the American Civil War until today, the industrial nations have released more than 185 billion tons of carbon into the atmosphere from burning massive amounts of fossil fuel.[35] Many scientists predict that the CO_2 content of the atmosphere will likely double by the middle part of the next century,

with temperatures rising beyond any levels we've experienced in recorded history.[36]

The burning of fossil fuels accounted for nearly two-thirds of the 8.5 billion tons of CO_2 added to the atmosphere in 1987.[37] The other one-third came from the increased burning of the earth's biomass.[38] Plants take in and store CO_2 in the process of photosynthesis. When they die or are burned, they release the stored-up carbon—often accumulated over hundreds of years—back into the atmosphere.[39] The amount of carbon contained in the biomass and soil humus of the world's forests exceeds the amount of carbon in the atmosphere by 1.3 and 4 times respectively.[40] The Amazon forest alone stores some 75 billion tons of carbon in its trees.[41] When the trees are cleared and burned to make room for cattle pastures, they emit a massive volume of CO_2 into the atmosphere. . . .

Still, the burning of biomass is only part of the story. Commercial cattle ranching contributes to global warming in other ways. Our highly mechanized agricultural sector uses up a sizable amount of fossil fuel energy. With 70 percent of all U.S. grain production now devoted to livestock feed, primarily for cattle, the energy burned just to produce the feed represents a significant addition to CO_2 emissions.[42]

It now takes the equivalent of a gallon of gasoline to produce a pound of grain-fed beef in the United States.[43] To sustain the yearly beef requirements of an average family of four people requires the consumption of over 260 gallons of fossil fuel. When that fuel is burned it releases 2.5 tons of additional carbon dioxide into the atmosphere—as much CO_2 as the average car emits in six months of normal operation.[44]

Moreover, to produce the feed crops for grain-fed cattle requires the use of petrochemical fertilizers, which emit nitrous oxide, another of the greenhouse gases. In the past forty years, the use of chemical fertilizers has increased dramatically from 14 million tons in 1950 to 143 million tons in 1989.[45] Nitrous oxide released from fertilizer and other sources now accounts for 6 percent of the global warming effect.[46]

Finally, cattle emit methane, a potent greenhouse gas. While methane is also emitted from peat bogs, rice paddies, and landfills, the increase in the cattle and termite population and the burning of forests and grasslands account for much of the increase in methane emissions over the past several decades. Methane emissions are responsible for 18 percent of the global warming trend.[47]

Reducing the cattle population to ecologically sustainable numbers will help facilitate an ecological restoration of nature on every continent. America's western range will slowly come to life again. Ancient rivers will flow, their waters bathing and healing thousands of damaged riparian zones across the great plains. Native wildflower and perennial bunchgrasses will sprout and bloom, spreading a verdant carpet across the western landscape. Cottonwood trees will shade the prairie once again, providing refuge for thousands of native birds. Streams and springs will come to life, bringing back freshwater trout and other native fish. The large mammals of the plains—elk, moose, pronghorn, antelope, bighorn sheep—will repopulate the western range once again, their numbers spreading out to fill the millions of acres of restored grassland. Predator species will thrive. Coyotes, wolves, bobcats, mountain lions, and lynx will steal their way back onto the great western range, performing their traditional role of culling big animal herds to ensure that native species do not exceed the carrying capacity of the plains ecosystems.

In Central and South America, the dissolution of the cattle complex will help idle tractors and bulldozers and diminish the familiar drone of thousands of machine saws cutting their way through the thicket of ancient forest ecosystems. Countless species of plants, insects, and animals will be granted a reprieve from what once appeared to be a sure death at the hands of cattle ranchers and multinational corporations. Millions of creatures, many of whom have inhabited this earth for millennia, will be given a chance to regroup, reproduce, and repopulate the forests. Future generations will have the opportunity to know, interact with, and appreciate these many diverse life forms; this multitude of wild and exotic creatures that creep, crawl, dart, fly over, swing through, and stalk the ancient forests, all fellow travelers in the unfolding evolutionary saga.

In Africa, the spreading desert will be slowed, allowing nature time to regenerate. Wildlife, once abundant in the sub-Sahara will slowly return. So too will the rich native flora. Wildebeest, elephants, zebras, rhinos, and lions will roam again over the open savannas, repopulating ancient habitats.

In Australia, New Zealand, and parts of Asia, the dissolution of the global cattle complex will foster a similar restoration of ancient forests and grasslands, as well as native flora and fauna.

Fewer cattle will lessen the strain on the world's remaining fresh water reserves and decrease the emission of global warming into the atmosphere. While the biosphere will still be choked with carbon dioxide from the burning of fossil fuels and the emissions of man-made chlorofluorocarbons, the worldwide reduction in cattle will significantly reduce methane emissions as well as carbon dioxide emissions resulting from the burning of forests and other biomass to provide pastureland.

As millions of Americans, Europeans, Japanese, and others make personal choices to reduce their beef consumption, the artificial protein ladder, erected during this century, will begin to collapse. The societal decision to reduce beef will profoundly affect the economics of human survival in the coming century. In the new world that is coming, millions of human beings will voluntarily choose to eat lower on the food chain so that millions of others may obtain the minimum food calories they need to sustain their lives. This grand redistribution of the earth's bounty, the most far-reaching in history, will unite the human race in a new fraternal bond. A new species awareness will begin where the rich meet the poor on the descending rungs of the world's protein ladder.

The decision to eat further down on the planet's food chain will force a wholesale reassessment of the entire grain-fed meat complex ranging from factory farm chickens to hogs. The collapse of the global cattle complex will likely precipitate a chain reaction, resulting in the elimination of other grain-fed meats from the human diet.

The dissolution of the commercial cattle complex will spare the rich and might help save the poor. Eliminating grain-fed beef and eating lower on the food chain will dramatically reduce the incidence of heart disease, cancer, and diabetes. Millions of human beings will enjoy better health and a longer life span. Billions of dollars in health care costs will be saved.

At the same time, more agricultural land and more grain will be potentially available to the poor. Liberating the land to grow grain for human beings could trigger a large-scale human migration out from the crowded urban shanty towns back to the countryside. Millions of displaced peasants would be able to return to their ancestral lands, where they could take up small-scale subsistence agriculture once again, providing their families with sustenance directly from the earth.

Of course, pressure will have to be put on ruling elites in developing countries to ensure an adequate redistribution of land so that the peasant populations can be self-sustaining. With access to land and grain, children of the poor will be able to survive infancy without falling victim to the range of parasitic and opportunistic diseases that now plague so many. Children will have a chance to grow up with sound bodies and minds capable of experiencing the fullness of human existence.

Moving beyond the beef culture is a revolutionary act, a sign of our willingness to reconstitute ourselves, to make ourselves whole. Restoring nature, resacralizing our relationship to cattle, and renewing our own being are inseparably linked. They are the essential implements of a new postmodern sensibility, the harbingers of a new earth-centered awareness. The dissolution of the modern cattle complex and the elimination of beef from the diet of the human race portends a new chapter in the unfolding of human consciousness. By doing battle with "the world steer," a new generation expresses its sensitivity to the biosphere and its regard for the plight of the poor. By eliminating beef from the human diet, our species takes a significant step toward a new species consciousness, reaching out in a spirit of shared partnership with the bovine and, by extension, other sentient creatures with whom we share the earth.

Notes

1. Cattle numbers come from Food and Agriculture Organization of the United Nations, *Production, 1989 Yearbook*, Vol. 43 (Rome, Italy: FAO, 1990), table 89.

2. Pieter Buringh, "Availability of Agricultural Land for Crop and Livestock Production," in David Pimentel and Carl Hall, eds., *Food and Natural Resources* (San Diego: Academic Press, 1989), 71. Pimentel estimates that a conversion of the present American grass/grain livestock system to a totally grass-fed system would free up in the United States alone about 130 million tons of grain for direct human consumption, enough to feed about 400 million people. David Pimentel, *Food, Energy and the Future of Society* (New York: Wiley, 1979), 26. Today, worldwide, about one-third of the 1.7 billion metric tons of total grain production is fed to livestock, which would suggest, using Pimentel's ratio, that a totally grass-fed livestock system worldwide might free enough grain up to feed over a billion people. U.S. Department of Agriculture, Economic Research Service, *World Agricultural Supply and Demand Estimates*, WASDE–256, July 11, 1991, table 256–6; World Bank, *Poverty and Hunger* (Washington, DC: World Bank, 1986), 24.

3. USDA, Economic Research Service, table 256–6; World Bank, *Poverty and Hunger*, 24.

4. Food and Agricultural Organization of the United Nations, *Production, 1989 Yearbook*, Vol 43 (Rome, Italy: FAO, 1990), table 92.

5. Marvin Harris, *The Sacred Cow and the Abominable Pig* (New York: Touchstone/Simon & Schuster, 1987), 109.

6. Jim Riley, "Where Are Beef's Potential Markets," *Beef*, July 1989, 30.

7. FAO, *Production*, table 92; Bureau of the Census, *Statistical Abstract 1990*, table 1161.

8. Judith Jones Putnam, "Food Consumption," *National Food Review* 13:3 (November 20, 1990).

9. Norman Meyers, *The Primary Source* (New York: W. W. Norton, 1983) 135; Bureau of the Census, *Statistical Abstract 1990*, table 1451.

10. *Choices*, Fourth Quarter 1989, 26.

11. Joe Vansickle, "A Tripling by Century's End," *Beef*, August 1990.

12. Jay Richter, "Washington Report," *Beef*, July 1989, 15.

13. Catherine Caulfield, "A Reporter at Large: The Rain Forests," *New Yorker*, January 14, 1985, 79.

14. James Parsons, "Forest to Pasture: Development or Destruction?" *Revista de Biologia Tropical* 24, Supplement 1, 1976, 124.

15. Norman Meyers, *The Primary Source*, 133; beef import figures from USDA, Foreign Agricultural Service as summarized.

16. Quoted in Tom Barry, *Roots of Rebellion* (Boston: South End Press, 1987), 84; quoted in Stephen Downer, "Cattle Ranchers Kill Mexican Rain Forests," *Daily Telegraph*, February 20, 1989.

17. Quoted in David Pimentel and Carl W. Hall, *Food and Natural Resources* (San Diego: Academic Press, 1989), 100–1.

18. World Commission on Environment and Development, *Our Common Future*, The Brundtland Commission Report (Oxford: Oxford University Press, 1987), 127.

19. Walter H. Corson, ed., *The Global Ecology Handbook* (Boston: Beacon Press, 1990), 77.

20. Paul Ehrlich and Anne Ehrlich, *The Population Explosion* (New York: Simon & Schuster, 1990), 127.

21. Robert Repetto, "Renewable Resources and Population Growth: Past Experiences and Future Prospects," *Population and Environment* 10:4 (Summer 1989), 228–29.

22. Sandra Postel, *Water: Rethinking Management in an Age of Scarcity,* Worldwatch Paper No. 62 (Washington, D.C.: Worldwatch Institute, 1984), 25.

23. Michael Fox and Nancy Wiswall, *The Hidden Costs of Beef* (Washington, D.C.: The Humane Society of the United States, 1989), 29; France Moore Lappé, *Diet for a Small Planet* (New York: Ballantine Books, 1982), 80.

24. David Pimentel, "Waste in Agriculture and Food Sectors: Environmental and Social Costs" (draft commissioned by the Gross National Waste Product Forum, Arlington, Va., 1989), 5.

25. Lappé, 80.

26. Based on animal unit monthly herbage consumption; Lynn Jacobs, "Amazing Graze: How the Livestock Industry is Ruining the American West," (United Nations Environmental Program, Desertification Control Bulletin 17, 1988), 14; John Lancaster, "Public Land, Private Profit," *Washington Post,* February 17, 1991, A1, A8, A9.

27. Jon Luoma, "Discouraging Words," *Audubon* 88 (September 1986): 104; Lancaster, A1, A8, A9.

28. John Lancaster, "Public Land, Private Profit," *Washington Post,* February 1991, A1, A8, A9.

29. Fox and Wiswall, 29; Lynn Jacobs, "Amazing Graze: How the Livestock Industry Is Ruining the American West," in *Desertification Control Bulletin 17* (Nairobi, Kenya: United Nations Environmental Program, 1988), 15.

30. Denzel Ferguson and Nancy Ferguson, *Sacred Cows at the Public Trough* (Bend, Ore.: Maverick Publications, 1983), 61; Jacobs, 15.

31. Ferguson and Ferguson, 61.

32. Ibid.

33. George Wuerthner, "The Price Is Wrong," *Sierra,* September/October 1990, 39.

34. Irving Mintzer, *A Matter of Degrees: The Potential for Controlling the Greenhouse Effect,* World Resources Institute Research Report No. 5 (Washington, D.C.: World Resource Institute, 1987), i; World Resources Institute et al., *World Resources 1990–91,* table 24.3, 350.

35. A. M. Solomon, "The Global Cycle of Carbon"; R. M. Rotty and C. D. Masters, "Carbon Dioxide from Fossil Fuel Combustion: Trends, Resources, and Technological Implications"; R. A. Houghton, "Carbon Dioxide Exchange Between the Atmosphere and Terrestrial Ecosystems"; cited in John R. Trabalka, "Atmospheric Carbon Dioxide and the Global Carbon Cycle" (Washington, D.C.: U.S. Government Printing Office, 1985).

36. V. R. Ramanathan, "Trace Gas Trends and Their Potential Role in Climate Change," *Journal of Geophysical Research* 90 (1985), 5547–66.

37. World Resources Institute et al., 346, table 24.1, 109.

38. Ibid.

39. Paul Ehrlich and Anne Ehrlich, *The Population Explosion,* 115.

40. Robert J. Buschbacher, "Tropical Deforestation and Pasture Development," *BioScience* 36, January 1986, 25.

41. Eugene Linden, "Playing with Fire," *Time,* September 18, 1989, 78.

42. David Pimentel, "Waste in Agriculture and Food Sectors: Environmental and Social Costs," paper for Gross National Waste Product, Arlington, Virginia, 1989, 9–10; Pimentel concludes that substituting a grass-feeding livestock system for the present grain and grass system would reduce energy inputs about 60 percent.

43. Alan B. Durning, "Cost of Beef for Health and Habitat," *Los Angeles Times,* 21 September 1986, p. 3.

44. Based on 65 pounds of beef consumed per person per year. The auto CO_2 emissions comparisons come from Andrew Kimbrell, "On the Road," in Jeremy Rifkin, ed., *The Green Lifestyle Handbook* (New York: Owl Book, 1990).

45. Lester R. Brown et al., *State of the World 1990* (Washington, D.C.: Worldwatch Institute; New York: W. W. Norton, 1990), 67.

46. Fred Pearce, "Methane: The Hidden Greenhouse Gas," *New Scientist,* May 6, 1990, 38.

47. Ibid.

Ecology in Our Backyards _____

Sara Stein

During the summer of 1991, one of our sons sent me the August 16 issue of the journal *Science,* which was devoted to land management policy. The many contributions to that issue made it abundantly clear that human civilization as we now know it, from grain fields to oil fields and from industrial to residential development, inevitably and inexorably reduces biological diversity. Throughout geological history, the "background" rate of extinction has been balanced by an equivalent rate of speciation: except during rare and drastic extinction episodes, Earth's number of species, though not its kinds, remained unchanged over billions of years. The recovery of biodiversity after major extinctions takes several million years. In the interval, the world is inhabited by a list of species more or less equivalent to ragweed and roaches.

Extinction is now approaching the rate prevalent during the catastrophe that killed the dinosaurs. For the first time in Earth's history, a major plant extinction is also under way.

Why this loss of biodiversity in both animal and plant life is potentially disastrous was stated most cogently in that issue of *Science* by Paul R. Ehrlich, an eminent population biologist at Stanford University and E. O. Wilson, an equally prominent entomologist at Harvard University. In their article "Biodiversity Studies: Science and Policy," they described the impact of human activity on global net primary productivity, which roughly means all the food available on land. Humans now directly use or in other ways make unavailable to other animals some 40 percent of the world's terrestrial food supply. The ecosystem services in which our burgeoning population will soon have appropriated a majority interest include waste disposal, water purification, pest suppression, and plant pollination as well as atmospheric regulation, nutrient recycling, flood and drought control, and soil manufacture. The reliable functioning of ecosystems depends exquisitely on the diversity of species—

plant, animal, and other—of which they are composed. As Ehrlich and Wilson wrote:

> The ecosystem services in which biodiversity plays the critical role are provided on such a grand scale and in a manner so intricate that there is usually no real possibility of substituting for them, even in cases where scientists have the requisite knowledge. In fact, one could conclude that virtually all human attempts at large-scale inorganic substitution for ecosystem services are ultimately unsuccessful, whether it be introductions of synthetic pesticides for natural pest control, inorganic fertilizer for natural soil maintenance, chlorination for natural water purification, dams for flood and drought control, or air-conditioning of overheated environments. Generally, the substitutes require a large energy subsidy, thereby adding to humanity's general impact on the environment, and are not completely satisfactory even in the short run.
>
> It is important to note that in supplying ecosystem services the species and genic diversity of natural systems is critical. One might assume that one grass or tree species can function as well as any other in helping control the hydrologic cycle in a watershed, or that one predator will be as good as another in controlling a potential pest. But, of course, organisms are generally highly adapted to specific physical and biotic environments—and organic substitutes, like inorganic ones, are likely to prove unsatisfactory.

In other words, we cannot go it alone. Nor may we pick and choose some few companions among the many to carry us into the future. If our species has preempted or co-opted Earth's own maintenance systems, those systems become our problem, to guard and tend at the peril of our own survival. As one who believes that in both biological and cultural evolution morality arises from necessity, this imperative struck me to the bone.

However, no contributor to that issue of *Science* had words of guidance for suburbia.

What is one to do on a quarter-acre lot?

The truth about those various colors by which an atlas theorizes the natural ecosystems of our land is that they are as lost to history as the flies and manure that once were the reality of Bedford's village green. We really occupy no color at all. There is no map tint for the peculiar—and peculiarly similar—patterns of flat lawns and bumpy shrubs, starlings and dandelions, that typify suburbia from one coast to the other. Everywhere the soil is poor, water scarce, growth weedy, succession sick, diversity a list of missing plants and animals. We are hemmed in by present realities: roads, neighbors, budgets, ordinances. We can't go back in time, either to the scythed meadows where wild lilies survived into the twentieth century, to the mosaic woodland that Indians sustained by fire, or to some primeval landscape as it might have been had humans never crossed the rims of melting glaciers. One can't advise Arizonans to plan their gardens around saguaro cacti that take forty years to reach chest height, insist to Kansans that prairie yards must annually be trampled by bison, sway Californians to the view that canyon fires are ecologically refreshing, or talk a Yankee into entertaining bears. The preservation or restoration of the wilderness is critical but not possible in one's own back yard.

One can, however, set aside a portion of this yard to plant, if not altogether naturally, then at least in a way not alien to the theoretical ecosystem in which one lives. The planting can be brought along through stages of succession or halted at a particular stage, and it can be encouraged to express apparent deficiencies in becoming ways that, since one is unaccustomed to the curly winter blades of switchgrass or the fuzzy yellow balls of a blossoming buttonbush, strike one as surprisingly exotic. So cleverly as to make one chuckle like a tickled baby, the suburban landscape can be teased to control its own pests, maintain its own soil, conserve its own water, support its own animal associates, and altogether mind its business with minimal interference from us.

But first one must make space.

The only way to do that is to take up less space oneself.

I read that the average lot size in suburban America has climbed to 10,000 square feet— roughly a quarter acre. Older lots tend to be smaller, but since house size has if anything grown faster than lot size, the pie of our land continues to be sliced pretty thin. On acreage subdivided into such portions, just the space required to maneuver excavating and roadbuilding equipment guarantees that little if anything will be left of the natural landscape; the cheapest way for a developer to leave the scene will be to throw grass seed in his wake. Into this intimidatingly blank surface the homeowner incises a bed that cringes along the foundation of the house and perhaps plants a weeping ornamental. The finished effect, in which the lawn serves as background for some baubles of exterior decoration, seems so normal to us that it is hard to view a piece of land in any other way.

It seemed so normal to us that even though we bought a glutton's portion—and there was no lawn at all—we immediately proceeded to "develop" it by clearing the brush and mowing. We started near the house. First, a back lawn, then lawn to either side, then a strip along the driveway, then loppings and mowings to roll the green rug over the land in all directions.

The first indication that we were doing something wrong was the disappearance of the pheasants. In those early days, we had planted behind the house a kitchen garden encircled by a hedge of currants whose brilliant berries were regularly enjoyed by a mother and father pheasant and all their little chicks. The distance from the hedge to the unmowed, tall grass cover was about twenty feet—a critical distance, it seems, for when we mowed a broader strip, the pheasants were cut off from their breakfast as though by an invisible fence. The more we extended the lawn, the less we saw of them, and finally we realized that there were none.

In this way we were introduced to a rather different concept of space than is implied by developers' and Realtors' use of "spacious." Spaciousness to us means not only roomy in area but visually open, expansive, uncluttered, uniform in texture, low in growth, without impediment to view. To others, "spacious" is closer to the biblical paradox, "My father's house has many mansions." The diversity and complexity of vegetation creates a spacious landscape for animals by offering each kind the opportunity to earn its living in its unique way. Remove the pheasant cover or the butterfly's flower and you have erased its space. The less variety of habitat the landscape offers, the less space there is until, when all is mowed, even an expanse the size of a golf course becomes just a hole in the world.

Suburbia has more holes already than a slice of imported Swiss, and the routes along solid ground are becoming more and more difficult for animals to negotiate. They (we, too) customarily take paths both for the efficiency that comes with familiar routes and, like pheasants under brush or us along bright streets, for safety from predators. When mother woodchucks place their children in separate dens, they visit them daily along a set itinerary. Mice and shrews take tiny paths through grass. Deer forged the trails that the Indians used and that later were often widened into roads. Certainly the pheasant family, exposed to hawks by our ignorant mowing, appreciated the "space" we created across their path about as much as I'd appreciate the space created by the Triborough Bridge's collapsing.

With animals' fear of exposure and fondness for paths in mind, we began to envision basic changes in our landscape. If ordinary garden design begins with the blank space of a lawn which is then cut here and there to create beds of taller plantings, we can aim for the obverse: a tall growth of grass, shrubs, and groves cut by mowed or mulched paths that occasionally open into clearings.

Once one begins to think in terms of paths, one realizes that they already exist, although invisibly. One doesn't walk across a lawn every which way, only in the particular ways that get one from place to place. Some of the places are spaces in the human sense of the word—open areas for sitting, eating, playing. These are the clearings. Others might be spaces in the more usual animal sense of resources that are visited regularly: garbage pail, woodpile, vegetable garden, sandbox.

It's astonishing how little land a family really uses and how much can be left as *Lebensraum* for others. Who ever uses the front yard? Who strolls along the fence? When does anybody sit in the corner of the yard?

I could have offered—indeed, I originally intended to—an illustration of a hypothetical sub-

urban lot planted the way I envision. I was saved the trouble of having to make that drawing from scratch by a letter from a reader, Michael McKeag, who had enjoyed *My Weeds*. Not knowing I was working on this book but realizing from the first one the direction of my own gardening, Michael sent a drawing of the landscape plan for his one-eighth-acre lot on a cul-de-sac in a tract house development in Oregon, along with a plant list and a map of the neighborhood.

Let's fill a back corner with a grove of trees and underplant the trees with shade-loving shrubs, I had already written before Mike's letter—and there it was on his plan, the pocket woodland that almost anyone can tuck into a corner.

Let's edge the grove with berry bushes of varying heights and species, wrap this hedgerow along the back boundary, and spill it into the other corner, I had continued in that early draft. This, too, Michael's land-

Michael McKeag's site plan for his lot in a tract development:

a. *meadow:*
   sedges,
   grasses,
   wildflowers

b. *artificial pond*

c. *wetland for*
   bog plants

d. *hedgerow,*
   mostly
   berrying
   species

e. *corner*
   woodland

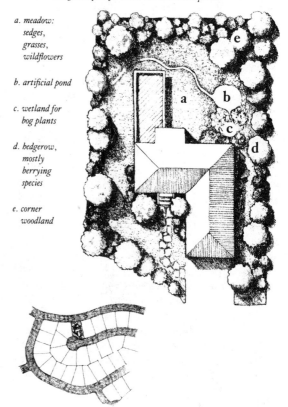

scape architect, Gretchen Vadnais, had already done with serviceberries and currants, hawthorns and hazelnuts—good foods for songbirds and small mammals.

Let's bring the hedgerow forth into the lawn with native grasses and meadow wildflowers, I had added. Can there be such a thing as transcontinental ESP? Mike's plan showed not only grass and wildflower meadow but also one of sedges and rushes around a small pool, to one side of which was a tiny bog complete with ferns and skunk cabbage. The moist areas are fed by a stream—artificial but not less appreciated by wildlife than any bit of water—that flows below the deck from which the family surveys this mini-wilderness. The entire landscape takes up half the lot, a sixteenth of an acre, yet includes three types of ecosystem: woodland, wetland, and grassland.

Let's keep a mowed strip along the sidewalk so the neighbors won't complain, I had sagely advised, but Michael chose instead a low stone wall that, if laid up without cement, can harbor toads and ground squirrels. Footpaths don't show up at the scale of this plan, but they are there, going where the family wishes to go by the routes they wish to take.

In a later letter, Michael wrote of his hope that his yard might influence his neighbors and perhaps, through publishing the plan in this book, even homeowners on distant cul-de-sacs. I swear he had not read this chapter, which now continues in its original form.

Let's see what happens when the neighbors, curious at first—perhaps a little disapproving that someone has planted something other than lawn and yew—come to covet your woodland path, your fruit, your flowers, your birds and butterflies, and begin to follow your trendy example.

Take the rectangle of land; reproduce it twenty times; lay the reproductions out in rows; place the rows back to back. See the pattern that emerges? This pattern of small woodlots edged with thickets, connected by hedgerows, and dotted with flowering meadows is the mosaic ecosystem suburbia could piece together over much of America, and each neighbor who thinks your place is comely and follows your example adds another rectangle to the overall design.

Were the larger landscape of suburbia to be reshaped in this way, as much as half the acreage could be returned to its former inhabitants, and, by sticking to our narrow human paths, we could let those of other animals cross ours in safety. It took fifty years to erase what Mrs. Dana saw. Perhaps it will take another fifty years to create something again worth seeing. The ecological history of suburbia has yet to be written, and I'd like to see it unfold well and richly toward a future worthy of another Mrs. Dana to arise and rhapsodize.

The gone goose died during Thanksgiving week. We didn't find the body. It simply disappeared as, sooner or later, all things that fall to the ground disappear. Perhaps in the wounded goose's case its disappearance was accelerated by a fox suddenly converting bird to mammal flesh and feces in the same way that the goose during its life had converted grass to bird meat and droppings (and goslings, too, of course), but why isn't the land heaped with corpses? Why isn't it buried in dead grass and manure? That all lives in whatever form eventually sink through the surface into the underworld should make us curious at least.

As a gardener I dutifully used to dig into the soil year after year dried manure, bonemeal, peat moss, and such without wondering what happened to it or how in the normal course of events cow

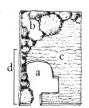

The mosaic ecosystem of future suburbia:
a. space for house and lawn or terrace
b. corner woodland
c. meadow
d. hedgerow

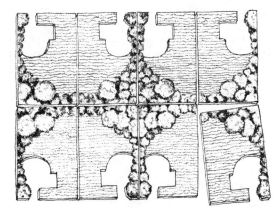

pats, steer skulls, or dead sphagnum disintegrate and burrow downward without the industry of fertilizer factories and forking gardeners. That millions of acres of grassland in Australia could be caked to death under mummified dung for lack of a necessary beetle to initiate decay certainly came to me as a surprise, and that ants and earthworms cultivate more organic material into the ground by far than gardeners do was also startling, and that every time I turned a forkful of soil I was turning the earth's stomach upside down hit me with the shock deserved by mass murderers.

This is how I came to leave the School of Neat and Clean.

I tried to reeducate Charlie, but he would have none of it. For many years he rented an apartment from my mother-in-law in the same house where Marty grew up in Queens, New York. Charlie boasted that the soil in the tiny plot he tended behind the row house grew currants as big as grapes, tomatoes the size of melons. This was a slight exaggeration—I believe he mistook gooseberries for currants—but the soil certainly was rich. And Charlie, living on a pittance, didn't begrudge impoverishing himself to make it so.

He stayed with us for a week one spring to help out. He couldn't be deterred from raking beds bare of winter litter. He was against stones as a matter of principle, no matter how small. He was for, in equal measure, cleanliness and dung.

This is the lecture I mentally prepared for Charlie but was helpless to deliver to that kindly and obstinate man.

Don't you realize, I raged internally, that plants eat stones? Where do you think minerals come from—those ions of such stuff as calcium and iron that roots absorb? From Earth's crust, of course, crumbled by frost, outgassed by volcanoes, dissolved by rain and groundwater, eroded by acid as tombstones are by the lichens that eat them. Can't you see that our northern soils are mineral-rich because glaciers ground our bedrock to a meal of stones and grit? That our wealth is not yet leached out as in the old stoneless soils to our south?

Leave the stones be, I say.

Here I imagine Charlie, never one to be taken for a fool, dropping a pebble into a glass of water, pointedly pretending to observe its dissolution.

Yes, Charlie. Rock dissolves very slowly. Not only that, but most of the minerals it releases promptly flow through bedrock's pores or along the surface and out to sea before plant roots can catch more than a tiny fraction of them. And true, too, that minerals aren't replaced anything like fast enough to support vegetation, vegetarians, or the entire food web that is life. Not even here, where the continent's granite body lies so close beneath our feet.

Still, dissolved stone is all plants eat.

This is as far as I got with my mental lecture. I would next have had to lead Charlie all the way back to the first lichens eating stone, maybe a billion years ago, and I knew he wouldn't follow me.

Lichens absorb minerals dissolving from the rocks they cling to and incorporate them into their cells as insoluble molecules—*organic* molecules, the stuff of grass and geese. Lichen—or any vegetation—thus becomes a mineral storehouse. Those that eat vegetation and those that eat vegetarians are also mineral storehouses. With exceeding slowness, but over the hundreds of millions of years since bare rock was first colonized, fantastic mineral wealth has been mined and banked in living tissue. Life itself, the tonnage of grass and forest and all the animals therein, is our mineral reservoir, and from it decayers recycle precious ions from old lives into new ones.

Decayers are soil organisms—most of them microscopic—that by digesting the fallen leaves and gone geese disassemble them step by step into their component minerals, which then become available once again to enter roots and ascend into life. The decayers' habitat is topsoil, which differs from the mix of crumbled rock and clay below in that it houses this teeming industry and the organic wherewithal to fuel it.

What you raked off the beds, Charlie, was my garden's recycling center.

What you stuck your fork into was its digestive system.

And, Charlie, if you hadn't raked and turned the soil, you wouldn't have had to feed the flowers, either.

My gardening primer warns, "Organic matter is not an addition you make just once and then forget about. It is always decomposing and being used by the plants; it must therefore always be replenished." That sounds sensible. But who was the gardener of Eden?

Such advice arises from post-paradise agricultural tribulations. When a piece of land is set aside to grow crops that will be harvested from it year after year, naturally the mineral wealth removed must be replaced. I have to do this with our vegetable garden, substituting in spring the manure Charlie favors for what we have taken the summer before and recycling back into the soil compost made over the year from weeds and crop residues. I don't like to do it, though: it isn't fun. And in more natural circumstances it isn't necessary.

Plants are capable of maintaining the fertility of their own soil and, indeed, of improving it. Imagine a bare bed of mineral subsoil with not a smidgen of mulch or fertilizer. Surely crabgrass will venture there. Crabgrass manages well on the spare mineral diet of such sterile soils. It efficiently absorbs the meager offering, incorporates it into its roots and leaves, goes to seed, and dies. Now what have we? The bed has a thin covering of dead grass at the surface and a skimpy network of dead roots below. Nickels and dimes, for sure, but the first organic deposit has been made.

As decayers mete out the interest on this deposit, dandelions, Queen Anne's lace, and foxtail grasses may find the soil good enough. Both of the wildflowers form tap roots that mine deeper minerals than the crabgrass could, and also serve as storage organs. The tops of the plants die in the fall, but, using the carbohydrates stored over the winter in their tap roots, the plants regrow the next spring. The foxtail grasses are annuals like crabgrass, and their fibrous roots mine poor soil with equal efficiency. But their top growth is luxurious: this second season's deposit has grown knee high.

And see the finches! Watch for mice! Foxtail's sumptuous heads of grain summon birds and small rodents that, by leaving high-nitrogen urine and rich droppings, further enrich the ground.

Probably by the third year the time is ripe for clover to arrive. Clover, like all legumes and a few other plants, has a special association with a bacterium that converts nitrogen molecules to an ion usable by plants. This is no mean trick. The gas, N_2, is pairs of atoms bound to one another so tightly that no plant or animal can remove the single nitrogen atoms it needs to manufacture proteins. The clover bacterium's rare chemistry pries apart the

gas, and each nitrogen atom attaches to oxygen atoms, forming the nitrate ion NO_3^-, which plant roots readily absorb.* All the nitrogen available in the soil and stored in plant and animal life has been "fixed" in this way, some by free-living bacteria, but most by species that infect legumes.

The association between the clover and its fixer is quite marvelous. As the seed sprouts, bacteria approach its root hairs. In response to their touch, the seedling grows to each a tiny tube through which the bacterium enters deeper into the root. The clover then grows round chambers where its bacteria, feeding on a carbohydrate specially prepared for them, rapidly multiply. In return for these favors, the plant receives a steady supply of nitrate during its life, and at its death the soil receives a large cache of nitrate from the root nodules the bacteria inhabited. A rich endowment has now been added to the growing mineral fund.

As organic material is deposited over the years, the subsoil near the surface becomes topsoil, first of a poor sort but growing ever richer—and thicker. Annual topdressings of dead plant material pile up; below, the roots of pioneer trees and shrubs now able to grow in this more fertile ground extend the zone of organic material downward. The more lavish and various the vegetation, the more opportunities there are for animals—more plants for caterpillars, more caterpillars for ants, more compost for earthworms, more earthworms for moles. Ants, worms, and burrowing mammals are the mixers and diggers, the forks and spades, the cultivators of this self-enriching garden.

The elaborate network of tunnels and chambers dug by a colony of red ants may extend beneath an entire yard and well into the subsoil. Ants carry the excavated dirt, laboriously dug out grain by grain, to the surface, where raindrops and footsteps mix it with plant litter. Earthworms, which tunnel by swallowing soil as they push through it, back up to deposit their castings on the ground. Their tunnels often reach three yards deep, and decaying roots may tempt them even farther.

---

* An ion is an atom or molecule that has lost or gained an electron and therefore carries an electrical charge. The nitrate ion has gained an electron and is therefore abbreviated NO_3^- to indicate its single negative charge. A calcium ion, which has lost two electrons, is abbreviated Ca^{++}.

No gardener turns a bed so deeply as these ant and earthworm cultivators, nor do we in our poor pokings tat so fine a lace of channels by which plants may receive a generosity of air and water.

Bring on the mice, moles, voles, and chipmunks! Let the woodchucks come!

It strains credulity, I know, that anyone should welcome woodchucks to the garden. They cost a lot of lettuce or the price of fencing the lettuce patch. But their excavation services are worth it. In New York State alone, woodchucks are estimated to bring to the surface 1.6 million tons of subsoil every year for conversion into topsoil. Let's do a little arithmetic. A local topsoil company sells its product—a mix of subsoil, sand, and leaf mulch—for $24 a cubic yard. One yard weighs one ton. The total for 1.6 million tons: more than $38 million.

Enough said.

But gardening books don't say it. We are led to believe that only our sweat, our mulch (our money!), can make a garden grow.

I had seen soil altogether wrongly. In my mind there was a sharp boundary, like a line drawn across a page, that separated underworld from upperworld, soil from litter. When I raked a bed clean, I defined the line exquisitely. When I dug compost in, I broke through it. But that image can't be right, for it suggests impermeability, a lack of natural movement through the boundary. If beyond one's clean garden beds detritus is continually raining down and plants are continually growing up, then there must be an active vertical transport system driving this recycling. It can't be otherwise; the interface between air and earth must be a blur of materials in motion.

Soil enrichment is inherent in the way all earthworms burrow: by ingesting soil at the front and egesting undigested remnants at the rear. Between entrance and exit, gut bacteria dining on organics the worm can't digest may multiply twentyfold, and they continue to feed and multiply in the worm's castings. There may be a thousand times more decayer bacteria in worm castings than in the surrounding soil, five times more nitrogen, seven times more phosphorus, and eleven times more potassium.

These, please note, are the very minerals one buys in bags of chemical fertilizer.

They're cheap, too: earthworms can defecate annually two hundred tons of castings per acre.

It occurred to me that the dictionary sense of the word "decay"—the destruction of some wholesome and perfect substance into a base, disintegrated form—is emotionally overwrought. Surely a lightsome calcium ion, dancily depicted Ca^{++}, is more pure than spinach leaves. The more degraded—the more like dirt—a thing becomes, the lighter and purer is its substance.

I like to think I do my part by eating salad that may be goose and passing on the crude leftovers for bacteria to refine. Although we call what we do digestion and what they do decay, I'm not sure I see the distinction. We eaters of whatever size are all in this together, this business of replenishing the soil. Without plants to eat, we all would die; without us to eat them, so would the plants.

But I realize now that to help one's garden overmuch is to hinder it. I must have been living in another world when I wrote, only a few years ago and with considerable satisfaction, of the view from my window of our gardens "bare to their bones, neat and clean, nicely edged, weed-free." Now I see that there is teeming life down there that, neatly and cleanly, I was starving. Why was I not replacing in their beds the limp bodies of weeds I had uprooted? What was I doing cutting flowers to the ground, raking them away, bagging grass clippings, blowing autumn leaves from underneath the hedge? I was robbing the life savings from my garden beds, exposing them to the elements to leach their lifeblood away.

I don't mean to say that we should hang up our shovels or trash our gardening books. Measure the ground's pH, by all means, but consider putting in plants that are adapted to that certain sweetness or sourness of soil. Recall, before laying down a mulch of pine bark, that each bush or tree is accustomed to a cover of its own dead leaves below it, and so are the decayers that refeed it. Keep a compost pile for kitchen wastes and cornstalks, but remember that fallen leaves, dead stems, and pulled weeds left in place supply a steadier source of humus than a once-in-a-springtime dole of rotted compost.

If such accommodations are unthinkable, then sure, fork in peat, spread mulch, give gifts of fertilizer. But realize that this deposit will gain interest only if the bed so started is thickly planted. The more webbed the soil is with roots, the more efficiently minerals will be harvested for storage. The more bulk of vegetation, the greater the storage capacity. The more kinds of plants there are, the more kinds of animals can live there, and the more competent the recycling business they can operate.

I mean to say that we should treasure the life in our garden both for the riches it holds and for the riches it sheds.

I mean to say that we should respect and trust our soil as a ecosystem which, if fairly treated, will thrive with minimal interference.

I mean to say that the gardener's role is neither to take nor to give: it is to plant.

A Lawn Doctor television ad proclaims, to admiring applause for a perfect expanse of green, that "great lawns like this one are made, not born." Quite true. What the ad fails to admit, however, is that the lawn so created is cut off from the life support systems on which the natural survival of grass depends, and it must therefore remain permanently in intensive care.

Lawn grasses are selected for their carpeting ability. Although each seed that germinates when the lawn is sown is an individual plant, the roots and stems soon form a feltlike mat from which the individual plants can no longer be untangled. The mat is seldom thicker than 4 inches; where developers have been stingy about replacing the topsoil they scraped away, the carpeting may be a mere 2 inches thick.

Naturally, so thin a skin dries quickly in the summer sun; unnaturally, we don't allow it to protect itself by tanning and taking its normal midsummer nap. To keep our grass green all summer, Lawn Doctor prescribed 1 inch of water a week, a total of 24 inches during the growing season, or more water than falls as rain from May through October anywhere in the United States.*

The manner of their growth puts lawn grasses in intense competition with one another. All the individual plants have the same mineral needs, all

are crammed together as tight as they can be, and all share the same thin zone of soil at the surface, where the minerals are most easily leached away by those weekly waterings that also keep the plants from ever ceasing their greedy growth. Lawn Doctor scheduled five feedings: in early spring, balanced phosphorus and potassium with a wallop of nitrogen; a coated form of nitrogen later in the spring, like a hard candy for the lawn to suck more gradually; a light meal in the first hot weeks of summer; then a rich dessert of nitrogen again in early fall, with sprinkles of the two P's as well. The feeding season ended appropriately at Thanksgiving with a *digestif* of phosphorus and potassium to prepare the grass for the next glut of nitrogen come spring.

This generous menu resulted in splendid growth that required weekly mowing from early in the chilly spring through the muggy heat of August and on into frost. Lawn Doctor prescribed, but didn't provide, that service, but it warned that any failure to remove the heavy clippings would likely smother the lawn. To these ends, we purchased a tractor and cart with which to cut off and take away the green growth in which the grass had stored the nutriment Lawn Doctor had supplied. The company did provide herbicide treatments to kill the clover and, having, thus purged the patient of this source of nitrogen, infused our naturally acid soil with lime to enhance the uptake of the petrochemicals that kept the grass growing as fast as we could mow it down and cart it off.

Continual amputation is a critical aspect of lawn care. Cutting grass regularly—preventing it from reaching up and flowering—forces it to sprout still more blades, more rhizomes, more roots, to become an ever more impenetrable mat until it is what its owner has worked so hard or paid so much to have: the perfect lawn, the perfect sealant through which nothing else can grow—and the perfect antithesis of an ecological system.

This is what Lawn Doctor did for us, and it was stunning.

That it looked so good was a credit to the doctor's art because only some portions of the lawn had been created in the proper way, on bare soil seeded with a mix of lawn grasses. Most of the expanse had been added by mowing whatever was already there, a procedure that will turn any sunny place into a lawn

---

* The annual precipitation in the Northeast averages 43 inches, most of it during the cold months of the year. Rainfall drops off westward: to 37 inches in Pittsburgh, 33 in Chicago, 14 in Denver and Santa Barbara. Seattle, in the rainforest area of the Pacific Northwest, receives an average of 39 inches.

of sorts. Intensive care did wonders even for what had once been rough goldenrod and brambles.

From a distance, one couldn't tell the difference between where we had sowed and where we had mowed. Close up, the sowed areas were finer and more uniform in texture than the areas that had merely been cut, but even in the roughest spots turf grasses spread at the expense of bunch grasses. Our native little bluestem (*andropogon scoparius*), a grass that grows in clumps, all but disappeared, to be replaced by creeping bluegrass. Mowed stands of goldenrod were immediately wiped out; clover took a little longer. But by the end of this, our brief Estate Age, we were the proud possessors of an acre of grass where not even a honeybee could find a flower to sip.

The spring following the year the pheasant family disappeared, we pulled the plug on the lawn that swept over the hillside and down the drive. By May the patient had arisen from its bed. By June it was in bloom, sparkling with buttercups. We cut what paths we needed, and waited to see how things would progress.

Over the next several years, the meadow intrinsic to lawn showed up rather rapidly on the neglected greensward. Without mowing or watering, the grass went to seed, faded to buff, and peacefully fell dormant during the summer heat. Clovers penetrated—red clover, white clover, and the yellow hop clover—followed by several vetches. These are all legumes, and all provided the grass with the nitrogen it craved to feed what had previously been its petrochemical dependence.

The legumes, and many of the other wildflowers that appeared, are deep-rooted. They excavated the earth, crumbling it to a texture more capable of holding moisture and more congenial to earthworms and decayers. Mining the soil much deeper than the lawn grass roots, they transferred precious minerals up into leaves and stems that, dying in the fall, deposited on the surface of the soil the richness they had delved. The grasses, greening and browning in their season, in turn contributed their plentiful thatch to their wildflower companions.

So the system began.

As it progressed, the soil improved. Unlike a lawn that, for all the years it is in place, can still be rolled back to reveal intact whatever the builder originally spread beneath it, meadows create topsoil and deepen the bed in which they grow.

The meadow also revealed differences in texture, chemistry, and moisture in ground that had seemed uniform when carpeted by a regularly watered lawn. A mosaic developed: a stand of coarse grass as high as my shoulder in one spot, in another an airy patch of pencil-high fine blades topped by feathery bloom, and here and there grasses whose seeds were oatlike or wheatlike among the original lawn grasses. A brilliant butterfly weed came up in a dry spot where yarrow also grew. Sedges shared damp ground with the lovely little flower called blue-eyed grass, though not in the quantity Mrs. Dana had observed. Pinks, daisies, milkweeds, buttercups, wild madder, devil's paintbrush, butter-and-eggs, two-flowered Cynthia, black-eyed Susan —each expressed some preference, each offered some gift.

That gifts were being offered was evident in the general hum and flutter of insect life. The meadow was audible with bees and crickets; the mowed grass was silent. The meadow waved and nodded in the wind; crowds of leaf hoppers leapt to the brush of a hand. The lawn was deadly still.

It began to seem a gap, a blank of no interest even to common cabbage butterflies. Its blankness extended up into air empty of the dragonflies that jeweled the meadow and, in autumn, of the finches that dropped by dozens to harvest its plentiful seeds. The cat would disappear into the tall grass, his tail twitching in anticipation of fat meadow voles. He never stalked the lawn. Friends left with wildflowers: Who would ask for a bouquet of lawn? When the meadow turned to gold and bronze set off by purple asters and yellow goldenrod, the lawn remained the tiresome green that it had been since May Day and would remain 'til Christmas. Even under the winter snow, the difference was footnoted by the tracks of rabbits, mice, and birds that went about their business in the meadow but shunned the lawn.

Out of stinginess, laziness, guilt, and curiosity, we ultimately withdrew all treatment from the remaining lawn except for necessary mowing. This was not an unqualified success. While it is true that clover helps to feed the grass, it also spreads at the lawn's expense. Various other creeping flowers bloom at less than the three-inch height to which we now set the mower's blade, giving the lawn a patchy, particolored, multitextured look. The grass is anyway not as green as greensward ought to be, certainly not as green as the moss that has taken over in some places. We mow less often and leave the scanty clippings to shrivel in the sun. During August droughts we seldom mow at all. That's when the lawn turns brown.

So we have reached a compromise. When, after several years on its own, the lawn has obviously suffered a major relapse, we give it a brief course of treatment—though not as lavishly as Lawn Doctor did—with organics instead of petrochemicals and with little enthusiasm (Lawn Doctor now offers an all-organic option). Since enjoying the robustness of a meadow, I resent the neediness of lawns. They don't behave in the tradition of the Graminae, the great and multitudinous family of grasses.

I'd like to tell my lawn a thing or two about its heritage, smack this pampered child with the hard facts about its pioneering family. How can it demand coddling when the very character of grass is to thrive on hardship?

Grasses sweep over the bitter, windblown steppes of Central Asia, creep with ice-nipped roots over the tundra's permafrost, arise in hummocks from black and stagnant swamps, tuft rock crevices in the mountains above the timberline, and green the desert in the rain shadow of the Rockies. They survive the frying heat of African savannas, sink roots deep into dry sand dunes and salt-washed tidal marshes, lead the way in the wake of forest fires, crowd into the polluted Jersey Meadows, germinate in city sidewalk cracks, grow eagerly beneath the hoofs of thundering herds, and positively enjoy a good burn. With leaves cropped by grazers and seeds consumed by birds and rodents, they still lift their blades for more.

I'd like my grass to realize its historical mission: to explore bare soil, to sink new roots in the most forbidding places, to boldly go where no trees can follow.

The Graminae are a family of more than 620 genera and 10,000 species that constitute the dominant biome occupying inhospitable land worldwide.

The first grasses appear in the fossil record in the early Cenozoic Era, when there were no polar ice caps, continents were entirely forested, and redwoods grew in Alaska. This balmy climate was what the world had known for the previous billion years. The family evolved during the next 50 million years against a background of unprecedented geo-logical upheavals that leavened the continents, created extensive drylands and deserts, dropped the average temperature at northern latitudes by fifty degrees F, and culminated in the final catastrophe of the Pleistocene Epoch when the Ice Age struck.

Dry grassland ecosystems date from at least midway through this period, 25 million years ago, when prairie grasses first appeared on the American Great Plains. The forests then were shrinking globally before the accelerating drought and cold. In California, magnolias became extinct. In Africa, apes evolved flat molars suitable for coarse grassland foods. In North America, horses left the forest to cross the plains on tiptoe, on hoofs, and in herds, exemplifying a pattern of physical and social adaptation to wide-open grassland that was followed in turn by the rest of the equid tribe and by bovines, caprids, camelids, and countless other large herbivores both extinct and extant.

Just short of 4 million years ago, two hominids left a trail of footprints at Laetoli, in the Rift Valley of East Africa, where there were also ostriches, rhinoceroses, pigs, hares, giraffes, elephants, and antelopes. The area was, and is, savanna.

The crossing of the threshold between hominid and human dates from about 3 million years ago, in the same grassland, at the beginning of the Pleistocene Epoch as the Ice Age opened. During that epoch, human populations multiplied to 5 million and occupied every continent except Antarctica. There was both vast deforestation and an equivalent spread of savanna, steppe, veldt, pampas, prairie, and tundra—grasslands all. Herds of horses 100,000 strong were common. There was a trend toward gigantism: mammoths, mastodons, giant ground sloths. The human brain tripled in size.

During the four thousand years following the last glacial retreat ten thousand years ago, agriculture was invented in the Middle East, North and South America, East Asia, Africa, and Papua New Guinea. Wheat, rice, barley, millet, rye, corn, sorghum, sugarcane, and bamboo are all grasses. Horses, camels, sheep, cows, caribou, water buffalo, and yaks are all grazers. Land that once supported 5 million now feeds 5 billion.

Lawn first appeared in the garden landscape five centuries ago.

An upstart.

What is meant by corridors, then, is not narrow strips along which animals might walk from one remote refuge to another, as our own young these days travel along the highways, but a continuity of living quarters among which movement is generational—by dispersal, not migration—from patch to patch along networks that may well originate in parklands or reservations but that must spread through all of our back yards.

The repopulation of each person's land therefore depends on neighbors, on whether they stop the flow of breeding—dampen bursts and snuff out sparks that would ignite new life beyond their boundaries—or feed the spread by what they plant and how they plant it. I enjoy my garden's private jokes, but animals don't perceive my land as private. They don't get this business of subdivisions. They are, as far as they know, on public ground. "My" butterflies need your flowers. "My" birds need your grain. The grouse I hope to welcome back must breed their way here through your switchgrass and raspberries. Thank you, whoever you are, for supporting the AWOL owl during our years-long scarcity of mice.

Last year I asked to join the local garden club. This was, it turned out, a social gaffe. One doesn't ask to join; one is invited. Nevertheless, permitted to go to one meeting, I immediately understood that even were an invitation forthcoming—which it was not—I would have been a misfit. The activity was arranging dried sprigs of this and that in mussel shells to decorate the trays of hospital patients on Thanksgiving Day. A nice thing to do, of course, but insufficient to a would-be member afflicted by wild turkeys on the brain.

I wanted to warn them against buckthorn and bittersweet. I wanted to offer to the annual plant sale species more critical than coleus to the ecology at large: infant hornbeams, little hollies, baby shadblow trees grown to transplant size and nicely potted up. I wanted to donate years of finding out and seeing how, regretting losses and celebrating returns. I wanted, I guess, to found a new chapter in the history of garden clubs.

And so, I hope, I have.

Again, Thanksgiving is approaching. The squirrels have nearly finished stocking nuts for winter. My pantry holds our share of fruit in half-pint jelly jars and quart containers. In the herb garden outside the kitchen, sage and rosemary will stay green just long enough to flavor the stuffing for our feast. In schools throughout the nation, teachers are again recounting the tales of pilgrims, pumpkins, corn, and turkeys—the great bird that has become the very symbol of plenty in the harvest season.

America is the homeland of the wild turkey, which once was widespread and abundant from western scrub to eastern forest. Now it survives only in scattered refuges. If Benjamin Franklin had had his way, our national symbol would have been the wild turkey instead of the bald eagle, a scavenger of dead meat. I think about that now. The near demise of eagles due to DDT galvanized the readers of Rachel Carson's *Silent Spring* to take action, and so powerfully that my children's generation, too, reverberates with alarm. Coming home from Maine, stalled in a traffic jam on a bridge above a bay, we saw a male bald eagle, white-crowned on vast wings, lift into the sky where thirty years ago his species was extinct. He held a fish in his talons. He was so big. I don't think our little pond or occasional dead goose could support that national emblem.

But had the turkey stood for America the Beautiful, we might have seen it as our civic duty to assure the gobbler a plentiful supply of nuts, grains, and fruits and of the beetles, spiders, snails, and centipedes that it also likes to eat. The turkey's natural habitat is "open woodlands with scattered natural or manmade clearings." We might, if we had more humbly stuck to our own paths, have kept our wild turkeys with us, sharing the promised land.

Perhaps wild turkeys can return; perhaps they can't. But when each of us, alone and in community, on acreage and in small back yards, for reasons of ecology, economy, or style has done all that can be done to restore the abundance of the land, many other animals surely will rejoin us.

Then it will work. Then there will be plenty. Then we will have reason for thanksgiving.

Enabling Environmental Practice

Anthony Weston

Environmental ethics has seldom viewed the development of values themselves as an evolutionary process. Actually, though, even our patron saint viewed them this way. "Nothing as important as an ethic is ever 'written'," insisted Aldo Leopold, and again: ethics "evolves in the minds of a thinking community."[1] This evolution, he adds, "never stops."

These lines come from the very same essay that ends with that all-too-familiar proposal, "A thing is right when it tends to preserve the integrity, stability, and beauty of the biotic community." Today that proposal is perpetually quoted as if it were a formula for a final and complete environmental ethic. Other philosophers have their own favorite formulae. Yet suppose instead that we took the more evolutionary Leopold—the tentative, provisional, nonformulaic Leopold—more seriously. Suppose that we view new sets of values as only gradually taking shape, as deeply interwoven with constantly-evolving institutions, experiences, and practices. How would environmental ethics look then?

It might seem that little would change. After all, a similar sociological view of the development of values is already widespread in contemporary mainstream ethics[2] which has nonetheless managed in practice to keep on plowing more or less the familiar old theoretical furrows. But there is a radical difference between mainstream ethics and environmental ethics. Mainstream ethics generally deals with sets of values that have long since consolidated. The familiar ethics of persons, for example, took shape several centuries ago with the rise of Protestantism and capitalism. Environmental ethics, by contrast, is only now entering what we could call an "originary" stage. Therefore, while mainstream ethics can perhaps ignore the evolutionary side of values, taking them for the most parts as "given," environmental ethics—so I will argue—cannot. The consequences of paying attention to these evolutionary processes turn out to be quite radical.

The Practice of Ethics at Originary Stages

Let us turn our attention to the appropriate *comportment* for ethics at the "originary states" of the development of values: stages at which new values are only beginning to be constituted and consolidated. Let us take as a working example the ethics of person just mentioned. We must try, then, to place ourselves back at the time when respect for persons, and indeed persons themselves, were far less secure: not at all so fixed, secure, or "natural" as they now seem, but strange, forced, truncated, the way they must have seemed to, say, Calvin's contemporaries. Our question then is: how should—how *could*—a proto-ethics of persons proceed in such a situation?

For one thing, the early stages in the development of such a new set of values require a great deal of exploration and metaphor in ethical notions. Only later can they be allowed to harden into analytic categories. For example, although the concept of "rights" of persons now may be invoked with a fair degree of rigor, through most of its history it played a much more open-ended role, allowing the possibility of treating whole new classes of people as rights-holders—slaves, foreigners, non-property-owners, women—in ways previously unheard of, and ways that, speaking literally, were misuses of the concept. ("'Barbarian rights'? But the very concept of 'barbarian' precludes being one of 'us,' i.e. Greeks, i.e. rights-holders . . . ") This malleable rhetoric of rights also *created* "rights-holders," and thus literally helped create persons themselves. To persuade someone that she has a right to something, for example, or to persuade a whole class or group that their rights have been violated, may dramatically change their behavior, and ultimately reconstructs their belief-systems and experiences of themselves as well. Even now the creative and rhetorical possibilities of the concept of rights are not exhausted. We might read the sweeping and inclusive notion of rights in *The United Nations*

Environmental Ethics, Vol. 14, No. 4 (Winter 1992), pp. 325, 329–338. Reprinted by permission of the author and the publisher.

Declaration of Human Rights in this light, for instance, rather than dismissing it, as do more legalistic thinkers, as conceptually confused.[3]

Moreover, the process of co-evolving values and practices at originary stages is seldom a smooth process of progressively filling in a kind of outline that is obvious from the start. Instead we see a variety of fairly incompatible outlines coupled with a wide range of protopractices, even social experiments of various sorts, all contributing to a kind of cultural working-through of a new set of possibilities. Those that ultimately prevail will, among other things, rewrite the history of the others, so that the less successful practices and experiments are eventually smoothed over, obscured—much as successful scientific paradigms, according to Kuhn, rewrite their own pasts so that in retrospect their evolution seems much smoother, more necessary, and more univocal than it actually was. Great moments in the canonical history of rights, for example, include the Declaration of Independence and the Declaration of the Rights of Man, capitalism's institutionalization of rights to property and wealth, and now the occasional defense of a non-positivistic notion of rights for international export. *Not* included are the utopian socialists' many experimental communities, which often explicitly embraced (what *became*) non-standard, in fact anticapitalistic notions of rights, or such sustained and massive struggles as the labor movement's organization around working-persons' rights or the various modern attempts by most social democracies to institutionalize rights to health care.

A long period of experimentation and uncertainty, then, ought to be expected and even welcomed in the originary stages of any new ethics. Remember that even the most currently familiar aspects of personhood co-evolved with a particular, complex, and even wildly improbable set of ideas and practices. Protestantism contributed not just a theology, and not just Calvin's peculiar and (if Max Weber is right) peculiarly world-historical "inner-world asceticism," but also such seemingly simple projects as an accessible Bible in the vernacular. Imagine the extraordinary impact of reading the holy text oneself, of being offered or pushed into an individual relation to God after centuries of only the most mediated access. Imagine the extraordinary self-preoccupation created by having to choose for the first time between rival versions of

the same revelation, with not only one's eternal soul in the balance but often one's earthly life as well. Only against such a background of practice did it become possible to begin to experience oneself as an individual, separate from others, autonomous, beholden to inner voices and something we now call "one's own values," and bearing the responsibility for one's choices. Only then, in short, did there appear on the scene not only the now-familiar ethics of persons but also persons themselves.

Rethinking Environmental Ethics

Again, we now look at the evolution of such values mostly from the far side. It is therefore easy to miss the fundamental contingency of those values and their dependence upon practices, institutions, and experiences that were for their time genuinely uncertain and exploratory. Reading a little sociology might restore some of that sense of contingency. In a way, though, that very turn to another discipline is also precisely the problem. We are too used to an easy division of labor that leaves philosophical ethics only the systematic tasks, articulating a set of values that is already solidified and middle-aged, and abandons originary questions to the social sciences.

Looking at such periods of uncertainty from the far side, as it were, tends to incapacitate us on the near side. Ethics itself no longer knows how to deal with values that are *now* entering an originary stage. Even when systematic ethics is out of its depth, we continue to imagine that it is the only kind of ethics there is. We continue to regard the contingency, open-endedness, and uncertainty of "new" values as an objection to them, ruling them out of ethical court entirely, or else as a kind of embarrassment to be quickly papered over with an ethical theory. We forget that every value that we now so confidently theorize about, as well as our theories themselves, had first a long period of gestation as well as a callow youth. Moreover, should we remember this much, we may simply want to tactfully withdraw from the scene: to wait a few centuries, with respect to the currently "new" values, before we think we can "do ethics" at all. But we do not always have that luxury.

The rest of the argument then is simple. *Environmental* values are in fact at an originary stage.

This I take to be the premise of most contemporary work in the field. But we can hardly confine ourselves to merely systematizing values that for the most part do not even exist. We also do not have the luxury of a few centuries' wait before we can break out the old familiar tools. We had better look for new tools instead. Whether any kind of latter-day theorizing is appropriate in environmental ethics is therefore very much an open question. Indeed, that we know how to proceed at *all* is very much an open question.

We might draw three conclusions paralleling those just drawn about ethics at previous originary stages. First and fundamentally, if environmental ethics is indeed at an originary stage, we can have only the barest sense of what ethics for a culture truly beyond anthropocentrism would actually look like. Calvinism and capitalism did not simply actualize some preexisting or easily anticipated notion of persons, but rather played a part in the larger *co-evolution* of respect for persons and persons themselves. What would emerge could only be imagined in advance in the dimmest of ways, or not imagined at all. Similarly, we are only now embarking on an attempt to move beyond anthropocentrism, and we simply cannot predict in advance where even another century, say, will take us.

When anthropocentrism is finally cut down to size, for example, there is no reason to think that what we will have or need in its place is something called "*non*-anthropocentrism" at all—as if that characterization would even begin to be useful in a culture for which anthropocentrism were indeed transcended. It may not be any kind of "centrism" whatsoever: i.e., some form of hierarchically structured ethics. It is already clear that hierarchy is not the only option.[4]

Second and correlatively, exploration and metaphor become crucial in environmental ethics. Only later can we harden originary notions into precise analytic categories. Any attempt to appropriate the moral force of rights-language for (much of) the transhuman world, for example, ought to be expected from the start to be *im*precise, literally "confused." ("'Animal rights'? But the very concept of 'animal' precludes being one of 'us', i.e., persons, i.e., rights-holders . . .") It need not be meant as a description of prevailing practice, but should be read instead as an attempt to *change* the prevailing practice. Christopher Stone's book *Should Trees Have Standing?—Toward Legal Rights for Natural Objects,* for example, is making a revisionist proposal about legal arrangements, not offering an analysis of the existing concept of rights.[5]

Something similar should be understood when we are invited to conceive not only animals or trees as rights-holders, but the land as a community and the planet as a person. Again, the force of all such arguments should be understood to be rhetorical, in a nonpejorative, pragmatic sense: the arguments are to be read as suggestive and open-ended sorts of challenges, even proposals for Deweyan kinds of social reconstruction, rather than attempts to demonstrate particular conclusions on the basis of premises supposed to be already accepted.[6] The force of these arguments lies in the way they open up the possibility of new connections, not in the way they settle or "close" any questions. Their work is more creative than summative; more prospective than retrospective. Their chief function is to provoke, to loosen up the language and correspondingly our thinking, to fire the imagination: to *open* questions, not to settle them.

The founders of environmental ethics were explorers along these lines. I want to return for a moment to Aldo Leopold: I think it is vital to reclaim him from the theorists. Bryan Norton reminds us, for example, that Leopold's appeal to the "integrity, stability, and beauty of the biotic community" occurs in the midst of a discussion of purely economic constructions of the land. It is best read, says Norton, as a kind of counterbalance and challenge to the excesses of pure commercialism, rather than as a grand criterion for moral action all by itself. John Rodman agrees, arguing that Leopold's work should be read as an environmental ethic *in process,* complicating the anthropocentric picture more or less from within, rather than as a kind of proto-system, simplifying and unifying an entirely new picture, that can be progressively refined in the way that utilitarian and deontological theories have been refined over the last century.[7] And I have already cited Leopold's own insistence that "the land ethic [is] a product of social evolution." He continues: "Only the most superficial student of history supposes that Moses "wrote" the Decalogue; it evolved in the minds of the thinking community, and Moses wrote a tentative summary of it. . . ."[8] Surely he thinks of himself as (merely) doing the same. It would be better to regard

Leopold not as purveying a general ethical theory at all, but rather as simply opening some questions, unsettling some assumptions, prying the door loose just far enough to lead, in time, to much wilder and certainly more diverse suggestions or ethical standards.

A third general conclusion is this. As I put it above, the process of evolving values and practices at originary stages is seldom a smooth process of progressively filling in a fairly obvious earlier outline. At originary stages, again, we should instead expect a variety of fairly incompatible outlines coupled with a wide range of proto-practices, even social experiments of various sorts, all contributing to a kind of cultural working-through of a new set of possibilities. In environmental ethics, then, we arrive at exactly the opposite view from J. Baird Callicott, for example, who insists that we attempt to formulate, right now, a complete, unified, "closed" (his term) theory of environmental ethics. Callicott even argues that contemporary environmental ethics should not tolerate more than one basic type of value, insisting on a "univocal" environmental ethic.[9] In fact, however, as I argued above, originary stages are the worst possible times to demand that we all speak with one voice. Once a set of values is culturally consolidated it may well be possible, perhaps even necessary, to reduce them to some kind of consistency. But environmental values are unlikely to be in such a position for a very long time. The necessary period of ferment, cultural experimentation, and *multi*-vocality is only *beginning*. So Callicott is right, perhaps, about the demands of systematic ethical theory at late cultural stages. But he is wrong—indeed wildly wrong—about what stage environmental values have actually reached.

Environmental Practice

Space for some analogues to the familiar theories does remain in the alternative environmental ethics envisioned here. I have argued that they are unreliable guides to the ethical future, but they might well be viewed as another kind of ethical experiment or proposal: rather like, for example, the work of the utopian socialists. However unrealistic, they may nonetheless play a historical and transitional role: highlighting new possibilities, inspiring reconstructive experiments, even perhaps

eventually provoking environmental ethics' equivalent of a Marx.

It should be clear, though, that the kind of constructive activity suggested by the argument offered here goes far beyond the familiar theories as well. Rather than systematizing environmental values, again, the overall project at this stage must be to begin to *coevolve* those values with practices and institutions that make them even *un*systematically possible. It is this point that I now want to develop. I offer one specific example of such a coevolutionary practice. I have to insist that is by no means the only example. Indeed the best thing that could be hoped, in my view, is the emergence of many others. But it is *one* example, and it may be a good example to help clarify how such approaches might look, and thus to clear the way for more.

A central part of the challenge is to create the social, psychological, and phenomenological preconditions—the conceptual, experiential, or even quite literal "Space"—for new or stronger environmental values to evolve. This is what I will call "enabling" such values; we may call the practical project *enabling environmental practice*. The specific example I propose is this. Consider the attempt to create actual, physical spaces for the emergence of trans-human experience: *places* within which some return to the experience of and immersion in natural settings is possible. Suppose in particular that certain places are set aside as quiet zones: places where automobile engines and lawnmowers and low-flying airplanes are not allowed, and yet places where people will live.

On one level the aim is modest: simply to make it possible to hear the birds and the winds and the silence once again. If bright outside lights were also banned, one could see the stars at night and feel the slow pulsations of the light over the seasons. A little creative zoning, in short, could make space for increasing divergent styles of living on the land: experiments in recycling and energy self-sufficiency, for example; mixed communities of humans and other species; serious "re-inhabitation," though perhaps with more emphasis on place and community than upon the individual re-inhabitors; the "ecosteries" that have been proposed on the model of monasteries; or other possibilities not yet even imagined.[10]

This is not a utopian proposal. Unplug a few outdoor lights, reroute some roads, and in some places of the country we could already have a first approximation. In gardening, meanwhile, we already experience some semblance of mixed communities. Practices like beekeeping already model a symbiotic relation with the "biotic community." It is not hard to work out policies to protect and extend such practices.

Enabling environmental practice is of course a *practice*. That does not mean that it is not also philosophical. "Theory"' and "practice" interpenetrate here. In the abstract, for example, the concept of "natural settings" just invoked has been acrimoniously debated, and the best-known positions are unfortunately more or less the extremes. "Social Ecologists" insist that no environment is ever purely natural, that human beings have already remade the entire world, and that the challenge is really to get the process under socially progressive and politically inclusive control. Some "Deep Ecologists," by contrast, argue that only wilderness is the "real world."[11] Both "deep" and "social" views have something to offer. But it may be that only from the point of view of practice, even so simple a practice as the attempt to create "quiet places," might we finally achieve the necessary distance to take what we can from the purely philosophical debate, and also to go beyond it toward a better set of questions and answers.

Both views, for example, unjustly discount "encounter." On the one hand, non-anthropocentrism should not become anti-anthropocentrism: the aim is not to push humans out of the picture entirely, but rather to open up the possibility of reciprocity *between* humans and the rest of nature. But reciprocity does require a space not wholly permeated by humans either. What we need to explore are possible realms of *interaction*. Probably we should say that both the wilderness and the city are "real worlds," if we must talk in such terms at all; but we must insist that there are still others also, and at present the most necessary of these are places where humans and other creatures, honored in their wildness and potential reciprocity, can come together, perhaps warily but at least openly.

As paradigmatic for philosophical engagement in this key we could take the work of Wendell Berry. Berry writes, for example, of what he calls "the phenomenon of edge or margin, that we know to be one of the powerful attractions of a diversified landscape, both to wildlife and to humans." "Margins" are places where domesticity and wildness meet. Mowing his small hayfield with a team of horses, Berry encounters a hawk who lands close to him, watching carefully but without fear. The hawk comes, he says,

> because of the conjunction of the small pasture and its wooded borders, of open hunting ground and the security of trees. . . . The human eye itself seems drawn to such margins, hungering for the difference made in the countryside by a hedgy fencerow, a stream, or a grove of trees. These margins are biologically rich, the meeting of two kinds of habitat.[12]

The hawk would not have come, he says, if the field had been larger, or if there had been no trees, or if he had been plowing with a tractor. Interaction is a fragile thing, and we need to pay careful attention to its preconditions. As Berry shows, this is a deeply philosophical and phenomenological project as well as a "practical" one—but nonetheless it always revolves around and refers back to practice. Without actually maintaining a farm, he would know very little of what he knows. The hawk would not—*could* not—have come to him.

Once again, this is only one example. Margins can't be the whole story. Many creatures avoid them; that is why the spotted owl's survival depends on large tracts of old-growth forest. Again, though it is *part* of the story, and a part given particularly short shrift, it seems, by all sides in the current debate.

There is no space here to develop the kind of philosophy of "practice" that would be necessary to fully work out these points. But we must at least note two opposite pitfalls in speaking of practice. First, again, it is not as if we come to this practice already knowing what values we will find or exemplify there. Too often the notion of "practice" in contemporary philosophy has degenerated into "application," i.e., of prior principles or theories. At best it might include a space for feedback from practice to principle or theory. Something more radical is meant here. Practice is the opening of the "space" for interaction, for the re-emergence of a larger world. It is a kind of exploration. We do not know in advance what we will find. Berry had to *learn*, for example, about "margins." Gary Snyder and others propose Buddhist terms to describe the necessary attitude: a kind of mindfulness, attentiveness: what Tom Birch is calling the "primary sense" of the notion of "consideration."[13]

On the other hand, this sort open-ended practice does not mean reducing our own activity to zero, as in some form of quietism. I do not mean that we must simply "open, and it will come," or that there is likely to be any single and simple set of values that somehow emerges once we merely get out of the way. Berry's view is that a more open-ended and respectful relation to nature requires constant and creative *activity:* in his case, constant presence in nature, constant interaction with his own animals, maintenance of a place that maximizes "margins." Others will (should, must) choose other ways. The crucial thing, again, is that humans must neither monopolize the picture entirely nor absent ourselves from it completely, but rather to try to live in interaction, to create a space for genuine encounter as part of our on-going reconstruction of our own lives and practices. What will come of such encounters, what will emerge from such sustained interactions, again, we cannot yet say.

No doubt it will be argued that Berry is necessarily an exception, that small unmechanized farms are utterly anachronistic and that any real maintenance of "margins" or space for "encounter" is unrealistic in mass society. Perhaps. But these are claims that are also open to argumentation and experiment, and one might even partially define an enabling environmental practice precisely by its having something practical to offer on the other side of these two automatically accepted commonplaces. Christopher Alexander and his colleagues, in *A Pattern Language* and elsewhere, for example, remind us how profoundly even the simplest features of houses, streets, and cities structure our experience of nature—and can be consciously redesigned to change those experiences. Windows on two sides of a room make it possible for natural light to suffice for daytime illumination. Buildings should be built on those parts of the land that are in the worst condition, not the best, leaving the most healthy and beautiful parts alone while improving the worse-off ones. On a variety of grounds they argue for the presence of still and moving water throughout the city, for extensive common land, "accessible green," sacred sites and burial grounds within the city as well, and so on. If we built mindfully, Alexander and his colleagues argue, main-taining and even expanding "margins," even with high human population densities, is not only possible but easy.[14] But we do have to put our theories to the side and begin to pay attention.

Notes

1. Aldo Leopold, *Sand County Almanac* (Oxford University Press, 1949), p. 225.

2. This point is argued at length in Part III of the full version of this paper, appearing in *Environmental Ethics* 14 (1992).

3. While Hugo Bedau (in "International Human Rights," in Tom Regan and Donald VanDeVeer, eds., *And Justice Toward All: New Essays in Philosophy and Public Policy* (Totowa, NJ: Rowman and Littlefield, 1982)) calls the *Declaration* "the triumphant product of several centuries of political, legal, and moral inquiry into . . . 'the dignity and worth of the human person'" (p. 298), he goes on to assert that "It is . . . doubtful whether the General Assembly that proclaimed the UN Declaration understood what a human right is," since in the document rights are often stated loosely and in many different modalities, such as "ideals, purposes, or aspirations" rather than just "as rights," and at the same time the Declaration allows considerations of general welfare to limit rights, which seems to undercut their function as protectors of individuals against such rationales (p. 302n). *Contra* Bedau, however, I am suggesting that the General Assembly understood "what rights are" very well. Rights-language is a broad-based moral language with multiple purposes and constituencies: in some contexts a counterweight to the typically self-serving utilitarian rhetoric or the powers that be; in others a provocation to think serious about even such much-mocked ideas as a right to a paid vacation; etc.

4. See for example Bernard Williams, *Ethics and the Limits of Philosophy* (Harvard University Press, 1985); Walzer's *Spheres of Justice* again; and Karen Warren, "The Power and Promise of Ecofeminism," *Environmental Ethics* 12 No. 2 (Summer 1990): 125–146.

5. Christopher Stone, *Should Trees Have Standing?—Toward Legal Rights for Natural Objects* (Los Altos: Wm Kaufmann, 1974). G. E. Varner, in "Do Species Have Standing?," *Environmental Ethics* 9, No. 1 (Spring 1987): 57–72, points out that the creation of new legal rights—as for example in the Endangered Species Act—helps expand what W. D. Lamont calls our "stock of ethical ideas—the mental capital, so to speak, with which [one] begins the business of living." There is no reason that the law must merely

reflect "growth" that has already occurred, as opposed to motivating some growth itself.

6. See Chaim Perelman, *The Realm of Rhetoric* (Notre Dame: University of Notre Dame Press, 1982) and C. Perelman and L. Olbrechts-Tyteca, *The New Rhetoric* (Notre Dame: University of Notre Dame Press, 1969) for an account of rhetoric that resists the usual Platonic disparagement.

7. Norton, "Conservation and Preservation: A Conceptual Rehabilitation," *Environmental Ethics* 8, No. 3 (Fall 1986): 195–220; Rodman "Four Forms of Ecological Consciousness Reconsidered," in Donald Scherer and Thomas Attig, *Ethics and the Environment* (Englewood Cliffs, N.J.: Prentice-Hall, 1983): pp. 89–92.

8. Leopold, *Sand County Almanac*, p. 225.

9. J. Baird Callicott, "The Case Against Moral Pluralism," *Environmental Ethics* 12, No. 2 (Summer 1990): 99–124.

10. On "ecosteries," see Alan Drengson, "The Ecostery Foundation of North America: Statement of Philosophy," *The Trumpeter* 7, No. 1 (Winter 1990): 12–16. On "reinhabitation" a good starting-point is Peter Berg, "What is Bioregionalism?", *The Trumpeter* 8, No. 1 (Winter 1991): 6–12.

11. See, for instance, Dave Foreman, "Reinhabitation, Biocentrism, and Self-Defense," *Earth First!* (1 August 1987); Murray Bookchin, "Which Way for the US Greens?" *New Politics* 11, No. 2 (Winter 1989); and Bill Devall, "Deep Ecology and its Critics," *Earth First!* (22 December 1987).

12. Wendell Berry, "Getting Along with Nature," in *Home Economics* (San Francisco: North Point Press, 1987), p. 13.

13. Gary Snyder, "Good, Wild, Sacred," in *The Practice of the Wild* (San Francisco: North Point Press, 1990); Tom Birch, "Universal Consideration," paper presented for the International Society for Environmental Ethics, American Philosophical Association, 27 December 1990; Jim Cheney, "Ecofeminism and Deep Ecology," *Environmental Ethics* 9, No. 2 (1987): 115–145. Snyder also speaks of "grace" as the primary "practice of the wild"; Doug Peacock (in *Grizzly Years*) insists upon "interspecific tact"; Berry writes of an "etiquette" of nature, Birch of "generosity of spirit" and "considerateness." All of these terms have their home in a discourse of manners and personal bearing, rather than moral discourse as usually conceived by ethical philosophers. We are not speaking of some universal categorical obligation, but of something much closer to us, bound up with who we are and how we immediately bear ourselves in the world—though not necessarily any more "optional" for all that.

14. Christopher Alexander, et al., *A Pattern Language* (New York: Oxford University Press, 1977). On windows, see sections 239, 159, and 107; on "site repair", section 104; on water in the city, sections 25, 64, and 71; on "accessible green," sections 51 and 60; on "holy ground," sections 24, 66, and 70.

EPILOGUE: CULTURAL DIVERSITY AND MORAL RELATIVISM

What is the relevance of the fact that around the planet there exists a wide variety of cultural viewpoints? Suppose by "a culture" we refer to a set of moral and empirical beliefs underlying a set of attitudes and broad viewpoints, a set embodied in a number of living persons, often, but not always, existing or having at one time existed in a continuous geographically identifiable region. Both with respect to some evaluative issues and some empirical matters, different cultures, by definition, have divergent views. Popular discussions of these matters tend to emphasize only differences, but members of different cultures are often in complete agreement about even fundamental questions and we need not fall into exaggeration here. They may be in complete accord about the morality of murder, robbery, the causes of anemia, the threat of nuclear war, the right to form one's own religious opinions, the harmful consequences of emotional abuse of children, and so on.

Perhaps, especially prior to the age of television, people were more ignorant of significant cultural differences, both in terms of beliefs and practices; it is less true today that one finds students emerging wide-eyed from their first encounter with an anthropology text, saying, "mon dieu, other people act in radically different ways and have beliefs wildly different from my own." Reflect: some people do believe in and practice polygamy (Africa, Asia, Utah), polyandry, cannibalism, slavery, bride-burning (for "insufficient" dowries in India), animal and human sacrifices for religious purposes (the Aztecs at one time, the Santerian religion in Florida), eating horses and dogs as a routine part of the diet (Korea, France, China), routine clitoridectomy of young nonconsenting females (Africa) and infanticide of normal female infants (India), routine coercive extraction of bribes to do business (the Near East); many do not.

We tend to notice practices that diverge from those familiar to us, and, in some contrast to those mentioned, we take note especially of those that seem attractive. Sometimes knowledge of other cultures offers us a novel way of looking at things, perhaps a new ideal to accept—one that we may think is deserving of acceptance and superior to our own way. We know that many native Americans did and do regard certain places as sacred, as special, to be preserved and not to be transformed for certain mundane purposes. We also may feel a loss when we see the gradual transformation of a beautiful valley free of wires, neon, cars, asphalt, garish advertising billboards, or golden arches into homogeneous hamburger alleys of a kind well-known in almost every college town. On reflection, we may come to think that we collectively do not value natural places as we should, that we give far too much free rein to market forces and that the so-called "primitive" outlook of certain other cultures is superior to our own.

Similarly, we may at first tend to discount the notions of other cultures (how could we not do so, of course, since our initial ideas tend to be the by-product of our absorption of ideas and ideals of the culture within which we have been raised); indeed, with little reflection, we often characterize such cultures as "primitive" or "backward" or "stone-age." So talk of the spirit of a mountain we classify as "animism"—as another scientifically uninformed superstition to be dismissed without further thought. But "animistic" or "pagan" beliefs may reflect the evaluation of certain nonhuman animals, plants, rivers, mountains as possessing a certain noninstrumental value, more than they involve the literal empirical belief that such entities embody nonnatural or divine spirits—perhaps, in the final analysis a bit of both. In this regard, it is worth recalling that Jesus is said to have driven evil demons into a group of pigs; arguably, then, a leading "first-world" religion embodies "animistic notions." Further the New Testament Greek word for "spirit" is (transliterated) *pneuma*, from which we get our expression "pneumatic tire." Some entities breathe air and are alive— not such a foreign idea.

This view held by some cultures may reflect, in part, a rejection of a widespread modern Western notion that nonhuman life possesses no value of its own, and when we dismiss such a view without reasonable argument, we may only be expressing our own cultural biases. So patient, charitable reflection on the views and assumptions of other cultures may foster critical reflection on our own views—and the possibility of transcending them. Imaginative literature may exercise a similar function for us and allow us to get outside of our own heads to some occasional and useful extent (see the poem reprinted here by Marge Piercy, a poem dedicated to roaches). Most people under 50 years in the United States have probably spent more time in enclosed shopping malls (the first generation in history to do so) than in a forest; perhaps we can learn something about the forests from the people who have spent more time in them or who literally know what it is like to live in them. Acquaintance with other cultures (or subcultures) can, then, be a positive resource for us.

Should we respect other cultures? Are the views of people of other cultures as meritorious as our own? The term *respect*, as a verb, might mean "fairly consider," "agree with," or

"not coercively prevent another from acting on." It may be characteristic of another culture to believe that:

Snakes are gods.

The world will end in the year 2222.

Nonhuman life is valuable for its own sake.

Ancient forests are the home of diverse, valuable life forms and should not be viewed as a crop to be harvested for the sake of preventing unemployment.

Female sexual pleasure should be minimized and, hence, surgical alteration of young females is obligatory.

Animal sacrifice to the gods is mandatory.

Recently-dead human bodies should not be displayed in public.

Automobiles should be made so that all parts are recyclable.

We deliberately chose a varied diet of examples; reflecting on them may help us avoid two extremes: an uncritical, romanticized acceptance of views thought to be pure, simple, untainted, non-Western, or "third-world" in outlook; or an uncritical, dismissive, almost cynical and arrogant "writing off" of outlooks not associated with what is modern, "efficient," "scientific," "sophisticated," and Western.[1]

We propose what seems a reasonable start on our questions about whether we must, in some sense, respect other cultures. First, surely we should fairly consider the views of other cultures—indeed *anyone's* views—be they from people held in disfavor by some, e.g., Moslem fundamentalists, Christian fundamentalists, used car salesmen, Serbian soldiers, communists, lawyers, atheists, academics, or the manager of the local whorehouse. Even Hitler was right about a few things, e.g., exercise is usually good for people. The right way to assess a view is, we judge, by assessing the reasons that can be marshaled in its favor, and against it, and not by indirect and often logically irrelevant considerations about the identity or group membership or background of the person espousing the views in question. Should we accept all the views of those from other cultures? Evidently doing so is not possible since they collectively are not compatible; that is, they are logically inconsistent with one another. Second, it is evident that in many cases, modern science provides compelling reason to reject the empirical assumptions of many cultures (including our own); we note the frequent denial of the process of evolution among many "modern Western" people, not to mention the lack of scientific support for the popular view that we may have lives after death. At least if one substantially accepts the canons of rational belief implicit in much of modern science (we think one should), then one has ground for rejecting much that is characteristic of various cultures, in spite of a current tendency to be so polite as to say nothing negative about another culture (or a member of it). That is surely a phony form of "respect," the kind involved in politely and falsely reassuring an alcoholic that one does not think that he or she has a problem.

If there is no compelling reason readily to agree with the defining assumptions of another culture (or subculture), must we at least not allow others to *act* on their own beliefs—beliefs that they may even regard as sacred or definitive of "who I am" as a Jew, as an African-American, an Irishman, a Catholic (Mafia member, Klan member, Nazi, skinhead, Blood, etc.)? The simplistic, easy response to this question is to say "of course, we must not interfere with those (competent adults) whose sincerely held beliefs differ from our own." This widely espoused view is incompatible with a great deal of sensible law and practice. Should we respect, in the sense of not coercively interfering with, the views of the sincere Nazi who wishes to make lampshades out of the skin of Jews? If we were to discover that Jeffrey Dahmer (a convicted serial killer in the United States in 1992) was simply motivated to kill and dismember his victims by a desire to be faithful to religious beliefs requiring human sacrifice, would we be forced to conclude that we must "live and let live" by way of respecting his beliefs, or those of some possible distinct culture to which he belonged? There indeed are some pedophiles who have a desire and right to engage in what most people classify as child abuse. Is it wrong to incarcerate (a paradigm example of coercive intervention) those who have sex with eleven-years-olds? Would doing so be a failure to respect the beliefs of the pedophiles in the "noninterference" sense of "respect"?[2] What about parents who insist on their right to keep their children out of public school and subject them to what some think of as a kind of religious brainwashing, arguably a serious form of psychological child abuse? Must we respect such parental rights?

One might say that one must not interfere with the beliefs of others so long as a person's acting on such beliefs does not cause harm to others. This is a plausible initial effort at providing an answer to our question of when we may interfere and when we may not. Several points are worthy of note here. First, the answer will not do for a number of reasons discussed in recent literature; indeed, we have come upon a serious and deep question of political philosophy, the answer to which turns out to be not at all simple.[3] Some of the difficulties surround the concept of harm. Some are related to the fact that we often consent to harm or the risk of such, and that often seems to be a relevant and complicating factor. In addition the tacit assumption is commonly made that *only* harm to humans is morally important, and that is precisely the central assumption that has been widely challenged in recent years in discussions of environmental ethics; at the very least, the assumption is not self-evident and needs to be defended.

The view that says we should interfere with actions proceeding from culturally alien norms when and only when one person harms another is, itself, on the face of it, *opposed* to a kind of moral relativism that insists that morality is relative (understanding the expression in the sense that all moral views or moral principles are equally plausible). One might ask, "why is it so opposed?" The short answer is that the view asserts that there is some universal, culturally invariant standard for deciding when it is permissible to interfere with the actions of others, even if those actions proceed from adherence to moral or other norms of other cultures (this view is then "anti-relativist" or "absolutist" in one sense of those elusive terms). One way to see this is to imagine someone who dissents from this principle and, when confronted with the claim, insists that it has no validity in his culture, and that in his culture killing a few people of an alien group is a valued and mandatory part of the rite of passage to achieving manhood. To claim that doing so is just murder and further that we have perfectly good reason to interfere with such actions is to reject the notion that we must not interfere with actions proceeding from, or defensible by, appeal to a moral principle definitive of another culture. To press a point a bit further, it is not clear why we should acquiesce to, say, child torture for purposes of pleasure, carried out by a person in our culture (but let us assume membership in a different subculture, say, the Marquis de Sade Pedophile Society) if we believe there is no rational justification for such actions. It is also not obvious why we should acquiesce and not interfere with such actions by a person of another culture even if that person can truly say that the norms of his or her culture imply that doing so is fine. It is one thing to fairly consider alternative and competing moral claims stemming from members of one's own culture or from another culture; it is another to accept them or to conclude that they deserve acceptance by any rational person. For reasons

we have elaborated, there is a third alternative to a naive capitulation to the norms of other cultures or, alternatively, a mindless, impulsive rejection of them.

Suppose that a specific type of act may be wrong on one occasion of its performance in one culture, *C1*, and all right on another occasion of its performance, say, in culture *C2*, i.e., the two *different performances* of the *same type* of act vary in moral value. For example, we might think that infanticide of a normal infant is wrong when carried out in an affluent culture but not wrong in a nomadic culture under conditions of severe scarcity. If there are cases so correctly evaluated, does this phenomenon support the view that morality is relative? The answer may be yes, if by "moral relativism" one means that *different performances of the same kind of action may vary in moral value* (perhaps across different cultures or perhaps within the same culture). Interestingly, the answer may be no, *if* by "moral relativism" one means there is no universally binding (across cultures) principle of morality; after all, if the consequences of the different performances of the acts are significantly different (and they may be), then the principle of utility (for example) would imply that the different performances have different moral values. Thus, there are principles of morality that may be rationally justifiable (we leave this open here of course) and binding on all people, which, in fact, implies that different performances of the same kind of act vary in moral value. That is, a certain relativism about specific actions is not only compatible with there being universally valid basic principles of morality, but is actually *implied by* this form of moral absolutism. Often, discussion of these matters fails to distinguish between a focus on basic moral *principle* and a focus on the morality of *particular acts*; the morality of specific performances of certain kinds of actions may vary (in that sense, morality changes across cultures or, simply, contexts) even if there are one or more valid and binding (across time and across space) principles of morality, ones that under-gird such judgments (in this sense, morality does not change). To make these few points is not to settle all the puzzles by a long shot; rather, it is intended to open the door for deeper reflection and discussion.

NOTES

1. Although Western European culture, or Anglo-Saxon culture carried in its train a substantive amount of racism and sexism, it is important to observe that this was characteristic of many other cultures, e.g., compare the practice of slavery found in Asia and in Africa and carried on by indigenous peoples. Further, certain democratic values in favor of tolerance, individual liberty and rights, and protection of minorities are, arguably, no better articulated anywhere historically than in the Western European moral and political thought, e.g., that of John Locke, Thomas Paine, Immanuel Kant, Jeremy Bentham, and John Stuart Mill, among others.

2. Not to generalize too quickly about such matters, there is a possible view that condones as permissible *only* adult sexual relations with children who consent and are *capable* of competent choice. Who is competent and capable of reasonable choice and about what are important matters. Sometimes "child" is defined as one under 18 years of age, but in some states it is legal for a person to marry at 14 years.

3. See Joel Feinberg, *Harm to Others* (New York: Oxford University Press, 1985).

BIBLIOGRAPHY

We wish to call special attention to the journal, *Environmental Ethics*, a pioneering periodical from the early days of an emerging field of study. The founding editor, Eugene Hargrove, as of 1994 was in the Department of Philosophy at the University of North Texas in Denton, Texas. We also wish to call attention to these periodicals: *Environmental Values, Between the Species, The Trumpeter, Environmental History Review, Journal of the Society for Conservation Biology,* and *Ecological Economics.* Other journals that occasionally focus on environmental issues are: *Inquiry, Monist, American Philosophical Quarterly, Ethics, Journal of Value Inquiry,* and *Philosophy and Public Affairs.*

Bibliographies are springboards to jump from; the materials cited here, incomplete in many respects, will lead the reader to other important works. Those interested will find the two annotated bibliographies drawn up by Eric Katz to be of great assistance. They are: "Environmental Ethics: A Select Annotated Bibliography 1983–1987," in *Research in Philosophy and Technology,* Volume 9, pp. 251–85; and "Environmental Ethics: A Select Annotated Bibliography: II: 1987–1990" in *Research in Philosophy & Technology,* Volume 12, pp. 287–324. In 1994 Katz was located at the New Jersey Institute of Technology, University Heights, Newark, New Jersey 07102 and was preparing a third bibliography. For both current bibliographic references, videotape information and current announcements about conferences on, or related to environmental ethics, see the lively and thorough *International Society for Environmental Ethics Newsletter* recently available by contacting Professor Laura Westra; Department of Philosophy; University of Windsor; Windsor, Ontario N9B 3P4; Canada. On a broad variety of topics in ethics, the excellent two-volume *Encyclopedia of Ethics* edited by Lawrence Becker and Charlotte Becker (New York: Garland Publishing Co., 1992) will prove extremely useful.

I. What We Are Doing

I-A. Human Population and Pressure on Resources

Bayles, Michael D., ed. *Ethics and Population* (Cambridge, MA: Schenkman, 1976).

Cole, H., *et al. Thinking About the Future: A Critique of The Limits to Growth* (London: Chatto & Windus and Sussex University Press, 1973).

Donaldson, Peter J. *Nature Against Us: The United States and the World Population Crisis* (Chapel Hill: University of North Carolina Press, 1990).

Ehrlich, Paul R. *The Population Bomb* (London: Pan Books/Ballantine, 1971).

Ehrlich, Paul R., and Anne H. Ehrlich. *Population, Resources, Environment: Issues in Human Ecology* (San Francisco: W. H. Freeman, 2nd ed., 1972).

———. *The Population Explosion* (New York: Simon & Schuster, 1990).

Hardin, Garrett. *Exploring New Ethics for Survival: The Voyage of the Spaceship Beagle* (New York: Viking Press. 1972).

Hartman, Betsy. *Reproductive Rights and Wrongs: The Global Politics of Population Control and Contraceptive Choice* (New York: Harper and Row, 1987).

Lappé, Frances Moore, and Joseph Collins. *World Hunger: Twelve Myths* (New York: Grove Press, 1986).

Malthus, Thomas Robert. *Population: The First Essay* (Ann Harbor Paperbacks/University of Michigan Press, 1959).

Orr, David, and Marvin S. Soroos. *The Global Predicament* (Chapel Hill, NC: University of North Carolina Press, 1979).

Partridge, Ernest, ed. *Responsibilities to Future Generations* (New York: Prometheus Books, 1981).

Sen, Amartya. *Poverty and Famines* (New York: Oxford University Press, 1981).

Simon, Julian L. *The Ultimate Resource* (Princeton: Princeton University Press, 1981).

Simon, Julian, and Herman Kahn, eds. *The Resourceful Earth* (Oxford: Basil Blackwell, 1984).

White, Rodney R. *North, South, and the Environmental Crisis* (Toronto: University of Toronto Press, 1993).

I-B. Forests and Wilderness

Agarwal, Bina. *Cold Hearths and Barren Slopes: The World Fuel Crisis in the Third World* (New Delhi: Allied Publishers Private Limited, 1986).

Barney, Daniel R. *The Last Stand, Ralph Nader's Study Group Report on the National Forests* (New York: Grossman Publishers, 1974).

Booth, Douglas. *Valuing Nature: The Decline and Preservation of Old Growth Forests* (Lanham, MD: Rowman and Littlefield, 1993).

Denslow, Julie, and Christine Padoch. *People of the Tropical Rain Forest* (Berkeley: University of California Press, 1988).

Dietrich, William. *The Final Forest: The Battle for the Last Great Trees of the Pacific Northwest* (New York: Simon and Schuster, 1992).

Frome, Michael. *Battle for the Wilderness* (New York: Praeger Publishers, 1974).

Gillis, M. D., and R. Repetto. *Public Policies and the Misuse of Forest Resources* (New York: Cambridge University Press, 1988).

Gradwohl, Judith, and Russell Greenberg. *Saving the Tropical Forests* (Washington, D.C.: Island Press, 1988).

Gregersen, Hans, Sydney Draper, and Dieter Elz, eds. *People and Trees: The Role of Social Forestry in Sustainable Development* (Washington, D.C.: World Bank Publications, 1989).

Guha, Ramachandra. *The Unquiet Woods: Ecological Change and Peasant Resistance in the Himalaya* (Berkeley: University of California Press, 1990).

Hurst, Philip. *Rainforest Politics: Ecological Destruction in South-East Asia* (London: Zed Books, 1990).

Mahar, Dennis J. *Government Policies and Deforestation in Brazil's Amazon Region* (Washington, D.C. World Bank, 1989).

Myers, Norman. *The Primary Source: Tropical Forests and Our Future* (New York: Norton Publishing, 1984).

Nash, Roderick. *Wilderness and the American Mind* (New Haven: Yale University Press, 1973).

———, ed. *American Environmentalism: Readings in Conservation History,* 3rd edition (New York: McGraw-Hill, 1990).

Nations, James D. *Tropical Rainforests, Endangered Environment* (New York: Franklin Watts, 1988).

Norse, Elliot A. *Ancient Forests of the Pacific Northwest* (Washington, D.C.: Island Press, 1990).

Ramakrishna, Kilaparti, and George M. Woodwell, eds. *World Forests for the Future* (New Haven: Yale University Press, 1993).

Repetto, R., and M. Gillis, eds. *Public Policies and the Misuse of Forest Resources* (New York: Cambridge University Press, 1988).

Routley, Richard, and Val Routley. *The Fight for the Forests* (Canberra: Australian National University Press, 1974).

Suess, Dr. *The Lorax* (New York: Random House, 1971).

Schwartz, William, ed. *Voices for the Wilderness* (New York: Ballantine Book, Inc., 1969).

Shiva, Vandana. *Forestry Crisis and Forestry Myths: A Critical Review of Tropical Forests: A Call for Action* (*Tropical Forest: A Call for Action* is a Joint Report of The World Bank, UNDP, and World Resources Institute.) (Malaysia: World Rainforest Movement, 1987).

I-C. Planetary Degradation

Abrahamson, D. *The Challenge of Global Warming* (Washington, D.C.: Island Press, 1989).

Benedick, Richard E., et al. *Greenhouse Warming: Negotiating a Global Regime* (Washington, D.C.: World Resources Institute, 1991).

———. *Ozone Diplomacy: New Directions in Safeguarding the Planet* (Cambridge: Harvard University Press, 1991).

Brown, Wilmette. *Roots: Black Ghetto Ecology* (London: Housewives in Dialogue, 1986).

Bullard, Robert D., ed. *Confronting Environmental Racism: Voices from the Grassroots* (Boston, MA: South End Press, 1993).

Dotto, Lydia. *The Ozone War* (Garden City, NY: Doubleday, 1978).

Fisher, David, E. *Fire and Ice: The Greenhouse Effect, Ozone Depletion, and Nuclear Winter* (New York: Harper & Row, 1990).

Edelstein, Michael R. *Contaminated Communities: The Social and Psychological Impacts of Residential Toxic Exposure* (Washington, D.C.: Island Press, 1988).

Gibson, Mary, ed. *To Breathe Freely: Risk, Consent, and Air* (Totowa, NJ: Rowman & Allanheld, 1985).

Hynes, H. Patricia. *The Recurring Silent Spring* (New York: Pergamon Press, 1989).

Leggett, Jeremy. *Global Warming: The Greenpeace Report* (New York: Oxford University Press, 1990).

MacLean, Doug, ed. *Energy and the Future* (Totowa, NJ: Rowman and Littlefield, 1983).

Michael, H. Brown. *The Toxic Cloud* (New York: Harper and Row, 1987).

Oppenheimer, M., and R. Boyle. *Dead Heat* (New York: Basic Books, 1990).

Pimentel, David, ed. *The Pesticide Question: Environment, Economics, and Ethics* (New York: Chapman and Hall, 1993).

Reid, Walter V. *Drowning the National Heritage: Climate Change and the U.S. Coastal Biodiversity* (Washington, D.C.: World Resources Institute, 1991).

———. *Keeping Options Alive: The Scientific Basis for Conserving Biodiversity* (Washington, D.C.: World Resources Institute, 1989).

Schneider, Stephen H. *Global Warming: Are We Entering the Greenhouse Century?* (San Francisco: Sierra Club Books, 1989).

Shrader-Frechette, K. S. *Nuclear Power and Public Policy* (Dordrecht, Holland: Reidel, 1989).

II. The Other Animals

Adams, Carol J. *The Sexual Politics of Meat: A Feminist-Vegetarian Critical Theory* (New York: Continuum, 1990).

The Animals Right's Agenda: The International Magazine of Animal Rights and Ecology. P.O. Box 6809, Syracuse, N.Y. 13217.

Between the Species. P.O. Box 254, Berkeley, Calif. 94701.

Bostock, Stephen St. C. *Zoos and Animal Rights: The Ethics of Keeping Animals* (London and New York: Routledge, 1993).

Cartmill, Matt. *A View to a Death in the Morning: Hunting and Nature Through History* (Cambridge, MA: Harvard University Press, 1993).

Cavalier, Paola, and Peter Singer, eds. *The Great Ape Project* (New York: St. Martin's Press, 1993).

Clark, Stephen. *The Moral Status of Animals* (Oxford: Clarendon Press, 1977).

Crosby, Alfred W. *Ecological Imperialism* (New York: Cambridge University Press, 1986).

Dawkins, Marian. *Animal Suffering: The Science of Animal Welfare* (New York: Routledge, Chapman, and Hall, 1980).

Ehrenfeld, D. *The Arrogance of Humanism* (New York: Oxford University Press, 1981).

Fox, M. W. *Returning to Eden: Animals Rights and Human Responsibility* (New York: Viking Press, 1980).

Fox, Michael, and Nancy Wiswall. *The Hidden Costs of Beef* (Washington, D.C.: Humane Society of the United States, 1989).

Frey, R. G. *Interests and Rights: The Case Against Animals* (Oxford: Clarendon Press, 1980).

———. *Rights, Animals and Suffering* (Oxford: Basil Blackwell Ltd., 1983).

Godlovitch, Stanley, Roslind Godlovitch, and John Harris, eds. *Animals, Men, and Morals* (London: Gallancz, 1971).

Hargrove, Eugene. *The Animal Rights/Environmental Ethics Debate: The Environmental Perspective* (Albany: State University of New York Press, 1992).

Harrison, Ruth. *Animal Machines: The New Factory Farming Industry* (London: Stuart, 1964).

Hawkins, Marion S. *Through Our Eyes Only: A Journey into Animal Consciousness* (New York: W. H. Freeman & Co., 1993).

Inquiry 22, nos. 1–2 (Summer 1979). Includes a useful bibliography; the entire issue is about animals.

Johnson, Edward. *Species and Morality*, Ph.D. dissertation in philosophy at Princeton University (1976); see University Microfilms International, 1977: Ann Arbor, Michigan.

Kroc, Ray. *Grinding It Out: The Making of McDonald's* (Chicago: Henry Regnery, 1977).

Lappé, Frances Moore. *Diet for a Small Planet* (New York: Ballantine Books, 1982).

Lappé, Frances Moore, and Joseph Collins. *Food First: Beyond the Myth of Scarcity* (New York: Ballantine Books, 1978).

Leahy, Michael P. T. *Against Liberation: Putting Animals in Perspective* (London and New York: Routledge, 1991).

Lovejoy, Arthur O. *The Great Chain of Being: A Study of the History of an Idea.* (Cambridge, MA: Harvard University Press, 1936).

Magell, Charles. *A Bibliography on Animal Rights and Related Matters* (Washington, D.C.: University Press of America, 1981).

Mason, Jim, and Peter Singer. *Animal Factories* (New York: Crown, 1980).

Midgley, Mary. *Animals and Why They Matter* (Harmondsworth, England: Penguin Books Ltd., 1983).

———. *Beast and Man* (Ithaca: Cornell University Press, 1979).

———. *Evolution as a Religion* (London: McThuen Ltd., 1985).

The Monist 70, no. 1 (January, 1987). Issue on animal rights.

Mowat, Farley. *Never Cry Wolf* (Toronto: Bantam Books, 1983).

Rachels, James. *Created from Animals: The Moral Implications of Darwinism* (Oxford and New York: Oxford University Press, 1990).

Regan, Tom. *All That Dwell Therein: Animal Rights and Environmental Ethics* (Berkeley: University of California Press, 1982).

———. *The Case for Animal Rights* (Berkeley: University of California Press, 1983).

———. *The Thee Generation: Reflections on the Coming Revolution* (Philadelphia: Temple University Press, 1991).

Regan, Tom, and Peter Singer, eds. *Animal Rights and Human Obligations* (Englewood Cliffs, NJ: Prentice-Hall, 1976).

Rifkin, Jeremy. *Beyond Beef: The Rise and Fall of the Cattle Culture* (New York: Dutton, 1992).

Rollin, Bernard. *Animal Rights and Human Morality,* rev. ed. (Buffalo: Prometheus Press, 1992).

———. *The Unheeded Cry: Animal Consciousness, Animal Pain and Science* (Oxford: Oxford University Press, 1989).

Rosenfield, Lenora. *From Beast-Machine to Man-Machine* (New York: Columbia University Press, 1968).

Ryder, Richard. *Victims of Science: The Use of Animals in Research* (London: Davis-Poynter, 1975).

———. *Speciesism: The Ethics of Vivisection* (Edinburgh: Scottish Society for the Prevention of Vivisection, 1974).

Serpell, James. *In the Company of Animals: Study of Human-Animal Relationships* (Oxford: Basil Blackwell, 1986).

Singer, Peter. *Animal Liberation* (New York: A New York Review Book, distributed by Random House, 1975).

———. *The Expanding Circle* (New York: Farrar, Straus, and Giroux, 1981).

———, ed. *In Defense of Animals* (New York: Basil Blackwell, 1987).

———. *Practical Ethics* (Cambridge: Cambridge University Press, 1979).

III. Constructing an Environmental Ethic

III-A. The Expanding Circle

Callicott, J. Baird, ed. *Companion to a Sand County Almanac: Interpretive and Critical Essays* (Madison: University of Wisconsin Press, 1987).

Engberg Robert, and Donald Wesling, eds. *John Muir: To Yosemite and Beyond: Writings from the Years 1863 to 1875* (Madison: University of Wisconsin Press, 1980).

Flader, Susan L. *Thinking like a Mountain: Aldo Leopold and the Evolution of an Ecological Attitude toward Deer, Wolves, and Forests* (Columbia: University of Missouri Press, 1974).

Hays, Samuel P. *Conservation and the Gospel of Efficiency: The Progressive Conservation Movement 1890–1920* (Cambridge, MA: Harvard University Press, 1959).

Hessel, Dieter T., ed. *After Nature's Revolt: Eco-Justice and Theology* (Minneapolis, MN: Augsburg Fortress, 1991).

Kellert, Stephen R., and Edward O. Wilson, eds. *The Biophilia Hypothesis* (Washington, D.C.: Island Press, 1993).

Lovelock, James. *Gaia: A New Look at Life on Earth* (New York: Oxford University Press, 1981).

Pinchot, Gifford. *The Fight for Conservation* (Seattle: University of Washington Press, 1910).

Marsh, George Perkins. *Man and Nature* (Cambridge, MA: Harvard University Press, 1965).

The Monist 75, no. 2 (April, 1992). Special issue on the intrinsic value of nature.

Schultz, Robert C., and J. Donald, Hughes, eds. *Ecological Consciousness: Essays from the Earthday X Colloquium, University of Denver, April 21–24, 1980* (Washington, D.C.: University Press of America, 1981).

Torrance, John, ed. *The Concept of Nature* (New York: Oxford University Press, 1993).

Wright, Larry. *Teleological Explanation* (Berkeley and Los Angeles: University of California Press, 1976).

III-B. Competing Visions

1. *Deep Ecology and Social Ecology*

Bookchin, Murray. *The Ecology of Freedom: The Emergence and Dissolution of Hierarchy* (Palo Alto, CA: Cheshire Books, 1982).

———. *The Philosophy of Social Ecology: Essays on Dialectical Naturalism* (Toronto: Black Rose Books, 1990).

———. *Post-Scarcity Anarchism* (San Francisco: Ramparts Press, 1971).

———. *Remaking Society: Pathways to a Green Future* (Boston: South End Press, 1990).

———. *Toward an Ecological Society* (Montreal: Black Rose Books, 1980).

Bradford, George. *How Deep Is Deep Ecology? A Challenge to Radical Environmentalists* (Ojai, CA.: Times Change Press, 1989).

Clark, John, ed. *Renewing the Earth: The Promise of Social Ecology* (London: Green Print, 1990).

———. *The Anarchist Moment: Reflections on Culture, Nature, and Power* (Toronto: Black Rose Books, 1984).

Devall, Bill. *Simple in Means, Rich in Ends, Practicing Deep Ecology* (Salt Lake City: Peregrine Smith Books, 1988).

Devall, Bill, and George Sessions. *Deep Ecology, Living as if Nature Mattered* (Salt Lake City: Peregrine Smith Books, 1985).

Drengson, Alan R. *Beyond Environmental Crisis: From Technocratic to Planetary Person* (New York: Peter Lang, 1989).

Evernden, Neil. *The Natural Alien* (Toronto: University of Toronto Press, 1985).

Fox, Warwick. *Toward a Transpersonal Ecology: Developing New Foundations for Environmentalism* (Boston: Shambhala, 1990).

Goldsmith, Edward. *The Way: An Ecological World View* (London: Rider, 1992).

Harbinger: *The Journal of Social Ecology.* P.O. Box 89, Plainfield, Vt. 05667.

Martin, Calvin Luther. *In the Spirit of the Earth: Rethinking History and Time* (Baltimore: Johns Hopkins University Press, 1992).

Mathews, Freya. *The Ecological Self* (London: Routledge, 1990).

McLaughlin, Andrew. *Regarding Nature: Industrialism and Deep Ecology* (Albany: State University of New York Press, 1993).

Merchant, Carolyn. *Radical Ecology: The Search for a Liveable World* (London and New York: Routledge, 1993).

Naess, Arne. *Ecology, Community, and Lifestyle* (Cambridge: Cambridge University Press, 1989).

Pepper, David. *Eco-socialism: From Deep Ecology to Social Justice* (London and New York: Routledge, 1993).

Reed, Peter, and David Rothenberg, eds. *Wisdom in the Open Air: The Norwegian Roots of Deep Ecology* (Minneapolis: University of Minnesota Press, 1993).

Rothenberg, David. *Is It Painful to Think? Conversations with Arne Naess* (Minneapolis: University of Minnesota Press, 1992).

Sale, Kirkpatrick. *Dwellers in the Land, The Bioregional Vision* (San Francisco: Sierra Club Books, 1985).

Seed, John, Joanna Macy, Pat Fleming, and Arne Naess. *Thinking Like a Mountain, Towards a Council of All Beings* (Philadelphia: New Society Publishers, 1988).

Snyder, Gary. *The Old Ways* (San Francisco: City Lights Books, 1977).

———. *Turtle Island* (New York: New Directions Books, 1977).

———. *The Practice of the Wild* (North Point, 1990).

Spretnak, Charlene, and Fritjof Capra. *Green Politics* rev. ed. (Santa Fe: Bear and Company, 1986).

The Trumpeter. LightStar: P.O. Box 5853, Victoria, B.C. Canada V8R 6S8.

Tobias, Michael, ed. *Deep Ecology* (San Diego: Avant Books, 1977).

2. Ecofeminism

Adams, Carol J., ed. *Ecofeminism and the Sacred* (New York: Continuum, 1993).

Allen, Paula Gunn. *The Sacred Hoop: Recovering the Feminine in American Indian Tradition* (Boston: Beacon Press, 1986).

Biehl, Janet. *Rethinking Ecofeminist Politics* (Boston: South End Press, 1991).

Brown, Wilmette. *Roots: Black Ghetto Ecology* (London: Housewives in Dialogue, 1986).

Caldecott, Leonie, and Stephanie Leland, eds. *Reclaim the Earth: Women Speak Out for Life on Earth* (London: The Women's Press 1983).

Diamond, Irene, and Gloria Feman Orenstein, eds. *Reweaving the World, The Emergence of Ecofeminism* (San Francisco: Sierra Club Books, 1990).

Easlea, Brian. *Science and Sexual Oppression: Patriarchy's Confrontation with Women and Nature* (London: Weidenfeld and Nicholson, 1981).

The Ecofeminist Newsletter: A Publication of the National Women Studies Association (NWSA) Ecofeminist Task Force, ed. Noel Sturgeon. Middletown, CT: Center for the Humanities, Wesleyan University.

Environmental Review 8, no. 1 (1984). Special issues on women and environmental history, guest editor, Carolyn Merchant.

Gaard, Greta, ed. *Ecofeminism: Women, Animals, Nature* (Philadelphia: Temple University Press, 1993).

Gray, Elizabeth Dodson. *Green Paradise Lost* (Wellesley, MA: Roundtable Press, 1979).

Griffin, Susan. *Women and Nature: The Roaring Inside Her* (New York: Harper and Row Publishers, Inc., 1978).

Heresies #13: Feminism and Ecology 4 (1981).

Hypatia 6 (Spring 1991). Special issue on ecological feminism.

Jaggar, Alison M., ed. *Living with Contradictions: Controversies in Feminist Social Ethics* (Boulder, CO: Westview Press, 1994).

Kolodny, Annette. *The Lay of the Land: Metaphor as Experience and History in American Life and Letters* (Chapel Hill: University of North Carolina Press, 1975).

LaChapelle, Delores. *Sacred Land, Sacred Sex: Rapture of the Deep* (Durango, CO: Vivaki Press, 1992).

List, Peter, C., ed. *Radical Environmentalism: Philosophy and Tactics* (Belmont, CA: Wadsworth Publishing Co., 1993).

Merchant, Carolyn. *The Death of Nature: Women, Ecology, and the Scientific Revolution* (New York: Harper and Row Publishers, Inc., 1983).

———. *Ecological Revolution: Nature, Gender, and Science in New England* (Chapel Hill: University of North Carolina, 1990).

———. *Radical Ecology: The Search for a Livable World* (NY: Routledge, 1992).

Mies, Maria, and Vandana Shiva. *Ecofeminism* (London: Zed Books, 1993).

The New Catalyst #10 (Winter 1987–88). Special issue: Women/Earth Speaking: Feminism and Ecology.

Plant, Judith, ed. *Healing the Wounds: The Promise of Ecofeminism* (Santa Cruz, CA: New Society Publishers, 1989).

Reuther, Rosemary Radford. *New Women, New Earth: Sexist Ideologies and Human Liberation* (New York: The Seabury Press, 1975).

Seager, Joni. *Earth Follies: Coming to Feminist Terms with the Global Environmental Crisis* (London and New York: Routledge, 1993).

Shiva, Vandana. *Staying Alive: Women, Ecology, and Development* (London: Zed Books, 1988).

Studies in the Humanities 15, no. 2 (1988). Special issue, Feminism, Ecology, and the Future of the Humanities. Edited by Patrick Murphy.

Tong, Rosemary, ed. *Feminine and Feminist Ethics* (Belmont, CA: Wadsworth Publishing Co., 1993).

III-C. Animal Liberation and Environmental Ethics

Hargrove, Eugene. *The Animal Rights/Environmental Ethics Debate: The Environmental Perspective* (Albany, NY: State University of New York Press, 1992).

III-D. The Value of Individuals, Species, and Ecosystems

Barbier, Edward, Joanne Burgess, Timothy Swanson, and David Pearce. *Elephants, Ivory and Economics* (London: Earthscan Publications, 1990).

Colinvaux, Paul. *Why Big Fierce Animals Are Rare* (Princeton University Press, 1978).

Ehrenfeld, David W. *Conserving Life on Earth* (New York: Oxford University Press, 1972).

———. *The Arrogance of Humanism* (New York: Oxford University Press, 1978).

Ehrlich, Paul, and Anne Ehrlich. *Extinction* (New York: Random House, 1981).

McNeely, J. A. *Economics and Biological Diversity* (Gland, Switzerland: International Union for the Conservation of Nature and Natural Resources 1988).

McNeely, Jeffrey A., Kenton R. Miller, Walter V. Reid, Russell Mittermeier, and Timothy B. Werner. *Conserving the World's Biological Diversity* (Washington, D.C.: WRI, 1990).

The Monist 75, no. 2 (April 1992). Special issue on the intrinsic value of nature.

Myers, Norman. *A Wealth of Wild Species: Storehouse for Human Welfare* (Boulder, CO: Westview Press, 1983).

Norton, Bryan, ed. *The Preservation of the Species* (Princeton: Princeton University Press, 1985).

———. *Why Preserve Natural Variety?* (Princeton: Princeton University Press, 1987).

Regenstein, Lewis. *The Politics of Extinction* (New York: Macmillan and Company, 1975).

Sober, Eliot. *Conceptual Issues in Evolutionary Biology* (Cambridge: MIT Press, 1984).

Wilson, E. O. ed., *Biodiversity* (Washington, D.C.: National Academy Press, 1986).

———. *Biophilia* (Cambridge: Harvard University Press, 1984).

———. *The Diversity of Life* (Cambridge: Harvard University Press, 1992).

Woodley, Stephen, James Kay, and George Francis, eds. *Ecological Integrity and the Management of Ecosystems* (Waterloo, Ontario: Heritage Resources Centre, University of Waterloo, and St. Lucie Press, 1993).

Wright, Larry. *Teleological Explanation* (Berkeley: University of California Press, 1976).

III-E. Land and Landscape

Ackerman, Bruce A., *Private Property and the Constitution* (New Haven: Yale University Press, 1977).

———, ed. *Economic Foundations of Property Law* (Boston: Little, Brown and Company, 1975).

Adams, Ansel. *The American Wilderness* (Boston: Little, Brown, and Co., 1991).

Becker, Lawrence C., *Property Rights: Philosophical Foundations* (London, Routledge and Kegan Paul, 1977).

Black Elk. *Black Elk Speaks* (New York: W. Morrow, 1932).

Blumenfeld, Samuel L., *Property in a Humane Economy* (La Salle, Ill., Open Court, 1974).

Brown, Joseph Epes, ed. *The Sacred Pipe* (New York: Penguin Books, 1973).

Capps, Walter Holden, ed. *Seeing With a Native Eye* (New York: HarperCollins, 1976).

Gewirth, Alan, *Human Rights: Essays in Justification and Application* (Chicago: University of Chicago Press, 1982).

Hardin, Garrett, and John Baden, eds. *Managing the Commons* (San Francisco: W. H. Freeman, 1977).

Hargrove, Eugene C., ed. *Religion and Environmental Crisis* (Athens: The University of Georgia Press, 1985).

Harris, Tom. *Death in the Marsh* (Covelo, CA: Island Press, 1991).

Hudson, Wendy E., ed. *Landscape Linkages and Biodiversity* (Covelo, CA: Island Press, 1991).

Hughes, J. Donald. *American Indian Ecology* (El Paso, TX.: Texas Western Press, 1983).

Kirk, Ruth, with Jerry Franklin. *The Olympic Rain Forest: An Ecological Web* (Seattle: University of Washington Press, 1992).

MacPherson, C. B. *The Political Theory of Possessive Individualism: Hobbes to Locke* (Oxford: Oxford University Press, 1962).

McCay, Bonnie J., and James M. Acheson, eds. *The Question of the Commons: The Culture and Ecology of Communal Resources* (Tucson: University of Arizona Press, 1991).

Nozick, Robert. *Anarchy, State, and Utopia* (New York: Basic Books, 1974).

Pennock, J. R., and Chapman, J. W., eds. NOMOS XXII: *Property* (New York: New York University Press, 1980).

Silko, Leslie Marmon. *Ceremony* (New York: Viking Press, 1977).

Suzuki, David and Peter Knudtson, eds. *Wisdom of the Elders: Sacred Native Stories of Nature* (New York: Bantam Books, 1992).

Vittachi, Anuradha. *Earth Conference One: Sharing A Vision for Our Planet* (Boston: Science Library, 1989).

Waldron, Jeremy. *The Right to Private Property* (Oxford: Clarendon Press, 1988).

Worster, Donald. *Nature's Economy: The Roots of Ecology* (San Francisco: Sierra Club Books, 1977).

IV. Economics, Ethics, and Ecology

IV-A. Environmental Policy Based on Willingness to Pay

Arthur, John, and William H. Shaw, eds. *Justice and Economic Distribution* (Englewood Cliffs, NJ: Prentice-Hall, 1978).

Berry, Wendell. *Home Economics* (San Francisco: North Point Press, 1987).

Bormann, F. H., and Stephen R. Kellert, eds. *Ecology, Economics, and Ethics: The Broken Circle* (New Haven: Yale University Press, 1991).

Brundtland, G. *Our Common Future* (New York: Oxford University Press, 1987).

Coleman, Jules. *Markets, Morals and the Law* (Cambridge: Cambridge University Press, 1988).

Costanza, Robert. *Ecological Economics* (New York: Columbia University Press, 1991).

Daly, Herman E. *Steady-State Economics: The Economics of Biophysical Equilibrium and Moral Growth* (San Francisco: W. H. Freeman, 1977).

Daly, Herman, and Cobb, John. *For The Common Good: Redirecting the Economy Toward Community, the Environment, and a Sustainable Future* (Boston: Beacon Press, 1989).

de la Court, Thijs. *Beyond Brundtland: Green Development in the 1990s* (New York: New Horizons Press. 1990).

Douglas, Mary, and Baron Isherwood. *The World of Goods* (New York: Basic Books, 1979).

Dryzek, John S. *Rational Ecology: Environment and Political Economy* (New York: Basil Blackwell, 1987).

Elkins, Paul. *Green Economics* (New York: Doubleday, 1992).

Elster, J. and E. Hylland, eds. *Foundations of Social Choice Theory* (Cambridge: Cambridge University Press, 1983).

English, Mary R. *Siting Low-Level Radioactive Waste Disposal Facilities* (New York: Quorum Books, 1992).

Freeman III, A. Myrick, Robert Haveman, and Allen Kneese. *The Economics of Environmental Policy* (New York: Wiley, 1973).

Fusfield, Daniel. *The Age of the Economist* (Glenview, IL: Scott Foresman and Company, 1986).

Goodland, Robert, ed. *Race to Save the Tropics: Ecology and Economics for a Sustainable Future* (Covelo, CA: Island Press, 1990).

Gupta, Avijit. *Ecology and Development in the Third World* (New York: Routledge, 1988).

Hardin, Garrett. *Living Within Limits: Ecology, Economics, and Population Taboos* (New York: Oxford University Press, 1993).

Jansson, Ann-Mari, ed. *Integration of Economy and Ecology* (Stockholm: University of Stockholm Press, 1984).

Kneese, A., S. Ben-David, and W. D. Shulze, eds. *The Ethical Foundations of Benefit-Cost Analysis* (Washington, D.C.: Resources for the Future, 1983).

Krutilla, John, and Anthony Fisher. *The Economic of Natural Environments* (Washington, D.C.: Resources for the Future, 1985).

Leonard, H. Jeffrey, et al. *Environment and the Poor: Development Strategies for a Common Agenda* (New Brunswick, NJ: Transaction Publishers, 1989).

MacDonnell, Lawrence J., and Sara F. Bates, eds. *Natural Resources Policy and Law: Trends and Directions* (Washington, D.C.: Island Press, 1993).

MacLean, Douglas, ed. *Values at Risk* (Totowa, NJ: Rowman and Littlefield, 1986).

MacNeil, Jim, Pieter Winsemius, and Taizo Yakushiju. *Beyond Interdependence* (New York: Oxford University Press, 1991).

Mishan, Edward J. *The Cost of Economic Growth* (Harmondsworth: Penguin Books, 1969).

Okun, Arthur M. *Equality and Efficiency: The Big Tradeoff* (Washington, D.C.: Brookings Institution, 1975).

Orr, David, W. *Ecological Literacy: Education and the Transition to a Environmental Postmodern World* (Albany: State University of New York Press, 1992).

———. *Blueprint for a Green Economy* (London: Earthscan Publications, 1989).

Perrings, Charles. *Economy and Environment* (Cambridge: Cambridge University Press, 1987).

Portney, Kent E. *Controversial Issues in Environmental Policy: Science vs. Economics vs. Politics* (Thousand Oaks, CA: Sage Publications, 1992).

Posner, Richard. *The Economics of Justice* (Cambridge, MA: Harvard University Press, 1981).

Rawls, J. *A Theory of Justice* (Cambridge, MA: Harvard University Press, 1971).

Sagoff, Mark. *The Economy of the Earth* (Cambridge: Cambridge University Press, 1988).

Schelling, Thomas. *Micromotives and Macrobehavior* (New York: Norton, 1978).

Schumacher, E. F. *Small Is Beautiful* (New York: Harper and Row, 1973).

Sen, A. K. *On Ethics and Economics* (New York: Basil Blackwell, 1987).

———. *Collective Choice and Social Welfare* (San Francisco: Holden-Day, 1970).

Seneca, Joseph, and Michael Taussig. *The Environmental Economics* (Englewood Cliffs, NJ: Prentice-Hall, 1979).

Shrader-Frechette, K. S. *Risk and Rationality* (Berkeley: University of California Press, 1991).

Stokey, Edith, and Zeckhauser, Richard. *A Primer for Policy Analysis* (New York: Norton & Company, 1978).

Tribe, Laurence H., Corinne S. Schelling, and John Voss, eds. *When Values Conflict: Essays on Environmental Analysis, Discourse and Decision* (Cambridge, MA: Ballinger Publishing Co., 1976).

Waring, Marilyn. *If Women Counted: A New Feminist Economics* (San Francisco: HarperCollins, 1988).

Winkler, Earl, and Jerrold R. Coombs, eds. *Applied Ethics: A Reader* (Cambridge, MA: Blackwells, 1993).

IV-B. Ecological Sustainability

Allen, Patricia, ed. *Food for the Future* (New York: John Wiley & Sons, 1993).

Anderson, Anthony B. *Alternatives to Deforestation: Steps Toward Sustainable Use of the Amazon Rain Forest* (New York: Columbia University Press, 1990).

Brown, Jennifer, ed. *Environmental Threats: Perception, Analysis and Management* (London: Belhaven Press, 1989).

Costanza, Robert, ed. *Ecological Economics: The Science and Management of Sustainability* (New York: Columbia University Press, 1991).

Eldredge, Niles, ed. *Systematics, Ecology, and the Biodiversity Crisis* (New York: Columbia University Press, 1992).

Elkington, John, and Jonathan Shopley. *The Shrinking Planet: U.S. Information Technology and Sustainable Development* (Holmes, PA: World Resources Institute, 1988).

Goodland, Robert, Herman F. Daly, and Salah El Serafy, eds. *Population, Technology, and Lifestyle* (Washington, D.C.: Island Press, 1992).

The Group of Green Economists. *Ecological Economics* (London: Zed Books, 1992).

Hawken, Paul. *The Ecology of Commerce* (New York: HarperCollins, 1994).

McIntosh, Robert P. *The Background of Ecology: Concept and Theory* (New York: Cambridge University Press, 1985).

Meeker-Lowry, Susan. *Economics As If Earth Really Mattered* (Santa Cruz, CA: New Society Publishers, 1988).

Milbrath, Lester. *Envisioning a Sustainable Society* (Albany, N.Y.: SUNY Press, 1989).

Miller, G. Tyler. *Living in the Environment*, 4th edition (Belmont, CA: Wadsworth Publishing Co., 1982).

National Commission on the Environment. *Choosing a Sustainable Future* (Washington, D.C.: Island Press, 1993).

Pearce, David, Edward Barbier, and Anil Markandya. *Sustainable Development: Economics and Environment in the Third World* (Brookfield, VT: Gower, 1990).

Primack, Richard B. *Essentials of Conservation Biology* (Sunderland, MA: Sinauer Associates, 1993).

Repetto, Robert, ed. *The Global Possible: Resources Development, and the New Century* (New Haven: Yale University Press, 1985).

Sachs, Wolfgang, ed. *Global Ecology* (London: Zed Books, 1993).

Shiva, Vandana. *Staying Alive: Women Ecology, and Development* (London: Zed Books, 1988).

Shrader-Frechette, Kristin S. *Burying Uncertainty: Risk and the Case Against Geological Disposal of Nuclear Waste* (Berkeley: University of California Press, 1993).

Slocombe, D. Scott, ed. *Tools for Sustainability: Explorations and Prospects* (Waterloo, Ontario: Wilfrid Laurier University Cold Regions Research Centre, 1991).

Walter, Bob, Louis Arkin, and Richard Crenshaw. *Sustainable Cities: Concepts and Strategies for Eco-City Development* (Los Angeles: Eco-Home Media, 1992).

Young, Michael D. *Towards Sustainable Agricultural Development* (New York: Columbia University Press, 1991).

V. Personal Choices and the Ecologically Good Life

Adams, Carol J. *The Sexual Politics of Meat* (New York: Continuum, 1990).

Alexander, Christopher. *A Pattern Language* (New York: Oxford University Press, 1977).

American Heart Association. *1991 Heart and Stroke Facts* (Dallas, TX: American Heart Association, 1991).

Barrett, James R. *Work and Community in the Jungle: Chicago's Packinghouse Workers* (Urbana: University of Illinois Press, 1987).

Berger, John J. *Restoring the Earth: How Americans Are Working to Renew Our Damaged Environment* (New York: Alfred A. Knopf, 1985).

Berry, Wendell. *Fidelity: Five Stories* (New York: Pantheon, 1992).

———. *What Are People For?* (San Francisco: North Point Press, 1990).

Boas, Max, and Steve Chain. *Big Mac: The Unauthorized Story of McDonald's* (New York: Dutton, 1976).

Brady, Nyle C. *The Nature and Properties of Soils,* 8th ed. (New York: Macmillan Publishing Co., 1974).

Campbell, Stu. *Let It Rot! The Home Gardener's Guide to Composting* (Pownal, VT: Garden Way Publishing/Storey Communications Inc., 1975).

Carson, Rachel. *Silent Spring,* 25th anniversary edition (Boston: Houghton Mifflin Co., 1987).

Creasy, Rosalind. *The Complete Book of Edible Landscaping: Home Landscaping with Food-Bearing Plants and Resource-Saving Techniques* (San Francisco and New York: Sierra Club Books/Random House, 1982).

Cross, John G., and Melvin J. Guyer. *Social Traps* (Ann Arbor: University of Michigan Press, 1980).

Druse, Ken. *The Natural Garden* (New York: Crown Publishers, 1987).

Eagan, David I., and David W. Orr, eds. *The Campus and Environmental Responsibility.* Theme issue of *New Directions for Higher Education* (San Francisco: Jossey-Bass Publishers, 1992).

The Earth Works Group. *50 Simple Things You Can Do to Save the Earth* (Earthworks Press, 1400 Shattuck Ave., Box 25, Berkeley, CA 94709, 1989).

Farallones Institute. *The Integral Urban House* (San Francisco: Sierra Club Books, 1979).

Fox, Michael, and Nancy Wiswall. *The Hidden Costs of Beef* (Washington, D.C.: Humane Society of the United States, 1989).

Glantz, Michael H., ed. *Desertification* (Boulder, CO: Westview Press, 1977).

Harris, Marvin, and Eric B. Ross. *Food and Evolution* (Philadelphia: Temple University Press, 1987).

Hiss, Tony. *The Experience of Place* (New York: Vintage, 1990).

Kroc, Ray. *Grinding It Out: The Making of McDonald's* (Chicago: Henry Regnery, 1977).

Lappé, Frances Moore. *Diet for a Small Planet* (New York: Ballentine Books, 1982).

List, Peter C., ed. *Radical Environmentalism: Philosophy and Tactics* (Belmont, CA: Wadsworth Publishing Co., 1993).

Milbrath, Lester W. *Envisioning a Sustainable Society: Learning our Way Out* (Albany: State University of New York Press, 1989).

National Research Council, Board on Agriculture. *Alternative Agriculture* (Washington, D.C.: National Academy Press, 1989).

Olsen, Jack. *Slaughter the Animals, Poison the Earth* (New York: Simon & Schuster, 1971).

Powell, Thomas, and Betty Powell. *The Avant Gardener* (Boston: Houghton Mifflin Co., 1975).

Repetto, Robert C. *The Forest for the Trees?* (Washington, D.C.: World Resources Institute, 1988).

Rifkin, Jeremy. *Biosphere Politics: A New Consciousness for a New Century* (New York: Crown, 1991).

———, ed. *The Green Lifestyle Handbook* (New York: Owl Book, 1990).

Robinette, Gary O. *Plants/People/and Environmental Quality* (Washington, D.C.: U.S. Department of the Interior, National Park Service, and American Society of Landscape Architects Foundation, 1972).

Rodale, Robert, ed. *The Basic Book of Organic Gardening* (New York: Ballantine, 1987).

Shane, Douglas R. *Hoofprints on the Forest: Cattle Ranching and the Destruction of Latin America's Tropical Forests* (Philadelphia: Institute for the Study of Human Issues, 1986).

Slatta, Richard W. *Cowboys of the Americas* (New Haven: Yale University Press, 1990).

Sussman, Vic. *Never Kiss a Goat on the Lips* (Emmaus, PA: Rodale Press, 1981).

U.S. Forest Service. USDA. *An Assessment of the Forest and Range Land Situation in the United States* (Washington, D.C.: Government Printing Office, 1988).

Wald, Johanna, and David Alberswerth. *Our Ailing Public Rangelands: Conditions Report—1989* (Washington, D.C.: National Wildlife Federation, October 1989).

Wallace, David Rains. *Life in the Balance* (New York: National Audubon Society, 1987).

Weston, Anthony. *Back to Earth: Tomorrow's Environmentalism* (Philadelphia: Temple University Press, 1994).

Whelan, Tensie. *Nature Tourism: Managing for the Environment* (Covelo, CA: Island Press, 1991).

Wolfe, Joan. *Making Things Happen: How To Be an Effective Volunteer* (Covelo, CA: Island Press, 1991).

World Commission on Environment and Development. *Our Common Future: The Bruntland Commission Report* (Oxford: Oxford University Press, 1987).

Zakin, Susan. *Coyotes and Town Dogs: Earth First! and the Environmental Movement* (New York: Viking, 1993).

Additional References: Ethical Theory and Environmental Ethics

A. Ethical Theory and Applied Ethics

Arthur, John, ed. *Morality and Moral Controversies* (Englewood Cliffs, NJ: Prentice-Hall, 1993).

Barcalow, Emmett. *Moral Philosophy: Theory and Issues* (Belmont, CA: Wadsworth Publishing Co., 1994).

Benjamin, Martin. *Splitting the Difference* (Lawrence, KS: University Press of Kansas, 1990).

Brandt, Richard. *Ethical Theory* (Oxford: Clarendon Press, 1979).

Feldman, Fred. *Introductory Ethics* (Englewood Cliffs, NJ: Prentice-Hall, 1978).

Luper-Foy, Stephen, and Curtis Brown. *The Moral Life* (Chicago: Harcourt Brace Jovanovich, 1992).

Manning, Rita C. *Speaking from the Heart: A Feminist Perspective on Ethics* (Lanham, MD: Rowman and Littlefield, 1992).

May, Larry, and Shari C. Sharratt. *Applied Ethics* (Englewood Cliffs, NJ: Prentice-Hall, 1994).

Miller, Harlan B., and William H. Williams, eds. *The Limits of Utilitarianism* (Minneapolis: University of Minnesota Press, 1982).

Narveson, Jan. *Moral Matters: An Introduction* (Lewiston, NY: Broadview Press, 1993).

Olen, Jeffrey, and Vincent Barry, eds. *Applying Ethics* (Belmont, CA: Wadsworth Publishing Co., 1992).

Rachels, James, ed. *The Right Thing to Do* (New York: Random House, 1989).

———. *The Elements of Moral Philosophy* (New York: McGraw Hill, 1993).

Regan, Tom, and Donald VanDeVeer, eds. *And Justice for All* (Totowa, NJ: Rowman and Littlefield, 1982).

Ruggiero, Vincent. *Thinking Critically About Ethical Issues* (Mountain View, CA: Mayfield Publishing, 1992).

Sen, Amartya, and Bernard Williams, eds. *Utilitarianism and Beyond* (Cambridge: Cambridge University Press, 1982).

Sher, George, ed. *Moral Philosophy* (San Diego: Harcourt Brace Jovanovich, Publishers, 1987).

Singer, Peter. *Applied Ethics* (Oxford: Oxford University Press, 1988).

———. *Practical Ethics* (Cambridge: Cambridge University Press, 1979).

Sterba, James. *Morality in Practice* (Belmont, CA: Wadsworth Publishing Co., 1988).

Taylor, Paul. *Problems of Moral Philosophy* (Belmont, CA: Dickenson Publishing Co., 1967).

B. Environmental Ethics

Armstrong, Susan, J., and Richard G. Botzler, eds. *Environmental Ethics: Divergence and Convergence* (New York: McGraw-Hill, 1993).

Attfield, Robin. *Environmental Philosophy: Principles and Prospects* (Avebury, England: Aldershot, 1993).

———. *The Ethics of Environmental Concern* (New York: Columbia University Press, 1983; 2nd edition, Athens: University of Georgia Press, 1991).

Barbour, Ian. *Technology, Environment, and Human Values* (New York: Praeger, 1980).

Berry, R. J. (Sam), ed. *Environmental Dilemmas: Ethics and Decisions* (London: Chapman and Hall, 1993).

Blackstone, William T., ed. *Philosophy and Environmental Crisis.* (Athens: University of Georgia Press, 1974).

Brennan, Andrew. *Thinking About Nature: An Investigation of Nature, Value and Ecology* (London: Routledge and Athens: University of Georgia Press, 1988).

Caldwell, Lynton Keith. *Between Two Worlds: Science, the Environmental Movement and Policy Choice* (New York: Cambridge University Press, 1990).

Callicott, J. Baird. *In Defense of the Land Ethic* (Albany: State University of New York Press, 1989).

Clark, Stephen R. L. *The Nature of the Beast: Are Animals Moral?* (Oxford University Press, 1982).

Cooper, David, E. and Joy A. Palmer, eds. *The Environment in Question: Ethics and Global Issues* (London: Routledge, 1992).

Coward, Harold, and Thomas Hurka, eds. *Ethics and Climate Change: The Greenhouse Effect* (Waterloo, Ontario: Wilfrid Laurier University Press, 1993).

Des Jardins, Joseph R. *Environmental Ethics: An Introduction to Environmental Philosophy* (Belmont, CA: Wadsworth, 1993).

Dobson, Andrew, and Paul Lucardie, eds. *Green Political Thought* (London: Unwin Hyman, 1990).

Dotto, Lydia. *Ethical Choices and Global Greenhouse Warming* (Waterloo, Ontario: Wilfrid Laurier University Press, 1993).

Dower, Nigel, ed. *Ethics and Environmental Responsibility* (Avebury, England: Aldershot, 1989).

Drengson, Alan R. *Beyond Environmental Crisis: From Technocrat to Planetary Person* (New York: Peter Lang Publishing Co., 1989).

Eckersley, Robyn. *Environmentalism and Political Theory: Toward an Ecocentric Approach* (Albany: State University of New York Press, 1992).

Elliot, Robert, and Arran Gare, eds. *Environmental Philosophy: A Collection of Readings* (University Park: Pennsylvania State University Press, 1983).

Goodin, Robert E. *Green Political Theory* (Cambridge: Polity Press, 1992).

Gruen, Lori, and Dale Jamieson, eds. *Reflecting on Nature: Readings in Environmental Philosophy* (Cambridge: Cambridge University Press, 1994).

Gunn, Alastair S., and Aarne Vesilind, eds. *Environmental Ethics for Engineers* (Cheldea, MI: Lewis Publishers, 1986).

Hanson, Philip P., ed. *Environmental Ethics: Philosophical and Policy Perspective* Vol. I (Burnaby, BC: Simon Fraser University, 1986).

Hargrove, Eugene. *Foundations of Environmental Ethics* (Englewood Cliffs, NJ: Prentice-Hall, 1989).

Hart, Richard E., ed. *Ethics and the Environment* (Lanham, MD: University Press of America, 1992).

Johnson, Lawrence, E. *A Morally Deep World: An Essay on Moral Significance and Environmental Ethics* (Cambridge: Cambridge University Press, 1991).

McCloskey, H. J. *Ecological Ethics and Politics* (Totowa, NJ: Rowman and Littlefield, 1983).

Miller, Alan, S. *Gaia Connections: An Introduction to Ecology, Ecoethics, and Economics* (Totowa, NJ: Roman and Littlefield, 1991).

Nash, Roderick, F. *The Rights of Nature: A History of Environmental Ethics* (Madison: University of Wisconsin Press, 1989).

Newton, Lisa, and Catherine Dillingham, eds. *Watersheds: Classic Cases in Environmental Ethics* (Belmont, CA: Wadsworth Publishing Co., 1994).

Norton, Bryan G. *Toward Unity Among Environmentalists* (New York: Oxford University Press, 1991).

Orr, David W. *Ecological Literacy: Education and the Transition to a Postmodern World* (Albany: State University Press of New York, 1992).

Passmore, John. *Man's Responsibility For Nature: Ecological Problems and Western Traditions* (New York: Charles Scribner's Sons, 1974).

Pojman, Louis P., ed. *Environmental Ethics: Readings in Theory and Application* (Boston: Jones and Bartlett, 1994).

Potter, Van Rensselaer. *Global Bioethics: Building on the Leopold Legacy* (East Lansing: Michigan State University Press, 1989).

Regan, Tom, ed. *Earthbound: New Introductory Essays in Environmental Ethics* (New York: Random House, 1984).

Rolston, Holmes, III. *Environmental Ethics* (Philadelphia: Temple University Press, 1988).

———. *Philosophy Gone Wild: Essays in Environmental Ethics* (Buffalo, NY: Prometheus Books, 1986).

Scherer, Donald. *Upstream/Downstream: Issues in Environmental Ethics* (Philadelphia: Temple University Press, 1990).

Scherer, Donald, and Thomas Attig, eds. *Ethics and the Environment* (Englewood Cliffs, NJ: Prentice-Hall, 1983).

Shabecoff, Phillip. *A Fierce Green Fire: The American Environmental Movement* (New York: Hill and Wang, 1993).

Shrader-Frechette, K. S., ed. *Environmental Ethics* (Pacific Grove, CA: The Boxwood Press, 1981).

Stone, Christopher F. *Earth and Other Ethics: The Case for Moral Pluralism* (New York: Harper and Row, 1987).

VanDeVeer, Donald, and Christine Pierce. *The Environmental Ethics and Policy Book* (Belmont, CA: Wadsworth Publishing Co., 1994).

Wenz, Peter, S. *Environmental Justice* (Albany: State University of New York Press, 1988).

Weston, Anthony. *Toward Better Problems: New Perspectives on Abortion, Animal Rights, The Environment, and Justice* (Philadelphia: Temple University Press, 1992).

Westphal, Dale, and Fred Westphal, eds. *Planet in Peril: Essays in Environmental Ethics* (Fort Worth: Harcourt Brace College Publishers, 1994).

Westra, Laura. *An Environmental Proposal for Ethics: The Principle of Integrity* (Lanham, MD: Rowman and Littlefield, 1993).

Worster, Donald, ed. *The Ends of the Earth: Perspectives on Modern Environmental History* (New York: Cambridge University Press, 1988).

Zimmerman, Michael, J. Baird Callicott, George Sessions, Karen J. Warren, and John P. Clark, eds. *Environmental Philosophy: From Animal Rights to Radical Ecology* (Englewood Cliffs, NJ: Prentice-Hall, 1993).